W9-APR-458

LIFE-SPAN HUMAN DEVELOPMENT

LIFE-SPAN HUMAN DEVELOPMENT

CAROL K. SIGELMAN

UNIVERSITY OF ARIZONA

DAVID R. SHAFFER

UNIVERSITY OF GEORGIA

Brooks/Cole Publishing Company
Pacific Grove, California

Brooks/Cole Publishing Company
A Division of Wadsworth, Inc.

Printed in the United States of America

10 9 8 7 6 5 4

Library of Congress Cataloging-in-Publication Data

Sigelman, Carol K.
Life-span human development / Carol K. Sigelman, David R. Shaffer.
p. cm.
Includes bibliographical references.
ISBN 0-534-12282-5
1. Developmental psychology. I. Shaffer, David R. (David Reed), 1946– . II. Title.
BF713.S53 1990
155—dc20 89-29685
CIP

Sponsoring Editors: Vicki Knight and Philip L. Curson
Marketing Representative: Mark Francisco
Editorial Assistants: Amy Mayfield and Heather Riedl
Production Coordinator: Fiorella Ljunggren
Production: Nancy Sjoberg, Del Mar Associates
Manuscript Editor: Lillian R. Rodberg
Permissions Editor: Elaine Kleiss
Interior and Cover Design: John Odam
Cover Art: *Seated Figures* (1940), by Henry Moore, has been reproduced by kind permission of the Henry Moore Foundation
Interior Illustration: Cyndie Clark-Huegel and Wayne Clark
Photo Researcher: Frankie Wright
Typesetting: TypeLink, Inc.
Cover Printing: The Lehigh Press, Inc.
Printing and Binding: R. R. Donnelley & Sons Company

(Credits continue on p. 707.)

Our purpose in writing this overview of life-span human development has been to create the book that we would most want our students to read—one that piques and satisfies their curiosity about how and why human beings change (and remain the same) from their beginnings as fertilized eggs to their last years of life, and one that shares the best theories, research, and practical advice that developmentalists have to offer. We want our students to understand that human development is an incredibly complex process that grows out of the interactions between a changing person and a changing world and that continues throughout the entire life span. We want them to appreciate how major theories of human development guide researchers but can also help anyone analyze the "real-life" issues that developing persons face. And we would like them to appreciate that the best advice about such matters as raising children, working with troubled adolescents, and aiding nursing home residents is based on research reports rather than on armchair speculation.

Guided by these goals, we have written a text that delves into important theoretical issues and incorporates the best of both classic and contemporary research from the several disciplines concerned with understanding developmental processes. But we also recognize that solid scholarship is of little benefit to students unless they want to read it and can understand it. Fortunately, our own excitement about human development has made it easy for us to bring our subject to life. We have done all that we can to write in a straightforward and informal manner, to clarify concepts through concrete examples or analogies, to amuse, to provoke thought, and to point out the relevance of material to students' lives and to the work of teachers, psychologists, nurses, day-care workers, and other human service professionals. In short, we have aimed for a book that is both rigorous and readable, both scholarly and practical.

Our Topical/Chronological Approach

The large majority of life-span development textbooks adopt a chronological or "age/stage" approach, carving the life span into age ranges and describing the prominent characteristics of individuals within each age range. By contrast, we use a topical approach blended with a chronological approach within topics. We focus on domains of development such as physical growth, cognition, and personality as we trace developmental trends in each domain from infancy to old age.

Why have we bucked the tide? Like many other instructors, we have typically favored topically organized textbooks when teaching child, adolescent, or adult development courses. As a result, it seemed only natural to use that same topical approach in introducing students to the whole life span. More important, a topical organization allows us to convey more effectively the flow of development—the systematic, and often truly dramatic, *transformations* that take place in the course of human life, as well as the *continuities* in development that make each individual a reflection of his or her past self. The topical approach also lends itself to a strong emphasis on developmental processes, so that students come away with a firm grasp of how nature and nurture contribute over time to normal developmental changes, as well as to differences among individuals.

Finally, a predominantly topical approach facilitates adopting a *life-span perspective* on human development. Happenings within any one period of the life span can be viewed from the vantage point of what comes before and what is yet to come. In chronologically organized textbooks, many topics are discussed only in connection with the age group to which they seem most relevant—for example, attachment in relation to infancy, play in relation to the preschool years, or sexuality in relation to adolescence and adulthood. As we have pursued our goal of writing a topical life-span text, we have repeatedly found ourselves grappling with intriguing questions that we might otherwise not even have asked. Consider the topic of attachment: Could what we know about infants' attachments to their parents also be useful in analyzing the attachments that children form to their best friends or that adults form to their romantic partners? Do securely attached infants later have a greater capacity to form and sustain friendships or romantic partnerships than infants whose early social experiences are less favorable? What are the consequences at different points in the life span of lacking someone to whom one is closely attached? Attachments are important throughout the life span, and we try to make that clear. Similarly, we have found it fascinating and instructive to ask how the young child's capacity for play is channeled later in life, or how mature sexuality evolves from the sexual curiosity evident even during infancy.

In short, we have adopted a topical approach because we consider it the best way to introduce the how and why of human development. However, we also appreciate the strengths of the chronological approach, particularly its ability to portray "the whole person" in each period of the life span. For this reason, we have integrated the age/stage approach within our topical organization—to have the best of both worlds.

Each topical chapter contains major sections on infancy, childhood, adolescence, and adulthood. The very existence of these sections is proof that we have indeed traced development in each of the domains we cover across the *whole* life span, although we do, of course, vary our emphasis on each period of the life span depending on its significance for the domain of development under consideration. These age/stage sections aid students in appreciating the distinctive qualities of each phase of life and make it easier for them to find material on any age period of particular interest to them. Moreover, they allow instructors who wish to move further in the direction of an age/stage approach to cover infancy, childhood, and adolescence in the first portion of the course and save all the material on adulthood for the end of the course.

To further emphasize the interrelatedness of developments within each age range, we have written a concluding chapter that summarizes major developments in each of seven periods of the life span, as well as broad themes in life-span development. This chapter serves as a handy reference for students who want to consolidate what they have learned so far or to strengthen their grasp of the "big picture." Finally, we have seized every opportunity along the way to highlight the intimate interrelationships among physical, cognitive, personal, and social development.

Organization of the Text

The book begins by orienting students to the scientific study of life-span development (Chapter 1) and to the central issues and theoretical perspectives that have dominated the field (Chapter 2). It then explores developmental processes in some depth, discussing genetic influences (Chapter 3) and environmental influences (Chapter 4) on development from a life-span perspective, showing how genes contribute to maturational changes and individual differences throughout the life span and how people are also the products of a prenatal environment and of postnatal experiences that vary as a function of age, culture, and historical period.

Chapters on the growth and aging of body and nervous system (Chapter 5) and on the development of sensory and perceptual capacities (Chapter 6) launch our examination of the development of basic human capacities. Chapter 7 introduces the Piagetian perspective on cognitive development and describes the development of language in relation to the development of thought; Chapter 8 views learning, memory, and problem solving from an information-processing perspective; and Chapter 9 explores the psychometric approach to cognition, delving into individual differences in intelligence and creativity.

The next three chapters concern the development of the self—changes in self-conceptions and personality (Chapter 10), in gender roles and sexuality (Chapter 11), and in personal priorities as they are reflected in motives and moral standards (Chapter 12). The self is set more squarely in a social context as we trace life-span changes in relationships and social competencies (Chapter 13), in roles and relationships within the family (Chapter 14), and in lifestyles as they are expressed in play, school, and work activities (Chapter 15). Finally, we offer a life-span perspective on developmental problems and disorders (Chapter 16), examine why people die and how they cope with death (Chapter 17), and highlight key trends and issues in life-span development (Chapter 18).

Chapter Organization

To ease the student's task, each chapter has been written in a standard format (with some deviations, we confess, in the first two chapters and the last) and contains, in this order:

A chapter outline that orients students to what lies ahead.

Introductory material that stimulates interest, lays out the plan for the chapter, and introduces key concepts, theories, and issues relevant to the area of development to be explored.

Four developmental sections that describe key changes and continuities, as well as the mechanisms underlying them, during four developmental periods—infancy, childhood, adolescence, and adulthood.

Applications, an examination of how knowledge has been applied to optimize development in the domain of development at issue. "Applications" sections deal with such topics as genetic counseling; recent innovations in care for premature babies; and programs designed to improve intellectual functioning, self-esteem, moral reasoning, social skills, and family functioning at different ages.

Reflections, a section in which we make some concluding observations and challenge students to step back from the material, appreciate its broader significance, or think about a chapter's themes in new ways. The "Reflections" sections help students see the larger picture—and contemplate the view.

Summary points that succinctly overview the chapter's main themes to aid students in reviewing the material.

Key terms, a list of the new terms introduced in the chapter. The terms are printed in boldface, defined when they are first presented in a chapter, and included in the glossary at the end of the book.

In addition, each chapter is sprinkled with photographs, tables, and figures. Although some of these are intended to stimulate interest or to entertain, they have a serious educational purpose as well: summarizing stage theories, presenting revealing research data, or illustrating concepts discussed in the chapter.

Similarly, the "boxes" in each chapter are integral parts of the text. They offer a closer look at selected topics, among them ways of combatting an infant's fear of strangers in the doctor's office, the effects of children on their parents, misconceptions about hyperactivity, the advantages and disadvantages of working part time during adolescence, cultural differences in the experience of menopause, problems facing middle-aged people who must care for their ailing parents, and interventions to increase the well-being of nursing home residents.

Finally, a word on referencing. Each chapter cites the authors and dates of publication for a large number of books and articles, which are fully referenced in the chapter-by-chapter bibliographies at the end of the book. Although some students may find these citations distracting, they are included for good reasons: because we *are* committed to the value of systematic research, because we believe in giving proper credit where credit is due, and because we want students to have the resources they need for pursuing their interests in human development.

Supplementary Aids

For the instructor, there is an instructor's manual that contains chapter outlines, learning objectives, and suggestions for class discussion, projects, films, videos, and additional readings. The test bank offers at least 60 multiple-choice and 10 true-or-false items for each chapter. The student study guide is designed to promote active learning by a guided review of the important principles and concepts in the text. The study materials for each chapter also include a comprehensive multiple-choice self-test and a number of "applications" exercises that challenge students to think about and to apply what they have learned.

Acknowledgments

A project of this magnitude cannot be carried out without the efforts of many people, all of whom deserve our deepest thanks. We are very grateful to the reviewers of the manuscript for their constructive criticism and useful suggestions. They are Freda Blanchard-Fields of Louisiana State University, Janet Fritz of Colorado State University, John Klein of Castleton State College, Rosanne Lorden of Eastern Kentucky University, Robin Palkovitz of the University of Delaware, Suzanne Pasch of the University of

Wisconsin at Milwaukee, and Katherine Van Giffen of California State University at Long Beach. We would also like to thank the many reviewers of the first and second editions of Shaffer's *Developmental Psychology: Childhood and Adolescence.* Their contributions to that book are reflected in the coverage of child development here.

For their help with some of the "drudge work" and for their enthusiasm about the book, we thank former students Susan McGurk, Sara Glisky, and Kelly Mansfield. Credit for excellent supplementary materials goes to Elizabeth Rider of Elizabethtown College, who prepared the study guide and material for the instructor's manual, and to Ariel Anderson of Western Michigan University, who prepared the test bank.

Producing this book required the joint efforts of Brooks/Cole and Del Mar Associates. We want to express our gratitude to Fiorella Ljunggren of Brooks/Cole for overseeing the whole process; to Nancy Sjoberg and her colleagues at Del Mar Associates for their creative and careful production work; and to Lillian Rodberg for all the thought and care she invested in copy editing and indexing. These pros were a joy to work with, and the book is much better because of them.

We are also deeply indebted to our sponsoring editors, C. Deborah Laughton and Vicki Knight. It was C. Deborah who saw the need for a life-span text like this one, pestered us unmercifully until we agreed to write it, and nurtured us as we began. It is unfortunate that she left Brooks/Cole before she could see her "baby" born, but we hope that she takes pride in the birth nonetheless. We are equally grateful to Vicki Knight, who joined Brooks/Cole when we needed her and skillfully shepherded the book through its final stages of development. Both C. Deborah and Vicki were more than splendid editors; they were invaluable sources of advice and moral support, as well as good friends.

Finally, we thank our families for all that they have contributed to our development and to our understanding of development. There is simply no way to thank Lee Sigelman enough for enduring a preoccupied spouse and a precipitous decline in the quality of his life without filing for divorce.

Carol K. Sigelman
David R. Shaffer

BRIEF CONTENTS

❦

1

2

3

THE GENETICS OF LIFE-SPAN DEVELOPMENT 67

4

ENVIRONMENT AND LIFE-SPAN DEVELOPMENT 99

17

The Final Challenge: Death and Dying 537

18

Fitting the Pieces Together 569

LIFE-SPAN HUMAN DEVELOPMENT

CHAPTER

1

UNDERSTANDING LIFE-SPAN HUMAN DEVELOPMENT

Dawn and Michael gaze down at their newly arrived daughter and wonder, as many new parents do, what their child's future will hold: How soon will she be toddling around the house and talking to us? Will she be popular in school and bring lots of friends home, or might she turn out to be a loner like her Uncle Dan? Will she be an "A" student and devoted daughter, or might she rebel, get caught up in drugs, and call from the police station in the middle of the night like the Harrison girl did? Will she go to college, achieve fame and fortune, and enjoy a happy marriage, or might she be one of those people whose lives are a never-ending series of false starts and disasters? And when she's grown, will she think we were good parents, keep in touch, and bring the grandchildren by? And when we're gone and she is old, what then?

Predicting the course of human lives is risky business, but it is the business of those of us who study the process of human development. This book is about development from conception to death. Among the many questions it addresses are the questions posed in Box 1.1. Have any of these questions occurred to you before? Do any of them intrigue you now? Probably so, for the simple fact is that we are all developing persons who interact daily with other developing persons. What *are* we interested in if not in ourselves and the people close to us? Most college students genuinely want to understand how they personally have been affected by experiences in their lives, how they have changed over the years, and where they may be heading. They are also curious about the behavior of people they know—for example, about why a 1-year-old nephew suddenly seems to be afraid of strangers, or why a roommate changes majors every month, or why Mom has started thinking about going back to school. Many students also have very practical motivations for learning about human development—for example, a desire to be a better parent or to work more effectively as a psychologist, nurse, teacher, or other human service professional.

In this introductory chapter, we lay the groundwork for the remainder of the book by addressing some questions about the nature of life-span human development and how knowledge of it is gained. What does it mean to say that people "develop" over the life span? How should the life span and its phases be viewed? How is our experience of the life span different from that of developing individuals in past eras or in other cultures? When did scientific studies of human development begin, why are they needed, and how exactly do today's researchers investigate how and why people change with age, and how their development can be channeled in positive directions?

WHAT IS DEVELOPMENT?

Let us define **development** as systematic changes in the individual occurring between conception and death, or from "womb to tomb." By describing these changes as "systematic," we imply that they are somehow orderly or patterned; changes due to unpredictable mood swings or random events are therefore excluded. Some scholars would want to restrict the concept of development to changes of a positive sort that make human beings more competent or more complex (Kaplan, 1983). Most developmentalists, though, argue that developmental change can take many forms: It may indeed be positive (as when a young child's speech becomes more and more adultlike), it may be negative (as when an elderly adult finds it more and more difficult to hear conversations), or it may simply represent a difference between earlier behavior and later behavior (as when a career woman who led a single life marries, or a boy who feared hairy monsters under the bed comes to fear child molesters instead).

The systematic changes of interest to developmentalists fall into three broad realms. *Physical development* includes the growth of the body and its organs during childhood, the appearance of physical signs of aging during adulthood, and the gains and losses in motor abilities that occur over the years. *Cognitive development* represents changes in mental processes involved in perception, language use, learning, and thought. And *psychosocial development* refers to changes in personal and interpersonal phenomena such as motives and emotions, personality traits, interpersonal skills and relationships, and roles played in the family and in the larger society.

Now, when in life are gains in the physical, cognitive, and psychosocial domains most likely, and when do negative changes usually occur? Many people picture the life span this way: First there are tremendous gains in capacity or positive changes from infancy to young adulthood; then there is little change at all from young adulthood through middle age; and finally there are disastrous declines in capacities in old age. This vision of the life span has some truth to it, particularly if we focus on biological change. Biologists typically define **growth** as the physical changes that occur from conception to maturity. Certainly one basic fact of human development is that we become more biologically mature—and just plain bigger—during the early part of the life span. Biologists traditionally use the term **aging** to refer to the deterioration of organisms (including human beings) that leads inevitably to their death. So from a biological perspective, development is indeed growth in early life and aging in later life.

Unfortunately, this biological view of development does not capture the whole truth. It ignores the fact that both positive and negative changes occur throughout the life span. For example, from early childhood to young adulthood, we certainly do gain many abilities, yet this is also a period in which suicide rates rise (Kagan, 1986). From our teenage years to our 40s, when we are supposedly not changing much, we actually seem to be gaining

Box 1.1
Some Questions about Human Development

Here are some of the questions that this book addresses. Do any of them intrigue you?

- What does the world look like to newborn infants? Can they make any sense of what goes on around them?
- Why do preschool children come out with wacky ideas such as the notion that the sun is alive and is following them around or that the dead can be revived if they are fed lots of chicken soup?
- Does experiencing the divorce of your parents when you are a child have any lasting effects on your personality or your relationships with other people?
- Would males and females still turn out to be different from each other even if they were treated the same by parents, teachers, and other people?
- When do children acquire a sense of right and wrong, and why do some people have higher moral standards than others do?
- Why do some teenagers become juvenile delinquents or drug abusers while others do not?
- Why are many college students unsure about what they want to do in life or unready to commit themselves to long-term relationships?
- How are adults affected by having a child, and how do they usually react when their children leave home to attend college or begin their careers?
- What should a person do to be a "good" parent, and how does "bad" parenting influence children's lives?
- Do adults really experience a "midlife crisis" in their forties that can make them as confused as teenagers often are about their lives?
- How is a person's sex life likely to change from age 20 to age 70?
- If I am dependent, shy, insecure, hostile, or otherwise less than perfect now, am I likely to remain that way through life or am I likely to "outgrow" my flaws?
- Why are some people friendly and outgoing while others are shy and reserved? Is personality shaped by experiences in the family? If so, why are children from the same family often so different from one another?
- What is it like to be old? How am I likely to be different at age 70 than I am now?
- How do elderly people really feel about dying? Are they afraid? Do they think about death a lot?
- How in the world does a fertilized egg evolve into a thinking, feeling, ever-changing adult?

self-confidence and other psychological strengths (Haan, 1981). And although many elderly adults do indeed find themselves becoming forgetful or hard-of-hearing, many of them are also still acquiring knowledge or even gaining a kind of wisdom about life that young people lack (Clayton & Birren, 1980). In short, development involves gains, losses, and just plain changes *at each phase of the life cycle* (Kagan, 1986). Above all, we should abandon the idea that aging involves only deterioration and loss. Developmentalists today prefer to use the term *aging* to refer to a wide range of changes, both positive and negative, in the *mature* organism (Birren & Zarit, 1985).

To grasp the meaning of life-span development more fully, we should also understand two important processes that underlie developmental change. **Maturation** is the biological unfolding of the individual according to a plan contained in the *genes*, or the hereditary material passed from parents to child at conception. Just as seeds systematically unfold to become mature plants, human beings "unfold" within the womb. Their genetic "program" then calls for them to walk and utter their first words at about 1 year of age, to achieve sexual maturity at about age 12 to 14, and so on. Since the brain undergoes maturational changes, maturation is partially responsible not only for many readily observable physical changes in human beings but for psychological changes such as an increased ability to solve problems or to understand what another person is feeling. It is even likely that we are biologically programmed to age and die. While heredity, or genetic makeup, surely contributes to differences among us in everything from eye color to intelligence, it also calls for all of us to undergo similar maturational changes over the life span.

The second critical developmental process is **learning**, or the process through which *experience* brings about relatively permanent changes in behavior. While a certain degree of physical maturation may be necessary before a child can become a great pianist, careful teaching and long hours of practice are also required. Many of our abilities and habits do not just "mature"; parents, teachers, and other important people show us how to behave in new ways, and we are changed by the events we experience during our lives. More generally, we change in response to the *environment* in which we develop—particularly in response to the actions of the people around us. As it turns out, many developmental changes are the products of *both* "nature" (genetic endowment and maturation) and "nurture" (environmental influences and learning). Many of the most exciting debates about human development revolve around exactly which process contributes more to specific developmental changes (see Plomin, 1990).

In summary, development is obviously a multifaceted and complex process. It can make us better, worse, or just different than we were before; it includes not only growth and aging but more; and it is brought about by both maturation and learning. As we shall now see, development also takes place in a historical and cultural context, a context that influences how the life span and its phases are viewed.

DIFFERENT CONCEPTS OF THE LIFE SPAN

People do not envision the life span as a single, long period between conception and death. Instead, they divide it into periods or phases, each of which is believed to be distinct in some way from the others. Table 1.1 lists the periods of the life span that many of today's developmentalists regard as distinct. You will want to keep these age ranges in mind as you read this book, for we will constantly be speaking of infants, preschoolers, school-aged children, adolescents, and young, middle-aged, and older adults. Remember that these ages are only approximate, and a person's age is only a rough indicator of his or her level of development: There are many differences among individuals of the same age. It is more useful to look at the

Table 1.1 An overview of periods of the life span

PERIOD OF LIFE	APPROXIMATE AGE RANGE
Prenatal period	Conception to birth
Infancy	First 2 years of life
Preschool period	2 to 5 or 6 years (some prefer to describe as "toddlers" children who have begun to walk and are age 1 to 3)
Middle childhood	6 to 12 or so (until the onset of puberty)
Adolescence	12 or so to 20 or so (when the individual is relatively independent of parents and assumes adult roles)
Early adulthood	20 to 40 years
Middle adulthood	40 to 65 years
Late adulthood	65 years and older

individual's functioning. For example, those 10-year-olds who have already experienced puberty might more usefully be classified as adolescents, and those teenagers who are fully self-supporting with children of their own function as young adults. Similarly, some 55-year-olds are physically and psychologically much "older" than some 75-year-olds.

The life span has not always been carved up into the same age periods contained in the table. In fact, even today, different cultures view the life span quite differently. The fact is that age, like gender and other significant human characteristics, means what a society chooses to have it mean. All societies appear to view age as a significant attribute, but each society has its own ways of dividing the life span and of treating the individuals who fall into different age groups. Each socially defined age group—called **age grade**, or age stratum—is assigned a different status and different roles, privileges, and responsibilities. We, for example, grant "adults" (18-year-olds, by law) a voting privilege that we do not grant to children, and we give senior citizen discounts to older adults but not to young or middle-aged adults. Just as high schools have their "elite" seniors and their "lowly" freshmen, whole societies are "layered" into age grades. So let us briefly examine how concepts of the life span and its age grades have evolved through history and how they vary from culture to culture in the world today.

Historical Changes in Phases of the Life Span

Every human being develops in a historical context: Being a developing person today is quite different from being a developing person in past eras. Moreover, the quick historical tour that we are about to take should convince you that the phases of the life span that we recognize today were not always perceived as distinct.

Childhood in Premodern Times

Imagine that you are a newborn baby boy in the ninth century B.C. in the city-state of Sparta. The Spartan elders soon inspect you and decide that you are strong and healthy enough to live; lucky for you, because otherwise you would have been taken into the wilderness and left to die (Despert, 1965). Having passed the test, you will now be exposed to a strict regimen designed to train you for the grim task of serving a military state. As an infant, you will take cold-water baths designed to "toughen" you (Despert, 1965). At 7 years of age, when children in our society today are entering the second grade, you will be taken from your home and raised in a barracks. You will be beaten often and may go for days at a time without food, all to instill in you the discipline you will need to become an able warrior and a credit to the Spartan nation (deMause, 1974; Despert, 1965).

Not all ancient societies treated their children as harshly as the Spartans did. And yet deplorable treatment of children has been the rule rather than the exception through much of recorded history (deMause, 1974). Well after the birth of Christ, children were still viewed as family "possessions" to be used as seen fit. In fact, it was not until the 12th century A.D. in Christian Europe that the law equated infanticide—the killing of children—with murder (deMause, 1974)! Yet the beatings continued. One mother in early America described a struggle with her 4-month-old infant: "I whipped him til he was actually black and blue, and until I *could not* whip him any more, and he never gave up one single inch" (deMause, 1974, p. 41).

Not only were children of past eras subjected to discipline that we would brand as child abuse, but they were expected to grow up fast. As an infant or toddler in medieval Europe, you would have been cared for until you could dress, feed, and bathe yourself, but you would hardly have been coddled (Ariès, 1962; deMause, 1974). At about age 6, you would have begun to wear miniature versions of adult clothing and would have begun a career working with adults (often a parent or relative) at home, at a shop, or in the fields. You would have participated in many of the same social and sexual activities that adults favored, and you would have discovered that the laws of the day made no distinction between children and adults. Had you, as a 10-year-old, been convicted of stealing, you would have been treated as a common thief and perhaps hanged for your crime (Kean, 1937).

Historian Phillippe Ariès (1962) concluded that European societies had no concept of "childhood" as we know it before 1600, or the start of the 17th century, and viewed children as miniature adults. Although medieval parents undoubtedly recognized that children were different from adults, they did view children as potentially evil beings and pressured them to overcome their deficiencies and

Although medieval children were pressured to abandon their childish ways as soon as possible, it is doubtful that they were viewed as nothing but miniature adults.

adopt adult roles as soon as possible (Borstelmann, 1983). During the 17th century, children came to be seen as more distinctly childlike—as innocent and helpless souls who should be protected, given a proper moral and religious education, and taught skills such as reading and writing so that they would eventually become good workers (Ariès, 1962). Although children were still considered economic possessions, parents were now discouraged from beating their children and were urged to treat them with more warmth and affection (Ariès, 1962; Despert, 1965).

And what is it like to be a child in our society today? Certainly we do not have to look hard to find ample evidence that child abuse and neglect continue to be serious problems. And yet the lives of most children are infinitely better than they were a few centuries ago. Modern industrial societies continue to regard children as a special class of human beings who need guidance and protection in order to develop well. Moreover, until the 20th century children were viewed as beings whose function was to serve their parents and society. Only in this century have we taken seriously the notion that *society* should serve children (Borstelmann, 1983).

The Invention of Adolescence

If modern concepts of childhood arose only in the 17th century, perhaps it is not surprising that adolescence did not come to be viewed as a distinct period of the life span in Western societies until the end of the 19th century (Kett, 1977). The spread of industry had a great deal to do with the emergence of adolescence. At first, developing industries in the United States and elsewhere needed cheap child labor, and children left the farms to work in factories. But as industry advanced and as immigrants began to fill the labor shortage in the late 19th century, children became economic liabilities rather than assets. What was needed now was an *educated* labor force. So laws restricting child labor and making schooling compulsory were passed. Now adolescents spent their days in school, separated from the adult world. They came to be regarded as distinct from adults, and they began to develop their own "peer culture" as they spent more time with their friends.

The adolescent experience has continued to change during the 20th century (Elder, 1980). Indeed, Kenneth Keniston (1970) once argued that a new stage of the life span that he called "youth" came into being after World War II as adolescents began to attend college and graduate school in large numbers. The age of entry into the adult world was now postponed even longer than it had been with the introduction of compulsory secondary education. Youth—those individuals who pursue an advanced education instead of going to work after high school—found themselves in an ambiguous territory between adolescence and adulthood, struggling to establish their own identity as a group. This distinct identity became particularly clear in the late 1960s and early 1970s: the days of student protests against violations of civil rights and the war in Vietnam, the days of hippies, flower children, and "acid-heads." Youth today may not be hippies, but they continue to take quite some time to strike out on their own as adults. Clearly the experiences of individuals who are approximately 12 to 20 years of age have changed considerably over history.

A Changing Adulthood

How is adulthood today different from adulthood in past eras? For one thing, more people are living longer now. In ancient Rome, the average age of death was about 20 to 30; in the late 17th century, the average life lasted 35 to 40 years (Dublin & Lotka, 1936). These figures, which are *averages*, are low mainly because so many individuals died in infancy. In medieval times, for example, one, and sometimes two, out of three babies did not make it through the first year (Borstelmann, 1983). Still, relatively few residents of ancient Rome or medieval Europe could have told us much about the experience of being 65 or older.

The average life expectancy has continued to increase dramatically during this century. At the turn of the century, a newborn in the United States could expect to live 47 years; today the average life expectancy for a newborn is 75 years (Pifer & Bronte, 1986). Again, most of this lengthening of the average life span has been due to major drops in infant mortality; fewer people have died young. However, people who do make it to adulthood are also living longer because disease prevention and health care have improved.

During the 20th century, the makeup of the United States population has also changed significantly. In 1900 about 4% of the population was 65 and older; today the figure is nearly 12%. Meanwhile, the percentage of the population under age 16 fell from 35% in 1900 to 22% in the mid-1980s (Pifer & Bronte, 1986). And we have not seen anything yet! The census takers are now watching the baby boom generation—the huge generation of people born between the close of World War II in 1946 and 1964—move into middle age. By 2035, when most baby boomers will have retired from work, 20% of the U.S. population—1 of 5 Americans—is expected to be 65 or older (Pifer & Bronte, 1986). No wonder the news media are discussing the strains on society that an ever-aging population will exert. This "graying of America" is largely due to major declines in the birth rate; fewer children are being born, so a larger proportion of the population is old. The fact that more adults are enjoying more years of life has also contributed.

What impacts have these social changes had on the experience of adulthood? Very possibly they have caused our society to create a newly distinct period of life called *middle age*, marked in part by the empty nest—the period after the children have left home. In the 19th century, when fewer people lived to a ripe old age and when people had larger families, many adults never experienced this phase of family life (Hareven, 1986). Now people have fewer children, and middle-aged adults today spend whole decades without children in the house (Neugarten & Neugarten, 1986).

Similarly, concepts of old age have changed over the past century. In the 19th century, relatively few men lived past 65. Those who did survive continued to work, literally until they dropped. Now both men and women work outside the home and then retire at 65 or often earlier. Old age has come to mean the retirement phase of the life span, the time when people over 65, like adolescents, are given few meaningful roles in the labor force, even though many of them are healthy, active, and capable (Rosenmayr, 1985).

In sum, one's age—whether it is 7, 17, or 70—means something quite different in each different historical era. Quite possibly, our society will see fit to identify new periods of the life span in the future, and the experience of being 7, 17, or 70 may be quite different in the 21st century from what it is now. It is clear that our modern way of "carving up" the life span into age grades is not the only way in which it can be done.

Cultural Differences in Phases of the Life Span

Just as the life span has been viewed differently in different historical eras, each culture has its own way of viewing the life span and dividing it into socially meaningful periods or age grades. In industrialized Western societies, the life span is often visualized as a straight line extending from birth to death. In certain other cultures, however, the recognized phases of the life span include a period before birth as well as an afterlife (Fry, 1985). In still other cultures, the life span is pictured as a circle, so that those who die are "recycled" and born again (Fry, 1985). The Hindu concept of reincarnation illustrates this concept of the life span. So does the Inuit Eskimo belief that the indestructible names of the dead wait in the underworld until they can reenter the world as newborns bearing the same names (Guemple, 1983).

Different societies also have different ways of forming age grades with distinct statuses in society. Jennie Keith (1985) reports, for example, that the St. Lawrence Eskimo simply distinguish between boys and men (or girls and women). By contrast, the Arusha people of East Africa have *six* socially meaningful age strata of males: youths, junior warriors, senior warriors, junior elders, senior elders, and retired elders. On top of that, all of the adolescent boys who are circumcised in coming-of-age ceremonies during a given five-year period are recognized as a distinct social group. Some societies clearly distinguish more age grades—

Box 1.2
Cultural Differences in the Meaning of Old Age

In our society, old age is widely defined as the period of life from age 65 on—an entirely arbitrary definition. How might it be different to be 65 years old in another culture?

For one thing, a 65-year-old would not have much company in many societies of the world. Just as people live longer today than they did in past eras, life expectancies are far higher in modern industrialized societies than they are in more traditional societies. Kenneth Weiss (1981) notes that in many hunter-gatherer societies, only about 10% of the people live past 60. Infant mortality rates are still startlingly high in underdeveloped countries, and people can die at any age from diseases, starvation, animal bites, and so on. By contrast, 75 to 85% of people in industrialized Western nations make it to age 65 or beyond. It is only in modern societies that we have come to view old age as the time in life for dying.

In most cultures, "old" is not defined in years. Most societies sensibly define old age in terms of a loss of *functional capacity* (Keith, 1985). For instance, among the !Kung hunter-gatherers of central Africa, one becomes old when one is no longer bearing and raising children (Biesele & Howell, 1981). Not many adults in our society would appreciate that definition of old age! Yet many people here also adopt a functional definition of old age, for they refuse to define themselves as old until they *feel* old.

and distinguish them more sharply—than other societies do. As Box 1.2 illustrates, people of the same age living in different cultures may have quite different lives indeed.

If there is anything universal in all of this, it is perhaps the tendency of all societies, past and present, to use age in *some* manner as a basis for categorizing people and assigning them privileges and responsibilities. Otherwise, we have no choice but to view human development within its particular historical and social context. Age simply does not have the same meaning across times and places; instead, each society settles on its own definition of the nature of the life span, the phases within it, and the lot of those individuals who fall in each phase. Most significantly, human development in one historical and cultural context is likely to differ from human development in another era and setting. This fact must continually be borne in mind by those who study development.

WHAT IS THE SCIENCE OF LIFE-SPAN DEVELOPMENT?

If development consists of systematic changes from conception to death, the science of development consists of the study of those changes. Actually, we should speak of the *sciences* of development, for the study of life-span development is a multidisciplinary enterprise. Table 1.2 lists some of the most important of these disciplines and the kinds of questions that they commonly raise. To acknowledge the multidisciplinary nature of the science of life-span development, we use the term *developmentalist* to refer to any scholar—regardless of discipline—who seeks to understand human development.

In this book, we draw on work from each of these disciplines because we believe that the mysteries of human development will be unraveled only if scientists from each of these disciplines join forces. On the basis of this belief, some universities have established human development programs that explicitly attempt to bring the perspectives of different disciplines together and to forge new, truly multidisciplinary perspectives. Even so, some disciplines have traditionally been more actively involved in the study of development than others have. This reality is reflected in this book, which draws most heavily on the field of **developmental psychology**, the branch of psychology concerned with understanding changes in individuals and their relationships with other people over the life span. Nonetheless, we believe that the study of life-span development *should* be multidisciplinary, and that researchers in any particular discipline will benefit by incorporating into their thinking the valuable insights gained in other fields.

What are the goals of developmentalists? Three major goals stand out: the description, explanation, and optimization of human development (Baltes, Reese, & Lipsitt, 1980). To achieve the goal of *description*, developmentalists characterize the behavior of human beings of different ages and trace how their behavior changes with age. Developmentalists attempt to describe typical (*normal*) development, as well as *individual differences* between people of

Table 1.2 Some disciplines that are part of the multidisciplinary effort to study human development

DISCIPLINE	MAJOR FOCUS/SAMPLE QUESTIONS OF INTEREST
Anthropology	The effects of culture on development: How much do such cultural practices as methods of rearing children or of caring for the frail elderly differ across societies, and what are the implications? Are there aspects of development that are universal, or evident in all known cultures?
Biology	The growth and aging of cells and organs: How does one fertilized egg become a fully developed human being? How does the functioning of human organs change as we age?
History	Changes in human development over the centuries: What has it been like to be a child or an elderly person in different historical periods? How is the family of today different from the family of the 19th century? How do major historical events affect people's lives?
Home economics or human ecology	Development within its family and societal context: What is the nature of the family as an institution, and how do family relationships contribute to the individual's development and adjustment?
Psychology	The functioning of the individual: How do mental abilities, personality traits, and social skills typically change with age? How stable or how changeable are each individual's qualities, and why?
Sociology	The nature of society and the individual's relationship to society: What does society expect of us at different ages? What roles do we play in the larger social system as we progress through life? How are we affected by social institutions and changes in these institutions?

the same age and individual differences in how people change over time. For instance, some researchers have devoted years to describing what newborn babies are typically like: How well can they see? Can they learn from experience or remember toys they have seen before? What do they usually do as they lie in their cribs? These same developmentalists have also noticed that individual differences are evident right from birth: Some newborns are more alert, active, and responsive to people than others are. Describing development after birth involves asking how infants, children, adolescents, and adults of different ages typically vary in aspects of physical, cognitive, and psychosocial development—and, at each phase of life, how much one person's development differs from another's.

Description is the starting point in any science, but ultimately scientists want to achieve the goal of *explanation* or understanding. In seeking to explain development, researchers ask why humans develop as they typically do and why some individuals turn out differently than others do. Again, developmentalists are interested in both typical changes *within* individuals and differences in development *between* individuals. For instance, descriptive studies tell us that teenagers typically become better able to think about abstract concepts such as truth, beauty, and love than they were as children. Why does this change in cognitive capacity occur, and why is it that the minds of some adolescents develop so much more rapidly than the minds of others? To answer such questions, we must try to identify learning experiences that might stimulate abstract thinking and must also consider the possibility that maturational processes contribute to cognitive growth. Obviously it is easier to describe development than to explain how it comes about!

Finally, the *optimization* of human development is the most practical goal of the science of life-span development. How can human beings be helped to develop in positive directions? How can their capacities be enhanced, and how can any developmental problems they suffer be overcome? Among the many important practical discoveries made by developmentalists are

- Ways to stimulate the normal growth of fragile, premature babies who must be kept in intensive care units after birth
- Ways to help children with learning problems achieve more success in school
- Ways to help adults cope with life crises such as the death of a spouse

The goal of optimizing development often cannot be achieved, however, until researchers are able to describe development and explain how it comes about.

In summary, the scope of this book, like the scope of

the science of human development, is large. We want to show you what developmentalists from multiple disciplines have learned about human development from conception to death—about typical physical, cognitive, and psychosocial changes and about individual differences in these interrelated aspects of development. Moreover, we will not be content with describing development; we also want to explain it and to show ways to optimize it or channel it in positive directions.

HOW THE STUDY OF HUMAN DEVELOPMENT HAS EVOLVED

Just as human development itself has changed through the ages, attempts to understand development have evolved over time. How did the scientific study of human development come about? How did pioneering efforts pave the way for today's sophisticated studies of development from conception to death?

A Science Is Born

Actually, the history of the scientific study of human development is quite brief. Philosophers have long expressed their views on the nature of human beings and the proper methods of raising children, but it was not until the 19th century that anything resembling scientific investigations of the developmental process was undertaken. At long last, for example, a number of people began to carefully observe the growth and development of their own children and to publish their findings in the form of **baby biographies**. Perhaps the most influential of these baby biographers was Charles Darwin (1809–1882), who made daily records of his own son's development (Darwin, 1877). Darwin's curiosity about child development stemmed from his theory of evolution. Quite simply, he believed that young, untrained infants share many characteristics with their nonhuman ancestors and that observing child development might provide insights into the evolutionary history of the human species.

Baby biographies left much to be desired as works of science. Different baby biographers emphasized very different aspects of their children's behavior, so that different baby biographies were difficult to compare. Then, too, parents are not always entirely objective about their own children, and baby biographers like Charles Darwin may also have let their assumptions about the nature of development bias their observations so that they "found" what they were looking for. Finally, each baby biography was based on a single child—and often the child of a distinguished individual, at that. Conclusions based on a single case may not hold true for other children.

We can give Charles Darwin and other eminent baby biographers much credit for making human development a legitimate topic of study. Still, the man who is most often cited as the founder of developmental psychology is G. Stanley Hall. Well aware of the shortcomings of baby biographies, Hall set out in the late 19th century to collect more objective data on large samples of individuals. He developed a now all-too-familiar research tool, the **questionnaire**, to explore "the contents of children's minds" (Hall, 1891). By asking children questions about every conceivable topic, he discovered that children's understanding of the world grows rapidly during childhood and that the "logic" of young children is often not very logical at all.

Hall went on to write an influential book titled *Adolescence* (1904) that was the first to call attention to adolescence as a unique phase of the life span. Influenced by evolutionary theory, Hall drew parallels between adolescence and the turbulent period in history during which barbarism gave way to modern civilization. Adolescence, then, was a turbulent period of the life span, a time of emotional ups and downs and rapid changes, a time of what Hall called **storm and stress**. Thus it is G. Stanley Hall we have to thank for the notion—a largely inaccurate notion, as it turns out—that most teenagers are just short of emotionally disturbed. Finally, this remarkable pioneer turned his attention to the end of the life span in his book *Senescence* (1922). G. Stanley Hall, then, does deserve much credit for founding the scientific study of human development.

The Study of Human Development Today

G. Stanley Hall was interested in all phases of the life span. In fact, a few brave scholars as early as the 18th century argued that human development during any period of the life span should be viewed in the context of the whole life span (Baltes, 1983; Reinert, 1979). Unfortunately, the science of human development began to break up into age-group specialty areas during the 20th century. Some researchers focused on infant or child development, while others specialized in adolescence, and still others formed the specialization called **gerontology**, the study of aging and old age. (Almost no one specialized in development during early and middle adulthood; after all, people supposedly do not change during those years!) Students of infancy, adolescence, and old age each went about their own work and rarely communicated with one another. Only since the 1960s and 1970s has a true **life-span perspective** on human development emerged (Baltes, 1983, 1987).

A Life-Span Perspective on Human Development

Paul Baltes, Hayne Reese, and Lewis Lipsitt (1980) have laid out five assumptions that are part of the newly emerging life-span perspective on human development:

1. *Development is a lifelong process.* Today's life-span developmentalists have moved beyond the traditional notion that development occurs only from conception to adolescence and that all we do in adulthood is lose everything we gained early in life. One is never too old to be a developing person.
2. *Development must be viewed in historical context.* We have already encountered ample justification for this assumption about human development. Not only is our development different from that of people in past eras, but we are affected by societal changes in our own time: by historical events such as wars, technological breakthroughs such as the development of the home computer, and social movements such as the women's movement. Each generation develops in its own way, and each generation changes the world for generations that follow. This has been demonstrated vividly by Glen Elder (1974, 1979; Elder, Liker, & Cross, 1984) in his fascinating studies of the effects of the Great Depression of the 1930s on child development. This economic crisis had lasting negative effects on some, though by no means all, children, especially those whose fathers became less affectionate and less consistent in disciplining them. Such children displayed many behavior problems (especially boys), had low aspirations and poor records in school as adolescents, and often became men who had erratic careers and unstable marriages or women who were seen by their own children many years later as ill-tempered. Clearly we can be affected by the times in which we grow up.

The child is not the only developing person in this photo. Younger members of the family can contribute to the ongoing development of their aging relatives.

3. *Development can take multiple directions.* Traditionally, developmental changes were often regarded as universal changes leading toward some "mature" form of functioning, as when predictable changes in children's thinking ultimately put them in a position to solve complex problems the way adults do. But as we have seen, today's developmentalists recognize that each person experiences both systematic gains and systematic losses throughout life. Moreover, some individuals can be gaining capacities while others of the same age are losing those same capacities, as when one older person seems to become more knowledgeable every day while another is becoming more and more forgetful.

Indeed, the differences among us seem to become wider and wider as we progress through the life span, because different people travel along different developmental paths (Baltes, Reese, & Lipsitt, 1980). Consider one rather frivolous example. As we will see in Chapter 5, all normal newborn babies behave in the very same way if you stroke the soles of their feet: Their toes automatically fan out in what is called the *Babinski reflex*. Now we ask you, what will happen if you stroke the feet of several 20-year-olds? There's no telling! Depending on the person, you may get a giggle, a bit of heavy breathing, or a swift kick. We suspect that the responses of 70-year-olds would be even more diverse, simply because each has been moving along his or her unique developmental path for many years. Because infants are only beginning to become different from one another, knowing an infant's age tells us a great deal about what that individual is like. By contrast, knowing that an adult is 70 years old may tell us almost nothing about how that individual will behave.

4. *Development is multiply influenced.* Some early developmental scholars believed development is almost entirely due to biologically programmed maturational processes—that our human genes dictate exactly how we will unfold from conception on. Other scholars believed just as strongly that how we develop is almost entirely the result of the unique experiences we have in life. Today's life-span developmentalists believe that both maturation and learning contribute to development. They maintain that humans develop through ongoing interactions between changing individuals and their changing world and that *a wide range of factors*, both inside and outside the person, affect development.

5. *Development in any one period of life can best be understood in the context of the whole life span.* Until quite recently, when the life-span perspective on human development emerged, developmentalists tended to specialize in studying one age group or another and were often unfamiliar with what was being learned about other portions of the life span. Although many developmentalists still specialize in a particular age group, they are now more inclined to think about their work in relation to that of other age specialists. Suppose you were interested in the question of how high school and college students go about deciding what they want to be in life. Wouldn't it be useful to know how children form ideas about their strengths and weaknesses, how they learn about different adult careers or society's expectations about "proper" vocations for men and women? After all, it seems likely that the choices adolescents make are related to their earlier experiences. And shouldn't we also know something about vocational development during adulthood? Do adults actually carry through with the vocational plans that they made as adolescents, or do they reformulate their life goals later on? Our understanding of adolescent development is bound to be richer if we concern ourselves with what led up to it and where it is leading.

In summary, by adopting a life-span perspective on human development in this book, we will be assuming that development (1) occurs throughout the life span rather than just in childhood, (2) is very much affected by the historical and cultural context in which it occurs, (3) can take many different directions, positive or negative, in different individuals or even in a single individual, (4) is influenced by many causal factors interacting with one another, and (5) can best be understood if changes during one period of life are viewed in relation to changes during other periods of life. Now, how can we gain understanding of this complex phenomenon called life-span development?

THE SCIENTIFIC METHOD

How *can* we gain knowledge of human development? The authors of this book are committed to the **scientific method** as the means of understanding development. There is nothing mysterious about the scientific method. It is really more of an *attitude* than a method: a belief that investigators should allow their systematic observations (or *data*) to determine the merits of their thinking. For example, for every "expert" who believes that psychological differences between males and females are largely biological in origin, there is likely to be another expert who just as firmly insists that the sexes differ because they are raised differently. Whom shall we believe? It is in the spirit of the scientific method to believe the data—for example, research findings regarding the effects of sexist and nonsexist learning experiences on the interests, activities, and personality traits of girls and boys. The scientist values conclusions that are based on factual evidence and is willing to abandon pet theories if data contradict them. Ultimately, then, the scientific method can protect the scientific community and society at large from flawed or erroneous ideas, even when those ideas are generated by great minds or "authorities."

As a particular method of acquiring knowledge, the scientific method involves a process of generating ideas and testing them by making observations. Often, casual observations provide the starting point for a scientist. Sigmund Freud, for example, carefully observed the psychologically disturbed adults whom he treated, attempting to gain insights into the nature and causes of their problems. From these observations, he concluded that many psychological problems in adulthood stem from experiences in early childhood; ultimately, Freud formulated his *psychoanalytic theory* of development. Theories are not the exclusive possession of scientists—everyone has theories! If someone were to ask you why males and females seem so similar at birth but so very different as adults, you would undoubtedly have something to say about the issue that reflects your own underlying theory of the origins of gender differences. So a **theory** is really nothing more than a set of concepts and propositions intended to describe and explain some aspect of experience.

How do scientists decide whether a theory is valid? By testing it. Theories generate specific predictions, or **hypotheses**, about what will hold true if we observe a phenomenon that interests us. Suppose, for example, that a theory states that psychological differences between the sexes are largely due to the fact that parents treat boys and girls differently. Based on this theory, a researcher might hypothesize that if parents grant boys and girls much the same freedoms, the two sexes will be similarly independent, whereas if parents allow boys to do many things that they will not permit girls to do, boys will be more independent than girls. What if the study designed to test this hypothesis indicates that boys are more independent than girls no matter how their parents treat them? Then the hypothesis would be disconfirmed by the research data, and the researcher would want to rethink this theory of sex-linked differences. If other hypotheses based on this theory were also inconsistent with the facts, the theory would have to be significantly revised or abandoned entirely. Researchers would then have to devise other theories to explain differences between the sexes and then test hypotheses based on those theories by collecting data.

This, then, is the heart of the scientific method—a persistent effort to put ideas to the test, to keep ideas that carefully gathered facts support, and to abandon those that carefully gathered facts contradict. Theories generate hypotheses that are tested through observation of behavior, and new observations of behavior indicate which theories are worth keeping (see Figure 1.1). Now let us look at the more specific ways in which researchers study human development—at the types of data they collect, the ways in which they seek to describe how human beings change with age, and the ways in which they try to explain developmental changes.

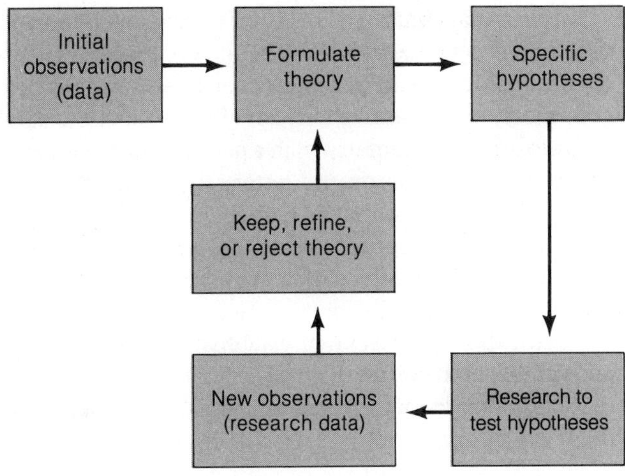

Figure 1.1 The scientific method in action.

MEASURING BEHAVIOR: DATA COLLECTION TECHNIQUES

No matter what aspect of human development we are interested in—whether it is the formation of bonds between infants and their parents, the origins of adolescent drug use, or the changes in communication that occur over time in a marriage—we must find a way to measure what interests us. Scientists insist that any measure should have two important qualities: **reliability** and **validity**. A measure is *reliable* if it yields consistent information from occasion to occasion. For example, if a personality test is supposed to measure the extent to which adults are assertive, the test score an individual receives one week should be similar to the test score he or she receives the next week rather than wildly different. Similarly, if two observers watch several adults in a situation in which they have the opportunity to act assertively toward a pushy salesperson, the two observers' assessments of each adult's degree of assertiveness should be consistent (that is, in agreement). If the observations of two or more observers or raters agree, or if the measurement of a trait can be made consistently from one testing to another shortly thereafter, the measure being used is reliable.

A measure is *valid* if it measures what it is supposed to measure. A personality scale intended to measure assertiveness could be very reliable or consistent and yet be a poor measure of assertiveness. For example, it could actually measure the extent to which a person wants to create a favorable impression on the tester rather than that person's true tendency to act assertively in everyday life. Researchers must demonstrate that they are actually assessing the trait they believe they are assessing rather than some other trait.

With the importance of establishing the reliability and validity of measures in mind, let us look at some of the quite different ways in which aspects of human development can be measured.

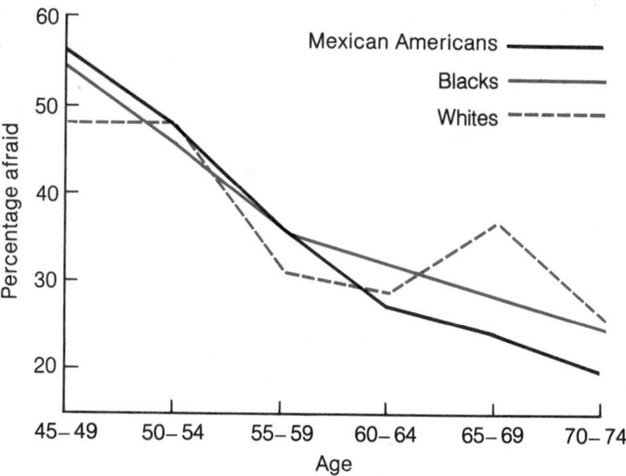

Figure 1.2 Percentage of adults interviewed who say they are "very afraid" and "somewhat afraid" of death. (From Bengtson, Cuellar, & Ragan, 1977)

Interviews and Questionnaires

Collecting information through an *interview* involves orally asking people questions about some aspect of their lives or psychological qualities. Collecting data via a *questionnaire* simply involves putting questions on paper and asking people to respond to them in writing. Both approaches can be used to inquire about any number of topics. Of course, interviews cannot be conducted with very young children who cannot understand or use speech very well, and questionnaires cannot be administered to children or adults who cannot read.

Consider this question asked in interviews with middle-aged and elderly adults in Los Angeles: "How afraid are you of death? Would you say you are: not at all afraid?/somewhat afraid?/or very afraid?" Vern Bengtson, Jose Cuellar, and Pauline Ragan (1977) used this and other questions to find out how much adults of different ages and ethnic groups fear death. Figure 1.2 shows what percentages of respondents reported that they were at least somewhat fearful of death. In this study, the interview used was a structured or *standardized* one; that is, all adults were asked exactly the same questions in the same order. The purpose of standardizing questions is to treat each person alike so that the responses of different people can be compared.

Other interviews are quite unstructured: The interviewer may start with a guiding set of questions but is free to pursue answers to questions with individually tailored follow-up questions and may, as a result, end up asking quite different questions of one person than of another person. Bengtson and his colleagues (1977) supplemented their standardized interviews about attitudes toward death by conducting unstandardized interviews with a sample of Mexican-American adults. These more freewheeling interviews suggested that many older adults had worked through their fears of death as they coped with difficult life events over the years, perhaps explaining why they seemed to face the prospect of death more calmly than many middle-aged respondents did. Unstructured interviews can often provide additional insights into each person's thinking that might be missed in a standardized interview. The disadvantage of unstructured interviews is that the responses of different individuals cannot as readily be compared.

Interviews and questionnaires are widely used to study human development and can often provide great insight into the thoughts, emotions, attitudes, and life circumstances of children and adults. Yet even the most well-designed and standardized interviews and questionnaires have their shortcomings. First, investigators must hope that the answers they receive are honest and accurate and that respondents are not just trying to present themselves in a positive or socially desirable light. For example, might many adults be reluctant to admit to a strange interviewer that they are highly anxious about dying? Second, investigators must be careful to ensure that children or adults of different ages and backgrounds interpret questions in the same way. If young children, for example, do not fully understand the questions asked of them, any differences between the responses of younger and older children might reflect differences in verbal understanding rather than real age differences in feelings, thoughts, and behaviors.

Psychological Tests

Who in our society is not familiar with tests? A *psychological test* is a set of questions or tasks used to determine a person's abilities, aptitudes, or personality traits. Among the most familiar tests are standardized tests of intelligence (IQ tests). Everything about these tests is standardized: the instructions the examiner must follow, the task materials used, and the methods of scoring answers. They are reasonably reliable and valid, and they allow testers to determine how any individual's intellectual performance compares to that of children or adults of the same age. We will be examining developmental changes in performance on these IQ tests in Chapter 9, where we explore such issues as whether an intelligent child is likely to grow up to be an intelligent and successful adult. In Chapter 10 we will see what personality tests have revealed about whether people's personalities change or remain the same over the years.

Psychological tests have their critics. For example, some feel that many tests are not actually valid. Some believe that test scores are too often used to make critical decisions about people's lives (for example, to place schoolchildren in low- or high-ability groups or to decide which job applicants to hire). Nonetheless, tests provide one useful source of information about the development of many abilities and traits.

Behavioral Observation

Many researchers prefer to study people's behavior directly rather than to ask them questions about it. **Naturalistic observation** is observing people in their common, everyday (that is, natural) surroundings. Ongoing behavior is observed in homes, schools, playgrounds, workplaces, nursing homes, or wherever people are going about their lives. Box 1.3 describes a study that involved naturalistic observation in a nursery school. Alternatively, behavioral (but not naturalistic) observations can be made in specially arranged settings (as when a researcher observes the teaching styles that parents use in a laboratory testing room to teach their children an unfamiliar game).

Naturalistic observation has been used more often to study child development than to study adult development. This is partly because infants and young children often cannot be studied through techniques that demand verbal skills, and partly because researchers can usually gain access to the settings in which children are found. The greatest advantage of naturalistic observation is that only it can tell us what children or adults actually do in everyday life (Willems & Alexander, 1982).

Yet naturalistic observation also has its limitations. First, some behaviors (for example, heroic efforts to help other people) occur too infrequently and unexpectedly to be observed in this manner. Second, many events are usually happening at the same time in a natural setting, and any of them may be affecting people's behavior. This makes it difficult to pinpoint the causes of the behavior or of any developmental trends in the behavior. Finally, the mere presence of an observer can sometimes make people behave differently than they otherwise would. Children may "ham it up" when they have an audience; parents may be on their best behavior. For this reason, researchers sometimes videotape the proceedings from a hidden location or spend time in the setting before they collect their "real" data so that the individuals they are observing become used to their presence and do not simply "perform" for them.

Case Studies

Any or all of the data collection methods we have described—interviews or questionnaires, tests, and behavioral observations—can be used to compile a detailed picture of a single individual's development through the **case study** method. The early baby biographies were a form of case study, and Sigmund Freud wrote many fascinating case studies of his patients. Using the case study approach, a psychologist might collect many types of information about a single individual such as family background, socioeconomic status, education and work history, health record, significant life events, and performance on psychological tests. Interviews with the individual are often the main source of data, but sometimes testing and naturalistic observation are also done. The case study approach has much to contribute to our understanding of the development of specific individuals. However, case studies have some of the same limitations that the early baby biographies had. In particular, we cannot always be confident that what we learn about specific individuals will apply to people in general.

Box 1.3
Naturalistic Observation in the Nursery School

Some years ago, Rosalind Charlesworth and Willard Hartup (1967) used the technique of naturalistic observation to find out whether nursery school children become more pleasant to one another as they grow older. These researchers first had to decide what behaviors were of interest to them and then had to develop and test out their observation scheme. They focused on instances in which children dispensed "positive social reinforcement" to each other. Examples of positive social reinforcement were specified in advance and included such behaviors as showing affection or approval, cooperating, sharing, and giving another child objects such as toys or snacks. Before the actual data were collected, different observers watched the same children to see if they could agree that instances of positive social reinforcement had occurred; that is, they established that their observational measure of positive social reinforcement was reliable. Observers also spent time learning the children's names and allowng these preschoolers to become accustomed to their presence. Then, over a five-week period, they systematically observed each child for a set amount of time.

Through this methodology, Charlesworth and Hartup were able to establish several important facts about social life in the nursery school. First, 4-year-olds gave more social reinforcers to peers than 3-year-olds did, suggesting that children become more responsive to peers as they grow older. Moreover, boys generally reinforced boys and girls reinforced girls; children this young already favored agemates of their own sex. Finally, children who gave the most social reinforcers got the most, and children who infrequently reinforced their peers received few niceties in return. In other words, these young children were already involved in the kinds of reciprocal, give-and-take exchanges that are common among adults. Naturalistic studies of this sort provide rich information about development in real-life settings, even if they typically cannot tell us *why* the observed behavior occurs.

These, then, are the most commonly used techniques of collecting data about human development. Since each method has its limitations, our knowledge is advanced the most when *multiple* methods are used to study the same aspect of human development and these different methods lead to the same conclusions.

DESCRIBING DEVELOPMENT: DEVELOPMENTAL RESEARCH DESIGNS

Assuming that developmental researchers have figured out what they want to measure and how they want to measure it, they can turn their attention to the goal of describing developmental changes. Two developmental research designs have been relied on extensively to achieve this descriptive goal: the cross-sectional design and the longitudinal design. A third design, the sequential study, has come into use in an attempt to overcome the limitations of the other two techniques. Let's first define the original two approaches and then explore their strengths and weaknesses.

The Cross-Sectional and Longitudinal Designs in Brief

In a **cross-sectional design**, the performances of different age groups of people are compared. A researcher interested in the development of language might record sentences spoken by a group of 2-year-olds, a group of 3-year-olds, and a group of 4-year-olds; calculate the average length of the sentences spoken by each age group; and compare these averages to describe how the sentences of children from age 2 to age 4 differ. A cross-sectional study of memory abilities in adulthood might use a memory test to compare the performance of adults in their 20s with that of adults in their 60s. In each case, what we learn about are *age differences*; from the differences in the performance of groups of different ages, we then attempt to draw conclusions about how performance changes with age.

In a **longitudinal design**, the performance of one group of individuals is assessed repeatedly over time. The language development study just described would be longitudinal rather than cross-sectional if we identified a group of 2-year-olds, measured the lengths of their sentences, waited a year until they were age 3 and measured the lengths of their sentences again, and did the same thing a year later when they were age 4. In any longitudinal study, whether it covers only 2 years or 20 or 50 years, the same individuals are studied *as they develop*. Thus the longitudinal design provides information about *age changes* rather than age differences.

Now, what difference does it make whether we choose the cross-sectional or the longitudinal design to describe development in some domain? Suppose that we were interested in adults' attitudes regarding the roles of men and women. How do attitudes about gender roles typically change over the adult years? Suppose we have a gender-role attitudes questionnaire that allows us to characterize any adult as having traditional attitudes about gender roles or as having liberated attitudes that emphasize equality of the two sexes. Suppose that in 1985 we conducted a cross-sectional study comparing the gender-role attitudes of adults 20, 40, and 60 years old. We were also clever enough to start a longitudinal study way back in 1945 with a group of 20-year-old men and women. We gave them the gender-role questionnaire at that time and again in 1965 when they were 40. We gave it a third time in 1985 when they were 60. Figure 1.3 outlines these two alternative designs, and Figure 1.4 portrays hypothetical age trends that they might generate.

What is going on here? The cross-sectional study seems to be indicating that, as people get older, their attitudes about gender roles become more traditional or conservative. The longitudinal study is suggesting precisely the opposite conclusion: As people get older, their attitudes about gender roles become more liberated. What are we to conclude about the development of gender-role attitudes? Why do the two studies yield totally different findings?

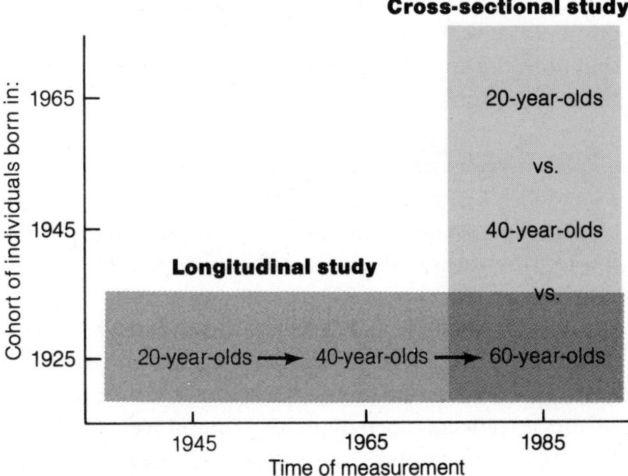

Figure 1.3 Cross-sectional and longitudinal studies of development from age 20 to age 60.

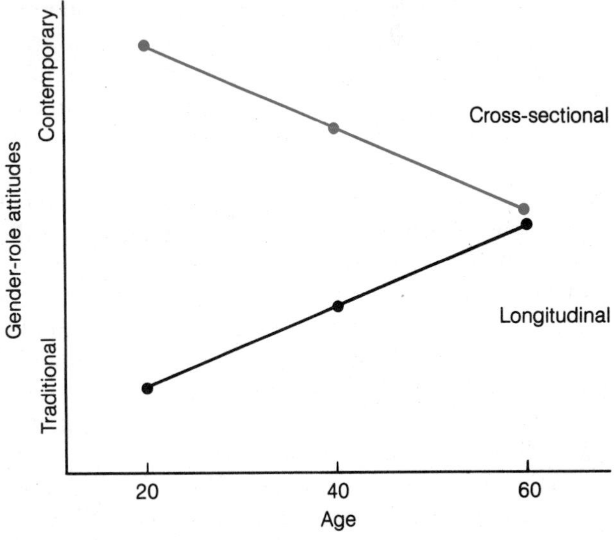

Figure 1.4 Conflicting findings of hypothetical cross-sectional and longitudinal studies of gender-role attitudes.

Age, Cohort, and Time of Measurement

To unravel the mystery we have posed, we must realize that the findings of developmental studies can actually be influenced by three factors: age, cohort, and time of measurement. *Age* is simple enough; after all, the whole purpose of our research is to describe how attitudes about gender roles change as a function of age during adulthood. The term **cohort** means a group of people born at the same time: either in the same year or within a specified, limited span of years. A cohort, in other words, consists of people born in a specified, limited span of years. People who are 40 years old today are not only older than 20-year-olds today, but they belong to a different cohort or generation. Finally, **time of measurement** is involved in any developmental study. Data are collected at some point (or points) in history, and therefore findings can be affected by the historical events and social climate of the times, whether they are the 1940s or 1980s. Once we are aware that age, cohort, and time of measurement can all influence developmental research findings, we are ready to appreciate that both the cross-sectional and the longitudinal designs have their problems.

Strengths and Weaknesses of the Cross-Sectional Design

In our cross-sectional study, the three age groups studied represent three different cohorts of people. The 60-year-olds were born in 1925, the 40-year-olds in 1945, and the 20-year-olds in 1965. Certainly these three groups had different formative experiences. The two older groups grew up in eras when traditional attitudes about the roles of the sexes were strongly held: Women were to stay at home and raise families, and men were to head the household and bring home the bacon. Perhaps, then, older adults' responses to the questionnaire in 1985 simply reflected the traditional views they learned early in life. The 20-year-olds are a different cohort entirely; they grew up when the women's movement was gaining momentum and when women were entering the labor force in huge numbers. Perhaps this led them to have relatively liberated attitudes. In short, the three age groups compared here not only differ in age but are members of different cohorts who had different growing-up experiences. The cross-sectional study *does* tell us how people of different ages differ, and this can be useful information. But the cross-sectional technique does not necessarily tell us how people develop *as a function of age.* Do 60-year-olds have more conservative gender-role attitudes than 20-year-olds do because they are older, or because they are members of a different cohort raised in a more traditional historical period? We cannot tell. *The effects of age and the effects of cohort differences are hopelessly tangled.*

This, then, is the central problem in cross-sectional designs, and it is a very real problem in studies designed to describe how adults develop over the years. As we shall see in Chapter 9, cross-sectional studies of performance on intelligence tests once appeared to indicate that we lose our intellectual faculties starting in middle age and perform quite poorly indeed in old age. Yet the older people who were being compared with younger adults in these studies were part of a cohort that grew up in a time when many people stopped their schooling before completing high school. Did these older people lose intellectual abilities in old age? Or did they perhaps have relatively low intellectual abilities throughout their lives? Suppose we do a cross-sectional study in which we ask people to rate dances on a scale of 1 to 10 and find that today's 40-year-olds rate the Twist higher than 20-year-olds do. Would we really want to conclude that as people get older they become fonder and fonder of the Twist? What we have discovered is a cohort effect, not a true developmental trend.

Despite this central problem, the cross-sectional design is still the design most often used by developmentalists. Why? Because it has the great advantage of being quick and easy; we can go out this year, sample individuals of different ages, and be done with it. Moreover, this design is likely to yield valid conclusions if there is little reason to believe that the cohorts studied have had widely different growing-up experiences. For example, we can compare children aged 3 and those aged 4 feeling confident that the world did not change in any major way during the year between the births of these two cohorts. It is when researchers attempt to make inferences about development over the span of many years that cohort effects are a serious problem.

The second major limitation of the cross-sectional design is this: It tells us nothing about the development of *individuals* because each person is observed at only one point in time. We can compare the average performances of the different age groups studied, but we do not watch a single person actually develop. We cannot, for example, see whether different people show divergent patterns of change in their gender-role attitudes over time, or if individuals who are especially liberated in their attitudes as 20-year-olds are later among the most liberated of the 60-year-olds. To address issues like these, we need longitudinal research.

Strengths and Weaknesses of the Longitudinal Design

At this point, the longitudinal design looks pretty wonderful. After all, it actually traces changes in individuals as they develop. It can tell us whether most people change in the same direction or whether different individuals show clearly different developmental paths. It can indicate whether traits remain stable over time so that the bright or aggressive or dependent young person retains those same traits in later life. And it can tell us whether experiences early in life predict traits and behaviors later in life. The cross-sectional design can do none of this.

What, then, are the limitations of the longitudinal design? Let's return to our longitudinal study of gender-role attitudes in which adults were first assessed at age 20 and then reassessed at age 40 and age 60. This study centers on *one cohort* of individuals: people who were 20 years old in 1945 (and therefore were members of the 1925 birth cohort). These people were raised in a particular historical context and then experienced changes in their social environment as they aged. Thus we must focus attention on the effects of *time of measurement* on the gender-role attitudes they expressed.

In 1945, these adults' responses were undoubtedly influenced by the prevailing traditional views of that time. By the time they were interviewed in 1985, as 60-year-olds, the times had changed immensely because of the women's movement and other social changes. Why, then, were their responses in 1985 more liberal than their responses in 1945? Perhaps it is not because people's gender-role attitudes generally become more liberal as they get older but only because changes in society from one time of measurement to the next affected the people we studied. Perhaps we would obtain entirely different "developmental" trends if we did this longitudinal study in an era in which sexism suddenly became the rage again!

In the longitudinal study, then, *the effects of age and the effects of time of measurement are tangled.* We cannot tell for sure in longitudinal research whether the age-related changes observed are true developmental trends or reflect historical events occurring between times of measurement or affecting responses at a particular time of assessment. Any cohort chosen for study will experience a different set of historical events over their lives than earlier or later generations experience. Thus we may not be able to generalize what we find for one cohort to people in general.

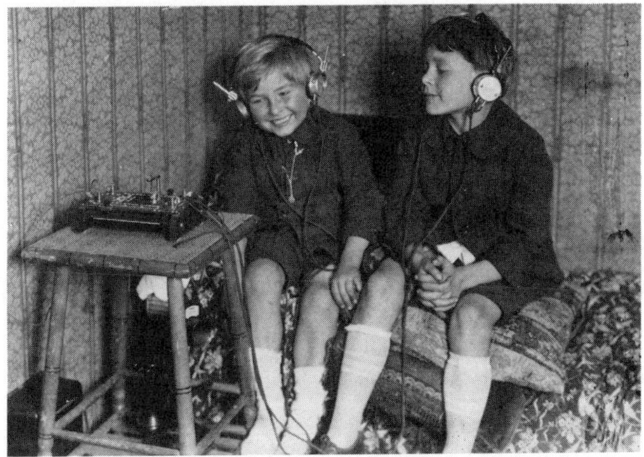

Children growing up in the 1930s had very different kinds of experiences from those of today's youth. Cross-generational changes in the environment may limit the results of a longitudinal study to the individuals who were growing up while the research was in progress.

This entanglement of age and time of measurement has been found to affect conclusions drawn from longitudinal studies of changes in intellectual performance over the adult years, as we will see in Chapter 9. As it turns out, members of recent cohorts who are repeatedly given IQ tests as they get older seem to retain their intellectual abilities longer than do members of earlier cohorts, perhaps because more recent cohorts are healthier and better educated (Schaie, 1983). Thus different conclusions can emerge from longitudinal studies depending on which cohort is studied.

There are still other disadvantages of the longitudinal design. One is fairly obvious: This approach is not at all easy; it is costly and time-consuming, particularly if it is used to trace development over a long span of time and at many points in time. Developmentalists are no lazier than most people, but when they simply do not have the resources to undertake a major longitudinal study, they sometimes rely on the far easier cross-sectional method. Second, because knowledge of human development is constantly changing, questions that seemed very exciting when a study was launched may seem rather trivial by the time the project ends, or researchers might wish that they had measured something that they did not originally anticipate would be important. Third, participants drop out of long-term studies; they move, or lose interest or, in studies of aging, die during the course of the study. The result is a smaller and less representative sample. For example, the aging adults in a longitudinal study of intellectual performance who die during the study are likely to be those in poor health. Final conclusions will then be based on an especially healthy (and perhaps especially mentally alert) group of survivors, people who are not typical of old people in general. Finally, researchers must be on guard for the effects that repeated testing may have on people. Sometimes, for example, simply taking a test improves performance on that test the next time around, or people remember what they said in one interview and try to make their answers on a second interview consistent with what they said previously.

Are both the cross-sectional and longitudinal designs hopelessly flawed, then? That would be overstating their weaknesses. As we have noted, the cross-sectional design is still very efficient and useful, especially when the cohorts studied are not widely different in age and formative experiences. Moreover, longitudinal studies are extremely valuable for what they can reveal about the actual changes in performance that occur as individuals get older—even though it must be recognized that the cohort studied may not develop in precisely the same way that an earlier or later cohort does. However, in an attempt to overcome the limitations of both cross-sectional and longitudinal designs, developmentalists have devised a new and more powerful method of describing developmental change: the sequential design.

Sequential Designs: The Best of Both Worlds

Sequential designs combine the cross-sectional approach and the longitudinal approach in a single study (Schaie, 1965, 1986). How might we conduct such a study to measure changes in attitudes about gender roles that occur as adults grow older? We might begin in 1945 with a sample of 20-year-olds (the 1925 birth cohort) and reassess these people's attitudes when they are 40 (in 1965) and 60 (in 1985). In 1965, we might launch a second longitudinal study with a sample of 20-year-olds (the 1945 cohort) and then reassess them every 20 years (in 1985 and 2005). Notice that there are actually *two* longitudinal studies here, each with a different cohort of people. Notice too that cross-sectional comparisons are also involved in this design; for instance, in 1965, we can compare the responses of 20-year-olds and 40-year-olds.

Now consider the three very different patterns of hypothetical findings displayed in Figure 1.5. In part A, the two cohorts studied (the 1925 birth cohort and the 1945 birth cohort) show almost identical patterns of change in their gender-role attitudes over the adult years. These data would suggest that adults, regardless of when they were born, show the same age-related changes; we seem to have uncovered a generalizable developmental trend. In part B of Figure 1.5, we see a different pattern of data—one that serves as an example of cohort effects in developmental research. Perhaps because of their differing growing-up experiences, individuals born in 1925 are considerably more

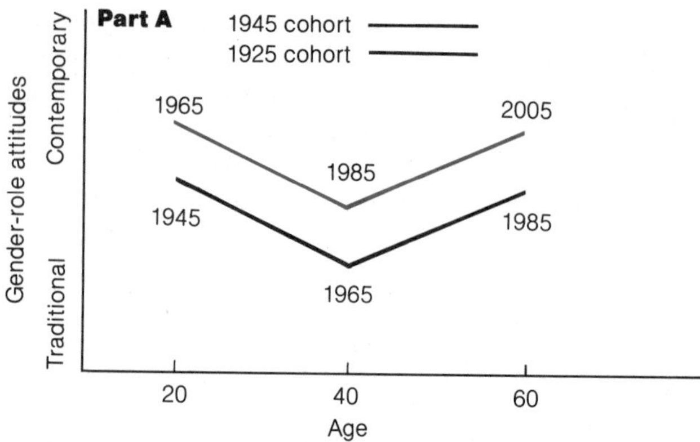

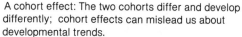

A generalizable age effect: Two cohorts develop similarly.

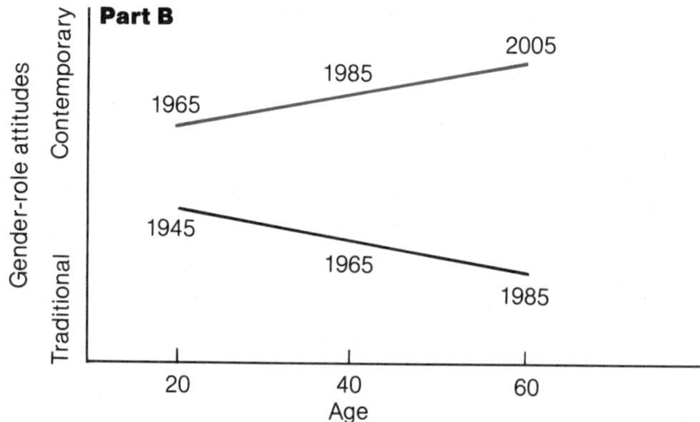

A cohort effect: The two cohorts differ and develop differently; cohort effects can mislead us about developmental trends.

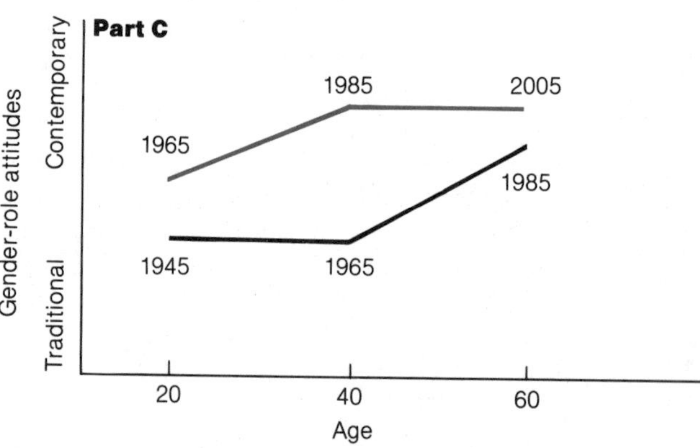

A time of measurement effect: Both cohorts are changed by historical events between the 1965 and 1985 times of measurement.

Figure 1.5 Hypothetical results of a sequential design.

conservative about gender roles than individuals born in 1945. Moreover, the two cohorts show divergent patterns of change over the years. In this case, then, attitudes about gender roles seem to be affected more by when a person was born than by how old that person is. Cohort effects like these are a nuisance when researchers are trying to identify basic developmental changes that everyone might experience. However, cohort effects are interesting in their own right, for they show that we are partly the products of the times in which we develop.

Finally, part C of Figure 1.5 shows still another possible pattern of results. Here *both* groups shift toward more liberal gender-role attitudes between 1965 and 1985. This shift appears to be a time-of-measurement effect. It does not seem to matter whether adults were 20 in 1965 or 40 in 1965; either way, their attitudes apparently became more liberated in response to social changes occurring between 1965 and 1985. It turns out that the trends portrayed in part C are not just hypothetical; it has been found that both college students and their parents adopted more liberated attitudes about women's roles during the 1970s (Helmreich, Spence, & Gibson, 1982).

This particular design is a very simple example of the sequential research strategy of combining the cross-sectional and longitudinal approaches (see Table 1.3 for a summary of these basic designs). We will encounter a much more complex sequential design in Chapter 9. It was used to study changes in intellectual performance during adulthood and involved assessing several different cohorts of adults on several occasions. The great advantage of sophisticated sequential designs is that they can begin to tell us:

Which age-related trends actually reflect how most people can be expected to develop over time

Which trends reflect instead the operation of cohort effects and suggest that each generation is affected by its distinct growing-up experiences

Which trends reflect the operation of "time-of-measurement" effects and imply that major historical events change people regardless of their age

Table 1.3 Summary of the cross-sectional, longitudinal, and sequential development designs

	CROSS-SECTIONAL METHOD	LONGITUDINAL METHOD	SEQUENTIAL METHOD
PROCEDURE	Observe people of different ages (or cohorts) at one point in time	Observe people of one age group repeatedly over time	Combine cross-sectional and longitudinal approaches; observe different cohorts on multiple occasions
INFORMATION GAINED	Describes age differences	Describes age changes	Describes age differences *and* age changes
ADVANTAGES	Demonstrates age differences in behavior; hints at developmental trends Takes little time to conduct; is inexpensive	Actually indicates how individuals are alike and different in the way they change over time Can reveal links between early behavior or experiences and later behavior	Helps separate the effects of age, cohort, and time of measurement Indicates whether developmental changes experienced by one generation or cohort are similar to those experienced by other cohorts
DISADVANTAGES	Age trends may reflect extraneous differences between cohorts rather than true developmental change Provides no information about change over time in individuals	Age trends may reflect historical (time-of-measurement) effects during the study rather than true developmental change Relatively time-consuming and expensive Measures devised may later prove inadequate Participants drop out Participants can be affected by repeated testing	Often complex and time-consuming Despite being the strongest method, may still leave questions about whether a developmental change is generalizable

In short, sequential designs can at least begin to untangle the effects of age, cohort, and time of measurement and to indicate which age trends are truly developmental in nature. Moreover, they are beginning to reveal that development is very much affected by the times in which people grow up and live (Schaie, 1986).

Cross-sectional, longitudinal, and sequential studies all contribute to our understanding of how people grow and change over time. We can be especially confident of conclusions when the results of different kinds of studies agree. And yet researchers are not content to describe development; they also attempt to achieve their goal of *explaining* it. Age and age differences, in themselves, do not explain a thing about development. We do not change *because* we get older; instead, we change because we are affected by maturational processes and learning experiences that occur as we get older. So how can researchers identify the factors responsible for developmental change?

EXPLAINING DEVELOPMENT: EXPERIMENTAL AND CORRELATIONAL METHODS

The most powerful method for explaining behavior or identifying the causes of developmental changes in behavior is the experiment. When experiments cannot be conducted, other research techniques may suggest answers to important "why" questions.

The Experimental Method

An **experiment** is a research technique in which the investigator manipulates or alters some aspect of people's environment in order to see what effect this has on their behavior. Let's examine an experiment conducted by Brian Coates and Willard Hartup (1969) to determine why preschoolers have more difficulty than older children do in learning new responses by observing someone else perform them. Coates and Hartup might have hypothesized that this age difference is due to the maturational changes in the brain or to the effects of schooling, but instead they hypothesized that young children do poorly because they do not spontaneously *describe* what they are watching as they watch it. Older children may do this kind of talking to themselves and consequently remember more of what they have seen. But what if preschoolers were prompted to use words to describe what they were watching? Would they then learn as much as older children?

To find out, Coates and Hartup "manipulated" the nature of the learning situation that children experienced. All children watched a short film in which an adult model displayed 20 novel behaviors, such as shooting at a tower of blocks with a pop gun, throwing a beanbag between his legs, and lassoing an inflatable toy with a Hula Hoop. Half the children were instructed to describe the model's actions as they watched the film; they were in the *induced-verbalization* condition of the experiment. The rest of the children (those in the *passive-observation* condition) were not given this special instruction; they simply watched the film and served as the *control group* in the experiment. These two treatments constitute the **independent variable** in the experiment. A *variable* is *any* quality that can vary or take on different values. Age, height, hair color, and score on an intelligence test are variables, and so is what we might call the type of treatment condition in this experiment (that is, instructions to describe what was seen versus no such instructions). The independent variable in any experiment is the aspect of the environment that the experimenter deliberately changes or manipulates in order to see what effect it has on behavior.

The whole idea of an experiment is to see whether the different treatments that form the independent variable have differing effects on the behavior being studied: the **dependent variable** in the experiment. The dependent variable that Coates and Hartup chose was the number of responses displayed by the adult model that a child could reproduce after viewing the film. The number of responses reproduced by a child could range from none to all 20 of them; the higher the number, the greater the amount of learning that had taken place. So we see that in an experiment the researcher manipulates an independent variable (here, instruction versus no instruction to describe what was seen) to see what effect this has on the dependent variable (amount of information learned).

Actually, Coates and Hartup performed a particular kind of experiment called an **age by treatment experiment**, one that allows researchers to determine if an experimental treatment has a different effect on one age group than it has on another. They tested two age groups: children aged 4 to 5 and children aged 7 to 8. In other words,

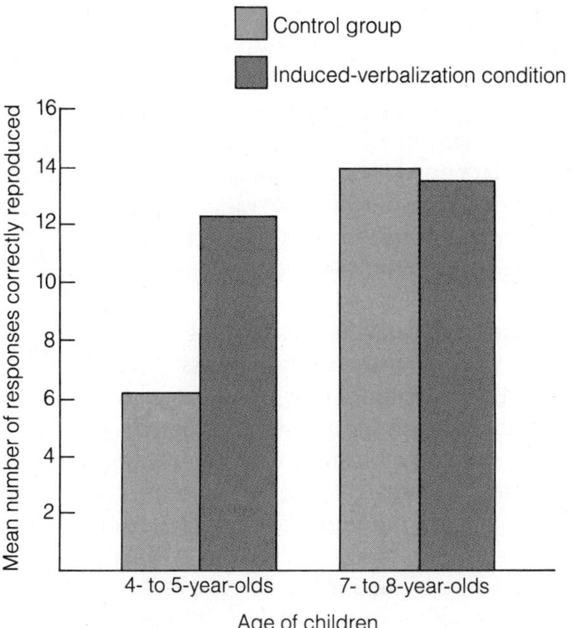

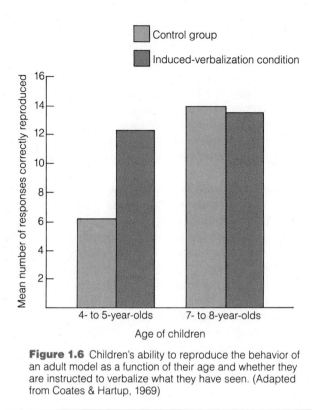

Figure 1.6 Children's ability to reproduce the behavior of an adult model as a function of their age and whether they are instructed to verbalize what they have seen. (Adapted from Coates & Hartup, 1969)

they made use of a cross-sectional design to study differences between younger and older children. But at each age level, half the children received the experimental treatment in which they were instructed to describe what they saw in the film as they viewed it, and half served as the control group receiving no such instructions.

Figure 1.6 shows the interesting findings that emerged from this experiment. First, the 4- to 5-year-olds who were *not* told to describe what they had seen learned very little. Comparing them to the 7- and 8-year-olds in the passive-observation control group, we see further evidence that preschoolers typically learn less than older children do from their observations. But notice that preschoolers who *were* instructed to describe what the model did learned just about as much as the older children did. It is clear that manipulating the independent variable (instructions) had a big impact on the learning performance of 4- and 5-year-old children: that young children *can* learn effectively if they describe what they watch. Finally, notice that the independent variable had little impact at all on the performance of 7- to 8-year-olds. Whether they were instructed to describe what they had seen or not, they learned a great deal, presumably because they spontaneously described what they saw even when they were not told to do so. In sum, the results of this experiment imply that 4- to 5-year-olds may generally learn less from watching social models than older children do because, unlike older children, they do not spontaneously produce verbal descriptions that would help them retain what they have observed.

The greatest strength of the experimental method is its ability to establish unambiguously that one thing *causes* another. Coates and Hartup were able to conclude that instructing young children to describe what they observe *causes* an improvement in their learning performance—or, to state this more generally, that manipulating the independent variable causes a change in the dependent variable. To be sure that a cause–effect relationship exists, however, we must make sure that *all other factors besides the independent variable are controlled or held constant*; that is, we must establish **experimental control**. In our example, achieving experimental control means that all children in the study must see the same film and must be tested in the same way. It also means that we must ensure that the children in the treatment group are similar to the children in the control group. This is achieved through **random assignment** of individuals to one treatment condition or the other, as by drawing their names from a hat in an unbiased manner. The experiment would be invalid if, for example, teachers chose their favorite students to be in the special treatment group and those children were brighter than children exposed to the control condition.

When experiments are properly conducted, they do indeed contribute to our ability to *explain* human development. Many experimental manipulations are far more elaborate than the simple instructions given to children by Coates and Hartup. Many experiments are also conducted with applications in mind. For instance, experiments discussed in a later chapter have shown that disadvantaged preschool children who participate in an intensive preschool education program later do better in school than similar children who receive no such program. Other experiments show that old people in nursing homes who are given control over everyday decisions become mentally and physically healthier than similar nursing home residents who have decisions made for them by facility staff. Thus experiments not only help explain development, but they contribute to the goal of *optimizing* it as well.

Does the experimental method have any limitations? Yes indeed! First, the findings of experiments may not invariably hold true in the real world because the situations created in laboratory experiments can be quite contrived and artificial—very unlike the situations that people encounter in everyday life. Urie Bronfenbrenner (1979) has been critical of the fact that so many developmental studies are contrived experiments. Indeed, he has charged that developmental psychology has become "the science of the strange behavior of children in strange situations with strange adults" (p. 19). Similarly, Robert McCall (1977) notes that experiments indicate what *can* cause a developmental change but not necessarily what actually *does* most strongly influence developmental change in natural settings. Both critics call for more *field experiments*—that is, experiments carried out in natural settings such as homes, schools, workplaces, and nursing homes rather than in laboratories. They also advocate the use of more nonexperimental studies that involve naturalistic observation, even though experimental control of events is lacking in such studies and researchers therefore cannot establish unambiguously that one thing causes another.

A second limitation of the experimental method is that it simply cannot be used to address many significant questions about human development. Suppose we were interested in how older women are affected by their husband's deaths? How could we study this question experimentally? Simple: We would identify a sample of women age 65 and older, randomly assign them to either the experimental group or the control group, and then shoot the husbands of all those women in the experimental group! Only textbook writers trying to make a point would propose such an outrageously immoral study. Ethical principles demand that developmentalists use methods other than experimentation to study many issues—notably correlational methods.

The Correlational Method

The **correlational method** involves determining whether two or more variables are related to one another. In an experiment, the researcher manipulates the independent variable that is believed to influence the dependent variable, and participants are randomly assigned to treatment conditions. In a correlational study neither of these steps is taken. Instead, the researchers take people as they find them—already "manipulated" by their life experiences—and attempt to see whether differences in people's experiences or characteristics are associated with differences in their behavior. Thus a correlational study of the effect of losing a husband on the psychological adjustment of older women might involve giving both widows and similar nonwidows a personality test to measure their adjustment. The "independent variable" (called a *predictor* in correlational research) is the person's marital status (widowed versus nonwidowed) and the dependent variable is psychological adjustment. The researcher has not manipulated marital status by killing off any husbands, and the women in the study were assigned by nature to their status as widows or nonwidows rather than randomly assigned to groups by an experimenter. The researcher would try to choose widows and nonwidows who are similar with respect to age, education, and so on. However, he or she would not have as much confidence that the two groups are alike in all respects except marital status as if random assignment had been possible.

Sometimes the experimental method and the correlational method can be applied to the same problem. Consider first an experiment designed to study the effects of different kinds of television programs on the behavior of preschool children. Friedrich and Stein (1973) randomly assigned children to one of three groups: One group watched violent cartoons like *Superman* and *Batman*, another group watched episodes of *Mister Rogers* that portrayed many helpful and cooperative acts, and a third group saw programs with neither aggressive nor altruistic themes. Using a complicated observation system, the researchers then counted instances of aggressive and helpful or friendly behavior in the nursery school setting. In this experiment, the children who watched violent programs—at least those who were already relatively aggressive—became more aggressive as a result of their TV watching. By contrast, many of the children who watched altruistic programs became friendlier and more helpful than children in the other experimental treatment groups. Thus this experiment demonstrated clear cause-and-effect relationships between the kind of television children watched and their later behavior.

How would a *correlational* study of the effects of television programs on preschool children be designed? Consider a project by Jerome and Dorothy Singer (1981). Here parents completed detailed logs describing the TV viewing habits of their preschool children: how much they watched and what they watched during a year's time. On four occasions, observers rated how aggressive the children were in interactions with other children in their nursery schools. In this manner, the researchers gathered data on the two variables of interest to them: amount of exposure to TV and degree of aggression. They were then able to calculate the **correlation** between these two variables—a measure of the extent to which individuals' scores on one variable are systematically associated with their scores on the other variable in either a positive or negative way. (Figure 1.7 shows how a correlation between these two variables can be displayed visually.)

Singer and Singer did indeed find a positive correlation between TV watching and aggression. Specifically, children who frequently watched action and adventure programs such as *Kojak* and *The Six Million Dollar Man* were more aggressive in the nursery school than children who rarely watched such programs. The type of TV watched clearly mattered, for children who frequently watched *Mister Rogers* and other nonaggressive programs were slightly less aggressive than children who rarely watched these kinds of programs.

Does this correlational study firmly establish that watching action-packed programs *causes* children to become more aggressive? No, it does not. Can you think of an alternative explanation for the correlation between TV watching and aggression? One possibility is that aggressiveness in children causes them to watch violent TV. Imagine that some of the children in the study were already aggressive little devils who sought out violence wherever they could get it, and that others were nonviolent little angels who shied away from watching violent programs. TV watching habits could then be the *effect* rather than the cause of aggression in children. Another possibility is that the association between TV watching and aggression is actually due to some third variable. For example, some children might have parents who are harsh and rejecting; these children might watch a lot of TV simply because there is nothing better to do in their homes and might also happen to be aggressive because they have watched their parents being aggressive or are acting out in the nursery school the negative feelings that have resulted from their being rejected. If this were the case, TV watching did not cause these children to become more aggressive than their peers; the treatment they received from their parents was the real cause.

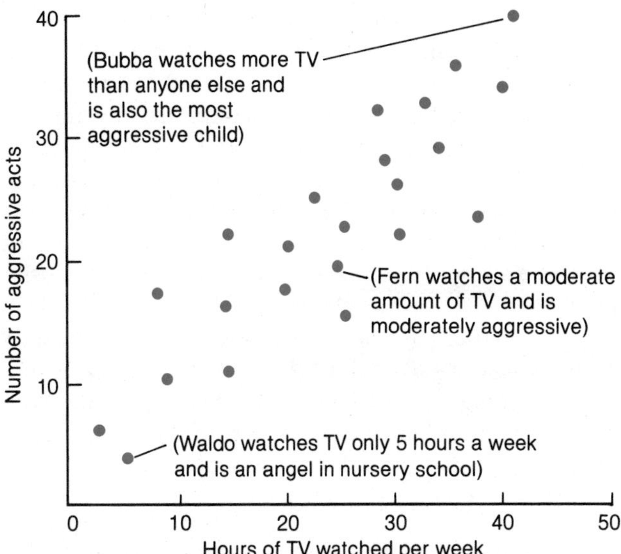

Figure 1.7 Plot of a hypothetical correlation between the amount of TV children watch and the number of aggressive acts they display. Each dot represents a specific child who watches a particular amount of TV and commits a particular number of aggressive acts. Here the correlation is positive: The more TV a child watches, the more aggressive he or she is.

Now that we have compared an experiment and a correlational study of the same topic, it becomes clear that the correlational method has one major limitation: *It cannot unambiguously indicate that one thing caused another.* However, correlational studies can *suggest* that a causal relationship exists. Indeed, Singer and Singer (1981) used complex statistical techniques to show that watching violent television probably did contribute to aggression in children and that several alternative explanations for the relationship between TV watching and aggression could probably be ruled out. Nonetheless, the experimental method can contribute more to the goal of explaining development than the correlational method can.

Despite this important limitation, the correlational method is very valuable. First, as already noted, certain problems can be addressed only through the correlational method because it would be unethical to conduct experiments. Secondly, correlational studies often have a "real world" quality that experiments lack. The Singer and Singer (1981) study, for example, says something about relationships between children's actual, everyday TV viewing habits and their behavior. Experiments sometimes expose children to only a short dose of violent TV in an artificial situation, making it difficult to be sure whether their behavior in such situations has any implications for their conduct in the natural environment. Finally, correlational studies and experimental studies supplement one another nicely. Indeed, our knowledge is advanced the most when the results of different kinds of studies *converge*: when experiments demonstrate a clear cause-and-effect relationship under controlled conditions *and* when correlational studies reveal that this very same relationship seems to be operating in everyday life (Miller, 1987). Through the use of both methods, then, developmentalists can hope to find answers to their many questions about why human beings develop as they do.

SOME THORNY ISSUES IN CONDUCTING DEVELOPMENTAL RESEARCH

Are you beginning to see that designing good developmental research is a difficult task? Researchers must first draw on theories and previous research to form a clear notion of what questions they want to answer and what hypotheses they want to test. They must then define the variables that interest them, decide how to measure those variables (for example, through interviews or through observation), and demonstrate that their measures are good ones (that is, that they are reliable and valid). And of course they must decide on a research design, choosing a cross-sectional, longitudinal, or sequential design if they are trying to describe age-related changes, and weighing the pros and cons of experimental or correlational methods if they wish to uncover possible influences on development. But there are many additional issues that researchers must grapple with. Here we will highlight three: choosing the individuals to be studied, figuring out how to measure the same trait at different ages, and protecting the rights of research participants.

Choosing Samples of People for Study

A research **sample** is simply a group of individuals chosen for study. Researchers are not interested solely in the sample they study; they hope to generalize their findings to a larger *population* of interest—for example, American high school students or nursing home residents. In many kinds of research, the ideal sample would be a **random sample**—that is, a sample that is formed by identifying all members of the larger population of interest and then, by a random means such as drawing names blindly, selecting a portion of that population to participate in the study. Random sampling increases confidence that the sample studied is representative or typical of the larger population of interest and therefore that conclusions based on studying the sample will hold true of the whole population.

In actual practice, developmentalists often draw their samples—sometimes random, sometimes not—from individuals who live near them. Thus if we were interested in drug use among American teenagers, we might survey a random sample of students at a local high school. Can you see a problem with this kind of sampling? Our ability to make statements about American teenagers in general might be quite limited if students at the high school we study are not typical of high school students in general—if, for example, our school is in a high-income suburb where drug use patterns are different than they might be in a low-income inner city area. Still, this is the way most research is done. As a result, researchers must be careful to describe the characteristics of the sample they studied and to avoid overgeneralizing their findings to populations that might be very different from their research sample.

When developmentalists conduct cross-sectional studies of development, one of their main challenges is to make sure that the age groups they study are similar to each other in all characteristics except age. Thus in a cross-sectional study of the development of memory abilities in childhood, we would not want to compare low-income 7-year-olds to high-income 11-year-olds. Instead, we might randomly sample children who attend the same school so that the two age groups we study are similar with respect to their average family income, intelligence, ethnic or racial background, and so on. But now suppose we want to compare the memory abilities of 20-year-olds and 60-year-olds. If we randomly sample people in these age groups, we encounter a major problem. As we have noted already, older adults today typically have had less education than young adults today have had. We would have no trouble at all showing that oldtimers do worse than the young people on our memory tests, but we would *not* be justified in blaming that poor performance on the aging process.

What is the solution? Many researchers cope with this

Box 1.4
A Cross-Cultural Comparison of Gender Roles

One of the greatest values of cross-cultural comparisons is that they can tell us whether a developmental phenomenon is or is not universal. Consider the roles that males and females play in society. In our culture, playing the masculine role has traditionally required traits such as independence, assertiveness, and dominance. By contrast, females are expected to be more emotional, passive, and sensitive to other people. Are these masculine and feminine roles universal? Could biological differences between the sexes lead inevitably to these sex differences in patterns of behavior?

Some years ago, anthropologist Margaret Mead (1935) compared the gender roles adopted by people in three tribal societies on the island of New Guinea. Although her observations were not rigorously scientific, they are certainly thought provoking. In the Arapesh tribe, both men and women were taught to play what we would regard as a feminine role: They were cooperative, nonaggressive, and sensitive to the needs of others. In

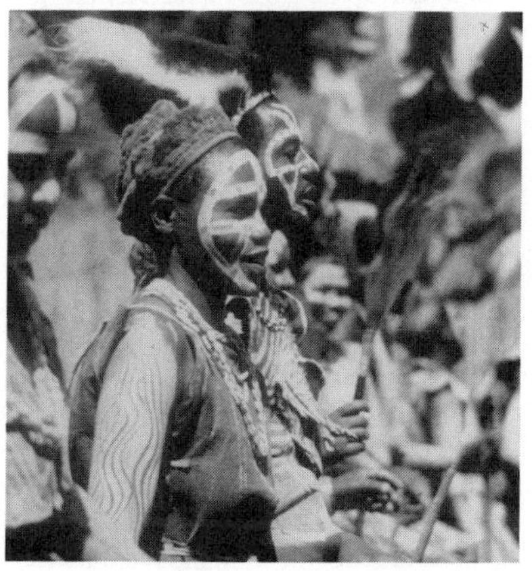

contrast, both men and women of the Mundugumor tribe were brought up to be hostile, aggressive, and emotionally unresponsive to other people: a masculine pattern of behavior by Western standards. Finally, the Tchambuli displayed a pattern of gender-role development that was the direct opposite of the Western pattern: Males were passive, emotionally dependent, and socially sensitive, whereas females were dominant, independent, and aggressive!

Mead's cross-cultural comparison suggests that cultural learning may have far more to do with the characteristic behavior patterns of men and women than biological differences between the sexes do. So we very much need cross-cultural comparisons such as Mead's. Without them, we might easily make the mistake of assuming that whatever holds true in our society holds true everywhere; with their help, we can begin to understand the roles of biology and environment in human development.

problem by selecting younger and older adults with equivalent years of education—for example, college graduates only. Then any performance differences between the age groups would not be the result of differences in the amount of education they have received. But notice that the samples chosen are no longer representative of their age groups. Statements about college-educated older people might not hold true of the large number of older adults who did *not* graduate from college. Again, researchers need to describe their samples carefully to make it clear that their findings might not generalize to other kinds of individuals.

Suppose we do a splendid job of sampling and feel confident that our findings would hold true of children or adults in the United States. Can we generalize to human beings in general? Not necessarily! In Chapter 4 and at other points throughout this book, we will be examining the extent to which human development differs from culture to culture. Some researchers deliberately conduct **cross-cultural comparisons** to find out if developmental phenomena that hold true in one culture also hold true in others. These cross-cultural comparisons demonstrate quite convincingly that human development is very much influenced by the cultural context in which it occurs (see Box 1.4 for an example).

Unfortunately, the vast majority of our knowledge of human development is based on studies of children and adults in Western societies in the 20th century. So bear in mind that we cannot just assume that findings based on children or adults in Peoria will also hold true of children or adults in Paris or Peking. What we learn about human development often depends on whom we sample.

Measuring the Same Trait at Different Ages

Even when developmentalists have excellent methods of measuring human traits and behaviors, they still may encounter problems in measuring age differences or age changes in those traits and behaviors (Schaie & Hertzog, 1985). The main problem is finding measures that are equally applicable and equally valid at all ages of interest.

Suppose, for example, that we want to trace how the trait we call "intelligence" changes with age. Intelligence tests developed for children ask them to define words, answer factual questions, construct designs with blocks, and so on. But tests designed for children often cannot be used with infants or adults. For example, because infants lack verbal abilities, entirely different kinds of tests have had to be devised to measure infant "intelligence." Therefore it is impossible to use one single test to trace the growth of intellectual abilities from infancy through adulthood.

Moreover, even if one test or measure can be used with several different age groups, it may not have the same

Box 1.5 Guidelines for Conducting Ethical Research

Drawing primarily on the principles of research ethics set forth by the American Psychological Association (1982), we can highlight some of the main ethical responsibilities that an investigator has. These responsibilities boil down to respecting the rights of research participants: allowing them to make informed and uncoerced decisions about taking part in research, protecting them from harm, and treating any information they provide as confidential (Miller, 1987).

Informed consent

Researchers generally should inform potential participants of all aspects of the research that might affect their decision to participate. The idea is to ensure that each person who chooses to participate in research has made a voluntary decision based on knowledge of what the research involves. But are young children or mentally impaired older adults capable of understanding what they are being asked to do and of giving their *informed* consent? Probably not (see Cooke, 1982; Ratzan, 1986). Therefore researchers who study such individuals should obtain informed consent from someone who can act on the individual's behalf: the parent or guardian of a child, school officials, superintendents, directors of institutions, or legal representatives. Even when someone else has provided consent, all prospective participants who have any ability to understand the request are typically given a chance to decide for themselves. Investigators also must not pressure anyone to participate and must respect any participant's right to refuse to participate in the first place, to drop out at any point during the study, and to refuse to have his or her data used by the investigator.

Protection from harm

Researchers are bound not to harm research participants either physically or psychologically. It may be difficult to predict whether any psychological harm is possible, but researchers must try to do so and should consult with others if they are in doubt. If harm to the participants seems likely, another way of obtaining the information should be considered or the research should be abandoned.

Debriefing people about any deception or concealment of information

Ideally, researchers are able to tell participants about the true purposes of the study in advance. However, in some cases doing so would make the study worthless. Suppose, for example, that we are interested in the moral development of children and adolescents and want to know if they would cheat if they thought they could get away with it. If we told all the participants in advance that the study was about cheating, do you think a single person would cheat? Instead, we might propose setting up a situation in which children have an opportunity to cheat and believe they are alone, but are actually being observed from behind a one-way mirror. Our ethical responsibility now is to *debrief* the participants—that is, to explain to them afterward what the true purpose of the study was and why they were misled about it. In this example, we would also have an obligation to make sure that children do not leave feeling upset about the fact that they cheated. A research ethics committee looks very closely at any study that involves deception to make sure that the deception is really necessary and is justified by the benefits of the research.

Confidentiality

Researchers also have an ethical responsibility to keep in confidence the information they collect. It would be unacceptable, for example, to tell a child's teacher that the child performed poorly on an intelligence test or to tell an adult's employer that he or she revealed a drinking problem in an interview. Only if participants give explicit permission to have information about them shared with someone else would that information be passed on. However, there are a few circumstances in which researchers must violate confidentiality. For example, many states now have laws that would prohibit an investigator from withholding the names of children who are believed to be the victims of child abuse. These are only a few of the considerations that researchers must keep in mind as they attempt to pursue knowledge while respecting the rights and welfare of individuals who help them gain this knowledge.

meaning at one age that it has at another. There is some evidence that adult intelligence tests may not measure quite the same thing in an older adult that they measure in a young adult (Cohen, 1957). For example, a young adult's performance on a test question designed to measure the ability to solve a problem may indeed measure problem-solving ability, but an elderly adult's performance on that same item is likely to be heavily influenced by that person's ability to remember the elements of the problem. Those old people who have retained their memory capacities will perform well, whereas those who have suffered memory declines will do poorly. Such items could mislead us about the development of intelligence if they do indeed measure the problem-solving abilities of young adults but inadvertently assess the memory abilities of old adults. Similarly, some tests and measures may be fairer to one age group than to another. It clearly would be unfair to elderly people, for example, to compare them to young adults on a memory test that includes only questions about the latest rock music.

In sum, developmentalists may encounter two special measurement problems when they attempt to describe development through the life span. First, they may be unable to find any single instrument or technique that is appropriate for all age groups of interest; they must then settle for using different measures with different age groups. Second, an instrument that seems employable with people of diverse ages could be measuring one trait at one age and a somewhat different trait at another age. Or it could be fairer to some age groups than to others. These problems make it challenging indeed to try to determine how important human attributes change over long stretches of the life span.

Protecting the Rights of Research Participants

Finally, developmental researchers sometimes also face thorny issues centering on **research ethics**, the standards of conduct that investigators are ethically bound to honor in order to protect their research participants from physical or psychological harm. Some ethical issues are easily resolved: One simply does *not* conduct experiments that will almost certainly cause physical or psychological damage—experiments in which children are physically abused or the husbands of elderly women are shot! Most ethical issues are far more subtle: Is it ethical to deceive people, for example, by telling them that they performed poorly on a test in order to create in them a temporary sense of failure? Is it an invasion of a family's privacy to ask children questions about the ways in which their parents punish them?

The American Psychological Association, the Society for Research in Child Development, the federal government, and many other agencies have established guidelines for ethical research with human beings (see Cooke, 1982; Miller, 1987). In addition, universities, research foundations, and government agencies that fund research have set up "human-subjects review committees" to determine whether proposed research projects conform to ethical standards. However, the ultimate responsibility for research ethics rests with the investigator. Deciding whether a proposed study is on safe ethical ground involves weighing the possible *benefits* of the research (gains in knowledge and potential benefits to humanity or to the participants themselves) against the potential *risks* to participants. If the potential benefits greatly outweigh the potential risks, and if there are no other, less-risky procedures that could produce these same benefits, the investigation will generally be approved and will be carried out. Box 1.5 describes some of the ethical issues that arise in developmental research and some of the ethical guidelines that researchers are urged to follow.

REFLECTIONS

Each upcoming chapter will close with a "Reflections" section that encourages you to think about larger themes and issues. Here, we'll keep it brief and simply emphasize what you have no doubt noticed already: Understanding life-span human development is an incredibly complex undertaking. Developmentalists must somehow make sense of continuities and changes in all facets of human functioning over entire lifetimes in response to numerous influences. Is this an impossible task? It would indeed be impossible if researchers merely conducted study after study without any guiding ideas. To understand human development, we need *theories* of human development. Theories guide research and bring order to the diverse facts that research establishes. They give us the "big picture," calling our attention to regularities in development and to critical processes underlying development. This is why we devote Chapter 2 to them.

SUMMARY POINTS

1. Life-span human development consists of systematic changes in the individual occurring between conception and death. Developmental changes can be positive, negative, or neutral and include growth, aging, and other changes; they occur through genetically programmed maturation as well as environmental influence or learning.

2. Concepts of the life span and its distinctive periods (or age grades) have changed greatly over history and vary greatly from culture to culture today. Until the 17th century, children were expected to assume adult roles very early and were treated quite harshly. In Western cultures, adolescence apparently did not come to be viewed as a distinct phase of the life span until the late 19th century, and a lengthening of the average life span and a decline in birth rates have led to a middle-aged "empty nest" phase and a period of old age in which people are retired.

3. The science of life-span development is a multidisciplinary enterprise with three goals: the description, explanation, and optimization of development. The scientific study of development got its start at the end of the 19th century with the first baby biographies. Although many developmentalists have specialized in studying one age group or another, today's developmentalists are increasingly adopting a life-span perspective and viewing development as a lifelong, historically embedded process that has many causes, takes many directions, and is best viewed as a whole.

4. The scientific method is, in part, the attitude that data, or systematic observations, should be used to decide which ideas are best. It involves formulating theories (sets of ideas) based on observations, testing specific hypotheses (predictions based on theory) by collecting new observations in research investigations, and using the data to evaluate the worth of theories.

5. To study human development, researchers must devise measures of the human attributes and behaviors and ensure that these measures are reliable and valid. The most widely used data collection techniques are interviews or questionnaires, tests, and behavioral observations (either naturalistic or nonnaturalistic). These techniques can be combined to study one individual in depth through the case study method.

6. Developmental researchers rely principally on the cross-sectional and longitudinal developmental research designs. The cross-sectional design, which compares different age groups (cohorts) at a single time of measurement, is easy to conduct but may be misleading if an age trend is actually due to differences in life experiences rather than to true developmental change. In the longitudinal design, one group (cohort) is assessed repeatedly as its members develop. However, participants in a longitudinal study may change over the years not as a function of age itself but in response to historical events. To counteract the limitations of cross-sectional and longitudinal designs, researchers use a sequential technique that combines the two approaches.

7. To achieve the goal of explaining (and often of optimizing) development, researchers rely primarily on experiments in which an independent variable is manipulated to see what effects this has on a dependent variable. If experimental control is achieved, an experiment can firmly establish that a cause-and-effect relationship exists between one variable and another. The alternative correlational method cannot yield firm conclusions about cause and effect but may be mandatory in some situations for ethical or practical reasons.

8. Developmentalists who want to conduct good research must decide such matters as selecting samples to study, ensuring that the different age groups studied are similar in everything but age, devising measures that are appropriate for use with younger and older individuals and that have the same meaning at different ages, and contributing to knowledge while adhering to standards of ethical research practice.

KEY TERMS

age by treatment experiment
age grades
aging
baby biographies
case study
cohort
correlation
correlational method
cross-cultural comparison
cross-sectional design
dependent variable
development
developmental psychology
experiment
experimental control
gerontology
growth
hypothesis
independent variable
learning
life-span perspective
longitudinal design
maturation
naturalistic observation
questionnaire
random assignment
random sample
reliability
research ethics
sample
scientific method
sequential design
storm and stress
theory
time of measurement
validity

CHAPTER

2

THEORIES OF HUMAN DEVELOPMENT

Sheila is an attractive 15-year-old whose relationship with James has become the center of her life. She gets by in school, but most of what goes on in the classroom bores her. Her relationship with her parents has been a bit strained lately, partly because her mother does not want her to spend so much time with James and nags her about homework and chores around the house. James, age 16, is also struggling at school as he tries to juggle his part-time job, family responsibilities, and time with Sheila. And these two teenagers have a far more serious problem: Sheila is pregnant. The sex "just happened" one night after a party about five months ago and continued thereafter. Neither Sheila nor James wanted a baby.

Here is a specific event in the lives of two developing individuals. How can we explain this unwanted teenage pregnancy? What is your theory? What explanations do the leading theories of human development offer? More practically, what can be done to reduce the high rate of teenage pregnancy in our society? Approximately 1 in 10 teenage females gives birth before the age of 18, and the consequences are sometimes an interrupted education, low income, and a difficult start for both new parent and new child (Brooks-Gunn & Furstenberg, 1989; Furstenberg, Lincoln, & Menken, 1981). What practical solutions to the problem of teenage pregnancy might different theorists offer? We will attempt to answer those questions in this chapter to illustrate the fact that different theories of human development often differ radically in their positions on the very same issue.

As we noted in Chapter 1, a *theory* is a set of ideas proposed to describe and explain certain phenomena. In other words, a theory is no more than a perspective on something (Kaplan, 1983). Theories of human development should give us insights into many developmental phenomena, including teenage pregnancy. Indeed, the beauty of theories is that they can organize our thinking about a wide range of specific facts or events. In science it simply is not enough to catalog fact after fact without somehow organizing this information around a set of concepts and propositions. We would soon be swamped by unrelated facts, becoming trivia experts who lack a big picture. A theory of human development provides needed organization; it offers us a lens through which we can interpret any number of specific facts or observations about human development. Once you grasp the major theories of human development, you will be in a position to draw on their concepts and propositions to make sense of new "facts" about your own development and that of people around you.

We all have at least half-baked theories about human development, ideas about the nature of developing persons and the important forces in development. However, scientific theories are expected to be more rigorous than our everyday theories. Good developmental theories should describe and explain a wide range of phenomena, but they should do so concisely. They should also be precise rather than vague so that they can generate explicit predictions about development—hypotheses that can be supported or disconfirmed by research. And finally, a theory's predictions should be borne out by the facts gathered through research. That is, a good theory should indeed help us better describe and explain human development (and even help us optimize it by solving practical problems such as the problem of teenage pregnancy). Theories that fail to meet these evaluation criteria need to be revised or, ultimately, discarded altogether.

In this chapter, we examine five major theoretical viewpoints:

Teenage pregnancy is one of many facts about human development waiting to be explained by theories.

The *psychoanalytic* viewpoint, as developed by Sigmund Freud and revised by Erik Erikson

The *cognitive-developmental* viewpoint associated with Jean Piaget

The *learning* perspective developed by B. F. Skinner, Albert Bandura, and others

The *ethological* theory associated with Konrad Lorenz, John Bowlby, and others

The newly emerging *contextual-dialectical* approach to human development across the life span.

Each theory emphasizes some aspects of human development more than others, and each makes particular assumptions or statements about the nature of human development. Let's set the stage by outlining some of the basic developmental issues on which theorists—and people in general, we should add—often disagree.

BASIC ISSUES IN HUMAN DEVELOPMENT

What are developing human beings like? How does development come about? What courses does it follow? Let us look at five major issues on which developmental theories often disagree.

The Nature of Human Beings: Good, Bad, or Neither?

Are people inherently good or inherently bad? Well before modern theories of human development were proposed, philosophers were taking stands on the nature of human beings. Thomas Hobbes and others portrayed children as inherently bad; it was society's task to control their selfish and aggressive impulses and teach them to behave in positive ways. Jean Jacques Rousseau took exactly the opposite stand: He believed that children were innately good, that they were born with an intuitive understanding of right and wrong and would develop in positive directions so long as society did not interfere with their natural tendencies. In the middle was the English philosopher John Locke, who believed that an infant is **tabula rasa** or "a blank slate" waiting to be written on by his or her experiences. Locke believed that children were neither innately good nor innately bad, that they could develop in any number of directions depending on their experiences, and so it was up to adults to help them develop good habits. Obviously these different visions of human nature—all of which are represented in one or more modern theories—have very different implications for how we should go about optimizing development.

Nature Versus Nurture

Is development primarily the result of nature (biological forces) or nurture (environmental forces)? Perhaps no controversy has been more heated than the **nature/nurture issue**. On the nature side of the debate have been those who emphasize the influence on human development of heredity, universal maturational processes guided by the genes, and biologically based predispositions. A strong believer in nature would claim that all normal children achieve the same developmental milestones at similar times because of maturational forces, and that differences among children or adults are largely due to differences in their genetic makeups. On the nurture side of the debate have been those who emphasize *environment*—forces outside the person including experiences in life, changes achieved through learning, and the influence of methods of child rearing, societal changes, and culture on development. A strong believer in nurture would argue, as John Locke did, that human development can take many different forms depending on which specific events the individual experiences over a lifetime. Other theorists take a middle ground and hold that human attributes such as intelligence and personality are the products of an involved interplay between biological and environmental forces (see Plomin, 1990).

Activity Versus Passivity

Are people active in their own development, or are they passively shaped by outside forces? Some theorists believe that children are curious, active creatures who in a very real sense orchestrate their own development by exploring the world around them or by shaping their own environments. For example, a 4-year-old girl who asks her mother for clothes to play "dress-up" and studiously watches how her teenage sister acts around boys would be viewed as actively contributing to her own sex-role development. Similarly, some theorists believe that adults take charge of their lives, influence those around them, and actively produce the developmental changes they experience. According to this view, developmental problems can also be partially attributable to the individual. The highly aggressive child may not just be the victim of poor parenting; this child may have helped create the climate in which he or she was raised by provoking punishment from Mom and Dad.

Others view humans as passive beings who are largely the products of forces beyond their control, usually environmental influences (or perhaps strong biological forces as well). From this vantage point, children are seen as gaining knowledge and skills only if adults provide them with the proper learning experiences, and old people who have become socially isolated might be viewed as the victims of an uncaring society. In short, theorists disagree about whether humans actively shape their own development or are passively shaped by external forces. The middle ground is to view humans and their environments as reciprocally influencing one another.

Continuity Versus Discontinuity

Is development continuous or discontinuous? The **continuity/discontinuity** issue is really three subissues (see Kagan, 1980). First, we can ask whether the changes we undergo over the life span are gradual or somewhat abrupt. *Continuity* theorists view human development as a process that occurs in small steps, without sudden changes. In contrast, *discontinuity* theorists picture the course of development as more like a series of stairsteps; children, for example, function at one stage of development, experience a rapid period of change and reorganization, and are then elevated to a new and presumably more advanced stage of development.

A second aspect of the continuity/discontinuity issue concerns whether changes are *quantitative* or *qualitative* in nature. Quantitative changes are changes in degree: A person becomes taller, or knows more pieces of information, or interacts with friends more or less frequently. By contrast, qualitative changes are changes in kind, changes that make the individual fundamentally different in some way from what he or she was like before. The transformation of a caterpillar into a butterfly or a tadpole into a frog is an example of such qualitative change. Similarly, we might regard the infant who lacks language as qualitatively different from the child who commands language, or the adult who can define concepts such as love abstractly as fundamentally different from the child who can offer only concrete examples of what people do when they are in love. Continuity theorists typically hold that developmental changes are gradual and quantitative, while discontinuity theorists hold that they are rather abrupt and qualitative. Discontinuity theorists are the ones who most often propose that we progress through **developmental stages**, each of which is a period of the life cycle characterized by a coherent set of abilities, motives, emotions, or behaviors. Each stage is perceived as quite different from the stage before or the stage after.

Finally, consider a third aspect of the continuity/discontinuity issue: Are there close connections between early development and later development, or does behavior early in life have little bearing on later behavior? As Jerome Kagan (1980) points out, continuity can mean that earlier and later development are connected in such a way that the achievements of an early stage carry over into later functioning. This would be the case, for example, if forming a close attachment to a parent during infancy provided the basis for participating in a mature love relationship during adulthood. Connectedness in development could also take the form of stability over time: The shy infant becomes the shy adult, the particularly alert and curious infant becomes the particularly intelligent adult. Either way, the roots of adult characteristics can be found in childhood.

Kagan, for one, believes that many later developments are *discontinuous* with, or unconnected to, earlier development. Sometimes a new behavior pattern simply replaces an old one without evolving from it, as when an infant who once smiled at everyone indiscriminately begins to cast a wary eye on any stranger, or when an adult who was a computer scientist switches careers and becomes a florist. The discontinuity position is that traits established in early childhood often do *not* carry over into adulthood and that people change in unpredictable ways.

In summary, the continuity/discontinuity issue has several facets. There is the issue of whether developmental change is gradual or abrupt, the issue of whether it is quantitative or qualitative in nature, and the issue of whether it is or is not connected to earlier development. Theorists do not always take the continuity position or the discontinuity position on all of these issues, but they do often lean predominantly in one direction or the other.

One Path or Many?

Do we all follow the same developmental path, or do we follow different paths? Developmental theorists often disagree about the extent to which developmental changes are *universal* (common to everyone) or *particularistic* (different from person to person). Stage theorists typically believe that the stages they propose are universal. For example, a stage theorist might claim that virtually all children enter a new stage in their intellectual development at about the time they start school, or that most adults, sometime around the age of 40, experience a "mid-life crisis" in which they raise major questions about their lives. From this perspective, development proceeds in certain universal directions. But other theorists believe that human development is far more varied than this. Paths of development followed in one culture may be very different from paths followed in another culture, and even within a single culture, one person may experience a quite different sequence of developmental changes than another does. As we saw in Chapter 1, this belief that development may proceed in many directions is part of the emerging life-span perspective on development.

These, then, are some of the major controversies about human development that different theories resolve in different ways. We invite you to clarify your own stands on these issues by completing the brief questionnaire in Box 2.1. At the end of the chapter, Box 2.8 indicates how the major developmental theorists might answer these same questions so that you can compare your own assumptions to theirs. For now, let's begin our survey of the theories, starting with Freud's psychoanalytic perspective.

FREUD'S PSYCHOANALYTIC THEORY

It is difficult to think of a theorist who has had a greater impact on Western thought than Sigmund Freud, the Viennese physician who lived from 1856 to 1939. This revolutionary thinker challenged prevailing notions of human nature and human development by proposing that we are driven by motives and emotions of which we are largely unaware and that we are shaped by our earliest experiences in life. His name is a household word, and his **psychoanalytic theory** continues to influence thinking about human development.

Human Nature: Instincts and Unconscious Motives

Central to Freud's psychoanalytic theory is the notion that human beings have basic biological urges or drives that must be satisfied. What kinds of urges? Undesirable ones! Freud viewed the newborn as a "seething cauldron," an inherently selfish creature "driven" by two kinds of **instincts**, or inborn biological forces that motivate behavior. The *life instincts* aim for survival: They direct life-sustaining activities such as breathing, eating, copulation, and the fulfillment of other bodily needs. The *death instincts* are destructive forces said to be present in all human beings and are expressed through such behavior as aggression, sadism, murder, and even masochism (harm directed against the self).

Freud strongly believed that human beings are often unaware that these instincts and other inner forces motivate their behavior. A teenage boy, for example, may not realize that his devotion to working out with weights could be a way of channeling his sexual or aggressive urges. Freud's concept of **unconscious motivation** refers to underlying forces and inner conflicts that influence thinking and behavior, even though they are not conscious or cannot be recalled. As Freud developed his psychoanalytic therapy, he came to rely on such therapy methods as hypnosis, free association (a quick spilling out of ideas), and dream analysis because he believed that only these techniques would uncover underlying unconscious motives. Our teenage boy's dreams, for instance, might re-

Box 2.1
How Do You Stand on Major Developmental Issues?

Choose one answer for each question and write down the corresponding letter or fill it in at the end of the box. Compare your results with Box 2.8 at the end of this chapter.

1. Children are
   a. creatures whose basically negative or selfish impulses must be controlled.
   b. neither inherently good nor inherently bad.
   c. creatures who are born with many positive and few negative tendencies.
2. Biological influences (heredity, maturational forces) and environmental influences (culture, parenting styles, learning experiences) are thought to contribute to development. Overall,
   a. biological factors contribute far more than environmental factors.
   b. biological factors contribute somewhat more than environmental factors.
   c. biological and environmental factors are equally important.
   d. environmental factors contribute somewhat more than biological factors.
   e. environmental factors contribute far more than biological factors.
3. People are basically
   a. active beings who play a major role in determining their own abilities and traits.
   b. passive beings whose characteristics are molded either by social influences (parents and other significant people, outside events) or by biological changes beyond their control.
4. Development proceeds
   a. through stages, so that the individual changes rather abruptly into a quite different kind of person than he or she was in an earlier stage.
   b. in a variety of ways, some stagelike, some gradual or continuous.
   c. continuously—in small increments without abrupt changes or distinct stages.
5. Traits such as aggressiveness or dependency in a person
   a. emerge in childhood and remain largely consistent over the years.
   b. first appear in childhood but often disappear or give way to quite different traits at some later time.
6. When we compare the development of different individuals, we see
   a. many similarities; children and adults develop along universal paths and experience similar changes at similar ages.
   b. many differences; different people often undergo different sequences of change and have widely different timetables of development.

	Question					
	1	2	3	4	5	6
Your pattern of answers:	_	_	_	_	_	_

veal deep desires for sex or power that he is unaware of or could not express in the light of day. So, we immediately see that Freud's theory is highly biological in nature: Biological instincts, forces that often provide an unconscious motivation for our actions, are said to guide human development.

Three Components of Personality: Id, Ego, and Superego

According to Freud (1933), each individual has a fixed amount of psychic (or mental) energy that can be used to satisfy basic urges or instincts. As the child develops, this psychic energy is divided among three components of the personality: the id, the ego, and the superego.

At birth, the personality is all **id.** The id's entire mission is to satisfy the instincts. It obeys the "pleasure principle," seeking immediate gratification, even when needs cannot be realistically or appropriately met. If you think about it, young infants do seem to be "all id" in many ways. When they are hungry or wet, they simply fuss and cry until their needs are met; they are not known for their patience. The id is the impulsive, irrational, and selfish part of the personality, and it is with us throughout the life span.

The second component of the personality is the **ego,** the rational side of the individual that operates according to the "reality principle" and tries to find realistic ways of gratifying the instincts. According to Freud (1933), the ego begins to emerge during infancy when psychic energy is diverted from the id to energize important cognitive processes such as perception, learning, and problem solving. The hungry toddler may be able to do more than merely cry when she is hungry; she may be able to draw on the resources of the ego to hunt down Dad, lead him to the kitchen, and say "Cake." However, toddlers' egos are still relatively immature; they want what they want NOW! As the ego matures further, children become more and more able to postpone their pleasures until a more appropriate time or to devise logical and realistic plans for meeting their needs. In order to find realistic ways to meet the id's basic needs, the ego must use some of its energy to block the id's irrational and impulsive thinking. Thus the ego is both servant and master to the id. It masters the id by delaying gratification until needs can be realistically met, but it also serves the id by weighing courses of action and selecting a plan that is most likely to satisfy the id's needs.

The third part of the Freudian personality is the **superego**, the individual's internalized moral standards. The superego develops from the ego and strives for *perfection* rather than for pleasure or realism (Freud, 1933). It begins to develop as 3- to 6-year-old children *internalize* (take on as their own) the moral standards and values of their parents. Typically, it grows stronger as children continue to absorb the values of adults. Once the superego emerges, children have a parental voice in their heads that tells them that it would be wrong to satisfy their ids by grabbing or stealing other children's snacks, and that voice makes them feel guilty or ashamed when they do violate society's rules and standards. The superego insists that we find socially acceptable or ethical outlets for the id's undesirable impulses.

Obviously the three parts of the personality do not see eye to eye! Conflict among the id, ego, and superego is inevitable. In the mature, healthy personality, a dynamic balance operates: The id communicates its basic needs, the ego restrains the impulsive id long enough to find realistic ways to satisfy these needs, and the superego decides whether the ego's problem-solving strategies are morally acceptable. The ego is clearly "in the middle"; it must serve two harsh masters by striking a balance between the opposing demands of the id and the superego, all the while accommodating to the realities of the external world.

According to Freud, psychological problems often arise when psychic energy is unevenly distributed among the id, the ego, and the superego. Because there is a fixed amount of psychic energy to be spent, too much energy devoted to one part of the personality inevitably means less to be channeled into the other parts. For example, the sociopath who routinely lies and cheats to get his way may have a very strong id, a normal ego, but a very weak superego, never having learned to respect the rights of other people. In contrast, the woman who is crippled by anxiety over the mere thought of having sex with her boyfriend may be controlled by an overly strong superego. Analysis of the balance among the three parts of the personality provided Freud and his followers with one means of understanding individual differences in personality and the origins of psychological disorders.

The three parts of the personality proposed by Freud are inevitably in conflict.

The Stages of Psychosexual Development

Freud viewed the sex instinct as the most important of the life instincts because he often discovered that the psychological disturbances of his patients revolved around childhood sexual conflicts. Childhood sex? Certainly the notion of childhood sexuality was one of the most controversial of Freud's ideas. Yet he used the term *sex* to refer to much more than what you are probably thinking of. Freud viewed many simple bodily actions such as sucking, biting, and urinating as "erotic" activities.

Although the sex instinct is presumably inborn, Freud (1940/1964) felt that its character changes over time as dictated by biological maturation. Freud's view was that the sex instinct's psychic energy, which he called **libido**, shifts from one part of the body to another over the years, moving the child into new stages of *psychosexual* development. Let's examine Freud's five stages of psychosexual development—oral, anal, phallic, latency, and genital—and then consider problems that might arise as the child passes through these stages.

The Oral Stage (Birth to 1 Year)

Freud was struck by the fact that infants spend much of their first year sucking, spitting, chewing, and biting, and he concluded that the sex instinct seeks pleasure through the mouth during this **oral stage**. There is no denying it: Young infants do suck, bite, or chew just about anything they can get their mouths on, even when they are not particularly hungry or thirsty. Freud went on to argue that later psychological development would be very much affected by how adequately the infant's oral needs were met and thus how closely attached the infant became to its mother. For example, the infant boy who was weaned too early or was fed only on a rigid schedule would be deprived of "oral gratification" and might later become a man who still craves "mother love" and becomes overdependent on his wife. In short, Freud argued that *early experiences may have a long-term effect on personality development.*

The Anal Stage (1 to 3 Years)

As the sphincter muscles mature in the second year of life, infants acquire the ability to withhold or expel fecal material at will. Voluntary defecation becomes the primary method of gratifying the sex instinct during the **anal stage**. Infants now face their first major conflict between biological urges and social demands, for parents insist that they control their bowels and become toilet trained. The way in which parents handle toilet training can leave lasting imprints on the personality. For example, the child who is harshly punished for mistakes or forced to sit for hours on the pottie seat may become an inhibited or stingy adult.

The Phallic Stage (3 to 6 Years)

Freud proposed that 4-year-old children have matured to the point that their genitals have become an interesting and sensitive area of the body. Preschoolers, Freud claimed, find pleasure in stroking and fondling their genitals. And—as if that were not controversial enough—Freud believed that preschool children develop a strong incestuous desire for the parent of the opposite sex. He called this period the **phallic stage** because he believed that the phallus (penis) assumes a critically important role in the psychosexual development of both boys and girls.

Consider the events of the phallic stage for boys. According to Freud, a 3- to 5-year-old boy, already strongly attached to his mother, develops an intense longing for her and begins to view his father as a rival for Mom's affection. Freud called this state of affairs the **Oedipus complex** after the legendary king of Thebes, Oedipus, who unwittingly killed his father and married his mother. The problem is that young boys, unlike Oedipus, are no match for their fathers. In fact, Freud proposed that they will come to fear that their fathers might castrate them as punishment for their rivalrous conduct.

When this *castration anxiety* becomes sufficiently intense, the boy will resolve his Oedipus complex. How? First, through **repression** of his incestuous and rivalrous desires (that is, the forcing of these anxiety-provoking thoughts out of conscious awareness), and second, by **identification** with his father (that is, emulating the father and taking on as his own the father's attitudes, attributes, and behaviors). Repression is clearly a defense against dangerous thoughts and feelings, but so is identification, for presumably a father would not retaliate against someone so much like himself. There are two important outcomes of the boy's identification with his father. First, he will become Daddy's "little man," learning his masculine sex role. Second, he will develop a superego by internalizing his father's moral standards.

What about preschool girls? Freud admitted that he was unsure about them. Once a 4-year-old girl discovers that she lacks a penis, she is believed to blame her mother for this "castrated" condition. She transfers her affection from her mother to her father, envies her father for possessing a penis, and hopes that he will share with her the valued organ that she lacks. (Freud assumed that her real underlying motive is to bear her father's child, especially a male child, to compensate for her lack of a penis.) This is the heart of the girl's **Electra complex**.

But how is the girl's conflict resolved? Boys fear castration, and that fear motivates them to identify with their fathers, but what do girls fear? After all, they supposedly believe that they have already been castrated. Freud (1924/1961) assumed that the Electra complex may simply fade away as the girl faces reality and recognizes the impossibility of possessing her father. The next best thing for her may be to identify with her mother, who *does* possess her father. However, Freud suggested that girls will develop weaker superegos than boys because they do not experience the powerful fear of retaliation (castration anxiety) that would absolutely force them to internalize the ethical standards of their parents. (As we will see in Chapter 12, Freud's suggestion that females are the moral inferiors of males not only is highly unpopular with women but is contradicted by most research.)

Although the inner conflicts of the phallic period may be more emotionally intense for a boy than for a girl, the similarities between the sexes are also clear. Children of each sex value the male phallus: Girls hope to gain one, and boys hope to keep theirs. Moreover, both boys and girls perceive the parent of the same sex as their major rival for the affection of the other parent. And finally, if development proceeds normally, both boys and girls resolve their conflicts by identifying with the parent of the same sex, thereby taking on a "masculine" or "feminine" role and developing a superego.

The Latency Period (Ages 6 to 12)

During the **latency period**, or the elementary school years, the child's sex instincts are relatively quiet. The conflicts of the phallic stage have been repressed, and libidinal energy is channeled into socially acceptable activities such as schoolwork and play with friends of the same sex. The ego and the superego continue to grow stronger as the child gains new problem-solving abilities and internalizes additional societal values. But this lull period in childhood sexuality will end abruptly with the coming of puberty.

The Genital Stage (Age 12 Onward)

With the onset of puberty comes the maturation of the reproductive system, a flooding of the body with sex hormones, and a reactivation of the genital zone as an area of sensual pleasure. The underlying goal of the sex instinct now becomes biological reproduction through sexual intercourse. But adolescents face conflicts in learning how to manage their new sexual urges in socially appropriate ways and how to form genuinely loving relationships. They may have difficulty accepting their new sexuality, and they may reexperience some of the conflicting feelings toward their parents that they felt during their preschool years as part of the Oedipal and Electra complexes.

Freud's theory of psychosexual development stopped with adolescence. Presumably adolescents and adults invest their libido in activities such as forming friendships, preparing for a career, courting, and marrying. They eventually satisfy the fully mature sex instinct by having children. Freud imagined that the individual remains in this **genital stage** throughout adulthood.

Early Experience, Defense Mechanisms, and Adult Personality

Freud's theory tends to emphasize nature more than nurture. He believed that inborn biological instincts drive behavior and biological maturation determines the child's progress through the five psychosexual stages. Much as he emphasized the role of biology in development, however, Freud also viewed nurture—especially early experiences within the family—as an important cause of individual differences in adult personality.

At each psychosexual stage, the id's impulses and social demands inevitably come into conflict. But parents can heighten this conflict and the child's anxiety by adopting certain methods of child rearing rather than others. To defend itself against this anxiety, the ego, without being aware of it, adopts **defense mechanisms** (Freud, 1940/1964). We all use these mechanisms, but some people become overdependent on them because of unfavorable experiences in early life.

Let's consider two defense mechanisms that have major developmental implications. **Fixation** is a kind of arrested development in which part of the libido remains tied to an early stage of development. Why might a child become fixated at the oral stage? Perhaps he or she was rarely allowed to linger at the breast, was prevented from mouthing and chewing objects around the house, or was otherwise deprived of oral gratification. This infant might become fixated at the oral stage to satisfy oral needs and to avoid the potentially even greater conflicts of the anal stage. For example, a child weaned too early might display an oral fixation by becoming a chronic thumbsucker and might, later in life, display this same fixation by chain-smoking, talking incessantly (as college professors are prone to do), or being overdependent on other people.

Another important defense mechanism, **regression**, involves retreating to an earlier, less traumatic stage of development. The child who is temporarily made insecure by the arrival of a new baby in the house may revert to childlike behavior—throwing temper tantrums, gooing like a baby, and wanting juice from a baby bottle. Similarly, the adult who is experiencing sexual conflicts and frustrations may regress to earlier modes of sexuality such as masturbation.

In summary, Freud insists that the past lives on. Early childhood experiences may haunt us in later life and influence our adult personalities, interests, and behaviors. Parents significantly influence a child's success in passing through the biologically programmed psychosexual stages. They can err by overindulging the child's urges, but more commonly they create lasting and severe inner conflicts and anxieties by denying an infant oral gratification, using harsh toilet-training practices with a toddler, or punishing the preschooler who is fascinated by naked bodies. Heavy reliance on fixation, regression, and other defense mechanisms may then become necessary just to keep the ego intact and functioning.

Now, what might Freud have said about the causes of teenage pregnancy and about the case of Sheila and James described at the start of the chapter? In Box 2.2, we speak for Freud. In this box and in boxes describing how other theorists would view teenage pregnancy, we have taken the liberty of speaking for the theorists, whether they are dead or alive. You might want to anticipate what each theorist might say before reading each such box to see if you can successfully apply the theories to a specific problem.

Strengths and Weaknesses of Freud's Theory

Are we really driven by sexual and aggressive instincts? Could we really have experienced Oedipus or Electra complexes and simply repressed these traumatic events? Or did Freud get carried away with sex? Could the sexual conflicts Freud thought so important have merely

Box 2.2 Psychoanalytic Theory Applied: Freud on Teenage Pregnancy

I welcome this opportunity to return to life to comment on the problem of teenage pregnancy. As you know, I was always fascinated by sex. This matter of teenage pregnancy is right up my alley! We must realize that teenagers experience intense conflicts during the genital stage of psychosexual development. Their new sexual urges are anxiety provoking and must somehow be managed. Moreover, the sexual conflicts of earlier psychosexual stages often reemerge during adolescence. Of course, I would need to find out more about the early childhood experiences and psychic conflicts of Sheila and James to pinpoint the specific causes of their behavior, but I can offer a few suggestions.

Since I've been back I have uncovered some revealing psychoanalytic studies of pregnant teenagers. In one study of 30 teenage girls,[1] many of them were found to be very dependent individuals who had weak egos and superegos. Perhaps Sheila and James did not have strong enough egos and superegos to keep their selfish ids in check; perhaps they sought immediate gratification of their sexual urges with no thought for future consequences or morality.

But it is also quite possible that these teenagers were motivated by inner conflicts that had their roots in infancy or the preschool years. For instance, many pregnant girls come from homes without fathers.[1] Perhaps Sheila never fully resolved the Electra complex of the phallic stage and was unconsciously seeking to possess her father by possessing James and having a baby. James, of course, might have been seeking to gratify his unconscious desire for his mother through Sheila. Teenagers often seem to distance themselves from their parents as a defense against reawakened Oedipal feelings of love for the opposite-sex parent.

All these possibilities suggest that Sheila and James may have had an especially difficult time dealing with their new-found sexuality. I'll bet my reputation that one or both of them has personality problems rooted in early childhood experiences. Without being consciously aware of what is motivating them, they may well be seeking to gratify needs that were never adequately met in their early years.

[1]For further information about the works "Dr. Freud" refers to, see Babikian & Goldman (1968), Hatcher (1973), and Schaffer & Pine (1973).

been reflections of the sexually repressive Victorian culture in which he and his patients lived? And could the lessons Freud learned from psychoanalyzing disturbed adults have little bearing on the development of normal children?

Few contemporary developmentalists accept all of Freud's theory. Indeed, research has failed to support many of his specific ideas (Fisher & Greenberg, 1977). For example, there is not much evidence that oral and anal experiences in childhood predict one's later personality. It also turns out that many 4- and 5-year-old children are so ignorant of male and female anatomy and of which genitals belong to which sex that it is hard to imagine that they could experience castration anxiety or penis envy (Katcher, 1955). Many developmentalists also fault Freud for proposing a theory that is difficult to test. How can one objectively study the workings of the id, ego, and superego, for example?

Despite the fact that some of Freud's specific ideas have not been supported by research or have proved difficult to test, many of his insights have stood up well. Perhaps Freud's greatest contribution was his concept of unconscious motivation. When psychologists were studying conscious aspects of experience such as perception, Freud boldly proclaimed that they were studying only the tip of the human iceberg, that much of our behavior is caused by forces and conflicts of which we are not consciously aware. Freud also deserves considerable credit for focusing attention on the potential importance of early experience in the family for later development. Debates continue about exactly how critical early experience is, but few developmentalists today doubt that early experiences *can* have lasting impacts. Finally, we might thank Freud for exploring the emotional side of human development: the loves, fears, anxieties, and other powerful emotions that play such an important role in our lives. Emotional development has often been slighted by developmentalists who have focused intently on observable behavior or on rational thought processes.

In sum, Freud was a great explorer who dared to navigate uncharted waters that his predecessors had not even thought to explore. In the process, he changed our views of human nature and human development, even though some of his specific ideas have not been well supported by research. Moreover, he inspired many disciples to contribute in their own right to our understanding of human development—including scholars who are writing to this day (see Reppen, 1985).

ERIKSON'S THEORY OF PSYCHOSOCIAL DEVELOPMENT

Freud's followers did not always agree completely with the master, and eventually some of them began to modify Freud's ideas. Among the best known of these *neo-Freudians* is Erik Erikson (1902–). Erikson studied with Freud's daughter, Anna, in Vienna, and emigrated to the United States when Hitler rose to power in Germany. His clinical work and studies focused on children, college students, victims of combat fatigue during World War II, civil rights workers in the South, and American Indians. These varied experiences help explain why he viewed social and cultural influences as critically important in shaping human development.

Freud and Erikson Compared

It is clear that Erikson (1963, 1968, 1982) was heavily influenced by Freud and agrees with him on a number of points. For example, he agrees that people are born with a number of basic instincts, that development proceeds through stages, and that the order of these stages is influenced by biological maturation. He agrees that the personality has three parts: the id, ego, and superego. In short, Erikson is clearly a psychoanalytic theorist.

However, Erikson's theory also differs from Freud's in several significant ways. First, Erikson places less emphasis on sexual urges and more emphasis on social influences than Freud did. True, Freud regarded social agents, particularly parents, as important, but Erikson insists that forces within the broader social environment—including peers, teachers, institutions such as schools and churches, and even the broader culture—are also highly important. Partly for this reason, he called his stages of development "psycho*social*" stages rather than "psycho*sexual*" stages. Erikson, then, leans more toward the "nurture" side of the nature–nurture issue than Freud did, viewing nature and nurture as equally important in development.

Second, Erikson's stages are broader in focus than Freud's are. Rather than focusing primarily on the child's seeking of bodily pleasure from one erogenous zone or another, Erikson considers a wider range of behaviors. Third,

Erikson puts less emphasis on the id and more emphasis on the ego. He assumes that human beings are basically rational creatures whose thoughts, feelings, and actions are largely controlled by the ego, and he is most interested in the development of the ego. Fourth, Erikson expresses a more positive view of human nature than Freud did. He believes that children are active explorers who seek to control their environment, not passive creatures who are driven by biological urges and molded by their parents. He also expresses more optimism than Freud did about our capacities for overcoming problems that originate in early childhood. Fifth and finally, his theory spans the entire life span. Whereas Freud's stages end with adolescence, Erikson believes that adults will continue to encounter critical conflicts that influence their future development.

With these similarities and differences between Freud and Erikson in mind, let's examine Erikson's eight stages of human development (see Table 2.1).

Eight Life Crises

Erikson believes that human beings face eight major crises, or conflicts, during their lives. Each conflict has its

Table 2.1 The stage theories of Freud, Erikson, and Piaget

FREUD (PSYCHOSEXUAL THEORY)		ERIKSON (PSYCHOSOCIAL THEORY)		PIAGET (COGNITIVE-DEVELOPMENTAL THEORY)	
Stage/age range	Description	Stage/age range	Description	Stage/age range	Description
Oral stage (birth to 1 year)	Libido is focused on the mouth as a source of pleasure. Obtaining oral gratification from a mother figure is critical to later development.	*Trust versus mistrust* (birth to 1 year)	Infants must learn to trust their caregivers to meet their needs. Responsive parenting is critical.	*Sensorimotor stage* (birth to 2 years)	Infants use sensory and motor schemes to explore and understand the world. At the start, they have only innate reflexes, but they develop ever more "intelligent" actions and eventually think before they act, using symbols.
Anal stage (1 to 3 years)	Libido is focused on the anus, and toilet training creates conflicts between the child's biological urges and society's demands.	*Autonomy versus shame and doubt* (1 to 3 years)	Children must learn to be autonomous—to assert their wills and do things for themselves—or they will doubt their abilities.		
Phallic stage (3 to 6 years)	Libido centers on the genitals, and curiosity about them abounds. Resolution of the Oedipus or Electra complex results in identification with the same-sex parent and development of the superego.	*Initiative versus guilt* (3 to 6 years)	Preschoolers develop initiative by devising and carrying out bold plans, but they must learn not to impinge on the rights of others.	*Preoperational stage* (2 to 7 years)	Preschoolers can use symbols (images and words) to understand the world. But their thinking is not yet logical; it is egocentric and heavily influenced by immediate perceptions.

Table 2.1 *(Continued)*

FREUD (PSYCHOSEXUAL THEORY)		ERIKSON (PSYCHOSOCIAL THEORY)		PIAGET (COGNITIVE-DEVELOPMENTAL THEORY)	
Stage/age range	Description	Stage/age range	Description	Stage/age range	Description
Latency period (6 to 12 years)	Libido is quiet; psychic energy is invested in schoolwork and play with same-sex friends.	*Industry versus inferiority* (6 to 12 years)	Children must master important social and academic skills and keep up with their peers or they will feel inferior.	*Concrete operations stage* (7 to 11 years)	School-aged children acquire logical operations that allow them to mentally classify and otherwise act on concrete objects in their heads. They can solve practical, real-world problems through a trial-and-error approach.
Genital stage (12 years and older)	Puberty reawakens the sexual instincts as youths seek to establish mature sexual relationships and pursue the biological goal of reproduction.	*Identity versus role confusion* (12 to 20 years)	Adolescents ask who they are and must establish social and vocational identities or else remain confused about the roles they should play as adults.	*Formal operations stage* (11 years and older)	Adolescents can think about abstract ideas, possibilities that do not exist, and long-range consequences. They can form hypotheses and systematically test them through experiments.
		Intimacy versus isolation (20 to 40 years)	Young adults seek to form a shared identity with another person, but may fear intimacy and experience loneliness and isolation.		
		Generativity versus stagnation (40 to 65 years)	Middle-aged adults must feel that they are producing something that will outlive them, either as parents or workers, or they will become stagnant and self-centered.		
		Integrity versus despair (65 and older)	Older adults must come to view their lives as meaningful in order to face death without worries and regrets.		

own time in life for emerging as the central psychological issue. Whether the conflict of a particular stage is fully resolved or not, the individual is pushed by both biological maturation and social demands into the next stage. At the same time, later conflicts will be mastered more successfully if earlier ones have been satisfactorily resolved. Table 2.1 summarizes the eight stages of psychosocial development, the Freudian stages that correspond to them, and the Piagetian stages to be discussed later.

Let's illustrate Erikson's thinking with a few examples, starting with his first stage, the conflict of **trust versus mistrust** in the first year of life. Freud emphasized the infant's oral activities during this period; Erikson does too, but he also takes interest in a broader range of infant activity. Just as infants "take in" or incorporate objects through the mouth, they "take in" objects by looking at them or feeling them with their hands. Freud emphasized the importance of a mother's feeding practices for later development. According to Erikson, what may be most important to later development is a caregiver's *general responsiveness* to the infant. To develop a basic sense of trust, infants must be able to count on their primary caregivers not only to provide food, but to relieve discomfort, to come when beckoned, to smile when smiled at. If caregivers neglect, reject, or respond inconsistently to the infant, the infant will mistrust other people. Yet Erikson believes that for development to proceed normally, a healthy balance must be struck between the terms of the critical conflict at each stage of life. For example, an infant who is overindulged may become too trusting (a gullible "sucker"); trust should outweigh mistrust, but the infant should acquire an element of skepticism to balance a solid sense of trust.

The development of trust provides the basis for healthy coping with the second conflict in life, the conflict of **autonomy versus shame and doubt.** Infants who have learned to trust other people also learn to trust themselves enough to assert their wills. During the "terrible twos" age period, toddlers loudly proclaim that they are developing wills of their own not only by resisting toilet training but by favoring two words above all others: "No" and "Me." The infant who has developed a sense of mistrust may not be capable of this kind of normal assertive behavior as a 2-year-old and, rather than becoming autonomous, will experience shame and doubt. Moreover, the toddler who is plagued by a strong sense of shame will have difficulty dreaming up and pursuing bold plans in the preschool stage of **initiative versus guilt** and may instead be too inhibited to build skyscrapers with blocks or to give finger painting a try.

In turn, the child who fails to acquire a strong sense of initiative may have difficulty mastering important academic and social skills and building a sense of self-confidence during the elementary school years (the stage of **industry versus inferiority**). He or she may also have difficulty in adolescence resolving the conflict of **identity versus role confusion** by settling on career goals, coming to grips with sexuality, developing a set of basic values, and otherwise figuring out who he or she is.

Erikson was one of the first theorists to propose systematic stages of adult development. Young adults face the conflict of **intimacy versus isolation**. They may want a love relationship while being afraid of giving up some of their newly won independence and sense of identity in the process. The task of achieving intimacy and making a long-term commitment to another person is all that much harder for the young adult who still suffers from role confusion and has a fragile sense of self. But most people do form a "shared identity" with a partner and then find themselves in middle age dealing with the issue of **generativity versus stagnation**. The term *generativity* means producing something that outlasts you, somehow leaving your mark on the world, and truly caring for future generations. Many adults achieve a sense of generativity as they see their parenting pay off in well-developed children; others may gain it by being teachers or mentors to young people, or by creating something like a book, an invention, or a new volunteer program that they can consider their lasting contribution to society. Other middle-aged adults become stagnated—unproductive and wrapped up in their own concerns.

Finally, Erikson viewed old age (**integrity versus despair**) as a time for facing the inevitability of death and making sense of one's life. Coming to the conclusion that one's life could not have been lived in any other way—that is, achieving a sense of integrity—puts the individual in a position to face death gracefully. This may be difficult for the adult who could never make a commitment to a lover or who was self-absorbed rather than caring as a middle-aged adult. The character Ebenezer Scrooge in Charles Dickens's *A Christmas Carol* illustrates these developmental problems well. Here was a self-centered, stagnated individual who had no intimate relationships and who was so caught up in greed that he ignored the needs of his young storekeeper, Bob Cratchit. Yet Scrooge's tale had a happy ending. By the end of the story he had acquired a sense of intimacy and generativity, and he was now ready to face life's final crisis without a sense of despair. An unlikely reversal? Not in Erikson's view. He maintains that "there is little that cannot be remedied later, there is much [in the way of harm] that can be prevented from happening at all" (1950, p. 104). Box 2.3 describes how Erikson might analyze the causes of teenage pregnancy.

Strengths and Weaknesses of Erikson's Theory

Many people find Erikson's emphasis on our rational, adaptive nature and on our social experience easier to accept than Freud's emphasis on irrationality and sexual instincts. Erikson highlights many of the social conflicts and

Box 2.3 Psychoanalytic Theory Applied: Erikson on Teenage Pregnancy

What do you think I, Erik Erikson, might have to say about teenage pregnancy? No, I am not as hung up on sexual issues as Dr. Freud was, but make no mistake about it: I see some merit in Freud's ideas. I agree that accepting one's sexual self is an important task of adolescence. I too might want to explore the earlier development of Sheila and James. For instance, Sheila's actions could have roots back in infancy, in my psychosocial stage of trust versus mistrust. Perhaps she had parents who were unresponsive to her needs and therefore never developed a strong sense of trust in others. Perhaps she could not trust James to stay with her, and sought to hang on to him by entering into a sexual relationship with him.

Even though each psychosocial conflict contributes to one's personality, we can gain a great deal of insight simply by focusing on the adolescent conflict of identity versus role confusion. Our society places considerable pressure on adolescents to find out who they are, to establish their identities as individuals and as members of society. Rapid changes in their bodies and minds also need to be incorporated in a new sense of self. Many adolescents seek a sense of identity by experimenting with different roles and behaviors to see what "fits." Some try drugs, wear bizarre clothes, change majors every other term, or join new groups or social movements: Adolescence is the time for this kind of exploration. I should know: I wandered all over Europe after high school, trying out a career as an artist and a number of other possibilities before I finally studied child psychoanalysis under Anna Freud and found my calling in my mid-20s.

So perhaps Sheila and James were searching for their identities when they began their sexual relationship. They may simply have been experimenting. When teenagers experiment, some mistakes are inevitable. Or they may have found their confusion about their identities very uncomfortable; in such cases, young people sometimes latch on to an identity prematurely, before they have really grappled with the issue of who they are, before they have engaged in serious experimenting. The teen who gets "lost in the crowd" or who joins a cult may be trying to gain an identity as part of a group. Similarly, Sheila may have been trying to find an easy resolution to her identity issues by becoming "James's girlfriend," and James may have sought his identity through Sheila. Here's what I said in my book *Identity*:[1]

> For where an assured sense of identity is missing, even friendships and affairs become desperate attempts at determining the fuzzy outlines of identity by mutual narcissistic mirrorying [sic]: to fall in love then often means to fall into one's mirror image, hurting oneself and damaging the mirror [p. 167].

If this is what Sheila and James were doing, I must be pessimistic about their future relationship. We know that many teenage marriages end in divorce; I think this may be because these young people try to form a "shared identity" before they have found themselves as individuals. Research supports me on this: Young adults who have already established their individual identities are more capable than those who have not of achieving the next developmental task in my stage theory—establishing intimate and committed relationships.[2]

"Dr. Erikson" is referring to Erikson (1968)[1] and Whitbourne & Tesch (1985).[2]

personal dilemmas that we remember, are currently experiencing, can easily anticipate, or can see affecting people we know.

Erikson does seem to have captured some central issues of life in his eight stages. We will return to him later in this book, for his theory has inspired some fascinating research, especially on the identity issues facing adolescents and on the course of adult development. At the same time, Erikson's theory has its shortcomings, many of which are similar to those of Freud's theory. In several respects, Erikson's theory is vague and difficult to test. How should we measure complex qualities such as initiative or integrity? What kinds of experiences must people have in order to cope with and successfully resolve psychosocial conflicts? How exactly does experience at one stage of the life span influence personality at a later stage? Erikson is simply not very explicit about these important issues. His theory is a *descriptive* overview of human social and emotional development that does not fully explain how or why this development takes place.

While psychoanalytic theories continue to influence the study of human development, other perspectives have come to dominate the field. Indeed, the emotional side of human development was largely ignored for many years as theorists turned their attention either to the rational mind and logical thinking or to the study of observable behavior. For example, Jean Piaget devoted his life to understanding how children become intelligent problem-solvers, whereas learning theorists initially decided that neither thought nor emotions could be studied objectively but that observable behavior could.

PIAGET'S COGNITIVE-DEVELOPMENTAL THEORY

No theorist has contributed more to our understanding of children's minds than Jean Piaget (1896–1980), a Swiss scholar who began to study children's intellectual development during the 1920s. This remarkable man developed quickly himself, publishing his first scientific article, about a rare albino sparrow, at the tender age of 10. His interest in zoology and the adaptation of animals to their environment was accompanied by an interest in philosophy. He finally put the two interests together by devoting his career to the study of how humans acquire knowledge and use it to adapt to their environments.

Piaget's life-long interest in cognitive development (the development of intellectual processes) emerged when he accepted a position in Paris at the Alfred Binet laboratories to work on the first standardized intelligence test. In this testing approach to the study of mental ability, an estimate of a person's intelligence is based on the number and types of questions that he or she answers correctly. Piaget soon found that he was more interested in children's *incorrect* answers than in their correct ones. He first noticed that children of about the same age were producing the same kinds of wrong answers. Then, by questioning children to find out how they were thinking about the problems presented to them, he began to realize that young children do not just know less than older children do; their thought *processes* are completely different. Eventually Piaget developed a full-blown theory to account for changes in thinking from infancy to adolescence.

Piaget's Basic Perspective on Intellectual Development

Influenced by his background in biology, Piaget (1950) viewed intelligence as a process that helps an organism adapt to its environment. The infant who can grasp a cookie and bring it to the mouth is behaving adaptively, as is the adolescent who can solve algebra problems or fix a broken fan belt. As children mature, they acquire ever more complex "cognitive structures" that aid them in adapting to their environments.

A cognitive structure—what Piaget called a **scheme** (often also called a *schema*)—is an organized pattern of action or thought that is used to deal with experiences. For example, 4-year-olds have been known to claim that the sun is alive because it moves. Such children are operating on the basis of a simple cognitive scheme: the concept that things that move are alive. The earliest schemes, formed in infancy, are simple motor habits—sucking, grasping, scooping, and so on. Simple as these behavioral recipes are, they allow the infant to manipulate toys and otherwise master the environment. Later in childhood, schemes take the form of "actions in the head" (for example, mental addition and subtraction) that allow children to manipulate information about the problems they encounter in everyday life. At any age, children rely on their current cognitive structures to understand the world around them. As a result, younger and older children may interpret and respond to the same events quite differently.

How do children develop more complex schemes and increase their understanding of the world? Piaget insisted that children are not born with innate ideas about reality, as some philosophers have claimed. Nor are they simply filled with information by adults. Instead, they *actively construct new understandings of the world based on their experiences.* How? By being the curious and active explorers that they are: by watching what is going on around them, by seeing what happens when they experiment on the objects they encounter, and by noticing it when their current understandings are faulty. The *interaction* of a biologically maturing child and his or her environment is responsible for cognitive development.

Return for a moment to the 4-year-old who believes that the sun is alive. Surely this idea was not something that the child learned from adults; it was apparently constructed by the child on the basis of experience. After all, many moving things *are* alive. So long as this child clings to this understanding, she will tend to regard any new object that moves as alive; that is, new experiences will be interpreted in terms of current cognitive structures, a process Piaget called **assimilation.** But suppose the child continues to encounter animate and inanimate objects in daily life and begins to notice that a wind-up toy and a paper airplane move but are not alive and that trees do not move from place to place but are alive. Now there is a contradiction or a "disequilibrium" between the child's understanding and the facts to be understood. It becomes clear to the child that the "objects-that-move-are-alive" concept needs to be revised. A new and more adequate understanding of the distinction between living and nonliving things will be constructed through the process of **accommodation**, an alteration of existing schemes so that they better fit new experiences.

So it goes throughout life. We bring the complementary processes of assimilation and accommodation to bear on our experiences. We naturally attempt to understand our experiences and solve problems using our current cognitive structures (through assimilation), but we sometimes find that our current understandings are flawed. This gives us reason to *revise* our understandings (through accommodation) so that our cognitive structures "fit" reality better (Piaget, 1952). Gradually, children who are exploring the world, developing new schemes, and reorganizing their knowledge of reality have progressed far enough to be thinking about old issues in entirely new ways; that is, they pass from one stage of cognitive development to the next.

Four Stages of Cognitive Development

Piaget proposed four major periods of cognitive development:

The sensorimotor stage (birth to age 2)

The preoperational stage (ages 2 to 7)

The concrete operations stage (ages 7 to 11)

The formal operations stage (ages 11 to 12 or later)

These stages form what Piaget called an *invariant sequence*; that is, all children progress through them in exactly the order in which they are listed. There is no skipping of stages, because each successive stage builds on the previous stage and represents a more complex way of thinking.

The key features of each stage are summarized in Table 2.1. The big message is that children of different ages think in very different ways. We will be exploring Piaget's theory in depth in Chapter 7, but for now let's look at one example of how children who are at different stages of cognitive development might approach the same problem. The problem is to figure out, given a number of objects and a bucket of water, why some objects float and others do not. This is one scientific problem used by Barbel Inhelder and Jean Piaget (1958) to explore the child's developing understanding of the physical world. They asked children to classify objects such as a wooden plank, a pebble, and a candle according to whether they would float or not

Piaget believed that children are naturally curious explorers who try to make sense of their surroundings.

and to explain their classifications. Then they allowed children to experiment with the objects and try to formulate a general law to explain why some objects float and others do not.

What might the infant in the **sensorimotor stage** do in this problem-solving situation? Inhelder and Piaget were not foolish enough to try to find out! The problem is obviously far beyond the grasp of infants who can deal with the world directly through their perceptions and actions but are unable to mentally devise solutions to problems. Lacking command of language, they will not even understand what the task is. What they *are* likely to do is to use their eyes, ears, and hands to actively explore the fascinating materials placed before them. A 6-month-old infant might use her "banging scheme" to bang a block of wood repeatedly against the bucket and listen to the clanking sound that results. A 1-year-old might experiment a bit with the materials, perhaps throwing and dropping objects into the water, carefully watching the splashes that are produced, and shrieking with delight. From the start, human beings are curious about the world; moreover, Piaget maintained, they learn about the world and acquire tools for solving problems through their sensory experiences and their actions (hence the label *sensorimotor* stage). So infants will not solve the floating bodies problem and may instead make a huge mess. However, their actions represent a kind of intelligence and at the same time stimulate their further intellectual growth.

The preschooler who has entered the **preoperational stage** of cognitive development has a great advantage over the infant, for he is now able to use symbols (gestures, images, or words) to stand for objects and events. But the preoperational thinker lacks the tools of logical thought and so is easily fooled by appearances. On the positive side, the 4- or 5-year-old can use language to talk about the task, can imagine doing something before actually doing it, and can think about what happened a few minutes ago rather than being limited, as the infant is, to the world that is immediately present. We can expect the preoperational child to take great interest in placing objects in the water to see what will happen. However, the child's "experiments" are likely to be completely unsystematic, and he is unlikely to form any general rule about floating objects. Being easily fooled by appearances, the preschooler may think that a large object will sink, even if it is light.

Inhelder and Piaget (1958) found that preoperational children offered a different explanation for each instance of floating or sinking they observed. They were not able to classify objects consistently along dimensions like weight and size, and they did not even seem to realize that some of their ideas contradicted others. So Tosc, at age 5, predicted that pebbles would float because they were small and that a plank would float because it was the same color as the bucket; Eli, age 6, decided that a candle would go to the bottom because it was round, and that a wooden ball would stay on top because it was round! Even when young children encounter evidence to contradict their ideas, they may not generalize to new situations and may cling to their incorrect ideas because they want them to be true:

> MIC (5 years) predicts that a plank will sink. The experiment which follows does not induce him to change his mind: [He leans on the plank with all his strength to keep it under the water.] *"You want to stay down, silly!"* — "Will it always stay on the water?" — *"Don't know."* — "Can it stay at the bottom another time?" — *"Yes"* [p. 22].

School-aged children who have advanced to the **concrete operations stage** are likely to seem much more logical in problem-solving situations. These children can perform a number of important actions, or *operations*, in the head. For example, they can mentally form categorization schemes. This helps them realize that either small or large objects can be heavy or light. They now begin to try to resolve contradictions such as the fact that a small object (a key) may sink while a large one (a plank) may float. They can also draw sound general conclusions based on what they observe. But they have difficulty formulating a general rule to explain why some large objects float and some small objects sink; they must depend instead on a trial-and-error approach to problem solving using the concrete materials before them. They are not able to propose a general "theory" of flotation and systematically test it out.

Adolescents who have reached the **formal operations stage** are able to do this. They can form hypotheses or predictions in their heads, plan in advance how to test their ideas, and imagine the consequences of their tests. Consider one 11-year-old:

> ALA (11; 9): "Why do you say that this key will sink?" — *"Because it is heavier than the water."* — "This little key is heavier than that water?" [The bucket is pointed out.] — *"I mean the same capacity of water would be less heavy than the key."* — "What do you

mean?"—*"You would put them* [metal or water] *in containers which contain the same amount and weigh them"* [p. 38].

This ability to imagine *possible* solutions to a problem and to test them out through systematic experiments is a key feature of formal-operational thought. It often takes some years beyond the age of 11 or 12 before adolescents can adopt a thoroughly systematic and scientific method of solving problems and can think through the implications of hypothetical ideas. However, once this kind of systematic hypothesis-testing strategy has developed, an adolescent might be able to formulate the general law of floating objects: the law that says that an object will float if its *density* is less than that of water. This same adolescent might also be able to devise grand theories about what is wrong with the older generation or the educational system!

Obviously the child's cognitive capacities change dramatically between infancy and adolescence as they progress through Piaget's four stages of cognitive development. Young children simply do not think as we do. But what might "Piaget" have to say about the issue of teenage pregnancy? See Box 2.4.

Strengths and Weaknesses of Piaget's Theory

Like Freud, Piaget was a true pioneer whose work has left a deep and lasting imprint on thinking about human development. Indeed, his cognitive-developmental perspective has dominated the field of human development for two or three decades. You will see his influence throughout this text, for the same mind that "constructs" understanding of the physical world also comes, with age, to understand sex differences, moral values, emotions, death, and a range of other important aspects of the human experience. The majority of developmentalists today accept Piaget's beliefs that thinking changes in qualitative ways during childhood, that children are active in their

Box 2.4 Cognitive-Developmental Theory Applied: Piaget on Teenage Pregnancy

You may be wondering what in the world I might have to say about teenage sexual behavior. After all, my main interest has been the development of the mind. And yet, don't you see, teenagers must *decide* whether or not to have sex and whether or not to use birth control. These decisions demand cognitive abilities.

Now you might think that an adolescent who has reached my stage of formal operations would be ready to consider all the possible consequences of his or her actions and make sound decisions. This is true. But different children achieve formal-operational thinking at different rates. I noticed that Sheila and James were not doing particularly well in school. It is possible that they are slow developers who still function in the stage of concrete operations and do not yet have the cognitive skills required to consider all the implications of a decision to have sex without protection.

I also find that many adolescents who show the beginning signs of formal-operational thought have not yet developed the full capacity to plan solutions to problems in advance and to consider all possible alternatives. This sometimes takes a few years. Moreover, adolescents just entering the stage of

formal operations often get carried away with their new cognitive powers. They sometimes begin to feel that they are unique and not subject to the laws of nature that affect others—for instance, "Other teenagers get pregnant, it won't happen to me." Studies show that teenagers fail to anticipate that they will need contraception, miscalculate their odds of becoming pregnant, do not think about the future consequences of their behavior, and are seriously misinformed about sex.[1]

I conclude, then, that the cognitive limitations and knowledge gaps of many teenagers have quite a bit to do with today's high rate of teenage pregnancy. These adolescents are not necessarily in the throes of personality conflicts, as Freud and Erikson would have you believe. They may simply be cognitively immature and uninformed.

[1]For further information about the studies "Dr. Piaget" cites, see: Cobliner (1974), Finkel & Finkel (1978), Morrison (1985), and Steinlauf (1979).

own development, and that development occurs through the interaction of person and environment. Piaget's description of intellectual development has been put to the test and has been largely supported (with some important qualifications that we discuss in detail in Chapter 7). And finally, Piaget's ideas have influenced education and child rearing by encouraging teachers and parents to make learning experiences concrete enough for the young child to understand and to stimulate children to discover concepts through their firsthand experiences.

In spite of these many contributions, Piaget has come in for his share of criticism. Some theorists, psychoanalytic theorists included, would fault Piaget for saying too little about the influences of motivation and emotion on thought processes. In addition, there is some question about whether Piaget's stages really "hang together" as the coherent modes of thinking that he believed they were. Children do not always act as though they were at only one particular stage. Other critics feel that Piaget may have been wrong to choose formal operations as the most "mature" mode of thinking and should have allowed for the possibility of cognitive growth beyond adolescence. And many have felt that Piaget *described* cognitive development well enough but did not fully explain how children progress from one stage of intellect to the next.

Among Piaget's harshest critics have been those who believe that we do not develop in a stagelike fashion at all—who believe that we are the products of whatever learning experiences we have in life. As we will see, these learning theorists paint a very different portrait of the developing person.

LEARNING THEORIES

> Give me a dozen healthy infants, well formed, and my own specified world to bring them up in and I'll guarantee to take any one at random and train him to become any type of specialist I might select—doctor, lawyer, artist, merchant, chief, and yes, even beggar-man and thief, regardless of his talents, penchants, tendencies, abilities, vocations, and race of his ancestors [Watson, 1925, p. 82].

There is a bold statement! It reflects a belief that nurture is everything and nature, or hereditary endowment, counts for nothing. It was made by John B. Watson, a strong believer in the importance of learning in human development and the father of the school of thought in psychology called behaviorism.

A basic premise of Watson's **behaviorism** is that conclusions about human development and functioning should be based on observations of overt behavior rather than on speculations about unconscious motives or cognitive processes that remain unobservable. Watson (1913) believed that the psychologists of his day were wasting their time studying subjective, "mentalistic" concepts such as sensation, emotion, and cognition. Psychologists should study observable stimuli and observable responses to them.

Moreover, said Watson, *learned* associations between external stimuli and observable responses are the building blocks of human development. Like John Locke, Watson believed that the infant is a *tabula rasa* to be written on by experience. Children have no inborn tendencies; how they turn out will depend entirely on the environment in which they grow up. So development depends on *learning*, the process through which experience (as opposed to biological maturation) produces relatively permanent changes in behavior. According to a behavioral perspective, then, it is a mistake to assume that children advance through a series of distinct stages partly programmed by maturation, as Freud, Erikson, and Piaget have argued. Instead, development is viewed as a continuous process of behavior change that can differ greatly from person to person.

Watson took a very extreme environmentalist stand on the nature/nurture issue, one that few developmentalists today would take. Perhaps that is because he lived in a time when most psychologists believed the opposite—that people's characteristics were primarily influenced by their hereditary endowment and that human development was a biological unfolding of capacities. To prove his point, Watson set out to demonstrate that children's fears are learned rather than inborn. He arranged the experiences of an infant named Albert in such a way as to make a child who was unafraid of white furry animals terrified of them (Watson & Raynor, 1920). It was relatively simple: He presented one stimulus (a white rat) to Albert at the same time that he produced another stimulus (a loud and frightening noise). Through learning, Albert formed an association between the white rat and the frightening noise and came to display a fearful response at the sight of white furry objects. Fears that are learned can be unlearned if feared objects such as the white rat come to be associated through learning with happy emotions. Thus response patterns can come and go over the years. Each individual will develop in his or her own directions and at his or her own speed depending on what is learned when.

Skinner's Operant-Conditioning Theory

B. F. Skinner, who is as well known as any contemporary psychologist, has done much to advance the behavioral learning theory pioneered by Watson. Through his research with animals, Skinner (1953) gained understanding of one very important form of learning. He would put a rat in a special cage called a "Skinner box." On one side of the box was a bar; pressing the bar caused a food pellet to be delivered. Upon entering the Skinner box, a rat does what rats normally do in a new environment: some moving around, sniffing, scratching, and so forth. The rat happens to press the lever and then happens to find a food pellet in the food receptacle. The rat goes on sniffing and exploring, hits the bar again in its meanderings, and again receives food. Through a series of such experiences, an association forms between the behavior of pressing the bar and its consequence, the delivery of a food pellet. Before long, the rat is no longer behaving as it was initially; it has formed a new habit and is pressing the bar as fast as its paws will let it!

This form of learning is called **operant** (or instrumental) **conditioning**. A learner's existing behaviors become either more or less probable depending on the consequences they produce. **Reinforcers** (such as the food pellets delivered to the rat) are consequences that increase the probability that a response will occur in the future. The rat formed a habit of pressing the bar frequently because that particular behavior was reinforced. Similarly, a boy may form a long-term habit of sharing food and toys with playmates if his parents reinforce generous behavior with praise, or a saleswoman may work harder at making sales if she receives a bonus for each sale. **Punishers**, on the other hand, are consequences that suppress a response and decrease the likelihood that it will occur in the future. If the rat who had been reinforced with a food pellet for pressing the bar were suddenly given a painful shock each time it pressed the bar, the "bar pressing" habit would begin to disappear. Similarly, a teenage girl whose car keys are confiscated every time she stays out beyond her curfew and a man who is criticized for interrupting people during meetings are likely to cut down on the responses that resulted in punishment. Very simply, we learn to keep doing the things that have positive consequences and to stop doing the things that have negative consequences.

Like Watson, then, Skinner believes that human development results from the individual's learning experiences. One boy's aggressive behavior may be reinforced over time because he gets his way with other children and his parents encourage his "macho" behavior. Another boy may quickly learn that aggression is punished. The two may develop in quite different directions based on their different histories of reinforcement and punishment. In this view, there is no cause for speaking of an "aggressive stage" in child development or an "aggressive drive" within human beings. Skinner does acknowledge that evolution has provided human beings with a brain that allows them to learn from experience and that even influences what they can learn most easily or what they find most reinforcing. However, he believes that the essence of human development is the continual acquisition of new habits of behavior and that these learned behaviors are controlled by *external* stimuli (reinforcers and punishers). Even if development seems stagelike, the cause need not be biological maturation. Instead, age-related changes in the environment—as when 6-year-olds enter school and are reinforced and punished in new ways by their teachers—could produce age-related changes in behavior (Bijou & Baer, 1961).

Most developmentalists appreciate that Skinner's operant conditioning is indeed one important mechanism of learning. They recognize that human development can take varied forms and that habits can emerge and disappear over a lifetime depending on whether they have positive or negative consequences. Yet some theorists believe that Skinner places too much emphasis on a single type of learning and too little emphasis on the role of cognitive processes such as attention, memory, and reflection in learning. Albert Bandura has proposed a cognitive social learning theory based in part on his reservations about Skinner's views.

Bandura's Cognitive Social Learning Theory

Albert Bandura's (1977, 1986, 1989) **social learning theory** claims that humans are cognitive beings whose active processing of information from the environment plays a major role in learning and human development.

Recently, he has termed his perspective a "social cognitive theory" to further emphasize the importance of cognition in human behavior (Bandura, 1986, 1989). To Skinner, the mind was a "black box" between external stimuli and responses. Because Skinner believed that the mind could not be studied objectively and felt that the causes of behavior lay in the environment rather than within the person, he paid little attention to cognitive processes. The same learning principles that shape the behavior of rats were also believed to shape the behavior of human beings.

But Bandura would argue that human learning *is* different from rat learning because humans have far more sophisticated cognitive capabilities. Bandura agrees with Skinner that operant conditioning is an important type of learning, but he notes that humans *think* about the connections between their behavior and its consequences, anticipate what consequences are likely to follow from their future behavior, and often are more affected by what they *believe* will happen than by the consequences they actually encounter. For example, a woman may continue to pursue an advanced degree despite many punishments and few immediate rewards because she *anticipates* a greater reward when she completes her studies. We are not just passively shaped by the external consequences of our behavior; we actively interpret past and present experiences and anticipate the future. We also reinforce or punish ourselves with mental "pats on the back" and self-criticism.

Nowhere is Bandura's cognitive emphasis clearer than in his decision to highlight **observational learning** as the most important mechanism through which human behavior changes. Observational learning is simply learning that results from observing the behavior of other people (called *social models*). A 2-year-old boy may discover how to pet the family dog merely by watching how his older sister does it. A teenager will learn the latest dress styles, dances, and "lingo" by watching and listening to other teenagers. A middle-aged man may learn how to use a computer by observing a colleague. Such observational learning could not occur unless cognitive processes were at work. We must, for example, pay attention to the model, actively digest what we observe, and store this information in memory if we are to imitate what we have observed at a later date.

Over the years, we are exposed to hundreds of social models and have the opportunity to learn thousands of behavior patterns (some good, some bad) simply by observing others perform them. We do not just imitate in a "monkey see, monkey do" fashion, either. We can learn abstract rules of behavior, as when the student watching a chemistry experiment in the lab learns not only how to perform that specific experiment but also how to go about performing experiments *in general*. Moreover, learning does not require that we be reinforced for imitating what we observe. We do, however, take note of whether the model's behavior has positive or negative consequences and use that information to decide whether to act on what we have learned.

Watson and Skinner may believe humans are shaped by the environment to become whatever those around them groom them to be, but Bandura does not. Because he views humans as active, cognitive beings, he holds that human development occurs through a continuous reciprocal interaction between person and environment—a perspective called **reciprocal determinism**. Consider the impacts of television on children's behavior (Bandura, 1986). It is clear that children can be influenced by their television "environment"; through their observation of models on the television screen they can, for example, learn aggressive acts such as slamming people against walls. And yet some children shy away from violent programs, whereas children who already have aggressive tendencies are especially likely to prefer and to select violent TV programs (Eron, Huesmann, Brice, Fischer, & Mermelstein, 1983). That is, the child actively shapes his or her TV viewing environment, which in turn may further strengthen preexisting aggressive tendencies. Our personal characteristics and our actions affect the social environment just as the social environment alters our personal characteristics and future behavior. Here Bandura sounds a bit like Piaget, who also believes that development occurs through the interaction of an active person with the environment.

But before we conclude that Bandura and Piaget see eye to eye, we had better ask what Bandura thinks about the idea of systematic and universal stages of human development. Clearly he is skeptical; instead, he thinks that development can proceed along many different paths depending on what kinds of social learning experiences the individual receives and helps to create. As in other learning theories, there are no "stages" of development; changes occur gradually through a lifetime of learning.

Bandura does acknowledge that children's cognitive

learning capacities mature over childhood. As they get older, for example, they can remember more about what they have seen and can imitate a greater variety of novel behaviors. And yet Bandura also believes that much development, especially the acquisition of complex knowledge, depends on experiences that are not universal—for example, on encountering specific material in school. Consequently, he doubts that all children develop through one universal set of stages as Piaget claimed (Bandura, 1986). Moreover, he thinks that Piaget did children a disservice by assuming that their capacities are limited and that they cannot learn certain things until they are maturationally ready. He prefers a more aggressive philosophy of child rearing and education: Adults should devise more sophisticated instructional techniques rather than waiting for children to make discoveries on their own.

Obviously there is a fundamental disagreement between stage theorists like Piaget or Erikson and the learning theorists. Stage theorists, even when they insist that experience is essential for normal development and contributes greatly to creating differences among individuals, still believe that universal maturational forces guide the development of all humans along similar paths—through the same stages. By contrast, learning theorists do not give us a general description of the normal course of human development because they insist that there is no such description to give. Instead, learning theorists give us a rich account of the mechanisms through which behavior can change over time. They ask us to apply basic principles of learning to understand how specific individuals change with age. So, can you apply learning principles to the matter of teenage pregnancy? Skinner's and Bandura's points of view appear in Box 2.5.

Strengths and Weaknesses of Learning Theory

Behavioral learning theories and Bandura's cognitive social learning theory have contributed immensely to our understanding of development. Learning theories are very precise and testable, and carefully controlled experiments have established that the learning processes these theories propose do in fact operate. Learning theorists have been able to demonstrate how we might learn everything from altruism to alcoholism. We will see the fruits of research on human learning throughout this text.

Moreover, the learning principles involved in operant conditioning, observational learning, and other forms of learning have been shown to operate *across the entire life span*. Stage theorists such as Freud and Piaget had little to say about adult development, but learning theorists can go about trying to understand middle-aged or older adults in the same way that they attempt to understand infants. Finally, learning theories have very practical applications; they have been the basis for many effective techniques for optimizing development and treating developmental problems. Parents and teachers can certainly be more effective when they systematically reinforce the behavior they hope to instill in children and when they serve as role models of desirable behavior. And many psychotherapists today apply behavioral and cognitive learning techniques to treat psychological problems.

At the same time, learning theories leave something to be desired as models of human development. Consider the following demonstration. Paul Weisberg (1963) reinforced 3-month-old infants with smiles and gentle rubs on the chin whenever they happened to babble. He found that these infants babbled more often than did infants who received the same social stimulation randomly rather than only after each babbling sound they made. But does this demonstration of the power of social reinforcement mean that infants normally begin to babble often *because* babbling is reinforced by their caregivers? Not necessarily. All normal infants babble at about 4 months of age even though some have more responsive parents than others do. Moreover, no matter what experiences were provided to a newborn, he or she would not be maturationally ready to begin babbling. We must suspect, then, that the maturation of the brain has more than a little to do with the onset of babbling during infancy.

This example really highlights two criticisms of learning theories as theories of human development. First, learning theorists rarely demonstrate that learning is actually responsible for commonly observed developmental changes; they often demonstrate only that learning *might have* resulted in developmental change. Second, learning theorists may have oversimplified their account of development by downplaying the influences of biology and maturation. Children simply cannot achieve certain developmental milestones until they are maturationally ready. And while individuals differ from each other partly because they have different experiences in life, they also differ from each other because they have different ge-

Box 2.5
Learning Theory Applied: Skinner and Bandura on Teenage Pregnancy

I ("B. F. Skinner") will get right to the point: Teenage pregnancy occurs because teenagers have *learned* to engage in sexual behavior! By the same token, teenagers also have not learned to practice contraception. My point has been made well by one team of researchers: "It is quite likely that if teenagers had to take a pill to become pregnant, early childbearing would quickly vanish as a social problem."[1] Let me offer a bit more detail. Sexual stimulation, like food, is naturally reinforcing; we tend to keep doing things that result in sexual pleasure. But other stimuli—for example, attention and positive comments from other people—become reinforcers through learning processes. Suppose that during their early dating history James was especially attentive and complimentary to Sheila each time she returned his kisses or responded positively to his attempts to fondle her, but became quite withdrawn and took her home early when she said "No." Reinforced for engaging in sexual activities and punished for refusing, Sheila's behavior would gradually be "shaped" in the direction of sexual intercourse. (If that sounds sexist, let me note that it could just as easily work the other way, attentive behavior on Sheila's part reinforcing James's sexual behavior.) Meanwhile, the use of contraception is an unlikely behavior because it detracts from the spontaneity of sex and has no immediate reinforcement value to speak of. Surely we need not assume that young people are riddled by inner conflicts or lack the cognitive capacities to make sound decisions about sex. It's much simpler to assume that the consequences of their past sexual behavior influenced their present sexual behavior.

I ("Albert Bandura") appreciate Professor Skinner's account of teenage pregnancy, but I believe that my social learning theory yields additional insights. Sheila and James have been learning a great deal about sexual behavior through observation. Today's adolescents live in a social world filled with messages about sex from their peers, the media, and, to a lesser extent, their parents. They actively process this information for future use. They learn that their friends are "doing it" and are enjoying themselves. They view sex on TV all the time—often exploitive sex, with never a mention of birth control and rarely a mention of consequences such as the strains of being a teenage parent.

In a recent study, adolescents were asked what people they regarded as models of "responsible sexual behavior" or of "irresponsible sexual behavior."[2] These teenagers had a hard time even thinking of positive sexual role models. Almost half of them named their parents as adults whom they *generally* respected as role models, but only about a quarter of them cited their parents as positive sexual role models. Most important, media personalities and friends readily came to mind as models of *irresponsible* sexual behavior. These findings suggest that adolescents today have more opportunities to learn sexually irresponsible behavior than to learn sexually responsible behavior through observation.

B. F. Skinner

Albert Bandura

"B. F. Skinner" is referring to Furstenberg, Lincoln, & Menken (1981),[1] and "Albert Bandura" is citing Fabes & Strouse (1984).[2]

netic endowments. Perhaps it is time to examine a theory that highlights the contributions of biology to human development.

ETHOLOGICAL THEORY

John Watson may have taken the extreme environmental stand he did partly because other theorists of his era took the equally extreme position that human development was almost entirely a matter of biological maturation guided by the genes. Prominent among these theorists was Arnold Gesell (1880–1961), an American physician and psychologist who collected some of the first systematic data on normal milestones in child development and influenced many parents with his popular books on child rearing (Gesell & Ilg, 1949). He was convinced that psychological development after birth, like the growth of the embryo before birth, was genetically controlled and highly predictable. Children, like plants, simply "bloomed" according to a timetable laid out in their genes; how their parents raised them was of little importance.

Today's developmentalists have largely rejected the position that all of development is laid out in the genes, much as they have rejected Watson's insistence that all is learned. However, the view that biological influences on development are significant is still with us in the form of the modern ethological perspective. Ethology is the study of the evolved behavior of a species in its natural surroundings. Ethologists have tended to focus on the ways in which members of a species are alike and develop in similar ways rather than on the ways in which they differ. Ethologists have also insisted that behavior be studied in its natural context (Hinde, 1983, 1989). After all, that is the context in which the behavior evolved and in which it has proved to be adaptive.

Ethological Studies of Attachment in Birds

Noted ethologists such as Konrad Lorenz and Niko Tinbergen have asked how behaviors that are species-wide (or at least universal in a segment of a species such as males or females or infants) might be adaptive in the sense that they contribute to survival. These sorts of "species-specific behaviors" are easy to recognize in animals. Birds, for example, seem to come biologically equipped to engage in instinctual behaviors such as following their mothers, building nests, and singing songs. But why do they do these things? During the course of evolution, birds with the genes responsible for these adaptive behaviors would be more likely to survive and pass on their genes to their offspring than birds without these genes. Eventually, the genes underlying these behaviors would become widespread in the species.

Consider Konrad Lorenz's classic work on **imprinting**, an innate or instinctual form of learning in which the young of certain species will follow and become attached to moving objects (typically their mothers) early in life. In his observations of goslings, Lorenz (1937) noted that

> imprinting is an automatic response; it is not learned but is simply "released" by the stimulus of a moving object;
>
> it occurs only within a narrowly delimited **critical period** shortly after the gosling has hatched, a period during which the organism is particularly sensitive to certain environmental influences, influences that will have little effect before or after the critical period.

During their critical period for imprinting, goslings readily attach themselves to the first moving object they encounter, even if that object is a human rather than a goose. If a gosling is separated from its mother during the critical period, it will miss the opportunity to form an attachment to her. The adaptive value of imprinting is obvious: Young birds stand a far better chance of surviving if they remain near a mother who can feed them and protect them from predators than if they wander through the reeds on their own. Because forming an attachment increases the chances of survival, the genetic program underlying this response has become widespread in geese, chickens, ducks, and other birds.

Although ethologists like Lorenz clearly emphasize the biological or genetic basis for behavior, they do *not* ignore environmental influences on development. Species-specific behaviors like the "following" response shown by young fowl have evolved because they have proved adaptive within the particular environment in which the species must try to survive. Other behaviors might prove more adaptive in a different environment. Moreover, responses like imprinting are not entirely inborn; they will not develop properly unless the right environmental stimulation (exposure to a moving object that "releases" the response) is provided.

Konrad Lorenz demonstrated that goslings would become imprinted to him rather than to their mother if he was the first moving object they encountered during their critical period for imprinting.

Ethology and Human Development

Do humans also display species-specific behaviors as they develop? Is there any similarity between imprinting in birds and parent/child attachment in humans? As we shall see in Chapter 13, a very influential ethological theory of the development of attachments between infants and their caregivers has been formulated by John Bowlby (1969, 1973). Bowlby believes that many infant behaviors that promote emotional attachments have evolved because they make it more likely that the infant will be cared for by adults and will therefore survive. Why, for example, do all normal human infants smile in response to human faces at about a month or two of age? What role might this play in survival? It is clear that adults have a hard time resisting a big grin from an infant; they are not as likely to warm up to and care for a sullen or unresponsive baby. Thus the social smile could well have become programmed into the genetic makeup of virtually all infants because it has adaptive value. Similarly, the infant's cry is quite adaptive, for it brings adults scurrying to meet the infant's needs. And once an infant becomes firmly attached to a caregiver at about 6 or 7 months of age, the infant, somewhat like a gosling, seems to be programmed to maintain proximity to this person. Adults, meanwhile, have perhaps evolved in ways that make them responsive to infants—for example, upset by the sound of an infant's cry.

Bowlby believes that the first three years of life may well be a kind of critical period for human beings in which they are uniquely ready to form close emotional ties and will suffer if they do not have the opportunity to do so. Normally, close attachments evolve in a stagelike manner; by the second half of the first year of life, most infants are clearly attached to someone. However, infants who are raised in understaffed and unstimulating institutions may not have the opportunity to "imprint" on any human being. As a result, Bowlby argues, they may miss the opportunity to acquire important social and emotional responses, and they may find it difficult later in life to form close and lasting relationships. Similarly, infants whose caregivers fail to respond consistently to them or even abandon them may later become insecure or overdependent in their relationships, afraid that partners will abandon them. In Bowlby's view, then, infants are biologically equipped to form close attachments early in life, but the quality of their early social experiences can leave a lasting stamp on their later development. Box 2.6 describes what John Bowlby might have to say about teenage pregnancy.

Strengths and Weaknesses of Ethological Theory

Because ethology grew out of the work of zoologists, more has been done to apply this perspective to the study of animals than to apply it to human beings. Bowlby's theory of attachment is the most ambitious ethological theory of human development to date, and ethologists have only fairly recently begun to study other aspects of human development (Hinde, 1983). Nonetheless, ethologists have already contributed to our understanding of human development by reminding us that human beings are biological creatures born with a number of genetically influenced predispositions. They encourage us to view every individual as the product of a long evolutionary history, and they stimulate us to ask how many of the behaviors that virtually all humans display might have aided our species in adapting to its environment. In addition, ethologists have shown us the value of studying human development in normal, everyday settings and of comparing human development to development in other species.

Like psychoanalytic theory, ethological theory has sometimes been criticized on the ground that it is difficult to test. It can indeed be difficult to prove that behaviors actually are inborn or actually do contribute to survival. In addition, ethological theory is sometimes criticized for offering after-the-fact explanations rather than predictions about what is likely to happen in the future. It is tempting, for example, to conclude that any behavior we commonly observe in humans *must* have a genetic basis. However, such a conclusion is unwarranted without evidence, particularly since human beings have such a great capacity to *learn* more adaptive behavior patterns and to teach them to their young. Finally, critics have raised questions about whether what holds true among other species really applies to humans. For instance, the concept of critical periods may not be very useful in analyzing human development; instead, it seems wiser to speak of *sensitive periods* during which some kinds of learning come a bit easier than they do at an earlier or later age (Hinde, 1983).

Despite these criticisms, the ethological perspective, with its emphasis on the biological roots of human development, provides a healthy balance to the environmental emphasis apparent in learning theories. Indeed, it seems

Box 2.6 Ethological Theory Applied: Bowlby on Teenage Pregnancy

I know that learning theorists such as Skinner and Bandura would like you to believe that teenagers such as Sheila and James learn through their experiences to engage in irresponsible sexual behavior, but let's look at this whole matter from a biological perspective. What behavior contributes to the survival of the species more than sexual behavior? Other species have been genetically programmed to engage in elaborate courtship rituals that ensure that they will attract biologically fit mates and reproduce. Why should we think that humans are any different? Aren't teenagers, by donning their designer jeans and flirting with each other in shopping malls, simply pursuing the biological goal of luring a suitable mate?

So let's at least consider the possibility that Sheila and James engaged in genetically influenced behavior with adaptive significance. Earlier in the history of our species, individuals whose genes called for early maturation and early sexual activity probably had an evolutionary advantage.[1] I'll admit that getting an early start may not be as adaptive in today's environment, where reproductive success as an adult may depend more on obtaining a good education in order to have the financial means to bear and raise children. Still, my point is that many teenagers may just be doing what comes naturally, given their biological heritage.

But let me also offer some comments about Sheila and James based on my theory of attachment. Like Freud, I believe that the quality of an infant's first relationship affects the quality of all later relationships. Even though infants and parents are biologically predisposed to form close emotional attachments, early social experiences will influence just how close and secure those attachments become. Imagine that Sheila and James, as infants, could never quite rely on their parents to come when called or to smile when smiled at. Or suppose that death or divorce caused one or both of these youngsters to suffer the loss of a parent to whom they were closely attached. I have theorized that young children form "working models" of attachment figures and of themselves based on their early experiences. Infants who receive inconsistent care or who are separated from a parent may well come to view attachment figures as unreliable and to view themselves as unlovable. If this were the case for Sheila and James, they might have engaged in sex to hang on to each other or to prove that they were lovable after all. Research is beginning to bear me out on this: Individuals who had insecure relationships with their parents tend to be insecure in their relationships with romantic partners as well.[2]

In short, teenage sexual behavior is, from an ethological perspective, behavior that is rooted in our evolutionary history and called for by our genetic endowment. At the same time, teenagers are not just the slaves of biologically based instincts; their experiences, especially with their parents, will also affect how their biologically based tendencies are expressed.

For further information on the studies cited by "Bowlby," see Weisfeld & Billings (1988)[1] and Hazan & Shaver (1987).[2]

that the more we learn about developmental processes, the more complex they seem, and the more we need to consider the full range of influences on development.

CONTEXTUAL-DIALECTICAL PERSPECTIVES ON DEVELOPMENT

Several theorists in the United States have been formulating new, more complex perspectives on development called **contextual-dialectical theories**. Very simply, these perspectives hold that development arises from the ongoing interrelationships between a changing organism and a changing world (for example, Lerner, 1982; Riegel, 1976, 1979; Sameroff, 1975, 1983). Changes in the person produce changes in his or her environment, changes in the environment produce changes in the person, and this interchange goes on continuously.

Actually, the importance of the social and historical context in which development occurs has been emphasized by Soviet psychologists ever since the Russian Revolution. Pioneering Russian theorist Lev Vygotsky (1962, 1978) entered into some lively debates with his contemporary, Jean Piaget, concerning the nature of cognitive development. As we have seen, Piaget believed that children expand their minds in the same universal directions as they go about exploring the world on their own. By contrast, Vygotsky insisted that children's minds are shaped by the particular social and historical context in which they live and by their interactions with adults.

Each society, for example, passes on to its children a particular language, which then colors their mental activities as they begin to think in words. Moreover, children are guided by adults toward acquiring the concepts and problem-solving techniques important in their culture. A 6-year-old girl who is given a set of construction blocks for Christmas, for example, may have no notion of how to build a house with it. But suppose her father demonstrates how to fit pieces together to make a roof and walls and then coaches his daughter as she tries it herself. She will eventually internalize the problem-solving techniques he shows her and, later, use them on her own. In Vygotsky's view, then, cognitive growth arises from the child's social interactions, and the knowledge and skills transmitted to children may be quite different in one culture and era than in another. A similar appreciation of the cultural and historical context of development is reflected in the dialectical theory of Klaus Riegel.

Riegel's Dialectical Theory

To illustrate the contextual-dialectical perspective more fully, let's consider the **dialectical theory** of development put forth by Klaus Riegel (1976, 1979). The term "dialectic" means a kind of dialogue or argument; dialectical theory holds that development results from continuous dialogues between a changing person and a changing world. Riegel questioned stage theories such as Piaget's because they seem to assume that we function at one stable and coherent stage or another for long periods of our lives. True, Piaget proposed that during transition periods between stages, children discover contradictions between their understandings and the reality of things. In these transition periods, person and environment are in disequilibrium or conflict, and the child is spurred on to devise more sophisticated understandings. But Piaget's child then moves to a new stage in which a good "fit" or an equilibrium between person and environment exists once more. By contrast, Riegel argues that while we seek harmony with our environments, we rarely achieve it. When person and world are in continual flux and conflict, there are no stable periods that can be described as stages.

Riegel focused attention on four major dimensions of development, two of them lying within the person and two of them lying outside the person:

1. An *inner-biological* dimension that involves such changes as the maturation of the nervous system, pubertal changes, menopause, wrinkling, and the onset of illnesses
2. An *individual-psychological* dimension that includes changing thoughts, emotions, and personality processes
3. An *outer physical* dimension, or the physical world of changing weather conditions, physical settings, and so on
4. A *cultural-sociological* dimension that includes a changing social environment, historical events, and cultural values

Each of these four dimensions is like a river, constantly changing, and each is interacting with the other dimensions and with other elements within the same dimension. So intimately intertwined are these dimensions that we really cannot easily separate person and environment.

Using Riegel's four dimensions, we can analyze the dialectics of growth and change—that is, the interaction between dimensions of development. According to Riegel, changes in one dimension of development inevitably lead to changes in other dimensions. Usually the adjustment process resembles a calm conversation between person and environment. For example, we easily adjust our steps as we confront curbs and stairs in the physical environment. Sometimes, however, we experience crises in which a major change in one dimension puts two or more of the dimensions "out of synch." We then seek to resolve the conflict if we can.

Let's look at the dynamic interplay of dimensions of development in the lives of Ed and Erma, a middle-aged married couple. Erma began working as a computer analyst five years ago and has just been offered a promotion—one that would require her to move to New Jersey. Ed is quite comfortable with his current job as a sales supervisor. Picture these two people at the dinner table carrying on a dialogue about the possibility of moving. Consider first the short-term development that may take place during their conversation. We immediately notice that what Ed says influences what Erma says next, and that what Erma says influences what Ed says. Ed and Erma affect and are affected by each other so much that we have to view them as a couple or unit rather than as two independent people. Moreover, there is a structure to their conversation: They take turns speaking (except when someone interrupts in the heat of debate), and their statements are related to what came before. Finally, unless one or the other stomps off in disgust, the whole dialogue may lead somewhere—perhaps to some meeting of the minds or to a new insight into their relationship. A dialogue like this, Riegel (1979) believes, is a good model of the developmental process.

To understand the longer-term development of Ed and Erma, we must place them in the context of changes that have been taking place in the cultural-sociological dimension of development. When Ed and Erma married, traditional gender-role beliefs prevailed in society; women were to be housewives or to subordinate their careers to those of their husbands. But Ed and Erma have been developing as individuals in a historical period of rapid change in beliefs regarding the roles of men and women (Hefner, Rebecca, & Oleshansky, 1975). This cultural-sociological change has helped create the present conflict in their lives; there would have been none if traditional ideas about gender roles had remained strong and Erma had been content as a housewife. Ed, who is content with his career and life, now experiences an *asynchrony*, or a lack of meshing, between the individual-psychological dimension of development (his own vocational goals and his traditional gender-role attitudes) and the cultural-sociological dimension of development (a social world that now asks him to view women as equals). Moreover, Ed's individual-psychological development now clashes with Erma's individual-psychological development. Erma is psychologically ready for new challenges in her career, while Ed wants to follow the career path he is already on. Marriage partners are constantly changing, and when changes in one partner do not mesh with changes in the other partner, the relationship can be thrown off balance.

Riegel argues that such conflicts between individuals and between the four dimensions of development affecting individuals produce developmental change. We cannot always predict in advance what the outcomes will be; that is, we cannot assume that development will inevitably move through a series of universal stages. Instead, we must analyze the ongoing transactions between people and their changing world. Perhaps Ed and Erma will simply decide to divorce. Or perhaps they will be able to forge a new agreement out of their disagreement—perhaps a plan to postpone the move until Ed has more time to locate a new job for himself. Whatever resolution is achieved, harmony or balance will not last long. Once resolutions to this conflict are achieved, new conflicts will inevitably arise in the lives of these two people. Riegel summarizes it this way:

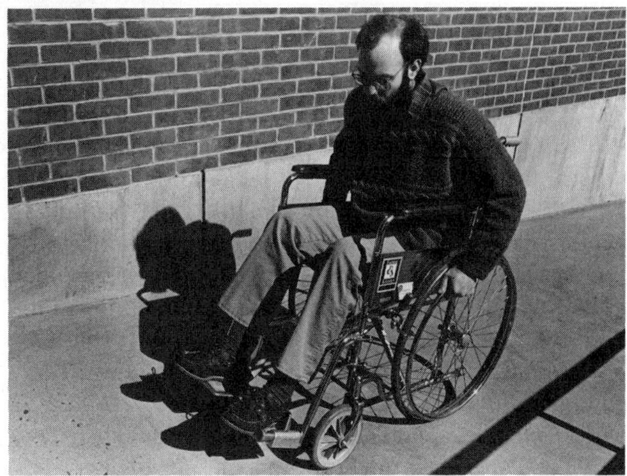

The inner-biological and individual-psychological dimensions of development proposed by Riegel can become "out of sync" when a person who loves sports becomes disabled. This disequilibrium may stimulate growth and change.

> Specifically, development is brought about by crises in these progressions [the four dimensions of development] which create discordance and conflicts. Through the actions of individuals in society, synchronization is reestablished and thereby progress achieved. But as such a coordination is attained, new discrepancies emerge producing a continuous flux of contradictions and changes [Riegel, 1979, p. 2].

In short, contextual-dialectical theorists believe that person and environment form a unit, that both are in continual flux, and that changes in one produce changes in the other (Lerner & Kauffman, 1985). We cannot ignore the fact that people develop in a changing historical context—something that Piaget and other stage theorists tend to do. Nor can we focus all of our attention on external events and ignore the effects of human beings on their environments—something that Skinner and other behavioral theorists tend to do. We must view development as consisting of changes in the *relationship* between person and environment. A contextual-dialectical perspective on teenage pregnancy is presented in Box 2.7.

Box 2.7
Contextual-Dialectical Theory Applied: Riegel on Teenage Pregnancy

To understand why Sheila and James are faced with an unintended pregnancy, we can start by analyzing their ongoing relationship. People select and shape their environments and therefore help to produce their own development. James and Sheila each influenced the other, just as each was influenced by the other. Their sexual behavior evolved over time through their ongoing "dialogue." Indeed, the most important influence on an adolescent's sexual behavior and use of contraceptives is his or her partner.[1]

Of course, I would also want to emphasize the relevant relations between these young people and the changing world in which they are developing. Our society has undergone a number of important historical, or cultural-sociological, changes that have had impacts on developing adolescents. Think of it: increased sexual permissiveness, more working mothers and therefore less supervision of teenagers, the introduction of the pill, the legalization of abortion, and more.[2] Sheila and James have undoubtedly been influenced by these social changes.

Moreover, the different dimensions of development are out of synchrony for today's teenagers. Teenagers are reaching sexual maturity earlier today than in past eras because of improved nutrition and health care (see Chapter 5); that is, their inner-biological development is proceeding rapidly. So today's young teenagers are biologically ready for sex, and society gives them plenty of messages to the effect that sex is desirable. And yet, in terms of the individual-psychological dimension of development, these young people may still be socially immature, overdependent on others, and psychologically unready for committed relationships.[3] In short, a conflict between the different dimensions of development exists for many teenagers like James and Sheila. They will take some action to reduce the conflict—perhaps in this case by convincing themselves that they are really psychologically mature enough for a sexual relationship.

My dialectical approach is also illustrated well by Beatrix Hamburg's[4] intriguing analysis of teenage pregnancy in high poverty areas. Many advantaged youth will postpone sexual pleasure for a time—or use birth control—because they are working toward long-term career goals. But what hope does the disadvantaged youth have when inner-city unemployment is rampant and educational systems are poor? Hamburg argues that many young women in such circumstances try to cope as best they can with their disadvantaged social environment by postponing work (since there are no jobs anyway) and instead having children. By having children, they mobilize their families to support them. Then, when the children are more able to care for themselves, and when their relatives are lined up to provide help with child care, they go back to school or begin working. Odd as it may seem, then, for some teenage girls getting pregnant may be an adaptive way of coping with a difficult sociocultural environment—and indeed of *changing* that environment in order to achieve personal goals.

For further information on the studies "Riegel" referred to, see Thompson & Spanier (1978),[1] Chilman (1986),[2] Lancaster & Hamburg (1986),[3] and Hamburg (1986).[4]

Strengths and Weaknesses of Contextual-Dialectical Theory

Contextual-dialectical perspectives on development have begun to emerge in recent years in response to some of the deficiencies of earlier stage theories and learning theories of development. They are complex, but that is because life-span human development appears to be far more complex than it once appeared to be. We can applaud Riegel and like-minded theorists for emphasizing some very important truths about human development. Development *does* occur in a context. People *do* change their environments and contribute to their own development, just as they are influenced by other people and by events outside them. And not all developmental changes lead inevitably to some "mature" end point such as the achievement of formal-operational thought. Instead, development takes many different directions, and we cannot always predict how lives will turn unless we look more closely at the ongoing transactions between the person and the environment.

The life-span developmental perspective introduced in Chapter 1 is contextual in its orientation. It emphasizes historical influences on development and the reciprocal relationship between person and environment. Life-span researchers have come to see that, while the development of infants and young children appears to be quite influenced by universal maturational processes, children, and especially adults, differ widely from one another because of the operation of social and historical forces. Thus a contextual perspective will prove to be important to us as we examine specific aspects of development in later chapters.

But perhaps you have noticed that the contextual-dialectical perspective does not give us a very clear picture of the course of human development. Indeed, there is no full-blown contextual-dialectical theory as yet. Klaus Riegel died before he could elaborate on his ideas, and other theorists are still working on theirs. Up to this point, these theorists have mainly alerted us to the need to examine how personal and environmental factors interact over time to produce developmental change. We could, therefore, criticize contextual-dialectical theory for being only partially formulated at this point. But a more serious criticism can be made: The contextual-dialectical perspective may never provide any coherent developmental theory. Why? Suppose we really take seriously the idea that development can take a wide range of forms owing to the influence of a wide range of factors both within and outside the person. How can we ever state generalizations about development that will hold up for most people? Must we develop separate theories for different subgroups of people: one theory for women born in 1920 and living in Kenya, another for men born in 1960 and living in the southeastern United States, and so on? If change over a lifetime depends on the ongoing transactions between a unique person and a unique environment, is each life span unique?

For these reasons, some theorists worry that the contextual-dialectical perspective will lead to a chaotic view of human development (Baltes, 1983). As an alternative, they suggest that we combine the contextual perspective with the best features of stage theories that propose universal developmental paths (Lerner & Kauffman, 1985). We might then see humans as moving in orderly and universal directions in some aspects of their development, yet we could also try to understand how that developmental course can be altered by a changing social and historical context. We might view such developmental attainments as formal-operational thinking not as inevitable achievements but as attainments that are more or less *probable* depending on the individual's life experiences (Lerner & Kauffman, 1985).

Whether contextual theorists will be able to develop useful theories of human development is not yet clear, but in the meantime the contributions of contextual-dialectical theorists have brought an increasing awareness that individual development must be studied in its larger social context.

THEORIES AND WORLD VIEWS

That completes our survey of the "grand" theories of human development. But these theories can be grouped into even grander categories, for each is grounded in a broader world view, or set of philosophical assumptions. By examining the fundamental assumptions that underlie different theories, we can better compare them and appreciate how deeply some of their disagreements run.

Hayne Reese and Willis Overton (Reese & Overton, 1970; Overton, 1984) have outlined two broad models or world views that underlie most developmental theories. The **mechanistic model** likens human beings to machines. More specifically, this model assumes that human beings (1) are a collection of parts (for example, they can be analyzed behavior by behavior, much as machines can be taken apart piece by piece), (2) are passive, changing only in response to outside stimulation (much as machines depend on outside energy sources to operate), and (3) change gradually or continuously as "parts," or specific behavior patterns, are added or subtracted. By contrast, the **organismic model** compares humans to plants and other living organisms. In this view, human beings (1) are whole beings who cannot be understood piece by piece because they are greater than the sum of their parts, (2) are active in the developmental process, behaving and changing under the guidance of forces springing from within themselves rather than being passively shaped by environmental events, and (3) evolve through distinct or discontinuous stages as they reorganize over time into a new and different whole beings.

Which theorists have adopted which model? Learning theorists such as Watson and Skinner clearly express a mechanistic world view, for they see human beings as passively shaped by environmental stimuli and they analyze human behavior response by response. Bandura's social learning theory, while it is still primarily mechanistic, does reflect the organismic assumption that humans are active beings who influence their environment (as they are being influenced by it). By contrast, psychoanalytic theorists such as Freud and Erikson, cognitive-developmental theorists of Piaget's persuasion, and ethologists such as Bowlby rest their theories primarily on the organismic model. Given some nourishment from their environments, human beings will evolve through stages that arise from forces lying within themselves — much as seeds evolve into blooming roses. And what about contextual-dialectical theories such as Riegel's? They may reflect still another broad world view, a contextual model that regards human development as an ongoing drama or interplay between changes within the organism *and* changes in the environment, or in the physical, social, and historical contexts in which individuals are embedded (Overton, 1984).

It is because different theories rest on different world views that they sometimes seem to offer such drastically different pictures of human development and its causes. Each world view contains unquestioned assumptions that determine what "facts" are considered important and how they are interpreted. Consequently, theorists who view the world through different lenses are likely to continue disagreeing even when the same "facts" are set before them. This is the very nature of science. And it means that our understanding of human development has changed and will continue to change as one prevailing world view gives way to another. As we will now see, different world views and theories also lead to different notions about how to optimize development.

APPLICATIONS: THERE'S NOTHING SO USEFUL AS A GOOD THEORY

One of the main functions of theories in any science is to guide attempts to gain knowledge through research. Thus Freud and Erikson stimulated researchers to study inner conflicts and the ego, while Skinner inspired them to analyze how behavior changes when its consequences change, and Piaget inspired them to explore children's thinking about every imaginable topic. Different theories stimulate different kinds of research and yield different kinds of "facts."

Theories also guide practice. For example, parents' beliefs about the nature of children and about child development guide their parenting behavior (McGillicuddy-DeLisi, 1985; Miller, 1988). As we have seen, each theory of human development represents a particular way of defining developmental issues and problems. Often how you define a problem determines how you attempt to solve it. To illustrate this point, let's take one last look at teenage pregnancy, which is clearly defined as a social problem in society today. As we have seen, different theorists hold radically different opinions about the causes of teenage pregnancy. How do you think each would go about trying to *reduce* the rate of teenage pregnancy?

Psychoanalytic theorists are likely to locate the "problem" within the person. Freud or Erikson might want to identify teenage girls who have especially weak egos, strained relationships with their mothers, or exceptional difficulties establishing their identities as they experience the many changes of adolescence. "High risk" teenagers might then be treated through psychoanalysis; the aim would be to help them resolve the inner conflicts that might "get them in trouble." This approach to solving the problem follows naturally from a psychoanalytic view of the causes of the problem. And it might well work with teenagers who are indeed emotionally disturbed. However, most pregnant girls are not psychologically disturbed; instead they are quite similar psychologically to their peers who do not get pregnant (Furstenberg, Lincoln, & Menken, 1981; Phipps-Yonas, 1980).

Perhaps Piaget's cognitive-developmental perspective has something better to offer to psychologically normal teenagers. Piagetians might be somewhat pessimistic about the chances of getting young teenagers to engage in long-term planning and rational decision making about sexual issues until they are solidly in the formal operations stage of cognitive development. And yet, as we will see in Chapter 7, researchers sometimes have been able to create learning experiences that help concrete-operational thinkers advance more quickly than usual to the stage of formal operations. Piaget would also want us to understand the kinds of misunderstandings that many adolescents have about their risks of pregnancy; we could then attempt to correct those mistaken ideas. His theory suggests that the solution to teenage pregnancy is teaching teenagers accurate information about sex and birth control options and helping students think clearly about the consequences of their sexual decisions — that is, improved sex education courses. Moreover, instead of just *telling* concrete-operational thinkers about the consequences of early pregnancy, we might make those consequences concrete instead of abstract for them (Proctor, 1986), perhaps by having students talk to teenage mothers and fathers about their lives or tend infants in a daycare center.

Most researchers concerned about teenage sexuality and pregnancy do indeed agree that improved sex education is an important part of the solution. And yet sex education courses often do little to change behavior. Adolescents who take them become more knowledgeable, but often their broader values and decision-making abilities do not change, and they do not become pregnant any less often (Kirby, 1985). True, there are some signs of progress: Sex-educated teenagers *do* practice contraception more consistently than teenagers who do not take sex education courses (Dawson, 1986; Marsiglio & Mott, 1986). Nonetheless, many teenagers who receive sex education have unintended pregnancies.

So possibly we need to consider solutions that locate the problem in the *environment* rather than in the individual's psychological weaknesses or cognitive deficiencies. Learning theorists strongly believe that changing the environment will change the person. In support of this belief, Douglas Kirby (1985) found that only one of the sex education projects he studied increased birth control use and decreased the rate of unintended pregnancies. It involved a major change in the school environment: the establishment of a health clinic in which students who were already sexually active could, in the strictest confidence, obtain specific information about how to use birth control devices and help in obtaining them. This program reflects a philosophy that the best way to change behavior is to teach and reinforce new behavior directly.

Albert Bandura's cognitive social learning theory also gives us some ideas about how to change the environment. Parents might be taught how to be better role models of responsible sexual behavior and how to communicate to their children about sex. Peers might be mobilized to serve as models of the advantages of postponing sex or engaging in "safe sex." Television programs might focus less on the joys of sex and more on its unwanted consequences. Through observational learning, teenagers might then develop sexually responsible habits. Learning theorists are generally more optimistic about the odds of changing behavior than ethological theorists are. Yet even though ethologists believe that teenage sexual behavior is a product of evolution, they would agree that teenagers might modify their behavior if their world were changed so that postponing parenthood became more adaptive than getting an early start on biological reproduction.

A similar thought might occur to contextual-dialectical theorists: The solution lies in changing the broader social context. Perhaps teenage pregnancy in poverty areas will not be significantly reduced until schools do more to motivate students, until jobs are made available, and until more disadvantaged young people gain hope that they can climb out of poverty if they pursue their education and postpone parenthood (Furstenberg, Brooks-Gunn, & Morgan, 1987). In other words, broader social changes may need to take place before individual teenagers will change their sexual practices.

We see, then, that the theoretical position that one takes has a huge impact on how one goes about attempting to optimize development. Yet, as we have also seen, each theory may have only a partial solution to the problem being addressed. In all likelihood, multiple approaches will be needed to make a serious dent in complex problems such as the high rate of teenage pregnancy—or to achieve the larger goal of understanding human development.

REFLECTIONS

More than all else, we hope that reading this chapter has made you realize that theories are not just speculative ideas with no practical use. Developmentalists need theories to guide their work. And *people in general* need theories to guide their behavior. Human beings simply cannot make sense of life unless they impose some order on it by making assumptions and forming generalizations. Every parent, teacher, human service professional, and observer of human beings is guided by *some* set of beliefs about how human beings develop and why they develop as they do. All things considered, it is better to be conscious of one's guiding beliefs than to be unaware of them. We hope that reading this chapter will stimulate you to clarify your own theories of human development. One way to start is by completing the exercise that appears in Box 2.8 and seeing which theorists' views are most compatible with your own.

You need not choose one theory and reject others. Indeed, because different theories often emphasize different aspects of development, one may be more relevant to a particular issue or to a particular age group than another. Today many developmentalists are theoretical **eclectics:** individuals who recognize that none of the major theories

Box 2.8
Match Wits with the Theorists on Developmental Issues

In Box 2.1, before you read this chapter, you were asked to indicate your positions on basic issues in human development by answering six questions. If you transcribe your answers below, you can compare your stands to those of the theorists described in this chapter (and also review the theories). With whom do you seem to agree the most?

	Question 1	2	3	4	5	6
Your pattern of answers:	__	__	__	__	__	__

Freud's psychoanalytic theory

a b b a a a

Freud held that biologically-based sexual instincts motivate behavior and steer development through five psychosexual stages. He believed that (1) the child's urges are basically selfish and aggressive, (2) biological changes are the driving force behind psychosexual stages (though he believed that parents influence how well these stages are negotiated), (3) children are passively influenced by forces beyond their control, (4) development is stagelike rather than continuous, (5) traits established in early childhood definitely carry over into adult personality traits, and (6) the psychosexual stages are universal.

Erikson's psychosocial theory

c c a a a a

Erikson theorized that humans progress through eight psychosocial conflicts as they mature biologically and attempt to adapt to their social environment. He holds that (1) we are born with basically good qualities, (2) both nature and nurture are important, (3) people are active in their own development, (4) development is stagelike, (5) there is carry over from early life to later life (though Erikson was more optimistic about the possibilities for overcoming early problems than Freud was), and (6) psychosocial stages are universal, though modified somewhat by culture.

Piaget's cognitive-developmental theory

c b a a b a

Piaget described four distinct stages in the development of intelligence that result as children attempt to make sense of their experience. He suggested that (1) we are born with positive tendencies such as curiosity, (2) maturation guides all children through the same sequence of stages, although experience is necessary as well and can influence the rate of development, (3) we are active in our own development as we "construct" more sophisticated understandings, (4) development is stagelike, (5) cognitive abilities change dramatically, and (6)

of human development can explain everything but that each has something to contribute to our understanding. In many ways, the emerging contextual-dialectical perspective on development is the broadest point of view yet proposed. There is no reason why many of the insights offered by Freud, Erikson, Piaget, Bandura, and others cannot be incorporated within this perspective to help us understand changing people in changing worlds.

In the remainder of this book, we take an eclectic and contextual approach to human development, borrowing from many theories in trying to draw a systematic and unified portrait of the developing person. We will also explore theoretical controversies, for these squabbles often produce some of the most exciting breakthroughs in the field. We invite you to join us in examining not just the specific "facts" of development but also the broader perspectives that have generated those facts and that give them larger meaning.

SUMMARY POINTS

1. A theory is a set of ideas proposed to describe and explain certain phenomena; it provides a perspective that helps organize a wide range of facts. Theories of human development address issues concerning the inherent nature of human beings, nature versus nurture, activity versus passivity, continuity versus discontinuity, and universality versus particularity.

2. According to Freud's psychoanalytic theory, humans are driven by inborn instincts of which they are largely unconscious; the id, which is purely instinctual, rules the infant; the rational ego emerges during infancy; and the superego, or conscience, takes form in the preschool years. Five psychosexual stages—oral, anal, phallic, latency, and genital—occur as the sex instinct matures; each stage is characterized by conflicts that create the need

everyone progresses through the same sequence of stages.

Learning theory: Skinner's version

b e b c b b

Skinner maintains that development is the result of learning from the consequences of one's behavior. In his view, (1) children are inherently neither good nor bad, (2) nurture or environment is far more important than nature, (3) people are passively shaped by environmental events, (4) development is gradual and continuous, as habits increase or decrease in strength, (5) early behavior may change dramatically later if the environment changes, and (6) development can proceed in many different directions depending on the individual's learning experiences.

Learning theory: Bandura's version

b d a c b b

Bandura's social learning theory states that humans change through cognitive forms of learning, especially observational learning. He argues that (1) children are inherently neither good nor bad, (2) nurture is more important than nature, (3) people influence their environments, and thus are active in their own development, (4) development is continuous rather than stagelike, (5) traits are unlikely to be stable if the person's environment changes, and (6) development can proceed in many directions depending on life experiences.

Ethological theory

c b b a a a

Bowlby emphasizes that children come biologically equipped with behavior patterns that have aided the species in adapting to its environment. He would say that (1) humans are born with many positive or adaptive tendencies, (2) nature is more important than nurture, (3) at least early in life, humans are guided by a biological program beyond their control (though they later become more active in their attachment relationships), (4) development is stagelike, marked by critical periods, (5) early experiences can have lasting effects on behavior, and (6) there are many similarities among members of the same species.

Contextual-dialectical theory

b c a b b b

Riegel and similar theorists believe that development results from the "dialogue" between a changing person and a changing physical and sociocultural context. These theorists appear to believe that (1) humans are inherently neither good nor bad, (2) nature and nurture, interacting continually, make us what we are, (3) people are active in their own development, (4) development probably involves some continuity and some discontinuity, some stagelike changes and some gradual ones, (5) early traits may be replaced by different traits if the environment changes, and (6) while some aspects of development may be universal, development generally varies widely from individual to individual.

for ego defense mechanisms and have lasting effects on the personality.

3. Erik Erikson emphasized a psychosocial approach to development, which he viewed as lifelong, progressing through eight stages of conflict resolution beginning with trust versus mistrust in infancy and concluding with integrity versus despair in old age. Each conflict must be resolved in favor of the positive trait (trust, for example) if development is to be healthy.

4. Jean Piaget's cognitive-developmental theory stresses universal, invariant stages in which children actively construct increasingly complex understandings by interacting with their environments: sensorimotor, preoperational, concrete-operational, and formal-operational.

5. Learning theorists hold that we change gradually through learning experiences and that we can develop in many different directions. John Watson advocated the study of overt behavior and strongly favored nurture over nature. B. F. Skinner advanced the behavioral perspective by demonstrating the importance of operant conditioning in human learning. Albert Bandura's social-learning theory differs from behavioral learning theories in emphasizing cognitive processes, observational learning, and a reciprocal determinism of person and environment.

6. Unlike learning theorists, ethological theorists emphasize nature more than nurture, studying the evolved behavior of different species in their natural settings. Konrad Lorenz used observations of young birds to demonstrate a genetically programmed imprinting response; John Bowlby has theorized that humans are also biologically equipped to form close attachments.

7. The newly emerging contextual-dialectical perspective on development, illustrated by Riegel's dialectical theory, emphasizes the study of the relations between a changing person and a changing world. Its world view differs from the mechanistic model expressed in learning theories or the organismic model expressed in stage theories.

8. Theories of human development guide not only research but practice; for Freud and Erikson, Piaget, learning theorists, ethologists, and contextual-dialectical theorists would each propose different approaches to the problem of teenage pregnancy.

9. No single theoretical viewpoint offers a totally adequate account of human development, but each contributes in important ways to our understanding.

KEY TERMS

accommodation
anal stage
assimilation
autonomy versus shame and doubt
behaviorism
concrete operations stage
contextual-dialectical theories
continuity/discontinuity issue
critical period
defense mechanisms
developmental stage
dialectical theory
eclectic
ego
Electra complex
ethology
fixation
formal operations stage
generativity versus stagnation
genital stage
id
identification
identity versus role confusion
imprinting
industry versus inferiority
initiative versus guilt
instinct
integrity versus despair
intimacy versus isolation
latency period
libido
mechanistic model
nature/nurture issue
observational learning
Oedipus complex
operant conditioning
oral stage
organismic model
phallic stage
preoperational stage
psychoanalytic theory
punisher
reciprocal determinism
regression
reinforcer
repression
scheme
sensorimotor stage
social learning theory
superego
tabula rasa
trust versus mistrust
unconscious motivation

CHAPTER

3

THE GENETICS OF LIFE-SPAN DEVELOPMENT

Oscar Stohr grew up in Czechoslovakia as a strict Catholic, loyal to the German Nazis during World War II. In middle age, he is now a loyal union member and factory supervisor in Germany. Jack Yufe, a store owner in California, was raised in the Caribbean by his Jewish father to fear and hate Nazis. Jack holds quite liberal attitudes, while Oscar is very conservative and traditional. Another bit of information: Oscar and Jack are identical twins with identical genetic makeups who were separated as babies and brought up on different sides of the earth (*Newsweek*, December 3, 1979).

It would seem that identical twins can become quite different sorts of people if they grow up in different environments and have different experiences in life. But there is more. The two men are part of a study of separated twins being conducted at the University of Minnesota by Dr. Thomas Bouchard, Jr., and his associates. They, like other identical twin pairs separated early in life, show some amazing similarities. Both Oscar and Jack excelled in sports at school but had difficulty with math. They have similar temperaments. And then there are the little things: a common taste for spicy food, a habit of flushing the toilet before and after using it, and an enjoyment of sneezing loudly to scare people! Perhaps the influence of **genes** on development must be taken seriously.

What, then, *are* the roles of heredity and environment in shaping the many physical and psychological characteristics that each of us possesses? That is the puzzle to be grappled with in this chapter. But before you read further, try the brief quiz on heredity in Box 3.1. We suspect that many of you have studied genetics and heredity before—and have also been exposed to some misconceptions about heredity that circulate in our society. Answers to the quiz will become clear as you read the chapter.

Most students the authors have taught are environmentalists at heart. They tend to believe that there is no such thing as a "bad seed," that proper parenting and a stimulating environment can make the development of virtually any child go well, and that most of the psychological differences between people are due to differences in their experiences over the course of a lifetime. Because many students are not equally appreciative of the contributions that genes make to development, we will emphasize those contributions first. Although we will also discover that genetic research has much to say about environmental influences on development, we will wait until Chapter 4 to put the environment on center stage.

We will begin by considering the ways in which genes make human beings alike in their characteristics and in their development. Then we will look more closely at what exactly is inherited at conception and at how an individual's traits can be influenced by this genetic endowment. At that point we will be ready to journey through the life span, stage by stage, asking how genes and environment make individuals different from one another in such aspects of behavior as intelligence and personality. This will put us in a position to draw some general conclusions about heredity and environment from a life-span perspective. Let's start by focusing on the genes that all humans share.

SPECIES HEREDITY, EVOLUTION, AND HUMAN DEVELOPMENT

Most discussions of heredity—and most of the remainder of this chapter—focus on the role of heredity in creating differences among people. Some inherit blue eyes, others brown eyes; some inherit blood type O, others blood type A or B. But isn't it remarkable that just about every one of us has two eyes and that we all have blood

Box 3.1
What Do You Know About Heredity?

Answer each question true or false.

1. It is the father's genetic contribution that determines whether a child is a boy or a girl.
2. Children born of the same two parents share exactly one half of their genes.
3. Two brown-eyed parents can have a blue-eyed child.
4. If a boy is color blind when it comes to distinguishing red and green, he can blame his mother.
5. The fact that people differ in genetic makeup is part of the reason that some perform better on tests of intelligence than others do.
6. Genes have nothing to do with what a person's personality is like.
7. Any characteristic that is highly influenced by genes cannot be altered by environmental forces.
8. The child whose mother or father has the severe psychological disorder known as schizophrenia has over a 50% chance of becoming schizophrenic.
9. Having a father who has criminal tendencies will not predispose a boy to crime if he grows up away from his father.
10. Every one of us carries several genes that are responsible for genetic defects.

(*Answers:* 1—T, 2—F, 3—T, 4—T, 5—T, 6—F, 7—F, 8—F, 9—F, 10—T. You might want to return to this quiz after you read the chapter to make sure that you understand the answers.)

coursing through our veins? And that virtually all of us develop in similar ways at similar ages—walking and talking at about 1 year, maturing sexually at about 12 to 14, and showing signs of aging in later life? These similarities are not coincidental. They are due to our **species heredity**—the genetic endowment that members of a particular species have in common. We can use language but cannot fly; birds can fly but cannot speak. Humans and birds each have their own distinct species heredity. Our shared human genetic endowment is responsible for maturational processes that all normal children experience—and it is also responsible for the fact that humans age and die at at least roughly similar times in life and live considerably longer than dogs, cats, and many other species do. Species heredity, then, is very important to our understanding of *universal* patterns of development and aging.

Where did we get this common species heredity? That's a question evolutionary theory can help us answer.

The Workings of Evolution

The theory of evolution proposed by Charles Darwin (1859), and modified somewhat over the years, attempts to explain how any species changes its characteristics over time or how new species can evolve from earlier species. The main argument is this:

1. *There is genetic variation in a species.* Some members of the species have different genes (and different genetically influenced characteristics and behaviors) than others do. If all members of the species were genetically identical, there would be no way for the genetic makeup of the species to change over time.

2. *Some genes aid in adaptation more than others do.* Suppose that some members of a species have genes that make them strong and intelligent, while others have genes that make them weak and dull. Surely those with the genes for strength and intelligence would be better able to adapt to their environment—for example, to win fights for survival or to figure out how to solve problems.

3. *Those genes that aid their bearers in adapting to the environment will be passed on to future generations more frequently than those genes that do not.* This is the principle of **natural selection**—the idea that nature "selects," or allows to survive and reproduce, those members of a species whose genes permit them to adapt to their environment. By contrast, those genes that somehow reduce the chances that an individual will survive and reproduce will become rarer and rarer over time because they will not be passed on to many offspring. Through natural selection, then, the genetic makeup of a whole species can slowly change over time.

Consider a classic example of speeded-up evolution. H. B. D. Kettlewell (1959) carefully studied moths in England. There is genetic variation among moths that makes some of them dark in color and others light in color. By placing light and dark moths in a number of different sites, Kettlewell found that in rural areas light-colored moths were more likely to survive than dark-colored moths. Just the opposite was true in the industrial areas of Birmingham, England: Dark moths were more likely to survive than light moths. The explanation? In rural areas, light-colored moths blended in well with light-colored trees and were better protected from predators by their camouflage. Natural selection favored them. However, in sooty industrial areas, light-colored moths stood out against the darkened trees, while dark moths were well disguised. Since industry came to England, the proportion of dark moths has increased, and it is currently higher in industrial areas than in rural areas. Interestingly, as pollution has been brought under control in some of the industrialized areas of England, the proportion of light-colored moths has increased somewhat (Bishop & Cooke, 1975).

Notice, then, that evolutionary theory is not just about genes. It is about the *match between genes and environment*. One genetic makeup may enhance survival in one kind of environment but prove maladaptive if the environment changes dramatically. Which genes are advantageous and which genes therefore become more common in future generations depends on what traits the environment demands.

If we take the evolutionary perspective seriously, we begin to suspect that humans, like any other species, are as they are and develop as they do partly because they have a shared species heredity that has passed the test of natural selection. And so long as some people are more likely to survive and have children than others are, biological evolution is slowly at work (Scarr & Kidd, 1983).

Perhaps the most significant aspect of human evolution is that we have been endowed with a powerful brain that allows us to learn almost anything from our experiences and to master a complex language so that we can communicate virtually anything to others. What could be more adaptive? As Sandra Scarr and Kenneth Kidd (1983) note, our species has not had to wait for biological evolution to give us furrier bodies to protect us from the cold. Humans have been able to use their brains to invent better and better clothing and heating systems and to communicate what they know to future generations. Most of the changes we see in society are due to this kind of *cultural evolution* rather than to biological evolution. What evolutionary biologists would want us to remember is that the ability to learn and the ability to teach others are themselves the products of biological evolution (Bonner, 1980).

Modern Evolutionary Theory: Sociobiology

Darwin's evolutionary theory continues to be influential today. Indeed, it has been given new life by a group of scholars who call themselves sociobiologists. **Sociobiology** has been defined by one of its pioneers, Edward O. Wilson (1975), as "the systematic study of the biological basis of all social behavior" (p. 4). Sociobiologists are thus interested in how many social behaviors—altruism, aggression, courtship rituals, parenting styles, and the like—might have evolved. Thus sociobiology is closely related to the field of ethology introduced in Chapter 2.

To the sociobiologist, as to Darwin, passing on genes to future generations is the name of the game in life. But Darwinian theory, with its emphasis on the survival of the "fittest" individuals, has always had some difficulty accounting for certain social behaviors. Why, for example, might a bird be biologically programmed to unselfishly risk its own life by warning its flock that a hawk is approaching? Such seemingly selfless or altruistic behavior could not possibly become built into a species' genetic code if the survival of the individual were all that mattered in evolution. Those whose genes predisposed them to perform altruistic acts would often cut their reproductive lives short through their noble actions. Their genes would therefore become rarer rather than more prevalent over time.

However, genes that predispose an individual to behave altruistically *could* become common in a species if altruism is the best strategy for ensuring that one's *family genes* are well represented in future generations (Hamilton, 1964; Trivers & Hare, 1976). More of the genes that a bird shares with close relatives might be passed along if this bird sacrifices its own genes by attracting the attention of the hawk than if it flees and leaves the whole group at the hawk's mercy. In other words, unselfishly helping one's relations can be seen as an evolved strategy that is adaptive because it ensures the survival of genes. Thus sociobiologists have advanced evolutionary theory by demonstrating that it is the survival of *genes*, which are shared with kin, rather than the survival of individuals, that matters in evolution.

Sociobiologists are beginning to examine human behavior and development from an evolutionary perspective (see MacDonald, 1988). To cite just one example, they are asking why women are often more involved in child care than men are, and why this is more true in some cultures than in others (Draper & Harpending, 1988). Sociobiologists would immediately point out that only women know for sure that their children are indeed theirs. From a genetic standpoint, then, a woman has good reason to devote her energies to child care so that her children can live to pass on the family genes to still another generation. By contrast, men can never be quite certain that their children are really their children. From a genetic standpoint, they should be more willing to care for children when they are assured that those children carry their own genetic formula than when they are uncertain who the father is. Indeed, sociobiologists have demonstrated that the males of some species are more involved in child care if they form a monogamous relationship with a female (Fuller, 1983).

Could similar principles be at work in human societies? Patricia Draper and Henry Harpending (1988) suggest that human beings learn early in life by watching adults whether it is more advantageous in their environment for men to be involved in nurturing the young or whether they should instead invest their energies in attracting as many women as they can. In cultures where food is plentiful and the survival of offspring is easily assured, it might make genetic sense for females to raise children largely without male help, and for males to roam from partner to partner. In cultures where male help in supporting children is more necessary to the survival of the young, the more adaptive strategy—adaptive in the sense of ensuring the survival of the family genes—may be to form lasting partnerships in which both parents contribute to child care.

Notice that sociobiologists do not claim humans are robots who simply act out behaviors dictated by their genes. Instead, they think humans have evolved in a way that makes them able to learn which patterns of social behavior are most biologically adaptive in the environment they encounter. At this point, sociobiological hypotheses about human beings such as those described here have not been adequately tested, partly because they are difficult to test conclusively. Until they are more fully tested, they will remain controversial (Lewontin, Rose, & Kamin, 1984). However, sociobiologists have already made an important point: Humans, like other animals, may behave as they do partly because those behaviors have proved adaptive in terms of ensuring the survival of genes.

In summary, our understanding of human behavior and development is enriched when we view it in the context of biological evolution. We begin to appreciate that we do indeed have a species heredity, a common genetic makeup that has evolved through natural selection because it has enabled humans to adapt to their environment. When we observe children all over the world progressing through similar maturational changes at similar times and when we note similarities in human behavior despite differences in cultural background and experiences, we are often observing the products of a lengthy process of biological evolution. Yet human beings are not all alike, partly because they have different genetic makeups and partly because they are influenced by the environment in which they develop. Let us now look more closely at the ways in which genes contribute to *differences* among us.

THE WORKINGS OF INDIVIDUAL HEREDITY

To understand the workings of heredity, we must start at **conception**, the moment when a woman's egg is fertilized by a man's sperm. Once we have established what is inherited at conception, we can examine the mechanisms through which genes translate into traits.

Conception and the Genetic Code

About once every 28 days, roughly midway between menstrual periods, human females ovulate. An ovum or egg cell ripens, leaves the ovary, and enters the fallopian tube. If a woman has sexual intercourse with a fertile male during or a few days before or after ovulation, the 300 to 400 million sperm cells contained in her partner's seminal fluid begin to swim, tadpole-style, in all directions. Of as many as 5,000 to 20,000 sperm that survive the long journey into the fallopian tubes, one may meet and penetrate the ovum that is descending from the ovary. A biochemical reaction occurs that repels other sperm, preventing them from repeating the fertilization process. Within a

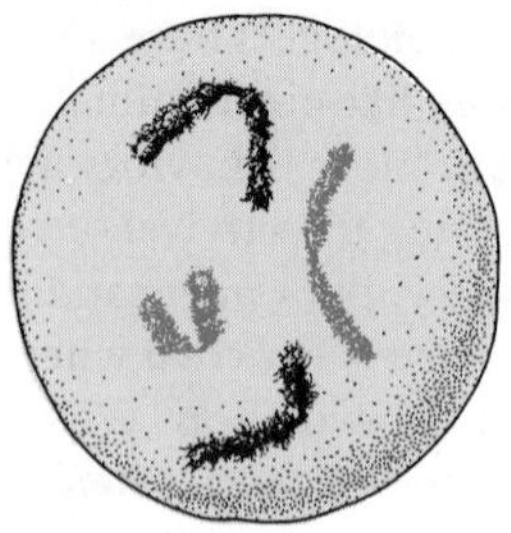

Step 1
Original parent cell (for illustrative purposes this cell contains but four chromosomes).

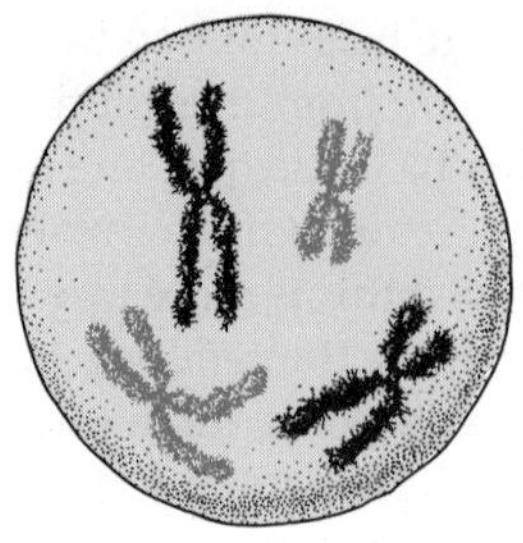

Step 2
Each chromosome splits lengthwise, producing a duplicate.

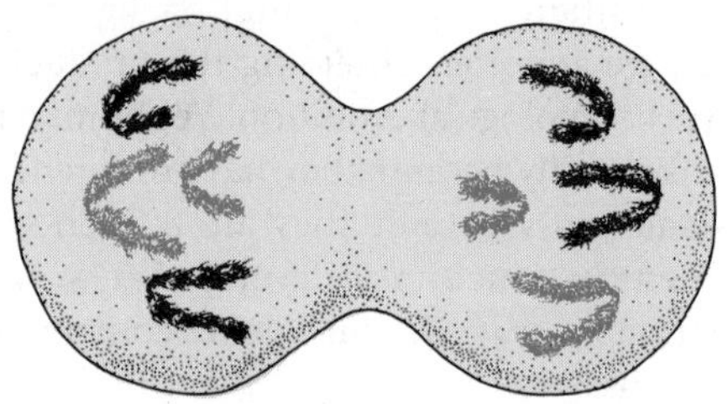

Step 3
The duplicate sets of chromosomes move to opposite ends of the parent cell, which then begins to divide.

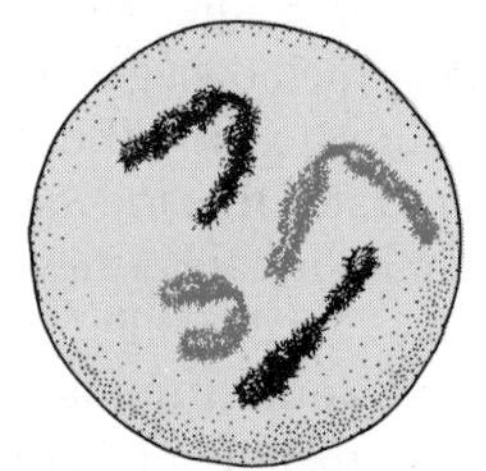

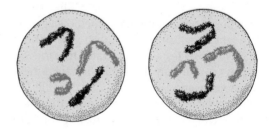

Step 4
The cell completes its division, producing two daughter cells that have identical sets of chromosomes.

Figure 3.1 Mitosis: The way cells reproduce themselves.

few hours, the sperm cell begins to disintegrate, releasing its genetic material. The nucleus of the ovum releases its own genetic material, and a new cell nucleus is created from the genetic material provided by mother and father. This new cell, called a **zygote**, is the beginning of a human being. Conception has occurred.

What is this genetic material contained in the new zygote? It is 46 threadlike bodies called **chromosomes**, which function as 23 pairs. Each member of a chromosome pair influences the same characteristics as the other member of the pair. Each chromosome is made up of thousands of **genes**, the basic units of heredity. Genes are actually stretches of DNA, the "double helix" molecule that provides a chemical "code" for development. Like chromosomes, genes function as pairs, the two members of each gene pair being located at the same sites on their corresponding chromosomes.

The sperm cell and the ovum each contributed 23 chromosomes to the zygote. Thus of each chromosome pair—and of each pair of genes on corresponding chromosomes—one member came from the father and one member came from the mother. Once formed, the single-celled zygote becomes a multiple-celled organism through a process of cell division called **mitosis**. During mitosis, a cell (and each of its 46 chromosomes) divides to produce two identical cells, each containing the same 46 chromosomes (see Figure 3.1). As the zygote moves through the fallopian tube toward its prenatal home in the uterus, it first divides into two cells, and the two then become four, the four become eight, and so on. Except for sperm and ova, all cells in the individual's body contain copies of the 46 chromosomes provided at conception. Mitosis continues throughout life, creating new cells that enable us to grow and replacing old cells that are damaged.

How is it that sperm and ova have only 23 chromosomes? It is because they are produced through a different process of cell division called **meiosis**. A reproductive germ cell in the ovaries of a female or the testes of a male contains 46 chromosomes, but it splits to form two 46-chromosome cells, and then these two cells split again to form 4 cells, each with 23 chromosomes. Each resulting sperm cell or ovum thus has only one member of each of the parent's 23 pairs of chromosomes.

Genetic Uniqueness and Relatedness

To understand how we are different from but like others genetically, let's look more carefully at those 46 chromosomes that contain the blueprint for the development of an individual human being. When a pair of parental chromosomes moves apart during meiosis, it is a matter of chance which of the two chromosomes will end up in a particular sperm or ovum. And because each chromosome pair segregates independently of all other pairs, each parent can produce many genetically unique sperm or egg cells. In fact, since each germ cell contains 23 pairs of chromosomes, a single parent can produce 2^{23}—more than 8 million—different sperm or ova. If a father can produce 8 million combinations of 23 chromosomes and a mother can produce 8 million, any couple could theoretically have 64 trillion babies without producing two children who inherited precisely the same set of genes!

In fact, the genetic uniqueness of children of the same parents is even greater than this because of a quirk of meiosis known as **crossing over**. When pairs of chromosomes line up before they separate, they cross each other and parts of them are exchanged, much as if you were to exchange a couple of fingers with a friend after a handshake. This crossing-over phenomenon actually alters the genetic composition of a chromosome and increases still further the number of distinct sperm or ova that an individual can produce. In other words, it is incredibly unlikely that there ever was or ever will be another human exactly like you genetically. The one exception is **identical twins** (or identical triplets, and so on). They originate from one fertilized ovum which later divides to form two or more genetically identical individuals. Identical twins thus share 100% of their genes.

How genetically alike are parent and child, or brother and sister? You and either your mother or father have 50% of your genes in common. Half of your chromosomes (and genes) do, after all, reside in the cells of your mother, while the other half reside in the cells of your father. But if you have followed our mathematics, you will see that siblings may have many genes in common or very few, depending on the luck of the draw of chromosomes during meiosis. Indeed, we can see for ourselves that some siblings seem to be alike in many ways, while others don't even seem to belong in the same family. Siblings do receive half of their genes from the same mother and half from the same father, so their genetic resemblance is 50%, like that of parent and child. The critical difference is that siblings share half of their genes *on the average*, some sharing more, others sharing less. The same applies to **fraternal twins**. Unlike identical twins, fraternal twins are the product of two ova that were fertilized by separate sperm at roughly the same time. Fraternal twins are no more alike genetically than brothers and sisters born at different times. Grandparent and grandchild, as well as half-brothers or sisters, have 25% of their genes in common on the average. Thus each of us (with the exception of identical twins) is genetically unique, but each of us also has genes in common with relatives. Genes provide for individuality, but they also make for family resemblances.

Determination of Sex

How is a child's sex determined? Of the 23 pairs of chromosomes that each individual inherits, 22 (called *autosomes*) are similar in males and females. Sex is determined by the 23rd pair, the sex chromosomes. A male child has one long chromosome called an **X chromosome** (based on its shape) and a short, stubby companion called a **Y chromosome**. Females have two X chromosomes. Figure 3.2 displays pairs of male and female chromosomes that have been photographed through a powerful microscope and then arranged and rephotographed in a pattern called a **karyotype**.

Which parent determines the child's sex, then? Since mothers have only X chromosomes to give, while a father's sperm cell will have either an X or a Y chromosome depending on how chromosomes sort out during meiosis, it is the father who determines a child's gender. If an ovum (with its one X chromosome) is fertilized by a sperm bearing a Y chromosome, the product is an XY zygote, a genetic male. If a sperm carrying an X chromosome reaches the ovum first, the result is an XX zygote, a genetic female. Pity the women who throughout history have been criticized,

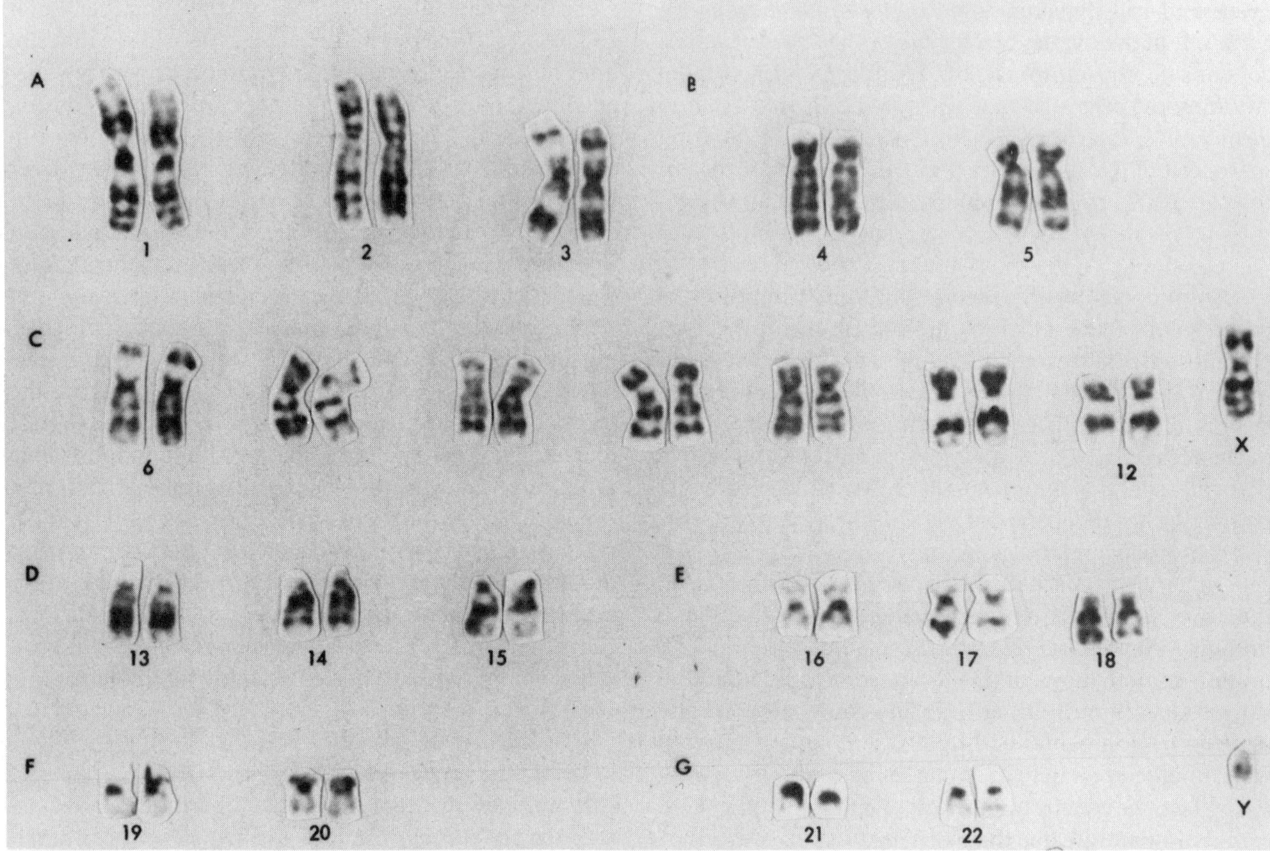

Figure 3.2 A male karyotype. This photographic arrangement shows the 22 pairs of autosomal chromosomes and the 2 sex chromosomes—an elongated X and a shorter Y chromosome.

tortured, divorced, and even beheaded for failing to bear their husbands a male heir!

So far, so good: We have a genetically unique boy or girl with about 500,000 genes in all on his or her 46 chromosomes. Now, how do genes influence the individual's characteristics and development? It is still a mystery, but we will first offer a solution that focuses on the nature of genes themselves.

Translation of the Genetic Code

Genes provide instructions for development. Specifically, they call for the production of chemical substances such as enzymes and other proteins that act on each other in such a way that cells are formed and function properly. Genes, for example, set in motion a process that results in the laying down of pigment called melanin in the iris of the eye. Some people's genes call for much of this pigment and the result is brown eyes; other people's genes call for less of it and the result is blue eyes. Genes also direct the formation of the brain and nervous system, potentially influencing intelligence in the process. No one, however, completely understands the biochemical events involved in how genes direct a single cell to become millions of diverse cells—blood cells, nerve cells, skin cells, and so on—all organized into marvelously effective human organs.

Nor does anyone fully understand how genes bring about certain developments at certain points in the life span. Apparently some genes direct the production of proteins that are in turn responsible for how the body is constructed and how it functions. However, other genes have the task of *regulating* the first set of genes. Current thinking is that specific gene pairs have specific messages to send, but that they are "turned on" or "turned off" by regulatory genes at different points in the life span (Scarr & Kidd, 1983). Thus genes responsible for directing the laying down of pigment in the eyes swing into action during the prenatal period, whereas genes that trigger the sexual maturation process during adolescence do not "turn on" until much later in development. An ever-changing pattern of genetic activity and inactivity, orchestrated by regulatory genes, occurs over the life span.

Finally, we must emphasize that environmental factors influence how the messages specified by the genes are carried out. Take the genes that influence an individual's height. One's genetic makeup is called one's **genotype**, and some people inherit genes calling for exceptional height while others inherit genes calling for a short stature. But genotype is different from **phenotype**, or the actual characteristics a person has (for example, a height of 5 feet 8 inches). The significant point here is that an individual whose genotype calls for exceptional height may or may not be tall. Certainly a child who is severely malnourished from the prenatal period on may turn out not to have a basketball player's build. So environmental influences combine with genetic influences to determine how a genotype is translated into a particular phenotype—the way a person actually looks, thinks, feels, and behaves.

Another way to approach the riddle of how genes influence us is to consider the major mechanisms of inheritance: the ways in which parents' genes influence their children's traits.

Mechanisms of Inheritance

There are three main mechanisms of inheritance: single gene-pair inheritance, sex-linked inheritance, and polygenic (or multiple gene) inheritance.

Single Gene-Pair Inheritance

Through **single gene-pair inheritance**, some human characteristics are influenced by only one pair of genes: one from the mother, one from the father. Although he knew nothing of genes, a 19th century monk named Gregor Mendel contributed greatly to our knowledge of single gene-pair inheritance by cross-breeding different strains of peas and watching the outcomes. His major discovery was a predictable pattern to the way in which two alternative characteristics (for example, smooth seeds or wrinkled seeds, green pods or yellow pods) would appear in the offspring of cross-breedings. He called some characteristics (for example, smooth seeds) "dominant" because they appeared more often in later generations than their opposite traits, which he called "recessive" traits. Among peas and among humans, an offspring's phenotype often is not simply a "blend" of the characteristics of mother and father. Instead, one of the parental genes often dominates the other, and the child will resemble the parent who contributed the dominant gene.

To illustrate the principles of Mendelian heredity, consider the remarkable fact that about three fourths of us can curl our tongues upward into a tubelike shape, whereas one fourth of us cannot. While the ability to curl one's tongue is of dubious value, this trait is determined by a single gene pair. It happens that the gene associated with tongue curling is a **dominant gene**. A weaker gene calling for the absence of tongue-curling ability is said to be a **recessive gene**. The person who inherits one "tongue-curl" gene and one "no-curl" gene would be able to curl his or her tongue (that is, would have a tongue-curling phenotype) because the tongue-curl gene overpowers the no-curl gene. Let's label the dominant, tongue-curl gene *T* and the recessive, no-curl gene *t*. We can now calculate the odds that parents with different genotypes for tongue curling would have children who can or cannot curl their tongues. Figure 3.3 shows two examples. In each part, we see that a father will contribute one or the other of his two genes to a sperm, and the mother will contribute one or the other of her two genes to an ovum. Each child inherits one of the mother's genes and one of the father's, so the four cells of each grid represent the four possible kinds of children that two parents, given their genotypes, could have.

Part A of Figure 3.3 is convincing evidence that dominant genes triumph over recessive genes. A tongue-curling father with the genotype TT is said to be **homozygous** for the trait of tongue curling because the two genes in his pair of genes are identical in their effects. Similarly, his wife, with the genotype tt, is homozygous (but can*not* curl her tongue). But each and every child they produce will necessarily be **heterozygous** for tongue curling—that is,

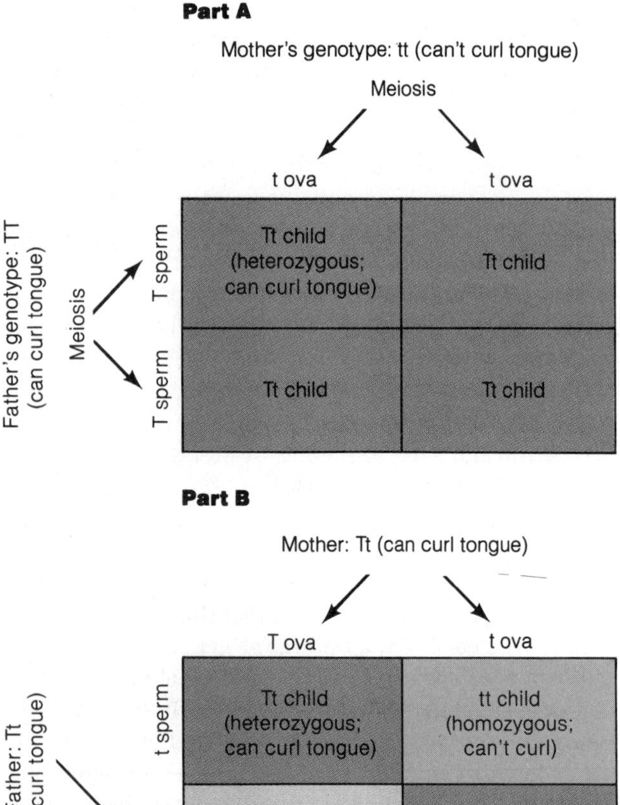

Figure 3.3 Two examples of the inheritance of the ability (or lack of ability) to curl one's tongue.

will have dissimilar genes, one for tongue curling, one for a lack of tongue curling (genotype Tt). Since the tongue-curl gene dominates, we can say that this couple has a 100% chance of having a tongue-curling child. Notice that two different genotypes—TT and Tt—both make for the same phenotype: an acrobatic tongue.

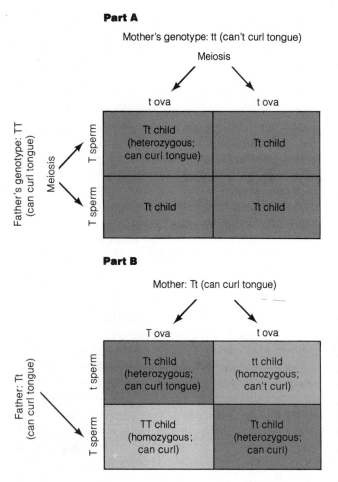

Part B of Figure 3.3 tells us that a tongue-curling man and a tongue-curling woman can surprise everyone and have a child who lacks this talent. These two parents are both heterozygous for tongue curling (the Tt genotype). If the father's recessive gene and the mother's recessive gene happen to unite in the zygote, a non-tongue-curling child (with the genotype tt) will be born. The chances are 25%—one out of four—that this couple will have such a child. Of course, the laws of conception are much like the laws of cards. This couple could either beat the odds and have a whole family of non-tongue-curling children or have no such children at all—just as the poker player could beat the odds and draw four aces or could draw none. Since people who cannot curl their tongues must have the tt genotype, two non-tongue-curling parents will have only non-tongue-curling (tt) children.

Table 3.1 lists a number of other examples of dominant and recessive traits associated with single gene-pair inheritance. In truth, many of the physical characteristics in this table such as eye color and hair color and curliness are actually influenced by more than the workings of a single pair of genes. However, it turns out that many genetically linked diseases and defects are entirely due to inheriting two recessive genes, one from each parent. Consider a common example: **sickle cell disease**.

Individuals with sickle cell disease have sickle-shaped blood cells that tend to cluster together and distribute less oxygen through the circulatory system than normal cells do. People with this disease have great difficulty breathing and exerting themselves, experience painful swelling of their joints, and often die from heart or kidney failure by adolescence. About 9% of blacks in the United States are heterozygous for this attribute (call their genotype Ss); they carry one gene that calls for round blood cells and one that calls for sickle-shaped blood cells (Thompson, 1975). Such people are also called **carriers** of the sickle cell disease because, while they do not have the disease, they can transmit the gene for it to their children. The child who inherits two recessive sickle cell genes (ss) has sickle cell disease. You might want to draw a diagram like those in Figure 3.3 to convince yourself that an Ss father and an Ss mother (two carriers) have a 25% chance of having a child with sickle cell disease.

An interesting feature of the sickle cell trait is that the dominant gene associated with round blood cells shows **incomplete dominance**—that is, it does not totally mask all the effects of the recessive sickle cell gene. Thus carriers of the sickle cell gene actually have many round blood cells but also some sickle-shaped cells (see Figure 3.4). When they are at high altitudes, are given anesthesia, or are otherwise deprived of oxygen, carriers may experience symptoms of sickle cell disease—very painful swelling of the joints and severe fatigue (Novitski, 1982). But under

Table 3.1 Examples of dominant and recessive traits

DOMINANT TRAITS	RECESSIVE TRAITS
Brown eyes	Gray, green, hazel, or blue eyes
Dark hair	Blond hair
Non-red hair (blond, brunette)	Red hair
Full head of hair	Pattern baldness[a]
Curly hair	Straight hair
Normal vision	Nearsightedness
Farsightedness	Normal vision
Normal vision	Color blindness
Roman nose	Straight nose
Broad lips	Thin lips
Short digits	Normal digits
Extra digits	Five digits
Double-jointedness	Normal joints
Immunity to poison ivy	Susceptibility to poison ivy
Pigmented skin	Albinism
Type A blood	Type O blood
Type B blood	Type O blood
Normal blood clotting	Hemophilia[a]
Normal hearing	Congenital deafness
Normal blood cells	Sickle cell disease[a]
Huntington's disease[a]	Normal brain and body maturation
Normal physiology	Phenylketonuria[a]
Normal physiology	Tay-Sachs disease[a]

[a]This condition is discussed elsewhere in the chapter.

normal circumstances, carriers do not experience these problems.

In still other cases of single gene-pair heredity, two genes influence a trait but neither dominates the other. This is called **codominance** because the phenotype of the heterozygous person is an exact compromise between the two genes that he or she has inherited. For example, the genes for blood types A and B each dominate the gene for blood type O, but neither dominates the other. The person who inherits one of each has both A antigens and B antigens in his or her blood. If you have the blood type AB, you illustrate this principle of genetic codominance. Single gene-pair inheritance is a bit more complex than it looks at first glance.

Several genetic defects besides sickle cell disease can be traced to a single pair of genes. Most of them are associated with recessive genes (we will examine some additional examples at the end of the chapter). All of us carry genes for several recessive genetic defects. However, there are a couple of thousand of them, and a couple is not at risk for having a child with such a defect unless *both of them are carriers of the same defective gene.* When both are carriers, they run a 25% risk each time they have a child that the child will inherit the disorder.

Can you figure out from this information why most societies have taboos against incest or laws against the marriage of first cousins? It is because relatives who mate share a common genetic heritage and run an especially high risk that the defective genes they possess will be the *same ones* their relative possesses. Perhaps for this genetic reason, many species of animals have evolved in ways that enable them to recognize their relatives so that they will not make the mistake of mating with them (Bateson, 1985).

Sex-Linked Inheritance

Some traits are called **sex-linked characteristics** because they are influenced by single genes located on the sex chromosomes rather than on the other 22 pairs of chromosomes we possess. Indeed, we could say "X-linked" rather than sex-linked because the vast majority of these sex-linked attributes are produced by genes located only on X chromosomes.

Let's ask why far more males than females have *red/green color blindness.* This inability to distinguish red and green is caused by a recessive gene that appears only on X chromosomes. If you'll recall, Y chromosomes are

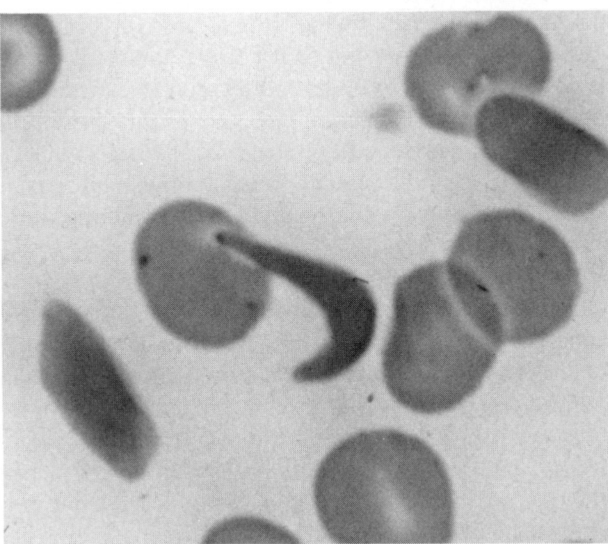

Figure 3.4 Normal (*left and right*) and "sickled" (*center*) blood cells from a carrier of sickle cell disease.

shorter than X chromosomes and have fewer genes. If a boy inherits the recessive gene on his X chromosome, there is no color vision gene on the Y chromosome that could potentially dominate the color blindness gene. He will be color blind. By contrast a girl who inherits the gene will usually have a normal color vision gene on her other X chromosome that will dominate the color blindness gene (see Figure 3.5). She would have to inherit two of the recessive color blindness genes (one from each parent) to be color blind herself. Who then should a boy blame if he is color blind? Definitely his mother, for she is the source of his X chromosome. *Hemophilia*, the so-called bleeder's disease, in which the ability of the blood to clot is deficient, is also far more common among males than females because it too is associated with a gene on X chromosomes. Other sex-linked traits include the Duchenne type of muscular dystrophy and certain forms of deafness and night blindness.

Many people believe that a man can tell if he will go bald by looking at the heads of his mother's male relatives; that is, they believe baldness is a sex-linked trait influenced by genes received from the mother. This belief is wrong. The most common form of baldness, pattern baldness, is influenced by a pair of genes that does not reside on the sex chromosomes. What happens is that a man who has but one of these recessive genes, received from either his father or mother, will go bald because his male hormones make the gene act as if it were dominant rather than recessive. A female's hormones protect her from this phenomenon, and she must have two of the "baldness" genes before her hair will thin (Burns, 1976). So a young man might want to look at the heads of older men on *both* sides of the family to estimate his odds of remaining hairy.

Polygenic Inheritance

So far we have considered only the influence of single genes or gene pairs on human traits. By looking at family histories and other evidence, it has been possible to figure out that a trait must be associated with a dominant or recessive gene. However, most important human characteristics are influenced by *multiple* pairs of genes; that is, they are **polygenic traits**. Examples of polygenic traits include height and weight, intelligence, personality, susceptibility to cancer, and a host of others. Imagine that intelligence were influenced by three pairs of genes, and that the gene pairs AA, BB, and CC would make for genius, while the genotype aa bb cc would make for low intelligence. Without going into the mathematics, there are 27 distinct genotypes that could result if we calculated all possible children that one couple of average intelligence (each with an Aa Bb Cc genotype, for example) could produce. Gene combinations that call for average intelligence would be more likely to occur than combinations associated with either very high or very low intelligence. When a trait is influenced by multiple genes, we would therefore expect many degrees of the trait in a population, and we would expect many people to be near the average and few to be extreme. This is exactly the way intelligence and many other measurable human traits are distributed in a large population.

Because polygenic inheritance is more complex than single gene-pair inheritance, we have no idea exactly how many gene pairs influence intelligence or other polygenic traits. At this point, all we can say is that unknown numbers and combinations of genes, interacting with environ-

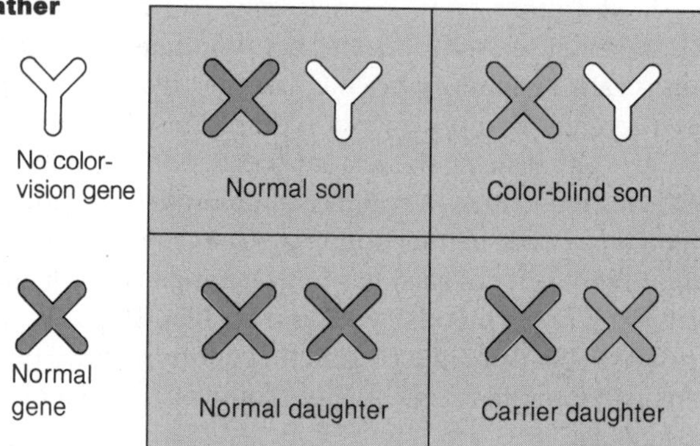

Figure 3.5 The workings of sex-linked inheritance of red/green color blindness. Notice that, in this example, a son has a 50% chance of being color blind, whereas a daughter has a 0% chance. A girl will be color blind only if her father is color blind *and* her mother is at least a carrier of the color-blindness gene.

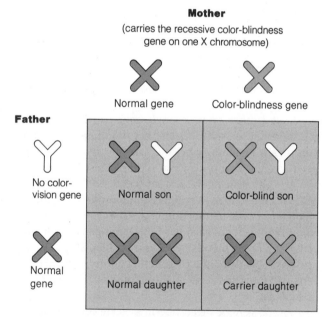

mental influences, create a wide range of individual differences in most important traits.

Mutations

We have now examined the three major mechanisms by which the genes inherited at conception influence traits. Occasionally, however, a new gene appears out of nowhere; it is not received from parents. A **mutation** is a change in the structure or arrangement of one or more genes that produces a new phenotype. Experts believe that the recessive gene for the sex-linked disorder hemophilia was first introduced into the royal families of Europe by Queen Victoria. Since no cases of hemophilia could be found in Queen Victoria's ancestry, the gene may have been a mutation that she then passed on to her offspring. In at least 30% of the cases of hemophilia, there is no family history of the disease, so these new cases are probably due to spontaneous mutations (Apgar & Beck, 1974).

Some mutations have beneficial effects and become more and more common in a population through the process of natural selection. The sickle cell gene is a good example. It probably arose originally as a mutation but became more prevalent in Africa, Central America, and other tropical areas over many generations because it protected those who had it from malaria and allowed them to produce children who also had the protective gene. People without the gene fell prey to malaria. Unfortunately, however, the sickle cell gene is not advantageous (and can be harmful) in environments where malaria is no longer a problem. Thus mutations can be either beneficial or harmful, depending on their nature and on the environment in which their bearers live.

Chromosome Abnormalities

A final way in which genetic endowment can influence human characteristics is through the occurrence of **chromosome abnormalities**—cases in which a child receives too many or too few chromosomes (or abnormal chromosomes) at conception. Most chromosome abnormalities are due to errors in chromosome division during meiosis. Through an accident of nature, an ovum or sperm cell may be produced with more or less than the usual 23 chromosomes. In most cases, a zygote with the wrong number of chromosomes is spontaneously aborted, but approximately 1 child in 200 is born with either 47 or 45 chromosomes rather than the normal 46 (Plomin, 1986).

Figure 3.6 Children with Down syndrome can live rich lives if they receive affection and encouragement from other people.

One of the most familiar chromosome abnormalities is **Down syndrome**, a chromosome disorder also known as *trisomy 21* because children with it receive three rather than two 21st chromosomes. Children with Down syndrome are mentally retarded and also have eyelid folds that give them an Oriental appearance (which is why they were once called "mongoloids"), short stubby limbs, and a thick tongue (see Figure 3.6). They can learn self-care as well as academic and vocational skills with special education, but they will remain mentally retarded through life.

What determines who has a Down syndrome child and who does not? Part of the answer is sheer chance. The errors in cell division responsible for Down syndrome can happen in any man or woman. However, the odds also increase dramatically as the age of the mother increases. As Table 3.2 reveals, the chances of having a baby with the syndrome become as high as 1 in 25 for mothers age 45 or older. Mothers who have already borne one Down syndrome child have an even higher risk, presumably because they are more susceptible to producing defective eggs than most women are.

Why is the older woman at high risk for producing a child with chromosome abnormalities? First, since ova actually begin to form during the prenatal period, it is possible that they degenerate and become abnormal over the years. Second, older women may have had more opportunities to become exposed to environmental hazards such as radiation, drugs, chemicals, and viruses that can damage ova. Most cases of Down syndrome can be traced

Table 3.2 Risk of Down syndrome as a function of mother's age

	PROBABILITY THAT THE CHILD WILL HAVE DOWN SYNDROME	
AGE OF MOTHER	At any pregnancy	After the birth of a child with Down syndrome
–29	1 in 1000	1 in 100
30–34	1 in 600	1 in 100
35–39	1 in 200	1 in 100
40–44	1 in 65	1 in 25
45–49	1 in 25	1 in 15

Source: Adapted from Pueschel & Goldstein, 1983.

to the mother's egg, but it has been found that 25% of these children received their extra 21st chromosome from their fathers rather than from their mothers (Magenis et al., 1977).

Most other chromosome abnormalities involve cases in which a child receives either too many or too few sex chromosomes. These *sex chromosome abnormalities*, like Down syndrome, can be attributed mainly to errors in meiosis that become increasingly likely as the ages of both father and mother increase. One well-known example is **Turner syndrome**, in which a female (about 1 in 3000) is born with a single X chromosome (XO). These girls remain small and often have stubby fingers and toes, a "webbed" neck, a broad chest, and underdeveloped breasts. They are sterile and typically favor traditionally feminine activities. Although they score about average on tests of verbal intelligence, their spatial reasoning abilities are often deficient (Rovert & Netley, 1982). Another example is **Klinefelter syndrome**, in which a male (1 in 200) is born with one or more extra X chromosomes (XXY). Klinefelter males tend to be tall and generally masculine in appearance, but they are sterile and develop feminine sex characteristics such as enlarged breasts at puberty. About 20 to 30% are mentally retarded (Burns, 1976).

We have now outlined the fundamentals of heredity. Each of us has a unique genetic makeup, or genotype, contained in his or her 23 pairs of chromosomes. Combinations of our parents' genes are passed to us at conception and influence our traits (phenotypes) through the mechanisms of single gene-pair, sex-linked, and polygenic inheritance. A small minority of individuals are also powerfully affected by genetic mutations or chromosome abnormalities. Now we are in a position to find out what researchers have learned about the extent to which psychological differences among us are influenced by differences in our hereditary endowments.

BEHAVIOR GENETICS: ACCOUNTING FOR INDIVIDUAL DIFFERENCES IN TRAITS

Behavior genetics is the scientific study of the extent to which genetic and environmental differences among people or animals are responsible for differences in their traits. Behavior geneticists recognize that it is impossible to say that one person's intelligence test score is, say, 80%, 50%, or 20% heredity and the rest environment. The individual would have no intelligence at all without *both* a genetic makeup and experiences. However, behavior geneticists can estimate the **heritability** of measured intelligence (IQ) or any other trait or behavior. Heritability is the amount of variability in a trait *within a large group of people* that can be linked to genetic differences among those individuals. To say that measured intelligence is "heritable" is to say that individual differences in IQ scores are to some degree—large or small—attributable to the fact that different individuals have different genes.

Individual differences in psychological traits are usually the result of both hereditary and environmental influences. When behavior geneticists tell us that a trait is or is not heritable, they also tell us about the extent to which differences in experience (for example, opportunities for intellectual stimulation) create psychological or behavioral differences among people. They can, therefore, provide us with some fascinating evidence about which existing differences among people are mostly genetic in origin and which differences are mostly environmental in origin (see Plomin, 1990). However, even when a trait proves to be highly heritable in a population, that does not in any way mean that the environment can have no impact on the trait or that special intervention programs are doomed to fail. Even if some children currently perform poorly on IQ tests partly because of their genetic makeup, they can still be stimulated to higher levels of intellectual performance if their environment is improved (Scarr & Carter-Saltzman, 1983).

To study the influence of genes on animal behavior, it is possible to set up experiments that involve breeding animals as one chooses or placing different breeds in environments of one's choice. This is clearly impossible with humans, so studies of human genetics must examine resemblances between people who vary in their **kinship**, or degree of genetic relatedness.

Experimental Breeding of Animals

Deliberately manipulating the genetic makeup of animals to study genetic influences on behavior is much like what Gregor Mendel did to discover the workings of heredity in plants. One of the most commonly used breeding experiments is **selective breeding**—deliberately determining whether it is possible to breed a trait selectively in animals. A classic example is R. C. Tryon's (1940) attempt to show that maze-learning ability is a heritable or genetically influenced attribute in rats. Tryon began by testing a large number of rats for the ability to run a complex maze. Rats that made few errors were labeled "maze bright"; those that made many errors were termed "maze dull." Then, across several generations, Tryon mated bright rats with bright rats and dull rats with dull rats. If differences in experience rather than differences in genetic makeup had accounted for the initial differences between bright and dull rats, this selective breeding would have had no impact. Instead, across generations the differences in learning performance between the maze-bright and maze-dull groups of rats became increasingly larger. Tryon had shown that maze-learning ability in rats is influenced by genetic makeup. Selective breeding studies have also shown that genes contribute to such attributes as activity level, emotionality, aggressiveness, and sex drive in rats, mice, and chickens (Plomin, DeFries, & McClearn, 1989).

Family Studies

People don't take kindly to the idea of being selectively bred by experimenters. An alternative procedure for studying genetic influences among humans is through family studies that determine the degree to which biological relatives possess similar traits. We might observe, for example, that intelligence tends to run in families: that members of some families generally score high on intelligence tests while members of other families generally score low. Can you see a potential weakness of this method? Isn't it possible that the parents of bright children provided them with a stimulating home environment rather than with genes for intelligence? Family members share not only genes but experiences.

Still, family studies have value. For example, it was by tracing the disease hemophilia through generations of the royal families of Europe that researchers discovered that boys were affected far more often than girls and that the disease must be sex-linked. Moreover, if we were to find that full siblings are more alike in a trait than half siblings, that would imply that the trait is heritable because full siblings are more genetically similar than half siblings. Finally, if we were to find that biological relatives are *not* any more similar in a trait than pairs of unrelated individuals, we can infer that genes must *not* have much to do with that trait. So even though family studies cannot always fully separate the effects of heredity and environment, they can at least tell us that differences in heredity *may* contribute to individual variations in any attribute we might choose to study.

Twin Studies

Twins have long been recognized as very important sources of evidence about the effects of heredity. The most common type of twin study involves determining whether identical twins reared together are more similar to each other than fraternal twins reared together. If genes matter, identical twins should be more similar, for they have 100% of their genes in common while fraternal twins share only 50% on the average. Box 3.2 shows how the similarity between twins or other pairs of individuals is measured so that the influences of heredity and environment can be estimated.

Both identical and fraternal twins are born at the same time into the same family, so it is assumed that the environments of identical twins are no more similar than the environments of fraternal twins. Is that really a safe assumption? After all, identical twins are often dressed alike and treated alike by anyone who has difficulty telling them apart. By contrast, fraternal twins look different and may be treated differently as a result. Perhaps "identical environments" rather than "identical genes" could make identical twins more similar in intelligence and other traits than fraternal twins are.

Identical twins are indeed perceived and treated more similarly than fraternal twins are (Lytton, 1977). Yet Lytton (1977) has suggested that parents react in a more similar fashion to identical twins than to fraternal twins because identical twins behave more similarly than fraternal

Box 3.2
Calculating the Influence of Heredity

Behavior geneticists rely on some simple and not so simple mathematical calculations to tell them whether or not a trait is genetically influenced and to estimate the degree to which heredity and environment can account for individual differences in the trait. When they study traits that a person either has or does not have (for example, a smoking habit or diabetes), researchers calculate and compare **concordance rates**—the percentage of pairs of people (for example, identical twins) in which *both* members display the trait of interest if one member has it. For example, suppose researchers locate 100 people who are identical twins and who have been hospitalized for severe depression, track down their twin siblings, and find that 60 of them also have had a major depression. If this concordance rate of 60% is higher than the rate for fraternal twin pairs, one can conclude that major depressive disorder is heritable. Since identical twins are *not* perfectly concordant, we can also conclude that their *experiences* must also have something to do with whether a person experiences major depression.

When a trait can assume many values (for example, height or intelligence), **correlation coefficients** rather than concordance rates are calculated. Any correlation coefficient (symbolized *r*) tells us the extent to which two variables or attributes "go together" so that as the value of one increases, the value of the other either increases or decreases in a systematic way. A medical researcher might want to know if people who get more exercise have fewer heart attacks. A behavior geneticist might want to know whether the IQ scores of twins "go together" with the IQ scores of their co-twins, so that if one twin is bright, the other is too. Suppose we had just five sets of identical twins and their IQ scores were determined to be as follows, on a scale where 100 is average:

	TWIN 1	TWIN 2
Pair A	165	170
Pair B	130	135
Pair C	105	100
Pair D	85	90
Pair E	60	55

The members of each twin pair are quite similar in their IQs, so the correlation coefficient would be very high: +.99, where the maximum positive correlation is +1.00. If, knowing the IQ of one twin, we would have no ability to predict whether the IQ of that person's co-twin would be high, average, or low, the result would be a correlation near zero. Correlations can also be negative (from −.01 to −1.00). To obtain a negative correlation in our twin example, a twin with a particularly high IQ would have to have a co-twin with a particularly low IQ—an unlikely outcome. Yet negative correlations are found in other kinds of research. For example, exercise is negatively correlated with the incidence of heart disease; people who exercise more are *less* likely to have heart attacks.

Now, suppose we find a correlation of +.80 between the IQ scores of identical twins and a correlation for fraternal twins of +.50. Although these correlations tell us that even fraternal twins resemble each other in IQ, they also indicate that identical twins are more similar to each other than fraternal twins are and thus suggest that heredity contributes to intelligence.

Behavior geneticists have proposed a formula to estimate the heritability of a trait based on a twin study:

$$H = (r \text{ identical twins} - r \text{ fraternal twins}) \times 2$$

In words, the heritability of an attribute *equals* the correlation between identical twins *minus* the correlation between fraternal twins, all multiplied by 2 (Plomin, DeFries, & McClearn, 1980).

Now we can estimate the contribution that heredity makes to variations in the trait of tested intelligence. If the correlation for identical twins is .80 and the correlation for fraternal twins is .50,

$$H = (.80 - .50) \times 2 = .30 \times 2 = .60.$$

This heritability quotient of .60 is moderately large on a scale ranging from .00 (not at all heritable) to 1.00 (totally heritable), so we might conclude that, *within the population from which our subjects were selected*, tested intelligence is influenced to some extent by hereditary factors. More specifically, 60% of the variability among people in tested intelligence can be attributed to differences in their genetic makeups. The heritability estimate would be much lower if identical twins were not much more similar in IQ than fraternal twins were. However, even in our example much of the variability among people (40%, to be more precise) is attributable to nonhereditary factors—that is, to environmental influences and to errors we may have made in measuring intelligence.

twins do. Moreover, Lytton contends that identical twins behave similarly because they have identical genetic makeups, not because they are treated similarly. In short, perceiving and treating identical twins similarly appears to be the *result* of their genetic similarity rather than the cause of their behavioral similarity. Most available evidence supports Lytton's argument and suggests that the twin method of study is basically sound (Loehlin & Nichols, 1976; Plomin, DeFries, & McClearn, 1989).

No single group of individuals has more to tell us about genetic influence than identical twins who have been separated early in life and grow up in very different environments. Thomas Bouchard (1984) and his colleagues have located 30 such pairs of twins, including Oscar Stohr and Jack Yufe, the twins described at the beginning of this chapter. Even though these twins were separated on the average at about 3 months of age, they have proved to be remarkably similar as middle-aged adults. The similarities show up in countless little ways: in their common dress styles, postures, and gestures (see also Farber, 1981). Moreover, these twins are very similar in height and fairly similar in weight, and they also perform quite similarly on measures of intelligence and personality. However, they do not perform identically, and this fact tells us that identical twins reared apart are also the products of their different experiences in life.

Adoption Studies

Finally, much can be learned about heredity and environment by studying individuals who are adopted early in life. Are adopted children similar to their biological parents, whose genes they share, or are they similar to their adoptive parents, whose environment they share? If they resemble their biological parents in intelligence or personality even though those parents did not raise them, genes must be influential. If they resemble their adoptive parents even though they are genetically unrelated to them, a good case can be made for environmental influence.

There are two problems with this approach. First, if children resemble their biological parents, it could be due to environmental influences before the adoption took place. The adoption method thus yields firmer conclusions when children are adopted immediately after they are born. Second, adoption agencies sometimes make selective placements. If, for example, they placed children whose biological parents were intelligent with intelligent adoptive parents and these children turned out to be intelligent themselves, how would we know whether it was due to their genes or to the stimulating environment that their bright adoptive parents provided? Fortunately, researchers can make corrections for any such selective placement when they estimate the contributions of genes and environment. All things considered, the adoption method is an excellent means of studying the influence of heredity and environment (Heath, Kendler, Eaves, & Markell, 1985).

Even if the family, twin, and adoption methods all have their limitations, we can be more confident in the results when evidence from all three types of studies agrees. Indeed, today's researchers often combine these techniques in a single study so that they can more fully explore the effects of heredity and environment (Plomin, 1990). And the information that they are gaining is important and often surprising, as we shall now see. Since our focus in this book is on life-span development, we would like to take you through the life span, stage by stage, sampling studies of the impacts of genes and environment on human characteristics such as intelligence, personality, and psychological disorders. With the help of Robert Plomin's (1986, 1990; Plomin & Thompson, 1988) excellent reviews of developmental behavior genetics, we will also ask whether the relative contributions of genes and environment change over the life span.

THE INFANT

Recall that from conception onward, genes are producing many important similarities among infants all over the world. This is due to the influence of *species heredity*—specifically, a universal, genetically programmed, maturational plan that is more powerful before birth and during infancy than it is later in life. Here we will ask how genes and environment contribute to differences among infants. Why is it that some infants achieve developmental milestones before others do, and why do babies have unique "personalities"?

Mental Ability

Infant intelligence is typically measured by testing infants to see if they have achieved certain milestones in motor behavior and can act adaptively to do such things as find hidden objects or follow simple instructions. In

Ronald Wilson's (1978, 1983) longitudinal study of twins, identical twins were no more similar than fraternal twins on a measure of infant mental development during the first year of life. But the picture changed starting at about 18 months of age. Individual heredity began to show itself, so that the correlation between the mental development scores of identical twins (.82) was higher than the correlation between the scores obtained by fraternal twins (.65). Moreover, at about this same age the profiles of change from one testing to the next were more similar for identical twins than for fraternal twins. For instance, if one identical twin had a big spurt in mental development between 18 months and 24 months of age, the other twin was likely to show the same spurt at the same time. Thus, the *course* of mental development was genetically influenced! Although likenesses between fraternal twins were not as great as those between identical twin pairs, they were great enough to suggest that sharing the same family environment contributes, along with sharing genes, to likenesses in infant intellectual development.

Adoption studies also suggest that both genes and environment contribute to individual differences in infant mental development. Robert Plomin and J. C. DeFries (1985) found that adopted infants who were relatively intelligent at age 2 had biological parents who were relatively intelligent. Since they did not grow up with these parents, genetic makeup seemed to make a difference. The mental development scores of these infants also correlated with the IQ scores of their adoptive parents, suggesting that environment also influenced infant mental development. Yet neither the IQs of biological parents nor the IQs of adoptive parents were strongly related to infants' scores (both of these correlations were only .10). Thus mental development in infancy was not yet strongly associated with either individual heredity or family environment. In summary, both twin and adoption studies suggest that individual heredity and environmental influences begin to show their effects on infant mental development during the second year of life. However, the influences of both factors are smaller than they will be later in life (Plomin, 1986).

Personality

As parents well know, different babies have different personalities. Hard as it may be to believe, genetic differences between infants have something to do with this fact. Researchers have focused on aspects of **temperament**: tendencies to respond in predictable ways that can be considered the building blocks of later personality. While different researchers have defined infant temperament in different ways, one scheme (Buss & Plomin, 1984) focuses on individual differences in *emotionality* (how easily and intensely upset an infant is by events), *activity* (the infant's typical vigor and pace of behavior), and *sociability* (a preference to be with others versus a tendency toward shyness and withdrawal).

In their study of twins, Ronald Wilson and Adam Matheny (1986) have found that genes have quite a bit of influence on an infant's emotionality: on whether he or she is easily upset and irritable or happy and animated, as reported by parents and as observed in the laboratory. Just as they found that differences among infants in mental development became more closely associated with genetic makeup at about 18 months of age, they noted that it was during the second year of life that identical twins begin to show more likeness in emotional tone than fraternal twins do. The sample developmental profiles in Figure 3.7 demonstrate what happened. Especially after 1 year of age, identical twins showed similar ups and downs in emotional tone from testing to testing. If one became more or less upsettable at 24 months than at 18 months, the other tended to develop in the very same direction. Meanwhile, fraternal twins were beginning to take their own distinct developmental paths and were becoming *less* similar in emotionality.

Similarly, genes have some influence on sociability. For example, identical twins are more alike than fraternal twins in the extent to which they show negative emotional reactions when a stranger approaches them (Goldsmith & Campos, 1986). And adopted infants who are shy tend to have biological parents who are relatively unsociable (Plomin & DeFries, 1985). Evidence that genes influence an infant's activity level is less consistent (Plomin & DeFries, 1985), but at least some studies suggest that it too is partly associated with genetic endowment (Goldsmith & Campos, 1986).

Overall, genetic differences among infants do indeed help explain why they differ from one another in physical growth, mental development, and temperament. The influence of individual heredity is often not apparent in the first year of life, but emerges in the second year. Differences among infants also derive from differences in their home environments. However, neither genetic differences nor environmental differences account very well for behavioral and psychological differences among infants. Robert McCall (1981) has suggested that this may be because all infants share a powerful maturational program that channels them along the same course of development. Unique hereditary endowment has little impact compared to this species heredity. Similarly, experience may temporarily deflect an infant from the path charted by species-wide genes, but environmental influence must be extremely powerful (as would be the case if an infant were seriously ill or deprived) to tamper much with nature's plan.

THE CHILD

After infancy, both individual heredity and experience begin to play more major roles in shaping consistent and long-lasting differences between individuals (Plomin, 1986). Consequently, each child develops a characteristic level of intellectual performance and a distinct personality.

Mental Ability

Evidence that a child's genes might matter more and more as the child develops comes from Wilson's longitudinal study of the intelligence test scores of pairs of identical and fraternal twins (Wilson, 1983). Identical twins become highly similar in their intellectual performances by the end of infancy and stay highly similar throughout childhood (the average correlation between the IQ scores of identical twins is about .85). Meanwhile, fraternal twins are most similar in IQ at about age 3 and become *less* similar over the years, so that by age 15 the correlation between their IQ scores drops to .54, about the same as that for nontwin siblings (see Figure 3.8). During childhood, identical twins' IQ scores also continue to change in similar directions at similar times; in other words, their developmental paths are similar. By contrast, members of fraternal twin pairs take their own distinct developmental paths, guided in part by their different genetic makeups.

This is not to say that environment has no impact, however. Wilson found that twins who experienced intellectually stimulating home environments had higher test scores than did twins whose homes were less stimulating. Similarly, adoption studies (see Plomin, 1986) indicate that the IQ scores of adopted children are correlated with measures of the intellectual abilities of both their biological parents (genetic influence) *and* their adoptive parents (environmental influence). Finally, even though intellectual differences among adopted children are related to the IQs of their biological parents, the *level* of intellectual performance that these children reach can be increased if they are adopted into intellectually stimulating homes.

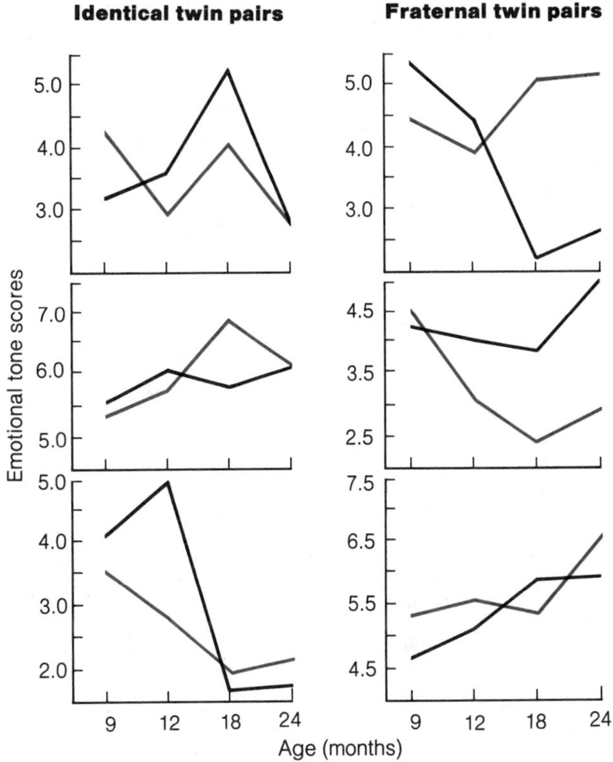

Figure 3.7 Changes in the emotionality of identical and fraternal twins during infancy. Starting in the second year of life, identical twins typically follow more similar development paths than fraternal twins do, as shown by these sample cases. (From Wilson & Matheny, 1986)

This was demonstrated by Sandra Scarr and Richard Weinberg (1976, 1983) in a study of black children adopted into the homes of white, middle-class, highly educated parents. These children scored about 20 points higher on IQ tests than would be expected if they had remained in the lower socioeconomic environments provided by their biological parents. Their actual IQ scores, in other words, were closer in value to those of their adoptive parents than

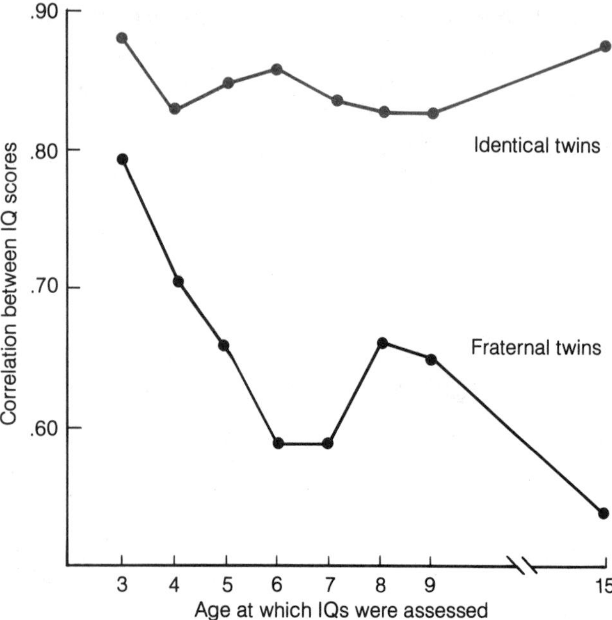

Figure 3.8 Changes in the correlations between the IQ scores of identical and fraternal twins over childhood. (Data from Wilson, 1983)

to those of their natural parents. Thus the improved home environment provided by middle-class adoptive parents boosts the IQs of adopted children as a group, even though genetic differences among them still make for IQ differences among them. Possibly, stimulating home environments help children realize whatever genetically based potentials they have (Wilson, 1983).

Personality

Do genes also influence a child's personality? One indication that they do comes from studies of childhood behavior problems. For example, some children seem to inherit a susceptibility to hyperactivity that makes it difficult for them to pay attention in school (Morrison & Stewart, 1973). Similarly, genes may predispose certain children to be bullies, to be restless or tense, or to get in trouble at school (O'Connor, Foch, Sherry, & Plomin, 1980). Thus we should not immediately assume that any behavior problem a child displays must be the result of faulty parenting.

Normal variations in personality are also partly influenced by genes, it seems. In a review of twin studies of personality, Arnold Buss and Robert Plomin (1984) report that if one identical twin displays a personality trait, the other one is likely to display it too. Average correlations between identical twins' traits were .63 for emotionality, .62 for activity, and .53 for sociability. The corresponding correlations for fraternal twins were near zero: what you would expect if these children were pairs of strangers living in different homes rather than twins who share half of their genes and the same home! Why is this? Scarr and Kidd (1983) suggest that while most parents push their children toward high intellectual and academic achievement, they allow their children's personalities to develop more freely, so children who live in the same home become more alike in IQ than in personality. Buss and Plomin also suggest that parents may distinguish between their children—especially fraternal twins—and try to treat them as distinct individuals with distinct personalities.

In sum, even though sharing a common home environment tends to make children more similar in their tested intelligence, it does little to make them similar in temperament or personality. Instead, family influences may conspire to make brothers and sisters *different* from each other in many personality attributes (Plomin, 1990). Meanwhile, genes are also creating differences among children. Indeed, genes appear to exert more and more influence over the years as they guide children along their own developmental paths (Goldsmith, 1983; Wilson, 1983).

THE ADOLESCENT

There are hints that individual differences among adolescents are even more closely linked to their genotypes than individual differences among children are. However, the experiences that adolescents seek out and encounter also affect their abilities and traits.

Mental Ability

Several studies suggest that genetic differences do even more to explain differences in tested IQ in adolescence than they did in childhood (Fischbein, 1981; Wilson, 1983). As we have seen, the IQs of adopted children are correlated with those of both their biological parents and their adoptive parents throughout childhood. During adolescence, the resemblance to biological parents remains evident, but adopted adolescents no longer resemble their adoptive parents in intellectual performance

It's no surprise that identical twins look alike and that parents dress them alike. The surprise in this photo is that identical twins—without any instructions—unconsciously put their hands in similar positions.

(Scarr & Weinberg, 1978). In other words, the association between the kind of home environment an individual experiences and his or her intellectual performance decreases from childhood to adolescence. Why is this? Very possibly, it is because children become more independent of their parents during adolescence and are increasingly influenced by environmental factors outside the home, such as the peer groups they join and the teachers they encounter (Scarr & Weinberg, 1978).

Personality

Are you beginning to wonder whether family environment has much impact on development? You should be, because we keep encountering evidence that as children get older there is less and less resemblance between individuals who grow up in the same house and share a neighborhood and community environment as well. Nowhere is this more apparent than in studies of personality. For example, despite the fact that biologically related adolescent siblings have 50% of their genes in common and share the same environment, the reported correlations between their personality traits are sometimes as low as .10 (Ahern, Johnson, Wilson, McClearn, & Vandenberg, 1982) and rarely above .20! Adopted siblings growing up in the same home hardly resemble each other at all (Scarr, Webber, Weinberg, & Wittig, 1981).

Does this mean that family environment counts for nothing? It does indeed suggest that the family environment does little to make siblings *similar* to each other. However, a very important message has emerged from recent research: Family environment *is* important in personality development, but it is important because it creates *differences* among children (Rowe & Plomin, 1981). If you think back to your own family experiences, you may recognize that there were ways in which your parents treated you and your brothers or sisters differently, in which you and your siblings had lopsided relationships in which one was more dominant or one was more giving, and in which you and your siblings traveled in different circles outside the home. Adolescent brothers and sisters do indeed report that they have different experiences (Daniels & Plomin, 1985; Dunn & Stocker, 1989).

What's more, differences in the experiences of siblings are systematically associated with differences in their personalities. Denise Daniels (1986), for example, surveyed biological and adoptive sibling pairs ranging in age from 12 to 18 about their relationships with their parents, siblings, and peers and gave them personality tests. As it turned out, the sibling in a pair who was more emotional than the other also experienced more antagonism and jealousy in the sibling relationship, and the sibling who was more sociable experienced more sibling closeness and belonged to more popular peer groups. Moreover, the adolescent who experienced more affection from his or her father had higher vocational aspirations than the sibling who experienced less paternal love. Very possibly, then, differences in experiences might help explain why brothers and sisters often have such different personalities.

In short, some of the most important environmental influences on development are *unique to the individual*. Even when siblings experience the same event such as a divorce or a visit to a space center, they may be affected very differently by it (McCall, 1983). And if you are not completely convinced yet, consider identical twins reared together. They share 100% of their genes and the same home and yet they have unique personalities. The correlation between their personality traits is often in the vicinity of .50. The difference between this correlation and a perfect correlation of 1.00 is a clear indication that *nonshared* or unique environmental influences are important contributors to their personality development (Rowe & Plomin, 1981).

We can conclude our discussion of the behavior genetics of adolescence by noting that some adolescent signs of mental or emotional disturbance can also be traced to genetic makeup (Plomin, 1986). Why, for example, are some adolescents more involved in delinquent behavior than others are? According to David Rowe (1983), genes are partly responsible, for the correlation between the delinquency rates of identical twins (about .70) is higher than that for fraternal twin pairs (about .50). However, the fact that identical twins are not completely similar tells us again that *unique* experiences matter. Even genetically identical adolescents living in the same home differ in their behavior.

In sum, we have ample evidence that adolescents differ in many attributes partly because they differ in genetic makeup. And we now know that, by adolescence, we can find little evidence that growing up in the same home makes adolescents similar to each other, but much evidence that their unique experiences, in and out of the home, make them different from each other.

THE ADULT

Do genetic differences among individuals continue to contribute to behavioral and psychological differences among them in adulthood? Or do the effects of experience eventually overshadow the effects of genes as the years pass? Let us summarize some of the main findings, and also examine the role of genes in the aging process.

Mental Ability

So far as we know, individual differences in individual intelligence remain strongly linked to individual genetic differences throughout adulthood (Plomin, 1986). We can summarize the contributions of genes and environment to individual differences in intelligence by examining the average correlations between the IQ scores of different types of relatives in Table 3.3. These averages are based on a review by Thomas Bouchard and Matthew McGue (1981) of studies involving 526 correlations based on 113,942 pairs of people. It is clear that these correlations become higher when people are more closely related genetically and are highest when they are identical twins. Can you also detect the workings of environment? For each level of kinship for which data are available, notice that:

Table 3.3 Average correlations between the intelligence scores of different pairs of individuals

	REARED TOGETHER	REARED APART
Identical twins	.86	.72
Fraternal twins	.60	.52
Biological siblings	.47	.24
Biological parent and child	.42	.22
Half siblings	.31	—
Adopted siblings	.34	—
Adoptive parent and adopted child	.19	—

Note: All but one of these averages were calculated by Bouchard and McGue (1981) based on studies of both children and adults. The correlation for fraternal twins reared apart was based on data reported by Pedersen, McClearn, Plomin, & Friberg (1985).

Pairs of individuals reared apart are somewhat less similar in IQ than pairs reared together.

Fraternal twins, who should have especially similar family experiences because they grow up at the same time, are often more alike than siblings born at different times.

The IQs of adopted children are related to those of their adopted parents (even though we have seen that this relationship may weaken over the years).

Most researchers now agree that at least 50% of the variability in IQ scores among individuals can be credited to genetic differences among these individuals (Plomin, 1986). The rest can be attributed to differences in experience.

Personality

What contributions do genes and environment make to adult personality? Much of the attention has centered on two broad and important personality dimensions. One is **extraversion/introversion**, or the extent to which a person is outgoing and socially oriented or shy, retiring, and uncomfortable around other people—a trait dimension that corresponds closely to the dimension of infant temperament called sociability. The second is **neuroticism**, or the extent to which a person is psychologically stable or unstable, anxious, and easily upset—a trait that can be likened to the aspect of infant temperament called emotionality.

In a large-scale study of twins in Sweden, correlations reflecting the likenesses between identical twin pairs on these two traits were only around .50 (Floderus-Myrhed, Pedersen, & Rasmuson, 1980). Obviously identical genes did not make for identical personalities, so the unique experiences of identical twins must have contributed to differences in their extraversion and neuroticism. The correlations for fraternal twins were even lower (about .20), however, so genes do seem to exert a significant influence on adult personality (see also Rose et al., 1988).

Overall, John Loehlin (1985) suggests that, of all the differences among adults in major dimensions of personality, about 40% of the variation may be due to genetic differences among them. Only 5% of it reflects the ways in which sharing a family environment can make family members similar to each other and different from people in other families. Indeed, adopted children, as adults, are no more like their adoptive parents in personality than they are like complete strangers (Loehlin, Willerman, & Horn, 1985). The remaining 55% of the variability in adult personalities is largely due to each individual's unique experiences—experiences that are not shared with other family members.

Finally, behavior geneticists have looked closely at the issue of whether some adults are more genetically predisposed to develop major psychological disorders than others are. Perhaps no disorder has been studied as much as **schizophrenia**, a serious mental illness that involves disturbances in logical thinking, emotional expression, and social behavior and often emerges in late adolescence or early adulthood.

Some people do indeed have genes that predispose them to schizophrenia. The average concordance rate (instances in which both twins have schizophrenia if one twin does) for identical twins is 57%, while the concordance rate for fraternal twins is only 13% (Gottesman & Shields, 1973). In addition, children who have one or more biological parent who is schizophrenic have an increased risk of schizophrenia, even if they are adopted away early in life (Heston, 1970). Thus it is genes, not experiencing the unusual family environment that a schizophrenic parent might provide, that put the children of schizophrenics at risk.

But let's put these findings in perspective. It is easy to mistakenly conclude that any child of a schizophrenic will become a schizophrenic. The rate of schizophrenia in the general population is about 1%. By comparison about 10% to 14% of children who have one schizophrenic parent develop schizophrenic symptoms themselves (Kessler, 1975). Although this figure does suggest that children of schizophrenics are at greater risk for schizophrenia than most children, notice that 86% to 90% of the children of one schizophrenic parent *do not* develop the disorder. Similarly, even if you are an identical twin whose co-twin develops the disorder, the odds are only about 1 out of 2 that you too will become schizophrenic! Clearly an individual's experiences must also be an important contributor to mental illness. In short, people do not inherit psychological disorders; instead, they inherit predispositions to develop disorders. Assuming that a person has inherited a genetic susceptibility to schizophrenia, it may take one or more stressful experience (for example, rejecting parents or a crumbling marriage) to trigger the illness.

Table 3-4. Percent of adopted sons who have criminal convictions

		BIOLOGICAL FATHER HAD CONVICTIONS?	
		Yes	No
ADOPTIVE FATHER HAD CONVICTIONS?	Yes	24.5	14.7
	No	20.0	13.5

Source: Figures from Mednick, Gabrielli, & Hutchings, 1984.

Much the same can be said for the many other problems of adulthood that appear to have some genetic basis. For example, as shown in Table 3.4, a man who was adopted in childhood is more likely to be convicted of crimes if his biological father had a criminal record than if he did not (Mednick, Gabrielli, & Hutchings, 1984; and see Baker, Mack, Moffitt, & Mednick, 1989, for evidence of a similar genetic contribution to women's criminal tendencies). Living with an adoptive father who had a criminal record has little impact. Yet, more than 75% of the men who had both their genes *and* their adoptive family environment predisposing them to crime had no convictions. Similarly, heredity contributes to alcoholism, depression, and a number of other psychological disorders, but it hardly makes those problems inevitable (Fuller & Thompson, 1978).

The Genetics of Aging

Finally, let us briefly examine the relationships between genes and aging. Do genes have anything to do with why some people age more quickly and die sooner than others do? If much of child development is guided by a genetic program, is there also a species-wide genetic program that makes all of us age and die?

Let's start with some convincing evidence that an individual's genes influence how that person ages. Many years ago, Franz Kallmann and Gerhard Sander (1949) launched a major study that involved repeatedly assessing both identical and fraternal twins as they aged. They found that identical twins still resemble each other physically late in life: They show visible signs of aging—graying and thinning of the hair, wrinkling, physical disabilities—at similar times. Moreover, identical twins in this study died on an average of 4 years apart, while fraternal twins died on an average of 5½ years apart (Kallmann & Jarvik, 1959). This finding suggests that individual genetic makeup, perhaps by influencing one's susceptibility to major diseases, may have a bearing on how long a person lives.

Identical twins also perform more similarly on IQ tests in later life than fraternal twins do (Kallmann & Jarvik, 1959). What's more, if one identical twin experiences a major drop in intellectual performance in later life, the other twin often does too (Jarvik & Bank, 1983). Finally, elderly identical twins, even those who were separated early in life, continue to be more alike than fraternal twins are in such aspects of personality as sociability, emotionality, and activity level (Plomin, Pedersen, McClearn, Nesselroade, & Bergeman, 1988). So we are probably safe in concluding that there is no point in adulthood at which one's genetic makeup ceases to affect one's physical and psychological characteristics.

Identical twins age similarly. Jack Yufe (*left*) and Oscar Stohr (*right*) are the separated twins described at the beginning of the chapter. Notice that they, like the twins on page 87, place their hands in similar positions.

Is it possible that there is a species-wide genetic program that calls for *all of us* to age and die? After all, human beings have a characteristic life span that is different from those of other species. There is much agreement that there must be some genetic basis for aging and dying. However, no specific "aging genes" have yet been identified, and it could be that there are no such genes. Instead, the genetic program that maintains life may simply run out (McClearn & Foch, 1985).

Researchers hope eventually to discover the genetic basis of aging and death by studying genetic defects that produce the symptoms of aging early in life. Certainly one of the most frightening of these disorders is **progeria**, a syndrome that involves premature aging starting in infancy (see Figure 3.9). As F. L. DeBusk (1972) describes it, growth slows down starting in infancy, hair loss and balding occur, the skin becomes covered with "age spots," joints stiffen, fat is lost, and bones degenerate and become fragile. Victims die on the average at age 13—some as early as 7, some as late as 27—often from the heart diseases that strike elderly people. The best guess is that progeria is associated with a single dominant gene but that the gene arises as a new mutation in each case of progeria (Brown, 1985).

Although research on progeria may tell us something about the genetics of aging, this disease does not perfectly mimic the normal aging process. For example, victims' bodies certainly age, but their nervous systems show no deterioration of the kind that humans often experience very late in life. It is as if the normally developing mind of a child were trapped in the deteriorating body of an aged adult. Actually, the chromosomal abnormality Down syndrome is perhaps the disorder that most closely mimics aging (Brown, 1985). Down's victims do show several symptoms of premature aging, including early graying and loss of hair, cardiovascular problems, and the early onset of *Alzheimer's disease*—the leading cause of "senility." (See Chapter 16 for evidence that this disease is caused in part by a gene on chromosome 21.)

Although none of the disorders that trigger premature aging includes *all* of the symptoms of normal aging (Brown, 1985; McClearn & Foch, 1985), it is possible that increased understanding of *several* of these "early aging"

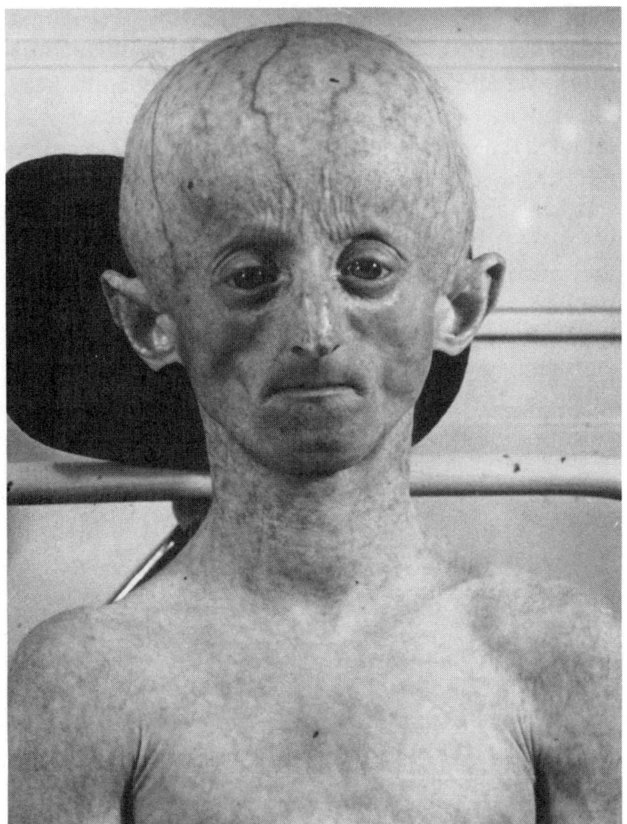

Figure 3.9 Progeria. This boy was a roly-poly, normal infant at 10 months but soon began to show the symptoms of premature aging associated with progeria. Fortunately, only about 1 in 8,000,000 people has this genetic disorder.

disorders will eventually help us unravel a very great mystery—why we age and die. There is no question that our human genes contribute to these final "developments," but there are many questions left unanswered about how they do so, as we will see in Chapter 17.

A LIFE-SPAN PERSPECTIVE ON GENES AND ENVIRONMENT

What should we conclude overall about the influences of genes and environment across the life span and about the ways in which these two great forces in development interact to make us what we are? The following general statements tie things together.

Both Genes and Environment Are at Work over the Entire Life Span

It should be clear by now that genes do not just orchestrate our growth before birth and then leave us alone. Instead, genes are "turning on" and "turning off" in patterned ways throughout the life span, and they are partly responsible for attributes and behavior patterns that we carry with us throughout our lives. Our shared species heredity makes us similar in the way we develop and age. Our unique individual genetic makeups cause us to develop and age in our own special ways.

However, environmental influences also impinge on us from conception to death. We have encountered some evidence that living in the same family can make people alike, even if they are genetically unrelated, especially in their performance on tests of intelligence. But we have also discovered perhaps even stronger evidence that living in the same family makes people *different,* especially in their personality traits. Thus we come to appreciate that experiences unique to the individual are a major factor in creating individual differences, even among members of the same family who have genes in common (Plomin, 1990).

The Relative Contributions of Genes and Environment Change over the Life Span

As we have also seen, the extent to which individual differences in traits can be attributed to differences in genetic makeup is greater at some points of the life span than at others. Perhaps because of strong species-wide maturational forces in early infancy, identical twins are often no more similar than fraternal twins at first. Later in infancy, and increasingly through the years of childhood and adolescence, our unique genetic blueprints seem to show themselves more and more in our behavior. Thus identical twins often remain similar to each other, but fraternal twins typically become less similar to each other as they get older. While we know little about the behavior genetics of old age, the current research suggests that there is little change over the adult years in the portions of the variation among people that can be linked to differences in their genes and environments.

At the same time, the environmental forces that make children in the same family alike seem stronger early in life than they do later in life (Plomin, 1986). As we move out of the home and into the larger world, we seem to be shaped more and more by our unique combination of experiences and develop along our own pathways.

Some Traits Are More Heritable Than Others

You may have gotten the impression that individual differences in virtually any human trait one cares to examine are strongly influenced by genes. But some traits are more heritable than others are. Let's attempt to rank human characteristics from the most to the least heritable.

Observable physical characteristics—from eye color to height—are very strongly associated with individual genetic endowment (Plomin, 1986). Even weight is heritable, for adopted children resemble their biological parents more than their adoptive parents in the weight they carry as adults (Stunkard et al., 1986). Aspects of physiological functioning are heritable, too. For example, identical twins have strikingly similar patterns of measured brain activity (Lykken, Tellegen, & Iacono, 1982), and their bodies react very similarly to alcohol (Martin, Oakeshott, Gibson, Starmer, Perl, & Wilkers, 1985; Neale & Martin, 1989). The fact that individual differences in these physical and physiological characteristics are strongly heritable does *not* necessarily mean that environmental forces have no effect on them. If, for example, one identical twin were well fed and the other starved throughout life, the first twin would clearly be taller than the second. Saying that height is a heritable trait simply means that the differences among people in a group of people studied—people who have grown up in whatever environments they have grown up in—can be accounted for to some extent by differences in their genetic makeups. However, the environment can affect the expression (or phenotype) of the vast majority of heritable attributes.

If physical and physiological characteristics can be described as strongly heritable, general intelligence seems to be moderately heritable. Perhaps half (or even more) of the variability among people in tested intelligence can be traced to genetic endowment, with the other half of the variation being due to differences in experience. Somewhat less influenced by genes are aspects of temperament and personality; here genetic influence is modest, but still evident.

Is there any trait that is *not* influenced by heredity? From one perspective, we should answer No. *All* human traits depend on having both a genotype and an environment. In this sense, genes and environment are both "100% important" (Hebb, 1970). But it is also the case that individual differences in some traits seem to have no relationship to variations in genetic endowment. Under the heading of mental abilities, for example, some researchers have found that neither the size of one's basic memory capacity nor the speed with which one can process visual information are heritable (Foch & Plomin, 1980). Also, identical twins are not much more alike with respect to how well they perform on tests of creativity than fraternal twins are (Plomin, 1990; Reznikoff, Domino, Bridges, & Honeyman, 1973). Twins of both types are similar in their degree of creativity, but this similarity must be due to their shared experiences. Thus some mental abilities are more heritable than others are.

Similarly, genes influence some aspects of personality more than they influence others. Genes seem to have a fair amount of influence on how sociable or extraverted and emotional or neurotic a person is. However, having certain personality traits that are stereotyped as "masculine" and being able to tolerate ambiguous situations are not notably heritable (Loehlin, 1982). Finally, an individual's social and political attitudes seem to be more influenced by experience than by heredity (Loehlin & Nichols, 1976). Thus we can conclude that some traits are especially influenced by genes and others are especially influenced by experience.

Heredity and Environment Truly Interact

The goal of much of the research discussed in this chapter has been to establish how much of the variation we observe in human traits such as intelligence can be attributed to differences in genetic makeup and how much can be attributed to differences in experience. Today, however, most behavior geneticists realize that it is overly simple to say that heredity contributes a set percentage to each human attribute and environment contributes the rest. The problem is that genetic and environmental influences on development are not independent. Instead, their influences interact throughout the life span. Instead of asking how much is due to genes and how much is due to environment, we should be asking *how* heredity and environment interact to make us what we are (Anastasi, 1958). Let's look more closely at what it really means to say that heredity and environment interact.

It should be clear by now that genes do not determine our actual characteristics; instead, they provide us with potentials, and the environments to which we are exposed then influence whether or not our potentials are actualized. Curt Stern (1956) likens genetic endowment to a rubber band and a person's actual traits to the length the rubber band reaches when it is stretched by the environment. Some people inherit shorter rubber bands than others do, but experiences can still have a major influence on eventual characteristics. Figure 3.10 illustrates this view. Notice that the person with a low genetic potential for intelligence might be "stretched" by an enriched environment to an intellectual level that exceeds that of the person with high potential raised in a deprived environment where his or her genetic endowment is never stretched. Individuals may display widely different levels of intellectual performance depending on the environments to which they are exposed. One's genotype helps set a range of possible outcomes for any particular trait, but the environment in which one develops may determine the point within that range where one will fall.

Now notice one more thing about Figure 3.10. It seems that those with high genetic endowment can be stretched further by environmental forces than those with low genetic endowment; the type of environment in which they grow up might make a difference of as much as 60 points in intelligence test scores. By comparison, those with low genetic endowment cannot be stretched as far; even the most stimulating program is unlikely to make the child with the genes for mental retardation a genius, even though intellectual enrichment will have beneficial effects.

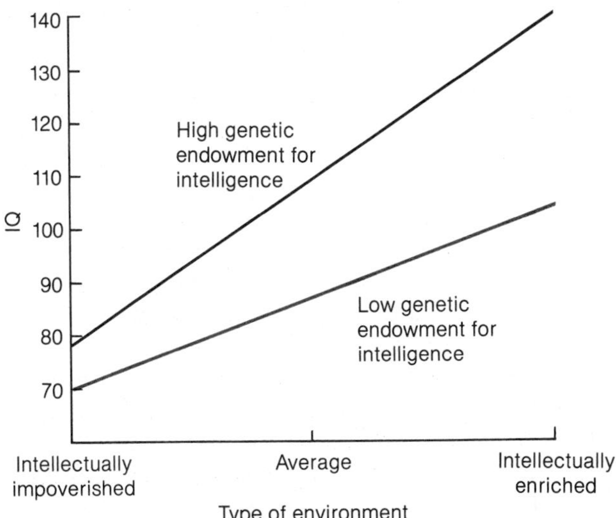

Figure 3.10 The rubber-band hypothesis. Individuals with different genetic potentials for intellectual development may exhibit widely varying levels of intellectual performance, depending on the environments to which they are exposed.

This fact of nature/nurture has been called the **range of reaction principle**—the idea that each genotype sets limits on the range of phenotypes that a person might display in response to different environments (Gottesman, 1963). Here the person with genes for high intelligence has a larger range of reaction than the person with genes for low intelligence. More generally, some people, because of their genetic endowment, are more susceptible to the effects of environment than others are. So it really works both ways: How our genotypes are expressed depends on what kind of environment we are exposed to, and how we respond to the environment depends on what kind of genes we have. *Genetic endowment and environment interact.*

However, even this rubber-band model of the interaction between heredity and environment is probably too simple. The influences of heredity and environment are so intimately intertwined throughout the life span that it is almost impossible to separate them. Each person's genetic makeup influences the kinds of experiences that he or she seeks out and actually has, and these experiences then strengthen or weaken genetically based tendencies. Sandra Scarr and Kathleen McCartney (1983), drawing on the theorizing of Plomin, DeFries, and Loehlin (1977), have proposed three ways in which genes and environment interact. To illustrate these interactions, let's imagine a child who has genes that make for sociability and a second child whose genes make for shyness and withdrawal.

Passive Genotype/Environment Interactions

The kind of home environment that parents provide for their children is influenced in part by the parents' own genotypes. And since parents also provide their children with genes, it turns out that the rearing environments to which children are exposed are correlated with (and are likely to suit) their own genotypes. This kind of correlation between genes and environment is termed passive because it is not the result of any deliberate action on the part of parents or children.

For instance, sociable parents not only transmit their "sociable" genes to their children but might, because they have "sociable" genes, create a very social home environment, inviting their friends over frequently and taking their children to many social events. Their children inherit genes for sociability, but they also receive an environment that suits their genes and that may make them even more sociable than they would otherwise be. By contrast, the child with shy parents receives genes for shyness and an environment without much social stimulation. When genotype and environment are correlated in this way, it is almost impossible to determine whether genes or home experiences have a greater influence on sociability.

Evocative Genotype/Environment Interactions

A child's genotype also evokes certain kinds of reactions from other people. The smiley, sociable baby gets more smiles and social stimulation than the withdrawn, shy baby does. We just can't help being attracted to such a baby. Similarly, a very bright child who is always asking questions is likely to receive more intellectual stimulation than a very dull child. So we see that genetic makeup may affect the reactions of other people to a child and, hence, the kind of social environment that the child will experience.

Active Genotype/Environment Interactions

Finally, a child's genotype influences what kinds of environments he or she actively seeks out. The child with genes for sociability is likely to seek out parties, invite friends to the house, and otherwise build a "niche" that is highly socially stimulating. The child with genes for shyness may actively avoid large group activities and instead develop interests in activities such as coin collecting that can be done alone.

Our examples so far are examples of *positive* correlations between a child's genes and a child's environment. The sociable child ends up in environments that match his or her genes and that would make for even greater sociability than genes alone might create, whereas the child with a genetic tendency toward shyness experiences environments that breed shyness. It's a case of the rich getting richer and the poor getting poorer. But as Scarr and McCartney (1983) note, gene/environment correlations can also be *negative*. For example, people might try extra hard to evoke social responses from the shy child and might even place a very shy child, but not a more sociable child, in a special program designed to teach social skills. Both positive and negative correlations between genes and environment may be important. Either way, our genotypes influence our environments, which in turn modify our genetically based predispositions.

Scarr and McCartney go on to suggest that the balance of passive, evocative, and active genotype/environment interactions shifts during development. Because infants are usually home-bound and tended by parents, their environment is largely influenced by their parents through passive genetic influences. As children develop, however, they become increasingly able to build their own niches, so active gene influences become more important. And when we actively choose our own environments, we are especially likely to pick ones that match our abilities and personalities well. The highly sociable adult rarely chooses a hermit's life, and the shy adult rarely chooses to be on center stage. Scarr and McCartney believe that this is one reason that fraternal twins and adopted children in the same family become less alike as they get older. They share an early home environment, but because they are genetically different, they increasingly build different niches as they get older and more independent. Identical twins, by contrast, may stay alike, even when separated, because their similar genes make them continue to seek out similar experiences. Finally, evocative influences continue to operate throughout life in much the same way. Summarizing their argument, Scarr and McCartney suggest that we are the products of "cooperative efforts of the nature/nurture team, directed by the genetic quarterback" (1983, p. 433).

In summary, both genes and environment are at work over the entire life span, but the relative contributions of these two forces do change with age. Similarly, some of our traits are more strongly influenced by our genetic makeups (or by our experiences) than others are. But we are missing the full story unless we appreciate how genes and environment interact and conspire to make us what we are. Environmental forces help determine whether we achieve our genetic potentials, and our genetic potentials help determine what experiences have a chance to affect us and how they affect us. Now you understand why today's developmentalists regard it as foolish to ask whether nature *or* nurture is responsible for human development. We are shaped by an incredibly complex interweaving of genetic and environmental influences from conception to death.

APPLICATIONS: GENETIC COUNSELING AND THE TREATMENT OF GENETIC DEFECTS

What are some of the practical applications of genetic research? There are a couple of thousand genetic defects associated with a single gene or gene pair, several kinds of chromosome disorders, and many polygenic susceptibilities to diseases and disorders such as schizophrenia. This information may be enough to drive parents-to-be crazy. All they want to know is whether their baby will be normal—and if not what they can do about it. Let's quickly note that about 95% of babies *will not* have genetic defects (Baird, Anderson, Newcombe, & Lowry, 1988; Hendin & Marks, 1978). Now let us see what is available for those parents who have some reason to suspect their future children are at risk.

Genetic counseling offers relevant information to people who fear that they or their unborn children are at risk for some genetically based problem. Suppose that a Jewish couple has heard that Tay-Sachs disease is especially common among Jewish children. This disease causes a degeneration of the nervous system and usually kills its victims by the age of 3. The couple might seek out a genetic counselor, who might be a medical researcher, geneticist, or physician.

Establishing the Likelihood of a Defect

Once the genetic counselor has established that the defect that concerns the parents is indeed hereditary in origin, he or she is likely to obtain a complete family history from each parent—one that may include information about the diseases and causes of death of relatives, the countries of origin of relatives (particularly since Tay-Sachs disease strikes most frequently among Jewish people of Eastern European ancestry), and previous problems in the child-bearing process. For some defects and disorders, family histories of this sort are the only basis for calculating the odds that a problem might occur.

However, specific tests are available to determine conclusively whether prospective parents are carriers for a number of hereditary defects. The number of such tests available is increasing at a staggering rate due to advances in genetic science (Schaeffer, 1987; Watson, Tooze, & Kurtz, 1983). For example, blood tests can determine whether a prospective parent carries the recessive gene for Tay-Sachs disease, as well as sickle cell disease, hemophilia, and many other conditions. Many chromosome abnormalities can also be detected by taking a small sample of each parent's skin and preparing karyotypes (chromosome analyses). And the children of a victim of **Huntington's disease** can finally find out whether they too will develop this frightening disorder that results in dementia (loss of intellectual function), emotional problems, loss of motor control, and premature death (see Box 3.3 for a description).

One couple who recently did request genetic counseling learned from the blood tests that they were both carriers of Tay-Sachs disease. The genetic counselor explained that there was a 1 in 4 chance that any child they conceived would inherit a recessive gene from each of them and have Tay-Sachs disease. There was also a 1 in 4 chance that the child would inherit two dominant (and normal) genes, and a 2 in 4 chance that any child would, like the parents themselves, be a carrier. The counselor also described Tay-Sachs disease and its tragic effects. After receiving this information, the young woman expressed strong reservations about having children, feeling that the odds were just too high to risk having a baby whose disease cannot be cured. The counselor told her that before making a final decision, she should be aware of screening procedures that can detect many genetic abnormalities, including Tay-Sachs disease, in the fetus.

Prenatal Detection of Abnormalities

The most familiar method of detecting chromosomal and genetic abnormalities during the prenatal period is **amniocentesis**. A needle is inserted into the abdomen of a pregnant woman in order to withdraw a sample of the amniotic fluid directly surrounding the fetus. Fetal cells in the fluid can be karyotyped to determine the sex of the fetus and the presence of chromosomal abnormalities such as Down syndrome. In addition, many genetic disorders such as Tay-Sachs disease can now be diagnosed through further analysis of fetal cells obtained in this way. While there is a slight risk of miscarriage associated with amniocentesis, the procedure is considered to be very safe (Fairweather, 1978; Schaeffer, 1987). It is now quite common for women over 35, who run increased risks of chromosome abnormalities, to have amniocentesis. In the vast majority of cases, they learn that their baby will be normal and can stop worrying.

The main disadvantage of amniocentesis is that it can-

Box 3.3
Huntington's Disease

Occasionally a genetic defect is associated with a single *dominant* gene. **Huntington's disease** is a famous (and terrifying) example. It first displays itself in middle age and is therefore considered an "early aging" disorder. The nervous systems of its victims steadily deteriorate; they lose both physical and mental abilities and die prematurely. Folk singer Woody Guthrie is a famous victim: What are the odds that his son Arlo will have the disease? Since he will have it if he received the dominant Huntington's gene rather than its normal counterpart gene from his father, the risk is 1 out of 2, or 50%! Fortunately the gene is very rare; 5 to 10 people in 100,000 develop the disease (Gusella et al., 1983).

What makes Huntington's disease especially frightening is that victims have often completed their families before they have any idea that they have the disease. And until recently there has been no test to identify who has the gene and who does not; children of a Huntington's disease victim had to wonder for most of their lives whether they inherited the Huntington's gene. The slightest signs of clumsiness, mood swings, or personality changes brought fears that the disease had struck. Some were afraid to marry or have children (Omenn, 1983).

Now the gene for Huntington's disease has been located on chromosome 4 (Gusella et al., 1983). A test can tell individuals at risk whether they have the gene (*60 Minutes*, October 26, 1986). But, if a test could tell you that you will certainly develop Huntington's disease, would you take it? Genetic counselor Gilbert Omenn (1983) asked this question of four siblings at risk for Huntington's disease. He got four different answers, ranging all the way from great interest to, "No way; you won't be seeing me again" (p. 185). Individuals at risk now must make a terribly difficult decision, not unlike that faced by people who fear they may be at risk for AIDS. However, knowing about the gene should help researchers find a treatment or even a cure for the disease. Imagine one small gene creating this much agony for a family!

not be performed before the 14th to the 16th week of pregnancy. Since the results may not come back for two or more weeks, parents have little time to consider a second-trimester abortion if the fetus is abnormal and abortion is their choice. A newer technique called **chorionic villus biopsy** is becoming more widely used because it permits the same tests that amniocentesis does but can be performed as early as the 10th week of pregnancy (Begley, Carey, & Katz, 1984). Here a catheter is inserted through the mother's vagina and cervix, and into the membrane called the *chorion* that surrounds the fetus, to extract cells. Still another prenatal diagnostic technique is **ultrasound**, a method for scanning the womb with sound waves to create a visual image of the fetus and detect at least the sorts of genetic defects that produce gross physical abnormalities.

For the parents whose tests reveal a normal fetus, the anxiety of undergoing the tests and waiting for the results gives way to relief. For those who learn that their fetus has a serious defect, the experience can be agonizing, especially if their religious or personal beliefs argue against the option of abortion. In the case of Tay-Sachs disease, for example, they must either violate their moral principles and terminate the pregnancy or face the prospect of watching their baby deteriorate and die. The genetic counselor not only informs the parents of their options but lends them support as they deliberate what to do. The situation is far happier when treatments or cures are available.

Treating Hereditary Disorders

One of the greatest success stories in genetic research is the story of **phenylketonuria**, or **PKU**, a disorder caused by a pair of recessive genes. Affected children lack a critical enzyme needed to metabolize phenylalanine, a component of many foods, including milk, and the main ingredient in aspartame, the sweetener used in many diet foods and beverages. As phenylalanine accumulates in the body, it is converted to a harmful acid that attacks the nervous system and causes children to be mentally retarded and hyperactive.

The great breakthroughs came in the mid-1950s, when scientists developed a special diet low in phenylalanine, and in 1961, when they developed a simple blood test that could determine if a child had PKU soon after birth—before any damage had been done. Newborn infants are now routinely screened for PKU, and affected children are immediately placed on the special (and unfortunately quite distasteful) diet. Research suggests that children with PKU must adhere to some form of the special diet until they are at least 8 years old to avoid brain damage (Holtzman, Kronmal, Van Doorninck, Azen, & Koch,

1986). Here, then, is a way to avert one of the many types of mental retardation. Here we have a wonderful example of the interaction between genes and environment: A child with PKU genes is mentally retarded with one diet (the usual one) but intellectually normal with another (the special diet).

Today many potentially devastating effects of genetic and chromosomal abnormalities can at least be minimized or controlled, if not cured. Children with Turner syndrome or Klinefelter syndrome can be given sex hormones to make them more normal in appearance; individuals with sickle cell disease can be given transfusions of blood containing the normal red blood cells they lack; and so on. Geneticists are hopeful that many serious genetic defects will become treatable in the near future through techniques that may eventually allow genetic engineers to replace genes that cause disorders with normal genes (Watson, Tooze, & Kurtz, 1983). Meanwhile, society as a whole will have to grapple with the ethical issues that have arisen as geneticists have gained the capacity to identify the carriers or potential victims of diseases and disorders, give parents information that might prompt them to decide on an abortion, and even experiment with techniques for altering the genetic code.

REFLECTIONS

It is impossible to study genetic influences on development without being struck by the countless ways in which identical twins are alike and those of us with unique genetic endowments are different from each other. We have even seen that one fourth of the population has inherited two recessive genes that render them incapable of curling their tongues into a tubelike shape! Genetic variation creates an incredible range of behavioral differences among us.

How do you feel about this? Genetic research has always been controversial. Some respected researchers continue to question the validity of the kinds of behavior genetics studies that we have surveyed in this chapter and doubt that the influences of genes and environment on individual differences can be cleanly separated (see Lewontin, Rose, & Kamin, 1984). Then there are people who resist the messages that this research contains. They want to believe that all people are created equal in all respects. Or they don't want to think that they're doomed to resemble their parents or limited in their potential to achieve anything they choose. Or it bothers them to think that parents, teachers, or governments cannot achieve everything they might want to achieve by improving the environments in which children develop. Perhaps you fall somewhere in this camp of skeptics and resisters.

If you do, let us lay out a more positive way of thinking about the implications of genetic research. First, it is quite possible to believe that people deserve equal rights and equal opportunities while still recognizing that they have different potentials sketched in their genetic codes. Indeed, it could be argued that society is richer when its members are diverse, when each has special strengths to contribute. Second, as we have stressed, the fact that individual differences in behavior in a group of people are partly or even largely due to differences in their genetic makeups does not mean that those traits are unalterable. Having an alcoholic parent, for instance, hardly means that one must become an alcoholic. Indeed, preventing alcoholism might become easier if those who are at risk know it and are helped to control their drinking. All things considered, today's genetic research offers much hope to those who wish to optimize development. A treatment for PKU would not have been discovered unless the PKU defect had been identified and understood by genetic researchers. Bearers of the PKU genes would simply become mentally retarded, as they did in the past. And there is nothing in genetic research to stop us from providing *all* children with the experiences that are most likely to allow them to develop their potentials to the fullest. Of course, providing children with optimal experiences depends on knowing which kinds of environments stimulate growth and which kinds of environments do not. Therefore, our next chapter takes a closer look at environmental influences on development.

SUMMARY POINTS

1. As humans, we share a species heredity that provides us with human characteristics and makes certain aspects of development and aging universal. This species heredity has arisen through the process of evolution and natural selection.

2. Each human also has an individual heredity provided at conception when sperm and ovum, each having retained 23 chromosomes at meiosis, unite to form a single-cell zygote that con-

tains 46 chromosomes (23 from each parent). Each child of the same parents receives only one or the other of each chromosome pair that each parent possesses, and because genetic material crosses over when the zygote is formed during meiosis, each child (with the exception of identical twins) is genetically unique but shares some genes with relatives.

3. Sex is determined by the sex (X and Y) chromosomes; since genetic males have an X and a Y chromosome while genetic females have two X chromosomes, the father determines the child's gender.

4. The genetic basis for development is not completely understood, but we do know that genes provide an instructional "code" that influences how cells are formed and how they function and that regulator genes turn these genes "on" and "off" throughout the life span.

5. Genotype (genetic makeup) does not always correspond exactly to phenotype (actual traits) because environmental factors also influence development.

6. There are three main mechanisms of inheritance: single gene-pair (Mendelian) inheritance, sex-linked inheritance, and polygenic (multiple gene) inheritance. Most important human traits are influenced by polygenic inheritance. Some children are also affected by noninherited changes in gene structure (mutations), while others, because of errors in meiosis, have chromosome abnormalities such as Down syndrome and a variety of sex chromosome abnormalities.

7. Behavior genetics is the study of how genes and environment contribute to individual differences in behavior. Human behavior geneticists analyze resemblances between people who are genetically related to different degrees by conducting family, twin, and adoption studies. Resemblances between pairs of people are expressed as concordance rates or correlation coefficients.

8. Infants are strongly influenced by a species-wide, genetically programmed, maturational plan, but individual differences in physical growth, mental abilities, and temperament are influenced by individual heredity. Neither individual heredity nor environment can account for many of the differences among infants as well as they can account for individual differences later in development.

9. During childhood, individual differences in mental ability become more consistent and more strongly reflect both genetic makeup and environmental influences that make members of the same family similar to each other and different from members of other families. Personality traits are also genetically influenced, but members of the same family often develop distinct personalities owing to nonshared aspects of their experiences.

10. Individual differences in mental ability continue to be quite strongly associated with differences in genetic endowment during adolescence; sharing a family environment appears to become less influential as adolescents become more independent and develop intellectually along their own paths and as differences in their experiences with parents, peers, and each other create differences in their personalities. Just as some children have a genetic susceptibility to problems such as hyperactivity, adolescent delinquency has some genetic basis.

11. During adulthood, the relative contributions of genes and environment to individual differences in mental ability and personality change very little.

12. Genetic makeup also influences how individuals age and when they die. The genetic basis of aging is not yet understood, but the study of early aging disorders such as progeria may provide clues.

13. Overall, both genes and environment (shared family environment as well as nonshared or unique experiences) are influential over the entire life span, although their relative influences change somewhat. Most important, hereditary and environmental influences interact, environment influencing how genes are expressed, and genes influencing the kinds of experiences people have with the environment.

14. Genetic counseling can help people calculate the risk that their unborn children may have for a genetic disorder. Blood tests can identify the carriers of many single gene-pair disorders, and abnormalities in the fetus can be detected through amniocentesis, chorionic villus biopsy, and ultrasound. As knowledge of the genetic code rapidly increases, many more genetic disorders are likely to become predictable, detectable, and treatable.

KEY TERMS

amniocentesis
behavior genetics
carriers
chorionic villus biopsy
chromosome
chromosome abnormalities
codominance
conception
concordance rate
correlation coefficient
crossing over
dominant gene
Down syndrome
extraversion/introversion
fraternal twins
genes
genetic counseling
genotype
heritability
heterozygous
homozygous
Huntington's disease
identical twins
incomplete dominance
karyotype
kinship
Klinefelter syndrome
meiosis
mitosis
mutation
natural selection
neuroticism
phenotype
phenylketonuria (PKU)
polygenic trait
progeria
range of reaction principle
recessive gene
schizophrenia
selective breeding
sex-linked characteristic
sickle cell disease
single gene-pair inheritance
sociobiology
species heredity
temperament
Turner syndrome
ultrasound
X chromosome
Y chromosome
zygote

CHAPTER

4

ENVIRONMENT AND LIFE-SPAN DEVELOPMENT

In 1970 a neglected and abused child named Genie came to the attention of authorities in Los Angeles, California. Her incredible story is well known to developmentalists (see Curtiss, 1977; Pines, 1981). Genie had been locked away in a back room as a toddler and had remained in solitary confinement until she was rescued at age 13. During her captivity, she had been tied down in a potty chair during the day and "caged" at night in a crib covered with wire. Genie's mother, who was nearly blind, would spend a few minutes with her every day as she fed the child. However, Genie's abusive father, who apparently hated children, would not permit anyone to talk to her. He would not tolerate television or any other noisemaking appliances. In fact, whenever Genie made a sound, her father was likely to come into her room and beat her while barking and growling like a wild dog.

What were the effects of this dreadful environment on Genie's development? About as disastrous as you might guess. Although Genie showed some signs of having experienced puberty when she was freed, she weighed less than 60 pounds and could not walk or even stand erect. Her vision and hearing were normal, but her intellectual performance was at roughly the level of a normal 1-year-old. She understood a word or two, but she could not speak. As you might expect, she was quite emotionally disturbed as well.

Now, what do you suppose happened once she was given her first chance at a stimulating environment—special education classes, help from a speech therapist after school, and nurturance as part of one therapist's family? Genie surprised everyone with her progress. Within eight months of her rescue, she had a vocabulary of 200 words and was already putting together the two-word sentences that are typical of young language learners. Her intelligence test scores steadily climbed over the years. At the age of 19, she could use public transportation and was functioning quite well in both her foster home and her special classes at school. And yet she was far from a normal young woman. Her speech was still less sophisticated than that used by a normal 5-year-old, and her intelligence test performance was still near the mental retardation zone. At last report, she was living in a home for mentally retarded adults who cannot live alone (Pines, 1981).

Obviously, environmental influences on development—for bad and for good—demand our serious attention. In Chapter 3 we emphasized genetic influences on development. We also stressed that genes and environment interact throughout the life span to make us what we are. If sharing a common genetic heritage can make different human beings alike in some respects, so can sharing similar environments. If having unique genes can make one person different from another, so can having unique experiences in life. But what is "environment," really? And what are some of the specific ways in which environmental factors influence development? In this chapter, we address those questions, in the hope that you will carry through the remainder of your study of life-span development an understanding of the workings of genes and environment.

First we will examine some ways in which we can conceptualize the environment. Then we will examine the impacts of environmental factors on very early development—that is, development *before* birth and in the period surrounding birth. Finally, we will focus on examples of the interrelationships between development and environment in each period of the life span, emphasizing that individual development always occurs in a cultural and historical context. We will, of course, be examining environmental influences on specific aspects of development throughout this text. But our job here is to grasp the concept of environment, and to examine some fascinating and important examples of how much one's environment matters.

WHAT IS ENVIRONMENT?

Let's start off with a modern definition of environment offered by Urie Bronfenbrenner and Ann Crouter (1983): **Environment** is "any event or condition outside the organism that is presumed to influence, or be influenced by, the person's development" (p. 359). Older concepts of environment tended to view it as a set of forces that shape the individual, as though the person were just a passive punching bag. Now, as Bronfenbrenner and Crouter emphasize, we understand that people also shape their environments and are, in turn, affected by the environments they have helped create. In other words, the relationship between person and environment is one of *reciprocal influence*. A woman, for example, may take a drug during her pregnancy that makes her newborn extraordinarily fussy. Environment has affected development. But a fussy baby is likely to affect the environment—for example, by irritating Mother. Mother now expresses her tenseness and irritability in her interactions with her infant, and this makes her infant all the more irritable and fussy, which of course aggravates Mother even more, which of course makes her baby even more cranky.

The interrelationships between a changing person and a changing environment are incredibly complex once we move beyond the simple notion that people are passively shaped by their experiences. But human development does in fact involve an ongoing transaction or exchange between changing person and changing environment (Valsiner & Benigni, 1986). Now let's briefly consider some ways of conceptualizing different types of environmental influence.

Physical Versus Social Environment

One way to view the environment is to distinguish between the physical (nonhuman) and social (human) environments. The physical environment includes everything from weather conditions to pollutants in the air, from the architectural design of one's house to the noise level in one's neighborhood. During prenatal development, the physical environment of the uterus and the tangible molecules that reach the fetus's bloodstream are crucial to early growth. Throughout the life span, we must adapt to the physical environments in which we find ourselves. Graham Rowles (1981) has suggested that the physical environment enlarges as the developing child moves out of the crib and home and then out of the immediate neighborhood to more distant settings—and that the physical environment shrinks again in later life as the older adult loses health and mobility and once more tends to center activity within the home front.

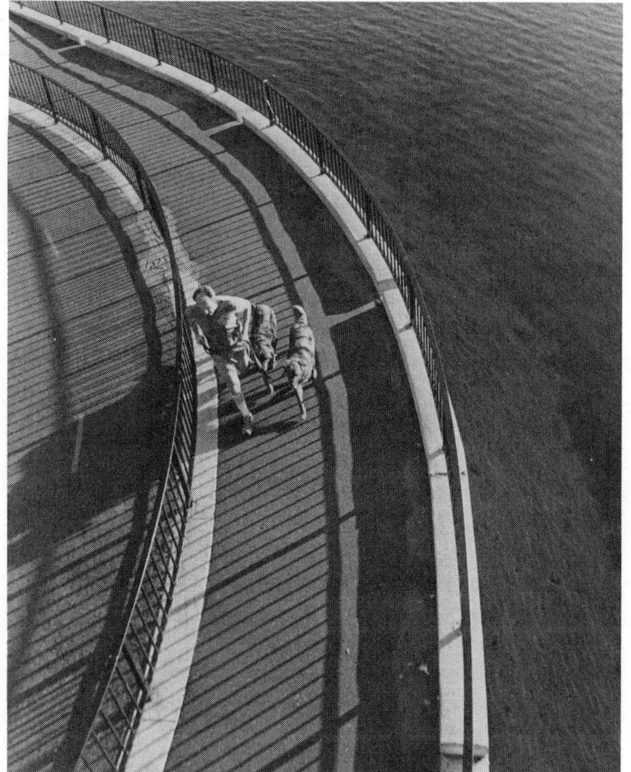

We are affected by the physical environments in which we develop.

Although the physical environment can be very influential, many developmentalists have been more concerned with the *social* environment in which development occurs: with the people in the individual's social world and with their day-to-day interactions with the developing person. Robert Kahn (1979) proposes that we move through the life span with a "social convoy," a group of significant others who affect our development and adjustment. The infant experiences a relatively small physical environment and usually has a small social convoy consisting mainly of parents and other caregivers. The social convoy enlarges as children develop close relationships with peers, grandparents, teachers, and others outside the home; it reaches its peak size as adults participate in a wide range of give-and-take relationships; and it may shrink again very late in life as mobility is lost and significant others die (Kahn, 1979). Similarly, we have few roles in society to play as young children, gain many roles during adulthood, and tend to lose roles as we retire or lose a mate in old age (Rosow, 1985). In sum, both the physical and the social environments are important, and both seem to change in systematic ways as the developing person changes.

The Environment as Life Events or Transitions

Another way to think about environmental influences on development is to focus on specific events or transitions during the life span: entering college, being in a car accident, moving, and so on. Whether we choose such events, they require short-term adaptations, and they can potentially affect long-term development. Some life events can be classified as **normative transitions**: transitions that most people in a society experience (see Datan & Ginsberg, 1975). Transitions such as starting school as a child, graduating from high school, marrying, having a child, and retiring from work are normative in our society. Each society also has expectations about what people should be doing or how they should behave at different points in the life span—expectations called **age norms**. Age norms are society's way of telling us how to act our age. The consensus in a society may be that 12-year-old girls are too young to date or that 70-year-old women are too old to wear bikinis. Age norms also tell us when it is appropriate to pass through normative transitions: We "should" marry when we are in our 20s; age 14 is too early, and age 50 is too late for a first marriage.

It is quite likely that we can detect regularities in psychological development over the life span partly because most people do experience the same events (normative transitions) at similar ages and are affected in similar ways by those events. Certainly normative transitions can have similar short-term effects on those who experience them—for example, by increasing stress and anxiety. Recently, Abigail Stewart, Michael Sokol, Joseph Healy, and Nia Chester (1986) examined the short-term impacts on the individual's psychological state of such normative transitions as entering elementary school, entering junior high school or high school, marrying, and having a first child. Interestingly, they found that both children and adults tended to become more passive, dependent on others, and insecure during these transitions. They temporarily felt a bit bewildered or uneasy about their abilities to cope. Later, as they adjusted, they appeared to regain their confidence and became more independent and assertive. But normative transitions can also have more lasting impacts, as we will see when we examine many of the most important ones in later chapters.

Finally, a "life events" approach to thinking about the environment requires that we also acknowledge the importance of **nonnormative transitions**—events that are idiosyncratic to the individual or that only a minority of people experience, such as developing a life-threatening disease or inheriting a large amount of money (see Callahan & McClusky, 1983, for studies of several nonnormative transitions). Experiencing the death of a child is certainly not normative, but it just as certainly can have devastating effects on parents that alter their future development. In sum, environment is partly the normative and nonnormative transitions an individual experiences over a lifetime, each transition requiring short-term adaptations and each potentially influencing longer-term development.

The Environment as a Series of Interrelated Systems

Finally, environment can be viewed as a series of settings or contexts for development ranging from immediate contexts such as the family to more remote contexts such as the broader culture. The **ecological approach** to development set forth by Urie Bronfenbrenner (1979, 1989) emphasizes that the developing person is embedded in a series of environmental systems that interact with one another and with the individual to influence development. Closest to the person is what Bronfenbrenner calls the **microsystem**, which consists of the immediate environments in which the person functions. The primary microsystem for a first-born infant is likely to be the family:

infant, mother, and father interacting with each other. This infant may also experience other microsystems such as a day care center or grandmother's house. As Jay Belsky and William Tolan (1981) stress, even though infants are relatively passive compared to older individuals, they are hardly lumps of clay, shaped by their companions. They contribute to their own development by affecting their parents, who in turn influence them in new ways. Indeed, even before they are born infants can shape their future environment—for example, by causing their parents to break up or to marry! Thus a microsystem like the family is indeed a system in which each person influences and is influenced by every other person.

Understanding the complex reciprocal influences of infant, mother, and father is enough of a challenge, but Bronfenbrenner insists that we cannot understand child development or family relations unless we also understand what he terms the **mesosystem**—the interrelationships or linkages between microsystems. Unpleasant experiences at the day care center (one microsystem) could certainly upset an infant and, in turn, disturb relationships within the family (another microsystem) and ultimately interfere with the infant's development. By the same token, a crisis in the family could make a child withdraw from staff members and other children at the day care center so that his or her experience there becomes less stimulating. On the other hand, a loving and stimulating home environment is likely to allow a child to benefit more from experiences in the day care center, or later in school.

According to Bronfenbrenner, the environment also includes the **exosystem**—social settings that the child never experiences directly but that can still influence his or her development. For example, children can be affected by whether or not their parents enjoy supportive social relationships, as well as by whether their parents' work is satisfying or stressful. In support of this notion, Cotterell (1986) discovered that mothers have difficulty providing a stimulating home environment when they have few friends to turn to for information and support and when their husbands work unusual shifts and are away from home a great deal. Similarly, children's experiences in school can be affected by their exosystem—by a racial integration plan adopted by the school board or by a plant closing in their community that results in a cut in the school system's budget.

Finally, we reach the broadest context in which development occurs—the **macrosystem**, or the larger cultural or subcultural context in which the microsystem, mesosystem, and exosystem are embedded. As we will illustrate in this chapter, this broader social environment can indeed have important effects on development. **Culture** can be defined as a system of meanings shared by a population of people and transmitted to future generations (Rohner, 1984). Those shared understandings include views about the nature of human beings at different points in the life span, about what children need to be taught to function in society, and about how one should lead one's life as an adult. Because culture changes or evolves over time, and because people developing in particular historical periods are affected by societal events such as wars or technological breakthroughs, each generation (or *cohort*) of individuals in a particular society develops in a distinct social context. In short, we cannot simply assume that development is the same in all cultures and historical periods. Moreover, we must adopt what anthropologist Ruth Benedict (1934) termed the principle of **cultural relativity**—the concept that human behavior cannot be properly understood unless it is interpreted within its larger cultural context. Laughing during a funeral, for instance, may be regarded as outrageously inappropriate in one society but entirely fitting in another.

The environmental systems proposed by Bronfenbrenner—each of them affecting and being affected by the developing person—are sketched in Figure 4.1. Each of us functions in particular microsystems linked to one another through the mesosystem and embedded in the larger context of the exosystem and the macrosystem. As we develop, settings such as the family or the broader culture evolve and change. Moreover, we move into new settings, as when a child progresses from preschool to elementary school to junior high school and also becomes involved in new peer groups and social organizations. As our environments change, we are likely to change.

In summary, understanding environmental influences on life-span development requires considering both the physical and the social environment; examining how life transitions, both normative and nonnormative, can alter development; and, perhaps most important, bearing in mind that individuals are shaped by and shape the many environmental systems with which they interact. We are now ready to examine some specific examples of the workings of environment over the life span. We will concen-

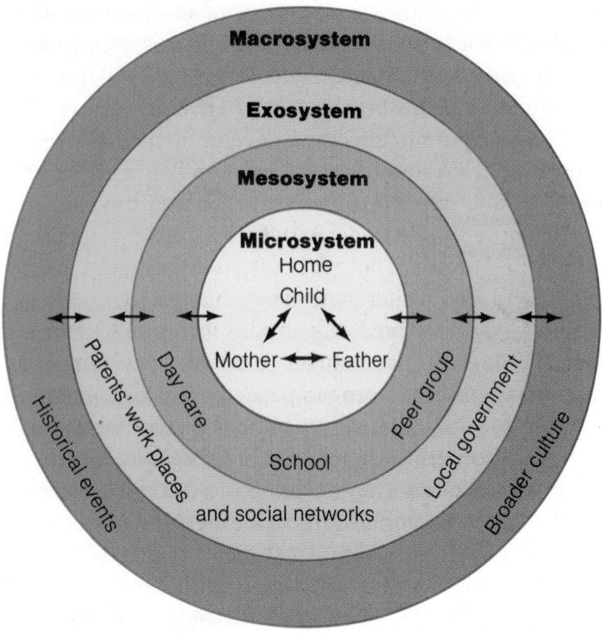

Figure 4.1 Bronfenbrenner's ecological model.

trate first on the physical environment and its crucial effects on development before birth; then we will see how the social environments associated with different cultures and historical periods—that is, how different "macrosystems"—affect development from birth to death.

PRENATAL DEVELOPMENT AND THE PRENATAL ENVIRONMENT

Perhaps at no time in the life span is development occurring faster—and is the environment more potentially important—than in the period between conception and birth. To understand how the **prenatal environment**, the physical environment of the womb, can affect development, we must first understand the maturational process that is occurring before birth.

Stages of Prenatal Development

When we left off in Chapter 3, conception had occurred and the product, a single-celled *zygote*, was working its way down the fallopian tube. It will take about 266 days (or about 9 months) for this one-celled zygote to become a fetus of some 200 billion cells that is ready to be born. Prenatal development is divided into three periods: the germinal period, the period of the embryo, and the period of the fetus.

The Germinal Period

The **germinal period** lasts for about 8 to 14 days, from conception until the **blastula**—a hollow ball of cells about the size of the head of a pin—is implanted in the wall of the uterus. The zygote first divides into two cells through mitosis; this cell division is then repeated many times, forming the blastula. When the blastula reaches the uterus, tendrils in its outer layer burrow into the blood vessels of the uterine wall. Actually this is quite an accomplishment in itself, as only about half of all fertilized ova are successfully implanted in the uterus (Roberts & Lowe, 1975). In addition, as many as half of all implanted embryos are abnormal in some way or burrow into a site incapable of sustaining them; they are miscarried (spontaneously aborted) and expelled (Adler & Carey, 1982). Apparently, then, only about 1 zygote in 4 will survive the initial phases of prenatal development.

The Period of the Embryo

The **period of the embryo** lasts from implantation at the end of the second week after conception to the end of the eighth week of prenatal development. In this short time, virtually all the major organs of the body take shape in at least a primitive form. Soon after implantation, the embryo secretes a hormone that prevents its mother from menstruating; this helps ensure its survival. The presence of this hormone in a woman's urine is taken as evidence of pregnancy in a common pregnancy test.

The layers of the embryo differentiate to form structures necessary to sustain development. The outer layer becomes the **amnion** (a watertight membrane that surrounds the embryo and fills with fluid that cushions and protects the embryo) and the **chorion** (a membrane that surrounds the amnion and becomes attached to the uterine lining to gather nourishment for the embryo). The side of the chorion that has rootlike villi to gather nourishment from the uterine tissues eventually becomes the lining of the **placenta**, a tissue that is fed by blood vessels from the mother and the embryo and is connected to the embryo by means of the embryo's lifeline, the **umbilical**

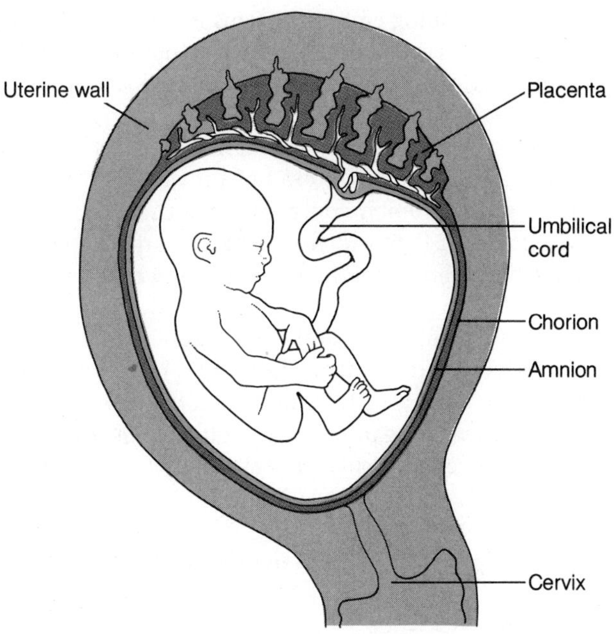

Figure 4.2 The embryo and its prenatal environment.

cord. Through the placenta and umbilical cord, the embryo receives oxygen and nutrients from the mother while eliminating carbon dioxide and metabolic wastes into the mother's bloodstream. A membrane called the *placental barrier* allows these small molecules (as well as more dangerous substances that we will discuss shortly) to pass through, but it prevents the quite large blood cells of embryo and mother from mingling (see Figure 4.2).

Meanwhile, the inner layers of the germinal cell mass are differentiating into an embryo. Cells, influenced by their environment of neighboring cells, cluster into groups, take on specialized functions, and become distinct organ systems (Sameroff, 1983). Development proceeds at a breathtaking pace. By only the fourth week after conception, a tiny heart has not only formed but has begun to beat. After the head forms, the eyes, ears, nose, and mouth rapidly take shape, and buds that will become arms and legs appear. During the second month, a very primitive nervous system is making newly formed muscles contract. At only 60 days after conception, at the close of the period of the embryo, the organism is a little over an inch long and has a distinctly human appearance.

In the seventh and eighth prenatal weeks, the important process of sexual differentiation begins. First, an undifferentiated tissue will become either the male testes or the female ovaries: If the embryo inherited a Y chromosome at conception, a gene on it will call for the construction of testes; in a genetic female with two X chromosomes, ovaries will form instead. The testes of a male embryo will then secrete **testosterone**, the primary male sex hormone and the hormone that will stimulate the development of a male internal reproductive system, as well as another hormone that inhibits the development of a female internal reproductive system. In the absence of these hormones, the embryo will develop the internal reproductive system of a female.

At three or four months after conception, another step in sexual differentiation is taken when testosterone secreted by the testes of a male stimulates the development of male external genitalia (a penis and scrotum). If testosterone is absent (as in normal females), female external genitalia will form. There is a rare sex-linked genetic disorder that makes the cells of a genetic male insensitive to the effects of male hormones, so that the fetus develops as a genetic male with undescended testes and with external genitals that resemble those of a female (Money & Ehrhardt, 1972). Obviously, then, each of us originally has the potential to develop either a male or a female reproductive system. Just as obviously, the period of the embryo is a dramatic and highly important period of development: the period when the structures that make us "human" evolve and take shape.

The Period of the Fetus

The **period of the fetus** lasts from the ninth week of pregnancy until birth. Organ systems that were formed during the period of the embryo continue their growth and begin to function. In the third month, distinguishable sex organs begin to appear, the bones and muscles rapidly develop, and the fetus becomes quite active. By the end of the third month, it is moving its arms, kicking its legs, making fists, and even turning somersaults (Apgar & Beck, 1974). During the *second trimester* (the fourth, fifth, and sixth months), even more refined activities such as thumbsucking appear, and by the end of this period the sensory organs are apparently functioning. We know this is so because premature infants as young as 25 weeks of age will become alert in response to a loud bell and blink in response to a bright light (Allen & Capute, 1986). At about

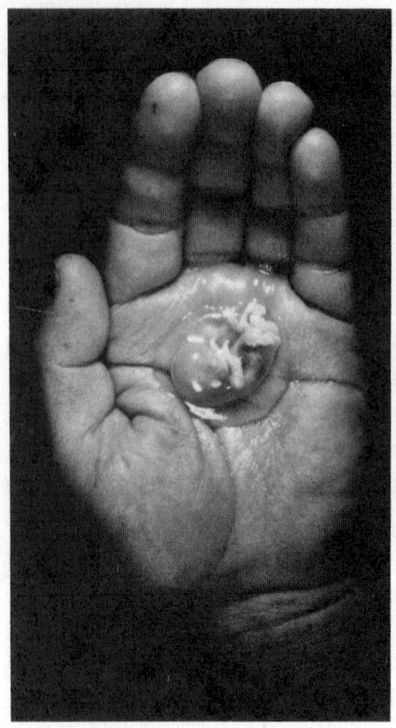

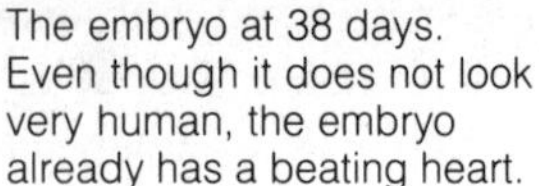

The embryo at 38 days. Even though it does not look very human, the embryo already has a beating heart.

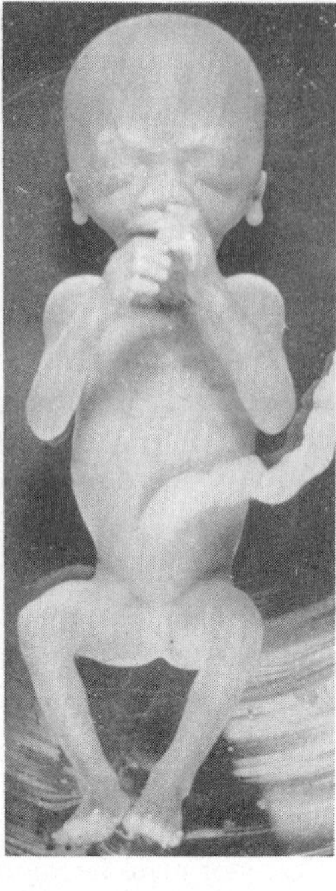

A human fetus at 210 days (7 months). By this age, survival outside the womb may be possible.

24 weeks of age, midway through the fifth month, the fetus reaches the **age of viability**, the point at which survival outside the uterus *may* be possible. Survival is "iffy" at this point, but the brain and respiratory system are well enough developed to make it possible in some cases. As medical techniques for keeping fragile babies alive have improved, the age of viability has decreased.

During the *third trimester* (the seventh, eighth, and ninth months), the fetus is gaining weight at a tremendously rapid rate. This is also a critical time in the development of the brain, for brain cells are rapidly multiplying. By the middle of the ninth month, the fetus is so large that its most comfortable position in cramped quarters is a head-down posture with the limbs curled in the so-called fetal position. At irregular intervals over the last month of pregnancy, the mother's uterus will contract. When these contractions become stronger, more frequent, and regular, the mother is entering the first stage of labor and the prenatal period is drawing to a close. Under normal circumstances, birth will occur in a matter of hours.

The developing embryo or fetus is a vulnerable little creature. How can its development be optimized? What hazards does it face? A number of odd ideas about the effects of the prenatal physical environment on growth have been offered by "experts" throughout history and well into the 20th century. For example, it was once believed that pregnant women could enhance their chances of bearing sons if they exercised (thereby stimulating the muscle development of their fetuses!) and that sexual activity during pregnancy (now recommended until a couple of weeks before delivery) would cause the child to be sexually precocious (MacFarlane, 1977). And until the early 1940s, it was widely believed that the placenta was a marvelous screening device that protected the embryo or fetus from nicotine, viruses, and all kinds of other hazards.

The Mother's Age, Emotional State, and Nutrition

The Mother's Age

At what age is it safest for a woman to become pregnant? Figure 4.3 shows us that there is a relationship between a mother's age and the risk of death for her fetus or **neonate** (newborn). The safest time to bear a child appears to be from about age 17 or 18 to age 35, although mothers under 20 are more likely to experience complications and to die during childbirth than those in their 20s (Planned Parenthood Federation of America, 1976). Why is this? One reason for increased fetal and infant mortality among teenage mothers is that the reproduction system of the very young teen may not be physically mature enough to sustain a fetus. However, the greater problem appears to be that teenagers often do not receive prenatal care. Teenage mothers and their babies are usually *not* at risk when they do receive appropriate prenatal care and medical treatment during the birth process (Baker & Mednick, 1984).

As for mothers over 40, as discussed in Chapter 3, they run a higher than average risk that their fetus will have chromosome abnormalities and may be spontaneously aborted as a result. The risks of complications during pregnancy and delivery are also higher in older women, perhaps in part because they, like adolescents, are less likely than women in their 20s and 30s to seek prenatal care early in their pregnancies (Brown, 1988). Even so, the vast majority of older women have normal pregnancies and healthy babies (Browne & Dixon, 1978; Leroy, 1988). Moreover,

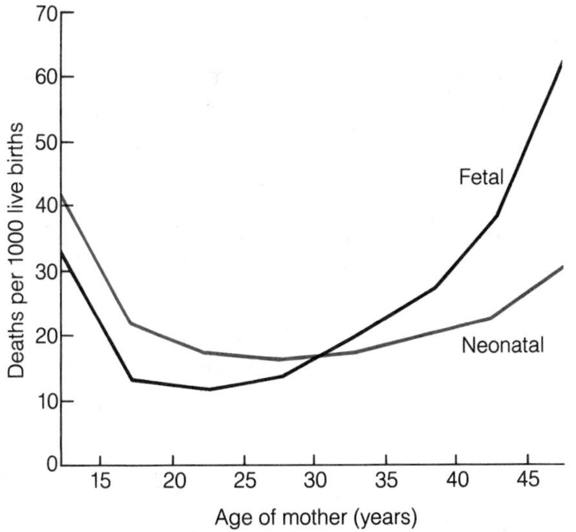

Figure 4.3 The relationship between the mother's age and the risk of death for the fetus or newborn. (From Kessner, 1973)

there is some evidence that older mothers are more responsive to their infants and more gratified by interacting with them than younger mothers are (Ragozin, Basham, Crnic, Greenberg, & Robinson, 1982).

The Mother's Emotional State

Does it matter how the mother feels about being pregnant? Although most women are happy about it, the fact remains that over half of all pregnancies are unplanned or unintended ("Half Our Pregnancies," 1983), and that single or unhappily married women are sometimes upset or depressed about their pregnancies (Browne & Dixon, 1978). Indeed, it is quite normal for any woman to experience at least some symptoms of anxiety and depression during her pregnancy (Kaplan, 1986). What effects might these negative emotions, or more severe emotional stresses, have on the fetus?

When a mother becomes emotionally aroused, her glands secrete powerful hormones such as adrenaline (also called epinephrine). These may cross the placental barrier and enter the fetus's bloodstream. At the very least, these hormones temporarily increase the fetus's motor activity (Sontag, 1941). However, a temporarily stressful experience such as falling or receiving a scare will generally not damage mother or fetus (Stott & Latchford, 1976). It is only when mothers experience *prolonged and severe* emotional stress and anxiety during their pregnancies that damage may be done. Chronically stressed mothers are at risk for such complications as miscarriage (spontaneous abortion), prolonged and painful labor, and premature delivery (Sameroff & Chandler, 1975). Moreover, Stott and Latchford (1976) discovered that infants whose mothers had experienced such prolonged stresses as marital problems, a move to a new location, economic worries, or the death of a parent were at risk for both physical and behavioral abnormalities. Others have found that the babies of highly stressed mothers tend to be hyperactive, irritable, and quite irregular in their feeding, sleeping, and bowel habits (Sameroff & Chandler, 1975). These behavioral difficulties appear to be directly related to the mother's prolonged stress during pregnancy. However, it is difficult to entirely rule out the possibility that the baby of an emotional mother is genetically predisposed to have a "difficult" temperament—or that the mother's emotional tensions affect her care of the infant after birth. Despite some uncertainty about how a mother's stress affects her infant, the woman who is highly distressed during her pregnancy might want to seek psychological help.

Nutrition

Forty years ago, doctors often advised mothers to gain no more than two pounds a month while pregnant and believed that a total gain of 15 to 18 pounds was quite sufficient. Today doctors are more likely to advise a gain of three to four pounds during the first three months of pregnancy and about a pound a week thereafter—a total increase of 24 to 28 pounds. Obstetricians now know that inadequate prenatal nutrition can be harmful, and severe malnutrition of the mother, as often occurs during famine, increases infant mortality and makes for small, underweight babies (Stein & Susser, 1976; Stein, Susser, Saenger, & Marolla, 1975). Such babies also tend to have fewer brain cells than babies born to well-nourished women and in some cases, though by no means all, have lasting intellectual deficiencies (Howard & Cronk, 1983; Winick, 1976). These harmful effects are most likely when the malnutrition occurs in the last trimester of pregnancy, for this is when the fetus is putting on most of its weight and when new brain cells are rapidly forming. Clearly it is important for mothers to receive a diet rich in proteins and vitamins and adequate in total calories.

Teratogens

A **teratogen** is any disease, drug, or other environmental agent that can harm a developing fetus (for example, by causing deformities, blindness, brain damage, or even death). The list of teratogens has grown frighteningly large over the years, making today's informed parents concerned about the many hazards their unborn children face. Before considering the many harmful consequences that teratogens can produce, let's emphasize that over 90% of babies are normal and that many of those with defects have mild, temporary, or reversible problems (Baird, Anderson, Newcombe, & Lowry, 1988; Heinonen, Slone, & Shapiro, 1977). Let us also lay out a few generalizations about the effects of teratogens so that we can then appreciate examples of these larger themes (Spreen, Tupper, Risser, Tuokko, & Edgell, 1984):

1. The effects of a teratogenic agent on an organ system are worst during the period when that organ system grows most rapidly.
2. Not all embryos and fetuses are affected, or affected equally, by a teratogen; susceptibility to harm is influenced by the unborn child's genetic makeup as well as by the quality of its early environment.
3. The same defect can be caused by different teratogens.
4. A variety of defects can result from a single teratogen.
5. The higher the "dose" of a teratogen, the more likely it is that serious damage will be done.

Let's look more closely at the first generalization, for it is very important. A period of rapid growth in an organ system can be viewed as a **critical period** for that organ system: a time during which the developing organism is particularly sensitive to environmental influences, positive or negative. As you'll recall, the organs take form during the period of the embryo (weeks 3 to 8 of prenatal development). As Figure 4.4 shows, it is during this time that most organ systems are most vulnerable to damage. Moreover, each organ has a critical period that corresponds to its own time of most rapid development. Once an organ or body part is fully formed, it often becomes less susceptible to damage.

However, as Figure 4.4 also indicates, some organ systems (the nervous system, for example) can be damaged throughout pregnancy. Indeed, many birth defects appear to be "anytime malformations"—problems that can arise at any point during the prenatal period (Heinonen, Slone, & Shapiro, 1977). Among the more common of these "anytime" problems are defects of the brain and spinal cord, dislocations of the hip, hernias, genital malformations, cataracts, and benign tumors. Because some defects are "anytime" defects, it might be better to speak of *"sensitive periods"* of prenatal development than to speak of critical periods. However, it is still the case that many teratogens have particularly devastating effects during the period of the embryo when the body's organs are rapidly taking form.

Diseases

The disease **rubella** (German measles) illustrates the critical period principle as well as other principles of teratology. Women affected by this single teratogen during their pregnancies often bear children who have a variety of defects, including blindness, deafness, heart defects, and mental retardation. Rubella is most dangerous during the first trimester of pregnancy, a critical period in which the eyes, ears, heart, and brain are rapidly forming. Yet not all babies whose mothers had rubella, even during the most critical period of prenatal development, will have problems. Studies have shown that birth defects occur in 50% to 80% of babies whose mothers had the disease in the first month of pregnancy, as compared with 25% of those infected in the second month and only 6% of those infected in the third month (Browne & Dixon, 1978; Fuhrmann & Vogel, 1976). Today doctors stress that a woman should not try to become pregnant unless she has already been immunized against this disease or has had it.

Now consider another teratogen, the sexually transmitted disease **syphilis**. Assuming that they live long enough to be born, the babies of mothers who have syphilis, like the babies of mothers who have rubella, often suffer from blindness, deafness, heart problems, or brain damage (Miller, 1976). Here is an example of the fact that two teratogens can be responsible for similar problems. The difference is that syphilis has its most damaging effects in the middle and later stages of pregnancy because syphilitic organisms cannot cross the placental barrier until the 18th prenatal week. This means that a mother-to-be who finds out she has the disease can be treated with anti-

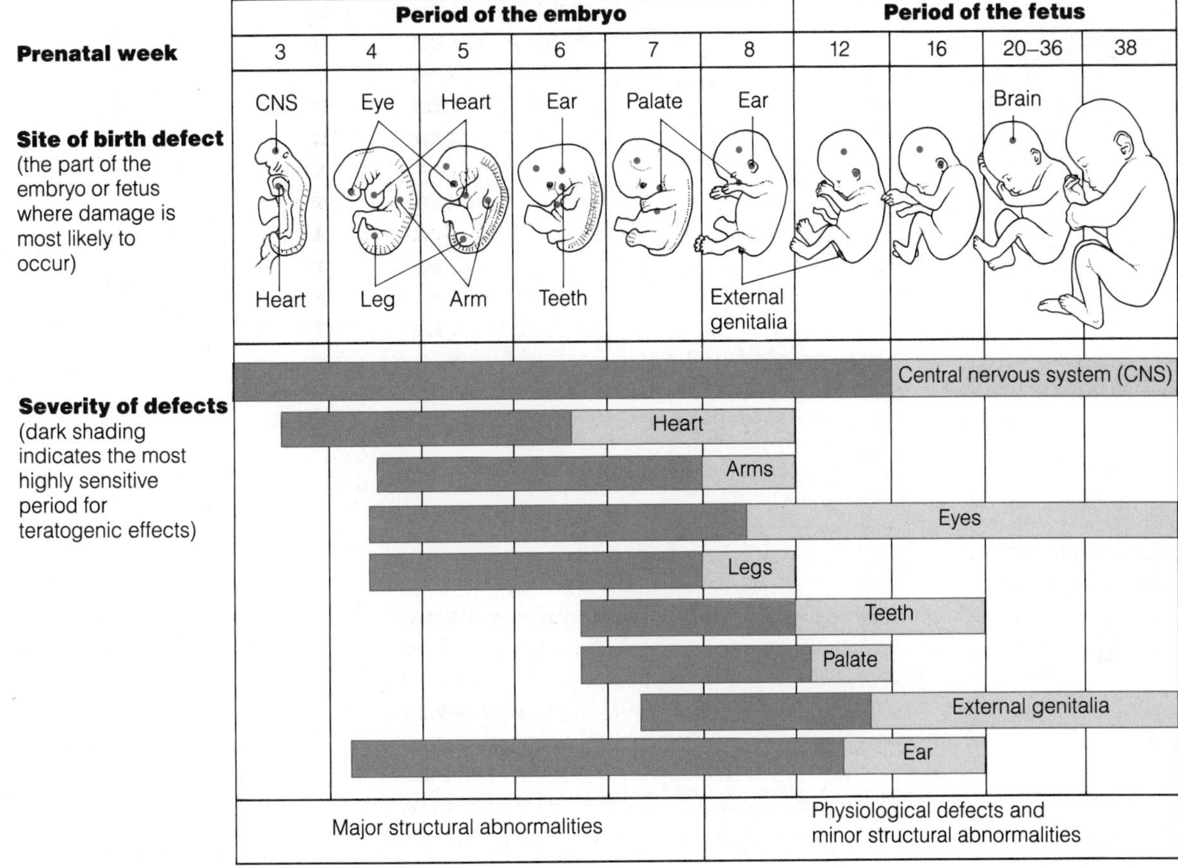

Figure 4.4 The critical periods of prenatal development. Teratogens are more likely to produce major structural abnormalities during the third through the eighth prenatal week. Note, however, that many organs and body parts remain sensitive to teratogenic agents throughout the nine-month prenatal period. (Adapted from Moore, 1977)

biotics long before the disease could harm her fetus. Table 4.1 describes a number of maternal conditions that may affect prenatal development.

Drugs

In 1960 a West German drug company began to market a mild tranquilizer, sold over the counter, that was said to relieve morning sickness (the periodic nausea that many women experience during the first trimester of pregnancy). Presumably the drug was perfectly safe, for it had no ill effects in tests on pregnant rats. The drug was **thalidomide**, the drug that more than any other alerted the world to the dangers of taking drugs during pregnancy.

Thousands of women who used thalidomide during the first two months of pregnancy were suddenly giving birth to babies with tragic defects—most notably, babies with all or parts of their limbs missing and with the feet or hands attached directly to the torso like flippers. Eyes, ears, noses, and hearts were also often badly deformed. It soon became clear that there were critical periods for different deformities. If the mother had taken the drug on or around the 35th day after her last menstrual period, her baby was likely to be born without ears. If she had taken it on the 39th through 41st day after last menstruation, the baby often had grossly deformed arms or no arms at all; if thalidomide was taken between the 40th and 46th day,

Table 4.1 Maternal diseases and conditions that may affect an embryo, fetus, or newborn

DISEASE OR CONDITION	EFFECTS
Sexually transmitted diseases	
Acquired immune deficiency syndrome (AIDS)	If transmitted from mother to child during birth, lowers defenses against disease and typically leads to death. Mothers can acquire it through sexual contact, blood transfusions, or the use of contaminated drug needles.
Gonorrhea	Attacks the eyes of the child during birth; blindness is prevented by administering silver nitrate eyedrops to newborns.
Herpes simplex (genital herpes)	May cause eye damage and serious brain damage unless mothers with active herpes undergo surgical deliveries to avoid infecting their babies through contact with the vaginal tract.
Syphilis	Untreated, can cause miscarriage or serious birth defects (see text).
Other maternal conditions or diseases	
Chicken pox	Can cause spontaneous abortion or premature delivery, though not malformations. Premature infants who are infected are weak and at risk of death.
Diabetes mellitus	Increases risks of stillbirth, death, and malformations, though the vast majority of babies of diabetic women survive.
Hepatitis	Disease can be transmitted from mother to child.
Hypertension (chronic high blood pressure)	Increases chances of miscarriage and infant death.
Influenza (flu)	The more powerful strains can cause spontaneous abortion or fetal abnormalities early in pregnancy.
Mumps	This relatively mild disease kills some fetuses.
Rubella	See text.
Smallpox	Increases risk of spontaneous abortion and stillbirth, even when the mother is immunized by vaccination.
Toxemia	Affecting about 5% of mothers in the third trimester, its mildest form, *preeclampsia*, causes high blood pressure and rapid weight gain in the mother. Untreated, preeclampsia may become *eclampsia* and cause maternal convulsions and coma or even death of mother and/or unborn child. Surviving infants may be brain damaged.
Toxoplasmosis	This mild and common disease, caused by a parasite present in raw meat and cat feces, can produce serious eye or brain damage or even death in the unborn child.

the child might have deformed legs or no legs. And if the mother waited until the 52nd day before using thalidomide, her baby was usually not affected (Apgar & Beck, 1974).

Pregnant women today do not take thalidomide, of course, but many of them do use another drug that is clearly teratogenic: alcohol (Vorhees & Mollnow, 1987). It was not so long ago—in 1973—that a cluster of symptoms dubbed **fetal alcohol syndrome** was identified (Jones, Smith, Ulleland, & Streissguth, 1973). The most noticeable physical symptoms are a small head and malformations of the heart, limbs, joints, and face (see Figure 4.5). Affected newborns are likely to display excessive irritability, hyperactivity, seizures, or tremors. They are smaller and lighter than normal, and their physical growth lags behind that of their age mates throughout childhood and adolescence. The majority of children with severe fetal alcohol syndrome score well below average on intelligence tests, and many are mentally retarded (Abel, 1981; Streissguth, Herman, & Smith, 1978).

How much drinking must a mother do to risk harming her baby? Clearly the symptoms of fetal alcohol syndrome are most severe when the "doses" of alcohol are highest—that is, when the mother is clearly an alcoholic. Heavy drinkers (those who consume five or more drinks a day) run a 30% or higher risk of having a child with fetal alcohol syndrome (Vorhees & Mollnow, 1987). However, even moderate alcohol consumption or "social drinking" (1–3 ounces a day) can lead to less serious fetal alcohol

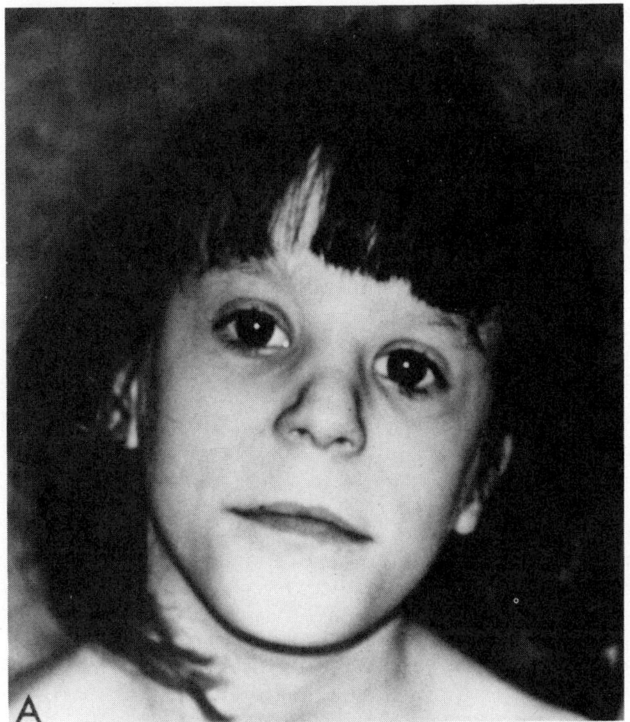

Figure 4.5 This girl's widely spaced eyes, flattened nose, and underdeveloped lip are three of the common physical symptoms of fetal alcohol syndrome.

effects, retarding physical growth, interfering with the normal development of the nervous system, and producing such problems as sluggishness in newborns, minor physical abnormalities, difficulty paying attention, and lower IQ scores (Abel, 1980; Streissguth, Barr, & Martin, 1983; Streissguth et al., 1989; Vorhees & Mollnow, 1987). Even a mother who drinks less than an ounce a day is likely to have a sluggish or placid newborn (Jacobson, Fein, Jacobson, Schwartz, & Dowler, 1984). Thus there appears to be no amount of drinking that is entirely safe, but the severity of the damage done by alcohol is clearly related to the "dose" of alcohol consumed (Vorhees & Mollnow, 1987).

Table 4.2 catalogs a number of other drugs and chemical substances and their known or suspected effects on the child. What do we make of these findings? Perhaps Virginia Apgar summarizes it all best: "A woman who is pregnant, or thinks she could possibly be pregnant, should not take any drugs whatsoever unless absolutely essential—and then only when prescribed by a physician who is aware of the pregnancy" (Apgar & Beck, 1974, p. 445). Unfortunately it has taken many tragedies such as the epidemic of thalidomide babies to bring this message home.

Environmental Hazards

A mother can control what she ingests, but sometimes she cannot control the physical environment surrounding her. Radiation is one potential hazard. After atomic bombs were dropped on Hiroshima and Nagasaki in 1945, not one pregnant woman who was within one-half mile of the blasts gave birth to a live child, and 75% of those who were within a mile and a quarter of the blasts had stillborn infants or seriously handicapped children who died soon after birth (Apgar & Beck, 1974). Unborn children who did survive this disaster have proved to have a higher than normal rate of mental retardation (Vorhees & Mollnow, 1987). Even clinical doses of radiation such as those used in X rays and cancer treatment seem to be capable of causing mutations, spontaneous abortions, and a variety of birth defects, especially if the mother is exposed during the first trimester of pregnancy. For this reason, expectant mothers are routinely advised to avoid X rays unless it is absolutely essential to their own survival, and women who work with X-ray equipment must take proper precautions.

Then there are the pollutants in the air we breathe and the water we drink. For example, "heavy metals" such as lead are discharged by smelting operations and other industries and may be present in paint or water pipes. These metals are known to impair the physical health and mental abilities of adults and children and to have teratogenic effects on developing embryos and fetuses, producing physical deformities and intellectual deficiencies (Miller, 1976; Rutter, 1980). The polluting chemicals called PCBs, now outlawed but still present in the environment, represent another hazard. Joseph Jacobson and his colleagues found that being exposed to low levels of PCBs when their mothers ate fish from Lake Michigan during pregnancy affected the neurological maturity of newborns (Jacobson, Jacobson, Fein, Schwartz, & Dowler, 1984). Some were also born small or born early.

Finally, a *father's* exposure to environmental toxins can affect a couple's children. How? It seems that a father's prolonged exposure to radiation, anesthetic gases used in

Table 4.2 Some drugs that affect (or are thought to affect) the fetus or newborn

SUBSTANCE	EFFECT
Antibiotics	Heavy use of streptomycin by mothers can produce hearing loss. Terramycin and tetracycline may be linked to premature delivery, retarded skeletal growth, cataracts, and a staining of the baby's teeth.
Alcohol	Small head, facial abnormalities, heart defects, low birth weight, and intellectual retardation (fetal alcohol syndrome; see text).
Aspirin	Used in large quantities, aspirin and other salicylates may cause neonatal bleeding and gastrointestinal discomfort. There is preliminary evidence that aspirin may be associated with low birth weight and lower intelligence test scores (Vorhees & Mollnow, 1987).
Barbiturates	In clinical doses, barbiturates cause the fetus or newborn to be sluggish. Large doses may cause anoxia (oxygen starvation) or interfere with breathing.
Hallucinogens	Research is inconclusive, but heavy use of marijuana may slow prenatal growth and lead to behavioral abnormalities in the newborn (Fried, 1980; Tinklenberg, 1975). LSD *may* cause congenital defects, including chromosome abnormalities, but this has not yet been firmly established (Schardein, 1985).
Narcotics	Addiction to heroin, codeine, methadone, or morphine increases the risk of premature delivery. The newborn is often addicted and experiences potentially fatal withdrawal symptoms unless ever smaller doses of the addictive drug are given after birth.
Sex hormones	Birth control pills containing female hormones have been known to produce heart defects and cardiovascular problems (Heinonen et al., 1977; Schardein, 1985), but today's pill formulas are safer. Progesterone in drugs used to prevent miscarriage may masculinize the fetus. Diethystilbestrol (DES), once also prescribed to prevent miscarriage, has been linked to reproductive problems and cervical cancer in exposed daughters (Hamm, 1981).
Stimulants	Caffeine use has been linked to prematurity, abnormal reflexes, and irritability at birth (Jacobson, Fein, Jacobson, Schwartz, & Dowler, 1984). The effects of cocaine are just being explored, but it may cause babies to be small, irritable, and susceptible to respiratory problems (Barol, 1986).
Tranquilizers	Tranquilizers other than thalidomide such as chlorpromazine and reserpine may produce respiratory distress in newborns.
Tobacco	Babies of smokers tend to be small and sometimes show long-term lags in physical and intellectual growth (U.S. Department of Health, Education and Welfare, 1979), but usually overcome early problems (Lefkowitz, 1981).
Vaccines	Immunization with live-virus vaccines should be avoided during pregnancy unless essential, for many of these viruses (for example, mumps, measles, smallpox) are powerful teratogens.

operating rooms, and other environmental toxins can damage his chromosomes and cause genetic defects in his children (Gunderson & Sackett, 1982). Clearly, there is a critical need for more research aimed at identifying a potentially huge range of chemicals, wastes, and other environmental hazards that could affect unborn children.

Summing Up

Surely, the message is clear: Factors present in the prenatal environment can often determine whether an embryo or fetus survives or how it looks and functions if it does survive. By becoming familiar with the material discussed here, and by staying abreast of new knowledge as it becomes available, parents-to-be can do much to increase the already high odds that their unborn child will be normal as it approaches its next challenge: the birth process.

THE PERINATAL ENVIRONMENT

The **perinatal environment** is the environment surrounding birth; it includes influences such as drugs given to the mother during delivery, delivery practices, and the social environment shortly after birth. Like the prenatal environment, the perinatal environment can greatly affect human development.

The Birth Process

Childbirth is a three-stage process. The first stage begins as the mother experiences *contractions* of the uterus spaced at 10-minute to 15-minute intervals and ends when her cervix has fully dilated so that the fetus's head can pass through. This phase of labor lasts an average of 8 to 14 hours for firstborn children and 3 to 8 hours for later-borns. The second stage of labor is *delivery*, which begins as the fetus's head passes through the cervix into the vagina and ends when the baby emerges from the mother's body. This is the time when the mother is often told to bear down (push) with each contraction to assist her baby through the birth canal. A quick delivery may take a half hour, whereas a long one may take more than an hour and a half. Finally, the third stage of the birth process is the *afterbirth*, or the expulsion of the placenta a few minutes after delivery.

When the birth process is completed, the mother (and often the father too, if he is present) is physically exhausted and relieved to be through the ordeal of giving birth. Meanwhile, the fetus has been thrust from its quite carefree existence into a strange new world. In the large majority of cases, the entire process goes smoothly, and parents and newborn quickly begin their relationship. Occasionally problems arise.

Hazards During the Birth Process

One clear hazard during the birth process is **anoxia**, or oxygen shortage. Anoxia can occur for any number of reasons—for example, because the umbilical cord becomes pinched or tangled during birth, because sedatives given to the mother reach the fetus and interfere with the baby's breathing, or because mucus lodged in the baby's throat prevents normal breathing. Why is anoxia dangerous? Largely because brain cells die if they are starved of oxygen for more than a few minutes. Severe anoxia can result in *cerebral palsy*, a motor disability in which the affected individual has difficulties controlling muscles of the arms, legs, or head (Apgar & Beck, 1974). Brain damage that results in mental retardation is also possible when anoxia is severe. Milder cases of anoxia make some children irritable at birth or delay their motor and cognitive development (Sameroff & Chandler, 1975). However, many victims, especially those whose environments after birth are optimal, become perfectly normal children (Sameroff & Chandler, 1975). In one study, for example, children who suffered from relatively brief anoxia scored below normal as a group on measures of intellectual development at age 3 but had average intelligence test scores by age 7 (Corah, Anthony, Painter, Stern, & Thurston, 1965). Only a minority of these children showed persisting problems. Thus prolonged anoxia can cause permanent disabilities, but the effects of milder anoxia are typically overcome as a child gets older.

Another bit of good news is that the chances of anoxia have been greatly reduced by the use of fetal monitoring procedures during labor and delivery. Doctors are now alert to the risk of anoxia if the fetus is not positioned in the usual head-down position, for then the birth process takes longer. If the baby is born feet or buttocks first (a **breech presentation**) delivery becomes more complex, although the vast majority of breech babies are normal (Apgar & Beck, 1974). A vaginal delivery is nearly impossible for the one fetus in a hundred lying sideways in the uterus. The fetus must be turned to assume a head-first position or be delivered by **Cesarean section**, a surgical procedure in which an incision is made in the mother's abdomen and uterus so that the baby can be removed.

And that leads us to the potential hazards associated with delivery procedures and technologies themselves. During the 19th century, many doctors believed that the routine use of *forceps* (an instrument resembling an oversized pair of salad tongs) was the best way to deliver babies (Edwards & Waldorf, 1984). Unfortunately, the use of forceps on the soft skull of the fetus sometimes caused serious problems, including cranial bleeding and brain damage. Now forceps are used with great care only when a baby is in danger.

As for the Cesarean section, it too has been controversial. Use of this alternative to normal vaginal delivery has prevented the death of many babies—for example, when the baby is too large or the mother is too small to permit normal delivery, when a fetus out of position cannot be repositioned, or when fetal monitoring reveals that a birth complication is likely. Medical advances have made Cesarean sections almost as safe as vaginal deliveries. However, mothers who have a "C-section" do take longer to recover from the birth process (Gottlieb & Barrett, 1986), and newborns born this way sometimes experience respiratory difficulties. Moreover, some observers question why Cesarean deliveries have become more common over the years, accounting for almost 23% of births in the United States (U.S. Bureau of the Census, 1987). Critics have argued that some doctors rely too heavily on this procedure because it is convenient and protects them from malpractice suits that might arise from complications in a vaginal delivery (Edwards & Waldorf, 1984).

Finally, concerns have also been raised about medications given to mothers during the birth process, as Box 4.1 reveals. Research suggests that these drugs can be beneficial in some cases, but they can also make an infant temporarily sluggish and have even interfered with the longer-term development of some children. Although today's drugs and dosage levels are far safer than those administered in the past, many women today opt for a drug-free delivery. Overall, it seems that birth technologies can have both positive and negative effects on the birth process and on development.

A few infants, however, are in great jeopardy at birth because of genetic defects, prenatal hazards, or perinatal damage. It is essential to their survival and well-being to identify them as early as possible. Today the **Apgar test** is routinely used to assess the newborn's heart rate, respiration, color, muscle tone, and reflexes immediately after birth and then 5 minutes later (see Table 4.3). Scores for each factor in this simple test range from 0 to 2, with a total possible score of 0 to 10. Infants who score 7 or higher are in good shape. However, infants scoring 4 or lower are at risk—their heartbeats are sluggish or nonexistent, their muscles are limp, and their breathing, if they are breathing, is shallow and irregular. These babies will immediately experience a different postnatal environment than the normal baby experiences, for they require medical intervention to survive. Later, we will take a closer look at patterns of intensive care for high-risk babies.

The Social Environment Surrounding Birth

The birth of a baby is a dramatic experience for the whole family. However, it was not that long ago that most hospitals barred fathers from the delivery room and snatched babies away from their mothers soon after delivery to place them in nurseries. Let us briefly look at the birth experience from a family perspective.

Box 4.1
Drugs During Delivery: Are They Harmful?

In modern times, mothers have been given a wide range of medications during the birth process—analgesics and anesthetics to reduce their pain, sedatives to relax them, and stimulants to induce or intensify uterine contractions. Yvonne Brackbill and her associates (Brackbill, 1979; Brackbill, McManus, & Woodward, 1985) have found that babies whose mothers received large doses of obstetrical medication were atypical in several ways. They smiled infrequently, were generally sluggish and irritable, and were difficult to feed or cuddle during the first few weeks of life. These effects may interfere with parents' involvement or emotional attachment to their infant (Murray, Dolby, Nation, & Thomas, 1981). Babies of heavily medicated mothers may even show deficits in motor and cognitive development for at least a year after birth (Brackbill, 1979). And even low doses of drugs may have subtle effects on the behavior of some newborns (Lester, Als, & Brazelton, 1982).

How can a single brief exposure to birth medications have such effects? First, a dose of medication large enough to affect the mother is likely to have much greater impacts on a fetus weighing only 7 pounds. In addition, newborns have immature circulatory and excretory systems, so powerful drugs may remain in their bodies for days or even weeks. Finally, sluggish and unresponsive babies get off to a slow start in their development and may take some time to catch up to their age mates who were not so heavily medicated at birth.

So should mothers go out of their way to avoid all obstetric medications? Perhaps that advice is too strong. For example, some women are at risk because of their size or body shape or because their babies are large. For such women, sedatives in appropriate doses can actually *reduce* the chances of some birth complications such as anoxia (Myers, 1980; Myers & Myers, 1979). By depressing the fetal metabolism, drugs prolong the brain's tolerance for oxygen deprivation; they also improve uterine blood flow and increase the supply of oxygen to the fetus.

There are many drugs, each with its own potential effects, and some are safer than others. The children most negatively affected by drugs have often been those whose mothers inhaled anesthetics such as nitrous oxide during the birth process (Brackbill & Broman, cited by Kolata, 1979). Doctors are more alert to the potentially negative effects of obstetric medications today than they once were, so they are more likely to use drugs only when clearly necessary and to use the least toxic drugs in the lowest effective doses at the safest times (Finster, Pedersen, & Morishima, 1984). Thus, taking obstetric medications is not as risky a business today as it once was, but it is still a decision that should be made cautiously.

Table 4.3 The Apgar test

	SCORE		
CHARACTERISTIC	0	1	2
Heart rate	Absent	Slow (less than 100 beats per minute)	Over 100 beats per minute
Respiratory effort	Absent	Slow or irregular	Good, baby is crying
Muscle tone	Flaccid, limp	Weak, some flexion	Strong, active motion
Color	Blue or pale	Body pink, extremities blue	Completely pink
Reflex irritability	No response	Frown, grimace, or weak cry	Vigorous cry

THE MOTHER

It is now clear that psychological factors such as the mother's attitude toward her pregnancy, her knowledge about the birth process, and the support she receives from her partner and other people are important determinants of her experience of the birth process and of her new baby. To begin with, the birth process itself goes more smoothly when the mother has social support. When the father or another supportive person is present during labor and delivery, women experience less pain, use less medication, and are likely to feel more positively about the whole birth process (Grossman, Eichler, Winickoff, & Associates, 1980; Henneborn & Cogan, 1975). Women who attend childbirth classes and are prepared for giving birth also have a more positive experience than those who do not receive instruction (Wideman & Singer, 1984).

The first minutes after birth can be a special time in which the mother can begin to love her newborn, provided she is allowed to get to know this little stranger. Marshall Klaus and John Kennell believe that the first 6 to 12 hours after birth are a sensitive period for the emotional *bonding* of a mother to her infant, a time when the mother is especially ready to develop a strong affection for her baby and when her baby is especially alert and responsive (Kennell, Voos, & Klaus, 1979). In a study testing their hypothesis, Klaus and Kennell (1976) had half of a group of new mothers follow what was then a traditional hospital routine: They saw their babies briefly after delivery, visited with them 6 to 12 hours later, and then had half-hour feeding sessions every four hours during their three-day stay in the hospital. Mothers in an "extended contact" group were allowed five "extra" hours a day to cuddle their babies, including an hour of skin-to-skin contact within three hours of birth.

A month later, mothers who had had extended contact with their infants appeared to be more involved with them and held them closer during feeding sessions. A year later, these mothers were still more soothing, cuddling, and nurturing than mothers who experienced the normal hospital routine. As for the 1-year-old infants, those who had had extended early contact with their mothers outperformed those who had not on tests of physical and mental development. Apparently, then, extended early contact promoted early mother/infant bonding, which may in turn have motivated mothers to interact in stimulating ways with their babies. This research has been partially responsible for changes in hospital policies about contact between mother and newborn.

But Klaus and Kennell may have gone too far when they claimed that parents who have little or no contact with their newborns during a sensitive period immediately after birth may never become as attached as they might have. In a careful review of many studies, Susan Goldberg (1983) found that "early contact" effects are not as large or as lasting as Klaus and Kennell found them to be. In one study, mothers who had not had much contact with their babies in the hours after birth caught up quickly to the early-contact mothers. Only 8 to 10 days after giving birth, they caressed and cuddled their babies just as much as the early-contact mothers did (Grossmann, Thane, & Grossmann, 1981). Moreover, Klaus and Kennell did not conclusively demonstrate that contact *immediately* after birth is beneficial, for they also allowed their "extended-contact" mothers more time with their babies over the next three days (Goldberg, 1983).

Overall, then, early contact can be a pleasant experience for both mother and baby, and it can help a mother *begin* to form an emotional bond to her child. However, attachments between infants and caregivers are not formed in a matter of minutes or hours. They develop slowly through social interactions taking place over many weeks and months (Rode, Chang, Fisch, & Sroufe, 1981; and see Chapter 13). Stated another way, early contact is neither crucial nor sufficient for the development of a strong parent/child relationship.

Finally, there is a "down side" to the mother's experience of birth: the potential for **postpartum blues**, or feelings of sadness, irritability, resentment, and depression, that as many as half of new mothers experience shortly after a birth (Kraus & Redman, 1986). As many as 10% to 15% experience clinical levels of depression and despair that may last for months (Dalton, 1980). Drugs taken during childbirth and the hormonal changes that occur as a mother returns from the pregnant state to a normal menstrual cycle can contribute to a temporary case of the blues (Dalton, 1980). A new mother might also feel overwhelmed by her new responsibilities and neglected if all the attention is showered on her baby. However, prolonged postpartum depression seems to be most likely among women who had negative feelings about their marriages or pregnancies before giving birth (Field et al., 1985). Such women need help and support, for when mothers are depressed, withdrawn, and unresponsive, their infants may develop similar depressive symptoms (Field, 1984; Field et al., 1985; Radke-Yarrow, Cummings, Kuczynski, & Chapman, 1985).

The Father

The birth process is also a significant event in the life of a father. He too may experience anxiety during his partner's pregnancy and during the birth process, and he too may find early contact with his baby special. He, like the mother, often shows an **engrossment** with the baby—an intense fascination and a desire to touch, hold, caress, and talk to this new member of the family (Greenberg & Morris, 1974; Peterson, Mehl, & Liederman, 1979). One young father put it this way: "When I come up to see [my] wife . . . I go look at the kid and then I pick her up and then I put her down. . . . I keep going back to the kid. It's like a magnet. That's what I can't get over, the fact that I feel like that" (Greenberg & Morris, 1974, p. 524). Some studies find that fathers who handle and help care for their babies in the hospital later spend more time with them at home than fathers who have not had these early interactions (Greenberg & Morris, 1974). Other studies fail to find these long-term effects on the father/infant relationship, but suggest that early contact with the newborn makes a father feel closer to his partner and more a part of a "family" (Palkowitz, 1985). Like mothers, however, fathers have much time later to learn to love their children even if they do not have much contact shortly after birth.

A Big Issue: Are Negative Effects of the Prenatal and Perinatal Environments Long Lasting?

We have now encountered many examples of what can go wrong during the prenatal and perinatal periods of development. Certainly some damaging effects are irreversible: The thalidomide baby will never grow normal arms or legs, and the child who is mentally retarded owing to fetal alcohol syndrome will always be mentally retarded. And yet there are countless adults walking around today whose mothers, unaware of many risk factors that concern us now, smoked and drank during their pregnancies, or received heavy doses of medication during delivery, and yet had children who turned out fine. As we have already emphasized, not all embryos, fetuses, or newborns exposed to hazards are affected by them. Is it also possible that some babies who are exposed and who are clearly affected recover from their deficiencies later in life?

Indeed it is! We now have longitudinal follow-up studies to tell us so (Kopp & Krakow, 1983). Consider these findings: Monroe Lefkowitz (1981) reported that 9 to 11 years after they were born, the children of mothers who smoked during pregnancy were no smaller, no less intelligent, no less achievement oriented, and no less socially adjusted than the children of nonsmokers. Zela Stein and her associates found that, as young adults entering the military, Dutch males whose mothers experienced famine during their pregnancies scored no lower on a test of intelligence than males who received adequate prenatal nutrition (Stein & Susser, 1976; Stein, Susser, Saenger, & Marolla, 1975).

And then we have the results of two major longitudinal studies of babies who were "at risk" at birth—for example, who had low birth weights, had been exposed to prenatal hazards, or suffered poor health (Baker & Mednick, 1984; Werner, 1989; Werner & Smith, 1982). These studies indicate that babies at risk—particularly those whose problems at birth are severe—have more intellectual and social problems as children and as adolescents than normal babies do. And yet these studies offer convincing evidence that many of these at-risk babies outgrew their problems with time. Emmy Werner and Ruth Smith (1982), in reporting on their follow-up of all babies born in 1955 on an island in Hawaii, went so far as to title their book *Vulnerable but Invincible*, so impressed were they by the "self-righting" tendencies that allow children to triumph over adverse environmental events and get back on a normal course of development. There simply is no direct link between early risks and later outcomes (Kopp & Krakow, 1983). Instead we must ask this: Why do some children recover from early deficiencies and why do others continue to have problems later in life?

There are probably two main reasons why some children are seemingly invulnerable to lasting damage and others are vulnerable (Garmezy, 1987; Werner, 1989). First, some children, in part because of their genetic makeup, may have greater personal strengths and recuperative powers than others do. For example, Werner and Smith (1982) noticed that some children who seemed to have everything—including their postnatal family environments—working against them had qualities such as social responsiveness and communication skills that helped to ensure that caregivers would love them. And that leads us to a second answer: The children who recover usually have favorable *postnatal* environments, whereas the children who do not recover often encounter additional stresses after they are born (Baker & Mednick, 1984; Werner & Smith, 1982).

Let's illustrate this by considering one at-risk group of babies: those with low birth weight. Until recently, the 8% to 9% of infants who weighed less than 2500 grams (5½ pounds) at birth were simply labeled premature. There are actually two subgroups of babies here. Some infants are small for their gestation age (time in the womb), even if they are born very close to their due dates, and are called **small for date** (Kopp & Parmelee, 1979). But most small babies are also born more than 3 weeks before their due dates and are called "preterm" or **short gestation babies**. Problems are especially likely among infants who not only arrive too early but are smaller than they should be considering the time they have been in the womb. As we have seen, a mother's smoking or drinking, fetal malnutrition, and a number of other factors can contribute to prematurity and low birth weight. Preterm and low birth weight babies are clearly at risk. They must first be helped to survive, for they are likely to develop infections, respiratory difficulties, and other problems. Assuming they do survive, they may be difficult to love because they are often tiny and wrinkled, as well as both unresponsive and irritable.

It doesn't sound good, does it? And yet, researchers are learning that preterm and low birth weight babies develop quite normally if they have favorable postnatal environments (Beckwith & Parmelee, 1986; Greenberg & Crnic, 1988; Wilson, 1985). Consider what Ronald Wilson (1985) found in his study of twins who were especially small at birth (weighing under 1750 grams, or less than about 3¾ pounds) and who were also small for their (short) gestation ages. Figure 4.6 shows that these babies were indeed deficient in mental development as infants. Notice, however, that they caught up over time. And notice too that those at-risk babies whose families had high socioeconomic status caught up *completely*; by age 6, their average IQ was normal (around 100). Problems were more lasting among at-risk twins who grew up in lower-class homes, though even they showed some self-righting tendencies. Similarly, Sarale Cohen, Arthur Parmelee, and

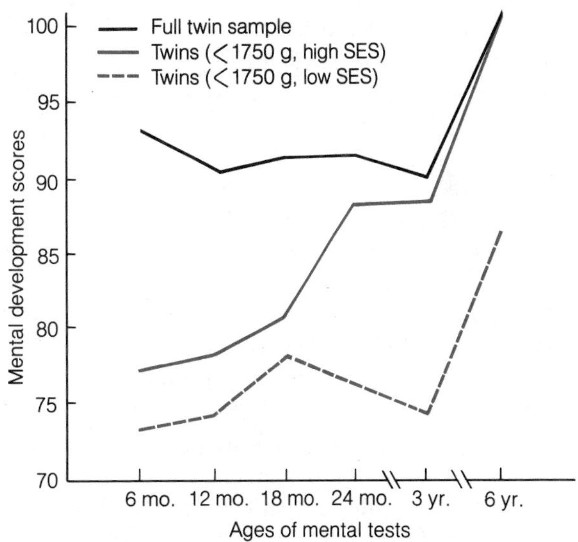

Figure 4.6 The mental development of low-birth-weight preterm twins in high and low socioeconomic-status (SES) homes. (From Wilson, 1985)

Box 4.2
Do We "Label" Premature Babies?

Quick—what comes to mind when you think of a premature infant? Small? Fragile? Relatively unattractive? Likely to be intellectually slow and socially backward? Do these stereotypes influence the ways in which mothers interact with a premature child? Marilyn Stern and Katherine Hildebrandt (1986) attempted to find out.

The catch was that the babies used in the study were all healthy, full-term infants about the same age as the women's own, 15- to 19-week-old babies. Half of the mothers were told that the unfamiliar infant with whom they would interact was premature; the other half were told that their partner was a full-term baby. Infants labeled premature were seen by these mothers as smaller, finer-featured, and less cute than full-term babies, and they were liked less. Although the women did not rate "preemies" as intellectually and socially delayed, they treated them as if they were. The "premature" infants were touched less than the infants described as full-term, and they were given the smallest and least complex of three rattles to play with, as though they could not handle more sophisticated toys. Moreover, the mothers' behavior apparently affected the infants. "Preemies" were less active than full-term babies during the interaction sessions, and college students could guess quite accurately by viewing videotapes of the sessions which babies had been labeled as premature. The danger here is clear: Mothers who expect their premature babies to be deficient may treat them as though they were deficient and possibly inhibit their development in the process.

their colleagues have found that preterm and low birth weight babies display normal intellectual functioning during childhood when they live in middle-class homes, when their mothers are relatively educated, and when their mothers are attentive and responsive when interacting with them but fare worse in less favorable environments (Beckwith & Parmelee, 1986; Cohen & Parmelee, 1983; Cohen, Parmelee, Beckwith, & Sigman, 1986).

Studies like these raise a larger issue about the importance of early experience. On one side of the issue are developmentalists such as Kevin MacDonald (1986) who take seriously the concept of critical (or sensitive) periods in early development. Those on the other side of the issue—for example, Jerome Kagan (1986)—stress the resilience of human beings, their ability to recover from early disadvantages and to respond to environmental influences throughout their lives (rather than primarily during so-called critical periods). Which is it?

We have encountered evidence in favor of both positions. Hazards during the important prenatal and perinatal periods *can* leave lasting scars, and yet many children show remarkable resilience. Isn't this the lesson we learn from the case of Genie described at the beginning of the chapter? Yes, she was permanently affected by extreme deprivation during sensitive periods of development early in life. Yet even she showed considerable resilience when her environment improved. There *do* seem to be some points in the life span, especially early on, in which both positive and negative environmental forces have especially strong impacts (Colombo, 1982). Yet at the same time, *environment matters throughout life*. Certainly it would be a huge mistake to assume that all children who show problems at birth are doomed (see Box 4.2). In short, early experience by itself rarely makes or breaks the developing person; later experience counts too.

It is time, then, to turn our attention to the *postnatal* environment. In chapters to come, we will have much to say about a wide range of environmental influences on development: influences of parents, peers, schools, workplaces, and so on. Here we want to focus most closely on the broader social environment in which development takes place—on the cultural context of development, or what Bronfenbrenner terms the macrosystem.

THE INFANT

How, you might ask, could culture have much to do with infant development? Isn't infant development mainly a matter of maturation programmed by the genes? Aren't infants too young to be exposed to much outside their immediate home environment? True, but their parents are products of the broader culture, and their learned beliefs about the nature of young children and notions about how to raise children can work their way into infants' daily lives.

Cross-cultural researcher Melvin Konner (1981) has summarized a great deal of evidence on cultural variations in the experience of infancy. He views parenting in the context of biological evolution, noting similarities between parenting among primates and other mammals and parenting in many nonindustrialized human societies in the world today. Then he shows how *cultural* evolution, or modernization, has led parents toward child-rearing styles that are quite different from those that biological evolution prescribed.

Let's get specific. What is it like to be an infant in a hunter-gatherer society today—one like the !Kung society in the Kalahari Desert of southern Africa? What is it like to be an infant in a modern industrialized country—the United States, for example? The contrasts are marked. Infant mortality is high among the !Kung, so babies are kept close at all times. They are carried upright in slings during the day, and they sleep in the same bed with their mothers at night. In the United States, infants are often left lying in their cribs alone; they often sleep in their own rooms. Because they do not go everywhere with their mothers, they probably receive less sensory stimulation than !Kung babies do. The !Kung infant is breast fed, suckles several times an hour as desired, and may not be weaned until the ripe old age of 4. Western babies? *If* they are breast fed, it tends to be done about every four hours; often they are switched to the bottle and then to solid food within a few months. In general, infants in hunter-gatherer societies are indulged considerably. Their mothers do little to restrain their natural desires and are in close physical contact with them from birth on. Infants in modern industrialized societies are expected to accommodate to their parents' schedules. Infant care practices in traditional agricultural societies fall somewhere in between, but vary considerably from one culture to another (Konner, 1981).

Clearly the experience of infancy differs from society to society. But what impacts do infant care practices have on child development? In many cases we do not know, but there are hints. Konner (1976), for example, finds that !Kung infants walk earlier than infants in our society do, perhaps because they spend so much time upright and have great freedom of movement in their slings. Ugandan babies, who also have close physical contact with their mothers, begin to protest separations from their mothers at only 5 or 6 months of age (Ainsworth, 1967); in our society, such separation anxiety is rarely observed before 7 months of age.

In addition, Dixon, LeVine, Richman, and Brazelton (1984) showed that mothers' teaching styles are affected by their culture and in turn affect their infants' behavior. In Kenya, mothers used a very physical style of teaching, pulling and pushing their infants here and there. They also took it for granted that their infants would be motivated to do what was expected of them. Their babies did not mind being tugged, and persisted on the task to please their mothers. By contrast, mothers in the United States used a verbal style of teaching and seemed to assume that they should motivate their infants to explore the task materials. Their infants were frustrated if they were tugged or restrained, had shorter attention spans, and spent more time than the African infants did simply playing with the task materials in varied ways. Thus cultural differences in mothers' teaching styles were associated with cultural differences in child behavior.

Finally, Charles Super and Sara Harkness (1981) provide a fascinating example of how an infant whose temperament is well suited for one child-rearing environment may be regarded as a "problem baby" in another cultural context. In Boston, mothers establish regular schedules for their infants with planned nap times, feeding times, bedtimes, and so on, whereas in Kokwet, a rural farming community in Kenya, mothers carry their babies with them during the day, sleep with them at night, and feed them on demand. Because of the demands their mothers place on them, Boston babies generally learn to sleep straight through the night earlier than Kokwet babies do, but a baby who cannot conform to a regular schedule is considered a "problem baby." The same baby is not viewed as difficult in Kokwet. After all, mothers are right there to feed their babies whenever they are ready to suckle. What drives a Kokwet mother up the wall is a baby who fusses when handed by the mother to someone else for a short time. In short, the baby whose temperament is mismatched to its cultural niche is likely to have a more difficult infancy than the baby who is temperamentally equipped to meet cultural demands.

In sum, infants are not too young to be affected by their cultural environments. But as children leave the relatively carefree period of infancy, they are even more explicitly taught to fit in to their cultural context.

THE CHILD

While infants must adapt to the physical and social environments in which they are raised, relatively few social demands are placed on them. After infancy, the demands increase, and cultural differences in the kinds of experiences that children have become more striking (Whiting & Edwards, 1988). **Socialization** is the process by which individuals acquire the beliefs, values, and behaviors judged important in their society. By socializing the young, society controls their undesirable behavior, prepares them to adapt to their environment and function effectively in it, and ensures that cultural traditions will be carried on by future generations. Parents, peers, schools, churches, and other people and institutions contribute to the socialization process.

Socialization Goals

What is it that parents hope their children will learn? What would *you* most want to instill in your children? There is much disagreement within this society, and much variation from society to society in the socialization curriculum. The parents of a !Kung boy might want him to learn hunting skills; the parents of a Chicago boy might want him to learn computer skills. Yet Robert LeVine (1974, p. 230) believes that parents everywhere have three very broad goals for their children:

1. The *survival goal*—to promote the physical survival and health of the child, ensuring that the child lives long enough to have children of his or her own.
2. The *economic goal*—to foster the skills and behavioral capacities that the child will need for economic self-maintenance as an adult.
3. The *self-actualization goal*—to foster behavioral capabilities for maximizing other cultural values (for example, morality, religion, achievement, wealth, prestige, and a sense of personal satisfaction).

Moreover, LeVine believes that these universal goals of parenting form a hierarchy. Until parents are confident that the child will survive, higher order goals such as teaching the child to talk, count, or follow moral rules are put on the back burner. And only when parents and other caregivers believe that their children have acquired many of the basic attributes that will eventually contribute to their economic self-sufficiency will they encourage such goals as self-actualization or self-fulfillment.

Because different societies must emphasize different parenting goals, child-rearing practices differ widely from society to society. As we have seen, in societies where infant mortality is high and the survival goal is hard to achieve, parents keep their infants close 24 hours a day to protect them. In some of these societies, babies are not even named until they seem likely to survive (Brazelton, 1979). These practices are not necessary in a society where

In many cultures, parents attempt to achieve the survival goal of parenting by keeping their babies close at all times.

infant mortality is low. As parents attempt to achieve the economic goal of parenting, they emphasize the values and skills that are most necessary to make a living in their society (Ogbu, 1981). A cross-cultural study of 104 traditional societies by Herbert Barry and his associates (Barry, Child, & Bacon, 1959) makes this point well. In societies with an agricultural or pastoral economy (those that accumulate food), parents stressed cooperation and obedience in raising their children because their agricultural activities demanded family teamwork. By contrast, hunting, trapping, and fishing societies (groups that do not accumulate food) stressed quite different values: independence, assertiveness, self-reliance, and other traits important in hunting.

Within any society, of course, parents differ widely in their specific socialization goals and parenting styles. For example, in the industrialized United States, many parents in lower socioeconomic strata emphasize obedience, neatness, and respect for power, while middle-class parents are more likely to stress ambition, creativity, and independence (Hess, 1970; Kohn, 1969). Why the difference? Perhaps it is because blue-collar workers expect that their children, like themselves, will have to work for a boss and defer to his or her authority, while middle-class professionals and business owners expect that their children, like themselves, will be self-employed or will manage other people and will need to be independent, self-assertive, creative, and so on. Being affluent and thus able to aid their children in achieving economic security, middle-class parents may also feel freer to encourage their children to pursue whatever interests them (LeVine's self-actualization goal).

Developmentalists have tended to view the child-rearing style used by white middle-class parents as a particularly good style. But as John Ogbu (1981) emphasizes, that style might do more harm than good in a culture or subculture that demands other attributes. If, for example, a family cannot survive unless children are obedient, it would be foolish to encourage children to "do their own thing." There is not one "right" way to socialize children. Instead, the definition of a competent parent depends on the particular qualities needed for success in a given culture or subculture. And it may also change as society changes. The broad goals of parenting may be universal, but the specific goals of socialization and the practices used by parents to achieve those goals differ widely from place to place, time to time, and individual to individual.

Cultural Variation and Our Understanding of Development

Perhaps it has occurred to you that if children are raised differently in different cultures and subcultures, our understandings of development might depend on which culture we study. This is the case, and here are some examples.

1. *Culture affects the behavior shown by children of a given age.* Children in many industrialized countries such as the United States are more competitive and less cooperative and helpful than their age mates in less developed countries such as Mexico (Kagan & Masden, 1972; Whiting & Whiting, 1975). It is quite likely that this is because we socialize children to be independent and assertive, while less industrialized cultures often teach children to cooperate within the family for the good of all.
2. *Culture affects the rate of development.* We have already seen that infants in hunter-gatherer societies learn to walk and protest separations from their mothers earlier than children in our society do.
3. *Culture affects the very direction of development.* Research in our society indicates that, as children get older and more intelligent, they are more and more able to pass up a small reward immediately and wait for a larger reward in the future (Mischel & Metzner, 1962). This ability to delay gratification is believed to be mature. Yet among the Aborigines of Australia, older and more intelligent children are *less* likely to delay gratification than younger and less intelligent children (Bochner & David, 1968). For nomadic hunters like the Aborigines who move frequently, it is maladaptive to be burdened by hoarded goods; older children have learned the value of consuming goods immediately. Examples like this are relatively rare, but they indicate that development *can* proceed in one direction in one society and in the opposite direction in another society.
4. *Culture affects our understandings of influences on development.* One team of investigators (Johnson, Teigen, & Davila, 1984) sought to determine whether a high level of anxiety in children is associated with a restrictive parenting style in which parents set many rules and strictly en-

force them or a permissive parenting style in which children are given considerable freedom to make their own decisions: an interesting question. In Mexico, a country where restrictive parenting was common, children whose parents were permissive were the most anxious. By contrast, in Norway, a country where parents are generally permissive, children whose parents were *restrictive* were the most anxious. Possibly, then, children are anxious when their parents use a style that is atypical in their particular society. Such findings obviously make it difficult to state general rules of good parenting!

The message is clear: We simply must view development in its social context. We must remind ourselves that most of the research reported in this textbook has been done with children and adults in North America and may not hold up in other societies. As Christine Fry (1985) puts it, "If you want your pet theory vetoed, ask an anthropologist" (p. 236).

THE ADOLESCENT

The adolescent's development is also shaped by the culture and subculture in which he or she lives. During adolescence, a child who has been socialized all along for adult life must actually make the transition to adulthood. Adolescence in our society is a time for moving out into the larger environment—for spending more and more time with friends, using a driver's license as a passport to distant locations, taking on part-time jobs, and, eventually, leaving the nest. Most important, it is a time of social redefinition, a time for shedding one's status as a child and gaining an identity as an adult.

The process of "dying" as a child and being "reborn" as an adult appears to be a universal experience. However, not all cultures recognize a period of the life span corresponding to our "adolescence," and the "coming of age" experience varies widely and occurs at widely different ages across cultures. In some societies, rituals have been developed to clearly mark the beginning of adulthood—rituals called **rites of passage** that signify the passage from one stage of life to another (in this case, the transition from childhood to adulthood). According to anthropologist Arnold van Gennep (1960), puberty rites involve a *separation* from the status of child, a *transition* during which the individual is prepared for adulthood, and an *incorporation* into society in one's new status as an adult. Box 4.3 shows how the rites of passage occur for boys and girls in one society in eastern Africa. Here we see no prolonged period of adolescence, no struggling for years to attain adult status in the eyes of society. In many nonindustrial societies, the adolescent rites of passage occur at about the time that boys mature physically and sexually and at the time that girls first menstruate—earlier than in our society. These rites make the transition to adulthood clear to the individual and to the whole society. They also serve political purposes—for example, ensuring that boys become loyal to their male elders and allowing a father to advertise his daughter's maturity so that he will obtain bridewealth when he transfers this valuable reproductive "property" to another man (Paige & Paige, 1981).

Now examine our society as an anthropologist might. When are you an adult? For some adolescents, a Bar or Bas Mitzvah or a confirmation ceremony signifies a sort of passage to adulthood, but these ceremonies do not apply to all and do not confer full adult status on youth. High school graduation is an important marker perhaps. But then again, our society has devised *many* legal ages—16 and up for driving, 18 for voting, and typically 21 for drinking—rather than one clear boundary between childhood and adulthood. Must one assume a full-time job or marry to fully establish one's credentials as an adult? In short, our society puts adolescents through a prolonged period—often lasting from age 10 or 12 to the early 20s—in which they are in limbo between childhood and adulthood (McKinney, 1984).

It was not always this way. The adolescent experience is shaped not only by culture, but by the historical context in which it occurs. According to historian Joseph Kett (1977), adolescents in the United States in the 18th century generally knew that they would remain on the farm and do what their parents did. By the early 19th century, the spread of industrialization was prompting many youths to leave the farms for the cities and factories. Children took on jobs as work apprentices or servants at an early age, and young people found themselves facing a far wider range of life choices than adolescents in the previous century had faced.

But as industry advanced further in the late 19th century, immigrants began to replace children in unskilled, low-paying jobs, while the need for an educated, skilled

Box 4.3 Rites of Passage Among the Kaguru

What is the adolescent experience like in other cultures? T. O. Beidelman (1971) gives us a closeup view of the coming of age process among the Kaguru of eastern Africa. Their puberty rites encompass separation, transition, and incorporation into the adult community.

The initiation ceremony for boys converts immature children into morally responsible adults. A group of boys, as young as age 10 to 12, are led into the bush, stripped of their clothes, and shaved of all hair, thereby experiencing a *separation* from their previous status as children. They then undergo a painful circumcision but are tended well during their recovery. Their elders make animal noises to warn them that they will be eaten by wild animals if they ever reveal the secrets of their initiation. The boys also learn about sexual practices and are taught ritual songs and riddles that instruct them in the ways of adulthood. After this *transition* period, they wash off the white ashes intended to "cool" them down during the circumcision process and are "anointed" with red earth, visually displaying their new status as adults. They are led back to the village and *reincorporated* into society with celebrations and feasts. They are even given new names as members of the community bless them. Now each youth is ready for sexual activity and marriage, as well as other adult roles.

The Kaguru girl is initiated by herself whenever she experiences her first menstruation. Unlike a boy, she does not become a more morally worthy person in the community's eyes; the prevailing view is that women are tainted creatures throughout life. The goal is to teach a girl to control her strong sexuality so that she will use it in appropriate ways to bear many children. The Kaguru do not surgically remove the clitoris as some societies do, but they do cut the girl's genital area as a mark of her new status. She too is separated from the community during her transition period so that she can be properly instructed, often by her grandmother. One of the songs both she and the boys learn goes, "The mouth of the wildcat is always open; let it be so, for it will never fill up" (p. 110). The message is that women (wildcats) are sexually insatiable and must remain so. After this transition period, the girl, like the boy, enjoys celebrations and feasts as she reenters society.

However these rites of passage may strike us, they serve a clear purpose for the Kaguru. A child dies and an adult is born; the conversion is evident to the individual and to the whole community. Moreover, the child is given clear instructions on how to play the role of an adult in Kaguru society. Unlike adolescents in our society, Kaguru youth need not struggle for years to find their place in the social order.

workforce was growing. Around the turn of the century, child labor laws and compulsory schooling laws were passed, and children and adolescents were kept in school and out of the workforce for longer periods. In effect, adolescents of the 20th century have been segregated from the adult world and encouraged to develop a peer culture of their own.

Not only do adolescents today often spend more time with peers than with adults, but they may find that adults are unable to prepare them adequately for the future. According to anthropologist Margaret Mead (1978), the rate at which society is changing greatly influences the adolescent experience. In nonindustrial societies with little social change, adolescents are socialized into their roles as adults by their elders, including their grandparents. In modern societies with rapid social change, where can adolescents turn for guidance? What their grandparents and parents know is likely to be obsolete: How many grandparents are "up" on the latest in computer technology or well versed in the effects of street drugs? In a rapidly changing society, youth must often look to their peers for guidance—or are left to their own devices to learn whatever they will need to know to function as adults. For many reasons, then, the adolescent experience in our society seems to be especially challenging.

In sum, adolescence is not just a matter of biological maturation and the development of new cognitive skills; it is a *social* process. The experience of adolescence and its impacts on later development and adjustment are influenced by how a particular society defines childhood and adulthood, by what demands and pressures it places on adolescents, and by what opportunities it provides them as they make their passage into adulthood. Unfortunately, most of our knowledge of adolescence is based on studies of adolescents in Western societies in the late 1900s. We must remind ourselves that we are learning about one kind of adolescent experience, the contemporary Western experience, not about *the* adolescent experience.

THE ADULT

Socialized throughout childhood and adolescence into the ways of our society, we finally become full-fledged members of that society. Quite clearly, the experience of adulthood is different for men and women who work in high-rise buildings and eat microwave dinners than it is for men and women who spend their days hunting and gathering in the rain forest. Moreover, the cultural and historical context in which adults develop influences the timing of major normative life transitions such as marrying, having children, and becoming a grandparent. Each society, through its age grades and age norms, informs its members what they should be doing when during their adult years and what they can expect of life when they become old.

Living Out Adult Lives: Age Norms and Life Transitions

During the 1960s, Bernice Neugarten, Joan Moore, and John Lowe (1965) tried to identify prevailing age norms by asking middle-class, middle-aged adults in Chicago questions about the "best ages" for major life transitions. They found that there was a great deal of consensus about when certain life transitions should ideally occur (see Table 4.4). Interestingly, David Plath and Keiko Ikeda (1975) found that age norms in Japan were quite similar to those in Chicago. But in nonindustrialized countries where people marry young, do not retire from productive roles unless they fall ill, and die at relatively early ages, quite different age norms would prevail. Members of different subcultures or social classes within a single society may also subscribe to different age norms. In the United States, for example, blue-collar men and women believe that transitions such as finishing school and marrying should occur earlier in adulthood than white-collar adults believe they should, suggesting that adults from lower socioeconomic groups are expected to "grow up" more quickly (Zepelin, Sills, & Heath, 1986–1987). It appears, then, that members of any particular culture or subculture share a set of age norms or expectations about how an adult life should be led.

More important, age norms influence how people lead their lives. Once age norms have been internalized, they serve as a **social clock**, a personal sense of when things should be done and when one is ahead of or behind the schedule dictated by age norms (Neugarten, 1968). Influenced by her social clock, for example, a 25-year-old woman in our society might begin to feel that, while her career is progressing right on schedule, she needs to think about getting married before she is "too old." Once she is married, her social "alarm clock" might go off in her mid-30s if she has not had children yet. Another woman may start a family, but then worry that she is not where she should be in her career. Meanwhile, young women in some other cultures are likely to feel that they are off schedule in their development if they are not already married and bearing children as teenagers.

Adults do indeed seem to know whether they are experiencing life transitions early, late, or on time as defined by their society. Age norms, then, as embodied in the social clock, provide people with a basis for evaluating how their adult development is progressing—and with reason to alter their lives if they are off schedule. Age norms and the social clock also affect how easily people adjust to life

Table 4.4 Age norms in our society: Age ranges most adults in the 1960s agreed are appropriate for different adult experiences

EXPERIENCE	AGE RANGE MOST PEOPLE DESIGNATED AS APPROPRIATE OR EXPECTED
Best age for a man to marry	20–25
Best age for a woman to marry	19–24
When most people should become grandparents	45–50
Best age for most people to finish school and go to work	20–22
When most men should be settled on a career	24–26
When most men hold their top jobs	45–50
When most people should be ready to retire	60–65
A young man	18–22
A middle-aged man	40–50
An old man	65–75
A young woman	18–24
A middle-aged woman	40–50
An old woman	60–75
When a man has the most responsibilities	35–50
When a man accomplishes most	40–50
The prime of life for a man	35–50
When a woman has the most responsibilities	25–40
When a woman accomplishes most	30–45
A good-looking woman	20–35

Source: Adapted from Neugarten, Moore, & Lowe, 1965, p. 712, Table 1.

transitions. Life transitions such as having children or retiring typically have more negative effects on us when they occur "off time" than when they occur "on time" (McLanahan & Sorensen, 1985).

As society changes, age norms often change. In fact, a new group of adults was recently asked the same questions about U.S. age norms that were posed 20 years ago (Passuth, Maines, & Neugarten, cited in Neugarten & Neugarten, 1986). Whereas almost 90% of the respondents in the 1960s thought the best age for a woman to marry was between 19 and 24, only 40% of the 1980s sample chose a "best" age in that narrow age range. In the 1960s study, a "young man" was generally believed to be 18 to 22 years old; in the 1980s study, a young man meant anyone from 18 to 40! Clearly something had changed. Specifically, Neugarten (1975, Neugarten & Neugarten, 1986) has argued that we are becoming an increasingly **age-irrelevant society**, a society in which age norms have loosened, boundaries between periods of the life span such as middle age and old age have become blurred, and people are experiencing major life transitions at a wider variety of ages. We *do* see some women today marrying in their early teens while others wait until their 30s after their careers are firmly established—or forgo marriage entirely. We do see mandatory retirement ages being done away with and older adults working, going back to college, jogging, and doing a variety of other things that do not seem to be consistent with more traditional age norms. While age is not yet entirely irrelevant in our society, the age norms that guide adult lives are indeed becoming less rigid (Zepelin et al., 1986–1987).

If our society is moving in the direction of becoming an age-irrelevant society, theories of adult development may need to be revised. Specifically, there would be less basis for claiming that adults progress through age-related stages of development. When, for example, most adults in a society start their careers and marry in their 20s, we can reasonably expect most 20-year-olds to be affected similarly by these experiences and to differ systematically from 30- or 40-year-olds, who are experiencing their own age-related life transitions. But if adults today experience major life transitions at diverse ages, age alone might tell us almost nothing about what an adult is like. We would have to focus instead on how adults are affected by whatever major life events and role changes they experience, *whenever they occur*. In other words, if age were irrelevant in society, it might also become irrelevant in developmental theories! More generally, patterns of adult development can be expected to differ depending on what age norms prevail in a society and how rigid or loose these norms are—another illustration of the importance of the social environment in which development occurs.

Growing Old in a Changing World

What can adults in different cultural settings look forward to when they become old? A few aspects of the aging experience may be universal. As we saw in Chapter 1, all societies seem to define some portion of the life span as old age, although the beginning of old age varies greatly from society to society (Amoss & Harrell, 1981). Moreover, many biological changes and diseases that eventually lead to frailty and dependence are universal. Other than that, the experience of being an old person varies dramatically from society to society and changes over time as a society changes. So, what about the widely held belief that old people were better off in the "old days" (or are better off in more traditional societies today) than they are in modern industrial societies?

Modernization and the Status of the Elderly

In some societies, to be old is to be honored and respected. In rural Taiwan, for example, birthday celebrations are held only when there is something worth celebrating—namely, the 60th, 70th, 88th (rather than 90th, because 9's are considered unlucky), and 100th birthdays (Harrell, 1981). The word for old (*lau*) is sometimes applied to middle-aged or even young adults to signify that they are as worthy of respect as the aged (Harrell, 1981). How many middle-aged adults do you know who would be delighted to be called "old"?

Is it true, then, that elderly people have higher status in traditional societies than in modernized societies? There is at least some truth to this (Finley, 1982; Fry, 1985; Keith, 1985). For example, young adults in less modernized societies such as Nigeria and India are more likely than young adults in more modern societies such as Israel to say that the young can learn much from old people and to say that they look forward to old age themselves (Bengtson, Dowd, Smith, & Inkeles, 1975). However, we can easily find examples of hunter-gatherer or agricultural societies in which the old have low status and modern societies in which they have high status (see Box 4.4).

Box 4.4
There's More Than One Way to Grow Old

There is no universal experience of old age. Consider differences in the aging experience in two traditional hunter-gatherer societies. Among the !Kung in southern Africa, people hunt and gather foods from a bountiful land. Older people are respected, and if they are in good health, they show a great deal of playfulness and vigor after they are relieved of their work roles (Biesele & Howell, 1981). As owners of a water hole and organizers of systems for sharing food, the old have leadership roles. They are valued for their knowledge of the local wildlife, kinship lines, and rituals, and they prepare their grandchildren for adulthood. As one young person said of an elderly woman, "She is an old person and knows everything" (p. 88).

Old age is not as pleasant for the Inuit Eskimo of Alaska, who must survive in a cold and barren environment (Guemple, 1983). Inuit men lose most of their status in society when they are too weak to hunt. The childless old are often verbally abused and fed only grudgingly. Even elderly people with children have sometimes been abandoned or "helped" to die, though Guemple does note that such practices

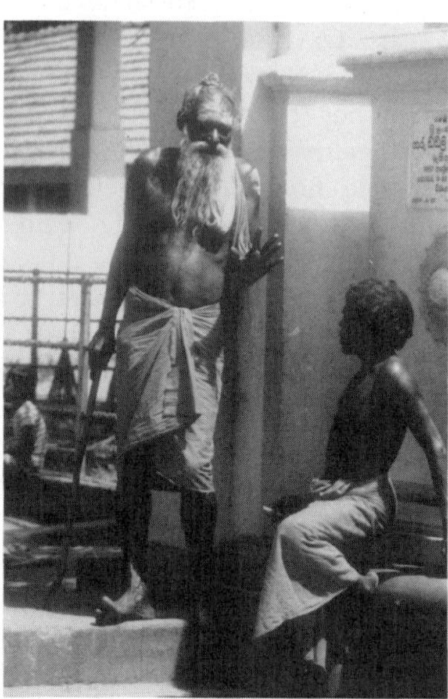

are not as heartless as they sound because the Inuit believe that people are reborn after death.

Just as we can find variation in the status of the old among hunter-gatherer societies, we can find it among modern nations—and even in our own society. For example, in both Japan and China, children have long been taught to hold their aging parents in high esteem and to provide for them. Chinese law actually punishes failures to care for aging parents (Goodstein & Goldstein, 1986). In the United States, older Japanese-Americans are apparently experiencing some strains as their children become more Americanized, but the traditional Japanese values of respect for aging parents are still strong (Osako & Liu, 1986). Elderly Mexican-American people also seem to enjoy especially strong family ties and are important sources of help and advice within the family (Dowd & Bengtson, 1978; Markides, Boldt, & Ray, 1986). Thus older members of minority groups are better off than Anglo-Americans in some respects, though they are also more likely than Anglo-Americans to suffer from disadvantages such as poverty and poor health (Dowd & Bengtson, 1978).

It is obvious from these examples that the aging experience is shaped by the social context in which it occurs. Moreover, different individuals within any culture or subculture grow old in their own unique ways.

What, then, determines the status of older people in a society? According to Pamela Amoss and Stevan Harrell (1981), two factors are critical. The first centers on the contributions that old people make to society, relative to the costs they represent to society. Old people will be valued to the extent that contributions exceed costs. So among the !Kung, old people play many useful roles in society, and, because food is plentiful, it is not too costly to society to provide for the dependent old. By contrast, in the harsh environment in which Eskimos live, an old man who cannot hunt can make little contribution, and if scarce food goes to his belly, the survival of younger members of society may be threatened.

The second factor emphasized by Amoss and Harrell (1981) is the degree of control over resources that older people have. When they own property and have control over inheritances, or when they fill leadership roles in the community, their status is likely to be high. What often, but not always, happens as a society undergoes the rapid social changes of modernization is that older people cannot make as many contributions to society as they once did and lose some of their power. Children turn to schools rather than to old people for the knowledge they need to fill jobs in industry; they give up traditional rituals; they move to cities and can support themselves without help from their elders (Amoss, 1981). Yet sometimes changes can take place in a modern society that improve the status of the elderly. In the 1970s, for example, younger Coast

Salish Indians in Washington State and British Columbia began to want to rediscover their heritage (Amoss, 1981). Suddenly old people, who knew that heritage thoroughly, regained much of the respect they had lost when the tribe first experienced modernization. Older people actively took advantage of this happy turn of events by reviving the old dances, leading them every winter weekend, and recruiting young people to the "old ways." They aggressively helped to create a social environment that was more favorable to them.

In short, social change in itself is not necessarily bad for the elderly. Social changes that increase the contributions of the old to society or give them new powers can increase their status; social changes that make their contributions obsolete, or that make them more costly to support, or that strip them of their power are likely to decrease their status. Since modernization often, though not always, involves these negative social changes, older people sometimes lose their status as their societies modernize. But it is too simple to think that old people are far more valued in nonindustrial societies than they are in modern industrialized societies, for in either kind of society the contributions and power of the elderly can be high or low.

Aging in Our Society

What is the status of older people in our own society? Tamara Hareven (1986) surveyed elderly people and their adult children in Manchester, New Hampshire. She concluded that things have changed in the last hundred years. In the "old days," families were larger and the nest never really emptied—or at least an adult child would feel obligated to remain at home to look after parents as they aged. Thus the elderly adults who were surveyed expected to be cared for by their children and viewed any kind of public assistance as a dreaded last resort. Their middle-aged children acknowledged the old norms and felt an obligation to care for their aging parents. However, they were very aware that times have changed and so did not expect their own children to support them when they became old.

Has the situation of old people deteriorated, then? Not necessarily. Hareven notes that it was not easy for 19th-century families to support their aging members, and that Social Security, pensions, and other sources of income have given older people today the means to live independently without burdening their children. It is true that family support of the old was more important then, and government support is more important now, but Hareven doubts that old people today are worse off. We may not be socialized to respect older people as much as people in some societies are, but our society provides most of them with sufficient financial support to make their aging experience tolerable, and the more advantaged members of the senior set, at least, have more opportunities for leisure and education than ever before (Achenbaum, 1985). These changes hint that the status of old people, while often low in the early stages of modernization, improves again after nations become highly industrialized and achieve a high standard of living (Finley, 1982; Keith, 1985).

In summary, there is no one experience of old age, any more than there is one experience of any other phase of the life span. We can certainly recognize our commonalities with developing individuals in other societies and times, but we must also marvel at the diversity of human experience, even within a particular society. Human development is surely influenced by the physical and social environments in which it occurs. And people of all ages, cultures, and historical periods help to *create* their own environments and to *produce* their own developmental change.

APPLICATIONS: GETTING LIFE OFF TO A GOOD START

The more we learn about important environmental influences on human development, the better able we are to optimize the environment and therefore to optimize development. Although the nature and quality of an individual's environment matters throughout the life span, it seems sensible to do as much as possible to get a baby's life off to a good start. Developmentalists have learned a good deal about how to optimize development in the important prenatal and perinatal periods.

Before Birth

For starters, it would be good for babies if more of them were planned and wanted. Once a woman is pregnant, she should seek good prenatal care so that she will learn how to optimize the well-being of both herself and her unborn child and so that any problems during the pregnancy can be managed appropriately. As we have seen, the guidelines for pregnant women are not that complicated, though they are often violated. They boil down to such practices as eating an adequate diet, protecting oneself against diseases, and avoiding drugs.

Today many couples are also enrolling in childbirth classes. The "natural childbirth" movement arose from the work of Grantly Dick-Read, in England, and Fernand Lamaze, in France. These two obstetricians discovered that many women could give birth painlessly, without medication, if they had been taught to associate childbirth with pleasant feelings and to ready themselves for the process by learning exercises, breathing methods, and relaxation techniques that make childbirth easier (Dick-Read, 1933/1972; Lamaze, 1958). The term "Lamaze" is by now practically a household word. Parents who learn the **Lamaze method** of *prepared* (rather than entirely natural) childbirth typically attend classes for six to eight weeks before the delivery. They learn a set of mental exercises and relaxation techniques, and the father or someone else becomes a coach who assists the mother to train her muscles and perfect her breathing for the event that lies ahead. He will usually be there to help his partner during delivery. Although research is scarce, it suggests that women who regularly attend Lamaze or similar childbirth classes are indeed more relaxed during labor, less often need medication, have an easier time delivering, and have more positive attitudes toward themselves, their families, and the childbirth process (Wideman & Singer, 1984).

Giving Birth

Today's women have more choices about how and where they want to give birth than women 20 years ago did. Gone are the days when almost all women gave birth

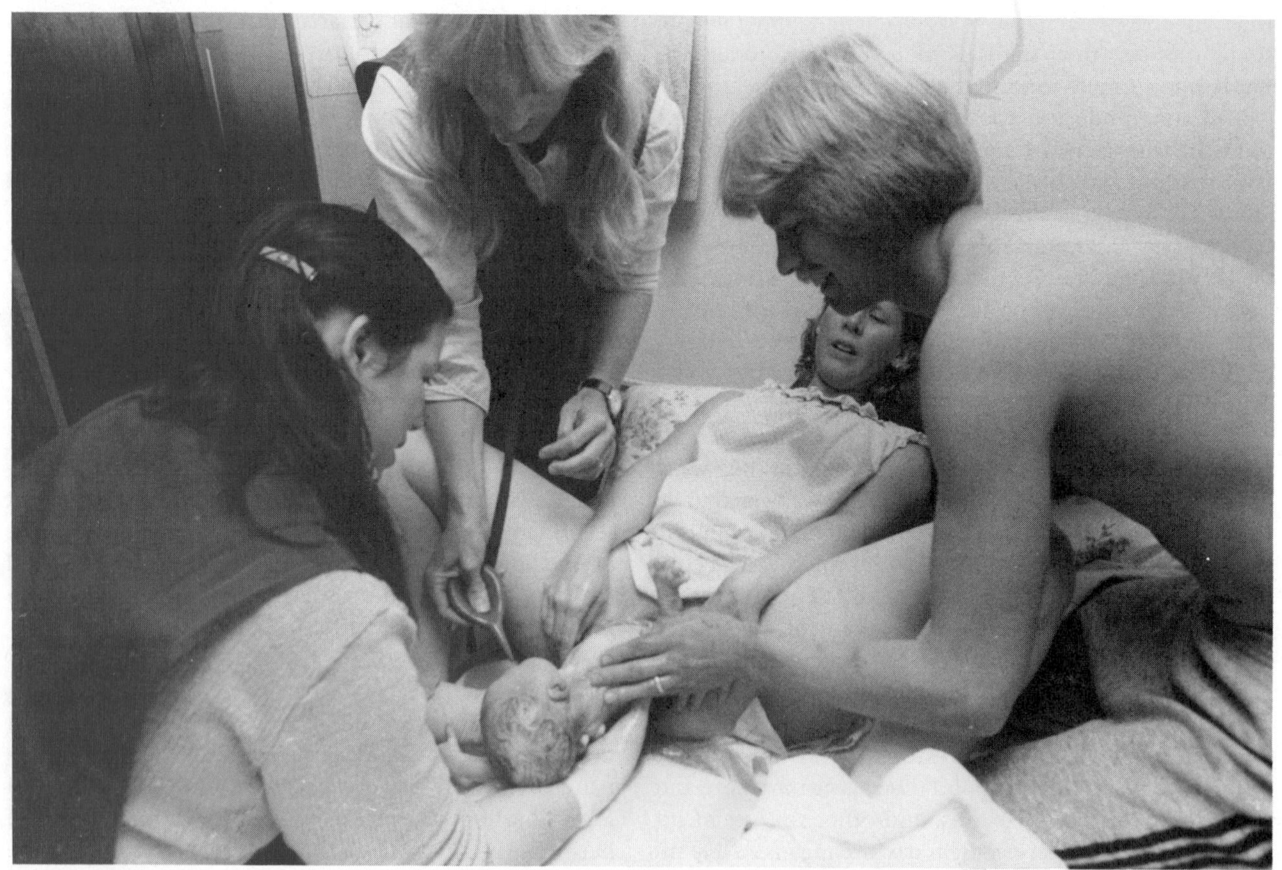

Birthing rooms provide many of the comforts of home within the protective walls of a hospital.

in a hospital, on their backs with their legs in stirrups, and under the influence of medication. For some years there has been a movement to return to the days when birth was a natural family event that occurred at home rather than a medical problem to be solved with high technology (Edwards & Waldorf, 1984).

Today, more and more couples are opting for home deliveries, often with the aid of one of the growing number of certified nurse-midwives who are trained in nonsurgical obstetrics. Those who favor home delivery argue that the relaxed atmosphere of the home setting calms the mother, making her delivery quicker and easier. Although the mothers who choose home delivery are usually those who can expect an easy time of it, the fact that mortality is low for infants born at home suggests that the risks of home deliveries are not great for healthy mothers who have received good prenatal care and who are at low risk for birth complications (MacFarlane, 1977).

Obstetricians in the United States have resisted the home birth movement, partly because they fear birth complications, and partly because home births threaten their monopoly in the childbirth field (Edwards & Waldorf, 1984). In response to criticisms of conventional delivery practices and the growing home birth movement, many hospitals have developed birthing rooms, or **alternative birth centers**, that provide a homelike atmosphere but still make medical technology available (Klee, 1986). Other birth centers have been developed independently of hospitals. In either case, mates or other close companions, and often even the couple's children, can be present during labor, and healthy infants can remain in the same room with their mothers (rooming-in) rather than spending their first days in the hospital nursery. Linnea Klee (1986) has found that mothers who choose alternative birth centers often want a more comfortable delivery but also want access to medical technologies "in case something goes wrong." By comparison, mothers who choose home delivery more often distrust the medical establishment. Today, the woman whose pregnancy is going smoothly has considerable freedom to give birth as she chooses.

After the Birth

So now that you have a baby, what do you do? New parents are often uncertain about how to relate to their babies and may find the period after birth stressful. T. Berry Brazelton (1979) believes that parents can be helped to appreciate their baby's competencies—and to feel competent themselves as parents. He has developed a newborn assessment technique, the *Brazelton Neonatal Behavioral Assessment Scale*, that is considerably more elaborate than the Apgar screening device. It assesses the strength of 20 infant reflexes as well as the infant's responses to 26 situations (for example, reactions to cuddling, general irritability, and orienting to the examiner's face and voice). This test can be used to identify infants with neurological problems, but it is also used to teach parents to understand their babies as individuals and to appreciate many of the pleasing competencies that they possess. During "Brazelton training," parents observe the test being administered and also learn how to administer it themselves to elicit pleasing responses such as smiles from their babies. Such training is believed to be especially appropriate for parents whose babies are sluggish or irritable and might be difficult to love.

Indeed, mothers of high-risk infants who receive Brazelton training become more responsive in their face-to-face interactions with their babies than mothers who do not, and their infants score higher on the Brazelton test one month later (Widmayer & Field, 1980). In addition, compared to untrained parents, trained parents are more knowledgeable about infant behavior, more confident of their caretaking abilities, and more satisfied with their infants (Myers, 1982). Although this brief intervention does not always accomplish wonders (see Belsky, 1985; Worobey & Brazelton, 1986), it appears to be a good way to help parents and babies get started right.

Giving the seriously premature or low birth weight infant a good start is a more difficult undertaking. Neonatal intensive care units have greatly increased the odds that babies who are at high risk will survive the perinatal period (Kopp & Krakow, 1983). Yet much is still being learned about how to optimize the rather abnormal environment in which these infants spend the first several weeks of life. For instance, while it has been known for some time that the high doses of oxygen that were formerly administered in intensive care units were damaging the immature eyes of babies and causing blindness, the damaging effects of bright lighting were discovered more recently (Glass et al., 1985).

Then there is the problem of providing high-risk infants with the stimulation they need in order to develop normally. Not long ago, these infants simply lay in their isolettes receiving little stimulation and little human contact. They were, in effect, deprived of the sensory stimulation that they would have received either in the womb or in a normal home environment. Today, their perinatal sensory environment is much improved, thanks to research on the effects of sensory stimulation programs. Many of these programs have centered on the "body senses" because much bodily stimulation is provided in the womb. So preterm infants have been stroked, held upright, rocked, and even put on waterbeds (see Schaefer, Hatcher, & Barglow, 1980). For example, Frank Scafidi and his colleagues (1986) provided preterm infants with just three 15-minute stimulation sessions a day over 10 days. These babies' bodies were massaged and their limbs were flexed and extended. Compared to control group infants, stimulated babies gained more weight, showed more mature behaviors on the Brazelton scale, and were able to leave the hospital sooner. Kathryn Barnard and Helen Bee (1983) found that preterm babies exposed to a combination of bodily and auditory stimulation in the hospital—15-minute doses of a rocking bed and a heartbeat sound—showed lasting benefits, for they scored higher than control infants on a measure of infant mental development at age 2. It appears that fairly simple and inexpensive environmental changes and special stimulation programs can help the high-risk infant develop normally.

High-risk infants can also benefit from programs that teach their parents how to provide them with sensitive and responsive care once they are home (Barrera, Rosenbaum, & Cunningham, 1986). One such program allowed low birth weight children to fully catch up to normal birth weight children in mental development by the age of 4 (Rauh, Achenbach, Nurcombe, Howell, & Teti, 1988). It is just as important to keep development on track after the perinatal period comes to a close as it is to get it started on the right track from the beginning.

REFLECTIONS

After studying Chapter 3 and this chapter, do you have a fuller appreciation of how both nature and nurture contribute to human development? We apologize if we have dwelt too much on what can go wrong—on the genetic defects, the prenatal risk factors, the birth complications, and so on. Certainly these sorts of problems show that the wrong genes or the wrong early environment can have profound impacts on development, but they make for depressing reading. Let's now emphasize the positive.

First, we know more about these problems today than ever before and can better prevent and treat them to allow more and more children to survive and thrive. Second, we can only marvel at the strengths of the human organism. The vast majority of us come into existence with an amazingly effective genetic program to guide our development. Most of us, whether in this culture or another, also receive the benefits of a normal human environment, an environment that joins forces with our genetic program to promote normal development. Perhaps most remarkably, it seems to take very adverse conditions over a long period of time—conditions like those experienced by Genie—to *keep* us from developing normally. Special interventions or a favorable home environment later in life can often get abnormal infants back on course, and even children who suffer all sorts of insults and indignities during their early years sometimes manage to become competent adults nonetheless. It's almost as if nature defies us to spoil her plan.

At the same time, we are clearly influenced by our experiences throughout the life span. Being a developing person today is not quite like being a developing person in the 15th or 19th centuries because we are partly shaped by the historical context in which we live. Being a developing person in central Africa is not quite like being a developing person in the United States because development is embedded in a social and cultural context. We will encounter numerous examples in the remainder of this text of the positive and negative impacts that environmental forces can have on the development of children and adults. But we will certainly want to keep in mind the idea that we are not just the passive recipients of environmental forces. Because we often choose our environmental niches, and because we affect those around us just as we are being affected by them, we are active players in our own developmental dramas.

SUMMARY POINTS

1. The environment of human development includes all events or conditions outside the person that affect or are affected by the person's development, including both the physical and the

social environment. As Bronfenbrenner's ecological model emphasizes, development depends on the ongoing *reciprocal* transactions between a changing person and a changing environment.

2. Environmental influences on development begin at conception as the zygote begins its passage through three stages of prenatal development: (1) the germinal period, (2) the period of the embryo, and (3) the period of the fetus.

3. The prenatal physical environment, as influenced by the age of the mother, her health, and a variety of teratogens, can significantly affect development, especially during sensitive periods when the embryo's organs are growing rapidly.

4. The perinatal environment surrounding birth, including the social environment, is also important. Childbirth is a three-step process consisting of the contractions of labor, delivery, and the afterbirth (expulsion of the placenta). Risks to the baby include anoxia and the effects of medications given to the mother.

5. Early emotional bonding, though pleasant, does not seem necessary for loving attachments to form.

6. Some problems created by prenatal and perinatal hazards are long-lasting, but many babies at risk show remarkable resilience and outgrow their problems.

7. Infants are not too young to be influenced by their cultural context; survival, economic, and self-actualization goals of parenting are universal, but parents in each culture or subculture emphasize the specific traits and skills most necessary for adult life in their particular societal context. Because child-rearing practices differ from society to society, findings regarding human development are influenced by the culture and time in which research is conducted.

8. During adolescence, children are socially redefined as adults, sometimes through rites of passage. In our society the passage to adulthood is prolonged and ill defined, and youth cannot always rely on adult guidance owing to rapid social change.

9. Many life transitions during adulthood are guided by the age norms that prevail in a society, although Bernice Neugarten has suggested that our society is becoming age-irrelevant.

10. The experience of growing old also varies widely across cultures and historical periods. The status of older adults largely depends on their contributions to society (relative to their costs) and on their control of resources.

11. In our own society, families provide less support to aging parents than they formerly provided, but government programs and an increased standard of living allow most elderly people to live comfortable and satisfying lives.

12. Ways of getting human lives off to a good start include prepared-childbirth classes, natural deliveries, and neonatal intensive care units that help at-risk infants survive. Some researchers are having luck with interventions designed to help parents understand and respond appropriately to their new babies.

KEY TERMS

age-irrelevant society
age norms
age of viability
alternative birth centers
amnion
anoxia
Apgar test
blastula
breech presentation
Cesarean section
chorion
critical period
cultural relativity
culture
ecological approach
engrossment
environment
exosystem
fetal alcohol syndrome
germinal period
Lamaze method
macrosystem
mesosystem
microsystem
neonate
nonnormative transition
normative transition
perinatal environment
period of the embryo
period of the fetus
placenta
prenatal environment
postpartum blues
rites of passage
rubella
short gestation baby
small for date
social clock
socialization
syphilis
teratogen
testosterone
thalidomide
umbilical cord

CHAPTER

5

THE PHYSICAL SELF

Steven's brain cells are dying at a rapid rate, and his muscles are weak. His heart does not function at peak efficiency. He has difficulty with the simple task of holding his head upright when he sits. He reacts slowly and does not learn or remember things well. What is your best guess about Steven's age and condition? Perhaps you guess that he is very old and has lost many of his capacities through normal aging. Or perhaps you figure that aging itself would not result in changes this extreme, and that Steven must therefore be an old man with Alzheimer's disease or some other senile brain disease or neurological disorder. But did it occur to you that Steven matches quite closely the description of a normal newborn baby?

This is not to suggest that young infants and old people with brain diseases are alike. It *is* saying that there will be some surprises in store in this chapter as we examine physical development over the life span. Brain cells do indeed die off in massive numbers early in life. They must do so to allow the development of an ever more sophisticated brain—a brain that regulates the heart and other organs to keep us alive even while it directs highly coordinated movements and engages in abstract thinking.

This chapter is about the development and aging of the human body. It traces changes in the body's size and proportions as well as changes within certain selected body systems. The nervous and endocrine systems get emphasis because we could not function at all without them. We will also look at the reproductive system: its maturation during adolescence and the changes it undergoes during adulthood. And we will examine the physical self in action: the development of motor skills and the changes in physical fitness and physical behavior that occur during adulthood. As we go, we will be trying to identify influences on physical development and aging, so that we can better understand why some children develop more rapidly than others do and why some older adults age more slowly than others do. To lay the groundwork for all of this, let us briefly examine the nature of the human body.

THE BODY'S SYSTEMS AND DEVELOPMENT

The human body is a marvelously complex system of organs working together to make the full range of human behavior possible. As we saw in Chapter 4, all the major organs of the body take shape during the prenatal period. Each bodily system—the digestive system, the circulatory system, the nervous system, the reproductive system, and so on—has its own orderly timetable of development. For example, the nervous system develops very rapidly, completing most of its important growth by the end of infancy. The reproductive system, by contrast, is slower to develop than most of the body's organs and systems and does not reach its time of rapid growth until adolescence (see Figure 5.1).

As a prelude to our discussion of physical development, it is useful to introduce two bodily systems that are critical in human growth and development. If we want to

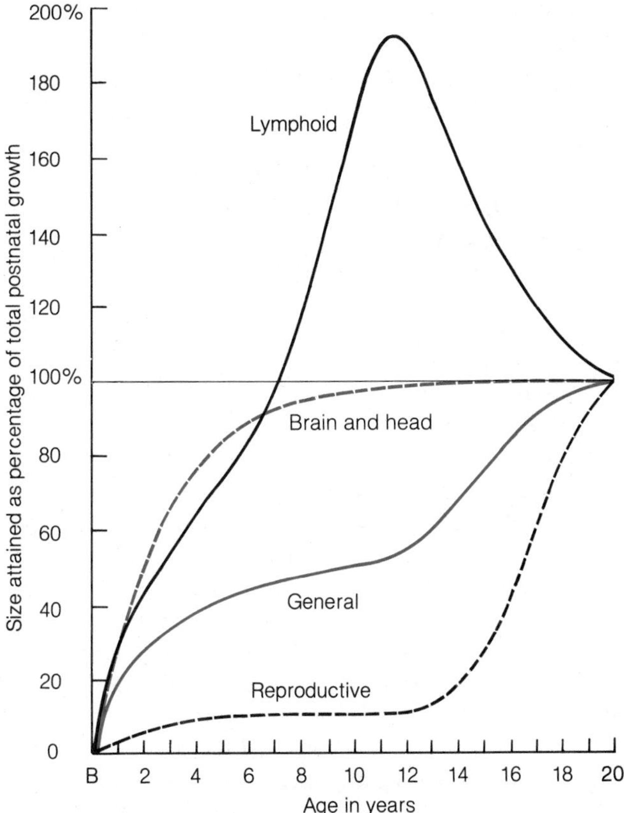

Figure 5.1 Growth curves for different body systems. Each curve plots the size of a group of organs or body parts as a percentage of their size at age 20. Thus size at age 20 is the 100% level on the vertical scale. The "general" curve describes changes in the body's size as well as the growth of respiratory and digestive organs and musculature. The brain and head grow more rapidly than the body in general, and the reproductive organs are the slowest to reach adult size. (The lymph nodes and other parts of the lymphoid system, which function as part of the immune system, also grow rapidly and actually exceed adult size during late childhood and adolescence.) (From Tanner, J. M., 1962)

understand physical growth and sexual maturation, we must understand the workings of the endocrine (hormonal) system. And if we want to know why adults are both physically and mentally more competent than infants are, we must understand the nervous system.

The Endocrine System and Growth

How *does* the human body grow? One way to answer that question is to point to the genes, for physical maturation is indeed guided by a genetic program. All humans have a distinctly human genetic makeup that makes them develop physically in similar directions and at similar rates. Individual heredity also influences the individual's rate of physical development and final size—in interaction, of course, with environmental factors such as whether a child's diet includes milk and other nutritious foods.

But how are genetic messages translated into action? It is here that the endocrine system plays its role. **Endocrine glands** secrete chemicals called *hormones* directly into the bloodstream. Perhaps the most critical of the endocrine glands is the **pituitary gland**, the so-called master gland located at the base of the brain. It is directly controlled by a part of the brain called the *hypothalamus*, and it triggers the release of hormones from all other endocrine glands by sending special hormone messages to those glands. Moreover, the pituitary produces **human growth hormone**, which stimulates the rapid growth and development of body cells. Children who lack this hormone are likely to stand only a little over four feet (or 130 cm) tall as adults (Tanner, 1978).

The *thyroid gland* also plays an important role in growth and development, as well as in the development of the nervous system. Babies who are born with a thyroid deficiency soon become mentally handicapped if their condition goes unnoticed and untreated (Tanner, 1978). Children who develop a thyroid deficiency later in life will not suffer brain damage since most of their brain growth has already occurred, but their growth will slow down drastically.

In Chapter 4, we encountered still another critical role of the endocrine system. A male fetus will not develop male reproductive organs unless (1) a gene on his Y chromosome triggers the development of the testes (which are endocrine glands), and (2) the testes secrete the most important of the male hormones, **testosterone.** Male sex hormones become highly important again during adolescence. When people speak of adolescence as a time when the hormones are flowing, they are quite right. The testes of a male secrete large quantities of testosterone and other male hormones (called **androgens**). These hormones trigger the adolescent growth spurt, as well as the development of the male sex organs, converting a boy into a man (Tanner, 1978). They also contribute to sexual motivation during adulthood.

Meanwhile, other endocrine glands in adolescent

girls — the *adrenal glands* — are secreting androgenlike hormones that result in their growth spurt, as well as in the development of pubic and bodily hair (Tanner, 1978). The ovaries (also endocrine glands) produce larger quantities of the primary female hormone, **estrogen**, and progesterone. These hormones are responsible for the development of the breasts and the female sex organs and for controlling menstrual cycles. The roles of different endocrine glands in physical growth and development are summarized in Table 5.1.

In adulthood, endocrine glands continue to secrete hormones under the direction of the hypothalamus and the pituitary to regulate bodily processes (Andres & Tobin, 1977). For example, thyroid hormones help the body's cells metabolize (break down) foods into usable nutrients, and the adrenal glands help the body cope with stress. Throughout the life span, then, the endocrine system works together with the brain and nervous system to keep the body on an even keel. As we will see in Chapter 17, some theorists even believe that changes in the functioning of the endocrine glands late in life bring about aging and death.

In short, the endocrine system is part of the reason we grow during childhood and mature during adolescence, why our bodily systems function effectively over the life span, and possibly why they do not function as well very late in life. The brain (particularly the hypothalamus) and the endocrine system work as a unit to accomplish these feats. But the brain has many other tasks to perform.

The Nervous System and Behavior

None of the physical or mental achievements that we regard as human would be possible without a functioning nervous system. By examining the basic structure of the nervous system here, we can ready ourselves to examine later in the chapter how it develops and ages.

The nervous system consists of the brain and spinal cord (central nervous system) and neural tissue extending into all parts of the body (peripheral nervous system). Its basic unit is a specialized cell called a **neuron**. Neurons have the most complex and varied shapes of any body cell. Figure 5.2 shows what a neuron in the spinal cord looks like. Suppose that this neuron were connected to a muscle in your right index finger. If you wanted to move that finger voluntarily, neurons in your brain would have to transmit signals to this neuron, which in turn would activate your muscle. Although neurons come in many shapes and sizes, they have some common features. *Dendrites* receive signals from other neurons. The *axon* of a neuron *transmits* signals — to another neuron or, in our example, directly to a muscle in your index finger. During development, axons become covered by a waxy material called **myelin**, which acts like insulation to speed the transmission of neural impulses. It is at the ends of axons that specialized chemicals called *neurotransmitters* are stored. The point at which the axon of one neuron makes a connection with another neuron is called a **synapse**. By releasing neurotransmitters, one neuron can either stimulate or inhibit the action of another neuron.

Table 5.1 Hormonal influences on growth and development

ENDOCRINE GLAND	HORMONES PRODUCED	EFFECTS ON GROWTH AND DEVELOPMENT
Pituitary	Activating hormones	Signal other endocrine glands to secrete their hormones
	Growth hormone	Helps regulate growth from birth through adolescence
Thyroid	Thyroxine	Affects growth and development of the brain and helps regulate growth of the body during childhood
Adrenal glands	Adrenal androgens	Stimulates the adolescent growth spurt, pubic hair, and axillary hair in females; supplements the adolescent growth spurt in males
Testes	Testosterone	Is responsible for differentiation of the male reproductive system during the prenatal period; triggers the male growth spurt and sexual maturation during adolescence
Ovaries	Estrogen Progesterone	Trigger sexual maturation in females and are responsible for regulating the menstrual cycle

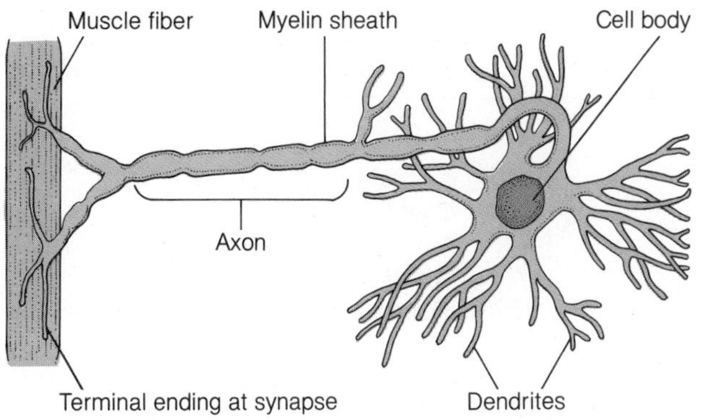

Figure 5.2 A neuron in the spinal cord. Its long axon, forming part of a bundle of nerve fibers or a nerve, connects with and stimulates a muscle. Other types of neurons form neuron-to-neuron connections or receive sensory information from the environment. Neurons have the most complex and varied forms of all body cells.

Now imagine a brain with as many as 100 billion of these neurons, each communicating through synapses to thousands of others (Cowan, 1979). The brain is complexly organized into systems of interconnected neurons. At birth, the most fully developed areas of the brain are the more primitive or "lower" portions such as the spinal cord, brain stem, and midbrain. These portions of the brain are adequate to control the infant's states of waking and sleeping, to permit simple motor reactions, and to regulate such biological functions as digestion, respiration, and elimination, making life possible. But we would be little different from snakes if the higher centers of the brain did not develop. It is the convoluted outer covering of the brain—the **cerebral cortex**—that is organized into areas that control voluntary body movements, perception, and higher intellectual functions such as learning, thinking, and speaking.

Now, why are young infants less physically and mentally capable than adults? Is it that adults have more neurons than infants do? More synapses connecting neurons? A more organized pattern of connections? And what happens to the brain in later life? If old people are forgetful or even "senile," does this mean that their neurons have died off or do not function as effectively as they once did? This chapter explores how the brain develops and ages, and how changes in the nervous system enable children to master new developmental tasks but may make it harder for some older people to function. It also explores three aspects of the physical self in each phase of the life span: the body (its size, composition, and functioning), the brain, and the use of body and brain in physical activities such as locomotion and finely controlled movements.

THE INFANT

Tremendous amounts of growth, brain development, and physical development occur during the two years of infancy. Understanding the newborn's capacities and limitations brings a fuller appreciation of the dramatic changes that take place between birth and adulthood.

A Profile of the Newborn

Newborns used to be viewed as helpless little organisms unprepared for the cold, cruel world. Now we know that they are far better prepared for life than that. What *are* the capabilities of the newborn?

Certainly one of the newborn's greatest strengths is a full set of useful **reflexes**. A reflex is an unlearned and automatic response to a stimulus, as when the eye automatically blinks in response to a puff of air. Reflexes can be contrasted with the newborn's spontaneous arm waving, leg kicking, and thrashing, movements that have no obvious stimulus. Table 5.2 lists some reflexes that can be readily observed in all normal newborns. These seemingly simple reactions are actually quite graceful, varied, and complex patterns of behavior (Prechtl, 1981).

Some reflexes are important to survival—for example, the breathing reflex (useful for obvious reasons), the eyeblink reflex (which protects against bright lights or foreign particles), and the sucking reflex (needed to obtain food). Other reflexes, so-called primitive ones, do not appear to be nearly as useful. Some are believed to be remnants of our evolutionary history that have outlived their purpose. The *Babinski reflex* is a good example. Why would it be adaptive for infants to fan their toes when the bottoms of their feet are stroked? We don't know. Other primitive reflexes may have some use, at least in some cultures. For example, the grasping reflex may help infants who are carried in slings or on their mothers' hips to hang on. And some primitive reflexes—for example, the grasping reflex

Table 5.2 Major reflexes present in full-term newborns

REFLEXES	DEVELOPMENTAL COURSE	SIGNIFICANCE
Survival reflexes		
Breathing reflex	Permanent	Provides oxygen and expels carbon dioxide
Eyeblink reflex	Permanent	Protects eyes from bright light or foreign objects
Pupillary reflex: Constriction of pupils to bright light; dilation to dark or dimly lit surroundings	Permanent	Protects against bright lights; adapts visual system to low illumination
Rooting reflex: Turning of cheek in direction of a tactile (touch) stimulus	Gradually weakens over the first 6 months of life	Orients child to breast or bottle
Sucking reflex: Sucking on objects placed (or taken) into mouth	Is gradually modified by experience over the first few months of life	Allows child to take in nutrients
Swallowing reflex	Is permanent but modified by experience	Allows child to take in nutrients and protects against choking
Primitive reflexes		
Babinski reflex: Fanning and then curling toes when bottom of foot is stroked	Usually disappears within the first 8 months–1 year of life	Presence at birth and disappearance in first year indicate normal neurological development
Grasping reflex: Curling of fingers around objects (such as a finger) that touch baby's palm	Disappears in first 3–4 months; is replaced by a voluntary grasp	Presence at birth and later disappearance indicate normal neurological development
Moro reflex: Loud noise or sudden change in position of baby's head will cause baby to throw arms outward, arch back, and then bring arms toward each other as if to hold onto something	Disappears over the first 6–7 months; however, child continues to react to unexpected noises or a loss of bodily support by showing a startle reflex (which does not disappear)	Presence at birth and later disappearance (or evolution into the startle reflex) indicate normal neurological development
Swimming reflex: Infant immersed in water will display active movements of arms and legs and involuntarily hold breath (thus staying afloat for some time)	Disappears in the first 4–6 months	Presence at birth and later disappearance indicate normal neurological development
Stepping reflex: Infants held upright so that their feet touch a flat surface will step as if to walk	Disappears in first 8 weeks unless infant has regular opportunities to practice it	Presence at birth and later disappearance indicate normal neurological development

Note: Preterm infants may show little or no evidence of primitive reflexes at birth, and their survival reflexes are likely to be irregular or immature. However, the missing reflexes will typically appear soon after birth and will disappear a little later than they do among full-term infants.

and the stepping reflex—may be forerunners of useful voluntary behaviors that develop later in infancy (Fentress & McLeod, 1986).

Primitive reflexes typically disappear during the early months of infancy. They are controlled by the lower, "subcortical" areas of the brain and are lost as the higher centers of the cerebral cortex begin to control behavior. Even if many primitive reflexes are not useful to infants, they have been extremely useful in diagnosing neurological problems. If such reflexes are *not* present at birth—or if they last too long in infancy—we know that something is wrong with a baby's nervous system. The existence of reflexes at birth tells us that infants come to life ready to respond to stimulation in adaptive ways. The disappearance of certain reflexes tells us that the nervous system is developing normally.

Another strength of newborns is their senses. As we saw in Chapter 4, the sensory systems are developing before birth, and as we shall see in Chapter 6, all of the major senses are functioning reasonably well at birth. Newborns do indeed see and hear, and they respond to tastes, smells, and touches in predictable ways too.

The sucking reflex is one of the newborn's most adaptive and frequently used innate reflexes.

Still another strength of newborns is that they are capable of learning from their experiences in simple ways. They can, for example, learn to suck faster if sucking produces a pleasant-tasting sugary liquid rather than plain water (Kron, 1966). In other words, they can change their behavior according to its consequences. The infant's learning capabilities are discussed in much greater detail in Chapter 8.

Finally, the fact that newborns have organized patterns of daily activity is considered another sign that they are well equipped for life. **Infant states** are the different levels of consciousness that newborns experience in a typical day; they range from sleeping to crying (see Table 5.3).

The fact that infants progress through these different states during a typical day suggests that their physiological processes are well organized. Infants rarely have problems establishing regular sleep cycles, for example, unless their nervous systems are abnormal in some way (Willemsen, 1979). Research on infant states also makes it clear that newborns have a good deal of individuality. In a study by Brown (1964), one newborn was in an alert state only 4% of the time, whereas another was alert 37% of the time. Similarly, one newborn cried only 17% of the time, but another spent fully 39% of its time crying. Such variations from infant to infant have obvious implications for parents. It is likely to be far more pleasant to tend a baby who is often alert and who rarely cries than it is to interact with a baby who is rarely attentive and frequently fussy.

During the first few days of life, newborns average about 70% of their time (16–18 hours a day) sleeping and only 2 to 3 hours in a state of alert inactivity in which they are actively taking in what is going on around them (Berg,

Table 5.3 Infant states described by Wolff (1966)

STATE	DESCRIPTION
Regular sleep	Babies lie still with their eyes closed and unmoving. Breathing is regular and the skin is pale. The infant does not respond to mild stimuli such as soft voices or flashing lights.
Irregular sleep	Babies breathe irregularly, and their eyes may move underneath their closed eyelids (in rapid eye movements, or REMs). The infant often grimaces, jerks, and twitches and may stir a bit in response to soft sounds or flashes of light.
Drowsiness	Drowsy babies who are just waking or falling asleep will intermittently open and close their eyes. They are fairly inactive, and their eyes have a glazed look when open. Breathing is regular but more rapid than in regular sleep.
Alert inactivity	Here we have a baby who scans the environment with interest. Head, trunk, and lip movements may occur, and breathing is fast and irregular. This is the state in which infants are most susceptible to learning.
Waking activity	Hungry or otherwise uncomfortable babies may wake suddenly and show sudden bursts of vigorous activity in which they twist their bodies and kick their legs. Their eyes are open, but they are not actively attending to their surroundings as they are in a state of alert inactivity. Breathing is irregular.
Crying	Babies often move from waking activity into a crying state in which they first whimper and then burst into loud, agitated cries accompanied by strong kicks and arm movements.

Adkinson, & Strock, 1973; Hutt, Lenard, & Prechtl, 1969). They normally take seven to ten daily naps of about 45 minutes to 2 hours each. Somewhere between 3 and 7 months of age, infants reach a milestone that parents appreciate: They begin to sleep through the night (Berg & Berg, 1979).

There is good reason to believe that young infants make good use of their sleep time. At birth, babies spend about half of their sleeping hours in a state of active, irregular sleep called **REM sleep** because of the rapid eye movements that occur during this phase. Yet infants older than 6 months spend only 25% to 30% of their total sleep in REM sleep, and the percentage drops to about 20% over the rest of the life span. During REM sleep, brain activity is more typical of wakefulness than of regular (non-REM) sleep, and adults awakened from REM sleep usually report that they were dreaming. Why, then, do young infants spend so much time in REM sleep? Are they dreaming? It is hard to know. Possibly REM sleep during the first months of life provides the nervous system with stimulation that enables it to mature (Boismier, 1977; Roffwarg, Muzio, & Dement, 1966). Newborns who are given extra stimulation while they are awake spend less time in REM sleep than infants who do not receive this stimulation (Boismier, 1977). Perhaps REM sleep declines so dramatically at 4 to 6 months of age because the brain has been rapidly maturing, the infant is becoming more alert, and the stimulation provided by REM activity is no longer needed.

Newborn infants are indeed competent and ready for life. They have a wide range of reflexes, functioning senses, a capacity to learn, and an organized pattern of waking and sleeping. But think for a moment about newborns in comparison to adults: Newborns are also quite limited beings. Their brains are not nearly as developed as they will be by the end of infancy. Yes, they move spontaneously and display a wide range of adaptive reflexes. They even reach in the direction of a moving object that they are watching, showing a primitive form of eye/hand coordination (Hofsten, 1982, 1984). But their capacity to move *voluntarily and intentionally*—for example, to grasp objects and bring them to their mouths—is limited, and they are not yet mobile. Consequently, they cannot meet their most basic needs. And although their senses are working, they just as certainly cannot *interpret* something like the images on a television screen in the way an older individual can. They can learn, but they are slow learners compared to older children, often requiring many learning trials before they make the connection between stimulus and response. And while we are faulting them, we might as well note that having a repertoire of cries is a far cry (so to speak) from having command of a human language that can express an infinite number of ideas. Newborns are clearly lacking important social and communication skills.

In short, newborns have *both* strengths and limitations. The strengths indicate that newborns are actively taking in what is happening around them, are able to adapt to their environments, and possess capacities that can serve as building blocks for later development. But the limitations of the newborn tell us that *much* remains to be accomplished during development.

The Body: Physical Growth

Newborns are typically about 20 inches long and weigh 7 to 7½ pounds. They do not remain tiny for long, for in the first few months of life they are gaining nearly an ounce of weight a day and an inch in length each month. By age 2, they have already attained about half of their eventual adult height and weigh 27 to 30 pounds. If they continued at their rapid pace of growth until age 18, they would stand about 12 feet 3 inches and weigh several tons!

You have probably noticed that young infants also seem to be all head. That is because growth proceeds in a **cephalocaudal** direction: literally, from the head to the tail. This pattern is clear in Figure 5.3: The head is way ahead of the rest of the body during the prenatal period and accounts for about 25% of the newborn's length. But the head accounts for only 12% of an adult's height. During the first year after birth, the trunk grows the fastest; in the second year, the legs are the fastest growing segment of the body.

While infants are growing from the head downward, they are also growing from the center outward to the extremities. This **proximodistal** direction of development can be seen during the prenatal period, when the chest and internal organs form before the arms, hands, and fingers. During the first year of life, the trunk is rapidly filling out while the arms remain short and stubby until they undergo their own period of rapid development. Overall, then, physical growth is orderly, obeying both the cephalocaudal and proximodistal principles of development.

Meanwhile, the bones and muscles are developing fast. At birth, most of the infant's bones are soft, pliable, and difficult to break. They are too small and flexible to allow newborns to sit up or balance themselves when pulled to a standing position. The soft cartilage-like tissues of the young infant gradually ossify (harden) into bony material as calcium and other minerals are deposited in them. More bones will develop, too, and they will become more closely interconnected. As for muscles, young infants are relative weaklings. They have all the muscle cells they will ever have, but strength will grow as muscles grow larger. Muscular development also proceeds in cephalocaudal and proximodistal directions.

The rapid physical and muscular growth that occurs during infancy helps make possible the drastic changes in motor development that we see during these two years. The other necessary ingredient is a more fully developed brain.

The Brain

Infants amaze us with their rapid development because their brains develop so rapidly. The brain develops at its fastest rate prenatally and in the early months after birth. Indeed, the last three months of prenatal life and the first two years after birth have been termed the period of the *brain growth spurt* (Brierley, 1976). First, new neurons are being formed rapidly during the prenatal period and this process continues for several months after birth (Rosenzweig & Leiman, 1982). Second, the brain is increasing in size and weight. At birth, a baby's brain is only 25% of its eventual adult weight. By age 2, it has already reached 75% of its adult weight. Third, the neurons are rapidly being covered with waxy myelin insulation that increases their ability to transmit signals effectively. Fourth, levels of neurotransmitters are increasing (Goldman-Rakic, Isseroff, Schwartz, & Bugbee, 1983). And fifth, neurons are organizing themselves into interconnected groups that take on specialized functions such as the control of motor behavior or visual perception.

However, neurons are dying off in massive numbers during this very period of most rapid brain development. Researchers estimate that almost *half* of the neurons produced in early life also die in early life (Janowsky & Finlay, 1986). Meanwhile, neurons are sprouting many dendritic branches and forming many synapses, or connections, with other neurons that later disappear. In one study, the number of synapses between cortical neurons grew to a peak at about age 1 or 2 and then declined thereafter (Hut-

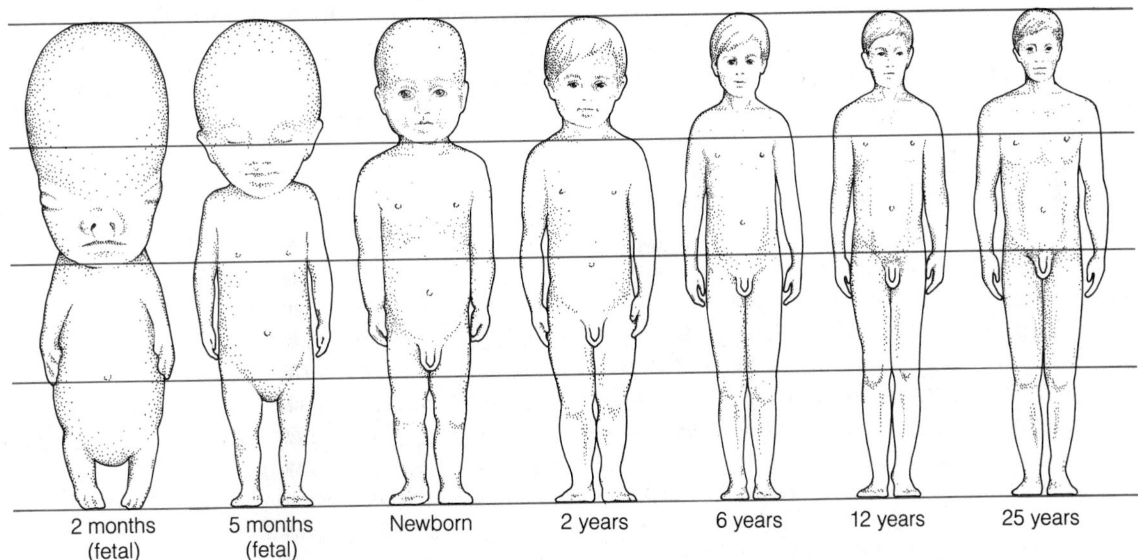

Figure 5.3 Changes in the proportions of the human body from the fetal period through adulthood.

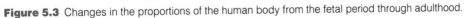

tenlocher, 1979). If we liken the developing brain to a house under construction, we must imagine that the builder decides to build many rooms and many hallways between rooms and later goes back and knocks about half of them out! It does not seem very efficient, but it is. Basically, neurons and synapses that get frequent use survive; those that are unused or faulty disappear (Cowan, 1979; Shepherd, 1988). It is like waiting to see which rooms and hallways get the most traffic before deciding which to retain in the final house. Losses of neural tissue apparently lead to developmental gains.

The brain of the fetus and young infant has a great deal of **plasticity**: Its cells are receptive to environmental influences, both damaging and growth-producing ones. We saw in Chapter 4 that the developing brain is very vulnerable to damage from drugs and diseases. But at the same time, this immature brain can recover from many injuries. Its cells are not yet fully committed to their specialized functions, so they can take over for brain cells that die (Spreen, Tupper, Risser, Tuokko, & Edgell, 1984). The immature brain is also plastic in the sense that it is highly responsive to environmental stimulation. Rats who grow up in enriched environments have larger, more effective brains than those of rats who grow up in deprived, barren environments (Bennett, Diamond, Krech, & Rosenzweig, 1964; Greenough, 1986). Normal sensory stimulation is essential if the young human brain is to form the interconnections among neurons that are required for normal human behavior. Experience "fine tunes" the brain, helping to determine which neurons and synapses survive (Greenough, 1986). Then, throughout life, the organization of synapses continues to change in response to experience, storing information for future use.

How are these early developments in the brain linked to infant development? We have seen that one of the strengths of newborns is a set of reflexes. These reflexes are made possible by the lower centers of the nervous system (the spinal cord, brain stem, and so on), which are relatively well developed at birth. And in the higher centers of the brain (the cortex), the sensory areas develop more rapidly than the portions of the cortex involved in thought and language. Thus the senses of newborns are in good working order, but newborns do not yet learn, remember, or think very effectively. Moreover, the steady development of the motor areas of the cerebral cortex converts the infant from a being who is largely incapable of moving voluntarily and deliberately to achieve goals to a 1- or 2-year-old who most definitely can.

Physical Behavior

Although the motor behaviors of newborns are far more sophisticated than they first appear to be (Prechtl, 1981), newborns are certainly not in a position to dance or thread needles! Yet by age 2, infants are toddlers, walking up and down stairs by themselves and using their hands to accomplish simple self-care tasks and to operate toys. How do the gross motor skills involved in walking and the fine motor skills involved in manipulating toys develop?

Basic Trends in Locomotor Development

Examine the motor milestones listed in Table 5.4. Column 2 presents the age at which 50% of U.S. infants master each skill (that is, the *developmental norm* for that skill); column 3 indicates when almost all infants (90%) have mastered each milestone. Can you recognize the workings of the cephalocaudal and proximodistal principles of development in these milestones?

Early motor development does proceed in a cephalocaudal direction because the neurons between the brain and the muscles myelinate in a head-to-tail manner. Thus infants can lift their heads before they can control their trunks enough to sit, and they can sit before they can

Table 5.4 Age norms (in months) for important motor milestones (based on Anglo-American, Hispanic, and black children in the United States)

SKILL	MONTH WHEN 50% OF INFANTS HAVE MASTERED THE SKILL	MONTH WHEN 90% OF INFANTS HAVE MASTERED THE SKILL
Lifts head 90° while lying on stomach	2.2	3.2
Rolls over	2.8	4.7
Sits propped up	2.9	4.2
Sits without support	5.5	7.8
Stands holding on	5.8	10.0
Walks holding on	9.2	12.7
Stands alone momentarily	9.8	13.0
Stands well alone	11.5	13.9
Walks well	12.1	14.3
Walks up steps	17.0	22.0
Kicks ball forward	20.0	24.0

Source: Adapted from Frankenburg & Dodds, 1967.

control their legs to walk. The *proximodistal* principle of development is a bit less obvious in Table 5.4, but is also evident in early motor development. Activities involving the trunk (rolling over, for example) appear before activities involving the extremities—arms, hands, and fingers; legs, feet, and toes. Long ago, Mary Shirley (1933) concluded that locomotor development is a maturational phenomenon. As the nerves and muscles mature in a downward and outward direction, infants gradually gain control over the lower and the peripheral parts of their bodies.

Life changes dramatically for infants and their parents when infants begin to crawl or creep at about 7 months of age. With this new mobility, infants can begin to explore the objects around them and to make contact with other people. Experience in moving through the spatial world contributes to cognitive development. For example, crawlers, as well as noncrawlers who are made mobile with the aid of special walkers, are more able to search for and find hidden objects than infants of the same age who are not mobile (Kermoian & Campos, 1988). Becoming mobile also increases the frequency of social interactions between infants and their parents (Gustafson, 1984). Thus motor development is linked to advances in both intellectual and social development.

Although parents must be on their toes when their infants first begin walking at about a year of age, they take great delight in witnessing this new milestone in motor development. Since walking is so significant, we look more closely at its development in Box 5.1.

Manipulating Objects

When we look at what infants can do with their hands, we also see a progression from reflexive activity to more voluntary, coordinated behavior. We saw that newborns come equipped with a grasping reflex that weakens at 2 to 4 months of age. During this period, infants cannot aim their grasps very well; they take swipes at objects, but they often miss or close their hands too early or too late (Bower, 1982).

By the middle of the first year, infants can once again grasp objects well, though they use a rather clumsy, clawlike grasp in which they press the palm and outer fingers together. Their eyes and hands are better coordinated so that they can correct their reach to obtain the target (Bower, 1982). The workings of the proximodistal principle of development can be seen when infants who could control their arms and then hands finally become able to control the individual fingers enough to use a **pincer grasp**. The pincer grasp involves only the thumb and the forefinger (or another finger) and appears at about 9 to 12 months (Halverson, 1931). Now, as they crawl about, infants can use their refined pincer grasp to corner bugs and turn dials on the television set.

By 16 months of age infants can scribble with a crayon, and by the end of the second year they can copy a simple horizontal or vertical line and even build towers of five or more blocks. They are rapidly gaining control of specific movements and then *integrating* those movements into whole, coordinated actions (Fentress & McLeod, 1986). Thus the infant comes to control the thumb and forefinger separately and then can use a pincer grasp as part of a meaningful sequence of movements; for example, reaching for a block, snatching it with a pincer grasp, laying it precisely on a tower of blocks, and releasing it.

Motor development during infancy is truly impressive. As the cortex of the brain develops to allow voluntary and coordinated actions, primitive reflexes disappear and skilled, deliberate actions take their place. And as body proportions change and the muscles develop, infants become able to balance themselves enough to walk, though with difficulty. Infants do not need to be taught these motor skills. Motor development depends on the maturation of body and brain, and infants all over the world progress through the same motor milestones in just about the same order and at just about the same times.

Yet experience also influences the rate of motor development. As we saw in Box 5.1, infants who practice their stepping reflex early in life or who grow up in cultures where babies are often held upright and carried in slings may walk somewhat earlier than the typical Western baby does. Moreover, today's Western babies progress through motor milestones faster than infants in the 1930s did; developmental norms established in the 1930s are therefore inaccurate when applied to today's infants. Possibly modern infants get more motor experience than their parents or grandparents did, and they may also develop faster because they mature faster.

Most important, *normal* freedom of movement is necessary for maturational processes to unfold. Wayne Dennis (1960) studied infants in institutional settings who had no toys and spent most of their time lying on their backs,

Box 5.1
How Do Infants Achieve the Ability to Walk?

Esther Thelen (1984) has observed early motor development closely and has performed and summarized much research concerning how the ability to walk emerges out of earlier motor capacities. Recall that newborns display a *stepping reflex* when they are held upright on a flat surface. They seem ready for walking at birth, and yet the stepping reflex disappears, and a full year will elapse before infants do indeed walk on their own. Why is this?

Thelen is not sure that the newborn's stepping action is really a reflex or that it disappears because the higher centers of the brain take over control of behavior. Instead, she suggests that the stepping action disappears because the growing infant's legs become too heavy for weak muscles to lift. Infants do *not* lose the ability to kick their legs spontaneously when they are lying down—when it is easier to move those fleshy things around. Moreover, the newborn's stepping and the older infant's kicking appear to be the same behavior patterns: spontaneous (not reflexive) action patterns that resemble walking motions. Through both their stepping and kicking, infants are practicing movements that will become part of walking later.

Why do infants take so long to walk, then? In Thelen's view, the basic motor patterns are there all along, as seen in early stepping and kicking, but infants must develop more muscle and

become less top-heavy before walking will be possible. Even when they first walk, they face a real challenge. They still have big heads and short legs, and that does not make for good balance. Steps are short; legs are wide apart; and hips, knees, and ankles are flexed. There is much teetering and falling, and a smooth gait and good balance will not be achieved for some time. Thelen's point is that we would walk funny too if we, like infants, were "fat, weak, and unstable" (Thelen, 1984, p. 246).

In support of Thelen's view, there is evidence that young infants who are allowed to exercise their primitive motor capabilities will walk somewhat earlier than usual. For example, one team of investigators found that 2- to 8-week-old infants who were held upright and encouraged to practice their stepping motion did not lose it as infants normally do (Zelazo, Zelazo, & Kolb, 1972). And these infants also walked at an earlier age than infants in a control group who did not receive this early training. Similarly, !Kung infants in the Kalahari Desert of Africa walk sooner than infants in our society do. Mothers there believe that motor skills must be taught and practiced, and so they keep their babies in an upright position a good deal of the time and carry them in slings that allow them plenty of arm and leg movement (Konner, 1976). It could be that these forms of exercise build the muscles.

Philip Zelazo (1984) believes that the cortex of the brain must also develop before the coordinated movements necessary for walking are possible—that it is not just a matter of gaining enough muscle and balance. Perhaps both Thelen and Zelazo are right. Infants may require *both* a stronger, more stable body and a more developed brain to finally get where they want to go on their own two feet.

often on hollowed-out mattresses that made it impossible for them even to roll over onto their stomachs. Of all infants aged 1 to 2, only 42% could sit alone, and *none* could walk. In fact, only 8% of the 2- and 3-year-olds and 15% of the 3- and 4-year-olds could walk alone! As Dennis concluded, maturation is certainly necessary for motor development, but it is not sufficient. Normal opportunities to practice motor behaviors are just as necessary.

THE CHILD

The development of the body, brain, and motor behavior during childhood is slower than it was during infancy, but it is steady. One need only compare the bodies and the physical feats of the 2-year-old and the 10-year-old to be impressed by how much change occurs over childhood.

The Body

From age 2 until puberty, children gain about 2 to 3 inches in height and 6 to 7 pounds in weight every year. During middle childhood (ages 6–11), children may *seem* to grow very little, probably because the gains are small in proportion to the child's size (4–4½′ tall and 60–80 pounds) and therefore harder to detect (Eichorn, 1979). The cephalocaudal and proximodistal principles of growth continue to operate. As the lower parts of the body and the extremities fill out, the child takes on more adultlike body proportions. The bones are continuing to grow and harden, and the muscles are becoming stronger.

The Brain

New neurons are no longer forming during childhood, but the brain is still developing. By a child's fifth birthday, the brain has achieved fully 90% of its adult weight, and the myelination of the nerves continues throughout childhood. Finally, different areas of the brain are becoming more specialized.

One important example of the developing organization of the brain is the **lateralization**, or specialization, of the two hemispheres of the cerebral cortex. In most people, the left cerebral hemisphere controls the right side of the body and is specially equipped to process language, whereas the right hemisphere controls the left side of the body and specializes in processing music and in carrying out such spatial activities as mentally visualizing designs. Lateralization also involves relying more on one hand or side of the body than on the other. About 90% or so of us rely on our right hands (or left hemispheres) to write and perform other motor activities. When exactly does the brain become lateralized?

Eric Lenneberg (1967) argued that lateralization takes place gradually throughout infancy and childhood and is not complete until adolescence. He cited evidence that children who suffer damage to the left hemisphere often recover their lost language capacities because the right hemisphere takes over the language functions that had been controlled by the left hemisphere. However, brain damage after puberty, when the brain has less plasticity, often means that people remain mute or only partially recover their linguistic abilities.

Despite Lenneberg's observations, quite a different picture of lateralization has emerged from recent research. In their review of the literature, Marcel Kinsbourne and Merrill Hiscock (1983) note that some signs of brain lateralization are evident at birth. For example, most newborns turn to the right rather than to the left when they lie on their backs, and these same babies later tend to reach for objects with their right hands (Michel, 1981). True, hand preference comes and goes over the months of infancy. Indeed, Douglas Ramsay (1984, 1985) has observed that in the very week that 6- or 7-month-old infants first begin babbling of the sort that involves repeating syllables (for example, "baba"), almost all show a clear preference for using their right hand. They did not favor either hand before, and they temporarily lose their right-hand preference afterward, only to regain it later.

Nonetheless, Kinsbourne and Hiscock (1983) argue that these early preferences for the right hand, even if they are not stable, tell us that the young brain is already organized in a lateralized fashion. Moreover, recent research suggests that the language capacities of young children who suffer damage to the left hemisphere do not recover quite as completely as Lenneberg thought (Goldman-Rakic et al., 1983). So, the brain seems to be lateralized quite early in life. However, as children develop they come to rely more and more consistently on one hemisphere or the other to carry out tasks; this involves a change in how the two sides of the brain are *used* rather than a fundamental change in the brain's structure (Kinsbourne & Hiscock, 1983; Witelson, 1987).

It is clear that children do rely increasingly on one hemisphere or the other to perform certain tasks as they get older. For example, Stanley Coren, Clare Porac, and Pam Duncan (1981) have shown that preferences for using one side of the body or the other become stronger between the preschool years and the high school years. They asked 3- to 5-year-olds and high school students to do such things as pick up a crayon, kick a ball, look into an opaque bottle to identify what was inside, or put an ear close to a box to hear sounds coming from it. In this way, they could see which hand, foot, eye, or ear each child favored. Although most preschoolers already preferred their right hands and feet, right eyes and ears were preferred more clearly by high school students than by the young children. Moreover, only about 32% of the preschoolers consistently demonstrated preference for the right side of the body on all tasks, but about 52% of the adolescents did.

Overall, then, the brain appears to be structured very early in life so that the two hemispheres of the cortex are capable of specialized functioning. As we develop, the large majority of us come to rely more on the left hemisphere to carry out language activities and more on the right hemisphere to do such things as perceive shapes and listen to music. We also come to rely more consistently on one hemisphere, usually the left, to control many of our physical activities.

Physical Behavior

Have you ever watched 3-year-olds try to catch a ball? Often their little arms clap together well after the ball has already bounced off their stomachs and dropped to the ground. According to Jack Keough and David Sugden (1985), infants are quite capable of controlling their movements in relation to a stationary world. What they still need to develop is the ability to move capably in a *changing* environment—when a ball is moving toward them, or when they must navigate on a crowded sidewalk. Those skills develop during childhood, when motor skills are also refined. For example, young children throw a ball only with the arm, but older children learn to step forward as they throw. Thus older children can throw farther than younger ones can, not just because they are bigger and stronger, but because they use more refined and efficient techniques of movement (Haywood, 1986).

The toddler in motion appears awkward compared to the older child, who takes steps in more fluid and rhythmical strides and is better able to avoid obstacles. And children quickly become able to do more than just walk. By age 3, children can walk or run in a straight line, though they cannot easily turn or stop while running. Four-year-olds can skip, hop on one foot, and run much farther and faster than they could a year earlier (Corbin, 1973). By age 5, children are becoming rather graceful. They pump their arms like adults do when they run, and their balance and coordination have improved to the point that some of them can ride a bicycle. With each passing year, school-age children can run a little faster, jump a little higher, and throw a ball a little farther (Herkowitz, 1978; Keough & Sugden, 1985).

At the same time, eye/hand coordination and control of the small muscles are improving rapidly so that children can make more and more sophisticated uses of their hands. Three-year-olds find it difficult to button their clothing, tie a shoe, or copy a figure on a piece of paper. By age 5, children can accomplish all of these feats and can even cut a straight line with scissors or copy letters and numbers with a crayon. By age 8 or 9, they can use household tools such as screwdrivers and have become skilled performers at games such as baseball and jacks that require eye/hand coordination. Children also become more and more able to intercept moving targets and win video games (Dorfman, 1977)!

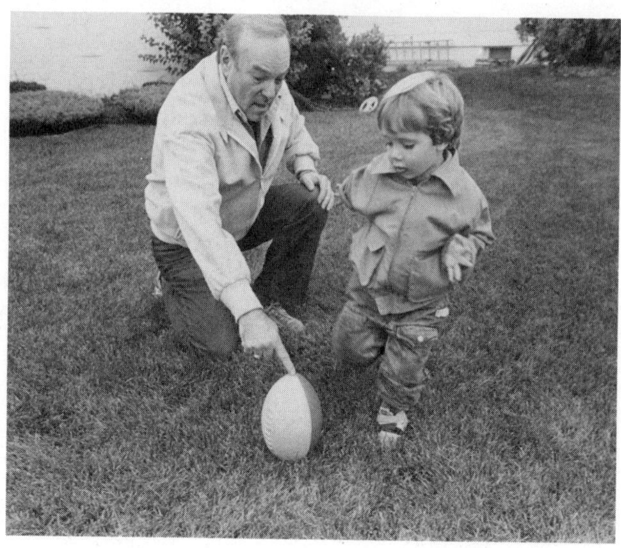

Preschool children are not as coordinated as they will be in a few years.

Finally, older children have quicker reactions than young children do. They can do something about it when basketballs suddenly fly toward their heads or when dogs run in front of their bikes. In studies of *reaction time*, a stimulus such as a light suddenly appears, and the subject's task is to respond to it as quickly as possible—for example, by pushing a button. These studies reveal that reaction time improves steadily throughout childhood (Thomas, Gallagher, & Purvis, 1981).

In short, no matter what aspect of physical growth and motor behavior we consider, we see steady and impressive improvement over the childhood years. But these changes are not nearly so dramatic as those that will occur during the adolescent years as the child becomes an adult.

THE ADOLESCENT

The Body: Physical and Sexual Maturation

Think back to the dramatic physical changes of adolescence and your reactions to them. You rapidly grew taller during the **adolescent growth spurt** and took on the body size and proportions of an adult. Moreover, you experienced **puberty**, the point in life when an individual attains sexual maturity and becomes capable of producing a child. The term *puberty*, by the way, is derived from a Latin word meaning "to grow hairy." Sprouting hair here and there is at least part of what it means to be an adolescent.

The Adolescent Growth Spurt

Typically, a girl's rapid growth begins at age 10½ and reaches a peak at age 12 (Tanner, 1981). Boys lag behind girls by about two years, so that their growth spurt typically begins at age 13 and peaks at age 14 (see Figure 5.4). As a result, there is a period in early junior high school when many boys appear "shrimpy" compared to many girls. Both sexes return to a slower rate of growth after the peak of their growth spurts.

Different parts of the body grow at different rates. One of the most disturbing aspects of growth for many adolescents is that the extremities of the body enlarge before the trunk and central areas do. Thus adolescents may be embarrassed by having huge feet or a protruding nose before the rest of their bodies have caught up. This direction of growth is the opposite of the proximodistal (center to extremities) direction of growth that characterizes early physical development.

Muscles also develop rapidly in both sexes, with boys normally gaining a higher proportion of muscle mass than girls do. Girls must be content with gaining some extra fat, for example, in the breasts. Total body weight increases in both sexes, but it is distributed differently. The hips broaden in young women, the shoulders in young men.

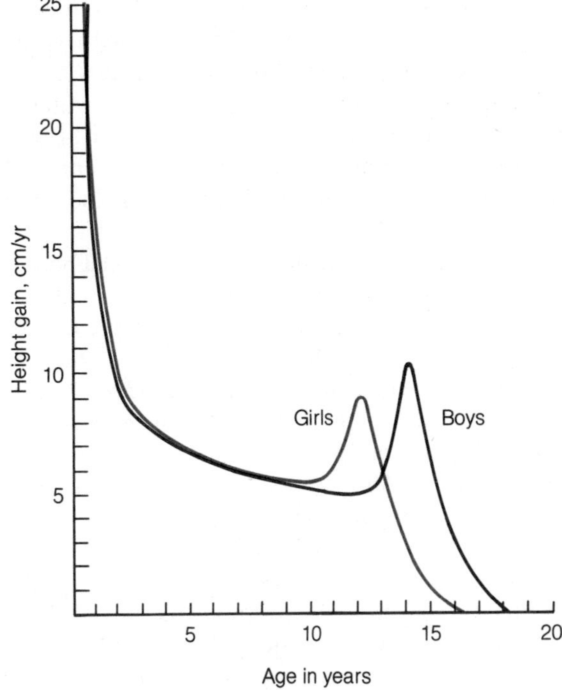

Figure 5.4 Gain in height per year by males and females from birth through adolescence. At about age 10½, girls begin their growth spurt. Boys follow some 2½ years later and grow faster than girls once their growth begins.

Sexual Maturation

For most girls, the first visible sign of sexual maturation is the accumulation of fatty tissue around their nipples, forming small "breast buds" at about age 11. Straight, soft pubic hair usually begins to appear a little later, although as many as one third of all girls develop some pubic hair before the breasts begin to develop (Tanner, 1978). As a girl enters her growth spurt, the breasts grow rapidly and the internal sex organs begin to mature. The most dramatic event in the sexual maturation process is the achievement of **menarche**—the first menstruation—at an average age in our society of about 12½ to 13 (Tanner, 1978). Young girls often menstruate without ovulating, so they *may* not actually be capable of reproducing for 12 to 18 months after menarche (Tanner, 1978). In the year after menarche, the breasts and kinky pubic hair also complete their development, and axillary (underarm) hair grows, only to be shaven off by most women in our society.

For the average boy, the sexual maturation process begins at about age 11 to 11½ with an initial enlargement of the testes and scrotum (the sacklike structure that encloses the testes). Unpigmented, straight pubic hair appears soon thereafter, and about six months later the penis grows rapidly at about the same time that the adolescent growth spurt begins. The marker of sexual maturation that is most like menarche in girls is a boy's first ejaculation—the emission of seminal fluid in a "wet dream" or while masturbating. It typically occurs at about age 13 or 14. Just as girls often do not ovulate until some time after menarche, boys often do not produce viable sperm until some time after their first ejaculation.

Somewhat later, boys begin to sprout facial hair, first at the corners of the upper lip and finally on the chin and jawline. A hairy chest may not appear until the late teens or early twenties, if at all. The voice lowers, providing many boys with the embarrassing experience of hearing their voices "crack" uncontrollably up and down between a squeaky soprano and a deep baritone, sometimes within a single sentence. And increased glandular activity makes for body odor and pimples in both boys and girls.

Variations in the Timing of Physical and Sexual Maturation

So far, we have been describing developmental norms, or the average ages when adolescent changes take place. But as Figure 5.5 suggests, there are great individual differences in the timing of physical and sexual maturation. An early-maturing girl may develop breast buds at age 8, start her growth spurt soon thereafter, and reach menarche at age 10½. Meanwhile, a late-developing boy may not begin to experience a growth of the penis until age 14½ or a height spurt until age 16. Within a junior high school, then, one will find a wide assortment of bodies, ranging from those that are entirely childlike to those that are fully adultlike. No wonder adolescents are self-conscious about their appearance!

What determines an adolescent's rate of development? Partly it is a matter of genetic influence. Identical twins typically experience changes at similar times, and early or late maturation tends to run in families (Tanner, 1978). In both sexes, the changes involved in physical and sexual maturation are triggered when the hypothalamus of the brain stimulates activity in the endocrine system (see discussion at start of chapter). Boys and girls have similar levels of both male and female sex hormones during childhood. But by the time sexual maturation is complete, males have larger quantities of male hormones (androgens) circulating in their blood than females do, while females have larger quantities of female hormones (estrogens and progesterone).

Physical and sexual maturation, then, are matura-

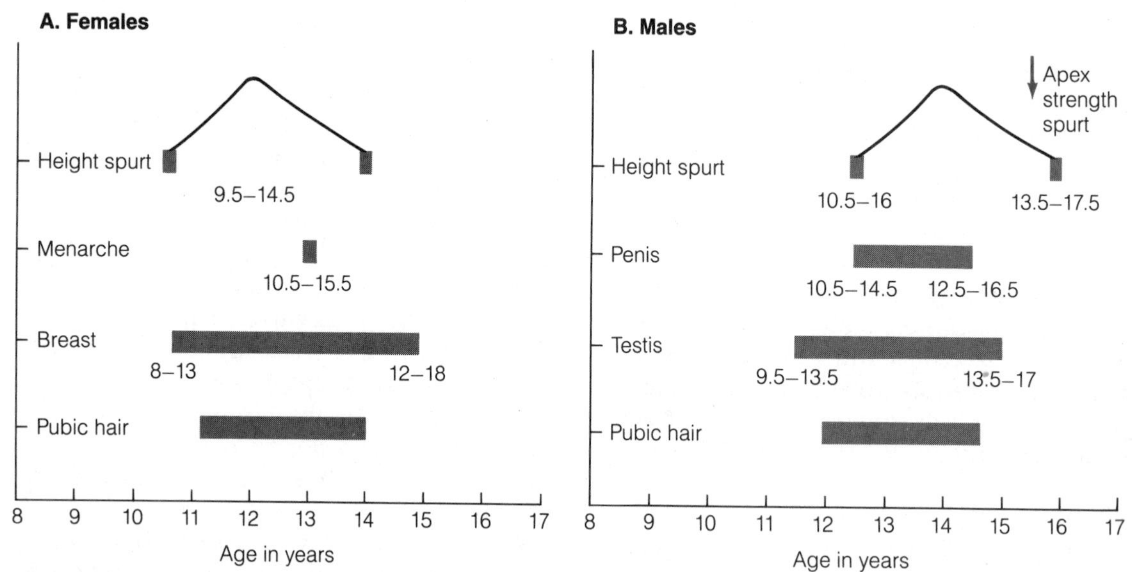

Figure 5.5 Sequence of events in the sexual maturation of females (A) and males (B). The numbers represent the variation among individuals in the ages at which each aspect of sexual maturation begins or ends. For example, we see that the growth of the penis may begin as early as age 10½ or as late as age 14½. (From Faust, 1977)

tional processes set in motion by the genes and executed by hormones. But environment also plays its part in the timing of maturation. This is dramatically clear in the **secular trend**, a historical trend in industrialized societies toward earlier maturation and greater body size. In 1880, for example, the average girl reached menarche at about age 16. In 1900, the age was down to about 14 to 15, and by the 1980s it was down to 12½ (Tanner, 1981). In addition, people have been growing taller and heavier over the past century: many adolescents are taller than their grandparents are, although the secular trend now appears to be leveling off in our society (Tanner, 1981). One can still find cultures where sexual maturity is reached much later than it is in industrialized nations. For example, in one part of New Guinea the average girl does not reach menarche until age 18 (Tanner, 1978). Many of the more prosperous Third World countries are now experiencing the secular trend.

What explains the secular trend? Better nutrition and advances in medical care seem to be most responsible (Tanner, 1978). Today's children are more likely than their parents or grandparents to reach their genetic potentials for maturation and growth because they are better fed and less likely to experience growth-retarding illnesses. Even within our own relatively affluent society, poorly nourished adolescents mature later than well-nourished ones do. It seems that a critical weight for one's height—or a critical proportion of body fat to total body weight—must be achieved before menstruation will occur (Frisch & McArthur, 1974). As a result, girls who engage regularly in strenuous physical activity and girls who suffer from anorexia nervosa (the life-threatening eating disorder that involves dieting to the point of starvation) often begin menstruating very late or stop menstruating after they have begun (Frisch & McArthur, 1974; Frisch, Wyshak, & Vincent, 1980). Similarly, undernourished boys grow slowly and are likely to produce fewer viable sperm than their well-fed peers do (Frisch, 1983). Truly, then, physical and sexual maturation are the products of an *interaction* between heredity and environment.

The Psychological Effects of Adolescent Development

Try to recall what it was like to watch your body and those of your friends changing before your eyes and to realize that you were achieving sexual maturity. What effects do these changes really have on adolescents?

In our culture, girls typically become quite concerned about appearance and worry about how others will respond to them (Greif & Ulman, 1982). One adolescent girl may think she is too tall, another that she is too short. One may try to pad her breasts, while another may hunch her shoulders to hide hers. Yet when breasts appear early in the maturation process, girls feel better about their bodies, their relationships with peers, and their abilities (Brooks-Gunn & Warren, 1988). Their emotional reactions to their first menstruation seem to be more mixed (Greif & Ulman, 1982). They are often a bit excited, but they are somewhat scared and confused as well, especially if they mature early or don't know what to expect (Ruble & Brooks-Gunn, 1982). Some develop poor body images because they are bothered by the gains in weight that typically accompany menarche (Duncan, Ritter, Dornbusch, Gross, & Carlsmith, 1985). Few are traumatized, but at the same time few express delight at becoming a woman (Ruble & Brooks-Gunn, 1982).

What about boys? They are more concerned with their body images than they might want people to believe. They hope to be tall, hairy, and handsome, and they are especially concerned about their physical and athletic prowess (Berscheid, Walster, & Bohrnstedt, 1973). As a result, while girls are lamenting the fact that they are gaining weight, boys welcome their weight gain (Duncan et al., 1985). Little is known about boys' reactions to their first ejaculation. However, Alan Gaddis and Jeanne Brooks-Gunn (1985) did interview a small sample of boys about this experience. Whereas girls typically tell their mothers immediately when they first menstruate, boys rarely tell anyone about their first ejaculation. Yet boys seem to react more positively to their first ejaculation than girls react to their first menstruation. Boys feel "excited" and "grown-up," though like girls they are also surprised by the experience and sometimes a bit scared. Thus sexual maturation seems to provoke mixed reactions in both males and females.

Adolescents who are physically and sexually maturing not only come to feel differently about themselves but come to be viewed and treated differently by other people. Laurence Steinberg (1981, 1988) has examined changes in family relations over a period of a year as boys and girls mature physically. Around the time that pubertal changes are peaking, adolescents become more autonomous or independent, less close to their parents, and more likely to experience conflicts with their parents, especially their mothers. When Steinberg (1981) observed family discussions over time, he found that the mothers of boys appeared to tire of the quibbling and gave up some of their own influence in the family to their more independent sons. Similarly, conflict between girls and their mothers heightens shortly after girls reach menarche and dies down later, though girls do not seem to gain as much influence in the family as boys do (Hill, 1988; Hill, Holmbeck, Marlow, Green, & Lynch, 1985). Once they have matured, boys and girls may also experience more pressure from both parents and peers to conform to their gender roles (Hill & Lynch, 1983). Thus, biological changes precipitate changes in the social environment that in turn influence how adolescence is experienced.

If "timely" maturation has psychological implications, what is it like to be an especially early or late developer? This question has aroused much interest. It turns out that the answer depends on whether we are talking about males or females and whether we examine their adjustment during adolescence or later on. Let's start with the more immediate impacts. Emmett is an early-developing boy, and Ludwig is a late developer. Other things being equal, Emmett should be at an advantage during the years when he is developed and Ludwig isn't. He's certainly more likely to star on the athletic field and have his way in fights, if nothing else. Mary Cover Jones and Nancy Bayley (1950) followed the development of early- and late-maturing boys over a six-year period. Early maturers were indeed at an advantage. They were poised and confident in social settings, were judged to be attractive, and often won athletic honors and student elections. By comparison, late-maturing boys tended to be more anxious and attention-seeking. And perhaps for good reason, late-maturing boys tend to feel unsure of themselves and inferior compared to their early-maturing peers (Livson & Peskin, 1980).

Now consider Ethel the early developer and Ludmilla the late developer. Traditionally, physical prowess has not been as important in girls' peer groups as in boys', so it is not clear that Ethel will gain much status from being larger and more muscled. In addition, since girls develop about two years earlier than boys do, Ethel will be somewhat of a "freak" for a time—the only one in her grade who is developed. She may be the target of some teasing. She may also find herself involved in the "teen scene" of dating and minor trouble-making before she is really ready (Magnusson, Stattin, & Allen, 1985). Perhaps for some of these reasons, the advantages of early maturation are not nearly so great for girls as they are for boys. Indeed, in the sixth grade, the early-maturing girl tends to be *less* popular than her prepubertal classmates (Faust, 1960; Jones & Mussen, 1958). In junior high school, the picture is reversed somewhat. Now the early maturer has more status than the late maturer, perhaps because girls see that the early-maturing girl already tends to be popular with boys (Faust, 1960). Late-maturing girls, like late-maturing boys, may experience some anxiety as they wait to mature, but they are not so disadvantaged as late-maturing boys.

Do these differences between early and late developers persist into adulthood? Basically, the differences fade over time. Yet there are some interesting twists in the plot. Jones (1965), for example, found that in their 30s

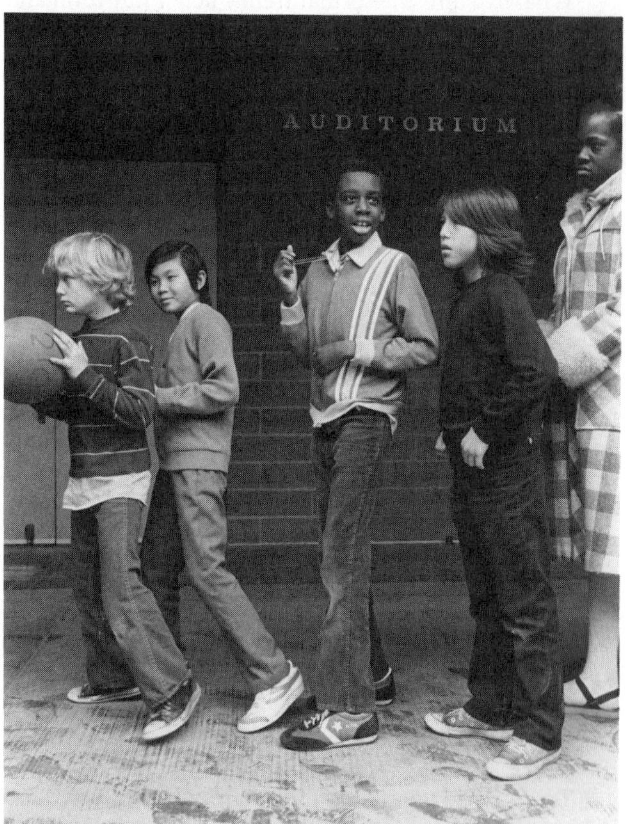

Bodies take all forms in adolescence.

early-maturing boys were still somewhat more sociable, confident, and responsible than their peers who had matured later in adolescence. So some of the advantages of early maturation had carried over into adulthood. Yet these early maturers also were more rigid and conforming than the late maturers, who as men seemed more able to be playful and innovative and to cope with ambiguous situations. Possibly their need to struggle with the problems of being late to mature created some strengths in late-maturing boys, while early-maturing boys were pushed into adult roles before they really had time to experiment much.

Similar hints that struggle stimulates growth appear in follow-up studies of girls. Harvey Peskin (1973) found that early-maturing girls have adjustment difficulties for a time during adolescence but at age 30 seem to be more self-directed and better able to cope with events than late-developing women. In short, those individuals who have a relatively easy time coping with physical and sexual maturation—especially early-developing boys—may retain some of their strengths in adulthood; however, late-developing boys and early-developing girls may learn through their struggles to cope with adversity and respond flexibly to change (Livson & Peskin, 1980).

Overall, then, the advantages of maturing early are greater for males than for females. In addition, the psychological differences between early and late maturers become smaller and more mixed in nature by adulthood. Finally, let us note that differences between early and late maturers are relatively small and that many other factors besides the timing of maturation influence whether this period of life goes smoothly or not.

The Brain

Adolescents are experiencing not only observable physical changes but mental changes as well. Through the ages, adults have noticed that teenagers suddenly begin to ask "what if" questions and to reason about weighty abstractions such as truth and justice. Can this shift to abstract thinking be tied to developments within the brain? Perhaps so, for the brain is completing its development during adolescence. By about age 16, it reaches its full adult weight; the myelination of its neural pathways continues into late adolescence (Tanner, 1978). This may help explain why infants, toddlers, and even school-aged children and young adolescents have shorter attention spans than do older adolescents and adults.

Herman Epstein (1974, 1980) has proposed that a spurt in brain development occurs at about age 10 to 12 and again at age 14 to 16. Indeed, his studies of head growth and brain-wave activity suggest that brain growth spurts occur at several points during infancy and childhood as well—and at just the ages at which children are believed by Jean Piaget and others to enter new stages of cognitive development (see also Fischer, 1987). So it is possible that adolescents develop the capacity for abstract thinking as their brains experience growth spurts. At this point, however, Epstein's intriguing findings are still controversial (Marsh, 1985), and developmentalists are not sure exactly why the mental capabilities of adolescents are so much more extensive than those of younger children.

Physical Behavior

Dramatic physical growth during adolescence makes teenagers stronger and more physically competent than children are. By age 14, adolescents can perform many motor activities as well as adults can (Keough & Sugden, 1985). Where they still often fall short compared to adults is in activities that require strength. Rapid muscle development over the adolescent years makes both boys and girls (but especially boys) noticeably stronger than they were as children (Faust, 1977). Their performance of large-muscle activities continues to improve: An adolescent can throw a ball farther, cover more ground in the standing long jump, and run much faster than a child can (Keough & Sugden, 1985). But as the adolescent years progress, the physical performances of boys continue to improve, while those of girls often level off—or worse yet, *decline* (see Figure 5.6).

What is going on here? It is easy to see that their larger muscles enable boys to outperform girls in activities that require strength. By the mid-20s, muscle accounts for 40% of the average man's body weight, compared to 24% of the average woman's (Marshall, 1977). But why would young women—who, after all, *do* experience physical and muscular growth—actually perform *worse* on some physical tests in later adolescence than they did in earlier adolescence? Gender-role socialization may be responsible (Herkowitz, 1978). As girls mature sexually and physically, they are often encouraged to be less "tomboyish" and to become more interested in traditionally "feminine" (and often more sedentary) activities. Let's note, however, that a study of world records in track, swimming, and cycling

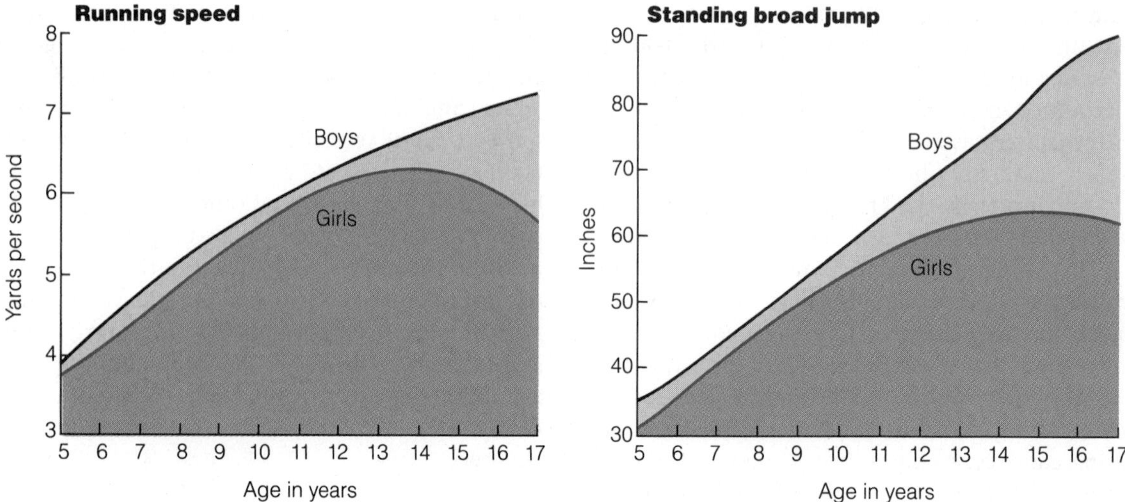

Figure 5.6 Age and sex differences in performance on two tests of large-muscle activity.

suggests that, as gender roles have changed since 1948, women have been improving their performances, and the male/female gap in physical performance has narrowed (Dyer, 1977). As girls participate more often in sports and other strenuous physical activities, their performance on tests of large-muscle activity is likely to improve during adolescence rather than decline.

Let us close by noting that adolescents within either sex differ widely in their physical abilities. Some are awkward, uncoordinated, and accident prone, while others are already setting world records in swimming or winning professional tennis tournaments. It takes much more than an adultlike body and adultlike musculature to turn in highly skilled physical performances. Those adolescents who excel in athletics undoubtedly have sound biological systems, but they are also motivated to develop their physical abilities and to train and practice hard (Keough & Sugden, 1985).

THE ADULT

Although the adolescent becomes physically, sexually, and mentally mature, changes in the physical self continue during the adult years.

The Body

The body of the mature adolescent or young adult is at its prime in many ways. It is strong and fit; its organs are functioning efficiently. But it is aging. Physical aging occurs slowly and steadily over most of the life span. It begins to have noticeable effects on physical appearance and functioning in middle age, and has had even more significant impacts by the time old age is reached.

Physical Appearance and Structure

Only minor changes in physical appearance occur in the 20s and 30s, but many people do notice signs that they are aging as they reach their 40s. The skin wrinkles, and the hair thins and turns gray (and may drop out by the handfuls in balding men). Middle-age spread may strike as people put on extra weight around the midsection and have the love handles and potbellies to prove it. Some people find these changes are difficult to accept, for they equate "old" with "unattractive."

The body shows additional effects of aging in old age. After gaining weight from their 20s to their 50s, people typically begin to lose it starting in their 60s (Shephard, 1978). A loss of fat in old age is usually coupled with a loss of muscle over the entire span of adulthood years (Montoye & Lamphiear, 1977; Murray et al., 1985). The result may be sagging flesh. "Age spots" also appear on the skin, which wrinkles and thins. The bones lose tissue so that the vertebrae collapse a bit, and many people get shorter as they age, though by only a half inch for the average man and an inch for the average woman (Adams, Davies, & Sweetnam, 1970). Older people may *seem* to shrink more than that as they age, but recall the secular trend: Old people today *are* relatively short in part because they grew up in a time when people did not grow so tall as younger people do today.

Extreme bone loss in later life results from the disease called **osteoporosis**, a serious loss of minerals that leaves the bones fragile and easily fractured. It is a special problem for older women, who never had as much bone mass as men to start with and whose bones tend to thin rapidly during menopause (Johnston, Hui, Witt, Appledorn, Baker, & Longcope, 1985). Women with osteoporosis often have the so-called dowager's hump, a noticeably rounded upper back (see Figure 5.7). Increased calcium intake, exercise, and taking estrogen and progesterone to compensate for hormone loss due to menopause (and also to relieve symptoms of menopause) have all been recommended to help prevent or slow osteoporosis (Soules & Bremner, 1982).

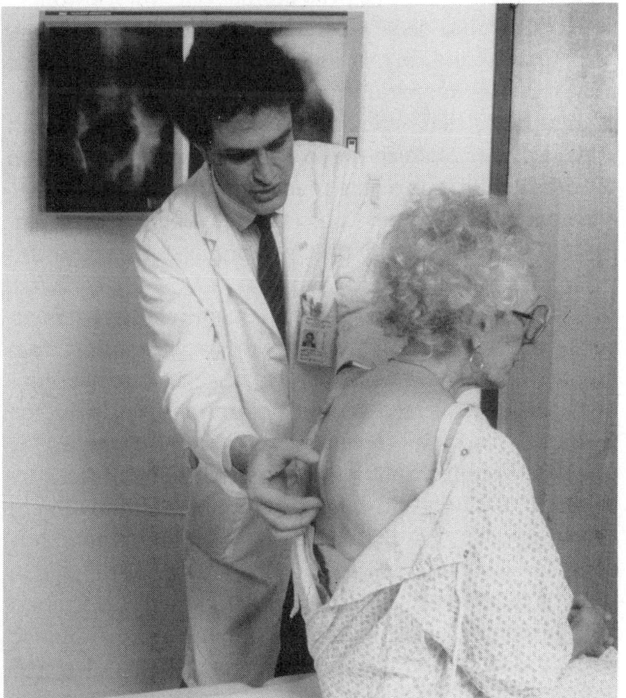

Figure 5.7 The "dowager's hump" associated with osteoporosis.

The joints are also aging over the adult years. The cushioning between bones wears out and the joints become stiffer. In its extreme, this normal aging process takes the form of *osteoarthritis*, a common disability in old age. The older person who can no longer button buttons, stoop to pick up dropped items, or even get in and out of the bathtub easily may feel incompetent and dependent (Whitbourne, 1985).

Bodily Functioning and Health

Aging also involves a gradual decline in the efficiency of most bodily systems from the 20s on (Whitbourne, 1985). No matter what physical function we look at—strength, the capacity of the heart or lungs to meet the demands of exercise, or the ability of the body to control its temperature—the gradual effects of aging are evident.

Consider what Harold Bafitis and Frederick Sargent (1977) discovered when they put together the results of several studies of physiological functioning over the life span. Figure 5.8 shows plots for two of the eight physiological measures they examined. *Vital capacity* is a measure of the volume of air that can be moved in and out of the lungs when a person breathes deeply. Thus it is an in-

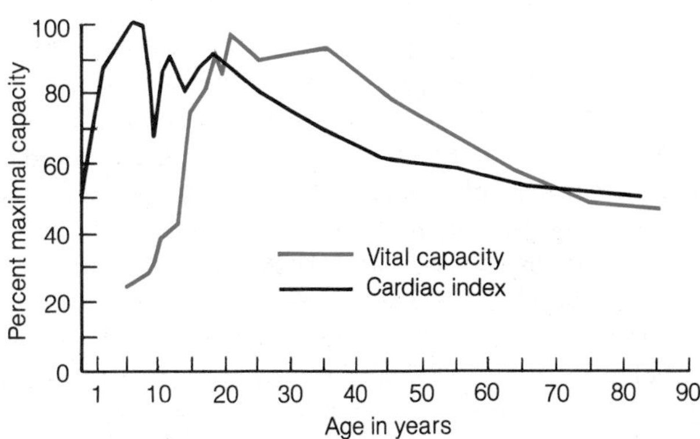

Figure 5.8 Changes in vital capacity and an index of cardiac functioning over the life span. (Data from Bafitis & Sargent, 1977)

dex of the functioning of the respiratory system. It increases over childhood, peaks at 18 to 20, and declines over the adult years. You can see that the measure of cardiac (heart) functioning peaks at about age 6, fluctuates until early adulthood, and declines thereafter.

Each system of the body seems to have its own timetable of development and aging. However, Bafitis and Sargent found that every measure they examined increased to a peak sometime between childhood and early adulthood and declined thereafter. In other words, aging actually begins in childhood rather than in later life. They also noted that during the peak years of physiological functioning, death rates are lower than they are in either infancy or later adulthood. Neither the infant nor the old person is well equipped to cope with stresses to the body such as pneumonia, extreme temperature changes, or exhausting activity. One final message of this review is also important: Individual differences in physiological functioning grow larger as age increases. For example, one would find more differences in vital capacity among 70-year-olds than among 20-year-olds. In other words, *different people age at different rates.* We should not assume that all older people have poor physiological functioning. What we can conclude is that the average old person is less physiologically fit than the average young person.

By the time people are 65 or older, it is hard to find many of them who do not have something or other wrong with their bodies. National health surveys indicate that 86% of the 65 and older age group have at least one chronic impairment: a sensory loss, a physical disability, or a degenerative disease (Harris, 1978). Arthritis alone affects 38%. About 20% have hypertension (high blood pressure), and about the same percentage have a heart condition (Harris, 1978). From these data, it appears that older adults are not healthy. But health is not just the absence of disease; it is also a sense of well-being and an ability to function (Shanas & Maddox, 1985). Data compiled by the National Center for Health Statistics show that from childhood on, more and more people view themselves as being less and less healthy as compared with others their age. Yet despite the fact that 86% of people age 65 or older have physical impairments, about two thirds of them describe their health as "good" or "excellent" as compared with their age cohorts (National Center for Health Statistics, 1983). Similarly, over 80% of old people are well enough to engage in major life activities such as work inside or outside the home, though many of them find such activities harder to perform (Harris, 1978). By their own standards, then, the majority of old people are healthy enough to keep their sense of well-being and ability to function.

The Reproductive System

During the adult years, people make good use of their reproductive systems. Most of them reproduce! The adult levels of sex hormones achieved during adolescence help ensure interest in sexual behavior. What other roles do these hormones play in early and middle adulthood?

Hormones and Adult Life

Although hormone levels fluctuate up and down in both sexes over time, hormone changes influence the lives of women more than they influence the lives of men. Hormone levels shift drastically each month as women progress through their menstrual cycles. Estrogen and progesterone levels rise to a peak at midcycle when a woman is ovulating and decline to a low as she approaches her menstrual period. Many women feel at their peak when they are ovulating, and experience more negative moods as their menstrual period approaches (Asso, 1983). Much attention has recently been focused on **premenstrual syndrome (PMS)**: breast tenderness, a bloated feeling, irritability, and moodiness occurring just before the menstrual flow. Cramps and other symptoms during menstruation are also of concern.

How much is the typical woman bothered by premenstrual and menstrual symptoms? Most women are far from incapacitated. We can quickly dispense with the sexist notion that a woman could not be president because she might fall apart if an international crisis fell at the wrong time of the month. Yet for a few women, the symptoms are so severe that life is disrupted each month and treatment may be necessary. For example, Nancy Fugate Woods, Ada Most, and Gretchen Kramer Dery (1982) asked 179 women aged 18 to 35 in the southeastern United States to report their premenstrual and menstrual symptoms. Table 5.5 shows the rates at which premenstrual symptoms were reported. Generally, fewer than 10% of the women felt that any particular symptom was severe or disabling. Many women experienced mild forms of these symptoms, but many other women did not experience them at all. Only irritability and mood swings in the premenstrual period

Table 5.5 Percentage of women reporting premenstrual symptoms

SYMPTOM	MILD/MODERATE	SEVERE/DISABLING
Weight gain	40.2	5.6
Crying	19.6	4.5
Lowered work or school performance	11.7	3.4
Takes naps	17.3	1.1
Headache	27.4	7.3
Skin disorders	32.4	6.7
Cramps	24.6	6.1
Anxiety	27.0	3.4
Backache	16.8	5.0
Fatigue	28.5	3.9
Painful breasts	27.9	7.6
Swelling	39.5	5.2
Irritability	44.2	12.2
Mood swings	46.5	4.7
Depression	29.7	7.0
Tension	34.3	7.6

Source: Data from Woods, Most, & Dery, 1982.

and cramps during menstruation were reported by at least 50% of the women.

Both biological and social factors contribute to premenstrual and menstrual symptoms. Some women may experience more severe hormonal fluctuations than other women do, or their bodies may react more to them (Asso, 1983). But social factors also affect the experience of menstrual cycle changes. For instance, college women report more symptom changes over a month if they know that their menstrual cycles are being studied than if they are just asked to report how they feel on specific days without knowing that the researchers are interested in menstrual cycles (Englander-Golden et al., 1986). This suggests that societal stereotypes of what women "should" experience at different phases of the menstrual cycle influence what is experienced and reported. In keeping with this hypothesis, women who have traditional female jobs outside the home or who are housewives experience more negative emotions during their premenstrual and menstrual phases of the month than do women in nontraditional occupations (Brown & Woods, 1986). Low levels of education and income are also associated with experiencing many symptoms (Woods, Most, & Dery, 1982). Possibly, then, less traditional and more highly educated women have shed many negative social stereotypes about menstruation.

In sum, we should not conclude that distress is "all in a woman's head" (Asso, 1983). But neither should we conclude that most women are seriously impaired for part of the month.

As for men, their hormone levels also fluctuate, but more on a daily than monthly basis. For example, testosterone levels are higher in the morning than in the afternoon, vary from day to day, and are high when a man is under stress (Harman & Talbert, 1985). And men with high testosterone levels are at least somewhat more sexually active than those with lower testosterone levels (Davidson et al., 1983). However, not enough is known yet to say whether men, like women, experience fluctuations in their moods or sense of well-being associated with fluctuations in their hormone levels.

The reproductive years do not continue forever. How do women react to the loss of their ability to bear children? And what happens to the reproductive system of men as they age?

Menopause

The ending of a woman's menstrual periods in midlife is called **menopause**. Consider the basic facts of this "change of life" (see Soules & Bremner, 1982). The average woman experiences menopause at about age 50, and the usual age range is from age 42 to 58. The process actually takes place over a number of years, as periods become either more or less frequent, and less regular (Sherman & Korenman, 1975). Levels of estrogens and other female hormones decline, so that the woman who has been through menopause has a hormone mix that is less "feminine" and more "masculine" than that of the premenopausal woman. When menopause is completed, a woman is no longer ovulating, no longer having periods, and no longer capable of conceiving a child.

The age at which a woman reaches menopause is unrelated to the age at which she reached menarche (Treloar, 1982). Although the age of menarche has declined over history as part of the secular trend, the age of menopause does not appear to have changed much and is similar from culture to culture (Greene, 1984). What *has* changed is that women are now living long enough to experience a considerable period of life in which they are postmenopausal.

Picture a woman who is experiencing menopause. The stereotyped image is this: She is even worse than the woman experiencing premenstrual syndrome; she is irritable and will scream at you or break into tears without provocation; she is depressed and emotionally unstable. How much truth is there to this stereotype? Not much at all. Only two menopausal symptoms have been directly tied to decreases in female hormone levels and affect most women (Greene, 1984). One symptom, affecting about two thirds of menopausal women in most studies, is **hot flashes**. These are sudden experiences of warmth and sweating that occur at unpredictable times, last for a few seconds or minutes, and are often followed by a cold shiver. The other symptom is **vaginal atrophy**. The walls of the vagina become thinner and dryer, and some women experience irritation or pain during intercourse.

What about the psychological symptoms—the irritability and depression? Once again, we discover that there is wide variation among women. Some experience menopause as nothing more than an ending of their periods. In one study, about 25% of the women studied reported no symptoms at all (Crawford & Hooper, 1973). Many other women experience some physical symptoms and mild psychological symptoms. Only a small minority experience severe psychological upset. And often when psychological symptoms such as depression are experienced, they are actually a continuation of problems that existed well before the age of menopause (Greene, 1984).

One good clue to the fact that menopause is not so bad is the fact that premenopausal women have a more negative view of it than postmenopausal women do (Neugarten, Wood, Kraines, & Loomis, 1963). Women who have been through menopause generally think it does little to change a woman and even improves her life. For most women, menopause also has no major effect one way or the other on sexual interest and activity, even though the frequency of sexual activity gradually declines during middle age (Greene, 1984). A minority of women may feel less feminine and desirable, but another minority find sex *more* enjoyable once they are free from the worry of becoming pregnant. Despite the stereotypes, menopause seems to be "no big deal" for most women.

Why do some women experience more severe menopausal symptoms than others do? Perhaps because some women experience greater biological changes than others do. But psychological and social factors are also involved, just as they were in influencing reactions to adolescent sexual maturation and to monthly menstrual cycles. For example, lower-income women and housewives—who, as we have seen, tend to experience menstruation negatively—have more negative attitudes toward menopause and more symptoms than women from higher socioeconomic backgrounds who work outside the home (Greene, 1984; Severne, 1982). And cultural factors are also involved (see Box 5.2). It would seem that the experience of menopause is influenced by the meaning it has to an individual woman and to the society in which she lives.

The Male Climacteric

Despite popular references to the "male menopause," men cannot experience menopause, since they do not menstruate. What they can experience is captured by the term **climacteric**—meaning "critical time," and, more specifically, the loss of reproductive capacity in either sex in later life. But women experience their climacteric within a relatively narrow age range around age 50; in contrast, men may lose the ability to father children around then, or much later, or maybe never: Men in their 90s have been known to father children. The sperm produced by older men may not be as active. Levels of testosterone and other male hormones also decrease over the adult years in most men (Soules & Bremner, 1982) though apparently not in extremely healthy men (Harman & Tsitouras, 1980). In sum, the changes associated with the climacteric in men are more gradual, more variable, and less complete than those in women (Soules & Bremner, 1982).

What are the psychological impacts of these changes? There are few. Because they occur gradually, changes in the reproductive system cannot really explain the "midlife crisis" that some men experience. As we shall see in Chapter 15, a midlife transition period in a man's 40s is related more to events in his career and personal life than to any changes in his hormones. The frequency of the average man's sexual activity does decline over the adult years, but this trend cannot easily be tied to decreased hormone levels either. Older men may need a minimum level of testosterone to remain sexually active, but they can become less sexually active over the years even if their testosterone levels remain high (Tsitouras, Martin, & Harman, 1982). As we will see in Chapter 11, reduced sexual activity in later life is probably related to factors other than low hormone levels.

For both sexes, then, changes in the reproductive system are a normal part of aging. Yet neither women nor men seem to suffer much as their ability to have children

Box 5.2
Cultural Differences in the Experience of Menopause

Menopause is universal, and most women around the world have at least some experience of hot flashes. Psychological symptoms, however, vary widely from culture to culture. For instance, Marcha Flint (1982) surveyed women of a high and socially advantaged caste in India and found that very few women experienced any symptoms at all. Women who had not reached menopause looked forward to it, and women who had reached it were pleased that they had. Why didn't these women express more of the negative emotional reactions that women in our own society often report? According to Flint, menopause brought social rewards to these Indian women. They were freed from the taboos associated with menstruation that had kept them veiled and segregated from male society as younger women. They could now mingle with men other than their husbands and fathers and even drink the local brew with the fellows. Moreover, they still had meaningful work roles and were seen as wise by virtue of their years. By comparison, Flint believes women in our society lose status when they reach menopause. As older women, they are viewed as less attractive than younger women and may find it difficult to get jobs or play other meaningful roles.

This is a fascinating example of the role of social attitudes in influencing adjustments to biological change. Yet Ann Wright (1982) warns us that adjustment to menopause is influenced by more than a society's views of menopause. For example, she expected Navajo women in the United States to have an easy time adjusting to menopause because postmenopausal Navajo women are freed from menstrual taboos, have meaningful roles in society, and become eligible to take on ceremonial roles. Instead, she found that menopausal complaints were about as common as they are among Anglo-American women. Why? Unlike Flint's advantaged women in India, American Indian women living on the reservation had low incomes and poor health and had to cope with hard physical labor. Perhaps, then, *several* aspects of the way of life in a culture must be considered to explain why its people respond relatively positively or relatively negatively to a life change. Within any culture, of course, individual women will also differ greatly in their responses.

wanes or disappears. Sexual activity becomes less frequent, but it remains an important part of life for most older adults.

The Aging Brain

Many people fear that aging means losing one's brain cells and ultimately becoming senile. As we shall see in Chapter 16, Alzheimer's disease and other causes of "senility" are *not* part of normal aging, and they affect only small minorities of old people. What *does* normally happen to the brain as we age?

Normal aging *is* associated with a loss of neurons and less effective functioning of many remaining neurons. We might call this the *degeneration model* of aging in the nervous system. In fact, neurons are dying throughout life, but it is possible that enough of them have died by old age that the loss begins to impair behavior. Just as brain weight and volume increase over childhood, they decrease over the adult years, especially after age 50 (Yamaura, Ito, Kubota, & Matsuzawa, 1980). Neuron loss seems to be greater in the areas of the brain responsible for sensory and motor activities than in either the association areas of the cortex, which are involved in thought, or the brain stem and lower brain, which are involved in basic physiological functions (Whitbourne, 1985). Before they die, many neurons atrophy, or shrivel, and function less effectively (Bondareff, 1985; Scheibel, Lindsay, Tomiyasu, & Scheibel, 1975).

Also, the levels of important neurotransmitter chemicals involved in such behaviors as learning and remembering decline over the adult years (Bartus, Dean, Beer, & Lippa, 1982). In addition, the formation of "senile plaques," hard areas in the tissue surrounding neurons, may interfere with neuronal functioning (Bondareff, 1985). Finally, blood flow to the brain is reduced even in healthy older people, and especially in those with cardiovascular diseases, so that some neurons become starved for oxygen and nutrients (Shinohara, 1985). Depressing as it is, aging implies degeneration within the nervous system.

However, recent research suggests that there is more to aging than degeneration: There is also growth. A *plasticity model* of the aging nervous system emphasizes that the brain can change in response to experience and develop new capabilities throughout the life span (Greenough, 1986). Consider the landmark findings of Stephen Buell and Paul Coleman (1979). They compared brain tissue collected from autopsies of middle-aged adults (age 44–55), normal elderly adults (68–92), and elderly adults who had senile brain disease. Like earlier researchers, they found signs of degeneration or neuron loss in old brains—and in middle-aged brains as well. But they also found that other neurons were growing longer, bushier dendrites and presumably making new connections, or synapses, with other neurons. Normal old people actually had more well-developed dendrites than either middle-aged adults or old people with senile brain diseases.

Similarly, Peter Huttenlocher (1979) found that the number of synapses in the area of the cortex that he studied increased dramatically in the first two years of life, dropped slightly between childhood and adulthood, but did not change greatly over the adult years until very late in life. Apparently, new connections were forming fast enough in later adulthood to keep up with neuron loss. Studies of animals provide even more convincing evidence of this kind of plasticity in the older brain (Bondareff, 1985; Greenough, 1986).

In part, this brain plasticity appears to be a compensation that allows the aging person to maintain abilities quite well despite some normal neural degeneration (Bondareff, 1985). However, brain growth in old age is also a direct response to stimulation or experience. William Greenough (1986) and his colleagues have demonstrated in several studies that adult rats who are trained to perform tasks such as running mazes will form new synapses—and form them in precisely the brain areas that are most involved in the specific type of learning they are experiencing. It has been known for some time that environmental stimulation promotes brain growth in young animals. The surprise has been the discovery that this plasticity continues in later life (Connor, Diamond, & Johnson, 1980). The aging brain may be less plastic, less influenced by environmental enrichment or deprivation than the infant brain is. But recent research suggests that the infant brain is less plastic and the old brain is more plastic than was previously believed (Spreen et al., 1984).

What are the implications of this research for the older person? It appears that both degeneration and plasticity, both losses and gains, characterize the aging brain (Bondareff, 1985). In some people, degeneration may win out, and declines in intellectual performance and other behaviors will occur. But in other people, plasticity may win out. That is, their brains may form new and adaptive neural connections faster than they are lost so that performance on some tasks actually *improves* with age, at least until very old age. As we shall see in Chapters 7, 8, and 9, there are wide individual differences among older adults in intellectual functioning. One key to maintaining or even improving performance in old age is to avoid diseases that can interfere with nervous-system functioning. Another key is to remain intellectually active. Certainly we want to get beyond the view that aging involves nothing but a slow death of the brain. Old brains *can* learn new tricks!

Physical Behavior

How well can older adults carry out physical activities? Obviously those who have severe arthritis may have difficulty merely walking or dressing themselves without pain, but here we focus on two more typical changes in physical behavior over the adult years: a slowing of behavior, and a decreased ability to engage in strenuous activities.

The Slowing of Behavior

You may have noticed, as you breeze by them on the sidewalk, that old people often walk more slowly than young people do. Indeed, their style of walking often resembles that of someone walking on a slippery surface (Murray, Kory, & Clarkson, 1969; and see Figure 5.9). Why is this? For one thing, the sensory systems involved in balance do not function as well in old age as they did in earlier years (Ochs, Newberry, Lenhardt, & Harkins, 1985). Elderly people, like young children, have difficulty performing tests in which they must try to keep their balance when they are placed on a moving platform or are given mis-

Figure 5.9 Compared to the young man, the average older man takes short strides, does not achieve so large an angle between heel and floor, and swings his arms less widely. He appears to tread cautiously. (Based on Murray, Kory, & Clarkson, 1969)

leading sensory feedback (Stelmach, Phillips, DiFabio, & Teasdale, 1989; Woollacott, Shumway-Cook, & Nashner, 1986). Thus, many older people may walk slowly to compensate for poor balance.

An old person's slow pace of walking may also be due to reduced cardiovascular functioning. Cunningham, Rechnitzer, Pearce, and Donner (1982) tested men aged 19 to 66 and found that the pace at which men of any age chose to walk and the fastest pace at which they could walk were associated with their cardiovascular capacity. Old people with strong hearts may walk very briskly, but those—probably the majority—who have cardiovascular limitations find themselves slowing down.

Finally, when we try to account for why old people do things slowly, we cannot overlook changes in the brain. James Birren has argued that *the* central change that comes about as we age is a slowing of the nervous system (see Birren, Woods, & Williams, 1980). It affects not only motor behavior but mental functioning, and it affects a majority of elderly people to at least some degree. We have already seen that young children have especially slow reaction times. Reaction times improve until the 20s and gradually become slower over the adult years (Wilkinson & Allison, 1989). Elderly adults are especially slow to react when tasks are complex: when any one of several stimuli might appear, and each of them requires a different response (Botwinick, 1984; Welford, 1984).

But some older adults remain quick. Physically fit old people and those who are free from cardiovascular diseases have quicker reactions than their peers who lead sedentary lives or have diseases (Spirduso, 1980). In addition, experience may help elderly people continue to perform well on familiar motor tasks despite a slowing of the nervous system (see Box 5.3). In short, we should not expect all old people to be slow in all situations, though most do slow down somewhat.

Performance of Vigorous Activity

Slowing of the nervous system and of motor performance is one important fact of aging. Another is that many people become out of shape. Typically, adults decrease their involvement in vigorous physical activity as they get older, females earlier than males (Shephard & Montelpare, 1988). By late adulthood, they may find that they get tired just climbing stairs or carrying groceries. Running a marathon is out of the question. Several researchers find that the body exhibits more signs of aging when it is asked to exert great effort than during more typical daily activities (Lakatta, 1985; Stones & Kozma, 1985). The heart, lungs, and muscles are all critical in performing physical tasks that require strength, speed, or endurance. During vigorous activity, the average older person tires quickly and needs considerable time to recover.

Yet some older people *can* perform vigorous physical activities. Michael Stones and Albert Kozma (1985) cite the examples of the 70-year-old woman who competed in the

Box 5.3
Are Older Typists Slow?

Timothy Salthouse (1984) examined the psychomotor performance of female typists from age 19 to 72. On average, and in keeping with the results of countless studies, the older women performed more slowly than younger women did on a "choice" reaction time task. Here they had to quickly press one typewriter key when the letter *R* appeared and another when the letter *L* appeared on a screen. In the graph, the diagonal line for choice reaction time shows the average performance of women of different ages, while each dot represents the reaction time of a particular woman. Longer reaction times (dots higher on the graph) mean slower performance. Yet notice that older women typed written material just as fast as the younger women did! Their reaction times during a typing exercise were *not* slowed by age.

How did they keep up their typing speed even though their nervous system's reactions had slowed? Through a careful analysis, Salthouse established that they did exactly what any highly skilled typist does. As they typed one letter, they were already processing information about the next letters to be typed, giving themselves more time to get ready for any particular stroke of the keys. They were planning farther ahead than the younger typists were. Thus, practice at a skill may allow older people who perform quite slowly on reaction time tasks in the laboratory to perform familiar motor tasks very quickly and effectively in everyday life.

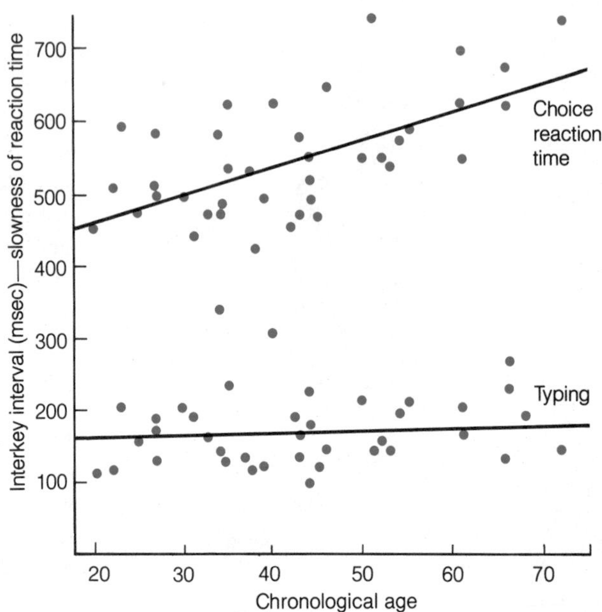

1972 Olympic equestrian events and the 98-year-old man who could run a marathon (26 miles) in 7½ hours! What if more older adults exercised vigorously? Can exercise slow the aging process? Regular exercise has many beneficial effects on the body at any age and can make an old body function more like a younger body. It can improve cardiovascular and respiratory functioning, slow bone loss, strengthen muscles, and enhance mental functioning (Buskirk, 1985; Clarkson-Smith & Hartley, 1989; Spirduso, 1980). Indeed, Roy Shephard (1978, 1985) estimates that regular fitness training at retirement age can delay the age at which a person becomes physically dependent by as many as eight years. What exercise cannot do is halt the inevitable aging process. Even the hearts of long-time athletes lose some of their capacity over time (Heath, Hagberg, Ehsani, & Holloszy, 1981; Stones & Kozma, 1985).

Aging, Disease, Disuse, and Abuse

We have now seen that many aspects of physical functioning decline over the adult years. But an important question arises: When we look at the old people of today, are we seeing the effects of aging itself or the effects of something else? The "something else" could be disease, disuse of the body, abuse of the body—or all three.

For instance, most old people have at least some chronic disease or impairment. How would an elderly person function if he or she could manage to stay completely disease free? James Birren and his colleagues (1963) addressed just this question in a classic study of men aged 65 to 91. Extensive medical examinations were conducted to identify two groups of elderly men: (1) those who were almost perfectly healthy and had *no* signs of disease at all and (2) those who had slight traces of disease-in-the-making but no clinically diagnosable diseases. Several aspects of physical and intellectual functioning were assessed in these men, and they were also compared to young men.

The most remarkable finding was that the healthier group of old men hardly differed at all from the young men. They were equal even in their capacity for physical exercise, and they actually beat the young men on measures of intelligence that require general information or knowledge of vocabulary words. Their main limitation was the slowing of brain activity and reaction time that seems to be so basic to the aging process. Overall, *aging itself in the absence of disease had little effect on physical and psychological functioning*. However, the men with slight traces of impending disease *were* deficient on several measures. Diseases that have progressed to the point of symptoms have more serious consequences for performance.

So, it is possible that disease rather than aging itself accounts for many declines in functioning in later life. We must note, however, that Birren and his colleagues had great difficulty in finding perfectly healthy old people. This means that most older people are experiencing *both* aging and disease, and we cannot neatly separate the effects of the two.

Since chronic diseases do become more common in old age, some experts even regard old age as a disease! John Rowe (1985) concludes that aging should not be equated with disease but that some aging processes are very diseaselike and harmful to the body. For example, arthritis and osteoporosis appear to be normal aging processes carried to an extreme. "Normal" changes in the blood vessels that make them stiffer directly cause high blood pressure. Thus the tendency to develop diseases is one part—and an important part—of normal aging. But it is also important to recognize that some older people remain much freer of disease than others do, and consequently function better. It would be a big mistake for an aging person to automatically assume that he or she is just "getting old" and therefore fail to seek medical treatment (Rowe, 1985).

Disuse and abuse of the body also contribute to declines in physical functioning. Masters and Johnson (1966) proposed a "use it or lose it" maxim to describe the fact that sexual functioning deteriorates if a person engages in little or no sexual activity. The same maxim can be applied to other systems of the body. Certainly muscles atrophy if they are not used, and the heart functions less well in the sedentary person than in the person who regularly exercises. Even the brain may need mental exercise to continue to function effectively in old age (Schaie, 1983). Most systems of the body seem to thrive on *use*. Finally, *abuse* of the body contributes to declines in functioning. Excessive alcohol consumption, a high fat diet, a sedentary lifestyle, and smoking are all clear examples. And while elderly adults are not often recreational drug abusers, many do take several prescribed medications. Drugs typically affect older adults more strongly than they do younger adults; drugs also interact with one another and with the aging body's chemistry to impair functioning (Cherry & Morton, 1989; Lamy, 1986).

Overall, then, poor functioning in old age may represent any combination of the effects of aging, disease, disuse, and abuse. Many of these factors can be controlled by adopting healthy lifestyles. To be sure, no one has discovered a way to stop the basic aging process from occurring. Nor can some diseases be prevented. But regular exercise, a nutritious diet, and the elimination of dangerous habits can have very positive effects, especially if these lifestyle changes are made early in life and continued throughout adulthood. Indeed, James Fries and Lawrence Crapo (1981) have suggested that most of us could survive to an average age of 85 in quite good health if we changed our lifestyles. We would then die a "natural" death when our bodies no longer have enough reserve capacities left to fight such insults as pneumonia. If today's young people are really getting the message about the effects of lifestyle on health, they should experience a longer and healthier old age than that experienced by older people today.

APPLICATIONS: NUTRITION ACROSS THE LIFE SPAN

"You are what you eat." Is that true? Since diet is one influence on physical growth and functioning that can be controlled, the answer has very practical implications. A

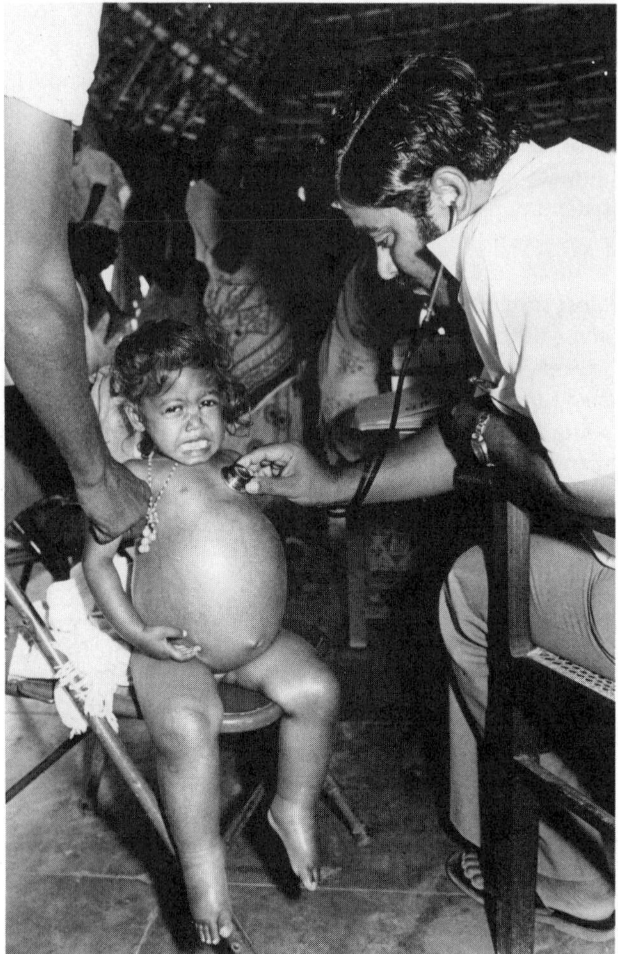

The lesions on this girl's skin and her swollen stomach are symptoms of a serious nutritional disease called *kwashiorkor*, which occurs when a child gets enough calories but little or no protein. In many poor countries, kwashiorkor develops after infants are weaned from the breast and lose their principal source of protein.

proper diet involves eating neither too little nor too much *and* obtaining sufficient amounts of important nutrients.

As we saw in Chapter 4, adequate nutrition is essential for normal prenatal development. The baby whose mother was severely malnourished during pregnancy is likely to be small, to have fewer than the normal number of brain cells, and to be at risk for other defects and even death. Diet continues to be essential during infancy, especially since the brain is still rapidly developing. Mothers who are breast feeding should continue on a nutritious diet with enough calories to supply both themselves and their infants. The effects of poor prenatal nutrition may be reversed if a child is well nourished after birth (Winick, 1976). However, prenatally malnourished infants may also need extra cognitive and social stimulation if they are to recover fully and achieve a normal level of intellectual development (Zeskind & Ramey, 1978, 1981).

Assuming that prenatal nutrition has been adequate, infants and young children seem to be able to cope with a temporary shortage of food. Although their growth is likely to slow down while they are malnourished, they grow much faster than normal when their diets become adequate again. James Tanner (1978) views this **catch-up growth** as a basic principle of physical development. After a period of malnutrition or serious illness, the child's body will struggle to get back on the growth course that it is genetically programmed to follow. But what if a child is seriously malnourished over a long time? We see many examples of this in famine-stricken countries. Many children die of starvation. But before they die, they are ravaged by serious nutrition-related diseases. Prolonged malnutrition during the first five years of life may seriously retard brain development and cause a child to remain smaller than normal throughout life (Tanner, 1978).

In the United States and other Western countries, malnutrition due to severe deficiencies in protein or total calorie intake is relatively rare. However, surveys suggest that many young children, especially in poverty areas, are not getting enough vitamins and minerals (Eichorn, 1979). Vitamin and mineral deficiencies may make children irritable and listless and slow their rate of growth. A child who is malnourished in this way is also less resistant to illnesses.

Then there are the young children who are *over*fed. The term *obesity* has been commonly used to describe individuals who are at least 20% above the "ideal" weight for their height, age, and sex; it has also been defined as an excessive proportion of fat to lean tissue. Obesity is a threat to health. Obese people do not live as long as their normal-weight peers, and they are at greater risk for such problems as heart and kidney disease, high blood pressure, diabetes, liver problems, and even arthritis. Generally, obesity is due to a combination of factors: heredity, overeating, and a low activity level.

Is an overweight infant or young child likely to remain overweight later in life? There is some evidence that this is the case (Neyzi et al., 1976; Zack, Harlan, Leaverton, & Cornoni-Huntley, 1979). However, there are many obese infants and young children who slim down as adults, and there are obese adults who were *not* overweight early in life (Roche, 1981). By the elementary school years, the relationship between early obesity and later obesity is stronger (Roche, 1981). Should chubby children be put on crash diets, then? No, for this may actually aggravate weight problems in the long run. Besides, once children are obese they often eat no more than their thinner peers (Mayer, 1975) but are less active. Many doctors suggest that obese children be encouraged to get more exercise rather than to severely restrict their diets. Overweight youngsters also need support from parents rather than criticism, especially since they face enough rejection and teasing from peers, who very early in the elementary school years develop negative stereotypes of their chubby age mates (Sigelman, Miller, & Whitworth, 1986; Staffieri, 1967).

Adolescence is another time of life in which nutritional needs change and proper diet is very important. Too much dieting may delay a girl's menarche. Improved nutrition over the past century is one reason for the secular trend toward earlier development and larger bodies. Yet many teenagers today seem to skip meals and choose junk food and fast food when they do eat. As a result, vitamin and mineral deficiencies are more common among 13- to 16-year-olds than among either younger children or older adolescents (McGanity, 1976). Teenagers also face increased risks of obesity because their rate of metabolism is slower than children's. Heightened concern with physical appearance during adolescence may make life especially difficult for the obese teenager (Mendelson & White, 1985).

Finally, new challenges arise in adulthood. As we have already seen, middle-aged adults, especially women, need to be especially concerned about getting enough calcium in their diets to help prevent osteoporosis. Middle-aged adults may find themselves gaining weight, especially if they become less physically active but keep eating as much as they did as younger adults (Weg, 1983). In addition, U.S. adults tend to eat too many fatty foods. This increases their chances of developing cardiovascular diseases and some cancers (Guigoz & Munro, 1985).

In old age, people tend to lose weight. For one thing, they seem to reduce their total calorie intakes (McGandy, Barrows, Spanias, Meredith, Stone, & Norris, 1966), in part because they become less physically active and therefore need less food. However, many experts worry that some older adults eat so little that they are not getting enough nutrients, and research does indeed suggest that older adults often suffer from deficiencies in needed vitamins and minerals (Guigoz & Munro, 1985). Maradee Davis and her colleagues (Davis, Murphy, & Neuhaus, 1988; Davis et al., 1985) have found that nutrition is especially inadequate among older people who have low incomes and live alone rather than with a spouse. Older adults who are malnourished not only may feel unwell and become susceptible to illnesses, they may even show symptoms of "senility" (Weg, 1983). Whether one is old or young, then, poor nutrition can threaten normal development and functioning.

REFLECTIONS

After reading this chapter, how would you describe the relationships between body and mind, between physiology and psychology? Did you notice how it seems almost impossible to distinguish body from mind? "Mind"—the nervous system—is, after all, part of the body, a system of cells interrelated to other systems of cells. Its functioning is affected by the capacity of the heart and lungs to supply it with oxygen and nutrients; at the same time, it regulates the functioning of these organs. It allows us to walk or run, yet it suffers if we do not do so regularly.

Moreover, changes in the body require psychological adjustments and bring psychological change. The newly mobile infant benefits psychologically from access to a larger physical and social world; the adolescent must adjust to physical and sexual maturation; the elderly adult may have to cope with disease and disability. At the same time, psychological attitudes influence reactions to physical changes. The teenage boy who values physical prowess above all things is especially discouraged if he matures late, and the woman who expects menopause to be difficult may indeed find it so.

In short, we must keep our focus on the *whole person*, body and mind, as we now turn toward the more "psychological" aspects of human development. And if we want to enhance development and functioning, it helps to know that sounder bodies mean sounder minds. We can see to it that our children get adequate nutrition and exercise, and we, as adults, can build preventive health practices into our own lifestyles. We cannot alter the basic processes of physical maturation and aging, but do we need to? It would, after all, be hard to improve on the elegant maturational plan that makes us increasingly effective, physically and mentally, over the years of infancy and childhood, and that converts children to adults during adolescence. And even biological aging—so long as it involves a minimum of disease, disuse, and abuse—is not to be dreaded. We will die, but we can surely increase the chances that we will remain physically and mentally fit until we do.

SUMMARY POINTS

1. Each of the many systems of the human body develops and ages at its own rate, guided by a genetic program set into action by the brain and hormones released by the endocrine system.

2. The nervous system, communicating by means of neurotransmitter chemicals, is central to all human functioning.

3. Newborns have a wide range of reflexes, working senses, a capacity to learn, and organized sleeping and waking states; they are competent but also limited creatures.

4. Infants grow physically in a cephalocaudal and proximodistal pattern; bones harden, muscles strengthen, and neurons proliferate and organize themselves into interconnected groups. The plasticity of the infant brain allows it to recover from injury and fine-tune itself in response to environmental stimulation.

5. As the motor areas of the brain's cortex mature, motor milestones are achieved in a predictable cephalocaudal and proximodistal order, permitting more controlled motions; maturation guides early motor development, but opportunities to practice motor behaviors are also necessary.

6. During childhood, the body steadily grows, neural transmission speeds up, lateralization becomes more firmly established, and control of large muscles and small muscles as well as reaction time improve.

7. The adolescent growth spurt and pubertal changes make adolescence a time of dramatic physical change: Girls reach menarche at an average age of 12½ or 13; boys experience their first ejaculation a bit later. Rates of maturation vary widely in part because of genetic makeup and in part because of nutrition and health status.

8. Most adolescent girls and boys react to the maturation process with mixed feelings and become concerned about their physical appearance or capabilities. The physical capabilities of boys improve during adolescence, while those of many girls level off or even decline, perhaps because of cultural factors that make girls less active physically. Advantages of early maturation are greater for boys than for girls, but the differences fade over time.

9. Most systems of the body reach a peak of functioning between childhood and early adulthood and decline steadily thereafter, but individual differences in the rate of aging are large.

10. During the reproductive years of adulthood, many women experience mood swings during the menstrual cycle, but few women are incapacitated. Men's hormone levels fluctuate, but there is little evidence their moods are affected.

11. Women reach menopause and lose their reproductive capacity at about age 50, and most experience hot flashes and vaginal atrophy, but few experience severe psychological symptoms. The reproductive systems of men age more gradually and less completely.

12. During adulthood, neurons in the brain atrophy and die, levels of neurotransmitters decrease, and blood flow to the brain decreases, but the aging brain is also plastic, forming new synapses to compensate for neural loss and reorganizing itself in response to learning experiences.

13. As people age, their motor and intellectual behavior appears to slow, possibly because of disease, disuse, and abuse as well as aging: Healthy old people perform much like young people. Although aging and disease are distinct, certain diseases are a fact of aging for most people.

14. One important aspect of a healthy lifestyle at any age is proper nutrition.

KEY TERMS

adolescent growth spurt
androgens
catch-up growth
cephalocaudal
cerebral cortex
climacteric
endocrine gland
estrogen
hot flashes
human growth hormone
infant states
lateralization
menarche
menopause
myelin
neuron
osteoporosis
pincer grasp
pituitary gland
plasticity
premenstrual syndrome (PMS)
proximodistal
puberty
reflex
REM sleep
secular trend
synapse
testosterone
vaginal atrophy

CHAPTER

PERCEPTION

You are a newborn, just entering the world. It is bright and noisy. You are sponged, swaddled, and handed to your mother. She says, "Oh, look at you," and gently strokes your head and shoulders. What do you make of all this sensory input? And how does your experience of this first encounter differ from your mother's? ❦

Psychologists have long distinguished between sensation and perception. **Sensation** is the process by which sensory receptor neurons detect information and transmit it to the brain. From birth, infants sense the environment. They detect light, sound, odor-bearing molecules in the air, and other stimuli. But do they make "sense" of it? **Perception** is the interpretation of sensory input: recognizing what you see, understanding what is said to you, knowing that the odor you have detected is sizzling steak, and so on. Does the newborn really perceive the world, or merely sense it? And what has happened to sensory and perceptual capacities by old age? Do the senses still work well, or do most people have visual or hearing impairments? Does the sensory world make as much sense as it did earlier in life?

Perhaps we should start with a more basic question: Why should you care about the development of sensation and perception? One of the authors (who shall remain nameless) asked this very question while taking an introductory psychology course in college. All that "stuff" about the anatomy of the eye and ear—that wasn't psychology. Fortunately, this unnamed college student wised up (though it took years). Sensation and perception are at the very heart of human functioning. Just try to think of one thing you do that does not depend on your perceiving the world around you. You certainly would have a tough time as a college student if you could neither read the printed word nor understand speech. Indeed, you would not be able to walk to class without certain body senses that control movement. Possibly one of the reasons that sensation and perception may not seem important is that they occur so effortlessly. We simply take them for granted—unless perhaps we are made to think about what it might be like to be blind or deaf. Then most of us are terrorized.

There is another reason to be interested in sensation and perception. For centuries, philosophers have asked questions about how we gain knowledge of reality, and their debates often center on perception. Let's briefly look at two issues that the early philosophers and contemporary developmental theorists have debated.

ISSUES IN PERCEPTUAL DEVELOPMENT

Empiricists such as the 17th century British philosopher John Locke (1690/1939) believed that infants enter the world as *tabulae rasae* (blank slates) who know nothing except what they learn through their senses and who are therefore the products of nurture rather than nature. Empiricists think infants perceive the world very differently from adults because they lack perceptual experience. In contrast, *nativists* argue that we come to the world with knowledge. For example, René Descartes (1638/1965) and Immanuel Kant (1781/1958) believed that we are born with an understanding of the spatial world. Presumably the infant does not need to learn that receding objects will appear smaller or that approaching objects will seem larger; perceptual understandings like these are built into the human nervous system, making the infant perceiver quite similar to the adult perceiver.

Today's developmental theorists take less extreme stands on the nature/nurture issue. They understand that the innate endowment of human beings, maturational processes, and experience or learning all contribute to perceptual development. Yet they still grapple with nature/nurture issues. They ask how early in life different perceptual capacities emerge and what kinds of experience help or hinder perceptual development.

Now consider a second issue that philosophers have debated: Is the coherent reality that we experience through the senses actually "out there," or is it something that we create by imposing meaning on otherwise ambiguous stimulation to the senses? This issue is hotly contested in two modern theories of perceptual development: enrichment theory and differentiation theory.

Enrichment theory, which has been associated with Jean Piaget (1954, 1960), argues that the stimulation received by sensory receptors is actually quite fragmented and confusing. We must add to it, or enrich it, if it is to make sense. You may look at a blurry camp photo, for example, and be able to recognize a particular camper because you can draw on your memory of who was at camp and who was friends with whom to mentally construct a recognized face. In this view, then, we bring much to our perceptual experience—notably stored knowledge—that helps us create order and meaning out of the bits and pieces of sensory stimulation that we receive (see Figure 6.1). Cognition "enriches" sensory experience. Cognitive development makes the child or adult more able to construct a meaningful world than the infant can.

By contrast, **differentiation theory** argues that all the information we could want is "out there" in the stimulation we receive. It is our task to differentiate that stimulation—to detect differences that were there all the time. Eleanor Gibson (1969, 1987; Gibson & Spelke, 1983) takes this view. Consider the world of dogs. At age 2, we may say "dog" when we see cats, dogs, and other small furry animals. We have not yet noticed the **distinctive features** of these types of animals. That is, we have not detected the critical differences in shape, size, and other qualities that would allow us to distinguish among them. Once we have this bit of perceptual learning taken care of, we might begin to differentiate breeds of dogs, noticing that bulldogs have squashed noses while Irish setters have long ones. Through continued perceptual learning, adults who serve as judges in dog shows are able to make fine distinctions among dogs of the same breed that the rest of us miss. Gibson's point is that the pieces of information needed in order to make these fine distinctions were always there in the dogs themselves. Similarly, the information that would permit us to recognize a dog as the same dog despite changes in our viewing angle is there all along. Although young infants seem to be sensitive to much of the information contained in the perceptual world, they will be able to extract even more such information as they get older.

Figure 6.1 Expectations influence perception. If you saw this drawing amid drawings of faces, you would be likely to perceive an elderly bald man with glasses. But look again with the idea of finding an animal, and you are likely to see a rat with large ears and its tail circling in front of its body. Cognition has a great deal to do with what we make of sensory stimulation. This is the position taken by enrichment theorists such as Jean Piaget. (Adapted from Reese, 1963)

Thus enrichment theorists such as Piaget and differentiation theorists such as Gibson disagee about how we come to perceive a more meaningful world as we get older. We either get better at adding information to sensory stimulation, or we get better at detecting information that is already contained in that stimulation. There is merit in both positions.

Philosophers were raising the kinds of issues about perception that Gibson and Piaget have raised long before anyone had conducted research on the perceptual capabilities of young infants. Now such research has been conducted, and it is some of the most exciting research in all of developmental psychology.

So let us get into it. We will want to look very closely at sensation and perception in infancy, for it is very early in life that we can see fundamental perceptual capacities emerge. We will also want to see how much more "intelligent" the senses become during childhood and adolescence. And we will want to confront the image of old age as a time when sensory abilities are lost to determine how much truth there is in this image. Finally, we will deal more explicitly with the issue of how nature and nurture contribute to perceptual development across the life span.

THE INFANT

The pioneering American psychologist William James (1890) doubted that young infants could make much sense of the sensory world: "To the infant, sounds, sights, touches, and pains, form one unanalyzed [blooming, buzzing] confusion" (Vol. 1, p. 496). James was actually noting that impressions from the several senses are fused rather than separable, but his statement has since been quoted to represent the view that the world of the young infant is hopelessly confusing.

Today the accepted view is that young infants have far greater perceptual abilities than James ever suspected. Their senses are functioning even before birth, and in their early months of life they show many signs that they are perceiving a coherent rather than a chaotic world. Why the change in views? It is not that babies have gotten any smarter. It is that researchers have gotten smarter. They have developed more sophisticated methods of studying exactly what infants can and cannot do. Infants, after all, cannot tell us directly what they perceive, so the trick has been to develop ways to let their behavior speak for them. We will see several examples of the ingenuity of modern research methods as we now explore perception in infancy.

Vision

Most of us tend to think of vision as our most indispensable sense. Because vision is indeed important, we examine its early development in some detail before turning to the other major senses.

Basic Capacities

The eye functions by taking in stimulation in the form of light and converting it to electrical-chemical signals to the brain. How well does the newborn's visual system work?

Quite well, in fact. From the first, the infant can detect changes in brightness; the pupils of newborns' eyes constrict in bright light and dilate (expand) in dim light (Pratt, 1954). The ability to discriminate between degrees of brightness develops rapidly. By only 2 months of age, infants can distinguish a white bar that differs only 5% in luminance from a solid white background (Peeples & Teller, 1975).

Very young infants also see the world in color, not in black and white as some early observers had thought. How do we know this? A widely used technique for studying perception relies on the fact that infants will lose interest in a repeatedly presented stimulus over time. This learning to be bored is called **habituation**. If an infant who has habituated to one stimulus regains interest when a somewhat different stimulus is substituted, we know that the two stimuli have been discriminated.

So suppose we habituate an infant to a blue disk. What will happen if we now present either a blue disk of a different shade or a green disk? As Marc Bornstein and his colleagues established, 4-month-old infants will show little interest in another blue disk but will be very interested in a green disk—even when the light reflected from these two stimuli differs in wavelength from the original blue stimulus by exactly the same amount (Bornstein, Kessen, & Weiskopf, 1976). Bornstein and his colleagues concluded that 4-month-olds discriminate colors and categorize portions of the continuum of wavelengths of light into basic color categories (red, blue, green, and yellow) in the same way that adults do. There are signs that infants younger than about 3 months of age may not yet be highly sensitive to blue colors (Powers, Schneck, & Teller, 1981). But there is agreement that by about 3 months of age color vision is very mature (Banks & Salapatek, 1983).

Do young infants see objects clearly, or are they blurry? This is a matter of **visual acuity**, or the ability to perceive detail. By adult standards, the newborn's visual acuity is poor. You have undoubtedly heard of 20/20 vision, as measured by the familiar eye chart (Snellen chart) with the big "E" at the top. Infants cannot be asked to read eye charts. However, they do prefer to look at a patterned stimulus unless it is so fine-grained that it looks no different than a blank. So by presenting more and more fine-grained striped patterns to infants, we can find the point at which acuity for the stripes is lost.

Although estimates differ, the newborn's vision may be as poor as 20/600, which means that the infant sees clearly at 20 feet what an adult with normal vision can see at 600 feet (Banks & Salapatek, 1983). Part of the reason for the newborn's poor acuity is difficulty with **visual accommodation**—that is, changing the shape of the lens of the eye to bring objects at different distances into focus. Until recently, it was thought that young infants could not accommodate and that they could see clearly only objects that were about 7 to 10 inches from their faces. Their lens shape was supposedly "set" for that distance. Now it seems that the ability to accommodate the lens develops very quickly, but that the eyes of young infants still do not produce sharp, clear images at *any* distance (Banks, 1980). Still, young infants can see quite well objects or patterns that are fairly large and have sharp light/dark contrasts—the faces of parents, for example (Banks & Salapatek, 1983). Visual acuity improves rapidly; by 6–12 months of age the infant sees as well as an adult does (Walk, 1981).

In short, the eyes of the young infant are not working at peak levels, but they are certainly working. Newborns can perceive light and dark, distinguish colors, and see patterns that are not too finely detailed. Now, does all this visual stimulation make any sense?

Very Early Pattern Perception

It is one thing to say that the young infants can see, but it is another to say that they can discriminate different patterns of visual stimulation. In the early 1960s, Robert Fantz conducted a number of pioneering studies to determine whether infants can discriminate forms or patterns. Babies were placed on their backs in an apparatus called a looking chamber and shown two or more patterns. An observer then recorded the amount of time that the infant gazed at each pattern. If infants gaze longer at one pattern than another, it demonstrates that they prefer one to the other, and they could not prefer one to the other unless they could distinguish them.

What did Fantz learn? Babies less than 2 days old could discriminate visual forms (Fantz, 1963). They preferred to look at patterned stimuli such as faces or concentric circles rather than at unpatterned disks. They also seemed to have a special interest in the human face, for they looked at a face longer than they looked at other patterned stimuli such as a bull's-eye or newsprint. However, Fantz (1961) also used his looking chamber to see whether young infants would prefer a face, a stimulus with facial features in a scrambled array, or a simpler stimulus with the same amount of light and dark as the normal face and the "scrambled" face. These infants clearly preferred both the face and the scrambled face to the unpatterned stimulus, but they were no more interested in the normal face than in the scrambled face. Here, then, was a hint that human faces are of interest to very young infants not because they are faces, but because they have certain physical properties that create interest, whether those properties show up in a real face or a scrambled face.

So the search began for the properties of patterns that "turn infants on." For one thing, infants are attracted to patterns that have a large amount of light/dark transition, or **contour**. Young infants are attracted to edges or boundaries between light and dark areas, especially if the light/dark contrast is sharp (Banks & Ginsburg, 1985). Since faces and scrambled faces have an equal amount of contour, they are equally interesting.

Second, young infants are attracted to movement. Newborns can and do track a moving target with their eyes, though their tracking is at first imprecise and is unlikely to occur unless the target is moving slowly (Kremenitzer, Vaughn, Kurtzberg, & Dowling, 1979). Newborns will also look longer at a rotating triangle than at a stationary one (Slater, Morison, Town, & Rose, 1985).

Finally, the *complexity* of a stimulus appears to influence early visual preferences. Fantz and Fagan (1975) exposed infants to two patterns of squares. The two stimuli had the same amount of light/dark contour, or light/dark border area, but they differed in complexity, or the number of elements or figures they contained. One had 8 squares, the other 32. One-month-old infants preferred the simpler pattern with 8 squares, while 2-month-olds preferred the more complex pattern. Putting this information together with other information, it seems that from birth infants are attracted to *moderately complex* patterns. They prefer a clear pattern of some kind (for example, an eight-square checkerboard) to either a blank stimulus or a very detailed or complex stimulus (for example, the 32-square array or a page from the *New York Times*). As infants mature, they come to prefer more and more complex stimuli.

In sum, we know that young infants have visual preferences and we know something about the physical properties of stimuli that attract their attention. They seek out contour, movement, and moderate complexity. As it happens, human faces have all of these physical properties. Martin Banks and his colleagues have offered a very simple explanation for these early visual preferences: *Young infants seem to prefer to look at whatever they can see well* (Banks & Ginsburg, 1985). Based on a very complex mathematical model, Banks has been able to predict what different patterns might look like to the eye of a young infant. Figure 6.2 gives an example. The young eye sees a highly complex checkerboard as a big dark blob. A moderately complex checkerboard still has pattern to it by the

Figure 6.2 What the young eye sees. By the time these two checkerboards are processed by eyes with undeveloped vision, only the checkerboard on the left may have any pattern left to it. Blurry vision in early infancy helps to explain a preference for moderately complex rather than highly complex stimuli. (From Banks & Salapatek, 1983)

time it is processed by the infant's eye. *Poor vision* would therefore explain why Fantz and Fagan (1975) found young infants to prefer moderate complexity to high complexity. Indeed, poor vision can account for a number of the infant's visual preferences. Young infants seem to actively seek out exactly the visual input that they can see well and that will stimulate the development of the visual centers of their brains (Banks & Ginsburg, 1985; Haith, 1980).

To this point, we have established that from birth, infants discriminate patterns and prefer some to others. But do they really perceive *forms*? For example, do they just see some lines or angles when they view a triangle, or do they see a triangular form that stands out from its background as a distinct shape? Do they perceive a coherent and whole form, or only parts of a form? Some research suggests that the newborn or 1-month-old is sensitive to information about whole shapes or forms (e.g., Slater, Morison, & Rose, 1983; Treiber & Wilcox, 1980). But most research points to an important breakthrough in perception starting at about 2 or 3 months of age.

Later Pattern and Form Perception

Even though the infant's accomplishments within the first couple of months of life are indeed impressive, important changes take place thereafter in the perception of patterns and forms. Part of the story is told in Figure 6.3, which shows what Philip Salapatek (1975; Maurer & Salapatek, 1976) discovered about the eye movements of 1-month-olds and 2-month-olds when they look at geometric figures or faces. Starting at about 2 months of age, infants no longer focus on some external boundary, as 1-month-olds do. Instead, they explore the interiors of figures thoroughly (for example, looking at a person's facial features rather than just at the chin, hairline, and top of head). It is as though they are no longer content to locate where an object starts and where it ends, as 1-month-olds tend to do; they seem to want to know *what it is.*

At about 2 or 3 months of age, infants also begin to prefer looking at a normal face rather than at a scrambled face (Kagan, 1971; Maurer, 1985). Recently, James Dannemiller and Benjamin Stephens (1988) convincingly demonstrated that at 3 months of age, but not at 6 weeks, infants even prefer a normal face drawing to an otherwise identical pattern in which areas that are normally dark on a face (facial features, hair) were made light, and areas that are normally light (the cheeks, for example) were made dark. Why does the human face seem to take on special significance at this age? Jerome Kagan (1971) proposed that infants are beginning to form mental representations or recipes—schemata—for familiar objects. The infant who has by now had some weeks of experience looking at human faces forms a schema or mental image of what faces generally look like. After about 2 or 3 months of age, the infant is in a position to compare objects to existing schemata for familiar objects. An object that is identical to an existing schema needs to be scanned only briefly to be matched to the schema. If it is greatly different from any existing schema, the infant will lose interest. If the stimulus is *moderately discrepant* from an existing schema, the infant will study it intently, as if trying to match it to the schema and therefore to interpret it in the context of existing knowledge.

From this perspective, a face drawing or a new face is especially attention-grabbing to infants 2 months old or

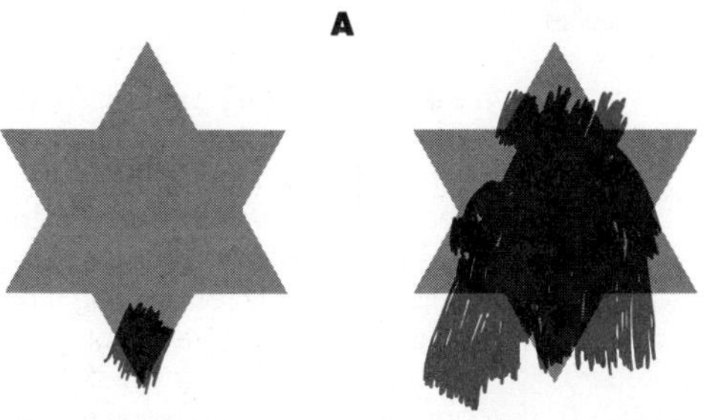

Visual scanning of a geometric figure by 1- and 2-month-old infants

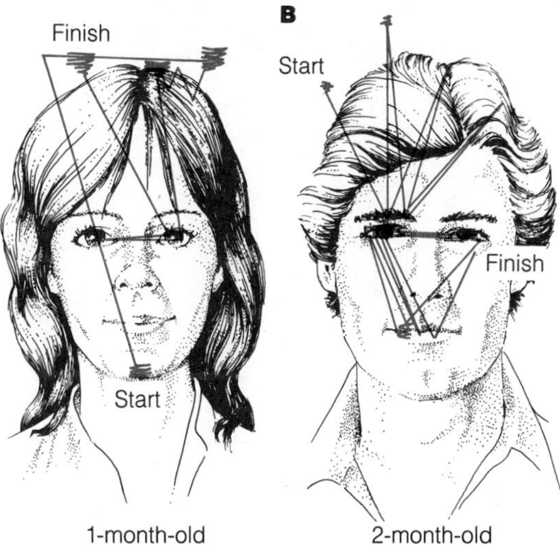

Visual scanning of the human face by 1- and 2-month-old infants

Figure 6.3 Visual scanning in early infancy. The 1-month-old seems to be trying to locate where an object begins and ends, whereas the 2-month-old seems to be on the way to figuring out what an object is by exploring it inside and out. (Adapted from Salapatek, 1975)

somewhat older. It is not quite like any face they have seen, but with some work they can experience the delight of recognizing it as a face—and infants do indeed express their pleasure when they can match what they see to an existing schema. At this point, infants are seeing a *face form*, not just an appealing patterning of light and dark. By contrast, a scrambled face may be too bizarre to interest an infant who has just struggled to form a mental model of the normal face. Now it is not just the physical properties of stimuli that matter; it is their *familiarity*.

Interestingly, it is at about this age that infants seem to recognize their parents' faces. Maria Barrera and Daphne Maurer (1981b) have shown that 3-month-old infants not only recognize photographs of their mothers' faces but prefer to look at their mothers rather than at strangers. They can also discriminate the faces of two strangers—strangers judged to be quite similar by a panel of adults (Barrera & Maurer, 1981a). Even more amazingly, 3-month-olds will look longer at faces that adults rate as attractive than at faces that adults rate as unattractive (Samuels & Ewy, 1985)! So by the tender age of 12 or 13 weeks, infants seem to have formed schemata to represent the human face in general and some faces in particular, have progressed beyond the point where strangers "all look alike," and even find some faces more appealing than others! The ability to discriminate and recognize faces improves rapidly in the following months (Cohen, DeLoache, & Strauss, 1979).

Infants of this age still have some work to do, however. For one thing, they must learn to perceive a world of distinct objects separated from other objects and from their backgrounds. How, for example, would a young infant know that a glass of milk in front of a cereal box on the kitchen table is not just part of the box? Philip Kellman and Elizabeth Spelke (1983; Kellman, Spelke, & Short, 1986) looked into this matter closely by presenting 4-month-old infants with a display consisting of a rod partially hidden by a block. As Box 6.1 reveals, these infants *did* perceive the rod as one whole rod, but only if it had moved around while they watched it, not if it was stationary. On the basis of such research, Eleanor Gibson and Elizabeth Spelke (1983) conclude that infants have an unlearned ability early in life to organize a visual scene into distinct objects. Some cues to the wholeness of an object, such as those provided by movement, are possibly even innate, for young infants seem to know more about objects when they are moving than when they are stationary (Gibson, 1987; Kaufmann-Hayoz, Kaufmann, & Stucki, 1986; Spelke, von Hofsten, & Kestenbaum, 1989). However, it takes longer for infants to learn to interpret other cues to an object's wholeness so that even a stationary scene can be organized into distinct objects, as shown in Box 6.1.

In the first half of their first year, infants also show an ability to perceive coherent patterns within a visual scene. Decades ago, Max Wertheimer (1923) and other **Gestalt**

Box 6.1
Perceiving Objects as Wholes

If you were to look at either the stationary hidden rod (display A) or the moving hidden rod (display B) below, you would readily perceive a whole rod, even though part of it is hidden from view. Do young infants also perceive a whole rod? To find out, Philip Kellman and Elizabeth Spelke (1983) habituated 4-month-olds to either display A or display B. Once the display was familiar, the infants were shown displays C (a whole rod) and D (two rod segments). Which did they now treat as "old hat"?

After habituating to a stationary rod, these infants showed no preference one way or the other for the whole rod or the rod segments. They had apparently not been able to use available cues—cues such as the fact that the two "parts" of the rod were oriented along the same line and were identical in width—to perceive a whole rod, or they would have preferred the novel display (D) to the now familiar whole rod (C). However, after watching a *moving* rod, these 4-month-olds showed far less interest in the full rod than in the two rod segments, apparently recognizing the full rod as familiar. They were able to make use of another cue to the fact that an object is a whole—common motion, or the fact that an object's parts move in the same direction at the same time. Thus infants seem to be able to recognize distinct objects in a visual scene quite early in life, especially if those objects move about.

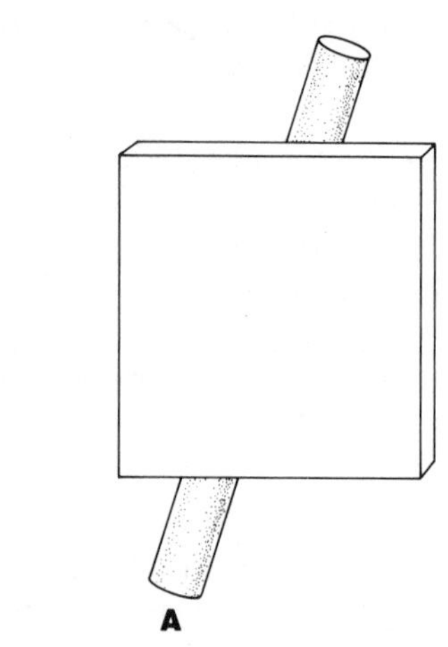

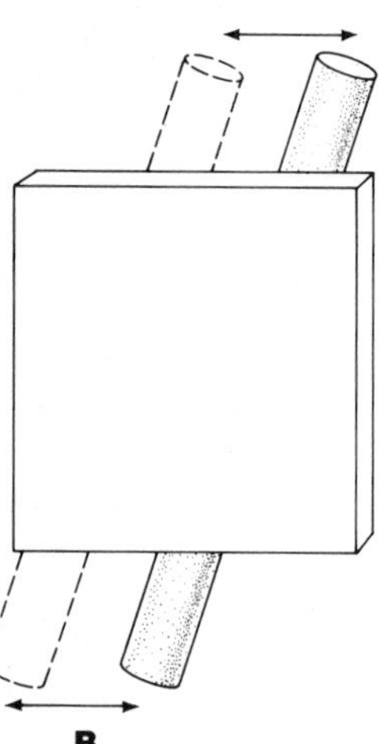

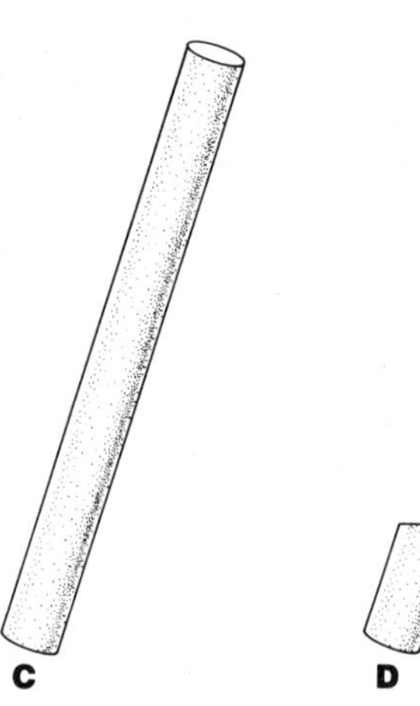

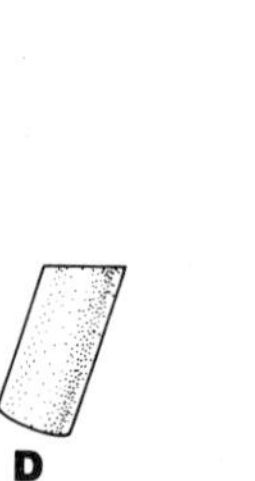

psychologists, emphasizing that there is an organization or patterning in all human experience, argued that human perception is guided by principles for imposing order and wholeness on sensory input. Shown arrays of numbers and letters, for example, humans will perceive as "belonging together" those that are near each other or that are similar in form. And if they are viewing letters arranged in the form of a triangle, humans will organize what they see into a well-formed, whole triangle, even if a letter or two is missing.

It seems that infants, at least by 3 or 4 months of age, operate according to some of these same Gestalt organizing principles (Aslin, 1987; Bertenthal, Profitt, Kramer, & Spetner, 1987; Bornstein, Ferdinandsen, & Gross, 1981; Van Giffen & Haith, 1984). For example, Katherine Van Giffen and Marshall Haith (1984) found that 3-month-olds, though apparently not 1-month-olds, will focus their attention on a small irregularity in an otherwise well formed circle or square pattern, as if they appreciated that it *is* a deviation from an otherwise well formed and symmetrical pattern. Early Gestalt psychologists believed that principles for organizing the perceptual world were innate; today's researchers are taking seriously the notion that infants do indeed perceive order and wholeness in their visual world very early in life.

Still another milestone in visual form perception is achieved at about the age of 1 year. Now, for example, infants often show more interest in a scrambled face than in a normal face. What has changed? According to Jerome Kagan (1971), infants now become interested in understanding stimuli that are highly discrepant from existing schemata. By now, he argues, their existing schemata are well developed, and they have the cognitive capacity to try to "explain" things that are very different from what they have come to expect. In fact, 2-year-olds who can talk will show that they are actively forming theories about a scrambled face. They say things like "Who hit him in the nose?" or "Who that, Mommy? A monster, Mommy?" (Kagan, 1971).

According to Kagan, experience with the visual world makes possible the meaningful interpretation of forms such as faces. Infants are at first attracted to objects on the basis of their physical properties. Then they are attracted to them because they are familiar enough that they can be matched to perceptual schemata. And finally, infants take interest in more complex and novel forms that are hard to interpret on the basis of previous knowledge. We could say that infants at first sense the physical properties of forms such as a face, then perceive those forms as recognizable wholes, and finally become able to interpret even novel sights intelligently.

Perception of Three-Dimensional Space

Another important aspect of visual perception involves perceiving depth and knowing when objects are near or far away. Do young infants perceive a three-dimensional spatial world?

Very young infants have some intriguing abilities to interpret spatial information. For example, they seem to know when an object is moving toward them and is about to hit them in the face. Thomas Bower and his associates (Bower, Broughton, & Moore, 1970b) slowly moved a foam rubber cube toward the faces of infants 6 to 20 days old. When the cube moved to within eight inches, the infants typically opened their eyes wide, threw their hands in front of their faces, and retracted their heads. Although other investigators have not always observed the strong defensive reactions that Bower saw, it does appear that infants 3 or 4 weeks old consistently blink when objects loom toward their faces (Yonas, Pettersen, & Lockman, 1979).

Somewhat later in infancy, babies also seem to operate by the principle of **size constancy**, the tendency to perceive an object as the same size despite changes in its distance from the eyes. We do not perceive friends as shrinking when they walk away from us, nor do we perceive them as swelling in size when they approach. Yet as distance changes, the size of the image cast on the retina changes. So if infants perceive an object as constant in size even when it is moved closer or farther away, this would suggest that their perception is three-dimensional. By 4 to 5 months of age, infants clearly recognize that a model of a human head is still the same old head when it is moved closer or farther away, but they treat a larger head substituted for the original head as novel and stare at it intently (Day & McKenzie, 1981). Size constancy is just one example of a number of early-developing perceptual constancies involving dimensions such as form, color, brightness, and shape.

Does this evidence of early spatial perception mean that young infants know enough about space to avoid crawling off a dropoff? The first attempt to examine depth perception in infants was carried out by Eleanor Gibson and Richard Walk (1960) using an apparatus called the **visual cliff**. This cliff (see Figure 6.4) consists of an elevated glass platform divided into two sections by a center board. On the "shallow" side, a checkerboard pattern is placed directly under the glass. On the "deep" side, the pattern is

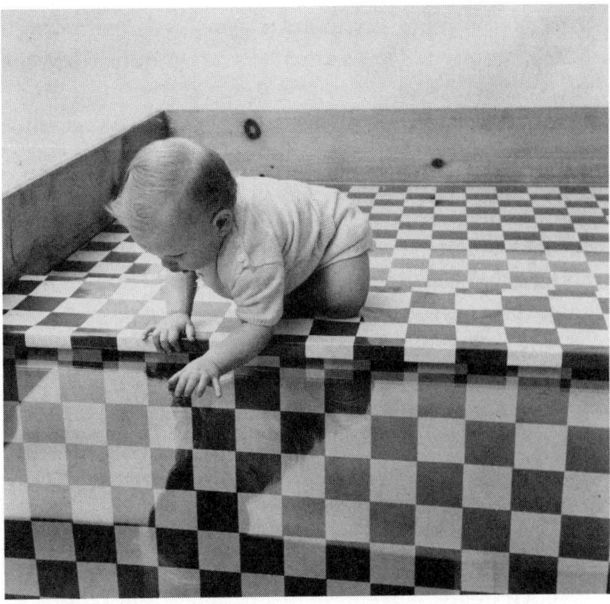

Figure 6.4 An infant on the edge of the visual cliff.

several feet below the glass, creating the illusion of a dropoff or "cliff." Infants are placed on the center board and coaxed by their mothers to cross both the "shallow" and the "deep" sides. Testing infants 6½ months of age and older, Gibson and Walk found that 27 of 36 infants would cross the shallow side to reach Mom, but only 3 of 36 would cross the deep side. Most infants of crawling age (typically 7 months or older) clearly perceive depth and are afraid of dropoffs.

But the testing procedure used by Gibson and Walk depended on the ability of infants to crawl. Would younger infants who cannot yet crawl be able to perceive a dropoff? Joseph Campos and his colleagues (Campos, Langer, & Krowitz, 1970) figured that the heart rates of young infants might tell them. So they lowered babies over the shallow and deep sides of the visual cliff. Babies as young as 2 months of age had a slower heart rate on the deep side than on the shallow side. Why slower? When we are afraid, our heart beats faster, not slower. A slow heart rate is a sign of interest. So 2-month-old infants perceive *some* difference between the deep and shallow sides of the visual cliff, but they have not yet learned to fear dropoffs. Perhaps, then, fear of dropoffs must be learned through experience crawling about—and perhaps falling now and then (Campos, Hiatt, Ramsay, Henderson, & Svejda, 1978).

Yet some infants who have crawled for some time have apparently not yet learned to fear dropoffs (Campos et al., 1978). They might shuffle right off the ends of beds or the tops of stairwells if they are not watched carefully! Nancy Rader and her associates (Rader, Bausano, & Richards, 1980) propose a maturational explanation for this. At about 6 or 7 months of age, they suggest, a "visual-motor program" matures that tells the infant, in essence, "Shift your weight forward only when your eyes tell you there's a solid surface ahead." For some early crawlers, this program may not yet have matured, so they may learn to rely on touch rather than vision as their guide. Therefore they may cross the deep side of the visual cliff because they feel the glass. Late crawlers are more likely to have the "believe your eyes" program in place by the time they crawl and so are not as likely to err. Thus *both* maturation and crawling experience may be required before infants will display a healthy respect for dropoffs.

In summary, perception of space develops rapidly in early infancy. The ability to see that an object is looming toward the face emerges earliest. The perception of size constancy despite variations in distance emerges by 4 or 5 months of age. By about 2 months of age, infants also seem to perceive some difference between an apparent dropoff and a solid surface. However, it is only in the second half of the first year that infants come to *fear* dropoffs through some combination of maturation and experience crawling.

Hearing

Hearing is at least as important to us as vision, especially if we want to communicate with others through spoken language. Sound striking the ear creates vibrations of the eardrum, which are transmitted to the cochlea in the inner ear and converted to signals to the brain. Newborns can hear quite well, better than they can see. They are startled by loud noises and will turn away from them, but they will turn in the direction of a less aversive sound (Field, Muir, Pilon, Sinclair, & Dodwell, 1980). This early ability to localize sound may, however, be a kind of reflex, for it disappears at 2 months and reappears in a more reliable form at about 4 months of age (Field et al., 1980; Muir, 1985).

Newborns appear to be a little less sensitive to very soft sounds than adults are (Aslin, Pisoni, & Jusczyk, 1983). As a result, a soft whisper may not be heard. However, newborns can discriminate among sounds within their range of hearing that differ in loudness, duration, direction, and frequency or pitch (Bower, 1982). These basic capacities improve rapidly during the first months of life.

Young infants seem to be well equipped to respond to human speech, for they can discriminate speech sounds very early in life. Peter Eimas (1975b, 1985) pioneered research in this area by demonstrating that infants 2 to 3 months old could distinguish consonant sounds that are very similar (for example, *ba* and *pa*). Indeed, infants seem to be able to tell the difference between the vowels *a* and *i* from the second day of life (Clarkson & Berg, 1983). These are impressive accomplishments.

Indeed, there are actually some speech sound discriminations that an infant can make better than an adult can. As we mature, we normally become especially sensitive to the sound differences that are significant in our own language and less sensitive to sound differences that are irrelevant to our own language. For example, infants can easily discriminate the consonants *r* and *l* (Eimas, 1975a). So can adults who speak English, French, Spanish, or German.

However, Oriental languages such as Chinese and Japanese make no distinction between *r* and *l*, and adult native speakers of those languages cannot make this particular auditory discrimination as well as infants can (Miyawaki, Strange, Verbrugge, Liberman, Jenkins, & Fujimura, 1975). Similarly, infants raised in English-speaking homes can make discriminations that are important in Hindi but nonexistent in English, but English-speaking adults have trouble doing so (Werker, Gilbert, Humphrey, & Tees, 1981).

By the end of the first year, as infants begin to master their first words, they are already becoming insensitive to sound contrasts that are irrelevant in their native language (Werker & Tees, 1984). In other words, the effects of their auditory experiences are starting to show. Interestingly, then, perceptual development, like so many aspects of life-span development, is not just a matter of adding new abilities; it is also a matter of *losing* unnecessary ones (Colombo, 1986), and this may apply to the old as well as to the young.

Do young infants recognize particular voices? Certainly parents sometimes sense that their newborns recognize their voices. Is this just wishful thinking? Anthony DeCasper and William Fifer (1980) found that babies can recognize their mothers' voices during the first 3 days of life. For half of the infants they studied, sucking faster than usual on a pacifier would activate a recording of the mother's voice, while sucking more slowly than usual would elicit a recording of a female stranger. Just the opposite was true for the remaining infants. These 1- to 3-day-old babies learned to suck either rapidly or slowly—whichever it took—to hear their mothers rather than strange women. It appears that babies know their companions "by ear" well before they know them by sight.

Indeed, the process of becoming familiar with mother's voice and with other sound patterns appears to begin prenatally. Anthony DeCasper and Melanie Spence (1986) had mothers recite a passage (for example, portions of Dr. Seuss's *The Cat in the Hat*) many times during the last six weeks of their pregnancies. At birth, the infants were tested to see if they would suck more to hear the story they had heard before birth or a different story. Sure enough, the familiar story was more reinforcing than a different story, whether it was read by the infant's mother or another baby's mother. Somehow their prenatal experience enabled these infants to recognize the distinctive sound pattern of the story they had heard in the womb. DeCasper and Spence suggest that auditory learning before birth could also explain why newborns prefer to hear their mothers' voices to those of unfamiliar women. Before we get carried away with the notion of educating youngsters before they are even born, however, we should bear in mind that the acoustics of the womb are poor and the nervous systems of fetuses are immature. Although some parents today seem willing to try almost anything to get their children's education off to an early start, it is doubtful that factual information can be instilled prenatally.

All of the evidence that we have presented thus far suggests that infants are especially attuned to perceive speech. Yet we now know that young infants are also very sensitive to the features of musical sounds (Aslin, Pisoni, & Jusczyk, 1983). For one thing, newborns seem to like music. For example, they will learn either to suck or to refrain

from sucking a pacifier if that is what it takes to have folk music played (Butterfield & Siperstein, 1972). By contrast, they will learn to do whatever it takes to *avoid* hearing nonrhythmic noise. By a few months of age, infants are also quite skilled at discriminating between melodies or recognizing the same tune despite changes in tempo or pitch (Chang & Trehub, 1977; Trehub, 1985). It is not yet clear whether infants prefer Muzak, Michael Jackson, or Mozart. But it *is* clear that they seem well equipped to perceive both speech sounds and musical sounds and to detect patterns of sounds.

In sum, hearing is well developed at birth, and auditory perception improves rapidly during infancy. Infants can recognize familiar sound patterns such as their mothers' voices soon after birth, and they are soon able to distinguish both speech sounds and musical patterns. As older infants begin to develop language, sound patterns take on additional meanings that they did not have earlier in infancy.

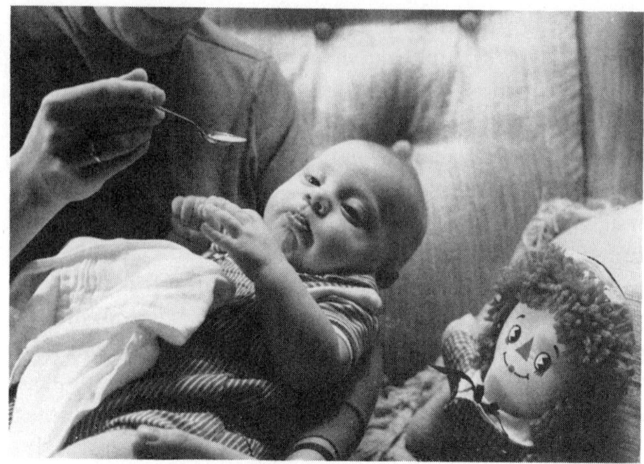

Newborns respond to tastes. In response to a sugar solution, newborns part their lips, lick their upper lips, make sucking movements, and sometimes smile. In response to bitter quinine, they purse their lips or open their mouths with the corners down. They even drool to get rid of the taste. Their faces tell us that they prefer sweet to bitter tastes.

Taste and Smell

Can newborns detect different tastes and smells? The sensory receptors for taste—taste buds—are mainly located on the tongue. In ways not fully understood, taste buds respond to chemical molecules and give rise to perceptions of sweet, salty, bitter, or sour tastes. We are apparently born with a sweet tooth, for shortly after birth babies will suck faster and longer for sweet (sugary) liquids than for bitter, sour, salty, or neutral (water) solutions (Crook, 1978). Different taste sensations also produce distinct facial expressions in the newborn. Jacob Steiner and his colleagues (see Ganchrow, Steiner, & Daher, 1983; Steiner, 1979) have found that newborns lick their lips and sometimes smile when they are tasting a sugar solution but purse their lips and even drool to get rid of the bad taste when they are given bitter quinine. Their facial expressions become more pronounced as a solution becomes sweeter or more bitter, suggesting that newborns can discriminate different concentrations of a substance.

The sense of smell, or **olfaction**, depends on sensory receptors in the nasal passage that react to chemical molecules in the air. It too is working well at birth. Newborns react vigorously to unpleasant smells such as vinegar or ammonia. At only a few hours of age, they will turn their heads away from an unpleasant smell (Rieser, Yonas, & Wilkner, 1976). Even more remarkable is evidence that babies can recognize their mothers by smell alone. Within a week, newborns who are breast-fed can already discriminate the smell of a pad from their mother's breast from that of an unused pad or a pad from another breast-feeding mother's breast (MacFarlane, 1977). Jennifer Cernoch and Richard Porter (1985) found that breast-fed 2-week-olds could also recognize their mothers' underarm odor, but babies who were bottle-fed could not, possibly because they have less contact with their mothers' bare skin. Thus the sense of smell we often take for granted may help babies and their parents get to know each other right from the start.

In sum, both the sense of taste and the sense of smell are working very well at birth. Later development is mainly a matter of learning to recognize what it is that is being tasted or smelled. As wine tasters illustrate, these senses can become highly educated indeed.

Touch, Temperature, and Pain

Receptors in the skin detect touch or pressure, heat or cold, and painful stimuli. We saw in Chapter 5 that newborns respond with reflexes if they are touched in appropriate areas. And even in their sleep, newborns will habituate to strokes of the same spot on the skin but respond again if the tactile stimulation is shifted to a new spot—from the ear to the lips, for example (Kisilevsky & Muir, 1984). So the sense of touch seems to be operating quite nicely at birth.

Later, infants become able to discriminate an object solely on the basis of their experience touching it. At 5 months of age, for example, infants will become habituated to a plywood shape after they have held it and explored it with their hands for a time without being allowed to see it. They then show more interest in touching a new shape than in touching the shape that has become familiar to them (Streri & Pecheux, 1986a).

Newborns are also sensitive to warmth and cold. They will try to maintain their body heat by becoming more active if the room temperature suddenly drops (Pratt, 1954). Infants even seem to be fascinated by thermal sensations. In one study, 6-month-olds were familiarized with a vial of a certain color and temperature (Bushnell, Shaw, & Strauss, 1985). When they were given a new vial of a different temperature, they treated it like a new object and explored it thoroughly with their eyes and hands. Yet when the color was switched but the temperature remained the same, they treated it as though it were the same old, and now boring, vial. These infants showed that they could remember a tactile sensation of warmth or coolness and that they found temperature sensations particularly interesting.

Finally, newborns clearly respond to painful stimuli, as any parent who has missed with a diaper pin knows. Even 1-day-old infants experience pain from pin pricks (like those administered in blood tests). Apparently, sensitivity to pain then increases over the first few days of life, for it takes much less aversive stimulation to bother a 5-day-old infant than a 1-day-old infant (Lipsitt & Levy, 1959).

For obvious ethical reasons, researchers have not exposed infants to severely painful stimuli. However, something has been learned about more intense forms of pain from the study of baby boys who undergo circumcision. Fran Porter, Richard Miller, and Richard Marshall (1986) analyzed the cries of such boys during different stages of the procedure. During the most painful stage, when surgical cutting without anesthesia was taking place, the babies' cries were short and high-pitched, occurring in a long series. These cries were similar to those of infants who are premature or neurologically abnormal in some way. Moreover, adults who heard the recordings judged these cries to be more urgent than those emitted during less painful parts of the circumcision procedure (for example, when the babies were being restrained or cleaned). Thus the quality of a baby's cry communicates to us how intensely painful an experience is. (If you are now wondering about the wisdom of circumcising males, Porter et al. [1986] assure us that infants recover quickly from their trauma.)

We have now seen that each of the major senses is operating in some form at birth, and that perceptual abilities that rely on each sense increase dramatically during infancy. Let us ask one final question about infant perception: Can infants put together information from the different senses?

Intersensory Perception

A friend tells you to close your eyes and then places a small, perfectly spherical object in your hand. As you finger it, you estimate that it is 1.5 to 2 inches in diameter, that it weighs at most a couple of ounces, and that it is very hard and is covered with little indentations, or "dimples." You suddenly have an "aha" experience and conclude that it is a ________.

A colleague who often conducts this exercise in class reports that most of his students easily identify the object as a golf ball—even if they have never touched or held a golf ball in their lives. This is an example of **cross-modal perception**: the ability to recognize through one sensory modality (in this case, touch) an object that is familiar through another (vision). It would be useful for the infant who is attempting to understand the world to be able to put together information gained from viewing, touching, sniffing, and otherwise exploring objects.

When are infants capable of cross-modal perception? There is some evidence that the senses are integrated at birth. For instance, newborns will look in the direction of a sound they hear, suggesting that vision and hearing are somehow linked from birth (Bower, 1982). Moreover, Bower and his colleagues (Bower, Broughton, & Moore, 1970a) demonstrated that infants 8 to 31 days old expect to feel objects that they can see. They were frustrated when Bower displayed a visual illusion that looked like a graspable object but proved to be nothing but air when they reached for it. Thus vision and touch and vision and hearing seem to be interrelated early in life. But we should note that young infants are not always upset by these kinds of visual/tactile or visual/auditory incongruities (Bower, 1982; Walk, 1981). Besides, these demonstrations do not establish that young infants are capable of recognizing through one sense an object that is familiar through another.

A vivid demonstration of cross-modal perception in early life involved familiarizing infants with an object through touch and then seeing if they could recognize the object by sight (Meltzoff & Borton, 1979). One-month-old infants were given one of two pacifiers to suck without being allowed to see what they were sucking. One pacifier was round and smooth, while the other had hard nubs on it. Infants then saw two styrofoam forms, one shaped like the smooth pacifier and the other like the nubbed pacifier. They tended to look more at the pacifier that they had sucked than at the unfamiliar one. They actually seemed to recognize by sight a stimulus that was familiar only through the sense of touch (see also Gibson & Walker, 1984).

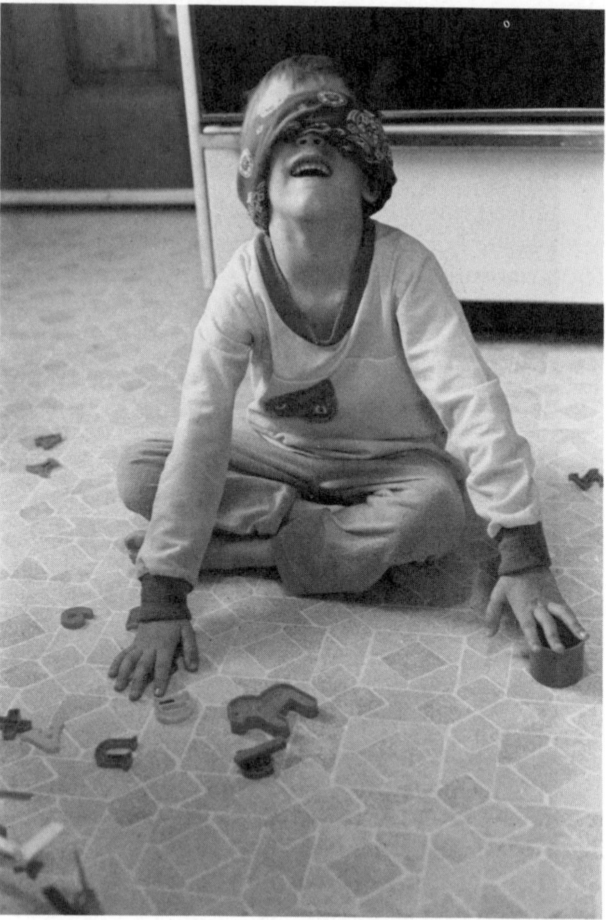

Intersensory perception. Children sometimes play games in which they must recognize familiar objects through touch alone. The ability to recognize through one sense (here, touch) what has been learned through another (vision) increases with age during infancy and childhood.

Is cross-modal perception innate, then? Perhaps not. Although oral-to-visual cross-modal transfer may be evident very early, other forms of cross-modal perception are not consistently or reliably displayed until about 4 to 6 months of age, if then (Gibson & Spelke, 1983; Rose, Gottfried, & Bridger, 1981; Streri & Pecheux, 1986b). Overall, it seems that very young infants respond globally to sensory stimuli and do not clearly distinguish visual experiences from auditory or tactile ones. The senses appear to be fused at birth, much as William James believed. During the first year, the senses begin to differentiate and continue to develop somewhat independently of one another. As each sense continues to develop, it becomes a more effective means of exploring objects. As a result, the infant becomes better able to recognize through one sense stimuli that are already familiar through another sense. The bulk of the evidence suggests that cross-modal perception does not reliably emerge until 4 to 6 months of age and then gradually improves with age, even into childhood and adolescence. Infants seem to progress from global perception to a differentiation of the several senses to an ability to consistently integrate information from the different senses.

The Infant in Perspective

What remarkable perceptual competencies even the very young infant has, and what remarkable progress is made within the first few months of life! All of the major senses begin working before birth and are clearly working at birth. Many perceptual abilities—for example, the ability to perceive depth through vision or to distinguish melodies through hearing—then emerge within just a few months of birth, so early that they often seem to be built into the genetic program. In later infancy, basic perceptual capacities are fine-tuned, and, importantly, infants become more and more able to *interpret* sensory experiences—recognizing a pattern of light as a chair or a spoon, for example. By the time infancy ends, many of the important aspects of perceptual development are complete. The senses and the mind are working to create a meaningful world of recognized objects, sounds, tastes, smells, and bodily sensations. But stay tuned.

THE CHILD

If most sensory and perceptual development is complete by the end of infancy, what is left to accomplish during childhood? Perceptual development during childhood is mostly a matter of learning to use the senses more intelligently. For example, children rapidly build knowledge of the world so that they can recognize and label what they sense, giving it greater meaning. In addition, much of perceptual development in childhood is really a matter of the development of **attention**, the focusing of perception and cognition on something in particular. For example, children become more able to use their senses deliberately and strategically to gather the information most relevant to a task at hand. Children also become more skilled at making the kinds of perceptual discriminations that are so important in complex cognitive tasks such as learning to read.

The Development of Attention

How do children deploy their sensory and perceptual abilities once they have them? One way to think about the development of attention is to describe the attention of the infant or very young child as captured by stimuli and the older child's attention as directed toward stimuli. Although they actively explore their surroundings, 1-month-old infants do not really deliberately choose to attend to a face; instead, a face captures their attention. Similarly, toddlers or preschoolers often seem to be caught up by one event and then quickly caught up by another. As children get older, their attention spans become longer, they become more selective in what they attend to, and they are better able to plan and carry out systematic strategies for using their senses to achieve goals.

Increased Attention Span

Young children do have short attention spans. Researchers know that they should limit their experimental sessions with young children to a few minutes, and nursery school teachers often switch classroom activities every 15 to 20 minutes. In one study of sustained attention, children were asked to put strips of colored paper in appropriately colored boxes (Yendovitskaya, 1971). Children aged 2½ to 3½ worked for an average of 18 minutes and were easily distracted. In contrast, children aged 5½ to 6 often persisted for an hour or more. Further improvements occur later in childhood. Preschoolers do sometimes become totally engrossed in an activity, but they often display a short attention span for activities we adults plan for them. And even when they are doing things they like, such as watching television, 2- and 3-year-olds often get up and move around the room or play with toys in between glances at the TV set; they spend far less of their "TV time" actually paying attention to the TV than school-aged children do (Anderson, Lorch, Field, Collins, & Nathan, 1986).

More Selective Attention

We have seen that infants are selective from the start in their perception. They have their preferences. But they are not very good at controlling their attention so that they deliberately concentrate on one thing while ignoring something else. With age, attention becomes more selective.

Convincing evidence of this comes from a study of visual perception conducted by George Strutt, Daniel Anderson, and Arnold Well (1975). They had 6-, 9-, 12-, and 20-year-olds sort cards with geometric designs on them as quickly as possible on the basis of some dimension (for example, whether the form on the card was a circle or a square). But in some trials, the cards also contained distracting information (for example, a star above or below the form). Younger children were generally slower at this card-sorting task than older children were, but the more important finding was that they were especially slowed up by irrelevant information on the cards. In other words, they were less inferior to older children when the only thing on the card was a circle or a square than when distractions were present. Although the older groups were also slowed down by irrelevant information, the effect was not nearly so strong. They were apparently better able to *selectively* focus their attention on the critical information and disregard the irrelevant information. Similarly, Eleanor Maccoby (1967) found that over the elementary school years children become better able to tune in one speaker while ignoring another speaker who is talking at the same time or to monitor two conversations at the same time and recall what was said. These findings suggest to the teachers of young children that performance will be better if distractions in task materials and in the room are kept to a minimum.

More Systematic Attention

Finally, as they get older children become more able to plan and carry out a systematic perceptual search. We have seen already that older infants are more likely than younger ones to thoroughly explore a pattern, both its exterior and its interior. Research with children in the Soviet Union reveals that visual scanning becomes more detailed or "exhaustive" over the first six years of life (Zaporozhets, 1965; and see Figure 6.5). But the really revealing findings come from studies of how children go about a *visual search*. Elaine Vurpillot (1968) recorded the eye movements of 4- to 10-year-olds who were trying to decide whether two houses, each with several windows containing various objects, were identical or different. Children aged 4 and 5 were not at all systematic. They often looked at only a few windows, and as a result often came to the wrong conclusion. In contrast, children older than 6½ were highly systematic. They checked each window in one house with the corresponding window in the other house, pair by pair. Older children also choose the strategy for scanning houses that best fits the instructions they are given. Thus 11-year-olds instructed to stop searching when they find one difference between houses will indeed stop when they find one difference, whereas 8-year-olds often continue their search needlessly after they have found one difference (Vlietstra, 1982).

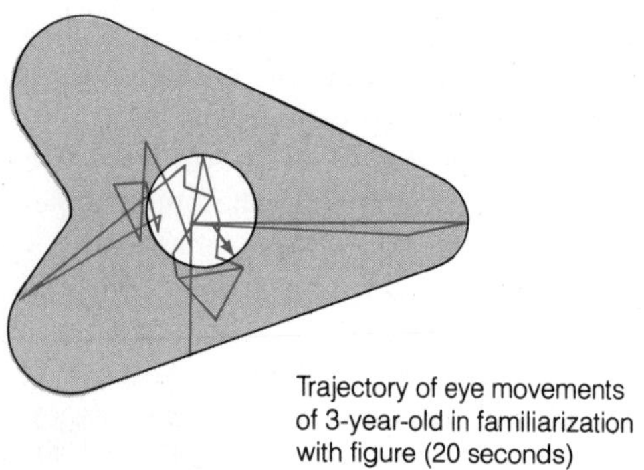

Trajectory of eye movements of 3-year-old in familiarization with figure (20 seconds)

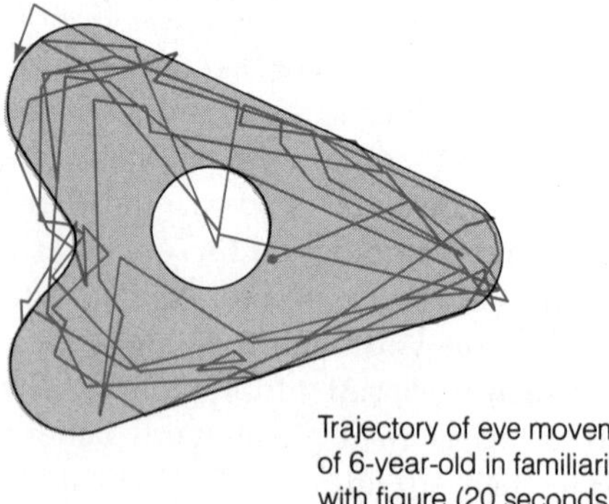

Trajectory of eye movements of 6-year-old in familiarization with figure (20 seconds)

Figure 6.5 Typical visual search patterns of 3- and 6-year-old children who scan an unfamiliar figure for 20 seconds. Note that the visual search of the 6-year-old is much more detailed and exhaustive. (Adapted from Zichenko, Van Chzhitsin, & Tarakanov, 1963)

Similarly, older children are more likely than younger children to plan a systematic strategy for searching for a lost item or retracing a route (see Wellman, 1985). And in a new situation, they more systematically survey the entire scene before deciding to direct their attention to something specific. Brian Vandenberg (1984), for example, set children aged 4 to 12 loose in a room that had six different toys in boxes: a wind-up bug, a water pump kit, and so on. The 4- to 6-year-olds tended to be "captured" by one interesting item and often did not get around to examining the rest. Older children behaved strategically: First they examined all six items, and then they returned to investigate the toys of most interest to them.

In summary, learning to control attention is an important part of perceptual development during childhood. Infants and young children are without question selectively attentive to the world around them, but they have not fully taken charge of their attentional processes. With age, children become more able to concentrate on a task for a long period, to focus on relevant information and ignore distractions, and to use their senses in a purposeful and systematic way to achieve goals.

Perception of Form and Learning to Read

One of the most challenging tasks that face children in our culture is learning to read. Reading involves many cognitive processes, but one of the most basic is the ability to recognize the form of letters and distinguish between letters such as *b* and *d*. Is the preschool child ready for this?

According to Eleanor Gibson (1969), reading readiness depends on learning to recognize the *distinctive features* of letters—that is, the specific elements that distinguish one

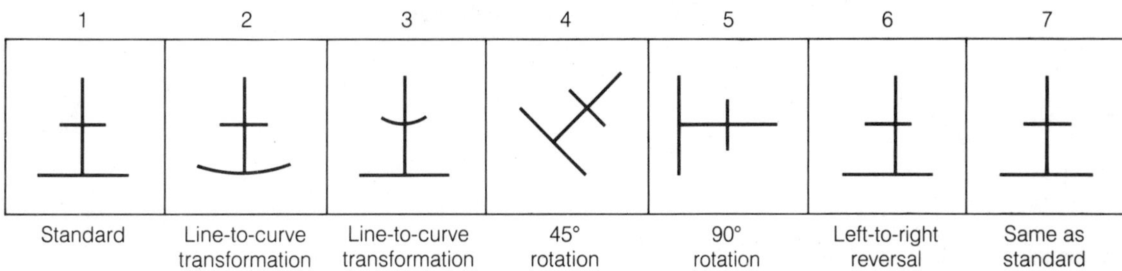

Figure 6.6 Examples of figures used to test children's ability to detect the distinctive features of letterlike forms. (Adapted from Gibson, Gibson, Pick, & Osser, 1962)

letter from another. So Gibson and her colleagues decided to see how well young children could distinguish different letterlike forms (Gibson, Gibson, Pick, & Osser, 1962). Children aged 4 to 8 were shown one "standard" form and asked to select those identical to the standard from among a set of similar forms (see Figure 6.6). The 4- and 5-year-olds often selected stimuli that were not identical to the standard. But the 6- to 8-year-olds were generally able to detect the distinctive features that differentiated the variations from the standard form. Given the responses of young children in Gibson's experiment, it is easy to appreciate that many preschoolers might have trouble learning to read if it requires noticing subtle differences such as that between the letters *b* and *d*.

To make sense of all those funny little squiggles on a printed page, of course, children must not only differentiate among them but must learn how they correspond to sounds in spoken language. Gibson and Harry Levin (1975) believe that children progress through three phases in learning to read, as Box 6.2 describes. Whether they are reading or performing other academic tasks, children make many important uses of their sensory and perceptual abilities as they progress through school.

THE ADOLESCENT

There is little to report about perception during adolescence, though we could perhaps talk of preferences for loud music and junk food and their implications for hearing and health. Some of the developments that occur during childhood are not quite completed until adolescence. For example, portions of the brain that help regulate attention are not fully myelinated until adolescence. Perhaps this helps explain why adolescents and young adults have incredibly long attention spans on occasion, as when they spend hours cramming for tests or typing term papers during the wee hours of the morning.

In addition, adolescents become still more efficient at ignoring irrelevant information so that they can concen-

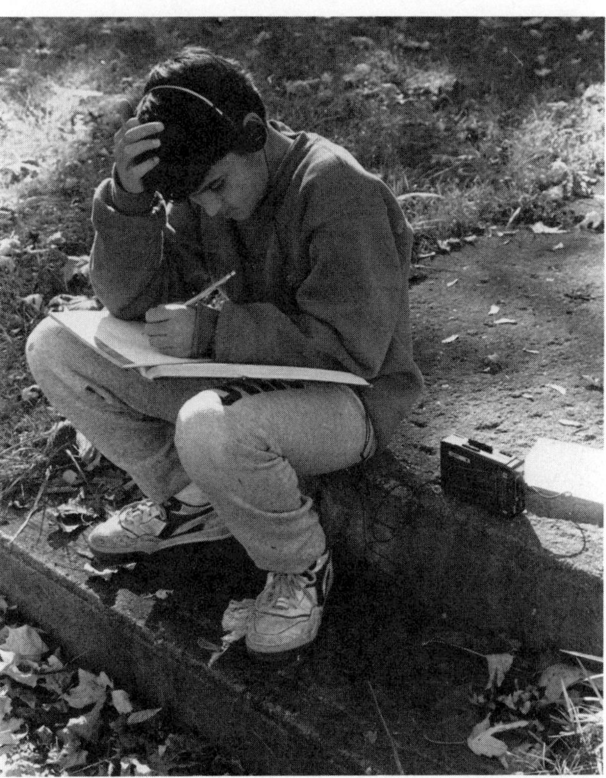

Adolescents are skilled at dividing their attention between two tasks.

Box 6.2
How Do Children Learn to Read?

Young children have mastered spoken language long before they are taught to read. How do they come to realize that the print on the page represents spoken words, and how do they then learn to translate print into spoken language? Eleanor Gibson and Harry Levin (1975) have identified three phases in learning to read.

First, children equate reading with storytelling: They may pick up a storybook and "read" very sensible sentences—most of which have no relation to the words on the page.

Next, children recognize that the squiggles on the printed page represent words. They may try to match the spoken words of a familiar story to the symbols on the page, though incorrectly (Smith, 1977). A 3-year-old who knows that the title of her storybook is *Santa Is Coming to Town* might try to "read" the cover by touching each letter and uttering a word or syllable, as illustrated below. Gradually, children learn that each letter is related to a particular sound and that combinations of letters (and sounds) make up printed words. However, the child who is just beginning to read may skip over words that are unfamiliar.

In the third and final phase of learning to read, children have become quite skilled at recognizing letters and sounds; they may try to "sound out" unknown words by breaking them into individual sounds or syllables. Children typically master the basic rules for translating letters into sounds by third or fourth grade (Morrison, 1984). However, the complexities of letter/sound correspondences in English give even older readers problems: For example, the *c* in *circle* is pronounced very differently from the *c* in *cannery*, and the *gh* in *ghetto* does not sound a bit like the *gh* in *rough*.

Poor readers are usually those who have had difficulty mastering these complex and irregular rules of letter/sound correspondence (Morrison, 1984). They have to devote so much mental effort to decoding the words that they have little attention to spare for interpreting and remembering the message. By contrast, good readers are quick at decoding letters and words so that they can direct their attention to comprehending the meaning. Evidence suggests that fewer children experience serious reading difficulties in countries where the letter/sound correspondence rules of the native language are simpler and more regular than those of English (Morrison, 1984).

How can children best be taught to read? The "phonics" approach teaches children to analyze words into their component sounds—that is, it systematically teaches them letter/sound correspondence rules. By contrast, the "whole word" approach teaches children to recognize specific words by sight. This approach assumes that young children perceive visual forms as wholes, and that the "parts" of printed words (the letters) are not as meaningful as the whole words. The merits of these two approaches have been debated for years. Some experts continue to think that the whole word approach is especially useful during the early phases of reading, when children are first learning that visual patterns such as CAT and TREE represent spoken words and therefore have meaning (Smith, 1977). However, many reading specialists believe that children must at some point have phonics training so that they can decode words they have not seen before (Chall, 1967). Perhaps because neither approach has proved to be clearly superior, many reading programs make use of both forms of instruction (Williams, 1979).

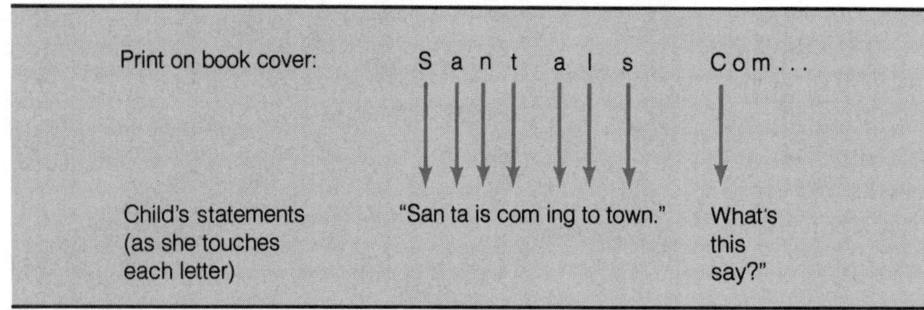
Print on book cover:
S a n t a l s
C o m . . .
Child's statements (as she touches each letter)
"San ta is com ing to town."
What's this say?"

trate on the task at hand. A study of 7-, 10-, and 13-year-olds by Patricia Miller and Michael Weiss (1981) illustrates this. The task was to remember the locations of animals that had been hidden behind different flaps. When they lifted each flap, children could also see a household object near the animal. Here, then, is a task that requires attending selectively to relevant information (the animals) and ignoring potentially distracting information (the household objects). When they were tested about the locations of the animals, 13-year-olds outperformed the younger groups. The more interesting finding was that these adolescents remembered *less* about the household objects than either 7- or 10-year-olds did. In other words, the adolescents were better than the children at centering their attention on relevant information *and* filtering out extraneous input that could interfere with their performance.

Adolescents can also divide their attention more systematically between two tasks. For example, Andrew Schiff and Irwin Knopf (1985) watched the eye movements of 9-year-olds and 13-year-olds during a visual search task with two parts. Children were to push a response key when particular symbols appeared at the center of a screen *and* remember letters flashed at the corners of the screen. The adolescents developed a strategy for switching their eyes back and forth from the center to the corners at the right times. The 9-year-olds had an unfortunate tendency to look at blank areas of the screen or to focus too much attention on the letters in the corners of the screen, thereby failing to detect the symbols in the center.

Adolescence appears to be a time of allocating one's attention and using one's senses efficiently and effectively to achieve goals—a time when basic sensory and perceptual capacities, as well as attentional skills, are at a peak. How long does the peak last?

THE ADULT

What becomes of sensory and perceptual capacities during adulthood? There is good news and bad news, and we might as well get the bad news out of the way first: Sensory and perceptual capacities decline with age in the normal person. Many declines begin in early adulthood and start to become noticeable in a person's 40s, giving middle-aged people a feeling that they are getting old. Further declines take place in later life, to the point that one would have a hard time finding a person age 65 or older who does not have at least some sensory or perceptual impairment. The good news (or the not so bad news) is that these changes are gradual and usually minor. Because changes are gradual, we can usually compensate for them, making small adjustments such as turning up the volume on the TV set or adding a little extra seasoning to food. Because losses are not severe, and because of the process of compensation, only a minority of old people develop serious problems such as blindness and deafness.

The losses we are talking about take two general forms. First, sensation is affected, as indicated by increases in **sensory thresholds**. The threshold for a sense is the point at which low levels of stimulation can be detected—a dim light can be seen, a faint tone can be heard, an odor can be detected, and so on. Stimulation that is below the threshold cannot be detected, so a raising of the threshold with age means that sensitivity to very low levels of stimulation is lost. (We saw that the very young infant is also insensitive to some very low levels of stimulation.)

Second, some changes during adulthood are more a matter of perception than of sensation. Even when stimulation is intense enough to be well above the detection threshold, older people often have difficulty processing sensory information. As we shall see, they may have trouble searching a visual scene, understanding rapid speech in a noisy room, or recognizing the foods that they are tasting.

So sensory and perceptual declines (with compensation) are typical during adulthood, though with individual variations. These declines involve both a raising of thresholds for detecting stimulation and a loss of some perceptual abilities.

Vision

Several changes in the eye and in the parts of the nervous system related to vision take place over the adult years, leading to vision problems in later life (see Corso, 1981; Kline & Schieber, 1985; Whitbourne, 1985). You may have noticed that the eyes of old people are often slightly discolored and dull. However, the more significant changes take place *within* the eye. The pupil of an old person normally is smaller than that of a young adult and does not change in size as much when lighting conditions change. The lens that focuses light to cast a sharp image on the retina has been gaining new cells from childhood on, making it denser and less flexible later in life: It cannot change shape, or accommodate, as well to bring objects at different distances into focus. The lens is also yellowing, and both it and the gelatinous liquid behind it are becoming less transparent. Finally, the sensory receptor cells in the retina and the complex nerves leading from the retina to the visual areas of the brain may die off over the years. Those that survive do not function as efficiently as they once did. What impacts do these physical changes have on visual sensation and perception?

Basic Changes in Visual Capacities

Gradual changes in the eye are often not noticeable until middle age. It is in the 40s that many people notice a nearly universal problem—a loss of near vision. This is a common sign of **presbyopia** (the term means "aging sight") and is related to a decreased ability of the lens to accommodate to objects that are close to the eye. Over the years, an adult may, without even being aware of it, gradually move newspapers and books farther from the eye to make them clearer—a form of compensation for presbyopia. But in the 40s, the arms may simply be too short to do the trick any longer! So middle-aged adults cope by getting reading glasses (or if they also have problems with distance vision, bifocals). In one study, only 4% of adults in their 20s and 30s wore glasses or lenses to correct their *near* vision; this figure jumped to 53% of adults in their 40s and 50s and about 80% of adults age 60 or older (Kosnik, Winslow, Kline, Rasinski, & Sekuler, 1988).

Many other gradual changes have no noticeable impact until old age. Now, consider the implications of some of these changes for driving. First consider age-related decreases in sensitivity to light and to changes in brightness. Older people have higher visual detection thresholds than younger adults do (Kline & Schieber, 1985). In other words, they are less sensitive to dim lights and may have trouble making things out in the dark. This would interfere with night driving, as well as navigating in a dark house. In addition, when we suddenly find ourselves in the dark, our eyes adapt and become more sensitive to even low levels of light in a few minutes through the process of **dark adaptation**. But for the older person, dark adaptation is not as successful at restoring vision. Thus the older person who is driving at night may have special problems when turning onto a dark road from a lighted highway.

It would seem that avoiding the dark is the way to compensate, but ironically many older adults also have difficulty with bright lights. Because the lens and fluid of the eye become cloudier with age, light is scattered on its way to the retina, and this produces glare when bright lights are encountered (Kline & Schieber, 1985). For example, many older adults do not cope with headlight glare as well as younger adults do (Pulling, Wolf, Sturgis, Vaillancourt, & Dolliver, 1980). Glare in a very bright room may interfere with clear vision, and old people may take some time to recover from sudden glares (for example, flashbulbs popping). In short, older people are in a bind: They cannot make things out well when illumination is low, but glare interferes with their vision when illumination is high.

For most of us, the heart of vision is the ability to see a clear image, not a blur. This is a matter of visual acuity. Does being old mean being blind? Because less light moves through the aged eye than through the younger eye and the light is scattered as it travels, visual acuity as measured by the familiar Snellen eye chart does decrease with age. Normally, what is measured is acuity with the best eye and with correction (glasses). Acuity seems to increase in childhood, peak in the 20s, stay quite steady through middle age, and steadily decline in old age (Pitts, 1982). But the changes in the average adult are minor. For example, in one major study of vision, even among 75- to 85-year-olds, 69% had corrected vision between 20/10 and 20/25 (Kahn et al., 1977). At worst, then, most of them could see at 20 feet what someone with standard acuity could see at 25 feet. Only 3.3% of them had corrected vision of 20/200 or worse—a cutoff commonly used to define legal blindness. Most of us need not fear becoming blind in old age, but most of us *will* wear corrective lenses (see Figure 6.7).

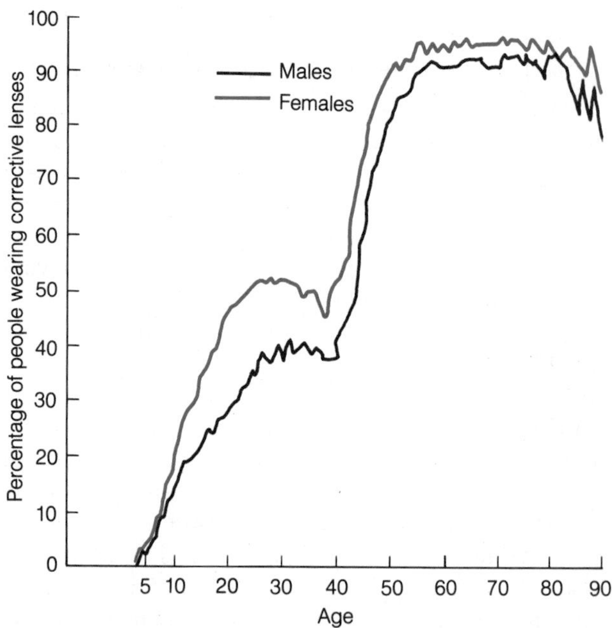

Figure 6.7 Percentage of Americans with corrective lenses. The percentage of people wearing glasses or contact lenses rises from less than 1% among 3-year-olds to 92% of those age 75 and older! Notice the steep rise during childhood and adolescence—and then another steep rise during the 40s, when many people find they need reading glasses because of presbyopia. (From National Center for Health Statistics, 1983)

The minority of elderly people who experience serious declines in visual acuity typically suffer from pathological conditions of the eye that become more prevalent in old age but are not part of aging itself (Pitts, 1982). For example, **cataracts**, opaque areas of the lens, are the leading cause of blindness in old age, affecting 5% to 7% of people over 65 (Corso, 1981; Greenberg & Branch, 1982). One contributing factor is lifelong heavy exposure to sunlight and its damaging ultraviolet rays (Kline & Schieber, 1985). Fortunately, cataracts can often be corrected surgically.

Even older adults without serious visual acuity problems may have difficulty perceiving the details of *moving* objects (Burg, 1966; Kosnik et al., 1988). Not unlike young infants, many older people have difficulty tracking fast-moving stimuli (Sharpe & Sylvester, 1978). This means that the standard Snellen eye chart may not fully detect problems that an older person might have while in motion. Indeed, in one study old adults who performed just as well as young adults on the Snellen acuity measure still had more trouble making out street signs while they were riding in a car in the dark (Sivak, Olson, & Pastalan, 1981). This would mean that the average old person has less time to react to a sign's message. Older adults also have more difficulty judging the speed of vehicles approaching an intersection than younger adults do (Hills, 1980).

Finally, perception of objects and events in space may become more difficult with age. For one thing, older adults have a smaller field of vision, or less peripheral vision (Burg, 1968). As a result, objects off to the side (a car coming from an intersecting street?) may not be detected until there is little time to react. In addition, depth perception may decrease slightly by old age, although so many cues are available to help us judge depth that the damage may not be great (Kline & Schieber, 1985; Pitts, 1982).

If you have come away with the impression that old people should not be allowed to drive, let us quickly note that the drivers who cause the most accidents are those under 25! When we take into account the fact that young people do more driving than elderly people do, it turns out that both elderly adults and young adults have more accidents *per mile driven* than middle-aged adults do (Planek, 1974; Williams & Carsten, 1989). At the same time, the driving records of older adults are not as bad as might be expected, because many of them compensate for visual losses and slower reactions by driving less frequently at night, during rush hour, or in the winter—or by being more cautious when they do drive (Planek, 1974). So young drivers might try to be patient the next time they find themselves behind a slow-moving elderly driver: He or she is doing everyone a favor by compensating for losses rather than denying them and driving fast.

Attention and Complex Visual Perception

As we saw when we examined perceptual development during infancy and childhood, perception is more than just seeing: It is using the senses intelligently and allocating attention efficiently. As we saw, the young child has more difficulty performing complex visual search tasks and ignoring irrelevant information than the older child does. Do older adults also have more difficulty than younger adults?

Dana Plude and William Hoyer (1981) asked young adults and elderly adults to sort cards containing from one to nine letters into two bins, depending on whether or not they contained specific target letters. Older adults were apparently more distracted by irrelevant information, for they were especially slow compared to young adults when the number of distractor letters on the cards was high. Yet this was true only in a condition in which the letters to be hunted for changed from session to session. When sorters got to practice over all six sessions with the same target letters, older adults were no longer especially bothered by having to search through many distractors. Similarly, older adults search more effectively when they know in advance where to look for a target in a larger display than when the location of a target is unpredictable (Farkas & Hoyer, 1980; Nissen & Corkin, 1985).

On the basis of findings like these, Plude and Hoyer (1985) propose that older adults have their greatest difficulties in processing visual information when the situation is *novel* (one is not sure exactly what to look for or where to look) and when it is *complex* (there is a great deal of distracting information to search through, or two tasks must be performed at once). By contrast, older adults have fewer problems if they have clear expectations about what they are to do and if the task is not overly complex. For instance, an older factory worker who has inspected radios for defects for years might perform just as well as a younger worker, for older adults often equal younger adults in performing familiar everyday tasks (Salthouse, 1982). However, this same worker might perform relatively

An older adult is likely to find the ice cream as efficiently as a younger adult in a familiar supermarket but may have difficulty with this visual search task if the supermarket is unfamiliar.

slowly if asked to examine unfamiliar products such as pocket calculators and look for a much larger number of possible defects—a novel and complex task.

In summary, it is normal for adults to experience a gradual loss of vision as they age and to experience special problems when they are in either darkness or bright light and when they or what they are viewing is moving. Performance on novel and complex visual perception tasks may also suffer in old age.

Hearing

There is indeed some truth to the stereotype of the hard-of-hearing older person. The older the age group, the greater the percentages of people who have at least some mild hearing loss: about 20% in the 45–54 age group and as many as 75% in the 75–79 age group (Butler & Lewis, 1977). In England, almost half of a sample of people 75 years of age or older reported difficulty understanding what is said when someone whispers to them in a quiet room (Davis, 1983). The good news is that most older people experience only mild hearing impairments.

Basic Capacities

Sources of hearing problems range from excess wax buildup in the ears to problems in the brain and nervous system. Most age-related hearing problems seem to originate in the inner ear, however (Olsho, Harkins, & Lenhardt, 1985). The cochlear hair cells that serve as auditory receptors, their surrounding structures, and the neurons leading from them to the brain degenerate gradually over the adult years. This leads to a set of problems called **presbycusis** (problems of the aging ear), the most common form of which is a loss of sensitivity to high-frequency (high-pitched) sounds. Thus the older person may have difficulty hearing a child's high voice or the flutes in an orchestra but may have less trouble with deep voices or tubas. Consonant sounds, especially *s* and *z*, are also harder to hear than vowels because they are higher in frequency (Whitbourne, 1985). To be heard by the average older adult, then, a sound—especially a high-pitched sound—must be louder than it needs to be to exceed the hearing threshold of a younger adult.

Presbycusis strikes earlier and harder in men than in women, though signs of it are noticeable in the 30s for both sexes (Corso, 1963). This could be because men age faster than women do, but it could also occur because men tend to experience more noise during their lives than women do. Although presbycusis seems to affect older people everywhere to some extent, men who have lived and worked in noisy industrial environments experience more hearing loss than do men exposed to lower levels of noise, and people in "noisy" cultures experience more loss than people in "quiet" societies (Bergman, 1980; McFarland, 1968, cited by Baltes, Reese, & Nesselroade, 1977). Fans of loud rock music, beware!

Yet performance on hearing tests may not tell us much about complex auditory perception in everyday life (Corso, 1981). By far the most important auditory perception task we perform is to understand speech. Are older adults handicapped in their ability to follow conversations?

Speech Perception

Understanding speech depends not only on the ability to hear but on complex cognitive processes. Under ideal listening conditions, older adults do seem to have more difficulty discriminating words that are read to them than younger adults do (Olsho, Harkins, & Lenhardt, 1985), perhaps because of degeneration within the ear. However, these problems are minor compared to the problems that older adults experience under *poor listening conditions*. Here the functioning of the brain is probably more important than the functioning of the ear (Corso, 1981).

For example, when you are trying to understand someone in the presence of loud background noise, you must keep your attention focused on what you are trying to hear and "hear between the lines," inferring what a word is from context when you cannot make it out completely. Memory is also required if you are asked to repeat what you heard.

Older adults are especially likely to have problems hearing if there is a great deal of background noise (Bergman, 1980; Hutchinson, 1989). The performance gap between them and younger adults is also greater when speech is otherwise "degraded"—for example, when it is fast, when it reverberates in a room, or when some of its frequencies are filtered out or distorted, as is the case in telephone conversations (Bergman, Blumenfeld, Cascardo, Dash, Levitt, & Margulies, 1976; and see Figure 6.8). Problems in understanding speech under these difficult conditions often become noticeable after about the age of 50 and more serious thereafter (Olsho, Harkins, & Lenhardt, 1985). Moreover, these problems can occur even in old people who do not have significant measured hearing loss (Bergman, 1980).

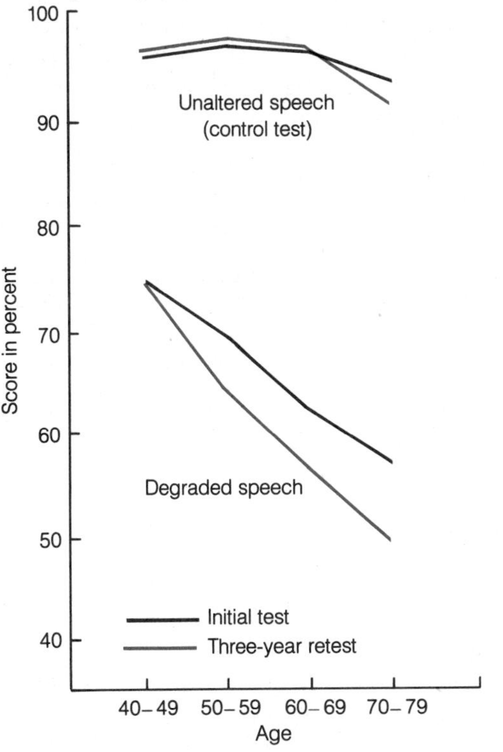

Figure 6.8 Age differences in hearing speech. Older adults have little difficulty understanding "unaltered speech"—sentences read aloud to them under excellent listening conditions. But, compared with younger adults, they do have difficulty in making out different forms of "degraded speech." In this study, they also experienced steeper declines in accuracy of hearing over a three-year period, especially when they listened to degraded speech.
(From Bergman, Blumenfeld, Cascardo, Dash, Levitt, & Margulies, 1976)

But let's note that some messages are easier to understand than others. Just as visual perception tasks are more difficult for older people when they are novel and complex, auditory perception tasks may be too (McDowd & Craik, 1988). In everyday situations, older adults can make good use of contextual cues to interpret what they hear (Hutchinson, 1989). In one study, for example, elderly adults were about as able as young adults to recall meaningful sentences they had just heard (Wingfield, Poon, Lombardi, & Lowe, 1985). However, they had serious difficulties in repeating back grammatical sentences that made no sense or random strings of words, especially when these meaningless stimuli were spoken rapidly. These findings suggest that older people may have less trouble following familiar, everyday conversations than following technical presentations on unfamiliar topics—especially if the speaker makes the task even harder by talking too fast.

Overall, then, most older adults have only limited hearing losses and only some difficulties understanding everyday speech, and they can compensate for them—for example, by reading lips. Novel and complex speech heard under poor listening conditions is likely to cause more difficulty. For those rarer older people who develop a significant hearing loss, the psychological effects can be serious (Herbst, 1983; Whitbourne, 1985). Imagine the frustration of no longer being able to follow conversations. The person trying to cope with a loss of hearing may find it easier to avoid social occasions than to struggle to understand what is said, and friends may also find it easier to avoid hearing-impaired people than to have to repeat themselves. But as we shall see at the end of this chapter, there are some highly effective, but also very simple, ways to help hearing-impaired older adults adjust. Moreover, our society offers people with sensory impairments access to many technologies that help them compensate for their losses. People in less developed countries are not so fortunate (Beall & Goldstein, 1986).

Taste and Smell

Does the older person become unable to appreciate tastes and aromas? Studies designed to measure taste thresholds suggest that with increasing age, many of us have more difficulty detecting weak taste stimulation—for example, a little bit of salt or citric acid in water (Corso, 1981; Whitbourne, 1985). Older people seem to remain more sensitive to faint sweet tastes than to other tastes (Spitzer, 1988). In addition, both middle-aged and older adults sometimes have difficulty consistently discriminating among tastes that are detectable but that differ in intensity. James Weiffenbach, Beverly Cowart, and Bruce Baum (1986), for example, found that older adults (aged 70 to 88) were less able than young adults (aged 23 to 39) to reliably judge one salt solution to be saltier than another. Similar difficulties in judging the bitterness of bitter tastes and the acidity of acid tastes were found, often starting in middle age. Degrees of sweetness could be distinguished effectively at all ages. Thus it seems that we are born with a sweet tooth and never lose it!

Similarly, the ability to detect odors appears to change somewhat with age. Sensitivity to weak odors rises from childhood to early adulthood and appears to remain high until it declines in old age (Doty et al., 1984; Stevens & Cain, 1987). The ability to distinguish among odors of different intensities appears to be somewhat greater in the years from middle childhood through middle age than in early childhood and old age (Rovee, Cohen, & Shlapack, 1975; Stevens & Cain, 1987). However, differences between age groups are usually small, and there are many older people who retain their sensitivity to both taste and smell quite well (Bartoshuk, Rifkin, Marks, & Bars, 1986; Engen, 1977; Whitbourne, 1985).

What *is* clear is that even modest declines in taste and smell, combined with other deficits, can reduce enjoyment of food in later life. This is not a matter of taste alone. As you know from the experience of having a stuffy nose, the sense of smell contributes greatly to the appreciation of food. Moreover, we recognize foods and appreciate them on the basis of their color and texture, so both vision and touch play some role too.

The ability to recognize different foods through taste and smell declines in old age. Susan Schiffman (1977), for example, blindfolded young adults (college students) and elderly adults (retired professors and their spouses and retirement home residents) and asked them to identify blended foods by taste and smell alone. As Table 6.1 reveals, the older people were less often correct than the college students. But was this due to a loss of taste sensitivity or a loss of smell sensitivity? Or was the problem neither taste nor smell, but instead a cognitive problem—recalling the right name for a food that was in fact sensed?

Claire Murphy (1985) attempted to shed light on these questions by presenting people aged 18–26 and age 65 and older with 12 of the blended foods used by Schiffman. First, she repeated Schiffman's finding: Elderly adults had more difficulty than young adults identifying what they were sniffing and tasting. Moreover, older men had more difficulty than older women, a finding that parallels the finding that men experience greater hearing loss in old age than women do. However, older people often came up with the wrong specific label but the right idea (identifying sugar as fruit or salt as peanuts, for example).

Table 6.1 Age differences in recognition of foods

	PERCENTAGE RECOGNIZING FOOD	
PUREED FOOD SUBSTANCE	College students (ages 18–22)	Elderly people (ages 67–93)
Apple	93	79
Banana	93	59
Pear	93	86
Pineapple	93	86
Strawberry	100	79
Walnut	33	28
Broccoli	81	62
Cabbage	74	69
Carrot	79	55
Celery	89	55
Corn	96	76
Cucumber	44	28
Green bean	85	62
Green pepper	78	59
Potato	52	59
Tomato	93	93
Beef	100	79
Fish	89	90
Pork	93	72
Rice	81	55

Elderly adults have more difficulty than young college students identifying most blended foods by taste and smell alone. Percentages of those recognizing food include reasonable guesses such as "orange" in response to "apple." Notice that some foods (for example, cucumber) are very difficult for people of any age to identify by taste and smell alone. Appearance and texture are important to our recognition of such foods.

Source: From Schiffman, 1977.

Thus at least some of their difficulty might have been cognitive in nature.

Finally, Murphy tested women who were blindfolded and had their nostrils blocked. Here was a chance to see whether age differences in recognition of foods were due mainly to the sense of smell or the sense of taste. Age differences in performance vanished; *both* young and elderly women did poorly when they had to rely on taste alone. Other research suggests that old people cannot discriminate foods as well as young adults can when they must rely on odor alone (Schiffman & Pasternak, 1979). Overall, then, Murphy and others have concluded that the reduced ability to identify foods in old age is due less to losses in the sense of taste than to losses in the sense of smell, and that cognitive difficulties are also involved.

How might losses in the senses of taste and smell affect an older person? Susan Whitbourne (1985) summarizes several implications. If foods do not have much taste, interest in eating may be lost and nutritional problems could result. Another possibility is to overuse seasonings such as salt and threaten health in still another way. (One of our students was horrified to see her grandmother dump most of a box of salt into the mashed potatoes on Thanksgiving Day!) Decreased sensitivity to odors can have effects beyond a loss of enjoyment of food (Whitbourne, 1985). Older people's social lives might suffer if they are not aware that their bodies or houses have unpleasant odors. More important, the inability to detect dangerous odors such as gas leaks or the smell of spoiled food threatens survival. Thus those older people who experience significant losses in sensitivity to tastes and smells may face a number of problems in everyday life.

Touch, Temperature, and Pain

By now, you are surely used to the idea that older adults are often less able than younger adults to detect weak sensory stimulation. Older adults are indeed less able to detect a soft touch or vibration on the skin. The detection threshold for touch increases and sensitivity is gradually lost from middle childhood on (Kenshalo, 1977; Verrillo & Verrillo, 1985). Older adults also sometimes judge the same tactile stimuli to be less intense than younger adults do (Verrillo, 1982). Also, their tactile perceptions may be less complete. For example, elderly people are less able than middle-aged or young people to match a form they explore with their right hand to one of several forms available to their left hand, possibly because they do not use effective search strategies (Kleinman & Brodzinsky, 1978). It is not clear that these minor losses in touch sensitivity have many implications for daily life, however.

Similarly, older people may be less sensitive to changes in temperature than younger adults are (Verrillo & Verrillo, 1985). For example, some elderly people keep their houses too cool because they are unaware of being cold and are then in danger if their already too cold bodies experience a temperature drop (Corso, 1981). Others may fail to notice it when the temperature becomes uncomfortably hot. Since older bodies are also less able than younger ones to maintain an even temperature, elderly people face an increased risk of death in heat waves or cold snaps (Rango, 1985; Whitbourne, 1985).

Finally, consider the perception of pain. It might seem only fair that older people should also be less sensitive to painful stimulation. This does seem to be the case, but age differences are not large or totally consistent (Kenshalo, 1977; Verrillo & Verrillo, 1985). The problem is that the experience of pain is highly subjective. Even if two people had actually experienced the same amount of pain, one person may report it as painful while another may "keep a stiff upper lip." Older men may be especially likely to hesitate to report experiencing pain, even when what they are feeling is probably painful (Clark & Mehl, 1971). It is difficult to accurately measure many of the sensory thresholds of older adults because they sometimes seem hesitant to report a sensation they are uncertain of (Botwinick, 1984).

Perhaps the more important part of pain perception is the ability to tolerate pain once it is felt. Although older people certainly experience more aches and pains than younger people do, it is not clear that they are less bothered by pain (Verrillo & Verrillo, 1985). For example, Stephen Harkins, Donald Price, and Michael Martelli (1986) subjected young (age 20–36), middle-aged (45–60), and older (65–80) adults to painful heats of different temperatures. Middle-aged and older adults judged the least intense heats to be less hot than the young adults did, suggesting that they were relatively insensitive to these weak pain stimuli. Yet they also tended to judge the hottest of the stimuli to be especially hot, suggesting that they definitely experienced highly painful stimuli as intense. In addition, judgments of the *unpleasantness* of these painful stimuli barely differed across age groups. Thus the researchers concluded that there are more similarities than differences between age groups in the experience of pain.

This research tells us little about the chronic pain that elderly people with arthritis and other conditions experience (Verrillo & Verrillo, 1985). We must guess, however, that older people respond to pain much as younger people do. The body senses that we have discussed here do not change with age nearly as much as the senses of vision and hearing do. Susan Whitbourne (1985) suggests that humans may remain sensitive to pain across the entire life span because it does so much to protect them. For example, the young infant who cries will bring an adult running, and the older person who feels pain is likely to turn down the hot water in the bath, stop lifting heavy boxes, or even go to the doctor.

A Summing Up

Of all the changes in sensation and perception during adulthood that we have considered, those involving vision and hearing appear to be the most important and the most nearly universal. Not only are these senses less keen, but they are used less effectively in such complex perceptual tasks as searching a cluttered room for a missing book or following rapid conversation in a noisy room. Declines in the other senses seem to be less serious and do not affect as many people.

Still, even the vision and hearing of most elderly adults are reasonably good. It is the minority of older adults with severe or multiple losses that we must worry about. In our complex society, difficulty driving, watching television, reading newspapers, and getting around can limit satisfaction and social interaction in old age. Sensory impairments even increase the risks of death, especially when deficits in vision and balance conspire to cause life-threatening falls (Ochs, Newberry, Lenhardt, & Harkins, 1985).

NATURE, NURTURE, AND PERCEPTUAL DEVELOPMENT

Now that we have surveyed perceptual growth and decline across the life span, let us return to the issue we raised at the start of this chapter: the debate about the roles of nature and nurture in perceptual development. Much of what we have learned about perceptual development in infancy supports the "nature" side of the nature/nurture debate. Many basic perceptual tendencies appear to be innate or to develop rapidly in all normal infants through maturational processes. Is experience relevant too?

Early Experience and Perceptual Development

What would visual perception be like in an infant who was blind at birth but later had surgery to permit vision? Research with animals gives some clues. In such research, young animals are temporarily deprived of sensory stimulation. If they later show a perceptual deficit, the experiences that they did *not* have must be necessary for normal perceptual development.

Nearly half a century ago, Austin Riesen and his associates found that chimpanzees raised in the dark experience a degeneration of the optic nerve that seriously restricts their vision (Riesen, Chow, Semmes, & Nissen, 1951). If the chimps spent no more than seven months in the dark, the damage could be reversed; otherwise it was permanent. If chimps were exposed to diffuse, unpatterned light for brief periods every day, damage to the optic nerves did not occur. Yet these visually deprived animals later had difficulty discriminating forms such as circles and squares—a task that normal chimps can easily master (Riesen, 1965).

In short, the visual system requires a minimal amount of stimulation early in life—including *patterned* stimulation—to develop normally in humans as well as in chimpanzees. Some babies are born with cataracts that make them nearly blind. Once surgery restores their sight, they, like Riesen's chimps, have difficulty, at least initially, discriminating common forms such as spheres and cubes (Walk, 1981).

Specific forms of visual stimulation appear to be necessary for development of certain neurons in the visual areas of the brain. Specific cells within the brain, for example, respond to either horizontal, vertical, or oblique (slanted) lines. If a kitten is fitted with goggles that allow it to view only vertical stripes, it develops an abundance of "vertical" cells but loses some of the cells that would enable it to detect horizontal and oblique lines (Stryker, Sherk, Leventhal, & Hirsch, 1978). Similarly, humans who have severe *astigmatism*—misshapen lenses that distort images—often have lasting difficulty seeing lines equally well in all orientations even after their vision is corrected (Mitchell, Freeman, Millodot, & Haegerstrom, 1973).

Suppose infants can see but are tied to cradleboards, as is done in some cultures, so that they cannot move? Would this confinement interfere with perceptual development? An early study of kittens suggested that it would (Held & Hein, 1963). However, Richard Walk (see Walk, 1981) suspected that young animals may not need to move independently if *objects in the environment* move. So he conducted an experiment in which he found that (1) kittens who grew up in restraining holders with no interesting movement to watch tended to doze off and showed no more depth perception than kittens raised entirely in the dark and (2) kittens who sat passively in their holders but watched cars streak around a racetrack had depth perception equal to that of kittens who were free to move around in a lighted environment.

If Walk's findings hold for humans, infants kept on cradleboards or physically disabled infants should suffer no perceptual deficits so long as they are regularly exposed to moving objects and pay attention to them. Of course, moving people and objects are very common in a typical home. Indeed, the main message of research on the effects of the early sensory environment is that *normal perceptual development requires normal sensory stimulation*—the kind of stimulation readily available to babies all over the world. It is only when such fundamental stimulation is lacking that perceptual development suffers.

Figure 6.9 Drawings used by William Hudson to study depth perception in pictures. South African adults and children indicated their understanding of depth and spatial cues by answering such questions as "Which animal is nearer the man?" and "What is the man doing (aiming at)?" Performance was poor among illiterate adults with little exposure to two-dimensional representations of space. (From Hudson, 1960)

Social and Cultural Influences on Later Perceptual Development

Do people who grow up in different societies and subcultures perceive the world in different ways? Perceptual preferences obviously differ from culture to culture. In some cultures, people think hefty women are more beautiful than slim ones, relish eating sheep's eyeballs or chicken heads, or delight in music that sounds to us like disorganized noise. But are more basic perceptual competencies also affected by socialization?

They seem to be (see Werner, 1979). For example, we have already seen that adults become far less sensitive than infants to sound contrasts that are not important in their own language. Another good example is cultural differences in the ability to interpret depth cues in a two-dimensional drawing or painting. William Hudson (1960) showed the drawings in Figure 6.9 to black and white children and adults in South Africa and asked them questions to see if they were making use of depth and spatial cues. To anyone in our Western culture, where two-dimensional representations of a three-dimensional world are common, the task is easy. However, many illiterate South African laborers of both races had great difficulty giving responses that indicated three-dimensional perception. In fact, they performed less well than schoolchildren and more like preschoolers. Hudson's findings suggest that both schooling and prior exposure to two-dimensional representations of space contribute to the ability to perceive depth and spatial relations in pictures. Although other researchers have suggested other reasons for cultural differences in spatial perception, there is agreement that such differences, as well as other perceptual differences, exist (Werner, 1979).

Perceptual Styles and Experience

Still another way in which experience can influence perception is revealed by research on **cognitive style**—each individual's characteristic ways of approaching problems and processing information. One important perceptual/cognitive style has been studied carefully by Herman Witkin and his colleagues (Witkin, 1959; Witkin & Goodenough, 1981). People who have a **field-dependent** style have perceptions that are dependent on or highly influenced by the surrounding context, while people who are **field independent** are less influenced by the surrounding context.

One way to identify an individual's perceptual style is to ask that person to locate a design that has been "embedded" in a complex background (see Figure 6.10). Field-independent individuals are more successful than field-dependent individuals at this task because they are more able to overcome the strong influence of the complex visual scene as they try to isolate the smaller figure embedded within it.

As children develop, they ordinarily become less field dependent and more field independent (Kogan, 1983; Witkin & Goodenough, 1981). This shift occurs gradually from childhood to adolescence (Witkin, 1959). Interestingly, people may once again become more field dependent in old age; at least, cross-sectional comparisons suggest that old people have more difficulty detecting embedded figures than young adults do (Axelrod & Cohen, 1961; Panek, 1985). Despite these developmental trends, however, some people at any age are more field independent than their age mates.

Where do these individual differences in perceptual style originate? Witkin traces them to both the home environment and the cultural environment. He and his associates believe that domineering parents who closely supervise their children's behavior and demand conformity to rigidly defined rules contribute to a field-dependent orientation. Parents who are less restrictive, less rule oriented, and more willing to allow children to take initiative foster the development of a field-independent orientation. In our society, parents have traditionally granted more freedom to boys than to girls, and this may explain why girls are often found to be less field independent than boys (Witkin & Goodenough, 1977). Similarly, people from some kinds of societies are more field independent than people from other societies (Witkin & Berry, 1975). Those in farming societies tend to work together, and children are expected to be obedient and cooperative and to place the needs of the group ahead of their own needs. As might be predicted, people from this kind of society were quite field dependent. By contrast, more field-independent styles were observed in hunter-gatherer societies, where people often work alone searching for food and are taught values of assertiveness, independence, and self-reliance.

Figure 6.10 Find the termite (there's only one).

Answer: The termite is in the third drawing, nestled in the curl at the bottom of the woman's hair.

Differences between field-independent and field-dependent individuals seem to extend beyond differences in their perceptions. For instance, field-dependent persons have been found to be very "people oriented"—interested in people, able to get along with others, and emotionally responsive (Witkin & Goodenough, 1977). By contrast, field-independent people tend to be more tolerant of ambiguous situations, more able to function independently, and more interested in achievement. Research on these cognitive styles tells us again that experiences—along with maturation and physiological aging—influence perceptual development. Is it possible, then, that the right experiences can improve the lives of individuals with sensory impairments?

APPLICATIONS: AIDING HEARING-IMPAIRED PEOPLE, YOUNG AND OLD

Sensory impairments can have many effects on people's overall development and adjustment. Yet much can be done throughout the life span to aid such individuals. Let us close this chapter by briefly examining interventions for children and adults who have hearing impairments.

In their book on hearing-impaired children, Fred Bess and Freeman McConnell (1981) alert us to the importance of identifying hearing impairments as early in life as possible. Hearing impairments often are not diagnosed until children are 2 or 3 or even older—that is, until it is obvious that their language development has been delayed. Think how much better it would be to detect such losses and help children early in the critical years of language learning. Testing the hearing of infants is challenging, but it can be done. One useful method, at least with infants 6 months old or older, is to observe the infant's ability to localize sound—that is, to turn in the direction of sounds of different intensities (Trehub, Bull, Schneider, & Morrongiello, 1986).

Once hearing-impaired infants are identified, interventions can be planned. Bess and McConnell (1981) describe in some detail the program offered by their own speech and hearing center in Nashville, Tennessee. Infants are first fitted with hearing aids that are carefully matched to their problems. Much effort is invested in helping both parents and children get used to the idea and in periodically checking to see that the aids are functioning properly. Then teachers come to the home to show parents how to make their children more aware of the world of sound by adding some emphasis to what parents naturally do when they are interacting with their children. For instance, the parent of a hearing child who hears the screech of a car's brakes outside might say, "That sounded terrible, didn't it?" The teachers suggest that parents of hearing-impaired children put their hands to their ears, rush the child to the window, and talk about the noise. Similarly, they urge parents to slam doors, deliberately rattle pots and pans, and create other such opportunities for the child to become alert to sounds. All the while, parents are using words to describe everyday objects, people, and events.

The combination of the right hearing aid and this auditory training in the home has been quite effective in improving the ability of hearing-impaired infants and preschoolers to hear speech. Some experts make the learning of sign language part of early intervention, but many agree that most hearing-impaired youngsters can make good use of their remaining hearing with proper hearing aids. There is also agreement that the important thing is to give hearing-impaired children *some* means of developing a language system, whether it is oral or visual, as early as possible.

Now let's turn to the other end of the life span. You may think that the problems of hearing-impaired old people can be readily solved with hearing aids. It is not quite that simple. First people are often reluctant to admit that they have a hearing problem and to seek help (Corso, 1981). Moreover, most hearing aids cannot really restore normal hearing; they tend to distort sounds and to magnify background noise as well as messages one might want to hear. And unfortunately, many older people have hearing aids that are of poor quality or that are poorly matched to their specific hearing problems (Corso, 1981).

But there are amazingly simple ways to help people with hearing losses compensate for their losses. For one thing, the environment can be altered to facilitate hearing. For example, furniture can be arranged to permit face-to-face contact, and noisy appliances can be moved away from areas where conversations normally take place (Olsho, Harkins, & Lenhardt, 1985). Then there are simple guidelines we can follow to make ourselves more understandable to the hearing-impaired person. One of the authors had great success with just one recommendation to a student who had started shouting at his grandmother to

Box 6.3
Guidelines for Talking to Hearing-Impaired People

Raymond Hull (1980) has recommended 13 simple steps that can be taken to make it easier for hearing-impaired elderly people to understand speech. Most of these measures are equally applicable to hearing-impaired people of any age.

- Speak slightly louder than usual.
- Use a normal rate of speech; avoid fast talk.
- Be within 3 to 6 feet of the listener.
- Make sure there's enough light so that the listener can see your lips and gestures well.
- Don't bother speaking if you're in the next room or otherwise not visible.
- Don't try if there is a great deal of background noise.
- Don't speak right into the person's ear. You won't be visible, and your speech will be distorted if it is too loud.
- Reword what you said if it is not understood; don't just repeat the same words.
- *Don't* use exaggerated articulations.
- Arrange the seating in a room so that conversants are close to each other and visible.
- Include hearing-impaired people in discussions concerning them.
- At meetings, make sure speakers use a microphone, even if no one asks.
- "Above all, treat elderly persons as adults. They, of anyone, deserve that respect" (p. 427).

make her understand him: Don't shout! Shouting not only distorts speech but raises the pitch of the voice—and high-pitched speech is more difficult for elderly people to hear than is speech spoken in a lower tone of voice. Several other recommendations for communicating effectively with hearing-impaired elderly people are presented in Box 6.3.

Hearing aid technologies are rapidly improving (Popelka, 1984) and society is helping through such technologies as captioning for the deaf on television. With or without better technologies, however, hearing-impaired people can be taught more effective ways of compensating for their hearing losses and *we* can make it easier for them to hear. Hearing impairments need not keep people of any age from a meaningful life.

REFLECTIONS

What are some of the larger messages that emerge from our survey of perceptual development over the life span? For one thing, we have seen that today's researchers have identified perceptual competencies in the very young infant that no one—except perhaps observant parents—even suspected were there. Have you ever noticed that Olympic swimming records seem to be broken every time a competition is held? Well, it often seems that each new study of infant perception tells us that some perceptual capacity emerges earlier than previous researchers thought. The lesson for researchers seems to be that the quality of knowledge gained in science depends on what researchers are looking for and what methods they use to look for it. The lesson for parents is that they should assume that their young infants are extracting a great deal of information from their sensory experiences—and should make opportunities for perceptual learning available. Parents need not teach perception; they need only avoid stunting its growth by denying infants sensory stimulation.

Recent research also provides us with a more optimistic picture of perception in old age. It's true that at least modest declines in the functioning of the senses seem to be part of normal aging. However, early research was often marred by the fact that older adults are sometimes more cautious than younger adults about reporting that they have detected a stimulus or sometimes use different criteria to judge stimuli (Botwinick, 1984). More recent research using more sophisticated methods of assessment sometimes suggests that declines are neither so steep nor so common as was once believed. In addition, researchers have begun to look for phenomena *other than* decline in perception—and have found them. They have shown, for example, that older adults may perform quite effectively when they are carrying out familiar perceptual tasks and can rely on expectations gained through experience. Contemporary researchers have also emphasized *compensation* for decline, or the many ways in which both aging individuals and society can prevent physiological losses from diminishing the quality of life.

We are about to turn our attention to cognitive development across the life span. Let's reemphasize, then, that perception is our primary means of obtaining knowledge. Jean Piaget rested his theory of cognitive development on the sensory and motor experiences of infancy for good reason. How *would* infants gain knowledge of the many objects in their physical world without being able to see them, finger them, and pop them into their mouths? How would infants develop the ability to talk about the world without hearing speech (or viewing sign language)? Perception is truly at the heart of human development. ❦

SUMMARY POINTS

1. *Sensation* is the detection of sensory stimulation; *perception* is the interpretation of what is sensed; developmentalists and philosophers differ about whether basic knowledge of the world is innate (the nativist position) or must be acquired through the senses (the empiricist position) and about whether sensory information needs to be embellished (enrichment theory) or is rich as it is (differentiation theory).

2. From birth, the visual system is working reasonably well. Infants under 2 months of age discriminate brightness and colors and are attracted to contour, moderate complexity, and movement. Starting at 2 or 3 months of age, they more clearly perceive whole forms or patterns. Spatial perception also develops rapidly, and by about 7 months infants fear dropoffs.

3. Young infants can recognize their mothers' voices and distinguish speech sounds, are sensitive to musical sounds, and soon learn to distinguish features of melodies.

4. The senses of taste and smell are also well developed at birth. Newborns avoid unpleasant tastes and enjoy sweet tastes, and they soon recognize their mothers by odor alone. Newborns are also sensitive to touch, temperature, and pain.

5. The senses are interrelated at birth, become more differentiated or distinct later, and gradually can be integrated to allow cross-modal perception. Most basic perceptual capabilities are in place by the end of infancy.

6. During childhood, we learn to allocate attention more effectively, to direct it selectively, and to ignore irrelevant information. Older children become able to detect subtle distinctions between letters as they learn to read. During adolescence, sensation and perception are at their peaks.

7. Over adulthood, sensory and perceptual capacities gradually decline, though many changes are minor and can be compensated for. Visual difficulties include presbyopia (especially a loss of near vision starting in middle age), problems perceiving motion, and difficulty performing novel and complex visual search tasks.

8. Hearing difficulty associated with aging (presbycusis) most commonly involves loss of sensitivity to high-frequency (high-pitched) sounds. Even elderly people without significant hearing losses often experience difficulty understanding novel and complex speech.

9. Many older people have difficulty recognizing or enjoying foods, largely because of declines in the sense of smell; touch, temperature, and pain perception also decline slightly.

10. Although many perceptual abilities appear to be innate or maturational, experience is also necessary for normal perceptual development and can influence perceptual styles.

KEY TERMS

accommodation (visual)
attention
cataracts
cognitive style
contour
cross-modal perception
dark adaptation
differentiation theory
distinctive feature
enrichment theory
field dependent
field independent
Gestalt psychology
habituation
olfaction
perception
presbycusis
presbyopia
sensation
sensory threshold
size constancy
visual acuity
visual cliff

CHAPTER

7

COGNITION AND LANGUAGE

Michael, at 6 months of age, is gazing intently at his father's keys. When Dad throws a dishcloth over the keys, Michael looks around aimlessly, as though the keys had never existed. Five-year-old Amy won't eat her rice because there are "too many." After her mother pushes the rice together in a more compact pile, Amy says, "Okay, that's a little many rices," and digs in. Nine-year-old Billy, asked by his art teacher to draw a person who has three eyes, protests: "I can't do it. Nobody has three eyes!"

Is there something wrong with these children's minds? Not at all. Their minds are working fine, for other children of their ages are likely to respond similarly. We must, then, seriously entertain the possibility that children think differently than adults do.

In this chapter, we begin an examination of the development of **cognition** — that is, the activity of knowing and the processes through which knowledge is acquired and problems are solved. Human beings are cognitive beings throughout the life span, but their minds change in important ways. The chapter concentrates on the very influential theory of cognitive development proposed by Jean Piaget. In addition, it traces the development of language and how language development is linked to the development of the mind. It also raises questions about the minds of adults and whether their problem-solving capacities diminish or improve or simply stay as they were in high school.

Cognitive development is viewed through only one lens here: that of Piaget and his many followers. Chapter 8 introduces an *information-processing approach* to the mind that focuses on specific mental activities such as paying attention, perceiving, storing relevant information in memory, weighing decisions, and so on. Moreover, Chapter 9 considers the mind from the perspective of intelligence testers and describes changes and individual differences in intellectual performance over the life span.

PIAGET'S APPROACH TO COGNITIVE DEVELOPMENT

Chapter 2 introduced the cognitive-developmental perspective associated with Jean Piaget. When Piaget worked on the development of standardized intelligence tests, he became disenchanted with an approach that seemed to be concerned only with determining the ages at which children could correctly answer certain questions. Piaget became intrigued by children's *mistakes*, for he noticed that children of the same age often made similar kinds of mistakes — errors that were typically quite different from those made by younger or older children. Could these age-related differences in error patterns reflect developmental steps, or stages, in intellectual growth? Piaget thought so, and then devoted his life to studying how children think, not just what they know (Flavell, 1963).

His studies started with close observation of his own three children as infants: how they explored new toys, solved simple problems that he arranged for them, and generally came to understand themselves and their world. Later Piaget began to study larger samples of children through what has become known as the **clinical method**. This method uses a question-and-answer technique to discover how children attack problems or think about everyday issues. Many contemporary researchers consider the method imprecise because it does not involve asking standard questions of all children tested, but Piaget (1929) believed the investigator must have the flexibility to pursue an individual child's line of reasoning so as to fully understand the child's mind. From his naturalistic observations of his own children and uses of the clinical method to explore children's understandings of everything from the rules of games to the concepts of space and time, Piaget formulated four major stages of cognitive development that will soon be examined in some detail.

What Is Intelligence?

Piaget defined **intelligence** as a basic life function that helps the organism to adapt to its environment. We observe adaptation as we watch the toddler figuring out how to work a jack-in-the-box, the school-aged child figuring out how to divide candies among friends, or the adult figuring out how to start a temperamental car. The newborn enters an unfamiliar world with few means of adapting to it other than working senses and reflexes. But Piaget viewed infants as active agents in their own development who learn about the world of people and things by observing, investigating, and experimenting (Cowan, 1978).

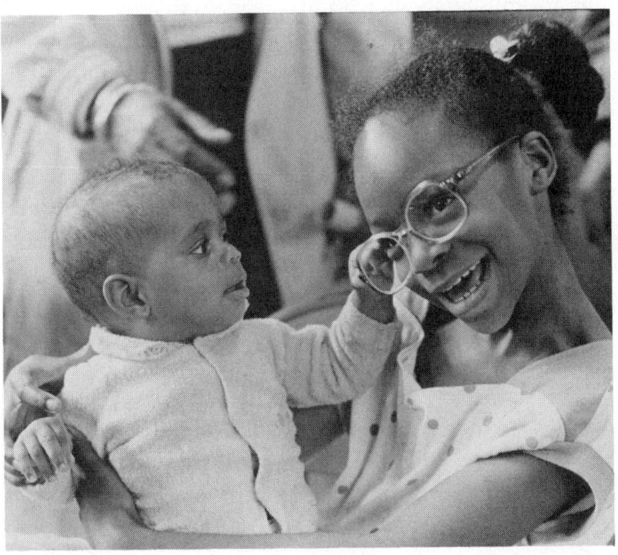

The grasping scheme. Infants have a range of behavioral schemes that allow them to explore new objects. Each scheme is a general pattern of behavior that can be adjusted to fit specific objects.

Knowledge gained through active exploration takes the form of one or another **scheme** (sometimes called a *schema* in the singular, *schemata* in the plural). Schemes are cognitive structures: organized patterns of action or thought that we construct to organize or interpret our experience (Piaget, 1952, 1977). For example, the infant's grasping actions and sucking responses are early *behavioral schemes*, for both are patterns of action used by infants to "adapt to" or deal with different objects. Piaget stressed that infant intelligence is *action*. During their second year, children develop *symbolic schemes*, or concepts. They use internal mental symbols such as images to represent or stand for aspects of experience, as when a young child sees a funny dance and carries away a mental model or image of how the dance was done. This symbolic capacity is clearly involved in language development, for words are symbols for things.

Finally, the thinking of children aged 7 and older progresses beyond the use of action schemes and symbolic schemes. It is characterized by a type of scheme called a **logical operation**, an internal mental activity performed on the objects of thought. Imagine that a young girl uses mental symbols to represent five apples and then mentally calculates how many apples would be left if she gave two of them to her brother. Logical operations include all the "actions" implied in mathematical symbols such as $+$, $-$, $\times$, and $\div$. They also make it possible for children to classify objects mentally into meaningful groups or to order objects from biggest to smallest. Intelligence in the older child is still action, but it is action performed *in the head*.

As children develop more sophisticated schemes or cognitive structures, they become increasingly able to adapt to their environments and solve problems. Because new schemes develop, children of different ages will deal with or understand the same stimuli differently. For example, the infant may get to know a shoe mainly as a "thing-to-chew," the preschooler may decide to let the shoe represent a telephone and put it to his or her ear, and the school-aged child may mentally count its shoelace eyelets.

How Does Intelligence Develop?

Piaget believed that all schemes, all forms of understanding, are created through the operation of two inborn intellectual functions that he called organization and adaptation. Through **organization**, children combine existing schemes into new and more complex ones. For example, the young infant who gazes, reaches, and grasps will organize these simple schemes into a complex structure, *visually directed reaching,* that allows actively seeking out objects for closer examination. Complex cognitive structures in older children grow out of reorganizations of more primitive structures.

Adaptation is the process of adjusting to the demands of the environment. It occurs through two complementary processes, assimilation and accommodation. Imagine that you are a 2-year-old, that the world is new, and that you see your first horse. What will you make of it? In all likelihood, you will try to relate it to something familiar. **Assimilation** is the process by which we interpret new experiences in terms of existing models of the world. Thus if you already have a scheme that mentally represents your knowledge of dogs, you may label this new beast "doggie." Through assimilation, we deal with the world in our own terms, sometimes bending the world to squeeze it into our existing categories. Throughout the life span, we rely on our existing cognitive structures to understand new events.

But what if you notice that this "doggie" is a bit bigger than most dogs and has a mane and has an awfully odd "bark"? You may then be prompted to change your understanding of the world of four-legged animals. **Accommodation** is the process of modifying existing cognitive structures to account for new experiences. Perhaps you will need to invent a new name for this horse or ask your mother what it is and revise your concept of four-legged animals accordingly (see Box 7.1).

If we always assimilated new experiences, our understandings would never advance. Piaget believed that all new experiences are greeted with a mix of assimilation and accommodation. Once we have schemes, we apply them to make sense of the world, but we also encounter puzzles that force us to modify our understandings through accommodation. Piaget believed that when new events seriously challenge old schemes, or prove one's existing understandings to be inadequate—as when a little girl sees a helicopter for the first time and is unsure what to make of it, or a man tries all the tricks he knows and still cannot get his car to start—we experience cognitive conflict. Cognitive conflict, or disequilibrium, then stimulates cognitive growth and the formation of more adequate understandings (Piaget, 1985). Thus Piaget assumed that human beings have a strong need to make better and better sense of their experience.

Intelligence, then, develops through the *interaction of the individual with the environment.* Piaget takes an interactionist position on the nature/nurture issue: Children's minds are not just programmed by learning experiences, nor are children born with innate ideas that impose order on reality. Instead, children *construct* reality. That is, they actively create knowledge of the world by acting on the world, physically or mentally.

In sum, Piaget views human beings as active creators of their own intellectual development. Their knowledge of

Box 7.1
Assimilation and Accommodation

Consider the possibilities when four-year-old Louise deals with a nearly empty soda bottle:

Assimilation: Louise imposes her schemes on this new object by pretending to drink from it as an infant would drink from a milk bottle, or by pretending it's a microphone and singing a song. Pretend play is mostly a matter of assimilating the world to whatever schemes one wishes to use.

Accommodation: Louise changes her schemes in response to new experience. Uncle Todd shows her how to blow into the bottle to make a whistling sound. She huffs and puffs and finally is able to imitate Uncle Todd. Imitation is mostly accommodation, for the child must change her action schemes to match what a model does.

Adaptation = Assimilation + Accommodation: Most intelligent behavior involves both processes. To drink what is left in the bottle (as any preschooler would want to do), Louise must assimilate the bottle to her schemes for grasping objects and then bringing them to her mouth; yet because this bottle has its own unique shape, she must accommodate her grasping action to fit this particular bottle.

the world, which takes the form of cognitive structures or schemes, changes as they organize and reorganize their existing knowledge and adapt to new experiences through the complementary processes of assimilation and accommodation. Through the interaction of biological maturation and experience, all normal human beings progress through four distinct stages of cognitive development, each one involving a qualitatively different adaptation to the world than the one that preceded it:

the *sensorimotor* stage (birth to 2 years)

the *preoperational* stage (2 to 7 years)

the stage of *concrete operations* (7 to 11 years)

the stage of *formal operations* (11 years and beyond)

These stages represent completely different levels of cognitive functioning and occur in an *invariant sequence*—that is, in the same order in all children. There is, however, room for a child's experience to speed up or slow down intellectual growth; the age ranges associated with stages are only suggested age norms.

Nowhere is the growing cognitive capacity of children more evident than in their mastery and use of language. Language reflects cognition; in turn, language serves humans well as a tool of thought and, of course, as an invaluable tool of communication.

MASTERING LANGUAGE

Although language is one of the most intricate bodies of knowledge we will ever acquire, all normal children master a language very early in life. Indeed, many infants are talking before they can walk. Can language be all that complex, then? It certainly can be. Linguists (scholars who study language) have yet to fully describe the rules of English or any other language, and so far computers cannot understand speech as well as most 5-year-olds can. What exactly is the task facing child language learners?

What Is Language?

Linguists define **language** as a system consisting of a limited number of signals—sounds or letters (or gestures in the case of the sign language used by deaf people)—that can be combined according to agreed-on rules to produce an infinite number of messages. Most of us might define it as a system of communication. *Any* human language is a marvelously versatile communication system that allows us to convey to our fellow humans virtually any thought or feeling we might have. To master a language such as English, a child must know what basic sounds are used to form words, what words mean, how to combine words to form meaningful statements, and how to use language effectively in their social interactions. That is, the child must master four aspects of language: phonology, semantics, syntax, and pragmatics.

Phonology is the sound system of a language, and the basic units of sound in any given language are its **phonemes**. The child in an English-speaking country must come to know the 45 phonemes used in English, which roughly correspond to the familiar vowel and consonant sounds, and must also know which ones can be combined in English and which ones cannot (for example, *st–*, but not *sb–*). Other languages have other basic sounds. Children must learn to hear and to pronounce the phonemes of their language in order to make sense of the speech they hear and to be understood when they speak (de Villiers & de Villiers, 1979).

Semantics is the aspect of language that concerns meanings. Words stand for, or symbolize, things, and the child must learn the connections between words and things. Since grasping semantics depends on understanding the world, cognitive development lays the groundwork for semantic development. The basic meaningful units of language are called **morphemes** rather than words. Words are indeed morphemes, but there are other morphemes that carry important meanings but are not words (for example, grammatical markers such as the *–ed* for past tense or the *–s* to signal a plural noun). Knowledge of semantics is also required to interpret whole sentences or speeches or paragraphs.

The language system also involves **syntax**, or the rules that specify how words are to be combined to form sentences. Consider these three sentences: (1) John Jane hit, (2) John hit Jane, and (3) Jane hit John. The first, as even very young children recognize, violates the rules of English sentence structure or syntax, although this word order would be perfectly acceptable in French. The second two sentences are grammatical English sentences that have very different meanings conveyed by the different word orders they use. Children must master rules of syntax to understand or use simple declarative sentences like these and then must master complex sentences with many phrases. Once these rules are understood, youngsters will have the capacity to express an infinite number of ideas—including ideas never expressed before—through language.

Finally, language learners must also master what has been termed **pragmatics**—rules specifying how language is to be used appropriately in different social contexts. To achieve their goals, children must learn when to say what to whom. They must learn to communicate effectively by taking into account who the listener is, what the listener already knows, and what the listener needs or wants to hear. "Give me that cookie" may be grammatical English, but the child is far more likely to win Grandma's heart (not to mention a cookie) with a polite, "May I please try one of your yummy cookies, Grandma?"

In short, mastering a human language is a staggering challenge, for it requires mastering phonology, semantics, syntax, and pragmatics. Moreover, human communication involves not only language use but *nonverbal communication* (facial expressions, tone of voice, gestures, and so on). Children must learn these nonverbal signals as well, for they often clarify the meaning of a verbal message and are an important means of communicating in their own right.

How Does Language Develop?

How do nature and nurture—biologically based capacities and experiences in conversing with others—enable children to become such capable communicators so rapidly? Well before they enter first grade, children can use well-formed sentences effectively to achieve their goals. Consider 3-year-old Sheila, a master of the pragmatics of language, who lobbied her adult companion to buy her ice cream by saying, "Yes, even when there's a babysitter, I get an ice cream" (Reeder, 1981, p. 135). Could Sheila have advanced this far this fast by simply imitating her parents or by learning from their efforts to correct her speech? Or should we assume that Sheila and other children could not achieve what they do without being somehow "prewired" with a special capacity to master language? What abilities must young children bring to the language-learning task, and what help must their companions provide them? We will address these questions later on. For now, keep the nature/nurture issue in mind as you read about how language development proceeds.

THE INFANT

During infancy, from birth to age 2, children are exploring the physical and social world around them and making tremendous progress in both cognition and language.

Cognitive Development: The Sensorimotor Stage

Piaget's **sensorimotor stage**, spanning the two years of infancy, involves coming to know the world through one's senses and actions. The dominant cognitive structures are *behavioral schemes*—patterns of action that evolve as infants begin to coordinate sensory input and motor responses (for example, by seeing and then grasping what is seen). At the start of the sensorimotor period, infants do not seem very intelligent, but watch for increasing signs of intelligent behavior as infants pass through the six substages of this stage. Infants will be transformed from *reflexive* creatures who do not seem capable of deliberate actions to *reflective* ones who can plan solutions to simple problems and carry them out.

Substage 1: Reflexive Activity (Birth to 1 Month)

During the first month of life, infants actively exercise and refine their innate reflexes such as sucking and grasping. New objects are assimilated to reflexive schemes; for example, the baby who initially sucks only nipples begins to suck blankets, fingers, and toys. The sucking reflex is altered in subtle ways as the infant accommodates it to different objects. Granted, this is not high intellect, but these primitive adaptations represent the beginning of cognitive growth.

Substage 2: Primary Circular Reactions (1 to 4 Months)

Increasingly, the infant seeks pleasurable stimulation. **Primary circular reactions** are pleasurable actions, centered on the infant's own body, that are discovered by chance and performed over and over. Thus Piaget's son Laurent brought his thumb to his mouth and sucked, apparently found it satisfying, and formed a habit of doing it. Repeatedly kicking one's legs or blowing bubbles is also a primary circular reaction—primary because it involves the body, circular because the pleasure these actions bring stimulates their repetition. Notice that the infant is actively exercising behavioral schemes and making things happen.

Substage 3: Secondary Circular Reactions (4 to 8 Months)

Secondary circular reactions are like primary circular reactions, except that they are centered on objects and events in the external environment. An infant may, for example, discover that a shake of the hand that grasps a rattle results in an interesting noise. The shaking action is then repeated over and over. Although this behavior seems intentional, Piaget argues that it is not, because there was no intended goal of making noise when the action was first performed.

Substage 4: Coordination of Secondary Schemes (8 to 12 Months)

True intentional behavior is seen when the infant can coordinate previously unrelated acts so that one serves as a *means* to achieving another. At 9 months of age, for example, Piaget's son Laurent was able to use a lifting scheme as the means to using his familiar grasping scheme: He lifted a cushion and then grasped the cigar case beneath it with his other hand (Piaget, 1952). It was evident to Piaget that the lifting action was intentional, that it served as a means to an end.

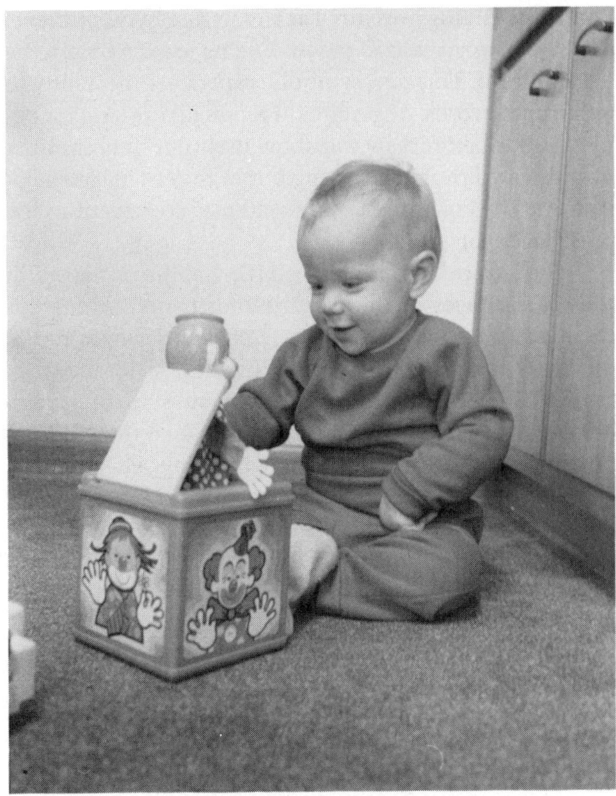

One-year-olds in the stage of tertiary circular reactions delight in discovering ways to make their toys respond in new and interesting ways.

Substage 5: Tertiary Circular Reactions (12 to 18 Months)

Notice that infants are gradually learning a great deal about the effects of their actions on the world. In Substage 5, the infant blossoms as a curious investigator of cause-and-effect relationships. **Tertiary circular reactions** involve devising *new* means of acting on objects to produce interesting results. The Substage 3 infant may find it satisfying to repeatedly squeeze a rubber duck to produce a quack, in a secondary circular reaction. The Substage 5 infant may explore other means to the same end. What happens if I step on the duck, or drop it, or bang it with my fist? What if I squeeze gently instead of firmly? Such tertiary circular reactions are trial-and-error schemes that reflect an active curiosity about the way the world works. Parents may be less than thrilled by this exciting cognitive advance when their infant explores new ways to mash food on the highchair tray!

Substage 6: Beginning of Thought (18 Months to 2 Years)

The crowning achievement of the sensorimotor stage involves internalizing behavioral schemes to construct mental symbols, or images, that can then guide future behavior. Now the infant can experiment *mentally* and may therefore show a kind of "insight" into how to solve a problem. For example, Piaget (1952) placed a bread crust out of reach on a table and laid a stick nearby to challenge his son, Laurent. Laurent was about to give up on reaching the bread, but then he "again looks at the bread, and without moving, looks very briefly at the stick, then suddenly grasps it and directs it toward the bread" (p. 335). This is not trial-and-error experimentation. Instead Laurent's "problem solving" occurred at an internal, symbolic level as he perhaps visualized the stick being used to obtain the distant bread. This new **symbolic capacity**—the ability to use images, words, or gestures to represent or stand for objects and experiences—will show itself not only in more sophisticated problem solving but in the language explosion and the enjoyment of pretend play so evident in the preschool years.

The advances in problem-solving ability reflected in the six substages of the sensorimotor period bring with them other important changes. Consider changes in the quality of infants' play activities. Infants are not really interested in manipulating toys until the substage of secondary circular reactions (4 to 8 months), when they may repeat an action like sucking or banging a toy over and over. When they reach the substage of tertiary circular reactions (12 to 18 months), they experiment in varied ways with toys, getting to know what these objects are all about. Reaching the final substage, the beginning of thought, opens up the possibility of letting one object represent or stand for another, so that a cooking pot can become a hat or a shoe can become a telephone. Such pretend play flourishes once infants acquire this capacity for symbolic thought. Table 7.1 summarizes the six stages and also indicates parallel developments in the capacity to imitate others and to understand that objects exist even when the infant is not experiencing them.

The Capacity for Imitation

An ability to imitate certain facial expressions may be inborn, but it apparently has little relation to the intentional imitation that is possible later in the first year (Field, Woodson, Greenberg, & Cohen, 1982; Meltzoff & Moore, 1983). Early in life, infants can imitate only actions that are already in their repertoire. When can they accommodate their behavior to imitate a novel action? Not until Substage 4, when the 8- to 12-month-old infant coordinates secondary schemes. And even then, imitation involves a great deal of struggle. Kenneth Kaye and Janet Marcus (1981) found that Substage 4 infants at first assimilate a novel response to an existing scheme and then gradually work up to a precise imitation over a period of weeks and months. Piaget's daughter Jacqueline, for example, spent quite a bit of time opening and closing her whole

Table 7.1 Summary of the substages and intellectual accomplishments of the sensorimotor period

SUBSTAGE	METHODS OF SOLVING PROBLEMS OR PRODUCING INTERESTING OUTCOMES	IMITATION	OBJECT CONCEPT
1. Reflex activity (0–1 month)	Exercise and accommodation of inborn reflexes	Some imitation of facial expressions	Tracks moving object but ignores its disappearance
2. Primary circular reactions (1–4 months)	Repeating interesting acts centered on one's own body	Repetition of own behavior that is mimicked by a companion	Looks intently at the spot where an object disappeared
3. Secondary circular reactions (4–8 months)	Repeating interesting acts on external objects	Same as in Substage 2	Searches for partly concealed object
4. Coordination of secondary schemata (8–12 months)	Combining actions to solve simple problems (first evidence of intentionality)	Ability to eventually imitate *novel* responses after crude initial attempts	Searches for and finds concealed object, but may err by searching site of last success
5. Tertiary circular reactions (12–18 months)	Experimenting to find new ways to solve problems or produce interesting outcomes	Systematic imitation of novel responses; deferred imitation of simple motor acts	Searches for and finds object where it was last seen
6. Beginning of thought (18–24 months)	First evidence of insight; child solves problems at an internal, symbolic level	Deferred imitation of complex behavioral sequences	Object concept is complete; searches for and finds objects that have been hidden through *invisible* displacements

hand before she could accommodate to and imitate her father's action of bending and straightening his forefinger (Piaget, 1951).

Voluntary imitation becomes more efficient at 12 to 18 months, but the greatest breakthrough comes in Substage 6 (18 to 24 months) with the emergence of the symbolic capacity. Now, according to Piaget, infants can engage in **deferred imitation**—that is, imitation of models who are no longer present—because they can create and later recall mental representations of what they have seen. Recent research suggests that as early as 9 months of age infants may be able to imitate novel actions involving unfamiliar toys after a one-day delay (Meltzoff, 1988b), and that 14-month-olds can remember and imitate such actions a week after they saw them (Meltzoff, 1988a). It seems, then, that the capacity for deferred imitation is present earlier in life than Piaget thought and may emerge before other symbolic skills do.

THE DEVELOPMENT OF OBJECT PERMANENCE

According to Piaget, infants are not born with the very fundamental understanding of the world that he termed the concept of **object permanence**. This is the understanding that objects continue to exist when they are no longer visible or otherwise detectable to the senses. For example, it has probably not occurred to you to wonder whether your coat is still in the closet after you shut the closet door (unless perhaps you have taken a philosophy course). But very young infants, because they rely on their senses, seem to operate as though objects exist only when they are perceived or acted on. According to Piaget, the infant must "construct" the notion that reality exists apart from one's experience of it.

Piaget believed that the concept of object permanence develops gradually over the entire sensorimotor period. Up through Substage 3, or roughly 4–8 months, infants will not search for a toy that has been fully covered by a cloth. In Substage 4, they seem to have that trick mastered, but Piaget (1954) demonstrated that they still rely very much on their perceptions and actions to "know" an object. After his 10-month-old daughter Jacqueline had repeatedly retrieved a toy parrot from one hiding place, Piaget put it in a new spot while she watched him. Amazingly, she looked in the original hiding place! She seemed to assume that her behavior determined where the object would appear; she did not treat the object as if it existed apart from her own actions. This tendency of 8- to 12-month-olds to search for an object in the place where they last had success finding it is called the **A, not B, error**.

In Substage 5, the young 1-year-old overcomes this error but continues to have trouble with *invisible* displacements—as when you hide a toy in your hand, move your hand under a pillow, and remove the hand. The infant will search where the object was last seen, seeming confused when it is not in your hand and failing to look under the pillow where it was deposited. Finally, by Substage 6 the infant is capable of *mentally representing* such invisible moves and so can master sophisticated hiding games. According to Piaget, the concept of object permanence is fully mastered at this point. However, recent research suggests that infants may develop some understandings of object permanence earlier than Piaget thought (see Box 7.2).

All in all, the child's intellectual achievements during the sensorimotor period are truly remarkable. By its end, they have become planful thinkers who can solve some problems in their heads, who can imitate actions they observed days ago, and who have developed not only the concept of object permanence but many other concepts as well. Moreover, they have begun to understand and use language.

Language Takes Root

For the first 10 to 13 months of life, infants are not yet capable of speaking meaningful words, but they are building up to that achievement.

PERCEIVING AND PRODUCING SOUNDS

As we learned in Chapter 6, newborns seem to "tune in" to human speech immediately. Moreover, very young infants can discriminate phonemes such as *b* and *p* or *d* and *t* (Eimas, 1975). Indeed, 7-month-old infants from homes where English is spoken are better than English-speaking adults at differentiating certain phonemes that are *not* used in English (Werker, Gilbert, Humphrey, & Tees, 1981).

What about producing sounds? Prelinguistic vocalizations develop in a stagelike pattern that is related to the maturation of motor control over the muscles involved in articulating sound (Sachs, 1985). At birth, infants produce at least three kinds of cries—a "hunger" cry, a "mad" cry, and a "pain" cry—that communicate their distress (Wolff, 1969). By the third week of life, infants also produce a

Box 7.2
Hiding Games: Early Understanding of Object Permanence

Are very young infants really as bound to their perceptions as Piaget believed? Do they really fail to grasp that objects exist even when they are not immediately visible to the eye? Thomas Bower (1982) doubts it, and his research illustrates a theme in much of the research that has been inspired by Piaget: Young infants may be more competent than Piaget thought.

Bower suggests young infants tested by Piaget failed to demonstrate object permanence merely because Piaget equated searching for the object with understanding. Instead, Bower had infants aged 1 to 4 months watch as a screen blocked a toy from view. A few seconds later, the screen was removed, revealing either the toy or an empty space where the toy had been. If these infants did not realize that the toy still existed once it was hidden from view, they should have been surprised when it was still there. Instead, they were puzzled when the toy was *not* there. Bower suggests that young infants have some sense of object permanence long before they are capable of searching for and finding a hidden object and that Piaget therefore underestimated their understanding. However, Bower agrees with Piaget that the ability to find hidden objects improves over the sensorimotor period as infants gain experience searching for objects that disappear from view (Wishart & Bower, 1985).

Similarly, recent research suggests that 8-month-olds who make the A not B error, looking for an object where they last found it rather than in its new hiding place, may know more than their seemingly misguided searching behavior reveals. Recently, Renee Baillargeon and Marcia Graber (1988) developed a task in which infants did not have to search for a hidden object to demonstrate their knowledge of its location. Eight-month-old infants watched as screens were placed in front of two placemats, one of which had a toy sitting on it. After a 15-second delay, a hand appeared and retrieved the toy from either the right hiding place or the wrong one. Would the infants be surprised to see the toy snatched from a place that was empty before the screens were put in place? Infants *were* surprised, as evidenced by their tendency to look longer when the seemingly impossible event occurred than when the toy was retrieved from the place in which it had originally been hidden.

This and other evidence suggests that infants who err by searching in spot A (the site of previous success) rather than in spot B (the new location) can remember, at least for a few seconds, that the object is now in B. However, they may not yet be able to act appropriately on this knowledge by searching in B (Baillargeon & Graber, 1988; Diamond, 1985). Perhaps they are merely unable to inhibit a tendency to reach for the spot they last searched. Indeed, Adele Diamond (1985) has observed that some of the infants who reach for spot A hardly look there, as though they know it is not the right place to be looking but cannot stop themselves.

In sum, it seems that babies sometimes know a good deal more about object permanence than they reveal through their actions when they are given the kinds of search tasks Piaget devised. Gradually, they become more skilled at acting on their knowledge and searching in the right spot, so that by the end of the sensorimotor period they are masters of even very complex "hide and seek" games.

"fake" cry that may be what Piaget would call a primary circular reaction—the repeating of an interesting noise for the sheer pleasure of making it (Wolff, 1969).

The next milestone in vocalization, at about 3 to 5 weeks of age, is **cooing**: repeating vowel-like sounds such as "oooooh" and "aaaaah." Cooing is associated with contented states rather than with distress. At about 3 to 4 months of age, infants expand their range of sounds considerably as they begin to produce consonants and then enter a period of **babbling**. Babbling, which appears between about 4 and 6 months of age, soon involves repeating consonant/vowel combinations such as "baba" or "dadadada," which sound like words but are not used meaningfully.

Up to about 6 months of age, infants all over the world, even deaf ones, sound pretty much alike, but the effects of experience soon show themselves. At roughly this age, deaf infants fall behind hearing infants in their ability to produce well-formed syllables (Oller & Eilers, 1988). When infants are about 8 months old, adults can recognize from their babbling sounds whether they have been listening to French, Chinese, or Arabic (De Boysson-Bardies, Sagart, & Durand, 1984). Advanced babblers begin to sound as though they are speaking the language they are hearing because they increasingly restrict their sounds to those that are phonemes in the language they are hearing and because they match their intonation patterns to those of that language (de Villiers & de Villiers, 1979; Weir,

1966). It seems that infants are "learning the tune before the words" (Bates, O'Connell, & Shore, 1987, p. 157).

In their quest to master the semantics of language, infants come to understand words before they can produce them. That is, comprehension is ahead of production, or expression, in language development. Before they really understand the specific words in a command, they will obey commands (e.g., "Get the ball") in familiar contexts (Benedict, 1979). This is probably because they can interpret tone of voice and context cues (Benedict, 1979). Shortly before speaking their first true words, however, or as they approach a year of age, they seem really to understand familiar words, for they look longer when commanded to look at an object labeled properly than they do when the command to look involves a nonsense word (Thomas, Campos, Shucard, Ramsay, & Shucard, 1981). From infancy on, we generally understand more words than we are able to control in our own speech or writing.

In their first year, infants are also learning basic lessons about the *pragmatics* of language. For example, during the first six months, they are most likely to coo or babble *while* a partner is speaking (Freedle & Lewis, 1977; Rosenthal, 1982). After that point, however, they seem to have mastered the rule of conversational turn-taking, for they vocalize when a partner has stopped talking. This marks a basic, highly important step in learning to use language appropriately in social interactions. Indeed, infants are learning a great deal about how to communicate before they ever utter a meaningful word.

The First Words: Holophrastic Speech

An infant's first meaningful word, spoken at about a year of age, is a special event for parents. First words have been called **holophrases** because a single word sometimes seems to represent an entire sentence's worth of meaning. These single-word "sentences" can serve different communication functions depending on how they are said and the context in which they are said (Greenfield & Smith, 1976). For example, 17-month-old Shelley used the word *ghetti* (spaghetti) in three different ways over a five-minute period. First, she pointed to the pan on the stove and seemed to be asking, "Is that spaghetti?" Later the function of her holophrase was to name the spaghetti when shown the contents of the pan, as in "It *is* spaghetti." Finally, she left little question that she was requesting spaghetti when she tugged at her companion's sleeve as he was eating it and used a whining tone.

There are limits to the amount of meaning that can be packed in a single word and its accompanying tone of voice and gestures, but infants in the holophrastic stage of language development do seem to have mastered basic language functions such as naming, questioning, requesting, and demanding. Moreover, 1-year-olds are showing that they are now capable of using symbols—not only words, but gestures (or behavioral schemes, in Piaget's terminology) such as pointing, raising their arms to signal "up," or panting heavily to say "dog" (Bates et al., 1987; Acredolo & Goodwyn, 1988).

What do 1-year-olds talk about? They talk about the very world that Piaget says they are rapidly coming to know. Katherine Nelson (1973) studied 18 infants as they learned their first 50 words and found that nearly two thirds of these early words referred to objects, including familiar people. Moreover, these objects were nearly all either manipulable by the child (for example, bottles, shoes) or capable of moving themselves (for example, animals, trucks). Certainly this fits well with Piaget's view of the infant as acting on the world and developing cognitively through his or her actions.

Initial language acquisition literally proceeds one word at a time. Three or four months may pass before the child has a vocabulary of 10 words (Nelson, 1973). But then the pace quickens, so that by 24 months of age children are producing an average of 186 words (Nelson, 1973).

One of the great challenges of early semantic development is to match the meanings that adults associate with words. Two kinds of errors are common. First, there is **overextension**, using a word to refer to too wide a range of objects or events, as when one 2-year-old called all furry, four-legged animals "doggie." The second, and opposite, error is **underextension**, as when the same child initially used the word "cookie" to refer only to chocolate chip cookies. Getting semantics right seems to be mainly a matter of discriminating similarities and differences—for example, categorizing animals on the basis of size, shape, the sounds they make, and other perceptual features (Clark & Clark, 1977; Prawat & Wildfong, 1980). But might children know more about the world than their semantic errors suggest? Yes! Two-year-olds who call all four-legged animals "doggie" can often point out a dog in a set of animal pictures when asked to do so (Thompson & Chapman, 1977).

It makes some sense that a child with a limited vocabulary might label a horse a "doggie" until other animal terms become available (de Villiers & de Villiers, 1979). Overextensions in word use may also be picked up from parents, who tend to use terms of intermediate generality like "dog," rather than more specific terms ("terrier") or general terms ("animal") when talking to infants or toddlers, while using more specific terms when talking with older children (Mervis & Mervis, 1982).

From Holophrases to Simple Sentences: Telegraphic Speech

The next step in language development, taken at about 18 to 24 months of age on the average, is combining two words into simple sentences. Toddlers all over the world use two-word sentences to express the same basic ideas (see Table 7.2). Early combinations of two or more words are sometimes called **telegraphic speech** because, like telegrams, many of them contain critical content words and omit frills such as articles, prepositions, and auxiliary verbs.

Now, it is ungrammatical in adult English to say "No wet" or "Where ball." However, two-word sentences are not just random word combinations or errors. They reflect children's *own* systematic rules for forming sentences. Psycholinguists have approached early child language as though it were a foreign language and have tried to describe the rules that young children seem to be using to form sentences. At first, psycholinguists such as Martin Braine (1963) focused on the order of the two words in two-word sentences, believing that children followed predictable rules of syntax. Now the emphasis has shifted to the *meanings* that children are attempting to convey.

Two-word sentences, like holophrases, serve several communication functions: naming, demanding, negating, and so on. Lois Bloom (1970) and others proposed that it is more appropriate to describe early language in terms of a **functional grammar**, one emphasizing the semantic relations between words, the meanings being expressed. For example, young children often use the same word order to convey different meanings. "Mommy sock" might mean "The sock is Mommy's" in one context and "Mommy is putting on my sock" in another. Word order sometimes does play a role: "Billy hit" and "Hit Billy" mean different things. Body language and tone of voice also communicate meanings, as when a child points and whines to emphasize a request for ice cream and not merely a noting of its existence (Wilkinson & Rembold, 1981). As it turns out, children from different cultures, and even different children within a single culture, differ con-

Table 7.2 Similarities in children's spontaneous two-word sentences in several languages

	LANGUAGE			
FUNCTION OF SENTENCE	English	German	Russian	Samoan
To locate or name	There book	Buch da (book there)	Tosya tam (Tosya there)	Keith lea (Keith there)
To demand	More milk Give candy	Mehr milch (more milk)	Yesche moloko (more milk)	Mai pepe (give doll)
To negate	No wet Not hungry	Nicht blasen (not blow)	Vody nyet (water no)	Le 'ai (not eat)
To indicate possession	My shoe Mama dress	Mein ball (my ball) Mamas hut (Mama's hat)	Mami chashka (Mama's cup)	Lole a'u (candy my)
To modify or qualify	Pretty dress Big boat	Armer wauwau (poor dog)	Papa bol'shoy (Papa big)	Fa'ali'i pepe (headstrong baby)
To question	Where ball	Wo ball (where ball)	Gde papa (where Papa)	Fea Punafu (where Punafu)

Source: Adapted from Slobin, 1979.

siderably in how they construct their two-word sentences and what sorts of words they include in them (Bates et al., 1987). Their communication goals may be much the same, but individual children devise their own ways of achieving them.

Overall, the functional grammar approach appears to be sound. Children learn to make combinations of words and accompanying body language perform basic communication functions as they interact with others. By the age of 2, they are typically understanding quite a bit, are using many words appropriately either alone or in two-word telegraphic sentences, and are positioning themselves for the language explosion that will occur from age 2 on.

THE CHILD

Once young children are talking, we have a better chance to see what is going on in their heads. No one has done more to make us aware of the surprising turns that children's minds can take than Jean Piaget, who has described how children enter the preoperational stage of cognitive development in their preschool years and progress to the concrete-operational stage as they enter their elementary school years. As children's minds develop, their language and communication skills expand dramatically.

The Preschool Child: Piaget's Preoperational Stage

The **preoperational stage** of cognitive development extends from roughly 2 to 7 years of age. Recall that the sensorimotor stage ended with the emergence of the symbolic capacity. This capacity runs wild in the preschool years and is the greatest cognitive strength of the preschooler compared to the infant. Imagine the possibilities: The child can now use words to refer to things, people, and events that are not physically present. Instead of being trapped in the immediate present, the child can refer to both past and future. Pretend or fantasy play flourishes at this age, as pots can stand for hats and cardboard boxes for houses. Some children invent imaginary friends and elaborate make-believe worlds. Some parents worry about such flights of fancy, but imaginative uses of the symbolic capacity contribute to both cognitive and social development, as we shall see in Chapter 15.

Yet the young child's mind is limited compared with that of an older child, and it was the limitations of preoperational thinking that Piaget explored most thoroughly. Preschoolers are freer of the immediate present than infants, but they are still highly influenced by their perceptions, and so they are easily fooled by appearances. We can illustrate this reliance on perceptions best by considering Piaget's classic tests of conservation.

Lack of Conservation

One of the many understandings about the physical world that children must develop is the concept of **conservation**, the understanding that certain properties of an object or substance do not change when its appearance is altered in some superficial way. So, find yourself a 4- or 5-year-old and try Piaget's conservation of liquid quantity task. Pour equal amounts of water into two identical glasses and get the child to agree that they have the "same amount to drink." Then, *as the child watches*, pour the water from one glass into a shorter, wider glass. Now ask whether the two containers—the tall, narrow glass or the shorter, broader one—have the same amount of water to drink or whether one has more water to drink. Children younger than 6 or 7 will usually say that the taller glass has more water than the shorter one (see Figure 7.1). Thus they are shown to lack the understanding that the volume of liquid is *conserved* despite the change in the shape it takes in different containers.

How can preschoolers be so easily fooled by appearances? Piaget thought it is because they lack the logical operations necessary for conservation. For instance, the preschooler lacks the cognitive operation called **decentration**, the ability to focus on two or more dimensions of a problem at one time. Consider the conservation task: The child must focus on height and width simultaneously *and* recognize that the increased width of the short, broad container compensates for its lesser height. Preoperational thinkers engage in **centration**—the tendency to center on a single aspect of the problem (here, focusing on height alone and concluding that the taller glass has more liquid). In other ways as well, preschoolers seem to have one-track minds. They may have trouble, for example, understanding that you can love and be angry at someone at the same time (Harter, 1982).

A second necessary cognitive operation is **reversibility**, the process of mentally undoing or reversing an action. Older children often display mastery of reversibility

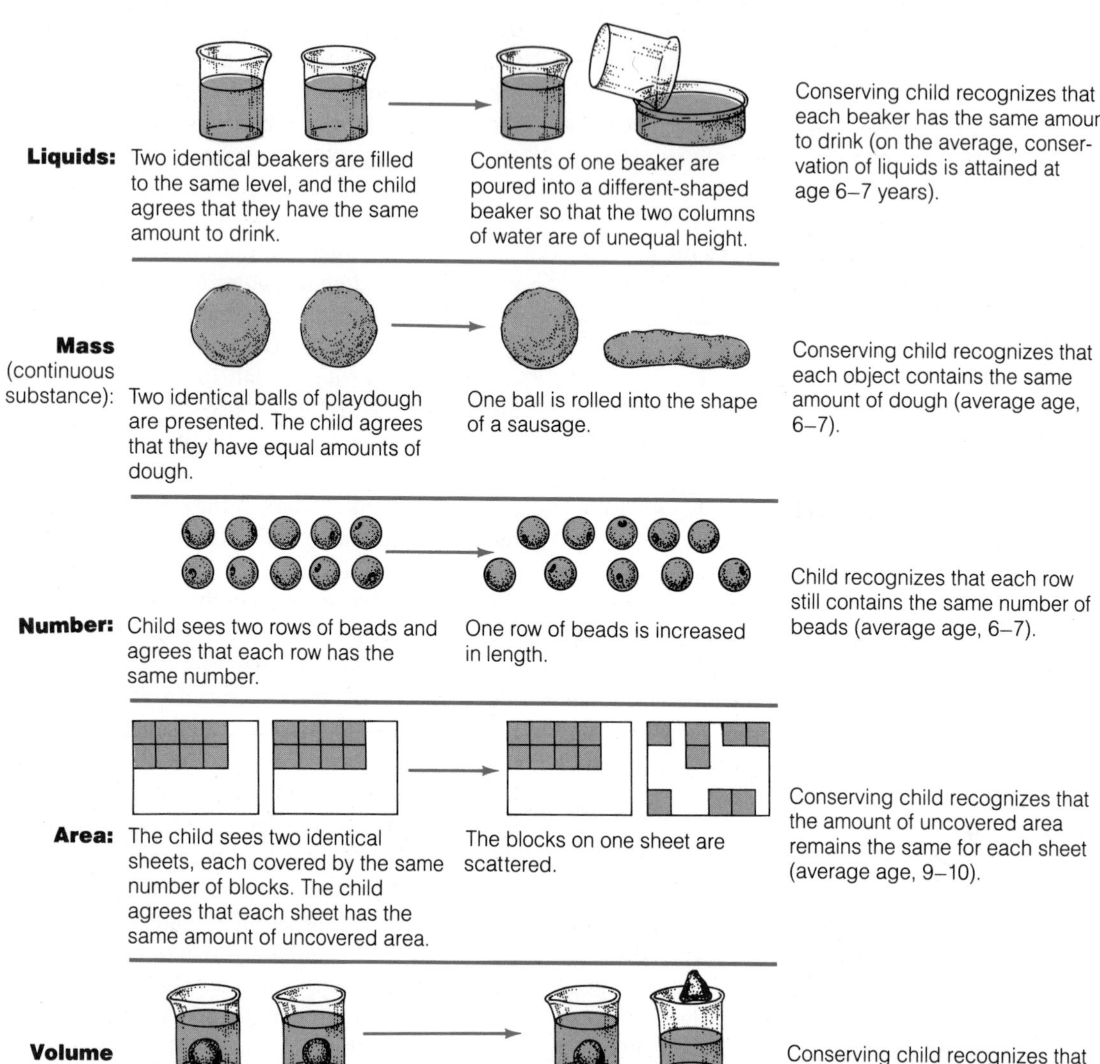

Liquids: Two identical beakers are filled to the same level, and the child agrees that they have the same amount to drink.
Contents of one beaker are poured into a different-shaped beaker so that the two columns of water are of unequal height.
Conserving child recognizes that each beaker has the same amount to drink (on the average, conservation of liquids is attained at age 6–7 years).
Mass (continuous substance): Two identical balls of playdough are presented. The child agrees that they have equal amounts of dough.
One ball is rolled into the shape of a sausage.
Conserving child recognizes that each object contains the same amount of dough (average age, 6–7).
Number: Child sees two rows of beads and agrees that each row has the same number.
One row of beads is increased in length.
Child recognizes that each row still contains the same number of beads (average age, 6–7).
Area: The child sees two identical sheets, each covered by the same number of blocks. The child agrees that each sheet has the same amount of uncovered area.
The blocks on one sheet are scattered.
Conserving child recognizes that the amount of uncovered area remains the same for each sheet (average age, 9–10).
Volume (water displacement): Two identical balls of clay are placed in two identical beakers that had been judged to have the same amount to drink. The child sees the water level rise to the same point in each beaker.
One ball of clay is taken from the water, molded into a different shape, and placed above the beaker. Child is asked whether the water level will be higher than, lower than, or the same as in the other beaker when the clay is reinserted into the water.
Conserving child recognizes that the water levels will be the same because nothing except the shape of the clay has changed—that is, the pieces of clay displace the same amount of water (average age, 9–12).

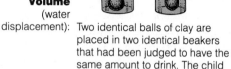

Figure 7.1 Some common tests of the child's ability to conserve.

by suggesting that the water be poured back into its original container to prove that it is still the same amount. The young child shows *irreversibility* of thinking and may insist that the water would overflow the glass if it were poured back. Finally, preoperational thinkers fail because they have trouble conceptualizing *transformations*, or processes of change from one state to another, as when water is poured from one glass to another or an object is dropped (see Figure 7.2). As a result, preoperational thinking is sometimes called *static thought*.

Preoperational children do not understand the concept of conservation, then, because they engage in centration, irreversible thought, and static thought. The older child, in the stage of concrete operations, has mastered decentration, reversibility, and transformational thought. The correct answer to the conservation task is now a matter of logic; there is no longer the need to rely on perceptions as one's guide. Indeed, a 9-year-old tested by one of our students grasped the logic so well and thought the question of which glass had more so stupid that she asked, "Is *this* what you do in college?!"

Egocentrism

Piaget believed that preoperational thought also involves **egocentrism**—a tendency to view the world solely from one's own perspective and to have difficulty recognizing other points of view. For example, he asked children to indicate what an asymmetrical mountain scene would look like from several different vantage points. Young children often chose the view from their own position (Piaget & Inhelder, 1956). Similarly, young children often assume that if they know something, other people do too (Ruffman & Olson, 1989). The same holds for desires: The 4-year-old who wants to go to MacDonald's for dinner may say that Mom and Dad want to go to MacDonald's, too, despite the fact that Mom's on a diet and Dad prefers Pizza Hut. Moreover, the preschool child's egocentric wishes sometimes bias his or her thinking, as when Sarah refuses to give up her belief that her wagon can float in the water, despite evidence to the contrary, because she wants so much to believe that it can.

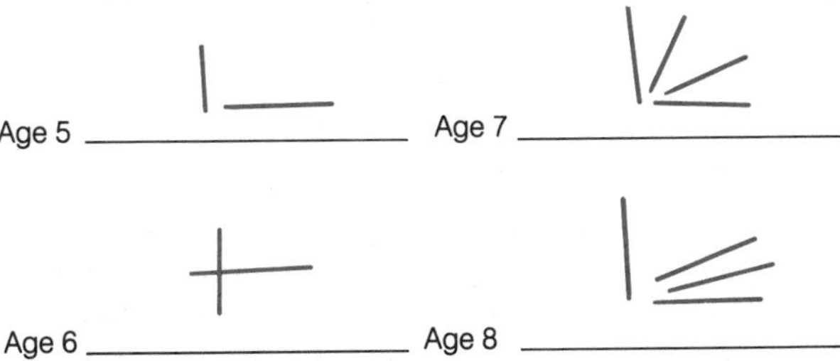

Figure 7.2 Preoperational thought is static. Slowly and repeatedly drop a pencil in front of a preschooler, and then ask the child to draw the falling of the pencil (or give the child a number of strips of paper to be arranged to show the falling of the pencil). Preoperational thinkers (the 5- and 6-year-olds) generally show you the before and the after but nothing in between. School-aged children are better able to conceptualize transformations like the falling of the pencil and so provide answers like those given by the 7-year-old and the 8-year-old also tested by one of our students.

Faulty Classification

The limitations of relying on perceptions and intuitions are also apparent when preoperational children are asked to think about classification systems. When 2- or 3-year-old children are asked to sort objects on the basis of similarities, they make interesting designs or change their sorting criteria from moment to moment. Older preoperational children are able to group objects systematically on the basis of shape, color, function, or other dimensions of similarity (Inhelder & Piaget, 1964). However, even children aged 4 to 7 have trouble thinking about relations between classes and subclasses, or wholes and parts. Given a set of wooden beads, most of which are brown but a few of which are white, preoperational children do fine when they are asked if all the beads are wooden and if there are more brown beads than white beads. That is, they can conceive of the whole class (wooden beads) or of the two subclasses (brown and white beads). However, when the question is, "Are there more brown beads or more wooden beads?," they usually say, "More brown beads." They cannot *simultaneously* relate the whole class to its parts, or they lack what Piaget termed the concept of **class inclusion**, the logical understanding that the parts are included within the whole. Notice that the child *centers* on the most striking perceptual feature of the problem—the fact that brown beads are more numerous than white ones, again being fooled by appearances.

Other Qualities of Preoperational Thought

Preoperational thought is also highly *concrete*. Simply ask a preschooler to tell you about love, death, or any other abstract or general concept and you will be convinced that young children can best understand concepts when they are illustrated very concretely. Piaget also noted that young children often have difficulty with concepts of causality. They sometimes show **transductive reasoning**, concluding that events that occur together cause each other. Thus Piaget's daughter reasoned, "I haven't had my nap, so it isn't afternoon." (We can see a touch of egocentrism here as well.) Finally, Piaget also noticed that young children sometimes display **animism**, a tendency to attribute life and lifelike qualities to inanimate objects. Thus the 4-year-old watching the setting sun says, "Look Daddy. It's hiding behind the mountain. Why is it going away? Is it angry?" (Cowan, 1978, p. 11). These qualities of preoperational thought make preschoolers a source of endless amusement for adults.

Did Piaget Underestimate the Preoperational Child?

Are preschool children really as illogical and egocentric as Piaget proposed? Perhaps not. At least it appears that many of Piaget's tasks were so complex that they could not reveal some of the capabilities of the young mind. Consider a few examples of the strengths uncovered by researchers using simpler tasks.

Rochel Gelman (1972) simplified Piaget's conservation of number task (which was shown in Figure 7.1, p. 210) and discovered that children as young as 3 have some grasp of the concept that number remains the same even when items are rearranged spatially. She first got children focusing their attention on number by playing a game in which two plates, one with two toy mice and one with three toy mice, were presented and the plate with the larger number was always declared the "winner." Then Gelman started introducing changes, sometimes adding or subtracting mice but sometimes just bunching up or spreading out the mice. Young children were not fooled by spatial rearrangements; they seemed to understand that number remained the same. However, they showed their limitations when they were given larger sets of numbers that they could not count.

Similarly, several researchers have demonstrated that preschool children are not as egocentric as Piaget claimed when tasks are reduced to the bare essentials. In one study, 3-year-olds were shown a card with a dog on one side and a cat on the other (Flavell, Everett, Croft, & Flavell, 1981). The card was held vertically between the child (who could see the dog) and the experimenter (who could see the cat). When children were asked what the experimenter could see, these 3-year-olds performed flawlessly. And finally, a review of more than 100 studies of children's causal reasoning revealed that even 3-year-olds understand some basic principles of causality such as the fact that causes precede rather than follow effects (Sedlak & Kurtz, 1981).

Studies like these have raised important questions about the adequacy of Piaget's theory and have led to a more careful consideration of the demands placed on children by tasks designed to assess their cognitive development. Piaget concluded that young children failed his tasks because they do not yet command logical operations such as reversibility. Other researchers have demonstrated that the cause of failure is often something else—for example, lack of attention to the relevant aspect of the task, memory limitations, or linguistic immaturity. It seems that young children may be developing sound intuitive understandings of the physical world earlier than Piaget thought. Yet they still seem to have difficulty grasping the logic behind concepts such as conservation. Moreover, they have difficulty applying their emerging understandings consistently to a wide range of tasks, especially to complex tasks that demand too many mental gymnastics.

The School-Aged Child: Piaget's Stage of Concrete Operations

At about the age that children start elementary school, their minds undergo a transformation. Piaget's third stage of cognitive development extends from roughly 7 to 11 or more years of age. The **concrete operations stage** involves mastering the *logical operations* that were missing in the preoperational stage—that is, becoming able to perform mental activities on the objects of thought, as when a child mentally adds or subtracts Halloween candies. For every limitation of the preoperational child, we can see a corresponding strength of the concrete operational child.

Conservation

Given the conservation of liquid quantity task (refer to Figure 7.1, p. 210), the preoperational child centers on either the height or width of the glasses, ignoring the other dimension, while the concrete-operational child can decenter and juggle two dimensions at once. Reversibility now allows the child to mentally reverse the pouring process and imagine the water in its original container. Transformational thought allows the child to better understand the process of change involved in pouring the water. Overall, armed with logical operations, the child now *knows* that there must be the same amount of water after the water in one glass is poured into a different container; he or she has logic, not just appearances, as a guide.

Looking back at the conservation tasks in Figure 7.1, you will notice that some forms of conservation (for example, mass and number) are understood sooner than others (area or volume). Piaget coined the term **horizontal decalage** to describe developmental inconsistencies like this—instances in which children can solve some but not all of the problems that supposedly require the same mental operations. He believed that horizontal decalage occurs because problems that appear quite similar may actually differ in complexity. Thus conservation of volume may emerge relatively late in the concrete-operational period because it actually requires coordinating the operations involved in conserving liquid quantities and conserving mass. Piaget maintained that operational abilities evolve in a predictable order as simple skills that appear early are reorganized into increasingly complex skills. Some studies support Piaget's view (Tomlinson-Keasey, Eisert, Kahle, Hardy-Brown, & Keasey, 1979), but others challenge his notion that different concrete-operational skills are mastered in the same order by all children (Case, 1985; Kuhn, 1988).

Relational Logic and Transitivity

To observe the powers of logical operations, consider the child's ability to think about relative size. A preoperational child given a set of sticks of different lengths and asked to arrange them in order from biggest to smallest is likely to struggle along, awkwardly comparing one pair of sticks at a time. Concrete-operational children are capable of **seriation**, which enables them to arrange items *mentally* along a quantifiable dimension such as length or weight. Thus they perform this seriating task quickly and correctly.

Concrete-operational thinkers also master the related concept of **transitivity**, which describes the necessary relations among elements in a series. If, for example, John is taller than Mark, and Mark is taller than Sam, who is taller, John or Sam? It follows *logically* that John must be taller than Sam, and the concrete operator grasps the transitivity of these size relationships. The preoperational child, lacking the concept of transitivity, will need to rely on perceptions to answer the question and might insist that John and Sam stand next to each other so that it can be determined which is taller. Some research using simplified tasks (Gelman, 1978; Trabasso, 1975) suggests that preoperational children have a better understanding of such transitive relations than Piaget gave them credit for. Other researchers, however, have demonstrated that preschool children may be able to solve simplified transitivity problems correctly without really grasping the logic of transitivity (Chapman & Lindenberger, 1988). It seems fair to conclude that preschool children, although they may have more understanding than Piaget believed, still cannot think about transitive relations as efficiently and effectively as older children do.

Other Advances in Cognition

The school-aged child overcomes much of the egocentrism of the preoperational period, becoming better and better at adopting other people's perspectives. Classification abilities improve as the child comes to grasp the concept of *class inclusion* and can bear in mind that subclasses (brown beads + white beads) are included in a whole class (wooden beads). Mastery of mathematical operations improves the child's ability to solve arithmetic problems, leading to an interest in measuring and counting things precisely (and fury when companions do not keep accurate score in card games). Overall, school-aged children strike us as more logical than preschoolers because they now possess a powerful arsenal of "actions in the head." But surely if Piaget proposed a fourth stage of cognitive development there must be some limitations to concrete operations. Indeed there are. This mode of thought is applied to objects, situations, and events that are real or readily imaginable (thus the term *concrete* operations). As we shall see later, concrete operators have difficulty thinking about abstract ideas and hypothetical propositions that have no basis in reality.

The Language Explosion of the Preschool Years

The capacity of preschool children to use symbols to represent the world around them is nowhere so evident as in their speech. In the short period from age 2 to 5, children come to speak sentences that are remarkably complex and adultlike. Table 7.3 gives an inkling of how fast things move within just 10 months. From the two-word

Table 7.3 Samples of one boy's speech at three ages

AGE	SAMPLE SENTENCES
28 months (telegraphic speech)	Somebody pencil Floor Where birdie go? Read dat Hit hammer, Mommy Yep, it fit Have screw
35 months	No—I don't know What dat feeled like? Lemme do again Don't—don't hold with me I'm going to drop it—inne dump truck Why—cracker can't talk? Those are mines
38 months	I like a racing car I broke my racing car It's broked You got some beads Who put dust on my hair? Mommy don't let me buy some Why it's not working?

Source: Adapted from McNeill, 1970.

stage of language acquisition children move on to three-word telegraphic sentences and then to still longer sentences, starting to master the little function words like articles and prepositions that were often missing in their early telegraphic sentences. They infer more and more of the rules of adult language.

How do we know when children are mastering new rules? Oddly enough, their progress sometimes reveals itself in new "mistakes." Consider the task of learning grammatical markers for plurals of nouns and past tenses of verbs. Typically this happens sometime during the third year. But a child who has been using the words "feet" and "went" may suddenly start to say "foots" and "goed." Does this represent a step backward? Not at all. The child was probably using the correct irregular forms at first by imitating what adults said without really understanding the meaning of plurality or verb tense. The use of "foots" and "goed" is a breakthrough: The child has now inferred the rule of adding *–s* to pluralize nouns and adding *–ed* to signal past tense. But at first, the child overapplies the rules to cases in which the adult form is irregular—a phenomenon known as **overregularization**. When the child masters exceptions to the rules, he or she will say "feet" and "went" once more. However, even 5- to 8-year-olds will occasionally overregularize unfamiliar words and say such things as "slided" rather than "slid" or "oxes" rather than "oxen" (Slobin, 1979).

Children must also master rules for creating variations of the basic declarative sentence; that is, they must master rules that allow them to convert a basic idea such as "I was eating pizza" into such forms as questions ("What was I eating?"), negative sentences ("I was not eating pizza"), and imperatives ("Eat the pizza!"). The prominent linguist Noam Chomsky (1968, 1975) drew attention to the child's learning of these rules by proposing that language be described in terms of a **transformational grammar** consisting of rules of syntax for transforming basic sentences into other forms.

How, for example, do young children learn to phrase the questions that they so frequently ask? The earliest questions often consist of nothing more than two- or three-word sentences with rising intonation (for example, "See kittie?"). Sometimes "wh" words like "what" or "where" appear (for example, "Where kittie?"). During the second stage of question asking, children begin to use auxiliary, or helping, verbs, but their questions are of this form: What Daddy is eating? Where the kittie is going? Their understanding of transformation rules is still incomplete (Dale, 1976). Finally, they learn the transformation rule that calls for moving the auxiliary verb ahead of the subject (as in the adultlike sentence, "What is Daddy eating?").

Meanwhile, children are starting to master complex sentences in which phrases or clauses serve as objects or subjects of sentences, as in "I remember *where it is*." By the end of the preschool period (age 5–6), children's sentences are very much like those of adults, even though they have never had a formal lesson in grammar. It's an amazing accomplishment. Yet there is more to accomplish.

Refining Language Skills in the School Years

Although 5-year-olds have learned a great deal about language in a remarkably brief period, quite a bit more work is left for the grade school years. Not only do schoolchildren improve their pronunciation skills, produce longer and more complex sentences, and continue to expand their vocabularies, but they also begin to think about and manipulate language in ways that were previously impossible.

Listening to preschool children talk, one is bound to notice that many of them have difficulty articulating certain phonemes; *sucker* may come out as *thucker, elephant* as *effalunt*. Many early articulation problems disappear during the school years (Owens, 1984). School-aged children also acquire many complex syntactical rules such as those for forming passive sentences and sentences with multiple clauses (Owens, 1984). Carol Chomsky (1969) demonstrated that not until the middle elementary school years do children master certain subtle differences in sentence constructions. The younger grade schooler, for example, may have difficulty with the distinction between "Ask Ellen what to feed the doll" and "Tell Ellen what to feed the doll." They often treat *ask* as if it meant *tell* and reply "hamburgers" or "eggs" instead of asking Ellen a question (Chomsky, 1969). School-aged children are gradually coming to grips with exceptions to grammatical rules and subtleties of complex sentence structure.

They are also expanding their knowledge of semantics. Thanks to the remarkable vocabulary spurt of the preschool period, 6-year-olds already understand some 8,000 to 14,000 words (Carey, 1977). They will continue to expand their vocabularies all their lives. Because concrete operations allow school-aged children to understand classification hierarchies, they also grasp relations among concepts and are able, for example, to label a leopard as a leopard, but also as a type of cat, an animal, and a living creature. They can also infer meanings that are not explicitly stated, as when a noisy 8-year-old recognizes that a teacher is being sarcastic in saying "My but you're quiet today" (Ackerman, 1982).

Moreover, school-aged children are rapidly developing **metalinguistic awareness**—an ability to think about language and its properties and uses. They come to enjoy the ambiguities, double meanings, and metaphors that language allows. In late elementary school, they begin to understand proverbs such as "When the cat's away, the mice will play" (Reynolds & Ortony, 1980; Saltz, 1979). Cognitive theorists have argued that the development of concrete operations may be responsible for both the growth of metalinguistic awareness and the child's increased understanding of humor. Nowhere are the signs of cognitive and metalinguistic growth more evident than in the school-aged child's delight in telling or hearing terrible jokes and riddles (see Box 7.3).

Finally, school-aged children become more able to communicate effectively because they are less cognitively egocentric and more able to take the perspective of their listener. Again, the preschool child is not hopelessly egocentric. But when the task is more challenging, the limitations of the younger child become apparent. Robert Krauss and Sam Glucksberg (1977), for example, had children from age 4 to 10 describe blocks with unfamiliar graphic designs on them to a peer on the other side of a screen. The speaker was to stack the blocks and tell the listener how to stack a duplicate set of blocks in the same order.

Kindergarteners failed miserably at this task. As shown in Table 7.4, they described designs in egocentric and idiosyncratic ways that could not mean much to their listeners. As a result, they did not get any better at communicating over the course of eight trials. By contrast, third and fifth graders gave more informative descriptions and were able to communicate nearly flawlessly by the end of the series of trials. School-aged children are better able to adjust their communication to the needs of their listeners—for example, by describing key differences among stimuli rather than merely giving each a name (Kahan & Richards, 1986) and by offering more information to a listener who is unfamiliar with the stimuli than to one who is already familiar with them (Sonnenschein, 1986). Older children are also more able to *evaluate* their messages and recognize when the content is ambiguous or uninformative, and they are also more likely to request clarifying information when someone else's message is ambiguous (Beal, 1987; Beal & Flavell, 1983; Patterson, O'Brien, Kister, Carter, & Kotsonis, 1981).

All things considered, then, we cannot help but be awed by the pace at which children master the fundamentals of a human language during their first five years of life, but we must also appreciate the continued growth that occurs during the elementary school years, particularly with respect to the practical problems of communicating effectively. It is time to ask how children acquire all of these remarkable language skills.

How Language Develops: Some Theories

Attempts to explain language acquisition have differed considerably in the stands taken on the nature/

Box 7.3
Children's Humor and Cognitive Development

Where does the fish keep its money?

Answer: In the riverbank.

Do you remember going through a phase in early elementary school of telling terrible jokes like this one? A preschooler hearing this joke may laugh at the silly idea of a fish having money, but if asked to rephrase the joke, the child is likely to say the answer was "In the bank." A child this age misses the whole idea that the humor of the joke depends on the double meaning of bank. Anything that looks or sounds silly may amuse preschoolers: Calling a "shoe" a "floo" or a "poo," for example. Once children realize that everything has a correct name, mislabeling things becomes funny (McGhee, 1979).

But with the onset of concrete-operational thought and the meta-linguistic awareness that accompanies it, children can really appreciate jokes and riddles that involve linguistic ambiguities. The riverbank joke boils down to a classification task: There is a large category of banks, with at least two subclasses, financial institutions and the banks of streams. School-aged children who have mastered the concept of class inclusion can keep the class and subclasses in mind at once and move back and forth mentally

between the two meanings of bank. Similarly, children cannot appreciate the punchline to "What has an ear but cannot hear?" unless they can mentally reclassify ears of the sort that grow on human heads as ears of the sort that grow on cornstalks, and hold both of these meanings in mind at once. Appreciation of such puns or plays on words is high among second graders (7- to 8-year-olds) and continues to grow until fourth or fifth grade (McGhee & Chapman, 1980; Yalisove, 1978).

Children's tastes in humor change again when they reach the beginning of Piaget's last stage of cognitive development at about age 11 or 12 (Yalisove, 1978). Simple riddles and puns are no longer cognitively challenging enough, it seems, and are likely to elicit groans (McGhee, 1979). Adolescents, who have entered the stage of formal operations, can appreciate jokes that involve an absurd or contrary-to-fact premise and a punchline that is quite logical if the absurd premise is accepted. The humor in "How can you fit six elephants into a VW?" depends on appreciating that "Three in the front and three in the back" is a perfectly logical answer only if one accepts the hypothetical premise that multiple elephants could fit in a small car (Yalisove, 1978). Reality-oriented school-aged children might simply judge this joke stupid; after all, elephants *can't* fit in cars. Clearly, then, children cannot appreciate certain forms of humor until they have the required cognitive abilities. Research on children's humor seems to suggest that children and adolescents are most attracted to jokes that challenge them intellectually by requiring that they use cognitive skills that they are just beginning to master (McGhee, 1979).

---

nurture issue. We can appreciate this by considering learning, nativist, and interactionist perspectives on language development.

The Learning Perspective

Ask most adults how children learn language and they are likely to say that children imitate what they hear and are praised when they get it right and corrected when they get it wrong. Different learning theorists emphasize different aspects of this view: Social-learning theorist Albert Bandura (1971) and others emphasize observational learning—learning by listening to and then imitating older companions. Behaviorist B. F. Skinner (1957) and others emphasize the role of reinforcement. As children achieve better and better approximations of adult language, parents and other adults praise meaningful speech and correct errors. Children are also reinforced by getting what they want when they speak correctly (Dale, 1976). In other words, learning theorists consider the child's social environment to be critical to what and how much the child learns.

How well does the learning perspective account for language development? Certainly it is no accident that children end up speaking the same language that their parents speak, down to the regional accent. Children *do* learn the words that they hear spoken by others—even on tele-

Table 7.4 Typical idiosyncratic descriptions offered by preschool children when talking about unfamiliar graphic designs in the Krauss and Glucksberg communication game

FORM	CHILD 1	2	3	4	5
	Man's legs	Airplane	Drapeholder	Zebra	Flying saucer
	Mother's hat	Ring	Keyhold	Lion	Snake
	Daddy's shirt	Milk jug	Shoe hold	Coffeepot	Dog

Source: Krauss & Glucksberg, 1977.

vision programs (Leonard, Chapman, Rowan, & Weiss, 1983; Rice & Woodsmall, 1988). In addition, young children are more likely to start using new words if they are reinforced for doing so than if they are not (Whitehurst & Valdez-Menchaca, 1988). And finally, children whose close companions frequently ask questions and make requests of them are more advanced in early language development, and even in later reading proficiency, than those whose parents are less conversational (Clarke-Stewart, 1973; Hoff-Ginsberg, 1986; Norman-Jackson, 1982; Price, Hess, & Dickson, 1981; Whitehurst et al., 1988).

However, learning theorists have had an easier time explaining the development of phonology and semantics than accounting for how syntactical rules are acquired. For example, after analyzing conversations between mothers and young children, Roger Brown, Courtney Cazden, and Ursula Bellugi (1969) discovered that a mother's approval or disapproval depended on the truth value or semantics of what was said, *not* on the grammatical correctness of the statement. Thus when a child looking at a cow says, "Him cow" (truthful but grammatically incorrect), Mom is likely to say, "That's right, darling," whereas if the child were to say, "There's a dog, Mommy" (grammatically correct but untruthful), Mom is likely to say, "No, silly—that's a cow." Similarly, parents seem just as likely to reward a grammatically primitive request ("Want milk") as a well-formed version of the same idea (Brown & Hanlon, 1970). Such evidence casts doubt on the idea that the major mechanism behind syntactic development is reinforcement.

Is imitation responsible for the acquisition of syntax? We have already seen that young children produce many sentences that they are unlikely to have heard adults using ("Allgone cookie," overregularizations such as "It broked," and so on). Also, an adult is likely to get nowhere in teaching syntax by saying "Repeat after me" unless the child already has at least some knowledge of the grammatical form to be learned. David McNeill (1970, pp. 106–107), for example, describes the child who said "Nobody don't like me." The child's mother attempted *ten times* to elicit, "Nobody likes me." Finally the child said, "Oh! Nobody don't likes me." Young children *do* frequently imitate others, and this may help them get to the point of producing new structures themselves, but it is harder to see how imitation can explain a child's grasping a new rule of syntax (Bloom, Hood, & Lightbown, 1974). Thus questions have been raised about whether reinforcement and imitation alone can account for the initial learning of grammatical rules (Slobin, 1979).

The Nativist Perspective

Nativists have made little of the role of the language environment and much of the role of the child's biologically programmed capacities in explaining language development. Linguists such as Noam Chomsky (1968, 1975) and David McNeill (1970) proposed that humans have an

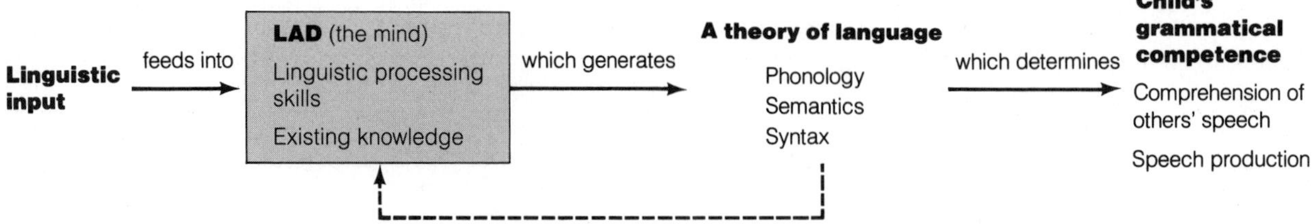

Figure 7.3 The language acquisition device (LAD).

inborn mechanism for mastering language called the **language acquisition device (LAD)**. To learn to speak, children need only hear other humans speak; using the LAD, they quickly grasp the "working rules" of whatever language they hear, much as Piaget's child can construct knowledge of the world (see Figure 7.3).

What evidence supports a nativist perspective on language development? For one thing, to master a communication system as complex and versatile as a human language would seem to require a very powerful brain as "standard equipment" (Molfese, 1977). Children do acquire language very fast, with no formal training. Moreover, they all progress through the same sequences at roughly similar ages, suggesting that language abilities unfold according to a species-wide maturational plan. Finally, early language development is similar in different cultures despite cultural differences in the styles of speech that adults use in talking to young children; this fact, too, supports the nativist view (Schieffelin & Ochs, 1983). Overregularizations and other universal features of early language surely say something about properties of the young human mind.

There are two major problems with the nativist perspective. First, attributing language development to a built-in language acquisition device does not really explain it. Explaining it requires knowing *how* such an inborn language processor sifts through language input and infers the rules of language. Second, nativists, in focusing on the defects of learning theories of language development, tend to underestimate the contributions of the child's language environment. The nativists base much of their argument on two assumptions: (1) that all children need to develop language is exposure to speech, and (2) that the speech children hear is so incredibly complex that only a highly powerful brain could possibly detect regularities in it. Both assumptions now seem to be inaccurate, and many language-development researchers currently believe that language development depends on an interaction of nature and nurture.

The Interactionist Perspective

Interactionists such as social-communication theorists Elizabeth Bates (Bates & MacWhinney, 1982) and Neil Bohannon (Bohannon & Warren-Leubecker, 1985) acknowledge that learning theorists *and* nativists are correct: Children's competencies *and* their language environment interact to shape the course of language development.

Many interactionists emphasize that acquiring language skills depends on and is related to acquiring many other capacities: perceptual, cognitive, motor, social, and emotional. They point out that the capacity for acquiring language is not really unique (as nativists who speak of the LAD claim); the same mind uses language and performs other sorts of cognitive activities, too (Bates, O'Connell, & Shore, 1987). Young children first begin to use words as meaningful symbols at a time when they are also displaying other new symbolic capacities such as the ability to engage in pretend play and to use tools to solve problems. The interactionists' position is not unlike that taken by Piaget (1970), for he believed that milestones in cognitive development pave the way for progress in language development, and that maturation and environment interact to guide both cognitive development and language development. Like Piaget (but unlike learning theorists), many interactionists argue that children can benefit from exposure to speech only if they are maturationally ready.

However, the interactionist position on language development, as developed by social-communication theorists, puts far more emphasis than Piaget did on the ways in which social interactions with adults contribute to both cognitive and linguistic development. Social-communication theorists note the interrelationships between language use and nonverbal forms of social communication such as nodding, pointing, and whining (Bates, O'Connell, & Shore, 1987). They emphasize that language is primarily a means of communicating—one that develops in the context of social interactions as children and their companions strive to get their messages across, one way or another.

Long before infants use words, their caregivers are showing them how to take turns in conversations, even if the most these young infants can contribute when their turn comes is a laugh or a bit of babbling (Bruner, 1983). As adults converse with young children, they create a supportive learning environment that helps children grasp the regularities of language (Bruner, 1983; Rondal, 1985). As children gain new language skills, adults adjust their styles of communication accordingly. Try conversing with a 2-year-old, and notice how you adapt your style of speaking. Language researchers use the term **motherese** to designate speech adults use with young children (see Gelman & Shatz, 1977): short, simple sentences, spoken slowly and in a high-pitched voice, often with much repetition, and with exaggerated emphasis on key words (usually words for objects and activities). For example, the mother trying to get her son to eat his peas might say, "Eat your peas now. Not the cookie. See those peas? Yeah, eat the *peas*." Calling this speech style motherese is actually sexist, for fathers as well as mothers use it, though perhaps with slight differences (Rondal, 1980). Moreover, it seems to be used by adults in all sorts of language communities (Grieser & Kuhl, 1988).

The nativists underestimated the contributions of environment to language development. Mere exposure to speech is not enough. Catherine Snow and her associates, for example, found that a group of Dutch-speaking children, despite the fact that they watched a great deal of German television, did not acquire any German words or grammar (Snow et al., 1976). Fortunately, virtually all children are provided with a rich language-learning environment in which parents and other companions converse with them daily in motherese about the objects and events that have captured their attention. By using this distinctive speech style, adults simplify the child's task of figuring out the rules of language (K. Nelson, Hirsh-Pasek, Jusczyk, & Cassidy, 1989; Rondal, 1985).

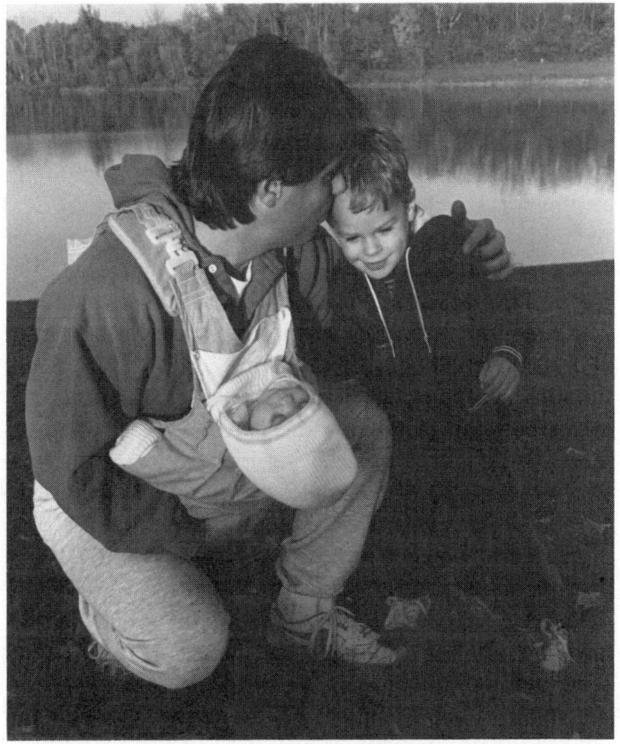

Motherese is used by fathers, too. Both mothers and fathers adapt their speech to young language learners.

Adults speaking to young children have additional strategies that foster language development. For example, they set up predictable routines or games that make it easier for children to learn the rules of language and communication (Bruner, 1983). Parents may go through their children's favorite picture books at bedtime asking, "What's this?" and "What's that?" This gives their children repeated opportunities to learn that conversing involves taking turns, that things have names, and that there are proper ways to pose questions and give answers. Soon the children are asking "What's this?" and "What's that?" themselves. Moreover, adults gradually increase the length and complexity of their sentences as their children's linguistic skills improve so that an adult's speech to a child is consistently slightly more complex than the child's own speech (Bohannon & Warren-Leubecker, 1985; Newport, Gleitman, & Gleitman, 1977; Shatz, 1983). Here, then, is a language environment that would seem to be ideal for learning ever more advanced language forms.

Finally, adults respond to children's communications in ways that may help them master grammar. If a child says "Doggie go," an adult may respond with an *expansion*—a more grammatically complete expression of the same thought ("Yes, the dog is going away"). Or the adult may *recast* what is said into a different grammatical form ("Where is the dog going?"). Adults use conversational techniques like motherese, expansions, and recasts mainly to improve communication, not to teach grammar (Penner, 1987), but these techniques expose children to new, more grammatical forms that they can build into their own speech (K. Nelson, 1977; Penner, 1987).

How can adults best facilitate young children's language learning? What capacities enable children to learn how language works by hearing it? Much remains to be learned about language development, but it does seem to require the interaction of a biologically prepared child with at least one willing conversational partner (Rondal, 1985).

THE ADOLESCENT

Although tremendous advances in both cognition and language occur from infancy to the end of childhood, still other transformations of the mind are in store for the adolescent. If teenagers become introspective, question their parents' authority, dream of perfect worlds, and contemplate their futures, cognitive development may explain why.

The Formal Operations Stage of Cognitive Development

Piaget set the beginning of the **formal operations stage** of cognitive development at age 11 or 12, or very possibly later. Recall that concrete operations are mental actions on *objects*—tangible things and events—as when an individual mentally classifies animals into categories. Formal operations are mental actions on *ideas*. Thus the adolescent who acquires formal operations can mentally juggle and think logically about ideas that can neither be seen nor heard, tasted nor smelled nor touched. In other words, formal-operational thought is more hypothetical and abstract than concrete-operational thought. It also may be viewed as involving more systematic and scientific approaches to problem solving (Keating, 1980).

Hypothetical and Abstract Thinking

If you could have a third eye and put it anywhere on your body, where would you put it, and why? That question was posed to 9-year-old fourth graders (i.e., concrete operators) and to 11- to 12-year-old sixth graders who were at the age when the first signs of formal operations often appear. In their drawings, all the 9-year-olds placed the third eye on their foreheads between their existing eyes; many thought the exercise was "stupid." The 11- and 12-year-olds were not as bound by the realities of eye location. They could invent ideas that were contrary to fact (for example, the idea of an eye in one's palm) and think logically about the implications of such ideas (see Figure 7.4). Thus concrete operators deal with realities, while formal operators can deal with *possibilities*, including those that contradict known reality.

Formal-operational thought is also more abstract than concrete-operational thought. The school-aged child might define the justice system in terms of police and judges; the adolescent might define it more abstractly as a branch of government concerned with balancing the rights of different interests in society. Or the school-aged child might be able to think logically about concrete and factually true statements, as in this syllogism: If you drink poison, you will die. Fred drank poison. Therefore Fred will die. The adolescent would be able to engage in such if-then thinking about either contrary-to-fact statements ("If you drink milk, you die") or symbols (If P, then Q. P. Therefore, Q).

Problem-Solving Strategies

Formal operations also permit systematic and scientific thinking about problems. One of Piaget's famous tests for formal-operational thinking is the pendulum task. The child is given a number of weights that can be tied to a string to make a pendulum and is told that he or she may vary the length of the string, the amount of weight attached to it, and the height from which the weight is released to find out which of these factors alone or in combination determines how quickly the pendulum makes its arc. How would you go about solving this problem?

The concrete operator is likely to jump right in without much advanced planning, using a *trial-and-error* approach. That is, the child may try a variety of different things, but fail to test out different hypotheses systematically—for example, the hypothesis that the shorter the

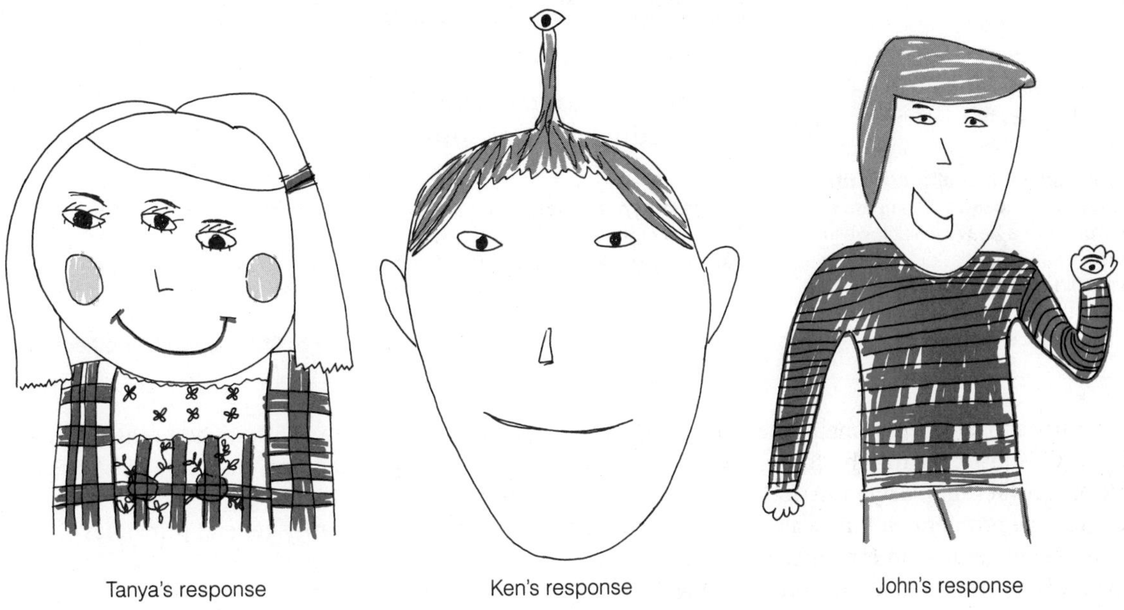

Figure 7.4 Where would you put a third eye? Tanya (age 9) did not show much inventiveness in drawing her "third eye." But Ken (age 11) said of his eye on top of a tuft of hair, "I could revolve the eye to look in all directions." John (also 11) wanted a third eye in his palm: "I could see around corners and see what kind of cookie I'll get out of the cookie jar." Ken and John show early signs of formal-operational thought.

string is, the faster the pendulum swings, all other factors remaining constant. Concrete operators are therefore unlikely to solve the problem. What they *can* do is draw proper general conclusions from specific observations—for example, from watching what happens if they stumble on a revealing test or if someone else demonstrates what happens if a pendulum with a short string is compared to a pendulum with a long string. This kind of reasoning, leading from specific observations to a general conclusion, is termed **empirical-inductive reasoning**.

What will the formal-operational individual do? In all likelihood, he or she will first sit and think, or *plan* an overall strategy for solving the problem. First, *all* the possible hypotheses should be generated; after all, the one that is overlooked may be the right one. Then, each hypothesis must be systematically tested. The trick is to vary each factor (for example, the length of the string) while holding the others constant (the weight, the height from which the weight is dropped, and so on). This is a matter of **hypothetical-deductive reasoning**, or reasoning from general ideas to their specific implications (see Box 7.4). In the pendulum problem, that means starting with a general hypothesis or idea about which factor matters and tracing the specific implications of the idea in an if-then fashion: "If the length of the string matters, then I should see a difference when I compare a long string to a short string while holding other factors constant." (It is, by the way, the length of the string that matters; the shorter the string, the faster the swing.)

In summary, formal-operational thought involves being able to think systematically about hypothetical ideas and abstract concepts. It involves mastering the hypothetical-deductive approach to problems that scientists use—forming many hypotheses and systematically testing them through an experimental method.

Progress Toward Mastery of Formal Operations

Can 11- and 12-year-olds really do all these sophisticated mental activities? In most cases, no. Piaget (1970) himself described the transition from concrete operations to formal operations as taking place gradually over several years. Many researchers have found it useful to distinguish

Box 7.4
Steps in Hypothetical-Deductive Reasoning

1. Form hypothesis: The weight of the bob might affect how fast the pendulum swings.

2. Trace specific implications of general hypothesis: If I compare a light weight to a heavy weight, while controlling all other factors, the pendulum should swing faster when the bob is heavy than when it is light (if my hypothesis is correct).

3. Test hypothesis: Try attaching a heavy weight and watch the rate of swing. Now attach a light weight to the *same* length string and drop the bob from the same height and with the same force so that all factors except the bob's weight are controlled, or constant. Watch again to compare the rates of swing for the heavy weight and the light weight.

4. Draw a conclusion: The weight of the bob has no effect; the pendulum moves through its arc as quickly with the heavy weight as with the light weight.

5. Come up with another hypothesis!

between early and late formal operations. For example, 11- to 13-year-olds just entering the formal operations stage are able to consider simple hypothetical propositions such as the three-eye problem. But most are not yet able to develop an overall game plan for solving a problem and to systematically generate and test hypotheses. These achievements are more likely later in adolescence.

Consider the findings of Suzanne Martorano (1977). She gave 80 girls in grades 6, 8, 10, and 12 a battery of ten Piagetian tasks. She included the pendulum problem to assess the ability to test hypotheses while controlling other factors. Other tasks included identifying all the possible combinations of chemicals that could produce a chemical reaction; figuring proportions to analyze how the behavior of a balance beam is affected by the heaviness of weights on the beam and their distances from the fulcrum or center; and thinking about the correlations between two variables.

This study, like several others, suggests that major progress toward advanced formal-operational thinking comes quite late. The sixth and eighth graders (ages 11–12 and 13–14) passed only two or three of the ten tasks on the average, and the tenth and twelfth graders (ages 15–16 and 17–18) passed an average of five or six. Thus even the twelfth graders did not consistently show formal operations across tasks; indeed, only 55% of them passed the pendulum problem, and they typically used concrete operations on some tasks and formal operations on others. Only two students in the whole study got all ten problems right.

Progress toward mastery of formal operations is obviously slow, at least as measured by Piaget's scientific tasks. These findings have major implications for secondary school teachers, who are often trying to teach very abstract material to students with a wide range of thinking patterns. Teachers may find that they need to give concrete thinkers extra aid by using specific examples and demonstrations to help clarify general principles.

Implications of Formal Thought

Formal-operational thought, even in its early forms, is a powerful tool that underlies other changes in adolescence, some good, some not so good. First the good news: As we shall see in Chapter 10, formal operations may pave the way for thinking about possible selves, gaining self-understanding, and forming a sense of who you are, or a sense of identity. And, as we shall see in Chapter 13, adolescents become skilled in understanding other people's personalities and taking others' perspectives. The formal-operational thinker is also better able to make sound decisions that involve weighing alternative actions and their possible consequences (see Chapter 12, for example, regarding moral reasoning). Thus advances in cognitive development help to lay the groundwork for advances in many other areas of development.

Now the bad news: Formal operations may also be related to some of the more painful aspects of the adolescent experience. Children tend to accept the world as it is and to heed the words of authority figures. The adolescent armed with formal operations can think more independently, imagine alternatives to present realities, and raise questions about everything from why parents set down the rules they do to why there is hunger in the world. Confusion, then, is one sometimes painful implication of formal operations. The more alternatives the adolescent can generate, the more likely it is that questioning will lead to confusion. Rebellion is also more likely in the formal-operational period. The ability to detect logical inconsistencies and flaws in the world as it is may turn into rebellious anger at parents or the government. In addition, some adolescents get carried away with idealism. They invent perfect worlds or envision perfectly logical solutions to problems they detect in the world around them and sometimes lose sight of practical considerations and real barriers to social change. Just as infants flaunt the new schemes they develop, adolescents sometimes go a bit overboard with their new cognitive skills, irritate their parents, and become frustrated when the world does not respond to their flawless logic.

One other painful change that may accompany formal operations is worth considering. David Elkind (1967) has proposed that the capacity for formal operations leads to **adolescent egocentrism**, a difficulty in properly differentiating one's own thoughts and feelings from those of other people. The young child's egocentrism is rooted in an unawareness that different people have different perspectives, but the adolescent's is rooted in an enhanced ability to engage in thinking about thinking, or **metacognition**. Elkind identified two types of adolescent egocentrism. The **imaginary audience** phenomenon involves confusing your own thoughts with the thoughts of a hypothesized audience for your behavior. Thus the teenage girl who spills Pepsi on her dress at a party may feel extremely self-conscious: "Look! They're all staring at me! I'm such a slob." She assumes everyone else in the room is as preoccupied with the stain as she is. Or the teenage boy may spend hours in front of the mirror getting ready for a date and then concern himself so much with how he imagines his date is reacting to him that he hardly notices her: "Why did I say that? . . . She looks bored . . . Did she notice my pimple?" (She, of course, is equally preoccupied with how she is "playing" to her audience. No wonder teenagers are often awkward and painfully aware of their every slip on first dates!)

The second form of adolescent egocentrism is the **personal fable**, a tendency to think that you and your thoughts and feelings are unique or special (Elkind, 1967). If the imaginary audience is a product of the failure to differentiate between self and other, the personal fable is a product of differentiating too much. Thus the adolescent who is in love for the first time imagines that no one in the history of the human race has ever felt such heights of emotion. When the relationship breaks up, of course, no one, least of all a parent, could possibly understand the crushing agony. Elkind suggests that the personal fable may also lead adolescents to feel that rules that apply to others do not apply to them. Thus, *they* won't be hurt if they speed down the highway without wearing seat belts; *they* won't become pregnant if they engage in sex without birth control.

Elkind hypothesized that the imaginary audience and the personal fable phenomena should increase when formal operations are first being acquired, then decrease as adolescents get older, gain fuller control of formal operations, and enter adult roles that require fuller consideration of others' perspectives. Self-consciousness associated with the imaginary audience does appear to be greater in early adolescence than later (Elkind & Bowen, 1979; Enright, Lapsley, & Shukla, 1979), but the relationship between the onset of formal operations and adolescent egocentrism is not yet clear (see Box 7.5). Nonetheless, Piaget's basic theme that adolescents think differently than children or adults do is well supported.

Language Skills in Adolescence

Language abilities are well developed by the end of childhood, but there is still room for growth in adolescence. Both spoken and written sentences become increasingly complex (Clark & Clark, 1977; Hunt, 1970). Vocabulary continues to grow, and the more advanced cognitive abilities of adolescents enable them to understand and use abstract concepts, metaphors, and analogies (Owens, 1984; Reynolds & Ortony, 1980; Saltz, 1979). In addition, adolescents continue to develop metalinguistic awareness of language and its uses. They grow better able to analyze jokes that depend on double meanings, sarcasm, and other linguistic ambiguities, and, as we saw in Box 7.5, their capacity for formal-operational thinking helps them appreciate absurd humor based on contrary-to-fact premises (Yalisove, 1978). Finally, adolescents make great strides in the pragmatics of language (Owens, 1984). For instance, they are more able to imagine an audience and tailor their written language to that audience (Fischer & Lazerson, 1984).

Thus advances in cognitive development are reflected in an increasing command of the complexities and subtleties of language. In their thinking, in their command of language, adolescents gradually come to be the intellectual equals of adults (Piaget, 1972). Or do they?

Box 7.5
"Nobody Understands Me": Research on Adolescent Egocentrism

To study adolescent egocentrism, researchers had to devise ways to measure it. The Imaginary Audience Scale (Elkind & Bowen, 1979) asks adolescents whether they would be uncomfortable in potentially embarrassing situations. Carla Lechner and Doreen Rosenthal (1984) questioned the validity of Elkind and Bowen's questions for identifying self-consciousness associated with an imaginary audience. They believed feelings of incompetence, weakness, or inadequacy might also be involved. Two items from their scale (p. 302, p. 304) are:

If on arrival at a party, you found a grease patch on your jeans, would you:

- Not worry?
- Go home because you think that everyone would notice?
- Go home because you don't feel right when you're dirty?

You can't avoid walking through a group of people standing chatting together. As you pass through, do you:

- Not think twice about it?
- Imagine that they are all looking at you?
- Feel bad because you have interrupted their conversation?

Only the second response option reflects the imaginary audience; the last option reflects self-consciousness due to feelings of inadequacy. Using their scale, Lechner and Rosenthal discovered that imaginary-audience responding was greater among students in grades 8 and 10 (13- and 15-year-olds) than among twelfth graders and adults, but that self-consciousness associated with feeling inadequate changed little at all with age.

Research on the personal fable has barely begun. Enright, Lapsley, and Shukla (1979) attempted to get at it by asking adolescents to rate the importance of things like "Trying to get other people to know what it is like being me" and "Communicating my unique feelings and viewpoints to others so they can at least get some idea about what I am like" (p. 689). They found that the personal fable faded less rapidly over the adolescent years than the imaginary audience did.

Studies of adolescent egocentrism typically find that it increases in early adolescence and declines in later adolescence. But does it really result from the emergence of formal operations? There is a good deal of confusion about this question (Lapsley et al., 1986). Some researchers even report that students who function primarily at the concrete-operational level actually show *more* self-conscious egocentrism than students who have command of formal operations—the reverse of what Elkind predicted (Gray & Hudson, 1984; Riley, Adams, & Nielsen, 1984).

What other factors might account for adolescent egocentrism, then? Riley, Adams, and Nielsen (1984) found that self-conscious egocentrism was more evident among adolescents whose parents were rejecting than among those whose parents were more supportive. Girls are also more self-conscious than boys are throughout the adolescent years (Elkind & Bowen, 1979; Gray & Hudson, 1984; Riley, Adams, & Nielsen, 1984), possibly because girls have traditionally been socialized to be highly concerned about their physical appearance.

Finally, adolescent egocentrism may be linked less to formal-operational thought than to the emergence of advanced social perspective-taking abilities that allow adolescents to contemplate how other people might perceive them or react to their behavior (Lapsley & Murphy, 1985). The truth is that researchers have not yet figured out precisely why young adolescents often feel that the whole world is watching them or that not one person in the world can truly understand them!

THE ADULT

Do adults think any differently than adolescents do? Does cognition change over the adult years? Until recently, developmentalists have not asked such questions. After all, Piaget indicated that the highest stage of cognitive development, formal operations, was fully mastered by most people by age 15 to 18. Why bother studying cognitive development in adulthood? As it turns out, it has been well worth the effort. Research has revealed limitations in adult performance that must be explained, but it also suggests that at least some adults progress to more advanced forms of thought beyond formal operations. Researchers have also gained insights into how adults *apply* their cognitive abilities to everyday life.

Limitations in Adult Cognitive Performance

If many high school students are shaky in their command of formal operations, do most of us gain fuller mastery after the high school years? Not necessarily, say studies of college students. Discouraging as it may be, research suggests that only about half of college students show firm and consistent mastery of formal operations on Piaget's scientific reasoning tasks (Neimark, 1975). Similarly, sizable percentages of American adults do not reason at the formal level, and there are some societies in which *no* adults solve formal-operational problems (Neimark, 1975).

Why don't more adults do well on Piagetian tasks? It does seem to take at least an average level of performance on standardized intelligence tests to reason at the formal level (Inhelder, 1966), but most college students meet this criterion. What seems more important than basic intelligence is formal education (Neimark, 1979). In cultures in which virtually no one solves Piaget's problems, people do not receive advanced schooling. But lack of formal education is not a problem for most college students, either. Perhaps a better explanation is that thinking in a formal-operational way requires *expertise in a domain of knowledge.*

Piaget (1972) himself suggested that adults may use formal operations in a field of expertise but use concrete operations in less familiar areas. That is, their use of formal operations is specialized rather than generalized. There is some support for this idea. For example, hunters in preliterate societies will often reason at a formal level when tracking prey, perhaps because this is an important and well-learned activity (Tulkin & Konner, 1973).

Looking at the relationship between expertise and formal operations among college students, Richard DeLisi and Joanne Staudt (1980) gave three kinds of problems—the pendulum problem, a political problem, and a literary criticism problem—to college students majoring in physics, political science, and English. As Table 7.5 illustrates, each group of majors did very well on the problem relevant to their field of expertise. On problems outside their fields, however, about half the students failed. Piaget's classic tasks all involve scientific problems that are more familiar to individuals with science and math training and expertise than to those in other fields (Blackburn, 1984). Thus studies using these tests may have underestimated the competencies of many adolescents and adults: People may have failed to use formal reasoning simply because the kinds of problems Piaget posed were unfamiliar to them.

Table 7.5 Expertise and formal operations

PROBLEM	PERCENTAGE OF STUDENTS DISPLAYING FORMAL THOUGHT		
	Physics majors	Political science majors	English majors
Pendulum problem	90	50	40
Political problem	60	80	40
Literary problem	40	40	90

College students show the greatest command of formal-operational thought in the subject area most related to their major.

Source: Data from DeLisi & Staudt, 1980.

As Kurt Fischer (1980; Fischer, Hand, & Russell, 1984) argues and demonstrates, each person may have an optimal level of performance that will show itself in familiar and well-trained content domains. However, actual performance across a diverse set of problems can be expected to be highly inconsistent unless the person has had a chance to build knowledge and skills in less familiar content domains. Fischer suggests that we can expect adults to be even more inconsistent across various tasks than children are. In part this is because adults choose careers and lifestyles and then use and strengthen formal modes of thinking *only in their areas of specialization.* It is unfortunate that we do not have more studies that assess the cognitive abilities of adults in their areas of specialization or in familiar, everyday contexts. For now, we can at least appreciate the importance of the individual's experience and the nature of the tasks he or she is asked to do as influences on cognitive performance across the life span (Rogoff & Lave, 1984).

Growth Beyond Formal Operations?

While some researchers have been asking why adults sometimes perform so poorly on cognitive tasks, others have been asking why certain adults sometimes perform so well. Take Piaget himself. Was his ability to generate a complex theory of development no more than the application of formal-operational thought? Or are there advances in cognitive development during adulthood that would better explain the remarkable cognitive achievements of some adults?

At this point, there are several intriguing ideas about what may lie beyond formal operations (see Commons, Richards, & Armon, 1984). First consider a rather negative profile of the adolescent who has attained formal operations. This adolescent, Waldo we'll call him, is carried away with his new powers of logical thinking. He does beautifully when we give him a Piagetian-like problem in which everything is given in the problem and the only task is to generate logically possible solutions and identify the one right solution. But he insists that there is a logically correct answer for every question, that if you simply apply logic you will arrive at absolute truths. Perhaps formal-operational adolescents like Waldo are not fully equipped for a real world in which you must figure out what the problem is instead of being handed one, or in which there simply is no one right answer (Cavanaugh, Kramer, Sinnott, Camp, & Markley, 1985; Labouvie-Vief, 1984). Let us consider some of the ways in which adults may be better equipped cognitively than adolescents are.

Problem Finding

Patricia Arlin (1975, 1977, 1984) has suggested that Piaget's formal operations is a *problem-solving stage* in which the individual can solve problems that are presented to him or her. She proposed that advanced thinkers go on to a **problem-finding stage**. That is, they can use their knowledge to rethink or reorganize existing knowledge and then ask important new questions or define totally new problems. Problem finding may not be a systematic stage of development beyond formal operations; it may just reflect a different use of a formal-operational mind. It does seem, however, that the ability to devise creative problems increases with age and cognitive development.

Relativism

Several researchers have suggested that adults are more likely than adolescents to adopt the position that knowledge is relative rather than absolute (Labouvie-Vief, 1984; Sinnott, 1984). **Relativism** in this sense means an understanding that knowledge depends on the subjective perspective of the knower. An *absolutist* assumes that truth lies in the nature of reality or that there is only one truth; a relativist assumes that one's own starting assumptions influence the "truth" that is discovered, and that there are multiple ways of viewing a problem.

Consider a logic problem given to preadolescents, adolescents, and adults by Gisela Labouvie-Vief and her colleagues (Labouvie-Vief, Adams, Hakim-Larson, & Hayden, 1983):

> John is known to be a heavy drinker, especially when he goes to parties. Mary, John's wife, warns him that if he gets drunk one more time she will leave him and take the children. Tonight John is out late at an office party. John comes home drunk [p. 5].

Does Mary leave John? Most preadolescents and many adolescents quickly and confidently said "Yes." They did not question the assumption that Mary would stand by her word; they simply applied logic to the information they were given. Adults were more likely to realize that different starting assumptions were possible and that the answer depended on which assumptions were chosen. One woman, for example, noted that if Mary had stayed with John for years, she would be unlikely to leave him now. This same woman said, "There was no right or wrong answer. You could get logically to both answers" (p. 12). Such adults were not just making more use of their real-world knowledge of marital relations; they were also seeing truth as relative and were aware of the importance of how the knower chooses to look at a problem.

In a study of cognitive growth over the college years, William Perry (1970) found that beginning college students often assumed that there were absolute, objective truths to be found if only they applied their minds or sought answers from their professors. As their college careers progressed, they often became frustrated in their search for absolute truths. They saw that many questions seemed to have a number of alternative answers, depending on the perspective of the answerer. Many took the extemely relativistic view that any opinion was as good as any other. They weren't sure how they could ever decide what to believe. Eventually, many understood that some opinions can be better supported than others; they were then able to commit themselves to specific positions while being fully aware that they were choosing among relative perspectives. Between adolescence and adulthood, then, many people begin as absolutists and become relativists; finally they are able to make commitments despite their more sophisticated awareness of the nature and limits of knowledge (see also Kitchener & King, 1981; Kitchener, King, Wood, & Davison, 1989; Labouvie-Vief, 1985).

Dialectical Thinking

Adults may also advance in their ability to engage in **dialectical thinking** (Basseches, 1984; Riegel, 1973), which involves the ability to uncover and resolve contradictions between opposing ideas. It reflects a view that thought is a process of creating ever-new orders in the face of conflicting ideas and a changing world (recall Chapter 2's discussion of the dialectical perspective on development). Real-world issues like the state of the economy or education are filled with inconsistencies that may be ignored by formal-operational adolescents who seek logical truths. But consider the college student asked by Michael Basseches (1984) to reflect on higher education. He first stated a *thesis*—that his college is a place where a special kind of exchange of knowledge goes on. He then detected an opposing idea, an *antithesis*—that people could exchange views as well at a cafe in Paris as at a college. Finally, he pulled the thesis and antithesis together into a *synthesis*, arguing that people at his college were more qualified to give opinions on certain subjects than people in a cafe were. Thus he reached a more sophisticated understanding by resolving one idea and its opposite. Basseches found that such dialectical thinking was more common among faculty than among college seniors, and more common among college seniors than among freshmen.

Relativism in the college years. Going to college means being exposed to new ideas and belief systems. Students who enter college thinking they know what they believe—or thinking they will soon discover "truths"—sometimes find themselves baffled instead. They may enter a period in which they view all knowledge and beliefs as relative and subjective. As one student said, "I am the type of person who would never tell anyone that their idea is wrong—if they searched, well, even if they hadn't searched, even if they just believed it—that's cool for them" (Kitchener & King, 1981, p. 96). Many of these students later decide that there are sound reasons for preferring some beliefs to others.

Basseches, Riegel, and others suggest that more advanced thinkers who have command of dialectical thinking do not ignore the real confusion of everyday life to make everything conform to formal logic. Instead, they thrive on detecting inconsistencies and paradoxes and then formulating new syntheses of theses and antitheses, only to repeat the process of changing their understandings again and again. According to Piaget, formal-operational thinkers have reached a state of cognitive balance, or equilibrium, in which all the pieces of the puzzle fit and the world makes sense. By contrast, dialectical thinkers are never in a state of equilibrium and seem to have a never-ending thirst for *disequilibrium* (Riegel, 1973)!

Thinking About Systems

Advanced thinkers also seem to be able to compare and contrast abstract systems of knowledge (Commons, Richards, & Kuhn, 1982; Fischer, Hand, & Russell, 1984; Labouvie-Vief, 1984; Richards & Commons, 1984). When a professor asks you to compare theories or, worse yet, to uncover overall principles behind several theories, you are being asked to reason about systems. Kurt Fischer and his associates have proposed that the ability to think about systems improves considerably beyond the age of 11 or 12. In one study (Kenny & Fischer, cited by Kenny, 1983), they asked subjects aged 8 to 20 to explain the basic mathematical operations of addition, subtraction, multiplication, and division. Concrete operators could use these operations but had difficulty defining them other than by example. At about age 10 to 11, children were more able to define any given math operation abstractly. At about age 16, students were more able to *compare* operations—for example, to recognize that addition and multiplication both involve combining numbers to produce larger ones and that multiplication is really addition repeated a specified number of times, so that, for example, $8 + 8 + 8$ and 8×3 both yield 24.

Only older subjects were able to engage in even more abstract thinking about the mathematics system—for example, to compare and contrast dissimilar operations like addition and division, and ultimately to identify abstract principles underlying all four math operations and accounting for their similarities and differences. Similarly, Michael Commons and his associates (1982) have found that graduate students are more able than undergraduates to compare and contrast systems of information and form supersystems to organize more specific systems. The adolescent is searching for one "right" system of thought, whether it is one solution to a problem, one theory, or one set of beliefs, but the more mature thinker can juggle multiple systems and integrate them into more abstract wholes.

So, What Lies Beyond Formal Operations?

It is not yet entirely clear which of these advanced cognitive abilities—problem finding, relativistic thinking, dialectical thinking, and thinking about systems—might really qualify as new and higher stages of cognitive development. The search for adult stages of cognitive development has only begun. If there are distinct stages of cognitive development beyond formal operations, they are likely to be most evident among adults with high intelligence and advanced education. Research does show, however, that cognitive development by no means stops in the adolescent years. During adulthood many people become better able to define and think through "real-life" problems that require making sense of contradictory and ambiguous information, that can be viewed from several perspectives, and that do not have one right answer.

What of the adult who has some command of formal-operational reasoning but does not show the advanced forms of thought that are believed to lie beyond it? Some psychologists believe that even if adults do not move into higher stages of development they may *use* whatever cognitive capacities they have differently from children and adolescents, as we see in Box 7.6. In other words, what may be most special about adult cognition is the ways in which cognitive structures are used. Adults use their minds for different purposes at different points in their lives, and they use their minds in more efficient ways as they gain expertise in their jobs and personal lives. Age does not tell

Box 7.6
How Adults Use Their Minds in Everyday Life

According to K. Warner Schaie (1977/1978), what is different about adult cognition is the uses to which the mind is put, not the stages at which the mind functions. Children and adolescents use their minds primarily for knowledge *acquisition*. They are, after all, asked to learn a good deal as they progress through school, so they ask themselves "What should I know?" and are open to all kinds of new ideas.

Young adults, still armed with concrete and formal operations, ask "How can I use what I know?" as they develop *achievement* goals. They use their minds to pursue the long-range vocational and personal goals to which they have become committed. Middle-aged adults increasingly use their minds to achieve *responsibility* (for example, to balance their own needs with the needs of family members or of employees and co-workers) and to engage in *executive monitoring* (keeping track of interrelated activities, as an executive must, in a complex

organization). Finally, Schaie proposes that elderly adults enter a period of cognitive *reintegration*. They reorganize their previously acquired knowledge and boil it down to the essentials; they save their minds for the most personally meaningful questions as they try to make sense of their lives; and they may be more likely than children or younger adults to ask "*Why* should I know?"

What kinds of problems *do* adults encounter in daily life and how do they go about solving them? Unfortunately, researchers have only recently begun to look at adult cognition in everyday contexts. It seems clear that many everyday problems do not really require formal-operational thinking and may even be solved more efficiently without it (Labouvie-Vief, 1985). After all, there is no point in considering all the logical possibilities when only a few of them are practical. In addition, as adults attempt to achieve goals in specific contexts like their work settings, and as they become experts in their areas of specialization, they develop shortcuts that save them the need to use more formal methods of thought (Scribner, 1984). A truck loader, for example, may simply know from experience how many boxes will fit in a truck and can dispense with any mathematical calculations. In sum, adults may think differently than adolescents do, and they may abandon problem-solving techniques that were useful in their school days in favor of specialized techniques that help them solve practical problems.

us much about how an adult thinks; life circumstances and the demands placed on adults to think at work, in the home, and in the community often tell us more.

Aging and Cognitive Performance

Do older adults retain or lose their ability to use Piagetian cognitive operations? Some mental abilities decline as the average person ages, and it appears that older adults often have trouble on Piagetian formal-operational tasks (Denney, 1982; Hooper & Sheehan, 1977). Older adults sometimes perform poorly even on *concrete*-operational tasks. Nancy Denney's (1982) review of research, for example, concludes that, on the average, older adults perform more poorly than younger adults on tasks involving classifying things and taking different spatial perspectives in a nonegocentric way. Difficulties with conservation tasks are less well documented but occur most often on conservation tasks that normally are mastered later in the concrete-operational period of childhood (for example, conservation of volume).

Does this really mean that elderly adults regress to immature modes of thought? Not necessarily. For one thing, these studies have used Piagetian tasks to make cross-sectional comparisons of different age groups. The poorer performance of older groups suggests—but does not prove—that cognitive abilities are lost as one ages. Consider, for example, that the average older adult today has had less formal schooling than the average younger adult has had and that level of education is usually far more predictive of success than age is (Labouvie-Vief, 1985; Selzer & Denney, 1980). Older adults who are college students are likely to perform just as well as younger college students on tests of formal operations (Blackburn, 1984; Hooper, Hooper, & Colbert, 1985).

Questions have also been raised about how the performance of older adults on Piagetian tasks should be interpreted (Labouvie-Vief, 1985). These problems are not only unfamiliar to many older adults, but they resemble the tasks that children confront in school, not those that most adults encounter in everyday contexts. Older people may not be very motivated to solve them. Also, they may rely on cognitive modes that have proved useful to them in daily life but that make them look cognitively deficient in the laboratory.

Consider this example. Kathy Pearce and Nancy Denney (1984) found that elderly adults, like children, often group two objects on the basis of some functional relationship between them (for example, putting a pipe and matches together because matches are used to light pipes) rather than on the basis of similarity (for example, putting a pipe and a saxophone together because they are similar in shape). Pearce and Denney suggest that this is not an immature classification strategy; in everyday life it makes sense to associate objects that are commonly used together. In school and in some job situations, people are more often asked to group objects according to similarities; perhaps this is why older children, adolescents, and young and middle-aged adults more often group objects on this basis. Such findings suggest that what appear to be deficits in older people may be mere differences in style. Also, elderly adults can quickly be taught to classify objects based on similarity and to succeed at other Piagetian tasks, so they may be far more competent than their performance on laboratory tasks sometimes indicates (Labouvie-Vief, 1985; Willis, 1985).

In sum, today's older adults appear not to perform concrete- and formal-operational tasks as well as their younger contemporaries do. Planners of adult education for senior citizens might bear in mind that some of their students, though by no means all, may benefit from more concrete forms of instruction. However, these age differences may be related to factors other than age, such as education or motivation; an actual age-related decline in operational abilities has not been established. Older adults who perform poorly on unfamiliar problems in laboratory situations often perform very capably on the sorts of problems that they encounter in everyday contexts (Cornelius & Caspi, 1987).

Language Skills in Adulthood

Because of the general assumption that language development is completed in childhood, we know little about how language abilities change in adulthood. The phonology of language seems to be mastered in childhood, and syntax is well mastered by the end of adolescence. Adults simply hold on to their knowledge of these aspects of language across the rest of the life span. However, knowledge of the semantics of language continues to *expand* in adulthood (Horn & Donaldson, 1980; Schaie, 1983). After all, adults gain experience with the world as they mature, so it is not surprising that their vocabularies continue to grow and that they better understand various

Language competencies are typically well maintained in old age.

meanings of the words they use. For example, in a study combining the cross-sectional and longitudinal approaches, K. Warner Schaie (1983) looked at intellectual change in different age groups over 14-year periods. Up until the mid-50s and mid-60s, adults increased their vocabularies from one testing to the next; only adults in their 70s displayed modest declines in vocabulary performance as they aged (see also Obler & Albert, 1985). Still, these late-life declines in verbal aspects of intelligence were not as steep as those observed in other aspects of intelligence (as we will see in Chapter 9).

Do elderly adults show no major deficiencies in language paralleling their deficiencies in cognitive performance? Some have difficulties. For example, hearing problems can interfere with oral communication, and older adults sometimes have trouble following rapid speech (Corso, 1977; Olsho, Harkins, & Lenhardt, 1985). Serious physical diseases, especially brain disorders such as Alzheimer's disease, also damage the linguistic abilities of a small minority of older people (Obler & Albert, 1985). Finally, difficulties in comprehending reading materials are sometimes observed in older adults, but these may be related to declines in *memory* skills rather than declines in basic linguistic competence (Belmore, 1981).

All things considered, language abilities, perhaps because they are so well exercised in everyday life and become so automatic, survive over the life span much better than less-practiced cognitive skills (Berg & Sternberg, 1985). Mainly, adults are diverse; some older adults lose linguistic skills, others remain superb communicators (Obler & Albert, 1985). When we know the age of an infant or young child, we know quite a bit about his or her cognitive and linguistic abilities. But as people mature through the life span their experiences steer them along different paths of development and aging. Age no longer tells us much.

PIAGET IN PERSPECTIVE

Now that Jean Piaget's theory of cognitive development and what it has to say about changes in thought over the life span has been examined, it is time to evaluate it. Let us start by giving credit where credit is due, and then consider challenges to Piaget's version of things.

Piaget's Contributions

Piaget is a giant in the field of human development. It is hard to imagine that we would know even a fraction of what we know about intellectual development without his groundbreaking work. One sign of a good theory is that it stimulates research. Piaget has been so stimulating to developmentalists that his cognitive-developmental perspective has now been applied to almost every aspect of development.

We can credit Piaget with some major insights into development that are widely accepted today. He showed us that human beings are active in their own development, that from the start they seek to master problems and to understand the incomprehensible. Similarly, Piaget taught us that young human beings do indeed think differently than older human beings and that there is great value in finding out how people of different ages reason, not just whether they give right or wrong answers.

Finally, and quite importantly, Piaget was largely right in his description of cognitive development. The developmental sequences he proposed seem to describe quite well the course and content of intellectual development for children and adolescents from the hundreds of cultures and subcultures that have now been studied (Cowan, 1978; Flavell, 1985). That is, although cultural factors do influence the *rate* of cognitive growth, the direction of development is always from sensorimotor thinking to preoperational thinking to concrete operations and, for many, to formal operations.

Challenges to Piaget

Partly because Piaget's theory has been so enormously influential, it has gotten more than its share of criticism. Developmentalists have asked: Was Piaget right about the timing of development? Did he pay enough attention to the distinction between competence and performance? Are his stages indeed coherent stages? Did he appreciate the relationships between thought, language, and social interaction? And, did he adequately explain cognitive development?

The Issue of Timing

One frequent charge is that individuals do not always enter a particular stage of development or master a concept when Piaget said they should. Specifically, Piaget may have been overpessimistic about the cognitive abilities of infants and young children and at the same time overoptimistic about the rate at which adolescents acquire formal operations and about the extent to which adults use them. Piaget's tasks often focused on unfamiliar concepts and relied on questioning procedures and phrasings that may have obscured the concept being tested. When researchers have used more familiar problems and reduced the task to its essentials, the hidden competencies of young children—and of adolescents and adults too—have been revealed.

Distinguishing Competence from Performance

Piaget was concerned with identifying the cognitive structures, or underlying competencies, that influence performance on cognitive tasks. But the distinction between competence and performance is an important one. An individual might know a concept but still fail a task—or pass a task without having truly mastered a concept (Flavell & Wohlwill, 1969). The age ranges Piaget proposed for some stages may have been off target in part because he largely ignored the many factors besides competence that can influence task performance: everything from the individual's motivation, verbal abilities, and memory capacity to the nature, complexity, and familiarity of a specific task. Piaget tended to assume that the individual who failed one of his tasks lacked the underlying concept he was testing. Yet researchers keep finding that individuals who fail one task often perform well on a slightly different task designed to assess the same cognitive ability (Kuhn, 1988). As we will see in Chapter 8, some developmentalists who adopt another perspective on intellectual development—the information-processing perspective—have tried to improve on Piaget by considering competencies *and* the many factors that determine whether or not those competencies are used in specific problem situations.

The Issue of Stages

Piaget maintained that each new stage of cognitive development is a coherent mode of thinking applied across a wide range of specific problems. Yet our review suggests that transitions in cognitive growth occur gradually and that there is often little consistency in the individual's performance on different tasks that presumably measure the abilities that define a given stage. For example, it may be years before a 7-year-old who can conserve number will be able to conserve volume, even though both tasks involve an understanding that quantity remains the same despite changes in appearance. So how much do we really say when we say a child is concrete-operational? More and more cognitive researchers are arguing that cognitive development is a matter of building skills in particular content areas (Fischer, 1980; Flavell, 1985). Thus one adolescent may well have progressed quite far along a predictable sequence of steps in the understanding of mathematical concepts, while being quite backward in a less familiar area of knowledge such as hypothesis testing. Perhaps, say the critics, cognitive development is too complex to be viewed as a progression from one coherent stage to another. Perhaps it is better to examine *sequences of development in specific domains of knowledge.*

Studies of adult cognitive development also raise questions about Piaget's stages. Specifically, critics have charged that Piaget may not have chosen the right model of mature thought when he described formal operations. Mature minds seem to be able to do more than think formally. Besides questioning the whole concept of stages in cognitive development, critics have asked whether Piaget stopped too soon or headed in the wrong direction in describing the later development of the mind.

Relationships Between Thought, Language, and Social Interaction

Piaget clearly felt that cognitive development preceded and laid the basis for language development, and most of his interest in language and communication was focused on how the egocentrism of young children influenced their speech (Piaget, 1926). Some critics have called for more attention to the ways in which language shapes thought. The Russian psychologist Lev Vygotsky (1962, 1978), for example, maintained that thought is forever altered once we begin "thinking in words."

Vygotsky also argued that language is an important means through which adults socialize children in thinking strategies and processes. Piaget may have given too little attention to the ways in which children's minds develop through their social interactions and communication with more competent adults. As we have seen, adults using intuitive strategies like motherese set up a supportive learning situation that makes the task of acquiring language simpler for their young children. Similarly, parents and teachers often demonstrate effective problem-solving strategies and then help children gradually internalize these strategies so that they can use them on their own (for example, see Rogoff & Wertsch, 1984). Even collaborating with peers can result in cognitive gains that a child might not achieve working alone (Gauvain & Rogoff, 1989). In short, Piaget tends to visualize the child as an isolated scientist exploring the world alone, when children in fact develop their minds in interaction with other people, and language and thought influence each other over the course of development (Rice & Kemper, 1984).

Explaining Development

Finally, Piaget's theory is not very clear about *how* we move from one stage to the next (Sternberg, 1984). Several psychologists suggest that Piaget did a better job of describing development than of explaining it (Brainerd, 1978; Kuhn, 1988). To be sure, Piaget did present his interactionist position on the nature/nurture issue. Presumably humans are always assimilating new experiences in ways that their level of maturation allows, accommodating their thinking to those experiences, and reorganizing their cognitive structures into increasingly complex modes of thought (Piaget, 1985). The problem is that this explanation is rather vague. We need to know far more about links between milestones in neurological development and cognitive change and about the specific kinds of experiences that contribute to important cognitive advances.

So, Piaget's theory of cognitive development might have been stronger if Piaget had devoted more attention to designing appropriate tasks to measure the competencies of a given age group more accurately; if he had explored the many factors besides underlying competence that influence actual performance; if he had been able to provide more convincing evidence that his stages are indeed coherent stages; if he had explored the implications of language and social interaction for thought; and if he had been more specific about *why* development proceeds as it does. It may be unfair, however, to expect an innovator who accomplished so much to have accomplished everything. It is, after all, Piaget himself who broke new ground and inspired so many others to look more carefully at cognitive development over the life span.

APPLICATIONS: IMPROVING COGNITIVE FUNCTIONING

Piaget was more concerned with describing and understanding development than with optimizing it. Indeed, he questioned the wisdom of American psychologists who kept asking how to speed up children's progress through his stages (Piaget, 1970). He believed that it is best for parents simply to provide young children with chances to explore their world and for teachers to use a discovery approach in the classroom that allows children to learn by doing. Given their natural curiosity and normal opportunities to try their hand at problems, children would construct ever more complex understandings on their own.

But psychologists and educators in the United States and Canada plunged ahead with attempts to train cognitive structures directly. Their motives were varied: to help children and adults function more effectively, to challenge Piaget's view that concepts like conservation cannot be mastered until the child is intellectually ready, or to identify the kinds of experiences that most directly stimulate cognitive growth.

What has been learned from these training studies? Generally they suggest that many Piagetian concepts can be taught to children who are slightly younger than the age at which the concepts would naturally emerge. Training is sometimes difficult, and it does not always generalize well to new problems, but progress can be achieved. For example, in an unusually effective intervention, Dorothy Field (1981) demonstrated that 4-year-olds could be trained to recognize the identity of a substance like a ball of clay before and after its appearance is altered—that is, to understand that although the clay looks different, it is still the *same* clay and has to be the same amount of clay. Field found that nearly 75% of the children given this identity training could solve at least three out of five conservation problems 2.5 to 5 months after training. Training in the concepts that Piaget insisted were requisites for conservation—reversibility and decentration—was not as successful, raising questions about whether these logical operations are really essential to conserving quantities.

Similar training studies have demonstrated that children who function at the late concrete operations stage can be taught formal operations (Keating, 1980; Nagy & Griffiths, 1982). In fact, for some children and adolescents who fail tests of formal operations, just a little exposure to the task materials is sometimes enough to improve performance (Stone & Day, 1978). Similarly, researchers have succeeded at improving the cognitive performance of older adults, sometimes with very simple interventions (Denney, 1982; Hooper & Sheehan, 1977; Willis, 1985). In her review of such studies, Nancy Denney (1982) concluded that mere practice is sometimes effective but that active training is more consistently effective. Modeling, or demonstrating how to solve problems, and giving feedback about the correctness of answers have proved especially effective. Such intervention studies suggest that some elderly individuals who perform poorly on problem-solving tasks simply need a quick "refresher course" to begin to show their underlying competence.

Make no mistake: *No one* has demonstrated that 2-year-olds can be taught formal operations. But at least these studies establish that specific training experiences can somewhat speed a child's progress through Piaget's stages or bring out more advanced capacities in an adult who is performing at a less advanced level. Moreover, they raise important theoretical questions about Piaget's notions about what accomplishments are necessary before other accomplishments are possible.

Meanwhile, many educators impressed by Piaget's ideas have built them into school curricula (see Gallagher & Easley, 1978). Piaget's hand has been especially noticeable in science classes, where some of his concepts are directly taught and where the discovery approach Piaget advocated has been used to encourage students to arrive at principles of science on their own. Many educators have also taken seriously Piaget's notion that children can understand best material that they can assimilate to their existing understandings. Finding out what the learner already knows and teaching accordingly is in the spirit of Piaget.

REFLECTIONS

Pause for a moment and consider the truly remarkable accomplishments that we have described in this chapter. The capacities of the human mind for thought and language are truly awesome. We can marvel at how an infant with no capacity for solving problems "in the head" and no speech can grow into an adult like Piaget or Chomsky who can invent abstract theories and communicate them to the rest of us—or into a typical adult who uses thought and language very effectively to live a life. Imagine not even grasping the fundamental concept that the rest of the world exists even when you are not directly experiencing it; imagine being able later in life to conceptualize hypothetical worlds that you have never experienced. Imagine progressing from a "vocabulary" of cries to a capacity to express an infinite number of ideas in language. Imagine, as you watch your next television program, how differently family members of different ages must interpret that same program, each with their own cognitive structures for interpreting events, each with their own vocabulary and language competencies.

Because the human mind is so complex, we should not be surprised that it is not yet understood. Piaget attacked only part of the puzzle, and only partially succeeded. Despite challenges to Piaget's theory, however, we urge you to master it well and give it a chance to change the way you view infants, young children, and adolescents. Try some conservation tasks on a preschooler: Seeing it is believing it! But you should also appreciate that humans are more than the rational problem-solvers and language-users that we have described here. After a period in which behavioral psychology dominated, psychology has returned to the study of the mind. It is perhaps unfortunate that huge progress in understanding the mind has meant, until very recently, a neglect of the emotional and motivational aspects of life-span development. Ah, but there is so much more to learn about the mind.

SUMMARY POINTS

1. Jean Piaget, through his clinical method, formulated four stages of cognitive development in which children construct more complex schemes through an interaction of maturation and experience. They adapt to the world through the inborn processes

of organization and adaptation (assimilating new experience to existing understandings and accommodating existing understandings to new experience).

2. To acquire language, children must master phonology (sound), semantics (meaning), and syntax (sentence structure), as well as learning how to use language appropriately (pragmatics) and to understand nonverbal communication.

3. According to Piaget, infants progress through six substages of the sensorimotor stage by perceiving and acting on the world: from reflexes to repeated actions (circular reactions) to experimentation and finally to the ability to engage in symbolic or representational thought. This symbolic capacity permits deferred imitation and full mastery of the concept of object permanence.

4. Meanwhile, infants begin to discriminate speech sounds and progress from crying, cooing, and babbling to one-word holophrases and then to telegraphic speech guided by a functional grammar that allows them to name things, make requests, and achieve other communication goals.

5. In Piaget's preoperational stage (ages 2–7), children make many uses of their symbolic capacity but are limited by their dependence on appearances, lack of logical mental operations, and egocentrism. They fail to grasp the concept of conservation because they engage in centration, irreversible thinking, and static thought. Recent research suggests that preschool capacities are greater than was supposed.

6. School-aged children enter the stage of concrete operations (ages 7–11) and begin to master conservation tasks; they can think about relations, grasping seriation and transitivity, and they understand the concept of class inclusion.

7. Language abilities improve dramatically in the preschool years, as illustrated by the appearance of overregularizations and new transformation rules. School-aged children refine their language skills, increase their metalinguistic awareness, and become less egocentric communicators. Theories of language development include learning theories, nativist theories, and interactionist theories that emphasize both the child's biologically based capacities and experience conversing with adults who use motherese.

8. Adolescents often show the first signs of formal operations at 11 or 12 and gradually master the hypothetical-deductive reasoning skills required to solve scientific problems. Cognitive changes result in linguistic and other developmental advances and may also contribute to confusion, rebellion, idealism, and adolescent egocentrism.

9. Adults are most likely to display formal-operational skills in their areas of expertise. Some may advance to cognitive stages beyond formal operations, displaying problem-finding abilities, relativism, dialectical thinking, and thinking about systems. Adults may also use their minds differently at different ages. Although aging adults often perform less well than younger adults on Piagetian tasks, factors other than age may explain this. Most older adults retain their language competencies remarkably well.

10. Piaget has made huge contributions to the field but has been criticized for inaccurately estimating the timing of cognitive changes, not considering factors besides competence that influence performance, failing to demonstrate that his stages have coherence, underestimating the role of language and social interaction in cognitive development, and offering vague explanations of development.

11. While Piaget believed in a discovery approach to learning, attempts to train cognitive structures suggest that development can be speeded up, though with some difficulty and with limits, and that older adults can be helped to use their cognitive competencies more effectively.

KEY TERMS

A, not B, error
accommodation
adaptation
adolescent egocentrism
animism
assimilation
babbling
centration
class inclusion
clinical method
cognition
concrete operations stage
conservation
cooing
decentration
deferred imitation
dialectical thinking
egocentrism
empirical-inductive reasoning
formal operations stage
functional grammar
holophrase
horizontal decalage
hypothetical-deductive reasoning
imaginary audience
intelligence
language
language acquisition device (LAD)
logical operation
metacognition
metalinguistic awareness
morpheme
motherese
object permanence
organization
overextension
overregularization
personal fable
phoneme
phonology
pragmatics
preoperational stage
primary circular reaction
problem-finding stage
relativism
reversibility
scheme (schema)
secondary circular reaction
semantics
sensorimotor stage
seriation
symbolic capacity
syntax
telegraphic speech
tertiary circular reaction
transductive reasoning
transformational grammar
transitivity
underextension

CHAPTER

8

LEARNING AND INFORMATION PROCESSING

"What did you learn in school today?"
"Where did you learn *that*?"
"I can't believe I remembered that."
"It's on the tip of my tongue."
"Sorry, I forgot."

Lines like these appear often in our conversations: learning and remembering, failing to learn and forgetting, are an important part of our daily lives. Moreover, individuals develop as they do partly because of what they have learned and remembered from their experiences. In this chapter, our examination of cognitive development continues, but from a different perspective than Piaget's. We first introduce traditional learning theories that describe basic learning mechanisms important at all ages. Then the chapter turns to an information-processing perspective on the mind that is useful in analyzing more complex forms of learning, memory, and problem solving. Finally, it examines how the capacities to learn, remember, and use stored information to solve problems change over the life span.

BASIC LEARNING PROCESSES

Learning is typically defined as a relatively permanent change in behavior (or behavior potential) that results from one's experiences. It is change—in thoughts, perceptions, or reactions to the environment—that is neither programmed by the genes nor due to maturation (Domjan & Burkhard, 1982). The capacity to learn is present at birth and strongly affects development and adaptation throughout the life span. Let us look at four fundamental and relatively simple types of learning: habituation, classical conditioning, operant conditioning, and observational learning.

Habituation

Students of infant development have attached much significance to a simple, often overlooked form of learning called **habituation**, or learning *not* to respond to a stimulus that is repeated over and over. Habituation might be thought of as learning to be bored by the familiar (for example, the continual ticking of a clock or the flickering of a fluorescent light). We might soon be overloaded if we reacted to everything that came along in life despite having seen it countless times before. It seems adaptive to reserve attention for novel experiences. From birth, humans habituate to repeatedly presented lights, sounds, or smells; such stimuli are somehow recognized as "old hat" (Willemsen, 1979; and see Chapter 6).

Classical Conditioning

In **classical conditioning**, a stimulus that initially had no effect on the individual comes to elicit a response through its association with a stimulus that already elicits the response. It is the new association between a stimulus and a response that is learned. To illustrate, consider how the Russian physiologist Ivan Pavlov originally discovered what is now called classical conditioning. In the course of his work on digestive processes in dogs, Pavlov noticed that his dogs would often salivate at the appearance of a caretaker who had come to feed them. Since it was unlikely that the dogs hoped to eat the caretaker, Pavlov sought another explanation. In the experiment he devised to test his idea, Pavlov sounded a bell just before the dogs were fed. The smell of food automatically makes dogs salivate. Therefore food is an **unconditioned stimulus (UCS)**—that is, a built-in and unlearned stimulus—for salivation, which in turn is an unlearned or **unconditioned response (UCR)** to food. During conditioning, the stimuli of the bell and the food were presented together several times. Afterward, Pavlov sounded the bell, withheld the food, and observed that the dogs now salivated at the sound of the bell alone. Their behavior had changed as a result of their experience. Specifically, an initially neutral stimulus, the bell, was now a **conditioned stimulus (CS)** for a **conditioned response (CR)**, salivation.

What role does classical conditioning play in human development? Perhaps less than the other basic learning processes discussed here, but it is highly involved in the learning of emotional responses. In a classic study, John Watson, founder of behavioral psychology, and Rosalie Raynor (1920) set out to demonstrate that fears can be learned—that they are not necessarily inborn, as was commonly thought at the time. Watson believed that all human behavior, with the exception of simple reflexes, is learned. A now famous 11-month-old named Albert was presented with a gentle white rat and showed no fear of it whatsoever until he was conditioned to fear it. Every time he reached for the white rat, Watson would sneak up behind him and bang a steel rod with a hammer. In this situation, the loud noise was the unconditioned stimulus for fear, the unconditioned response: Infants are naturally upset by a loud noise. But through learning, the white rat became a conditioned stimulus for a conditioned fear response.

By today's standards, Watson's experiment would be viewed as unethical, especially since Albert left the hospital where he was taught to fear before his fear could be eliminated. Nonetheless, Watson had made his point: Emotional responses can be learned.

Perhaps you can identify a fear or phobia you learned when an object or event that is not fearsome in itself became associated with a frightening experience. To this day, one of the authors shivers at the sight (or even the thought) of antiseptic cotton, undoubtedly because cotton just happened to be there when the iodine swabbed on a skinned knee caused painful shivers.

Fortunately, responses that are learned through classical conditioning can be unlearned through the same process, called **counterconditioning**. Thus Mary Cover Jones (1924) demonstrated that a 2-year-old named Peter could be helped to overcome his fear of furry things by the same technique used to condition Albert to fear them. Peter was exposed to a rabbit (for him, a CS for fearful responses) while he ate some of his favorite food (a UCS for pleasant feelings). Through such a pairing, Peter came to associate the rabbit with pleasurable rather than fearful feelings until he was gradually able to hold the rabbit calmly. Positive emotional reactions *can* be learned through classical conditioning. Indeed, it is undoubtedly involved when infants learn to respond positively to their parents, who at first may be neutral stimuli but who become associated with the positive sensations of receiving milk, being rocked, and being comforted. And classical conditioning surely is involved when adults find that certain songs on the radio, scents, or articles of clothing "turn them on."

Operant (Instrumental) Conditioning

A third, highly important form of basic learning is **operant conditioning**. In classical conditioning, responses are elicited or provoked by a stimulus. In operant conditioning, a learner first *emits* a response, or behaves in some way, and then comes to associate this action with the positive or negative consequences that ensue. B. F. Skinner (1953) made this form of conditioning famous. The basic principle makes a good deal of sense: We tend to repeat behaviors that have pleasant consequences and cut down on behaviors that have unpleasant consequences.

Possible Consequences of Behavior

In the language of operant conditioning, *reinforcement* occurs when a consequence *strengthens* a response, or makes it more likely to occur in the future. If a child cleans his room and then receives a hug, the hug will probably provide **positive reinforcement** for room cleaning and make it more likely in the future. *Positive* here means that something has been *added* to the situation, and *reinforcement* means that the behavior is strengthened. Thus a positive reinforcer is an event that, when introduced following a behavior, makes that behavior more probable in the future. **Negative reinforcement** also involves the strengthening of some behavioral tendency, but the behavior is strengthened because something negative or unpleasant is *removed* from the situation, or is escaped or avoided, after the behavior occurs. Have you been in a car in which an obnoxious buzzer sounds until you fasten your seat belt? The idea is that your "buckling up" behavior will become a stronger habit through *negative reinforcement*, because buckling up allows you to escape the unpleasant buzzer. No candy or hugs follow the buckling up, so it is not positive reinforcement that makes you likely to buckle up. It is negative reinforcement.

We are likely to keep doing things that allow us to escape or avoid unpleasantness, so we learn many habits through negative reinforcement. If a child finds that flattering Mom is the secret to stopping her nagging, the child will keep right on flattering. If you find that you can avoid visits from someone you find incredibly boring by going running around 6 P.M., you'll become a faithful jogger! In each case, a behavior is strengthened through negative reinforcement—through the removal or elimination of something unpleasant.

The point about negative reinforcement has been labored because there is a common, and absolutely incorrect, tendency to think that the term *negative reinforcement* is a fancy name for punishment. Contrast reinforcement, whether it is positive or negative, with punishment: Whereas reinforcement increases the strength of the behavior that preceded it, **punishment** decreases the strength of the behavior that preceded it. There are two forms of punishment paralleling the two forms of reinforcement. Either an unpleasant event can be added to the situation following the behavior (for example, a cashier is criticized for coming up short of cash at the end of the day), or something pleasant can be removed from the situation following the behavior (the amount she was short is deducted from her pay).

These four possible consequences of a behavior are summarized in Figure 8.1. Also, some behavior is simply ignored; that is, it has no particular consequence. Behavior that is ignored, or that is no longer reinforced, tends to weaken, a process called **extinction**. Indeed, a good alternative to punishment, at least for behavior that is not dangerous, is to ignore it while reinforcing desirable behavior that is incompatible with it. All too often, the well-behaved child is ignored, and the misbehaving child gets the attention—which serves as positive reinforcement for the misbehavior! Skinner and other behavioral theorists emphasize the power of positive reinforcement in child rearing. The approval of loving parents is a powerful reinforcer even in adulthood. But parents who feel that punishment is necessary can use the guidelines in Box 8.1 to make it more effective.

	Positive stimulus (pleasant)	Negative stimulus (unpleasant)
Administered	POSITIVE REINFORCEMENT (strengthens the behavior) "Thanks, Moose." Approval added to Moose's life makes cleaning up more likely in the future.	PUNISHMENT (weakens the behavior) "Call Action News! Moose is helping out for once!" Ridicule makes cleaning less likely in the future.
Withdrawn	PUNISHMENT (weakens the behavior) While he is in the kitchen, his daughter gobbles up his pie.	NEGATIVE REINFORCEMENT (strengthens the behavior) When he goes to the kitchen, his son stops begging him for the car keys and an unpleasant ordeal ends.

Figure 8.1 Possible consequences of behavior. Moose, uncharacteristically, starts to clear the dishes from the table after dinner. Here are four possible consequences of his behavior. Consider both the type of consequence—whether it is a positive or negative stimulus—and whether it is administered ("added to") the situation or withdrawn.

Behavior Modification

Life does not always arrange the consequences of behavior systematically to strengthen desirable behavior and weaken undesirable behavior, so both good and bad habits are learned. Many human service professionals use techniques of **behavior modification**, the systematic application of learning principles to change behavior in desirable directions. For example, the technique of **shaping**, which involves reinforcing successively closer approximations of the behavior that is ultimately desired, is often used to teach mentally retarded and other developmentally delayed children new skills. To teach a boy to put his shirt on by himself, a teacher might first reinforce him with praise or a bit of cereal for simply getting his arms into the sleeves, even if he does not button up; then reinforce him only when he also buttons a button or two; and finally reinforce him only when he gets all the buttons properly buttoned.

The timing of reinforcement has proved important in behavior modification efforts and in daily life. A reinforcer is most effective when it occurs during or immediately after a response (Domjan & Burkhard, 1982). This is especially true of infants and young children; older children and adults are better able to recall the acts that led later to pleasant or unpleasant outcomes. Frequency of reinforcement also makes a difference. Early in a training effort, it is best to provide **continuous reinforcement**, reinforcing the new behavior every time it occurs so that a habit is

Box 8.1 Using Punishment Effectively

Although operant researchers emphasize positively reinforcing good behavior, most parents use punishment at least occasionally. They can use it more effectively by following these guidelines, derived from the research literature (Domjan & Burkhard, 1982; Parke, 1977):

- **Punish as soon as possible.** It is best to punish as the child prepares to misbehave or at least during the act. Postponing punishment ("Wait til Daddy comes home") is bad practice. Young children may conclude that Daddy is punishing them for whatever they are doing at the moment—for example, putting toys back in the toy box. Delayed punishment can be effective with older children if the punisher explains why the child is being punished (Verna, 1977).
- **Punish with intensity (but not too much intensity).** Laboratory research with young children suggests that intense punishment, in the form of loud buzzers or noises, is more effective than mild punishment; that is, a loud "No" is likely to be more effective than a soft "No." But we should not be tricked into thinking that severe physical punishment is a good idea. Severe spankings have several disadvantages: They create high anxiety that can interfere with "learning one's lesson," they may make the child learn to fear and avoid the punisher, and they teach the child that aggression is an appropriate way of dealing with problems. So intense punishment can be effective as long as it is not so intense that it has these sorts of negative side effects.
- **Punish consistently.** Acts that are punished only now and then persist. After all, the child is then being reinforced part of the time for the (usually fun) misbehavior.
- **Be otherwise warm.** Children respond better to punishment from a person who is otherwise affectionate than to punishment from someone who is usually cold.
- **Explain yourself.** Explaining why the behavior was wrong and is being punished helps children learn to control their own behavior in the future (for example, to recall why the behavior would be unwise). Older children and adolescents, in particular, want and benefit from explanations that point out the social consequences of misbehavior.
- **Reinforce alternative behavior.** Since punishment alone tells a child what not to do but not *what to do*, it makes sense to strengthen acceptable alternatives to the misbehavior. The parent who does not want a toddler to play with an expensive vase might punish that behavior but also reinforce play with an unbreakable plastic pot.
- **Consider alternative responses to misbehavior.** Although spanking seems to be the first thing that many parents think of when a child misbehaves, punishment can also involve taking away desirable stimuli (for example, TV privileges). And a highly effective alternative to punishment is a procedure called **time out**, or time out from the opportunity to have one's misbehavior positively reinforced. The boy who is throwing toys around the room might be sent for a few minutes to a quiet room where he is cut off from the pleasure of creating havoc. When misbehavior is no longer reinforced, it weakens.

formed. However, if a child is always reinforced in the training situation but is not reinforced after the training has ended, extinction (fading) of the behavior will occur. The best method for maintaining desirable behavior over long periods is **partial reinforcement**, in which only some of the occurrences of an act are reinforced, ideally on an unpredictable schedule. An analogy makes this clear. If you've found water every time you've gone to a certain well, you'll give up on the well if you find it dry once or twice (rapid extinction following continuous reinforcement). But if the well has produced water, say, 60% of the time, you will not be dismayed by a "dry" trip or two, or even by many more such unreinforced trips (slow extinction following partial reinforcement).

Continuous reinforcement may be a good way of getting a new behavior started, but partial reinforcement is an effective way of getting the new behavior to continue when all reinforcement ceases. This is good news for the typical parent, who is inconsistent and simply cannot praise good deeds every time they occur. Of course, the same principle also applies to bad behavior. The parent who occasionally gives in to a child's whining for candy in the supermarket can expect more whining in the future.

Observational Learning

The form of basic learning we will consider last is **observational learning**, which results from observing the behavior of other people. Almost anything can be learned by watching (or listening to) other people. The child may learn how to speak the language and how to tackle math problems, as well as how to swear, snack between meals, and smoke in imitation of parents. As we saw in Chapter 2, this form of learning is emphasized in the modern social learning theory developed by Albert Bandura (1977, 1986) and others.

Bandura set out to demonstrate that people could learn a response that was neither elicited by a conditioned stimulus (classical conditioning) nor performed and then strengthened by a reinforcer (operant conditioning). His classic experiment involved the learning of aggressive behavior by nursery school children (Bandura, 1965). Children watched a short film in which an adult *model* attacked an inflatable Bobo doll, hitting the doll with a mallet while shouting "Sockeroo," throwing rubber balls at the doll while shouting "Bang, bang, bang," and so on. There were three experimental conditions:

1. Children in the *model-rewarded* condition saw a second adult give the aggressive model some candy and a soft drink for a "championship performance."
2. Children in the *model-punished* condition saw a second adult scold and spank the model for beating up on Bobo.
3. Children in the *no-consequences* condition simply saw the model behave aggressively.

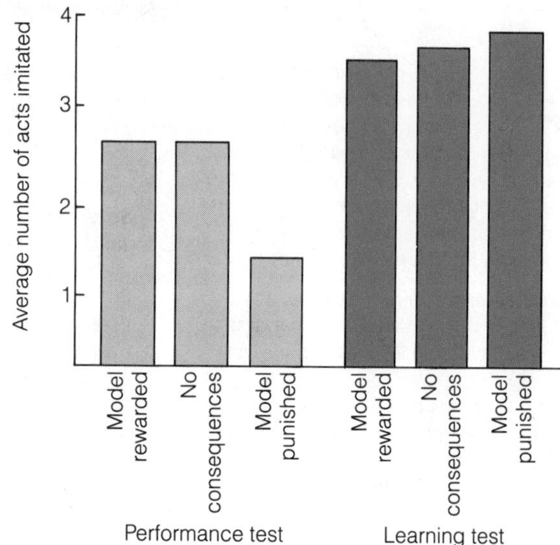

Figure 8.2 Average number of aggressive responses imitated during the performance test and the learning test for children who had seen a model rewarded, punished, or receiving no consequences for his actions. (Adapted from Bandura, 1965)

After the film ended, it was the children's turn to be in a playroom with the Bobo doll and many of the props the model had used to work Bobo over. What did children in the three conditions learn from observing the model in the film?

As the left side of Figure 8.2 shows, children in the model-rewarded condition and the no-consequences condition imitated more of the model's aggressive acts than children who had seen the model punished for aggression. But Bandura also devised a learning test in which he encouraged children to reproduce all of the model's behavior they could remember. The results of this test, which appear in the right-hand portion of Figure 8.2, indicate that children learned about the same amount from observing the model no matter what experimental condition they were in. Apparently children who saw the model punished imitated fewer of the model's behaviors on the initial "performance" test because they had learned from the film that they might be punished for striking Bobo. Nonetheless, these children learned a great deal about how to behave aggressively, knowledge that could be acted upon in the future if their expectation and fear of punishment were not as great.

Children do learn new behavior simply through observing a model—even though they have not tried out the aggressive behaviors before and have not been reinforced for performing them. Moreover, the study demonstrates that children can learn from observation without performing or imitating the learned responses. The distinction between *learning* and *performing* is therefore an important one. Children learn from the consequences to the model—a process called *vicarious reinforcement*—and this influences whether they perform what is learned. Similarly, children can learn by observing even without being reinforced, but reinforcing them for imitating will increase the chances that they will perform behavior learned through observation.

Social learning theorists are far more cognitively oriented than behavioral theorists such as John Watson and B. F. Skinner. Observational learning, unlike classical and

In Bandura's classic experiment, children who had watched an adult model show aggression toward a Bobo doll in several unusual ways (*top row*) performed similar acts themselves (*middle and bottom rows*), even though they hadn't been reinforced for committing such acts.

operant conditioning, requires a mind that attends to, remembers, and interprets information about other people's behavior. To learn anything, the learner must first pay attention to a model. In real life, some models are more influential than others because they capture more attention. People who are warm and nurturant and/or powerful and competent are most likely to be imitated by children (Bandura, 1977). Parents, teachers, older siblings, and popular peers often fit these descriptions. As people mature, they prefer models who are similar to themselves in some way—these models might include friends, or people in the same occupation, ethnic group, political party, and so on (Bandura, 1986).

Cognitive processes are also involved in storing information about what was observed. Somehow the learner must mentally represent or symbolize what the model did or said. These symbolic representations might be *images* of the model's action or *words* that describe and summarize what was seen. Finally, learners also process information about the consequences of behavior, form expectations about the likelihood of reinforcement or punishment in the future, and even *mentally* reinforce or punish their own actions—all very cognitive activities.

Basic Learning Processes in Perspective

Many of the changes in behavior that occur as people develop result from basic learning processes. Humans of all ages do learn not to respond to the highly familiar (habituation). They learn positive and negative emotional associations to a wide range of stimuli (classical conditioning). They form habits, good and bad, by being influenced by the reinforcing or punishing consequences of what they do (operant conditioning). And they change their own understandings and behaviors after watching other people behave (observational learning). Bandura's social learning theory comes the closest of any learning theory to viewing human learners as cognitive beings who actively select information from their environment and manipulate it mentally. Yet other psychologists have looked even more closely at the cognitive processes involved in learning complex material of the type studied in school, remembering it, and using it to solve problems.

THE INFORMATION-PROCESSING APPROACH

As the behavioral perspective gained a firm hold among psychologists, it became unfashionable to study mental events that could not be directly observed. According to Howard Gardner (1985), the "cognitive revolution" in psychology could not have occurred without (1) a demonstration of the inadequacies of the behaviorist approach, and (2) the rise of computer technology.

Demonstrating inadequacies in the behaviorist approach was easiest when such approaches were applied to complex learning and memory tasks. Consider learning from this textbook. Obviously some very complex processes occur between your registering of the pattern of print and your writing an essay on an exam. To hope to account for complex cognitive processes, behaviorists had to posit chains of mental stimuli and responses between the external stimulus (for instance, the printed page) and the overt response. This approach proved cumbersome at best.

Then came the computer with its capacity for systematically converting input to output. For information theorists in the mid-1950s, the computer seemed to provide a good analogy to the human mind (Gardner, 1985; Newell & Simon, 1961). Any computer has a limited capacity for processing information, associated with its hardware and software. The *hardware* is the machine itself—its keyboard (or input system), its storage capacity, and so on. The mind's "hardware" is the nervous system, including the brain, the sensory receptors, and their neural connections. The computer's *software* consists of the programs used to manipulate stored and received information: word-processing and statistics programs and the like. The mind, too, has its "software," mental "programs" that represent the ways information is registered, interpreted, stored, retrieved, and analyzed.

The computer, then, was the basis for the **information-processing approach** to human cognition, which emphasizes the fundamental mental processes involved in attention, perception, memory, and decision making. When the information-processing approach began to affect studies of development, the hardware and software of the mind were thought to change over the life span. Just as today's more highly developed computers have greater capacity than those of the past, maturation of the nervous system plus experience presumably enable adults to remember more than young children do and to perform more complex cognitive feats with greater accuracy (Klahr & Wallace, 1976).

Figure 8.3 presents a simplified and slightly altered version of an information-processing model. Imagine that your history professor says that the U.S. Constitution was ratified in 1789: This statement is an environmental stimulus. Assuming that you are not lost in a daydream, your **sensory register** will log it, holding it for a fraction of a second as a kind of afterimage (or in this example, a kind of echo). Much that strikes the sensory register quickly disappears without further processing. However, if you think you may need to remember 1789, it will be moved into **short-term memory**, or working memory, which can hold a limited amount of information (perhaps only about 7 items or chunks of information) for several seconds. For example, short-term memory can hold on to a telephone number while you dial it. Short-term memory is involved in temporarily storing information and in actively operating on or doing something to it (for example, consciously thinking about the meaning of the term "ratify").

To be remembered for any length of time, information must be moved into **long-term memory**, a relatively permanent store of information that represents what most people mean by memory. More than likely, you will hold the professor's statement in short-term memory just long enough to record it in your notes. Later, as you study your notes, you will rehearse the information or use other memory strategies to move it into long-term memory so that you can retrieve it the next day when you are taking the test.

This simplified model shows what you must do to

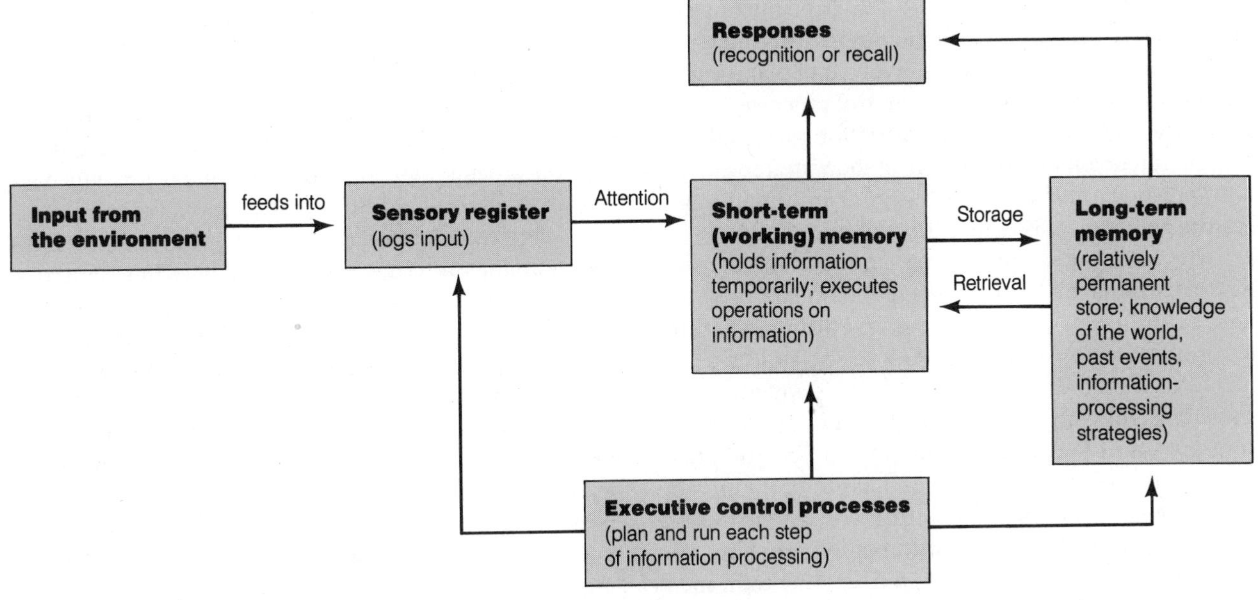

Figure 8.3 A model of information processing. (Adapted from Atkinson & Shiffrin, 1968)

learn and remember something. The first step is **encoding** the information: getting it into the system, learning it, moving it from the sensory register to short-term memory to long-term memory while organizing it in a form suitable for storing. If it never gets in, it cannot be remembered. Then there is **storage**, or the holding of information in the long-term memory store. Memories fade over time unless they are appropriately stored in long-term memory. And finally, there is **retrieval**, or getting information out again when it is needed. If you are asked a multiple-choice question about when the Constitution was ratified, you need not actively retrieve the correct date; you merely need to recognize it among the options. This is an example of **recognition memory**.

Now, suppose you were asked, "When was the Constitution ratified?" This would be a test of **recall memory**, which requires active retrieval without the aid of cues. Most people find questions requiring recognition memory easier to answer than those requiring recall. This is true across the life span, suggesting that many things that we have apparently encoded or learned are "in there someplace," but we have trouble retrieving them. Breakdowns in remembering can involve difficulties in initial encoding, storage, or retrieval.

Now imagine that you are asked how many years passed between the signing of the Declaration of Independence (1776, remember?) and the ratification of the Constitution. Here we have a simple example of **problem solving**, or use of the information-processing system to achieve a goal or to arrive at a decision (in this case, to answer the question). Here, too, the information-processing model describes what happens between stimulus and response. The question will move through the memory system. You will need to draw on your long-term memory to understand the question, and then you will have to search long-term memory for the two relevant dates. Moreover, you will need to locate your stored knowledge of the mathematical operation of subtraction. You will then transfer this stored information to short-term, or working, memory so that you can use your subtraction "program" (1789 minus 1776) to derive the correct answer.

Notice that processing information successfully requires both knowing what you are doing and making decisions. This is why the information-processing model includes *executive control processes* involved in planning and monitoring what is done. These control processes run the show, guiding the selection, organization, manipulation, and interpretation of information all the way along. Stored knowledge about the world and about information processing guides what is done with new information.

The information-processing approach to cognition has the advantage of focusing attention on *how* people remember things or solve problems, not just on what they recall or what answer they give. A young child's performance on a problem could break down in any number of ways: The child might not be paying attention to the relevant aspects of the problem; might be unable to hold all the relevant pieces of information in short-term memory long enough to do anything with them; might lack the strategies for transferring new information into long-term memory or retrieving information from long-term memory as needed; might simply not have enough stored knowledge to understand the problem; or might not have the executive control processes needed to manage the steps in problem solving. If we can identify how information processes in the younger individual differ from information processes in the older individual, we will have gained much insight into cognitive development.

Many information processes typically improve between infancy and adulthood and then decline somewhat in old age, although this pattern is not uniform for all processes. For example, Figure 8.4 shows how many numbers in sequence people of different ages can recall immediately after hearing strings of digits read to them quickly. This *memory-span* task, which at least partly reflects the capacity of short-term memory, is included on many IQ tests. Describing age trends like this is not nearly as fun as trying to determine why they occur—our task as we now examine changes in learning, memory, and problem solving over the life span.

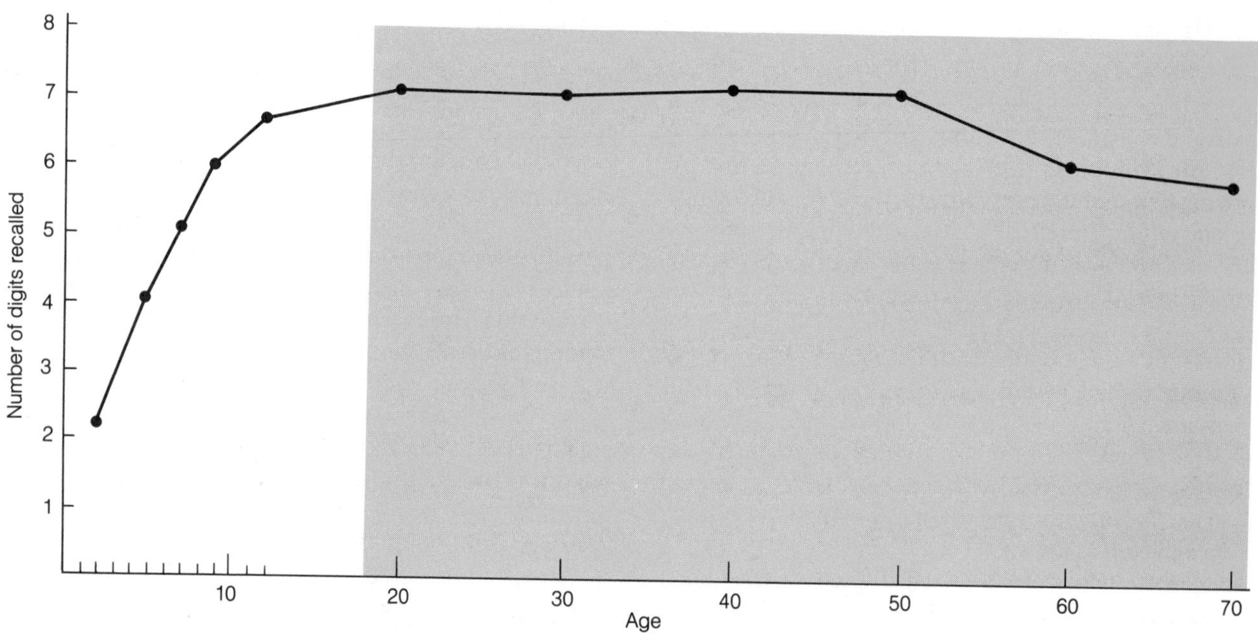

Figure 8.4 Age differences in memory for strings of digits. The average number of sequential digits that can be remembered immediately increases in childhood and decreases somewhat in old age. [Child data reflect Dempster's summary of several studies (1981); adult data are from a study by Botwinick and Storandt (1974)]

THE INFANT

We have already seen that infants explore the world thoroughly through their senses. But are they learning from their sensory experiences and remembering anything?

Can Young Infants Learn?

Infants can learn at birth and even before birth (Rovee-Collier, 1987). After they are repeatedly exposed to a stimulus, newborns show habituation to it, ceasing to be interested any longer and preferring something novel (Friedman, 1972). Newborns can also be classically conditioned, although not always easily (Fitzgerald & Brackbill, 1976). Lewis Lipsitt and Herbert Kaye (1964) paired a musical tone with the presentation of a nipple (an unconditioned stimulus for sucking). After several of these conditioning trials, 2- to 3-day-old infants began to suck at the sound of the tone, which had become a conditioned stimulus (CS) for the sucking response. Operant conditioning is also possible. At the tender age of 1 day, infants will learn to suck faster on a nipple when their sucking is positively reinforced by sugary rather than plain water (Kron, 1966).

Whether observational learning exists at birth is controversial. Newborns apparently can imitate certain facial expressions, such as surprise and sadness, and actions, such as sticking out the tongue or pursing the lips (Field, Woodson, Greenberg, & Cohen, 1982; Meltzoff & Moore, 1983; Reissland, 1988). However, this response is probably quite different from the older child's ability to imitate a novel act or store a representation of what a model did. Eugene Abravanel and Ann Sigafoos (1984) were able to get 1-month-old infants to imitate only one of several actions (tongue protrusion) reliably, suggesting that imitation does not come easily. In addition, older infants in the study (up to 5 months of age) *did not* imitate actions. This suggests that imitation in the newborn may be an involuntary, automatic, reflexlike action that disappears with age, just as many of the newborn's reflexes do, to be replaced later by more voluntary imitation as the cortex of the brain develops (see also Kaitz, Meschulach-Sarfaty, Auerbach, & Eidelman, 1988; Vinter, 1986).

So newborns can learn. But are they competent learners? In some respects they are, especially when they are learning responses that result in food or are otherwise significant biologically (Rovee-Collier, 1987). However, they are less competent learners than they will be later in infancy. For one thing, newborns are often slow to learn. They may need nearly 200 conditioning trials to learn to turn their heads at the sound of a bell in order to be reinforced with milk (Papousek, 1967). By 3 months of age, infants need only about 40 trials to learn the same response, and by 5 months of age they need fewer than 30. Second, the range of responses that a newborn can learn and perform is quite limited. Only a few reflexes (such as sucking and blinking) can be classically conditioned to a neutral stimulus (Fitzgerald & Brackbill, 1976). Similarly, operant conditioning and observational learning have been demonstrated only for behaviors already within the newborn's repertoire; entirely new behaviors cannot be learned. As infants develop, they rapidly become able to learn more kinds of responses, and to learn them faster.

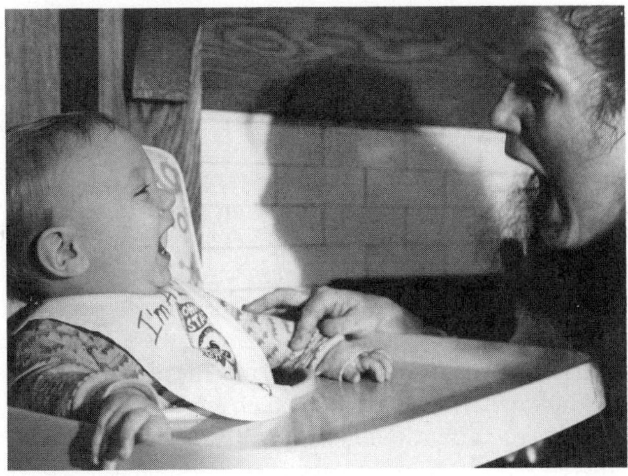

Infants perfect their observational learning skills as they get older.

How Well Do Infants Remember What They Have Learned?

Assessing infant memory has required ingenuity, since infants cannot just tell us what they recall. An infant's habituation to a repeatedly presented stimulus, for example, tells us that the stimulus is recognized as something experienced before: Preferring to look at a novel stimulus rather than a familiar one is a sign of recognition memory. Newborns do show recognition memory, preferring something new to something they have seen many times (Fagan, 1984). By about 5 months of age infants need less "study time" before a stimulus becomes old hat, and they can *retain* what they have learned longer—for up to two weeks (Fagan, 1984).

Another method of establishing the existence of memory early in infancy has relied on operant-conditioning techniques. Babies are taught to jiggle an overhead mobile by kicking it, an action that is very reinforcing. Then the mobile is presented at a later time to see if the infant will kick. To succeed at this task, the infant must recognize the mobile and "recall" that the thing to do is to kick, a feat that seems to require both recognition memory and at least a primitive form of recall. Research by Carolyn Rovee-Collier and her colleagues suggests that infants 2 to 3 months of age will indeed remember to kick two or three weeks later (Davis & Rovee-Collier, 1983; Sullivan, 1982). In a 2-month-old, memory is "iffy"; it seems to depend on exactly how the initial training was done and how much the infant noticed about the situation during training (Vander Linde, Morrongiello, & Rovee-Collier, 1985). It seems, then, that recall memory in the presence of cues (in this case, the presence of the mobile) may emerge during the first months of life. Indeed, research now suggests that infants in their first months of life display some learned responses hours and even days after they learned them (Little, Lipsitt, & Rovee-Collier, 1984; Rovee-Collier, 1987).

But what about actively retrieving something from memory when it is no longer present? At about 8 to 12 months of age, infants will search for and find a hidden toy in tasks like those used to test for Piaget's concept of object permanence (Sophian, 1980). This is evidence of recall (Sophian, 1980). The ability to imitate a novel act after a delay—deferred imitation—also provides evidence of recall memory. As early as 9 months of age, many infants can imitate novel actions (for example, pushing a button on a box to produce a beep) after a 24-hour delay (Meltzoff, 1988). More and more of them will be able to imitate single actions by 18 months of age, when many also start to imitate combinations of novel actions (Abravanel & Gingold, 1985). The ability to imitate a model's behaviors after a delay continues to improve thereafter (McCall, Parke, & Kavanaugh, 1977).

Such laboratory experiments may underestimate how much infants can remember in everyday, involving situations (Daehler & Greco, 1985). Daniel Ashmead and Marion Perlmutter (1980) used a technique in which parents kept diaries to study recall in 7- to 11-month-old infants. Consider 7-month-old Anne, as described by her mother:

> Trying to change Anne's diaper and dress her in A.M. on changing table. She immediately turns over and crawls to top edge of table and reaches over edge several times. Today I had picked up the pink lotion so it wasn't where she expected it to be. Anne paused, looked back and forth and looked at me puzzled. Her eyes brightened when she saw the bottle—immediately took it from me [p. 11].

By age 2, infants seem to be able to recall events that happened months ago. Katherine Nelson (1984), for example, taped the monologues of a bright 2-year-old as the infant was falling asleep. Here, at 24 months of age, Emily reconstructs a trip to the library with her grandmother that took place four months previously: "Go library. I sat in Mormor's lap. I went to the library. Probably that's what we did. Probably we did in the *bus*!" (p. 122).

What remarkable progress is made during the two years of infancy! Infants begin with an ability to learn only certain kinds of associations, often very slowly, but soon become more and more polished learners. They can recognize the familiar from birth and can recall with the aid of cues by about 2 to 3 months of age. As they get older, they can retain information longer and longer. More advanced recall memory, which requires actively retrieving an image of an object or event that is no longer present, appears to emerge toward the end of the first year. And by age 2, infants seem able to consciously and deliberately try to recall something that happened long ago. By then, they are beginning to do what you and I do when we speak of "remembering." And yet, though infants store memories, the infant years are a blank for most of us. Box 8.2 explores this mystery.

Basic Learning Processes After Infancy

The basic learning processes that develop in infancy continue to operate throughout the life span in much the same way. To be sure, some advances in learning ability occur. For example, the older child's ability to learn through observation is greater than the younger child's. Watching a televised model, older children will use words to describe what they have seen and thus retain more (Coates & Hartup, 1969). And rather than recalling mainly what actors have done, older children will absorb more about the reasons these actions were undertaken and the

Box 8.2
Where Did the Early Childhood Memories Go?

Though infants are quite capable of remembering, most people remember almost nothing that happened to them before the age of about 3—or if they do have memories, some of them turn out to be pure fiction! This lack of memory for the early years of life has been termed **infantile amnesia**. For example, Karen Sheingold and Yvette Tenney (1982) questioned college students about the birth of their younger brothers or sisters—who took care of them, what presents they and the baby got, what time of day their mothers returned from the hospital, and so on. Students who were at least 3 or 4 at the time recalled a great deal, as did children who were asked these questions when they were as young as 4 years old. However, only 3 of 22 college students who were younger than 3 at the time of a sibling's birth remembered anything at all about the event. Why?

Sigmund Freud thought infantile amnesia was a matter of blocking out or repressing from consciousness highly emotional events, but contemporary researchers have developed more cognitive explanations. For example, infants do not use language and adults do, so it is possible that early memories are stored in some nonverbal code that we cannot retrieve once we are verbal adults (Sheingold & Tenney, 1982; White & Pillemer, 1979). Or possibly infants do not have enough space in working memory to hold the multiple pieces of information about actor, action, and setting that are needed to encode a specific event (White & Pillemer, 1979). It has also been suggested that children must first develop general expectations about events (or "scripts" describing, for example, what they usually do when they get up in the morning) before deviations from the script (for example, the morning Mom went to the hospital to have the baby) become memorable as distinct events (Nelson, 1984). It is difficult to pinpoint the precise reasons for infantile amnesia, but it is clear that a period of life that is highly important to later development is a blank for most of us (Perlmutter, 1986).

consequences they produce (Collins, Wellman, Keniston, & Westby, 1978). Thus a 4-year-old may notice that a man put a gun in someone's bureau drawer, but a 10-year-old may realize that the villain is trying to conceal his guilt—and that he gets his comeuppance after the commercial.

For the most part, however, basic forms of learning are both evident and important at *all* ages. The young adult habituates to the familiar, might develop a classically conditioned fear of flying after a very rough flight, might cease to work hard on the job after receiving the punishment of a pay cut, and might learn a new cooking method by watching Julia Child cooking on television. An old person in a nursing home might become more and more dependent because staff members are unknowingly reinforcing dependence, but could be helped to become more independent by systematic reinforcement of independence (Baltes & Barton, 1979). In all of us, changes are partly the result of our learning experiences.

THE CHILD

The 2-year-old is already a highly capable information processor, as evidenced by the rapid language learning that takes place at this age. But dramatic improvements in learning, memory, and problem solving take place over the childhood years, as children learn everything from how to flush toilets to how to work advanced math problems.

Learning and Memory over the Childhood Years

In countless learning situations, older children learn faster and remember more than younger children do. But *why*? Four main hypotheses about why learning and memory improve, patterned after those formulated by John Flavell and Henry Wellman (1977), are summarized in Box 8.3.

Do Basic Capacities Change?

Since the nervous system continues developing in the early years of life, it seems plausible that older children remember more than younger children do because they have a better "computer"—a larger or more efficient information-processing system. However, we can quickly rule out the idea that the storage capacity of long-term memory enlarges. There is no consistent evidence that it changes after the first month of life (Perlmutter, 1986). In fact, both young and old have more room for storage than they could ever possibly use. Nor does the capacity of the sensory register to take in stimuli seem to change much (House, 1982). Possibly more short-term or working mem-

Box 8.3
Hypotheses About Developmental Changes in Memory

- **Basic capacities:** Older children and young adults have higher-powered "computers" than young children or elderly adults do. They have more "work space" for manipulating information and/or they can do it faster.
- **Memory strategies:** Older children and young adults have learned and consistently use effective methods for getting information into long-term memory and retrieving it when they need it.
- **Knowledge about memory:** Older children and young adults know a great deal about memory. They know how long they must study to learn things thoroughly, which kinds of memory tasks take more effort, which strategies best fit each task, and so on.
- **Knowledge about the world:** Older children and young adults know more about the world in general than young children and elderly adults do. Their knowledge makes many learning materials familiar, and familiar material is easier to learn and remember than unfamiliar material. They are experts rather than novices.

ory space becomes available with age so that older children and adults can keep more things in mind at once and perform more simultaneous mental operations than a young child can.

This idea has been featured in revisions of Piaget's theory of cognitive development proposed by two neo-Piagetians who have been strongly influenced by the information-processing approach. Juan Pascual-Leone (1970, 1984) and Robbie Case (1984, 1985) both propose that more advanced stages of cognitive development are made possible by increases in working memory space. For example, Piaget stressed the preschooler's tendency to *center* on one aspect of a problem and lose sight of another (for example, to attend to the height of a glass but ignore its width, or vice versa). Perhaps young children simply do not have enough working memory space to keep both pieces of information in mind at once. Similarly, it is possible that young children do poorly on memory tasks because they cannot keep the first items on a list in mind while processing newer ones or fail mathematical problem-solving tasks because they cannot keep the facts of the problem in mind while they are performing calculations.

At this point, it has not been shown that the *total* capacity of short-term memory for storing and operating on information changes with age (Dempster, 1985), but older children do appear to have more working memory space available for constructive *use* (Case, 1984; Kail, 1988). In other words, as children develop they become faster or more efficient at executing basic mental processes, and this frees space in working memory for other purposes. For instance, the reason older children can immediately recall more digits than younger children can, may be that they can identify the digits sooner when they hear them. Thus they can devote more of their available working memory to trying to remember the digits (Dempster, 1981, 1985; Howard & Polich, 1985).

Many information processes that are time consuming and effortful early in life become *automatized*—that is, they can be done with little thinking or effort—later in life. This change need not be related to the maturation of the brain. It could be that older children are simply more familiar with things like numbers, or that they are more able to allocate working memory space to the most important aspects of a task (Flavell, 1985; Whitney, 1986).

Do Memory Strategies Change?

Steady improvements in memory over childhood may also reflect increasingly effective strategies for remembering. Susan Somerville, Henry Wellman, and Joan Cultice (1983) tested young children's ability to deliberately remember everyday things. They had mothers say things like "Remind me to buy candy at the store" to 2-, 3-, and 4-year-olds. Even the 2-year-olds would, without prompting, remind their mothers within a few minutes of being told to do so—if the task was of high interest. Even the next morning, they did quite well at reminding their mothers of such important tasks as buying candy, though they did quite poorly at remembering such low-interest tasks as bringing in the laundry. But even though toddlers can deliberately remember important information when they are highly motivated to do so, their stategies are quite primitive compared to those of older children. Consider what happened when 3-year-olds were asked to remember which of four cups had a toy dog hidden under it (Wellman, Ritter, & Flavell, 1975). When the experimenter left the room, the behavior of these youngsters was observed through a one-way mirror. Many children looked at or touched the cup the toy was beneath, and these strategies paid off in later recall. By contrast, older children would probably not need to touch the right cup; they would use a more mature strategy such as repeating to themselves, "It's in the second cup."

A good sign of the memory limitations of young children is the fact that their recognition memory is way ahead of their recall memory. If 4-year-olds were shown the 12 items in Figure 8.5, they would *recognize* nearly all of them if asked to select the objects they had seen from a larger set of pictures (Brown, 1975). But if asked to *recall* the objects, they might remember only two to four of them, a far cry from the seven to nine items that an 8-year-old would recall or the ten to eleven an adult would recall several minutes later. What specific strategies evolve during childhood to permit this dramatic improvement in performance?

One important strategy is **rehearsal**, or repeating the items one is trying to learn and remember. To learn the objects in Figure 8.5, you might say over and over, "Apple, truck, grapes, . . ." Another is **organization**, or classifying items into meaningful groups. You might lump the apple, the grapes, and the hamburger into a category of "foods" and form other categories for "animals," "vehicles," and "baseball equipment." You would then rehearse each category and recall it as a cluster. Another organizational strategy, *chunking*, is used when we break a long number (6065551843) into manageable subunits (606-555-1843, a phone number). Finally, there is the strategy of **elaboration**, or the active creation of meaningful links between items to be remembered. Elaboration is achieved by adding something to the items, in the form of either words or images. A sentence like "The apple fell on the horse's head" would help you remember two of the items in Figure 8.5; visualizing this idea, with or without a sentence, would also help. Elaboration is especially helpful in learning foreign languages. For example, one might link the Spanish word *"pato"* (pronounced pot-o) to the English word "duck" by imagining a duck in a pot of boiling water.

Figure 8.5 Memory task. Imagine that you have 120 seconds to learn the 12 objects pictured here. What tricks or strategies might you devise to make your task easier?

The development of rehearsal illustrates children's progress in controlling and using memory strategies. John Flavell and his associates (see Flavell, 1985) have demonstrated that the use of rehearsal increases with age. In one study, they asked children to watch as the experimenter pointed to three pictures in an array of seven pictures and to remember which pictures were pointed to in what order (Flavell, Beach, & Chinsky, 1966). Both talking aloud and moving the lips were taken as signs that rehearsal was being done. Only 10% of the 5-year-olds rehearsed, but more than half of the 7-year-olds and 85% of the 10-year-olds did so. As usual, the amount remembered increased with age. By about age 7, most children use rehearsal effectively, though not on all kinds of tasks.

Older children develop even more effective rehearsal strategies. For example, 8-year-olds will rehearse a list of words presented one at a time in just that way—one at a time. Twelve-year-olds are more likely to rehearse clusters of words, repeating, for example, the first and second words when they are rehearsing the third word (Ornstein, Naus, & Liberty, 1975). Rehearsing clusters is more effective than rehearsing one item at a time, but the young grade school child may not be able to manage this if words are presented one at a time. In one study, 7-year-olds rehearsed each new item by itself unless the researchers both taught them to rehearse clusters of items *and* visually displayed earlier items so that they did not have to retrieve them from memory themselves (Ornstein, Medlin, Stone, & Naus, 1985). Twelve-year-olds could rehearse groups of items effectively even without having earlier items displayed visually. Effective use of advanced rehearsal strategies, then, may depend on mastery of other basic competencies such as the ability to retrieve relevant material from memory.

Flavell (1985) has concluded that rehearsal and other memory strategies develop through three stages:

1. *Mediation deficiency.* At this stage the child lacks the basic cognitive skills to execute or benefit from the strategy; attempts to coach the child in its use will be ineffective.
2. *Production deficiency.* Now the child can use the strategy and can benefit from its use, but does not often use it. This is what is meant by the term **production deficiency**. At this stage, prompting or coaching the child to employ the strategy may pay off in more effective recall.
3. *Mature strategy use.* Finally, the strategy is used *spontaneously* and effectively to aid learning and memory. Now coaching is a waste of time. Thus as children gain fuller control of a strategy, they seem to recognize more easily that it is relevant to a task, and they independently apply it to a wider variety of tasks.

Use of the strategy of *organization* develops through these same stages but is mastered a bit later in childhood than the relatively simple strategy of rehearsal. Until about age 9 or 10, children are not much better at recalling lists of items that lend themselves readily to grouping than they are at recalling lists of unrelated words (Flavell & Wellman, 1977). And even when young schoolchildren begin to use organization as an aid to recall, the categories they develop are often not as logical and useful as those developed by adults (Liberty & Ornstein, 1973). Coaching in organization, like coaching in rehearsal, may increase use of the strategy among children who are in the production-deficiency stage of mastery, at about 6 to 8 years of age (Kee & Bell, 1981). Finally, the *elaboration* strategy is rarely used spontaneously before adolescence (Pressley, 1982).

Using effective memory strategies to learn material is only half the battle. *Retrieval strategies* can influence how much is recalled, even when effective memory strategies were used initially. Indeed, retrieving something from memory can often be a complex adventure in problem solving, as when you try to remember when you went on a trip by searching for cues that might trigger your memory (''Well, I still had long hair then, but it was after Fred's party, and . . .''). Consider this example of the young child's problem with retrieval. Michael Pressley and Joel Levin (1980) prompted 6- and 11-year-olds to elaborate on 18 pairs of stimuli they were trying to learn. When it was time for the recall test, half the children were told to use their elaborate images to help them remember, while the other half were given no special instructions. The 11-year-olds recalled more of the items than the younger children did, and they performed well regardless of whether they were told to use their images as an aid. In contrast, the 6-year-olds recalled nearly twice as many items when given retrieval instructions than when left to their own devices (see Figure 8.6). Strange as it may seem, it apparently did not occur to the young children to use the images they had worked so hard to create as part of their retrieval strategy (see also Kee & Bell, 1981). The message here is important: Even when younger schoolchildren are shown how to organize or elaborate while they are learning, they may still do less well than older children because they fail to exploit the results of those strategies during retrieval.

Does Knowledge About Memory and Other Cognitive Processes Change?

The term **metamemory** refers to knowledge of memory and memory processes. It is knowing, for example, what one's memory limits are, which memory strategies are more or less effective, and which memory tasks are more or less difficult (Flavell, 1985). Metamemory also includes being able to plan and control memory processes consciously as one is learning and remembering (Brown, 1975). Metamemory is part of *metacognition*, knowledge of the human mind and of the whole range of cognitive processes. Your store of metacognitive knowledge might include an understanding that you are better at word problems than at math problems, that it is harder to pay attention to what you are trying to learn when there is distracting noise in the background than when it is quiet, and that it is wise to check out a proposed solution to a problem before concluding it is correct.

When do children show evidence of metamemory? The study by Wellman, Ritter, and Flavell (1975) demonstrated that 3-year-olds could use simple memory strate-

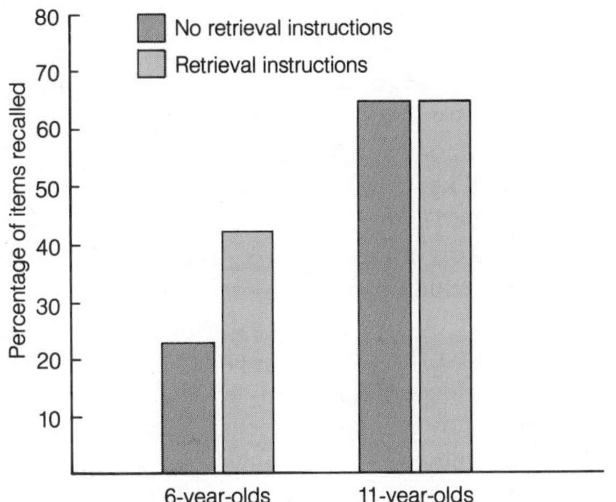

Figure 8.6 Young children need coaching in retrieval. Even when they had been coached to use an elaboration strategy in learning, young children benefited from being instructed to use the images they had formed at retrieval time. Older children do this spontaneously.

gies such as looking at or touching a cup that hid a toy dog, but the children used such strategies only when explicitly told to remember where the dog was. Children told only to wait with the dog until the experimenter returned did not use memory strategies as often. In a second experiment, the same task was tried with 2-year-olds. (Actually, the delay interval had to be made shorter because 2-year-olds tended to become squirmy and leave the room otherwise!) These 2-year-olds did nothing different when told to remember than when told to wait. It would seem that by about age 3 children have acquired at least one simple bit of knowledge about memory: To remember something, one must work at it!

Indeed, young children learn a good deal about memory during their preschool years (Cunningham & Weaver, 1989; Schneider & Sodian, 1988; Wellman, 1977). Still, they have much left to learn. For instance, they do not always know their own memory limitations. In one study (Yussen & Levy, 1975) preschoolers, third graders, and adults were asked to estimate whether they would be able to recall sets of pictures ranging from small numbers to large numbers of items. Preschoolers' estimates were highly unrealistic, as if to say, "I can remember anything!" Third graders made more realistic estimates after being told of a peer's average performance on the items, but preschoolers were unfazed by such information, continuing to overestimate their memory capacities.

Much growth in metamemory occurs during the school years. For instance, up to about age 7, most children do not seem to realize that related items or those that can be organized into categories are easier to recall than unrelated items (Kreutzer, Leonard, & Flavell, 1975). Young elementary schoolchildren are also less aware of which memory strategies are superior. For example, Elaine Justice (1985) asked second, fourth, and sixth graders (ages 7, 9, and 11, respectively) about the merits of different strategies. All realized that rehearsing or categorizing would be better than just looking at items or naming them, but only sixth graders consistently preferred categorization to rehearsal.

Are increases in metamemory a major contributor to improved memory performance over the childhood years? Actually, the evidence is mixed. In their review of research, John Cavanaugh and Marion Perlmutter (1982) concluded that there was only a weak relationship between metamemory and memory performance. Good metamemory apparently is not required for good recall (Bjorklund & Zeman, 1982). Moreover, children who know what to do do not always do it, so good metamemory is no guarantee of good recall (Salatas & Flavell, 1976). Still, there seems to be at least some link between metamemory and performance, enough to suggest the merits of teaching children more about how memory works and how to make it work more effectively for them.

Does Increased Knowledge of the World in General Contribute to Improvements in Memory?

Ten-year-olds obviously know considerably more about the world in general than 2-year-olds do. Metamemory may be the form of knowledge most relevant to memory performance, but the individual's knowledge of a content area to be learned, or **knowledge base** as it has come to be called, might also be involved in learning and memory. Think about the difference between reading about a topic that you already know well and reading about a new topic. In the first case, you can read quite quickly because you can quickly link the information to the knowledge you have already stored. All you really need to do is check for any new information or information that contradicts what you already know. Learning about a highly unfamiliar topic is more difficult. You may even sigh "It's Greek to me" and learn almost nothing.

Perhaps the most dramatic illustration of the powerful influence of knowledge base on memory was provided by Michelene Chi (1978). She demonstrated that children could outperform adults at a memory task—something that children virtually never do. How? She simply recruited children who were expert chess players and compared them to adults who were familiar with the game but lacked expertise. On a test of memory for sequences of digits, children recalled fewer than adults did, as is typical. But on a test of memory for the locations of chess pieces, the children beat the adults (Figure 8.7). Because they were experts, these children were able to form more and larger meaningful mental "chunks" or groups of chess pieces, and that was what allowed them to remember more.

Pause to consider the implications: On most tasks, young children are the novices and older children or adults are the experts. Perhaps older children and adults recall longer strings of digits only because they are more familiar with numbers than young children are. Perhaps they recall more words in word lists because they have more familiarity with language. Perhaps memory improves in childhood simply because older children know more about all kinds of things than younger children do (Perlmutter, 1986).

In their areas of expertise, whether the topic is math or dinosaurs, children appear to develop highly specialized and effective strategies of information processing, just as the young chess players studied by Chi apparently had (Chi, Hutchinson, & Robin, 1989; Keil, 1984). Indeed, children with low general intellectual ability but high expertise sometimes understand and remember more about stories in their area of expertise than children with higher intellectual ability but less expertise (Schneider, Korkel, & Weinert, 1989). It seems that the more one knows, the more one *can* know. It also seems that how well a child does on a memory task depends not only on age but on familiarity with the specific task at hand.

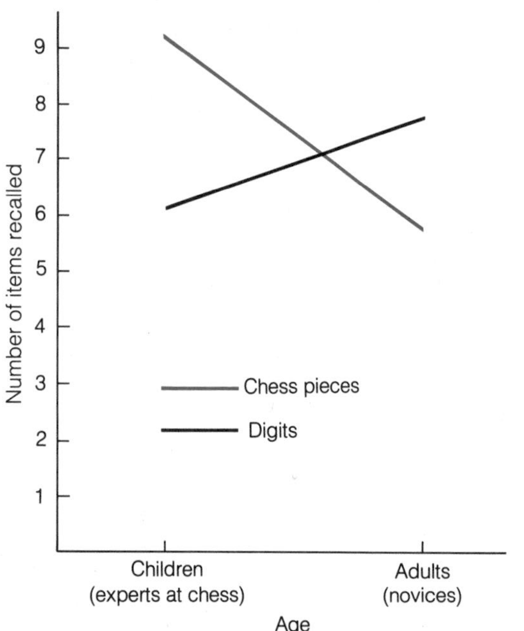

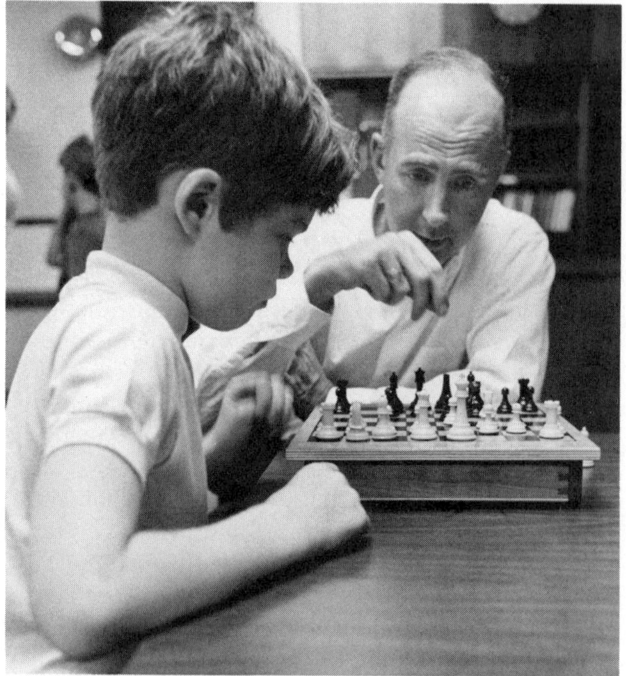

Figure 8.7 Effects of expertise on memory. Michelene Chi found that child chess experts outperformed adult chess novices on a test of recall for the location of chess pieces (though, in keeping with the usual developmental trend, these children could not recall strings of numbers as well as adults could).

A SUMMING UP

We can now draw four conclusions about the development of learning and memory:

1. Older children have a greater information-processing *capacity* than younger children do, particularly in the sense that they have automatized certain basic information processes to leave room in working memory for other cognitive processes.
2. Older children use more effective *memory strategies* in encoding and retrieving information.
3. Older children know more about memory, and their *metamemory* may allow them to choose appropriate strategies and control and monitor their learning.
4. Older children know more in general, and their larger *knowledge base* improves their ability to learn and remember.

Can we choose a best hypothesis? Probably not at this point. All these phenomena may contribute something to the dramatic improvements in learning and memory performance that occur over the childhood years. They may also interact. For example, the automatization of certain information processes may leave the child with enough working memory space to use effective memory strategies that were just too draining earlier in childhood (Bjorklund, 1987; Guttentag, 1985). Or increased knowledge may permit faster information processing. We will return to these same four hypotheses when we consider changes in learning and memory in adulthood.

Problem Solving in Childhood

To solve a problem, one must process information about the task, as well as use stored information, to achieve a goal. How do problem-solving capacities change during childhood? A kind of problem that was originally studied by behavioral learning psychologists provides a good example of how the behavioral and information-processing perspectives differ. It also shows us something about changes in problem solving between early and later childhood. Examine the pairs of objects on the left in Figure 8.8. If you were being tested on this discrimination learning task, you would be given such pairs of objects pair by pair in a series of trials, would guess which member of the pair the experimenter had in mind as the "right one," and would then be told whether you are right or wrong (the one with the plus sign above it is right in each trial). Your goal is to figure out what value on what dimension (size, color, left/right position on the page) the experimenter has decided is the right one so that you are no longer just guessing but are making the correct choice consistently. From a behavioral perspective, this is a simple matter of operant conditioning; after a series of trials in which the larger object is consistently reinforced, the tendency to "pick large" should be gradually strengthened.

Now assume that a group of children has learned that "large" is right and begins a new series of trials in which "small" is right. This is called a **reversal shift** problem because the learner must now respond to the opposite or re-

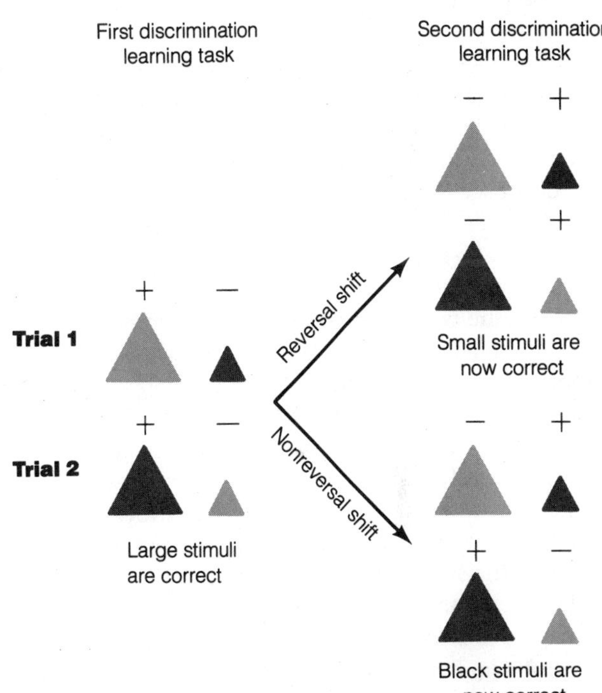

Figure 8.8 Discrimination learning and reversal and nonreversal shifts; + indicates the correct (rewarded) stimuli and − indicates the incorrect (nonrewarded) stimuli. All subjects first learn to respond to large stimuli on the training task and then are switched to a second problem set in which either small stimuli are reinforced (reversal learning) or black stimuli are reinforced (nonreversal learning). (Adapted from Kendler & Kendler, 1962)

verse end of one stimulus dimension (in this case size). But let us put other children who originally learned to pick "large" in a **nonreversal shift** condition, one in which they must now switch to another dimension entirely (for example, by learning to choose the black object; see the right side of Figure 8.8). Which of these two new problems, the reversal shift or the nonreversal shift, do you think should be easier to learn?

According to operant conditioning theory, the nonreversal shift should be easier. Since the large stimuli that were rewarded during the original training trials were black half the time, the response "pick black" was partially reinforced. However, the response "pick small" was *not* reinforced, so that should make the reversal shift (from large to small) harder. What actually happens? Both animals and young (nursery school) children do indeed find it easier to solve nonreversal problems (Kendler & Kendler, 1975). However, Tracy and Howard Kendler (Kendler, Kendler, & Leonard, 1962) reported that half of their 5- to 6-year-olds and a clear majority of their 8- to 10-year-olds learned *reversal* shifts ("large" to "small") more easily than nonreversal shifts. Here was one piece in a growing collection of evidence suggesting that older children do not conform to simple operant principles. It was evidence of what has come to be called the **5-to-7 shift**, a dramatic change in the way children learn and solve problems at about the age they enter school. Many theorists, Piaget among them, have noticed a qualitative change in behavior during this period of childhood.

What is behind the 5-to-7 shift? One view is that children of this age become capable of using language as a tool of thought—a phenomenon called **verbal mediation** in thought (Luria, 1961). The child begins to give labels to aspects of the stimuli that seem important (for example, thinking, "It's the large one"). Once the child has used language to identify one end of a dimension in the reversal shift problem, figuring out that "small," the other end of the same dimension, is now correct becomes easier. In contrast, nonreversal shifts are more difficult because the child has to switch verbal mediators (from size labels to color labels).

The 5-to-7 shift may also be seen as a shift to a more cognitive approach to problem solving, one that involves forming and testing hypotheses (T. S. Kendler, 1979). It is this idea that has been pursued most vigorously by researchers adopting an information-processing approach. Their goal is to understand what hypotheses children of different ages are forming and how they are responding to evidence about the correctness of their hypotheses. Children 3 or 4 years old sometimes form hunches, but they are not very effective hypothesis-testers. For example, they often abandon hypotheses after being told that their choice was *right* or stick with wrong hypotheses after being told that they are wrong (Tumblin & Gholson, 1981). Five-year-olds overcome these problems but do not keep good track of hypotheses they had previously rejected, so they sometimes waste their time checking out incorrect rules over again (Kemler, 1978). Older children are more efficient and effective hypothesis-testers.

We can conclude, then, that important changes in problem-solving strategies do occur at roughly the time of the 5-to-7 shift, and perhaps even earlier. Instead of being passively shaped by reinforcement, children become active formulators and testers of hypotheses. Instead of proceeding in a haphazard, trial-and-error way, children of about kindergarten age begin to formulate logical plans for solving problems (Klahr & Robinson, 1981). Problem solving on these kinds of tasks then improves during the elementary school years.

The information-processing approach to problem solving has picked up where behavioral psychologists left off, and in addition it has provided a richer understanding of how children go about solving the kinds of complex problems that interested Jean Piaget. Consider the problem of predicting what will happen to the balance beam in Figure 8.9 when weights are put on each side of the fulcrum, or balancing point. The goal is to decide which way the balance beam will tip when it is released. To judge correctly, one must take into account both the number of weights and their distances from the fulcrum. Piaget never provided a very full account of how children approached this problem and why they typically failed it before their adolescent years. Robert Siegler (1981) has done so. He be-

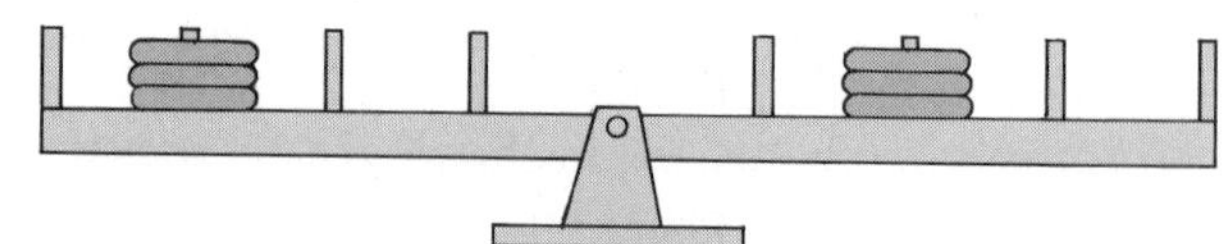

Figure 8.9 The balance-scale apparatus used by Siegler to study children's problem-solving abilities.

lieves that children faced with a problem first gather information and then formulate a rule to account for that information. The rule formed will depend on exactly what information has been encoded about the problem. Siegler proposed that four rules were possible in the balance-beam problem:

> *Rule 1:* The child predicts that the arm with more weight will drop, ignoring the distance of weights from the center.
>
> *Rule 2:* Weight is still the most important factor, but if the weights on each arm are equal, the child will consider the distance of the weights from the fulcrum to break the tie.
>
> *Rule 3:* Both weight and distance are considered, but if one side has more weight while the other has its weights farther from the fulcrum, the child is confused and will simply guess.
>
> *Rule 4:* Using this mature rule, the child knows that the pull on each arm is a function of weight times distance. For example, if there are three weights on the second peg to the left and two weights on the fourth peg to the right, the left torque is $3 \times 2 = 6$ and the right torque is $2 \times 4 = 8$, so the right arm will go down.

Table 8.1 presents six problems that Siegler devised to identify exactly which of the four rules each problem-solver was using. For example, children using rule 1 and encoding only weight should be able to solve problems 1, 2, and 4 but will think the arms should balance in problem 3, even though one set of weights is farther from center than the other. Similarly, they should think the right arm will drop on problems 5 and 6. A distinctive pattern of successes and failures is associated with each of the other possible rules.

When Siegler (1981) administered these tasks to subjects aged 3 to 20, he found that 91% appeared to be using one or the other of the four rules, but with pronounced age differences. Almost no 3-year-olds used any kind of rule, again showing us that the very young child has limited problem-solving skills. By contrast, 4- and 5-year-olds were rule governed, more than 80% of them using rule 1 and encoding weight but ignoring distance. By age 8, children were generally using rule 2 or 3; by 12, the vast majority had settled on rule 3. And, although most 20-year-olds continued to use rule 3, 30% of them had discovered the weight times distance principle reflected in rule 4.

Imagine how effective teachers might be if they, like Siegler, could accurately diagnose the information-processing strategies of their learners to know exactly what each child is noticing (or failing to notice) about a prob-

Table 8.1 Six balance-scale problems and the patterning of answers that follows from using each of four rules for solving problems

		SIEGLER'S RULE			
PROBLEM	CORRECT ANSWER	1	2	3	4
1. 	Balance	100% correct	100% correct	100% correct	100% correct
2. 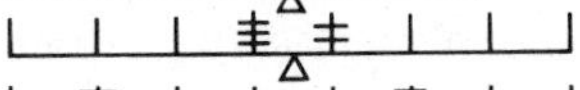	Left down	100% correct	100% correct	100% correct	100% correct
3. 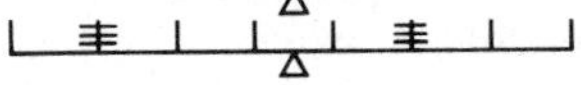	Left down	0% correct (will say balance)	100% correct	100% correct	100% correct
4. 	Left down	100% correct	100% correct	33% correct (chance responding)	100% correct
5. 	Left down	0% correct (will say right down)	0% correct (will say right down)	33% correct (chance responding)	100% correct
6. 	Balance	0% correct (will say right down)	0% correct (will say right down)	33% correct (chance responding)	100% correct

lem and exactly what rules or strategies each child is using. This same rule-assessment approach has in fact been used to identify exactly why individual children make errors on arithmetic problems (see Mayer, 1985). For example, the child who works the subtraction problem 24 − 18 and gets 16 rather than 6 is not just making a random mistake but is using a faulty rule—one that does not yet include the rule for "borrowing." Helping this child requires instruction quite different from that appropriate for the child who makes a different kind of error.

THE ADOLESCENT

Parents who feel they have to nag their adolescents continually to do their chores may wonder whether teenagers process any information at all! Actually, learning, memory, and problem solving continue to improve during the adolescent years. First, new learning and memory strategies emerge; it is only during adolescence that the memory strategy of elaboration is mastered (Pressley, 1982). Adolescents also develop and refine advanced learning and memory strategies that are highly relevant to school learning—for example, note taking and underlining. Ann Brown and Sandra Smiley (1978) looked at the performance of students from the fifth grade (age 11) to eleventh and twelfth grade who were asked to recall a story. Some learners were asked to recall the story immediately; others were given an additional five minutes to study it before they were tested. Amazingly, fifth graders gained almost nothing from the extra study period, except for those few who used the time to underline or take notes. Junior high school students benefited to an extent, but only in senior high school did most students use underlining and note taking effectively to improve their recall. When some students were told to underline or take notes if they wished, fifth graders still did not improve, largely because they did not use these strategies to highlight the most important points. (Many underlined almost everything!) Thus strategies for studying readings and then identifying important points improve considerably between elementary school and high school (see also Brown, Day, & Jones, 1983).

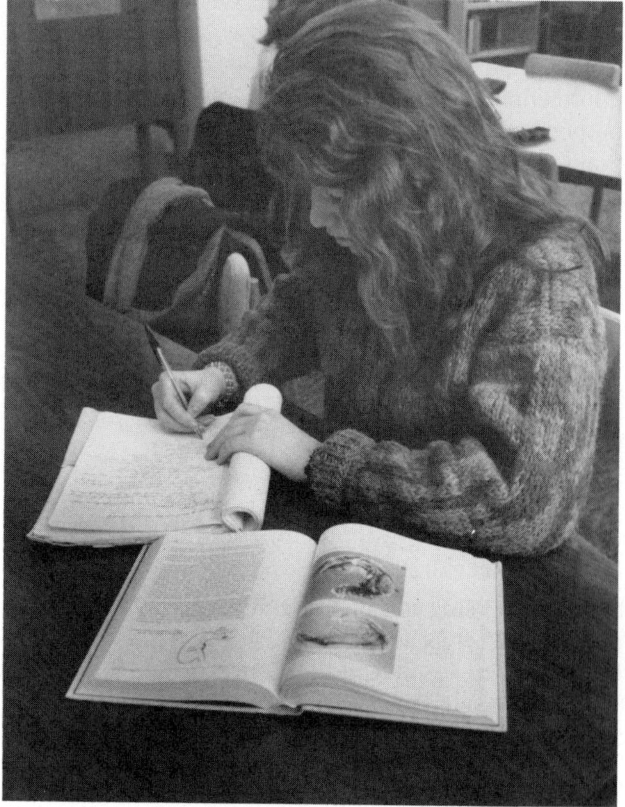

Note taking is an effective study strategy. As adolescents mature, they become more likely to take notes and become better at identifying the important main ideas.

As they get older, adolescents also seem to make *more deliberate* use of strategies that younger children use more or less unconsciously (Bjorklund, 1985). For example, they may deliberately organize a list of words instead of simply making use of any natural organization or grouping that happens to be there already. And they use existing strategies more *selectively* (Bray, Hersh, & Turner, 1985; Bray, Justice, & Zahm, 1983; Miller & Weiss, 1981), for example, memorizing the material on which they know they will be tested and deliberately forgetting the rest. Patricia Miller and Michael Weiss (1981) asked children to remember the locations of animals that had been hidden behind flaps but also placed a household object near each animal. Fewer 7- and 10-year-olds than 13-year-olds could recall where the animals had been hidden, but the younger children remembered *more* than 13-year-olds did about task-irrelevant information (the locations of the household objects). Norman Bray and his colleagues (1985) suggest that between ages 7 and 11, children get better at distinguishing between what is relevant and what is irrelevant information, but that during adolescence they advance even farther by selectively using their memory strategies only on the relevant material. In short, adolescents do not bother with material after being told, in effect, "This won't be on the test."

Other strides are made in adolescence. Basic capacities continue to improve so that adolescents can remember more digits in memory-span tests than children can (Dempster, 1981). Of course, adolescents also continue to expand their knowledge base, so they may do better on some tasks than children do simply because they know more about the topic. The more specific kind of knowledge called metacognition also improves (Brown, Bransford, Ferrara, & Campione, 1983). Poor readers and younger readers appear to have a variety of metacognitive limitations (Baker & Brown, 1984). For example, they have trouble tailoring their reading strategies to different purposes (studying versus skimming). They may also have difficulty realizing when they don't understand and doing something about it. Growth in strategies, basic capacities, knowledge base, and metacognition probably also helps explain the growth in everyday problem-solving ability that occurs during the adolescent years (Berg, 1989).

As Brown, Bransford, Ferrara, and Campione (1983) have concluded, development between grades six and twelve on school tasks such as reading and writing seems to parallel development during elementary school on simpler memory tasks. Students at first use effective study strategies only here and there; that is, they show production deficiencies. But as they mature and as their metacognitive abilities improve, they begin to master the strategies more fully so that they can apply them *deliberately and spontaneously* across a wider variety of tasks.

THE ADULT

If you are about age 20, you will be pleased to know that the young adult college student has served as the standard of effective information processing against which all other age groups are compared. Although information processes are thought to be most efficient in young adults, some growth occurs during the adult years before aging begins to take a toll on some memory and problem-solving capacities.

Adult Learning, Memory, and Problem Solving: Developing Expertise

Young adults still have some mental skills to learn. Comparisons of people who are new to their chosen fields of study with those who are more experienced make this clear. At Piaget's highest stage of cognitive development, formal operations, adults often perform better in their areas of specialization than in unfamiliar areas. Similarly, adults often learn, remember, and solve problems best in their areas of expertise. Experts process information differently than novices do; that is, knowledge base influences both the nature and effectiveness of information processing.

Consider the effects of knowledge base on memory. How might adults who are baseball experts and adults who care little for baseball perceive and remember the same game? George Spilich and his associates (1979) had college students who knew a great deal or very little about baseball listen to a tape of half an inning of play. Experts recalled more of the information central to the game—the important plays and the fate of each batter, in proper order—whereas novices were caught up by less central facts such as the threatening weather conditions and the number of people attending the game. Experts also recalled more central details—for example, noting that a double was a line drive down the left-field line rather than just a double.

Now consider the impact of increased expertise in one's career on the ability to solve problems. Alan Lesgold (1984) and his associates observed how radiologists at different stages of career development interpret X-rays and make diagnoses based on them. Lesgold emphasizes that these physicians were developing and using schemata, or organized networks of knowledge stored in long-term memory, to guide their perceptions of X-rays and their ultimate decisions. Resident radiologists recently out of medical school seemed to rely on general, relatively simple schemes and principles of diagnosis (for example, noting all the abnormalities one can and then looking for a disease that fits). These novices often did not consider additional information such as the patient's medical condition or the exact location of a dark spot on the film, factors that could mean the difference between seeing a collapsed lung and seeing a tumor. Experienced physicians did consider these sorts of complexities. They had more complete schemes and could quickly, surely, and almost automatically call up just the specific knowledge they needed to make an accurate diagnosis. Interestingly, residents who were fairly experienced but were not yet experts seemed to perform less well than "rookie" residents on occasion. Lesgold suggests that these moderately experienced doctors may have been in the process of forming more complex schemes but were not yet automatizing them.

In short, experts know more, and they use specific stored knowledge to solve problems, quickly detecting how new problems stack up against old problems (Chi, Glaser, & Rees, 1982). In effect, experts do not need to think much—like experienced drivers who can put themselves on "autopilot," free to use their minds for more than driving unless some new situation occurs. Organized knowledge allows them to use well-learned routines quickly and accurately. Although adults continue to use general learning and memory strategies to deal with problems outside their expertise, they also develop highly effective, specific, and automatized information-processing routines that help them learn, remember, and think very effectively in their areas of specialization.

Do You Lose It in Old Age?

Many people worry that aging means losing your memory. Indeed, many older adults feel that they are becoming forgetful (Sunderland, Watts, Baddeley, & Harris, 1986). No less an expert on learning than B. F. Skinner has complained about memory problems (see Box 8.4)! In one study, young and elderly adults kept diaries of their problems with memory in everyday life (Cavanaugh, Grady, & Perlmutter, 1983). The older adults reported more such problems, especially when it came to remembering names, routines like filling the car with gas, and objects such as the book that they would need later. Older adults were also more upset by their memory lapses, perhaps because they viewed them as signs of aging.

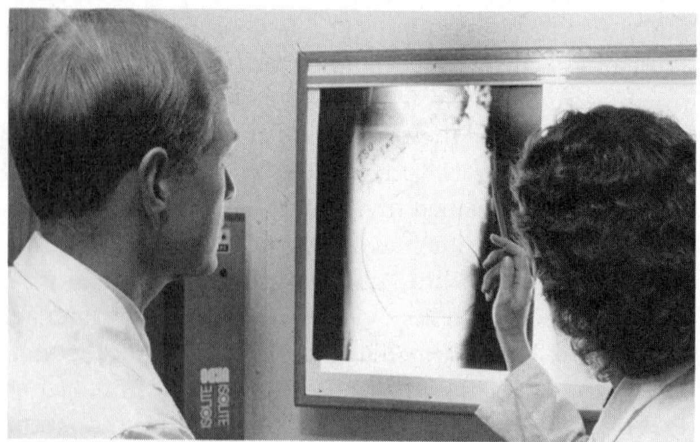

As adults learn the ropes of their chosen fields, they can draw from their well-organized knowledge bases to find just the right information to fit the problem at hand. Solving problems becomes automatic and effortless.

Declines in Learning and Memory

Does research support the idea that learning and memory capabilities decline in old age? Much of it does, but the following qualifications are important:

- Most of the research is based on cross-sectional studies comparing age groups, which suggests that the age differences detected could be related to factors other than age.
- Declines, when observed, do not occur until the late 60s and the 70s and are slight.
- Only some older people have memory problems.
- Old people do poorly on some tasks but well on others (for example, poorly on meaningless tasks but well on meaningful everyday tasks).

Of the types of memory stores examined earlier—the sensory register, short-term memory, and long-term memory—which is most likely to decline in old age? Just as children show little improvement with age in the functioning of the sensory register, declines in this component of the memory system are very modest in old age, and their significance is unclear (Poon, 1985). Short-term memory capacity, as indicated by the number of digits or letters that can be immediately recalled, improves over childhood and declines modestly in late adulthood (Botwinick, 1984). *Long-term memory*—the aspect of memory that shows the greatest growth during childhood—shows the greatest decline in old age.

"Ah," you may say, "but I have a grandmother who can remember every detail of what happened years ago." Most of us do know an older person with a seemingly phenomenal memory for the distant past. And many older people feel that they can remember events of the distant past vividly but forget what happened yesterday. But are these impressions to be trusted? After all, it is likely that older people's stories of the past are well rehearsed or often repeated accounts of events highly important to them

Box 8.4
B. F. Skinner Fights an Aging Mind

As he neared 80, B. F. Skinner (1983) reflected on his own aging and shared his tactics for remaining intellectually active. From his perspective as an operant learning theorist, he viewed old age as a time when reinforcement becomes scarce (for example, food doesn't taste as good, symphonies don't sound as good, and rewards for professional achievement don't come as often). Not surprisingly, he saw the key to successful aging as a matter of changing one's environment so that staying involved in things is reinforced and therefore is worth the effort. For example, turning up the volume on the stereo can make listening to music more reinforcing.

As for his mental life, Skinner, like many older people, had suffered at least modest memory loss: "One of the more disheartening experiences of old age is discovering that a point you have just made—so significant, so beautifully expressed—was made by you in something you published a long time ago" (p. 242). His coping device? Plenty of use of memory aids—for example, leaving his umbrella on the doorknob or attached to his briefcase so that he would remember to take it, keeping a notepad near the bed to write down ideas for later use, and keeping books within easy reach while writing. He and his wife even worked out ways to hide their memory lapses when they were introduced to someone whose name they could not remember: "If there is any conceivable chance that she could have met the person, I simply say to her, 'Of course, you remember . . . ?' and she grasps the outstretched hand and says, 'Yes, of course. How are you?' The acquaintance may not remember meeting my wife, but is not sure of his or her memory, either" (p. 240).

Thus by making small changes in his environment, Skinner was able to compensate for intellectual losses and remain an active and productive scholar. Most of us wish we could do half as well!

(Schaie & Willis, 1986). Some of those stories may not even be accurate. Older adults who feel they can recall the distant past as though it were yesterday—and yesterday as though it had not happened—are being unfair to themselves, comparing important or vivid events of the distant past with mundane recent events such as watching television or eating dinner (Erber, 1981).

Memory researchers have more recently tried to distinguish objectively between memory for the distant past, or **remote long-term memory**, and immediate long-term memory (for example, memory for what happened yesterday or last week). For example, Leonard Poon and his associates tested recognition memory for public events occurring from the 1910s to the 1970s (Poon, Fozard, Paulshock, & Thomas, 1979). People from their 30s to their 60s recognized events from the 1950s, 1960s, and 1970s about equally well. Memory of events from earlier decades was actually better among older persons than among 30-year-olds (though here the comparison was not entirely fair because older adults had been alive at the time but younger ones had not). In such research, it is hard to control for how and when knowledge of past events was gained, and findings are somewhat inconsistent. Overall, though, older adults do not seem to remember significant events from the remote past less well than younger adults do (Lachman & Lachman, 1980).

Like people of any age, elderly adults have more trouble remembering a given event as more time passes (Botwinick, 1984). Thus they will generally remember an important event that took place a year ago better than an equally important event that took place 20 years ago. However, older adults are most likely to show memory deficits when their immediate rather than remote long-term memory is tested—that is, when they are asked to learn *new material* and then retrieve it from long-term memory (Poon, 1985). Might this be because most studies of adult memory have involved asking people to learn unfamiliar material in a laboratory setting? Such studies seem to indicate that the aspects of learning and memory in which older adults look deficient in comparison to young and middle-aged adults are some of the same areas in which young children look bad in comparison to older children (for reviews, see Botwinick, 1984; Craik, 1977; Guttentag, 1985; Perlmutter, 1986; Poon, 1985). Here are some of the major weaknesses—and, by implication, strengths—of the average older adult:

On the average, older adults are slower at learning and retrieving information than younger adults are; they may need to go through the material more times to learn it equally well and need more time to respond when their memory is tested. Thus they are hurt by time limits, whereas allowing them to set their own pace during learning or testing helps them close the gap between themselves and younger adults (Botwinick, 1984; Canestrari, 1963).

Older adults sometimes do not process new information as deeply or elaborately as younger adults do, thinking about its meaning (Erber, Herman, & Botwinick, 1980). Jerome Yesavage, Terrence Rose, and Gordon Bower (1983) were able to help elderly people associate names with faces by getting them to encode the information very elaborately—for example, learning who "Mr. Whalen" was by changing his name to "whale," forming an image of a whale in his mouth (his most prominent facial feature), *and* thinking about the pleasantness of this image. Some older adults fail to retrieve information on occasion because they never thoroughly encoded or learned it in the first place.

Older adults fare especially poorly when the material is unfamiliar—when they cannot tie it to their existing knowledge. The gap between younger and older learners is therefore greater when the material is meaningless or unfamiliar to both groups than when it is meaningful or familiar. In a vivid demonstration of how familiarity influences memory, Barrett and Wright (1981) had young and old adults examine modern words likely to be most familiar to young adults (for example, dude, disco, and bummer) and words from the past likely to be most familiar to older adults (for example, pompadour, gramophone, and vamp). Sure enough, young adults outperformed older adults on the "new" words, but old adults outperformed young adults on the "old" words, demonstrating the effects of differences in knowledge base. Unfortunately, many laboratory tasks involve learning material that is both meaningless and unfamiliar, making older adults look worse than they do in more meaningful everyday contexts (Poon, 1985).

Many older adults *seem less likely to use effective memory strategies* as often as younger adults do; most are capable of using strategies such as organization and elaboration but show *production deficiencies.* As a result, coaching in memory strategies sometimes benefits older adults more than younger adults (Hultsch, 1971; Poon, 1985). Perhaps older adults are just out of practice.

Older adults are likely to be *more deficient in recall memory than in recognition memory.* Age differences in recognition memory are minimal, but age differences in recall are often sizable. In a study of memory for high school classmates (Bahrick, Bahrick, & Wittlinger, 1975), even adults who were almost 35 years away from graduation still could recognize which of five names matched a picture in their yearbook about 90% of the time. However, the ability to recall names of classmates when given only their photos as cues dropped considerably as the age of the rememberer increased. Basically, some older people have difficulty retrieving information that is "in there" when they are asked to recall it. Thus problems in retrieval, along with problems in encoding new material, contribute to memory difficulties.

Finally, older adults seem to have *more difficulty on tasks that require conscious or deliberate information processing* than on tasks that are more automatic (Hasher & Zacks, 1979, 1984; Mitchell & Perlmutter, 1986; Rabinowitz, 1986). Consider this example of automatic learning: You know, without ever having tried to learn it, that the word *result* appears more frequently in speech and writing than the word *insult.* Lynn Hasher and Rose Zacks (1979) have discovered that young children, older adults, and young adults are equally accurate at estimating how frequently they have encountered objects or words presented to them. This ability to remember how frequently something has occurred seems to be automatic and effortless at all ages (Ellis, Palmer, & Reeves, 1988). By contrast, actively recalling the specific items in a list of unrelated words requires effortful use of strategies.

Now consider the fact that well-practiced tasks can be performed more automatically than less-practiced tasks. For example, over the years readers get lots of practice in asking themselves whether what they have just read follows from what came before, or makes sense in context; they rarely perform the more effort-consuming task of deciding whether specific sentences appeared in passages they have read (unless, of course, they are taking tests in school). Sure enough, Lynne Reder, Cynthia Wible, and John Martin (1986) found that elderly adults were just as good as young adults at judging whether sentences could be plausibly based on the story they had read. This was a well-practiced, automatic activity. However, older adults were deficient when it came to deliberately searching their memories to judge whether specific sentences had or had not appeared in the story (see Figure 8.10). Thus, age differences are generally smaller when well-practiced (and more automatic) skills are assessed than when less-practiced (and more effort-consuming) skills are assessed (Denney, 1982).

Overall, these findings do suggest that older adults are likely to do less well than younger adults in just about the same areas in which young children do less well than older children. Does the older adult simply function like the young child when it comes to learning and memory, then? Not really. We must ask *why* some older adults have difficulty with some learning and memory tasks, using the hypotheses about learning and memory thought to explain childhood improvements in performance. These hypotheses center on basic capacities, strategy use, metamemory or metacognition, and knowledge base.

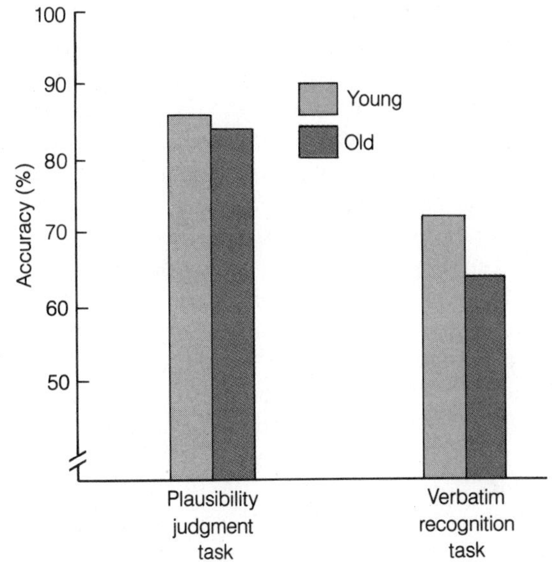

Figure 8.10 Older people don't always do worse than younger people. Comparing college students and college alumni of retirement age, Reder, Wible, and Martin (1986) found that the old were no worse than the young at judging whether statements were plausible according to a story they had read. This may be a well-practiced and automatic cognitive activity. Older adults did do worse at judging whether statements had actually appeared in the story, a less well-practiced task for adults who have been out of school for years. (Adapted from Reder, Wible, & Martin, 1986)

Explaining Declines in Learning and Memory in Old Age

Let's start with the hypothesis that differences in *knowledge base* explain differences between older and younger adults. We immediately encounter a problem: Young children may be ignorant, but elderly adults are not. As we have seen, older adults apparently retain a great deal of information about the past very well. It *is* possible that younger adults know more about the material in some academically oriented laboratory tasks than do older adults whose school experiences are long past. Still, older adults must be viewed as generally at least as knowledgeable as young adults. Deficiencies in knowledge base are probably not the source of most of the memory problems that older adults display.

Perhaps elderly adults, like young children, are deficient in the specific knowledge called metamemory. Marilyn Zivian and Richard Darjes (1983), for example, noted that middle-aged adults who were in college knew more about which memory strategies are most effective, and performed better on a recall test, than did middle-aged adults who were not in school. Both middle-aged adults and older adults who were out of school favored simple rehearsal over superior strategies such as organization. Perhaps knowledge of some of the strategies that prove useful in school—and that also prove useful in laboratory memory tasks—is a bit rusty in many old people. Yet Roger Dixon and David Hultsch (1983a, b) have found that older adults are not deficient in all areas of metamemory; moreover, their actual recall performance is related more to motivational aspects of metamemory (such as the belief that they can control their memory and prevent memory loss in old age) than to factual aspects (such as knowing which memory strategies are best or which memory tasks are hardest). For the most part, then, we can conclude that the ignorance of memory processes that plagues the young child is not a great problem for the older adult (Guttentag, 1985). Chances are that knowledge of memory has more to do with the growth of memory capacity during childhood than with the decline of memory in old age (Perlmutter, 1986). However, it seems that some older adults *believe* that their memories are failing and perform poorly partly as a result (Cavanaugh & Poon, 1989; Hertzog, Hultsch, & Dixon, 1989).

What about the hypothesis that failure to use effective *memory strategies* accounts for deficits in old age? As we have seen, many older adults do show production deficiencies; that is, they do not spontaneously use strategies such as organization. This may indeed be part of the problem. But *why* do many older adults fail to use effective strategies?

According to Robert Guttentag (1985), the answer might lie in our fourth hypothesis—the notion that *basic processing capacities* change with age. Evidence suggests that both young children and old adults need to devote more mental effort and time (more space in short-term, or working, memory) to certain mental operations than older children or young adults do. Tasks that require a great deal of mental effort or the performance of several mental operations at once are likely to cause difficulty. Carrying out a deliberate strategy such as organization or elaboration may use up working space needed for the material being learned.

Unquestionably, the speed of mental operations often declines in old age, possibly because of changes in the brain (Cerella, 1985; Salthouse, 1985; and see Chapter 5 on the slowing of the nervous system in later life). Moreover, we have seen that both younger children and older adults do relatively well when learning and remembering can take place automatically—that is, when mental effort is *not* required. To this point, then, we might conclude that many older adults, while they have a vast knowledge base and a good deal of knowledge about learning and memory, perform basic mental operations relatively slowly, and therefore might not have enough memory capacity left to use mentally taxing memory strategies. But before we accept this conclusion, we should consider some additional hypotheses—hypotheses suggesting that age differences in learning and memory may be due to factors *other than* a decline in basic memory capacities in old age.

One alternative hypothesis is that cohort differences can explain the apparent decline of some learning and memory skills in old age. Elderly people today are less educated, on average, than younger adults are, and they are farther away from their school days. Education is an important influence on learning and memory. Indeed, in one study in Morocco, *only* those individuals who had had formal schooling used the memory strategy of verbal rehearsal, presumably because they learned it in the classroom (Wagner, 1978). Moreover, older adults who are highly educated or who have high verbal ability often perform just as well as younger adults do (Cavanaugh, 1983), and adults who are presently in college outperform those who have been out of school for years and who may have become rusty at the sorts of learning and memory skills required in school (Zivian & Darjes, 1983). Similarly, cohort differences in health might help explain age differences in memory performance, for older adults are more likely than younger adults to have chronic or degenerative diseases, and even mild diseases can impair performance (Barrett & Watkins, 1986). In sum, ill health or educational differences could account for apparent declines in learning and memory in old age.

It is also possible that older adults sometimes perform poorly not because of deficient abilities but because of motivational factors, which are important at all ages. Sometimes old people appear forgetful only because they have been asked to learn and remember material that is of no interest or use to them. In one study in which adults were to learn nonsense syllables, for example, fully 80% of the elderly subjects simply dropped out of the study; they saw no point in learning such nonsense (Hulicka, 1967)! Elderly adults seem to be more likely than young adults to ask whether information is potentially useful to them before they invest energy in learning it (Schaie, 1977/1978).

In addition, some elderly adults adopt a cautious style of responding in the laboratory, not giving an answer unless they are firmly convinced that it is correct (Botwinick, 1984). Some of these individuals may doubt their abilities (Bellucci & Hoyer, 1975) or may respond cautiously to reduce anxiety related to the testing situation (Botwinick, 1984). If elderly adults are rewarded for giving answers of *some kind*, whether right or wrong, they become more motivated to offer guesses and their performance on word-learning tasks improves (Leech & Witte, 1971).

Finally, we must consider the hypothesis that older adults display learning and memory deficits mainly because the tasks that have typically been presented to them are far removed from the everyday contexts in which they normally learn and remember. Consider the difference between remembering a list of food terms in the laboratory and remembering what to buy at the grocery store. In learning a list, the learner may have no choice but to use mental memory strategies such as organization and elaboration. But in everyday life, neither young nor old adults rely on such internal strategies nearly so much as they rely on *external aids*—notes, lists, and the like (Cavanaugh et al., 1983). After all, why conjure images to help one remember what to buy at the supermarket when one can simply write out a shopping list?

In the everyday task of grocery shopping, the job of remembering where to find the baking powder or cream cheese is simplified immensely because one can draw on one's previous experience in the store (one's knowledge base). Moreover, items are embedded in a meaningful context such as the baking section or the dairy section, so cues are available in the store to help one remember. In one demonstration of the importance of such contextual cues (Waddell & Rogoff, 1981), older adults did just as well as middle-aged adults at remembering the locations of objects (toy cars, pieces of furniture, and so on) that had been placed in a meaningful landscape consisting of a parking lot, houses, a church, and other landmarks. They had difficulty only when these items were stripped of a meaningful context and were placed in cubicles. In everyday situations, then, elderly adults can place new information in the context of what they already know and can make use of situational cues to help them remember. As a result, they can often remember as well as or better than younger adults (Poon, 1985).

Impressed by the influence of such factors as educational experience, motivation, and task characteristics on the performance of elderly adults, many researchers are adopting a *contextual perspective* on learning and memory (Hultsch & Dixon, 1984; Labouvie-Vief & Schell, 1982; Poon, 1985). They emphasize that performance on learning and memory tasks derives from an interaction between characteristics of the learner such as goals and motivations, characteristics of the particular task at hand, and characteristics of the broader context in which a task is performed. They are not convinced that older adults lack basic learning and memory capacities, for old people's performance is influenced by the context in which their performance is assessed. Most important, older adults who appear to be deficient in the laboratory often perform very capably on tasks that are highly motivating and presented in a meaningful context. Findings like these cast doubt on the notion that cognitive skills inevitably decline in old age because of a universal biological aging process.

Some researchers even suggest that apparent deficits in older adults may instead be adaptive styles of processing information (Labouvie-Vief & Schell, 1982; Perlmutter, 1986; Poon, 1985). It may, for example, make sense for many older adults to adopt a slower, more cautious style of responding, or to let some cognitive skills grow rusty in order to maintain and strengthen those skills that are most useful to them in everyday life. Marion Perlmutter (1986) suggests that while older adults may know less than younger adults about how to approach the tasks that experimenters have been fond of presenting to them, they may know more than younger adults do about using their stored knowledge effectively in daily life. Children improve their memory for all kinds of things; older adults may improve their memory for relevant things and forget the rest!

In summary, some adults, late in life, experience difficulty on some learning and memory tasks. Changes in basic information-processing capacities may contribute, but so may such factors as limited education, low motivation, and the irrelevance of many laboratory tasks to everyday life.

Problem Solving in Later Adulthood

Just as young children perform more poorly than older children on problem-solving tasks in the laboratory, older adults typically perform more poorly than young adults do. Adults, for example, have been given the same kinds of discrimination learning problems that we illustrated back in Figure 8.8 (p. 253), in which they must figure out which of several attributes of geometric figures is the one the experimenter has in mind. Offenbach (1974) compared children aged 7 to 11, young adults, and old adults on such a task. Performance peaked in young adulthood, and elderly adults sometimes looked bad even in comparison to children. Like children, they often abandoned a good hypothesis after being told their choice was correct, and they sometimes stuck with bad hunches despite evidence to the contrary. However, David Arenberg (1982) found the original task to be confusing to older adults. Instead, he gave men the more realistic task of solving a mystery by determining which of eight foods was always part of a series of meals that had poisoned diners. Among groups of men ranging in age from their 20s to their 80s, average performance decreased steadily as the age of the group increased. However, Arenberg was one of the few researchers to collect longitudinal data, giving these men the same tasks at least six years later. Interestingly, young and middle-aged men tended to improve the second time around; only men who had been in their 70s when first tested showed any decline as they aged, suggesting that very late in life it may become more difficult to sift through a large amount of information to test hypotheses.

Other insights into problem solving over the life span come from research using the twenty-questions task. Subjects are given an array of items and asked to find out, in as few yes/no questions as possible, which item the experimenter has in mind (see Figure 8.11). Nancy Denney (1985) has summarized considerable research on how both children and adults solve this task. The soundest problem-solving strategy, used by both older children and young adults, is to ask **constraint-seeking questions**, questions that rule out more than one item (for example, "Is it an animal?"). Young children and older adults tend to pursue specific hypotheses ("Is it a cow?"). Consequently, they must ask more questions to identify the right object. However, older adults do far better if the task is altered to make it more familiar; they then draw on their knowledge base to solve the problem. For example, when Denney (1980) used an array of playing cards, older adults asked plenty of constraint-seeking questions ("Is it a heart?" or "Is it a face card?"). Thus older adults seem to be able to use effective problem-solving strategies, but often do not use them—still another example of a production deficiency. Because of their underlying knowledge they can be quickly taught through modeling to ask constraint-seeking questions (Denney, Jones, & Krigel, 1979).

Once again we see that the average old person does not perform many laboratory information-processing tasks as well as young and middle-aged adults typically do. Yet the gap can be wide or nonexistent depending on the specific requirements of a problem-solving task (Reese & Rodeheaver, 1985). Problem solving in daily life has barely been explored, but there are hints that the ability to deal with everyday problems such as deciding which purchases to make or how to resolve conflicts with family members improves from early adulthood to middle age and well into old age (Cornelius & Caspi, 1987). Finally, the amount of education a person has had is at least as important as age in determining success at problem solving in the adult years (Denney, 1985).

APPLICATIONS: IMPROVING MEMORY

Have you noticed that the material in this chapter has great potential value to educators? Skinner's operant conditioning principles have long been widely applied to improving classroom learning and motivation. More recently, the information-processing perspective has yielded improved methods for diagnosing learning problems and improving instruction.

Researchers are also learning that there is almost no limit to what the human mind can remember with sufficient training and practice. Ericsson, Chase, and Faloon (1980), for example, put an average college student to work on improving the number of digits he could recall. He practiced for about an hour a day, three to five days a week, for more than a year and a half—over 200 hours in all. His improvement? He went from a memory span of 7 digits to one of 79 digits! His method involved forming meaningful associations between strings of digits and running times—for example, seeing 3492 as "3 minutes and 49 point 2 seconds, near world-record mile time" (p. 1181). It also involved chunking numbers into groups of three or four and then organizing the chunks into large units.

Now, what about the young children and older adults who show memory difficulties? We have already seen that they can often benefit from coaching in the use of effective memory strategies. Forrest Scogin, Martha Storandt, and Leeanne Lott (1985) created a self-study manual from which elderly adults could learn strategies such as using

Figure 8.11 A 20-questions game. You can try the 20-questions game on a young child or a friend by thinking of one item in the matrix and asking your testee to find out which it is by asking you yes/no questions. Look for constraint-seeking questions (for example, "Is it animate?"), and note the total number of questions that must be asked to identify the correct item.

imagery to associate names with faces and chunking or categorizing the information to be remembered. Adults who worked through the 16 one-hour study units still complained about memory problems but improved their performance on memory tests. Yet coaching in strategies like organization and elaboration sometimes improves learning in a specific situation but does not carry over well to new situations (Pressley, Forrest-Pressley, Elliott-Faust, & Miller, 1985). What is missing?

Leading researchers claim that transfer of skills requires that students be explicitly trained to plan and control their use of strategies (Campione, Brown, & Bryant, 1985; Paris & Oka, 1986; Pressley et al., 1985)—in other words, metacognition must be taught. Scott Paris and Evelyn Oka (1986) undertook a major project designed to teach third and fifth graders how to plan and use effective reading strategies—for example, to set reading goals ("My goal is to learn the main causes of the American Revolution"); to stop along the way to paraphrase what they had read; and to check to see whether the reading was making sense to them or needed to be reviewed. The training approach involved group discussion of texts the students were reading. With guidance from an adult expert, students gradually became better able to think about reading strategies and to apply the strategies to their reading activities. The training was very effective in teaching these metacognitive skills (see also Baker & Brown, 1984). It is perhaps odd that with all that teachers attempt to teach, they rarely do much to teach students how to learn!

An entirely different approach to memory improvement is to change the learning situation rather than the learner (Pressley, 1983). If, for example, young children or some older adults do not spontaneously organize the material they are learning to make it more meaningful, one can organize it for them. If the material is unfamiliar, one can use examples or analogies that will help learners tie it to something that is familiar (for example, teaching a senior citizens' group about the federal budget by likening it to their personal budgets). If young children and older adults need more time, let them set their own pace. Surely the best of all possible worlds for the learner would be one in which these two approaches are combined, so that materials and teaching techniques are tailored to the learner's information-processing capacities *and* training is offered in how to stretch those capacities.

REFLECTIONS

We have covered a lot of ground in this chapter. Reflecting on the development of learning and information-processing capacities, it strikes us that the information-processing approach can provide a rich account of why people of different ages succeed or fail in their efforts to learn, remember, and think. This approach is popular among developmentalists today, and its potential is just being realized.

It also strikes us that research on information processing does not paint a very pretty picture of either the very young child or the elderly adult. Infants start life with a capacity to learn, but learning is quite a struggle at first. Even by preschool age, children learn many things slowly, remember incompletely, and have difficulty solving complex problems. Capacities improve, only to become shakier in old age, when many adults do have a feeling that they are getting more forgetful and once again struggle to solve problems in the laboratory. But the laboratory and the real world are not the same. Recall that this same "incompetent" preschooler is, after all, acquiring language in no time at all and absorbing knowledge like a sponge. Surely the more deliberate and organized information-processing strategies can wait until later in childhood! And those "less competent" older adults also have many things down quite nicely. They've become experts at living their lives, able to draw on stored knowledge and automatized processing routines to do the tasks they need to do. And if they become a little forgetful as they age, most compensate quite well with such tricks as notes on the refrigerator (Cavanaugh, Grady, & Perlmutter, 1983). In short, humans seem well adapted to do with their minds exactly what is most important for them at each stage of the life span. In this sense, then, the human mind is remarkable at any age. ❦

SUMMARY POINTS

1. Learning, a relatively permanent change in behavior resulting from experience, is the process by which new information, attitudes, abilities, and habits are acquired.

2. The four basic types of learning are habituation, classical conditioning, operant conditioning, and observational learning. Habituation is learning not to respond to a repeatedly presented

stimulus. In classical conditioning, an initially neutral stimulus is repeatedly paired with an unconditioned stimulus that always elicits an unconditioned response; consequently, the neutral stimulus becomes a conditioned stimulus for the response. Many emotional responses are acquired this way.

3. In operant conditioning, what is learned is an association between a response or behavior and the consequences that it produces. In reinforcement (positive or negative), consequences strengthen behavior. Punishment decreases the strength of behavior, and extinction occurs when no consequences follow the behavior. Both the timing and frequency of reinforcement are important. In behavior modification, learning techniques such as shaping are applied to teach and strengthen desirable habits.

4. In observational learning, the individual learns from observing another person (a model). Learning may occur in the absence of reinforcement even if performance (imitation) does not. However, the consequences of the action for the model or the learner can affect the likelihood of performance. Observational learning is cognitive learning, involving selective attention and symbolic representation of what was seen.

5. The behaviorist perspective has given way to the more cognitive information-processing approach. The human "computer" takes in information into a sensory register, short-term memory, and long-term memory (the encoding process); stores it; retrieves it (demonstrating either recognition or recall memory); and uses it to solve problems.

6. Infants are capable of learning from the start. They show recognition memory at birth, simple recall in the presence of cues at 2 or 3 months, recall in the absence of cues toward the end of the first year, and deliberate attempts to retrieve something by age 2. Basic learning processes improve considerably over infancy and into childhood and continue to operate throughout the life span.

7. Learning and memory continue to improve during childhood: (a) Basic information-processing capacity increases as the brain matures and fundamental processes are automatized, (b) memory strategies improve, leading finally to their spontaneous use, (c) metamemory improves, and (d) the general knowledge base grows, improving the processing of new information in areas of expertise.

8. During the "5-to-7 shift," children become more able to use verbal mediation and improve their ability to form and test hypotheses. Even young children use rules to solve problems but fail to solve problems correctly so long as their rules fail to encompass all the relevant aspects of the problem.

9. Adolescents master advanced learning strategies such as elaboration, note taking, and underlining; use their strategies more deliberately and selectively; and use their increased metacognitive abilities to guide their learning and remembering.

10. As adults gain expertise, they develop large and organized knowledge bases as well as specialized, highly effective, and automatized ways of using their knowledge.

11. Many older adults perform less well than young adults on some kinds of memory tasks. Functional declines of the sensory register and short-term memory are minor compared to declines in long-term memory, especially when immediate (rather than remote) long-term memory is assessed. Compared with younger adults, many older adults are, at least on many laboratory tasks, slower learners; do not encode material as thoroughly; have special difficulties with unfamiliar or meaningless material; often show production deficiencies; are more at a disadvantage on recall than on recognition memory tasks; and are especially deficient on tasks that require "effortful" processing or unpracticed skills.

12. Older adults retain their knowledge base well and have only limited deficiencies in metamemory. Possibly a late-life decrease in basic processing capacity slows the performance of many elderly adults and impedes use of memory strategies. Contextual factors such as cohort differences, low motivation, and the irrelevance of many laboratory tasks to everyday life may also account for age differences in learning and memory.

13. On average, older adults also perform less well than younger adults do on some problem-solving tasks, but everyday problem-solving skills are likely to be maintained well in old age.

14. Basic learning theories and the information-processing approach can be applied to improve education: Practice improves memory skills; coaching in strategy use combined with systematic teaching of metacognitive skills can benefit both young children and old people, as can altering instruction to better match the capacities of the learner.

KEY TERMS

behavior modification
classical conditioning
conditioned response (CR)
conditioned stimulus (CS)
constraint-seeking questions
continuous reinforcement
counterconditioning
elaboration
encoding
extinction
5-to-7 shift
habituation
infantile amnesia
information-processing approach
knowledge base
learning
long-term memory
metamemory
negative reinforcement
nonreversal shift
observational learning
operant conditioning
organization (as a memory strategy)
partial reinforcement
positive reinforcement
problem solving
production deficiency
punishment
recall memory
recognition memory
rehearsal
remote long-term memory
retrieval
reversal shift
sensory register
shaping
short-term memory
storage
time out
unconditioned response (UCR)
unconditioned stimulus (UCS)
verbal mediation

CHAPTER

9

Mental Abilities

When he was 3 years old, the 19th-century English philosopher John Stuart Mill began to study Greek under his father's direction. At age 6½, he wrote a history of Rome. He tackled Latin at age 8, and before age 9 he was reading original Latin works. At 8 he also began his study of geometry and algebra. Mill's IQ score has been estimated at 190, where 100 is average (Cox, 1926).

At the age of 35, Michael continues to live in an institution for the mentally retarded. He has been labeled profoundly retarded and has an IQ score of 17, as nearly as it can be estimated. Michael responds to people with grins and is able to walk in a fashion, but he cannot feed or dress himself and does not use language.

As these examples indicate, the range of human cognitive abilities is immense. So far, our exploration of cognitive development has focused mainly on what human minds have in common, not on how they differ. Piaget, after all, was interested in identifying *universal* stages describing the ways in which thought is structured or organized by all normal humans as they develop. Similarly, the information-processing approach has been used mainly to understand the basic cognitive processes that all people use to learn, remember, and solve problems.

This chapter continues exploring how the human mind normally changes over the life span, but with a greater emphasis on individual differences in cognitive abilities. It introduces still another approach to the study of the mind: the *psychometric*, or testing, approach to intelligence that has led to the creation of intelligence tests. It examines how performance on intelligence tests changes over the life span, touching on the hereditary and environmental influences that make one person more "intelligent" than another. It views both the gifted and the mentally retarded individual from a life-span perspective. Finally, it considers forms of intellectual ability that are not typically measured by intelligence tests, especially creative abilities.

WHAT IS INTELLIGENCE?

Piaget defined intelligence as "adaptive thinking or action" (Piaget, 1950). Other experts have offered different definitions, many of which have centered in some way on the ability to think abstractly or to solve problems effectively (Sternberg & Berg, 1986). Early definitions of intelligence tended to reflect the assumption that intelligence is innate intellectual ability, genetically determined and thus fixed at conception. It has now become clear that intelligence is *not* fixed. Instead, it is changeable or subject to environmental influence, for an individual's intelligence test scores may vary—often considerably—over a lifetime. Bear in mind that understandings of this complex human quality have changed since the first intelligence tests were created at the turn of the century—and that there is still no single, universally accepted definition of intelligence.

The Psychometric Approach to Intelligence

The research tradition that spawned the development of standardized tests of intelligence is the **psychometric approach**. According to its theorists, intelligence is a trait or a set of traits that characterizes some people to a greater extent than others. The goals, then, are to

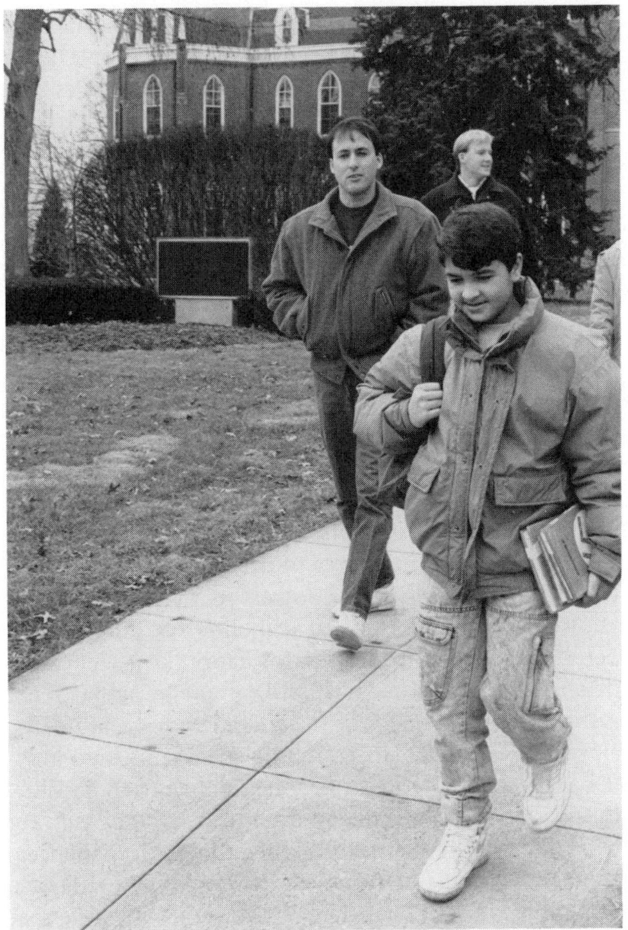

Gifted children in college? A special program at the University of Washington allows highly selected gifted children as young as 10 to thrive as college students (Robinson & Robinson, 1982). Some minds develop faster and farther than others.

identify these traits precisely and to measure them so that differences among individuals can be described. But from the start, experts could not agree on whether intelligence is one general cognitive ability or many specific abilities.

Is Intelligence a Single Attribute or Many Attributes?

One way of trying to determine whether intelligence is a single ability or many abilities is to ask a group of subjects to perform a large number of mental tasks and then to analyze their performance using a statistical procedure called **factor analysis**. This technique identifies clusters of tasks or test items (called *factors*) that are highly related with one another and unrelated to other items. Suppose, for example, that the items given to a group include many that require verbal skills (for example, defining words) and many that require mathematical skills (solving arithmetic puzzles). Now suppose that people who do well on any verbal item also do well on other verbal items, and people who do well on any math problem also do well on other math problems, but that people who do well on verbal problems may perform either poorly or well on math problems, and vice versa. In this case, math performance does not correlate highly with verbal performance, and factor analysis would reveal a "verbal ability factor" that is distinct from a "math ability factor."

There would seem to be two separate abilities here, and we could not predict from someone's verbal ability score how high that person's math ability score would be. If, by contrast, correlations among the items revealed that those people who do well on any item in the test tend to do well on others as well, it would seem that one general ability factor is involved in performance on both verbal and math problems. This research method has been used to try to understand whether intelligence is one ability or many abilities.

Charles Spearman (1927) was among the first to use factor analysis to study intelligence. He concluded that a general mental ability (called *g*) contributes to performance on many different kinds of tasks. However, he also noticed that a student who excelled at most tasks might also score very low on a particular measure (for example, memory for words). So he proposed that intelligence has two aspects: *g*, or general ability, and *s*, or special abilities, each of which is specific to a particular kind of task.

When Louis Thurstone (1938; Thurstone & Thurstone, 1941) factor-analyzed test scores obtained by eighth graders and college students, he identified seven fairly distinct factors that he called *primary mental abilities*: spatial ability, perceptual speed (the quick noting of visual detail), numerical reasoning (arithmetic skills), verbal meaning (defining words), word fluency (speed in recognizing words), memory, and inductive reasoning (forming a rule to describe a set of observations). Thus Thurstone concluded that Spearman's general ability factor should be broken into several distinct mental abilities.

The controversy was not over. J. P. Guilford (1967) proposed that there are as many as 120 distinct mental abilities! He argued that there are four kinds of intellectual *contents* (things that people can think about such as ideas or the behaviors of other people); five types of mental *operations* or actions on these contents (such as recognizing, remembering, or evaluating); and six kinds of intellectual *products* or outcomes of thinking (such as a concept or an inference). His **structure-of-intellect model** therefore allows for as many as 120 abilities if one considers all the possible combinations of the contents, operations, and products ($4 \times 5 \times 6 = 120$). For example, among the many kinds of items that Guilford created was the one in Figure 9.1, which measures "social intelligence." The test taker must act on a *behavioral* content (the figure's facial expression), using the operation of *cognition*, to produce a particular product, the likely *implication* of that facial expression.

Obviously the use of factor analysis has not exactly settled the question of what intelligence is! The specific methods of factor analysis used by various researchers have differed, and the results of a factor analysis depend on how many different kinds of tasks are included in the group of tasks given to test takers. Moreover, the researcher's own interpretations of the resulting patterns of correlations influence how factors are labeled. There does seem to be agreement that intelligence is more than just one general ability that determines how well people do on *all* cognitive tasks. On the other hand, most studies suggest that there are considerably fewer mental abilities than Guilford's 120 (Brody & Brody, 1976).

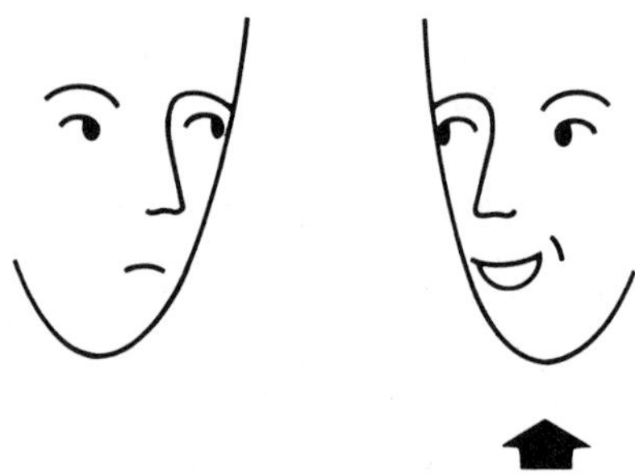

1. I'm glad you're feeling a little better.
2. You make the funniest faces!
3. Didn't I tell you she'd say "No"?

Figure 9.1 An item from one of Guilford's tests of social intelligence. The task is to read the characters' expressions and to decide what the person marked by the arrow is most probably saying to the other person. You may wish to try this item yourself (the correct answer appears below). (Adapted from Guilford, 1967)

Answer: 3.

A Contemporary Psychometric View of Intelligence

Raymond Cattell and John Horn have greatly influenced current research by proposing that Spearman's *g* and Thurstone's seven major mental abilities can be divided into two major dimensions of intellect: fluid intelligence and crystallized intelligence (Cattell, 1963; Horn & Cattell, 1967; Horn, 1982). **Fluid intelligence** is the ability to use one's mind actively to solve novel problems—for example, to solve verbal analogies, remember unrelated pairs of words, or recognize relationships among geometric figures. The skills involved are not taught and are believed to be relatively free of cultural influences. **Crystallized intelligence**, in contrast, is the ability to use knowledge acquired through schooling and other life experiences. Tests of general information ("At what temperature does water boil?"), word comprehension ("What is the meaning of *duplicate*?"), and numerical abilities are all measures of crystallized intelligence. Thus fluid intelligence seems to involve using one's mind in new and flexible ways, while crystallized intelligence involves using what one may have already learned through experience.

The concepts of fluid and crystallized intelligence have proved useful, but there are those who believe that none of the psychometric theories of intelligence have fully described what it means to be an intelligent person. Let us examine a way of thinking about intelligence that is quite different from regarding it as some specified number of intellectual factors. Doing so will help us capture the nature of intelligence—and help us bear in mind the limitations of the IQ tests used to measure it.

A Modern Information-Processing Theory of Intelligence

Robert Sternberg (1985) has recently proposed a **triarchic theory of intelligence** that emphasizes three aspects of intelligent behavior: context, experience, and information-processing components. First, Sternberg argues that what is defined as intelligent behavior depends on the sociocultural *context* in which it is displayed. Intelligent people adapt to the environment they are in (for example, a job setting), or they shape that environment to suit them better, or they find a better environment. Such people have "street smarts." Psychologists, according to Sternberg, must begin to understand intelligence as behavior in the real world, not as behavior in taking tests.

This perspective views intelligent behavior as varying from one culture or subculture to another, from one period in history to another, and from one period of the life span to another. For example, Sternberg describes attending a conference in Venezuela and showing up at 8:00 A.M. sharp, only to find that he and four other North Americans were the only ones there. A behavior that is "intelligent" in North America proved to be rather "dumb" in a culture where expectations about punctuality are different. Sternberg also notes that what is intelligent can change over time. Numerical abilities once played an important role in intelligent behavior in our own society but may no longer be as important now that calculators and computers are widely used. And certainly the infant learning how to master new toys shows a different kind of intelligence than the adult mastering a college curriculum. Thus our definition of the intelligent infant must differ from our definition of the intelligent adult.

To understand what our particular culture considers to be intelligent, Sternberg and his colleagues asked both experts and average people about what behaviors they think reflect intelligence (Sternberg, Conway, Ketron, & Bernstein, 1981). Although there were some differences, experts and lay people agreed that intelligence boils down to three main abilities: problem-solving ability, verbal ability, and social competence (for example, being sensitive to other people's needs). Of course, this is a view of how intelligence is defined *in our culture*. The outcome might be different if people in Nepal, Botswana, or Thailand were surveyed (Jayanthi & Rogoff, 1985).

The second aspect of the triarchic theory focuses on the role of *experience* in intelligence. What is intelligent when one first encounters a new task is not the same as what is intelligent after extensive experience with that task. The first kind of intelligence, *response to novelty*, requires active and conscious information processing. Sternberg believes that relatively novel tasks provide the best measures of intelligence—so long as they are not so totally foreign that one has no chance to bring one's knowledge to bear on them (for example, calculus problems presented to a 5-year-old). Novel tasks get at the individual's ability to come up with good ideas or fresh insights.

In daily life, however, people also perform more or less intelligently on tasks they have done over and over (reading the newspaper, for example). This second kind of intelligence reflects **automatization**, or an increased efficiency of information processing with practice. It is intelligent to develop little "programs in the mind" for performing common everyday activities like driving efficiently and unthinkingly. To assess a test-taker's behavior, says Sternberg, it is important to know how familiar a task is to that person. Giving people of two different cultural groups an intelligence test in which the items are familiar to one group and novel to the other introduces **culture bias**, making it difficult to obtain a fair assessment of the groups' relative abilities.

The third aspect of the triarchic theory focuses on *information-processing components*. As an information-processing theorist, Sternberg believes that the theories of intelligence underlying the development of IQ tests ignore *how* people produce intelligent answers. He argues that the components of intelligent behavior range from identifying the problem to carrying out strategies to solve it, and that a full picture of intelligence includes not only the number of answers people get right but the processes they use to arrive at answers and the efficiency with which they use those processes.

So, fully assessing how intelligent Harry and Huang are requires consideration of the *context* in which they perform (their age, culture, and historical period); their previous *experience* with a task (whether their behavior reflects response to novelty or automatized processes); and their information-processing approach. In addition, we might also recognize that individuals can be more or less able in managing their environments, dealing with the novel or the familiar, and carrying out logical thought processes. Unfortunately, the widely used tests of intelligence do not reflect this sophisticated view of intelligence.

HOW IS INTELLIGENCE MEASURED?

When psychologists first began to devise intelligence tests at the turn of the century, their concern was not with defining the nature of intelligence but with the more practical task of determining which schoolchildren were likely to be slow learners. Consequently, many tests had no precisely defined theory of intelligence behind them and were originally intended for assessing intelligence in children, not in adults.

Alfred Binet and the Stanford-Binet Test

Alfred Binet and a colleague, Théodore Simon, produced the forerunner of our modern intelligence tests. In 1904 they were commissioned by the French government to devise a test that would identify "dull" children who might need special instruction. Binet and Simon devised a large battery of tasks measuring the skills believed to be necessary for classroom learning: attention, perception, memory, reasoning, verbal comprehension, and so on. Items that discriminated between normal children and children described by their teachers as slow were kept in the final test.

The test was soon revised so that items were *age graded.* For example, a set of "6-year-old" items could be passed by most 6-year-olds but few 5-year-olds; another group of items could be passed by most 12-year-olds and were said to measure the intellectual skills of the average 12-year-old. This permitted the testers to describe a child's **mental age (MA)**, the level of age-graded problems that the child is able to solve. Thus a child who passes all items at the 5-year-old level but does poorly on more advanced items — regardless of her actual age — is said to have a mental age (MA) of 5.

Binet's efforts to develop a test of intelligence are still with us, in the form of the *Stanford-Binet Scale.* In 1916 Lewis Terman of Stanford University translated and published a revised version of Binet's test for use with American children. It contained age-graded items for ages 3 to 13 (see Table 9.1 for some sample problems). Moreover, Terman made use of a procedure that had been developed for comparing mental age to chronological age. It is one thing to have a mental age of 10 when one is chronologically only 8, but another thing entirely to have that same mental age when one is 15. The **intelligence quotient**, or **IQ**, was originally calculated by dividing mental age by chronological age and then multiplying by 100:

$$IQ = MA/CA \times 100$$

Notice that an IQ score of 100 indicates average intelligence; the child is passing just the items that age mates typically pass, and mental age is equal to chronological age. The child of 8 with a mental age of 10 has a higher IQ (specifically, 125); the child of 15 with a mental age of 10 has an IQ of only 67 and is clearly below average compared to children of the same age.

A revised version of the Stanford-Binet is still in use (Thorndike, Hagen, & Sattler, 1986). Its **test norms** — standards of normal performance reflecting average scores and the range of scores around the average — are based on the performance of a large and representative sample of people (2-year-olds through adults) from many socioeconomic and racial backgrounds. The concept of mental age is no longer used to calculate IQ; instead individuals

Table 9.1 Some performance criteria from the Stanford-Binet test

AGE	CHILD SHOULD BE ABLE TO
3	Point to objects that serve various functions such as "goes on your feet"
	Name pictures of objects such as *chair, flag*
	Repeat a list of 2 words or digits—for example, *car, dog*
4	Discriminate visual forms such as squares, circles, and triangles
	Define words such as *ball* and *bat*
	Repeat 10-word sentences
	Count up to 4 objects
	Solve problems such as "In daytime it is light; at night it is . . ."
6	State the difference between similar items such as a *bird* and a *dog*
	Count up to 9 objects
	Solve analogies such as "An inch is short; a mile is . . ."
9	Solve verbal problems such as "Tell me a number that rhymes with *tree*"
	Solve simple arithmetic problems such as "If I buy 4 cents' worth of candy and give the storekeeper 10 cents, how much money will I get back?"
	Repeat 4 digits in reverse order
12	Define words such as *skill* and *muzzle*
	Repeat 5 digits in reverse order
	Solve verbal absurdities such as "One day we saw several icebergs that had been entirely melted by the warmth of the Gulf Stream. What is foolish about that?"

Source: Adapted from Terman & Merrill, 1972.

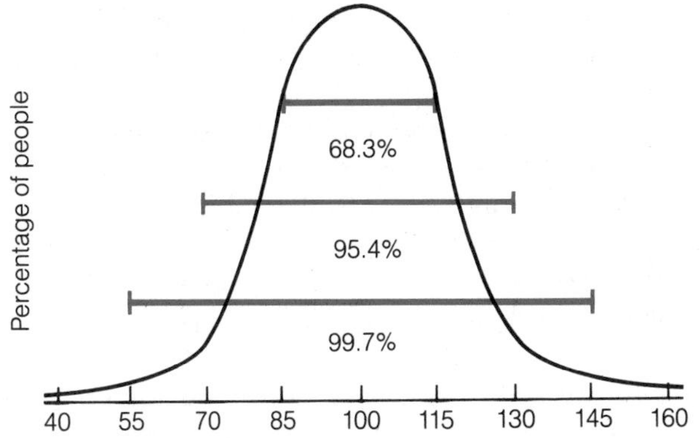

Figure 9.2 The approximate distribution of IQ scores.

receive scores that reflect how well or poorly they do as compared with other people of the same age. An IQ of 100 is still average, and the higher the IQ score an individual attains, the better the performance is in comparison to peers.

The Wechsler Scales

David Wechsler constructed a set of intelligence tests that is also in wide use. The Wechsler Preschool and Primary Scale of Intelligence (WPPSI) is for children between the ages of 4 and 6½ (Wechsler, 1967). The Wechsler Intelligence Scale for Children–Revised (WISC–R) is appropriate for schoolchildren aged 6 to 16 (Wechsler, 1974), and the Wechsler Adult Intelligence Scale–Revised (WAIS–R) is used with adults (Wechsler, 1981). Wechsler developed his tests in part because he believed that the Stanford-Binet had too many items requiring verbal skills and too few requiring nonverbal abilities. The Wechsler tests yield a *verbal IQ* score based on items measuring vocabulary, general knowledge, arithmetic reasoning, and the like, and a *performance IQ* based on such nonverbal skills as the ability to assemble puzzles, solve mazes, reproduce geometric designs with colored blocks, and rearrange pictures to tell a meaningful story. As with the Stanford-Binet, a score of 100 is defined as average performance for one's age. A person's *full-scale IQ* is a combination of the verbal and performance scores. A large discrepancy between verbal IQ and performance IQ may indicate a learning disorder (for example, children who have trouble learning to read often do worse on the verbal section than on the performance section).

The Distribution of IQ Scores

To more fully interpret an IQ score of 130 or 85, it helps to know how IQ scores are distributed in the population at large. Scores for large groups of people form a **normal distribution**, or a symmetrical, bell-shaped, spread around the average score of 100 (see Figure 9.2). Scores around the average are common; the more distant the score from 100 on either side the rarer it is. Over two thirds of the people have IQs between 85 and 115. Fewer than 3% have scores of 130 or above, a score that has often been used as one criterion of giftedness. John Stuart Mill, with his estimated IQ of 190, was very rare indeed! Similarly, fewer than 3% have IQs below 70, a cutoff that is commonly used today to define mental retardation.

Intelligence Testing Today

Traditional IQ tests continue to be used, but new ones are continually being developed. For example, the authors of the recently developed *Kaufman Assessment Battery for Children* (K-ABC) have included both minority groups and handicapped children in their norm samples and have deliberately tried to make their test fairer to such children than they believe either the Stanford-Binet or the Wechsler tests are (Kaufman & Kaufman, 1983). Others have taken more radical approaches based on their dissatisfaction with the way in which intelligence has traditionally been defined and measured. Reuven Feuerstein (1979), for example, has argued that, even though intelligence is often viewed as a *potential* to learn from experience, tests typically assess *what has been learned*, not what can be learned. Feuerstein's *Learning Potential Assessment Device* asks children to learn new things with the guidance of an adult who provides increasingly helpful instruction and cues. This test interprets intelligence as the ability to learn quickly with minimal guidance. Robert Sternberg (1985) finds this approach compatible with his triarchic theory of intelligence. To better understand the information processes involved in verbal ability, for example, Sternberg does not ask people to define words they learned in the past, as IQ testers so often do. Instead, he places an unfamiliar word in a set of sentences and asks people to *learn*, from context, what the new word means, just as they must do in real life.

Despite their vast influence, IQ tests have been roundly criticized. A single IQ score certainly does not do justice to the complexity of human mental abilities. Indeed, Piaget devised his theory of cognitive development partly because he was dissatisfied with the psychometric approach to assessing intelligence. And, as Sternberg and others note, it is high time to study *how* humans process information in order to understand why some people do better than others on IQ tests. In sum, the nature of intelligence is still poorly understood. We do, however, have a vast store of information about how IQ scores change over the life span and about the implications for development and achievement of having a low or high IQ.

THE INFANT

As we saw in Chapters 7 and 8, the mind develops very rapidly in infancy. But how can an infant's intellectual growth be measured? Is it possible to identify infants who are more or less intelligent than their age mates? And does high (or low) intelligence in infancy predict high (or low) intelligence in childhood and adulthood?

Developmental Quotients

None of the standard intelligence tests can be used with children much younger than 3 because the test items require verbal skills and attention spans that the infant does not have. Some developmentalists have tried to measure infant intelligence by assessing the rate at which infants achieve important developmental milestones. Perhaps the best known and most widely used of the infant tests is the *Bayley Scales of Infant Development* (Bayley, 1969). This test, designed for infants aged 2 to 30 months, has three parts:

1. The *motor* scale (which measures the infant's ability to do such things as grasp a cube and throw a ball)
2. The *mental* scale (which includes adaptive behaviors such as reaching for a desirable object, searching for a hidden toy, and following directions)
3. The *infant behavioral record* (a rating of the child's behavior on dimensions such as goal-directedness, fearfulness, and social responsivity)

On the basis of the first two scores, the infant is given a **DQ**, or **developmental quotient**, rather than an IQ. The DQ summarizes how well or poorly the infant performs in comparison to a large norm group of infants the same age.

Infant Intelligence and Later Intelligence

As they grow older, infants do progress through many developmental milestones of the kind assessed by the Bayley Scales, so such scales are useful in charting infants' developmental progress. They are also useful in diagnosing neurological problems and mental retardation—even when these conditions are fairly mild and difficult to detect through standard pediatric or neurological examinations (Escalona, 1968; Honzik, 1983). But does DQ predict later IQ? Can we identify which infants are likely to be gifted, average, or mentally retarded during the school years? Apparently not. Correlations between infant DQ and child IQ are very low, sometimes close to zero, as illustrated in Figure 9.3, which plots correlations between test scores in infancy and early childhood and IQ at age 8. The infant who does well on the Bayley Scales or other infant

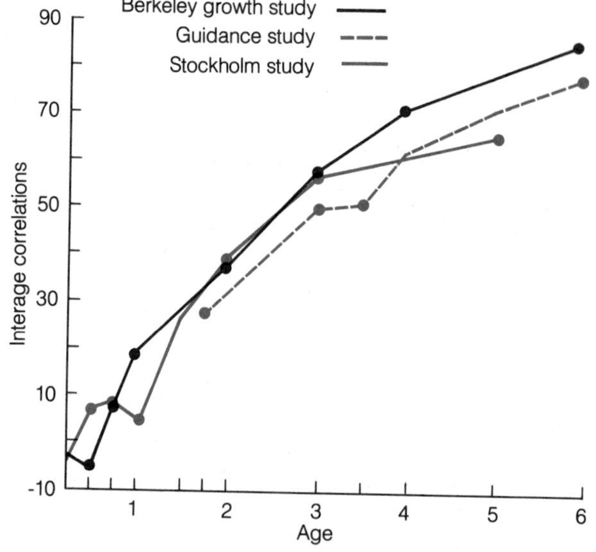

Figure 9.3 Correlations between early intelligence test scores and IQ at age 8. Notice that scores on infant tests are not highly correlated with IQ at age 8. High- or low-scoring infants will not necessarily maintain those standings when they reach childhood. Preschool IQ scores predict later IQ scores better. (From Honzik, 1983)

tests may or may not obtain a high IQ score later in life (Honzik, 1983; McCall, 1983; Rose, Feldman, Wallace, & McCarton, 1989). In fact, developmental standing at a given point during infancy often has little relationship to developmental standing later in infancy. The one exception seems to be that the infant who scores very low on an infant test often turns out to be mentally retarded. As you can see, the correlations between early test scores and IQ at age 8 become higher and higher as age at which the early test is given increases.

Why don't infant development scales do a better job of predicting children's later IQs? Perhaps the main reason is that infant tests and IQ tests tap very different kinds of abilities. The failure of infant tests to predict later IQ has led some researchers to the broader conclusion that the nature of intelligence changes qualitatively from infancy to childhood and even within infancy (McCall, Eichorn, & Hogarty, 1977). Piaget would undoubtedly approve of this argument. Infant scales focus heavily on the sensory and motor skills that Piaget believed are so important in infancy; IQ tests such as the Stanford-Binet and WISC emphasize more abstract abilities such as verbal reasoning, concept formation, and problem solving.

Robert McCall (1981, 1983) offers another explanation, arguing that the growth of intelligence during infancy is highly influenced by powerful and universal maturational processes. Maturational forces pull infants back on course if environmental influences cause them to stray. For this reason, higher or lower infant test scores are likely to be mere temporary deviations from a universal developmental path. As the child nears age 2, McCall argues, maturational forces become less strong, so individual differences become larger and more stable over time. Consistent differences related to both individual genetic makeup and environment now begin to emerge.

Should we give up on trying to predict later IQ on the basis of development in infancy? Perhaps not yet. The information-processing approach has given new life to the issue of continuity in intelligence from infancy to childhood. Joseph Fagan and others have found that certain measures of infant attention predict IQ during the years from 2 to 8 better than infant intelligence tests do (Bornstein & Sigman, 1986; Fagan & McGrath, 1981; Fagan & Singer, 1983; Rose et al., 1989). Specifically, the speed with which an infant *habituates* to a repeatedly presented or constant stimulus and the strength of the infant's tendency to prefer a novel stimulus to a familiar one assessed in the first six months of life have an average correlation of .46 with IQ in childhood, particularly verbal IQ (Bornstein & Sigman, 1986). Perhaps we can characterize the "smart" infant as one who quickly gets bored by the same old thing, seeks out novel experiences, and soaks up information quickly—in short, as an efficient information processor.

It appears there *is* some continuity between infant intelligence and childhood intelligence. Although such Bayley Scale accomplishments as throwing a ball are unlikely to carry over into vocabulary learning or problem-solving skills in childhood, the extent to which the young infant processes information quickly can predict the extent to which a child learns quickly. In addition, some continuity has been demonstrated between some components of a developmental quotient and *similar* components of later IQ. For example, Lewis and Enright (reported by Lewis & Michalson, 1985) found that language items on the Bayley Scales predicted verbal IQ at age 6. By contrast, the Bayley Scales could not be used to identify which infants would turn out to be mathematically gifted. So, at least some of the seeds of later intellectual functioning do seem to be laid in infancy.

THE CHILD

Over the childhood years, children become able to answer more questions, and harder questions, on IQ tests. That is, their mental ages increase. What about a child's IQ score, which reflects how that child compares with peers? And what does an IQ really tell us about a child?

How Stable Are IQ Scores During Childhood?

It was once assumed that a person's IQ reflected his or her mental *capacity*—a capacity that was genetically determined and therefore would remain quite stable over time. In other words, a child with an IQ of 120 at age 5 was expected to obtain a similar IQ at age 10, 15, or 20.

Is this idea supported by research? As we have seen, infant tests do not predict later IQ test scores at all well. However, starting at about age 4 there is a fairly strong relationship between early IQ and later IQ, and the relationship grows even stronger by middle childhood. Table 9.2 summarizes the results of a longitudinal study of more

Table 9.2 Correlations of IQs measured during the preschool years and middle childhood with IQs measured at ages 10 and 18

AGE OF CHILD	CORRELATION WITH IQ AT AGE 10	CORRELATION WITH IQ AT AGE 18
4	.66	.42
6	.76	.61
8	.88	.70
10	—	.76
12	.87	.76

Source: From Honzik, Macfarlane, & Allen, 1948.

than 250 children (Honzik, Macfarlane, & Allen, 1948): The shorter the interval between two testings, the higher the correlation between children's IQ scores. But even when a number of years have passed, IQ seems to be a very stable attribute. After all, the scores that children obtain at age 6 are clearly related to those they obtain twelve years later at age 18.

There is something these correlations are not telling us, however. They are based on a large *group* of children, and they do not necessarily mean that the IQs of *individual children* will remain stable over the years. As it turns out, many children show sizable ups and downs in their IQ scores over the course of childhood. Robert McCall and his associates looked at the IQ scores of 140 children who had taken intelligence tests at regular intervals from age 2½ to age 17 (McCall, Applebaum, & Hogarty, 1973). More than *half* of these children showed wide fluctuations in IQ over time, and the average range of variation in their scores was a whopping 28.5 points. One child in seven showed changes of at least 40 points, and one child shifted by 74 IQ points!

How do we reconcile the conclusion that IQ is relatively stable with this clear evidence of instability? We can still conclude that, within a group of children, children's standings, high or low, in comparison with peers stay quite stable from one point to another during the childhood years. But at the same time, many individual children experience drops or gains in IQ scores from testing to testing. Apparently IQ is reasonably stable for some children, but it is highly variable for many others during childhood.

Some wandering of IQ scores upward or downward over time is just random fluctuation—for example, a good day at one testing, a bad day at the next testing. Yet it is interesting to note that children whose scores fluctuate the most tend to live in unstable home environments—that is, their life experiences had fluctuated between periods of happiness and turmoil (Honzik et al., 1948). Moreover, some children are likely to gain IQ points over childhood and others are likely to lose them. Who are the gainers, and who are the losers?

Gainers seem to have parents who foster achievement and are neither too strict nor too lax in child rearing (McCall et al., 1973). On the other hand, noticeable drops in IQ with age often occur among children who live in poverty. Otto Klineberg (1963) proposed a **cumulative-deficit hypothesis** to explain this: Impoverished environments inhibit intellectual growth, and these negative effects accumulate or snowball over time. There is some support for the cumulative-deficit hypothesis (Jensen, 1977). In fact, a cumulative deficit among disadvantaged children may start to appear during infancy. In a very effective intervention effort at the University of North Carolina, Craig Ramey and Ron Haskins (1981) were able to maintain normal rates of mental development in disadvantaged infants whose mothers were relatively uneducated and low in IQ. Starting before their third month of life, the babies attended a day-care center every weekday. At the center, they participated in activities designed to stimulate their intellectual development. Similar infants who did not attend the center nor receive training started to show declines in Bayley scores after 1 year of age and suffered declines in Stanford-Binet IQ scores between ages 2 and 3. As we discovered in Chapter 5, lack of intellectual stimulation early in life can inhibit the formation of neural connections and could well interfere with normal brain development and produce cumulating intellectual deficits.

How Well Do IQ Scores Predict School Achievement?

The original purpose of IQ testing was to estimate how well children would do in school. Do IQ test scores indeed predict school achievement? Apparently. The average correlation between children's IQ scores and their current grades in school is about .50 (Minton & Schneider, 1980). Correlations between IQ and future academic success—as measured by grades, teachers' ratings, or scores on standardized achievement tests—are about the same. Yet these correlations are far from perfect. Factors such as the student's work habits, interests, and motivation to succeed also affect school achievement and are reflected in grades. In addition, children who have similar IQ scores often have quite different styles of problem solving that influence their school achievement (see Box 9.1). As it turns out, the best single predictor of a student's future grades is not an IQ score but the student's earlier grades (Minton & Schneider, 1980).

Box 9.1
Cognitive Styles and IQ

Cognitive differences among children include more than differences in their IQ scores. For one thing, individuals differ in their *cognitive styles*—their characteristic and preferred ways of approaching problems and processing information. In addition to differing in field independence/field dependence, which was discussed in Chapter 6, children differ on a dimension called reflectivity/impulsivity (Kagan, Rosman, Day, Albert, & Phillips, 1964). **Impulsive** children seem to respond to problems quickly, favoring the first hypothesis they think of. **Reflective** children have a slower conceptual tempo; they take their time and evaluate many possible hypotheses before arriving at an answer.

The illustration (*right*) is from the *Matching Familiar Figures Test*, which is used to assess reflectivity/impulsivity. The child is to select from six alternatives the figure that exactly matches the "standard" figure at the top. An individual may be slow or fast, accurate or inaccurate. Typically, a child who is fast and inaccurate is identified as impulsive, one who is slow and accurate is identified as reflective.

A reflective style would seem superior; for many problems, accuracy is valued, regardless of speed. Also, children generally become more reflective as they get older, suggesting that reflectivity is more developmentally mature than impulsivity (Salkind & Nelson, 1980). Therefore, some researchers are convinced that reflective individuals are simply more competent at processing information than impulsive individuals are (Block, Gjerde, & Block, 1986).

However, there is still considerable debate and confusion about whether tests of reflectivity/impulsivity measure differences in ability or differences in style—or both (Kogan, 1983; Smith & K. Nelson, 1988). If impulsive children are just developmentally slow compared to their more reflective peers, there should be some point in development at which everyone becomes reflective. But there is no such point; differences along this dimension can be found even among adults (Zelniker & Jeffrey, 1979). Zelniker and Jeffrey (1976, 1979) argue that impulsive individuals are different but not necessarily deficient. Reflective individuals analyze details carefully—just the strategy that is needed to avoid making errors on the sample problem. Impulsive individuals take in the global picture, considering stimuli as wholes. In tasks for which a global analysis is appropriate—for example, to quickly determine if one overall shape matches another—impulsive children sometimes excel. Which strategy is best then depends on the task, and impulsive children should not be viewed as intellectually inferior to reflective children (Zelniker & Jeffrey, 1979).

Perhaps this is why children who are reflective have only somewhat higher IQs on the average than children who are impulsive (Messer, 1976). And yet, given the demands of our schools for accuracy, reflective children generally have an easier time with reading, memorizing, and other academic activities and do better in school as a result (Messer, 1976). Apparently, impulsive children do not lack general intellectual ability but invest too little effort in their work and make careless errors, even on tasks where a global style of processing is appropriate (Smith & K. Nelson, 1988). In sum, cognitive style seems to be a matter of *both* style and ability (Smith & K. Nelson, 1988).

Answer to sample problem: The first bear in the first row matches the standard.

THE ADOLESCENT

Intellectual growth is very rapid during infancy and childhood. What happens during adolescence?

Continuity Between Childhood and Adulthood

Intellectual growth continues to be rapid in early adolescence and then slows down (Bayley, 1968). By adolescence, IQ scores have become even more stable and predict IQ in middle age very well (Eichorn, Hunt, & Honzik, 1981). This does not mean that individuals no longer show changes in their scores from testing to testing. They do.

IQ scores also continue to predict school achievement. Adolescents with higher IQs obtain higher grades in junior and senior high school. They are also less likely to drop out of high school and more likely to go on to college than their peers with lower IQs (Brody & Brody, 1976). However, IQ scores do not predict college grades as well as they predict high school grades (Brody & Brody, 1976). This is probably because most college students have at least the average intellectual ability needed to succeed in college. Actual success is therefore more influenced by personal qualities such as motivation.

So far, no surprises. Patterns that emerged in childhood continue in adolescence. However, some intriguing research suggests that the timing of puberty during adolescence may influence at least one mental ability that is often measured by IQ tests.

The Timing of Puberty and Mental Abilities

Starting in early adolescence, females outperform males on tests of verbal ability, whereas males outperform females on tests of mathematical ability and visual/spatial ability (for example, the ability to recognize a complex geometric figure that has been rotated in three-dimensional space or to navigate using a map; see Figure 9.4). Why? Deborah Waber (1977) proposed that these sex differences might be related to the earlier maturation of females. Specifically, she proposed that early maturation in adolescents of either sex would cut short the process by which the two sides of the brain take on specialized or lateralized functions (see Chapter 5). Verbal ability would consequently be high, but visual/spatial abilities would remain underdeveloped. In other words, late maturers would have more years in which brain specialization could be completed and would therefore excel in spatial ability.

Waber may have been at least half right. The timing of puberty did not affect verbal ability, but both late-maturing girls and late-maturing boys outperformed early maturers on measures of visual/spatial ability. Waber also was able to link this finding to separate evidence of a greater specialization of the two sides of the brain among late maturers.

Several studies have supported Waber's finding that, on the average, late maturers have greater visual/spatial ability than early maturers do. This difference is still evi-

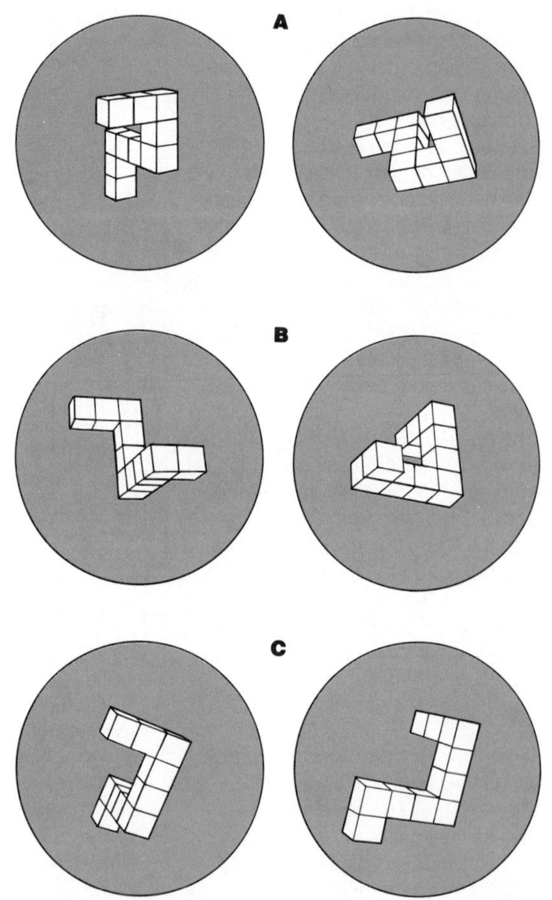

Figure 9.4 A spatial ability task. Decide whether the two figures in each pair are alike or different. (From Shepard & Metzler, 1971)

Answer: The two figures in items A and B are the same, but the two in item C are different.

dent at college age, though it is small (Sanders & Soares, 1986). However, it has proved difficult to explain this finding or use it to explain sex differences in visual/spatial ability (Newcombe, Dubas, & Baenninger, 1989). For example, some studies suggest that sex differences in spatial ability actually show up *before* puberty, weakening Waber's argument (Linn & Petersen, 1985). Even when differences in spatial ability between early and late maturers are found, they are not always accompanied by the differences in brain specialization that are supposed to underlie them (Linn & Petersen, 1985; Newcombe & Bandura, 1983). Finally, sex differences in spatial ability might have as much to do with sex differences in socialization as with the timing of puberty. Females who excel on spatial ability tasks often distinguish themselves from other females by showing more interest in traditionally "masculine" intellectual areas such as math and science (Newcombe & Bandura, 1983) or by participating more often in "masculine" activities that require spatial skills such as soccer and carpentry (Baenninger & Newcombe, 1989; Signorella, Jamison, & Krupa, 1989). Females who adopt a more traditional feminine role may gain less experience in spatial thinking.

In sum, individual differences in at least one important mental ability, spatial skills, do seem to be related to the timing of puberty in both sexes, but it is not yet clear why. Nor is it clear how other factors such as involvement in masculine-stereotyped activities might contribute to sex differences in spatial ability.

THE ADULT

Do IQ scores predict achievement after people have left school? How does performance on IQ tests change during the adult years? And do IQ scores decline in old age, as performance on Piagetian cognitive tasks and performance on memory tasks appear to do?

Does IQ Affect Occupational Success in Adulthood?

There is indeed a relationship between IQ and occupational status. This was demonstrated in an early study of World War II military personnel (Harrell & Harrell, 1945). Table 9.3 shows the rank order (from most prestigious to least prestigious) of civilian occupations these men had. The average IQ score for an occupation increases as the prestige of the occupation increases. The reason for this relationship is clear: It undoubtedly takes more intellectual ability to complete law school and become a lawyer than it does to be a farmhand. But also notice the "range of IQ" column. There were some very bright men working in some of the lower status occupations. Apparently a high IQ is no guarantee that one will be working in a prestigious job.

Now a second question: Are bright lawyers, electricians, or farmhands more successful or productive than their less intelligent colleagues? Erness and Nathan Brody (1976) have concluded from the research that it depends on the type of job. In high status occupations where high IQs are required for entrance, there is no relationship between IQ and job performance. Scientists with IQs of 150 may publish no more articles than their colleagues with IQs of 115, and extremely bright lawyers may win no more cases than their merely "above average" colleagues. Every-

Table 9.3 Average IQs and range of IQs for enlisted military personnel who had worked at various civilian occupations

OCCUPATION	AVERAGE IQ	RANGE OF IQS
Accountant	128.1	94–157
Lawyer	127.6	96–157
Engineer	126.6	100–151
Chemist	124.8	102–153
Reporter	124.5	100–157
Teacher	122.8	76–155
Pharmacist	120.5	76–149
Bookkeeper	120.0	70–157
Sales manager	119.0	90–137
Purchasing agent	118.7	82–153
Radio repairman	115.3	56–151
Salesman	115.1	60–153
Artist	114.9	82–139
Stock clerk	111.8	54–151
Machinist	110.1	38–153
Electrician	109.0	64–149
Riveter	104.1	50–141
Butcher	102.9	42–147
Bartender	102.2	56–137
Carpenter	102.1	42–147
Chauffeur	100.8	46–143
Cook and baker	97.2	20–147
Truck driver	96.2	16–149
Barber	95.3	42–141
Farmhand	91.4	24–141
Miner	90.6	42–139

Source: From Harrell & Harrell, 1945.

body (well, almost everybody) who gains entrance to the field is reasonably bright. By contrast, IQ scores do seem to predict job success in occupations of intermediate status in which cognitive skills are helpful and the range of IQs is large. For example, bright bookkeepers outperform their relatively less intelligent colleagues. Finally, when we consider low status occupations, the relationship between IQ and job performance once again vanishes, probably because routine jobs make few intellectual demands on people. More intelligent workers do tend to be dissatisfied with these jobs and to leave them if they can.

In sum, it appears that IQ scores do have some bearing on occupational success. However, they do not predict an adult's occupation as well as they predict a child's school achievement, and they do not predict how well an adult performs a given job as well as they predict what kind of job he or she obtains (Brody & Brody, 1976).

How Do Intellectual Abilities Change with Age?

Perhaps no question about adult development has been studied as thoroughly as the question of how intellectual abilities change with age. Early cross-sectional studies comparing different age groups of adults yielded disturbing findings—disturbing at least to people over 20. For example, extensive testing during World War I using the *Army Alpha Test* showed that scores on this IQ-type test steadily decreased from the young groups of 20 years of age or less to the older groups of up to 50 and 60 years of age (Yerkes, 1921). Does this finding mean that we're brightest at 20 and it's downhill from there? Not necessarily. In longitudinal follow-up studies, the scores of a group of middle-aged people on the Army Alpha Test were compared to the scores these same people obtained when they were college freshmen. The middle-age scores were *higher* on every subtest except the one dealing with arithmetic (Owens, 1953)! This finding shook psychologists accustomed to assuming that intellectual performance peaked at about age 20 (Cunningham & Owens, 1983). Longitudinal studies also suggested that only modest decline occurs in old age.

Why the big discrepancy? As already discussed, both cross-sectional and longitudinal studies have their problems. Cross-sectional studies compare people of different cohorts who have had different levels of education and different growing-up experiences because they were born at different times. Yet longitudinal studies are also flawed. People die or drop out of such studies. Those who are left—those whose scores can be charted across the years—tend to be those with better health and higher intellectual functioning, the very people who may be most likely to improve their abilities in earlier adulthood and maintain them in old age (Schaie, 1983).

So neither kind of study is entirely adequate in determining how IQ test performance changes with age, though both have value. For example, cross-sectional studies *do* tell us that the average older person today performs more poorly on IQ tests than the average younger person. This information may be useful in planning adult education programs. And the longitudinal studies have told us a great deal about change over time in at least a select segment of the population and have revealed that individual differences in IQ scores are quite stable over the adult years. Still, the best information about changes in intellectual abilities has come from sophisticated *sequential studies*, which combine the cross-sectional and longitudinal approaches. Let us look closely at the findings of one major sequential study, the Seattle Longitudinal Study directed by K. Warner Schaie (see Schaie, 1983; Schaie & Hertzog, 1983, 1986).

The Seattle study began in 1956 with a sample of members of a health maintenance organization ranging in age from 22 to 70. They were given a revised test of primary mental abilities that yielded scores for five separate mental abilities (see Box 9.2). Seven years later, as many of them as could be found were retested. In addition, a new sample of adults ranging in age from their 20s to their 70s was tested. These two samples made it possible to determine how the performance of the same individuals changed over a period of 7 years *and* to compare the performance of people who were 20 years old in 1956 with that of a different cohort of people who were 20 in 1963. This same strategy was repeated in 1970 and 1977, giving the researchers a wealth of information about different cohorts, including longitudinal data on some of the same people over a 21-year period.

What has this study revealed? First, it seems that when a person was born has at least as much influence on intellectual functioning as age does. In other words, cohort or generational effects on performance were evident, confirming the suspicion that cross-sectional comparisons of different age groups yield too grim a picture of declines in

Box 9.2
The Primary Mental Abilities Measured in Schaie's Seattle Study

- **Verbal meaning:** One must recognize the meaning of a word by identifying the best synonym for it from a list of four words. This ability comes in handy in reading and understanding speech.
- **Space:** This is the ability to imagine how an object would look if it were rotated in space. Given one figure (an F, for example), one must quickly determine whether six other figures are or are not the F at another angle (for example, upside down). Spatial ability would aid in reading maps or assembling pieces of equipment.
- **Reasoning:** The test of reasoning involves foreseeing the pattern in a series of letters. Given the pattern "b c r c d r d e r," one would have to figure out that the next letter should be "e." Reasoning enters into solving problems in real life, as when one analyzes a situation on the basis of past experience and plans an appropriate future course.
- **Number:** This is the ability to deal with basic arithmetic problems quickly. Given an addition problem that has been worked to yield a sum, one must decide whether it has been worked correctly. Although mathematics abilities may be less useful today now that we have calculators, they still play a role in daily life.
- **Word fluency:** Finally, the word fluency test measures the quick recall of words. One must write down as many words as possible during a 5-minute period that begin with the letter *s*. Presumably this ability enters into talking and reading easily.

Source: These descriptions are based on those provided by Schaie (1983, pp. 73–74) of the following test: Thurstone, L. L., & Thurstone, T. G. (1948). *SRA Primary Mental Abilities, Ages 11–17, Form AM.* Chicago: Science Research Associates, Inc.

intellectual abilities during adulthood. Schaie compared the scores obtained by people who were born at different times when they were the same ages. Compared to the most recently born cohort in the study (people born in 1952), earlier generations did poorly on the tests of reasoning and verbal meaning, the two tests that Thurstone viewed as most relevant to educational aptitude. Today's elderly people are especially disadvantaged in these and other areas; on the test of numerical ability, people born between 1903 and 1924 actually performed better than both earlier and later generations. So different generations may have a special edge in different areas of intellectual performance, and growing-up experiences do affect intellectual abilities.

What happened to mental abilities of these individuals as they aged? Table 9.4 charts average performance in five areas at various ages as a percentage of performance at age 25. These data have been corrected to eliminate some of the problems such as dropouts that can make longitudinal data misleading. Numbers higher than 100 indicate that performance exceeded that at age 25. For the most part, only modest changes in abilities occur until after age 67, and modest gains can be seen in most areas in the 30s, 40s, and even 50s. Peak performance in some categories is reached *after* age 25, though modest declines in others occur in middle age. Only in the 60s and 70s do abilities decline substantially. In other words, decline in intellectual performance comes later in life than was previously thought. By the age of 80, significant declines in several abilities are evident. Before that age, the average older person functions within the normal range of ability for young adults.

But another important message of the Seattle study, and other research as well, is that patterns of aging differ for different abilities. For one thing, *fluid intelligence* (those abilities requiring active thinking and reasoning applied to novel problems, as measured by tests like the

Table 9.4 Mental abilities at different ages as a percentage of performance at age 25[a]

AGE	VERBAL MEANING	SPACE	REASONING	NUMBER	WORD FLUENCY	OVERALL INTELLECTUAL ABILITY
32	105	103	100	107	105	105
39	109	105	103	110	105	108
46	109	107	102	120	104	109
53	113	106	103	122	94	111
60	111	105	101	126	90	110
67	107	103	91	122	83[a]	104
74	97	90	81[a]	109	81[a]	92
81	87	79	73[a]	90	62[a]	80[a]

[a]These average performances fall in the lowest 25% of the distribution for 25-year-olds. Thus they represent the most substantial declines in performance in old age.
Source: Modified from Schaie, 1983.

primary mental abilities tests of reasoning and space) usually declines earlier and more steeply than *crystallized intelligence* (those abilities involving the use of knowledge acquired through experience, as in answering the verbal meaning test used by Schaie). Consistently, older adults appear to lose some of their ability to grapple with new problems, but they maintain their "crystallized" general knowledge and vocabulary quite well and sometimes even improve on them (Dixon, Kramer, & Baltes, 1985; Horn, 1982).

A similar phenomenon has been noticed when the Wechsler test (WAIS) is used. Performance IQ scores (which often involve nonverbal and novel materials) decline earlier than verbal IQ scores do (Busse & Maddox, 1985). Such age-related declines in performance may be due in part to a slowing of response in old age (Hertzog, 1989). Tests of fluid intelligence and performance IQ are often timed (Schaie & Hertzog, 1986), and performance on speeded tests does decline more in old age than performance on unspeeded tests does (Jarvik & Bank, 1983). Also, these kinds of IQ items may be more unfamiliar to older adults than to younger ones—that is, the tests may be subtly biased against older adults (see Box 9.3). For all these reasons, an overall IQ score tells relatively little about the growth or decline of mental performance among adults.

We now have an overall picture of intellectual functioning in adulthood. Age-group differences in performance suggest that older adults today are at a disadvantage on many tests compared to younger adults today, partly because of deficiencies in the quality of education they received during early life. But actual declines in intellectual abilities associated with aging are generally minor un-

Box 9.3
Are IQ Tests Fair to Older Adults?

As we will see shortly, it has been charged that IQ tests are biased against members of some cultural or subcultural groups. Could they also be biased against adults, especially older ones? After all, they do not include the sorts of problems that adults are most likely to encounter in everyday life (Labouvie-Vief, 1985).

J. A. Demming and S. L. Pressey (1957) were skeptical of early cross-sectional studies showing that average IQ scores declined with age from the early 20s onward, so they set out to design information tests more relevant to adult life. Among their items were questions about where to look in the yellow pages to find an Airedale, what to call the document that disposes of a person's property at death, and what to call the person who baptizes babies.

The findings were interesting: On these "adult" information tests, 20-year-olds were no longer the superstars. Instead, average scores *increased* from age group to age group, so that adults in their 30s, 40s, or 50s and older generally outperformed adults in their 20s, as well they might if they had been gaining knowledge about practical, everyday issues over the years.

Also suspecting that traditional IQ tests might be biased against older adults, Steven Cornelius (1984) hypothesized that the kinds of items used to measure crystallized intelligence (for example, vocabulary items) remain familiar across the adult years, but that items used to measure fluid intelligence (for example, figuring out what letter comes next in a series of letters that has a system to it) are quite foreign to adults who have been out of school for a long time. The typical aging pattern, of course, involves the maintenance of crystallized abilities and the decline of fluid abilities. So, Cornelius had young, middle-aged, and elderly adults take tests of both crystallized and fluid intelligence and also rate each item for familiarity, difficulty, effortfulness, and demands for speed.

As expected, tests of crystallized intelligence were perceived about the same across age groups, but elderly adults typically judged tests of fluid intelligence to be more unfamiliar, difficult, effortful, and speeded than younger adults did. This study does not prove that older adults show declines in fluid intelligence only because they are "rusty" or out of practice on the kinds of items used to measure fluid intelligence. As Cornelius acknowledged, it is possible that declines in fluid abilities in later life make tests of these abilities look difficult. Still, we must wonder again whether traditional IQ tests give older adults a fair chance to show what they can do.

Until IQ tests designed explicitly for older adults are constructed, it makes sense to try to make traditional IQ tests as fair as possible. Even minor changes—doing away with computer-scored answer sheets, increasing the size of the print to help those with visual problems, and arranging items more clearly on the page—can significantly increase the IQ scores of older adults (Popkin, Schaie, & Krauss, 1983). It seems, then, that increased sensitivity to the issue of age bias in intelligence testing is warranted—at least if we hope to give people of all ages the fullest opportunity to display whatever intellectual abilities they possess.

til people enter their 60s or 70s. And even in old age, declines in fluid and performance abilities are more apparent than declines in crystallized or verbal abilities, and declines on speeded tests are steeper than declines on unspeeded tests.

One last message of this research is worth special emphasis: *Declines in intellectual abilities are not universal.* In later life, many people maintain their abilities very well or even *gain* ground, while others experience modest declines in ability and still others experience steep ones (Dixon, Kramer, & Baltes, 1985).

What Factors Are Associated with Declining Intellectual Abilities in Old Age?

Who is most likely to experience declines in intellectual performance in old age? In Schaie's (1983) Seattle study, *poor health*, not surprisingly, was one sign of potential problems. People with severe cardiovascular diseases were particularly at risk, perhaps because these diseases reduce oxygen flow to the brain. Even diseases such as arthritis that do not directly affect brain functioning tended to be associated with intellectual decline in some individuals; pain, depression, drug side effects, reduced physical exercise, and decreased involvement in certain intellectually stimulating activities could all potentially contribute. People who retain their physical and mental health typically maintain their intellectual skills well in old age (Manton, Siegler, & Woodbury, 1986; Schaie, 1983; Siegler & Costa, 1985).

The importance of health is also evidenced by the tendency of people within a few years of dying to experience a rapid decline in intellectual abilities (Kleemeier, 1962; and see Botwinick, 1984; Hayslip, Fish, & Wilson, 1989). This phenomenon has been given the depressing label **terminal drop**. By noticing the warning signs of cognitive deterioration in elderly people, one might even be able to identify those who have undetected health problems (Jarvik & Bank, 1983). Perhaps there really is something to the saying, "Sound body, sound mind"!

A second factor in decline is an *unstimulating lifestyle.* Schaie and his colleagues found that the biggest intellectual declines were shown by elderly widows who had low social status, engaged in few activities, and were dissatisfied with their lives (Gribbin, Schaie, & Parham, 1980; Schaie, 1984). Such women were alone and had apparently disengaged themselves from life. Many of the people who tended to maintain their performance or even show gains were of average or high social status, had intact families, and were engaged in many physical and mental activities. Other studies suggest that highly educated people are the most likely to maintain their intellectual abilities (Jarvik & Bank, 1983), possibly because they maintain an intellectually stimulating lifestyle over the adult years (Schaie, 1983).

The moral is "Use it or lose it!" This rule, which applies to muscular strength and sexual functioning, seems also to apply to intellectual functioning in later life (Schaie, 1983). Like infants and children, older adults need chances to exercise their minds. The plasticity of the nervous system throughout the life span enables elderly individuals to benefit from intellectual stimulation and training, to maintain the intellectual skills most relevant to their activities, and to compensate for the loss of less exer-

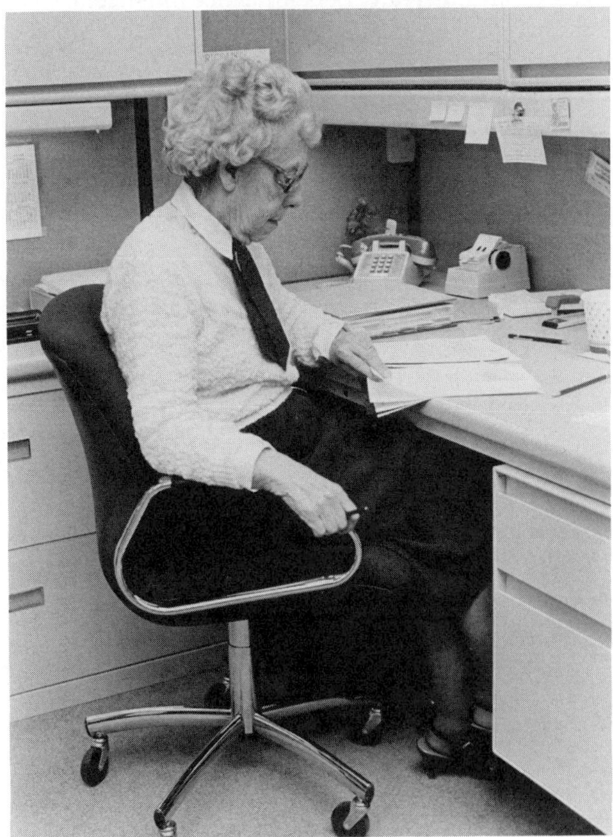

When it comes to intellectual functioning, "use it or lose it" seems to be the rule.

cised abilities (Dixon, Kramer, & Baltes, 1985). There is still much to learn about why different people travel different developmental paths in later life. What is more certain is that most of us can look forward to many years of optimal intellectual functioning before *some* of us experience losses of *some* mental abilities in later life.

FACTORS THAT INFLUENCE IQ SCORES

Why do children or adults who are *the same age* differ in IQ? The pioneers of the IQ testing movement had a ready answer. If, as they generally believed, intelligence is an inherited trait, individual differences in IQ exist simply because some people get better genes at conception than others do. Even though IQ scores are now known not to be fixed at birth, heredity does influence intelligence. Perhaps half of the variation in IQ scores within a group of people can be linked to genetic differences among individuals (Plomin & DeFries, 1980; see also Chapter 3). But this leaves about half attributable to differences in the environments in which people develop. In short, heredity and environment interact to influence intellectual performance.

Here we look more closely at environmental influences on IQ. This will involve examining the home environment in infancy and early childhood to detect factors that stimulate or inhibit intellectual development. Then we will see how far information about early home environments can take us in explaining individual differences in IQ scores associated with birth order and family size, socioeconomic status, and racial or ethnic group.

Home Environment and IQ

Bettye Caldwell and Robert Bradley have developed a widely used instrument for determining how intellectually stimulating or impoverished a home environment is (Caldwell & Bradley, 1978; Bradley & Caldwell, 1984). The **HOME inventory** (*H*ome *O*bservation for *M*easurement of the *E*nvironment) comes in both infant and preschool versions; the six subscales (and sample items) of the preschool version are displayed in Table 9.5 (Caldwell & Bradley, 1978).

Table 9.5 Subscales and sample items from the HOME inventory

SUBSCALE	SAMPLE ITEMS
I: Emotional and Verbal Responsivity of the Mother (11 items)	Mother responds to child's vocalizations with a verbal response Mother's speech is clear, distinct, and audible Mother caresses or kisses child at least once during visit
II: Avoidance of Restriction and Punishment (8 items)	Mother neither slaps nor spanks child during visit Mother does not scold or derogate child during visit Mother does not interfere with the child's actions or restrict child's movements more than three times during visit
III: Organization of Physical and Temporal Environment (6 items)	Child gets out of house at least four times a week Child's play environment appears safe and free of hazards
IV: Provision of Appropriate Play Materials (9 items)	Child has push or pull toy Parents provide learning equipment appropriate to age—mobile, table and chairs, highchair, playpen, and so on Mother provides toys or interesting activities for child during interview
V: Maternal Involvement with Child (6 items)	Mother "talks" to child while doing her work Mother structures the child's play periods
VI: Opportunities for Variety in Daily Stimulation (5 items)	Father provides some caretaking every day Mother reads stories at least three times weekly Child has three or more books of his own

Source: From Caldwell & Bradley, 1978.

Do scores on the HOME predict children's cognitive functioning? Indeed they do (Bradley et al., 1989). In fact, both Bradley and Caldwell (1976) and Helen Bee and her associates (1982) found that the quality of the home environment measured when children were either 6 or 12 months of age is a better predictor of their IQs at ages 3 and 4 than is their own first-year performance on tests of infant intelligence. Moreover, the quality of a child's home environment at both age 2 and age 10 is associated with his or her school achievement in fourth or fifth grade (Bradley, Caldwell, & Rock, 1988).

What aspects of the home environment matter most? Allen Gottfried (1984) has compiled the results of several longitudinal studies that have used the HOME instrument to predict IQ in early childhood. The most important factors appeared to be parental involvement with the child, provision of appropriate play materials, and opportunities for a variety of stimulation. There is apparently such a thing as too much stimulation, for in overcrowded homes the quality of the HOME environment tends to be low (Bradley & Caldwell, 1984). Other researchers (e.g., Crockenberg, 1983) would add that the sheer amount of stimulation parents provide to their young children may not be as important as whether that stimulation is responsive—that is, whether it is in reaction to the child's own behavior (a smile in return for a smile, an answer in return for a question). Many researchers would also stress that stimulation should be matched to the competencies of the child—neither too simple nor too challenging—something that depends on the parent's knowing the child's capacities well (Hunt & Paraskevopoulos, 1980; Miller, 1986). In short, an intellectually stimulating home is one in which parents are eager to be involved with their children and are responsive to their developmental needs and behavior (MacPhee, Ramey, & Yeates, 1984).

Do differences in stimulation in the home really *create* individual differences in IQ? Some have argued that intelligent children simply received genes for intelligence from their genetically bright parents. Did those parents just happen to provide stimulating home environments but influence their children mainly at conception (Longstreth et al., 1981)? Keith Yeates and his colleagues (Yeates, MacPhee, Campbell, & Ramey, 1983) evaluated this hypothesis in a longitudinal study of 112 mothers and their children aged 2 to 4. They measured the mothers' IQs, the children's IQs from age 2 to age 4, and the families' HOME environments. Of the factors measured, the best predictor of a child's IQ at age 2 was the mother's IQ, just as a genetic hypothesis would suggest; home environment had little effect on its own. But the picture changed by the time children were 4 years old, when the quality of the home environment *did* correlate significantly with IQ. Moreover, the researchers established statistically that differences in the quality of the home environment influenced children's IQ regardless of the IQ of their mothers (see also Gottfried & Gottfried, 1984). The argument that genetic influences can fully explain the apparent effects of home environment on IQ does not hold up, at least after age 2. This is consistent with Robert McCall's (1981) idea, touched on earlier, that a child's environment becomes more influential after the strong maturational forces of infancy wane.

Birth Order, Family Configuration, and IQ

It has long been noticed that first-born children, only children, and children from small families obtain somewhat higher IQ scores than later-born children and children from large families. A massive study in Holland, for example, examined the military records of 386,114 men and reported the remarkable findings displayed in Figure 9.5 (Belmont & Marolla, 1973). Controlling for both social class and birth order, the researchers found that brighter men tended to come from smaller families. In addition, within any given family size, first-borns outperformed second-borns, who outperformed third-borns, and so on down the line. Notice that these are very small differences; the entire graph in Figure 9.5 spans only 6 IQ points. Also bear in mind that these are group averages; all first-borns are not brighter than all later-borns. Nonetheless, these findings are not unique to Dutch males; they have been repeated many times (Berbaum & Moreland, 1980; Falbo & Polit, 1986; Markus & Zajonc, 1977; Zajonc & Markus, 1975).

Why the differences? It seems that first-borns and children from smaller families receive more high quality intellectual stimulation from their parents than do later-borns and children from large families (Falbo & Polit, 1986). Indeed, this is precisely what Bradley and Caldwell (1984) have found using the HOME inventory to assess the home environment during infancy. In addition, Mary Rothbart (1971) asked mothers to supervise the performance of their 5-year-olds on a series of achievement tasks. Half were first-borns and half were second-borns, all from two-child families. Mothers of first-borns gave more

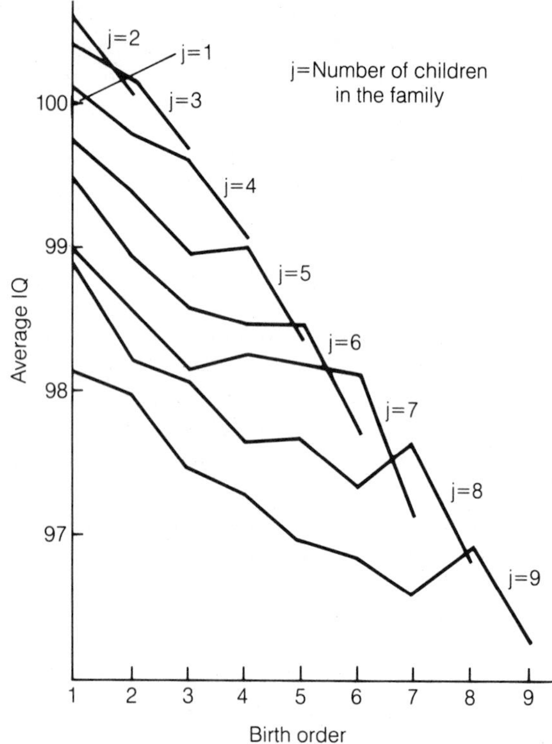

Figure 9.5 Average scores on a nonverbal measure of intelligence as a function of the examinee's birth order and the size of his family. Both early birth order and small family size tend to be associated with higher IQs. (From Belmont & Marolla, 1973)

complex technical explanations to their children, they put more pressure on them to succeed, and they were more anxious about their performance. Perhaps as a result, first-borns attained higher scores than second-borns on all but one of the tasks. Thus first-borns and children from small families seem to receive both more intellectual stimulation during infancy and more direct achievement training in the preschool years.

Social Class Differences in IQ

Another reliable finding is that children from lower- and working-class homes average some 10 to 20 points below their middle-class age mates on IQ tests. Moreover, improving the economic conditions of children's homes can improve their IQs. For example, investigators have charted the intellectual growth of adopted children who had been placed in their new homes before their first birthday (Scarr & Weinberg, 1977, 1983; Skodak & Skeels, 1949). Many of these children came from disadvantaged family backgrounds with biological parents who were poorly educated and somewhat below average in IQ. They were placed in middle-class homes with adoptive parents who were highly educated and above average in intelligence. By the time they were 4 to 7 years old, these adoptees were scoring well above average on standardized IQ tests (about 110 in Scarr and Weinberg's study and 112 in Skodak and Skeels's).

Could social class differences in IQ be due to differences in the quality of the home environment that parents of different socioeconomic levels provide? Yes, at least partially. Scores on the HOME inventory are higher in middle-class homes than in lower-class homes, indicating that middle-class homes tend to be more intellectually stimulating (Gottfried, 1984). However, social class is still correlated with intellectual development even when social class differences in home environment are controlled for (Gottfried & Gottfried, 1984). Other factors that tend to be more common in lower than in higher socioeconomic environments—for example, poor nutrition or disruptive family experiences that undermine the motivation to succeed on tests—may also contribute to the social class gap in IQ.

Racial and Ethnic Differences in IQ

Racial and ethnic differences in IQ scores have also been observed. In the United States, for example, children of black, Native American, and Hispanic ancestry tend to score below Anglo-American norms on IQ tests (Minton & Schneider, 1980). Most of the attention has focused on comparisons of black and white children. Black children living in the southeastern United States seem to do especially poorly, but even black children living in the North or in metropolitan areas of the South have tended to attain average IQs about 12 to 15 points lower than those of their white age mates (Loehlin, Lindzey, & Spuhler, 1975). Of course, it is essential to keep in mind that these are differences in *group averages*. Like the IQ scores of white children, those of black children run the whole range from the mentally retarded zone to the gifted zone, and many black children have higher IQs than most white children do. We certainly cannot predict an individual's IQ merely on the basis of racial or ethnic identity.

Having said that, we must ask why these average

group differences exist. If you are thinking about the social class differences we just described, your answer is likely to be that minority group children simply grow up in less advantaged environments. This is true. But before we consider an environmental explanation for racial and ethnic group differences, let us consider the following alternative ideas: (1) bias in testing hurts members of minority groups, (2) minority group members are not highly motivated in testing situations, and (3) group differences in IQ may have a hereditary basis.

One possibility is *test bias*, or the idea that IQ tests are more appropriate for children from white middle-class backgrounds than for children from other subcultural groups. Black and Hispanic children who speak a different dialect of English than that spoken by middle-class Anglo children may not understand the test instructions or items as well. Their experiences may not allow them to become familiar with some of the information that is called for on the tests (for example, "What is a 747?").

But even though standardized IQ test items sometimes have a middle-class flavor, group differences in IQ cannot be traced solely to test bias. *Culture-fair IQ tests* include items that should be equally unfamiliar (or familiar) to people from all ethnic groups and social classes. Yet racial differences still emerge on such tests (Jensen, 1980). Translating existing tests into the Black English dialect spoken by urban black children also does not appear to increase their scores (Quay, 1971). And finally, IQ tests seem to predict future school achievement as well for blacks and other minorities as they do for whites (Cole, 1981; Oakland & Parmelee, 1985; Reynolds & Kaufman, 1985). IQ tests have indeed been *used* in discriminatory ways to make decisions about children's educational placements, but the tests themselves do not appear to be unfair.

Another possibility is that minority children are not highly motivated in testing situations (Zigler, Abelson, Trickett, & Seitz, 1982). They may be wary of strange examiners and may see little point in trying to do well. Disadvantaged children do indeed do some 7 to 10 points better when they are given time to warm up to a friendly examiner or are given a mix of easy and hard items so that they do not become discouraged by a long string of difficult items (Zigler et al., 1982). Even though middle-class children also do better with a friendly examiner (Sacks, 1952), this argument may still have some merit (Moore, 1986).

Perhaps no idea in psychology has sparked more heated debate than the suggestion that racial and ethnic differences in IQ scores are due to group differences in genetic makeup. Perhaps the strongest proponent of this view is Arthur Jensen (1969, 1980). There is evidence that differences in genetic makeup contribute, along with environment, to IQ differences within either the white or the black population (see Chapter 3). Jensen went on to suggest that IQ differences *between* groups may be hereditary—that the white race may have more of the genes that contribute to high intelligence than the black race does. Without pointing out the many limitations of the data on which Jensen based his hypothesis or the complexities of the controversy Jensen has stirred, we will say that most psychologists do not think that evidence that heredity contributes to within-group differences says much at all about the reasons for between-group differences.

Lewontin (1976) makes this point with an analogy. Suppose that corn seeds with different genetic makeups are randomly drawn from a bag and planted in two fields—one that is barren and one that has fertile soil. Since all the plants within each field were grown in the same soil, their differences in height would have to be due to differences in genetic makeup. A genetic explanation would fit. But if the plants in the fertile field are generally taller than those in the barren field, this *between-field* variation must be entirely due to environment. Similarly, even though genes partially explain individual differences in IQ *within* black groups and white groups, the average difference *between* the racial groups may still reflect nothing more than differences in the environments they typically experience. There is currently no basis for concluding that differences in genetic makeup between the races account for average group differences in IQ.

So it is time to return to an environmental hypothesis about racial and ethnic differences in IQ. The research by Sandra Scarr and Richard Weinberg (1977, 1983) on adopted children is very relevant. The adopted children whose IQs ended up averaging 110 in their study were in fact black children adopted into advantaged white, middle-class homes. Placement in advantaged homes allowed these children to exceed the average IQ in the general population by 10 points and to exceed the IQs of comparable black children raised in more disadvantaged environments by 20 points. They did as well on tests and in school as white children adopted into similar middle-class families—that is, adopted into the "culture of the tests and the schools" (Scarr & Weinberg, 1983, p. 261). Scarr and Weinberg (1983) conclude that this could not have happened if black children were genetically deficient.

Recently, Elsie Moore (1986) has pursued the research of Scarr and Weinberg by comparing black children adopted into middle-class white homes with similar black children adopted into middle-class black homes. Average IQs were above average in both groups by the time children were tested at age 7 to 10. Again, improving the socioeconomic environment seems to increase the IQ scores of minority group children. However, even though the two groups were both economically advantaged, black children placed in white homes had an average IQ of 117, higher than the 104 average of the black children placed in black homes.

Moore tried to find out why by carefully observing the children during the IQ testing session and by observing their mothers interacting with them. She found what she believes are cultural differences in styles of test taking and styles of parenting even within the same social class. The children who had been placed in white homes seemed to enjoy the testing situation more than the children who had been placed in black homes. They were more willing to try to answer questions, they stuck to the tasks longer, they more often elaborated on their reasons for answering as they did, and they seemed more confident. The children from black homes often seemed to want to escape the testing situation and sometimes shook their heads as if to say they did not know the answer before the question was even completed.

These contrasting styles of test taking seemed to be linked to the styles of interaction the children's mothers used with them in a problem-solving situation that Moore set up. Compared to the black mothers, the white mothers provided a great deal of positive encouragement. They joked to relieve tension and they even cheered or applauded when their children made progress. The black mothers more often showed their displeasure with their children. Perhaps that is why their children were less comfortable and motivated in the IQ testing situation than the children adopted by white women were.

Don't misunderstand: Neither Scarr and Weinberg, nor Moore, nor we are suggesting that white parents are better parents all around than black parents or that black children would be better off if they were adopted into white homes. The major message of all this research is that children, whether they are black or white, perform better on IQ tests when they grow up in more intellectually stimulating, often middle-class, environments. Unfortunately, more black than white children continue to live in poverty, and socioeconomic differences between the races continue to explain part of the average IQ difference between the races. Moore's (1986) findings further hint that even when children of different racial and ethnic groups all grow up in advantaged homes, there may be subtle cultural differences in parenting styles that still make for group differences in IQ test performance. But as Scarr and Weinberg (1976) insist, there are other human traits besides a high IQ score that should be valued, and some of them may not be fostered as well by white middle-class parents as by other parents.

If the goal is to increase IQ scores, we have already identified aspects of the home environment that help stimulate the intellectual growth of both black and white children. There are also signs, based on scores on the Scholastic Aptitude Test (SAT), a commonly used college entrance test, that the test performance gap between whites and blacks has been narrowing in recent years (Jones, 1984). Perhaps the issue of racial and ethnic differences in IQ will largely disappear as economic conditions and opportunities for minority groups improve.

THE EXTREMES OF INTELLIGENCE

Although we have identified some of the factors that contribute to individual differences in intellectual performance, we cannot fully appreciate the magnitude of these differences without considering people at the extremes of the IQ continuum. Just how different are gifted individuals and mentally retarded individuals? And how different are their lives?

Giftedness

The gifted child used to be identified solely by an IQ score—one that was 130 or 140 or higher. Programs for gifted children still focus mainly on children with very high IQs, but there is increased recognition that some children are gifted because they have special abilities rather than because they have high general intelligence. So today's definitions emphasize that **giftedness** involves having a high IQ *or* showing special abilities in areas valued in our society such as creativity, mathematics, the performing and visual arts, or even leadership (Coleman, 1985).

None other than Lewis Terman, developer of the Stanford-Binet test, launched a major longitudinal study of gifted children back in 1922 (Fincher, 1973; Terman, 1954; Terman & Oden, 1959). The subjects were more than 1500 California schoolchildren who were nominated by their teachers and who had IQs of 140 or higher.

It soon became apparent that these high-IQ children were exceptional in many respects other than intelligence. For example, they weighed more at birth and had learned to walk and talk sooner than most toddlers. They reached puberty somewhat earlier than average and had better-than-average health. Their teachers rated them better adjusted and more morally mature than their less intelligent peers. And although they were no more popular than their classmates, they were quick to take on leadership responsibilities. Taken together, these findings destroy the stereotype that most gifted children are frail, sickly youngsters who are socially inadequate and emotionally immature (see also Janos & Robinson, 1985). (This generalization may not hold true among the few children with extremely high IQ scores of 180 or higher, however. A fairly high proportion of these youngsters—perhaps a quarter—are poorly adjusted psychologically and socially, perhaps because they are so much more mature than their age mates and are often bored by what goes on in their classrooms [Janos & Robinson, 1985].)

A convincing demonstration of the personal and social maturity of most gifted children comes from a study by Nancy Robinson and Paul Janos (1986). These researchers studied gifted children who, at the age of 14 or younger, entered the University of Washington as part of a special program to accelerate their education. Contrary to the common wisdom that gifted children will suffer socially and emotionally if they skip grades and must fit in with much older students, these youngsters showed no signs at all of maladjustment. Indeed, on several measures of psychological and social maturity and adjustment, they equalled their much older college classmates, as well as similarly gifted students who attended high school.

What becomes of gifted children as adults? Most of Terman's gifted children were still remarkable in many respects. Fewer than 5% were rated as seriously maladjusted, and their rates of such problems as ill health, mental illness, alcoholism, and delinquent behavior were but a fraction of those observed in the general population (Terman, 1954). They were as likely to marry as members of the general population, and they were more likely to be satisfied with their marriages and less likely to divorce. Owing to the influence of gender-role norms during the period covered by the study, many gifted women did not pursue careers outside the home, but the occupational achievements of the men were impressive. The vast majority (86%) were working in professional or semiprofessional jobs by age 40. As a group, they had taken out more than 200 patents and written some 2000 scientific reports, 100 books, 375 plays or short stories, and more than 300 essays, sketches, magazine articles, and critiques.

Gifted children have either high IQ scores or special abilities.

In short, Terman's gifted children moved through adulthood as healthy, happy, and (in many cases) highly productive individuals. But was it their giftedness that accounted for these happy outcomes? As David McClelland (cited by Fincher, 1973) pointed out, it could be that these gifted individuals succeeded because most of them also happened to have come from advantaged family backgrounds. Indeed, when Terman (1954) contrasted the gifted individuals who were most successful in their careers with those who were less successful, he found that the fathers of the successful subjects had more education and better jobs than the fathers of the less successful subjects. Their homes also had a more intellectual climate when they were growing up (as indexed by the number of books present and the parents' involvement in the child's learning activities). And finally, only half as many of them had experienced the disruption of parents' divorce. Perhaps because of these differences in home environment, the scores of the successful group had remained quite stable over the years, while those of the less successful group had declined since childhood, even though both groups started out with IQs averaging about 150.

High IQ may predict good health, happiness, and success, but it does not guarantee them (see Box 9.4). Even among a select sample of children with high IQs, the quality of the home environment still contributes in important ways to future outcomes and accomplishments.

Mental Retardation

What about the other extreme of the IQ continuum? **Mental retardation** is currently defined by the American Association on Mental Deficiency as "significant subaverage general intellectual functioning resulting in or associated with concurrent impairments in adaptive behavior and manifested during the developmental period" (Grossman, 1983, p. 1). Translated, this means that to be diagnosed as mentally retarded an individual must show, before adulthood, an IQ score below 70 *and* have difficulties meeting age-appropriate expectations in everyday life.

Four levels of mental retardation are recognized, each of them representing a portion of the IQ range below 70: mild, moderate, severe, and profound. A *mildly retarded* adult (IQ 55 to 69 on the Wechsler tests) is likely to have a mental age comparable to that of an 8- to 12-year-old child. Mildly retarded persons can learn both academic and practical skills in school with special instruction, and they can potentially work and live independently or with occasional help as adults. *Moderately retarded* individuals

Box 9.4 What Became of the Child Prodigies?

Two recent books in the popular literature add to the insights that Terman's study gives us about gifted children. The first, *Whatever Happened to the Quiz Kids?* was written by Ruth Feldman (1982) about the later lives of children who, like her, appeared on the program *Quiz Kids* in the 1940s and 1950s, awing radio (and later TV) audiences with their knowledge. Feldman interviewed some former Quiz Kids and sent questionnaires to as many others as she could trace. They were a highly successful group—even more so than Terman's group. The most famous of them was James Watson, winner of the Nobel Prize for his part in unlocking the structure of the genetic material DNA. Nearly all were college graduates, and many had advanced or professional degrees. Perhaps because they were of a later generation, a larger percentage of female Quiz Kids than female "Termites," as Terman's subjects were nicknamed, worked outside the home for most of their adult lives. Failure was rare.

But failure can come, even to the most gifted of the prodigies, as Amy Wallace's (1986) biography of William Sidis, *The Prodigy*, makes clear. Sidis was the son of a brilliant Harvard psychologist (we regret having to report this) and the godson of the pioneering psychologist William James. From infancy, "Billy" was the subject of an experiment designed by his father to prove that magnificent talents can be developed in any child. Given the most enriched of early environments (and probably some good genes as well), Billy could read the newspaper at 18 months of age and had learned eight languages by the time he reached school age. His school years were brief, however, for he entered Harvard at age 11 and was teaching mathematics at Rice University by age 17! But his parents had invested so much energy in developing his mind that they apparently neglected his social development. His social incompetence and odd habits were as widely publicized as his intellectual feats, and finally William Sidis had apparently had enough of it all. He quit the academic life, took a series of menial jobs, and lived as a hermit, writing about obscure topics and jumping at every opportunity to show children his prodigious collection of streetcar and subway tickets. Sidis seemed content with his life of obscurity, but he certainly did not achieve the greatness that might have been predicted. He died of a stroke at age 46.

William Sidis was clearly the exception to all we know about gifted children and their outcomes. Nonetheless, his story reminds us that early blooming is no guarantee of later flowering. And it works the other way, too: Late blooming does not rule out eminence in adulthood. We need only cite the case of Albert Einstein, whose name is synonymous with genius. Einstein didn't speak until age 4, could not read until age 7, and was judged by his teachers to have little future at all (Feldman, 1982)!

(IQ 40–54) can also learn basic academic skills and many life skills, but they are more likely than mildly retarded people to need supervision and support in order to hold jobs and live in the community. *Severely retarded* persons (IQ 25–39) typically can learn many basic self-help skills and communication skills, but they typically master few academic skills and need a good deal of continuing training and support as adults. Finally, *profoundly retarded* persons, with IQs below 25 and mental ages below 3 years, show major delays in all areas of development and require basic care, often in an institutional setting, though they, too, can benefit from training. Obviously, then, there are important differences among mentally retarded individuals.

Mental retardation has many causes. More severely retarded persons often have what is called **organic retardation**; that is, their retardation is due to some identifiable biological cause associated with hereditary factors, diseases, or injuries. *Down syndrome*, which is associated with an extra chromosome, is a familiar example of organic retardation (see Chapter 3). Many other forms of organic retardation are associated with prenatal risk factors—an alcoholic mother, exposure to rubella, and so on (see Chapter 4). Such children, because they are seriously delayed and often have physical defects, can often be identified at birth or during infancy. However, the most common form of mental retardation, **cultural/familial retardation**, is not usually recognized until a child performs poorly on an IQ test in school. It appears to be related to some combination of low genetic potential and a poor environment. Culturally/familially retarded children are generally mildly retarded, come from poverty areas, and have a parent or sibling who is also retarded (Westling, 1986). Probably 75% to 85% of mental retardation is of this type: exact cause unknown (Baumeister, 1973).

What becomes of mentally retarded children as they grow up? For one thing, their mental ages continue to increase well into adulthood because they are developing at a slower-than-normal pace (Fisher & Zeaman, 1970), but for the same reason, their IQs remain low. As for their outcomes in life, consider a follow-up study of individuals who had been put in segregated special education classes for the mentally retarded during the 1920s (the time when Terman began his study of the gifted) and 1930s (Ross, Begab, Dondis, Giampiccolo, & Meyers, 1985). These subjects had a mean IQ of 67 (most were either mildly retarded or had IQs from 70–80). They were compared with their siblings and with nonretarded peers about 35 years later.

Generally, these mentally retarded adults had poor life outcomes in middle age in comparison with nonretarded groups. About 80% of the retarded men were employed, but they usually held semi-skilled or unskilled jobs that required little education or intellectual ability (as was true in Terman's gifted sample, women tended to marry and become housewives). Compared with nonretarded peers, retarded men and women fared worse on other counts as well. For example, they had lower incomes, less adequate housing, poorer adjustment in social relationships, and a greater dependency on others.

Yet the authors of the study still found grounds for optimism. These individuals did much better during adulthood than stereotyped expectations of mentally retarded persons would predict. Most did work and marry, after all, and about 80% reported having no need for public assistance in the 10 years before they were interviewed. This study, like others before it, suggests that many children who are labeled mentally retarded by the schools—and who do indeed have difficulty with the tasks demanded of them in school—"vanish" into the general population after they leave school. Apparently they can adapt to the demands of adult life. As the authors put it, "It does not take as many IQ points as most people believe to be productive, to get along with others, and to be self-fulfilled" (Ross et al., 1985, p. 149).

CREATIVITY AND SPECIAL ABILITIES

Despite their happy outcomes, not one of Terman's high-IQ gifted children became truly eminent. Recall that teachers nominated bright children for the study. Is it possible that they overlooked some children who were gifted with special talents but who were not "teachers' pets" (Fincher, 1973)? We know that Terman excluded children with IQs below 140, some of whom may have had special talents. Recent definitions of giftedness include not only a high IQ but the ability to accomplish in a particular area such as music, art, or writing. The word "creativity" pops to mind.

What Is Creativity?

Creativity may be more important than IQ in allowing a Michelangelo or a Mozart to break new ground. But what is creativity, and what do we know about creativity over the life span?

Defining creativity has provoked as much controversy as defining intelligence (see Mumford & Gustafson, 1988). However, **creativity** is often defined as the ability to produce *novel* responses or works. Moreover, it is not enough for these products to be outlandish; they must in some way be appropriate in context or valued by others. In his structure-of-intellect model, J. P. Guilford (1967) captured the idea of creativity by proposing that it involves divergent thinking rather than convergent thinking. **Divergent thinking** requires coming up with a variety of ideas or solutions to a problem when there is no one right answer. Indeed, the most common measure of creativity, at least in children, is what is called **ideational fluency**—the sheer number of different, including novel, ideas that one can generate when asked, for example, to think of all the possible uses for a cork (Kogan, 1983). **Convergent thinking** involves "converging" on the one best answer to a problem and is precisely what IQ tests measure.

Research indeed suggests that creativity and divergent thinking are distinct from general intelligence and convergent thinking. For example, Getzels and Jackson (1962) gave more than 500 students, in grades 6 to 12, intelligence tests and five creativity tests:

1. A word-association test in which students were asked to give as many definitions as possible for fairly common words
2. A test of alternate uses, in which students were asked to think of as many uses as they could for familiar objects
3. A hidden-shapes test that required them to find geometric figures hidden in more complex figures
4. A fables test in which they furnished the last line for an unfinished fable
5. A make-up-problems test in which they were to make up a variety of mathematical problems from a large amount of numerical information.

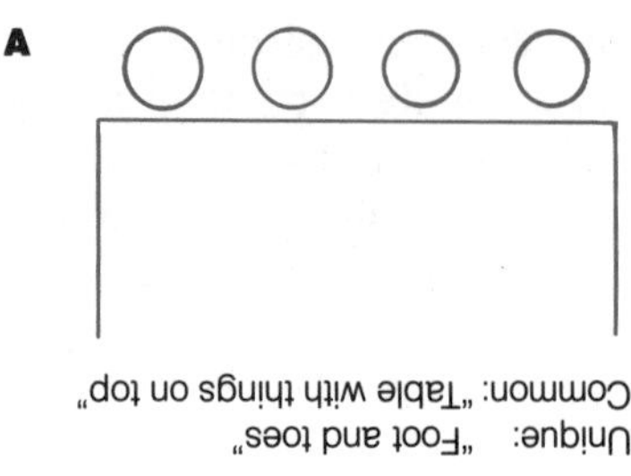

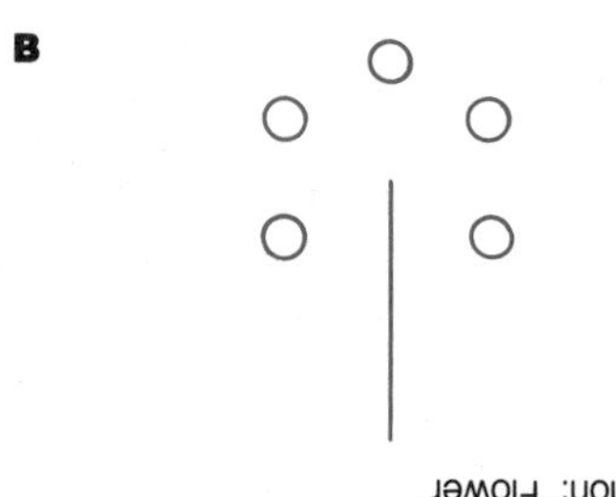

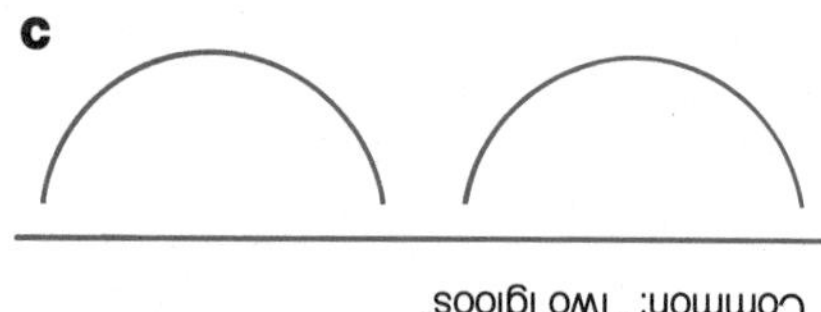

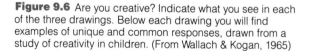

Figure 9.6 Are you creative? Indicate what you see in each of the three drawings. Below each drawing you will find examples of unique and common responses, drawn from a study of creativity in children. (From Wallach & Kogan, 1965)

Scores on these creativity measures and scores on IQ tests correlated very little. Thus creativity seems to be largely independent of general intelligence as defined by IQ tests (Kogan, 1983). At the same time, highly creative people rarely have below-average IQs, so a *minimum* of intelligence is probably required for creativity (Wallach, 1971, 1985). Among people with above-average IQs, an individual's IQ score cannot predict his or her level of creativity. (Test yourself on Figure 9.6.)

Creativity in Childhood and Adolescence

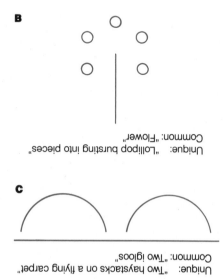

What is the child who scores high on tests of creativity like? Getzels and Jackson (1962) compared children who had high creativity scores but normal-range IQ scores with children who scored high in IQ but not creativity. Personality measures suggested that the creative children showed more freedom, originality, humor, violence, and playfulness than the high-IQ children. Perhaps as a result, the high-IQ children were more success-oriented and received more approval from teachers. Compared with their less creative peers, creative children also engage in more fantasy or pretend play in interaction with other children (Kogan, 1983). Such play often involves inventing new uses for familiar objects and new roles for oneself. Possibly parents contribute to such creative tendencies, for the parents of creative children and adolescents tend to accept their children as they are and grant them a good deal of freedom to explore new possibilities on their own (Harrington, Block, & Block, 1987). Surprisingly, there seem to be no consistent differences in scores on creativity tests between children of different races and social classes (Kogan, 1983). Again we see evidence that creativity must be quite distinct from the cognitive abilities measured on IQ tests.

How does performance on creativity tests change with age? There is remarkably little information (Kogan, 1983). Overall, creativity seems to increase over the childhood and adolescent years, but there appear to be certain ages along the way when it drops off temporarily. Summarizing his cross-cultural research, Paul Torrance (1975) has suggested that creativity in our society may drop at about age 5, when children enter school; then at about age 9; and again at about age 13, when adolescents experience pressures to conform. In other cultures, however, he found that creativity scores dipped downward at somewhat different ages (see also Smith & Carlsson, 1985). Overall, then, the developmental course of creativity is not like the predictable increase in mental age seen on IQ measures. Instead, creativity seems to wax and wane with age, possibly because of the demands that a specific culture places on children at specific ages (Torrance, 1975), or possibly because children go through cycles of being relatively free and "young at heart" at some points in development and more inhibited at other points (Smith & Carlsson, 1985).

Now an important question: How well does performance on tests of creativity predict actual creative accomplishments such as original artwork or outstanding science projects? There may be some links. For example, Harrington, Block, and Block (1983) found that the quality of preschoolers' answers on a test of ideational fluency predicted their teachers' ratings of their creativity in sixth grade. More important, some researchers have found that scores on creativity tests administered in either elementary or secondary school predict actual creative achievements in adulthood (Howieson, 1981; Torrance, 1988). However, the overall picture is still somewhat discouraging. From his review of the research, Nathan Kogan (1983) concluded that scores on creativity tests are better predictors of *current* creative achievements than of *later* accomplishments. Later accomplishments are more closely associated with earlier accomplishments *in the same field* (Richards, Holland, & Lutz, 1967).

On the basis of such data, Michael Wallach (1985) suggests that, just as it was a mistake to expect IQ to predict creative accomplishments, it may have been a mistake to expect tests of creativity to do so. Why? Because both kinds of tests attempt to measure *general* cognitive abilities. Instead, there seem to be many *specific talents*, and each of them (artistic, mathematical, musical, and so on) requires distinct skills and experiences (Gardner, 1983; see Box 9.5).

This is exactly the direction that researchers are now taking, looking at those individuals who do indeed show exceptional talent in a particular field and trying to determine the basis of their accomplishments. David Feldman (1980, 1982, 1986), for example, has studied children who are "prodigies" in such areas as chess, music, and mathematics. These children were generally similar to other children in areas outside their areas of special talent. What contributed to their special achievements? They were, of course, talented, but they also seemed to have a powerful motivation to develop their special talents, a real passion for what they were doing. The Olympic gymnast Olga Korbutt put it well: "If gymnastics did not exist, I would have invented it" (Feldman, 1982, p. 35). Moreover, these achievers were blessed with an *environment* that nurtured their talent and motivation (see also Hennessey & Amabile, 1988). They were strongly encouraged and supported by their families and intensively tutored or coached by experts. As Feldman sees it, the child with creative potential in a specific field must become intimately familiar with the current state of the field if he or she is to advance or transform it, as the ground-breaking artist or musician does. As Howard Gruber (1982) puts it, "Insight comes to the prepared mind . . ." (p. 22). To further emphasize the importance of environment, Feldman notes that child prodigies were lucky enough to live in a culture and time that recognized and valued their special abilities. Olga Korbutt's talent might not have bloomed if gymnastics had not been highly valued in the Soviet Union when she was growing up.

Box 9.5
The Many Sides of Intelligence

Howard Gardner is one psychologist who is not fond of describing people with a single IQ score. In his book *Frames of Mind*, Gardner (1983) argues that there are many intelligences, not one; he proposes the following intellectual abilities as distinctive: *Linguistic intelligence* (shown by the poet's facility with words); *musical intelligence* (based on an acute sensitivity to sound patterns); *logical-mathematical intelligence* (the kind of abstract thinking shown by mathematicians and scientists and emphasized by Piaget); *spatial intelligence* (most obvious in great artists who can perceive things accurately and transform what they see); *bodily-kinesthetic intelligence* (the "intelligent" movement shown by dancers and athletes); and at least two forms of *personal intelligence* (both the ability to understand one's own inner life and social intelligence, or exceptional sensitivity to other people). Notice that traditional IQ tests emphasize linguistic and logical-mathematical intelligence, but ignore most of the other forms.

Gardner does not claim that this is *the* definitive list of intelligences. But he does make his case that each is distinct. He argues, for example, that a person can be exceptional in one ability but poor in others. Indeed, this is dramatically clear in individuals known as **idiot savants**, people who have an extraordinary talent but who are otherwise mentally retarded. Leslie Lemke is one such individual (*Lexington Leader*, November 21, 1980). He is blind, has cerebral palsy, and is mentally retarded, and he could not talk until he was an adult. Yet he can hear a musical piece once and play it flawlessly on the piano or imitate songs in German or Italian perfectly even though his own speech is still primitive.

Gardner also notes that each intelligence has its own distinctive developmental course. Many of the great composers, for example, revealed their genius in childhood, whereas logical-mathematical intelligence often shows up later in life. Each of Gardner's intelligences can also be linked to a specific area of the brain.

It perhaps says something about our culture that some of Gardner's intelligences seem to be valued more than others. We do, for example, provide gifted programs to nurture the abilities of children who score high on traditional IQ tests or who show talent in math or science. But do we try to identify and nurture the talents of children who show exceptional social skills and sensitivity to other people? Social intelligence is now being studied seriously, and it appears to consist of multiple abilities (social skills, empathy, and so on) that are unrelated to general intelligence (Marlowe, 1986). However, we have a long way to go before we know as much about the specialized intelligences that Gardner identifies as we know about the kind of intelligence reflected in IQ scores.

In summary, there are many forms of giftedness, many "intelligences." Efforts to study creativity have revealed that performance on creativity tests is distinct from performance on IQ tests. Yet neither tests of general intelligence nor tests of general creativity are very good at predicting which children will show exceptional talent in a *specific* field. Instead, that kind of talent seems to be related to characteristics of the individual, including exceptional motivation, *and* characteristics of the environment, especially support and prolonged training in the field.

Creative Achievement During Adulthood

By the time people are adults, their creative accomplishments are apparent. Examinations of creativity during the adult years have therefore focused on that very small number of people who have become giants in their fields—art, music, science, philosophy, and so on. The big question has been this: *When* in adulthood are such individuals most productive and most likely to produce their best works? Is it early in adulthood, when they can benefit from youth's enthusiasm and freshness of approach? Or is it later in adulthood, when they have fully mastered their field and have the experience and knowledge necessary to make a breakthrough in it? And what becomes of eminent creators in old age?

A pioneer of this kind of research was Harvey Lehman (1953). He used historical materials to determine when notable contributors in a broad variety of fields produced their most notable works. He found that in most fields creative production increased steeply from the 20s to the 30s, when it peaked. There was a gradual and steady decline with age in the production of quality works thereafter. Wayne Dennis (1966) criticized Lehman for, among other things, failing to take into account the fact that some creative achievers died early and so could produce works only in their younger years. In Dennis's own study, among noted individuals who lived into old age, productivity did indeed rise in early adulthood, but it continued at high levels for many years after the 30s, declining only in old age.

One thing Lehman and Dennis did agree on is that peak times of creative achievement vary from field to field. For example, Figure 9.7 shows that the productivity of scholars in the humanities (for example, historians and philosophers) continues well into old age and actually peaks in the 60s, possibly because creative work in these fields often involves integrating knowledge that has "crystallized" over the years. By contrast, productivity in the arts (for example, music or drama) does peak in the 30s and 40s and declines quite steeply thereafter, perhaps because artistic creativity depends on a more "fluid" or innovative kind of thinking. Scientists seem to be intermediate, peaking in their 40s and declining only in their 70s. Even within the same general field, differences in peak times have been noted. For example, poets reach their peak before novelists do, and mathematicians peak before other scientists do (Dennis, 1966; Lehman, 1953).

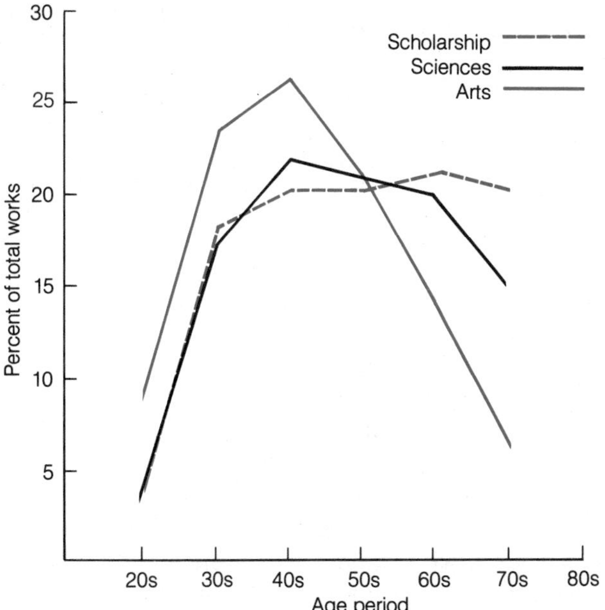

Figure 9.7 Percentage of total works produced in each decade of the lives of eminent creators. The "scholarship" group includes historians and philosophers; the "sciences" include natural and physical scientists, inventors, and mathematicians; and the "arts" category includes architects, musicians, dramatists, poets, and so on. (Data from Dennis, 1966)

Still, in many fields (including psychology, by the way), creative production rises to a peak in the late 30s or early 40s, and there are some declines in both the total number of works and the number of high quality works thereafter (Horner, Rushton, & Vernon, 1986; Simonton, 1984). This pattern seems to hold up well across different cultures and historical periods (Simonton, 1975). Even so, many creators are still producing outstanding works in old age—sometimes their greatest works (Lehman, 1953). Michelangelo, for instance, was in his 70s and 80s when he worked on St. Peter's Cathedral. Indeed, the truly eminent among the eminent seem to start early and finish late (Simonton, 1984).

How can we account for this relationship between age and creative achievement? One explanation, proposed long ago (Beard, 1874, cited by Simonton, 1984) is that creative achievement requires both enthusiasm and experience. In early adulthood the enthusiasm is there, but the experience is not; in later adulthood the experience is there, but the enthusiasm or vigor has fallen off. The individual between 30 and 40 has it all. Dean Simonton (1984, 1989) has proposed another theory: Each creator may have a certain potential to create that is realized over the adult years, and as potential is realized, less is left to be realized. Ideas must first be generated, and then they must be carried through to produce actual works (a poem, a piece of art, a scientific publication). After a career was launched, some time would elapse before any ideas were generated or works actually completed. This would explain the rise in creative achievement between the 20s and 30s. Some kinds of work take longer to formulate or complete than others. This might help explain why a poet (who can generate and carry out ideas quickly) might reach a creative peak earlier in life than, say, a historian (who may need to devote years to the research and writing necessary to complete a book).

Why does creative production eventually begin to taper off? Simonton (1985) charted when in their careers the major (often cited) works and more obscure works of 10 distinguished psychologists were done. (The 10 included B. F. Skinner, Albert Bandura, and J. P. Guilford, by the way.) The *percentage* of works that were major or significant ones did not change with age. In other words, psychologists in later life were not just producing trivial publications after doing all their really important works in early adulthood or middle age; they continued to produce highly valued works (see also Over, 1989). Simonton suggests that older creators may simply have used up much of their total stock of potential ideas earlier in life. They never totally exhaust their creative potential, but they have less of it left to realize. This account also fits nicely with evidence that younger creators often generate many fresh ideas, whereas older creators often build on existing ideas (Mumford & Gustafson, 1988).

What about mere mortals like us? We may not produce the Great American Novel, but we show more modest signs of creativity in daily life, some of us more than others. Do ordinary adults of different ages differ in creativity? Here, because so few adults are eminent creators, researchers have fallen back on tests designed to measure creativity. Alpaugh and Birren (1977), for example, gave a test of divergent thinking to teachers ranging in age from their 20s to their 80s. Divergent thinking decreased from age group to age group, starting in the 30s. Similarly, in a study combining the cross-sectional and longitudinal approaches, divergent thinking abilities appeared to decrease at least modestly after about age 40 and to decrease even more steeply starting at about 70 (McCrae, Arenberg, & Costa, 1987). By contrast, Gail Jaquish and Richard Ripple (1981) found that divergent thinking scores did not fall off at all until old age. In fact, middle-aged adults (40–60) had a slight edge on younger adults. The elderly subjects were not as different from younger adults in the originality of their ideas as they were in the sheer number of ideas they generated. In addition, among both middle-aged and elderly adults, but not among younger adults, people with high self-esteem excelled at divergent thinking. Overall, then, these researchers suspected that low self-esteem might inhibit many older adults from fully using creative abilities that they still possess. So, these studies disagree about exactly when creative abilities might decline in normal adults, but they agree with the studies of eminent achievers at a broad level: Creative behavior, while possible throughout the adult years, becomes less frequent in later life.

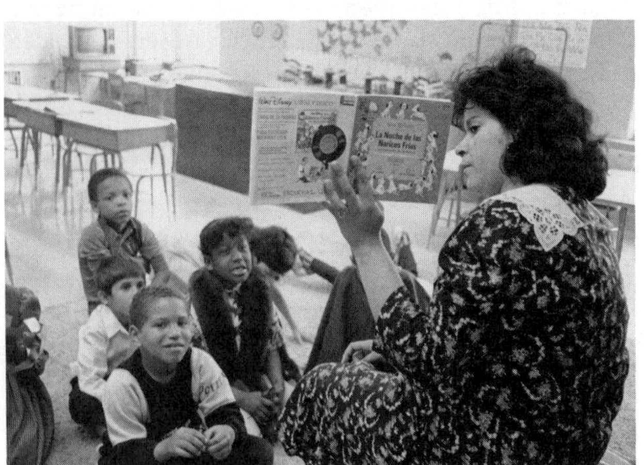

Head Start programs aim to stimulate the intellectual development of disadvantaged preschoolers.

APPLICATIONS: BOOSTING INTELLECTUAL PERFORMANCE ACROSS THE LIFE SPAN

How much can special training improve performance on tests of intelligence? Is special training effective only early in life when intellectual growth is most rapid, or can it also work later in life? Some intervention studies have explored how plastic or moldable intelligence is in early childhood, adolescence, and old age. Most of these interventions have been offered to those most in need of them—disadvantaged infants and preschoolers, mentally retarded individuals, and adults whose intellectual abilities are declining in old age.

During the 1960s, a number of programs were launched to enrich the early learning experiences of disadvantaged preschoolers. *Project Head Start* is perhaps the best known of these interventions. The idea was to provide a variety of social and intellectual experiences that might better prepare these children for school. At first, Head Start and similar programs seemed to be a smashing success. Children in the programs were posting average gains of about 10 points on IQ tests. But then discouragement set in: By the time children reached the middle years of grade school, their IQs were no higher than those of control-group children (e.g., Gray, Ramsey, & Klaus, 1982). Such findings led Arthur Jensen (1969, p. 2) to conclude that "compensatory education has been tried and it apparently has failed."

But that was not the end of it. Children in some of these programs have now been followed into their teens and even 20s. Irving Lazar and Richard Darlington (1982) reported on the long-term effects of 11 early intervention programs. These long-term studies indicate the following:

1. Children who participate in early intervention programs show immediate gains on IQ tests, whereas nonparticipants do not. But, indeed, the cognitive gains rarely last for more than three or four years after the program has ended. Programs that begin early and teach parents how to stimulate their children's intellectual growth so that they can continue to do so after the special intervention has ended may achieve somewhat longer-lasting IQ gains (Levenstein, 1970). Still, IQ gains tend to fade. Impacts on measures other than IQ are more encouraging.
2. Participants tend to score somewhat higher than nonparticipants on tests of reading, language, and mathematics achievement. In addition, this "achievement gap" seems to widen over the years.
3. Compensatory education seems to improve children's attitudes about achievement. When asked to describe something that has made them feel proud of themselves, program participants are more likely than nonparticipants to mention scholastic achievements or (in the case of 15- to 18-year-olds) job-related successes.
4. Program participants are more likely to meet their school's basic requirements than nonparticipants are. They are less likely to be assigned to special education classes, to be retained in a grade, or to drop out of high school. Graduates of the highly successful Perry Preschool Program, for example, were less likely than control youth to experience failure in school or to be involved in delinquent behavior as adolescents (Berrueta-Clement, Schweinhart, Barnett, Epstein, & Weikart, 1984).

In sum, longitudinal evaluations suggest that compensatory education has been tried and *apparently it works*! Early intervention also works with handicapped and mentally retarded youngsters (White, 1985–1986). It will be of interest to see if differences between participants and nonparticipants survive through the adult years. It will also be of interest to see if disadvantaged children who receive special interventions starting in infancy (e.g., Ramey & Haskins, 1981) fare better later in life than those whose programs started in the preschool years.

These findings are indeed encouraging, but is it too late to intervene after the years of infancy and early childhood have passed? Not at all, says Israeli psychologist Reuven Feuerstein. Early in this chapter, we described Feuerstein's innovative approach to testing intelligence by directly testing the potential to learn with guidance. He has also developed cognitive training programs for culturally disadvantaged and mentally retarded adolescents and young adults (Feuerstein, Miller, Hoffman, Rand, Mintzker, & Jensen, 1981). His theory is that such individuals are not learning as much from their direct experiences as more advantaged learners are. What they need, then, is a "mediator," a guide who structures and interprets the environment for them at first. They will then learn how to learn more from their experiences on their own. Feuerstein's program leads students through several cognitive tasks, teaching them the concepts and cognitive strategies they need to perform well. It also attempts to increase their motivation to learn.

Participants in one intervention study were 12- to 15-year-old mentally retarded and nearly mentally retarded adolescents who were 3 to 4 years behind their peers academically (Feuerstein et al., 1981). Compared to a control group that received a general enrichment program, participants in Feuerstein's special program showed immediate gains on intellectual and cognitive measures. Moreover, participants were still ahead of nonparticipants two years later when they had been drafted into the Israeli Army and took a military intelligence test and the Primary Mental Abilities test. Even more impressively, benefits of the training appeared to *increase* over this two-year period, rather than fading away as the gains of intervention programs often do. This kind of cumulative effect is precisely what Feuerstein expected. After all, his whole approach is aimed at helping students to learn more in the future from their own experiences.

Finally, what about old age? Can you teach old dogs new tricks? And can you reteach old dogs who have suffered declines in mental abilities the old tricks they have lost? K. Warner Schaie and Sherry Willis (1986) focused on spatial ability and reasoning, two of the fluid mental abilities that are most likely to decline in old age. Within a group of older people ranging in age from 64 to 95 and participating in the Seattle longitudinal study of intelligence, they first identified individuals whose scores on one or the other of the abilities had declined over a 14-year period, as well as individuals who had remained stable over the same period. The goal with the decliners would be to restore lost ability; the goal with those who had maintained their ability would be to improve it. Participants were exposed to five hours of training in either spatial ability or reasoning and took pretests and posttests on measures of both abilities. The spatial training involved learning how to rotate objects in space, at first physically and then mentally. Training in reasoning involved learning how to examine a series of stimuli (for example, musical notes) and detect a recurring pattern in the series in order to identify what the next stimulus in the sequence (for example, the next note) should be.

Figure 9.8 shows the effects of the training. Those who were trained in an ability clearly showed greater gains in that ability than did those who were trained in the other ability. And both those who had suffered ability declines and those who had maintained their abilities prior to the study improved, though decliners showed significantly more improvement in spatial ability than nondecliners did. Schaie and Willis estimated that between 40% and 62% of the decliners gained enough through training to bring them back up to the level of performance that they had achieved 14 years earlier before decline set in.

The larger messages? You *can* teach old dogs new tricks—and reteach them old tricks—in very little time. Similar studies suggest that the benefits of training persist, at least for the periods for which follow-up data exist (Hayslip, 1989; Willis, 1985), and that older adults can even improve on their own by practicing relevant skills (Baltes, Sowarka, & Kliegl, 1989). Schaie and Willis warn that they worked with a healthy group and that their findings do not mean that elderly people with brain disorders can be aided to this degree. But they do emphasize that for many older adults, "observed cognitive decline is not irreversible, is likely to be attributable to disuse, and can be subjected to environmental manipulations involving relatively simple and inexpensive educational training techniques" (p. 231). In sum, we are delighted to conclude that the minds of healthy human beings have a good deal of plasticity over the entire life span!

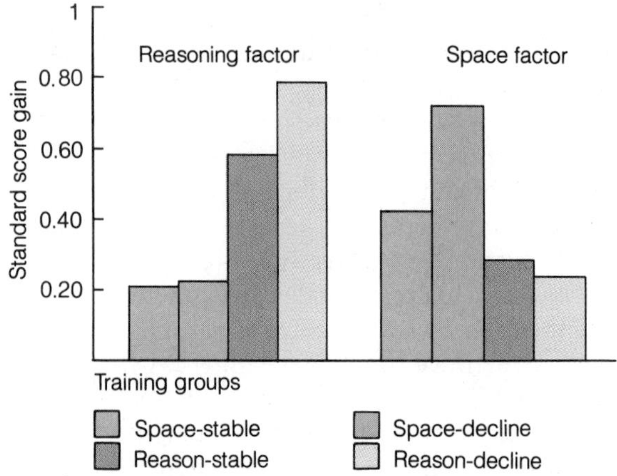

Figure 9.8 Effects of training on the spatial ability and reasoning of elderly adults. To interpret the size of the gains in, for example, the reasoning factor (left side of the figure), bear in mind that those trained in spatial ability (both those whose abilities declined before the training study and those whose abilities had remained stable) did not receive training in reasoning. Therefore they are the untrained control group when the changes in scores on the reasoning tests are considered—but they are the trained group when scores on spatial ability tests are considered. (From Schaie & Willis, 1986)

REFLECTIONS

Our account of cognitive development over the life span is now complete. We hope you appreciate that each of the three major approaches to the mind that we have considered—the Piagetian cognitive-developmental approach discussed in Chapter 7, the information-processing approach discussed in Chapter 8, and the psychometric or testing approach discussed here—offers something of value. Perhaps we can summarize it this way: Piaget has shown us that comparing the thought of a preschooler to the thought of an adult is like comparing a tadpole and a frog. Modes of thought change qualitatively with age. The information-processing approach has put the thinking process under a microscope so that we can understand more precisely why the young child cannot remember as much information or solve problems as successfully as the adult can. Finally, the psychometric approach has told us that if we look at the wide range of tasks to which the mind can be applied, we can recognize distinct mental abilities that each person consistently displays in greater or lesser amounts. We need not choose one approach and reject the others. Our understanding of the mind is likely to be richer if all three approaches continue to thrive.

Indeed, the three approaches have led us to some of the very same conclusions. No matter how we have looked at cognitive development, we have seen that dramatic cognitive growth in infancy, childhood, and adolescence is followed by relative stability during early adulthood and middle age, and finally by modest decline in old age for at least some individuals. We have also seen that cognitive performance can be improved at any age. And finally, we have seen that *cognition becomes specialized*. Adults are most likely to use Piaget's formal operational thought in their areas of specialization. They develop specialized knowledge bases and information-processing strategies that allow them to think most effectively in the areas they know best. And, as we have seen here, they may have plenty of one mental ability but little of another, or may gain ground in one ability over time while losing ground in another. One's age, immediate environment, and larger cultural and historical contexts influence which abilities prosper and which do not.

There are truly many "intelligences." And from today's vantage point, it seems foolish indeed to think that a single IQ score can possibly describe the complexities of human cognitive development.

SUMMARY POINTS

1. The psychometric or testing approach to cognition defines intelligence as a set of traits that allows some people to think and solve problems more effectively than others do. Sternberg's contemporary triarchic theory of intelligence offers an alternative view.

2. Intelligence tests such as the Stanford-Binet and the Wechsler scales compare an individual's performance on a variety of cognitive tasks with the average performance of age mates. IQ scores in the population form a normal or bell-shaped distribution with an average score of 100.

3. In infancy, mental growth is rapid and is measured by developmental quotients derived from tests such as the Bayley Scales. However, infant scores do not predict later IQ well; rapid habituation and novelty seeking do.

4. During childhood, mental growth continues and IQs at one age predict IQs at later ages quite well; however, many individuals show wide variations in their IQ scores over time. Those who gain IQ points often have favorable home environments, while disadvantaged children often show a cumulative deficit.

5. In adolescence, IQs continue to be relatively stable over time and to predict school achievement. The timing of puberty is related to performance on measures of spatial ability but may not explain sex differences in this intellectual skill.

6. IQ is related to the status or prestige of an adult's occupation, but it predicts success within a given occupation only for intermediate-status jobs. Both cross-sectional studies and longitudinal studies tend to distort the picture of age-related change. Sequential studies suggest that (a) date of birth (cohort) influences test performance, (b) no major declines in mental abilities occur until the 60s or 70s, (c) some abilities decline more than others do, and (d) not all people's abilities decline. Decline is most likely in those who have poor health and unstimulating lifestyles.

7. Individual differences in IQ at a given age may be linked to qualities of the early home environment, birth order, family size, and social class. The low average scores of some minority groups on IQ tests may be explained by disadvantaged environments or cultural differences in test taking. Black children perform much better if they grow up in stimulating homes.

8. Children identified as gifted on the basis of a high IQ score have been found to be above average in virtually all ways; mentally retarded individuals show varied levels of functioning depending on their IQs and the causes of their retardation. Mildly retarded individuals appear to meet the demands of adult life better than those of school.

9. Creativity, the ability to produce novel and socially valued works, is a distinct mental ability that demands divergent rather than convergent thinking; it is largely independent of IQ once a minimum IQ is exceeded. Eminent creators are typically most productive during their 30s and 40s. Creative capacities survive into old age; but average older adults perform less well on creativity tests than younger adults do.

10. Attempts to boost performance on IQ tests suggest that mental abilities are plastic throughout the life span.

KEY TERMS

automatization
convergent thinking
creativity
crystallized intelligence
cultural/familial retardation
culture bias
cumulative-deficit hypothesis
developmental quotient (DQ)
divergent thinking
factor analysis
fluid intelligence
giftedness
HOME inventory
ideational fluency
idiot savant
impulsivity
intelligence quotient (IQ)
mental age (MA)
mental retardation
normal distribution
organic retardation
psychometric approach
reflectivity
structure-of-intellect model
terminal drop
test norms
triarchic theory of intelligence

CHAPTER

10

SELF-CONCEPTIONS, PERSONALITY, AND EMOTIONAL EXPRESSION

Roger, age 54: I think back to what I was like as a teenager and just laugh. I was so shy I could hardly carry on a conversation with anyone except my brother. And girls—forget it. I couldn't get near them without panicking. I had no confidence at all back then, but I'm a totally different person now. I'm much more relaxed and outgoing. I deal with people every day at work and think nothing of it, and I'm not afraid to tell my boss exactly what I think.

Kay, age 48: I'm really not any different today than I was in college. I've always liked being around people and having a good time, and I've always believed you've got to stand up for what you believe. I had a temper back then, and that's still true today. "Same old Kay"—that's what my friends say.

Both of these adults seem to have a clear sense of what they are like as individuals. Yet one perceives that his personality has changed dramatically over the years, while the other feels strongly that her past and present selves are one and the same. This chapter is about the ways in which our personalities, and our perceptions of those personalities, change—and remain the same—over the life span.

CONCEPTUALIZING THE SELF

How would you describe yourself as a person? If you are like most adults, you would probably respond by mentioning your noteworthy interpersonal characteristics (for example, honesty, friendliness, or kindness), your religious or moral preferences, and your interests and values. In doing so, you would be describing that elusive concept that psychologists call the personality. **Personality** can be defined as the organized combination of attributes, motives, values, and behaviors that is unique to each individual. Most often, people (psychologists included) try to describe personalities in terms of *personality traits*—dispositions such as sociability, independence, dominance, anxiety, and so on, which are assumed to be relatively consistent across different situations and over time. Thus if you peg a classmate as insecure, you expect this person to behave insecurely at school and at work, now and next year. Similarly, psychologists who adopt the *psychometric approach* to personality, and who therefore attempt to measure aspects of personality through the use of tests and scales, assume that an individual's personality traits do not change from day to day. Whether or not our personality traits do in fact remain highly consistent across situations and times is a question that this chapter examines in some detail.

Theories of Personality Development

How does the personality develop? Is it formed in childhood so that we enter adulthood with a consistent set of predispositions that last a lifetime? Or is it something far more changeable, something that can take dramatic turns at any point in life? To get some feel for current debates about the nature of personality development, let us examine some striking differences between two major theoretical perspectives on the nature of personality and personality development.

Psychoanalytic Theory

Sigmund Freud was concerned with the development and inner dynamics of three parts of the personality: the selfish id, the rational ego, and the moralistic superego (see Chapter 2). Freud strongly believed that biological urges residing within the id push all children through universal stages of psychosexual development, starting with the oral stage of infancy and ending with the genital stage of adolescence when sexual maturity is attained. Freud apparently did not believe that the personality continues to develop after adolescence, since he did not propose stages of adult psychosexual growth. In fact, Freud believed that the personality was formed in infancy and early childhood—during the first five years of life, essentially—and changed little thereafter. His view was that anxieties arising from harsh parenting and other unfavorable early experiences would leave a permanent mark on the personality and reveal themselves in adult personality traits.

Erik Erikson, a neo-Freudian theorist, also proposed stages of personality development but thought that the personality *does* continue to change and grow during adulthood. As individuals successfully resolve the central conflict of each stage of psychosocial development, they gain new personality strengths—for example, a sense of purpose as a preschooler, life goals as an adolescent, or a greater concern for future generations as a middle-aged adult (see Table 10.1). Individual differences in personality presumably reflect the different experiences individuals have as they struggle to cope with the challenges of each life stage. Evidence bearing on Erikson's theory of psychosocial development is considered in this chapter.

Recently, other stage theorists have followed in the footsteps of Erikson by proposing systematic changes in personality during adulthood. In this chapter, for example, we will encounter the work of George Vaillant, a psychoanalytically oriented theorist who has built on Erikson's theory. Another psychoanalytically influenced theorist, Daniel Levinson, is one of the leading proponents of the view that most adults experience a predictable "midlife crisis" stage of development during their 40s. (His views are examined in Chapter 15.) These theorists do not agree with Freud that the personality is essentially "set in stone" during early childhood. Yet they and others continue to pursue the psychoanalytic notion that people everywhere progress through systematic stages of development, undergoing similar personality changes at similar ages.

Social Learning Theory

Social learning theorists such as Albert Bandura question the whole idea of universal stages of human development. Instead, they emphasize that we can change at any time in life if our environments change. An aggressive boy can become a warm and caring man if his aggression is no longer rewarded; a woman who has been socially withdrawn can become more outgoing if she begins to interact closely with friends who serve as models of outgoing, sociable behavior. From this perspective, personality is a set of behavior tendencies very much influenced by the specific social situations in which we find ourselves and by our interactions with other people.

Believing strongly in situational influences on behavior, social learning theorists have tended to doubt that people have enduring tendencies called personality traits that show themselves consistently in a wide range of situations over long stretches of the life span. True, this kind of consistency could occur if the individual's social environment remained the same, as might be the case for a rancher who continues to do the same ranching on the same ranch in the same small town for a lifetime. However, most of us experience a series of changes in our social environments as we become older. Just as we behave differently when we are in a library than when we are at a party, we may become "different people" as we take on new roles in life, develop new relationships, or move to new locations. To the social

Table 10.1 Erikson's stages of psychosocial development in brief

AGE RANGE	STAGE	EMERGING PERSONALITY STRENGTH
Birth to 1 year	Trust vs. mistrust	Hope
1 to 3 years	Autonomy vs. shame and doubt	Will (a sense of self)
3 to 6 years	Initiative vs. guilt	Purpose (goal setting)
6 to 12 years	Industry vs. inferiority	Competence
12 to 20 years	Identity vs. role confusion	Fidelity (ability to commit self)
20 to 40 years (early adulthood)	Intimacy vs. isolation	Love
40 to 65 years (middle adulthood)	Generativity vs. stagnation	Care (investment in future generations)
65 or so on (late adulthood)	Integrity vs. despair	Wisdom

learning theorist, then, personality development is a very individual process whose direction depends on each person's social experiences. Other nonstage theorists, including those who adopt the contextual-dialectical perspective introduced in Chapter 2, make similar assumptions.

Obviously stage theorists and nonstage theorists do not see eye to eye about how the personality develops! Stage theorists propose universal, age-related personality changes, while nonstage theorists propose that change may occur any time in life and can proceed in many directions. Moreover, some theorists, notably Freud, assume that personality development is essentially completed early in life and that our traits remain largely stable thereafter, whereas other theorists suspect that we never stop changing as individuals.

Self-Concept and Self-Esteem

When you describe yourself, you may not be describing your actual personality so much as you are revealing your **self-concept**—your *perceptions* of your unique attributes or traits. We all know people who seem to have unrealistic self-conceptions—the fellow who thinks he is "God's gift to women" (who don't agree) or the woman who believes she is a dull plodder but is actually very bright. A closely related aspect of self-perception is **self-esteem**—a person's overall evaluation of his or her worth as a person. The self-concept is cognitive in nature, consisting of many different beliefs about the self. By contrast, self-esteem is a person's overall emotional or evaluative reaction to those beliefs. Like self-concept, self-esteem is not necessarily an accurate reflection of "objective" personality. One person may have high self-esteem despite possessing many undesirable qualities, while another may have low self-esteem despite being a thoroughly admirable person.

Because self-concept and self-esteem may or may not be accurate reflections of a person's objective characteristics, this chapter concerns the development of objective personality traits as well as more subjective self-conceptions and evaluations. When do infants become aware of themselves as distinct individuals, and when do they begin to display their own unique personalities? What do children of different ages focus on when they describe themselves, and to what extent do their personality traits predict what they will be like as adults? How do adolescents go about "finding themselves" as individuals? Do people's personalities and self-perceptions systematically change over the adult years, or do they remain essentially the same? Having answered some of these questions, we will take a closer look at the development of one particularly fascinating facet of personality—the way in which we experience and express emotions.

THE INFANT

If you could somehow peek inside the mind of an infant, do you think you would find a "self"? Do infants have any awareness that they exist or any sense of themselves as distinct individuals? Let's explore this issue and then see if it makes any sense to say that infants display unique "personalities."

The Emerging Self

Many developmental theorists believe that infants are born without a sense of self. Margaret Mahler (Mahler, Pine, & Bergman, 1975) likens the newborn to a "chick in an egg" who has no reason to differentiate itself from the surrounding environment. After all, every need that the baby has is soon satisfied by companions, who are simply "there" and have no identities of their own. When, then, do infants first come to gain a sense of themselves as beings separate from the world around them?

This is not an easy question to answer, but it is helpful to recall Piaget's description of cognitive development during early infancy. It is between about 4 and 8 months of age (the stage of secondary circular reactions) that infants stop restricting their activities to parts of their own bodies (for example, by repeatedly kicking their legs) and begin to act on *external* objects (for example, by repeatedly shaking a rattle). Thus by the middle of their first year, infants seem to have learned something about the limits of their own bodies and have come to recognize that they can operate on objects external to this "physical self." Indeed, the first glimmers of this capacity to distinguish self from environment can be detected in the first month or two of life (Stern, 1983).

Once infants know *that they are* (that they exist independently of other entities), they are in a position to find out *who* or *what* they are (Harter, 1983). When do infants recognize themselves as distinct individuals and become able to tell themselves apart from other infants? To find out, Michael Lewis and Jeanne Brooks-Gunn (1979) used an ingenious technique first used with chimpanzees: Mother daubs a spot of rouge on the infant's nose and then places the infant in front of a mirror. If infants have some mental image of their own faces and recognize their mirror images as themselves, they should soon notice the red spot and reach for or wipe their own noses rather than the nose of the mirror image. When infants 9 to 24 months old were given this rouge test, the youngest infants showed no self-recognition: They seemed to treat the image in the mirror as if it were "some other kid." Signs of self-recognition were evident among a few of the 15-month-olds, but only among the 18- to 24-month-olds did a large majority of infants touch their noses, apparently realizing that they had a strange mark on their faces that warranted investigation. They knew exactly who that kid in the mirror was!

To recognize their own facial features, infants seem to have to categorize the people they encounter in daily life and then place themselves into the social categories they are forming. According to Lewis and Brooks-Gunn, infants begin to form a **categorical self** as they classify themselves along socially significant dimensions such as age and sex, figuring out what is "like me" and what is "not like me." By the end of the first year, infants are already able to distinguish between strange babies and strange adults or between strange women and strange men (Lewis & Brooks-Gunn, 1979; Brooks-Gunn & Lewis, 1981). They become aware that they are like other babies rather than like adults and like either males or females. Before they are 18 months of age, infants are more able to tell themselves apart from opposite-sex babies or from older individuals than they are able to distinguish between photos of themselves and other infants of the same gender. As they approach age 2, they also master this task. Overall, then, if an infant girl 18 months of age could respond verbally to the question "Who am I?" she might well say, "I look like a baby and I look like a girl."

In sum, self-recognition and self-awareness develop gradually during the two years of infancy so that by 18 to 24 months of age most infants definitely have an awareness of who they are—at least as a physical self with a unique appearance and as a categorical self belonging to specific age and gender categories. To what can we attribute this emerging self-awareness? First, the ability to recognize the self depends on cognitive development. By about 18 to 24 months of age, infants fully master the concept that objects have a permanent existence, and they become capable of mentally representing the world around them through images (see Chapter 7). Indeed, the development of object permanence and the development of self-recognition are closely related (Berthenthal & Fischer, 1978). Interestingly, children who are mentally retarded are slow to recognize themselves in a mirror but can do so once they have attained a mental age of at least 18 to 20 months (Hill & Tomlin, 1981).

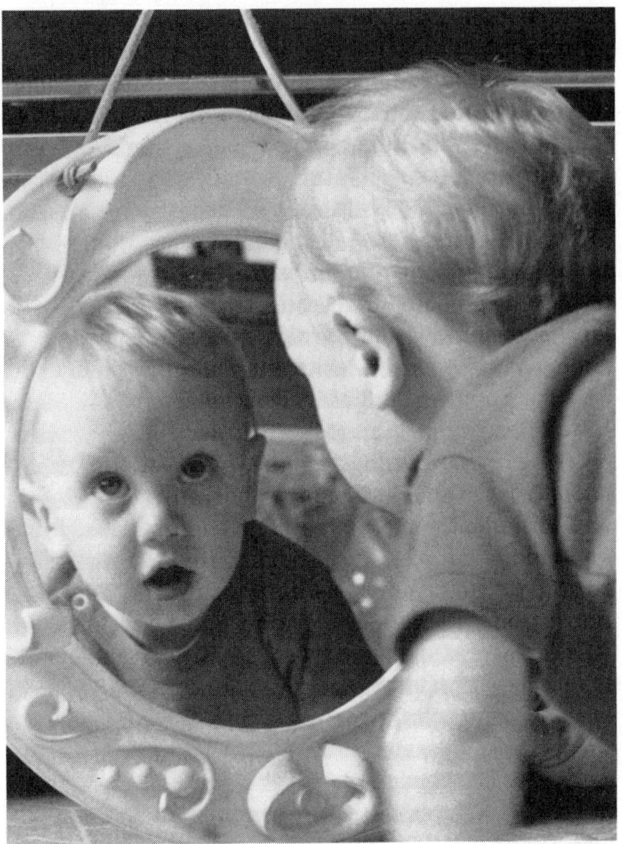

Recognizing one's mirror image is an important milestone in the development of the self.

Self-awareness also seems to depend on social experience. Chimpanzees who have been raised in complete isolation, unlike those who have had contact with other chimps, fail to recognize themselves in a mirror (Gallup, 1979). The critical role of social interaction in the development of the self was appreciated long ago by Charles

Cooley (1902) and George Herbert Mead (1934). Cooley used the term **looking-glass self** to emphasize that our understanding of self is a reflection of how other people respond to us; that is, our self-concepts are the images cast by a social mirror. Through their actions and words, parents and other companions communicate to infants that they are babies and are also either girls or boys. Later, social feedback helps children determine what they are like and what they can and cannot do well. Throughout life, we forge new self-concepts through our social interactions. Thus the development of the self and social development are closely intertwined, beginning in infancy.

The Budding Personality

Even though it takes infants some time to become aware of themselves as individuals, they *are* individuals with their own distinctive personalities from the first weeks of life. The study of infant personality has centered on dimensions of **temperament**, or tendencies to respond in predictable ways to events—tendencies that can be considered the building blocks of personality. Although temperament has been defined and measured in a number of different ways, there is much agreement that babies differ in their temperaments from an early age (Goldsmith et al., 1987).

For example, Arnold Buss and Robert Plomin (1984) have found that some babies are more *emotionally reactive* (or easily and intensely irritated by events) than others are; that some are highly *active* while others are quite sluggish; and that some are very *sociable*, or interested in and responsive to people, while others are standoffish (Buss & Plomin, 1984). Because identical twin infants are more similar in these aspects of temperament than fraternal twin infants are, there is good reason to believe that temperament is partly influenced by genetic endowment.

Another revealing approach to the study of temperament has been developed by Alexander Thomas, Stella Chess, and their colleagues (Chess & Thomas, 1984; Thomas, Chess, & Birch, 1970; Thomas & Chess, 1977, 1986). These researchers gathered information about nine dimensions of infant behavior (for example, activity level, typical mood, regularity or predictability of feeding and sleeping habits, and adaptability to new experiences or changes in routine). They were able to place most infants into one of three categories according to the overall patterning of their temperamental qualities:

1. *The easy child.* Easy infants are even-tempered, are typically content or happy, and are quite open and adaptable to new experiences such as the approach of a stranger or their first taste of strained plums. They have regular feeding and sleeping habits, and they tolerate frustrations and discomforts well.
2. *The difficult child.* Difficult infants are active, irritable, and irregular in their habits. They often react very negatively (and vigorously) to changes in routine and are often slow to adapt to new people or situations. They cry frequently and loudly and often have tantrums when they are frustrated by such events as being restrained or having to live with a dirty diaper.
3. *The slow-to-warm-up child.* Slow-to-warm-up infants are quite inactive, somewhat moody, and only moderately regular in their daily schedules. Like difficult children, they are slow to adapt to new people and situations, but they typically respond in mildly rather than intensely negative ways. For example, they may resist cuddling by looking away from the cuddler rather than by kicking or screaming. They do eventually adjust, showing a quiet interest in new foods, people, or places.

Among the infants in New York studied longitudinally by Thomas and Chess, 40% (happily) were easy infants; 10% were difficult infants; 15% were slow-to-warm-up infants; and the remaining third could not be clearly placed in one category or another because they shared qualities of two or more categories. Thomas and Chess also found that infants who were easy, slow-to-warm-up, or difficult at 2 months of age often fell into the same category later in infancy.

Does an infant's early temperament predict his or her later personality? Jerome Kagan, Steven Reznick, and their colleagues have been investigating one aspect of early temperament that they believe is highly significant—the tendency to be inhibited or uninhibited in the face of new experiences (Kagan, 1989; Kagan, Reznick, Snidman, Gibbons, & Johnson, 1988; Reznick et al., 1986). At the age of 21 months, inhibited children could be identified by their tendency to take time to warm up to a strange examiner, to retreat from unfamiliar objects such as a large robot, and to fret and cling to their mothers. At ages 5½ and 7½, differences between inhibited and uninhibited children were still evident. Children who had been inhibited toddlers were more likely than children who had been uninhibited at 21 months to be shy with peers and to be cautious in new situations. Kagan and his colleagues have also found that inhibited youngsters become physiologically aroused (as indicated by their high heart rates) in situations that barely faze other children. The researchers suspect that this early behavioral style may be genetically influenced and that at least some inhibited children grow up to be introverted and anxious adults who do not deal well with job interviews or other potentially stressful situations.

Could it be that our personalities are largely sketched out at conception and that we carry through life the temperamental qualities that we first display as young infants? It is not that simple. Instead, early temperamental qualities *may or may not* carry over into childhood and adulthood depending on the interaction between the individual's predispositions and his or her social environment. Alexander Thomas and Stella Chess have demonstrated this point well by showing how babies' temperaments can affect their parents and how parents in turn can affect their children's future personalities. We explore this fascinating and important research in Box 10.1.

In sum, by the time the first two years of life come to a close, infants have become very aware of themselves as individuals. Toddlers recognize themselves in the mirror, refer to themselves by name, and understand that they are physically distinct from other human beings. Cognitive development and experiences with the social looking glass make this new self-awareness possible. Moreover, each toddler has his or her own personality, based in part on temperamental qualities that are genetically influenced and that are apparent early in infancy. However, the personality is by no means set in infancy; temperamental traits sometimes carry over into later life, but they sometimes have little bearing on later personality (Moss & Susman, 1980). Children's personalities will continue to form, and they will acquire much richer understandings of themselves as individuals, as they continue to experience cognitive growth and continue to interact with other people after their infant years.

THE CHILD

Ask children of different ages to tell you about themselves. You'll find their responses amusing, and you'll learn something about how children get a better grasp on what they are like as individuals.

Elaborating on a Sense of Self

Once toddlers begin to talk, they can tell us about their emerging self-concepts—and do! By age 2, some toddlers are already using the personal pronouns *I, me, my,* and *mine* (or their names) when referring to the self and *you* when addressing a companion (Lewis & Brooks-Gunn, 1979). This linguistic distinction suggests that 2-year-olds now have a firm concept of "self" and "others" (who are also recognized as selves). Toddlers also show us that they are developing a categorical self when they describe themselves in terms of age ("I this many"), size and gender ("I big girl now"), and types of activities ("Davie runner—zoom"). During the preschool years, children gain more and more understanding of which social categories they belong to.

However, the preschool child's self-concept is very concrete and physical (Damon & Hart, 1982). When asked to describe themselves, preschoolers dwell on their physical characteristics ("I have brown hair"), their possessions ("I have a bike"), and the physical actions they can perform ("I can jump"). In one study (Keller, Ford, & Meachum, 1978), 3- to 5-year-olds were asked to say ten things about themselves and to complete the sentences "I am a ________" and "I am a boy/girl who ________." Fully half of the children's responses were *action* statements such as "I play baseball" or "I walk to school." Very few of these young children made any mention of their psychological traits or inner qualities. Adults who describe themselves in such concrete, physical terms are considered more than a bit shallow!

Dramatic changes in self-descriptions are apparent by about the age of 8 (Livesley & Bromley, 1973). Now children seem to be capable of looking beneath the surface and describing their enduring inner qualities or traits ("I'm friendly," "I'm funny," and so on). They now understand that an inner world of thoughts and feelings exists and sets them apart from other individuals (Damon & Hart, 1982). Moreover, while many of their self-descriptions still center on their actions, they now describe not just what they typically do or what they can do but how their abilities compare with those of their companions (Secord & Peevers, 1974). The preschooler who claims to be able to throw a ball now becomes the third grader who claims to be able to throw one farther than any of her classmates can. What has changed? For one thing, children who have entered the concrete-operational stage of cognitive development are capable of forming generalizations about their characteristic behavior, of detecting their consistent traits. For another, they are more capable of engaging in social comparison—of noticing how they stack up compared with other individuals and using that information to judge themselves. They then define and judge themselves in terms of whether they are more or less competent than other children.

Social comparisons help school-aged children understand both how they are like others and how they are different from others. On the one hand, elementary school children are more likely than preschoolers to define them-

Box 10.1 Early Temperament, Parenting, and Later Development

In their longitudinal study of temperament from early infancy to early adulthood, Alexander Thomas and Stella Chess tried to find out whether an infant's temperament predicts what he or she will be like as a child, adolescent, or young adult (Chess & Thomas, 1984; Thomas & Chess, 1986). They found that early temperamental patterns do indeed persist to some extent and affect an individual's adjustment later in life: Difficult infants who had often fussed when they could not have more milk often became children who fell apart if they could not work math problems correctly. Moreover, while temperament during *infancy* had little bearing on adjustment during adulthood, being difficult (or easy) in temperament as a 3- or 4-year-old actually predicted being difficult (or easy) in temperament and being poorly or well adjusted as a young adult.

Even so, early and later temperament were not so strongly linked as this discussion might imply, and the longer the time span, the weaker the relationship. Some easy children turned into maladjusted adults—and some difficult children outgrew their behavior problems. What, then, determines whether or not temperamental qualities persist?

Much may depend on how parents respond to their children. The parents of difficult children can easily take it personally when their babies cry all the time and may even become resentful and hostile. Thus the infant's own qualities may bring out impatience, irritation, and punitive attitudes in parents who might have been far more affectionate interacting with an easy baby. In turn, a tense and punitive parent is likely to make the child all the more difficult, and a sort of vicious cycle will be set in motion. Chess and Thomas found that difficult children were especially likely to display behavior problems later in life if their parents had been impatient, inconsistent, and demanding.

Difficult infants whose parents adapted more successfully to their temperaments and gave them more time to adjust to new experiences became able to master new situations effectively and energetically. The case of Carl illustrates this process. Early in life, Carl was one of the most difficult children Chess and Thomas encountered: "Whether it was the first bath or the first solid foods in infancy, the beginning of nursery and elementary school, or the first birthday parties or shopping trips, each experience evoked stormy responses, with loud crying and struggling to get away" [1984, p. 188]. Carl's mother became convinced she was a bad mother, but fortunately Carl's father, an easygoing man himself, recognized and even delighted in Carl's "lusty" behavior and patiently and supportively waited for him to adapt to new situations.

This patient father helped his wife adopt his own patient style, and Carl did not develop serious behavior problems. Carl's difficult temperament did come out in force when he entered college. He became very frustrated and began to take a dim view of school, but he reduced his course load and got through this difficult period successfully. By age 23, he was no longer considered by the researchers to have a difficult temperament.

In the same way, slow-to-warm-up children fare much better when their parents are patient and reassuring than when their parents either pressure them to adapt too quickly to new situations or become overprotective of these apparently timid souls, denying them needed learning opportunities.

In sum, the roots of later personality seem to sprout very early in life, but personality is by no means set in stone in infancy and there is plenty of room for change in later years. Healthy personality development seems to depend on the "goodness of fit" between child and environment and on the mutual influences of parents and child on one another (Thomas & Chess, 1977; and see Lerner & Lerner, 1983, for similar evidence that adjustment in school is influenced by the fit between a child's temperament and a teacher's demands). The moral for parents is clear, then: Get to know your baby as an individual and allow for his or her special personality quirks.

selves as part of social units ("I'm a Kimball, a second grader at Oakhill School, a Brownie Scout"). They are forming a social identity that ties them to similar others (Damon & Hart, 1982). On the other hand, children also take special notice of how they differ from others. A black girl in a largely white school, for example, is more likely to mention her race when she is asked to tell about herself than is a black girl in an all-black school (McGuire, McGuire, Child, & Fujioka, 1978). Why? Simply because children do attempt to discover the ways in which they can distinguish themselves from their peers.

Self-Esteem

As children amass a wide range of perceptions of themselves and engage in social comparisons, they begin to evaluate their overall worth. Susan Harter (1982b) has developed a self-perception scale that asks children to evaluate their competencies in four areas:

1. Cognitive competence (for example, feeling smart, doing well in school)
2. Social competence (being popular, feeling liked)
3. Physical competence (being good at new games, excelling at sports)
4. General self-worth (feeling like a good person, and wanting to stay the same)

When this scale was given to third through ninth graders, it became obvious that even third graders had well-defined positive or negative feelings about themselves. Moreover, children make important distinctions between their competency in one kind of situation and their competency in another. That is, children do not just have generally high or generally low self-esteem. One child may feel very competent in sports but incompetent in the classroom, while another child may feel on top of things in academic and social situations but hopelessly inferior on the playground or athletic field.

Finally, children's self-ratings seem to be relatively accurate reflections of how others perceive them; for example, children with high cognitive self-esteem are rated as cognitively competent by their teachers, and children with high physical self-esteem are frequently chosen by peers in sporting events. In Harter's study, the accuracy of self-evaluations increased over the elementary school years. Moreover, when Harter revised her scale for use with preschoolers, she discovered that the self-evaluations of 4- to 7-year-old children are not yet as accurate as those of older children (Harter & Pike, 1984). The self-esteem scores of young children may reflect their *desires* to be liked or to be "good" at various activities as much as their actual competencies. Thus self-evaluations become more realistic as children mature. At the same time, children are increasingly realizing what they "should" be like, and forming an ever-grander "ideal self." The gap between the real self and the ideal self therefore increases with age (Glick & Zigler, 1985).

The emergence of concern with social comparison at about age 7 or 8 also has important implications for self-esteem. Preschoolers often seem to be rather oblivious to information about how they compare to others (Ruble, 1983). They have a delightful tendency to believe that they are the greatest, even in the face of direct evidence that they have been outclassed by their peers. Even kindergartners in the classroom rarely behave in ways that suggest they are trying to evaluate themselves in comparison to others (Frey & Ruble, 1985). They do watch their classmates and sometimes even make social comparisons ("Same lunchbox—we're twinsies!"), but they seem to be doing this out of an interest in being sociable and making friends. They are simply noting similarities between themselves and other children.

By contrast, first-grade children begin to seek information that will tell them whether they are more or less competent than their peers; they glance at each other's papers, ask "How many did you miss?" and say things like "I can't write as well as Beth can" (Frey & Ruble, 1985). Older elementary school children are more subtle than first graders about making potentially embarrassing social comparisons out loud, but they sneak looks at other children's papers and are highly attentive to information about where they stand in the classroom pecking order. Unfortunately, many children inevitably come out on the short end of these social comparisons and come to lose some of the inflated self-esteem that they had as preschoolers (Dweck & Elliott, 1983). One of the reasons that some children have higher self-esteem than others do, then, is that some are in fact more competent and socially attractive than others are and therefore fare better in social comparisons.

Why else might some children develop higher self-esteem than others do? As you might guess, parents can play a critical role. Stanley Coopersmith (1967) has discovered that boys with high self-esteem have mothers who are highly loving and accepting and who enforce clearly stated rules of behavior while allowing their children to express their opinions and participate in decision making. We cannot be sure that this loving and democratic parenting style *causes* high self-esteem, but we can imagine such a causal process at work. Certainly the extent to which parents express approval and acceptance of their children is likely to affect how those children think about themselves (Isberg et al., 1989). Sending the message that "You're a good kid" promotes high self-esteem; saying, in effect, "You're no good; why can't you be like Susie?" is likely to have the opposite effect. This is the concept of the looking-glass self in action: Children will form self-concepts that reflect the evaluations of significant people in their lives.

But perhaps love and approval alone are not enough. A clear system of rules and consistent discipline provided in a spirit of democracy may also contribute to self-esteem by giving children a firm basis for evaluating whether their behavior is good or bad and also by sending them the message that their opinions are respected. Teachers, peers, and other significant individuals probably contribute to self-esteem in much the same way that parents do—by communicating their judgments of a child. These judgments, along with all the information that children gain by watching their behavior and comparing it with that of their peers, shape their overall self-evaluations. Once a child has high or low self-esteem, it tends to remain quite stable over the grade school years (Coopersmith, 1967). Most important, how children feel about themselves appears to be related to their adjustment. High self-esteem is associated with good performance in school, popularity, and many other positive attributes (Coopersmith, 1967).

The Personality Stabilizes

Although some aspects of an infant's temperament predict his or her later personality, other early personality tendencies do not seem to persist into childhood. For this reason, we cannot always be very confident that the sociable or irritable infant will remain that way as a child or adult. It seems that several important dimensions of personality do not "gel" until the elementary school years (Moss & Susman, 1980). The Fels Institute conducted a longitudinal study of development from birth to early adulthood reported by Jerome Kagan and Howard Moss (1962). In this study, some traits that first stabilized in childhood remained evident in adulthood while other traits changed considerably (see Figure 10.1). Achievement orientation, sex-typed (or sex-appropriate) activity, and spontaneity were reasonably stable over time in both males and females. For example, children who were highly achievement oriented were still highly achievement oriented as young adults, whereas their less academically oriented peers turned into adults with little motivation to achieve. By contrast, tendencies toward anger or aggression and initiation of activities with the other sex were stable for males but not for females, whereas tendencies to react passively in stressful situations and to be dependent on other people were much more stable for females.

How can we explain this pattern of results? Kagan and Moss (1962) suggest that the stability of a personality trait over time depends on its being valued by society and consistent with society's prescribed gender roles. Only then will it be reinforced. Parents, peers, teachers, and other agents of socialization do indeed value achievement in both sexes, so early socialization experiences encourage both boys and girls to remain achievement oriented. Society also encourages sex-typed activities for both boys and girls. But aggressive tendencies may persist more in boys, and passivity and dependence may be more stable in girls, because our society has traditionally not allowed aggressive girls to remain aggressive or dependent boys to remain dependent.

Overall, then, childhood behaviors that are socially valued may endure, whereas traits that conflict with cultural norms may be discouraged and may fail to persist into adulthood. It is clear that children do develop distinctive personalities; moreover, *some* of their traits stay with them over the years.

The Self and Erikson's Stages of Psychosocial Development

Let's conclude our discussion of childhood personality development by applying Erik Erikson's (1963, 1982) theory of psychosocial development. Erikson would not be at all surprised by the sorts of developmental changes in

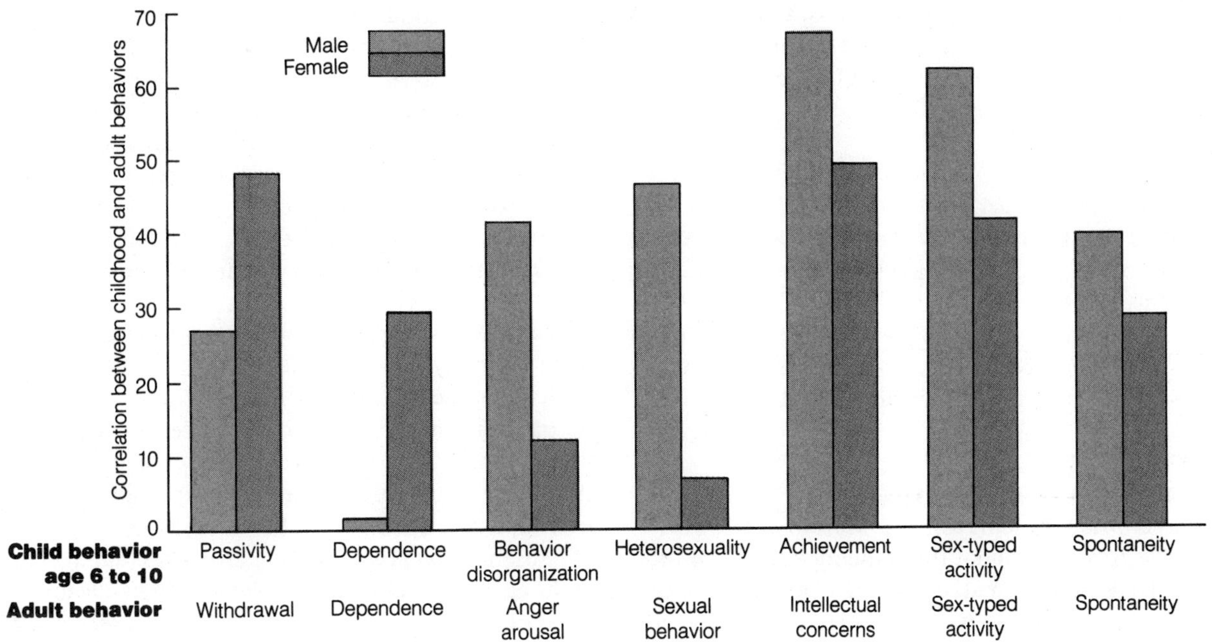

Figure 10.1 Stability and change in seven classes of behavior between childhood and early adulthood. *Note:* Each bar shows the correlation between child behavior and adult behavior. The higher the correlation, the more the individual's standing within the group on the trait remains consistent over time. (Adapted from Kagan & Moss, 1962)

self-conceptions and self-evaluations that have been described. Erikson proposed that infants face the psychosocial conflict of basic **trust versus mistrust** (see Chapter 2). During this period, they begin to recognize that they are separate from the caregivers who respond to their needs; as we have seen, infants do indeed learn to distinguish self from other (typically mother).

Toddlers, or those "terrible" 2-year-olds, acquire an even clearer sense of themselves as individuals as they struggle with the psychosocial conflict of **autonomy versus shame and doubt**. They are determined to do things themselves to demonstrate their independence and their control over their parents. They say "me, me, me," and "no," even when they really mean "yes," loudly proclaiming that they have wills of their own. Notice that this quest for autonomy is happening at the very age when children recognize themselves in the mirror. Four- and 5-year-olds who have achieved a sense of autonomy enter Erikson's stage of **initiative versus guilt**. In these years of imaginative play, children acquire new motor skills; devise grand plans to build sand castles, bake cakes, or conquer the "bad guys" in their fantasies; and take great pride in accomplishing the goals they set. Isn't it understandable, then, that these preschool children would define themselves in terms of their physical activities and abilities?

A sense of initiative, Erikson believes, will pave the way for success when elementary schoolchildren face the conflict of **industry versus inferiority**. To gain a sense of industry, children must master the important cognitive and social skills—reading, writing, cooperative teamwork, and so on—that are necessary to win the approval of both adults and peers. It seems natural that they would measure themselves against their peers to determine how competent they are becoming—that is, that they would use social comparison to evaluate themselves. According to Erikson, children who successfully master each of these psychosocial conflicts gain new ego strengths—a trust in themselves and the future, a strong and independent will, a sense of purpose and adventuresomeness, and a feeling of basic competence. Moreover, they put themselves in a position to pose the question "Who am I?"—and, if all goes well, to answer it—during adolescence.

THE ADOLESCENT

Perhaps no period of the life span is more important to the development of the self than adolescence. Adolescence is truly a time for "finding oneself," for getting to know very intimately the person one has become, and for struggling to determine the person one will be.

The Self-Concept: Becoming a Personality Theorist

Raymond Montemayor and Marvin Eisen (1977) learned a great deal about the self-concepts of children and adolescents from grade 4 to grade 12 by simply asking students to write 20 different answers to the question "Who am I?" Box 10.2 shows the answers of a 9-year-old, an 11-year-old, and a 17-year-old. Notice how self-conceptions become less concrete and more abstract with age, and recall Piaget's theory that children begin to shift from concrete-operational to formal-operational thinking at about age 11 or 12. Younger children (9- to 10-year-olds) are capable of describing their psychological traits but often describe themselves in quite concrete terms, much as even younger children do, mentioning their physical attributes and favorite activities. Children entering adolescence (11- to 12-year-olds) more often generalize about their inner qualities or personality traits. High school students' self-descriptions are even more abstract, focusing not only on personality traits, but often on important values and ideologies or beliefs.

Moreover, adolescents reflect more about what they are like; they are *more self-aware* than children are (Selman, 1980). Their new cognitive ability to think about their own and other people's thoughts and feelings can make them painfully self-conscious. Finally, older adolescents seem to be able to paint a *more integrated* or coherent self-portrait than children or young adolescents can. Instead of merely listing traits, they try to organize their self-perceptions, including those that seem contradictory, into a coherent picture (Bernstein, 1980; Harter, 1986).

Susan Harter (1986) and her associates found that until the age of about 14 to 16, adolescents are quite unaware of inconsistencies within themselves or at least are not bothered by them. By ninth grade, a girl who likes to think of herself as a happy person may become upset because she is often depressed at home; or a boy may become confused about why he is so nervous on dates when he seems to be so relaxed in other situations. It is not until their later high school years, however, that adolescents are able to integrate such conflicting perceptions into a more coherent view of themselves. Thus a 17- or 18-year-old boy

Box 10.2
Three Children Answer the Question "Who Am I?"

9-year-old

My name is Bruce C. I have brown eyes. I have brown hair. I love! sports. I have seven people in my family. I have great! eye site. I have lots! of friends. I live at . . . I have an uncle who is almost 7 feet tall. My teacher is Mrs. V. I play hockey! I'm almost the smartest boy in the class. I love! food . . . I love! school.

11½-year-old

My name is A. I'm a human being . . . a girl . . . a truthful person. I'm not pretty. I do so-so in my studies. I'm a very good cellist. I'm a little tall for my age. I like several boys . . . I'm old fashioned. I am a very good swimmer . . . I try to be helpful . . . Mostly I'm good, but I lose my temper. I'm not well liked by some girls and boys. I don't know if boys like me . . .

17-year-old

I am a human being . . . a girl . . . an individual . . . I am a Pisces. I am a moody person . . . an indecisive person . . . an ambitious person. I am a big curious person . . . I am lonely. I am an American (God help me). I am a Democrat. I am a liberal person. I am a radical. I am conservative. I am a pseudoliberal. I am an Atheist. I am not a classifiable person (i.e., I don't want to be).

Source: From Montemayor & Eisen, 1977, pp. 317–318.

might conclude that it is perfectly understandable to be relaxed and confident in most situations but nervous on dates when one has not yet had much dating experience.

In sum, self-understandings become more abstract and more integrated, and self-awareness increases, from childhood to adolescence and over the course of adolescence. Truly, the adolescent becomes a sophisticated personality theorist who reflects upon and understands the workings of his or her personality and who also has a richer understanding of other people.

Adolescent Self-Esteem

The founder of developmental psychology, G. Stanley Hall, characterized adolescence as a time of emotional turmoil and psychological *storm and stress* (see Chapter 1). By this account, adolescents might be expected to experience wild "ups and downs" in self-esteem. Moreover, the very fact that adolescents become more self-aware or self-reflective could easily lead them to doubt themselves.

Does research support the view that adolescents have low self-esteem? To some extent it does. For instance, in a comparison of children who were ages 8 to 11, 12 to 14, and 15 or older, it was found that self-image problems were greatest among the 12- to 14-year-olds (Simmons, Rosenberg, & Rosenberg, 1973). These early adolescents had relatively low self-esteem, were highly self-conscious, and reported that their self-perceptions were highly changeable. Girls who are making the transition to junior high school, coping with pubertal changes, and beginning to date all at the same time are especially likely to suffer a drop in general self-esteem (Simmons, Blyth, Van Cleave, & Bush, 1979). Some of us do indeed remember seventh grade as a year we would like to forget!

But before we conclude that adolescence is hazardous to the self, we should note that most adolescents emerge from this period with essentially the same degree of self-esteem they had at the outset (Dusek & Flaherty, 1981). They seem to revise their self-concepts in fairly minor ways as they experience physical, cognitive, and social changes. In addition, even though some young people do experience self-doubts as they enter adolescence, gradual, modest increases in self-esteem occur in later adolescence (Marsh, 1989; McCarthy & Hoge, 1982; O'Malley & Bachman, 1983; Savin-Williams & Demo, 1984). Brief "ripples" in self-esteem smooth out. G. Stanley Hall's description of adolescence as a stormy time for the self seems to fit only a minority of adolescents (Offer, Ostrov, & Howard, 1984).

Forming a Sense of Identity

Like G. Stanley Hall, Erik Erikson viewed adolescence as a time of major changes in the self. It was Erikson (1963, 1968, 1982) who characterized adolescence as a critical period in the lifelong process of forming one's **identity** as a person and who proposed that adolescents experience the psychosocial conflict of **identity versus role confusion**. The concept of identity is slippery, but it refers mainly to a self-definition—a firm and coherent sense of who you are, where you are heading, and where you fit into society. To achieve a sense of identity, the adolescent must somehow integrate the many separate perceptions that are part of the self-concept into a coherent sense of self and must feel that he or she is, deep down, the same person yesterday, today, and tomorrow, at home, at school, or at work. The search for identity involves grappling with many important questions: What kind of career do I want? What religious, moral, and political values can I really call my own? Who am I as a man or woman and as a sexual being? Where do I fit in the world? What do I really want out of my life?

Can you recall struggling with such issues yourself? Are you currently struggling with some of them? If so, you can appreciate the uncomfortable feelings that adolescents may experience when they cannot seem to work out their identity issues. Erikson believed that many young people in modern society experience a full-blown and painful "identity crisis."

As we have already hinted, there are many reasons why adolescents might begin to think seriously about who they are and to find themselves confused about identity issues. As their bodies change, they must revise their body images (a part of their self-concept) and become accustomed to being sexual beings. We all know that a bodily change such as a new haircut or a weight gain can very much affect how we feel about ourselves as people. Then there is the fact that adolescents are changing cognitively. Entering Piaget's stage of formal-operational thought allows adolescents to think abstractly and to entertain hypothetical possibilities. The school-aged child is likely to accept the self as it is, but the adolescent can imagine possible future selves and form abstract concepts of the self. Indeed, adolescents who think in complex and abstract ways are more likely to raise and resolve identity issues than adolescents who are less cognitively mature (Slugoski, Marcia, & Koopman, 1984; Waterman, 1984).

Finally, we cannot ignore social demands on adolescents that prompt them to confront identity issues. Most notably, parents and other agents of society quite bluntly ask adolescents to "grow up"—to decide what they want to do in life and to get on with it. According to Erikson (1968), our society supports youth by providing them with a period when they are relatively free of responsibilities and are given permission to experiment with different roles in order to find themselves. Society even provides settings such as colleges and universities in which such experimentation can take place.

Developmental Trends in Identity Formation

When is a sense of identity actually achieved? James Marcia (1966) stimulated much research on this question by developing an interview that allows investigators to classify adolescents into one of four *identity statuses* based on what they say about making occupational, religious, and political choices. The key questions are whether or not an individual has experienced a *crisis* (or has seriously grappled with identity issues and explored alternatives) and whether or not he or she has achieved a *commitment* (that is, a resolution of the questions raised). According to whether there is crisis and commitment, the individual is classified into one of the four identity statuses shown in Table 10.2.

We can get a good sense of when identity is formed from Philip Meilman's (1979) study of college-bound boys between 12 and 18, 21-year-old college males, and 24-year-old young men (see Figure 10.2). Most of the 12- and 15-year-olds were in either the identity diffusion or the foreclosure status. At these ages, many adolescents simply have not thought yet about who they are and either have no idea or know that any ideas they do have are very likely to change (the **diffusion status**, with no crisis and no commitment). Other adolescents may say things like "I'm going to be a doctor like my dad" and appear to have their acts together. However, it becomes apparent that they have never really thought through *on their own* what suits them best and have simply accepted identities suggested

Table 10.2 The four identity statuses, as shown by current religious beliefs

	NO CRISIS EXPERIENCED	CRISIS EXPERIENCED
NO COMMITMENT MADE	DIFFUSION STATUS The person has not yet thought about or resolved identity issues and has failed to chart directions in life. *Example:* "I haven't really thought much about religion, and I guess I don't know what I believe exactly."	MORATORIUM STATUS The individual is currently experiencing an identity crisis and is actively raising questions and seeking answers. *Example:* "I'm in the middle of evaluating my beliefs and hope that I'll be able to figure out what's right for me. I like many of the answers provided by my Catholic upbringing, but I've also become skeptical about some teachings and have been looking into Unitarianism to see if it might help me answer my questions."
COMMITMENT MADE	FORECLOSURE STATUS The individual seems to know who he or she is but has latched on to an identity prematurely, without much thought (e.g., by uncritically becoming what parents or other authority figures suggest they should). *Example:* "My parents are Baptists and I'm a Baptist; it's just the way I grew up."	IDENTITY ACHIEVEMENT STATUS Individual has resolved his or her identity crises and made commitments to particular goals, beliefs, and values. *Example:* "I really did some soul-searching about my religion and other religions too and finally know what I believe and what I don't."

to them by their parents or other people (the **foreclosure status**, involving a commitment without a crisis).

As Figure 10.2 indicates, progress toward identity achievement becomes more evident starting at age 18. Notice that more individuals now begin to fall in the **moratorium status**, in which the individual is currently experiencing a crisis, or is actively exploring identity issues. Presumably, entering the moratorium status is a good sign, for if the individual can find answers to the questions raised, he or she will move on to the identity achievement status. Yet notice that only 20% of the 18-year-olds, 40% of the college students, and slightly over half of the 24-year-olds in Meilman's study had achieved a firm identity based on a careful weighing of alternatives (the **identity achievement status**).

Is the identity formation process different for females than it is for males? In most respects, no (Waterman, 1982). Females usually achieve a clear sense of identity at about the same ages that males do. However, one intriguing sex difference has been observed: Although today's college women are just as concerned about establishing a career identity as men are, they attach greater importance to the aspects of identity that center on interpersonal relationships, gender role, and sexuality (Bilsker, Schiedel, & Marcia, 1988; Kroger, 1988; Waterman, 1982). Perhaps we can see the continuing influence of traditional gender roles here.

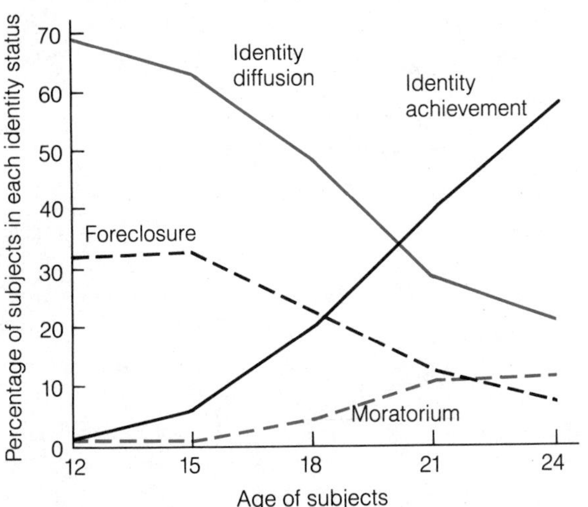

Figure 10.2 Percentages of subjects in each of Marcia's four identity statuses as a function of age. Note that only 4% of the 15-year-olds and 20% of the 18-year-olds had achieved a stable identity. (Based on Meilman, 1979)

Judging from such research, identity formation takes quite a bit of time. Not until late adolescence—during the college years—do many young men and women move into the moratorium status and then achieve a sense of identity (Waterman, 1982). But this is by no means the end of the identity formation process. Many adults are *still* struggling with identity issues or have reopened the question of who they are after thinking they had all the answers earlier in life (Waterman, 1982, 1988).

Moreover, the process of achieving identity is quite uneven (Archer, 1982; Kroger, 1988). For example, Sally Archer (1982) assessed the identity statuses of sixth to twelfth graders in four areas: occupational choice, gender-role attitudes, religious beliefs, and political ideologies. Only 5% of her adolescents were in the same identity status in all four areas, and more than 90% were in two or three categories across the four areas. Apparently, then, adolescents often achieve a sense of identity in one area while still floundering in another area. In fact, college students appear to make great progress from their freshman to senior years in establishing career goals, but they often seem to end their college careers more confused about their religious values than they were when they entered college (Waterman, 1982). Thus, certain aspects of identity may take shape earlier or remain more stable than others do.

Social Influences on Identity Formation

The adolescent's progress toward achieving identity is related to his or her social experiences. Some of the apparent identity confusion and backsliding that seems to occur during college, for example, may stem from being exposed to diverse ideas in a college environment and being encouraged to think things through independently. Youth who begin working after high school make faster progress than college students do toward establishing religious and political identities, even though the two groups are similar in their achievement of vocational identities (Munro & Adams, 1977).

Social influences on identity formation are also suggested by links between adolescents' identity statuses and their relationships with their parents. In his review of the literature, Alan Waterman (1982) concludes that adolescents in the diffusion status are more likely than adolescents in the other categories to be neglected or rejected by their parents and to be distant from them. Perhaps it is difficult to forge one's own identity without first having the opportunity to identify with respected parental figures and take on some of their desirable qualities. At the other extreme, adolescents categorized as being in the identity foreclosure status appear to have the closest relationships with their parents. Is it possible that these parent/child relationships are so close that the foreclosed adolescent never questions parental authority or feels any need to forge a separate identity?

By comparison, students who are classified in either the moratorium or identity achievement statuses appear to have a solid base of affection at home combined with considerable freedom to be individuals in their own right (Campbell, Adams, & Dobson, 1984; Grotevant & Cooper, 1986). In family discussions, for example, these adolescents experience a sense of closeness and mutual respect while feeling free to disagree with their parents; they are encouraged to compare their perspectives to those of other family members (Grotevant & Cooper, 1986). It appears, then, that the search for a separate identity may go best when parents provide love and guidance but also give their children room to define themselves as separate, independent individuals. Recall that this is the same kind of parenting that seems to help children gain a strong sense of self-esteem.

Finally, identity formation is influenced by the broader social and historical context in which it occurs—a point that Erikson himself strongly emphasized. The whole notion that adolescents should choose a personal identity after carefully exploring many options may well be peculiar to Western societies in the 20th century (Cote & Levine, 1988). As in past centuries, adolescents in many non-Western societies today, and even in some segments of our own society, simply adopt the adult roles they are expected to adopt, without any soul-searching or experimentation. For many of the world's adolescents, what Marcia calls identity foreclosure is probably the most adaptive route to adulthood (Cote & Levine, 1988). Obviously, the specific life goals that adolescents establish will also depend on what options are available and valued in their society.

All signs suggest that in Western society, at least, the adolescent who is able to raise serious questions about the self and answer them—that is, the individual who achieves identity—is better off for it.

Identity achievement seems to be associated with psychological well-being and high self-esteem, complex thinking about moral issues and other matters, a willingness to accept other people, and a variety of other psychological strengths (Waterman, 1984). By contrast, those individuals who fail to achieve a sense of identity may find themselves lacking self-esteem and drifting aimlessly, trapped in the identity diffusion status. Alternatively, they may take on what Erikson calls a *negative identity* as a "black sheep," "delinquent," or "loser" because it seems better to become everything that one is not supposed to become than to have no identity at all. Erikson recognized

Adolescents sometimes experiment with a variety of looks in their search for a sense of identity.

that identity issues can and do crop up later in life even for those people who form a positive sense of identity during adolescence. Nonetheless, he quite rightly marked the adolescent period as the key time in life for defining who we are.

THE ADULT

As we enter adulthood, we have gained a great deal of understanding of what we are like as individuals and most definitely have our own unique personalities. What happens during the adult years? Are self-conceptions and actual personality traits highly changeable, or do they remain much the same?

Self-Esteem and Self-Conceptions in Adulthood

Let's first ask whether self-concepts and levels of self-esteem change over the adult years. If we take Erik Erikson's perspective, we might expect that many adults gain self-esteem as they cope successfully with the challenges of establishing a family and career and as they work toward a sense of integrity or meaning in old age. But consider the diseases and physical impairments that become more likely as adults age, and some of the losses of roles and relationships that occur in later life: One might expect elderly adults to have lower self-esteem than young and middle-aged adults.

Which is it? As it turns out, neither. For example, Joseph Veroff, Elizabeth Douvan, and Richard Kulka (1981) compared young, middle-aged, and elderly adults in national surveys conducted in 1957 and 1976 and found no evidence at all that any of these age groups had higher self-esteem than any other. Their review of several studies of self-esteem in adulthood led Bengtson, Reedy, and Gordon (1985) to conclude that the self-esteem of elderly adults at least equals, and is sometimes greater than, that of younger adults. So we can toss out the stereotype that most older adults suffer from a poor self-image! Apparently most elderly people feel good about themselves despite the difficulties that aging may create for them.

But might younger and older individuals have different reasons for feeling good about themselves? Veroff and his colleagues think so. In their study, young adults were more likely than older adults to distinguish themselves from others by describing their unique personality traits while emphasizing their ties to other people. Perhaps this is because they were struggling with the identity and intimacy issues that Erikson believes are important during this period of adulthood. Middle-aged adults often found self-esteem by priding themselves on being good parents, husbands or wives, or workers—by pointing out their successful performance of adult roles. Finally, elderly adults were less likely to characterize themselves in terms of social roles, probably because they had retired from work and their children were grown. Instead they seemed to derive self-esteem from thinking of themselves as highly moral and religious, as if they had started thinking about the big questions that are part of Erikson's quest for a sense of integrity in old age. In sum, adults of different ages appear to feel equally good about themselves, but they may differ in the weight they attach to various aspects of the self.

Despite this intriguing hint of age differences, we still must conclude that younger and older adults are more similar than different in the ways they conceptualize themselves (Bengtson et al., 1985). Regardless of age, adults most frequently describe themselves in terms of their unique personal qualities and their social roles (George & Okun, 1985). Moreover, individual adults tend to maintain much the same favorable or unfavorable self-concepts over time (Mortimer, Finch, & Kumka, 1982). On balance, then, self-conceptions seem to change relatively little during adulthood, though they certainly can change. Perhaps we need to feel that we are basically the same people over the years and distort our self-perceptions to maintain such an image. Or perhaps we actually don't change much and therefore have no reason to change our self-perceptions.

Stability and Change in Adult Personality

How do our objective personality traits change over a lifetime? Is there some point in childhood or adolescence at which our personalities become set, to change little thereafter? Or do personality traits change significantly during adulthood as people launch careers and families as young adults, deal with major responsibilities and evaluate their lives in middle age, face threats to health in old age, or encounter their own unique crises throughout adulthood? If you are shy or moody at age 20, will you still

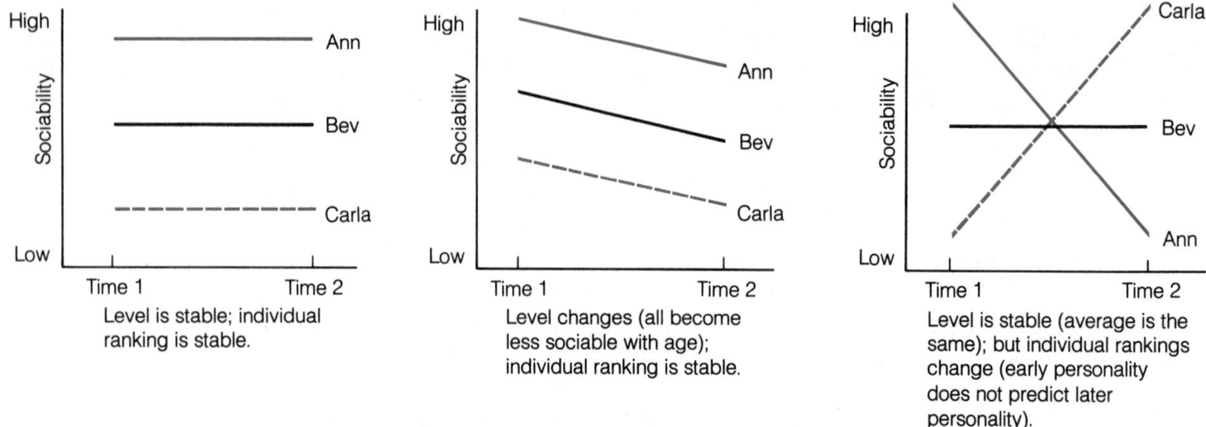

Figure 10.3 Possible patterns of stability and change in the personality trait of sociability: The simple case of Ann, Bev, and Carla.

be that way at age 40 or age 80? And are there any ways in which all of us change in similar directions as we age?

The question is really whether there is continuity (stability) or discontinuity (change) in the personality. And the issue is more complex than it may appear at first glance, partly because there are at least two senses in which we can be stable or changeable. First, stability in personality can mean stability over time in an *individual's ranking* within a group on a personality trait or dimension. If the most sociable children turn into the most sociable adults, and the least sociable children turn into the least sociable adults, then each person's standing on the dimension of sociability would be stable from childhood to adulthood. But if knowing how sociable or unsociable a person is early in life provided no basis for predicting how sociable that individual will be in later life, individuals apparently change unpredictably, some becoming more sociable, some becoming less sociable, than they were earlier.

The second meaning of personality stability and change centers on whether there is stability in the *average level* of a trait in a group. Level of sociability would be stable during adulthood, for example, if older people were no more or less sociable than younger people on the average, but changeable if elderly adults, as a group, were consistently less sociable than younger adults—or if most people became less sociable as they aged. Stability in individual rankings and stability in average trait levels are clearly distinct; one can exist without the other. Figure 10.3 graphs some of the patterns of stability and change that could potentially be found. Now let's see what *has* been found.

Do People Retain Their Rankings on Trait Dimensions over the Years?

Paul Costa, Robert McCrae, and their colleagues have closely studied the personalities of men who participated in the Baltimore Longitudinal Study of Aging (Costa, McCrae, & Arenberg, 1983; McCrae & Costa, 1984). Economically advantaged and well educated men ranging in age from their 20s to their 90s have been recruited into the study since 1958 and have been given a personality test about every six years. The test asks them to agree or disagree with statements such as "Often I get angry with people too quickly." Much of the focus has been on two major dimensions of personality, each of which consists of several traits:

Extraversion: the degree to which one is active, sociable, assertive, and so on rather than introverted.

Neuroticism: the degree to which one is emotionally unstable, anxious, depressed, easily upset, and hostile, rather than calm and emotionally well-balanced.

Extraversion is related to the aspect of infant temperament called sociability, and neuroticism can be likened to infant emotionality.

Are individual rankings on traits related to extraversion and neuroticism stable over the years? Apparently so, at least across intervals of 6 or 12 years (Costa, McCrae, & Arenberg, 1980, 1983). In other words, the adult who tends to be extraverted or emotionally stable now is likely to remain extraverted or emotionally stable compared to peers several years from now. The correlations between personality trait scores on two occasions 12 years apart were in the range of .70 to .80, suggesting some room for change in certain individuals, but also considerable consistency over time. These researchers have reported almost identical results in a study that also included women (Costa & McCrae, 1988).

Since Costa and his colleagues assessed changes over time in adults of different ages, they had a chance to see whether the personalities of older people were any more stable or unbendable over time than those of younger people. It makes some sense to think that as we try out different jobs, marry, and raise children in early adulthood, our personalities might change, but that as we settle into later life we might become more locked into consistent ways of behaving. As it turned out, elderly adults were no more "rigid" in their personality traits than younger adults were; young or old, stability or consistency over time was the rule. However, Stephen Finn (1986) found that college students tested in their 20s had changed quite a bit by age 50, whereas the personalities of middle-aged adults tested in their 40s and then tested again in their 70s were more stable. Perhaps Finn's findings differ from those of Costa because adult personalities are not fully formed in college and stabilize only after the early 20s (Costa & McCrae, 1988). Whatever the reasons, we cannot yet be sure that people's personalities become even more firmly set after midlife than they were in early adulthood.

We should note that Costa and his colleagues found greater stability of personality traits than many other researchers have found (e.g., Finn, 1986; Haan, 1981; Leon, Gillum, Gillum, & Gouze, 1979). When stability coefficients are in the neighborhood of .50 or less, as they more typically are, they are open to varying interpretations. Our own conclusion is that there is considerable, though far from perfect, consistency and predictability over time in certain important dimensions of personality. Moreover, this consistency is not due simply to a desire on the part of adults to *think* they remain the same, for it also shows up when their spouses are asked to rate them over the years (Conley, 1985; Costa & McCrae, 1988).

In sum, research has so far confirmed the notion that relatively enduring personality traits exist. Perhaps this explains why we often perceive ourselves as being the same basic people we used to be and why people we have not seen for years often seem not to have changed much at all. If this is bad news for people who are dissatisfied with their current personalities, it is good news if we want to predict what we and other people will be like in the future. Indeed, McCrae and Costa (1984) offer preliminary evidence that knowing a person's personality is highly useful in predicting how he or she will respond to life events. Whether the event is marriage, retirement, or the death of a loved one, for example, individuals who score high on measures of neuroticism may consistently have more difficulty coping than more emotionally stable individuals do.

Individuals can and do change, however, and some aspects of personality are less consistent over time than others. Extraversion and neuroticism—the broad personality dimensions on which Costa and his colleagues focused—appear to be more stable than many other aspects of personality (Bengtson, Reedy, & Gordon, 1985). Interests, attitudes, levels of self-assurance, and behavior patterns associated with the many roles we take on and shed during our lives seem to be quite a bit more changeable (Bengtson et al., 1985; Mussen, Eichorn, Honzik, Beiber, & Meredith, 1980).

But even if individuals' rankings on many personality dimensions remain quite stable during adulthood, it is still possible that most people systematically change in certain common directions. You may be consistently more extraverted than I over the years, and yet both of us, along with our peers, could become less extraverted at age 70 than we were at age 20. So let us examine the second major aspect of continuity and discontinuity in personality: the matter of stability and change in *average* levels of traits.

Do the Personalities of Adults Change Systematically?

Do older adults, as a group, have different personalities than younger adults do? Cross-sectional studies suggest that they do in some respects. For example, Bernice Neugarten and her colleagues, in their pioneering Kansas City studies of adult life, found that elderly men and women were more introverted, introspective, and attuned to inner feelings than middle-aged adults were (Neugarten, 1977). They seemed less concerned with demands placed on them by other people and more attuned to voices within themselves (see also Costa, McCrae, & Arenberg, 1983; Costa et al., 1986). Older adults also seem to be somewhat more emotionally stable but also less open to new experiences (Costa et al., 1986).

The problem is that many of these age-group differences appear to be *generational*, or cohort, differences rather than true maturational changes. We learn from these age-group comparisons that people's personalities are considerably affected by when they were born and by what sorts of experiences they had in their formative years (Schaie & Parham, 1976). For example, today's older men have been found to be more restrained about expressing their feelings and less assertive than today's young men, but when they are assessed repeatedly over the years, there is no sign that men *become* more restrained or less assertive (Douglas & Arenberg, 1978). Possibly, then, elderly people grew up in a time when free self-expression was less strongly encouraged than it has been in more recent times.

It is quite another question to ask whether people's personalities actually become different *as they age*. Norma Haan (1981) has summarized many of the key findings on personality development from adolescence to middle age that have emerged from two longitudinal studies of development conducted in Oakland and Berkeley, California. These studies suggest that there is significant personal growth from adolescence to middle age. Professional judges rated men's and women's traits on the basis of their responses to lengthy interviews and tests administered during adolescence and then again when subjects were in their 30s and 40s. Both men and women in these studies became more cognitively invested in life (more intellectual and interested in achievement), more open to the self (self-aware and introspective), more self-confident (satisfied with themselves, assertive), and more nurturant toward others (giving, sympathetic). For many, this growth toward greater psychological freedom and maturity in middle age occurred after a period of backsliding between early and late adolescence. During this period, many people temporarily became less nurturant toward other people, more concerned with their own welfare, and less self-confident.

Similarly, Jeylan Mortimer, Michael Finch, and Donald Kumka (1982) found that some self-rated traits such as a sense of well-being and competence dipped in late adolescence (senior year of college, to be exact) but then rose to higher levels during the 10 years after college. Men and women also seem to become more achievement oriented and autonomous between their 20s and their 40s (Stevens & Truss, 1985). In these studies and others, trait levels changed despite considerable stability in individuals' rankings on the same trait dimensions. These changes make a great deal of sense when we realize that adolescence is a somewhat unsettled period that involves many life changes, but that adults have opportunities to become more confident and independent as they actually get their lives off the ground and settle into specific work and family roles.

What about the period from middle age to old age? There are only a few signs that most people change in similar ways during this period. Adults' activity levels (their tendencies to be energetic, fast working, and action oriented) tend to decline after age 50 (Douglas & Arenberg, 1978). Some longitudinal studies also reinforce the idea that people become somewhat more introspective, or preoccupied with physical and psychological concerns, in old age (Leon et al., 1979). However, most personality traits do *not* seem to change in systematic directions in later life (Costa & McCrae, 1988).

Where do we stand, then? Most evidence suggests this:

1. Different generations of people often have somewhat distinctive personality profiles as groups, indicating that the historical context in which people grow up affects their personality development.
2. There is some personality growth from adolescence to middle adulthood — a strengthening of qualities such as self-confidence, autonomy, and nurturance; evidently we do not stop developing as individuals once adolescence ends.
3. There are very few ways in which the personality traits of adults systematically change in similar directions as they progress from middle adulthood to later adulthood, though some decreases in activity level and increases in introspectiveness may be observed.

Overall, then, whether we look at individuals' relative positions on trait dimensions or at the average levels of different traits for younger and older adults, there seems to be substantial stability in personality during adulthood — along with some change, especially in early adulthood.

Why Do People Change or Remain the Same?

Having figured out that there is both stability and change in personality traits over the life span, developmentalists are beginning to ask why some people stay much the same and others change. What makes a personality stable? First, the influence of genetic inheritance might be at work (see Chapter 3). It is possible that heredity influences temperamental qualities that show up early in infancy and gives rise to enduring personality traits such as extraversion and neuroticism. Second, childhood experiences may have lasting effects that promote stability of personality. We have seen that at least some personality traits take shape in childhood and persist into adulthood, and we have seen that children's experiences within the family can leave lasting imprints on their personalities (Chess & Thomas, 1984; Moss & Susman, 1980).

Third and finally, we must consider the possibility that our traits remain stable because our environments remain stable. Here the argument is not just that early experiences have lasting effects—it is that *both early and later experiences* promote personality stability. Imagine that Wilma, because of some mix of genes and early experience, shows an early tendency to be extraverted, whereas Wanda is a shy introvert from the start. Wilma's friendliness is likely to elicit friendliness from other people throughout her life. Moreover, as an extravert, she will seek out and create environments to her liking, placing herself in crowds, at parties, and in jobs where she can socialize. In these environments, Wilma is likely to maintain or even strengthen her initial tendency to be extraverted. Wanda, meanwhile, might go out of her way to avoid parties, keep to herself, and therefore remain an introverted individual, comfortable with herself and her lifestyle. In short, we are exposed to, seek out, and actively create social environments later in life that are likely to sustain our early personality predispositions.

What, then, might be responsible for significant changes in personality? Biological maturation and aging could contribute. For example, cognitive maturation contributes to changes in self-conceptions during childhood and adolescence, and biological aging could have some effect on the personalities of adults. A more likely possibility, however, is that adults change in response to changes in their social environments or in response to major life events (Belsky, 1990; Wells & Stryker, 1988). For example, adults who land good jobs with high incomes and much freedom to make decisions either maintain their initial sense of competence or gain confidence after college, whereas those who face job insecurity and unemployment in their early careers lose some of their sense of competence (Mortimer, Finch, & Kumka, 1982). In this way, life events (in this case, job experiences) help determine whether traits evident in early adulthood persist or change. If their lives change dramatically enough, adults can become very different people than they were earlier in life.

Who Changes and Who Does Not?

Some types of people are more likely to change over the years than others are. Longitudinal research led Jack Block (1971, 1981) to conclude that asking whether adult personality is continuous or discontinuous is rather silly: Some adults remain very predictable over the years while others change so much that they become unrecognizable. Block has described several personality "types," each with a distinctive set of traits, and he has shown that some of these types of people change more than others do. Generally, the people who are the most changeable from adolescence to middle age are the ones who were the least well adjusted initially.

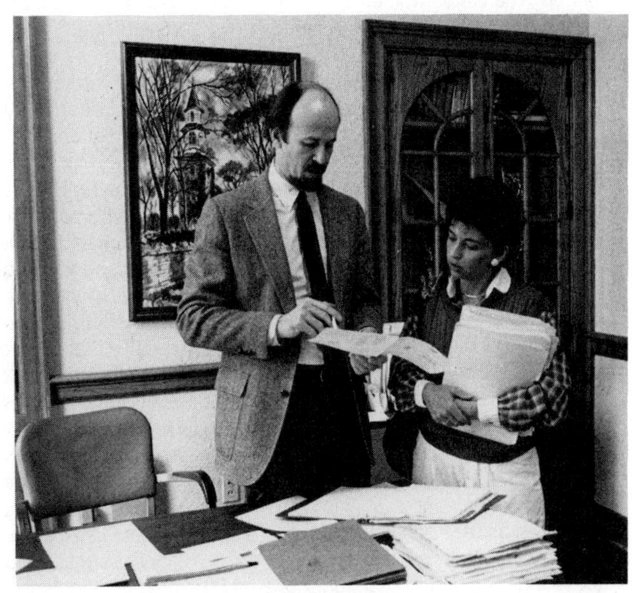

Starting a new job is the kind of life event that can potentially change an adult's self-conceptions.

The notion that some people are more changeable than others is nicely illustrated by the fascinating findings of Florine Livson described in Box 10.3. This research also suggests that people are most likely to change when the goodness of fit between their personalities and their environments (or lifestyles) is very poor.

A Summing Up

Is personality stable or changeable during adulthood? It is both. Research suggests, however, that stability tends to prevail, and that change usually occurs gradually within this context of basic stability (Costa, McCrae, & Arenberg, 1983). Important dimensions of personality do tend to remain much the same from one age to another, although there is still ample room for specific individuals to change. Moreover, there are only a few ways in which personalities change systematically with age.

Genes, early childhood experiences, and the tendency to seek out or end up in environments that match and reinforce earlier predispositions all contribute to stability. On the other hand, change in personality becomes more likely if people's environments change considerably or if they find themselves in situations that are mismatched to the traits they might naturally express. Moreover, some

Box 10.3
Personality "Fit" and Personality Change

Using data from the Oakland longitudinal study of human development, Florine Livson (1976) studied women who were mentally healthy at age 50 and tried to determine how they got that way. Some women were psychologically healthy at both age 40 and age 50, while others improved dramatically during that same period. The stable women and the improvers proved to be two distinct types of people.

"Traditional" women were conventional and fit well into the stereotypically feminine role. They were outgoing and popular as teenagers, and continued to express these same traits in adulthood, changing little at all. By contrast, "independents" did not fit traditional feminine roles as well. As teenagers, they tended to be unconventional, introspective, and motivated to achieve. During adulthood, these nontraditional women, like most women of their era, abandoned careers to pursue the lives of housewives and mothers, but they then found themselves confronting a midlife crisis at about age 40. They were depressed and up in the air about what to do with their lives as their children prepared to leave the nest. By age 50, however, these independent women rediscovered the intellectual skills that had been so evident in their teenage years and rebounded toward a level of psychological health equal to that of the traditional woman.

Two cases illustrate these contrasts well. Mrs. T, a traditional woman, simply maintained her outgoing personality and love of mothering after her daughters left home and married. She thrived on the frequent visits of her daughters, their children, and their friends and cousins. Mrs. I, a nontraditional or independent woman, had interrupted a promising career to become a wife and mother. She became increasingly distressed as the departure of her youngest child approached. She was overweight, tired, depressed, and so passive that she was reluctant to go out of the house alone. However, she eventually got involved with a charitable organization and worked her way into an administrative position that gave her a chance to use her intellectual skills effectively. She lost weight, her self-esteem rose, and she became a more equal partner in her marriage. She had changed immensely, becoming more like the person she was as a teenager than like the woman she was at age 40.

Livson (1981) discovered a remarkably similar pattern among men. Mentally healthy men who fit the traditional male role by being self-disciplined, emotionally controlled, and achievement-oriented adolescents experienced little in the way of midlife turmoil, although they did start being more emotionally expressive by age 50. However, "nontraditional" men, who were emotionally expressive and rebellious as teenagers, experienced a difficult time in adulthood, probably because they were pressured to conform to the traditional masculine role; at 40, they were trying to suppress their emotional sides but were angry and stress-ridden as a result. They then rebounded to a higher level of psychological adjustment at age 50 when they were perhaps freed from role demands and could allow their more "feminine" side to emerge once more.

Certainly one moral of Livson's study is that some types of people are more likely to change during adulthood than others are. But perhaps a more important message is that the *fit* between person and environment is critical in personality development—the very message that has emerged from the research on children with easy, difficult, and slow-to-warm-up temperaments conducted by Thomas and Chess (1986; Chess & Thomas, 1984).

types of individuals are more changeable than others are. Finally, even if personalities often remain basically the same for long stretches of the life span, this does *not* mean that they cannot change—as, for example, with the help of a skilled psychotherapist (Kagan, 1983). Powerful experiences have the capacity to alter us at any stage of life.

It is perhaps significant that researchers who conclude that adults hardly change at all over the years typically study personality by administering standardized personality scales. Researchers who interview people in depth about their lives often detect more change and growth (Belsky, 1990; Wrightsman, 1988).

Psychosocial Growth During Adulthood

Erikson was one of the first to claim that adults experience stagelike changes in personality during adulthood. Does research support his ideas?

Establishing Intimacy

As Erikson saw it, young adulthood is a time for dealing with the psychosocial conflict of **intimacy versus isolation**. He theorized that one must achieve a sense of individual identity before becoming able to commit oneself to a *shared identity* with another person—that one must know oneself before one can love someone else. The young adult who has no clear sense of self may be threatened by the idea of entering a committed, long-term relationship and being "tied down" or may become overdependent on a partner as a source of identity.

To test Erikson's view that identity paves the way for genuine intimacy, Susan Whitbourne and Stephanie Tesch (1985) measured identity status and intimacy status among college seniors and 24- to 27-year-old alumni from the same university. The researchers interviewed people about their closest relationships and placed each person in one of six intimacy statuses ranging from being a social isolate with no close relationships to being involved in a genuinely intimate relationship (see Table 10.3). With respect to identity formation, more alumni than college students fell in either the moratorium (active questioning) or achievement identity statuses, indicating that progress toward achieving identity continues to be made *after* college graduation, most likely as young adults face the demands of launching careers and assuming other adult roles. College graduates had also progressed farther than college seniors in resolving intimacy issues; more of them were involved in long-term, committed relationships. Finally, and most important, the college graduates who had well-formed identities were more likely than those who did not to be capable of genuine and lasting intimacy—precisely what Erikson theorized.

Table 10.3 Intimacy statuses

INTIMACY STATUS	DESCRIPTION
Isolate	No close relationship
Stereotyped	Shallow relationship with little communication or involvement
Pseudointimate	Relationship is long-lasting but stereotyped or lacking in depth
Preintimate	Relationship rates high on communication and involvement; what is missing is a long-term commitment to one's partner
Merger	Close to intimate, for there is high involvement and open communication, but partners are not co-determining (e.g., one is over-dependent on the other and has no separate identity)
Intimate	Has it all—high involvement, open communication, mutual determination, and long-term commitment

Source: Used in a study by Whitbourne & Tesch (1985) and largely based on the work of Orlofsky, Marcia, & Lesser (1973).

Other researchers have come to the same conclusion (Orlovsky, Marcia, & Lesser, 1973; Raskin, 1986). Indeed, Kahn and his colleagues (1985) discovered that men who lacked a sense of identity in college were less likely to be married 18 years later than men who had achieved an identity in college. Perhaps because of prevailing social expectations, women in this study married with or without a clear sense of personal identity. However, women who lacked a sense of identity in college were less likely than identity-achieving women to have had a stable marriage during early adulthood.

So far, so good, then. As Erikson claimed, we apparently must know ourselves before we can truly love another person. More generally, there seems to be considerable growth after adolescence in the aspects of the self that concerned Erikson. In the 10 years after college, for example, individuals gain considerably in the Eriksonian personality attributes of industry, identity, and intimacy (Whitbourne & Waterman, 1979).

Middle Age and Generativity

Is there continuing psychosocial growth in middle age? George Vaillant (1977), a psychoanalytic theorist, conducted an in-depth longitudinal study of mentally healthy Harvard men covering the years from college to middle age, as well as a longitudinal study of blue-collar workers with little education (Vaillant, 1983; Vaillant & Milofsky, 1980). One of his important findings has been that men come to rely on more mature ego defense mechanisms as they get older.

As young adults, for example, many men coped with crises in their lives by escaping reality or blaming other people for their deficiencies. In middle age, these men were more likely to rely on such mature coping methods as realistic planning and a healthy sense of humor to get them through difficult times. Those middle-aged men who had grown the most and who relied most heavily on mature ego defense mechanisms were among the happiest, healthiest, most successful, and most well adjusted in the sample.

In addition, Vaillant found that Erikson's stages fit the men he studied quite well, though he felt the need to insert a new stage between intimacy versus isolation and Erikson's middle-age stage of generativity versus stagnation. Most men were indeed concerned with intimacy issues in their 20s, but they appeared to enter a new psychosocial stage in their 30s that Vaillant called *career consolidation,* during which they focused most of their energies on advancing in their careers and were not very reflective or concerned about others. Vaillant likened these 30-year-olds to elementary school children in the stage of industry versus inferiority, striving hard to conform to other people's expectations of them and rarely asking themselves if what they were doing was worthwhile. It was as if they had merely traded their lunchboxes for briefcases!

In their 40s, many men then became more concerned with the issue of **generativity versus stagnation**, which involves gaining the capacity to produce something that outlives you and to become genuinely concerned about the welfare of future generations. True, some middle-aged men continued to be the "colorless" workaholics of the career consolidation stage or had never moved beyond struggling with intimacy issues. However, many others expressed more interest than they had previously in passing on something of value, either to their own children or to younger people at work. They reflected on their lives and experienced the kind of intellectual vitality that adolescents sometimes experience as they struggle with identity issues. Vaillant discovered that few of these men experienced a full-blown and turbulent midlife crisis, just as few had experienced a severe identity crisis as college students. Nonetheless they were growing as individuals, often becoming more caring and self-aware as they entered their 50s. One of these men expressed the developmental progression Vaillant detected perfectly: "At 20 to 30, I think I learned how to get along with my wife. From 30 to 40, I learned how to be a success in my job. And at 40 to 50, I worried less about myself and more about the children" (1977, p. 195).

Thus Vaillant offers evidence that men progress through stages of intimacy, career consolidation, and generativity in order, though he warns against attaching rigid age ranges to these stages. Far less is known about the psychosocial development of women, although they, too, appear to gain a stronger sense of generativity in middle age (Ochse & Plug, 1986; Ryff & Heincke, 1983). Such research suggests that the psychosocial growth that Erikson envisioned during middle adulthood may indeed occur for many men and women.

Old Age and Integrity

Do elderly adults continue to grow psychologically as they confront Erikson's psychosocial issue of **integrity versus despair**—that is, as they try to find a sense of meaning in their lives that helps them face the inevitability of death? Surprisingly little is known. However, noted gerontologist Robert Butler (1963, 1975) has proposed that elderly adults engage in a process he calls **life review**. They reflect on unresolved conflicts of the past in order to come to terms with themselves, find new meaning and coherence in their lives, and prepare for death.

Do elderly people in fact engage in life review, and does it help them achieve a healthy sense of integrity? Although most of us know elderly people who seem preoccupied with the "old days," there is surprisingly little support for the idea that elderly people spend more of their waking hours thinking about the old days than younger people do (Gambria, 1979–1980). However, there are signs that the old, more than the young, use reminiscence to evaluate and integrate the pieces of their lives (Molinari & Reichlin, 1984–1985). Those who use the life-review process to confront and come to terms with their failures

What is generativity? It is singer Cissy Houston saying this about her highly successful singing daughter, Whitney: "To be singing with someone you brought into the world, who you cradled in your arms—it's nice. It's wonderful to see something you do that comes out halfway right."

seem to have a stronger sense of ego integrity than those who do not (Boylin, Gordon, & Nehrke, 1976).

Believing that life review can be beneficial in later life, Robert Butler has used it as a form of therapy, asking elderly adults to reconstruct and reflect on their lives with the help of photo albums and other memorabilia. There are signs that participation in life-review therapy can indeed help elderly adults feel less anxious and more content with themselves and their lives (Haight, 1988; Molinari & Reichlin, 1984–1985).

On balance, we must conclude that Erikson's theory of psychosocial development during adulthood is partially, though not fully, supported. The evidence is quite convincing that adolescence is a time for struggling with identity issues and that achieving a sense of identity paves the way for forming a truly intimate relationship with another person as a young adult. Moreover, gaining a sense of generativity does seem to be an issue in middle age (Ryff & Heincke, 1983). Still, when adults of different ages are tested for Eriksonian strengths such as intimacy and generativity, it is not always clear that particular strengths really emerge in the order Erikson proposed (Ochse & Plug, 1986; Tesch, 1985). However, we can certainly agree with Erikson on one thing: People are capable of personal growth and change throughout the life span.

THE EMOTIONAL SELF

Although many aspects of the self and the personality are worthy of a closer look, one of the most important is our experience of emotions—joy, sadness, pride, shame, and all the other feelings that reflect our responses to events and motivate and regulate our behavior. Emotional development is multifaceted; among other things, it includes acquiring basic capacities for and personal styles of experiencing, expressing, and controlling feelings. Do infants experience the same emotions that adults experience? What do children learn about emotions and about how to express (or hide) them? Why do some people scream with delight and shout in anger while others keep their emotions under strict control? Do our emotional "personalities" change during adulthood? If so, how? Here, we will examine only selected aspects of emotional development, saving the important topic of emotional attachments and love until Chapter 13.

The Emergence of Emotions in Infancy

Until recently, most researchers believed that infants did not really have emotional lives, or at least that their emotional expressions were only globally positive or negative in nature. Parents, by contrast, have long felt that their babies' faces reveal a wide range of specific emotions. In one study, more than half the mothers of 1-month-old infants said that their babies displayed distinct emotional responses indicating interest, surprise, joy, anger, and fear (Johnson, Emde, Pannabecker, Stenberg, & Davis, 1982). Carroll Izard (1982) and his colleagues have now confirmed that parents are basically right. Izard has videotaped infants' responses to such events as grasping an ice cube, having a toy taken away, or seeing their mothers return after a separation. By analyzing specific facial movements such as the raising of the brows and the wrinkling of the nose and by asking raters to judge what emotion a baby's face revealed, Izard has established that infants do indeed express distinct emotions and that adults can readily interpret which emotions they are expressing.

Izard concludes that a number of facial expressions of emotion appear in a predictable order over the first two years. At birth, babies show interest, distress in response to pain, disgust, and the suggestion of a smile. Angry expressions appear at 3 to 4 months—at about the same time that infants acquire enough control of their limbs to push unpleasant stimuli away. Sadness emerges at about this same time, with fear making its appearance at age 5 to 7 months, shame and shyness appearing shortly thereafter, and complex emotions such as contempt, pride, and guilt appearing only in the second year. These basic emotional expressions seem to be biologically programmed, since they emerge in all normal infants early and at roughly the same ages. Moreover, facial expressions of basic emotions such as joy, sadness, and fear are displayed and interpreted similarly in all cultures, suggesting that they are wired in to the human species (Izard, 1982).

Although they may be biologically programmed, emotional expressions are soon shaped by sociocultural forces. One of the first lessons babies in our culture learn is that positive emotions such as joy and interest are more welcomed than negative emotions. Carol Malatesta, Jeanette Haviland, and their colleagues have carefully observed the face-to-face interactions of mothers with infants in their first year of life (Malatesta, Grigoryev, Lamb, Albin, & Culver, 1986; Malatesta & Haviland, 1982). Like Izard, they find that young infants display a wide range of positive and negative emotions, changing their expressions with lightning speed (once every 7 seconds) while their mothers do the same. Mothers, however, restrict themselves mainly to displays of interest, surprise, and so on, thus serving as models of positive emotions. What's more, mothers respond selectively to their babies' expressions; over the early months, they become increasingly responsive to their babies' expressions of interest and less responsive to their babies' expressions of pain (Malatesta et al., 1986). Through basic learning processes, then, infants are trained to show more pleasant faces and fewer unpleasant faces—and they do just this over time. They begin to learn which emotional expressions are acceptable in their culture and in their own particular homes, and they develop styles of emotional expression that match those of their parents (Denham, 1989).

What we do *not* know is precisely what is going on inside as infants display emotions. Among adults, there is often a difference between the observable emotional expression and the inner emotional state (or bodily feeling of anger, fear, and so on). An angry adult can, for example, hide that anger behind a smile. But most researchers assume that emotional states and expressions match during infancy (Cole, 1985). In other words, it is assumed that when infants show a mad face they have been hurt or frustrated in some way; they simply aren't thought to be capable of putting on a face that is inconsistent with their inner state. Yet we might still wonder whether the psychological experience of anger or sadness in an infant is really like the same emotional experience in an adult. Adults, after all, think as they feel. However, the baby in the doctor's office who displays a face of anger after being given a shot is hardly likely to be thinking, "Boy, I'm mad at this lady; she'd better not stick me again." Infants may well need to acquire the capacity for symbolic thought and a sense of self-awareness before they can mentally represent their own emotional experiences and can *consciously* interpret

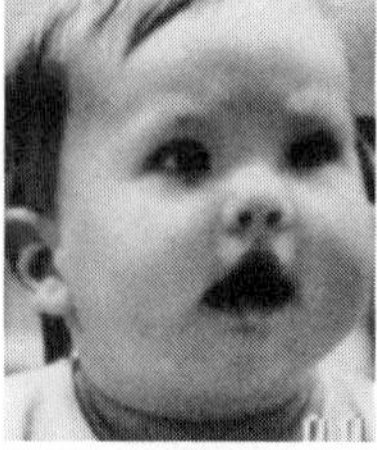

Interest: brows raised; mouth may be rounded; lips may be pursed.

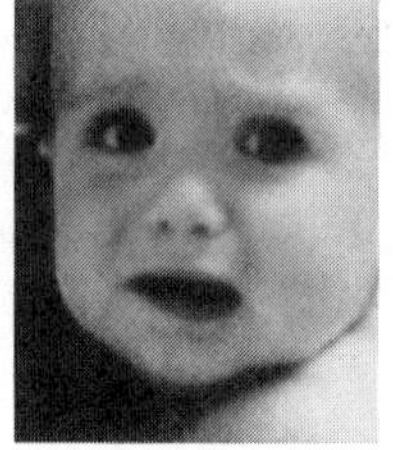

Fear: mouth retracted; brows level and drawn up and in; eyelids lifted.

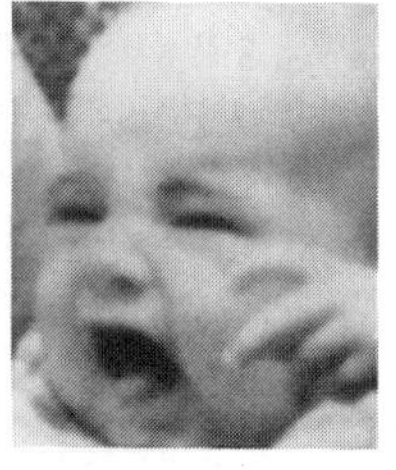

Disgust: tongue protruding; upper lip raised; nose wrinkled.

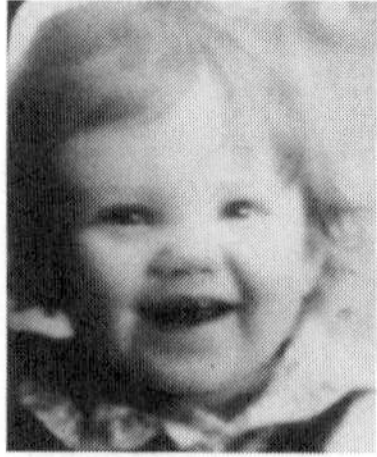

Joy: bright eyes; cheeks lifted; mouth forms a smile.

Sadness: corners of mouth turned down; inner portion of brows raised.

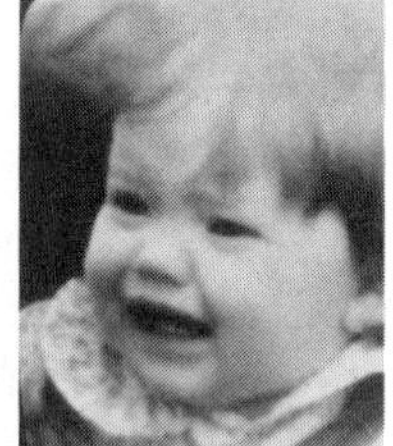

Anger: mouth squared at corners; brows drawn together and pointing down; eyes fixed straight ahead.

Infants express a wide range of emotions.

the emotions that their faces and physiological states reveal (Lewis & Michalson, 1983; Lewis, Sullivan, Stanger, & Weiss, 1989; Stipek, 1983). Similarly, although infants can discriminate among facial expressions of emotion within a few months of birth, it takes them a good deal longer to demonstrate that they know what these expressions mean, avoiding, for example, the animal that provokes fear in their companions (Nelson, 1987).

Learning About Emotions and How to Control Them

During the preschool and elementary school years, children do become more conscious of their emotions, learn a great deal about how to interpret emotions, and begin to exert some control over their expressive behavior. By the age of 2, children already have some awareness of which faces are "happy" or "sad" faces and which faces fit which situations. Linda Michalson and Michael Lewis (1985) found that 70% of 2-year-olds could already pick out a happy face as the face that is appropriate at a birthday party. Knowledge of negative emotions comes more slowly, perhaps because these expressions are discouraged and are therefore observed less often than positive emotions, but such understanding expands rapidly during the preschool years (Michalson & Lewis, 1985). Nonetheless, preschoolers have much left to learn. Susan Harter (1982a, 1986), for example, finds that children younger than about 9, because of their cognitive limitations, have difficulty understanding that a person can experience two conflicting emotions at the same time. According to Harter, this lack of understanding can have serious consequences. For example, the young child who views mother as "all mad" rather than both mad and loving at the same time may become very upset and afraid.

From the age of 2 on, children also begin to use emotional expressions more consciously and deliberately as communication signals, as when a child falls but does not break into tears until Mom is in sight (Cole, 1985). Moreover, preschoolers can at least try to control the expression of their emotions, as when they fight back the tears after being told not to cry or even mask their true feelings in an effort to deceive someone (Lewis, Stanger, & Sullivan, 1989). Now inner state and outer expression are not quite so closely matched as they were in infancy. Still, preschoolers are quite inept compared with older children at disguising their true feelings; they typically wear their feelings on their faces and express those feelings freely (Cole, 1985).

It is in elementary school that children become truly skilled in the art of deceit! What happens is that children are gradually learning a set of **display rules** for emotion—cultural rules specifying what emotions should or should not be expressed under what circumstances. They are also learning the more specific display rules that prevail in their own families, for some parents tolerate outbursts of anger or shrieks of delight more than other parents do (Halberstadt, 1984). As children learn display rules, the gap between what they are experiencing inside and what they express to the world widens (a nicer way of saying that they become more skilled in the art of deceit).

Consider a study by Carolyn Saarni (1984). Children aged 7, 9, and 11 participated in a preliminary research session in which they were rewarded for their labors with an attractive gift—a can of juice, a candy bar, and 50 cents. At the close of a second research session, when they were expecting a nice gift, they instead got a boring baby toy—for instance, a plastic key on a ring. Here, then, was a situation in which our culture's display rule reads something like this: "Look pleased, despite receiving a disappointing gift." Were children aware of this social rule? Could they control their behavior enough to hide their disappointment or even feign delight?

Saarni coded the children's behavior into three categories: positive (an enthusiastic "thank you," a broad smile), negative (a failure to say "thank you," a wrinkled nose, an "ugh," a shrug, and so on), and "transitional" (or middle-range behaviors reflecting a partial attempt to control one's responses as in a mumbled "thank you" or a distressed smile). Figure 10.4 shows the frequency of outright positive reactions to a lousy gift. Clearly the youngest children, especially boys, were not very positive in this situation; their inner disappointment showed through. Older children, especially girls, were more able to conform to the display rule by hiding their true negative feelings and even expressing pleasure. Possibly they had more knowledge of the display rule than the younger children did, or possibly they were more able and willing to follow it by hiding their disappointment.

School-aged children and adolescents increasingly understand that there is an inner world of emotional expe-

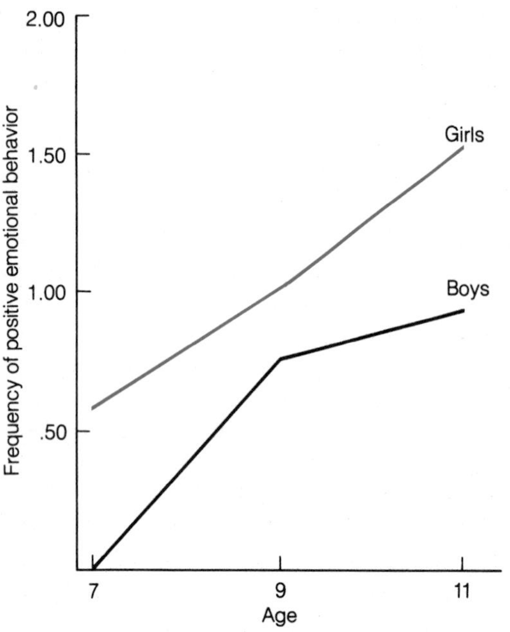

Figure 10.4 With age, children are more able to display positive emotional reactions after receiving a disappointing gift. (Based on Saarni, 1984)

rience that can be quite different from visible emotional signals (Harris, Olthof, & Terwogt, 1981). Moreover, they become increasingly able to control their outward emotional expressions as they learn how they should feel in particular situations and how they should express (or hide) what they feel in accordance with display rules. In all likelihood, this "socialization of emotions" works for the good of society—at least all societies appear to have established emotional display rules of some kind. We may not like the idea that children become more and more able to mask and alter their true feelings as they grow older, but life might be unbearable if adults were typically as honest about their feelings as most preschoolers are!

Emotions in Adult Life

Over the course of infancy, childhood, and adolescence, our emotional lives become richer as we experience a wider range of different emotions and become more aware of our emotional experience. We also enter adulthood with our own distinctive emotional "personalities," partly influenced by our experiences in the family (see Box 10.4).

How do our emotional lives change during adulthood? The most popular hypothesis has been that aging brings with it a blunting of both emotional expression and inner emotional experience (see Malatesta, 1981). The idea is that elderly people do not show much emotion and, in fact, do not react with as much emotional intensity to events as younger and middle-aged adults do. A related view is that when elderly adults *do* feel emotions, they are often negative ones. Several early studies seemed to support these views, but the studies were flawed. Most notably, they often involved institutionalized elderly people, who are likely to have more restricted and unhappy emotional lives than healthy individuals do (Malatesta, 1981).

Carol Malatesta and her colleagues reopened the issue of age differences in adult emotional experience. In one study (Malatesta & Kalnok, 1984), they questioned young, middle-aged, and older adults about their emotional experiences and expressions. The message of this study was that the emotional lives of adults of different ages are far more similar than different. There was no sign that elderly people experience more negative emotions than younger people do, or that emotions are any less important in their lives, or that they experience emotions any less intensely. Moreover, the faces of young, middle-aged, and elderly women are about equally expressive when they recall events that provoked various emotions in them. If there is any difference, it is that older women's faces tend to con-

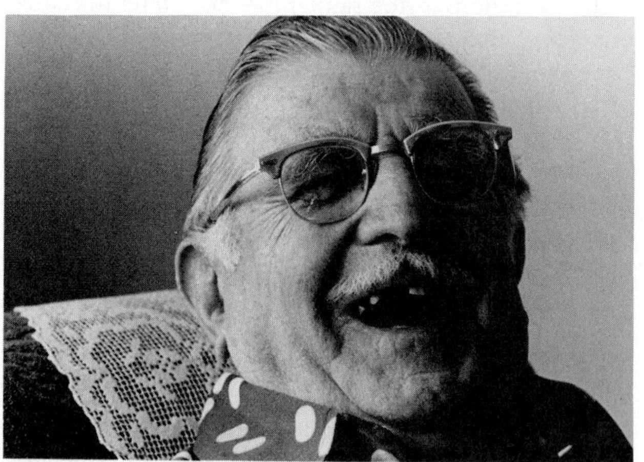

People continue to experience strong emotions in old age.

Box 10.4
Learning How to Express Emotions in the Family

Why is it that some adults keep their feelings under tight control while others let us know exactly what they are feeling? As we have seen already, children in our society are generally taught to control and hide their negative emotions in accordance with our culture's display rules. Consequently, most adults are less outwardly expressive of their emotions than the majority of preschool children are. Yet Amy Halberstadt (1984) suspected that strong displays of emotion are far more acceptable in some families than in others and that the display rules that prevail in our families have much to do with our own emotional behavior later in life.

Halberstadt asked college students and their mothers to report on how emotionally expressive their families were during the students' childhood years. Was it acceptable, for example, to spontaneously hug another family member or to criticize someone for being late? How intense and frequent were emotional displays like these? Once Halberstadt had information about

the emotional expressiveness of each student's family, she asked the students to perform a number of tasks that required them to express and understand emotions.

Halberstadt found that different families did indeed vary considerably in the extent to which they valued and permitted open expressions of emotion. Moreover, the expressive style that a student experienced in the family as a child was associated with his or her ability to express and interpret emotions as a college student. Specifically, students whose families were highly expressive were able to communicate emotions more clearly or accurately than students whose families were more emotionally restrained. Meanwhile, students from unexpressive families were superior on tasks requiring them to *interpret* emotional displays. Why? It is not surprising that the child who has permission and many opportunities to express emotions will become an adult who expresses emotions freely and unambiguously. But why are those who grow up in emotionally unexpressive families particularly good at reading emotional signals? Perhaps it is because they simply must learn to be keen observers of the subtleties of emotional communication if they are to understand how their "poker-faced" parents and siblings are feeling. It would not do to miss the barely visible tightening of the lips that means Mom is mad! Far more research is needed, but it seems quite likely that we develop our own distinct emotional "personalities" in the context of the family.

vey mixed signals more often and may be somewhat harder to read as a result (Malatesta, Izard, Culver, & Nicolich, 1987).

Although more research is needed, it appears that we would be making a mistake in assuming that most elderly people no longer experience strong emotions or experience mostly negative ones. Instead, it seems that old people, like young people, differ considerably in their emotional "personalities" and lead complex emotional lives.

APPLICATIONS: BOOSTING SELF-ESTEEM THROUGHOUT THE LIFE SPAN

Much of this chapter has centered on our self-conceptions and the sense of self-esteem that they generate. We all know that children and adults who lack self-esteem suffer for it. So what do we know about the possibilities for boosting self-esteem when it is low?

Earlier in this chapter, we noted that parents can do a great deal to foster high self-esteem in their children. Specifically, parents who blend acceptance or love with democratic and consistent discipline nourish self-esteem. Such parents are able to express their disapproval of a child's misbehavior while conveying the message that the child is a valuable and lovable person. They set clear guidelines for behavior and yet allow their children to express their own views and become individuals in their own right. These parental practices are associated with both high self-esteem and the achievement of identity in adolescence.

Susan Rosenholtz (1977, 1985) believes that teachers can also have a major impact on children's self-evaluations. Too often, she argues, educational experiences are set up so that children are ranked on a global dimension of academic competence. For instance, youngsters are placed in high or low reading groups, teachers publicly give students positive or negative feedback, and children make their own social comparisons with classmates. Children soon come to view themselves as either *generally* competent or *generally* incompetent individuals. The problem, of course, is that half the children in *any* classroom will always end up below average! These children then carry their low self-esteem and low expectations of success into their interactions with more capable students, and the more capable students also expect them to be incompetent. Thus poor performance may become a way of life (Rosenholtz, 1985).

Rosenholtz argues that children would be far better off in a *multidimensional* classroom—one in which many different abilities (rather than one general ability dimension) are recognized. She has experimented with a curriculum that teaches children that different abilities are all important and that everyone has strengths of some kind. Low-ability students who are exposed to such a curriculum appear to gain confidence, for they become more likely than children in a traditional classroom to speak out and exert influence when they work with their classmates (Rosenholtz, 1977). As we discovered in Chapter 9, there are in fact many kinds of intelligence. The child who is deficient in the reading skills that prove so critical to the pecking order in most traditional classrooms may well shine in mechanics, music, art, athletics, or leadership skills. When only generalized academic ability counts in school, it may be difficult indeed for many children to recognize a talent that could become a source of pride and self-esteem.

Individuals who enter adulthood with high self-esteem may still face challenges maintaining it in the face of life events such as job failures, moves, divorces, and illness. Adults are likely to manage the tasks of early, middle, and late adulthood more successfully if they *are* able to sustain positive self-concepts. Not surprisingly, researchers have wondered whether aging itself is a threat to self-esteem. Although we have seen that older adults as a group have self-esteem no lower than that of younger adults, some older adults do have low opinions of themselves. Could part of the problem be that they have internalized or taken to heart society's negative views of old age? **Ageism** is the term used to describe prejudice against elderly people (Butler, 1975). "Ageists" believe the stereotypes implying that old people are sickly, cranky, dependent, forgetful, and otherwise incompetent or unpleasant, and they seek to keep old people at a distance. Knowing that ageism exists in our society, Russell Ward (1977) expected that elderly people would try to avoid labeling themselves as "elderly" or "old" and would have lower self-esteem if they did accept these labels than if they distanced themselves from old age by referring to themselves as "middle-aged" or "young." Although almost 45% of the 65-and-older adults in this study did in fact label themselves as middle-aged rather than elderly, how people labeled themselves was not related to their self-esteem. Instead, elderly people who were low in self-esteem simply held more negative attitudes toward old people in general than did elderly people with high self-esteem.

After demonstrating to their own satisfaction that many elderly people do share society's negative views of their own age group, Judith Rodin and Ellen Langer (1980) set out to boost the self-esteem of nursing home residents. These researchers discovered that 80% of these people, a week after entering the nursing home, blamed physical aging for many of their difficulties in functioning. It did not occur to them that the nursing home environment could be a source of these problems; they were, they thought, incompetent because they were old. In an experiment designed to change these views, Rodin and Langer exposed one group of residents to new explanations for their problems. According to this new "theory," the fact that they found walking difficult was not because they were old and feeble; it was because the nursing home floors were tiled and therefore very slippery for people of all ages. The fact that they grew tired in the evening was not the weariness of old age; instead, anyone would be tired after being awakened at 5:30 in the morning.

Compared to an untreated control group and a group that merely received medical information to the effect that physical aging was not the major source of their difficulties, the group that learned to attribute difficulties to their environment rather than to their old age fared well. They became more active and sociable, and even more healthy, than the other groups. The moral? Elderly people who can avoid taking negative stereotypes of old people to heart and who can avoid blaming almost any difficulty they encounter on the ravages of old age—that is, older adults who can avoid thinking like ageists—appear to have a good chance of feeling good about themselves in later life. Perhaps the worst thing about old age is thinking the worst about old age!

REFLECTIONS

What a complex picture of change and stability emerges when we think about the development of the self across the life span. Before adulthood, considerable change occurs. Infants who only dimly perceive that they exist as separate beings become preschoolers impressed with their physical feats but barely aware of their inner psychological traits, and these youngsters ultimately become adolescents or young adults who have developed elaborate theories of the workings of personality and who have forged unique, complex identities. Moreover, despite some early stability in personality, many of the personality traits of infants and children give way to quite different traits later in life.

If children seem like ever-growing seedlings, adults are more like durable oaks. They seem to carry with them through the years fairly consistent self-conceptions, characteristic levels of self-esteem, and important personality traits. We exaggerate a bit; there is indeed change and even growth in the self after adolescence. But we find it intriguing that many adults change as little as they apparently do.

Perhaps there really is something to be said for having a stable and consistent sense of who we are and of being able to predict how we will behave in the future. Indeed, we seem to work hard throughout our lives to maintain a positive view of ourselves, even in the face of crises and challenges, and we take comfort in knowing that there is a link between what we were, what we are, and what we will become. Susan Whitbourne (1986), for example, has shown that adults strive extremely hard, using self-deception where necessary, to maintain an image of themselves as "loving, competent, and good." It is not tolerable to most of us to admit that we don't care about family members, are incompetent at work, or have all the wrong values and priorities. Nor is it pleasant to lack the sense that a "real me" exists, to feel like many different people in the same body.

And yet who wants to be the "same old person" all the time? The individual whose personality is completely stable sounds like a person in a rut, a person whose growth has been stunted. We also want to feel that we are improving ourselves, "getting better every day," and that if we have character defects or problems we can overcome them. In a classic demonstration of this desire to believe that we grow psychologically over the years, Diana Woodruff and James Birren (1972) had middle-aged adults take a personality test and fill out a second test indicating how they would have responded when they were in college. These adults depicted themselves as quite pitiful creatures in their college years; they genuinely believed that they had gained many personality strengths over the 25 years since their college days. In fact, this personality test had actually been given to them during college, and they had hardly changed at all over the years!

In view of our desire to think that we maintain our strengths and also improve on them, the research findings we have discussed in this chapter couldn't be more reassuring. They tell us that we have a sound basis for feeling a sense of continuity between past, present, and future selves. And yet these findings also tell us that psychological growth can and does occur for many people during adulthood. And even if we do not yet actually possess all the desirable traits that we would like to possess, we can still convince ourselves that we do—or that we soon will!

SUMMARY POINTS

1. Stage theorists like Freud maintain that we experience similar personality changes at similar ages; Erik Erikson and other psychoanalytic theorists argue that stagelike changes in personality continue during adulthood. By contrast, social learning theorists and other nonstage theorists maintain that people can change in any number of directions at any time in life if their social environments change. Self-concept (perceptions of one's attributes) and self-esteem (overall evaluations of one's worth) do not always coincide with objective personality traits.

2. Quite early in their first year, infants acquire some sense that they exist separately from the world around them; by 18 to 24 months of age, they display self-recognition and can categorize themselves by age and gender. Even young infants display distinctive temperaments partially influenced by genetic endowment but also shaped by the interaction between child and environment.

3. The self-concepts of preschool children are very concrete and physical. By about age 8, children begin to describe their inner psychological traits and evaluate their competencies through social comparison processes. Children are most likely to develop high self-esteem if they fare well in social comparisons

and if their parents are both loving and democratic in enforcing rules. During middle childhood, personality traits become more consistent and enduring than they were earlier in life, especially if they are culturally valued and consistent with sex-role standards.

4. During adolescence, self-concepts become more abstract and integrated, and self-awareness increases, though most adolescents experience no more than temporary disturbances in self-esteem at the onset of adolescence.

5. The most difficult challenge of adolescence is resolving Erikson's conflict of identity versus role confusion. From the diffusion and foreclosure identity statuses, many college-aged youth progress to the moratorium status and ultimately to the identity achievement status. Identity formation is an uneven process that often continues into adulthood and that is influenced by social experiences such as interactions with loving parents who encourage individuality.

6. During adulthood, self-conceptions and self-esteem change relatively little, although adults of different ages may have slightly different reasons for feeling good about themselves. Individuals' rankings on important dimensions of personality remain quite stable over the years.

7. From adolescence to middle adulthood, many people appear to gain confidence, independence, and other personal strengths; from middle age to old age only a few systematic changes occur (for example, decreased activity and increased introspectiveness).

8. Stability of personality may be influenced by genetic makeup, early experience, the fact that people seek out and encounter experiences that reinforce their earlier personalities, and the "fit" between person and environment.

9. Erikson's theory of psychosocial development is supported by evidence that a sense of identity lays a foundation for achieving a sense of intimacy. Vaillant's research suggests stages of intimacy versus isolation, career consolidation, and generativity versus stagnation. The process of life review may help elderly people resolve Erikson's issue of integrity versus despair.

10. The development of the emotional self begins in infancy; biologically-based emotions become socialized in the first year through modeling and reinforcement by parents and others. Children rapidly become more knowledgeable about emotions, begin to use emotional expressions deliberately as tools of communication, and learn display rules governing emotional expression.

11. Emotions continue to be important in adulthood, and there is little evidence that elderly people experience fewer emotions or more negative emotions than younger adults do.

12. Children's self-esteem can be strengthened by parents who blend acceptance with democratic and consistent discipline and by teachers who establish multidimensional classrooms in which many different abilities are valued. The self-esteem of older adults can be increased by reducing their tendency to internalize ageist attitudes.

KEY TERMS

ageism
autonomy versus shame and doubt
categorical self
diffusion status
display rules
foreclosure status
generativity versus stagnation
identity
identity achievement status
identity versus role confusion
industry versus inferiority
initiative versus guilt
integrity versus despair
intimacy versus isolation
life review
looking-glass self
moratorium status
personality
self-concept
self-esteem
social comparison
temperament
trust versus mistrust

CHAPTER

11

GENDER ROLES AND SEXUALITY

"Is it a boy (or a girl)?" When proud new parents telephone to announce a birth, that is the first question friends and family tend to ask (Intons-Peterson & Reddel, 1984). It's not long before children know they are girls or boys. Many little girls acquire a taste for frilly dresses and dollhouses, while little boys race their toy cars across the carpet or wrestle each other on the lawn. As adults, we never lose our awareness of being either men or women. We define ourselves partly in terms of our "feminine" or "masculine" qualities, and we play roles in keeping with our society's view of what a woman or a man should be. In short, being female or male is a highly important aspect of the self throughout the life span.

In this chapter, we will be looking at how the characteristics and life experiences of male and female humans differ—and why. We will try to determine just how similar and how different males and females are during different periods of the life span. We will see how girls and boys learn to play their parts as girls or boys and how they are groomed for their roles as women or men, and we will consider some of the ways in which adult men and women are steered along different developmental paths in our society. In addition, we will take a look at an aspect of development that ultimately becomes quite central to our concepts of ourselves as males or females—the development of human sexuality.

MALE AND FEMALE: SORTING OUT THE DIFFERENCES

What are the implications of being a male or a female? We can think in terms of physical differences, psychological differences, and differences in roles played in society. The physical differences are undeniable. A zygote that receives an X chromosome from each parent is a genetic (XX) female, whereas a zygote that receives a Y chromosome from the father is a genetic (XY) male. Chromosomal differences result in different prenatal hormone balances in males and females, and hormones are responsible for the facts that the genitals of males and females differ and that only females can bear children. Moreover, males typically grow to be taller, heavier, and more muscular than females, while females may be the hardier sex in that they live longer and are less susceptible to many physical disorders. Some theorists argue that biological differences between males and females are ultimately responsible for psychological and social differences between the sexes (for example, that the male hormone testosterone predisposes males to be more aggressive than females). Later in the chapter, we will explore the notion that certain differences between the sexes have a biological basis.

However, there is much more to being male or female than biological heritage. Virtually all societies expect the two sexes to adopt different **gender roles**, the patterns of behavior and traits that define how to act the part of a female or a male in a particular society.[1] Characteristics and behaviors viewed as desirable for males or females are

[1]We use the term *sex* when we are referring to the distinction between biological males and biological females and the term *gender* when we are discussing masculine and feminine traits and behavior patterns that develop as social influences interact with biology. Although many developmentalists speak of *sex roles* or *sex-role stereotypes* where we speak of *gender roles* or *gender-role stereotypes*, we believe that it is useful to emphasize through our use of terms that most differences between the sexes are not purely biological but instead are related to socialization experiences.

specified in **gender-role norms**—that is, society's expectations or standards concerning what males and females *should* be like (Pleck, 1981). Each society's norms generate **gender-role stereotypes**, overgeneralized and largely inaccurate beliefs about what males and females *are* like (Pleck, 1981). Through the process of **gender typing**, children not only become aware that they are biological males or females but acquire the motives, values, and patterns of behavior that their culture considers appropriate for members of their biological sex. Through the gender-typing process, for example, little Susie might learn a gender-role norm stating that women should strive to be good mothers and gender-role stereotypes indicating that women are more skilled at nurturing children than men are. As an adult, Susan might then adopt the traditional feminine role by quitting her job when her first child is born and devoting herself to the task of mothering.

We would be very mistaken, then, to credit any differences that we observe between girls and boys or women and men to biological causes. They could just as easily be due to differences in the ways in which males and females are perceived and raised. But before we try to explain sex differences, perhaps we should find out what these differences are believed to be and what they actually are.

Gender Norms and Stereotypes

Which sex is more likely to express emotions? to be tidy? to be competitive? to use harsh language? If you are like most people, you undoubtedly have some ideas about how men and women differ psychologically and can easily answer these questions.

The female's role as childbearer is largely responsible for the gender-role norms that have prevailed in our society. Girls have typically been encouraged to assume an **expressive role** that involves being kind, nurturant, cooperative, and sensitive to the needs of others (Parsons, 1955). These psychological traits, it is assumed, will prepare girls to play the roles of wife and mother—to keep the family functioning and to raise children successfully. By contrast, boys have been encouraged to adopt an **instrumental role**, for as a traditionally defined husband and father, the male faces the tasks of providing for the family and protecting it from harm. Thus boys are expected to become dominant, independent, assertive, and competitive. Similar norms for males and females apply in many, though certainly not all, societies. In most nonindustrial societies, for example, boys are pressured more strongly than girls to become achievement oriented and self-reliant, and girls are more strongly encouraged than boys to become nurturant, responsible, and obedient (Barry, Bacon, & Child, 1957). All of these traits are typically valued in both sexes, but the emphasis placed on each depends on the sex of the child (Zern, 1984).

When cultural norms demand that females play an expressive role and males play an instrumental role, we naturally assume that females actually possess expressive traits and males possess instrumental traits. That is, we form stereotypes of males and females and then make assumptions about what people are like solely on the basis of knowing they are male or female (Broverman, Vogel, Broverman, Clarkson, & Rosenkrantz, 1972). If you are thinking that these stereotypes have disappeared as attention to women's rights has increased and as more women have entered the labor force, you are wrong. Although change has occurred, many adolescents and young adults still endorse many traditional stereotypes about masculinity and femininity and prefer individuals who conform to these stereotypes (Lewin & Tragos, 1987; Ruble, 1983; Shaffer & Johnson, 1980; White, Kruczek, Brown, & White, 1989). Might these notions have a basis in fact, then? Let's see.

Actual Psychological Differences Between the Sexes

In a classic review of more than 1500 studies comparing males and females, Eleanor Maccoby and Carol Jacklin (1974) concluded that only four common gender stereotypes are reasonably accurate (that is, are consistently supported by research):

1. Females have greater *verbal abilities* than males. Girls tend to develop verbal skills at an earlier age than boys, but sex differences are not always clearcut until adolescence, as indicated by measures of such things as vocabulary, reading comprehension, and speech fluency.
2. Males outperform females on tests of *visual/spatial ability* (for example, arranging blocks in patterns, identifying the same figure from different angles). Although Maccoby and Jacklin concluded that these differences emerge only in adolescence, they can be detected in childhood and then persist across the life span (Linn & Petersen, 1985).
3. Similarly, males outperform females on the average

on tests of *mathematical reasoning*, starting in early adolescence (ages 12 to 13).

4. And finally, males are more physically and verbally *aggressive* than females, starting as early as age 2.

Where is all the evidence that males possess instrumental traits and females possess expressive traits? Maccoby and Jacklin conclude that most of our stereotypes of males and females are just that—overgeneralizations unsupported by fact. Some of these unfounded beliefs are described in Table 11.1. Why do they persist? Perhaps because we, as the holders of male/female stereotypes, are biased in our perceptions. We are more likely to notice and remember examples of behavior that confirm our beliefs than to notice exceptions such as independent behavior in a woman, or emotional sensitivity in a man (Martin & Halverson, 1981).

Since the publication of Maccoby and Jacklin's monumental review, some researchers have argued that there are more true sex differences than Maccoby and Jacklin claimed (for example, Block, 1976). In support of this point of view, recent studies show that boys are more physically active than girls, starting in infancy (Eaton & Enns, 1986). Moreover, Maccoby and Jacklin themselves identified some sex differences that are at least partially supported by the evidence. For example, females are often no more timid or fearful than males when they are observed in fear-provoking situations, but they *report* feelings of fear more often. Similarly, girls are no more compliant with their peers than boys are, but they do comply more often with the requests of parents and teachers. Finally, some studies find that males tend to be more dominant and competitive, or that females tend to be more nurturant or empathic, in at least some situations.

Other research supports the contrasting view that even the largest psychological differences between the sexes are trivial. For example, if you imagine all the differences among children or adults in the degree to which they are aggressive, from the most aggressive to the least aggressive person in a group, it turns out that only 5% of that variation can be traced to whether a person is a male or a female (Hyde, 1984). Apparently the remaining 95%

Table 11.1 Some unfounded beliefs about sex differences

BELIEF	FACTS
1. Girls are more "social" than boys.	The two sexes are equally interested in social stimuli, equally responsive to social reinforcement, and equally proficient at learning from social models. At certain ages, boys actually spend more time than girls with playmates.
2. Girls are more "suggestible" than boys.	Most studies of children's conformity find no sex differences. However, sometimes boys are more likely than girls to accept peer-group values that conflict with their own.
3. Girls have lower self-esteem than boys.	The sexes are highly similar in their overall self-satisfaction and self-confidence throughout childhood and adolescence. However, men and women differ in the areas in which they have their greatest self-confidence: females rate themselves higher in social competence, while males see themselves as dominant or potent.
4. Girls are better at simple repetitive tasks, whereas boys excel at tasks that require higher-level cognitive processing.	The evidence does not support these assertions. Neither sex is superior at rote learning, probability learning, or concept formation.
5. Boys are more "analytic" than girls.	Overall, boys and girls do not differ on tests of analytic cognitive style or logical reasoning, although boys do excel if the task requires visual/spatial abilities.
6. Girls lack achievement motivation.	Perhaps the myth of lesser achievement motivation for females has persisted because males and females have generally directed their achievement strivings toward different goals.

Source: Adapted from Maccoby & Jacklin, 1974.

of the variation is due to other differences between people besides whether they are male or female. In other words, *average* levels of aggression for males and females may be noticeably different, but within each sex there are both extremely aggressive and extremely nonaggressive individuals: It is impossible to predict accurately how aggressive a person is simply by knowing his or her gender. The sex differences in cognitive and verbal abilities that Maccoby and Jacklin identified are also small (Caplan, MacPherson, & Tobin, 1985; Hyde, 1981; Hyde & Linn, 1988). Moreover, these sex differences appear to be even smaller today than they used to be (Feingold, 1988; Hyde & Linn, 1988). Finally, sex differences that are evident in one social context often are not evident in another context (Deaux, 1984). For example, the sex differences in abilities found in our culture do not appear among kibbutz dwellers in Israel, suggesting that they are not biologically inevitable and that contextual influences on male and female development are very important (Safir, 1986).

What should we conclude from this research on psychological differences between the sexes? There is bound to be some disagreement among different scholars about which psychological differences between the sexes are real and which are not. Despite their quibbles, however, most developmentalists can agree on this: *The vast majority of gender stereotypes are not supported by fact.* In truth, males and females are far more psychologically *similar* than they are different, and even the most well-documented differences seem to be modest.

Yet it *does* make a very real difference in our society whether one is a male or a female. First, gender norms and stereotypes, even when they are unfounded, do affect how we perceive ourselves and other people. So long as people expect females to be less competent than males, for example, females are likely to lack confidence in many achievement situations, especially those stereotyped as masculine endeavors (Hannah & Kahn, 1989; Lenney, 1977, 1981). Moreover, the belief that women are less competent than men may help explain why employers who must choose between equally qualified men and women often offer a more advanced position or a higher salary to a man (Forisha & Goldman, 1981; Terborg & Ilgen, 1975). The fact that many stereotypes are unfounded does not make them any less potent.

In addition, even though males and females are not very different psychologically, they are still steered toward different *roles in society* (Ruble, 1988). In childhood, girls and boys conform to their gender roles by segregating themselves by sex and developing different interests and play activities (Huston, 1985). As adolescents and adults, males and females pursue different lifestyles. Although more women are entering male-dominated fields today than in the past, men are not entering female-dominated fields, and most high school students continue to aspire toward occupations that are dominated by members of their own sex (Hannah & Kahn, 1989; Lueptow, 1981; Reid & Stephens, 1985). If you go to a college graduation ceremony today, you will still see relatively few women among the engineers and few men among the nursing graduates. And while more men are sharing child-rearing and household responsibilities with their spouses today, most couples still divide the labor along traditional lines so that she is primarily responsible for child care and housework, while he is primarily responsible for earning money and managing it (Hiller & Philliber, 1986). When we think about who asks whom out on a date, who stays home from work when a child is sick, or who sews the buttons back on shirts, we come to the conclusion that traditional gender roles are alive and well, despite significant social change!

In short, we continue to live in a society where, for better or worse, being male or female *matters*. The psychological differences between the sexes may be few and small, but the physical differences are always visible, and the roles that most men and women play in society continue to differ. So now let's trace how girls and boys master their "gender-role curriculum" and how they apply what they learn throughout their lives.

THE INFANT

At birth there are very few differences, other than the obvious anatomical ones, between males and females (Maccoby & Jacklin, 1974). Female infants are said to be hardier, to mature faster, to talk sooner, and to be more sensitive to pain than male infants, whereas larger, more muscular males tend to sleep less, to cry more, and to be somewhat more active and irritable than female infants (see Bell, Weller, & Waldrip, 1971; Hutt, 1972; Maccoby, 1980; Moss, 1967). Even these few differences tend to be small and inconsistent. Nonetheless, it does not take long at all after newborns are labeled as girls or boys for gender stereotypes to affect how they are perceived and treated—and for infants themselves to notice that males and females are different.

Sex Differences and Early Gender-Role Learning

While the baby is still in the hospital delivery room or nursery, parents tend to call an infant son "big guy" or "tiger" and to comment on the vigor of his cries, kicks, and grasps. Girl infants are more likely to be labeled "sugar" or "sweetie" and described as soft, cuddly, and adorable (Maccoby, 1980; MacFarlane, 1977). Even when objective examinations reveal no such differences between boys and girls at birth, parents perceive boys as strong, large-featured, and coordinated, while viewing girls as weaker, finer-featured, and more awkward (Rubin, Provenzano, & Luria, 1974). Soon boys and girls are decked out in either blue or pink and provided with "sex-appropriate" toys and room furnishings (Rheingold & Cook, 1975). In one study (Condry & Condry, 1976), college students watched a videotape of a 9-month-old infant who was introduced as either a girl ("Dana") or a boy ("David"). Influenced by their internalized stereotypes, students interpreted "David's" strong reaction to a jack-in-the-box as "anger," but students who watched "Dana" concluded that the very same behavior was "fear." This stereotyping of boys and girls from birth could be partly the effect of biological differences between the sexes, but more likely it is the *cause* of later behavioral differences between the sexes (Lewis & Weinraub, 1979).

Gender-role socialization begins very early as parents provide their infants with "gender-appropriate" clothing, toys, and hairstyles.

However, infants are not merely the passive targets of other people's reactions to them. They are also actively trying to get to know the social world around them, as well as themselves. By the end of the first year, infants can already distinguish between strange women and strange men (Brooks-Gunn & Lewis, 1981; Lewis & Brooks-Gunn, 1979). As they begin to categorize other people as males and females, they also establish which of these two significant social categories they themselves belong to. By 18 months of age, most infants seem to have a primitive knowledge that they are either like other males or like other females, even if they cannot verbalize it (Lewis & Weinraub, 1979). Almost all children give verbal proof that they have acquired a firm **gender identity**, or an awareness that they are either a boy or a girl, by the age of 2½ to 3 (Thompson, 1975).

Yet even before they are conscious of their gender identity, infant boys are already beginning to behave differently than infant girls. Boys aged 14 to 22 months usually prefer trucks and cars to other playthings, while girls of this age would rather play with dolls and soft toys (Smith & Daglish, 1977). As they approach the age of 2, then, infants are already beginning to behave in ways that are considered gender appropriate in our society. Infant boys and girls are not as different in their interests and preferences as they will become during the preschool years. However, the two years of infancy lay the groundwork for later gender-role development. Because their sex is important to those around them, and because they see for themselves that males and females differ in appearance, infants at least begin to form categories of "male" and "female," to establish a gender identity, and to pursue "gender-appropriate" pasttimes (Lewis & Weinraub, 1979). Is it also possible that these young boys and girls are beginning the process of becoming sexual beings?

Infant Sexuality

It was Sigmund Freud (see Chapter 2) who made the seemingly outrageous claim that human beings are sexual beings from birth onward. We are born, he said, with a reserve of sexual energy that is redirected toward different parts of the body as we develop. Freud may have been wrong about many things, but he was quite right about the fact that infants are sexual beings.

Infants are, of course, biologically equipped at birth with the chromosomes, hormones, and genitals that characterize either males or females. Moreover, young infants in Freud's oral stage of development *do* appear to derive pleasure from sucking, mouthing, biting, and other oral activities. But the real clincher is this: Both male babies (Kinsey, Pomeroy, & Martin, 1948) and female babies (Bakwin, 1973) have been observed to touch and manipulate their genital areas, to experience physical arousal, and to undergo what appear to be orgasms. For example, female infants less than a year old have been observed rubbing against objects or manipulating themselves; grunting, flushing, and becoming agitated; and then sweating, relaxing, and turning paler. It is not uncommon for male infants to have erections and in some cases to progress through changes that look remarkably like sexual arousal, orgasm, and a return to an unaroused state.

What should we make of this infant sexuality? It seems obvious that the infant's experience of masturbation is very different from the adult's experience of it. Infants feel bodily sensations, but they are hardly aware that their behavior is "sexual." How unfortunate, then, that the mother of one infant girl studied by Bakwin was apparently shocked by this "immoral" behavior and slapped and scolded her innocent child (to no avail). Infants are sexual beings primarily in the sense that their genitals are sensitive and their nervous systems allow sexual reflexes. They are also as curious about their bodies as they are about the rest of the world. It will not be too long, however, before they begin to learn what human sexuality is about and how the members of their society regard it.

THE CHILD

Much of the "action" in gender-role development takes place during the toddler and preschool years. Meanwhile children are expressing curiosity about their bodies and learning about human sexuality.

Gender-Role Development

Very young children rapidly acquire (1) a gender identity, the knowledge that they are boys or girls (and that they will be that way for life), (2) gender stereotypes, or ideas about what males and females are supposedly like, and (3) gender-typed behavior patterns, or tendencies to favor "gender-appropriate" activities and behaviors over those typically associated with the other sex.

Understanding the Gender Concept

A critical milestone in gender-role development is acquiring a gender identity. As we have noted, almost all children can accurately label themselves as either boys or girls by the age of 2½ to 3 (Thompson, 1975). It will take longer for them to grasp the fact that a person's biological sex remains the same despite superficial changes. Many 3- to 5-year-olds think that boys can become mommies or girls daddies if they really want to do so, or that a person who changes hairstyles or clothing can become a member of the other sex (Marcus & Overton, 1978; Slaby & Frey, 1975). Children normally begin to understand that sex is an unchanging quality between the ages of 5 and 7. Once children have a "stable" identity as a male or female, they do in fact retain that same identity for life (except in very rare cases, as when a transsexual male begins to feel he is a woman trapped in a male body).

Acquiring Gender Stereotypes

Remarkable as it may seem, toddlers begin to learn society's gender stereotypes at about the same time they become aware of their basic identities as boys or girls. Deanna Kuhn and her associates (Kuhn, Nash, & Brucken, 1978) showed a male doll ("Michael") and a female doll ("Lisa") to children aged 2½ to 3½ and asked each child which of the two dolls would engage in various sex-stereotyped activities. Even among the 2½-year-olds, many boys and girls agreed that girls talk a lot, never hit, often need help, like to play with dolls, and like to help their mothers with chores such as cooking and cleaning. Boys, of course, like to play with cars, like to help their fathers, like to build things, and are apt to say, "I can hit you." Apparently toddlers are well on their way to becoming sexists!

Over the next several years, children's heads become filled with considerably more "knowledge" about how males and females differ. As we saw in Chapter 10, during the elementary school years children begin to describe themselves in terms of their underlying psychological traits, rather than merely in terms of their observable physical characteristics and activities. Similarly, elementary school children begin to understand stereotypes describing the supposed *psychological* traits of males and females. For example, Deborah Best and her colleagues (1977) found that fourth and fifth graders in England, Ireland, and the United States generally agreed that women are weak, emotional, soft-hearted, sophisticated, and affectionate, while men are ambitious, assertive, aggressive, dominating, and cruel.

How seriously do children take the gender-role expectations that they are rapidly learning? William Damon (1977) told children 4 to 9 years old a story about a little boy named George who insists on playing with dolls, even though his parents have told him that dolls are for girls and that boys should play with other toys. Children were then asked a number of questions to assess their impressions of gender roles.

Four-year-olds believed that doll play and other cross-sex behaviors are okay if that is what George really wants to do. As 4-year-old Jack put it, "It's up to him" (Damon, 1977, p. 249). By age 6, about the time they understand that their sex will remain constant, children become extremely rigid in their thinking and intolerant of anyone who violates traditional gender-role standards. These norms now have the force of absolute moral laws and must be obeyed. Consider the reaction of 6-year-old Michael to George's doll play:

> *(Why do you think people tell George not to play with dolls?)* Well, he should only play with things that boys play with. The things that he is playing with now is girls' stuff. . . . *(Can George play with Barbie dolls if he wants to?)* No sir! . . . *(What should George do?)* He should stop playing with girls' dolls and start playing with G.I. Joe. *(Why can a boy play with G.I. Joe and not a Barbie doll?)* Because if a boy is playing with a Barbie doll, then he's just going to get people teasing him [Damon, 1977, p. 255; italics added].

The oldest children in Damon's sample were more flexible in their thinking and less chauvinistic (see also Alpert & Breen, 1989; Martin, 1989). Note how 9-year-old James distinguishes between moral rules that we are obligated to obey and gender-role standards or customs that do not have this same moral force:

> *(What if . . . he kept playing with dolls? Do you think [his parents] would punish him?)* No. *(How come?)* It's not really doing anything bad. *(Why isn't it bad?)* Because . . . if he was breaking a window, and he kept on doing that, they could punish him, because you're not supposed to break windows. But if you want to you can play with dolls. *(What's the difference . . . ?)* Well, breaking windows you're not supposed to do. And if you play with dolls, you can, but boys usually don't [Damon, 1977, p. 263; italics added].

Why do 6- or 7-year-olds interpret gender stereotypes as though they were absolute moral rules rather than social conventions? Perhaps it is because they view any rule or custom as a natural law like the law of gravity that must always be correct (Carter & Patterson, 1982). Or perhaps these young children must exaggerate gender roles in order to "get them cognitively clear" (Maccoby, 1980). Once their gender identities are more firmly established, perhaps they can afford to be more flexible in their thinking about what is "for boys" and what is "for girls."

The Development of Gender-Typed Behavior

Finally, children rapidly come to behave in "gender-appropriate" ways. As we have seen, preferences for gender-appropriate toys are detectable in infancy. Apparently, children develop clear preferences for "boy" toys or "girl" toys even before they have established clear identities as males or females or can correctly label toys as "boy things" or "girl things" (Blakemore, LaRue, & Olejnik, 1979; Fagot, Leinbach, & Hagan, 1986)! Moreover, chil-

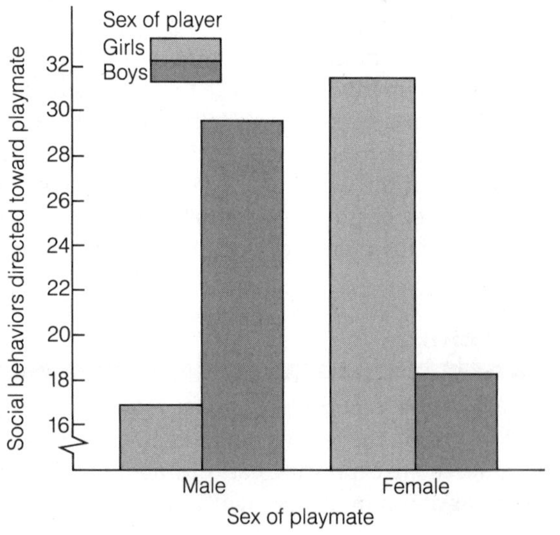

Figure 11.1 Do toddlers prefer playmates of their own sex? Apparently so, for boys are much more sociable with boys than with girls, whereas girls are more outgoing with girls than with boys. (Based on Jacklin & Maccoby, 1978)

dren quickly come to favor same-sex playmates. In one study (Jacklin & Maccoby, 1978), pairs of 33-month-old toddlers (two boys, two girls, or a boy and a girl) were placed in a laboratory playroom and observed to see how often they engaged in solitary activities and how often they engaged in social play. As we see in Figure 11.1, boys were more sociable with boys than with girls, while girls were more sociable with girls than with boys. During the elementary school years, boys and girls develop even stronger preferences for peers of their own sex and segregate themselves into boys' and girls' peer groups much of the time (Thorne & Luria, 1986). This is true in a variety of cultures (Whiting & Edwards, 1988).

Boys face stronger pressures to adhere to gender-role expectations than girls do. As early as age 2, boys already show a stronger preference for gender-appropriate toys than girls do (Blakemore et al., 1979). And recently, John Richardson and Carl Simpson (1982) recorded the toy preferences of 750 children aged 5 to 9 years as expressed in their letters to Santa Claus. Although both boys and girls expressed gender-typed preferences, we see in Table 11.2 that more girls than boys asked for "opposite-sex" items. Moreover, young girls often wish they were boys, but it is rare indeed for a boy to wish he were a girl (Goldman & Goldman, 1982). Just ask your female classmates if they were "tomboys" when they were young, and you're likely to find that most were (Hyde, Rosenberg, & Behrman, 1977). But we defy you to find many male classmates who are willing to admit that they were "sissies" in their youth! The masculine role is very clearly defined in our society; as a result, a major developmental task facing boys is to learn how not to be girls (Emmerich, 1959). Since girls are given more leeway to engage in cross-sex activities and since they soon discover that the masculine role has greater status in society and that many "male" activities are fun, it is understandable that many of them are drawn to masculine activities during childhood.

Table 11.2 Percentages of boys and girls who requested popular "masculine" and "feminine" items from Santa Claus

ITEMS	PERCENTAGE OF BOYS REQUESTING	PERCENTAGE OF GIRLS REQUESTING
Masculine items		
Vehicles	43.5	8.2
Sports equipment	25.1	15.1
Spatial-temporal toys (construction sets, clocks, and so on)	24.5	15.6
Race cars	23.4	5.1
Real vehicles (tricycles, bikes, motorbikes)	15.3	9.7
Feminine items		
Dolls (adult female)	.6	27.4
Dolls (babies)	.6	23.4
Domestic accessories	1.7	21.7
Dollhouses	1.9	16.1
Stuffed animals	5.0	5.4

Source: Based on Richardson & Simpson, 1982.

In sum, gender-role development proceeds with remarkable speed. By the time they enter school, children have long been aware of their gender identities as boys or girls, have acquired many stereotypes about how the sexes differ, and have come to prefer gender-appropriate activities and same-sex playmates. During middle childhood, their knowledge continues to expand as they learn more about gender-stereotyped psychological traits, and they become more flexible in their thinking about gender roles. Yet their *behavior* becomes even more gender-typed, especially if they are boys, and they segregate themselves from the other sex. Now the most intriguing question: How does all this happen so fast?

Theories of Gender-Role Development

Several theories have been proposed to account for sex differences and the development of gender roles. Some theories emphasize the role of biological differences between the sexes, others emphasize social influences on children. Some emphasize what society does to children, others what children do to themselves as they try to understand gender and all its implications. Let's briefly examine a biologically oriented theory and then consider the more "social" approaches offered by psychoanalytic theory, social learning theory, and cognitive-developmental theory.

Money and Ehrhardt's Biosocial Theory

Once, many theorists believed that behavioral differences between males and females were the inevitable result of biological differences between the sexes. More recently, even biologically oriented theorists have come to recognize that biological and social influences interact. For example, the biosocial theory proposed by John Money and Anke Ehrhardt (1972) differs from most theories of gender-role development in calling attention to the ways in which biological events influence the development of boys and girls. But it also focuses on ways in which early biological developments influence how people *react* to a child and suggests that these social reactions then have much to do with children's assuming gender roles.

Money and Ehrhardt stress that receiving either male (XY) or female (XX) chromosomes at conception is merely a starting point in biological differentiation between the sexes. A number of critical events affect a person's eventual preference for the masculine or the feminine role. If a Y chromosome is present, a previously undifferentiated tissue develops into testes as the embryo develops; otherwise it develops into ovaries. At a second critical point, the testes of a male embryo normally secrete the male hormone *testosterone*, which stimulates the development of a male internal reproductive system, and another hormone that inhibits the development of female organs. Without these hormones, the internal reproductive system of a female will develop from the same tissues. At a third critical point, three to four months after conception, secretion of testosterone by the testes normally leads to the growth of a penis and scrotum. If testosterone is absent (as in normal females) or if a male fetus's cells are insensitive to the male sex hormones he produces, female external genitalia (labia and clitoris) will form. Finally, testosterone alters the development of the brain and nervous system. For example, it signals the male brain to stop secreting hormones in a cyclical pattern so that males do not experience menstrual cycles at puberty. Clearly, then, fertilized eggs have the potential to acquire the anatomical and physiological features of either sex. Events at each critical step in the sexual differentiation process determine the outcome.

Once a biological male or female is born, social factors immediately enter the picture. Parents and other people label and begin to react to the child on the basis of the appearance of his or her genitals. If a child's genitals are abnormal and he or she is mislabeled as a member of the other sex, this incorrect label will have an impact of its own on the child's future development. For example, if a biological male were consistently labeled and treated as a girl, he would, by about age 3, acquire the gender identity (though not the biological sex) of a girl. Finally, biological factors enter the scene again at puberty when large quantities of hormones are released, stimulating the growth of the reproductive system, the appearance of secondary sex characteristics, and the development of sexual urges. These events, in combination with one's earlier self-concept as a male or female, provide the basis for adult gender identity and role behavior. The complex series of choice points that Money and Ehrhardt propose is diagrammed in Figure 11.2.

How much influence *do* biological factors have on the behavior of males and females? Corinne Hutt (1972) believes that genetic differences between the sexes may help explain why boys are more vulnerable to problems such as reading disabilities, speech defects, several emotional disorders, and certain forms of mental retardation. For example, since genetic males have but one X chromosome, they are more susceptible to X-linked recessive disorders because they need but one defective gene from their mothers to display the disorder, whereas a female would have to inherit a recessive gene from each of her parents (see Chapter 3). Psychological theories of gender typing cannot easily explain why males often appear to be the "weaker sex," susceptible to many developmental disorders.

Biological influences on development are also evident in studies of children who are exposed to the "wrong" hormones prenatally (Ehrhardt & Baker, 1974; Money & Ehrhardt, 1972). Before the consequences were known, some mothers who had had problems carrying pregnancies to term were given drugs containing progestins, which are converted to the male hormone testosterone by the body. These drugs had the effect of masculinizing female fetuses so that, despite their XX genetic endowment and female internal organs, they were born with external organs that resembled those of a boy (for example, a large clitoris that looked like a penis and fused labia that resembled a scrotum). Several of these **androgenized females** (girls exposed to androgens) were recognized as genetic females, underwent surgery to alter their genitals, and were then raised as girls.

Did early exposure to male hormones then have any effect on the development of these girls? It seemed so. Compared with their sisters and other girls, many more of the androgenized females were tomboys. They preferred to dress in slacks and shorts, showed almost no interest in jewelry and cosmetics, and clearly favored vigorous athletic activities (and male playmates) over traditionally

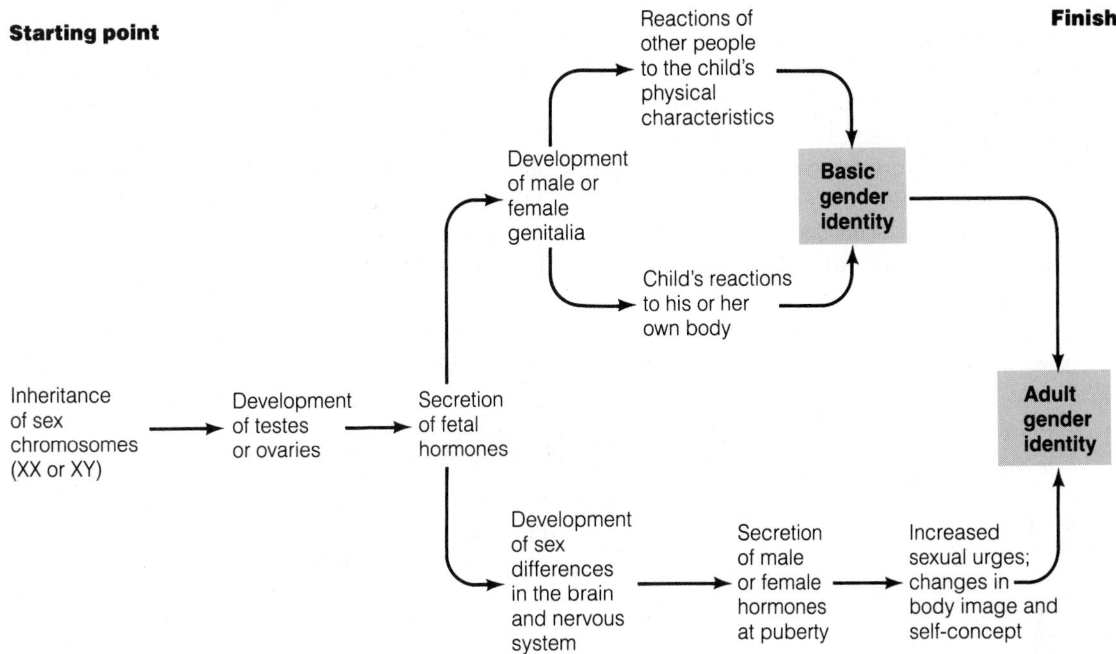

Figure 11.2 Critical events in Money and Ehrhardt's biosocial theory of gender typing. (From Money & Ehrhardt, 1972)

feminine pursuits. And while they expressed an interest in dating boys, marrying, and having children, they began dating somewhat later than other girls and felt that marriage should be delayed until they had established their careers. It could be argued that family members may have reacted to these girls' abnormal genitals and treated them more like boys than like girls, even though interviews with the girls' parents suggested that this was not the case (Ehrhardt & Baker, 1974). It is also possible that the cortisone treatments many of these girls received did more to increase their activity level than prenatal exposure to androgen did (Huston, 1983). Nonetheless we must take seriously the possibility that prenatal exposure to male hormones can affect later attitudes, interests, and activities.

Similarly, some researchers believe that prenatal hormones have something to do with the fact that boys are more aggressive than girls from the age of about 2 on (Maccoby & Jacklin, 1980). The evidence is quite convincing when experiments are conducted with animals. For example, female rhesus monkeys exposed prenatally to the male hormone testosterone often threaten other monkeys, engage in rough-and-tumble play, and try to "mount" a partner as males do at the beginning of a sexual encounter (Young, Goy, & Phoenix, 1964). By contrast, genetically male rat pups that are castrated and cannot produce testosterone display female sexual behavior (Beach, 1965).

What about humans? When androgenized females and their sisters fight, it is most often the masculinized girl who starts it (Ehrhardt & Baker, 1974). Moreover, 16-year-old boys who label themselves physically and verbally aggressive appear to have higher testosterone levels than boys who view themselves as nonaggressive (Olweus, Mattsson, Schalling, & Low, 1980). We must be cautious in interpreting these findings, however. For one thing, hormone levels are not just the cause of behavior; they are also the result of experience. For example, the testosterone levels of male rhesus monkeys rise after they win a fight and fall after they are defeated (Rose, Bernstein, & Gordon, 1975). As a result, it is difficult to establish unambiguously that high concentrations of male hormones *cause* aggressive and otherwise "masculine" behavior (Maccoby & Jacklin, 1980).

In addition, we must give serious consideration to the *social* aspect of Money and Ehrhardt's biosocial theory.

How a child is labeled and treated can have a considerable impact on gender development. For instance, some androgenized females were labeled as boys at birth and raised as such until their abnormalities were detected. Money and Ehrhardt (1972) report that the discovery and correction of this condition (by surgery and relabeling as a girl) caused few if any adjustment problems if the sex change took place *before the age of 18 months.* After age 3, sexual reassignment was exceedingly difficult because these genetic females had experienced prolonged masculine gender typing and had already labeled themselves as boys. These sorts of findings led Money to conclude that there is a *critical period* between 18 months and 3 years of age for the establishment of gender identity. Box 11.1 presents further support for this critical-period concept, as well as evidence that it might better be termed a *sensitive* period.

In sum, Money and Ehrhardt's biosocial theory stresses the importance of early biological developments that influence how parents and other social agents label a child at birth and that possibly also affect behavior more directly. However, the theory also holds that whether children are socialized as boys or girls strongly influences their gender-role development—in short, that biological and social factors interact (Huston, 1983).

Box 11.1
Is Biology Destiny?

When biological sex and social labeling conflict, which wins out? Consider the fascinating case of a male identical twin whose penis was damaged beyond repair during circumcision (Money & Tucker, 1975). The parents agreed to a surgical procedure that made their 21-month-old boy anatomically a girl. Then they treated him as a girl. By age 5, this boy-turned-girl was quite different from her genetically identical brother. She most certainly knew that she was a girl; had developed strong preferences for feminine toys, activities, and apparel; and was far neater and daintier than her brother. This, then, is a vivid demonstration that the most decisive influence on gender-role development is how a child is labeled and treated. Or is it?

Milton Diamond (1982) describes what happened when the BBC attempted to produce a program about this girl after Money and Tucker had completed their study. As a teenager, she was quite maladjusted, according to her psychiatrists. She apparently was unhappy, uncomfortable in her female role, and rejected by her peers, who were put off by her masculine appearance and walk and had been known to call her "cavewoman." Perhaps, then, we should back off from the conclusion that social learning is all that matters. Apparently biology matters too.

A second source of evidence is a study of 18 biological males in the Dominican Republic with a genetic condition that makes their cells insensitive to the effects of male hormones (Imperato-McGinley, Peterson, Gautier, & Sturla, 1979). They had begun life with ambiguous genitals, were mistaken for girls, and so were labeled and raised as females. However, under the influence of male hormones produced at puberty, they sprouted beards and became entirely masculine in appearance. How in the world does a person adjust to becoming a man after leading an entire childhood as a girl?

Amazingly, 16 of 18 of these individuals seemed able to accept their late conversion from female to male and to adopt masculine lifestyles, including the establishment of heterosexual relationships. One retained a female identity and sex role, while the remaining individual switched to a male gender identity but still dressed as a female. Obviously this research casts some doubt on the notion that socialization during the first three years is critical to later gender-role development and suggests that hormonal influences may be more important than social influences. Yet the study has been criticized (see Ehrhardt, 1985). Little information was reported about how these individuals were raised, for example. It is possible that Dominican adults, knowing that this genetic disorder was common in their society, treated these girls-turned-boys differently from other "girls" when they were young. The "girls" themselves may have recognized early on that they belonged to a special class of youngsters and may never have fully committed themselves to being girls.

Considering all of this evidence, is social experience during the first three years of life (Money's critical period) really so powerful that it overrides biological influences? What studies of individuals with genital abnormalities appear to teach us is this: to view the first three years of life as a *sensitive* rather than a critical period for gender-role development, while recognizing that *both* biology and society influence a child's gender identity and gender-role development.

And if you are beginning to wonder whether your friends are really the males or females you thought them to be, perhaps we should emphasize that the kinds of disorders we have been discussing are *extremely* rare!

Freud's Psychoanalytic Theory

Freud viewed both biology (the sex instinct that is rechanneled toward different parts of the body with age) and environment (especially the ways in which parents treat a child) as responsible for sex-role development (see Chapter 2). More specifically, the 3- to 6-year-old child in the phallic stage of development harbors a biologically based love for the parent of the opposite sex, experiences internal conflict and anxiety as a result of this incestuous desire, and resolves the conflict through a process of **identification** with the same-sex parent. According to Freud, a boy experiencing his Oedipus complex loves his mother, fears that his father will retaliate by castrating him, and ultimately is forced to identify with his father, thereby emulating his father and adopting his father's attitudes and behaviors. Freud believed that a boy would show weak masculinity later in life if his father was inadequate as a masculine model, often absent from the home, or not sufficiently dominant and threatening to foster a strong identification based on fear.

Meanwhile, a preschool-aged girl is said to experience an Electra complex involving a desire for her father and a rivalry with her mother. However, since she supposedly believes herself to have been castrated already, she is not as strongly motivated to identify with her mother as her brother is motivated to identify with his father. Nonetheless, a girl does identify with her mother and also receives reinforcement from her father for "feminine" behavior that resembles that of her mother. Freud believed that a girl would fail to adopt her feminine role if she did not identify with her mother or had a mother who proved inadequate as a feminine model. Thus Freud's theory emphasizes the role of emotions (love, fear, and so on) in motivating gender-role development and argues that children adopt their roles by patterning themselves after their same-sex parents.

We can applaud Freud for identifying the preschool years as a critical time for gender-role development. In addition, his view that boys have a more powerful motivation to adopt their gender role than girls do is consistent with the finding that boys seem to learn gender stereotypes and gender-typed behaviors faster and more completely than girls do. Finally, the notion that fathers play an important role in the gender typing of their daughters as well as their sons has now been confirmed (Huston, 1983; Lamb, 1981).

However, on other counts psychoanalytic theory has not fared well at all. Many preschool children are so ignorant of male and female genitals that it is hard to see how most boys could fear castration or most girls could experience penis envy (Bem, 1989; Katcher, 1955). Moreover, Freud assumed that a boy's identification with his father is based on fear, but most researchers find that boys identify most strongly with fathers who are warm and nurturant rather than overly punitive and threatening (Hetherington & Frankie, 1967; Mussen & Rutherford, 1963). Finally, children are not especially similar psychologically to their same-sex parents (Maccoby & Jacklin, 1974). Apparently other individuals besides parents influence a child's gender-related characteristics. And apparently we must look elsewhere for more complete explanations of gender-role development.

Social Learning Theory

According to social learning theorists such as Albert Bandura (1977) and Walter Mischel (1970), children learn masculine or feminine identities, preferences, and behaviors in two ways. First, through *differential reinforcement*, children are encouraged and rewarded for sex-appropriate behaviors and punished for behaviors considered more appropriate for members of the other sex. And second, through *observational learning*, children adopt the attitudes and behaviors of same-sex models. In this view, a child's gender-role development depends on which of his or her behaviors people reinforce or punish and on what sorts of social models are available. Change the social environment, and you change the course of gender-role development.

Parents clearly provide differential reinforcement to boys and girls. Beverly Fagot (1978), for example, observed families with children only 20 to 24 months of age. Daughters were reinforced for dancing, dressing up (as women), following their parents around, asking for assistance, and playing with dolls; they were discouraged from manipulating objects, running, jumping, and climbing. On the other hand, boys were reprimanded for "feminine" activities (playing with dolls, seeking help) and encouraged to play with "masculine" toys such as blocks, trucks, and push-and-pull toys. Fathers are even more likely than mothers to reward both boys and girls, and especially boys, for playing with gender-appropriate toys and to punish play with toys considered appropriate for the other sex (Huston, 1983; Langlois & Downs, 1980). Because fathers do this, they are an especially important influence on the gender-role development of their sons and daughters.

Similarly, peers reinforce and punish boys and girls for different behaviors. And they start early! Beverly Fagot (1985) discovered that boys only 21 to 25 months of age belittle and disrupt each other for playing with "feminine" toys or with girls, and girls express their disapproval of girls who choose to play with boys. Later in childhood, peers become even more likely to reinforce what they consider to be sex-appropriate behavior and punish cross-sex behavior (Huston, 1983). Meanwhile, teachers provide different kinds of feedback to their male and female students and in this way may unwittingly contribute to sex differences in achievement, as we see in Box 11.2.

Observational learning also contributes to gender typing, for children see which toys and activities are "for girls" and which are "for boys" and imitate individuals of their own sex. It takes some years, however, before children pay more attention to same-sex models than to other-sex models. John Masters and his associates (Masters, Ford, Arend, Grotevant, & Clark, 1979) found that preschool children are more concerned about the gender-appropriateness of the behavior they are observing than the sex of the model who displays it. For example, 4- to 5-year-old boys will play with objects labeled "boys' toys" even after they have seen a girl playing with them, but they avoid "girls' toys" that boy models have played with earlier. At about the age of 6 or 7, children do begin to pay closer attention to same-sex models than to opposite-sex models and will avoid toys and activities that members of the other sex seem to enjoy (Ruble, Balaban, & Cooper, 1981). Sometimes children are also reinforced for imitating same-sex models, as when the proud father says, "That's my boy; you're just like daddy!"

Not only do children learn by watching the children and adults with whom they interact, but they learn from the media—radio, television, movies, magazines—and even from their picture books and elementary school readers. In the world of television, for example, males are often dominant characters who work at a profession, whereas many females are passive, emotional creatures who usually manage a home or work at "feminine" occupations such as nursing (Liebert & Sprafklin, 1988). Children who watch more than 25 hours of television a week

Box 11.2
Teaching Boys to Be Boys and Girls to Be Girls in the Classroom

Teachers often treat girls and boys in subtly different ways, and this differential treatment may help explain why girls ultimately tend to excel in language arts and reading while boys tend to excel in math and science (see Wilkinson & Marrett, 1985). For instance, Carol Dweck and her colleagues (Dweck, Davidson, Nelson, and Enna, 1978) found that elementary school teachers often react to academic successes by praising girls for their effort or hard work and boys for their problem-solving strategies or ability. By contrast, when students perform poorly, teachers are likely to communicate to girls that their intellectual shortcomings were responsible, whereas they criticize boys for being sloppy or not trying hard enough. The pattern of feedback that girls often receive is likely to lead them to believe that they lack ability, to underestimate their chances of future success, and even to become helpless in the face of failure (Dweck & Elliott, 1983; Dweck et al., 1978).

Disturbingly, it is often the *brightest* females who most underestimate their abilities and chances of success (Dweck & Elliott, 1983). Jacquelynne Parsons and her associates (Parsons, Kaczala, & Meese, 1982) looked at how elementary school teachers praised students in classrooms where boys and girls clearly differed in their achievement expectancies. These teachers were more likely to praise girls whom they expected to do *poorly* than girls whom they expected to do well. It was the opposite for boys: The more the teacher expected of a boy, the more he was praised. Perhaps you can see how a gifted girl who is rarely praised for her achievements might eventually conclude that she must lack ability or that academic success is not very important for girls, particularly when both the gifted boys *and* her less competent female classmates receive far more praise than she does. By reacting differently to girls and boys, then, teachers may teach lessons that they never consciously intended to teach—lessons that can cause girls to doubt their academic abilities.

are more likely to choose gender-appropriate toys and to hold stereotyped views of males and females than their classmates who watch little television (Frueh & McGhee, 1975; McGhee & Frueh, 1980). As more women play detectives and more men raise families on television, children's notions of female and male roles are likely to change; indeed, watching *The Cosby Show* and other nonsexist programs is associated with holding *less* stereotyped views of the sexes (Rosenwasser, Lingenfelter, & Harrington, 1989).

In sum, there is much evidence that differential reinforcement and observational learning contribute to gender-role development. However, social learning theorists have often portrayed children as the passive recipients of external influences: Parents, peers, characters on television, and other people show them what to do and reinforce them for doing it. Perhaps this perspective does not put enough emphasis on what children themselves contribute to their own gender socialization. For example, children do not receive gender-stereotyped Christmas presents simply because their parents foist those toys upon them. Instead, parents tend to select gender-neutral and often educational toys for their children, while their boys beg for machine guns and their girls for tea sets (Robinson & Morris, 1986)!

Cognitive-Developmental Theory

Lawrence Kohlberg (1966) has proposed a cognitive theory of gender typing that is quite different from the other theories we have considered and helps explain why boys and girls adopt traditional gender roles even when their parents may not want them to do so. Among Kohlberg's major themes are these:

1. Gender-role development depends on cognitive development, for children must acquire certain understandings about gender before they will be influenced by their social experiences.
2. Children actively socialize themselves; they are not merely the passive targets of social influence.

According to both psychoanalytic theory and social learning theory, children are first influenced by their companions to adopt "male" or "female" roles and *then* come to view themselves as girls or boys and to identify with (or habitually imitate) same-sex models. Kohlberg suggests that children *first* come to understand that they are girls or boys and then *actively* seek out same-sex models and a wide range of information about how to act like a girl or a boy. To Kohlberg, it's not "I'm treated like a boy; therefore I must be a boy." It's more like "I'm a boy; therefore I'll do everything I can to find out how to behave like one."

What understandings are necessary before children will teach themselves to behave like boys or girls? Kohlberg believes that children progress through the following three stages as they acquire an understanding of what it means to be a female or male:

1. **Gender identity.** By about the age of 3, the child recognizes that he or she is a male or a female.
2. **Gender stability.** Somewhat later, the child also comes to understand that this gender identity is stable over time. Boys invariably become men and girls grow up to be women.
3. **Gender consistency.** The gender concept is complete when the child realizes that one's sex is also stable across situations. Children of age 6 or 7 are no longer fooled by appearances. They know, for example, that one's sex cannot be altered by superficial changes such as dressing up as a member of the other sex or taking up cross-sex activities.

As we saw earlier, 3- to 5-year-olds often do lack the concepts of gender stability and gender consistency; they often claim that a boy could become a mommy if he really wanted to, or that a girl could become a boy if she cut her hair and wore a cowboy outfit. As children enter the concrete-operational stage of cognitive development and realize that physical quantities such as an amount of liquid are conserved despite changes in appearance, they also realize that gender is conserved despite changes in appearance (Marcus & Overton, 1978). The fact that children progress through Kohlberg's three stages in a variety of cultures suggests that cognitive maturation is an important influence on the child's emerging understanding of gender (Munroe, Shimmin, & Munroe, 1984). Gaining knowledge of male and female anatomy may also contribute (Bem, 1989).

The most controversial aspect of Kohlberg's theory has been his claim that children's behavior changes dramatically once they fully grasp that their biological sex is unchangeable. It is then, Kohlberg argues, that they will actively seek out same-sex models and imitate them. Starting at the age of 5 to 7, then, they become highly motivated to acquire values, interests, and behaviors that are consistent with their cognitive judgments about themselves. Their mature understanding of gender is the *cause*, rather than the consequence, of attending to same-sex models.

As we have seen, children do become more attentive to same-sex models at just this age (Ruble et al., 1981). What is the problem, then? It is that children have already learned many gender-role stereotypes and have developed clear preferences for same-sex activities and playmates long before they master the concepts of gender stability and gender consistency and begin to attend more selectively to same-sex models.

Carol Martin and Charles Halverson (1981) have proposed a somewhat different cognitive theory (actually, an information-processing theory) that overcomes this problem. Like Kohlberg, they believe that children are intrinsically motivated to acquire values, interests, and behaviors that are consistent with their cognitive judgments about the self. However, Martin and Halverson argue that this "self-socialization" begins as soon as children acquire a *basic* gender identity at the age of 2 or 3. According to their *schematic-processing model*, children acquire **gender schemas**—organized sets of beliefs and expectations about males and females that influence the kinds of information they will attend to and remember.

First, children acquire a simple "in-group out-group" schema that allows them to classify some objects, behaviors, and roles as for males and others as for females (for example, cars are for boys, girls can cry but boys should not, and so on). Then they seek out more elaborate information about the role of their own sex, constructing an "own-sex schema." Thus, a young girl who knows her basic gender identity might first learn that sewing is for girls and building model airplanes is for boys. Then, because she is a girl and wants to act consistently with her own self-concept, she gathers a great deal of information about sewing to add to her own-sex schema, while largely ignoring any information that comes her way about how to build model airplanes.

Consistent with this schematic processing theory, children do appear to be especially interested in learning about objects or activities that fit their own-sex schemas. In one study, 4- to 9-year-olds were given boxes of gender-neutral objects (hole punches, burglar alarms, and so on) and were told that the objects were either "girl" items or "boy" items (Bradbard, Martin, Endsley, & Halverson, 1986). Boys explored "boy" items more than girls did, and girls explored "girl" items more than boys did. A week later, children easily recalled which items were for boys and which were for girls; they had apparently sorted the objects according to their "in-group out-group" schemas. In addition, boys recalled more in-depth information about "boy" items than did girls, whereas girls recalled more than boys about these very same objects if they had been labeled "girl" items. If children's information-gathering efforts are indeed guided by their own-sex schemas in this way, we can easily see how boys and girls might acquire very different stores of knowledge as they develop.

Once gender schemas are in place, children will actually distort new information so that it is consistent with their schemas. Martin and Halverson (1983), for example, showed 5- and 6-year-olds pictures of children performing gender-consistent activities (for example, a boy playing with a truck) and pictures of children performing gender-inconsistent activities (for example, a girl sawing wood). A week later, children easily recalled the sex of the actor when activities were gender-consistent, but when an actor's behavior was gender-inconsistent, children often distorted the scene to make it gender-consistent (for example, by saying that it was a boy, not a girl, who had chopped wood). Thus this research gives us some insight into why inaccurate gender stereotypes persist. The child who believes that women cannot be doctors can be exposed to a female doctor but is likely to remember seeing a nurse and will still insist that women cannot be doctors!

An Attempt at Integration

It is likely that some combination of the biosocial, social-learning, and cognitive approaches provides the most accurate explanation of sex differences and gender-role development (Huston, 1983; Ruble, 1988). The biosocial model offered by Money and Ehrhardt acknowledges the importance of biological developments that influence how people label and treat a child. Kohlberg's cognitive-developmental theory and Martin and Halverson's gender schema approach convince us that cognitive maturation plays a part in early gender-role development. Once children acquire at least some understanding that they are boys or girls, they become highly motivated to learn their appropriate roles. When they finally grasp, at age 5 to 7, that their sex will never change, they become even more highly motivated and pay special attention to same-sex models. Even parents who try hard to avoid teaching their children to adopt traditional gender roles are often amazed at how their children seem to become little "sexists" all on their own.

And yet we cannot ignore evidence that socialization agents are influencing children well *before* they understand that they are boys or girls. By age 2, for example, a boy already prefers "boys'" toys and activities because parents, siblings, and even young peers reinforce him for doing "boy things" and discourage behaviors they consider feminine. In other words, social learning theorists were correct in concluding that children behave in gender-consistent ways because other people encourage them to do so. Differential reinforcement and observational learning continue to influence children later in childhood. Differences in learning experiences may help explain why, even though virtually all children form gender concepts and schemas, *some* children are far more gender-typed in their preferences and activities than others are (Serbin & Sprafkin, 1986).

In short, children are born with a male or female biological endowment, are influenced by other people from birth on to become "real boys" or "real girls," and also actively socialize themselves to behave in ways that seem consistent with their understandings that they are either boys or girls. All theories of gender-role development would agree that what children actually learn about how to be males or females depends greatly on what their particular society offers them in the way of a gender "curriculum." Thus we must view gender-role development from a contextual perspective and appreciate that there is nothing inevitable about the patterns of male and female development that we observe in our own society today. In another era, in another culture, the process of gender-role socialization can produce quite different kinds of boys and girls.

Childhood Sexuality

How are boys and girls preparing for the day when they will participate in mature sexual relationships? They are learning a great deal about sexuality and reproduction, are continuing to be curious about their bodies, and are gradually interacting with the other sex in ways that will prepare them to begin dating in adolescence.

Knowledge of Sex and Reproduction

How much do children know about anatomical differences between the sexes and about reproduction? When Ronald and Juliette Goldman (1982) asked children aged 5 to 15 in four countries how they could tell a boy newborn from a girl newborn, young children (5- to 7-year-olds) typically said that they could tell from the baby's clothes or count on the nurse to tell them. Other children knew that sexual anatomy was the key differentiator between males and females and had acquired a more correct and explicit vocabulary for discussing sexual organs.

Anne Bernstein and Philip Cowan (1975) have traced how children's understandings of how people get babies change from age 3 to age 12. These researchers, adopting a Piagetian cognitive-developmental perspective, demonstrated that the sophistication of children's explanations of reproduction is linked to their level of cognitive development. Young children often seemed to assume either that babies were just there all along or that they were somehow manufactured, much as toys might be. According to Jane, age 3½, "You find [the baby] at a store that makes it. . . . Well, they get it and then they put it in the tummy and then it goes quickly out" (p. 81). And a young boy, making what he could of a book about reproduction in the animal world, created his own delightful scenario:

> *[How would the lady get a baby to grow in her tummy?]* Um, get a rabbit . . . they just get a duck or a goose and they get a little more growned . . . and then they turn into a baby. *[A rabbit will turn into a baby?]* They give them some food, people food, and they grow like a baby. *[If I asked you to tell me just one way that people get babies, what would you say?]* I would say, a store, buy a duck. . . . [Bernstein & Cowan, 1975, p. 87; italics supplied].

Aren't preschoolers fascinating?! These young children apparently invent their own understandings of reproduction before they are told the "facts of life." Even if they are given information, they interpret it as best they can in terms of concepts that they do understand (such as buying items at the store). Between the ages of 9 and 11, most children are beginning to understand that sexual intercourse plays a role in the making of babies (Goldman &

Goldman, 1982). By 11 or 12 years of age, most children have integrated information about sexual intercourse with information about the biological union of egg and sperm (Bernstein & Cowan, 1975). Yet even then many of them think that the baby was originally contained in either the sperm or the egg rather than created from the union of the two. Perhaps it is not surprising that children have many mistaken ideas about reproduction when we consider how secretive adults are about the whole matter. As children mature cognitively, they are able to construct ever more accurate understandings of sexuality and reproduction from the information they do receive.

Sexual Behavior During Childhood

According to Freud, preschoolers in the *phallic stage* of psychosexual development are actively interested in their genitals and seek bodily pleasure through masturbation. School-aged children, by contrast, enter a *latency period* in which they repress their sexuality and turn their attention instead to schoolwork and friendships with same-sex peers. Freud was partly right and partly wrong.

Freud was correct to propose that preschoolers are highly curious about their bodies, masturbate, and engage in both same-sex and cross-sex sexual play. He was wrong to believe that such activities occur infrequently among school-aged children. Analyzing interviews with children age 4 to 14 gathered by Alfred Kinsey and his associates, James Elias and Paul Gebhard (1969) found that:

- Fifty-six percent of the boys and 30% of the girls reported that they had masturbated before reaching puberty.
- Fifty-two percent of the boys and 35% of the girls had engaged in some form of sexual play with same-sex peers (exhibition of genitals, manipulation of one another's genitals, and so on).
- Thirty-four percent of the boys and 37% of the girls reported similar forms of heterosexual play.

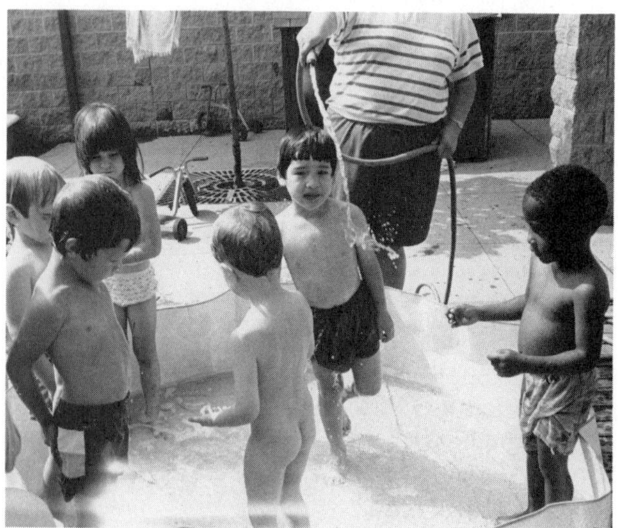

Preschoolers are naturally curious about the human body.

Such sexual experimentation, which is more common among boys than among girls, appears to *increase* with age, rather than decreasing with age as Freud claimed (Rosen & Hall, 1984). Perhaps Freud was misled by the fact that preschoolers, often unaware of society's rules of etiquette, express their sexual curiosity in public more often than older children do (Rosen & Hall, 1984). Latency-period children may be more discreet than preschoolers, but they have by no means lost their sexual curiosity.

Perhaps Freud was also misled because the Victorian society in which he lived was especially restrictive about sexuality. Whether children do or do not engage in various sexual behaviors is very much influenced by the society in which they live, as well as by their own parents' attitudes about sexuality. In all societies, children undergo a process of sexual socialization in which they learn which sexual behaviors are and are not permissible in childhood and expected in adulthood. Judging from the anthropological research of Clellan Ford and Frank Beach (1951), the diversity in sexual attitudes and behaviors among cultures of the world is staggering. In *restrictive* societies, children are not allowed to express any sexuality. In New Guinea, for example, Kwoma boys were not allowed to touch themselves, and a boy caught having an erection was likely to have his penis beaten with a stick. Kwoma parents were careful to avoid letting their children see them having intercourse. Some restrictive societies relaxed the rules after children reached puberty, but others did not do so until young people married. In *semirestrictive* societies, formal rules prohibiting childhood masturbation and sex play existed, but they were frequently violated and adults rarely punished children unless the violations were flagrant.

How different it was in *permissive* societies, where children were free to express their sexuality and were even encouraged to prepare for their roles as mature sexual beings. In some of these societies, adults sexually stimulated infants and young children to soothe them. Children were permitted to masturbate and play their sexual games publicly, and they imitated the adult sexual behaviors that their parents frequently allowed them to witness.

Where does our own society fall on this continuum of sexual restrictiveness and permissiveness? Ford and Beach (1951) placed the United States in the "restrictive" category. Perhaps today we could argue that "semirestrictive" is a more fitting label, but our society continues to try to keep children ignorant of sexuality and sexually inactive. For example, today's parents are aware that children masturbate, but 30% to 40% of them still think it is wrong (Gagnon, 1985). Some time ago, Margaret Mead (1928) contrasted the permissive sexual socialization of children and adolescents in Samoa with the more restrictive regimen of our society. She concluded that we make the transition to adulthood harder than it need be by denying children opportunities to prepare for sexual relationships later in life.

However, children in our society do receive some preparation for adolescent and adult sexuality as they engage in masturbation and sexual play and learn more about sexuality and reproduction with each passing year. Moreover, as Box 11.3 indicates, even though school-aged

Box 11.3
Before the First Date: Relationships Between the Sexes During Childhood

School-aged children are by no means as uninterested in sexuality and the opposite sex as Freud claimed. Yet relationships between boys and girls in the childhood years are a bit of a puzzle. They appear to be love/hate relationships. On the one hand, children seem to realize that they will eventually date and marry and take special interest in particular members of the other sex. In a survey of Pennsylvania children ages 10 to 12, Carlfred Broderick and George Rowe (1968) found that 71% of the girls claimed to have a boyfriend and 56% of the boys claimed to have a girlfriend. Moreover, about half of the youngsters admitted that they had been "in love" at some time, and almost a quarter had even had "dates." True, many of these "puppy love" relationships are one-sided. Jennie might love Tim, but Tim might be unaware of it, aware of it but unreciprocating, or even thoroughly appalled by the idea. Still, these pre-adolescent attractions may prepare children for dating in adolescence.

Similarly, Barrie Thorne and Zella Luria (1986), who observed 9- to 11-year-old children extensively in and around their schools, concluded that boys and girls were learning sexual "scripts" that would be played out in adolescence and adulthood. Boys were readying themselves for the excitement of sexuality, perhaps, by daringly using taboo words and reading *Playboy* and *Penthouse*. Girls, meanwhile, seemed to be learning about the emotional aspects of relationships by forming close friendships with other girls and swapping intimacies, often about which boys they "liked" or thought "cute."

At the very same time, relationships between the sexes during the elementary school years are often quite hostile. Boys and girls do live in largely segregated social worlds during these years. They often openly express negative opinions of the other sex, girls describing boys as "dirty" and "noisy," boys complaining bitterly about the way girls "carry on" (Goldman & Goldman, 1982). Moreover, Thorne and Luria found that children sometimes used the term "like" to insult each other, as in, "Jennie likes [that kid we all know is a nerd]" or "[That kid we all know is a nerd] likes Jennie." In addition, a favorite pasttime is kiss-and-chase games. Most often, the girls, sometimes viewed by the boys as "cooties" laden with germs, chased and attempted to kiss unfortunate boys, though it sometimes worked the other way as well. It is often a case of the war of one whole sex against the other: "Tony, help save me from the girls" (Thorne & Luria, 1986, p. 187).

So what are children learning for future use from their love/hate relationships with the other sex? For one thing, they are learning that dating and marriage are most probably ahead of them in life and are becoming attracted to the idea (Broderick & Rowe, 1968). And yet, judging from Thorne and Luria's findings, they are also learning that relationships with the other sex hold the potential not only for enjoyment but for danger. Members of the other sex, they discover, are both desirable partners and "the enemy." As they go about both loving and hating each other, kissing and running away, so-called latency-stage children make it clear that they are sexual beings grooming themselves for more explicitly sexual—but still often ambivalent—heterosexual relationships later in life (Thorne & Luria, 1986).

children spend most of their time in same-sex peer groups, they nonetheless show considerable interest in the other sex and rehearse "scripts" for boy/girl relationships that they will play out more fully during adolescence.

THE ADOLESCENT

How do adolescents prepare to adopt the masculine or feminine roles that they will be asked to play in adulthood? How do they come to grips with their transformation into sexually mature men and women? Adolescence is a period in which the challenges and pressures are great.

Adhering to Gender Roles

We observed earlier that young elementary schoolchildren are highly rigid in their thinking about gender roles, viewing gender norms as akin to moral laws that cannot be violated. In middle childhood, children begin to think more flexibly about gender norms, recognizing that they are not absolute laws. And in adolescence? Curiously, teenagers once again seem to become highly intolerant of certain role violations and stereotyped in their thinking about the proper roles of males and females. They are more likely than somewhat younger children to make negative judgments of peers who violate expectations by engaging in cross-sex behavior or expressing cross-sex interests (Carter & McCloskey, 1983–1984; Emmerich & Shepard, 1982; Sigelman, Carr, & Begley, 1986; Stoddart & Turiel, 1985).

Consider a study by Trish Stoddart and Elliot Turiel (1985) that involved children in kindergarten and third, fifth, and eighth grades (ages 5 to 13). These children were asked questions about a boy who either wears a barrette or puts on nail polish and about a girl who either sports a crew cut or wears a boy's suit. As Figure 11.3 reveals, both the kindergartners and the adolescents judged these behaviors to be very wrong, while third and fifth graders viewed them far more tolerantly. Like the elementary schoolchildren, eighth graders clearly understood that gender-role expectations are just social conventions that can easily be changed and do not necessarily apply in all societies. However, these adolescents had also begun to conceptualize gender-role violations as a sign of psychological abnormality and could not tolerate them. Budding adolescents apparently do not want to interact with "deviants" and are prone to calling them names such as "fag" or "queer" (Carter & McCloskey, 1983–1984).

Why do adolescents show a heightened concern with conformity to gender roles? Phyllis Katz (1979) sees it this way: Adolescents increasingly find that they must conform to traditional gender norms in order to succeed in the dating scene and prepare for adult family and career roles. For example, a girl who was a tomboy and thought nothing of it may find during adolescence that she must dress and behave in more "feminine" ways to attract boys, and a boy may find that he is more popular if he projects a more sharply "masculine" image. Social pressures on adolescents to conform to traditional roles may even help explain why sex differences in verbal, mathematical, and spatial abilities sometimes become clearcut only during the adolescent years (Hill & Lynch, 1983). Whatever the precise reasons, it is fascinating indeed that the rigidly sexist views about many gender-role issues held in early childhood fade away only to make a comeback during adoles-

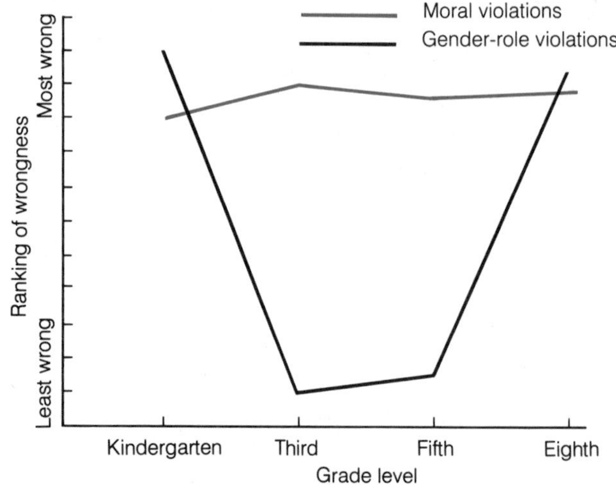

Figure 11.3 Children's rankings of the wrongness of gender-role transgressions (such as a boy's wearing nail polish) and violations of moral rules (such as pushing another child from a swing). Notice that children of all ages deplore immoral acts, but that only kindergartners and adolescents view gender-role violations as wrong. Elementary school children come to think about gender-role standards in a more flexible way than they did earlier in life, but adolescents become concerned about the psychological implications of deviating from one's "proper" role. (Adapted from Stoddart & Turiel, 1985)

cence. As adolescents then become more comfortable with their identities as men and women, they can perhaps afford to be more flexible in their thinking. Indeed, adults are less rigidly stereotyped in their thinking about gender roles than high school students are (Urberg, 1979).

Adolescent Sexuality

Although infants and children are sexual beings, sexuality assumes far greater importance once sexual maturity is achieved. Adolescents must now incorporate into their identities as males or females concepts of themselves as *sexual* males or females. Moreover, they must figure out how to express their sexuality in the context of interpersonal relationships. As adolescents attempt to form their identities as individuals, they raise questions about their attractiveness to the opposite sex, their sexual values, and their goals in close relationships. They also experiment with sexual behavior—sometimes with good outcomes, sometimes with bad ones. What are the sexual values of today's teenagers? What is "normal" sexual behavior during adolescence? The psychological aspects of dating relationships are explored further in Chapter 13; here, let's focus on the sexual aspects.

Teenage Sexual Morality

Have today's teenagers adopted a "new morality" that is dramatically different from traditional standards of sexual behavior? The sexual attitudes of adolescents have indeed changed dramatically during this century, especially during the 1960s and 1970s. And yet even before the AIDS epidemic came along, few teenagers had totally abandoned the "old values."

In a review of the literature on teenage sexuality, Philip Dreyer (1982) characterizes some of the most important changes that have occurred in sexual attitudes. First, most adolescents seem to believe that *sex with affection is acceptable*. This means that most adolescents no longer accept the traditional belief that premarital intercourse is always morally wrong, although a minority still do. In contrast, today's adolescents do not go so far as to view casual sex as acceptable, and they strongly disapprove of exploitative sex. They insist that the partners be "in love" or feel a close emotional involvement with each other.

A second important change is the *decline of the* ***double standard***. According to the double standard, sexual behavior that is viewed as appropriate for males is viewed as inappropriate for females, or the standards for the two sexes otherwise differ. Thus in the "old days," a young man was expected to "sow some wild oats," while a young woman was expected to remain a virgin until she married. (Apparently, there were a few "bad girls" willing to accommodate all those eager young men!) The double standard has not entirely disappeared. For example, college students still tend to believe that a woman who has many sexual partners is more immoral than a man who does the same thing (Robinson & Jedlicka, 1982). However, our society has been moving for some time toward a single standard of sexual behavior used to judge both males and females.

A third change might be described as *increased confusion about sexual norms*. As Dreyer notes, the "sex with affection" norm is more than a little ambiguous. Must one be truly in love, or is some degree of liking enough to justify sexual intercourse? It is now up to the individual to answer such questions. In addition, adolescents continually receive mixed messages about sexuality. They are encouraged to be popular and attractive to the other sex, and they watch countless television programs and movies that glamorize sexual behavior. Lamenting the strong peer pressure on her to become sexually active, one girl offered this amusing definition of a virgin: "an awfully ugly third grader" (Gullotta, Adams, & Alexander, 1986, p. 109). Yet teenagers are also told to value virginity and to fear and avoid sexually transmitted diseases, pregnancy, and bad reputations. According to teenagers, many parents do convey double messages, communicating that sexuality is a natural way of expressing love, but also saying that nice individuals (and especially nice girls) wait until marriage (Darling & Hicks, 1982). Of course, members of the parent world also disagree among themselves, some insisting that all sexual behavior outside marriage is immoral, others helping their children to obtain contraceptives.

As a result of all these conflicting signals, adolescents are often quite confused about how to behave. The standards for males and females are now more similar, and adolescents tend to agree that sexual intercourse in the context of emotional involvement is acceptable, but teenagers still find they must forge their own codes of behavior, and they differ widely in what they decide.

Sexual Behavior

If attitudes about sexual behavior have changed, has sexual behavior itself changed? Yes, it has. Indeed, it is dif-

Today's adolescents are involved in sexual activity very early.

ficult to identify any aspects of sexual behavior that have *not* changed. It does appear that experimentation with homosexual activity, typically most common among young adolescent boys, may actually have decreased slightly over the years (Dreyer, 1982). In one study, 14% of teenage boys and 11% of girls indicated that they had had a sexual experience with someone of their own sex, and far fewer said that they were likely to be involved in a homosexual relationship in the future (Hass, 1979).

Otherwise, today's adolescents are involved in more, and more intimate, forms of sexual behavior at earlier ages than adolescents of the past were (Dreyer, 1982). More adolescents report that they masturbate and more regard it as normal than in past eras (Dreyer, 1982), though many still feel guilty or uneasy about it (Coles & Stokes, 1985). About three-fourths of adolescent boys and half of adolescent girls masturbate (Hass, 1979). Adolescents are also involved in several forms of petting at younger ages than they used to be. Typically, teenagers progress through a predictable sequence of behaviors as they get older that ranges from kissing and necking to light petting to heavy (or genital) petting to intercourse and oral sex (DeLamater & MacCorquodale, 1979).

Finally, more adolescents today are having sexual intercourse. Figure 11.4 shows the percentages of high school and college students who have experienced premarital intercourse in each of three historical periods (Dreyer, 1982). This figure illustrates several phenomena. First, rates of sexual intercourse increase with age over the adolescent years. As recently as 1979, only a small minority of teenagers under age 15 had had intercourse, about half had experienced it by the end of high school, and a large majority had experienced it by the end of the college years (or by around age 20 or 21 if they did not attend college). Second, much social change has occurred; the percentages of both males and females who have had intercourse have increased during this century. Third and finally, notice that the sexual behavior of females has changed a good deal more than the sexual behavior of males has (Wielandt & Boldsen, 1989). The decline of the double standard is clearly not just a matter of changes in attitude. As a result, recent cohorts of college women have been about as likely to have had sexual intercourse as college men (Darling, Kallen, & VanDusen, 1984).

Despite these significant social changes, we can still see hints that the effects of the double standard persist, not so much in the rates of sexual behavior as in the attitudes surrounding it. For example, teenage girls appear to be more insistent than teenage boys that sex and love go together (Coles & Stokes, 1985), and they are more often engaged to or going steady with their first sexual part-

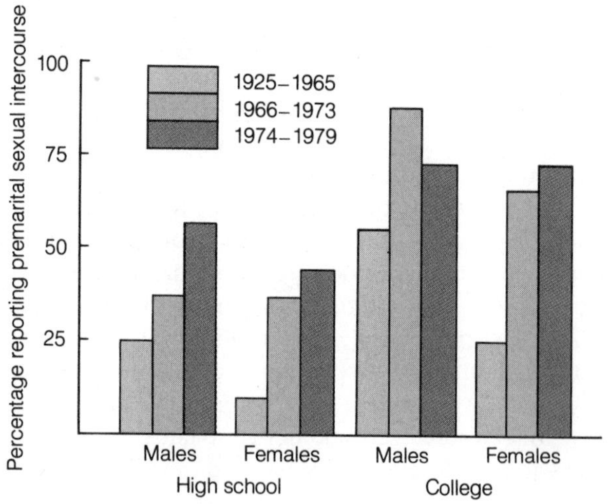

Figure 11.4 Historical changes in the percentages of high school and college students reporting premarital sexual intercourse. (Adapted from Dreyer, 1982)

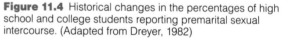

ners (Zelnik & Shah, 1983). When asked if emotional involvement is a prerequisite for intercourse, 85% of college women say "always" or "most of the time"; only 40% of college men do (Carroll, Volk, & Hyde, 1985). Apparently, then, females continue to be more likely than males to associate physical intimacy with emotional intimacy. This continuing gap between the sexes can sometimes create misunderstanding and hurt feelings, and it may partly explain why females are more ambivalent about their first sexual experiences than males are (Coles & Stokes, 1985).

In sum, both the sexual attitudes and the sexual behaviors of adolescents have changed considerably in this century. Sexual involvement is now part of the normal adolescent's experience—part of his or her search for identity and emotional fulfillment (Dreyer, 1982). Most adolescents seem able to adjust successfully, but there have also been some casualties among those who are psychologically immature or who end up as part of the statistics on sexually transmitted disease and unwanted teenage pregnancy.

Unfortunately, large proportions of sexually active adolescent couples fail to practice birth control, partly because they are cognitively immature and fail to take seriously the possibility that their behavior could have unwanted consequences (Morrison, 1985; and see our discussion of teenage pregnancy in Chapter 2). For the 1 teenage girl out of 10 who gives birth before she reaches the age of 18, the consequences of teenage sexuality are likely to include an interrupted education, low income, and a difficult start for both new parent and child (Furstenberg, Lincoln, & Menken, 1981). This young mother's life situation and her child's developmental status are likely to improve later on, especially if she goes back to school and limits her family, but she is likely to remain economically disadvantaged compared with her peers who postpone parenthood until their 20s (Furstenberg, Brooks-Gunn, & Morgan, 1987). Meanwhile the AIDS epidemic continues, but adolescents show few signs of having adopted safer sexual practices in response to this threat (Carroll, 1988). No wonder many educators are now calling for a stronger program of sex education and counseling in the schools. If teenage sexuality is here to stay, then there is little chance of preventing its unwanted consequences unless both boys and girls begin to behave in more sexually responsible ways.

THE ADULT

You might think that once children and adolescents have learned their gender roles, they simply play them out during adulthood. Instead, as people face the challenges of adult life, their gender roles and concepts of themselves as men and women change. So do their sex lives.

Sex Differences in the Achievement of Identity and Intimacy

As we saw in Chapter 10, Erik Erikson's theory of psychosocial development proposes that late adolescence is a time for establishing an identity (or self-definition), whereas early adulthood is a time for establishing intimacy (or the ability to commit oneself to a long-lasting relationship). If you think about it, the task of forming an identity, especially when it centers on establishing career goals, is a "masculine"—that is, instrumental—endeavor (Livson, 1983). It involves separating from one's parents and defining oneself as an autonomous and independent person. The task of achieving intimacy, by contrast, seems to require "feminine"—that is, expressive—qualities (the ability to care, express feelings, and so on). Might men and women differ, then, in their quests for identity and intimacy?

There are signs that males and females go about resolving identity and intimacy issues in different ways. First, males have traditionally been more likely to focus on issues of vocational goals and personal ideologies in forming an identity, while females have been more likely to raise and resolve questions about their sexual values, gender roles, and interpersonal relationships (Douvan & Adelson, 1966; Hodgson & Fischer, 1979). Today, women emphasize career goals as much as men do, but they continue to attach more importance to interpersonal aspects of identity and less to ideological aspects (Bilsker, Schiedel, & Marcia, 1988). For women, then, issues of identity and intimacy are often more intertwined (Hodgson & Fischer, 1979).

Second, although some females appear to follow the male developmental path of achieving identity before intimacy, other females take quite different developmental paths. Among college men, for example, the achievement of genuine intimacy is unlikely unless identity has been achieved (Schiedel & Marcia, 1985). Thus Jeff may not feel psychologically ready for marriage or even a serious relationship: He wants to figure out where he is headed, finish school, and perhaps even launch his career first. Martha, who is highly serious about her career, may follow the same identity-before-intimacy route followed by most men. But Sue, like many college women over the years, wants to resolve intimacy issues before she addresses the question of who she is as an individual (Hodgson & Fischer, 1979; Schiedel & Marcia, 1985; Tesch & Whitbourne, 1982). This was an even more common pattern in the past: Many women established "reflected" identities by becoming wives and mothers but postponed establishing *personal* identities until their children were more self-sufficient and they could begin to think about their own interests (O'Connell, 1976). Finally, still other women tackle both identity and intimacy tasks at once. Sarah, for instance, may forge a personal identity that largely centers on her intimate relationships and her desire to be a caring person. In short, Erikson's theory seems to fit men better than it fits women because women differ more in the ways they go about dealing with identity and intimacy issues.

Is this picture changing as more women pursue independent career goals and postpone marriage? It seems to be. Among today's college women, for example, those with liberated attitudes about the roles of women are farther along in the search for a personal identity than those who hold more traditional attitudes (Stein & Weston, 1982). Moreover, women (and men too) who describe themselves as having many masculine-stereotyped traits such as assertiveness and independence are more likely to have achieved a personal identity than women who view themselves as having traditionally feminine personality traits (Grotevant & Thorbecke, 1982; Schiedel & Marcia, 1985). We can speculate, then, that as more women adopt feminist attitudes and place greater emphasis on establishing their own careers and less emphasis on preparing for traditional roles as wives and mothers, sex differences in the paths to identity and intimacy may decrease.

Gender Roles in Adulthood

Although males and females play out their masculine or feminine roles throughout their lives, the specific content of those roles changes considerably over the life span. The young boy, for example, plays his masculine role by playing with trucks or wrestling with his chums, while the man may play his role by holding down a job. Moreover, the degree of difference between male and female roles also changes. Although children and adolescents do adopt behaviors consistent with their "boy" or "girl" roles, the two sexes otherwise adopt quite similar roles in society—namely, the roles of children and students. Even in early adulthood, the roles that men and women play often do not differ much, as members of both sexes are often single and in school or working.

However, the roles of men and women become more distinct when they marry and especially when they have children. Even among newlyweds, for example, the wife typically does the lion's share of the housework and specific tasks tend to be parceled out along traditional lines (Atkinson & Huston, 1984). This is true even if the wife works outside the home, although it is even more true if she does not and if she and her husband have traditionally gender-typed personal traits. Moreover, the birth of a child tends to make even quite "liberated" couples divide their labors in more traditional ways than they did before they

had a child (Cowan & Cowan, 1987). It is she who becomes primarily responsible for child care and household tasks; he tends to emphasize his role as "breadwinner" and center his energies on providing for the family. Even as men today increase their participation in child care and housework, they still tend to play a "helper" role (Baruch & Barnett, 1986), and about two-thirds of what gets done at home is still done by women (Pleck, 1985). Moreover, there is still a tendency to view a wife's career as secondary.

What happens after the children are grown? Older people do seem to hold more traditional attitudes about the roles of men and women than younger people do (Markides & Vernon, 1984), and they divide the labor at home in traditional ways (Richmond-Abbott, 1983). However, in some respects the roles played by men and women become more similar again starting in middle age, when the nest empties and child-rearing responsibilities end, and continuing into old age, when work roles end and when men and women play similar roles as grandparents and lead more similar daily lifestyles. It would seem, then, that the roles of men and women are fairly similar before marriage, maximally different during the parental years, and more similar again later on.

Do these sorts of shifts in the roles played by men and women during adulthood affect them psychologically? Do adults become more psychologically "masculine" in work roles that require assertiveness and independence or more "feminine" when they must nurture young children?

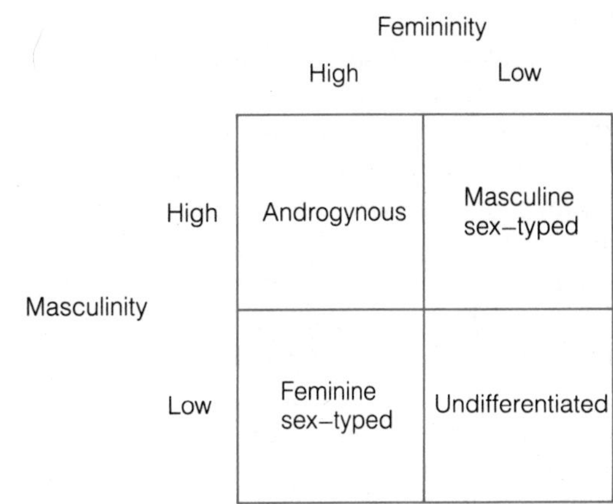

Figure 11.5 Categories of gender-role orientation based on viewing masculinity and femininity as separate dimensions of personality.

Masculinity, Femininity, and Androgyny

For many years, psychologists assumed that masculinity and femininity were at opposite ends of a single dimension. If one possessed highly masculine traits, one must be very unfeminine; being highly feminine implied being unmasculine. Sandra Bem (1974) challenged this assumption by arguing that individuals of either sex can be characterized by psychological **androgyny**—that is, can possess *both* masculine-stereotyped traits (for example, being aggressive, analytical, forceful, and independent) and feminine-stereotyped traits (for example, being affectionate, compassionate, gentle, and understanding). In Bem's model, then, masculinity and femininity are *two separate dimensions* of personality. A male or female who has many masculine-stereotyped traits and few feminine ones is defined as a *masculine sex–typed* person. One who has many feminine- and few masculine-stereotyped traits is said to be *feminine sex–typed*. The androgynous person possesses both masculine and feminine attributes, whereas the *undifferentiated* individual lacks both of these kinds of attributes (see Figure 11.5).

Do androgynous people really exist? Bem (1974, 1979) and other investigators (Spence & Helmreich, 1978) have developed inventories that contain both a masculinity scale and a femininity scale that ask people how they perceive themselves. In one large sample of college students (Spence & Helmreich, 1978), roughly 33% of the test takers were "masculine" men or "feminine" women; 27% to 32% were androgynous, and the remaining individuals were either undifferentiated (low on both scales) or "sex-reversed" (masculine sex–typed females or feminine sex–typed males). So androgynous individuals do indeed exist, and in sizable numbers. Now we can ask whether perceived masculinity, femininity, and androgyny change over the adult years.

Gutmann's Hypothesis About Sex Differences in Adulthood

David Gutmann (1975, 1977) has offered the intriguing hypothesis that the demands of parenthood, which he calls the **parental imperative**, not only pressure mothers and fathers into different roles but affect them psychologically. Drawing on his own cross-cultural research and that of others, he suggests that in many cultures young and middle-aged men must emphasize their "masculine" qualities in order to feed and protect their families, while young and middle-aged women must express their "feminine" qualities in order to nurture children and meet the emotional needs of their families. Thus men need to be dominant, independent, assertive, and even aggressive, while women need to be nurturant, emotionally sensitive, submissive, and so on.

According to Gutmann, all this changes dramatically starting in midlife when men and women are freed from the demands of the parental imperative. Men become less active and more passive, take less interest in community affairs, and take more interest in religious contemplation and family relationships. They sometimes do "women's work" after they are no longer able to hunt, farm, or otherwise fulfill their masculine roles. Meanwhile, women are changing in precisely the opposite direction. After being quite passive and submissive as younger women, they become more active, domineering, and assertive in later life. In many cultures, they take charge of the household after being the underlings of their mothers-in-law as young women, and they become freer to participate in community affairs and rituals. In short, Gutmann proposes that over the course of adulthood psychologically "masculine" men become "feminine" men, while "feminine" women become "masculine" women. During later adulthood, both sexes express the parts of their personalities that were suppressed in early adulthood. Similar ideas were proposed some time ago by the psychoanalytic theorist Carl Jung (1933).

Does Research Support Gutmann's Hypothesis?

Several studies at least partially support Gutmann's hypothesis. Barbara Abrahams, Shirley Feldman, and Sharon Nash (1978) gave Bem's androgyny inventory to young adults who were either living with someone, married but without children, expecting their first child, or new parents. Men and women who were parents were the most highly sex-typed (least androgynous) of the four groups. These findings suggest that taking on the role of parent leads men to perceive themselves as more masculine in personality while causing women to perceive themselves as having predominantly feminine strengths. So far, so good for Gutmann's hypothesis that the demands of parenting exaggerate the psychological differences between men and women.

In an even more ambitious study, Feldman, Biringen, and Nash (1981) gave the Bem inventory to individuals at eight different stages of the family life cycle—from single adolescents and young adults to grandparents. Although men scored higher on the masculinity scale and lower on the femininity scale than women did at all stages of life, once again parents had more traditionally sex-typed personality traits than adolescents and young adults without children. Moreover, in the *postparental* phases of the life cycle, especially among grandparents, sex differences in self-perceptions decreased.

For example, grandfathers were especially tender and compassionate compared with younger men, and grandmothers were more autonomous than women in other life situations. Contrary to Gutmann's hypothesis, however, grandfathers did not replace their masculine traits with feminine traits while grandmothers were becoming less feminine and more masculine. Instead, both sexes were androgynous: Grandfathers retained their masculine traits while gaining some feminine attributes, and grandmothers retained their feminine traits while adding some masculine attributes. This finding is particularly interesting in view of the fact that today's older people should, if anything, be *more* traditionally gender-typed than younger adults who have grown up in an era of more flexible gender norms. Indeed, today's college men and women have highly similar personality profiles as groups, while past generations of college men and women were quite dissimilar (Stevens & Truss, 1985).

Overall, then, it seems that young adults who are not parents are relatively androgynous, that parenting brings out traditionally sex-typed traits in both men and women, and that androgyny once again emerges when the parenting years are over. These findings all involve cross-sectional comparisons of younger and older adults and all focus on *self-perceived* personality traits; however, longitudinal studies in which people's traits are rated by researchers rather than by themselves also suggest that there is a shift toward androgyny during later midlife (Livson, 1983), though more men than women appear to experience this shift (Livson, 1983; Turner, 1982).

These fluctuations in gender-role orientations during adulthood appear to be related more to changes in roles or social demands than to age alone. For example, young parents are more psychologically sex-typed than nonparents of the same age (Feldman, Biringen, & Nash, 1981). In addition, employment outside the home may make at least as much difference as parenthood in determining how sex-typed or androgynous adults are (Cunningham & Antill, 1984). Finally, because cultural learning also influences personality, it is unlikely that Gutmann's "parental imperative" is truly imperative or universal. Long ago, for example, Margaret Mead (1935) identified one cultural group in which *both* men and women were cooperative, nonaggressive, and sensitive to the needs of others; another group in which members of both sexes were hostile, aggressive, and emotionally unresponsive; and still another group in which men possessed the presumably "feminine" traits of passivity, emotional dependence, and social sensitivity, while women were dominant, independent, and aggressive! Again we must adopt a contextual perspective on gender-role development and appreciate that males and females can develop in any number of different directions depending on their social, cultural, and historical context.

Are There Advantages to Being Androgynous?

When we think about the idea that a person can be both assertive and sensitive, both independent and understanding, we can't help but think that being androgynous is psychologically healthy. Certainly Sandra Bem (1975, 1978) believes that androgyny is desirable. And Florine Livson (1983) has suggested that middle-aged adults who achieve androgyny have reached the pinnacle of gender-role development, transcending stereotypes and becoming far freer to express the different sides of their personalities.

Are androgynous people "better" people? Bem has shown that androgynous men and women are more flexible in their behavior than more sex-typed individuals. For example, androgynous people, like masculine sex-typed people, can display the "masculine," instrumental trait of independence by resisting social pressure to judge very unamusing cartoons as funny just because their peers do. Yet they are as likely as feminine sex-typed individuals to display the "feminine," expressive quality of nurturance by interacting positively with a baby. In addition, androgynous individuals sometimes appear to enjoy higher self-esteem and are perceived as more likeable and better adjusted than their traditionally sex-typed peers (Major, Carnevale, & Deaux, 1981; Massad, 1981).

Before we jump to the conclusion that androgyny is a thoroughly desirable attribute, however, let's add a couple of footnotes. First, it appears that it is the possession of "masculine" traits rather than androgyny per se that tends to be most strongly associated with high self-esteem and good adjustment (Orlofsky & O'Heron, 1987; Whitley, 1983). Both masculine sex-typed and androgynous individuals have higher self-esteem than feminine sex-typed or undifferentiated persons do—whether they are men or women. Second, although androgynous adults appear to raise children who also blend masculine and feminine attributes (Orlofsky, 1979), at least one study suggests that the children of traditionally sex-typed parents may be somewhat more socially responsible, socially assertive, and otherwise competent than the children of androgynous parents are, possibly because their parents are firmer

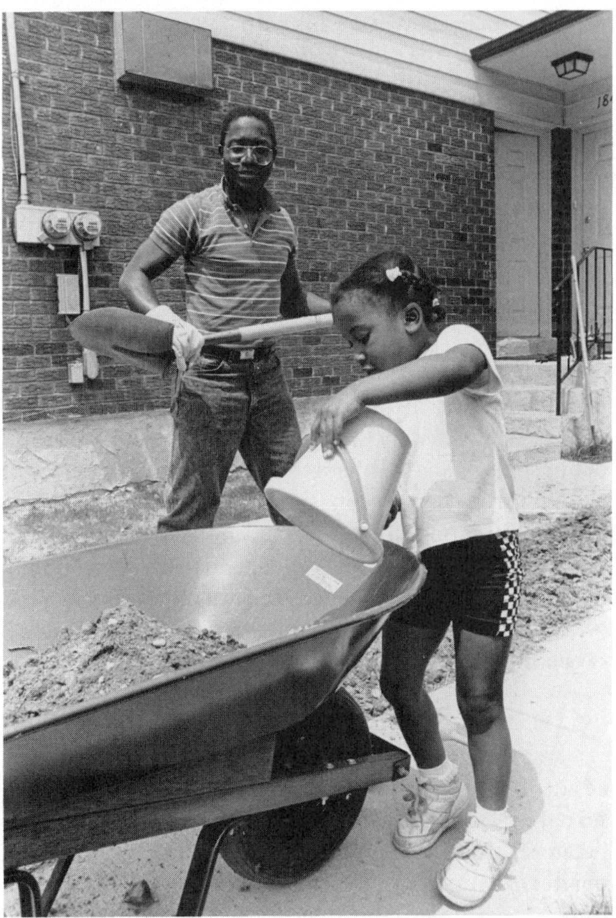

Children are likely to become androgynous if their parents do not restrict them to stereotypic roles.

and more demanding than androgynous parents are (Baumrind, 1982). Finally, even though we might expect that androgynous older people enjoy being freed from the confining roles they played as younger adults, androgynous elderly people seem to be no more satisfied with life than their traditionally sex-typed peers (Windle, 1986).

In sum, it may be premature to conclude that one is better off in *all* respects to be androgynous than to be either masculine or feminine in orientation. Still, the very fact that androgynous individuals exist reminds us again that males and females are far more similar than they are different psychologically. Moreover, androgynous females are not perceived as any less feminine, nor androgynous men as any less masculine, simply because they combine their sex-typed traits with traits considered more appropriate for the other sex (Major, Carnevale, & Deaux, 1981). Nor do androgynous people show any signs of maladjustment merely because they do not conform to traditional masculine/feminine orientations (Orlofsky & O'Heron, 1987). Thus we can at least conclude that it is unlikely to be damaging for men to become a little more "feminine" or for women to become a little more "masculine."

Adult Sexuality

Adults are sexual beings, and their perceptions of themselves as sexual beings become an important part of their identities as men and women. Like adolescents, adults have been affected by the increased sexual permissiveness of our society, and it is hard to tell whether what we know about current generations of adults will apply to future generations raised in more sexually permissive times. Let's conclude our discussion of gender and adult development by briefly examining changes in sexuality over the adult years and some fascinating and significant differences between men and women.

Sexual Activity in Adult Relationships

As part of their quest for identity and intimacy, young adults define themselves as sexual beings and establish sexual preferences. Most adults establish an exclusively heterosexual sexual preference. About a third of men and a quarter of women report a homosexual experience at some time in their lives (Hunt, 1974), but fewer than 5% develop an exclusive preference for partners of their own sex (Maier, 1984). Just as the sexual preferences of adults are varied, so are their sexual lifestyles. Some adults remain single—some of them actively seeking a wide range of partners, others having one partner at a time, and still others leading celibate lives. Yet over 9 of 10 Americans marry at some point, and most adults are married at any given time. As a result, most of our knowledge of adult sexuality pertains to heterosexual married couples.

Apparently today's adults enjoy more varied and active sex lives than adults of previous generations did (Hunt, 1974; Westoff, 1974). However, it quickly becomes clear that the frequency of sexual activity declines over the course of a marriage. The honeymoon appears to end quickly, within two or three years (Greenblat, 1983; Jasso, 1985)! Cathy Greenblat (1983) found that couples married for a year or less had intercourse an average of 15 times a month, though some couples were far more active than others. Among couples married for six years, the average rate had dropped to six times a month, with those who were sexually active at the start of their marriages remaining relatively active in comparison to other couples later in their marriage. Couples cited such factors as work pressures, children, fatigue, and familiarity with each other as reasons for their diminished activity, but they continued to view sexual activity as important in their marriages.

For quite a large number of married couples, difficulties in the marital relationship lead to extramarital sexual activity. In their groundbreaking survey of sexual behavior, Alfred Kinsey and his associates (1948, 1953) found that half of married men and a quarter of married women had had an extramarital affair by age 40. All signs suggest that the double standard pertaining to extramarital sex is weakening, that more young women are having affairs, and that soon approximately half of both women and men will have experienced extramarital sex (Thompson, 1983).

What becomes of people's sex lives in late middle age and old age? Many young people can barely conceive of their parents or, heaven forbid, their grandparents as sexual beings! In fact, the frequency with which the average couple has sexual intercourse does continue to decline over the years, and in late middle age and old age increasing numbers of people cease to have intercourse (Broderick, 1982; Mobarak & Shamoian, 1985). Moreover, older married people are less likely than younger married people to rank "sexual and affectional activity" among their favorite leisure activities (Mancini & Orthner, 1978). Are people right, then, when they view elderly people as sexless or asexual people?

No, they are not! People continue to be sexual beings throughout the life span. Perhaps the most amazing discoveries about sex in late adulthood are those of Bernard Starr and Marcella Weiner (1981), who surveyed 800 elderly volunteers aged 60 to 91. In this group, over 90% claimed to like sex, almost 80% were still sexually active, and 75% said that their sex lives were the same as or better than they had been when they were younger. One 70-year-old widow, asked how often she would like to have sex, was not bashful at all about replying, "Morning, noon, and night" (p. 47).

Obviously it is quite possible for people to remain highly interested in sex and be sexually active in old age. Yet Starr and Weiner's findings are likely to exaggerate the rate of sexual activity among the elderly since only the most sexually active people may have agreed to complete such a survey. A study by Linda George and Stephen Weiler (1981) traced changes in the frequency of sexual intercourse over a period of six years among married adults who were 46 to 71 years of age at the start of the study. Questions about sexual behavior were only a small part of a much larger study, so it is likely that the participants are more representative of older people than those studied by Starr and Weiner.

Table 11.3 Involvement in sexual intercourse over a six-year period among middle-aged and elderly married people*

PATTERN OF CHANGE	AGE AT START OF STUDY 46–56	56–65	Over 65
Men			
Stable activity	66.6	63.5	42.4
Decreasing activity	15.9	14.9	21.2
Increasing activity	4.8	4.1	9.1
Continuous abstinence	0.0	9.5	12.1
Other: Unpredictable fluctuations	12.7	8.0	15.2
Women			
Stable activity	61.4	55.6	33.3
Decreasing activity	15.8	30.5	33.3
Increasing activity	3.6	2.8	0.0
Continuous abstinence	5.3	5.5	33.3
Other: Unpredictable fluctuations	13.9	5.6	0.0

*In these data reported by George and Weiler (1981), the frequency with which married adults had sexual intercourse was measured four times over a six-year period. Those who showed "stable activity" did have intercourse and maintained the same frequency of intercourse throughout the study period. "Decreasing activity" involved either becoming less active or ceasing activity, while increasing activity involved either resuming sex after being abstinent or increasing one's rate of activity over the six-year period.

As Table 11.3 shows, the majority of middle-aged people, and sizable minorities of people over age 65, were not only sexually active but had maintained the same level of activity they had enjoyed at the start of the six-year period. A few people even became more sexually active. At the same time, sizable minorities of individuals, especially among those who were 65 or older at the start of the study, either had intercourse less often or stopped entirely during the course of the study. Overall, about 70% of the 65-and-older men and 67% of the elderly women had sexual intercourse *some* time during the six-year period, but elderly women were more likely than elderly men to reduce or curtail their involvement in sexual intercourse.

In sum, most people do not end their sex lives when they get old. Just as obviously, there is *some* decrease with age in sexual activity, especially among women, although many older adults who no longer have sexual intercourse or have it less frequently continue to be sexually motivated and turn to masturbation as an alternative (Kinsey et al., 1948, 1953; Weizman & Hart, 1987). Finally, we should appreciate the immense variety among elderly adults, who range from those who are every bit as sexually active as they ever were to those who have entirely lost interest.

Explanations for Declining Sexual Activity

How can we explain the decline in sexual interest and activity that many adults, especially women, seem to experience over the years? And why do some people remain sexually active while others do not?

Consider first the physiological changes in sexual capacity that occur with age, as revealed by the pioneering research of William Masters and Virginia Johnson (1966, 1970). Males are at their peak of sexual responsiveness in their late teens and early 20s and gradually become less responsive thereafter. A young man is easily and quickly aroused; his orgasm is intense; and he may have a refractory, or recovery, period of only minutes before he is capable of sexual activity again. The older man is likely to be the slower man—slower to arouse, slower to ejaculate after being aroused, and slower to recover afterward. Men over 60 often require 12 to 24 hours between erections and do not ejaculate during every sexual episode as a young man typically does. Finally, as we discovered in Chapter 5, levels of male sex hormones decline gradually with age in many men, although researchers generally do not believe that these hormonal changes are sufficient to explain the changes in sexual behavior that most men experience.

Physiological changes in women are far less dramatic. Women reach their peak of physiological responsiveness to sexual stimulation later than men do, often not until their late 30s. Women are capable of more orgasms in a given time span than men because they have little or no refractory period after orgasm. This capacity is retained into old age. Moreover, as we discovered in Chapter 5, menopause does not seem to reduce sexual activity and interest for most women. However, like older men, older women typically are slower to become sexually excited. Moreover, some experience discomfort associated with decreased lubrication.

All things considered, the physiological changes that men and women experience cannot take us far in understanding why many of them become less sexually active in middle age or old age. Masters and Johnson concluded that both men and women are physiologically capable of sexual behavior well into old age. Most men can function into their 60s and a minority into their 70s and even 80s (Broderick, 1982). Women retain their physiological capacity for sex even longer than men. Yet they are the ones who are less sexually active in old age!

Apparently we must turn to factors other than biological aging to explain changes in sexual behavior. In summarizing these factors, Pauline Robinson (1983) quotes Alex Comfort (1974): "In our experience, old folks stop having sex for the same reason they stop riding a bicycle—general infirmity, thinking it looks ridiculous, and no bicycle" (p. 440). Under the category of infirmity, any number of diseases and disabilities, as well as the drugs prescribed for them, can limit sexual functioning. This is a particular problem for men, who may become impotent when they are in poor health. *Mental* health problems are also very important: Many cases of impotence among middle-aged and elderly men seem to be attributable to psychological causes such as stress at work and depression rather than to physiological causes (Felstein, 1983).

The second source of problems is social attitudes that view sexual activity in old age as "ridiculous," or at least inappropriate. Old people are stereotyped as sexually unappealing and sexless (or as "dirty old men") and are discouraged from expressing sexual interests. These negative attitudes may lead a person's adult children or the staff of a nursing home to interfere in an older person's attempts to find sexual satisfaction or may cause elderly people to suppress their sexuality (Robinson, 1983). Moreover, older women are even further inhibited by a double standard rooted in tradition: Old women, our society insists, are especially sexually unattractive, and it is especially improper for them to express sexual needs or make sexual advances.

Third, there is the "no bicycle" part of Comfort's analogy—namely, the lack of a partner, or at least of a willing and desirable partner. Among older married couples, both husband and wife most frequently attribute declines in their sexual activity to *his* difficulties—impotence, poor health, and so on (Pfeiffer, Verwoerdt, & Davis, 1972). So elderly married women sometimes find themselves without a "bicycle." However, the greater problem is that most older women are widowed, divorced, or single and face grave difficulties finding partners. The elderly woman searching for a partner confronts the reality that for every 100 women there are only 69 men; moreover, most of these men are married, and those who are single are very often looking for a younger partner (Robinson, 1983). Lack of a partner, then, is *the* major problem for elderly women, many of whom continue to be interested in sex, physiologically capable of sexual behavior, and desirous of love and affection.

We might add just one more element to Comfort's bicycle analogy: lack of previous cycling experience. Masters and Johnson (1966, 1970) proposed a "use it or lose it"

Most older adults continue to be sexual beings who seek love and affection.

principle of sexual behavior to reflect two findings. First, level of sexual activity early in adulthood predicts level of sexual activity in later life. The relationship is not necessarily causal, by the way; it could simply be that some people are more sexually motivated than others are throughout adulthood. A second element of the "use it or lose it" rule may well be causal, however: Middle-aged and elderly adults who experience a long period of sexual abstinence often experience difficulty regaining their sexual capacity afterwards.

In summary, sexual behavior does decline with age, but most older people continue to be sexual beings who, like younger people, seek love and affection as well as physical intimacy. Elderly people can continue to enjoy an active sex life if they retain their physical and mental health, do not allow negative attitudes surrounding sexuality in later life to stand in their way, have a willing and able partner, and can avoid long periods of abstinence. It seems likely that elderly people of the future, influenced by the increased sexual permissiveness of our society during this century, will be freer than the elderly people of today to express their sexual selves.

APPLICATIONS: CHANGING GENDER-ROLE ATTITUDES AND BEHAVIOR

Today many people believe that the world would be a better place if sexism were eliminated and if boys and girls were no longer socialized to adopt traditional "masculine" or "feminine" roles, interests, and behaviors. Children of both sexes would then have the freedom to be androgynous; women would no longer suffer from a lack of assertiveness and confidence in the world of work, and men would no longer be forced to suppress their emotions. Just how successful are efforts to encourage more flexible gender roles and eliminate sexist attitudes?

In a number of projects designed to change gender-role behavior, children have been exposed to nonsexist films, encouraged to imitate models of cross-sex behavior, reinforced by teachers for trying out cross-sex activities, and provided with nonsexist educational materials (see Katz, 1986). One particularly ambitious educational program was undertaken by Marcia Guttentag and Helen Bray (1976). Kindergarten, fifth-grade, and ninth-grade students were exposed to age-appropriate activities and readings designed to teach them about the problems created by stereotyping and sexism and about the potentials of women. This program worked quite successfully with the younger children, especially the fifth-grade girls, who were already quite open-minded and became outraged by what they learned about sexism. However, it actually had a boomerang effect among the ninth-grade boys: They seemed to resist the new ideas they were being taught and actually expressed more stereotyped views after the training than before. Even the adolescent girls, while they believed that more occupations should be open to women and took many lessons to heart, tended to cling to the idea that women should run the family and men should be the primary breadwinners.

This study and others suggest that efforts at change are more effective with younger children than with older children and with girls than with boys (Katz, 1986). It makes sense that it is easier to alter children's thinking before it has fully crystallized than after. And girls, after all, have much to gain from adopting masculine-stereotyped interests and behaviors, whereas boys may know all too well that they stand to lose if they become too "feminine" or give up the advantages of the male role (Katz, 1986).

But the barriers to change do not stop here. Sometimes change efforts work but fail to have lasting or generalizable effects. For example, Marlaine Lockheed (1986) sought to break down the rigid sex segregation of the middle childhood years by having fourth and fifth graders participate in small, mixed-sex work groups in the classroom. In the experimental classes as compared with traditional classes, children became more receptive to such interactions and did indeed interact more with their classmates of the other sex. And yet when children were asked who their favorite classmates were, they continued to choose children of their own sex almost exclusively. One suspects, then, that despite this exposure to cross-sex cooperation and interaction, these children were going to go right back to their sex-segregated worlds. Indeed, one group of 4-year-old children who were praised by their teachers for cross-sex play immediately reverted to same-sex play as soon as the reinforcement program ended (Serbin, Tonick, & Sternglanz, 1977).

Apparently new gender-role attitudes and behaviors *can* be taught to children, but it is not at all easy to achieve lasting change that generalizes well to new situations. Perhaps the greatest obstacle to change is that children have been groomed for their traditional gender roles ever since they were born and continue to be bombarded with traditional gender-role messages every day. A short-term intervention project may have little chance of succeeding in this larger context. It may be that more substantial change in the way in which boys and girls view themselves and behave must await further change in society. Social changes have already had an impact on children (see, for example, Etaugh, Levine, & Mennella, 1984). Judith Lorber (1986) sees much hope in her 13-year-old's response when Lorber inquired whether a new mother of their acquaintance delivered a boy or a girl: "Why do you want to know?" this child of a new era asked (p. 567).

REFLECTIONS

This chapter raises some provocative questions about what it really means, or should mean, to be a male or a female. Clearly the answer depends on many factors—one's culture, the times in which one lives, one's own unique predispositions and experiences, and, of course, one's age. We are struck by how much the meanings of masculinity and femininity change over the life span. Children meet the demands of their gender roles by choosing the "right" toys and by playing with others of their own sex. Adults conform to their masculine or feminine roles by choosing the "right" lifestyles and by establishing sexual relationships with partners of the other sex. We have also seen that the psychological and behavioral gap between males and females narrows and widens over the life span. At birth, it seems, there are few differences between the sexes, but it is not long before toddlers and preschoolers master gender stereotypes and seek to be either "real" boys or "real" girls. The differences between the sexes then cumulate, reaching their peak when adults become parents and finally lessening again in late middle age and old age. We picture Great-Grandma and Great-Grandpa on the porch, possibly grumbling about "women's lib," unisex dress styles, or other fads, and yet very possibly being more alike in many ways than they were as younger people.

If males and females start out much alike and become more similar again at the end of the life span, one almost wonders why society devotes so much effort in the intervening years to making them different from each other! Certainly we have encountered little support for the notion that gender differences are biologically inevitable. And if, despite considerable social pressure to develop in different directions, males and females are still more psychologically similar than different, perhaps it is damaging to demand that they suppress some of their capacities while exaggerating others.

Indeed, Joseph Pleck (1981) has argued that traditional gender roles have done a great deal of damage. He views today's emphasis on androgyny as a step in the right direction if it helps us overcome the tendency to force girls and boys into narrow molds that represent our ideals of masculinity and femininity. Pleck believes that this only makes most of us feel inadequate because we are not "masculine" or "feminine" enough. And yet he may also have a point when he notes that a new ideal of androgyny may create problems similar to those created by the traditional ideals—too much pressure on children and adults to live up to an unattainable model of psychological adjustment, this time one in which they must blend masculine and feminine traits. Some suggest that the solution is to move away from the whole notion that there are "masculine" and "feminine" traits (Lott, 1985). Then people would just be people. What would our lives be like if a person's biological sex were of approximately the same significance to us as a person's eye color, just one of many characteristics to be noticed and then largely ignored? That, surely, would be the most radical social change of all!

SUMMARY POINTS

1. Differences between males and females can be detected in the physical, psychological, and social realms; some gender differences are biological in origin and others arise as males and females learn their gender roles (including gender-role norms and stereotypes).

2. Research comparing males and females indicates that the two sexes are far more similar than different psychologically: The average male is more aggressive and better at spatial and mathematical tasks but less adept at verbal tasks than the average female, but these and other sex differences are small.

3. During infancy, boys and girls are very similar, but adults treat them differently. By age 2, infants have gained a primitive knowledge of their own gender identity and display "gender-appropriate" play preferences. Infants are also sexual beings from the start, responding physiologically to genital stimulation even though they have no awareness that their responses are "sexual."

4. Gender typing progresses most rapidly during the toddler and preschool years; school-age children know that sex is unchanging and are at first quite rigid in their thinking about gender roles.

5. The biosocial theory proposed by Money and Ehrhardt emphasizes prenatal biological developments but also stresses the interaction of biological and social influences.

6. From Freud's psychoanalytic perspective, gender-role development results from the child's identification with the same-sex parent; social learning theorists focus on differential reinforcement and observational learning; and Kohlberg's cognitive-developmental theory and the schematic-processing perspective hold that children socialize themselves as they construct gender concepts.

7. Contrary to Freud's theory, sexual curiosity continues into the latency stage. Societies differ considerably in how they prepare children for mature sexual relationships.

8. Adolescents initially become quite intolerant of gender-role violations. During this century, the view that sex with affection is acceptable has come to prevail, the double standard has weakened, conflicting norms have increased confusion among teenagers, and more adolescents are engaging in sexual behavior at earlier ages than in the past.

9. Adults continue to be influenced by the changing demands of gender roles; women more often than men link identity with intimacy and often do not follow the male identity-before-intimacy path of development. Marriage and parenthood appear to cause men and women to adopt more traditionally sex-typed roles. Postparental adults tend to experience a shift toward androgyny, blending masculine-stereotyped and feminine-stereotyped traits (though not switching personalities).

10. Most adults marry and become less sexually active over the course of their marriages. Declines in the physiological capacity for sex cannot fully explain declines in sexual activity; poor physical or mental health, lack of a partner, negative societal attitudes, and periods of sexual abstinence also contribute.

11. Attempts to change the gender-role attitudes and behaviors of children have been partially successful but often fail to have lasting effects, perhaps because socialization into traditional roles is so pervasive. Yet societal pressure to adopt narrowly defined gender roles appears to be lessening.

KEY TERMS

androgenized females
androgyny
double standard
expressive role
gender consistency
gender identity
gender-role norms
gender roles
gender-role stereotypes
gender schemas
gender stability
gender typing
identification
instrumental role
parental imperative

CHAPTER

12

CHOICES: MOTIVES AND MORALS

Will Sharon help Ted out by letting him copy from her test paper, or will she turn him down because she believes that cheating is wrong?

Will Bruce take the new job he has been offered in New York, or will he stay in Kansas City to keep his relationship with Abby alive?

When her parents ask Julie if she has used drugs, will she admit that she has or will she lie about it?

Will Sam run for Student Senate so that he can have some influence on campus, or will he decide to concentrate on improving his grade point average? ❦

These questions are a sampling of the choices we face as human beings—choices that reflect our priorities, values, and standards. Some of these choices are moral ones: for example, the choice between cheating or not cheating, lying or telling the truth. Others are not issues of right or wrong so much as matters of preferences and priorities. They reveal which of our motives—for example, the motive to achieve or the motive to affiliate with other people—are the strongest.

In the previous two chapters, we have been examining the development of the self. In this chapter, we continue that process by exploring how we acquire the predominant motivations and moral outlooks that help define us as individuals. How do children acquire motives such as a strong need for achievement, and how do motivations change over the life span? When and how do children acquire a sense of right and wrong, a set of moral standards? How do our ways of dealing with moral choices change over the life span? These are the issues that will concern us in this chapter, all of them centering on priorities and choices and how they change from infancy to old age. Let's set the stage by looking at the nature of human motivation and offering some perspectives on morality.

HUMAN MOTIVES

A **motive** is usually defined as an energizing state that directs a person's behavior toward a particular kind of goal. The traveler who has not eaten for hours, for example, will be governed by the hunger motive and will therefore be more preoccupied with finding a restaurant than with viewing the scenery. *Physiological motives* include hunger, thirst, and sex, along with the need for rest, the need to escape pain, and so on. We will not be concerned with these motives here, but it is important to recognize that they are part of our nature throughout the life span. It is when we lack food, water, rest, or other biological essentials that we become aware of the power of these motives to govern us. We literally *need* to obtain what we lack.

Psychological motives, the motives that do concern us here, also energize behavior in pursuit of a goal. Some psychologists would argue that certain psychological motives such as a need to feel competent are almost as basic to human nature as the need for food (Deci & Ryan, 1985; White, 1959). However, most psychological motives are not biologically compelling; rather, they are learned motivations or acquired tastes. We do not *need* to earn an "A" or land a prestigious job in the same biological sense that we need food when our hunger motive is aroused. Yet psychological motives can still be compelling, as when an ambitious young adult is willing to sacrifice almost everything to "make it" in a career.

This chapter examines several important psychological motives: needs for mastery, achievement, affiliation with other people, power or influence, and so on. Because these motives are partly the products of learning experiences, each of them operates more strongly in some people than in others. It will be of interest, then, to determine when different psychological motives emerge and what specific learning experiences strengthen or weaken them. Moreover, we will be concerned with how predominant motives change as life situations change.

PERSPECTIVES ON MORAL DEVELOPMENT

Among a person's characteristic motivations is often a motivation to act in responsible and moral ways, to think of oneself and to be thought of by others as a moral individual (Blasi, 1984; Hoffman, 1988). Moreover, we must sometimes choose between gratifying our own needs and doing what is "right," as when a student who is strongly motivated to achieve nonetheless refrains from cheating on the final.

Although we might debate endlessly about what **morality** really is, most of us might agree that the term implies *an ability to distinguish right from wrong and to act on this distinction.* Psychologists have identified three basic components of morality:

1. An *affective*, or emotional, component that consists of the feelings that surround right or wrong actions and that motivate moral thoughts and actions
2. A *cognitive* component that centers on the way we conceptualize right and wrong and make decisions about how to behave
3. A *behavioral* component that reflects how we actually behave when, for example, we experience the temptation to cheat, steal, or lie

As it turns out, each of the three major theoretical perspectives on moral development has focused on a different component of morality. So let's briefly see what psychoanalytic theory has to say about moral affect, what cognitive-developmental theory has to say about moral cognition or reasoning, and what social learning theory can tell us about moral behavior.

Moral Affect: Psychoanalytic Theory

What kinds of **moral affects**, or emotions, do you feel if you contemplate cheating or engaging in some other behavior that you know to be wrong? Chances are you experience negative feelings such as shame, guilt, anxiety, and fear of being detected. By contrast, when you know you have done the right thing, you may feel pride or self-satisfaction. Obviously, then, both positive and negative emotions are an important part of morality, for we will be motivated to avoid negative emotions and experience positive ones by acting in moral ways.

Assuming that young infants are unlikely to feel these sorts of moral emotions, when do they arise? Freud's (1935/1960) psychoanalytic theory offered an answer (see Chapter 2). Freud believed that the mature personality has three components: the selfish and irrational id, the rational ego, and the moralistic superego. The *superego*, or conscience, has the important task of ensuring that any plans formed by the ego to gratify the id's urges are morally acceptable. Infants and toddlers, Freud claimed, lack a superego and are essentially "all id." They will therefore act on their selfish motives unless their parents control them. During the phallic stage (ages 3–6), when children are presumed to experience an emotional conflict over their love for the other-sex parent, the superego is formed. To resolve his *Oedipus complex*, a boy identifies with and patterns himself after his father, particularly if his father is a threatening figure who arouses fear. Not only does he learn his masculine role in this manner, but he takes on as his own, through the process called **internalization**, his father's moral standards. Similarly, a girl resolves her *Electra complex* by identifying with her mother and internalizing her mother's moral standards. However, Freud believed that girls, because they do not experience the intense fear of castration that boys experience, develop weaker superegos than males do.

Learning to resist temptation is an important part of moral development.

Having a superego, then, is like having a parent inside your head—always there, even when your parents are not, to tell you what is right or wrong and to arouse emotions such as shame and guilt in you if you so much as think about violating the rules. We can applaud Freud for pointing out that emotion is a very important part of morality and for noting that children must somehow internalize moral standards if they are to behave morally even when no authority figure is present to detect and punish them. However, the specifics of Freud's theory are largely unsupported. Cold, threatening, and punitive parents, as we shall see later, do *not* raise morally mature youngsters; males do *not* appear to have stronger superegos than females; and children who are 6 or 7 years of age, and who have presumably achieved moral maturity by resolving their Oedipal conflicts, have *not* completed their moral growth. Although Freud's broad themes have some merit, it is perhaps time to lay the particulars of his theory of moral development to rest.

Moral Reasoning: Cognitive Developmental Theory

Cognitive developmentalists study morality by looking at the development of **moral reasoning**—that is, the thinking process that occurs when we are deciding whether an act is right or wrong. These theorists assume that moral development depends on cognitive development. Moral reasoning is said to progress through an *invariant sequence*, or a fixed and universal order, of stages, each of which is a consistent way of thinking about moral issues that is different from the stages preceding or following it. To cognitive-developmental theorists, what is really of interest is *how we decide* what to do, not what we decide or what we actually do. A young child and an adult might both decide not to steal a pen that is there for the taking, but the reasons they give for their decision might be entirely different.

A cognitive-developmental perspective on moral development was first outlined by Jean Piaget (1932/1965). He studied children's concepts of the nature of rules by asking Swiss children about their games of marbles. He also studied children's concepts of justice by presenting them with moral dilemmas in the form of stories. For example, he told of two boys, John and Henry. John, after being called to dinner, goes through the door to the dining room. Although he could not have known it, there is a chair with a tray of 15 cups on it behind the door, and when the door swings open, all 15 cups break. Henry, by contrast, was trying to reach some jam in the cupboard when his mother was out and knocked over a single cup. Having heard the two stories, children were asked "Are these children equally guilty?" and "If not, which child is naughtier? Why?"

From the ways in which children answered such questions, Piaget formulated a theory of moral development that includes a premoral period and two moral stages. During the **premoral period** (the preschool years), children show little concern for or awareness of rules and are not considered to be moral beings. Between the ages of 6 and 10, children are usually in the stage of **heteronomous morality** ("heteronomous" meaning being under the rule of another). Children of this age believe that rules come from parents and other authority figures and are sacred and unalterable. They also believe that rule violations are wrong to the extent that they have damaging consequences, even if the violator had good intentions (as the boy who broke 15 cups did). Finally, at the age of 10 or 11 most children enter the stage of **autonomous morality**. They now view rules as agreements between individuals—agreements that can be changed through a consensus of those individuals. In judging actions, they pay more attention to whether an actor's intentions were good or bad, viewing the misbehaving boy who broke one cup as naughtier than the well-intentioned boy who broke 15. According to Piaget, progress through these stages depends on cognitive maturation and social experience, particularly the experience of resolving differences of perspective that arise in discussions with peers. Several features of Piaget's two stages of moral development are summarized in Table 12.1.

Inspired by Piaget's pioneering work, Lawrence Kohlberg (1963, 1981, 1984) formulated the cognitive-developmental theory that has come to dominate the study of moral development.[1] He began his work by asking 10-, 13-, and 16-year-old boys questions about various "moral dilemmas" to assess how they were thinking about them. Careful analysis of the responses led Kohlberg to conclude

[1]Lawrence Kohlberg was born in 1927 and died in 1987. He put his own moral principles into action as a youth by helping to transport Jewish refugees from Europe to Israel after World War II, devised his theory of moral development as a doctoral student at the University of Chicago, and then spent most of his career at Harvard studying moral development and promoting moral education (Green, 1989).

Table 12.1 Piaget's two major stages of moral development

ASPECT OF MORALITY	STAGE OF MORAL REASONING: Stage of heteronomous morality (ages 6 to 10)	STAGE OF MORAL REASONING: Stage of autonomous morality (ages 10 or 11 and up)
Conception of rules	*Rules are moral absolutes.* Heteronomous children develop a strong respect for rules and believe they must be obeyed at all times. Rules are laid down by authority figures such as God, the police, or parents. They are sacred and unalterable.	*Rules are agreements among individuals.* Children now realize that the rules of games are not handed down from adult authority figures but are constructed through a consensus of players and can therefore be changed through consensus. Similarly, laws in society are agreements that can be changed with the consent of the people they govern.
Basis for judging acts	*Consequences matter more than intentions.* An act is wrong to the extent that it has damaging consequences. Thus John, who accidentally broke 15 cups while performing a well-intentioned act, is often judged naughtier than Henry, who broke 1 cup while stealing jam.	*Intentions matter more than consequences.* Children's judgments of right or wrong now depend more on the actor's intent to deceive, cause harm, or violate rules than on the magnitude of the damage done. Ten-year-olds reliably say that Henry, who broke 1 cup while stealing jam, is naughtier than the well-intentioned John, who broke 15 cups accidentally. And unlike an inflexible 6-year-old, a 10-year-old might allow that it is morally defensible to break the speed limit when one is rushing to the hospital in a medical emergency.
View of punishment	*Punishment is for the sake of punishment.* Heteronomous children favor punishment for its own sake rather than as a means of helping the rule-violator understand the implications of the transgression. Thus a 6-year-old might favor spanking a boy who has broken a window rather than making him pay for the window from his allowance.	*The punishment should fit the crime.* Autonomous children try to tailor punishments to the act. Making a boy who deliberately breaks a window pay to have it replaced teaches him that windows cost money and that wrongs should be righted.
Nature of justice	*Justice is immanent in the world.* Heteronomous children believe in **immanent justice**: the idea that rule violations will invariably be punished. So if a 7-year-old girl were to fall and skin her knee shortly after stealing cookies, she might conclude that this injury was the punishment she deserved for her crime. The forces of justice reside in the universe and will get you one way or another!	*Justice is less than perfect.* Perhaps because they have learned from experience that wrongdoing often goes undetected and unpunished, autonomous children no longer believe in immanent justice.

that moral growth progresses through a universal and invariant sequence of three broad moral levels, each of which is composed of two distinct stages. Each stage grows out of the preceding stage and represents a more complex way of thinking about moral issues. Kohlberg insists that a person cannot skip any stages and that once a person has reached a higher stage, he or she will not regress to earlier stages.

Think about how you would respond to the following moral dilemma posed by Kohlberg and his colleagues:

> There was a woman who had very bad cancer, and there was no treatment known to medicine that would save her. Her doctor, Dr. Jefferson, knew that she had only about 6 months to live. She was in terrible pain, but she was so weak that a good dose of a pain killer like ether or morphine would make her die sooner. She was delirious and almost crazy with pain, and in her calm periods she would ask Dr. Jefferson to give her enough ether to kill her. She said she couldn't stand the pain and she was going to die in a few months anyway. Although he knows that mercy killing is against the law, the doctor thinks about granting her request [Colby, Kohlberg, Gibbs, & Lieberman, 1983, p. 79].

Should Dr. Jefferson give her the drug that would make her die? Why or why not? Should the woman have the right to make the final decision? Why or why not? These are among the questions that people are asked after hearing the dilemma. Remember, Kohlberg's goal is to understand how an individual thinks, not whether he or she is for or against providing the woman with the drug. Individuals at each stage of moral reasoning might well endorse *either* of the alternative courses of action, but for different reasons.

How cognitively sophisticated is your moral reasoning? Kohlberg's three levels of moral reasoning, and the two stages within each level, are as follows:

At the level of **preconventional morality**, rules are really external to the self rather than internalized. The child conforms to rules imposed by authority figures in order to avoid punishment or to obtain personal rewards. The perspective of the self dominates: What is right is what one can get away with or what is personally satisfying.

> *Stage 1: Punishment-and-obedience orientation.* The goodness or badness of an act depends on its consequences. The child will obey authorities to avoid punishment but may not consider an act wrong if it will not be punished. The greater the harm done or the more severe the punishment, the more "bad" the act is.
>
> *Stage 2: Instrumental hedonism.* A person at the second stage of moral development conforms to rules in order to gain rewards or satisfy personal needs. There is some concern for the perspectives of others, but it is ultimately motivated by the hope of benefit in return. "You scratch my back and I'll scratch yours" is the guiding philosophy.

At the level of **conventional morality**, the individual *has* internalized many moral values. He or she strives to obey the rules set forth by others (such as parents, peers, and the government) in order to win their approval and recognition for good behavior or to maintain social order. The perspectives of other people besides the self are clearly recognized and given serious consideration.

> *Stage 3: "Good boy" or "good girl" morality.* What is right is now that which pleases, helps, or is approved by others. People are often judged by their intentions, "meaning well" is valued, and it is important to be "nice."
>
> *Stage 4: Authority and social-order-maintaining morality.* Now what is right is what conforms to the rules of legitimate authorities. The reason for conforming is not so much a fear of punishment as a belief that rules and laws maintain a social order that is worth preserving. Doing one's duty and respecting law and order are valued.

At the third and final level of moral reasoning, **postconventional morality**, the individual attempts to define what is right in terms of broad principles of justice that have validity apart from the views of particular authority figures. The individual may distinguish between what is morally right and what is legal, recognizing that some laws—for example, the racial segregation laws that Dr. Martin Luther King, Jr., challenged—violate basic moral principle. Thus the person transcends the perspectives of particular social groups or authorities and begins to take the perspective of *all* individuals.

> *Stage 5: Morality of contract, individual rights, and democratically accepted law.* At this "social contract" stage, there is an increased understanding of the underlying purposes served by laws and a concern that rules be arrived at through a democratic consensus so that they express the will of the majority or maximize social welfare. Whereas the person at stage 4 is unlikely to challenge an established law, the stage 5 moral reasoner might call for democratic change in a law that compromises basic rights. The principles embodied in the U.S. Constitution illustrate stage 5 morality.
>
> *Stage 6: Morality of individual principles of conscience.* At this "highest" stage of moral reasoning, the individual defines right and wrong on the basis of self-chosen principles that are broad and universal in application. The stage 6 thinker does *not* just make up whatever principles he or she happens to favor but instead arrives at abstract principles of respect for all individuals and their rights that *all* religions or moral authorities might view as moral. Kohlberg (1981) described stage 6 thinking as a kind of "moral musical chairs" in which the person facing a moral dilemma is able to take the perspective or "chair" of each and every person or group that could potentially be affected by a decision and arrive at a solution that would be regarded as just from every "chair." Stage 6 is Kohlberg's vision of ideal moral reasoning, but it is so rarely observed that Kohlberg stopped attempting to measure its existence.

Box 12.1
Responses to the Mercy-Killing Dilemma at Kohlberg's Three Levels of Moral Reasoning

Preconventional morality

Pro: At this level of moral reasoning, a person might argue that Dr. Jefferson should give the terminally ill woman a drug that will kill her because there is little chance that he will be found out and punished (stage 1). Besides, he might benefit from the gratitude of her family in the long run and should think of it as the right thing to do if it serves his purposes (stage 2).

Con: Other individuals, however, might argue just as forcefully that the doctor runs a big risk of losing his license and being thrown in prison (stage 1). Besides, he really has little to gain personally by taking such a big chance. If the woman wants to kill herself, that's her business (stage 2).

Conventional morality

Pro: We might expect many individuals who reason at the conventional level of morality to disapprove of mercy killing, either because they believe that most people would disapprove of it (stage 3) or because it is against the laws that we as citizens are obligated to uphold (stage 4). A stage 3 conventional moral reasoner might emphasize that Dr. Jefferson would lose the respect of his colleagues and friends if he administered the drug. A stage 4 reasoner might say: "The Bible says, 'Thou shalt not kill,' and the law clearly forbids mercy killing. Dr. Jefferson simply can't take the law into his own hands; instead, he has a duty to uphold the law."

Con: Yet it is also possible to argue in favor of mercy killing at the conventional level of moral reasoning. A stage 3 conventional moral reasoner might argue that most people would understand that the doctor was motivated by concern for the woman rather than by self-interest and would be able to forgive him for what was essentially an act of kindness. A stage 4 thinker might appeal to the authority of the Hippocratic oath, which spells out a doctor's duty to relieve suffering.

Postconventional morality

A postconventional moral reasoner might approach the mercy-killing dilemma by asking about the *morality* of the mercy-killing act, not just whether it will be punished or is socially acceptable and legal (stage 5). And by considering the perspectives of *all*—the doctor, the dying woman, other terminally ill people, people in general—in order to arrive at a decision that would uphold a broad moral principle and would be viewed as just from any vantage point (stage 6).

Pro: The postconventional moral reasoner operating at stage 5 is likely to think about the moral purposes served by laws against mercy killing and ask whether these laws truly maximize the good of all. This stage 5 thinker might decide that the doctor's act of mercy killing is a morally justifiable means of relieving human suffering, but may also insist that the doctor be willing to be held legally accountable for his action. The stage 6 thinker is likely to take an even broader perspective, considering how all humans everywhere will be affected by the doctor's action. This individual might argue that everyone has a basic right to dignity and self-determination, so long as others are not harmed by one's decisions. Assuming that no one else will be hurt, the dying woman has a right to live and die as she chooses. From this perspective, the doctor is doing right by respecting her integrity as a person and saving the woman, her family, and all of society from needless suffering.

Con: After carefully analyzing the rationale behind laws against mercy killing, a stage 5 postconventional reasoner might decide that those laws do indeed protect citizens' rights and should be upheld. If the laws were changed through the democratic process, that might be another thing, but right now the doctor can best serve society by adhering to them. A stage 6 thinker might say: "If we truly adhere to the principle that human life should be valued above all else, it is morally wrong to 'play God' and decide that some lives are worth living and others are not. Before long, we would have a world in which no life has value."

In Box 12.1, we present examples of how people at the preconventional, conventional, and postconventional levels of moral reasoning might reason about the mercy-killing dilemma. Notice that progress through Kohlberg's stages of moral reasoning depends in part on the development of perspective-taking abilities (Selman, 1980). Specifically, as individuals become more able to consider perspectives other than their own, moral reasoning progresses from a rather egocentric focus on personal welfare at the first of the three moral levels, to a concern with the perspectives of other people (parents, friends, and even members of the society in which one lives) at the second level, and, ultimately, to a concern with what is right from the perspective of *all* people at the third level.

Moral Behavior: Social Learning Theory

Social learning theorists such as Albert Bandura (1986), Walter Mischel (1974), and Justin Aronfreed (1976) have been primarily interested in the behavioral component of morality—in what we actually do when faced with temptation. These theorists claim that moral behavior is learned in the same way that other social behaviors are learned: through the operation of reinforcement and punishment and through observational learning. They also consider moral behavior to be strongly influenced by the nature of the specific situations in which people find themselves: It is not at all surprising to see a person behave morally in one situation but transgress in another situation or to proclaim that nothing is more important than honesty but then lie.

To highlight the difference between social learning theory and other perspectives, let's see how different theorists might attempt to predict whether a teenager (Bubba, we'll call him) will cheat on his upcoming math test. Freud would certainly want to know whether Bubba identified strongly with his father in early childhood. If he did, presumably he has developed a strong superego as part of his personality and therefore will be less likely to cheat, lie, or steal than a child with a weak superego (unless, of course, his father had a weak superego).

Kohlberg, meanwhile, would be interested in Bubba's level of cognitive development and, specifically, in the stage at which he reasons about moral dilemmas. Although Kohlberg insists that one's level of moral reasoning does not necessarily predict which decision one will make, Kohlberg would at least expect Bubba's mode of making decisions to be consistent across many moral situations. If he thinks in a conventional way about mercy killing, he is also likely to think at the conventional level in deliberating whether or not to cheat on a test. Moreover, since Kohlberg believes that each higher moral stage is a more adequate way of making moral decisions, he might expect the child whose moral reasoning is advanced to be at least somewhat less likely to cheat than the child who still thinks at the preconventional level.

Notice, then, that both the psychoanalytic perspective and the cognitive-developmental perspective view morality as a kind of personality trait—a quality that each of us possesses that consistently influences our judgments and actions.

What might social learning theorists say about Bubba? They would be curious about the moral habits he has learned. If Bubba's parents, for example, have consistently reinforced him when he has behaved morally and punished him when he has misbehaved, he will be more likely to behave in morally acceptable ways than a child who has not had adequate moral training. Bubba is also likely to be better off if he has been exposed to many models of morally acceptable behavior rather than brought up in the company of liars, cheaters, and thieves.

And yet social learning theorists are skeptical of the notion that morality is a single highly consistent trait or mode of thinking that will show itself in all situations. Bubba's parents might have taught him to follow rules of honesty, for example, but perhaps that learning does not generalize well to the math class when Bubba faces an opportunity to cheat. Moreover, *situational* influences in the math class might have more influence on Bubba's behavior than his prior learning. What if it is obvious to him that he stands no chance of being caught and punished? What if his friend Willard promises to get him a date on Friday night (a powerful reinforcer) if he enters into a cheating conspiracy? What if he observes his classmates cheating on the test and sees that they are getting away with it?

In sum, the social learning perspective on moral development holds that morality is *situation-specific behavior* rather than a generalized trait such as a strong superego or a postconventional mode of moral reasoning. Influenced by specific learning experiences, we do acquire relatively strong or relatively weak sets of habits that express themselves in situations in which it is possible to cheat, lie, steal, help a person in need, and so on. And yet each specific moral situation we encounter also affects our behavior. As a result, behavior is often inconsistent from situation to situation.

We are now ready to trace the development of motivation and morality from infancy to old age. Our coverage concentrates on the self as a motivated being, channeling energies in certain directions rather than others. Moreover, it charts the development of the self as a moral being, examining moral affect, cognition, and behavior as they have been conceptualized by psychoanalytic, cognitive-developmental, and social learning theorists.

THE INFANT

We do not often think of infants as strongly motivated to achieve goals, and we certainly do not think of them as having a motivation to behave morally. Yet developmentalists are beginning to appreciate that the foundations for many important motives and for the learning of moral standards are established very early in life.

What Motivates Infants?

It seems obvious that infants come equipped with a variety of physiological needs and are therefore motivated to obtain food and water, escape pain and discomfort, and otherwise ensure their survival and well-being. It may not be so obvious that infants possess psychological motivations. Yet they do appear to have at least two very important psychological motives: an achievement-related motive to master the environment, and a socially oriented motive to affiliate with other human beings.

Mastery Motivation

Some time ago, psychoanalyst Robert White (1959) proposed that human beings are intrinsically motivated from infancy onward to master their environment. He called this **effectance motivation**, or competence motivation—a desire to have an effect on or to cope successfully with the world of objects and people. This effectance, competence, or mastery motive can be seen in action when infants struggle to open kitchen cabinets, stack blocks, or figure out how new toys work—and derive pleasure from their efforts. Indeed, young infants seem to take more pleasure from striving to achieve a goal than from actually achieving it (MacTurk, McCarthy, Vietze, & Yarrow, 1987). White argued that it is the nature of human beings to seek out challenges just for the joy of attempting to master them.

Elaborating on the concept of mastery motivation, Martin Ford and Ross Thompson (1985) have suggested that infants form important beliefs about their ability to master the world, and these beliefs influence their future efforts to pursue goals and conquer challenges. Specifically, they form perceptions of *competence* (notions of their own ability or inability to achieve goals) and perceptions of *control* (beliefs about whether the environment will respond to their mastery efforts). The infant who rifles through Mom's purse to find her keys and succeeds, for example, not only derives pleasure from this experience but may learn a larger lesson: I have skills (perceived competence), and the world around me responds to my efforts to display competence and to have effects (perceived control).

Of course, there is abundant evidence that infants are curious, active explorers who are constantly striving to understand and to exert control over the world around them. Jean Piaget certainly insisted that infants are intrinsically motivated to explore and understand the world around them. In many ways, then, a striving for mastery or competence appears to be inborn and will display itself in the behavior of all normal infants without any prompting from parents. Even so, some infants appear to be more mastery oriented than others. Given a new push toy, for example, one baby may simply look at it, while another may mouth it and bang it and even push it back and forth across the floor. Why might some infants have a stronger effectance motive than others do?

Three influences on mastery motivation appear to be important: appropriate stimulation, a responsive environment, and a secure relationship with a caregiver.

Leon Yarrow and his associates (1984) observed both mothers and fathers interacting with their infants at 6 months and 12 months of age. The researchers measured mastery motivation by giving infants new toys to explore and observing how actively they explored them and by giving them problems to solve (for example, how to get to a toy behind a Plexiglas screen). Infants who were highly mastery oriented on these tasks were those whose parents frequently stimulated their curiosity by providing *sensory stimulation* designed to arouse and amuse them (tickling, games of pat-a-cake, bouncing, and so on).

Other research suggests that the *responsiveness* of the environment is important and that mastery motivation will blossom if infants have plenty of opportunities to see for themselves that they can control their environments (Ford & Thompson, 1985). Parents who return smiles and coos or respond promptly to cries show infants that they can affect people around them. Similarly, when 8-week-old babies see that their actions can make a brightly colored mobile rotate, they smile and coo and take far more interest in the mobile than infants who have no control over its movements (Watson & Ramey, 1972). Later, they learn new responses more quickly than infants who have not had opportunities to be in control (Finkelstein & Ramey, 1977).

Finally, *a secure and loving attachment* to parents seems to promote mastery motivation. Infants who are securely attached to their mothers at 12 to 15 months of age are more likely than those who are insecurely attached (1) to venture away from their mothers to explore a strange environment and (2) to display a strong sense of curiosity, self-reliance, and eagerness to solve problems some four years later in kindergarten (Arend, Gove, & Sroufe, 1979; Cassidy, 1986; Matas, Arend, & Sroufe, 1978; and see Chapter 13).

Does an infant's level of mastery motivation affect his or her later development? Apparently it does. Babies who actively attempt to master challenges at 6 and 12 months of age have been found to score higher on a test of mental development at age 2½ than their less mastery-oriented peers (Messer et al., 1986). In other words, infants are intrinsically motivated to master challenges; parents may contribute to strengthening this inborn motive by stimulating their infants appropriately, responding to their actions, and developing a secure relationship with them; and the strength of an infant's effectance or mastery motivation may well influence how much the child learns from experiences and how well he or she functions intellectually later in childhood.

The Affiliation Motive

Another important psychological motivation that is evident in infancy is an **affiliative motive**—a desire to interact with other human beings. Early social behavior and the formation of close attachments to parents are examined in Chapter 13; here, it is enough to say that infants are social beings from the start. By the age of 6 weeks, infants clearly prefer social stimulation to nonsocial stimulation, and they will protest when any adult puts them down or walks off and leaves them alone (Schaffer & Emerson, 1964). Starting at about 7 months of age, when they form their first attachments, infants display a special and very powerful motivation to be close to and to interact with the lucky individuals who are the objects of their love. Their interest in socializing only grows stronger over the first two years of life.

During infancy, then, the roots of two important motivations that remain central to humans throughout the life span are plain to see: a desire to be competent and effective as individuals, and a desire to form and maintain social relationships. The infant's mastery motivation may be converted into later needs for achievement, power, and self-assertion, whereas early attachments to parents may provide the basis for later concerns with gaining approval, a sense of belonging, and intimacy (Veroff & Veroff, 1980).

Moral Development in Infancy

Do infants have any sense of right or wrong? If an infant takes a toy that belongs to another child, would you label the act stealing? If an infant had hit another child in the head with a toy, would you insist that the infant be put on trial for assault? Chances are you would answer these questions "No." Adults in our society, including psychologists, tend to view infants as **amoral**—that is, lacking any sense of morality. Since we do not believe that infants are capable of evaluating their behavior in the light of moral standards, we do not hold them morally responsible for any wrongs they commit (although we may certainly attempt to prevent them from harming others). Nor do we expect them to be "good" when we are not around to watch them.

Yet even though infants are largely amoral, it is now clear that children begin to learn "moral" lessons during their first two years of life. Roger Burton (1984) provides a delightful example of the moral socialization of his 1½-year-old daughter Ursula. It seems that Ursula was so taken by the candy that she and her sisters had gathered on Halloween that she snatched candy from her sisters' bags. The sisters immediately said "No, that's mine," and conveyed their outrage in the strongest terms. A week later, the sisters again found some of their candy in Ursula's bag and raised a fuss, and it was their mother's turn to explain the rules to Ursula. The problem continued until finally Burton himself came upon Ursula in one of her sister's rooms looking at the forbidden candy. Ursula looked up and said, "No, this is Maria's, not Ursula's" (p. 199).

Burton believes it is through such specific social learning experiences, cumulated over the years, that we come to understand the meaning of stealing in a more general way. Moreover, we learn from our unpleasant experiences to associate the act of stealing with negative emotional responses. Eventually, we do not even have to think about it; we simply ignore opportunities to steal. So moral learning does begin in infancy as children experience positive or negative reactions to their behavior.

It is also becoming clear that infants are not quite so selfish and unconcerned about other people as Freud and many other theorists have assumed. Perhaps the strongest evidence that infants have something akin to a moral sense comes from studies of empathy and altruism. **Empathy** is the vicarious experiencing of another person's feelings (for example, smiling at the good fortune of another

Children learn very early that some acts have negative consequences.

or experiencing another person's distress), and **altruism** is behavior such as helping or sharing that is motivated by a concern for the welfare of others rather than by self-interest. Amazingly, even newborns display a very primitive form of empathy. They are distressed by the cries of other newborns; moreover, they are *not* distressed in the same way by hearing their own taped cries or the cries of chimpanzees, so their response to the distress of other infants is more than an aversion to any unpleasant noise (Martin & Clark, 1982).

It is unlikely that newborns really distinguish between another infant's distress and their own, for they have not yet distinguished themselves from the rest of the world. Moreover, they are not yet capable of acting on their primitive empathy by behaving altruistically to relieve another's distress (Hoffman, 1981). Yet older infants *do* seem to realize that it is someone else rather than themselves who needs help and will try to provide it, at least toward the end of their second year. Consider the reaction of 21-month-old John to his distressed playmate, Jerry:

> Today Jerry was kind of cranky; he just started . . . bawling and he wouldn't stop. John kept coming over and handing Jerry toys, trying to cheer him up. . . . He'd say things like "Here Jerry," and I said to John "Jerry's sad; he doesn't feel good; he had a shot today." John would look at me with his eyebrows wrinkled together like he really understood that Jerry was crying because he was unhappy. . . . [Zahn-Waxler, Radke-Yarrow, & King, 1979, pp. 321–322].

Overall, then, infants are amoral in many respects, particularly when it comes to making judgments of right and wrong or resisting temptations to engage in prohibited behaviors. Yet at the same time, their "moral socialization" has begun. Moreover, they already show the rudiments of empathy for other people and a motivation to help others in distress. Drawing on this evidence, Martin Hoffman (1981, 1988) has argued that empathy is built into the very nature of human beings and serves as an important motivator of moral behavior. Why, Hoffman asks, would we set aside our own selfish motives to help other people or to avoid harming them unless we had the capacity to share their emotions?

THE CHILD

During the years from age 2 to age 12, children's motives are shaped by the society in which they live. And while children do not become fully mature in their moral affect, thought, and behavior, they do internalize many important moral values.

Motivation During Childhood: A Look at Achievement Motivation

What motivates children? Like infants, children are motivated to affiliate with others, both adults and peers. In addition, the mastery motive that is so evident during infancy provides a foundation for later achievement motivation. Once they pass the age of 2, children are even more goal-oriented than they were as infants. They not only enjoy stacking blocks, but if an adult shows them how to construct a particular tower of blocks, they will struggle to do it just that way, correct themselves if they make a mistake, and become quite frustrated if they cannot achieve their goal (Bullock & Lutkenhaus, 1988).

Our society is a highly achievement-oriented one—some might say too much so (Spence, 1985). For this reason perhaps, developmentalists in North America have been more interested in achievement motives than in other motives. Let's see why some children are more likely than others to try hard in school and to take pleasure in mastering math, language arts, and other academic tasks.

What Is Achievement Motivation?

David McClelland and his associates (McClelland, Atkinson, Clark, & Lowell, 1953; McClelland, 1985) defined the **need for achievement** as a motive to compete and strive for success whenever one's behavior can be evaluated against a standard of excellence. In other words, people with a high achievement motivation take pride in their ability to meet high standards and are motivated by this sense of self-fulfillment to work hard, be successful, and outperform others when faced with new challenges.

To measure achievement motivation, McClelland and his colleagues gave children or adults pictures and asked them to compose stories about them. Assuming that people will project their own motives onto the pictured situation, counting the achievement-related themes in the stories provides a measure of an individual's need for achievement. In responding to the scene portrayed in Figure 12.1, for example, a person with a high need for achievement might say that the men have been working for months on a new scientific breakthrough that will revolutionize medicine, whereas a person with a low need for achievement might say that the workers are glad the day is over so that they can go home and watch television.

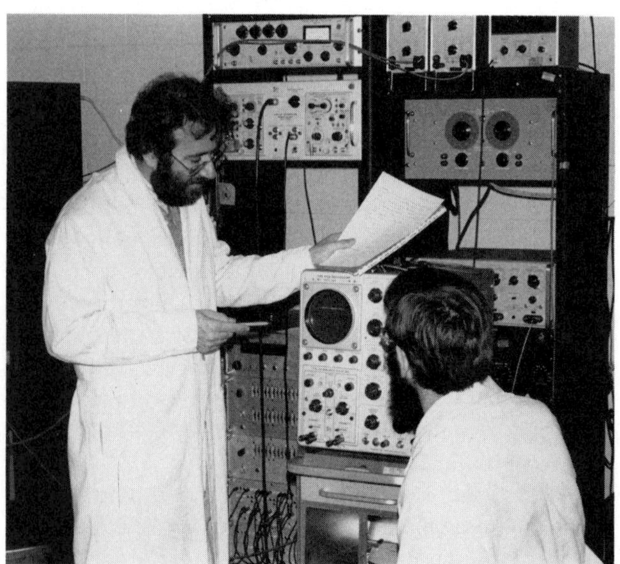

Figure 12.1 Scenes like this one were used by David McClelland and his associates to measure achievement motivation.

Elaborating on the concept of an achievement motive, Susan Harter (1981) suggests that children may strive to achieve for either of two reasons: (1) to satisfy their own needs for competence or mastery (an *intrinsic orientation* very much like White's effectance motivation and McClelland's need for achievement) or (2) to earn external incentives such as grades, prizes, approval, or high-paying jobs (an *extrinsic orientation*). Harter asked children whether the reasons they performed various activities were intrinsic (I like challenging tasks; I like to solve problems myself) or extrinsic (I do things to get good grades, to win the teacher's approval). She found that children who are intrinsically oriented toward achievement are more likely than extrinsically oriented children to prefer challenging problems over simpler ones and to view themselves as highly competent at academic tasks.

Although some adults may not care *why* children strive for success, most parents and educators would like to see children develop an intrinsic orientation toward achievement—that is, a strong need for achievement based on joy and pride in mastery. Individuals who score high in need for achievement do indeed tend to receive better grades than those who score low (McClelland et al., 1953). How might this motive be instilled? McClelland suggests that parents stress independence (doing for oneself) at an early age and reinforce self-reliance; research bears this out (Grolnick & Ryan, 1989; Winterbottom, 1958). Directly encouraging children to do things well also fosters achievement motivation (Rosen & D'Andrade, 1959).

Will a high need for achievement ensure that a child achieves to his or her potential? Many researchers, while recognizing that the concept of need for achievement has value, also believe that it tells only part of the story. Perhaps it is too simple to assume that one global motive will predict behavior in all achievement situations. Among the other important factors to be considered are the value placed on achieving a particular goal, the individual's perceived competence and expectancies of success, and the individual's sense of control over outcomes and his or her theories about the reasons for success or failure.

The Value Placed on Achievement in a Particular Situation

John Atkinson (1964) insisted that the *value* of success to the individual (as well as the aversiveness of failing) is an important influence on achievement outcomes. It seems obvious that we are more likely to strive hard for a goal we really care about than for a goal that is unimportant. Thus it may be too simple to think that a person who scores high in overall need for achievement will be motivated to succeed in all situations; a strong need for achievement predicts success only when the value placed on achievement is high (Raynor, 1970).

Perceived Competence and Expectancies of Success

We are also more likely to work hard when we think we have a reasonable chance of succeeding than when we see no hope of attaining a goal. Expectations of success matter (Atkinson, 1964). For example, children with high IQs and low expectancies of academic success often earn poorer grades than their classmates who have lower IQs but higher expectancies (Battle, 1966; Crandall, 1967). Children who perceive themselves as competent and expect to achieve often do succeed, whereas those who expect to fail may spend little time and effort pursuing goals that they believe to be out of reach.

Perceived Control and Explanations of Success and Failure

Researchers have also discovered that children's achievement behavior depends on how they interpret their successes and failures and whether they think they can control these outcomes. Bernard Weiner (1974, 1986) has proposed an **attribution theory** of motivation in which he argues that the explanations (causal attributions) we offer for our outcomes influence our future expectancies of success and our future motivation to succeed. Weiner has emphasized four causes of success or failure: ability (or lack thereof), effort, task difficulty, and luck (either good or bad).

Two of these causes, ability and effort, are internal causes or qualities of the individual, whereas the other two, task difficulty and luck, are external or environmental factors. In other words, Weiner proposes that causal attributions can be grouped along a locus dimension (internal versus external). Here Weiner's thinking corresponds to earlier work on a dimension of personality called **locus of control** (Crandall, 1967, 1969). Individuals with an *internal locus of control* assume that they are personally responsible for what happens to them. For example, they might credit an A grade on a paper to superior writing ability or hard work. Individuals with an *external locus of control* believe that their outcomes depend more on luck, fate, or the actions of others than on their own abilities and efforts. They might say that their A's are due to luck (the teacher just happened to like this one), indiscriminate grading, or some other external cause. Children with an internal locus of control earn higher grades and higher scores on academic achievement tests than children with an external locus of control do (Findley & Cooper, 1983), perhaps because they believe their efforts will pay off and therefore work harder.

Weiner also claims that causes differ along a *stability* dimension. Ability and task difficulty are reasonably stable or unchangeable. If one has low math ability today, one is likely to have the same low ability tomorrow, and if a math problem is particularly difficult, similar problems are also likely to be difficult. By contrast, the amount of effort one expends and the workings of luck are highly unstable or variable from situation to situation. Thus Weiner categorizes causes of success or failure along both a locus of causality and a stability dimension, as shown in Table 12.2.

Why is it useful to use both locus of causality and stability to distinguish attributions? Mainly because it is not *always* adaptive to attribute what happens to internal causes, as research on locus of control would lead us to believe. It is indeed healthy to conclude that your successes must be due to high ability; this will not only make you feel proud but will lead you to expect more successes in the future, since ability is relatively stable and should

Table 12.2 Weiner's classification of the causes of achievement outcomes (and examples of how you might explain a terrible test grade)

	Locus of Causality	
	Internal Cause	External Cause
Stable Cause	*Ability* "I'm hopeless in math."	*Task difficulty* "That test was incredibly hard and much too long."
Unstable Cause	*Effort* "I should have studied more instead of going out to play."	*Luck* "What luck! Every question seemed to be about the one day of class I missed."

therefore continue to affect future performance. But is it healthy to conclude after a failure that you are hopelessly incompetent, miserably lacking in ability? Hardly! Low ability may be an internal cause of poor performance, but because it is also a stable cause, attributing failure to low ability is an admission that you can do little to improve on your lousy performance. Not only would you have low expectancies of future success and little motivation to strive, but you would lose self-esteem by admitting that you are "dumb."

As it turns out (see Dweck & Elliott, 1983; Dweck & Leggett, 1988), high achievers tend to attribute their successes to internal and stable causes such as high ability, but they blame their failures either on external factors beyond their control ("That test was impossibly hard." "That professor's grading is biased") or on internal causes that they can easily overcome (such as the unstable factor of insufficient effort). They do *not* blame the internal but stable factor of low ability ("I'm terrible at this and will never do any better"). Students with this healthy attributional style have been termed *mastery oriented* because they persist in the face of failure, believing that their increased effort will pay off (Dweck, 1978).

Children who tend to be low achievers often attribute their successes either to the internal cause of hard work or to external causes such as the easiness of the task or luck. Thus they do not experience the pride and self-esteem that come from viewing oneself as highly capable. Yet they often attribute their failures to an internal and stable cause—namely, lack of ability—which may cause them to have low expectancies of success and to give up (Dweck & Elliott, 1983). Carol Dweck (1978) has characterized this attributional style as a form of **learned helplessness**, or a crippling inability to act when it seems that one cannot control unpleasant or frustrating events. Helpless children, because they believe that their failures stem from personal inadequacies, will not even try to improve after they have experienced failure—and so they perform even less well than they did before they failed. They seem to view failures as proof of their incompetence rather than as opportunities to increase their competence by mastering a challenge (Dweck & Leggett, 1988).

Surprisingly perhaps, even many high-ability students adopt this unhealthy attributional style (Dweck, 1978; Phillips, 1984). Teachers and parents may foster it by praising children for being neat or working hard when they succeed but criticizing them for lacking intelligence or understanding when they fail. Unfortunately, girls receive this helplessness-producing pattern of feedback more often than boys do (Dweck, Davidson, Nelson, & Enna, 1978; Dweck & Elliott, 1983; and see Chapter 11).

Can children with a "helpless" attribution style be helped to overcome their self-defeating attributions? Yes, indeed. Carol Dweck (1975) exposed children who had become helpless in the face of repeated failure on math problems to a simple *attribution retraining* treatment. Over 25 sessions, these children experienced some successes and were told after each of several prearranged failures that they had not worked fast enough and should have tried harder. After this retraining, they tended to attribute their failures to lack of effort rather than to low ability and performed much better on the math problems than they had initially. By contrast, helpless children who were given nothing but success experiences during their treatment sessions never learned to cope with failure and retained their helpless ways. It seems that parents and teachers can do much to foster healthy attribution styles by helping children to view themselves as competent ("You're really good at this, aren't you?") and as capable of overcoming difficulties ("You'll get it if you keep trying").

Interestingly, much of what we have said about the importance of attributions for success and failure may not apply to very young children. Before the age of 7 or so, children seem almost oblivious to the negative implications of failure. Even after repeated poor performances, they almost invariably think that they have high ability and that they will do well in the future (Dweck & Elliott, 1983; Stipek, 1984). Nor do they give up or become helpless in the face of failure as older children often do (Miller, 1985). In short, young children are unrealistically optimistic.

Why is this? It is partly a matter of wishful thinking; the more young children want to succeed, the more they believe that they *will* succeed, even if they have failed in the past (Stipek, Roberts, & Sanborn, 1984). In addition, young children are protected from damaging self-perceptions because they do not yet fully understand the concept of ability (Nicholls, 1978; Nicholls & Miller, 1984). They do not recognize that some failures are due to the relatively enduring attribute called low ability rather than to lack of trying, and that low ability can prevent even the hardest worker from succeeding. It is not until age 10 or so that children fully understand this—and become more vulnerable to feelings of helplessness after repeated failures. These changes are probably related both to cognitive development—especially an increased ability to analyze the causes of events and to infer enduring traits from behavior—and to an accumulation of feedback in school about one's deficiencies (Stipek, 1984).

A Summing Up

Obviously, achievement motivation and achievement behavior involve far more than just a global need for achievement. Children do differ in their characteristic motives to achieve, but the *value* of success to the individual must also be considered. Why act on any motive to achieve if the goal seems unimportant or irrelevant to one's other goals? Moreover, an individual's perceived competence and *expectancies* of success also count, for there may be little point in striving if one lacks confidence that one can meet the challenge. And finally, drawing on attribution theory, we must recognize that achievement behavior is very much affected by the ways in which an individual interprets successes and failures in life. Only by considering all of these factors will we be able to predict how children will actually behave and what they will actually accomplish when they confront tasks.

Moral Development During Childhood

Just as children's characteristic motives are shaped by their experiences in the family, at school, and in society at large, their standards of morality and their motivation to live up to these standards grow out of their social experiences. Research on moral development during childhood has explored how children of different ages think about moral issues. It has also told us a good deal about how children actually behave when their moral values are tested.

Kohlberg's View of the Moral Reasoning of the Child

The hypothetical moral dilemmas that Lawrence Kohlberg devised to assess stage of moral reasoning (for example, the mercy-killing dilemma presented earlier) are too complex for young children to understand. When school-aged children are tested, they generally reason at the preconventional level, taking an egocentric perspective on morality and defining as right those acts that are rewarded and as wrong those acts that are punished (Colby et al., 1983). At best, they are beginning to make the transition to conventional moral reasoning by displaying a stage 3 concern with being a "good boy" or a "good girl" who gains the approval of others. In short, from Kohlberg's perspective, most children, but especially young ones, are not really moral beings yet, for they have not yet internalized conventional societal values as their own. Thus Kohlberg's stages of moral reasoning seem to be more useful in describing the moral reasoning of adolescents and adults than they are in describing the moral reasoning of young children.

However, other researchers have looked more closely at the moral reasoning of young children and find that they *do* engage in some fairly sophisticated thinking about right and wrong and are more than egocentrically amoral beings.

Research on Piaget's Theory of Moral Reasoning

How accurate is Piaget's view that children progress from a stage of heteronomous morality to a stage of autonomous morality at about the age of 10? Consider first Piaget's claim that young children judge acts as right or wrong on the basis of their consequences rather than the intentions that guided them. He found that children in the heteronomous stage of moral reasoning (ages 6 to 10) usually judged John, the well-intentioned boy who broke 15 cups accidentally, naughtier than Henry, who broke one cup while reaching for some forbidden jam. The problem is that this moral-decision story confused the issue by asking if the individual who causes a small amount of harm in the service of bad intentions is naughtier than the person who causes a large amount of damage despite good intentions.

Sharon Nelson (1980) overcame this flaw in an interesting experiment with 3-year-olds. Each child listened to stories in which a character threw a ball to a playmate. The actor's motive was described as *good* (his friend had nothing to play with) or *bad* (the actor was mad at his friend), and the consequences of his act were either *positive* (the friend caught the ball and was happy to play with it) or *negative* (the ball hit the friend in the head and made him cry). To make the task even simpler, Nelson showed children drawings of what happened (see Figure 12.2 for an example).

How did these 3-year-olds judge the "goodness" or "badness" of the actor's behavior? As we see in Figure 12.3, they did judge acts that had positive consequences

Figure 12.2 Examples of drawings used by Nelson to convey an actor's intentions to preschool children. Here, there are negative intent and a negative consequence. (From Nelson, 1980)

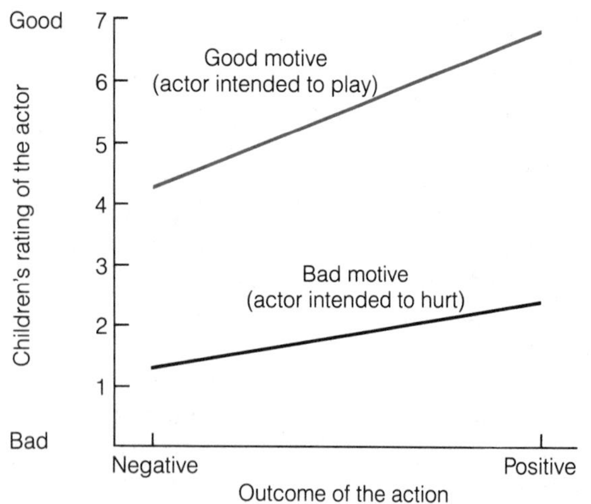

Figure 12.3 Average ratings of an actor's behavior for actors who had either good or bad intentions and produced either positive or negative outcomes. (From Nelson, 1980)

more favorably than acts that had negative consequences. Yet the more interesting finding was that the well-intentioned child who had wanted to play was evaluated much more favorably than the child who intended to hurt his friend, *regardless of the consequences of his actions.* Apparently, then, even very young children can base their moral judgments on an actor's intentions (see also Nelson-Le Gall, 1985). Indeed, if you listen to young children, you may hear them try to escape punishment by pleading, "I didn't mean it! I didn't mean it!"

Apparently, then, Piaget's rather difficult tasks underestimated the ability of young children to weigh both consequences and intentions in making moral judgments. Piaget may also have underestimated social influences on children's moral decisions. It is now clear that young children differ greatly from each other in the extent to which they emphasize intentions or consequences (Helkama, 1988). What's more, it turns out that the weights that a child places on consequences and intentions mirror almost exactly the weights that a child's mother places on these factors in making moral judgments (Leon, 1984). Even so, Piaget was correct to an extent: In many situations, young children do tend to assign more weight to consequences and less weight to intentions than older children do, even though both younger and older children consider both motives and outcomes in judging acts (Surber, 1982).

Piaget also claimed that children in the heteronomous stage of moral development view rules as sacred prescriptions laid down by respected authority figures. These moral absolutes cannot be questioned or changed. However, Elliot Turiel (1978, 1983) observed that children actually encounter two kinds of rules: (1) **moral rules**, or standards that focus on the basic rights and privileges of individuals, and (2) **social-conventional rules**, standards determined by social consensus that tell us what is appropriate in a particular social setting. Moral rules include rules against hitting, stealing, lying, and otherwise harming others or violating their rights. Social-conventional rules are more like rules of social etiquette than like moral laws and include the rules of games as well as school rules that forbid eating snacks in class or using the restroom without permission.

Apparently children learn quite early that moral and social-conventional rules are different, and that moral rules are more compelling and "sacred" (Nucci & Nucci, 1982; Smetana, 1985, 1989). Judith Smetana (1981) discovered that preschool children as young as age 2½ regard moral transgressions such as hitting, stealing, or refusing to share as much more serious and deserving of punishment than social-conventional violations such as not staying in one's seat in nursery school or not saying grace before eating. Even more remarkable is what these youngsters said when asked if a violation would be okay if there were no rule against it: They claimed that it was always wrong to hit people or commit other moral transgressions, rule or no rule, but they felt that it would be perfectly okay for children to get out of their seats at nursery school or violate other social conventions in the absence of any explicit rules. Moreover, 6- to 10-year-old children, who should be in Piaget's heteronomous stage of morality, are quite capable of questioning adult authority (Tisak, 1986). These children claim that the moral rules that parents set are legitimate, but they believe that it can be inappropriate and unjustifiable for parents to arbitrarily require children to perform household chores or to restrict their children's friendships.

Clearly, then, children younger than about 10 years of age are considerably more sophisticated in their moral thinking than Piaget believed. They are quite capable of judging acts as right or wrong according to whether the actor's intentions were good or bad, even though they do often place more weight on an act's consequences and less weight on the motives behind an act than older children do. They do not view *all* rules as absolute, sacred, and unchangeable. Instead, they realize that social-conventional rules are far more arbitrary and less binding than moral rules. Moreover, even 5- and 6-year-olds have already formed quite sophisticated concepts of what is fair and what is not and will try to act fairly by dividing rewards equally among themselves (Damon, 1977, 1984). Overall, then, Piaget charted many interesting patterns of moral growth, but it seems that children grow much more rapidly than either he or Kohlberg imagined.

Resisting Temptation: Children's Moral Behavior

Most adults are less interested in how children think about moral dilemmas than in how they actually behave. To most people, the ultimate goal of moral socialization is to produce a child who can resist the temptation to violate moral rules even when there is little chance of detection and punishment (Hoffman, 1970). This individual has not only internalized moral values but is motivated to abide by them. Can children be trusted to abide by rules? Will they cheat if they think they can get away with it? What factors influence whether or not a child will behave morally? These are just the sorts of questions that social learning theorists have asked, and their findings add greatly to our understanding of moral development and how it can be fostered.

Consider a classic study of moral behavior reported by Hugh Hartshorne and Mark May (1928–1930). The purpose was to investigate the moral character of 10,000 children (aged 8–16) by tempting them to lie, cheat, or steal in a variety of situations. It readily became apparent that almost all children espoused "sound" moral values, claiming that honesty was good, that cheating and stealing were wrong, and so on. Yet the most noteworthy findings of this massive investigation were that (1) children who cheated or violated other moral rules in a particular situation were just as likely as those who did not to state that cheating is wrong, and (2) most children *did* violate their own moral rules in at least one situation. In other words, Hartshorne and May had a tough time finding children who not only espoused the right values but consistently acted according to those values. Instead, the moral behavior of most children was quite inconsistent with their values and was also inconsistent from situation to situation. Morality seemed to be largely specific to the situation rather than a stable character trait.

Reanalyses of these data and new investigations suggest that children are somewhat more consistent in their behavior than Hartshorne and May concluded (Burton, 1963; Nelson, Grinder, & Mutterer, 1969; Rushton, 1980). Across a set of situations, some children tend to be more honest, more likely to resist temptation, or more helpful than other children are. Still, moral thought, affect, and behavior are not so closely interrelated in childhood as they will be by adolescence or adulthood (Blasi, 1980).

Why are children relatively inconsistent in their moral behavior? One explanation may be that they tend to reason at Kohlberg's preconventional level of moral reasoning. When punishment and reward are the primary considerations in defining acts as right or wrong, perhaps it is not surprising that the child may see nothing much wrong with cheating when the chances of detection and punishment are slim. In addition, moral inconsistency results from *situational* influences on behavior. A child's willingness to lie, cheat, or violate other moral prohibitions is definitely influenced by a variety of situation-specific factors such as the importance of the goal that can be achieved by transgressing, the probability of being detected, and the amount of encouragement provided by peers for deviant behavior (Burton, 1976). Social learning theorists have identified many important situational influences on moral behavior, so let's briefly see what they have learned that might aid parents and other socialization agents in raising a child who can be counted on to behave morally.

WHO RAISES MORALLY MATURE CHILDREN?

As noted at the start of the chapter, social learning theorists believe that habits of moral behavior are learned in the same way that many other social behaviors are learned—through reinforcement and punishment and through observational learning. Thus, social learning theorists would advise parents to reinforce moral behavior, punish immoral behavior, and serve as models of moral behavior rather than as bad examples.

Reinforcement and punishment do indeed play a role in moral development. Positive moral behaviors such as sharing can be encouraged if adults reinforce these acts (Fischer, 1963). Unfortunately, adults often fail to recognize that a child has resisted a temptation or passed up an opportunity to break a rule and deserves praise, so many parents rely heavily on punishment of misdeeds to teach children not to commit forbidden acts. The problem with this is that punishment can breed anger and resentment, especially if it is harsh. And, at best, it will only temporarily suppress the unwanted behavior; when the odds of being detected and punished are low, the behavior is likely to recur. Nonetheless, punishment can contribute to moral growth if it is not overly harsh, if it teaches children to associate negative emotions with their wrongdoing, and if it is accompanied by efforts to encourage and reinforce more acceptable behavior (Parke, 1977; Perry & Parke, 1975; Sears, Maccoby, & Levin, 1957; and see Chapter 8).

Social learning theorists would also emphasize that parents should serve as models of moral behavior. Children are often quick to imitate rule-breakers, especially if these models of misbehavior are not punished (Rosenkoetter, 1973). On the other hand, children will follow the example of an adult who resists temptation (Toner, Parke, & Yussen, 1978). Moreover, they are especially likely to do so if models verbalize the rule they are following and state a rationale for not committing the prohibited act (Grusec, Kuczynski, Rushton, & Simutis, 1979). Finally, the explanations or rationales offered by adults seem to work best when they are tailored to the developmental level of the child. Rule-following models whose rationales match the child's own level of moral reasoning are more influential than models whose rationales are beyond the child's level of moral understanding (Toner & Potts, 1981). Thus, a girl who reasons at the preconventional level might respond well to the argument that swiping other children's belongings will get her in big trouble with the teacher, whereas a conventional thinker might be swayed by an argument that focuses on the rights and feelings of classmates.

We gain additional insights into how to foster not only moral behavior but moral thought and affect from the important work of Martin Hoffman (1970, 1983, 1988). Several years ago, Hoffman (1970) reviewed the child-rearing literature to determine which parental approaches were associated with high levels of moral development. Three major approaches were compared:

1. **Love withdrawal** (withholding attention, affection, or approval after a child misbehaves—or, in other words, creating anxiety by threatening a loss of reinforcement from parents)
2. **Power assertion** (the use of power to administer spankings, take away privileges, and so on—in other words, the use of punishment)
3. **Induction** (explaining to a child why the behavior is wrong and should be changed by emphasizing how it affects other people)

Suppose that little Ronnie has just put the beloved family cat through a cycle in the clothes dryer. Using love withdrawal, a parent might say, "How could any child of mine do something like that? I can't even bear to look at you." Using power assertion, a parent might say, "Get to your room this minute; you're going to catch it." Using induction, a parent might say, "Ronnie, look how scared Fluffy is. You could have killed her, and you know how sad we'd all be if she died." Induction, then, is a matter of providing rationales or explanations that focus special attention on the consequences of wrongdoing for other people (or cats, as the case may be).

Which approach best fosters moral development? As you can see in Table 12.3, induction is more often positively associated with children's moral maturity than either love withdrawal or power assertion is. The use of power assertion is actually more often associated with moral *immaturity* than with moral maturity! Love withdrawal has been found to have positive effects in some studies but negative effects in others. Why is induction particularly effective? When parents explain *why* an act was wrong, they provide their children with cognitive rationales for evaluating their own behavior; that is, induction helps children internalize their parents' standards. And by pointing out how others are affected by the child's

Table 12.3 Relationships between parents' use of three disciplinary strategies and children's moral development

DIRECTION OF RELATIONSHIP BETWEEN PARENTS' USE OF A DISCIPLINARY STRATEGY AND CHILDREN'S MORAL MATURITY	TYPE OF DISCIPLINE		
	Power assertion	Love withdrawal	Induction
+ (positive correlation)	7	8	38
– (negative correlation)	32	11	6

Note: Table entries represent the number of occasions on which a particular disciplinary technique was found to be associated (either positively or negatively) with a measure of children's moral affect, reasoning, or behavior.

Source: Adapted from Brody & Shaffer, 1982.

actions, parents help the child take the perspective of others and empathize with them. Induction also allows parents to talk about moral affect (guilt and shame) and even to explain what the child should have done instead. In short, induction illustrates the cognitive, affective, and behavioral aspects of morality and may help children to integrate them.

Hoffman (1983) realizes that parents often combine power assertion, love withdrawal, and induction rather than using a single approach. In fact, he believes that prudent use of power assertion or love withdrawal as an accompaniment to induction in disciplinary encounters can help motivate the child to pay attention to the message being communicated. Still, Hoffman's work suggests that children must be taught why immoral acts are wrong if they are ever to truly internalize the moral values that adults would like them to acquire. His work provides a fairly clear picture of how parents can best contribute to the moral growth of their children and prepare them to resist the temptations that await them in adolescence.

THE ADOLESCENT

As adolescents gain the capacity to think about abstract and hypothetical ideas and as they chart their future identities, many of them devote a good deal of reflection to their values and priorities, their motivations and moral standards. What is it that I really want out of life? What moral values can I claim as my own? Reflection sometimes fosters growth.

Achievement Motivation During Adolescence

You might think that adolescents would become even more dedicated to academic success as they begin to realize that they need a good education in order to succeed as adults. It is not that simple. In fact, research presents a somewhat disheartening picture of achievement motivation during adolescence. Consider Deborah Stipek's (1984) conclusions from studies of the development of achievement motivation from early childhood to adolescence:

> On the average, children value academic achievement more as they progress through school, but their expectations for success and self-perceptions of competence decline, and their affect toward school becomes more negative. Children also become increasingly concerned about achievement outcomes and reinforcement (e.g., high grades) associated with positive outcomes and less concerned about intrinsic satisfaction in achieving greater competence [p. 153].

Many of the negative trends Stipek describes become especially apparent during the junior high school years. More and more youths become quite alienated from school and display little motivation for academic tasks. Many other adolescents continue to work hard at their studies but have what Susan Harter (1981) calls an *extrinsic* orientation rather than an intrinsic orientation toward achievement. They are more concerned with the rewards they can gain from their efforts than with the pleasure of mastery for mastery's sake.

By adolescence, some students have little motivation to achieve.

How can we explain these trends? According to Stipek, they are partly due to cognitive growth. As we saw earlier, children increasingly understand the implications of the feedback they receive from teachers and begin to distinguish between ability and effort. Inevitably, this means that they gain more realistic perceptions of their own abilities (Benenson & Dweck, 1986; Nicholls, 1978). As a result, some exuberantly confident young children become adolescents who are fully aware that they lack academic ability in certain areas. Stipek also emphasizes that the nature of the feedback children receive changes over the years. Teachers of young children often reinforce or punish children according to how hard they try rather than how good their work is. As Stipek puts it, it would be unthinkable for an adult to say to a 5-year-old exhibiting a drawing, "What an ugly picture, you sure can't draw very well" (p. 156). The positive feedback young children receive for their efforts may contribute to their sense that hard work can overcome any barrier (Rosenholtz & Simpson, 1984). Over the school years, however, teachers increasingly base their grades on the quality of the work and will criticize poor work when they see it. Those students who receive negative feedback are often being told, in effect, that they lack academic ability.

Finally, it is possible that some adolescents lose interest in academic achievement because other motives take priority. James Coleman (1961) once asked high school students how they would like to be remembered. Only 31% of the boys and 28% of the girls wanted to be remembered as bright students. Many of the boys (45%) were more concerned about their reputations as athletic stars; others (24%) wanted to be remembered as popular. Girls wanted to be remembered as leaders of extracurricular activities (37%) or as popular students (35%). Not coincidentally, these students also regarded athletic skills and social skills as more relevant than academic accomplishments to being in the leading crowds. Since peer acceptance is highly important to most adolescents, perhaps it is not surprising that some of them emphasize academic goals less and social goals more, particularly if they attend schools where few students are highly achievement oriented.

Not all or even most adolescents care little about academic achievement, however. Some of the general trends just described are negative, but adolescents still range from those who are striving hard and enjoying their work to those who are dropping out of school. Much depends on the social context in which they develop. In some families, schools, and neighborhoods, academic achievement is highly valued; in others, getting high marks in school is not particularly encouraged and can even brand a boy unmasculine and a girl unfeminine (Weiner, 1980). It is perhaps more accurate to say that adolescents become *diverse* in their academic achievement motivations, some consciously making achievement their top priority, others losing interest as their frustrations with school mount, as they become more aware of their limitations, and as the values of those around them influence their own priorities.

Moral Development in the Teen Years

Although most teenagers break the law now and then, adolescence is actually a period of considerable growth in moral reasoning and a time when many individuals become increasingly motivated to behave morally. Consider first the results of a 20-year longitudinal study that involved repeatedly asking the 10-, 13-, and 16-year-old boys originally studied by Kohlberg to respond to moral dilemmas (Colby et al., 1983). Figure 12.4 shows the percentage of judgments offered at each age that reflected each of Kohlberg's six stages.

A number of interesting developmental trends can be seen here. Notice that the preconventional reasoning (stage 1 and 2 thinking) that dominates among 10-year-olds decreases considerably during the teen years. During the adolescent years, conventional reasoning (stages 3 and 4) is becoming the dominant mode of moral thinking. So, among 13- to 14-year-olds most moral judgments reflect either a stage 2 (instrumental hedonism) approach—"You scratch my back and I'll scratch yours"—or a stage 3 ("good boy"/"good girl") concern with being nice and earning approval. Over half of the judgments offered by 16- to 18-year-olds embodied stage 3 reasoning, but about a fifth were scored as stage 4 (authority and social-order-maintaining morality) arguments. These older adolescents were beginning to take a broad societal perspective on justice and were concerned about acting in ways that would help maintain the social system.

Where are all the postconventional moral reasoners? Although Kohlberg's early work indicated that a small proportion of adolescents had progressed to the postconventional level of thought, his more recent research based on a more rigorous scoring system indicates that postconventional reasoning does not appear *at all* until early adult-

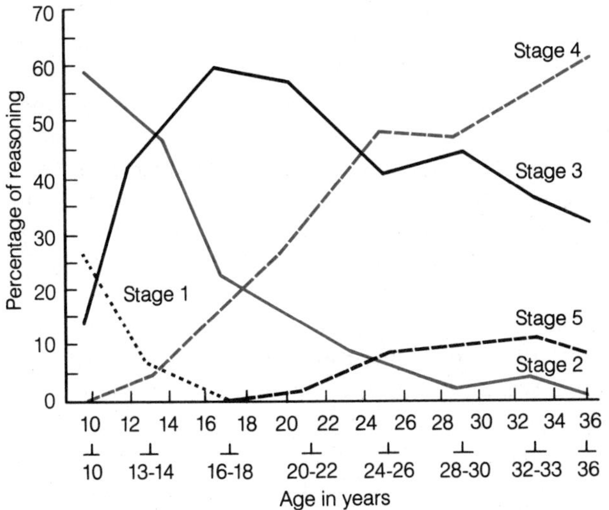

Figure 12.4 Average percentage of moral reasoning at each of Kohlberg's stages for males from age 10 to age 36. (From Colby, Kohlberg, Gibbs, & Lieberman, 1983)

hood. In short, the main developmental trend in moral reasoning during adolescence is a shift from preconventional thinking to more conventional reasoning. It is during adolescence that most individuals seem to rise above a concern with external rewards and punishments and begin to express a genuine concern with living up to the moral standards that parents and other authorities have taught them and ensuring that laws designed to make human relations orderly and fair are taken seriously and maintained.

William Damon (1984) observes another interesting breakthrough in moral development during adolescence: an increased tendency to view morality as something that contributes to a positive identity or self-definition. Because adolescents are more sensitive than children are to the expectations of those around them, they are more motivated to establish reputations as moral and caring individuals and to feel good about their moral values. To the child, being "good" often means sacrificing one's real interests and desires in order to stay on the "good side" of adults; to the adolescent, being "good" often becomes a way of *advancing* one's self-interest by bolstering one's sense of being a worthy individual. In support of Damon's argument, Perry, Perry, and Weiss (1986) found that most children believe that a girl who helped her father unload the car at the beach would be less happy than a girl who immediately ran to the shore to play; only adolescents (eighth graders) claimed that a helpful individual is likely to be happier than a selfish one. In short, most adolescents have clearly internalized at least some of society's moral values, and many are highly motivated to be the kinds of moral beings that people around them want them to be, even if they do not always behave in the most moral ways.

THE ADULT

During adulthood, we continually make decisions that have consequences for ourselves and those around us, decisions that are influenced by our motives and moral values. The adult whose affiliation motive is strong may turn down a promotion in order to maintain a close relationship, while the adult who is highly achievement oriented may sacrifice relationships in order to climb the career ladder. And because adults have responsibilities as employers or work supervisors, parents, or community leaders, their moral decisions affect those around them. Here we will try to understand how the strengths of different motives change over the adult years, how the moral thinking of adults differs from that of children or adolescents, and how adults attempt to find a larger meaning in their lives.

Motivations During the Adult Years

An adult's characteristic motives can have much to do with his or her decisions and life outcomes. For instance, women who have a strong need to achieve are more likely to work outside the home than women who are less achievement oriented (Krogh, 1985). Moreover, adults who are high in the need for achievement are more competent workers than adults who have little concern with working hard and mastering challenges (Helmreich, Sawin, & Carsrud, 1986; Spence, 1985).

Characteristic motives such as a high need for achievement typically take shape during childhood. The child who has a strong need for achievement is likely to remain an achievement-oriented adult (Kagan & Moss, 1962), and the highly achievement-oriented young adult is likely to remain relatively achievement oriented in middle age (Stevens & Truss, 1985). However, this kind of individual consistency does not necessarily mean that middle-aged adults are as highly achievement oriented as young adults are. It would be possible for most adults to lose some of their drive over the years, even though some of them are consistently more achievement oriented than their peers. Are middle-aged or older adults generally less achievement oriented than younger adults? Do needs for affiliation change over the adult years? How do changes in work or family situations affect the strengths of important motives?

Let's explore these questions by examining a study of adult motivations conducted by Joseph Veroff, David Reuman, and Sheila Feld (1984). These investigators reported on two national surveys of American adults, one conducted in 1957 and the other in 1976. Asking respondents to tell stories in response to pictures, Veroff and his associates measured four motives:

1. The *motive to achieve,* or to attain standards of excellence
2. The *motive to affiliate,* or to form and maintain close relationships
3. The *motive for power as fear of weakness,* or a concern with avoiding being controlled or having low status compared to others
4. A *motive for power as hope of power,* or a disposition to have an impact on the world

One interesting finding of this study—one that highlights the importance of contextual factors in development—was that adults of certain cohorts appeared to have distinctive lifelong motivations. Women who were adolescents or young adults during World War II, for example, appeared to be more achievement oriented when tested in 1957 and again in 1976 than earlier or later generations of women. Possibly this is because they took on major work responsibilities during the war. In studying age differences and similarities in characteristic motives, Veroff and his associates identified those age trends that were consistent in both the 1957 and 1976 surveys. These trends differed for men and women, so we'll discuss the two sexes separately, drawing on related studies in trying to picture how motivations might change during adulthood.

As Figure 12.5 shows, young, middle-aged, and older men in the Veroff studies were about equally motivated to achieve, to affiliate with others, and to avoid appearing weak. Here, then, we find no support at all for the stereotyped idea that older adults are "unmotivated" or have ceased to pursue goals, and we see that performing well and having close relationships are important goals throughout the adult years. However, middle-aged men, especially those aged 50 to 54, were more motivated by the hope of power than either younger or older men. Veroff suggests that middle-aged men may reach a point in life at which they strongly desire to have an impact through their work but perhaps worry that they cannot do so.

Not all studies of men's motives are consistent (Heckhausen, 1986). For example, although Veroff et al. (1984) found that achievement motivation changed little with age, some studies indicate that it increases from young adulthood to middle adulthood (Stevens & Truss, 1985; Veroff, Atkinson, Feld, & Gurin, 1960) and then tapers off in later middle age and old age (Veroff et al., 1960). Moreover, different individuals show different patterns of

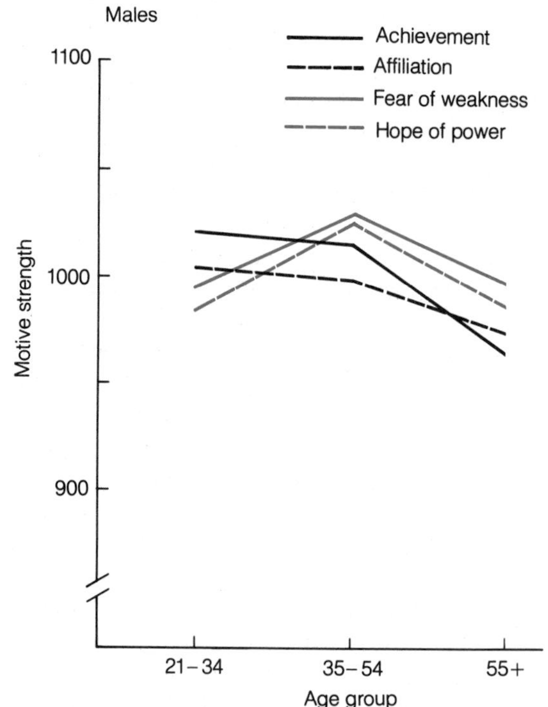

Figure 12.5 Strength of different motives in men of different ages: 1957 and 1976 data combined. A score of 1000 is average overall. (Data from Veroff, Reuman, & Feld, 1984)

change. Why? As Joel Raynor (1982) suggests, this may be because different men follow different career paths. The man who has career goals but fails to achieve them would be expected to lose some achievement motivation over the years as a result of repeated failure. Surprisingly, the man who has clear goals and step-by-step moves closer to fulfilling them might also lose achievement motivation if he has nothing further to strive for. If Harry always wanted to own his own company and finally succeeds, he may feel quite bored and aimless once his company is running smoothly. Other men may be able to maintain a strong achievement orientation throughout their adult lives if they continually devise new goals to replace the goals that they achieve.

In short, achievement motivation might increase, remain steady, or decrease depending on whether the individual's efforts meet with success or failure and whether the individual is able to form new goals once old goals are attained. Thus no one pattern of changing achievement motivation fits all.

How do women's motives change over the years? Veroff and his associates (1984) found that younger and older women were equal in their needs for power. However, the affiliation and achievement motives of younger and older women did differ, as shown in Figure 12.6.

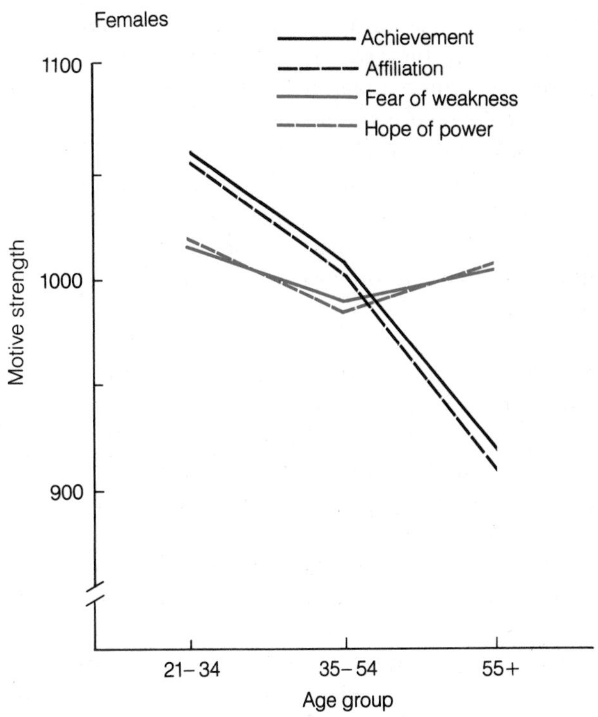

Figure 12.6 Strength of different motives in women of different ages: 1957 and 1976 data combined. A score of 1000 is average overall. (Data from Veroff, Reuman, & Feld, 1984)

The motive to affiliate diminished with age. Veroff proposed that young women were likely to be highly concerned with finding a marriage partner and establishing a friendship network and therefore were especially insecure about their relationships; older women had found ways to satisfy these affiliative needs and were therefore less preoccupied with them. This "feminine" pattern of a decline in the affiliation motive was not evident among women who had high-prestige careers, but it *was* evident among men who held low-prestige jobs and perhaps were not as work oriented as most men or as career-oriented women. Veroff believes that highly career-oriented adults of both sexes continue to face uncertainties in their relationships and so continue to have strong affiliation needs.

The second major age trend in female motivations was a decline in achievement motivation (see also Mellinger & Erdwins, 1985). This trend pertained exclusively to *career-related* motivations; older women were just as concerned as younger women with performing daily tasks competently. Possibly, then, older adults of both sexes may become less motivated to pursue long-term career goals but may remain highly motivated to perform *today's* tasks as competently as possible (Maehr & Kleiber, 1981).

It makes sense to think that a woman might set aside career-achievement goals as she invests her energies in nurturing children. Indeed, this seems to be the case; most mothers place higher value on nurturing their children than on meeting their own achievement needs (Krogh, 1985). However, highly educated women appear to regain a strong motive to achieve outside the home once their children are older and they can invest more energy in outside work. For example, among highly competent young female Radcliffe students, the need for achievement was high during and immediately after college, dropped off during the primary child-rearing years, and increased once again when the women were in their late 30s and their children were more independent (Baruch, 1967; Malatesta

& Culver, 1984). By contrast, less-educated women are less likely to regain their career-related achievement motivation as their children mature; instead, their need for individual achievement simply declines over the years (Baruch, 1967). Apparently, then, women are especially likely to be motivated to achieve when they have the educational background that would allow them to pursue attractive career goals and when they are not preoccupied by other needs—the motive to affiliate or to nurture children, for example.

From this evidence it appears that adults' motives are more affected by their life situations or social contexts than by the aging process. Adults of different ages are often more alike in their most pressing motives than they are different, and there is little evidence that elderly people lose their motivation. Moreover, the *individual's* characteristic motives tend to remain fairly stable or consistent over the years, much as many personality traits do. When motives *do* change over the adult years, the change is often related to specific life experiences—for example, a history of failures, a realization that one cannot progress any further in a career, or a release from child-rearing responsibilities. Even an increased opportunity to satisfy a motive may make that motive less compelling. Predominant motives can and do change during adulthood, but most of us seek to demonstrate competence, maintain close relationships, and influence other people throughout our lives. We also retain our motivation to make morally sound decisions.

Moral Development During the Adult Years

How does moral thinking change during adulthood? As we have discovered already (see Figure 12.4, p. 389), Kohlberg's postconventional moral reasoning appears to emerge *only* during the adult years, if it emerges at all. In Kohlberg's 20- year longitudinal study (Colby et al., 1983), the large majority of adults in their 30s still reasoned at the conventional level, although many adults had shifted from stage 3 to stage 4. A minority of individuals—one-sixth to one-eighth of the sample of men—had begun to use stage 5 postconventional reasoning, showing a deeper understanding of the basis for laws and distinguishing between just and unjust laws. There is clearly moral growth in early adulthood (Walker, 1989). Do these growth trends continue into later adulthood, or do older adults instead revert to less mature forms of moral reasoning?

In previous chapters, we have encountered evidence that elderly people do not perform as well as young and middle-aged adults do on many cognitive tasks. In keeping with this evidence, one of the first studies of moral reasoning in adulthood (Bielby & Papalia, 1975) indicated that the average elderly person reasoned at a less mature stage of moral reasoning than the average young or middle-aged adult did. More recent studies paint a very different picture, however. They suggest that there are no real age differences in stage of moral reasoning, at least when relatively educated adults are studied and when the age groups compared have similar levels of education (Chap, 1985–1986; Pratt, Golding, & Hunter, 1983; Pratt, Golding, & Kerig, 1987). Although no longitudinal studies are available, these cross-sectional comparisons suggest that moral thinking does not deteriorate in old age.

Indeed, some researchers are uncovering hints that elderly adults (and, to a lesser extent, middle-aged adults as well) may be *more* morally sophisticated than young adults. Older adults appear to have firmer opinions about what is morally right and wrong (Chap, 1985–1986). Moreover, Michael Pratt and his associates have found that elderly adults reformulate the issues raised by moral dilemmas in their own ways (Pratt, Golding, Hunter, & Norris, 1988), reflect more on these issues (Pratt et al., 1987), and, perhaps as a result, are sometimes more consistent in their moral reasoning from dilemma to dilemma than younger adults are (Pratt et al., 1983).

However we look at these findings, we can find little evidence that people regress in old age to more self-centered or immature perspectives on moral issues. Instead, older people usually seem to maintain the level of moral reasoning they developed earlier in adulthood and may even integrate their thinking into a more coherent moral philosophy. Kohlberg (1973) himself argued that experience confronting moral issues and taking responsibility for one's decisions during a lifetime may help adults form more coherent moral outlooks (see also Gibbs, 1979). Certainly the interesting possibility that moral growth continues throughout adulthood deserves more attention.

KOHLBERG'S THEORY OF MORAL DEVELOPMENT IN PERSPECTIVE

We have now seen that children think about hypothetical moral dilemmas primarily in a preconventional manner, that adolescents adopt a conventional mode of moral reasoning, and that a minority of adults progress to the postconventional level of reasoning in Kohlberg's system. Kohlberg appears to have discovered an important developmental progression in moral thought. But let's now complete our discussion of moral reasoning by evaluating Kohlberg's theory, examining both the evidence that supports the theory and the criticisms that have been made of it.

Evidence Supportive of Kohlberg's Stage Sequence

Recall that Kohlberg claims that his stages form an invariant and universal sequence of moral growth. Do all people progress through the stages in precisely the order Kohlberg specified? It appears that they do, to a point. Several longitudinal studies of moral growth that have tracked the same individuals over time demonstrate this—for example, studies in the United States (Colby et al., 1983; Walker, 1989), one in Turkey (Nisan & Kohlberg, 1982), and one in Israel (Snarey, Reimer, & Kohlberg, 1985). Regardless of their culture, individuals do not skip stages. Moreover, only about 5% of them regress from a higher stage to a lower stage from one testing to the next, and these instances of regression are so few that they probably reflect scoring errors. However, the idea that everyone progresses through stages 1 to 4 in order is better supported than the idea that people continue to progress from stage 4 to stages 5 and 6. Stage 3 or 4 is the end of the developmental journey for most individuals.

Factors That Promote Moral Growth

How much support is there for Kohlberg's thinking about the factors that contribute to moral growth? Basically, he has argued, as Piaget did, that two influences are most important: cognitive growth and relevant social experiences.

Cognitive Growth

What kind of cognitive growth is necessary? The preconventional reasoner adopts an egocentric, very concrete perspective on moral issues. To reach the conventional stage of moral reasoning and become concerned about living up to the moral standards that significant others transmit, an individual must be capable of taking other people's perspectives (Walker, 1980). Gaining the capacity for postconventional or "principled" moral reasoning requires still more cognitive growth—namely, a solid command of formal-operational thinking (Tomlinson-Keasey & Keasey, 1974; Walker, 1980). The person who bases moral judgments on abstract principles must be able to reason abstractly and take all possible perspectives on a moral issue. Both perspective-taking abilities and more general cognitive abilities appear to be *necessary but not sufficient* for moral growth, however. In other words, not all proficient role-takers have reached the conventional level of moral reasoning, and not all formal operators progress to the *post*conventional level of moral reasoning, but these milestones in moral development cannot be achieved without the requisite cognitive skills.

Relevant Social Experience

The second major influence on moral development proposed by Kohlberg is relevant social experience. What social experiences matter? Kohlberg stressed the need for experiences that require people to take the perspectives of others so that they can appreciate that they are part of a larger social order and that moral rules are a consensus of individuals in society. Interacting with people who hold views different from one's own also creates *cognitive disequilibrium*, or a conflict between existing cognitive structures and new ideas, which in turn stimulates new ways of thinking.

One sure way to experience differences in perspective is to interact with peers. Like Piaget, Kohlberg felt that interactions with equals probably contribute more to moral growth than one-sided interactions with adult authority figures in which children are expected to defer to the adults. Children do seem to think more deeply about their own and their partners' moral ideas in discussions with peers than in talks with their mothers (Kruger & Tomasello, 1986). Moreover, popular children who often take part in social activities and who assume positions of leadership in the peer group tend to make mature moral judgments (Keasey, 1971). Presumably college students who engage in many "bull sessions" with their friends, debating the pros and cons of the burning issues of the day, are contributing to their moral growth (see the "Applications" section at the end of this chapter). And for women, at least, the simple experience of hashing out everyday decisions jointly with one's spouse seems to contribute to moral growth (Walker, 1986).

A second important kind of social experience is receiving an advanced education. For example, students who go on to college experience more moral growth after leaving high school than those who do not (Boldizar, Wilson, & Deemer, 1989; Rest & Thoma, 1985). It is likely that advanced educational experiences not only contribute to cognitive growth but give students opportunities to be exposed to the diverse ideas and perspectives that produce cognitive conflict and soul-searching.

Finally, still another relevant social experience is living in a complex, diverse, and democratic society. Just as we learn the give-and-take of mutual perspective taking by discussing issues with our friends, we learn in a diverse democracy that the opinions of many groups must be weighed and that laws reflect a consensus of the citizens rather than the arbitrary rulings of a dictator. Indeed, cross-cultural studies of moral reasoning suggest that postconventional moral reasoning emerges primarily in Western democracies. By contrast, it is not at all unusual to find that people in rural villages in underdeveloped countries show absolutely no signs of postconventional reasoning (Harkness, Edwards, & Super, 1981; Snarey, 1985; Tietjen & Walker, 1985). People in these homogeneous communities may have less experience with the kinds of political conflicts and compromises that are necessary in a more complex society and so may never have any need to question conventional moral standards. By adopting a contextual perspective on development, we can appreciate that the conventional (mostly stage 3) reasoning displayed by adults in these societies is adaptive and mature within their own social systems (Harkness et al., 1981).

Adults in many rural societies seem to have no need for postconventional moral reasoning.

In sum, Kohlberg not only devised a stage sequence that appears to have universal applicability but he correctly identified some of the major factors that determine how far an individual progresses in the sequence. Advanced moral reasoning is most likely if the individual has acquired the necessary cognitive skills (particularly perspective-taking skills and, later, the ability to reason abstractly). Moreover, an individual's moral development is highly influenced by social context, particularly by opportunities to interact with individuals who express a variety of opinions and perspectives (through discussing issues with peers as well as through receiving advanced schooling or participating in a democracy made up of diverse groups with diverse perspectives). It seems that individuals everywhere progress from the preconventional to the conventional level of moral reasoning, but that only those individuals who have sophisticated formal-operational skills and particular kinds of social experiences ever reach the postconventional level of moral judgment.

Is Kohlberg's theory of moral development sound, then? Not entirely, say the critics. Whenever a theory arouses the enormous interest that Kohlberg's has aroused, you can bet that it will also provoke an enormous amount of criticism. Many of the criticisms have centered on the possibility that Kohlberg's theory is biased against certain groups of people and on the fact that it says much about moral reasoning but little about moral affect, motivation, and behavior.

Is Kohlberg's Theory Biased?

Some critics have charged that Kohlberg's theory reflects a cultural bias, a liberal bias, and/or a sexist bias. Charges have been made that the stage theory unfairly makes people from non-Western cultures, people with conservative values, or the half of the human race that is female appear to be less than morally mature.

Although research indicates that children and adolescents in the cultures that have been studied proceed through the first three or four stages in order, we have seen that postconventional reasoning simply does not exist in some societies. Critics charge that Kohlberg's highest stages reflect a Western ideal of justice, and that the stage theory is therefore biased against people who live in non-Western societies or who do not value individualism and individual rights highly enough to want to challenge society's rules (Gibbs & Schnell, 1985). People in societies that emphasize social harmony and place the good of the group ahead of the good of the individual may be viewed as conventional moral thinkers in Kohlberg's system but may actually have very sophisticated concepts of justice (Snarey, 1985; Tietjen & Walker, 1985).

Similarly, critics charge that a person must hold liberal values—must, for example, oppose capital punishment or support civil disobedience in the name of human rights—in order to be classified as a postconventional moral reasoner. In one study (de Vries & Walker, 1986), 100% of the college students who showed signs of postconventional thought opposed capital punishment, while none of the men and only a third of the women who were transitional between stage 2 and stage 3 moral reasoning opposed capital punishment. As de Vries and Walker (1986) note, it could be that opposition to capital punishment actually is a more valid moral position than support of capital punishment in that it involves valuing life highly. However, it could also be that the theory is unfair to conservatives who emphasize "law-and-order" principles (Lapsley, Harwell, Olson, Flannery, & Quintana, 1984).

These criticisms may have some merit. However, no criticism of Kohlberg has stirred more heat than the charge that his theory is biased against women. Carol Gilligan (1977, 1982) has been disturbed by the fact that Kohlberg's stages were based on interviews with males and that, in some studies, women seemed to be the moral inferiors of men, reasoning at stage 3 of Kohlberg's stage sequence when men usually reasoned at stage 4. She proposes that females develop a distinctly *feminine* orientation to moral issues, one that is no less mature than the orientation adopted by most men and incorporated in Kohlberg's theory. Gilligan suggests that boys are traditionally raised to be independent, assertive, and achievement oriented and consequently come to view moral dilemmas as inevitable conflicts between the rights of two or more parties and to view laws and other social conventions as necessary for resolving these conflicts (a perspective reflected in Kohlberg's stage 4 reasoning). By contrast, girls are brought up to be nurturant, empathic, and concerned about the needs of others—in short, to define their sense of "goodness" in terms of their concern for other people. These experiences, Gilligan argues, should encourage females to think of moral dilemmas as conflicts between one's own selfishness and the needs or desires of others (a perspective that approximates stage 3 in Kohlberg's scheme). The differences boil down to the difference between a "masculine" *morality of justice* (in which laws defining rights and responsibilities prevail) and a "feminine" *morality of care* or responsibility (in which the welfare of the people involved is most central).

Gilligan derived stages in the development of a morality of care by analyzing interviews with 29 pregnant women facing the difficult dilemma of deciding whether to continue their pregnancies or have abortions. In the first stage, self-interest guides decisions; in the second, a woman is willing to sacrifice self-interest for the welfare of other people; and in the third, a woman adopts a complex morality of care in which the goal is to avoid hurting *either* the self or other people. This mature morality of care is reflected in the thinking of one 25-year-old: "I would not be doing myself or the child a favor by having this child. . . . I don't need to pay off my imaginary debts to the world through this child, and I don't think that it is right to bring a child into the world and use it for that purpose" (1977, p. 505).

At this point, there is little support for Gilligan's claim that Kohlberg's theory is systematically biased against females, for most studies indicate that women reason just as complexly about moral issues as men do when their answers are scored by Kohlberg's criteria (Thoma, 1986; Walker, 1984, 1989). Nor is it clear that women think entirely differently about moral dilemmas than men do. However, Gilligan's work has increased our awareness that *both* men and women often think about moral issues—especially real life as opposed to hypothetical moral issues—in terms of their responsibilities for the welfare of other people (Ford & Lowery, 1986; Lyons, 1983; Walker, 1989). Perhaps Kohlberg has emphasized only one way, a very legalistic way, of thinking about right and wrong, and there is merit in tracing the development of *both* a morality of justice and a morality of care (Brabeck, 1983).

Is Kohlberg's Theory Incomplete?

Another major criticism of Kohlberg's theory is that it focuses so much on moral reasoning that it almost entirely ignores moral affect and moral behavior. The charge, then, is that it provides an incomplete view of moral development (Gibbs & Schnell, 1985; Haan, Aerts, & Cooper, 1985). For example, Norma Haan and her colleagues (1985) insist that moral dilemmas in everyday life arouse powerful emotions. We care about moral issues and about the people who will be affected by our decisions; we agonize about what to do; we very much want to feel that we are moral beings, and our egos are threatened when we act immorally. Such emotions play a central role in morality by motivating our actions, and any theory that overlooks the role of emotions and motivations in morality is incomplete. Moreover, Haan argues, what we should ultimately be interested in when we study morality is how people actually behave in specific situations. It may be interesting to know what moral principles people hold or how they think about moral issues, but since people often do not act according to their principles, we should be more concerned with figuring why they act as they do.

There is no question that Kohlberg has been primarily concerned with moral reasoning rather than with moral affect and behavior. Moreover, as already noted, a person might decide to uphold or to break a law at any of the stages of moral reasoning. What distinguishes one stage from the next is the complexity or structure of a person's reasoning, not the specific decisions he or she reaches. Nonetheless, Kohlberg has argued that more advanced moral reasoners are more likely to behave in accordance with widely accepted moral standards than less advanced moral reasoners are. He would predict, for example, that the preconventional thinker might readily decide to cheat on a test if the chances of being detected were small and the potential rewards high. The postconventional thinker would be more likely to appreciate that cheating is wrong in principle, regardless of the chances of detection, because it infringes on the rights of others and undermines social order.

How well *does* a person's stage of moral reasoning predict that person's behavior? Many researchers have found that the moral judgments of young children do *not* predict what they will do when they are given a chance to cheat or violate other moral norms (Nelson, Grinder, & Biaggio, 1969; Santrock, 1975; Toner & Potts, 1981). However, studies of older grade school children, adolescents, and adults often find at least some consistency between moral reasoning and conduct. Individuals at higher stages of moral reasoning are more likely than individuals at lower stages to behave altruistically and conscientiously and are less likely to cheat or engage in delinquent or criminal activity (see Blasi, 1980; Kohlberg & Candee, 1984; Linn, 1989). Kohlberg (1975), for example, found that only 15% of students who reasoned at the postconventional level cheated when given an opportunity to cheat, compared with 55% of the students at the conventional level of moral reasoning and 70% of those at the preconventional level (see also Malinowski & Smith, 1985).

Just as Kohlberg expected, however, the relationship between stage of moral reasoning and moral behavior is far from perfect. For example, even though juvenile delinquents are more likely than nondelinquents to function at the preconventional level of moral reasoning, a sizable number of delinquents are capable of conventional moral reasoning but break the law anyway (Blasi, 1980). This lack of a strong correspondence between moral cognition and moral behavior suggests that many personal qualities besides level of moral reasoning, and many situational or contextual factors as well, also influence whether a person will behave morally or immorally in daily life (Haan et al., 1985; Kurtines, 1986).

In sum, Kohlberg's theory of moral development has become prominent for good reason. It does indeed describe a universal sequence of changes in moral reasoning extending from childhood through adulthood. Moreover, the evidence supports Kohlberg's view that both cognitive growth and social experiences contribute to moral growth. However, there is also some merit to criticisms of the theory. The theory may indeed be somewhat biased against people who live in non-Western societies, who hold values other than individualistic and democratic ones, or who emphasize a "morality of care" rather than a morality of abstract rights. Moreover, because Kohlberg's theory focuses entirely on moral reasoning, we must rely on other perspectives such as social learning theory to understand how moral affect and moral behavior develop, and how thought, emotion, and behavior interact to make us the moral beings we ultimately become.

RELIGIOUS DEVELOPMENT AND THE SEARCH FOR MEANING IN LIFE

Many people cannot think about morality without thinking about the religious beliefs that they have come to hold. Even people who do not consider themselves religious often develop philosophies of life that give them a sense of meaning and direction. Let us briefly examine the spiritual side of human development by asking two questions: First, to what extent do people of different ages care about and participate in religious activities? And second, how do the ways in which we make sense of our existence change over the life span?

Involvement in Religion

Children's levels of participation in religious activities are often influenced by their parents' wishes; adults more often make their own choices. How does involvement in religion change over the adult years? A stereotype of elderly people has it that they become highly religious as they prepare for death. The stereotype is reflected in this conversation between two children: "The first asked 'Why is Grandma spending so much time reading the Bible these days?' 'I guess she is cramming for final exams,' the second replied" (Blazer & Palmore, 1976, p. 82). On the other hand, it might be predicted that elderly people become *less* involved in religion as they begin to experience health problems or disengage themselves from social activities.

Which is it? It depends on what we mean when we describe a person as religious. If we mean attending church and participating in other organized religious activities, it appears that older adults are less religiously involved than younger adults (Ainlay & Smith, 1984; Blazer & Palmore, 1976; Moberg, 1965). As elderly people become less socially active generally, they often reduce their participation in organized religious activities. However, being religious means more than attending services and meetings. In their 20-year longitudinal study of religiosity in later life, Dan Blazer and Erdman Palmore (1976; Palmore, 1981) periodically asked adults who were age 60 to age 94 at the start of the study questions about both their religious activity and their religious attitudes. Religious activity (attending church, reading the Bible, and so on) did decline among these adults as they aged, especially among those who were already age 70 or older at the start of the study. However, there was no change at all in religious attitudes (viewing religion as very important and as a great comfort).

Notice that these findings offer no support at all for the view that people "get religion" or cling to it more strongly in old age. However, Ainlay and Hunter (cited by Ainlay & Smith, 1984) report that while participation in organized religious activities does indeed decrease from middle age to old age, involvement in *private* religious activities—prayer and Bible study, for example—increases with age (see also Young & Dowling, 1987). The message? The importance of religion does not change much at all with age, and elderly adults may substitute private or informal religious activity for more formal observances.

Does being highly religious contribute in any way to an adult's well-being? It appears that it does, although we cannot be sure that religious involvement actually *causes* increased well-being. Adults who emphasize the importance of religion and who are religiously active feel happier, better adjusted, and more useful (Blazer & Palmore, 1976), and have a stronger sense of meaning in their lives (Tellis-Nayak, 1982), than less religious individuals do. More generally, adults appear to be highly motivated to make sense of life or to find meaning in it, and those who do achieve a firm sense of purpose and meaning experience greater physical and psychological well-being than

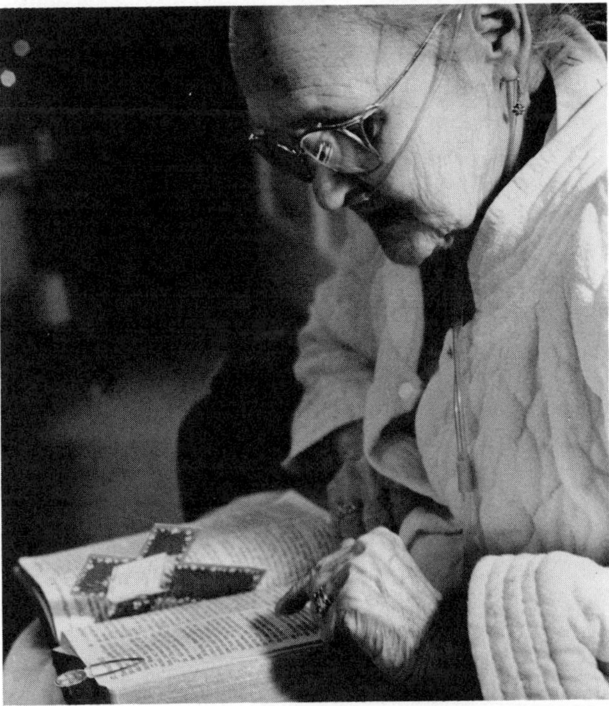

Participation in organized religious activities declines in old age, but interest in religion does not.

those who do not (Reker, Peacock, & Wong, 1987). It is useful, then, to look more closely at the ways in which people of different ages go about their quest for meaning.

Age Differences in the Nature of Faith

James Fowler (1981) has taken on the challenging task of describing the development of **faith**—by which he means the ways in which we make or find meaning in our lives. Faith, then, is much broader than a set of specific religious beliefs and need not have much to do with organized religion. Fowler claims that the quest for meaning is universal: "We do not live by bread alone, sex alone, success alone. . . . We require meaning. We need purpose and priorities; we must have some grasp on the big picture" (p. 4).

Fowler proposed six stages of faith based on the theories of Piaget, Erikson, and Kohlberg, as well as on interviews with individuals ranging in age from 3 to 84. These stages, as outlined in Box 12.2, show some striking parallels to Kohlberg's stages of moral reasoning. Like Kohlberg, Fowler believes that progress through his stages depends on both cognitive development and social experiences (especially life crises that force us to reflect). Basically, Fowler pictures the development of faith during childhood and adolescence as a movement from concrete images of God to more abstract systems of meaning, most often based on the religious beliefs that we have been taught. In early adulthood, at least some people who have solid command of formal-operational thought progress to the stage of **individuative-reflective faith**. For the first time, they engage in serious reflection about the meaning of life and develop a philosophy that is uniquely their own, whether it is like or unlike the conventional belief system that they held as children or adolescents. According to Fowler, a few adults progress even farther and begin to perceive a oneness in all religions and philosophies.

Fowler's cross-sectional comparison of children and adults of different ages supports his stages and the age ranges he attaches to them. Unfortunately, no longitudinal research has yet been conducted to determine if people actually progress through these stages in order as they get older. Still, Fowler's fascinating ideas about the development of faith add to our knowledge of the development of the self. It does indeed seem that we are motivated throughout the life span to make sense of our existence and to find purpose and direction in our lives.

APPLICATIONS: STIMULATING MORAL DEVELOPMENT

As we think about how human beings acquire important values that guide their behavior, we naturally come to a very practical question: How can we encourage children and adolescents to develop "good" values and become highly moral beings? Earlier, we saw that parents can contribute considerably to their children's moral development by being good role models, reinforcing moral action and punishing immoral action, and using the discipline technique of induction so that children understand why their misbehavior is wrong. But what might peers be able to contribute to an individual's moral development? If, as both Piaget and Kohlberg claim, peers are at least as important as parents in stimulating moral growth, perhaps the most direct way in which to raise levels of moral thought is to harness "peer power."

This is precisely what many psychologists and educators have attempted to do. They have put individuals together in pairs or small groups to discuss hypothetical moral dilemmas. The rationale is quite simple: Exposure to forms of moral reasoning more mature than one's own will stimulate advances in moral reasoning. Cognitive disequilibrium will be produced when students experience discrepancies between their own thinking and that of other individuals. This cognitive imbalance will motivate them to devise more mature modes of thinking. Ideally, then, groups should be composed of students who do indeed reason at different stages of moral development rather than students who reason alike.

Does participation in group discussions produce more mature moral reasoning? The many studies reviewed by Andre Schlaefli, James Rest, and Stephen Thoma (1985) say yes. Average changes that are the equivalent of about four to five years of natural development can be achieved in programs lasting for about three to twelve weeks. Thus it does seem possible to speed the rate at which individuals progress through Kohlberg's stages of moral reasoning.

Moreover, researchers have learned something about what kinds of discussion are most helpful. For example, it is indeed important that students be exposed to reasoning that is slightly more mature than their own (Berkowitz, 1985). Even more interesting is evidence that moral growth is most likely to occur when students become involved in particular kinds of dialogues or transactions.

Box 12.2
Fowler's Stages of Faith

James Fowler (1981) maintains that a lifelong quest for meaning begins when infants learn to trust their caregivers. In these earliest interactions, they learn that they are separate from but dependent upon others and begin to sense that powerful adults can protect them from dangers such as the threat of separation. Fowler's six stages of faith build on this foundation:

1. **Intuitive-projective faith** (early childhood). Young preoperational children, with their great imaginative capacities, pick up fragments of religious stories and invent their own images of good and evil forces in the world. Their descriptions of God are very concrete: "He has a light shirt on, he has brown hair, he has brown eyelashes" (Fowler, 1981, p. 127). They do the best they can to make sense of religious teachings. Yet we must wonder what it all means to the young child—for example, to the young girl from Connecticut whose version of the Lord's Prayer went, "Our Father who art in New Haven, Harold be they name" (Fischer & Lazerson, 1984, p. 332).

2. **Mythic-literal faith** (the school-aged child). As they gain capacities for logical thought (concrete operations), children develop more coherent, but still very concrete, ways of ordering the world. Religious teachings are interpreted literally, and God is often likened to a parent figure, a loving disciplinarian who rewards the good and punishes the bad. Some adolescents and adults continue to function at this concrete level.

3. **Synthetic-conventional faith** (adolescence). As they acquire even more advanced, formal-operational cognitive abilities, adolescents take what they have been taught and synthesize it into a coherent belief system that expresses their identity and ties them to other people. Although synthetic-conventional faith is more abstract than earlier forms of faith, the individual is largely conforming to the values of significant others and has not yet seriously reflected about alternative ideologies.

4. **Individuative-reflective faith** (early adulthood). Through serious questioning and analysis of alternative beliefs and values, some adults find a sense of meaning that is their own unique philosophy rather than one they have adopted quite uncritically from other people. One person at this level might continue to accept many of the beliefs of the religion in which he or she was brought up—but only after a period of thoughtfully evaluating what really matters and what does not. Another might construct a philosophy of life or ideology that has little to do with organized religion—for example, the young man described by Fowler who, as a result of his military experience, began to see a world in which the rich and powerful oppress the poor and powerless. According to Fowler, the transition to individuative-reflective faith is unlikely unless a person is uprooted from his or her familiar environment and exposed to new ideas—possibly by going off to college!

5. **Conjunctive faith** (middle age). A few adults establish an even more abstract and complex sense of meaning that allows them to deal with paradoxes and interpret reality in multiple ways. Whereas the stage 4 adult tends to have the world neatly defined in terms of a coherent ideology of his or her own making, the stage 5 adult is more open to new experiences. A 78-year-old woman interviewed by Fowler expressed this complex world view: "Whether you call it God or Jesus or Cosmic Flow or Reality or Love, it doesn't matter what you call it. It is there. And what you learn directly from that source will not tie you up in creeds . . . that separate you from your fellow man" (Fowler, 1981, p. 192).

6. **Universalizing faith** (middle age or beyond). Finally, just as Kohlberg believes that there is an ideal form of moral reasoning described by his sixth stage (Universal Principle), Fowler believes that a few individuals such as Mahatma Gandhi or Mother Teresa somehow transcend specific belief systems and life's mysteries to achieve a sense of oneness with all beings and a commitment to breaking down the barriers that divide people. You'll have to read Fowler's fascinating book to get the full flavor of this stage!

Fowler finds that adults can fit into any of the stages from stage 2 to stage 6. However, the most common forms of faith during adulthood are the synthetic-conventional and the individuative-reflective. Conjunctive faith does not appear before age 30 and remains rare even in later life, and only one person Fowler interviewed met the requirements of stage 6. Much work remains to be done to test the validity of Fowler's provocative theory, but he makes one point very convincingly: No matter what our age, we seem to need to impose some sense of meaning on life.

Marvin Berkowitz and John Gibbs (1983) have identified the kinds of transactions that are particularly useful. Rather than merely talking past one another or paraphrasing each other, the students who benefit the most from discussions actively transform, analyze, or otherwise act upon what their conversation partners have said. They say things such as "You're missing an important distinction here," "Let me elaborate on your view," and "Here's some-

Box 12.3
The "Just Community" Approach to Fostering Morality

Lawrence Kohlberg (1985) and his colleagues attempted to create a special moral environment called the "Just Community" in selected high schools—to have students and teachers jointly decide on rules, discuss the real moral issues facing them, and democratically decide how to handle discipline cases. Instead of talking about hypothetical moral issues, the community of students and teachers talks about and formulates rules concerning pressing problems of drug use, race relations, cheating, and student apathy. The Just Community is obviously quite different from a traditional school in which rules are handed down by school authorities, and it is designed to help students see themselves as part of a larger community, to understand and respect the perspectives of others, and to care about the welfare of the entire community. The program was launched in a lower-income area of Cambridge, Massachusetts, as well as in the wealthy suburb of Scarsdale, New York.

Not all the data are in, but the Just Community experience appears to have an impact on moral reasoning similar to that of group discussions of hypothetical moral issues. However, Kohlberg's goal was not merely to push students from one stage to the next, but to change the entire moral atmosphere of the school. He reported that the approach has been successful at doing just that—at creating a real sense of community in which the prevailing peer norms are supportive of moral behavior (see also Power, 1985). In Scarsdale, for example, teachers wanted students to stop cheating, but students felt pressure from home to get good grades, were unconcerned about cheating, and were not about to "squeal" on their friends. Through lengthy discussion during a community meeting, the group finally decided that cheating was indeed harming noncheaters and undermining trust between teachers and students. The community decided to institute a plan in which anyone who observed an instance of cheating had a responsibility to confront the cheater and to report the behavior to the disciplinary committee if the cheater did not do so first. It was very difficult for students to "rat" on their friends at first, but they began to see that they had an obligation to each other to do so. Perhaps it will take ambitious efforts such as the Just Community approach to produce enduring commitments to moral action among today's students.

thing I think we can both agree on." It is when discussion partners really do something cognitively with what they hear others say that they experience moral growth.

Although discussion of moral issues can stimulate moral growth, Kohlberg (1985) and his colleagues decided that more significant and lasting changes might be achieved by altering the entire moral atmosphere of a school to create a democratically governed and caring community. This **Just Community** approach to moral education is described in Box 12.3. Demonstrations like these suggest that parents, peers, and schools can all contribute to the making of more moral and caring citizens.

REFLECTIONS

We hope that this chapter has stimulated you to think about your own priorities—about whether your achievement motive or your affiliation motive is stronger, about whether you are studying right now for the sake of learning or for the sake of a grade, and, of course, about which of Kohlberg's stages of moral reasoning fits you best and about what moral values guide your decisions. We'll leave you to your own reflections—though we do hope you'll go out and engage your friends in some stimulating discussion of the moral issues of our time!

What we will note here is that we have now completed our series of chapters on the development of the self, or the person as an individual. In Chapter 10, we looked at the development of self-conceptions and distinctive personality traits. We established that some personality traits are quite stable over the years, but we also discovered that our understandings of what we are like as individuals change immensely from infancy to adulthood. In Chapter 11, we centered attention on our identities as males or females, exploring the many implications of sex and gender roles for the individual's development. It seems there is not a day when we are not aware of being either a man or a woman. Moreover, many of the choices we make in life are influenced by social norms that tell us what a man or a woman should be. In the present chapter, of course, we have concentrated on the ways in which our identities as individuals partly reflect our characteristic motives and moral standards. Overall, then, we emerge from childhood and adolescence as unique individuals with our own distinctive personalities and abilities, conceptions of ourselves, driving motivations, and moral values and habits. We continue to evolve as individuals during adulthood as we enter new roles and face new social demands.

But individual development does not occur in a vacuum; it must be viewed from a contextual perspective. Repeatedly, we have described the ways in which parents, peers, and other socialization agents help shape each individual's development. We have seen that the individual's development may take different forms depending on the historical and social context in which it occurs. Our task in upcoming chapters will be to put the individual even more squarely in a social context. We will examine the development of social relationships in the next chapter, starting with the infant's formation of an attachment to a parent. In Chapter 14, we'll put the individual in a family context, exploring what it means to be a family member during each phase of the life span and how the family itself develops and changes over time. Finally, Chapter 15 will give us an opportunity to view the individual in interaction with other individuals in play, school, and work settings. It should become clear that throughout our lives we are both independent and interdependent—distinct and autonomous individuals, and yet beings whose lives are intimately entwined with those of other distinct and autonomous individuals. ❦

SUMMARY POINTS

1. Our priorities are reflected in motives, or energizing states that direct behavior toward goals, and in morality, or the ability to distinguish between right and wrong and to act on that distinction.

2. Freud's psychoanalytic theory describes moral development in terms of the formation of the superego and a sense of guilt. Cognitive-developmental theorist Jean Piaget proposed that children's moral thinking progresses through premoral, heteronomous, and autonomous stages, and Lawrence Kohlberg proposed three levels of moral reasoning—preconventional, conventional, and postconventional—each with two stages. Social learning theorists have focused on how moral behavior is influenced by past learning and situational pressures.

3. Early in life, infants display a mastery or effectance motivation and affiliative motivations. Although infants are amoral in many respects, they begin learning about right and wrong and display primitive forms of empathy and altruism.

4. From age 2 to age 12, characteristic motives take form. Some children develop a stronger need for achievement than others do, but achievement is also influenced by the value placed on success and expectancies of success. High achievers tend to have a mastery-oriented rather than a helpless attributional style.

5. Most children operate at the preconventional level of moral reasoning, but both Kohlberg and Piaget may have underestimated the moral sophistication of young children. Situational influences contribute to moral inconsistency, and reinforcement, modeling, and the disciplinary approach of induction can foster moral growth.

6. During adolescence, achievement motivation sometimes wanes; a shift from preconventional to conventional moral reasoning is evident.

7. An individual's characteristic motives often remain relatively consistent from childhood to adulthood, and adults of different ages are quite similar in their motivations. Men's power (and possibly their achievement) motives may peak in middle adulthood, whereas some women experience declines in affiliation and achievement motives.

8. Some adults progress from the conventional to the postconventional level of moral reasoning; elderly adults do not "regress" in their moral thought and may even form more coherent moral philosophies. Kohlberg's stages form an invariant sequence, with progress through them influenced by cognitive growth and social experiences, but it has been charged that his theory is biased and says little about moral affect and behavior.

9. Religious commitment changes little during adulthood and is associated with well-being. James Fowler suggests that humans progress through stages of faith development in their efforts to make sense of their existence.

10. Attempts to foster moral development through group discussions of moral dilemmas and the Just Community approach can be effective.

KEY TERMS

affiliative motive
altruism
amoral
attribution theory
autonomous morality
conventional morality
effectance motivation
empathy
faith
heteronomous morality
immanent justice
individuative-reflective faith
induction
internalization
Just Community
learned helplessness
locus of control
love withdrawal
moral affect
moral reasoning
moral rules
morality
motive
need for achievement
postconventional morality
power assertion
preconventional morality
premoral period
social-conventional rules

CHAPTER

13

PARTICIPATION IN THE SOCIAL WORLD

She is greeted by doctor, nurse, and parents in the delivery room as her life begins. As an infant, she becomes very attached to her mother and father, following them around the house and whimpering when they leave her. As a child, she continues to love her parents and to spend enjoyable hours with them, but she also plays happily with other children and becomes friends with the little girl who lives at the end of the block. During her elementary school years, she is well accepted by her classmates and inseparable from her best friend. As a teenager, she begins to have crushes on boys, goes on dates, and tells her best friend all about them. After finishing college, she finds the man for her, marries, and has children. At age 50, she and her husband enjoy visiting with their children and grandchildren and socializing with their friends. At 75, she is a widow, but she continues to enjoy spending time with her family and friends and reminiscing about all the people who have been important to her during her life. ❦

This is not an unusual life story, although we might have built in a bit more of the pains that come from worrying about relationships or seeing them end. What would make this life story or any life story unusual is to remove the people from it—to picture an infant unattached to any adult, a child who has no friends and rarely plays with other children, or an adult who lives alone, sees no one, and loves no one. Indeed, it is impossible to conceive that a human being could develop normally in a social vacuum. As the poet John Donne wrote, "No man is an island, entire of itself." We might add that no human being can *become* entire without interacting with other human beings.

This chapter traces the development of human beings as social beings, centering attention on such questions as these: What sorts of social relationships are especially important during different phases of the life span, and what is the character of these relationships? When and how do we develop the social competence it takes to interact smoothly with other people, to understand them as individuals, and to enter into intimate relationships with them? What are some of the implications for human development of being deprived of close relationships at different points in life? We begin with some broad perspectives concerning the significance of social relationships for human development.

PERSPECTIVES ON THE SIGNIFICANCE OF RELATIONSHIPS IN LIFE-SPAN DEVELOPMENT

What is it, really, that social relationships contribute to our development? And what relationships are especially significant? Let's briefly see what developmental theorists have had to say.

What Do We Gain from Social Relationships?

No doubt you have your own ideas about why you value your relationships with family and friends. One thing we surely gain from relationships is sheer enjoyment. From infancy to old age, we are attracted to other people and take pleasure from our interactions with them. But how do these enjoyable relationships contribute to our development? Perhaps we can summarize it by saying that other people provide us with learning opportunities and social support.

The *learning experiences* social interactions provide affect virtually all aspects of our development. This has been one of the major messages of social learning theory, as we have seen in Chapter 2 and elsewhere. We acquire language as young children, for example, because the people around us converse with us, serving as models of how to communicate and reinforcing our communication attempts. We learn to adopt a masculine or feminine role partly because parents and peers show us how "real boys" or "real girls" behave and reinforce us for behaving that way. Social interactions also contribute in important ways to cognitive development (Vygotsky, 1978). The parent who helps a child fix a broken toy or work a math problem is actually imparting problem-solving strategies that will become part of the child's own cognitive tool kit. And most certainly, it is other people who teach us social skills and patterns of social behavior. The infant learns from face-to-face interactions with a parent how to take turns with a social partner, the child learns through other children that expressing interest in what someone is doing is a better way to make friends than picking a fight, and the adult continues to look to other people for guidance about how to behave as a lover, parent, worker, or group leader.

A second major function of special relationships is to provide us with **social support**, or emotional and practical help that bolsters us as individuals and protects us from stress. Robert Kahn and Toni Antonucci (1980) have described three important forms of social support: *affect* (or love and affection), *affirmation* (or expressions of approval and agreement, acknowledgment of our worth, and so on), and *aid* (or direct assistance in the form of information, advice, assistance, money, and so on). After Grace is in a minor car accident, for example, her husband may give her a big hug (affect), agree with her that it was the other driver's fault (affirmation), and phone the insurance company (aid). As Kahn and Antonucci see it, having reliable sources of social support benefits us both by increasing our sense of well-being and by protecting us from the potentially negative effects of stressful life events.

Although many researchers use the term *social network* to describe the array of significant individuals who serve as sources of social support, Kahn and Antonucci prefer to describe these significant people as a *social convoy* to convey the idea that social supports change over the life span. An infant's convoy may consist only of parents, but the social convoy enlarges over the years as friends, supportive teachers, colleagues, and other significant people join it. As new members are added, others drift away. Still other people remain in the convoy, but we learn to interact with them in new ways, as when the infant son who is thoroughly dependent on his mother becomes the adolescent son clamoring for his independence—and later the middle-aged son who helps his mother manage her money and care for her lawn. Thus an individual's social convoy is an ever-changing source of social support.

In sum, other people are important to us for an endless range of reasons, but their most critical roles in the developmental process are as teachers and as sources of social support. We could not learn our culture's patterns of social behavior without them, and we could not meet life's challenges as well without the affection, affirmation, and aid provided by our social convoys.

Which Relationships Are Most Critical to Development?

Many noted developmental theorists have felt that no social relationship is more important to human development than the very first—the bond between parent and infant. Sigmund Freud (1905/1930) left no doubt about his opinion: A stable mother/child relationship, he maintained, is essential for normal personality development. His follower Erik Erikson tended to agree. So has John Bowlby (1969, 1973, 1980), an ethological theorist whose views on early parent/infant attachments we will be examining later. Bowlby, for instance, has claimed that the caregiver/infant relationship becomes a "working model" for later intimate relationships. The infant who learns from positive experiences with parents that he or she is lovable and that people can be trusted is likely to carry those attitudes into future relationships. The infant who is neglected, rejected, or treated inconsistently and unreliably by a caregiver may become an adult who is either overdependent on others and insecure in relationships or aloof, too independent, and unable to form close relationships. As we shall see in this chapter, the parent/infant relationship *is* important and has been studied extensively for good reason.

And yet, some theorists argue that relationships with **peers** are equally significant. At the least, these researchers

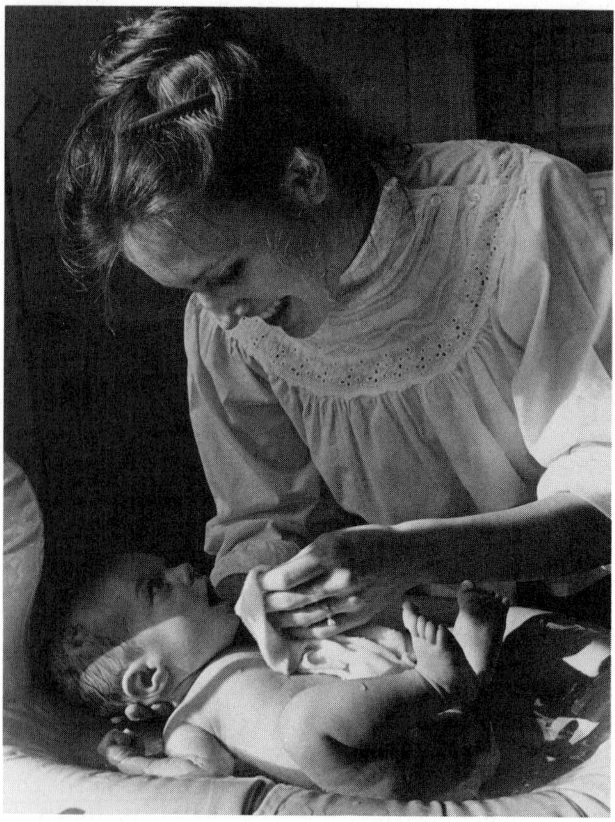

Relationships with caregivers start us on our way as social beings.

think there are "two social worlds of childhood," one involving adult/child relationships and the other involving peer relationships, and that these two worlds contribute differently to development (Youniss, 1980). Who is a peer? Someone who is one's social equal, someone who functions at a similar level of behavioral complexity, often someone of similar age (Lewis & Rosenblum, 1975). As Jean Piaget (1932/1965) observed, relationships with peers are quite different from relationships with parents. Parent/child relationships are lopsided. Because parents have more power than children do, children are in a subordinate position and must defer to adult authority. By contrast, two children have equal power and influence and must learn to appreciate each other's perspectives, to negotiate and compromise, and to cooperate with each other if they hope to get along. Thus Piaget believed that peers can make a unique contribution to child development that adult authority figures cannot make. As we saw in Chapter 12, for example, give-and-take experiences with peers appear to contribute in a special way to moral development.

Another theorist who believed that peer relationships contribute significantly to development was Harry Stack Sullivan (1953), a neo-Freudian (and see Buhrmester & Furman, 1986; Youniss, 1980). Sullivan believed that interpersonal needs are important throughout life but that these needs change with age and are gratified through different kinds of social relationships. According to Sullivan, the parent/child relationship is indeed central up to about age 6, for infants need tender care and nurturance from their parents and preschool children need their parents to serve as playmates and companions. From about age 6 on, however, peers become increasingly central in children's lives. At first, children need peers as companions or playmates; then they need to be accepted by peers; and then, around the age of 9 to 12, they begin to need intimacy in the form of a close friendship.

Indeed, Sullivan placed special emphasis on the developmental significance of **chumships**, or close friendships with peers of the same sex that emerge at about age 9 to 12. It is with their close chums, Sullivan believed, that children become capable of truly caring about another person and learn the importance of trust, loyalty, and honesty in relationships. In fact, Sullivan believed that participating in a close chumship could do much to make up for any insecurities caused by a poor parent/child relationship. Moreover, the lessons about intimacy learned in the context of same-sex chumships would then carry over into the intimate romantic relationships formed during adolescence and adulthood. The child who never had a chum would be at a clear disadvantage later in life.

Debates about the relative significance of parents and peers for later development continue to rage, some developmentalists sharing Freud's belief that the quality of an infant's attachment to an adult is the most significant influence on later personality and social development, others sharing the belief of Piaget and Sullivan that early relationships with peers are at least as significant. And to add to the confusion, still other theorists suspect that *neither* early relationships with parents nor early relationships with peers decisively determine the quality of adult relationships, for these relationships are very much influenced by subsequent life circumstances and experiences (Lerner & Ryff, 1978).

THE INFANT

Human infants are social beings from the start, but the nature of their social relationships changes dramatically as they form close attachments to parents or other companions and as they develop the social skills that allow them to coordinate their own activities with those of other infants.

Attachment: The Emergence of the First Relationship

According to John Bowlby (1969), an **attachment** is a strong affectional tie that binds a person to an intimate companion. For most of us the first attachment we form is to a parent. How do we know when an infant boy is attached to his mother? He will try to maintain proximity to her—crying, clinging, approaching, following, doing whatever it takes to maintain closeness. Moreover, he will prefer her to other individuals, reserving his biggest smiles for her and seeking her out when he is upset, discomforted, or afraid. In short, he will show many of the same symptoms that we might observe in an adult who is "in love." True, close emotional ties are expressed in somewhat different ways, and serve somewhat different functions, at different points in the life span. Adults, for example, do not usually feel compelled to follow their mates around the house, and they look to their loved ones for more than comforting hugs and smiles. Nonetheless, there are basic similarities between the infant attached to Mother, the child attached to a best friend, and the adult attached to a mate or lover. Throughout the life span, the objects of our attachments are special people with whom we are motivated to maintain contact (Ainsworth, 1989).

Like any relationship, the parent/child attachment relationship is reciprocal. Parents become attached to their infants; infants become attached to their parents.

The Caregiver's Attachment to the Infant

Parents have an edge on infants: They can begin to form an emotional attachment to their infants from the moment of birth—or even during pregnancy. As we saw in Chapter 4, Marshall Klaus and John Kennell (1976) have argued and demonstrated that mothers who have an opportunity for skin-to-skin contact with their babies may form a bond to their infants during the first few hours after birth. Indeed, these researchers found that mothers who had such early contact continued, a year later, to be more nurturing than mothers who had limited contact with their babies after birth. However, other researchers have discovered that the effects of early contact are not so large or so long-lasting as Klaus and Kennell believed (Goldberg, 1983). Moreover, adoptive parents and parents whose babies are premature or ill and must be separated from them during their stay in intensive care still form close attachments to their infants (Rode, Chang, Fisch, & Sroufe, 1981; Singer, Brodzinsky, Ramsay, Steir, & Waters, 1985). In short, parents *can* become highly emotionally involved with their infants during the first few hours after birth, but early contact is neither crucial nor sufficient for the development of strong parent-to-infant attachments. Instead, these attachments seem to build during parent/child interactions that take place over many weeks and months.

Why do parents become attached to their infants? After all, young infants drool, spit up, fuss, cry, dirty their diapers on a regular basis, and often require a lot of attention at all hours of the day and night. Yet they also have their endearing qualities, and it is these features that help ensure that their parents will love them. For starters, babies are "cute"; their chubby cheeks and rounded profiles appeal to adults (Alley, 1981). Moreover, babies behave in ways that are endearing and that make them seem responsive to adults. Early reflexive behaviors such as sucking, rooting, grasping, and smiling may help convince parents that their infants enjoy their company (Bowlby, 1969; and see Box 13.1). Moreover, newborns are responsive to human voices, particularly high-pitched "feminine" voices (see Chapter 6). And when infants begin to coo and babble, their parents can enjoy back-and-forth "conversations" with them (Stevenson, VerHoeve, Roach, & Leavitt, 1986).

Over the weeks and months, caregivers and infants develop synchronized routines much like dances, in which the partners take turns responding to each other's leads. Daniel Stern (1977) describes one such "dance" that occurred as a mother was feeding her 3-month-old infant:

> This silent and almost motionless instant continued to hang until the mother suddenly shattered it by saying "Hey!" and simultaneously opened her eyes wider, raising her eyebrows further, and throwing her head up toward the infant. Almost simultaneously, the baby's eyes widened. His head tilted up and, as his smile broadened, the nipple fell out of his mouth. Now she said, "Well, hello! . . . Heello . . . Heelloo," so that her pitch rose and

Box 13.1
The Asocial Smile Becomes a Social Smile

What is more appealing than a baby's smile? Infants smile from birth, and John Bowlby (1969) argues that smiling is one of the biologically programmed behaviors that foster the formation of affectional ties between parents and infants. However, the newborn's first smiles are not necessarily "social." Soft sounds, changes in brightness, and the appearance of a new visual pattern are examples of nonsocial stimuli that can elicit smiles from very young infants (Ambrose, 1963; Bower, 1982). Basically, early smiles are *reflexive* responses to a variety of external or internal events.

True *social* smiling begins as early as 3 weeks of age, when the sound of a female voice may produce a grin. In the fifth or sixth week of life, the human face

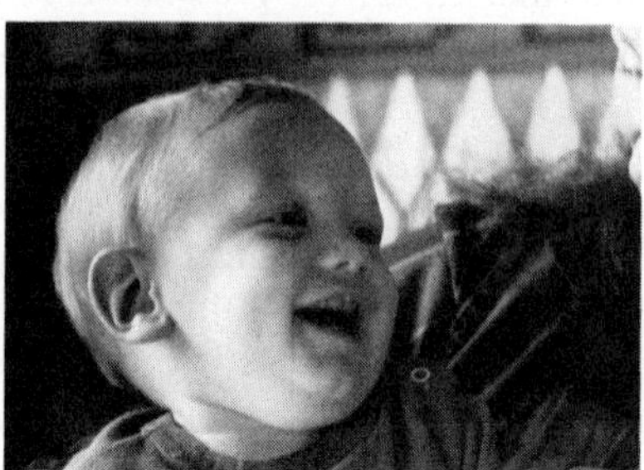

(particularly the eyes) replaces the female voice as the most potent elicitor of smiling (Wolff, 1963). By 3 or 4 months of age, infants are apt to crack broad smiles in response to either a familiar or a strange face, although they may be quicker to smile at familiar companions (Bowlby, 1969).

As infants form attachments at 6 or 7 months of age, they begin to reserve their best smiles for the objects of their love. As parents watch the emergence of true social smiling, they often sense that their infants are becoming "real people." The typical response of adults to an infant's smile is to smile back (Gewirtz & Gewirtz, 1968); similarly, infants smile all the more when their smiles are reciprocated (Brackbill, 1958). Normally, then, assuming that both partners in the caregiver/infant relationship are responsive to one another, reciprocal smiling becomes more frequent and helps build a special relationship. And a delightful time is had by all!

the "hellos" became longer and more emphatic on each successive repetition. With each phrase, the baby expressed more pleasure, and his body resonated almost like a balloon . . . filling a little more with each breath. The mother then paused and her face relaxed. They watched each other expectantly for a moment . . . then the baby suddenly took an initiative. . . . His head lurched forward, his hands jerked up, and a fuller smile blossomed. His mother was jolted into motion. She moved forward, mouth open and eyes alight, and said "Oooooh . . . ya wanna play do ya . . . yeah?" And off they went [p. 3].

In sum, parents form attachments to their infants partly because babies are physically appealing, come equipped with a number of reflexes that promote the formation of an attachment, and are highly responsive to people and capable of synchronizing their behavior with that of their "dance partners." As caregiver and infant practice their interaction routines and as infants gain new social skills, the parent/infant relationship should become more satisfying to both parties and should eventually blossom into a fully reciprocal attachment.

Yet we should not assume that all parents invariably become closely attached to their infants. In the first place, some babies are hard to love. Adults have a difficult time establishing stable and synchronized routines with irritable and unresponsive infants (Greene, Fox, & Lewis, 1983; Thoman, Acebo, & Becker, 1983). Mothers of infants who cry a good deal, for example, are quite willing to attend to their babies' basic needs, but they spend less time in playful and affectionate exchanges than mothers whose babies are less fretful and more responsive to social play (Greene, Fox, & Lewis, 1983).

Second, some adults have difficulty responding to infants. Parents who were themselves unloved, neglected, or abused as children sometimes feel rejected when their babies are irritable or inattentive. These insecure adults may then withdraw their attention—sometimes to the point of neglecting the child or becoming physically abusive (Rutter, 1979; Steele & Pollack, 1974). In addition, mothers who do not want to be parents or who are depressed sometimes have difficulty forming close attachments (Matejcek, Dytrych, & Schuller, 1979; Radke-Yarrow, Cummings, Kuczynski, & Chapman, 1985).

Finally, some parents appear to have difficulty reading their babies' signals and therefore fail to establish smoothly synchronized relationships with them (Sprunger, Boyce, & Gaines, 1985). For example, babies are quite capable of letting adults know when they are overstimulated; they will look away or express displeasure. However, if caregivers are insensitive to these signals and keep right on providing more stimulation than their infants can handle, their infants learn to avoid them (Belsky, Rovine, & Taylor, 1984; Isabella, Belsky, & von Eye, 1989).

In addition, the broader social context surrounding caregiver and infant can affect how they react to each other. For example, mothers who must care for several small children with little or no assistance may find themselves unwilling or unable to devote much attention to their newest baby, particularly if the infant is at all irritable or unresponsive (Belsky, 1980; Crockenberg, 1981), and parents who are unhappy in their marriages may have difficulty interacting responsively with their infants (Belsky, 1981). The larger cultural context may also matter; for example, more infants in Western European countries than in other cultures seem to ignore or avoid their parents when they are reunited with them after a separation (IJzendoorn & Kroonenberg, 1988). In short, while most new parents quickly form strong attachments to their infants, characteristics of the baby, the caregiver, and the surrounding social environment can clearly affect the strength of parental love for child.

The Infant's Attachment to the Caregiver

Infants require some time before they are developmentally ready to form a genuine attachment to another human being. Infants progress through the following phases as they develop close ties with their caregivers (Ainsworth, 1973; Bowlby, 1969):

1. *Undiscriminating social responsiveness* (birth to 2 or 3 months). Very young infants are responsive to voices, faces, and other social stimuli, but *any* human is of interest to them. They do not yet show a clear preference for one person over another.
2. *Discriminating social responsiveness* (2 or 3 months to 6 or 7 months). Now infants are beginning to express preferences for familiar companions (e.g., Watson, Hayes, Vietze, & Becker, 1979). They are likely to direct their biggest grins and most enthusiastic babbles toward those companions, though they are still quite friendly toward strangers. An attachment is beginning to take shape.
3. *Active proximity seeking* (6 or 7 months to about age 3). At about 6 or 7 months of age, infants clearly become attached to particular people, often their mothers. Able to crawl now, an infant will follow along behind its mother to stay close, protest when she leaves, and greet her warmly when she returns. Within weeks after forming their first genuine attachments, about half of the infants in Schaffer and Emerson's (1964) study of Scottish infants were becoming attached to other people (fathers, siblings, grandparents, regular babysitters). By 18 months of age, very few infants were attached to only one person, and some were attached to five or more.

Yet infants no sooner experience the pleasures of love than they experience the discomfort of fear. One form of fear, **separation anxiety**, is actually a sign that an attachment has formed. Once attached to a parent, infants often become wary or fretful when separated from that parent and will try to avoid separation if they can by following behind. Separation anxiety normally appears at the time that infants are forming their first genuine attachments, peaks at 14 to 18 months, and gradually becomes less frequent and less intense throughout infancy and the preschool period (Kagan, 1976; Weinraub & Lewis, 1977).

A second fearful response that often emerges once an attachment is formed is **stranger anxiety**, a wary or fretful reaction to the approach of an unfamiliar person. Most infants react positively to strangers until they form their first attachment, and then become wary of strangers shortly thereafter (Schaffer & Emerson, 1964). Wary reactions to strangers—often mixed with signs of interest—become common at 8 to 10 months of age, continue through the first year, and gradually decline in intensity over the second year (Sroufe, 1977). Box 13.2 describes the circumstances under which stranger anxiety is most and least likely to occur and suggests how healthcare professionals can use this knowledge to head off outbreaks of fear and trembling in their offices.

Finally, the formation of a strong attachment to a caregiver has another important consequence: It facilitates the development of exploratory behavior. Mary Ainsworth (Ainsworth et al., 1978) emphasizes that an attachment figure serves as a **secure base** for exploration, a point of safety from which an infant can feel free to venture away. Thus a securely attached infant visiting a neighbor's home with Mom may be comfortable exploring the living room and dining room so long as he or she can check back occasionally to see that Mom is still there. Infants are indeed more likely to explore an unfamiliar setting if their attachment figures are present than if they are not (Sroufe, 1977). Paradoxical as it may seem, then, in-

Box 13.2
Combatting Stranger Anxiety: The Case of the Doctor's Appointment

It is not unusual for 1- or 2-year-olds visiting the doctor's office to break into tears and cling to their parents. Toddlers who remember previous visits may be suffering "shot anxiety" rather than stranger anxiety, but some infants are undoubtedly bothered by nothing more than the approach of strange adults. Stranger-wary infants often stare at the stranger for a moment and then turn away, whimper, and seek the comfort of their parents. Occasionally, infants become terrified and highly upset. Obviously it is in the interests of doctors and nurses—and babysitters and other "strangers" as well—to be able to prevent such negative reactions. What might we suggest?

First, stranger anxiety is less likely to occur if an attachment figure is nearby. In one study, fewer than one-third of 6- to 12-month-olds were wary of an approaching stranger when they were seated on their mothers' laps (Morgan & Ricciuti, 1969). Yet about two-thirds of these infants frowned, turned away, whimpered, or cried if they were seated only four feet from their mothers. Clearly doctors and nurses would do well to avoid separating parent and child in the doctor's office unless it is unavoidable.

Second, stranger anxiety is less likely to occur if the caregiver responds positively to the stranger. Beginning in the second half of the first year, infants try to read other people's emotional reactions to uncertain situations and are able to use this information to guide their own behavior. Because infants engage in this process of **social referencing**, they respond much more favorably to a stranger's approach if their mothers have either spoken positively to the stranger or issued a warm greeting than if their mothers have reacted neutrally or negatively toward this person (Boccia & Campos, 1983; Feinman & Lewis, 1983). It might not hurt, then, for medical staff to try to start a pleasant exchange with the mother of a young child—or with the father, for infants look to their dads as much as to their mothers for social-referencing cues (Dickstein & Parke, 1988).

Third, stranger anxiety is less likely to occur in familiar settings than in unfamiliar ones. So, for example, stranger wariness may be rare in the home but common in an unfamiliar laboratory (Sroufe, Waters, & Matas, 1974). Although the doctor's office is *not* home, some physicians have deliberately decorated their offices to make them seem more homelike. This should help. Moreover, an unfamiliar environment can become a familiar one if infants are given the time to get used to it. Alan Sroufe and his colleagues (1974) found that over 90% of 10-month-olds became upset if a stranger approached within a minute after they had been placed in an unfamiliar room; only 50% did so when they had had 10 minutes to become accustomed to the room.

Fourth, and not surprisingly, an infant's response to a stranger depends on the stranger's behavior (Sroufe, 1977). The meeting is likely to go best if the stranger initially keeps his or her distance and then approaches slowly while smiling, talking, and offering a familiar toy or suggesting a familiar activity (Bretherton, Stolberg, & Kreye, 1981; Sroufe, 1977). Intrusive strangers who approach quickly and force themselves on the child (for example, by trying to pick children up before they have time to adjust) probably get the response they deserve.

Fifth and finally, stranger anxiety is affected by the physical appearance of a stranger. Jerome Kagan (1972) claims that infants form *schemas*, or mental representations, for the faces they encounter in daily life and are most likely to be afraid of people whom they cannot match to their existing schemas. We might infer from this that professionals who have unusual physical features such as beards *or* who dress in unusual outfits might elicit more wariness than those who resemble the people infants encounter every day. Pediatric professionals may not be able to change their physical features, but they can and often have exchanged their starkly white uniforms for more familiar clothing, thus allowing their young patients to more readily recognize them as members of the human race. Babysitters who favor the "punk" look might also heed this advice!

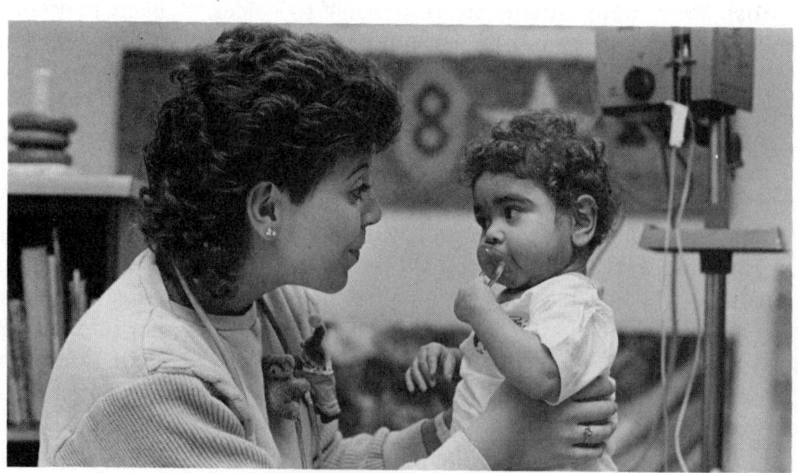

fants apparently need to rely on another person in order to feel confident about acting independently.

The timetable for the formation of attachments is now clear, and we have seen that the emergence of a specific attachment often brings with it both uncertainty (separation and stranger anxiety) and confidence (a willingness to use the attachment figure as a secure base for exploration). It is time to explain *why* attachments form and why an infant might choose one person rather than another as a love object.

Theories of Attachment

Four major theories of the development of parent/infant attachments have been offered: psychoanalytic theory, learning theory, cognitive-developmental theory, and ethological theory. Let's examine the main arguments of each theory and then see how well each theory fits the facts.

Psychoanalytic Theory: I Love You Because You Feed Me

According to Freud, infants in the oral stage of psychosexual development will become attached to any person who provides oral pleasure. Since mothers usually feed infants, they are typically the objects of infants' affections. A secure attachment will form if a mother is relaxed and generous in her feeding practices. Erik Erikson also believed that a mother's feeding practices would influence the security of an infant's attachment. However, he emphasized that a mother's *general responsiveness* to her child, not just her tendency to gratify oral needs, would affect the strength of the attachment. According to Erikson, a caregiver who consistently responds to an infant's needs breeds a sense of *trust* in other people and in the self that is essential to later development.

Learning Theory: I Love You Because You're Reinforcing

For quite different reasons, learning theorists have also assumed that infants will form attachments to the individuals who feed them and meet their other needs. As a caregiver provides food, fresh diapers, tender touches, and other pleasant experiences, the infant comes to associate that person with pleasurable sensations. Through learning, then, caregivers become a source of reinforcement, and infants will do whatever is necessary to attract their attention and remain near these rewarding individuals.

Cognitive-Developmental Theory: I Love You Because I Know You

Proponents of Piaget's cognitive-developmental theory believe that the ability to form attachments depends in part on the infant's level of intellectual development or knowledge of the surrounding world. Before an attachment can form, the infant must be able to *discriminate* between social and nonsocial stimuli and then among social stimuli (familiar persons versus strangers, one familiar person versus another). Moreover, the infant must recognize that close companions continue to exist even when they are absent; otherwise, there would be no cause for separation anxiety when a caregiver leaves the room (Kohlberg, 1969; Schaffer, 1971). In other words, infants will not form attachments until they have acquired some concept of *person permanence* (a form of the object-permanence concept discussed in Chapter 7). So cognitive-developmental theorists claim that attachments form naturally as infants come to know the social world around them, begin to discriminate familiar companions, and understand that these companions have a permanent existence.

Ethological Theory: I Love You Because I Was Born to Love

An influential ethological theory of attachment proposed by John Bowlby (1969, 1973, 1980) argues that infants (and parents, too) are biologically predisposed to form attachments. Ethologists assume that all species, including human beings, are born with a number of innate behavioral tendencies that have in some way contributed to the survival of the species over the course of evolution. It makes sense to think, for example, that young birds have tended to survive if they stay close to their mothers so that they can be fed and be protected from predators—but have perished, and failed to pass their genes to future generations, if they have strayed away. Thus chicks, ducks, and goslings may have gradually evolved so that they engage in **imprinting**, an innate form of learning in which the young will follow and become attached to a moving object (usually the mother) during a critical period early in life (see Chapter 2). The imprinting response observed by Konrad Lorenz (1937) is an example of a species-specific and largely innate behavior that has survival value.

What about human infants? Human infants may not become imprinted to their mothers in the same way that young fowl do, but they most certainly follow their love objects around. Moreover, Bowlby argues that they come equipped with a number of other behaviors besides following that help ensure that adults will love them and tend to them. Among these behaviors are sucking, clinging, smiling, and vocalizing (crying, cooing, and babbling). Moreover, Bowlby argues that adults are biologically programmed to respond to an infant's signals, just as infants are programmed to respond to the sight, sound, and touch of their caregivers. It is difficult indeed for an adult to ignore a baby's cry or to fail to warm up to a baby's big grin. In other words, both human infants and human caregivers have evolved in ways that predispose them to form close attachments, and this ensures that infants will receive the care, protection, and stimulation they need to survive and thrive.

If it sounds to you as though ethologists believe that attachments form automatically, we should correct that impression. Bowlby believes that the quality of an attachment will be influenced by the ongoing interaction between infant and caregiver and by the ability of each partner to respond to the other's signals. The infant's preprogrammed signals to other people may eventually wane if they fail to produce favorable reactions because a caregiver is unresponsive (Ainsworth et al., 1978). In addition, infants themselves must learn to react sensitively to their caregiver's signals so that they can adjust their own behavior to mesh well with the behavior of their love object. So while Bowley believes that humans are biologically prepared to form attachments, he also stresses that mutual learning processes contribute to the unfolding of a secure relationship.

What Does the Evidence Say?

Each of the four major theories of attachment has something to contribute to our understanding, but some hypotheses about attachment are better supported by research than others.

For instance, researchers have tested Freud's claim that feeding experiences play a central role in the formation of attachments. A classic study conducted by Harry Harlow and Robert Zimmerman (1959) examined the relative importance of feeding and tactile stimulation to infant monkeys. Monkeys were reared with two surrogate mothers: a wire "mother" and a cloth "mother" wrapped in foam rubber and covered with terrycloth (see Figure 13.1). Half the infants were fed by the cloth mother, and the remaining half by the wire mother.

Figure 13.1 The "wire" and "cloth" surrogate mothers used in Harlow's research. This infant remains with the cloth mother even though it must stretch to the wire mother in order to feed.

The research question was simple: Would these infants become attached to the "mother" who fed them, or would they instead prefer the cuddly terrycloth "mother"? There was no contest, really: Infants clearly preferred the cloth mother, *regardless of which mother had fed them*. Even if their food came from the wire mother, they spent more time clinging to the cloth mother, ran to "her" when they were upset or afraid, and showed every sign of being attached to her. Harlow's research demonstrated that what he called **contact comfort**, or the pleasurable tactile sensations provided by a soft and cuddly "parent," is a more powerful contributor to attachment in monkeys than feeding and the reduction of hunger.

We have no reason to believe that feeding is any more important to human infants than to baby monkeys. Schaffer and Emerson (1964) asked mothers how they scheduled their feedings and when they weaned their infants. The generosity of a mother's feeding practices simply did not predict the strength of her infant's attachment to her. In fact, for 39% of these infants, the person who usually fed, bathed, and changed the child (typically the mother) was not even the child's primary attachment figure!

In short, we must reject Freud's psychoanalytic theory of attachment, even though we can applaud him for stressing how significant early attachments to caregivers are. Infants do not seem to form an attachment to an adult simply because that person capably satisfies the infant's hunger. Yet caregivers do many other nice things for infants. Could it still be that infants are most likely to attach themselves to adults who are generally responsive to their needs? Indeed it could! Infants become attached to caregivers who, from the start, are highly sensitive to the babies' signals, emotionally expressive, and fond of close contact with their charges (Ainsworth, 1979; Ainsworth et al., 1978; Goldsmith & Alansky, 1987). Relationships are less secure when a caregiver is inconsistent, responding enthusiastically sometimes but ignoring the infant other times—or when a caregiver is typically unresponsive and neglecting or even rejecting. The infant's characteristics also have a bearing; for example, an attachment is less likely to be secure if the infant is by temperament fearful and easily distressed (Goldsmith & Alansky, 1987). However, it appears that the caregiver's temperament and behavior have more to do with whether or not a secure attachment forms than do characteristics of the infant (Goldberg, Perrotta, Minde, & Corter, 1986; Weber, Levitt, & Clark, 1986).

Here, then, is some support for Erikson's psychoanalytic theory, for he claimed that responsive parenting contributes to the development of trust. These findings are also consistent with some versions of learning theory, for a highly responsive adult should be more reinforcing to an infant than a neglectful or aloof one. Between Erikson's theory and learning theory, then, we gain some understanding of why infants might attach themselves to one available adult rather than to another.

Cognitive-developmental theory does not have much to say about which adults are most likely to appeal to infants, but it does alert us to important interrelationships between cognitive development and social development. In truth, infants are not developmentally ready to form attachments and protest separations until they have at least some conception of object permanence (or person permanence) and have begun to search for and find hidden objects (Lester, Kotelchuck, Spelke, Sellers, & Klein, 1974). Thus, infants apparently need to construct understandings of the world around them before they can recognize a caregiver and enter into a special relationship with her or him.

Finally, Bowlby's ethological theory of attachment is quite well supported by research evidence, perhaps because it is a broad theory that draws not only on ethological research with animals but on psychoanalytic and cognitive theories as well. Although it is difficult to prove that behaviors such as smiling or grasping contribute to the survival of the species, it is likely that many infant behaviors that are innate or maturational in nature do contribute to the formation of attachments. Moreover, Bowlby acknowledges that biological preparedness is not enough to guarantee a firm attachment. The *experiences* of caregivers and infants as they interact strongly influence the quality of the relationship that forms. In sum, psychoanalytic, learning, cognitive-developmental, and ethological theories *all* contribute something to our understanding of attachment.

How Does the Quality of Early Attachments Affect Later Development?

From Freud on, almost everyone has assumed that the quality of a child's relationship to a parent figure is very important in shaping future development. Just how important *is* a secure attachment for later development? Two lines of research offer us an answer.

The Effects of Social Deprivation in Infancy

Experiments with monkeys leave no question that social isolation early in life has disastrous effects on development (Harlow & Harlow, 1977). Of course, experiments of this sort cannot be conducted with humans, but studies of infants in deprived institutional settings suggest that what is true of monkeys is also true of humans (Goldfarb, 1943, 1945, 1947; Provence & Lipton, 1962; Spitz, 1945). In the kinds of institutions studied, it was not unusual for one caregiver to be responsible for 8 to 12 infants. Adults rarely saw the infants except to bathe and change them or to prop a bottle against their pillows at feeding times. Often the infants had few or no crib toys and few opportunities to get out and practice motor skills. Thus they were often deprived of both social and sensory stimulation.

What are such infants like? Actually, they develop

quite normally until about 6 months of age; from that point on, they seldom cry, coo, or babble; become rigid when they are picked up; have few language skills; and often appear either forlorn and uninterested in their caretakers or emotionally starved and insatiable in their need for affection. Do these negative effects persist? William Goldfarb (1943, 1947) compared children who left an understaffed orphanage during the first year of life with similar children who spent their first three years at the orphanage before departing for foster homes. By assessing these children periodically from age 3½ to age 12, Goldfarb found that the children who spent three years in the orphanage were behind in almost all aspects of their development. They performed poorly on tests of intelligence, were socially immature and highly dependent on adults, and were prone to language and speech problems, as well as behavior problems such as aggression and hyperactivity. By adolescence, they were often loners and had a difficult time relating to peers or family members. Similarly, Barbara Tizard (1977; Hodges & Tizard, 1989) found that children who had spent at least four years in institutions were much less popular and much more restless and disobedient in school at age 8 and more emotionally troubled and antisocial at age 16 than children adopted early in life. The institutions Tizard studied were adequately staffed and apparently provided the stimulation necessary for normal intellectual development. However, because children were cared for by 50 to 80 different caregivers in their early years, they rarely became attached to any one adult.

What really causes these negative effects of institutional deprivation on development? It is probably not just the lack of sensory stimulation, for institutionalized children who lack contact with adult caregivers but who have plenty of toys and can see and hear other infants are still developmentally delayed (Provence & Lipton, 1962). Nor is it the lack of a single "mother figure." In *adequately staffed* institutions in the Soviet Union, the People's Republic of China, and Israel, infants cared for by several responsive caregivers appear to be quite normal in all respects (Bronfenbrenner, 1970; Kessen, 1975; Levy-Shiff, 1983). Apparently, then, normal development depends on *sustained interactions with responsive caregivers, whether one or several.*

Can infants who are deprived of responsive social stimulation recover? Often they can, if they are placed in homes where they receive ample doses of individual attention from affectionate and responsive caregivers (Clarke & Clarke, 1976; Rutter, 1979). Recovery seems to be especially speedy and complete if deprived children are placed with highly educated, relatively affluent parents (Clark & Hanisee, 1982; Hodges & Tizard, 1989). Full recovery is also more likely if the period of deprivation is relatively short. Children whose deprivation lasts for the first three years or more of life are likely to have lasting social, emotional, and intellectual difficulties, even though they make progress after their deprivation ends (Dennis, 1973; Goldfarb, 1943, 1947; Hodges & Tizard, 1989; Rutter, 1979). However, we cannot be sure what could be accomplished with such children if they were rehabilitated in optimal environments.

The Later Development of Securely and Insecurely Attached Infants

Now consider infants raised at home: Does the quality of their relationships to their parents affect their later development? Most investigations of this question have relied on a technique for measuring the quality of an attachment developed by Mary Ainsworth and her associates (see Ainsworth et al., 1978). Ainsworth's **Strange Situation test** consists of a series of eight episodes designed to gradually escalate the amount of stress infants experience as they react to the approaches of an adult stranger and the departures and returns of their mothers. On the basis of an infant's pattern of behavior across the episodes, the quality of his or her attachment to mother is characterized as one of the three types described in Box 13.3: **secure attachment, insecure/resistant attachment**, and **insecure/avoidant attachment**.

Now the question of primary interest to us: Are securely attached infants likely to become children who are more competent than their age mates who experience insecure (either resistant or avoidant) attachments? Everett Waters and his associates (Waters, Wippman, & Sroufe, 1979) measured the quality of infants' attachments to their mothers at 15 months of age and then observed these children in nursery school at age 3½. Children who had been securely attached as infants were social leaders in the nursery school setting: They often initiated play activities, were sensitive to the needs and feelings of other children, and were popular with their peers (see also Jacobson & Wille, 1986). Moreover, securely attached infants became children whose teachers described them as curious, self-directed, and eager to learn. By contrast, children who had been insecurely attached at age 15 months became 3½-year-olds who were socially and emotionally withdrawn and were hesitant to engage other children in play activities. These children were also less curious, less interested in learning, and less forceful in pursuing their goals than securely attached children. By age 4 to 5, children who had been securely attached as infants were still more curious, more responsive to peers, and less dependent on adults than classmates who had been insecurely attached (Arend, Gove, & Sroufe, 1979; Sroufe, Fox, & Pancake, 1983).

We see, then, that a secure attachment in infancy may have implications for both social and intellectual development. It is possible that their pleasant relationships with responsive caregivers teach securely attached infants how to interact smoothly with other people and also to expect others to react positively to their social gestures. Perhaps they become curious and independent problem solvers because their parents provided them with a secure base for exploration.

Despite these indications that a secure attachment to a mother figure in infancy predicts later competence, we must avoid concluding that infants who are insecurely attached to their mothers are doomed. First, affectionate ties to *fathers* (or perhaps siblings or grandparents) can com-

Box 13.3 Three Types of Attachment Displayed in Ainsworth's Strange Situation

1. Secure attachment

About 70% of 1-year-olds in our society are securely attached (Ainsworth et al., 1978).[1] The securely attached infant actively explores the room when alone with the mother because she serves as a secure base for exploration. The infant may be upset by separation but greets the mother when she returns and welcomes physical contact with her. The child is outgoing with a stranger while the mother is present. As we have seen, Mary Ainsworth (1979) and others find that mothers of securely attached infants are likely to be responsive and emotionally sensitive.

2. Insecure/resistant attachment

About 10% of 1-year-olds show ambivalent reactions to their mothers. The insecure/resistant infant is quite anxious and unlikely to explore while the mother is present but becomes very distressed when she departs, often showing stronger separation anxiety than the securely attached infant. Yet when the mother returns, the infant is ambivalent: He or she may try to remain near the mother but seems to resent her for having left and may resist if she tries to make physical contact. Insecure/resistant infants are also quite wary of strangers, even when their mothers are present. It seems, then, that resistant or ambivalent infants are drawn to their mothers but lack a sense of trust. When Mom leaves the room, such an infant may wonder whether she'll ever come back! Some babies may show a resistant pattern of attachment because they have an irritable and unresponsive temperament (Waters et al., 1980). Yet the mothers of such children may breed ambivalence by being inconsistent in their caregiving, reacting enthusiastically or indifferently depending on their moods (Ainsworth, 1979).

3. Insecure/avoidant attachment

Insecure/avoidant infants (about 20% of 1-year-olds) seem uninterested in exploring, show little distress when separated from their mothers, and avoid contact when their mothers return. These infants are not particularly wary of strangers but sometimes avoid or ignore them in much the same way that they avoid or ignore their mothers. Avoidant infants, then, seem somewhat detached from their parents. Their mothers tend to be impatient, unresponsive to the infant's signals, and resentful when the infant interferes with their own plans (Ainsworth, 1979; Egeland & Farber, 1984)—or else they are overzealous, providing high levels of stimulation even when their children do not want stimulation, and therefore causing their children to avoid them (Belsky et al., 1984; Isabella et al., 1989). Perhaps because they receive inconsistent care involving both overstimulation and understimulation, abused or maltreated infants frequently display a "disorganized" pattern of attachment that combines features of the resistant and avoidant styles (Carlson, Cicchetti, Barnett, & Braunwald, 1989). They will seek their mothers out but then become apprehensive or avoidant when their mothers approach them.

[1] The proportions of infants falling in each attachment category vary somewhat from culture to culture and from subgroup to subgroup within a particular society (Van IJzendoorn & Kroonenberg, 1988). Nonetheless, more babies around the world fall in the secure-attachment category than in either of the others.

pensate for insecure mother/infant relationships. Many infants who are insecurely attached to their mothers are securely attached to their fathers—and are, as a result, more sociable than infants who are not securely attached to either parent (Main & Weston, 1981). Also, an initially insecure attachment may have no negative long-term consequences because it becomes a secure attachment later on. Unlike diamonds, attachments are not forever. Although most children experience the same kind of attachments to their parents in childhood that they experienced in infancy (Main & Cassidy, 1988), changing family circumstances can convert insecure attachments into secure ones—or secure attachments into insecure ones. In one study, almost half of the infants assessed experienced a change in the security of their attachment to their mothers in the short period between 12 and 19 months of age (Thompson & Lamb, 1984). A secure attachment may become insecure if a mother withdraws from caregiving activities because of stresses such as marital problems, financial woes, or a lack of emotional support from friends and family members. When a mother returns to work and places her infant in day care, the parent/infant attachment may also take a turn for the worse, though it sometimes becomes *more* secure (Thompson & Lamb, 1984; and see Chapter 15 for a fuller discussion of the effects of day care). Meanwhile, initially insecure infants are likely to become securely attached if the lives of their close companions become less stressful (Vaughn, Egeland, Sroufe, & Waters,

Box 13.4
Do Securely Attached Infants Become Socially Competent Adults?

Our award for the longest longitudinal study of the implications of early attachments goes to Arlene Skolnick (1986). Using longitudinal data from the Berkeley Guidance Study, she sought to determine whether there was any consistency in the quality of an individual's social relationships from infancy to middle age. The question was this: Does the infant who is securely attached to his or her mother at 21 to 30 months of age become the child who is well liked, warm, socially perceptive, and otherwise socially competent . . . and become the adolescent who is popular and a leader among peers . . . and become the adult who is sociable, psychologically healthy, and happily married? Skolnick analyzed ratings of the quality of each individual's age-appropriate relationships for each of these four periods of the life span.

One interesting finding of this study was that only a little over a fourth of the participants had either consistently favorable or consistently poor interpersonal relationships across all four periods of life. In other words, it was typical for people to have high-quality relationships at some points in life but lower-quality relationships at others.

One important implication of this finding is this: "Secure attachment to the mother does not make one invulnerable to later problems and socioemotional difficulties, and poor early relations with the mother do not doom a person to a life of loneliness, poor relationships, or psychopathology" (Skolnick, 1986, p. 193).

Skolnick did find that security of attachment in infancy was at least modestly related to some aspects of later social competence—for example, to a girl's social adjustment as a child and to a boy's adjustment as an adult. Similarly, Mary Main and her associates (Main, Kaplan, & Cassidy, 1985) have found that adults who recall their own relationships with their parents in positive ways are more likely than adults who have unpleasant memories of childhood to have achieved secure relationships with their own infants. Main argues that the early parent/child relationship can affect an adult's view of relationships in general, although she, like Skolnick, concludes that later experiences apparently help many individuals overcome unpleasant early experiences with their parents and go on to enjoy positive social relationships. Indeed, in Skolnick's study, adult outcomes were actually better predicted by *peer relations*, especially during adolescence, than by parent/infant interactions that had taken place many years earlier. Adolescents who had positive relationships with peers often grew up to be adults who were socially well adjusted, whereas youngsters who had poor relations with peers more often became adults who were unmarried or unhappily married, relatively unsociable, or saddled with personal problems.

Overall, then, these findings challenge Freud's strong claim that the quality of an infant's relationship with his or her mother establishes a pattern of personality and social behavior that decisively determines the quality of all future relationships. There is *some* carryover from the infant/parent bond to adult social relationships, but we apparently have plenty of time to learn new social skills and different attitudes toward relationships in our later interactions with peers.

1979). Clearly, the quality of attachment in infancy is unlikely to have long-range effects on development unless the *same* quality is maintained consistently over a reasonably long period (Lamb, 1987).

Finally, we must appreciate that an individual's social relationships *after* infancy affect his or her ultimate social adjustment (Lamb, 1987). Box 13.4 explores the long-range implications of early attachments, illustrating that both early relationships with parents and later experiences with peers have a bearing on how well adjusted people are as adults. In short, the quality of attachment during infancy is important, but it is only *one* influence on later social development. Thus we must supplement our discussion of parent/child relations with a look at the "second world of childhood"—the world of peer relations.

Peer Relations During Infancy

Developmentalists have viewed the caregiver/infant relationship as so central to development that they have neglected infants' relationships with age mates until fairly recently. If two infants are placed together on the floor, can they interact in a meaningful way? Do infants become attached to familiar playmates as they become attached to caregivers?

Examining the evidence, Dale Hay (1985) concludes that peer interaction skills develop quite early in life, but that infants display social skills in their interactions with adults earlier than they display the same skills in their relations with other infants. Hay believes that this is because adult partners are more socially skilled than infant partners and can therefore adjust their own behavior to create a smooth "dance" or give-and-take routine with an infant. By contrast, when two socially unskilled infants interact, neither may have the social competence to coordinate his or her own behavior smoothly with that of a partner. Many friendly babbles and offers of toys go unnoticed and unreciprocated, and the interaction often has a fragmented or disorganized quality. Indeed, Deborah Vandell and Kathy Wilson (1987) find that there are more turn-taking exchanges when mother and infant interact than when an infant interacts with either an older sibling or another infant. Moreover, those infants who engage in a great deal of turn-taking with their mothers later engage in more turn-taking with peers than do infants who have not had as many opportunities to learn social skills with the help of a skilled adult.

Infants show an interest in other infants from the first months of life, but they do not really interact until about the middle of the first year. By then, infants will often smile at their tiny companions, vocalize, offer toys, and gesture to one another (Hay, Nash, & Pedersen, 1983; Vandell, Wilson, & Buchanan, 1980). Yet investigators have still wondered just how social some of these early peer relations are. Edward Mueller and his associates (Mueller & Lucas, 1975; Mueller & Vandell, 1979) have suggested that infants pass through three stages of early sociability from age 1 to age 2. At first, in the *object-centered* stage, two infants may jointly focus on a toy but will pay more attention to the toy than to each other. During the second, or *simple interactive* stage, infants more obviously influence one another and respond appropriately to each other's behavior. Consider this example:

> Larry sits on the floor and Bernie turns and looks toward him. Bernie waves his hand and says "da," still looking at Larry. He repeats the vocalization three more times before Larry laughs. Bernie vocalizes again and Larry laughs again. This same sequence . . . is repeated twelve more times before Bernie . . . walks off [Mueller & Lucas, 1975, p. 241].

At this stage, it is possible that infants merely act toward peers as if they were little more than particularly responsive "toys" to be controlled (Brownell, 1986). However, as early as 16 to 18 months of age, infants progress to a third, or *complementary interactive*, stage in which their interactions are even more clearly social. When they smile or vocalize, one can see that they intend to influence their playmates and fully expect a response (Kavanaugh & McCall, 1983). Moreover, they adopt roles in their play and can reverse roles. Thus the toddler who receives a toy may immediately offer a toy in return, or the toddler who has been the "chaser" can become the "chasee" in a game of tag. By the end of the second year, infants become far more proficient at this kind of turn-taking and reciprocal exchange (Brownell, 1986). Almost inevitably, they also get into more conflicts with their playmates (Hay, 1985; Shantz, 1987).

Surprising as it may seem, infants also form special, though not necessarily long-lasting, relationships with preferred playmates—"friendships," if you will. In their second year, infants increasingly distinguish among infants, just as they distinguish among adults. Moreover, they behave more sociably in the company of a familiar

With age, infants' interactions with one another become increasingly skilled and reciprocal.

playmate than they behave in the company of a strange playmate (Hay, 1985). Finally, at least some infant pairs establish a mutual preference for one another's company (Howes, 1983). On Israeli kibbutzim where children are cared for in groups, Martha Zaslow (1980) discovered that many pairs of infants as young as 1 year of age became especially attached to one another. Hadara and Rivka, for instance, consistently sought each other out as playmates, mourned one another's absence, and disturbed everyone with their loud babbling "conversations" when they were confined to their cribs!

In sum, the caregiver/infant relationship is not the only important social relationship that develops during infancy, although it is the relationship that comes first and that has the potential to steer social development in either adaptive or maladaptive directions. Through their interactions with significant adults *and* their interactions with peers, infants begin to acquire the social competencies that will permit them to become even more sociable beings during childhood.

THE CHILD

Children's social relationships change tremendously from infancy to later childhood. In part, this is because children are experiencing a good deal of cognitive growth and are gaining an ever-deeper understanding of other people. Let us look at this cognitive growth and then see how it is reflected in children's actual social relationships over the years: Who are the important members of children's social networks, and with whom do they spend the most time? What draws children together as friends? Why are some children more popular than others? And just how important are children's social relationships to their overall development?

Growth in Social Cognition

Doesn't it make sense to think that the quality of children's relationships with both parents and peers should improve as they come to understand other people more fully? The infant is just beginning to acquire knowledge of other people—coming to know parents or siblings by looks, forming expectations about how familiar companions will behave, and beginning to categorize people according to sex, age, and other observable characteristics. However, an infant cannot analyze the personalities of other people or recognize that their companions have their own distinct needs, feelings, and thoughts.

These skills are part of the larger domain of **social cognition**—thinking about the thoughts, feelings, motives, and behaviors of the self and other people. Among other things, social-cognitive skills allow children to figure out how to get themselves invited to birthday parties, to understand why their mothers are furious at them, and to realize that not all seemingly friendly strangers can be trusted. Growth in social cognition is distinct from, but intimately intertwined with, growth in the sorts of cognitions about the physical world that so fascinated Jean Piaget (Flavell, 1985). We have already touched on some important aspects of social-cognitive development in this book, seeing, for example, that older children think differently than younger children do about what they are like as individuals, about how males and females differ, and about why it is wrong to cheat or steal. Here let's focus on developmental changes in how children characterize their companions as individuals and in how well they can adopt other people's perspectives.

Person Perception

In studies of *person perception,* or impression formation, children are asked to describe familiar people: parents, friends, disliked classmates, and so on. As we discovered in Chapter 10, children younger than 7 or 8 describe themselves in very concrete and physical terms. They describe other people that way too (Livesley & Bromley, 1973; Peevers & Secord, 1973). Five-year-old Jenny, for example, says: "My daddy is big. He has hairy legs and eats mustard. Yuck! My daddy likes dogs—do you?" Not much of a personality profile there! Young children perceive others in terms of their physical appearance, possessions, and activities. When psychological terms are used, they are often global terms such as "nice" or "mean" rather than more specific trait labels (Livesley & Bromley, 1973). Moreover, traits are not yet viewed as enduring qualities that can predict how a person will behave in the future (Rholes, Jones, & Wade, 1988; Rholes & Ruble, 1984). The 5-year-old who describes a friend as "dumb" may only be using this trait label to describe that friend's recent "dumb" behavior and may well expect "smart" behavior tomorrow.

At the age of 7 or 8, children begin to "get below the surface" of human beings and describe them in terms of their enduring psychological traits. Ten-year-old Kim describes her friend Jill: "She's funny and friendly to everyone, and she's in the gifted program because she's smart, but sometimes she's bossy." As children reach the age of 11 or 12, they even begin to make social comparisons and contrasts on important psychological dimensions, noting that one classmate is smarter or shyer than another (Barenboim, 1981). As children get older, they also make more use of psychological traits to explain why people behave as they do, claiming that Mike pulled the dog's tail *because* he's cruel (Gnepp & Chilamkurti, 1988). Clearly, then, children become more "psychologically minded" as their emerging social-cognitive abilities permit them to make inferences from the concrete behavior they observe in the people around them.

Social Perspective Taking

Another important aspect of social-cognitive growth involves outgrowing the egocentrism that Piaget believed characterizes young children and developing *role-taking or perspective-taking skills*: the ability to assume another person's perspective and understand his or her thoughts and feelings in relation to one's own. Robert Selman (1976, 1980; Yeates & Selman, 1989) established that role-taking abilities unfold through a series of stages during childhood and adolescence by posing questions about interpersonal dilemmas:

> Holly is an 8-year-old girl who likes to climb trees. She is the best tree climber in the neighborhood. One day while climbing down from a tall tree, she falls . . . but does not hurt herself. Her father sees her fall. He is upset and asks her to promise not to climb trees anymore. Holly promises.
>
> Later that day, Holly and her friends meet Shawn. Shawn's kitten is caught in a tree and can't get down. Something has to be done right away or the kitten may fall. Holly is the only one who climbs trees well enough to reach the kitten and get it down but she remembers her promise to her father [1976, p. 302].

To assess how well a child understands the perspectives of Holly, her father, and Shawn, Selman asks: Does Holly know how Shawn feels about the kitten? How will Holly's father feel if he finds out she climbed the tree? What does Holly think her father will do if he finds out she climbed the tree? What would you do in this situation? Children's responses to such questions led Selman to conclude that role-taking abilities develop in a stagelike manner, as shown in Table 13.1.

Preschool children are largely egocentric. Unaware of any perspective other than their own, they assume that they and other people see eye to eye. As concrete-operational cognitive abilities emerge, children become better able to consider another person's point of view (Keating & Clark, 1980). Later in childhood, they can simultaneously think about their own thoughts and the thoughts of another person, and they realize that their companions can do the same. Finally, adolescents who have reached the formal-operational stage of cognitive development become capable of mentally juggling multiple perspectives, including the generalized perspective of "most people."

What implications do these sorts of advances in social cognition have for children's actual relationships? Important ones!

Children's Social Networks

The Parent/Child Attachment

How does the parent/child attachment change during childhood? Relationships within the family are examined in more detail in Chapter 14, but here let's simply emphasize that affectional ties to parents remain highly important and continue to contribute to development during childhood and well beyond childhood. At the same time, children become increasingly independent of their par-

Table 13.1 Selman's stages of social perspective taking

STAGE	TYPICAL RESPONSES TO THE "HOLLY" DILEMMA
0. *Egocentric or undifferentiated perspective* (roughly 3 to 6 years): Children are unaware of any perspective other than their own. They assume that whatever they feel is right for Holly to do will be agreed on by others.	Children often assume that Holly will save the kitten and that her father will be "happy because he likes kittens." In other words, these children like kittens themselves, and they assume that Holly and her father also like kittens.
1. *Social-informational role taking* (roughly 6 to 8 years): Children now recognize that people can have perspectives that differ from their own but believe that this happens *only* because these individuals have received different information. The child is still unable to think about the thinking of others and know in advance how others will react to an event.	When asked whether Holly's father will be angry because she climbed the tree, the child may say "If he didn't know why she climbed the tree, he would be angry. But if he knew why she did it, he would realize that she had a good reason." Thus, the child is saying that if both parties have exactly the same information, they will reach the same conclusion.
2. *Self-reflective role taking* (roughly 8 to 10 years): Children now know that their own and others' points of view may conflict even if they have the same information. They consider the other person's viewpoint. They also recognize that the other person can put himself in their shoes. However, the child cannot consider his own perspective and that of another person at the same time.	If asked whether Holly will climb the tree, the child might say "Yes. She knows that her father will understand why she did it." In so doing, the child is focusing on the father's consideration of Holly's perspective. But if asked whether the father would want Holly to climb the tree, the child usually says no, thereby indicating that he is now assuming the father's perspective and considering the father's concern for Holly's safety.
3. *Mutual role taking* (roughly 10–12 years): The child can now simultaneously consider her own and another person's points of view and recognize that the other person can do the same. At this point, each party can put the self in the other's place and view the self from that vantage point before deciding how to react. The child can also assume the perspective of a disinterested third party and anticipate how each participant (self and other) will react to the viewpoint of his or her partner.	At this stage, a child might take the perspective of a disinterested third party and indicate that she knows that both Holly and her father are thinking about what each other is thinking. For example, one child remarked: "Holly wanted to get the kitten because she likes kittens, but she knew that she wasn't supposed to climb trees. Holly's father knew that Holly had been told not to climb trees, but he couldn't have known about [the kitten]."
4. *Social and conventional system role taking* (roughly 12 to 15 and older): The young adolescent now attempts to understand another person's perspective by comparing it with that of the social system in which he operates (that is, the view of the "generalized other"). In other words, adolescents expect others to consider and typically assume perspectives on events that most people in their social group would take.	A Stage 4 adolescent might think that Holly's father would become angry and punish her for climbing the tree because fathers generally punish children who disobey. However, adolescents sometimes recognize that other people may have a personal viewpoint quite discrepant from that of the "generalized other." Thus the reaction of Holly's father may depend on the extent to which he is unlike other fathers.

Source: Adapted from Selman, 1976.

ents. John Bowlby (1969) believes that by about the age of 3 children enter a new phase of parent/child attachment and become capable of participating in a **goal-corrected partnership**. Partly because they have more advanced social-cognitive abilities, they can now take the goals and plans of a parent into consideration and adjust their behavior accordingly. Thus, a 1-year-old cries and tries to follow when Mom leaves the house to talk to a neighbor, whereas the 4-year-old child probably understands where Mom is going and can control the need for her attention until she returns. Increasingly, parent and child become true partners sensitive to one another's needs and perspectives. This phase of attachment lasts a lifetime.

Observational studies suggest that 2- to 3-year-olds are more likely than 4- to 5-year-olds to remain near an adult and seek physical affection (Hartup, 1983). Older preschoolers still seek attention and approval from their parents and rush to them for comfort when they are frightened or hurt, but they also begin to spend more time with peers and increasingly seek *peer* attention and approval. Within children's social networks, then, parents continue to be important sources of affection, affirmation of worth, and aid, but peers increasingly meet needs for companionship (Furman & Buhrmester, 1985).

Peer Relations

Over the years from age 2 to age 12, children spend more time with peers and less time with adults. This trend

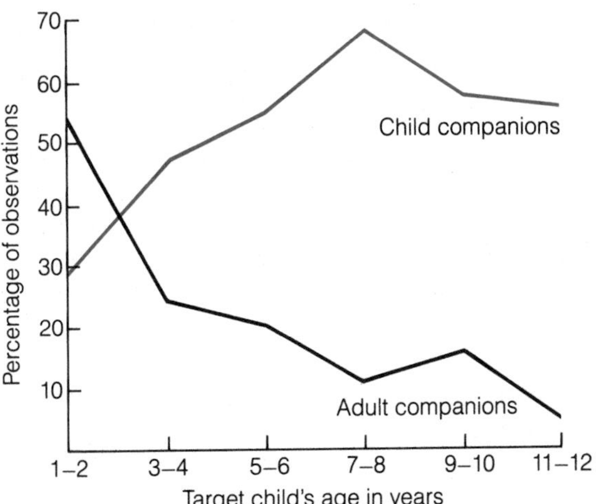

Figure 13.2 Developmental changes in children's companionship with adults and other children. (From Ellis, Rogoff, & Cromer, 1981)

is shown vividly in Figure 13.2, which summarizes what Sharri Ellis and her colleagues (Ellis, Rogoff, & Cromer, 1981) found when they observed 436 children playing in their homes and around the neighborhood. Interestingly, this same study revealed that youngsters of all ages spent *less* time with age mates (defined as children whose ages were within a year of their own) than with children who were more than a year older or younger than they were. Apparently we must take seriously the idea that peers are not merely age mates but rather "social equals."

Another finding of this study is a familiar one: Even 1- to 2-year-olds were playing more often with same-sex companions than with other-sex companions, and this like-sex bias became increasingly strong with age. Segregation of the sexes may occur later in other cultures, though it eventually occurs in most societies (Whiting & Edwards, 1988). For example, boys and girls in Kokwet, Kenya, spend no more time with same-sex peers than they spend with other-sex peers until they are about age 6, when they become freer to choose their own companions and begin helping their parents with tasks that are clearly either "men's work" or "women's work" (Harkness & Super, 1985). In addition, boys tend to form "packs," whereas girls form "pairs"; that is, a boy often plays competitive games or team sports in groups, whereas a girl more often establishes an exclusive relationship with one friend (Lever, 1976; Tietgen, 1982).

Overall, then, children spend an increasing amount of time with peers, and those peers are typically *same*-sex children who are only *roughly similar* in age but who enjoy the same sex-typed activities. Some of these peers will become special, for they will become a child's close friends.

Children's Friendships

Close friends are an especially important part of the child's social world. Through their attachments to friends, children learn a good deal about how to relate to other people and receive a good deal of emotional support. But what qualifies someone as a friend? The answer to that question seems to depend very much on a child's level of social-cognitive development (Selman, 1980). To the preschool child, a friend is "Terry, who lives next door and plays with me." The principal basis for friendship is *common activity*. Young children form relatively short-lived friendships with peers who are similar to themselves in observable characteristics such as age, sex, and racial or ethnic group—and who participate in and enjoy similar activities (Dickens & Perlman, 1981). As children begin to recognize that playmates may have different motives and feelings than they do, they increasingly define friends as individuals who do nice things for them and do not hurt them. However, they self-servingly put the emphasis on what their friends can do for them. Finally, as 8- to 10-year-old children enter Selman's second stage of social perspective taking or role taking, they begin to understand that friendships are *reciprocal relationships* in which two people act with mutual respect, kindness, and affection (Furman & Bierman, 1983; Selman, 1980): "Terry and I like each other and stick by each other no matter what."

In short, children become more selective about whom they call a friend as they begin to understand others as psychological beings. No longer are physical and behavioral similarities sufficient; as children appreciate how their own interests and perspectives and those of their peers are similar or different, they also insist that their friends be *psychologically* similar to themselves. Moreover, they come to appreciate that *each* partner in a friendship must be sensitive to the other's perspective. Perhaps because they rest on a firmer basis, the friendships of older children are more long-lasting than the friendships of younger children (Berndt & Hoyle, 1985).

Some children have more advanced social-cognitive skills than others do, and this helps explain why some children have an easier time making friends than others do. It is likely that experience interacting with peers sharpens role-taking skills, and that, in turn, sophisticated role-taking skills help make a child a more sensitive and desirable companion. For whatever reasons, children whose role-taking skills are advanced are more likely than age mates who perform poorly on tests of role taking to be sociable and popular and to have established close friendships with others (Gnepp, 1989; Kurdek & Krile, 1982; LeMare & Rubin, 1987; McGuire & Weisz, 1982). Good role takers are in a position to infer the needs of others so that they can respond appropriately; they can, for example, figure out that another child is confused and needs help with a project even though the other child does not explicitly ask for help (Hudson, Forman, & Brion-Meisels, 1982). Moreover, they are skilled at figuring out how to resolve the disagreements that inevitably arise when children play together (Shantz, 1987; Yeates & Selman, 1989). It is easy to see how their social-cognitive skills might contribute to their popularity. Why are some children more popular with their peers than others are—and why does it matter?

Peer Acceptance and Popularity

Typically, researchers study peer-group acceptance through **sociometric techniques**—methods for determining who is liked and disliked in a group. In a sociometric survey, children in a classroom may be asked to nominate several classmates whom they like and several whom they dislike, or they may be asked to rate all of their classmates in terms of their desirability as companions. According to John Coie and his associates (Coie, Dodge, & Coppotelli, 1982), it is important to find out who is liked *and* who is disliked, for this allows children to be classified into four quite distinct categories of social status: the *popular* (well-liked by most and rarely disliked), the *rejected* (rarely liked and often disliked), the *neglected* (isolated children who are neither liked nor disliked but seem instead to be invisible to their classmates), and the *controversial* (children who are liked by many but also disliked by many—for example, the fun-loving child with leadership skills who also has a nasty habit of fighting).

Why are some children more popular than others, and why are some children rejected by their peers? Box 13.5 addresses this question, considering everything from a child's name to his or her social skills. What may be most important is a child's *social competence*—the ability to apply social-cognitive skills successfully in initiating social interactions, responding positively to peers, resolving interpersonal conflicts, and so on. Many of these same skills continue to be associated with social acceptance later in life.

Do the outcomes of such popularity polls really matter? Yes—especially for children who are actively rejected by their peers. Children who are neglected by their peers often gain greater peer acceptance later, but children who are rejected tend to maintain their rejected status from grade to grade (Coie & Dodge, 1983), perhaps in part because they have established reputations as undesirable companions and enter new situations expecting to be disliked (Rabiner & Coie, 1989). Rejected children are also at risk of engaging in antisocial or delinquent behavior and displaying psychological and emotional disorders as adolescents or adults (Cowen, Pederson, Babigian, Izzo, & Trost, 1973; Roff, Sells, & Golden, 1972).

A Summing Up: The Contributions of Peers to Child Development

Long aware of the many contributions that parents make to child development, developmentalists now appreciate that peers may be every bit as important. In a classic set of experiments, Harry Harlow and his associates (Alexander & Harlow, 1965; Suomi & Harlow, 1975, 1978) assessed the development of rhesus monkeys deprived of contact with either their mothers or their peers early in life. Monkeys who grew up with their mothers but who were deprived of peer contact failed to develop normal patterns of social and sexual behavior. When finally exposed to age mates, these social misfits avoided them or, if they did approach them, were inappropriately aggressive. Monkeys who were raised *only* with peers formed strong attachments to one another and generally displayed normal patterns of social behavior within their peer group. They did prove to be aggressive toward monkeys from ouside their peer group and were easily upset by minor stresses. Otherwise, however, the social and emotional adjustment of monkeys raised only with peers was generally superior to that of monkeys raised only with their mothers.

Interestingly, Anna Freud and Sophie Dann (1951) discovered that six young children who lived essentially by themselves in a German concentration camp were strikingly similar to Harlow's "peer only" monkeys. These children were strongly attached to one another, so much so that they could not bear to be separated, and they inter-

Box 13.5
Who Is Popular and Who Is Not?

Which children are liked by many classmates and disliked by few or none? Popularity is affected by some personal characteristics that a child can do little about. For instance, children with names that are judged to be attractive are more popular than children whose names are unattractive (McDavid & Harari, 1966). Thus Steven or Susan are likely to gain more peer acceptance than Herman, Chastity, or Moon Unit. Moreover, physically attractive children are likely to be more popular than physically unattractive children (see Langlois, 1986). As early as the preschool years, children have learned a "beauty is good" stereotype that leads them to believe that physically attractive peers are friendlier, nicer, smarter, and better in almost every way than their less attractive counterparts (Stycynski & Langlois, 1977).

It is quite likely that parents, teachers, and peers contribute to self-fulfilling prophecies by subtly or not so subtly communicating their expectations to attractive and unattractive children (Langlois, 1986). That is, their behavior may cause the attractive child to become more confident, outgoing, and friendly, while causing the physically unattractive child who is expected to be unpleasant and antisocial to take on just these qualities.

A child's *competencies* also influence popularity. For example, children who are relatively intelligent and achieve well in school tend to be more socially accepted than those who are less intelligent (Green, Forehand, Beck, & Vosk, 1980). But even more relevant to peer acceptance are *social* competencies. We have already seen that children who experienced secure attachments to their parents as infants tend to be popular as preschoolers. Mothers who are friendly and agreeable in their interactions tend to have children who are the same way (Putallaz, 1987). Moreover, we have seen that children who have advanced role-taking skills are likely to be popular. Generally, popular children are socially skilled children—cooperative and responsive rather than argumentative and disruptive (Coie, Dodge, & Coppotelli, 1982; Ladd, Price, & Hart, 1988).

We can appreciate how social skills contribute to popularity if we consider what happens when children try to enter and gain acceptance in play groups (Coie & Kupersmidt, 1983; Dodge, 1983; Putallaz & Gottman, 1981; Putallaz & Wasserman, 1989). Children who are ultimately accepted by unfamiliar peers are effective at initiating social interactions and at responding positively to others' bids for attention. When they want to join a group's activity, for example, socially skilled children first hold back and figure out what is going on and then smoothly blend into the group, commenting pleasantly about whatever the other children are discussing. By contrast, children who are eventually rejected by their peers tend to be pushy and disruptive. Jimmy, for example, may sit beside two boys who are playing checkers and distract them by talking about a TV program he saw the night before. Worse, he may criticize the way the boys are playing checkers, or even threaten violence if he is not allowed to play. Children who end up being neglected by their peers often hover around a group without taking any positive steps to initiate contact and shy away from peers who attempt to make contact with them.

In sum, popularity is affected by many factors. It may help to have a desirable name or an attractive face, but it is probably more important to have advanced social-cognitive skills and to behave in socially competent ways.

acted with one another in very caring and socially mature ways. Although they were at first highly suspicious of and hostile toward the adults who attempted to help them at the war's end, they gradually warmed up to these outsiders and went on to lead normal, productive lives as middle-aged adults (Hartup, 1983).

The conclusion that emerges from these studies is that parents and peers each contribute something different and perhaps unique to social development. Parents may provide a sense of emotional security that enables infants to explore their environment and to appreciate that other people can be interesting companions. Meanwhile, contact with peers may be especially critical to the learning of social skills and normal patterns of social behavior.

But the influences of peers extend far beyond the realm of social development. For one thing peers—especially close friends—make important contributions to emotional development and adjustment. Friendships teach children how to participate in emotionally intimate relationships and offer them emotional support and comfort that can help them feel better about themselves and weather stressful events such as a divorce or illness in the family (Norris & Rubin, 1984). But that's not all. Interactions with peers also contribute to both physical and cognitive development (Athey, 1984). Children often learn from other children how to hit baseballs, perform cartwheels, or build model planes, and they practice new motor skills every day in their play. Moreover, just as children must have social-cognitive skills in order to interact smoothly with their peers, their social interactions stimulate new cognitive growth. Children's minds are stretched when they use them to pretend they are explorers sailing across the Atlantic or to reach a compromise because one of them wants to sail across the Atlantic but another wants to go to the bathroom. In short, peers have a hand in virtually all areas of child development.

Childhood is indeed a period of rapid and significant social development. As they get older, children develop the basic social-cognitive skills that allow them to understand others as individuals, spend more time with peers but maintain their attachments to parents, form close friendships with similar others, and establish reputations as either popular or unpopular companions that can affect their later adjustment. Normal child development seems to require not only close attachments to adults but also close attachments to peers.

THE ADOLESCENT

Although children are already highly involved in peer activities, adolescents spend even more time with peers and less time with parents (Buhrmester & Furman, 1986). Some parents see so little of their teenagers that they sometimes wonder if they have changed addresses! Moreover, the *quality* of peer relations changes during adolescence. For one thing, adolescents begin to form boy/girl friendships and go on dates. Moreover, they become more capable of participating in truly deep and intimate attachments.

Social Cognition

Adolescents experience tremendous growth in their ability to understand other people, growth that allows them to form deeper relationships. When asked to describe people they know, adolescents offer personality profiles that are even more psychological than those provided by children (Livesley & Bromley, 1973; O'Mahony, 1986). They are more able to describe people as unique individuals with distinctive personality traits, interests, values, and feelings. Moreover, they are able to create more integrated, or organized, person descriptions, analyzing how a person's diverse and often inconsistent traits fit together and make sense as a whole personality. Dan, for example, may notice that Karen brags about her abilities at times but seems very unsure of herself at other times, and he may integrate these seemingly discrepant impressions by concluding that Karen is basically insecure and boasts only to hide her insecurity. Some adolescents spend hours psychoanalyzing their friends and acquaintances, trying to figure out what really makes them tick.

Adolescents' role-taking skills are also more sophisticated than those of children (Selman, 1980; Yeates & Selman, 1989). As Table 13.1 (p. 420) showed, many adolescents become mental jugglers, keeping in the air their own perspective, that of another person, *and* that of an abstract "generalized other" representing a larger social group. Suppose that 14-year-old Beth is arguing with her parents about whether she should be allowed to go on single dates. Although self-interest can always interfere with mature thinking, Beth may realize that her parents are motivated by a concern for her welfare *and* imagine how "parents in general" and "teenagers in general" would view

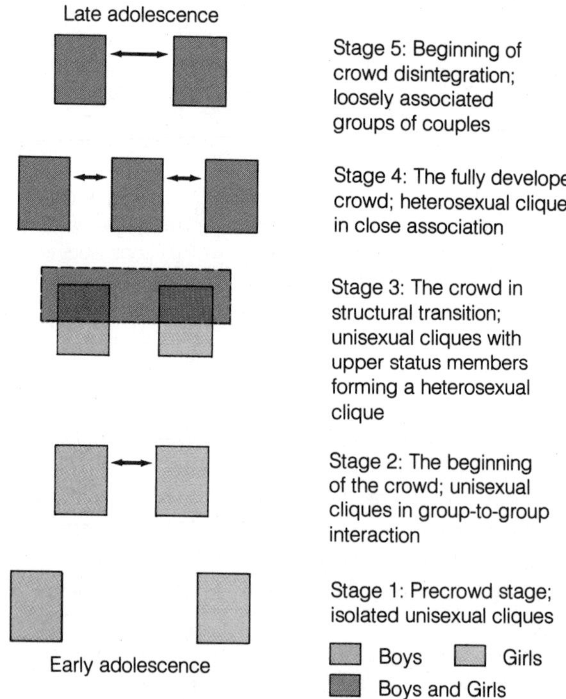

Figure 13.3 Stages in the evolution of the peer group during adolescence: from same-sex cliques (*bottom*) to dating couples (*top*). (From Dunphy, 1963)

the issue. Instead of merely pushing her own perspective or trying to manipulate her parents, she may be able to integrate multiple perspectives in a solution that is best for *the relationship*. Thus she may decide that going on double dates until she demonstrates that she is responsible is the best way to balance, for the good of the parent/child relationship, her interest in freedom and her parents' concerns for her welfare. Not all 14-year-olds are this sophisticated, but Robert Selman finds that considerable growth in the ability to understand and resolve interpersonal conflicts occurs during the adolescent years (Selman, Beardslee, Schultz, Krupa, & Podorefsky, 1986).

Social-cognitive growth during adolescence helps explain why young adolescents often seem preoccupied with how others will respond to them. Their improving social-cognitive skills make them better able to contemplate how their behaviors might "go over," and they become more egocentrically self-conscious as a result (Elkind, 1980). As their social-cognitive growth continues, they become more skilled at distinguishing between their own thoughts and those of other people and overcome some of their preoccupation with what other people might be thinking about them. And as they gain new social-cognitive skills, their relationships also change.

Social Networks: The Transition from Same-Sex Peer Groups to Dating Relationships

One of the most important tasks of adolescence is to learn how to relate to members of the other sex. As we learned in Chapter 11, elementary school children are interested in the other sex and are gradually preparing themselves for heterosexual relationships. Still, how do boys and girls who live in their own, gender-segregated worlds arrive at the point of dating "the enemy"?

Some time ago, Dexter Dunphy (1963) offered a plausible account of how peer-group structures change during adolescence to pave the way for dating relationships. The steps in the process are outlined in Figure 13.3. It begins in late childhood, when boys and girls are members of same-sex **cliques**, or small friendship groups, and have little to do with the other sex. Next, members of boy cliques and girl cliques begin to interact with each other more frequently. Same-sex cliques provide what we might call a secure base for exploring how to interact with members of the other sex. Talking to a girl when your buddies are there is far less threatening than doing so on your own. In the third stage, the most popular boys and girls form a *heterosexual* clique. As less popular peers also enter into heterosexual cliques, a new peer group structure, the **crowd**, completes its evolution. The crowd, a collection of up to about four heterosexual cliques, comes into play mainly as a mechanism for arranging organized social activities on the weekend—parties, outings to the lake or mall, and so on. Those adolescents who do become members of a mixed-sex clique and a crowd have many opportunities to get to know members of the other sex. Eventually, however, interacting with the other sex in group settings is not enough. Couples form, sometimes double-dating or spending time with other couples, and the crowd disintegrates after having served its purpose of bringing boys and girls together.

In a junior or senior high school, different crowds typically form, each consisting of individuals who are similar to one another in some way. In a recent study of adolescent crowds, B. Bradford Brown and Mary Jane Lohr (1987) found that about two-thirds of students in grades 7 to 12 were identified by their peers as members of one crowd or another. The "jock" crowd and the "popular" crowd typically had higher status than crowds composed of "druggies," "toughs," or "nobodies." Moreover, while being part of some crowd appeared to be a source of self-esteem, self-esteem was higher among members of high-status crowds than among members of low-status crowds. Thus mixed-sex adolescent crowds serve to give teenagers a social identity, but they also continually remind them of whether their status among their peers is high or low.

As adolescents begin dating, the attachments they form to romantic partners become among their most important social ties. Adolescents in our society go on their first dates at about the age of 14 on average, though there is much variation (Dickinson, 1975; Miller, McCoy, & Olson, 1986). Dates have increasingly become a matter of boy and girl informally getting together rather than boy formally asking girl out (Murstein, 1980). How do you remember your first dates? If they were typical, they were probably quite awkward and superficial (Douvan & Adelson, 1966; Place, 1975). Boy and girl both want to succeed in the dating scene and may be so concerned with playing a role to impress their partner that they cannot really relax and be themselves. A deeper relationship sometimes evolves as dating partners get to know each other better: Most adolescents do go steady with someone at some time.

In one study, for example, about 80% of white high school students and 68% of black high school students reported that they either were going steady at present or had gone steady at some time (Dickinson, 1975). Of course, the vast majority of these first loves do not survive. It may take until the end of high school—or even longer—for dating partners to achieve a more genuine emotional intimacy (Douvan & Adelson, 1966). Meanwhile, adolescents are preparing for this day by participating in same-sex friendships.

Adolescent Friendships

If friendships in early childhood center on common activities, and friendships in late childhood center on loyalty and mutual aid, then adolescent friendships increasingly hinge on *mutual intimacy and self-disclosure* (Tesch, 1983). Adolescents continue to form friendships with peers who are similar to themselves. However, they increasingly choose friends whose *psychological qualities*—interests, attitudes, values, and personalities—seem to match their own. Now friends are like-minded individuals who can confide in one another (Berndt, 1982).

The transition to intimate friendships based on a sharing of thoughts and feelings occurs earlier among girls than among boys (Berndt, 1982; Burhmester & Furman, 1986). Elizabeth Douvan and Joseph Adelson (1966) described several notable changes in girls' same-sex friendships during adolescence. Between the ages of 11 and 13, girlfriends mainly enjoyed doing things together. In the 14 to 16 age range, friendships became far more emotionally close. Best friends confided their deepest thoughts and feelings to one another and trusted one another to keep secrets. Indeed, teenage girls who are best friends are almost like "lovers," intensely attached to one another and inseparable. This intimacy does have its costs. Friends of this age are sometimes overdependent on each other—possessive, jealous, and outraged by any betrayal of their trust (Douvan & Adelson, 1966). Girls' friendships become more relaxed starting at about age 17 or 18. As they become more autonomous, gain social-cognitive skills, and become more involved in dating, girls become less emotionally dependent on a best friend and more able to accept and even appreciate differences between themselves and their friends.

What happens to boys' friendships during this period? Douvan and Adelson found that boys' friendships were less emotionally intense. Like the friendships of 11- to 13-year-old girls, those of 14- to 16-year-old boys were based largely on an enjoyment of common activities and a willingness to come to one another's aid. This sex difference in friendships does not necessarily mean that boys' friendships are less intimate in all ways than those of girls, however. For example, knowledge of what one's friends are like psychologically increases from childhood to adolescence among *both* boys and girls, and adolescent boys seem to know as much as adolescent girls do about such things as their friends' favorite school subjects and major worries (Diaz & Berndt, 1982). Possibly, then, girls who are best friends talk more about their feelings than boys do, but boys nonetheless get to know their friends quite well by doing things with them (Berndt, 1982).

Although same-sex friendships remain important throughout adolescence, teenagers increasingly enter into close cross-sex friendships. How do these cross-sex friendships compare with same-sex friendships? Ruth Sharabany, Ruth Gershoni, and John Hofman (1981) asked fifth to eleventh graders to assess their same- and cross-sex friendships in terms of such aspects of intimacy as spontaneity, trust and loyalty, sensitivity to the other's feelings, attachment, and so on. As you can see in Figure 13.4, same-sex friendships were highly intimate in most respects throughout this age range, but cross-sex friendships did

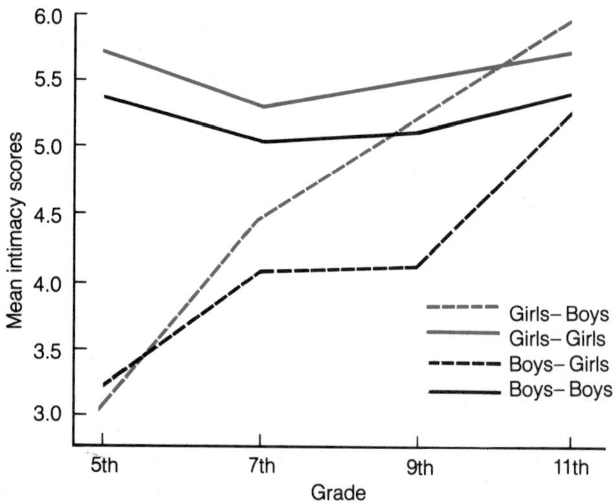

Figure 13.4 Changes during adolescence in the intimacy of same-sex and cross-sex friendships. (From Sharabany, Gershoni, & Hofman, 1981)

not attain this same high level of intimacy until eleventh grade. We can also observe interesting sex differences: All along, girls tended to report higher degrees of intimacy in their friendships than boys did; moreover, girls experienced intimacy in their friendships with boys sooner than boys experienced intimacy in their relationships with girls. These findings offer some support for Harry Stack Sullivan's view that children learn lessons about intimate attachments in their same-sex chumships that they only later apply in their heterosexual relationships. They also reinforce the finding that boys are somewhat slower than girls to achieve emotional intimacy in their close relationships.

Parent and Peer Influence on Adolescents

Quite obviously, adolescents become more and more involved in both same-sex and cross-sex relationships with peers as they get older. Should parents worry about this? Will they lose influence over their children? Will the values of the peer group replace the values that parents have worked so long to instill in their children?

One approach to answering these questions has been to study **conformity** to parents and peers, or the tendency to go along with the opinions of one or the other. For example, Thomas Berndt (1979) asked children in the third through twelfth grades to judge how much they would be likely to bend to parent or peer pressure in a number of hypothetical situations—for example, if peers advocated *antisocial* behavior such as soaping windows on Halloween or if the child were urged to choose one *prosocial* behavior (for example, helping a brother with homework) over another favored by the child (visiting a sick friend) or to choose one *neutral* act (going for a walk) rather than another (playing cards).

Conformity to pressure from adults to engage in prosocial or neutral acts decreased gradually and steadily with age. Conformity to peer pressure to perform positive acts did not change with age. Instead, the most striking developmental trend was an increase in conformity to peers who urged *antisocial* behavior. This trend reached a peak in ninth grade (see also Bixenstine, DeCorte, & Bixenstine, 1976; Steinberg & Silverberg, 1986). Apparently, then, parents have some grounds for worrying that their adolescents may get themselves in trouble by going along with the crowd, especially at around the age of 15. Peer pressure is particularly strong at this age, and being accepted by peers is particularly important (Gavin & Furman, 1989).

But conformity to peers advocating misconduct *decreased* by the end of high school. Why is this? As adolescents make progress in their quest for autonomy, they become less dependent on *both* parents and peers for guidance and more able to make their own choices. Laurence Steinberg and Susan Silverberg (1986) argue that increased dependence on peers may even be a necessary step in the development of autonomy. Adolescents who are trying to become more independent of their parents may need the security that peer acceptance provides before they are ready to become truly autonomous in later adolescence. They are unlikely to achieve this acceptance if they conform too closely to adult rules and values (Allen, Weissberg, & Hawkins, 1989). The parent whose teenager ends up at the police station may not be totally comforted by this thought, but it does seem that a period of high conformity to peers may pave the way for later independence.

Even though midadolescence is a time of high susceptibility to negative peer pressure, parents typically need not be unduly worried about losing their adolescents to the peer group. Moreover, they should not think of adolescence as a time of warfare between parents and peers. Adolescents who have good relationships with their parents are less susceptible to peer pressures and are less likely to experience conflicts between parents and peers than are adolescents whose family relationships are poor (Bixenstine et al., 1976; Brook, Whiteman, & Gordon, 1983). When parents are warm, neither too controlling nor too lax, and consistent in their discipline, adolescents are likely to have internalized their parents' values. They also have less need to rebel or to seek acceptance in the peer group because they cannot obtain it at home. Fortunately, most adolescents *do* enjoy close relationships with their parents and very much want their parents' approval (Youniss & Smollar, 1985).

In addition, parent/peer wars are often kept to a minimum because parents and peers tend to exert their influences in distinct realms. Hans Sebald (1986), for example, has asked adolescents whether they would seek the advice of their parents or the advice of their peers on a number of different issues. Peers were likely to be more influential than parents when it came to such decisions as what dress styles to wear and which clubs, social events, hobbies, and other social activities to choose. By contrast, adolescents claimed that they would depend more on their parents in

It is no accident that teenagers dress alike. Peers exert more influence on dress styles than parents do.

deciding which courses to take, whether or not to go to college, which occupations to select, and how to spend money. Apparently, then, peers tend to influence the *current* lifestyles, social activities, and tastes of adolescents, but parents continue to be the major shapers of *future* educational and vocational decisions and important values (Sebald, 1986; Wilks, 1986).

A final reason that we should not think of parents and peers as adversaries is this: Even when parents and peers influence the same aspects of behavior, their influences often work in the same direction (Hartup, 1983). In other words, it is not really typical for adults to be saying one thing while peers are saying the opposite. This makes sense: After all, parents exert some influence on their children's friendship choices, if only by choosing a neighborhood in which to live (Rubin & Sloman, 1984). Moreover, adolescents themselves typically choose friends who come from backgrounds similar to their own. In many adolescent crowds, especially those consisting of "jocks" or "populars," peer pressure is actually exerted on adolescents to *refrain* from misconduct and to get more involved in school activities (Clasen & Brown, 1985). Thus, adolescents often find that their parents and their peers value many of the same things.

In short, adolescent socialization is not a continual war of parents *versus* peers; instead, these two important sources of influence *combine* to affect development. As their teenage children become more involved in activities with peers or more susceptible to peer pressures, parents usually continue to be important forces in their children's lives. Most parents have good relationships with their teenagers; parents and peers often influence distinct aspects of behavior and decision making; and parents and peers often see eye to eye on many important issues: These factors usually keep parent/peer warfare to a manageable minimum. Most parents know how important it is for children and adolescents to have close relationships with their social equals; after all, these friendships help develop many of the aspects of social competence that allow people to form and maintain good relationships as adults.

THE ADULT

Relationships with family and friends seem to be no less important during adulthood than they are earlier in life, but they take on different qualities over the adult years.

Social Cognition

As adults go about the business of interacting with both intimates and acquaintances, they rely on their social-cognitive skills to make sense of other people. Do important social-cognitive skills such as the ability to analyze other people's personalities or adopt their perspectives change during adulthood? Surprisingly little is known, but we can offer some hints (Kramer, 1986). As you may recall from Chapter 7, *non*social cognitive abilities such as those used in testing scientific hypotheses may actually improve during early and middle adulthood. Compared with adolescents, who seem to want to force facts into one neat and logical system, some adults become better able to accept contradictions in the real world and are more aware that problems can be viewed from a number of different perspectives. However, cognitive researchers also find that many elderly people seem to perform poorly on Piagetian tasks assessing nonsocial cognition (Denney, 1982).

Might these same developmental trends apply to social cognition? It does make sense to think that adults, through their years of social experience, might increasingly become experts in the social domain (Roodin, Rybash, & Hoyer, 1986). Fredda Blanchard-Fields (1986a) has compared the answers of adolescents and adults who were asked to judge how responsible actors in stories were for their actions. She found that adolescents tend to stick to a single answer based on the facts they are given, whereas adults tend to read between the lines, adopt more than one perspective (for example, a moral perspective and a legal one), and express an awareness that their own perspective on life influences their conclusions and is only one of many that could be taken. Similarly, she found that when young and (especially) middle-aged adults are presented with a conflict between a teenage boy and his parents, they are better able than adolescents to integrate the perspectives of *both* son and parents into a workable solution (Blanchard-Fields, 1986b). Here, then, are some hints that the social-cognitive skills of adults may continue to expand after adolescence. Through a combination of social experience and cognitive growth, adults have the potential to become quite sophisticated students of human psychology.

Do elderly people continue to display sophisticated social-cognitive skills? Here the answers are mixed. Some researchers find that elderly people have difficulty adopting perspectives different from their own (Denney, 1982), but others find that elderly people perform as well as younger adults on many social-cognitive tasks. For example, there seem to be few differences in the way young, middle-aged, and elderly adults describe people (Fitzgerald & Martin-Louer, 1983–1984). At all ages, adults emphasize the psychological qualities that make an individual unique.

It is becoming clear that the social-cognitive abilities of adults depend far more on the extent and nature of their social experiences than on their age. For example, Lenise Dolen and David Bearison (1982) asked subjects ranging in age from 65 to 89 to perform three social-cognition tasks: a person-perception task in which they described two people they knew well, an interpersonal problem-solving task in which they had to devise alternative ways to bring about a story's outcome, and a perspective-taking task in which they were to retell a story from the vantage point of each of three characters. Age was completely unrelated to performance on these tasks. Instead, the elderly adults who performed well in comparison with their peers were those who were socially active, particularly those who were deeply involved in meaningful social roles such as those of spouse, grandparent, church member, and worker.

In sum, adults may actually gain social-cognitive abilities during adulthood that they did not possess as adolescents, learning to analyze interpersonal issues in highly complex ways from a number of perspectives. Moreover, most adults seem to maintain their social-cognitive skills quite well in old age, even though many of them perform quite poorly on many *non*social cognitive tasks. Although elderly people may grow rusty at solving physical science problems because they have been out of school for years, they may continue to display sophisticated social-cognitive skills so long as they continue to practice those skills every day in their social interactions. Possibly it is only when elderly people become socially isolated or inactive that they experience difficulties thinking in complex ways about personal and interpersonal issues. How many people *do* become socially isolated in old age? Perhaps we should find out by examining how people's social networks change over the adult years.

Social Networks

Whom do adults interact with and how socially active are they? For most adults, a marriage partner becomes a central part of the social landscape, and interactions with one's children soon become important as well. Adults also maintain close relationships with their parents and other relatives. Moreover, most adults enjoy many nonfamily ties. They have close friends, associate closely with colleagues and co-workers, and often become members of "peer groups" devoted to such activities as poker, softball, car pooling, or child care.

Do the social networks of younger and older adults differ? Young adults are busily forming romantic relationships and friendships with both men and women, typically choosing to associate with people who are similar to them in important ways, just as children and adolescents do. Young singles seem to have more ties to friends and fewer to family than older and married adults do (Fischer & Phillips, 1982; Fischer, Sollie, Sorell, & Green, 1989). Young adults derive great pleasure from their social ties, but they are also more likely than older adults to express concerns about their relationships or to wish they had more of them (Kahn & Antonucci, 1983, cited by Antonucci, 1985; Veroff, Douvan, & Kulka, 1981).

As adults marry, have children, and take on increasing responsibilities in their jobs, their social networks appear to shrink somewhat. Middle-aged adults have close ties to many relatives, but they often have fewer close friends than younger adults do, perhaps because they have less time for friendship (Fischer & Phillips, 1982; Shulman,

1975). And what about elderly people? Do their social networks deteriorate? Apparently not. Older adults, especially men, do have fewer friends, but they have about as many close relationships with relatives as middle-aged adults do (Babchuk, 1978–1979; Fischer & Phillips, 1982). Moreover, they seem to receive about as much social support from relatives and friends as middle-aged adults do (Kahn & Antonucci, 1983, cited by Antonucci, 1985). In other words, adults' social networks do shrink some in total size from early adulthood to very old age (Morgan, 1988), but most elderly adults still have rich social networks.

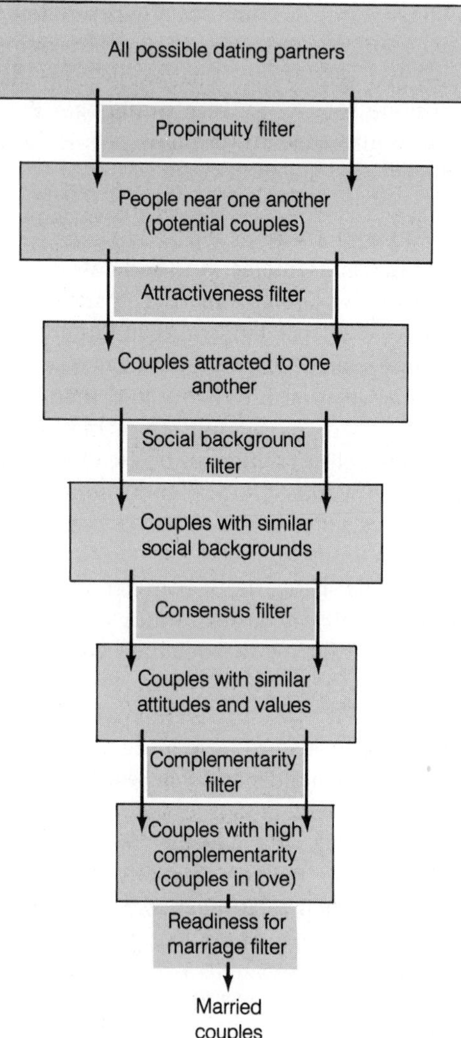

Figure 13.5 Udry's filter model of mate selection: Start with all possible partners and narrow the field down to one. (From Udry, 1971)

But aren't most old people socially isolated and lonely, you ask? Louis Harris and associates (1981) report that fully 65% of U.S. adults aged 18 to 64 *believe* that loneliness is a "very serious problem" for most old people. Yet when elderly adults themselves were asked about their "very serious problems," only 13% cited loneliness! Older people spend more time alone than younger adults do (Larson, Zuzanek, & Mannell, 1985), but it is *young* adults who more often report feelings of loneliness (Parlee, 1979). Perhaps young adults, because they are less secure in their relationships, are anxious when they are not with other people; perhaps elderly adults have learned that being alone need not mean being lonely and can enjoy time to themselves. Whatever the reasons, we must rid ourselves of the myth that most older adults suffer from a lack of close attachments and are lonely.

Romantic Relationships

For many adults, the most important member of the larger social network is a spouse or romantic partner. As Erik Erikson has emphasized, early adulthood is an important time for establishing truly intimate and committed love relationships—marriages or other enduring emotional attachments. What is love? Robert Sternberg and Susan Grajek (1984) note that it has been defined in countless ways, but their own research suggests that love for a romantic partner, love for parents and siblings, and love for a best friend have something in common—namely, a sense of mutual communication, sharing, and support. Beyond that, romantic love relationships are typically more passionate, more exclusive and preoccupying, and more potentially distressing than friendships are (Davis, 1985).

Partner Selection

Why do we choose one romantic partner rather than another? Richard Udry (1971) has captured many of the messages of research on this topic in his **filter model of mate selection** (Figure 13.5). Udry asks us to imagine that mate selection is a process of sifting through all potential partners to find one chosen partner. The first filter in Udry's model, *propinquity*, reflects the truth that we are most likely to become involved with someone who lives nearby. Although your perfect mate may be living in Outer

Mongolia, there is little chance that you will ever meet this person, much less fall in love! The next filter, the *attractiveness* filter, reminds us of what we have discovered already: People are attracted to physically attractive people from an early age. Since unattractive people face low odds of linking up with attractive people, what typically happens is that we select people whose level of attractiveness is near our own and who are physically appealing to us. Next we screen people based on *social background*, favoring as romantic partners those who match us in such characteristics as socioeconomic background, education, racial or ethnic group, and religious affiliation.

Assuming that a potential partner passes through these larger, coarser "screens," *consensus*, or similarity, with respect to values, attitudes, and interests may help determine whether the relationship endures or crumbles. If potential mates are psychologically similar, they may then favor a relationship in which there is also *complementarity*, or a meshing of strengths and weaknesses that somehow makes each person more complete. Jerry and Fran, for example, may be similar in most important ways but may also find that they complement each other well because Jerry is better at planning social activities than Fran is, while Fran offers Jerry a cool head when Jerry might otherwise become emotionally upset about events at work. Finally, Udry notes that all the compatibility in the world is unlikely to lead to marriage unless both partners possess a *readiness for marriage* (or for a lasting commitment of some kind).

Although Udry concentrated on bases for marital choice, we can readily apply the model to any romantic relationship, whether heterosexual or homosexual, whether aimed toward marriage or aimed toward a lasting commitment. The model may sound rather "cold and clinical," as though it somehow misses the intangible qualities of love or likens selecting a mate to selecting a stereo system. Moreover, dating relationships probably do not evolve in an orderly, chronological manner from one filter to the next, with each filter in turn determining whether or not the relationship will continue (Huston, Surra, Fitzgerald, & Cate, 1981). Nonetheless, the factors that Udry includes in his model *are* very influential in the formation of romantic relationships. The most important theme is that we gravitate toward those who are similar to ourselves in a wide range of important ways (Buss, 1985). In this sense, choosing a mate as an adult very much resembles choosing a friend as a child. It is also interesting to observe that just as infants progress from a general responsiveness to people to an exclusive relationship with one attachment figure, adolescents and adults progress from a period of dating many partners to the selection of *one* special partner.

Love as Attachment: Styles of Loving

Several researchers have become intrigued by parallels between an infant's attachment to a parent figure and a young adult's love for a romantic partner (Hazan & Shaver, 1987; Kahn & Antonucci, 1980; Lerner & Ryff, 1978). Obviously parent/infant attachments and adult romantic attachments are not identical. Yet the adult who is in love, like the infant who is attached to a parent, experiences strong affection for his or her partner, wants to be close, takes comfort from the bond, and may even experience the sorts of fears of separation that an infant experiences.

Cindy Hazan and Phillip Shaver (1987) have demonstrated that adults can be classified into the same three categories of attachment—secure, insecure/resistant, and insecure/avoidant—that have been used to characterize parent/infant attachments. Box 13.6 shows how Hazan and Shaver have translated the three types of infant attachments into adult terms.

What implications do these different styles of attachment have for adults? From studies of college students and of adults who responded to a newspaper ad, Hazan and Shaver conclude that an adult's style of attachment is related to the quality of that individual's romantic relationships. For example, adults with a *secure* attachment style experience a good deal of trust and many positive emotions in their current love relationships, and their relationships last longer than those of adults who fit either of the insecure attachment categories. Both *avoidant* and *resistant* adults report a great deal of jealousy and emotional extremes of love and pain in their love relationships and are dubious that lasting love can be found. In addition, avoidant lovers seem to fear intimacy, whereas resistant individuals tend to be obsessed by their relationships and overdependent on their partners. Resistant individuals, and to a lesser extent avoidant ones as well, also report more loneliness than secure respondents do.

How do these styles of attachment take form? Hazan and Shaver suspected that they may be formed during

Box 13.6
Three Adult Attachment Types: Which Best Describes Your Feelings?

Secure attachment (56% of adults)
I find it relatively easy to get close to others and am comfortable depending on them and having them depend on me. I don't often worry about being abandoned or about someone getting too close to me.

Insecure/resistant attachment (19% of adults)
I find that others are reluctant to get as close as I would like. I often worry that my partner doesn't really love me or won't want to stay with me. I want to merge completely with another person, and this desire sometimes scares people away.

Insecure/avoidant attachment (25% of adults)
I am somewhat uncomfortable being close to others; I find it difficult to trust them completely, difficult to allow myself to depend on them. I am nervous when anyone gets too close, and often, love partners want me to be more intimate than I feel comfortable being.

Source: Modified from Hazan & Shaver, 1987.

childhood and may be related to the quality of the individual's attachment to parents. Indeed, there were at least weak associations between how respondents recalled their early relationships with their parents and how they characterized their current attachment style. Securely attached adults reported that their relationships with their parents and their parents' relationship to each other had been warm, but adults in the insecure attachment categories tended to remember their parents as unfair, critical, or cold. Hazan and Shaver emphasize that these links between past and present were weak and that adults' styles of loving are undoubtedly very much influenced by their experiences in romantic relationships. Nonetheless, this research suggests that at least some of us may develop styles of intimacy as infants and children that continue to affect the nature and quality of our intimate attachments as adults (see also Kobak & Sceery, 1988).

Relationships with spouses or romantic partners remain central throughout adulthood. We will postpone our discussion of how these relationships evolve and change until Chapter 14. For now, let us consider another attachment that is highly important during adulthood: the friendship bond.

Adult Friendships

Although young adults typically have more friends than older adults do, friends remain an important part of the social convoy throughout the adult years. One noteworthy message of research on the quality of adults' friendships is that men and women continue to display the differences in styles of friendship that they displayed as adolescents. As Paul Wright (1982) puts it, female friends typically interact "face to face," whereas male friends typically interact "side by side." In other words, female friends spend a great deal of time talking about their feelings and problems, while male friends enjoy doing things together (Winstead, 1986). Most likely, sex differences in friendship styles are rooted in early gender socialization (Winstead, 1986). Moreover, they persist into old age (Fox, Gibbs, & Auerbach, 1985; Roberto & Kimboko, 1989). In addition, elderly men are less likely than elderly women to have intimate friendships outside the family (Babchuk, 1978–1979; Field & Minkler, 1988; Powers & Bultena, 1976). Often their most important friends are their wives (Kendig, Coles, Pittelkow, & Wilson, 1989).

Friendships come and go over the years. As people move or experience other life changes, they lose some friends and acquire others. Perhaps for this reason, elderly adults especially value friendships that have lasted a lifetime (Adams, 1985–1986; Matthews, 1986; Shea, Thompson, & Blieszner, 1988). Imagine having a friend whom you have known for 50 or more years—since, as one man put it, you were "knee-high to a duck" (Matthews, 1986). Imagine sharing a lifetime of experience with someone who knows you inside and out. Almost three-fourths of the women Rebecca Adams interviewed claimed that "old friends are the best friends." Many of these women felt emotionally closer to friends from the past who were geographically distant than to newer friends who lived nearby. However, most elderly people seem to have close friends nearby as well as close friends far away, and they remain quite capable of making new friends late in life (Adams, 1985–1986; Matthews, 1986; Shea et al., 1988).

One potential problem that may arise in friendships in later life is that one friend may develop health problems or other difficulties and become overdependent on his or her partner. Social psychologists have long emphasized the importance of **equity**, or a balance of contributions and gains, in relationships between spouses, friends, and other intimates (Walster, Walster, & Berscheid, 1978). Generally, relationships are perceived as more satisfying when they are equitable than when they are inequitable. A person who receives too much from a relationship is likely to feel guilty, while a person who gives a great deal and receives little in return often feels angry or resentful (Walster et al., 1978).

Is equity important in later-life friendships? Karen Roberto and Jean Scott (1986) report that elderly adults experienced less distress in friendships they perceived as equitable than in friendships they perceived as inequitable. Interestingly, *overbenefited*, or dependent, friends experienced more distress than underbenefited, or support-giving friends. Elderly adults who find themselves unable to contribute equally to a friendship may feel especially uncomfortable in their dependent role, while friends who find themselves in the helper role may take some comfort from knowing they are capable of giving. Ultimately, friendships may crumble if they become too inequitable (Allan, 1986). This may be why elderly people seem to call on family before they call on friends when they need help or emotional support (Chatters, Taylor, & Jackson, 1986; Kendig et al., 1989). As a result, they usually manage to maintain very equitable relationships with their friends (Ingersoll-Dayton & Antonucci, 1988).

Close friendships that have lasted for years are particularly important to adults.

In sum, adults of all ages seem to enjoy close friendships and often are able to carry with them through life—as part of their social convoy—old friends with whom they can share a lifetime of experiences. Yet most elderly people also supplement old friends with new friends and feel most satisfied with those relationships in which there is equity or a balance of giving and taking.

Adult Relationships and Adult Development

We have emphasized throughout this chapter that close attachments to other people are essential to normal cognitive, social, and emotional development. Children who lack close relationships to parents and peers clearly suffer for it (Norris & Rubin, 1984). Is this also true in adulthood?

It seems to be. Adults are better off in many ways if they enjoy meaningful relationships. Much attention has been centered on the significance of social networks and social support to elderly people—possibly because researchers, like members of the general public, have incorrectly assumed that elderly adults are usually socially isolated! The major generalization that has emerged from this research is this: It is the *quality* rather than the quantity of an individual's social relationships that is most closely related to that person's sense of well-being or happiness (Arling, 1987; Holahan & Holahan, 1987; Liang, Dvorkin, Kahana, & Mazian, 1980; Ward, Sherman, & LaGory, 1984).

Consider what Russell Ward and his colleagues (Ward, Sherman, & LaGory, 1984) found when they surveyed adults aged 60 and older about their social networks and social supports. They inquired about *objective* aspects of people's social ties: how many close relationships they had, how often they saw relatives and friends, and how much practical aid and emotional support they received. However, these researchers also asked about *subjective* perceptions of support: about whether these adults felt that they saw important others enough and received enough practical help and opportunities to share their feelings with others. Individuals who had many ties and received a great deal of practical and emotional support tended to have a greater sense of well-being than those who were more socially deprived in an objective sense. And yet, the more important contributor to well-being was the *perception* of having positive social ties and sources of support (see also Krause, Liang, & Yatomi, 1989). Just as people can feel lonely even though they are surrounded by other people, adults can apparently feel deprived of social support even though they receive a considerable amount of it—or can have quite restricted social networks and yet feel satisfied with their relationships.

Similarly, other researchers find that the size of an adult's social network is not nearly so important as whether it includes at least one **confidant**—a spouse, relative, or friend to whom the individual feels an especially close attachment and with whom thoughts and feelings can be shared (de Jong-Gierveld, 1986; Lowenthal & Haven, 1968; Snow & Crapo, 1982). Still others, agreeing that quality is more important than quantity, find that supportive friends may contribute more to well-being in old age than children or other relatives do (Arling, 1976; Pihlblad & Adams, 1972). In short, a small number of close and harmonious relationships can do much to make negative life events more bearable and improve the overall quality of an adult's life. Whatever our ages, it seems, our development hinges considerably on the quality of our ties to fellow humans.

APPLICATIONS: HELPING THE SOCIALLY ISOLATED

Developmentalists have naturally become interested in applying what they have learned about social development to the task of helping individuals who are socially isolated and lonely to develop richer social relationships. They have been quite successful.

Children who are isolated from their peers typically lack basic social and social-cognitive skills, such as those involved in successfully initiating play activities; cooperating; communicating their needs; giving help, affection, and approval; and resolving interpersonal conflicts (Asher, 1986). One popular method of teaching them social skills is called *coaching*. An adult therapist models or displays social skills, explains why they are useful, allows children to practice them, and then offers feedback to help children improve on their performances.

Sherrie Oden and Steven Asher (1977) coached third- and fourth-grade social isolates in four important social skills: how to participate in play activities, how to take turns and share, how to communicate effectively, and how to give attention and help to peers. Not only did the children who were coached become more outgoing and positive in their social behavior, but a follow-up assessment a year later revealed that they had achieved even further gains in their sociometric status within the classroom (see also Bierman, 1986; Ladd, 1981).

Another successful approach to helping isolated and withdrawn children grew out of research on monkeys who had been socially isolated from birth. After six months of such isolation, infant monkeys emerge terrified of other monkeys and lacking in the most basic of social skills (Harlow & Harlow, 1977). They clutch themselves and bury their heads as if to shut out a strange new social world; engage in abnormal behaviors such as self-biting, rocking, and pulling out tufts of their hair; and allow themselves to be abused by normal age mates. As adults, they seem to

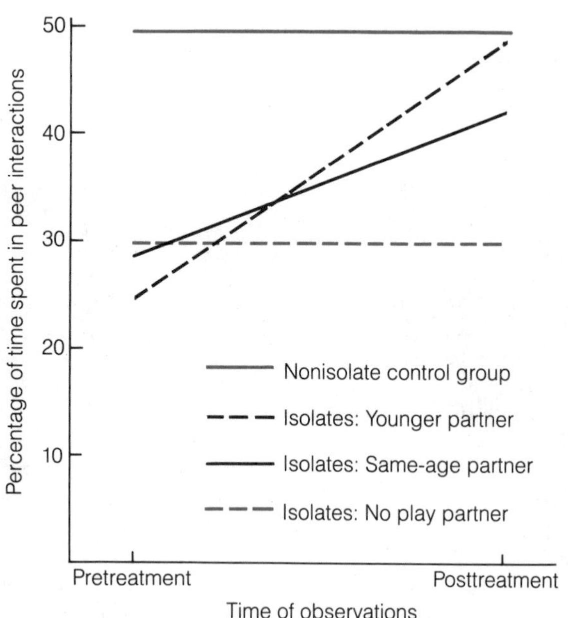

Figure 13.6 Percentages of time that children spent interacting with peers before and after engaging in play sessions with a younger or a same-age partner. (Data from Furman, Rahe, & Hartup, 1979)

have no idea of how to go about mating. However, Stephen Suomi and Harry Harlow (1972) discovered that these social isolates could learn normal social skills if they interacted with *younger* monkeys. Whereas age mates simply would not put up with these maladjusted loners, younger monkeys would cling to the isolates and attempt to play rather than working them over. By the end of 26 weeks of contact with a younger "therapist," isolates had come out of their shells, and follow-up studies revealed that they turned out to be socially and sexually competent adults (Novak, 1979).

Heartened by this research, Wyndol Furman, Don Rahe, and Willard Hartup (1979) tried the same approach with children who had been identified as social isolates in a day-care setting. Some children experienced play sessions with a child 18 months younger than they were, others played with a partner of the same age, and still others participated in no play sessions. As Figure 13.6 shows, withdrawn children who had played with a partner became much more socially outgoing in their classrooms than social isolates who had not taken part in any play sessions. Moreover, the improvements were greatest for those who had played with a *younger* partner. Perhaps, then, some socially withdrawn children need to gain social skills and confidence with their social *un*equals before they are ready to interact comfortably with their social equals.

Lonely college students are not entirely unlike socially withdrawn children. In many cases, they too have social-skills deficits that make it difficult for them to make contact with people, carry on meaningful conversations, and build more intimate relationships (Rook, 1984). For instance, Warren Jones and his associates (Jones, Hobbs, & Hockenbury, 1982) discovered that lonely college students are less likely than nonlonely ones to give positive attention to their conversation partners by referring to them, pursuing topics they bring up, and asking questions. These researchers used a form of coaching to teach a group of lonely college men to be more attentive to female conversation partners. Trainees listened to tapes modeling appropriate conversational behaviors, practiced the skills they observed, and received feedback about their skills. Compared with students who received no coaching or who simply interacted with a partner without benefit of training, the trained students became more able to offer reinforcing attention to women. Moreover, they left the program reporting that they were less lonely, shy, and self-conscious.

However, not all individuals who are lonely and socially isolated are socially incompetent. For some individuals, the real problem is a restricted social environment, a lack of opportunities for forming close relationships (Rook, 1984). Such was the case for the socially isolated elderly people described by Marc Pilisuk and Meredith Minkler (1980). Living in inner-city hotels in San Francisco, these individuals were often prisoners of their rooms because of disability, poverty, and fear of crime. To change things, public health nurses began to offer free blood pressure checkups in the lobby of one hotel. As the nurses got to know residents, they were able to link individuals who had common interests and draw residents into conversations. After about a year, the residents formed their own activities club; organized discussions, film showings, and parties; and were well on their way out of their social isolation. The trick was to change their social environment rather than their social skills.

Since development is influenced by both individual and environmental factors, it makes sense to think that socially isolated and lonely children and adults can be helped most through efforts to improve their own social skills and confidence in social situations *and* to change their environments in order to increase their opportunities for meaningful social interaction. Indeed, one research team found that unpopular children were helped the most when they received social-skills coaching *and* were put in a new social situation, one in which they had opportunities to work cooperatively with peers to achieve common goals (Bierman & Furman, 1984). In short, multiple approaches may be needed to enrich social lives and enhance social development across the life span.

REFLECTIONS

We like the notion that each of us travels through life accompanied by an ever-changing social convoy. It's a comforting thought, at least for the majority of us who have rich social networks. It also reminds us that any individual's development is intimately intertwined with that of other individuals. In this chapter, we have concentrated mainly on how we as individuals benefit from close attachments—from having a secure bond with at least one caregiver as an infant, close friendships and accepting peers as a child or adolescent, and intimate romantic relationships and friendships as an adult. Remember, though, that we not only have convoys but are also part of the social convoys of other people. Thus we can contribute to the development of those closest to us by being understanding and supportive friends, warm and responsive parents for our children, or caring supporters of our aging parents. Unfortunately, we not only have the potential to help one another cope with problems, but we sometimes *are* one another's problems. The love and social stimulation, the mistreatment and rejection—all are part of being a social being!

If we take seriously the idea that each of us affects and is affected by significant members of our social convoys throughout the life span, it is worthwhile to study the development of *relationships* rather than the development of isolated individuals. In the next chapter, we will attempt to determine how relationships within the family change over the life cycle as people play out their roles as children, parents, and grandparents. So far, developmentalists have only scratched the surface in their attempts to understand how relationships change and how partners in relationships shape each other's development as they journey together through time.

SUMMARY POINTS

1. Social relationships contribute immensely to human development, primarily by providing us with critical learning opportunities and social support (affect, affirmation, and aid). The developmental significance of early parent/child relationships was underscored by Freud, that of peer relationships by Piaget and Sullivan.

2. Before infants are ready to form attachments to their caregivers, parents typically become attached to their infants, although some parents have difficulty doing so for personal or social reasons.

3. In forming attachments, infants progress through phases of undiscriminating social responsiveness, discriminating social responsiveness, and active proximity seeking; the formation of attachments at about 6 or 7 months of age is accompanied by separation anxiety and stranger anxiety.

4. Although the Freudian view that infants become attached to those who feed them lacks support, Erik Erikson and learning theorists were correct to emphasize the caregiver's responsiveness and reinforcing qualities, cognitive-developmental theorists to emphasize cognitive requisites for attachment, and ethological theorist John Bowlby to stress biological predispositions coupled with social experience. A secure attachment contributes to later competence, but insecurely attached or socially deprived infants are not inevitably doomed to a lifetime of poor relationships.

5. Infants increasingly become able to coordinate their own activity with that of their small companions to participate in give-and-take exchanges.

6. During the years from 2 to 12, social-cognitive abilities, including person-perception and role-taking skills, improve immensely; children participate in goal-corrected partnerships with their parents and spend increasing amounts of time with peers, especially same-sex ones, forming friendships on the basis of common activity and then reciprocal caring. Both physical attributes and social skills contribute to popularity, and children who are rejected by their peers are at risk for future problems.

7. During adolescence, heterosexual cliques and crowds facilitate the transition from same-sex peer groups to dating relationships, and same- and cross-sex friendships increasingly involve emotional intimacy and self-disclosure. Although susceptibility to negative peer pressures peaks at about age 15, adolescence is not a continual war of parents versus peers.

8. Adults often have more sophisticated social-cognitive abilities than adolescents do and apparently keep these skills in old age unless they become socially inactive; most adults of all ages have rich social networks.

9. In forming romantic attachments, adults screen potential partners through a set of filters, favoring partners similar to themselves. Adults have either secure, resistant, or avoidant styles of loving that may be rooted in their early attachment experiences.

10. Although adults are highly involved with their spouses or romantic partners, they continue to value friendships, especially long-lasting and equitable ones. Well-being is more influenced by the quality than the quantity of relationships.

11. Socially withdrawn individuals can be helped through social-skills training and exposure to more social-interaction opportunities.

KEY TERMS

attachment
chumship
clique
confidant
conformity
contact comfort
crowd
equity
filter model of mate selection
goal-corrected partnership
imprinting
insecure/avoidant attachment
insecure/resistant attachment
peer
secure attachment
secure base
separation anxiety
social cognition
social referencing
social support
sociometric techniques
Strange Situation test
stranger anxiety

CHAPTER

14

THE FAMILY

Burnam and Addie Ledford hosted the yearly Ledford family reunion at their home in Lancaster, Kentucky, in 1978 (Egerton, 1983). He was 102, she 93. They had married in 1903 and were nearing 75 years of married life. They had 13 children, 9 of them still surviving, the oldest age 69; 32 grandchildren, the oldest age 42; and 39 great-grandchildren, so many that Burnam marveled, "It's like planting seeds. . . . They keep coming up" (p. 4). John Egerton, preparing a history of the Ledford family, marveled at the clan gathered at the reunion: "They were short and tall, stout and thin, plain and pretty, long-haired and bald-headed. They were outgoing and reserved, as close as brothers and sisters, as distant as strangers" (p. 3). He marveled too at how much Burnam and Addie recalled about their parents and more distant ancestors, and at how much they valued their bonds to past, present, and future generations of Ledfords.

The Ledfords are an unusual family, but their emphasis on family ties is not at all unusual. We are all bound to families. We are born into them, work our ways toward adulthood in them, start our own as adults, and remain connected to them in old age. We are part of our families, and they become part of us. This chapter examines the family and its diverse and important roles in human development throughout the life span. We begin by characterizing the nature of the family and tracing recent trends in family life and then try to capture the experiences of developing individuals in developing families. We'll examine the family experiences of infants, children, and adolescents, asking how children are affected by their relationships with their parents and siblings. Then we'll shift to an adult's perspective on the family, tracing the implications for adult development of such family transitions as marrying, becoming a parent, watching children leave the nest, and becoming a grandparent. Finally, we'll look at the diversity of today's family lifestyles, considering families that remain childless or experience a divorce.

UNDERSTANDING THE FAMILY

The Family as a System

Family theorists conceptualize the family as a social system embedded in larger social systems. To say that the family is a system means that the family, like the human body, is truly a whole consisting of interrelated parts, each of which affects and is affected by each other part, and each of which contributes to the functioning of the whole. In the past, developmentalists did not adopt this systems perspective. They typically focused almost entirely on the mother/child relationship; moreover, they assumed that the only process of interest within the family was the mother's influence on the child's development. Mothers were viewed as shapers and molders, children as lumps of clay. What does this simple view of the "family" leave out? How about the fact that the family system usually includes a man who is husband to his wife and father to his child? That the family usually includes more than one child? That children can affect their parents, just as they are affected by their parents?

Four generations of the Ledford family.

The **nuclear family** consists of husband/father, wife/mother, and at least one child. Jay Belsky (1981) draws our attention to how complex even a simple man, woman, and infant "system" can be. An infant interacting with his or her mother is already involved in a process of *reciprocal* influence, evident even when we notice that an infant's smile is likely to be greeted by a mother's smile, and that a mother's smile is likely to be reciprocated by an infant's grin. However, the presence of *both* parents "transforms the mother–infant dyad into a *family system* [comprising] a husband–wife as well as mother–infant and father–infant relationships" (Belsky, 1981, p. 17).

One implication of the fact that the family is a system is that the relationship between any pair in the family will be different according to whether the third person is present or not. For example, fathers talk less to their toddlers when their wives are present (Stoneman & Brody, 1981), and mothers are less likely to play with or hold their youngsters when their husbands are around (Belsky, 1981). Similarly, in early adolescence, mother/son interactions are less conflict-ridden when the father is present, whereas the entry of the mother into father/son interactions seems to cause the father to withdraw and become less involved in the boy's activities (Gjerde, 1986). Finally, the quality of the marriage relationship can and does affect the relationship between either parent and the child, and, in turn, each parent's experience with the child can affect the quality of the marriage. In short, every individual and every relationship within the family affects every other individual and relationship through reciprocal influence (see Figure 14.1). Now you see why it was rather naive to think that the family could be understood by studying only the ways in which mothers mold their children.

Now think about how complex the family system becomes if we add another child or two to it and must attempt to understand the unique relationships between each parent and each of these children, as well as relationships between siblings. Or consider the complexity of an **extended family** household, in which parents and their children live with other kin—grandparents or aunts, uncles, nieces, and nephews. Such extended-family households are common in many cultures of the world and are also common among black Americans, as when a disadvantaged mother with children lives with and depends on her mother for help in child rearing (Wilson, 1986). Even when nuclear families do not live in the same household with other relatives, they most certainly affect and are affected by these kin.

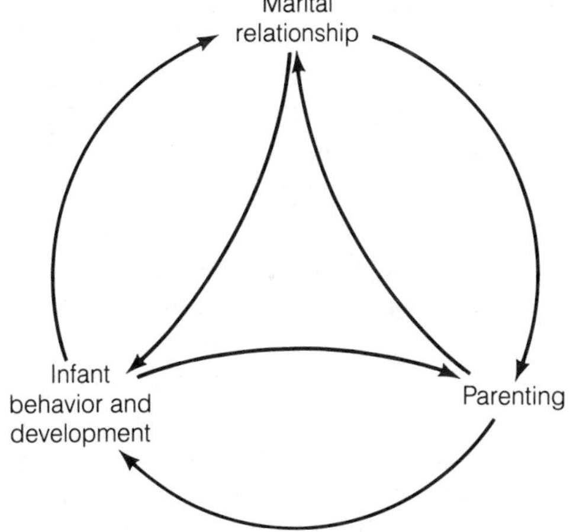

Figure 14.1 A model of the family as a social system. As implied in the diagram, a family is bigger than the sum of its parts. Parents affect infants, who affect each parent and the marital relationship. Of course, the marital relationship may affect the parenting the infant receives, the infant's behavior, and so on. Clearly, families are complex social systems. As an exercise, you may wish to rediagram the patterns of influence within a family after adding a sibling or two. (From Belsky, 1981)

Finally, whether a family is of the nuclear or the extended type, we cannot think of it as a unit that exists in a vacuum. As we discussed in Chapter 4, the family system is embedded in larger social systems such as a neighborhood, a community, a subculture, and a broader culture (Bronfenbrenner, 1979, 1989). The family experience in our culture is quite different from that in cultures where new brides become underlings in the households of their mothers-in-law, or where men can have several wives. There is an almost infinite variety of family forms in the world, and a correspondingly wide range of developmental experiences within the family.

The Family as a Changing System: The Family Life Cycle

It would be difficult enough to study the family as a system if it kept the same members and continued to perform the same activities over and over again for as long as it existed. But obviously, this is not the case. The membership changes as new children are born and as grown children leave the nest. Moreover, the individuals within the family are all developing individuals, and the *relationships* between husband and wife, parent and child, and sibling and sibling also develop in systematic ways over time. Since the family is truly a system, changes in family membership or changes in any individual or relationship within the family are bound to affect the dynamics of the whole. Somehow we have to view the family itself as a developing organism.

One popular way of describing the family as a developing system is to characterize stages of the **family life cycle**, the sequence of changes in family composition, roles, and relationships that occur from the time people marry until they die. Family theorist Evelyn Duvall (1977) has outlined eight stages of the family life cycle (see Table 14.1). In each stage, family members play distinctive roles and carry out distinctive developmental tasks—for example, the tasks of establishing a satisfying relationship as newlyweds, adjusting to the demands of new parenthood in the childbearing phase, and adapting to the departure of children in the launching-center phase. In this chapter, we will look at the impacts of these family transitions on adults, and we will examine how the child's experience of the family changes as he or she develops. We will also come to appreciate that an increasing number of people do not experience the traditional family life cycle.

Table 14.1 Stages of the family life cycle

STAGE	AVAILABLE ROLES
1. Married couple (without children)	Wife Husband
2. Childbearing family (oldest child birth to 30 months)	Wife–mother Husband–father Infant daughter or son
3. Family with preschool children (oldest child 30 months to 6 years)	Wife–mother Husband–father Daughter–sister Son–brother
4. Family with school-aged children (oldest child up to 12 years)	Wife–mother Husband–father Daughter–sister Son–brother
5. Family with teenagers (oldest child 13 to 20 years)	Wife–mother Husband–father Daughter–sister Son–brother
6. Family launching young adults (first child gone to last child gone)	Wife–mother–grandmother Husband–father–grandfather Daughter–sister–aunt Son–brother–uncle
7. Family without children (empty nest to retirement)	Wife–mother–grandmother Husband–father–grandfather
8. Aging family (retirement to death)	Wife–mother–grandmother Husband–father–grandfather Widow or widower

Source: Adapted from Duvall, 1977.

A Changing Family System in a Changing World

Not only is the family a system, and not only is it a developing system, but it exists and develops in a changing world. During the 20th century, several dramatic social changes have altered the makeup of the typical family and have changed the quality of family experience. Drawing on several analyses of U.S. Census data and other surveys (Aizenberg & Treas, 1985; Glick, 1984b; Nock, 1987; Norton & Moorman, 1987; Rossi, 1986; Sweet & Bumpass, 1987), we will highlight the following trends:

1. *Increased numbers of single adults.* More adults are living as singles today than in the past. However, don't be deceived into thinking that marriage is out of style, for about 90% of today's young adults can still be expected to marry at some time in their lives (Norton & Moorman, 1987).

2. *Postponement of marriage.* Many adults are not rejecting marriage but are simply delaying it while they pursue educational and career goals. Although the average age of first marriage decreased during the first half of the century, it has now risen again, to about 23 for women and 25 for men (Nock, 1987), despite high rates of teenage pregnancy.

3. *Decreased childbearing.* Today's adults are not only waiting longer after they marry to have children, but they are having fewer of them. The Baby Boom period after World War II was an unusual departure from an otherwise consistent trend toward smaller family sizes. Increasing numbers of young women will remain childless throughout their adult lives. However, the more impressive trend is that those couples who do have children are typically limiting their families to only about two children.

4. *Increased female participation in the labor force.* Owing to a truly dramatic social change, most women, including the majority of those with children, now work outside the home. Although women still carry the lion's share of child-rearing and housework responsibilities, fewer and fewer children have a mother whose full-time job is to be a mother.

5. *Increased divorce.* It is well known that the divorce rate has been increasing over the past decades, to the point that 40% to 50% of newly married couples can expect to divorce at some point in their marriage (Glick, 1984b). However, it appears that the Baby Boom generation is the group most prone to divorce, and that new cohorts, like earlier generations, may have a somewhat lower divorce rate than this (Norton & Moorman, 1987).

6. *Increased numbers of single-parent families.* Partly because of a rising rate of out-of-wedlock births, but mostly because of the rise in divorce rates, it is projected that 40% to 50% of all children born in the 1980s will spend some time in a single-parent family (Glick, 1984b). At present, about 20% to 25% of children live in such a family, 9 times out of 10 with their mothers.

7. *Increased remarriage.* Simply because more married couples are divorcing, more adults (about 75% of divorced individuals) are remarrying. Often they are forming new **reconstituted families** that involve at least a parent, a stepparent, and a child, and that sometimes blend multiple children from two families into a new family. Stepparent homes represent about 11% of all American households (Santrock, Warshak, Lindbergh, & Meadows, 1982).

8. *Increased years without children.* Because modern couples are compressing their childbearing into a shorter time span, because some divorced individuals do not remarry, and because people are living longer, adults today spend more of their later years as couples or as single adults without children in their homes. In the past, adults who had large families often did not live long enough to experience the "empty nest," and they often died before many of their grandchildren were born. Today, more children know their grandparents. Moreover, almost half of the elderly adults who have had children not only live to become grandparents but live to become great-grandparents (Shanas, 1980)! And finally, "many more parents and children are finding themselves growing old together" (Aizenberg & Treas, 1985, p. 173).

We'll leave it to you to decide what is good and what is bad about these trends. Our main point is this: The American family is more diverse than ever before. Our stereotyped image of the family—the traditional *Leave It to Beaver* nuclear family with a breadwinning father, housewife-mother, and children—is just that: a stereotype. By one estimate, this "ideal" family represented 70% of the families in 1960 but only 12% in 1980 (Klineberg, 1984). Although the family is by no means dying, we must broaden our image of it to include the many dual-career, single-parent, reconstituted, and childless families that exist today. Bear that in mind as we begin our excursion into family life at the beginning—with the birth of an infant.

THE INFANT

Children begin to affect their parents even before they arrive, for expectant parents will often plan ahead by selecting names for the infant, decorating a nursery, moving to larger quarters, and changing or leaving jobs (Grossman, Eichler, Winickoff, & associates, 1980). In a later section, we will see just what effects a new baby has on first-time parents. Here, we'll concentrate on the emerging relationships between mothers and fathers and their infants.

The Mother/Infant Relationship

In Chapter 13, we discussed at length the mother/infant attachment and its significance for later development. There is a simple reason that the mother/infant relationship has received far more attention than the father/

infant relationship: Mothers have traditionally been the primary caregivers for infants. As we saw in Chapter 13, it is when mothers are warm, sensitive, and responsive that infants become securely attached to them (Ainsworth, 1979). A new mother need not be a wizard at reading her baby's cues for her baby to develop normally. However, infants are most likely to form secure relationships with mothers (or other primary caregivers) who really seem to enjoy interacting with them, who can read their infants' signals accurately, and who respond appropriately and promptly to those signals. By fostering a secure attachment, a warm, sensitive, and responsive parent contributes to other positive outcomes as well—for example, to later social competence in interactions with peers, an interest in exploring the world, and rapid intellectual growth (for example, Bradley, Caldwell, & Elardo, 1979; Cassidy, 1986; Waters, Wippman, & Sroufe, 1979).

At the same time, let's give infants some credit for affecting their mothers. Even an otherwise socially skilled woman may find it difficult to love a baby who cries endlessly. Indeed, "easy" babies seem to make sensitive and responsive parenting easy, whereas difficult babies who are unresponsive and irritable can sometimes help "produce" rather unaffectionate mothers (Greene, Fox, & Lewis, 1983). Mothers do have considerable influence on infant development. However, the mother/child relationship takes on its distinctive character as a result of the *reciprocal* contributions of mother and infant.

The Father/Infant Relationship

Now that developmentalists have taken seriously the idea that the family is a system, they have discovered that fathers are part of the family too. How do the roles of father and mother typically differ? What contributions do fathers make to their children's development?

Let's begin with this question: Are fathers as capable as mothers of nurturing an infant? Gender stereotypes would suggest that fathers are not cut out to care for young children, but the evidence suggests otherwise. Overall, fathers and mothers seem to be more similar than different in the ways they interact with infants and young children. In one study, for example, mothers and fathers were observed while they fed their infants (Parke & Sawin, 1976). Fathers were no less able than mothers to perform this caregiving task effectively and to ensure that the milk was consumed, nor were they any less sensitive to the infant's cues during the feeding session. Similarly, fathers, just like mothers, become objects of their infants' love, know how to soothe and comfort them, and serve as secure bases for their explorations (Lamb, 1981). We really have no basis for thinking that mothers are uniquely qualified to parent or that men are hopelessly inept around young children. However, the fact that fathers are *capable* of sensitive parenting does not necessarily mean they play the same roles in their children's lives that mothers do (Parke & Tinsley, 1984). Fathers and mothers do differ in both the quantity and quality of the parenting they provide.

Consider first the matter of quantity. Mothers simply spend more time with children than fathers do. This seems to be the case even when we take into account the fact that fathers sometimes have less time available to be with their children (Parke & Tinsley, 1984). Several years ago, Freda Rebelsky and Cheryl Hanks (1971) attached microphones to 10 infants and recorded how often their fathers spoke to them between the ages of 2 weeks and 3 months. On an average day, the fathers addressed their infants only 2.7 times for a total of approximately 40 seconds! But aren't today's fathers more involved in child rearing, especially since so many of their wives work? To an extent, they are more involved, especially if their wives not only work but hold nontraditional views of what the male role should be (Barnett & Baruch, 1987). On the other hand, there has not been nearly the increase in father involvement that you might expect. Indeed, one study revealed that fathers in 1975 participated no more frequently in child care and housework tasks than fathers in 1965 did, despite the dramatic increase in the number of working mothers during those years (Coverman & Sheley, 1986). Mothers spent less time on family tasks, but fathers did little to compensate for their wives' decreasing involvement. It is still the case, then, that mothers spend considerably more time parenting than fathers do.

Now consider the issue of quality: Just how do mothers and fathers differ in their typical styles of interacting with young children? When mothers interact with their children, a large proportion of their time is devoted to providing care: offering food, changing diapers, wiping noses, and so on. After all, they are typically the primary caregivers, and their husbands typically play a secondary role by helping with child-care duties. Compared to mothers, fathers spend a greater proportion of their time with children in *play* (Parke & Tinsley, 1984). Moreover, a father's *style* of playing with his infant is typically different from a mother's. Specifically, fathers are more likely than mothers to provide playful and rowdy physical stimulation and to initiate unusual or unpredictable games (Lamb, 1981). Fathers seem to specialize in tickling, poking, bouncing, and surprising infants, whereas mothers adopt a quieter style of play that involves playing more traditional games and holding, hugging, talking to, and soothing infants.

Another commonly found difference between fathers and mothers is that fathers seem to treat boys and girls more differently than mothers do (see Chapter 11). For one thing, fathers often spend more time with sons than with daughters (Barnett & Baruch, 1987; Parke, 1979). In addition, they are more likely than mothers to encourage boys to play with masculine-stereotyped toys, to encourage girls to play with feminine-stereotyped toys, and to discourage play that is considered more appropriate for the other sex—even when their children are only a year old (Snow, Jacklin, & Maccoby, 1983). Thus mothers tend to be "equal opportunity" parents, treating girls and boys much the same, while fathers seem to alter their parenting style according to whether they are interacting with sons or daughters.

In view of the roles that fathers play in their children's lives, what are their unique contributions to child development? Certainly if a mother is for some reason unresponsive or rejecting, a father might be crucial to providing the security that infants need so much. Interestingly, Mary Main and Donna Weston (1981) have found that many infants are securely attached to both parents, but some are securely attached to their mothers but not to their fathers, and others are securely attached to their fathers but not to their mothers. Moreover, infants who are securely attached to at least one parent, whether mother or father, are more socially responsive than infants who are attached to neither parent—and infants who are securely attached to *both* parents are even more socially responsive (Main & Weston, 1981). Clearly, then, development gets off to a better start if fathers establish close relationships with their infants.

In the longer term, involved fathers contribute in several ways to their children's social and intellectual development. For example, boys who have warm and nurturant fathers are more likely to adopt a masculine role than boys who have cold, uninvolved fathers (Hetherington & Frankie, 1967). Fathers have more influence on their sons' gender development than on their daughters' (Stevenson & Black, 1988), but they also contribute to the feminine gender-typing of girls (Lamb, 1981). Moreover, children of both sexes, but especially boys, benefit intellectually and achieve more in school when they have involved and nurturant fathers than when they do not (Belsky, 1981; Lamb, 1981). In short, fathers richly deserve the increased respect they have been getting from developmentalists lately. They are not only capable of sensitive and responsive parenting, but they can contribute in many positive ways to their children's development when they *use* their competencies and take an active part in child rearing.

Mothers, Fathers, and Infants: The System at Work

So far, we have considered mother/child and father/child relationships without viewing the new family as a *three-person* system. Researchers have begun to show that the mother/child relationship cannot be understood without adding the father to the picture, nor can father/child interactions be understood without examining how mothers influence that relationship. In other words, parents have **indirect effects** on their children through their ability to influence the behavior of their spouses. More generally, indirect effects within the family are instances in which the relationship between two individuals is mod-

Fathers contribute to the gender-role development of both sons and daughters.

ified by the behavior or attitudes of a third family member.

Consider how a father might indirectly influence the mother/infant relationship. If husband and wife are experiencing tension in their marriage, his negative behavior toward her will disrupt her caregiving routines and interfere with her ability to enjoy her infant (Belsky, 1981). Indeed, both parents are likely to be unresponsive and negative toward their infant if they are experiencing strife in their own relationship (Pedersen, Anderson, & Cain, 1977). Indirect effects within families can also be positive. For example, fathers whose wives believe that a father should play an important role in a child's life are more likely to be involved with their infants (Palkovitz, 1984). Fathers' involvement is also greater when the two parents talk frequently about the baby (Belsky, Gilstrap, & Rovine, 1984; Lamb & Elster, 1985). Possibly, then, mothers exert an indirect and positive influence on the father/infant relationship by encouraging their mates to become more involved fathers. In sum, both mothers and fathers can affect their children indirectly through their interactions with their *spouses*. And overall, children appear to be best off when couples provide *mutual* support and encouragement that allows both of them to be more sensitive and responsive parents (Crnic, Robinson, Ragozin, Robinson, & Basham, 1983).

Now, perhaps, you can appreciate that even the simplest of families is a true social system that is bigger than the sum of its parts. Not only does each family member influence every other family member directly, but the relationship that any two family members have can indirectly affect the relationships between other members of the family. Because mothers, fathers, and children all affect one another, socialization within the family is obviously not a one-way street in which influence flows only from parent to child. Indeed, family socialization is not merely a two-way street; it is more like the busy intersection of many avenues of influence.

THE CHILD

As children reach the age of 2 or 3, parents continue to be caregivers and playmates, but they also become more concerned with teaching children how to behave (and how not to behave), and they use some approach to child rearing and discipline to achieve this end. Siblings also serve as socialization agents and become an important part of the child's experience of the family.

Dimensions of Child Rearing

How can I be a good parent? Certainly that question is a significant one to parents. Yet we probably cannot offer an answer that is good for all times and all social contexts. As John Ogbu (1981) stresses, a "competent" parent in one cultural or subcultural context could well be an incompetent one in another setting where the skills required for success as an adult are quite different. For example, parents in inner-city ghettos are often extremely affectionate with their infants but tend to use harsh and inconsistent punishment with their children. From a middle-class perspective, such practices are frowned upon; it is better, middle-class parents and many researchers would say, to be warm, to reason with children rather than slap them around, and to enforce rules consistently. Yet Ogbu argues that harsh and inconsistent discipline is likely to foster such traits as assertiveness, self-reliance, and a mistrust of authority figures—traits that are likely to be very useful if a youngster wants to survive in the street culture of the ghetto. So let's bear in mind that "good parenting" is really parenting that prepares children to meet the demands of the specific culture or subculture in which they live.

Having said that, we can draw some conclusions about the ingredients of good parenting, at least in middle-class homes in Western societies. We can go far in understanding what parenting styles are effective by considering just two dimensions of parenting: **warmth/hostility** and **permissiveness/restrictiveness** (c.f., Maccoby & Martin, 1983; Schaefer, 1959). Warm parents often smile at, praise, and encourage their children, expressing a great deal of affection, even though they are critical when a child misbehaves. Hostile or rejecting parents are often quick to criticize, belittle, punish, or ignore their children and rarely communicate to children that they are loved and valued. The *permissiveness/restrictiveness dimension* of parenting concerns the amount of autonomy that parents allow their children. Restrictive parents are controlling; they impose many demands, set many rules, and monitor their children to ensure that the rules are followed. Permissive parents make few demands of their children and allow them a great deal of autonomy in exploring the environment, expressing their opinions and emotions, and making decisions about their own activities. By crossing these

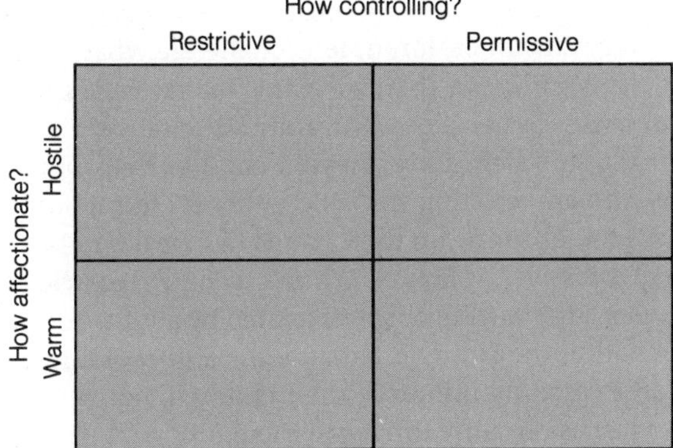

Figure 14.2 The dimensions of parenting.

two dimensions, we actually have four basic patterns of child rearing to consider: warmth combined with restrictiveness, warmth combined with permissiveness, hostility combined with restrictiveness, and hostility combined with permissiveness (Figure 14.2).

We assume that you have no difficulty deciding that warmth or love is preferable to coldness or rejection. Countless studies demonstrate that parental love is a powerful contributor to healthy cognitive, social, and emotional development (Maccoby & Martin, 1983). Children want to please loving parents and so are motivated to do what is expected of them and learn what their parents would like them to learn. By contrast, consider a group of "unwanted" Czechoslovakian children whose mothers had tried repeatedly to gain permission to abort them (Matejcek, Dytrych, & Schuller, 1979). Compared with "wanted" children from similar family backgrounds, the unwanted children had less stable ties to their mothers and fathers; were described as anxious, emotionally frustrated, and irritable; had more physical health problems; made poorer grades in school; were less popular with their peers; and were more likely to require psychiatric attention for serious behavior problems. Children simply do not thrive when they are rejected.

Now, what about the permissiveness/restrictiveness dimension of parenting: Is it better for parents to be highly controlling or to grant considerable autonomy to their children? Here we need to get more specific about degrees of restrictiveness and permissiveness, and we can do so by considering the three patterns of parental control identified by Diana Baumrind (1967, 1977):

1. **Authoritarian parenting:** This is a highly restrictive parenting style in which adults impose many rules, expect strict obedience, rarely explain why the child should comply with rules, and often rely on power tactics such as physical punishment to gain compliance.
2. **Authoritative parenting:** Authoritative parents are more flexible. They allow their children a fair amount of freedom but also set clear rules. They explain the rationales for their rules and restrictions, are responsive to their children's needs and points of view, and consistently enforce whatever rules they establish.
3. **Permissive parenting:** This is a lax pattern of parenting in which adults make relatively few demands, encourage their children to express their feelings and impulses, and rarely exert firm control over their behavior.

When Baumrind (1967) linked these three parenting styles to the characteristics of the preschool children who were exposed to each style, she found that authoritative parenting was most likely to be associated with positive outcomes for the child. Children of authoritative parents were cheerful, socially responsible, self-reliant, achievement oriented, and cooperative with adults and peers. Children of authoritarian parents tended to be conflicted and irritable; that is, they were moody and seemingly unhappy, easily annoyed, relatively aimless, and not very pleasant to be around. Finally, children of permissive parents were often impulsive and aggressive, especially if they were boys; they tended to be bossy and self-centered, rebellious, lacking in self-control, rather aimless, and quite low in independence and achievement. When Baumrind (1977) reassessed these children at ages 8 to 9, children of authoritative parents still had an edge on their peers with respect to both cognitive criteria (that is, shows originality in thinking, has high achievement motivation, likes intellectual challenges) and social criteria (for example, is sociable and outgoing, participates actively and shows leadership in group activities). Indeed, the strengths of children exposed to authoritative parenting are still evident in adolescence (see Maccoby & Martin, 1983).

Now let's put the warmth/hostility and permissiveness/restrictiveness dimensions back together again. In Baumrind's study, most parents were warm and loving rather than hostile. Thus it appears that warmth combined with *moderate* parental control—as opposed to warmth combined with either extreme restrictiveness or extreme permissiveness—is most closely associated with healthy child development. Children apparently need love *and* limits—a set of rules to help them structure their behavior. Without such guidance, they may not learn self-control and may become quite selfish, unruly, and lacking in clear achievement goals. And if they receive too much guidance? Then children may have few opportunities to learn self-reliance and may lack confidence in their own decision-making abilities (Grolnick & Ryan, 1989).

The very least successful parenting styles are those that combine hostility or rejection with either extreme permissiveness *or* extreme restrictiveness (Becker, 1964; Schaefer, 1959). Children whose parents are rejecting and highly controlling are often found to be extremely withdrawn and inhibited. Sometimes they even show masochistic or suicidal tendencies, possibly because they must bottle up the anxieties and resentments that their harsh and unloving parents have created within them. By contrast, children of permissive and rejecting parents tend to be hostile and rebellious and are likely to engage in delinquent acts such as alcohol and drug abuse and a variety of criminal offenses (Patterson & Stouthamer-Loeber, 1984; Pulkkinen, 1982). These children have parents who in effect say, "I don't care about you and I don't care what you do." It seems quite natural, then, that the children might act out their resentments by striking back at authority. In short, the undesirable effects of either extremely restrictive (authoritarian) or extremely permissive parenting are multiplied when parents are also cold, aloof, or unconcerned.

Assuming that parents are loving, how much parental control is optimal depends greatly on the age and competence of the child. Normally, parents gradually become less restrictive as their children mature and become more capable of making their own decisions (Schaefer & Bayley, 1963). That is as we might expect. It makes a good deal of sense for parents to call many of the shots for a 2-year-old, for 2-year-olds are not known for their sound judgment. Ultimately, however, children cannot learn how to make decisions and govern their own behavior if every decision is made for them and they are rarely given a chance to try things on their own. So ideally, parents will gradually shift their authoritative approach from a moderately restrictive to a moderately permissive one as a child matures.

Now that we have laid out some guidelines about which parenting styles are most and least likely to foster positive traits in children, let's challenge what we have said. Isn't it possible that easygoing, manageable children *cause* their parents to be warm and authoritative? Couldn't difficult, stubborn, and aggressive children help mold parents who are rejecting and who either try to rule with an iron hand or throw up their hands in defeat and become overpermissive? As Box 14.1 shows, a child's behavior *does* influence the way he or she is treated by adults. Socialization within the family is a matter of reciprocal influence: Parents certainly influence their children, but their children just as certainly influence them.

Sibling Relationships

A family system consisting of mother, father, and child is perturbed by the arrival of a new baby and becomes a new—and considerably more complex—family system.

A New Baby Arrives

Judy Dunn and Carol Kendrick (1982) have studied how children adapt to a new baby in the house, and the account they provide is not an entirely cheerful one. Mothers typically devote less warm and playful attention to their first-borns after the new baby arrives than before (see also Stewart, Mobley, Van Tuyl, & Salvador, 1987). Partly for this reason, first-borns often find being "dethroned" a stressful experience. They typically become more difficult and demanding or dependent and "clingy," and they often develop problems with their sleeping, eating, and toileting routines. Most of their battles are with their mothers, but a minority of them are not above hitting, poking, and pinching their younger brothers or sisters. Although positive effects such as an increased insistence on doing things independently are also common, it is clear that first-borns are not entirely thrilled to have an attention-grabbing new baby in the house. They resent losing their parents' attention, and their own difficult behavior may alienate their parents even further.

Thus **sibling rivalry**—a spirit of competition, jealousy, or resentment between siblings—often begins as soon as a younger brother or sister arrives. Can it be minimized? Dunn and Kendrick (1982) find that the adjustment process is easier if the first-born had positive relationships with both parents before the younger sibling arrived. After the baby arrives, parents seem best advised to

Box 14.1
Child Effects on Parents

Richard Bell (Bell & Chapman, 1986; Bell & Harper, 1977) has done much to focus attention on "child effects" within the family. In one study, he and Barbara Keller (Keller & Bell, 1979) challenged the finding (reported in Chapter 12) that a parent's use of the discipline technique of *induction* (explanations emphasizing the consequences of a child's behavior for other people) fosters moral maturity in a child. Isn't it possible instead that children who are already "good" are more likely than less responsive children to elicit inductive explanations from adults?

Keller and Bell (1979) had female college students attempt to convince 9-year-old girls to behave altruistically (for example, to spend more time sewing a pillow for a handicapped child than sewing a pillow for themselves). The trick was that the girls had been taught to act in one of two ways: (1) attentively, looking at the college student's face, smiling, and answering questions promptly; or (2) inattentively, looking at the task materials and pausing before they answered. As expected, the subjects who were confronted with an attentive child used a great deal of induction, pointing out how other children might feel if the child were selfish. By contrast, college students who interacted with an inattentive child were more likely to use power-assertion techniques such as promising rewards for altruism and threatening penalties for selfishness.

An even more dramatic demonstration of child effects has been provided by Kathleen Anderson, Hugh Lytton, and David Romney (1986). They studied mothers of boys who were officially diagnosed as having conduct disorders—boys who were aggressive and had histories of fire setting, truancy, temper outbursts, and other serious problems. The researchers had each of these mothers interact with her own conduct-disordered son, another mother's conduct-disordered son, and a normal boy. Meanwhile, mothers of normal boys also interacted with their own sons and both normal and conduct-disordered boys. The findings were clear: Whether a mother's own child was conduct-disordered or well-behaved, she behaved more negatively and made more demands and requests when she was paired with a conduct-disordered boy than when she interacted with a normal boy. In this study, then, there was little evidence that the mothers of conduct-disordered boys were generally colder than the mothers of normal boys or that their "bad parenting" was responsible for their sons' behavior problems. Instead, these boys seemed to be so noncompliant and difficult that they brought out "bad parenting" in every mother with whom they interacted.

These demonstrations of "child effects" within the family are tremendously important. We simply cannot take it for granted that parents are solely responsible for whether their children are "good" or "bad." Studies such as Diana Baumrind's that report correlations between parenting styles and child development do not unambiguously prove that parents *cause* their children to behave as they do. It now seems more likely that both parenting behavior and child behavior gradually evolve as parent and child *mutually* influence one another. It is probably still true that parents have more influence on their children than their children have on them, if only because parents' personalities have already taken shape and they wield more power in parent-child interactions than children do. Nonetheless, we must remind ourselves that the family is a *system* whose members socialize one another.

maintain positive relationships with their first-born and to guard against ignoring her or him. They should set aside time to let their first-born know that she or he is still loved and considered important; they should also try to maintain the child's routines as much as possible. Yet Dunn and Kendrick (1981) find that older girls whose parents become *overly* attentive to them are the ones who played the *least* with and were *most negative* toward their baby brothers or sisters 14 months later. Thus parents may have to tread a thin line between two traps: becoming so attentive to the new baby that they deprive the older child of attention and love, and becoming so indulgent of the first-born that he or she becomes resentful of any competition.

Sibling Relationships Over the Course of Childhood

Fortunately, most older siblings adjust fairly quickly to having a new brother or sister and stop displaying many of the behavior problems that they displayed at first (Dunn & Kendrick, 1982). Children whose early reactions were relatively affectionate continue to be more affectionate at age 6 than children who were initially upset and hostile (Stilwell & Dunn, 1984, cited by Dunn, 1984). Moreover, brothers and sisters are likely to get along if their parents get along (MacKinnon, 1989). Yet even in the best of sibling relationships, conflict is normal. Quarrels often become more frequent and intense once the younger child reaches 18 to 24 months of age and is better able to retali-

Coercive and rivalrous conduct between siblings is a normal part of family life.

ate by hitting or teasing, or by making sure parents notice the older sib's bad behavior (Dunn & Munn, 1985). Jealousies, skirmishes, bouts of teasing, and shouting matches continue to be part of the sibling relationship throughout childhood.

However, we are dwelling too much on the negative. Sibling relationships are truly paradoxical because they involve *both* closeness and conflict. For example, Wyndol Furman and Duane Buhrmester (1985a, 1985b) found that school-aged siblings who were similar in age (especially if they were of the same sex) reported more warmth and closeness than other sibling pairs—but that, at the same time, they were most likely to experience friction and conflict (especially if they were of the opposite sex). Moreover, children perceived their sibling relationships to be more conflict ridden and less satisfying than their relations with parents, grandparents, and friends. And yet siblings were also viewed as more important and more reliable than friends! These findings make perfect sense when we realize that acts of kindness and affection between brothers and sisters are typically more common than hateful or rivalrous acts (Abramovich, Corter, Pepler, & Stanhope, 1986; Baskett & Johnson, 1982).

What positive roles do siblings actually play in one another's development? One of their important roles is to provide *emotional support*. Brothers and sisters confide in each other and protect and comfort one another in rough times. Even preschoolers jump in to comfort their infant siblings when their mothers leave them or when strangers appear (Stewart & Marvin, 1984). Second, older siblings often provide *caretaking* services for younger siblings. Indeed, in a study of 186 societies, older children were the *principal* caregivers for infants and toddlers in 57% of the groups studied (Weisner & Gallimore, 1977). In our society as well, older siblings, especially girls, are frequently asked to babysit or tend their younger sibs (Cicirelli, 1982).

Finally, older siblings serve as *teachers* of new behavior (Summers, 1987). During infancy, children are already becoming very attentive to their older siblings, often imitating their actions or taking over toys that they have abandoned (Abramovich, Corter, & Pepler, 1980). Older siblings continue to serve as models later in childhood. Moreover, when older siblings "play school" with their younger siblings and teach them important lessons such as the ABCs, younger siblings have an easier time learning to read (Norman-Jackson, 1982).

It may seem that younger siblings are receiving all the benefits of the relationship. However, as teachers and college professors can appreciate, teaching is an excellent learning experience. Children who tutor younger children in school actually show significant gains in their own academic achievement (Feldman, Devin-Sheehan, & Allen, 1976). Moreover, the more younger siblings a college woman has (up to three), the higher she is likely to score on the SAT, or Scholastic Achievement Test (Paulhus & Shaffer, 1981). So it appears that *both* older and younger siblings learn when older siblings take on the role of teacher.

In sum, there is a good deal of reciprocal influence in families that contain preschool or school-aged children. Parents, by adopting particular styles of child rearing with each of their children, are influencing their youngsters' development. Children are exerting influence on their parents, often influencing the extent to which their parents are warm or hostile, restrictive or permissive. And, once a couple has a second child, the family system changes, and sibling relationships take on a life of their own. Although rivalry and conflict seem to be a normal part of such relationships, siblings also provide one another with emotional support, caretaking, and teaching.[1]

THE ADOLESCENT

Conjure an image of the relationship between adolescents and their parents. Perhaps you envision a teenage boy who is out all the time with friends, groans when his parents suggest that he do anything with them, and resents the slightest attempt by his parents to cramp his freedom . . . a "sassy" teenage girl who thinks her parents don't know a thing and argues with them about virtually everything . . . and parents who wring their hands in despair and wonder if they'll ever survive their children's adolescent years. Many people believe that the period of the family life cycle in which parents have adolescents in the house is a particularly stressful time. They believe that a huge gap between the values of parents and youth emerges and that pleasant parent/child relationships deteriorate into bitter struggles. Let's see how much truth there is to these characterizations.

The Generation Gap: Is There One?

Some of those who characterize adolescence as a period of parent/child conflict assume that the problem lies in the **generation gap**—the discrepancy between the values and attitudes of the different generations. Is there a generation gap? Yes, but it is not nearly so wide as is often assumed (Steinberg, 1985). It is inevitable that middle-aged parents and their teenage children have somewhat different priorities and preoccupations simply because they are at different points in the life span and face different developmental issues. For example, teenagers are likely to see all the time in the world ahead of them, whereas middle-aged parents may be feeling that time is running out; teenagers may be idealistically imagining a perfect future, whereas parents may be realistically dealing with the task of keeping the family out of debt. In addition, we must remember that parents and adolescents are members of different cohorts or generations, each with their own distinctive socialization experiences. Thus, for example, today's youth tend to hold more liberal attitudes about the roles that women should play in society than their parents do, partly because the parent generation grew up in more traditional times (Helmreich, Spence, & Gibson, 1982).

So parents and their children do differ on some issues, partly because they are at different points in the life cycle, and partly because they had different socialization experiences. However, parents and their adolescents more often see eye to eye than is typically assumed. Adolescents are highly influenced by their parents when it comes to basic values such as the importance of education or the kinds of careers that are most suitable (see Chapter 13). It is in areas where peer influence is particularly strong—issues of dress, preferred social activities, and other matters of taste—that parents and teenagers do not always agree. Although sparks can fly when parents and teenagers argue about which clothes a teen can and cannot wear or whether he or she can go to see the latest "sick" movie, these differences are really quite trivial in comparison to the more fundamental agreements between teenagers and their parents.

How Do Adolescents Feel About Their Parents?

Many observers have also argued that adolescents distance themselves from their parents, lose respect for them, and somehow love them less completely than they did as children. These beliefs do not hold up any better than the belief that the generation gap is a yawning chasm.

For example, Daniel Offer, Eric Ostrov, and Kenneth Howard (1981) found that most teenagers described their family relationships as harmonious. Table 14.2 shows how many high school students agreed with a number of statements about their relationships with their parents. There is no doubt about it: The great majority of these teenagers felt good about their relationships with their parents. Notice too that boys and girls feel similarly, and that there is

[1]Important as siblings can be, only children do not appear to be damaged by not having them. Indeed, only children equal first-borns and second-borns in two-child families on measures of intelligence, achievement, adjustment, character, and sociability, and these three groups outperform later-born children in large families on measures of intelligence, achievement, and character (Falbo & Polit, 1986). Only children, like children with only one sibling, enjoy the advantages of a good deal of attention and stimulation from their parents, and apparently gain through friendships outside the home whatever they may miss by not having brothers or sisters.

Table 14.2 Percentages of adolescents endorsing different statements about their family relationships

STATEMENT	PERCENTAGE CONCURRING			
	Males 13–15	Males 16–18	Females 13–15	Females 16–18
My parents are usually patient with me.	84	79	80	76
I can count on my parents most of the time.	78	76	74	77
I feel I have a part in making family decisions.	71	72	70	73
When my parents are strict, I feel that they are right even if I get angry.	54	54	58	58
Understanding my parents is beyond me.	18	17	21	18
Very often I feel that my father is no good.	16	17	18	16
Very often I feel that my mother is no good.	11	12	12	10

Source: Adapted from Offer, Ostrov, & Howard, 1981.

no sign that adolescents grow increasingly disenchanted with their parents as they get older.

So far, then, it appears that parent/adolescent relationships are really not much different than parent/child relationships. The generation gap is narrow, and most adolescents feel good about their parents and their relationships with their parents. Yet the parent/child relationship *does* change during adolescence—not in its degree of closeness so much as in the balance of power between parents and adolescents. To understand these changes, we must ask what adolescents are really supposed to achieve as they make the transition to adulthood.

The Quest for Autonomy: Renegotiating the Parent/Child Relationship

Most developmental theorists agree that a critical developmental task of adolescence is to achieve **autonomy**. This complex concept has two major components: (1) *emotional autonomy*, or an ability to serve as one's own source of emotional strength rather than childishly depending on parents to provide comfort, constant reassurance, and emotional security, and (2) *behavioral autonomy*, or an increased ability to make decisions independently, take care of oneself, and govern one's own affairs (Steinberg, 1985). If adolescents are to "make it" as adults, they can't be rushing home to Mom for solace and loving hugs after every little setback, or depending on parents to get them to work on time and manage their checkbooks. Parents want their adolescents to become autonomous, and adolescents want the freedom to become autonomous.

What happens within the family system as adolescents become more physically and cognitively mature and more capable of acting autonomously? Conflicts between parents and children become more frequent. Laurence Steinberg (1981) observed boys' interactions with their mothers and fathers in family discussions as these youth began to experience the changes of puberty. The boys asserted themselves more, interrupted their parents more, and became more argumentative as they reached the period of greatest pubertal growth. Similarly, conflict between girls and their mothers heightens when girls reach puberty (Brooks-Gunn & Zahaykevich, 1989; Hill, Holmbeck, Marlow, Green, & Lynch, 1985; Steinberg, 1988). Parent/adolescent conflicts are usually not severe, but squabbles over such matters as disobedience, neglect of schoolwork, and household chores are common (Montemayor, 1982).

What are the outcomes of these conflicts or power struggles? Steinberg (1981) found that boys gained power within the family as they reached puberty. Although they did not achieve the degree of influence in family decisions that their fathers commanded, they did gain power in the family at the expense of their mothers. More generally, as adolescents assert themselves more, as parents turn over more power to them, the parent/child relationship changes from one in which parents are dominant to one in which parents and their sons and daughters are on a more equal footing (Feldman & Gehring, 1988; Steinberg, 1981; Youniss & Smollar, 1985). Moreover, this shift in the balance of power seems to facilitate the adolescent's development. Adolescents grow psychologically when they are free to disagree with their parents in a family climate of mutual support (Grotevant & Cooper, 1986).

In the past, many theorists assumed that achieving autonomy meant separating from parents—cutting the cords. Now researchers are appreciating that there is a second important task facing adolescents: *maintaining* a close attachment with their families, even as they are gaining autonomy and preparing to leave the nest (Grotevant & Cooper, 1986; Youniss & Smollar, 1985). The challenge for parents is really quite similar: to nurture autonomy while still maintaining a positive relationship with their teenagers. Autonomy *and* attachment, or independence *and* interdependence, are the goals. There is no need for adolescents to become emotionally detached from parents in order to become autonomous (Ryan & Lynch, 1989). Indeed, high self-esteem and psychological maturity are more characteristic of adolescents who emphasize the positive side of autonomy—the quest for self-governance—than of adolescents who believe that their primary mission is to break away from their parents (Moore, 1987).

From their interviews with teenagers, James Youniss and Jacqueline Smollar (1985) learned that parents gradually loosen the reins as their school-aged children become adolescents, but they by no means cease to set rules and monitor their children's behavior. They give adolescents more freedom to be out with their friends away from parental eyes, but they still watch closely to see that their children are doing well in school and are not developing any serious problems. Viewing their children as more mature, parents not only give them more freedom but also demand more of them. Adolescents, meanwhile, stop seeing their parents as the all-knowing, all-powerful figures they once seemed to be and ask their parents to give reasons for their rules. Yet they still respect their parents and want their approval. In short, "the bond to parents is not severed so much as it is transformed" during adolescence (Youniss & Smollar, 1985, p. 92).

If we were to plot an ideal scenario, we could not have envisioned one much better than the one described in these findings. Adolescents are most likely to become autonomous if their parents keep their rules to a reasonable minimum, explain them, *and* continue to be warm and supportive (Kandel & Lesser, 1972). In other words, the winning combination is a blend of parental warmth and a style of control that is neither too permissive nor too restrictive. In Baumrind's terms, it is an authoritative style of parenting—the same style that appears to foster healthy child development. It gives adolescents opportunities to strengthen their independent decision-making skills while still having the benefit of their parents' guidance and advice.

It is when parents are rejecting and overstrict or rejecting and overlax that teenagers are most likely to rebel and get into trouble (Balswick & Macrides, 1975). Of course, we must once again remind ourselves that parents and children influence each other reciprocally. It is unfair to blame adolescent problems such as rebelliousness and delinquency entirely on "bad parenting." Instead, it is quite likely that responsible and levelheaded adolescents "produce" parents who are loving and reasonable in setting rules, and that this positive parenting further contributes to adolescent autonomy. By contrast, parents who are confronted with a teenager who is rude, hostile, and aggressive may become hostile in return and further compound their child's problems.

The parent/adolescent relationship is truly a partnership, and its quality depends on what both parents and their children do to renegotiate their relationship. Apparently, most parents and their teenagers do not experience a large generation gap and maintain positive feelings for one another. Yet they also rework their relationship so that it becomes more equal. As a result, most adolescents are able to achieve autonomy while also shifting to a more mutual or friendlike attachment to their parents.

THE ADULT

So far, we have concentrated on the child's experience of family life. Let's now ask how adults develop and change as they progress through stages of the family life cycle.

Establishing the Marriage

In our society, well over 90% of adults choose to marry, and young adults marry for love. In contrast, parents in colonial America exerted far more influence on when and even whom a child married (Nock, 1987). Even today, marriages in many cultures are not formed on the basis of love but are arranged by leaders of kin groups who are concerned with acquiring property, new allies, and the rights to any children produced by a couple. As Corinne Nydegger (1986) puts it, "These matters are too important to be left to youngsters" (p. 111). So in reading what follows, remember that our way of establishing families is not the only way.

Marrying is a life transition: It involves taking on a new role (as husband or wife) and adjusting to life as a couple. We rejoice at weddings and view newlyweds as supremely happy beings. Yet individuals who have just been struggling to achieve autonomy now find that they must compromise with their partners and adapt to each other's personalities and preferences. What happens to couples as they settle into their married lives? Ted Huston and his colleagues (Huston, McHale, & Crouter, 1986) suggest that the honeymoon may be short. In their longitudinal study of 100 newlywed couples, these researchers discovered that several aspects of the marital relationship took turns for the worse from 3 months to 15 months after the marriage ceremony. For example, couples became less satisfied with the marriage and with such aspects of it as their sex lives; they less frequently said, "I love you," complimented each other, or disclosed their feelings to each other; and, although they spent only somewhat less time with each other, more of that time was spent getting tasks done and less was spent having fun or just talking. The couples whose relationships deteriorated the most severely were those who engaged in a great deal of mutual criticism and other negative behaviors from the start.

Although Huston and his colleagues found most couples far more satisfied than dissatisfied with their relationships after the "honeymoon" was over, their findings do suggest that there are some strains involved in adapting to marriage. Blissfully happy relationships evolve into still happy but more ambivalent ones. Perhaps couples begin to see "warts" that they did not notice before marriage. Perhaps they stop trying to be on their best behavior. Or maybe they simply begin to take each other for granted. Whatever the reasons, marital relationships no sooner begin than they change in systematic ways.

Pregnancy adds to the challenges faced by newlyweds, who are trying to adjust to life as a couple.

New Parenthood and the Child-Rearing Family

Many couples have children within a few years of the marriage ceremony. How does the arrival of a child affect wife, husband, and the marital relationship? One popular view holds that having children draws a couple closer together; other people believe that children introduce additional strains into a relationship. Which is it? And how do parents' lives change when they have additional children?

Becoming a Parent

On average, new parenthood is a stressful life transition that involves both positive and negative changes. Most parents claim that having a child improves their lives—that their new "bundle of joy" offers them love, companionship, and enjoyment, and makes them feel more self-fulfilled or grown up (Hoffman & Manis, 1979). But let's stop to analyze the situation more closely. Couples have added new roles (as mothers and fathers) to their existing roles (as spouses, workers, and so on). As we will see in Chapter 15, parents often experience strain as they attempt to juggle work and family responsibilities, and these role conflicts are especially acute for today's working women. New parents not only have an incredible amount of new work to do as caregivers, but they lose sleep, worry about whether they are doing the right things for their baby, find that they have less time to themselves, and often feel a strain on their checking accounts as well. Thus new parents often find themselves under stress. And even egalitarian couples who previously shared household tasks begin to divide their labors along more traditional lines; she specializes in the "feminine" role by becoming the primary caregiver and housekeeper, often quitting her job or reducing her work hours to do so, while he is likely to become even more involved in his "masculine" role as provider (Cowan & Cowan, 1987).

What is the outcome of these stresses and of the tendency of husband and wife to establish somewhat separate lifestyles? The findings of Jay Belsky and his associates (Belsky, Lang, & Rovine, 1985) are fairly typical. On average, marital satisfaction declines from before to after the birth, contradicting the notion that husband and wife will become closer if they have a child. This decline in marital satisfaction is steeper among women than among men, undoubtedly because the burden of child-care responsibilities typically falls more heavily on the mother. Indeed, it seems that mothers generally experience new parenthood more intensely than fathers do; they not only feel more of the stress, but they enjoy more of the pleasures (Wilkie & Ames, 1986).

However, there are wide individual differences in adjustment to new parenthood: Some new parents experience the transition as a bowl of cherries, others experience it as the pits, as a full-blown crisis in their lives. What might make this life event easier or harder to manage? We can answer that question by focusing on the nature of the event itself, the individual who must cope with it, and the outside resources that the individual has available. The event is the baby, and we have already seen that infants who are difficult (for example, irritable and fussy) create more stresses and anxieties for parents than infants who are quiet, sociable, responsive, and otherwise easy to love (Sirignano & Lachman, 1985; Wilkie & Ames, 1986; Wright, Henggeler, & Craig, 1986).

As for the person, some adults are better equipped than others are to cope with stress and with conflicts between roles. They find adaptive ways to restructure their social lives and work roles to accommodate a new baby (Myer-Walls, 1984). In addition, parents who are older, conceive after the marriage ceremony, and wait longer once they are married to have children have an easier time than parents who are young and possibly immature or who must adjust to each other at the same time they are adjusting to a new baby (Belsky, 1981). Finally, parents who recall their own parents as warm and accepting are likely to experience a smoother transition to new parenthood and less marital discord than couples in which either spouse was raised in an aloof or rejecting manner—a sign that parents may affect their children's capacity to deal with the challenges of parenthood (Belsky & Isabella, 1985).

Outside resources can also make a great deal of difference to the new parent. Most important of all is spouse support. For example, things go considerably better for a new mother when she has a good relationship with her husband and when her husband shares the burden of child-care and housework responsibilities with her (Tietjen & Bradley, 1985). By contrast, the transition to new parenthood is likely to be especially trying for the woman who has no partner or an unsupportive one. Social support from friends and relatives can also help the new parent cope (Stemp, Turner, & Noh, 1986). Thus, it seems that parents who have an easy baby to contend with, who possess positive personal qualities, and who receive reliable support from their spouses and other intimates are in the best position to cope adaptively with the stresses of new parenthood.

The Second Child Arrives

What becomes of married couples as they have a second child (or even more) and as their children grow older? As you might suppose, the arrival of a second child means additional stress (Kreppner, Paulsen, & Schuetze, 1982). Parents not only must devote time to the new baby, but they must deal with their first-born child's normal anxieties about this change in lifestyle. Because the workload is

Parents can find keeping up with young children draining.

heavier, fathers often become more involved with their children (Stewart et al., 1987). And what about the mother whose husband is not highly involved in family life or who is raising children as a single parent? She may find herself without a moment's rest as she tries to keep up with two active, curious, mobile, and needy youngsters.

In view of the strains that a second child creates, it is not surprising that marital satisfaction remains somewhat depressed as additional children are added to the family (Rollins & Feldman, 1970). Marital problems are sometimes particularly acute among low-income working mothers with preschool children—most likely because these mothers are simply overwhelmed with responsibilities (Schumm & Bugaighis, 1986). And, offensive as these findings may be to male readers, one study has revealed that mothers who had two boys experienced poorer marital adjustment than either childless women or mothers of girls, suggesting that boys may be especially demanding (Abbott & Brody, 1985).

Again, let's bear in mind that most parents are satisfied with their marriages and take great pleasure from their relationships with their children. Indeed, both men and women view their roles as spouses and parents as the most important part of their identities (Whitbourne, 1986). However, it is still the case that children complicate their parents' lives by demanding everything from fresh diapers and close monitoring to chauffeuring services and the money for college. By claiming time and energy that might otherwise go into nourishing the marital relationship and by adding stresses to their parents' lives, children do seem to have a negative, though typically only slightly negative, effect on the marital relationship (Glenn & McLanahan, 1982).

The Empty Nest

As children reach maturity, the family becomes a launching center that fires adolescents and young adults off into the world to work and start their own families. The term **empty nest** describes the family after the departure of the last child. Clearly the emptying of the nest involves changes in role and lifestyle for parents, particularly for mothers who have centered their lives on child rearing. How are parents affected by this transition?

Quite positively, it seems! Just as the entry of children into the family seems to cause modest decreases in marital satisfaction, their departure seems to cause modest *increases* in marital satisfaction and perceived quality of life (Glenn, 1975; Lee, 1988; Olson & Lavee, 1989; Rollins & Feldman, 1970). After the nest empties, parents feel that their marriages are more equitable and that their spouses are more accommodating to their needs (Menaghan, 1983). Mothers are especially likely to feel somewhat better about themselves and their lives in general when they no longer have children in the house (Harkins, 1978; McLanahan & Sorenson, 1985; Neugarten, 1970). Asked how she would feel about her adult children moving back home, one woman may have spoken for many: "Oh, God, I wouldn't like it. It would be awful. I'm tired of waiting on people" (Aldous, 1985, p. 131). So much for the belief—one that was common among developmentalists in the not too distant past—that the empty nest creates feelings of emptiness!

True, a minority of parents, mothers *and* fathers, find this transition very disturbing, and others have mixed feelings about it. For example, women who experience the transition "off-time"—who feel that their departing children are not yet ready to leave—are likely to experience the event negatively (Harkins, 1978). And fathers who have poor marriages but who appear to have very close relationships with their children may also suffer (Lewis, Freneau, & Roberts, 1979). Still, hard as it may be for departing children to believe, children appear to cause more stress to their parents when they arrive in the family than when they depart.

Why do parents generally react positively to the empty nest? Possibly it is because they have fewer roles and responsibilities and therefore experience less stress and strain. If parenting is a little like beating one's head against a wall, there is surely some relief when one stops! But we need not view parenthood as self-abuse to understand that empty nest couples have more time to focus on their marital relationship and to enjoy activities together. Indeed, marital satisfaction is highest during the empty nest transition when couples *do* participate in activities together rather than leading separate social lives (Orthner, 1975). Moreover, parents are likely to view the emptying of the nest as evidence that they have accomplished the ultimate goal of parenting. They expect and want their children to launch adult lives and take pleasure in having done their job well. Finally, as we shall see, parents by no means lose contact with their children after the nest empties, so it is not as though they are really losing their children.

To appreciate the positive side of the empty nest transition, consider 44-year-old Donna, a housewife–mother who was constructively preparing for the empty nest. She had already taken a job, was considering going back to school to obtain a degree in counseling, and was very much looking forward to the next 20 years. She also expressed what Erik Erikson would call a sense of generativity: "I have five terrific daughters that didn't just happen. It took lots of time to mold, correct, love, and challenge them. . . . It's nice to see such rewarding results." For a parent like Donna, the emptying of the nest means the achievement of an important goal and an opportunity to set new goals as an individual and as a couple. No wonder it is typically an easy transition to make.

Grandparenthood

What is your image of grandparents? Are they white-haired, jovial elders offering cookies and hugs? Actually, that image is a bit off the mark. If the nest is typically emptying when parents are in their 40s and 50s, most parents become grandparents in that age range—when they are middle-aged, not elderly, and when both Grandma and Grandpa are likely to be highly involved in careers and community activities. Moreover, because there are few firm rules about how to play the grandparent role, some grandparents fit our stereotyped image but others adopt quite different styles of relating to their grandchildren.

The diversity of grandparents is illustrated by the results of a national survey of grandparents of teenagers conducted by Andrew Cherlin and Frank Furstenberg (1986). These researchers determined the prevalence of three major styles of grandparenting:

1. *Remote.* Remote grandparents (29% of the sample) were symbolic figures seen only occasionally by their grandchildren. Primarily because they were geographically distant, they were emotionally distant as well.
2. *Companionate.* This was the most common style of grandparenting (55% of the sample). Companionate grandparents saw their grandchildren frequently and enjoyed sharing activities with them. They only rarely played a parental role; their goal was enjoyment rather than giving and receiving practical aid. Moreover, like most grandparents, they operated according to a "norm of noninterference," hesitating to meddle in the way their adult children were raising their children. They were quite happy to leave the child-care responsibilities to their children. As one put it, "You can love them and then say, 'Here, take them now, go on home'" (p. 55).
3. *Involved.* Finally, 16% of the grandparents assumed a parentlike role. Like companionate grandparents, they saw their grandchildren frequently and were playful with them, but unlike companionate grandparents they also often helped with child care, gave advice, and played other practical roles in their grandchildren's lives. Some involved grandparents were truly substitute parents who lived with and tended their grandchildren because their daughters were unmarried or recently divorced and worked outside the home.

We see, then, that grandparenting can take many forms. Nonetheless, most grandparents often see at least some of their grandchildren and prefer a role that is high in enjoyment and affection but low in responsibility. How do grandparents feel about their role? Again, there is much diversity, but the vast majority find being a grandparent very gratifying (Cherlin & Furstenberg, 1986). Remote grandparents are the least satisfied, largely because they wish they lived closer to their grandchildren and could see them more often. Grandmothers tend to be somewhat more satisfied than grandfathers (Thomas, 1986), and relationships between grandchildren and their maternal grandmothers tend to be especially close (Matthews & Sprey, 1985). Traditional gender roles may help explain this, for women often serve as "kin-keepers" in the family, keeping up contacts and ensuring that close, affectionate relationships are maintained (Atkinson, Kivett, & Campbell, 1986; Cherlin & Furstenberg, 1986; Hagestad, 1985).

A major point to recognize about the grandparent role is that it is not entirely voluntary. Adults can decide when to become parents, but they become grandparents, ready or not, when their children have babies. Some women become grandparents in their 30s or even late 20s because their teenage daughters have children; these women tend to be far less enthusiastic about the role than grandmothers who become grandmothers "on time" (Hagestad & Burton, 1986). In addition, once adults become grandparents, their access to their grandchildren depends on their relationship with their adult children and their children's spouses. When their children's lives change, their roles can change dramatically. As Gunhild Hagestad (1985) puts it, grandparents are "the family national guard"

(p. 46); that is, they are on alert and come to the rescue when there is a crisis in the family. For example, when an adult child divorces, grandparents are often drawn into a more highly involved role as they help a child (usually a daughter) cope with divorce, diminished income, and child-care responsibilities (Cherlin & Furstenberg, 1986; Gerstel, 1988; Matthews & Sprey, 1984). Yet if their own child does not obtain custody, grandparents' access to their grandchildren may be reduced or even cut off, causing them much anguish.

The grandparent role changes in predictable ways as grandchildren change. Cherlin and Furstenberg (1986) conclude that the time when grandchildren are young is the "fat part of grandparenting," a time when enjoyment and involvement are especially high. The fact that both grandchildren and grandparents are relatively young at this time may explain why young grandparents have been found to be more "fun-seeking" and less formal in their role than older grandparents are (Neugarten & Weinstein, 1964). As grandchildren become teenagers, grandparents, like parents, see less and less of them. Finally, as grandchildren launch out on their own as adults, grandparents today often become great-grandparents. Because few adults in the past lived long enough to play the great-grandparent role, it is even fuzzier than the grandparent role. Although great-grandparents often feel a sense of pride when their families extend to four generations, they are not as often involved in the lives of their great-grandchildren (Cavanaugh, 1990; Cherlin & Furstenberg, 1986).

In short, grandparenthood seems to be important in the lives of middle-aged and elderly adults, though it takes many forms depending on such factors as the grandparents' preferences, the geographical distance between grandparents and grandchildren, and changes in the lives of grandchildren and their parents. Moreover, children view grandparents as important figures in their lives (Furman & Buhrmester, 1985a). Indeed, all three generations seem to benefit from maintaining close ties.

Changing Family Relationships During Adulthood

It is clear that relationships develop and change with time, so let's see what becomes of relationships between spouses, siblings, and parents and their children during the adult years.

The Marital Relationship

What have you concluded about changes in marital relationships over the family life cycle? Basically, we have seen that marital satisfaction, while generally high for most couples, dips somewhat after the honeymoon period is over, dips still lower in the new-parenthood phase, continues to drop as new children are added to the family, and does not seem to recover until the children leave the nest. These are precisely the trends discovered by Boyd Rollins and Harold Feldman (1970) when they surveyed adults in the eight different phases of the family life cycle about their marital happiness (see Figure 14.3). Moreover, their findings reinforce another point we have been making: Women, because they have traditionally been more involved than men in rearing children, tend to be more strongly affected by family life transitions than men are.

As we have also seen, these average trends fit some families much better than others, depending on such factors as the difficulty of a child's temperament and the extent to which both parents contribute to child rearing. Moreover, these trends are quite weak, and knowing the stage of the family life cycle an adult is experiencing really does not allow us to predict very well how satisfied that adult is with marriage. To do that, we have to consider many additional factors. For example, happily married people, as compared with unhappily married people, tend to have positive personality traits such as self-confidence, social maturity, and an ability to nurture others (Skolnick, 1981). Moreover, their personalities are similar; it is when "opposites attract" and find their personalities clashing day after day that marital problems tend to arise (Skolnick, 1981). Finally, happily married partners genuinely like each other and enjoy each other's company; they do not just stay together because it is convenient, because they believe marriage should be a lifelong commitment, or because they think it is best for the children (Lauer & Lauer, 1986; Skolnick, 1981).

Without question, the marital relationship is centrally important to adult development. Adults feel generally good about their lives if their marriages are satisfying (Campbell, 1981). Indeed, both adults and children seem to thrive when a couple is able to maintain a close and committed partnership over the years. And, as we shall see shortly, adults and children alike suffer when a marriage dissolves.

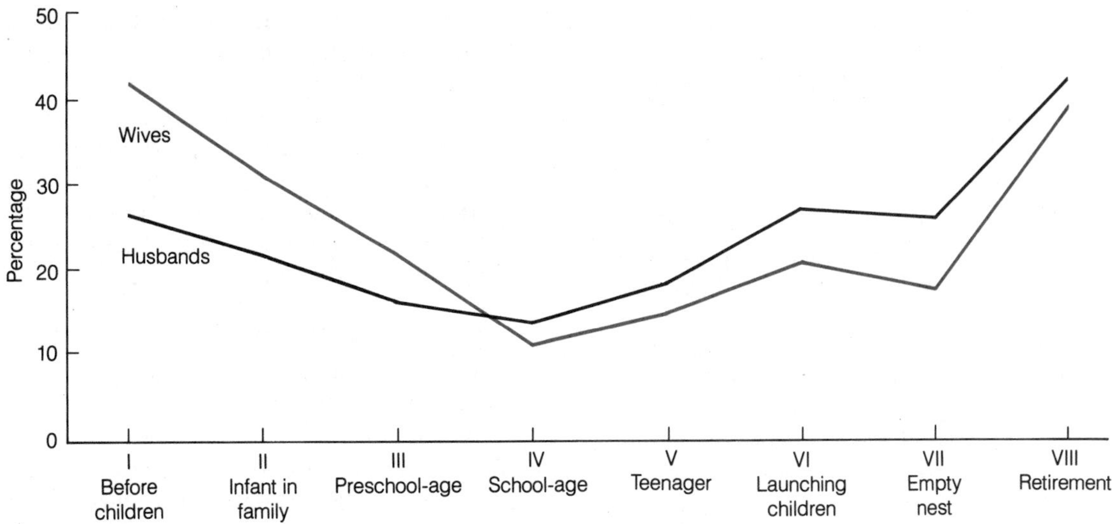

Figure 14.3 Percentages of wives and husbands at different stages of the family life cycle who say their marriage is going well "all the time." (From Rollins & Feldman, 1970)

Sibling Relationships

How do the relationships between brothers and sisters change once they no longer live together in the same house and have launched their own separate lives? Contact between siblings decreases over the adult years (Dunn, 1984; Goetting, 1986). After all, adults normally marry and develop their own friendship networks, and they often move away from their hometowns. According to Victor Cicirelli (1982), adult siblings typically see each other several times a year and communicate through phone calls or letters about how they are getting along. Most of them rarely discuss intimate problems with each other, nor do they help each other much except in times of crisis. The sibling relationship is less intense than it was during childhood and adolescence when sibs were living in the same house (and sometimes the same bedroom) and were intimately involved in each other's daily lives.

Yet the same ambivalence that characterizes sibling relationships during childhood seems to carry over into adulthood. A great deal of caring and emotional closeness persists, despite infrequent contact (Gold, 1989). Siblings may grow even closer in old age; in Cicirelli's (1982) survey, 68% of middle-aged adults but 83% of elderly adults described their relationships with siblings as either "close" or "extremely close." The potential for sibling rivalry and conflict also persists, however. Although conflict is far less frequent than during childhood, old rivalries can and do flare up again during adulthood.

Helgola Ross and Joel Milgram (1982) discovered from interviewing adults ranging in age from 22 to 93 that sibling relationships can become warmer or cooler in response to specific life events. Siblings typically became closer if one moved geographically nearer to the other, became sick, lost a spouse, or divorced. Yet relationships sometimes deteriorated when one sibling moved away or got married, or when differences between siblings in educational or employment status or values became large. When parents became ill or died, some siblings rallied together, while others became hostile toward one another. It turned out that siblings who had enjoyed a close relationship during childhood were likely to become even closer after many significant life events, whereas siblings who had had poor relationships during childhood were likely to become even more rivalrous in response to the same life events.

The sibling relationship is typically the longest-lasting relationship we have, linking us to individuals who share many of our genes and experiences (Goetting, 1986). It is a relationship that can be very close, very tense and conflictual, or, for many people, some of both. When it remains close, older adults are likely to feel better about themselves and their lives (Cicirelli, 1989).

Relationships Between the Generations

It is now amply clear that the different generations in most families are in close contact and enjoy affectionate give-and-take relationships. As young adults leave the nest, they by no means sever ties with their parents; instead, they and their parents negotiate a new relationship, sometimes a more intimate one in which they move beyond playing out their roles as "child" and "parent" (Greene & Boxer, 1986; Richards, Bengtson, & Miller, 1989). For example, Kenneth and Anna Sullivan (1980) monitored the family relationships of males who went away to college and males who remained at home and commuted to college. Those who left home actually experienced more affection for and closer communication with their parents than those who remained at home. Moreover, their mothers felt more affectionate toward them than they had before their sons went off to school. Similarly, Kathleen White, Joseph Speisman, and Daryl Costos (1983) found that some young adults, as they become individuals in their own right, begin to see their parents as individuals in their own right rather than merely as parent figures. Daughters, especially married ones, were more likely to establish a new and more mutual relationship with their mothers than sons were. One young woman expressed the transformation well:

> I am understanding her now more than I ever did before. I have started to understand that I had to stop blaming her for everything in my life. I felt she had been a lousy parent. Now, I'm more understanding that my mother is a person and that she has her own problems and her own life . . . I accepted her as a mother—but she actually is a human being. . . . [White, Speisman, & Costos, 1983, p. 73]

Apparently, then, there are opportunities for parent/child relationships to become even more affectionate and intimate after the nest has emptied if adult children and their parents begin to see each other in new ways. What happens when children become middle-aged and their parents elderly? In Chapter 13, we exploded the myth that most elderly people are socially isolated and lonely. In large part, they are not lonely because they maintain close ties with their families. According to national surveys, 80% of people over 65 have living children, about half either live with a child (18%) or live within 10 minutes of at least one child (34%), and about three-fourths had seen at least one child in the week before they were interviewed (Shanas, 1980). Middle-aged children continue to feel very close to their parents (Belsky, 1990; Richards, Bengtson, & Miller, 1989).

So much for the myth that today's families have abandoned the elderly! These findings indicate that the predominant family form in the United States is neither the isolated nuclear family nor the extended family household; instead it is what has been called the **modified extended family**—an arrangement in which nuclear families live in their own separate households but have close ties and frequent communication and interaction with their other kin (Litwak, 1960). Most elderly people prefer just this pattern and do not want to have to live with their children if they can avoid it (Brody, Johnsen, & Fulcomer, 1984; Okraku, 1987).

Relationships between the generations are not only close and affectionate, but they are generally quite equitable as well. That is, each generation gives something and each generation receives something in return. Among Mexican-American clans, for example, intergenerational give and take seems to be especially common (Markides, Boldt, & Ray, 1986). Elders receive a great deal of advice and practical help about everything from personal problems to home repairs from their middle-aged children, *and* their middle-aged children turn to them for advice and help. Similarly, different generations within the family mutually influence one another. Parents not only transmit their values to their children, but adult children also shape their parents' attitudes and values (Glass, Bengtson, & Dunham, 1986). Thus relationships within the family system continue to be reciprocally influential throughout the life span.

At the same time, middle-aged adults often give more in the way of social support and tangible aid to the younger and older generations than they receive in return. Indeed, Elaine Brody (1981, 1985) uses the phrase "**middle generation squeeze**" to convey the idea that middle-aged adults sometimes experience heavy demands from both the younger and the older generations. Imagine that you are a 47-year-old woman immersed in your career, mar-

Box 14.2
The Sandwich Generation: Adults Who Care for Aging Parents

More and more adults with children are finding themselves caring for their aging parents, "sandwiched" between the younger and older generations and experiencing middle generation squeeze. Elaine Brody (1985) estimates that about 5 million Americans are providing parent care at any given time, and that many more of us will do it at some time or another in our adult lives, often for many years. Most of these caregivers are daughters in their 40s and 50s playing out their roles as "kin-keepers"—women whose nests are no sooner emptied of children than they are refilled with aging parents. Yet the geriatric center with which Brody is affiliated receives calls for help from all kinds of caregivers:

> An exhausted, 70-year-old woman who could no longer go on caring for her disabled, 93-year-old mother; . . . a divorcee of 57 who was caring for two disabled sons, a 6-year-old grandchild, and an 87-year-old wheelchair-bound mother; and a young couple in their early 30s, about to have a first child, who had taken two older people into their home—the wife's terminally ill mother and the confused, incontinent grandmother for whom the mother had been caring [p. 23].

As you might imagine, these caregivers experience many strains: emotional, physical, and financial (Belsky, 1990; Brody, 1985). A woman who is almost wholly responsible for a dependent elder often feels angry and resentful because she has no time for herself and little freedom to pursue her own goals. She may become socially isolated or experience strain in her other relationships because she has little energy left to give to her husband, employer, or children. Some women find that they must quit their jobs or reduce their work hours in order to cope. Strains are especially severe among adults who are living with and caring for a mentally impaired parent who not only has difficulties with memory and judgment but engages in disruptive and socially inappropriate behavior (Deimling & Bass, 1986). And yet most of these caregivers still feel guilty about not doing enough for their parents (Brody, 1985)!

One thing is evident in all of this: Young and middle-aged adults today continue to feel a strong sense of responsibility to care for their ailing parents (Brody, Johnsen, & Fulcomer, 1984; Okraku, 1987). Neither adult children nor aging parents want to have to live together or want to see younger generations overburdened with bills and responsibilities. Yet all generations agree that aging parents deserve emotional support and practical aid. Again, then, we can abandon the myth that today's elderly people are abandoned by their families.

As Brody (1985) sees it, adults have never before been called upon to provide so much help for so many years to aging parents and grandparents, and they are doing their best to meet the challenge. At the same time, these caregivers are a group at risk, and they may need help from the government if they are to continue to provide the bulk of emotional support and care that physically and mentally impaired elders receive (Brody et al., 1984).

riage, and social life. You could well be asked to cope at the very same time with menopause, a teenager in the house, a young adult child who needs money for college or help in launching or caring for his or her own family—*and* a widowed mother who has had a stroke and cannot manage her own home anymore. That is "middle generation squeeze"! Box 14.2 demonstrates that middle-aged adults who must foster their children's development while tending to their own development *and* caring for aging parents can usually find their burdens quite overwhelming.

In sum, generations within a family maintain close relationships throughout adulthood, mutually supporting and influencing one another. Yet the quality of parent/child relationships often changes over the life span. The child who is dependent on parents becomes the adult child who can truly be interdependent with parents—and in some cases ultimately becomes the person on whom aging parents depend.

VARIATIONS ON THE FAMILY THEME

Useful as it is, the concept of a family life cycle simply does not capture the diversity of adult lifestyles and family experiences. Many of today's adults do not progress in a neat and orderly way through the eight stages of the family life cycle—marrying, having their children, watching them leave the nest, and so on. A small number never marry; a larger number never have children; and a still larger number move in and out of married life by marrying, divorcing, and remarrying. So, to underscore the diversity of today's lifestyles, let's briefly examine some of these variations on "normal" family themes.

Singles

Single adults are often pictured as being young and leading an active social life. Because adults are postponing marriage, there is indeed a growing number of young, single adults. Yet it is nearly impossible to describe the "typical" single adult, for this category also includes middle-aged and elderly people who have experienced divorce or the death of a spouse, as well as adults who have never married.

It *is* typical to start adulthood as a single person; a majority of adults in the 18 to 29 age range are unmarried (Sweet & Bumpass, 1987). Although young singles are busy preparing for their careers or getting them off the ground, they are also busy building social networks. They are likely to be more socially active and to have a wider circle of friends than they will have in later years (Fischer & Phillips, 1982). For women, though not for men, postponing marriage and childbearing is likely to pay off in later career success, for it means staying in school longer (Haggstrom, Kanouse, & Morrison, 1986).

A growing number of young single adults are living with a romantic partner without being married. Such **cohabitation** is more common than it used to be; about 10% of single adults in their 20s and early 30s cohabitate (Sweet & Bumpass, 1987). Cohabitation has become a part of the courtship process for a substantial minority of college students and other young adults, including many who have already married and divorced (Spanier, 1983). It is typically not a substitute for marriage; instead, it is usually a temporary arrangement, sometimes seen as a test of compatibility, that leads either to marriage or to a break-up (Macklin, 1978; Newcomb, 1979; Tanfer, 1987). In most respects, cohabiting couples experience the same satisfactions and the same problems as married couples, although they often keep their own bank accounts and put more emphasis on self-sufficiency and independence (Blumstein & Schwartz, 1983).

It makes some sense to think that couples who live together before marrying would have more opportunity than those who do not to determine whether they are truly compatible. Yet couples who live together and then marry seem, if anything, to be *more* dissatisfied with their marriages (DeMaris & Leslie, 1984) and *more* likely to divorce (Bennett, Blanc, & Bloom, 1988) than couples who do not live together before marrying. It is unlikely that the experience of cohabitation itself is responsible. Instead, it seems that the kinds of people who choose to live together may be somewhat more susceptible to marital problems or less committed to marriage than the kinds of people who do not. They tend, for example, to be less religious and less conventional in other respects (DeMaris & Leslie, 1984; Newcomb, 1979). Moreover, cohabiting couples who marry are less similar in age, previous marital status, race, and occupational level than couples who do not live together before marriage (Gwartney-Gibbs, 1986). Possibly, then, their dissimilarities make achieving a harmonious marriage more difficult than it otherwise might be. For these and other reasons, we end up with no support for the notion that cohabitation enables people to select their mates more wisely.

What of the adults who never marry? How do they fare later in adulthood when most of their peers are married? Not badly at all, it seems, despite stereotypes suggesting that they are miserably lonely and maladjusted. Although single adults who have been through a divorce tend to be lonelier than married adults, never-married adults are not, even in old age (Cargan, 1981; Essex & Nam, 1987; Stull & Scarisbrick-Hauser, 1989). Single adults as a group do typically have a lower overall sense of well-being or happiness than married adults do (Campbell, 1981; Veroff, Douvan, & Kulka, 1981), but Norval Glenn and Charles Weaver (1988) have discovered that the "happiness gap" between never-married adults and married adults has narrowed since the 1970s. (Divorced single adults have remained a relatively unhappy group.) These findings hint that the single life is becoming a more satisfying lifestyle, and that marriage may not be quite so gratifying as it once was.

Box 14.3
Gay Men and Lesbian Women

Roughly 2% to 5% of adults in the United States are thought to be exclusively homosexual, and it is likely that this estimate is on the low side (Paul & Weinrich, 1982). Despite society's tendency to stereotype gay men as effeminate and lesbian women as too "mannish," gay and lesbian adults have the same wide range of psychological and social attributes that heterosexual adults do. No one would think of drawing a character sketch of a person based solely on the knowledge that he or she has a heterosexual sexual orientation, yet many people persist in assuming that knowing a person prefers same-sex romantic partners gives them the "whole story."

The lifestyles that gay men and lesbian women adopt are as diverse as they are. In a major study of homosexuals, Alan Bell and Martin Weinberg (1978) found that some lived monogamously, much like happily married couples; others, especially men, lived with a roommate but actually sought sexual relationships outside of their partnership. Still others were either "swingers"—single adults who attempted to find partners but were frequently lonely—or individuals who lived asexual lives and did little to find partners. A sizable minority—fewer than a fifth of the gay men but over a third of the lesbian women—had been married at some point, but most remained single and did not experience the transitions of the family life cycle.

So far as can be determined, gay or lesbian couples are far more similar to heterosexual couples than they are different. Their relationships evolve through the same stages of development and are generally just as satisfying as those of married or cohabiting heterosexuals (Kurdek & Schmitt, 1986). Contrary to myth, gay and lesbian couples do not "play roles," one consistently adopting the dominant "husband" role and the other adopting the more submissive "wife" role (Larson, 1982; Peplau & Amaro, 1982). Instead, homosexual couples are likely to have more egalitarian relationships than married couples do (Blumstein & Schwartz, 1983). Whereas married couples typically divide the labor according to traditional gender stereotypes, there are no clear guidelines in homosexual relationships about who should do what, so partners tend to work out a division of labor through trial and error based on who is especially talented at what or who hates doing what (Blumstein & Schwartz, 1983).

If anything makes the adult development of gay and lesbian adults different from that of heterosexuals (other than the obvious fact that most do not marry and have children), it is the prejudice they face. For many, the process of admitting that they have a homosexual orientation and establishing a positive identity in the face of negative societal attitudes is a long and torturous one (Berger, 1982). Many realize in childhood that they are "different" and struggle for years to accept their homosexuality. Even after accepting their sexual orientation, many must lead secret lives for fear of persecution. The AIDS epidemic has only compounded the challenges that gay men face. However, most eventually do come to accept themselves as they are and appear to be no less satisfied with their lives in middle age and later life than heterosexuals are (Berger, 1982).

In sum, gay men and lesbian women typically do not lead their lives according to the family life cycle, but they, like heterosexual adults, pursue such a wide range of different lifestyles that it is grossly inaccurate to stereotype them. If we can generalize at all, we can perhaps say that most gay and lesbian adults, like most heterosexual adults, want to feel good about themselves, want to participate in close relationships, and are largely successful at achieving those goals.

Finally, the category of single adults also includes individuals who have a homosexual orientation: gay men and lesbian women. Although a minority of homosexual adults marry (and typically divorce), most remain single throughout their lives and so do not experience the events of the family life cycle. Box 14.3 examines the lifestyles of these adults. Like other single adults, homosexual adults are a widely diverse group who cannot be stereotyped.

Childless Married Couples

Another increasingly large group of adults who do not experience the usual stages of the family life cycle are dual-career couples who remain childless. Many of these individuals want children but cannot have them, but a growing number voluntarily decide to put off having children or avoid having them at all (Bloom & Pebley, 1982). In the past, married couples who did not have children were often regarded as selfish or even psychologically disturbed. Although some of that stigma persists, it is increasingly acceptable to choose a childless (or, as childless couples prefer to put it, "childfree") life (Veroff, Douvan, & Kulka, 1981).

How are childless couples faring while their peers are having, raising, and launching children? Generally, quite well. Their marital satisfaction is somewhat higher than that of couples with children during the child-rearing years (Abbott & Brody, 1985; Glenn & McLanahan, 1982). But don't childless adults suffer in old age when they lack children to help them and offer them emotional support? For the most part, middle-aged and elderly childless couples seem to be no less satisfied with their lives than parents whose children have left the nest (Glenn & McLanahan, 1981; Rempel, 1985). However, elderly women who are childless *and* widowed do appear to be relatively dissatisfied with their lives compared with elderly women who have adult children (Beckman, 1981; Singh & Williams, 1981). Possibly, then, childless couples derive a good deal of satisfaction from their marriages but may eventually suffer from a lack of social support when those marriages end.

Families Experiencing Divorce

Orderly progress through the family life cycle is disrupted when a couple divorces. It is estimated that somewhere between 40% and 50% of recent marriages will end in divorce (Glick, 1984b; Sweet & Bumpass, 1987). Thus divorce has almost become a normative transition in the family life cycle, though it can occur at any point in a marriage. Divorce is *not* just one life event; instead, it is a series of stressful experiences for the entire family that begins with marital conflict before the divorce and includes a whole complex of life changes afterward. As Mavis Hetherington and Kathleen Camara (1984) see it, families must often cope with "the diminution of financial resources, changes in residence, assumption of new roles and responsibilities, establishment of new patterns of intrafamilial interaction, reorganization of routines and schedules, and eventually the introduction of new relationships into the existing family" (p. 398).

Why do people divorce? What effects does divorce typically have on family members? And how can we explain the fact that some adults and children eventually thrive after a divorce whereas others experience persisting problems?

Before the Divorce

The processes within the family that ultimately cause couples to divorce are largely unknown (Kitson, Babri, & Roach, 1985). Nor is it known why many unhappy couples stay together, while some seemingly well-adjusted couples nonetheless divorce. However, Gay Kitson and her colleagues (1985) have pieced together a portrait of the couples at highest risk for divorce. Generally they are young adults, in their 20s and 30s, who have been married for an average of about seven years, which means that they often have preschool-aged or school-aged children (Glick, 1984b; Sweet & Bumpass, 1987). They are especially likely to divorce if they married as teenagers, had a short courtship, or conceived a child before marrying—all factors that might suggest an unreadiness for marriage and unusually high financial and psychological stress accompanying new parenthood. Finally, they are more likely to be low in socioeconomic status than high, although there is intriguing evidence that highly educated and highly paid career women are also especially prone to divorce. This profile cannot take us far, however, because all kinds of couples are divorcing today.

Contrary to the notion that today's couples do not really give their marriages a chance to work, research suggests that most divorcing couples experience a few years of marital distress and often try out separations before they make the final decision to divorce (Kitson et al., 1985). Although the stated reasons for divorcing are varied, they are no longer restricted to severe problems such as nonsupport, alcoholism, or abuse (Kitson & Sussman, 1982). Instead, couples today typically divorce because they feel their marriages are lacking in communication, emotional fulfillment, or compatibility.

After the Divorce: Crisis and Reorganization

Most families going through a divorce experience a crisis period with considerable disruption that often lasts for a year or more (Hetherington, 1981, 1987, 1989; Hetherington, Cox, & Cox, 1982; Wallerstein & Kelly, 1980). Typically, both spouses experience emotional as well as practical difficulties. The wife, who usually obtains custody of any children, is likely to be angry, depressed, moody, lonely, and otherwise distressed, although often relieved as well. The husband is also likely to be distressed, particularly if he feels shut off from his children. Both individuals must manage the difficult task of revising their identities to become single people rather than married people. Both sometimes feel socially isolated from former friends and unsure of themselves as they attempt to establish new romantic relationships. Women with children are likely to face the added problems of coping with a seriously reduced income, moving to a lower-income neighborhood, and trying to work and raise young children singlehandedly.

Because of all these stresses, divorced adults, much like widowed adults, are at high risk for depression, physical health problems, and even death (Stroebe & Stroebe, 1986). Although research has typically focused on young adults, divorced adults over 50 appear to experience even more distress than younger adults do, often feeling very uncertain and pessimistic about what lies ahead of them (Chiriboga, 1982). For most adults, divorce is a very negative experience.

As you might suspect, psychologically distressed adults do not make the best of parents. Moreover, children going through a divorce do not make the best of children, for they are suffering too. They are often angry, fearful, depressed, and guilty, especially if they are preschoolers who fear that they are somehow responsible for what happened (Hetherington, 1981). They are likely to be whiney and dependent, disobedient, and downright disrespectful. Parent/child relationships at this time are best described as a vicious circle in which the child's behavior problems and the parent's ineffective parenting styles feed on each other.

Mavis Hetherington and her associates (1982) find that custodial mothers, overburdened by responsibilities and by their own emotional reactions to the divorce, often become edgy, impatient, and insensitive to their children's needs. In terms of the dimensions of child rearing we have discussed, they become less warm and loving, and they also become more inconsistent in their discipline, sometimes trying to seize control of their children with a heavyhanded or restrictive style of parenting, but also failing to carry through in enforcing rules and making fewer demands that their children behave maturely. Noncustodial fathers, meanwhile, are likely to be overpermissive, indulging their children during visits. This is not the formula for producing well-adjusted, competent children. The behavior problems that children display undoubtedly make effective parenting difficult, but a deterioration in parenting style undoubtedly aggravates children's behavior problems.

The low point in mother/child relations comes about a year after the divorce and is particularly severe when the child is a boy. One divorced mother described her family's ordeal as a "struggle for survival," while another characterized her experiences with her children as like "getting bitten to death by ducks" (Hetherington, Cox, & Cox, 1982, p. 258). Not surprisingly, the stresses associated with the divorce and a breakdown in effective parenting often lead not only to behavior problems at home but to a disruption of a child's relations with peers and academic problems at school, especially when a child is young at the time of the divorce (Allison & Furstenberg, 1989; Hetherington et al., 1982; Kinard & Reinherz, 1986).

How long do these negative consequences last? Hetherington and her colleagues find that families are beginning to pull themselves back together two years after the divorce. It is not yet clear whether women or men suffer most in the long term (Kitson & Raschke, 1981), but some evidence suggests that boys recover more slowly than girls. Girls normally recover from their social and emotional disturbances by the end of the second year, to a point where they are quite indistinguishable from girls in intact families (Hetherington et al., 1982). Although boys improve dramatically during this same period, many of them continue to show signs of emotional distress and problems in their relationships with parents, siblings, teachers, and peers, even six years after the divorce (Hetherington, 1987).

Why might boys have more persistent problems? Possibly they are exposed to more parental conflict and offered less social support than girls are (Hetherington et al., 1982). Moreover, they may be more likely than girls to suffer from separation from their fathers and restricted access to male role models. Indeed, it could be that boys look bad because most researchers have studied the most common family arrangement after divorce—mother-headed homes. Interestingly, those few boys whose fathers assume custody seem to fare better than boys who live with their mothers; in fact, children of both sexes appear to be better adjusted when they live with their same-sex parent (Peterson & Zill, 1986; Santrock & Warchak, 1979; Zaslow, 1989).

Although many of the emotional and behavioral disturbances that parents and children experience typically fade away after about two years, the whole event is not entirely forgotten. Judith Wallerstein (1984) finds that adolescents who are 10 years away from their parents' divorce recall few of the events that transpired when they were preschoolers but often continue to be negative about what the divorce has done to their lives and harbor fantasies that their parents will reconcile. One girl whose parents had both remarried was quite blunt: "I wish my stepfather would go back to his first wife, I wish my stepmother would go back to her first husband, and I would like my mom and dad to get together again" (Wallerstein, 1984, p. 452). Interestingly, Wallerstein (1984, 1987) finds that young adults who were school-aged children or adolescents when their parents divorced suffered less than preschoolers at the time of the divorce but were even more burdened by painful memories ten years afterward. Moreover, they were more likely to fear that they would be unable to find happiness in marriage. There may well be some truth to that fear, for adults whose parents divorced are more likely to experience divorce themselves than adults from intact families (Glenn, 1985; Keith & Finlay, 1988).

In sum, divorce is a difficult experience for all involved. Problems reach crisis proportions about a year after the divorce, and while most of them disappear over the next couple of years, young children, especially boys, may have persistent problems, and even many years later children of both sexes are still carrying painful feelings.

But now let us offset this gloomy picture of the typical divorce with more encouraging messages. In the first place, a conflict-ridden two-parent family is clearly more detrimental to a child's development than a stable single-parent family. Indeed, many of the behavior problems that children display after a divorce are actually evident well *before* the divorce and may be related to long-standing family conflict rather than to divorce itself (Block, Block, & Gjerde, 1986; Demo & Acock, 1988). Children may actually benefit if the ending of a stormy marriage ultimately reduces the stress they experience and enables either or both parents to be more sensitive and responsive to their needs (Hetherington, 1981; Wallerstein & Kelly, 1980). So much for "staying together for the good of the children"!

Second, not all families experience all the difficulties we have described. Indeed, some adults and children manage this transition quite well and even thrive afterward (Hetherington, 1989). What factors, then, might facilitate a positive adjustment to divorce? Box 14.4 addresses this question.

Remarriage and Reconstituted Families

Within 3 to 5 years of a divorce, about 75% of single-parent families will experience yet another major change when the parent remarries and the children acquire a stepparent—and sometimes new siblings as well (Glick, 1984b). Remarriage shortly after divorce contributes further to a "pile-up" of stressors and means starting a second family life cycle (Hill, 1986). Although most remarried adults are satisfied with their second marriages, second marriages are somewhat more likely to end in divorce than first marriages (Glick, 1984b). Imagine, then, the stresses for adults and children who find themselves in a recurring cycle of marriage, marital conflict, divorce, single status, and remarriage (see Brody, Neubaum, & Forehand, 1988)!

How do children fare when their custodial parents remarry? Interestingly, just as boys seem to suffer more than girls when they live with a single-parent mother, boys seem to benefit more than girls when they gain a stepfather, enjoying higher self-esteem, being less anxious and angered, and overcoming most of the adjustment problems they displayed before their mothers remarried (Clingempeel, Ievoli, & Brand, 1984; Hetherington, 1987; Santrock et al., 1982; Zaslow, 1989). Less is known about the transition from a father-headed single-parent home to a two-parent family with a stepmother, but it appears that this transition is also more difficult for girls, especially if their biological mothers maintain frequent contact with them (Clingempeel & Segal, 1986). It seems that girls are often so closely allied with their mothers that they are bothered by either a stepfather competing for their mother's attention or a stepmother attempting to play a substitute-mother role. Yet, girls do adjust over time to being part of a reconstituted family (Clingempeel & Segal, 1986; Hetherington, 1987).

In the end, remarriage generally works out well for adults and children alike. Adults gain the satisfactions of companionship, and children gain stepparents who generally appear to play the parent role quite well (Santrock et al., 1982). Compared with boys in single-parent homes, boys in reconstituted families appear to fare well, while girls are probably no worse off—and possibly better off eventually—than they would be in a single-parent home. Even so, the transition from a single-parent family to a reconstituted family involves a period of adjustment and disruption as family members get used to one another and adopt new roles.

Even this quick examination of the diverse experiences of today's families should convince us that it is difficult indeed to generalize about the American family. We can gain many insights by tracing the progression of developing human beings through the stages of the family life cycle, but we must also recognize that an increasing

Box 14.4
Smoothing the Bumpy Path to Recovery After Divorce

Some adults and children thrive after a divorce, whereas others suffer many negative and long-lasting effects. Although the individual's temperament and coping skills influence how well he or she adjusts (Hetherington, 1989), several factors can make the individual's task easier:

Adequate financial support

Families fare better after a divorce if their finances are not seriously undermined (Desimone-Luis, O'Mahoney, & Hunt, 1979; Menaghan & Lieberman, 1986). Unfortunately, many mother-headed families experience a precipitous drop in income and then must cope with the additional challenges of moving to a lower-income area and struggling for survival. Recent efforts to ensure that more noncustodial parents pay their child support payments may help the cause.

Adequate parenting by the custodial parent

The custodial parent obviously plays a critical role in what happens to the family. If she or he can continue to be warm, authoritative, and consistent, children are far less likely to experience problems (Hetherington & Camara, 1984; Kline, Tschann, Johnston, & Wallerstein, 1989). It is difficult to be an effective parent when one is depressed and under stress, but parents who understand the stakes involved may be more able to give their children the love and guidance they need.

Emotional support from the noncustodial parent

If parents continue to squabble after the divorce and are hostile toward each other, both are likely to be upset, the custodial parent's parenting is likely to suffer, and children will feel torn in their loyalties and experience behavior problems (Kline et al., 1989; Long, Slater, Forehand, & Fauber, 1988). Children also suffer when they lose contact with their noncustodial parent. Unfortunately, about a third of children living with their mothers lose all contact with their fathers (Seltzer & Bianchi, 1988). By contrast, regular contact with *supportive* fathers helps children (particularly sons) make a positive adjustment to life in a single-parent home (Hess & Camara, 1979; Rosen, 1979). Ideally, then, children should be able to maintain affectionate ties with *both* parents and should be protected from any continuing conflict between parents.

Additional social support

Divorcing adults are less depressed if they have close confidants (Menaghan & Lieberman, 1986). Moreover, children benefit from peer support programs in which they and other children of divorce can share their feelings, correct their misconceptions, and learn positive coping skills (Pedro-Carroll & Cowen, 1985; Stolberg & Garrison, 1985). Adolescents in single-parent homes also appear to be less likely to engage in delinquent behavior if a second adult (a grandmother, for example) lives in the home than if one parent bears the sole responsibility for child rearing and supervision (Dornbusch et al., 1985). In short, friends, relatives, peers, school personnel, and other sources of social support outside the family can do much to help families adjust to divorce.

A minimum of additional stressors

Generally, families respond most positively to divorce if additional disruptions are kept to a minimum—for example, if parents do not have to move, go through court hearings, get new jobs, cope with the loss of their children, and so on (Buehler, Hogan, Robinson, & Levy, 1985–1986). It only makes sense that it is easier to deal with a couple of changes than a mountain of stressors. Although families cannot always control events, they can perhaps strive to keep their lives as simple as possible.

Here, then, we have the first steps in the path toward a positive divorce experience. We also have still another good example of how the family is a social system embedded in larger social systems. Mother, father, and children will all influence each other's adjustment to divorce, and the family's experience will also depend on its interactions with the surrounding world.

number of individuals depart in some way or another from that traditional pattern.

APPLICATIONS: CONFRONTING THE PROBLEM OF FAMILY VIOLENCE

Just as family relationships can be our greatest source of nurturance and support, they can be our greatest source of anguish. Nowhere is this more obvious than in cases of family violence. Child abuse is perhaps the most visible form of family violence. Every day, infants, children, and adolescents are burned, bruised, beaten, starved, suffocated, sexually abused, or otherwise mistreated by their caretakers. Other children are not the targets of physical violence but are victims of psychological maltreatment—rejected, verbally abused, and even terrorized by their par-

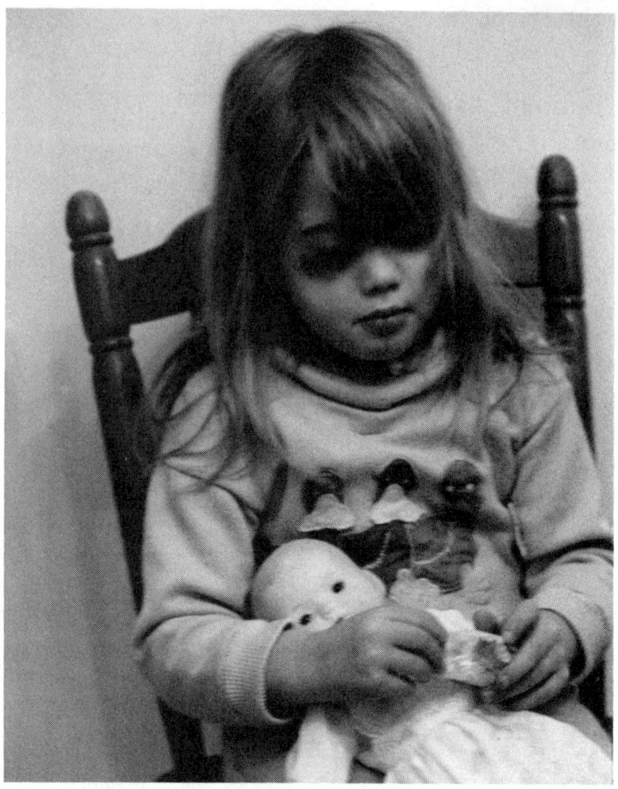

Child abuse is only one of the many forms of family violence that pose a grave problem in our society today.

ents (Hart & Brassard, 1987). Still others are neglected and deprived of the basic care and stimulation that they need to develop normally. In 1985, over 1.9 *million* reports of child maltreatment of all sorts were filed in the United States (American Humane Association, cited in U.S. Bureau of the Census, 1989). In a survey of two-parent families, Murray Straus and Richard Gelles (1986) found that almost 11% of the children had been kicked, bitten, punched, hit with an object, beaten up, or threatened with a knife or gun by their parents in the past year.[2] Since many cases of child abuse and neglect are not detected or reported, this may be only the tip of the iceberg.

The abuse of children by their caregivers is only one form of family violence. Much of the violence children experience, some of it life-threatening, is inflicted by their own siblings (Straus, 1980). And *spouse abuse* is also rampant. Marital violence is often mutual, but since husbands often do more severe damage to wives than wives do to husbands, we hear more about wife-battering. Straus and Gelles (1986) estimate that almost 16% of married couples in the United States experience some form of marital violence in a year's time—often "only" a shove or a slap, but violence nonetheless. Almost 6% of the couples they surveyed reported at least one instance of severe violence (kicking, punching, and the other behaviors that these same researchers defined as severe forms of child abuse). Indeed, dating partners appear to get a head start on marital violence, for alarmingly high percentages of high school students (Henton et al., 1983) and college students (Sigelman, Berry, & Wiles, 1984) experience violence in their dating relationships.

Margaret Hudson (1986) has noted that child abuse and neglect, while they have always existed, were "discovered" as social problems in the 1960s; that spouse abuse came to the public's attention in the 1970s; and that finally in the 1980s it became clear that elderly people are also the targets of family violence. Frail or impaired older people are physically or psychologically mistreated, neglected, financially exploited, and stripped of their rights—typically by adult children or other relatives serving as their major caregivers. No one really knows how many elderly people are abused, but the estimates range from about 1% to 10% (Hudson, 1986).

It is not a pretty picture. Here we have a social problem of major dimensions that causes untold suffering and inhibits the development of family members of all ages. What can be done to prevent it or to stop it once it occurs? To answer that applied question, we must first try to gain some insight into why family violence occurs in the first place.

Why Does Family Violence Occur?

Child abuse has been studied the longest, and there are similarities between the various forms of family violence. Therefore, let's see what has been learned about the causes of child abuse.

Anyone examining a badly beaten child might imme-

[2]When Straus and Gelles omitted from their definition hitting a child with an object (because it is something that many parents believe to be an appropriate way of disciplining children), the rate of what they considered to be severe child abuse dropped to a little less than 2%.

diately conclude that the abuser must be a psychologically disturbed individual who needs professional help. Strange as it may seem, only about 1 child abuser in 10 appears to have a severe mental illness (Kempe & Kempe, 1978). Instead, child abusers come from all races, ethnic groups, and social classes, and many of them appear to be rather typical, loving parents—except for their tendency to become extremely irritated with their children and to do things they will later regret.

Yet there are at least some differences between parents who abuse their children and parents who do not. An unusually high proportion of child abusers were abused, neglected, or unloved themselves (Belsky, 1980; Egeland, Jacobvitz, & Sroufe, 1988; Steele & Pollack, 1974). However, the cycle of abuse can be broken if these individuals receive emotional support from parent substitutes, therapists, or spouses and are spared from severe stress as adults (Egeland, Jacobvitz, & Sroufe, 1988). Moreover, abusive and nonabusive mothers differ in their reactions to young children. For example, Byron Egeland (1979; Egeland, Sroufe, & Erickson, 1983) found that when infants cry to communicate needs such as hunger, nonabusive mothers treated these cries as signs of discomfort (correct interpretation), whereas abusive mothers often inferred that the baby was somehow criticizing or rejecting them. Indeed, abusive parents seem to find even an infant's smile unpleasantly arousing (Frodi & Lamb, 1980). In short, abusive parents seem to find caregiving more stressful and ego-threatening and less enjoyable than other parents do (Trickett & Susman, 1988). Still, it has been difficult to identify a particular kind of person who is highly likely to turn into a child abuser.

Could some children bring out the worst in their parents? An abusive parent often singles out only one child in the family as a target; this offers us a hint that child characteristics might matter (Gil, 1970). No one is suggesting that children are to *blame* for being abused, but some children do appear to be more at risk than others. For example, infants who are emotionally unresponsive, hyperactive, irritable, or ill are far more likely to be abused than quiet, healthy, and responsive infants who are easy to care for (Egeland & Sroufe, 1981; Sherrod, O'Connor, Vietze, & Altemeier, 1984). Similarly, defiant children may elicit stronger and stronger forms of physical punishment from their caregivers—until the line between spanking and abuse is crossed (Parke & Lewis, 1981). Yet many difficult children are not mistreated, while other seemingly easy children are. Just as characteristics of the caregiver cannot fully explain why abuse occurs, neither can characteristics of children, though it is quite likely that the *combination* of a high-risk parent and a high-risk child spells trouble (Bugental, Blue, & Cruzcosa, 1989).

But even the match between child and caregiver may not be enough to explain abuse. We should, as always, consider the social context surrounding the family system. Quite consistently, abuse is most likely to occur in families under stress. If, for example, a relatively young, poorly educated mother is overburdened with responsibilities and receives little assistance from the father or any other sources of social support, she stands an increased risk of becoming abusive (Egeland et al., 1983). Moreover, some neighborhoods have higher rates of abuse than other neighborhoods with the same demographic and socioeconomic characteristics. These high-risk areas tend to be deteriorating neighborhoods where families are socially isolated and have little in the way of community services or informal social support (Garbarino & Sherman, 1980). Finally, ours is a culture in which many forms of violence are common and in which the use of physical punishment as a means of controlling children's behavior is widely accepted. Cross-cultural studies reveal that children are rarely abused in societies that discourage physical punishment (see Belsky, 1980).

As you can see, child abuse is a complex phenomenon with a multitude of causes and contributing factors (Figure 14.4). The very same is true of spouse abuse, elder abuse, and other forms of family violence. What does this say about the prospects for preventing or stopping abuse?

How Do We Solve the Problem?

The very fact that family violence has so many causes is a bit discouraging. Where do we begin to intervene, and just how many problems must we correct before we can prevent or stop the violence? Yet despite the complexity of the problem, progress has been made.

Consider first the task of preventing violence before it starts. This requires identifying high-risk families—a task that is greatly aided by the kinds of studies we have reviewed. For example, once we know that an infant is at risk for abuse because he or she is particularly irritable or unre-

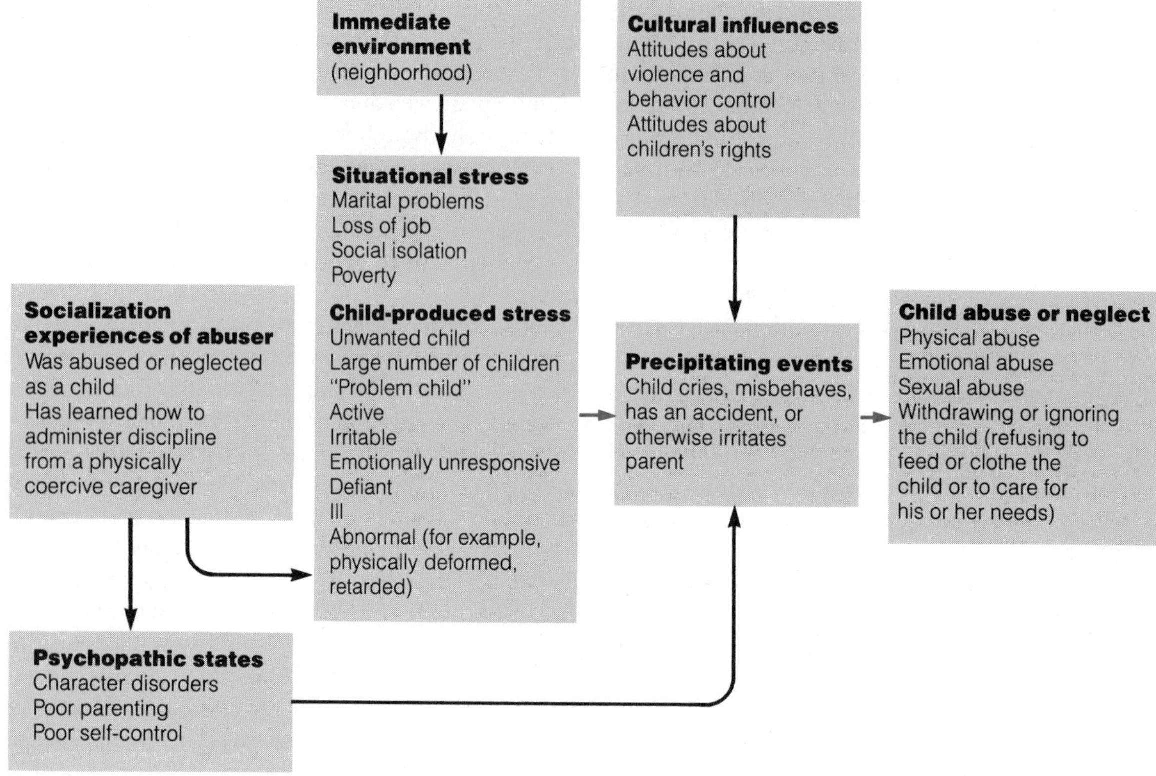

Figure 14.4 A social–ecological model of child abuse. (Adapted from Gelles, 1973)

sponsive, it makes sense to help the child's parents appreciate the infant's positive qualities and learn to bring them out. Indeed, learning how to elicit smiles, reflexes, and other positive responses from preterm infants makes parents more responsive in their interactions with their babies and, in turn, helps their babies develop more normally (Widmayer & Field, 1980).

Other efforts to prevent abuse have been directed at high-risk parents. Steven Schinke and his associates (1986), for example, decided to teach better techniques for managing problems and coping with stress to one high-risk group of mothers—teenagers who were single parents under a great deal of stress. They tried to teach a wide range of stress-management skills: problem-solving strategies, self-praise for handling difficult situations, communication skills such as refusing unreasonable demands and requesting help, relaxation techniques, and even techniques for building a stronger social support network. Three months later, the mothers who received the training outperformed the control group on several measures. They had improved their problem-solving skills, had established stronger social support networks, enjoyed higher self-esteem, and were more confident about their parenting skills. It seems likely that high-risk parents who have learned effective techniques for coping with stress will be better able to deal with the sometimes overwhelming challenges they face without resorting to violence. Such parents can also benefit from efforts to teach them effective child management skills (Wolfe, Edwards, Manion, & Koverola, 1988).

What about the parents who are already abusive? Here, the problem is more thorny, largely because our social institutions are very reluctant to intervene in the family unless a child is repeatedly and severely abused. What does seem clear is that a few visits from a social worker are unlikely to solve the problem (Oates, 1986). More promising is Parents Anonymous, a self-help approach based on

Alcoholics Anonymous that is available to help caregivers understand their problems and to give them the emotional support they often lack.[3] Ultimately, however, a comprehensive approach is likely to be most effective. Abusive parents need emotional support and the opportunity to learn more effective parenting and coping skills, and the victims of abuse need help in overcoming the cognitive, social, and behavioral problems associated with abuse (Oates, 1986). In short, the ultimate goal in attempting to decrease child abuse and other forms of family violence must be to convert a pathological family system into a healthy one.

REFLECTIONS

If you do not yet fully appreciate the awesome significance of the family for human development across the life span, think for a moment about how very badly things can go when the family does not fulfill its many important functions. Start with the infant who is neglected and who does not experience anything faintly resembling warm, sensitive, and responsive parenting. How is this infant to form the secure attachments that serve as foundations for later competence? Think about the child or adolescent whose parents are downright hostile—who either provide no guidance at all or bury the child in rules and severely punish every misstep. How is this child to learn how to care about other people, fit into society, or function as an autonomous adult?

And why stop there? Adults are also developing individuals, and they too are greatly affected by their family experiences. Picture the young adult who desperately wants an intimate relationship but cannot seem to find one—or the adult who marries full of high hopes only to become the target of unrelenting criticism, anger, and even physical violence. Then there are the trials and tribulations of child rearing. How does a parent develop as an individual when *nothing* seems to quiet a distressed baby, stop a preschooler's violent outbursts, keep an adolescent off cocaine, or get a 30-year-old "child" away from the television set and out into the world? How does an elderly parent thrive when an adult child is hateful and abusive?

You get the picture. Fortunately, most of us fare much better than this, and our development is constantly nourished rather than poisoned by our family relationships. Moreover, most of us seem to appreciate just how important our families are. Children *know* that their parents are their primary sources of affection and aid (Furman & Buhrmester, 1985a), and adults who are asked to describe what is most important in their lives almost universally speak of their families (Whitbourne, 1986). While we change, and our families change, as we get older, it seems that we never cease to be affected by, or to affect, those people we call "family." ❦

SUMMARY POINTS

1. The family, whether it is nuclear or extended in form, is best viewed as a changing social system embedded in larger social systems that are also changing. Social trends affecting family life today include greater numbers of single adults; the postponement of marriage; a decline in childbearing; more female participation in the labor force; more divorces, single-parent families, and remarriages; and more years with an empty nest.
2. Infants affect and are affected by their parents, and developmental outcomes are likely to be positive when *both* parents are involved with their children and also have positive *indirect* effects on their children by virtue of their influence on each other.
3. Child rearing can be described in terms of the dimensions of warmth/hostility and permissiveness/restrictiveness; generally, children are most socially and cognitively competent when their parents adopt an authoritative style of parenting, though children also exert reciprocal influence on their parents.
4. When a second child enters the family system, mothers typically become less attentive to their first-borns, first-borns find the experience stressful, and sibling rivalry—accompanied by much affection—characterizes sibling relationships.
5. The "generation gap" is much smaller than has often been assumed, and adolescents are most likely to gain autonomy when parents grant their teenagers freedom but continue to be loving and supportive guides.
6. Marital satisfaction declines somewhat as newlyweds adjust to each other, declines still further as couples face the stresses of new parenthood and child rearing, then often increases again after the empty nest transition. Most adults seem to view the empty nest phase more positively than negatively and to take pleasure from becoming grandparents, most often playing a companionate role rather than a remote or involved role.

[3]Chapters of Parents Anonymous are now located in many cities and towns in the United States. (For locations, one can consult a telephone directory or write to Parents Anonymous, 6733 South Sepulveda Blvd., Suite 270, Los Angeles, CA 90045.) Not only is there no charge for participation in these self-help groups, but many cities and counties provide free family therapy to abusive parents.

7. Although marital satisfaction declines during the parenting years, especially among women, it depends on many additional factors.

8. In adulthood, siblings have less contact but normally continue to feel emotionally close. Young adults sometimes establish more mutual and intimate relationships with their parents, and middle-aged adults continue to experience mutually supportive relationships with their elderly parents, though some experience the stresses of "middle generation squeeze."

9. Among the adults whose lives are inadequately described by the family life cycle are heterosexual and homosexual single adults, some of whom cohabitate, and childless married couples, who do not seem to suffer from a lack of children unless they find themselves widowed and lacking in social support.

10. Divorce significantly disrupts family life for a year or two; some children (especially boys) experience long-lasting social and academic problems, though many factors influence adjustment. Most single-parent families adapt well to becoming part of a reconstituted family.

11. Family violence, which occurs in all possible relationships within the family, includes child abuse; parent characteristics, child characteristics, and social-contextual factors all contribute to the problem and must be considered in formulating solutions.

KEY TERMS

authoritarian parenting
authoritative parenting
autonomy
cohabitation
empty nest
extended family
family life cycle
generation gap
indirect effects
"middle generation squeeze"
modified extended family
nuclear family
permissive parenting
permissiveness/restrictiveness dimension
reconstituted family
sibling rivalry
warmth/hostility dimension

CHAPTER

15

LIFESTYLES: PLAY, SCHOOL, AND WORK

Just for the fun of it, draw a large circle or "pie" to represent all the waking hours available to you in a typical week. Now carve up the pie to show how you allocate your time among different activities. What portion of your time is spent attending classes or studying? Working? Engaging in hobbies, sports, and other recreational activities? Socializing? Performing chores and personal-care tasks? Watching television? Are you satisfied with how you spend your time, or would you be better off in the long run if you rebudgeted your time?

All of us, in each phase of the life span, have characteristic lifestyles—ways in which we divide our time among activities such as work, play or leisure, and schooling. The lifestyle of an infant is quite clearly different from that of a middle-aged adult! Moreover, within any age group, there are individual differences in lifestyles, differences that have the potential to shape later development. The central question addressed in this chapter is: What do we do with our time in different phases of the life span, and how do our activities affect our development?

PLAY AND WORK

What is the difference between play and work? If you ask people on the street, you might hear that play is the "fun stuff" that children do, whereas work is the "serious business" of making a living as an adult. Play is "useless," work is "useful." Play is for children, work is for adults. These commonsense definitions contain an element of truth. However, developmentalists define **play** as activity that is enjoyable and absorbing, is intrinsically motivated (done for the sheer enjoyment of doing it rather than to achieve some practical goal), and has an unrealistic or "pretendlike" quality (see Rubin, Fein, & Vandenberg, 1983). By contrast, **work** is goal-directed activity that is aimed toward producing something of use or contributing to subsistence (Neff, 1985). These definitions apply to any age.

We recognize that young children are clearly playing when they line up the dining room chairs to create a "boat" and exuberantly make motorboat sounds as they scout for whales. They are caught up in the pleasure of their activity, they have no intention of producing anything of use, and they are quite aware that they are pretending and need not fear drowning in their imaginary ocean. But perhaps because play is commonly viewed as childish and frivolous, we tend to describe adults as engaging in "leisure activity" rather than play. **Leisure** is time that is one's own, free of obligations—time that potentially provides the opportunity for true play (Bammel & Burris-Bammel, 1982). Adults may seldom create the elaborate fantasy worlds that young children do, but they certainly can lose themselves in intrinsically motivating activities, whether they are envisioning themselves as superstars on the tennis court or playing around with offbeat ideas as they lie by the swimming pool. If play is basically a state of mind, adults, like children, are capable of playing.

The clearest example of work in our society is paid employment. Yet our definition of work also includes the homemaker's productive activity in the home, for the homemaker, although unpaid, is contributing to the family's subsistence and welfare. It also seems entirely reasonable to say that children are working as they pursue their education. Indeed, witness the terms we use: school*work*, home*work*, *work*books. The ultimate goal of education is to provide children with the skills they need *in order to* become productive members of society. Schoolwork, then, is not done just for the sake of doing it; rather, it is often instrumental to the achievement of practical goals.

It is not always this easy to distinguish between work and play. For example, a golfer may be working rather than playing if she is actually out on the golf course to make business contacts rather than to have fun. By the same token, the man sitting at his computer terminal may appear to be working but may instead be playfully experimenting with a graphics program with no particular goal in mind. As they say, "One man's work is another man's [or woman's or child's] play." The meanings of work and play are elusive because we must ask not only what people are doing but why they are doing it and how they feel about it.

The balance of work and play in our lives changes over the life span. It is difficult to think of infants as working, but they do acquire the capacity for play. Children obviously spend a good deal of time playing, but as they get older, they are increasingly drawn into the world of work through their activities at school and chores at home. Indeed, in many of the world's cultures, as in earlier times in the United States, children begin to make significant contributions to the family's subsistence at about the age of 6 or 7, when they are given responsibilities for tending younger children, gathering food, and watching herds of cattle (Weisner, 1984). During adolescence, youth in our society are asked to take their schooling seriously and to prepare for a career, and they often work part time while they attend school. Among adults, especially middle-aged adults, a common complaint is that there is simply not enough time for having fun because work and family responsibilities consume so much time (McGuire, Dottavio, & O'Leary, 1986). We detect what might be viewed as a depressing developmental trend here, then: Less play and more work as we get older! Yet the emptying of the nest and retirement offer older adults more leisure time than they had earlier in adulthood—and perhaps new opportunities to play.

Children in some cultures participate in work at an early age.

So our activities do change over the life span. More important, our activities *change us*. As we will see, children gain competencies by playing and by attending school, and adults fare well or poorly depending on how they work and play.

THE INFANT

It may sound odd to speak of an infant's lifestyle, but infants certainly do have characteristic patterns of daily activity. Infants log a large number of hours of sleep, but they also spend a good deal of very constructive time exploring the world around them, playing with people and things, and acquiring new competencies in the process. Some infants pursue these activities at home, while others today do so in alternative care settings.

Play

Jean Piaget (1962) was fascinated by the infant's play because he believed it provided a glimpse of the child's emerging cognitive abilities in action. He viewed play as an opportunity for children to practice whatever cognitive competencies they possessed and to strengthen them in the process. We now have a fairly clear picture of how the play of infants changes as they progress through the stages of Piaget's sensorimotor period.

At first, infants play with their own bodies, for example, by kicking their legs or sucking their fingers. At about 4 to 8 months, they take a greater interest in toys and will repeatedly suck, bang, or shake rattles and toy animals. During these early months, they derive great pleasure from using the behavioral schemes that they have acquired to explore everything in reach. When infants reach their first birthdays, new cognitive capacities allow them to experiment with playthings, performing novel actions rather than merely repeating the same action over and over. They also begin to learn about the functions of objects and use them more appropriately, as when an infant turns the dial on a toy phone rather than just patting or banging it (Belsky & Most, 1981). So infants acquire ever more sophisticated ways of interacting with playthings. They also become increasingly sophisticated partners in social games such as pat-a-cake and peek-a-boo (Ross & Lollis, 1987).

Perhaps the most exciting breakthrough in the infant's play is the emergence of **symbolic play**—pretend play in which one actor, object, or action represents another. Piaget emphasized that the infant's thought changes immensely when he or she acquires the capacity to make one thing stand for or represent another. This **symbolic capacity** is involved in pretend play (where, for example, a clump of mud might symbolize a pie), in language use (where words symbolize or stand for things and events), in delayed imitation (where a mental image symbolizes the behavior that will be imitated), and in problem solving (where solutions can be conjured mentally).

When does symbolic or pretend play first emerge? At about 9 or 10 months of age, infants may put an empty cup to their lips, showing some recognition of the cup's function (McCune-Nicolich & Fenson, 1984). As early as 1 year of age, the same act is likely to become more clearly symbolic of real drinking. Now the infant may smile, give mother or father a knowing glance, or make loud lip-smacking sounds (Nicolich, 1977). In other words, the 1-year-old is not merely recognizing that cups are for drinking but is quite aware that these drinking actions stand for or symbolize real drinking. The earliest forms of symbolic play are actions just like this: The infant pretends to engage in familiar activities such as eating, sleeping, or washing, using appropriate props.

These are fairly simple forms of pretense, however; symbolic play becomes considerably more sophisticated between the ages of 1 and 2. Three major developmental trends have been identified (Corrigan, 1987; McCune-Nicolich & Fenson, 1984): decentration, decontextualization, and integration. *Decentration* refers to the increased tendency of infants and young children to adopt roles other than that of the self in their pretend play. Thus the infant who has at first pretended to drink from a cup might later pretend to be a mother giving a doll a drink or put the cup in the doll's hands and make the doll play the role of drinker. Gradually, then, symbolic play involves more than merely playing oneself doing the things one normally does. It increasingly involves getting outside the self and symbolizing the actions of others.

Decontextualization means that play actions become more independent of a concrete context of real objects. Infants progress from using realistic materials in familiar ways to using increasingly unusual substitutes for the real thing. So, for example, an infant may first pretend to drink from a cup and later pretend to drink from a block. In other words, pretend drinking can occur even when a real cup is not available, and an object like a block can be used to stand for something quite different from itself.

Finally, the increased *integration* in play activities seen during the second year of life is a shift from pretending to engage in single acts to pretending to perform multiple acts in meaningful sequences. So, for example, a young infant may give a doll a drink, whereas an older infant may say to the doll, "Drink milk," repeatedly raise the cup to the doll's mouth, burp the doll, and wipe its mouth! Interestingly, this ability to combine actions in meaningful ways during pretend play emerges at the same time that 18- to 24-month-olds are becoming capable of combining words into short sentences and imitating two or three actions in a series (Brownell, 1988; Shore, 1986; Shore, O'Connell, & Bates, 1984). Thus all of these breakthroughs may be associated with a more general advance in cognitive abilities.

In sum, symbolic play develops very rapidly indeed in the second year of life. Infants begin to play the roles of agents other than the self (decentration), they become less dependent on realistic props and more able to use objects to stand for things very different from what they are (decontextualization), and they become able to combine actions to create coherent "plots" (integration). Parents can foster this development by providing infants with a secure base of affection and by playing along with their little dramas (O'Connell & Bretherton, 1984; Slade, 1987). As they leave the sensorimotor period at age 2, infants have acquired the symbolic capacity they will need to let their imaginations run wild and free during the preschool years.

Alternative Care Settings and Infant Development

In recent years an important question has arisen about the ways in which infants in our society spend their time: Should infants be cared for at home by a parent, or can they pursue their developmental agendas just as well in a day-care setting? Although "infant schools" were quite popular in the early 19th century, once women were no longer needed in the labor force the belief arose that infants must spend their time with a single caregiver—namely, a mother—in order to develop normally (Pence, 1986). Now that over half of the mothers in the United States work outside the home at least part time, more and more infants and young children are receiving alternative forms of care. Where are these infants? According to one national survey, 34% are in their own homes, usually with a relative or sometimes with a sitter; 20% are in the homes of relatives; 23% are in day-care homes (typically run by a woman who takes a few children into her own home for payment); and only about 5% are in large day-care centers (Klein, 1985).

Do infants who attend day-care homes or centers suffer in any way compared to infants who stay at home with a parent? Much research to date suggests that they do not (Clarke-Stewart & Fein, 1983; Etaugh, 1980; Scarr, 1984). Jerome Kagan and his associates (Kagan, Kearsley, & Zelazo, 1978), for example, found that infants who attended a high quality, university-affiliated day-care center were no less securely attached to their mothers than infants who were raised at home. Moreover, day-care infants were generally indistinguishable from home-reared infants on measures of cognitive, linguistic, and social development. Apparently, then, day care is not *necessarily* damaging to children.

However, this broad generalization does not tell the full story. First, the *quality* of a particular day-care setting clearly matters. Just as some parents are highly nurturant while others are neglecting or abusive, some day-care experiences are beneficial and others are dreadful. It is not difficult to see that an infant will suffer in many ways if he or she ends up with a babysitter who snoozes all day in front of the TV set or must fight for adult attention as one of many infants in a large center with high staff turnover. As Sandra Scarr (1984) puts it, the important thing is that infants receive good care: "The who and the where are much less important than the what" (p. 33). Much of the research concerning day care and home care has investigated high-quality centers—centers in which well-trained caregivers have very few infants to tend and spend a good deal of time in one-to-one interaction with them, much as a mother might. It is this one-to-one interaction with familiar and competent adults that infants seem to need, *wherever they are* (Belsky, 1984; Phillips, McCartney, & Scarr, 1987; Scarr, 1984).

Also, some infants fare better in alternative care than others do. Infants from disadvantaged homes who are at risk of delayed development actually experience *faster* intellectual growth if they attend a high quality day-care program especially designed to meet their needs than if they stay at home (Ramey, Bryant, & Snarez, 1985). It also seems that infants who have already formed attachments to their parents may adjust better than young infants who are just forming their first attachments. Infants who spend many hours with babysitters or family day-care providers before they reach the age of 1 are more likely to be insecurely attached to their mothers and fathers than are infants who are tended primarily by their mothers (Barglow, Vaughn, & Molitor, 1987; Belsky & Rovine, 1988; Vaughn, Gove, & Egeland, 1980). This negative effect of alternative care on young infants is especially likely to be observed in boys, particularly those with difficult temperaments (Belsky & Rovine, 1988).

Finally, the effects of alternative care depend greatly on parents' attitudes and behaviors. Outcomes are likely to be better if a mother has positive attitudes about working and about being a mother and if she has the personal qualities it takes to provide warm and sensitive care (Belsky & Rovine, 1988; Benn, 1986). It also helps if her partner is supportive of her working (Spitze, 1988). Ultimately, the quality of parenting that infants receive at home may have more to do with their development than the kind of alternative care they receive when they are not at home (Lamb et al., 1988).

In sum, we cannot draw pat conclusions about the effects of alternative care on infant development, for these effects range from the beneficial to the damaging. It does seem, however, that alternative care is least likely to disrupt development if infants are old enough to have already formed attachments to their parents and if they interact with *both* responsive substitute caregivers and responsive parents.

Meanwhile, parents who work struggle to find and keep competent sitters or high quality day-care placements. The U.S. government has been less willing than the governments of many European countries to finance day care. Sandra Scarr (1984) finds this puzzling, since our government is quite willing to invest in children once they are old enough to attend public school. Increasingly, employers are realizing that it is in their best interest to help workers obtain quality day care, and a few have even established day-care centers at the work site (Burud, Aschbacher, & McCroskey, 1984). Until more options are available, however, working parents will continue to face the challenges of finding the very best alternative care they can afford.[1]

THE CHILD

When infancy is behind them, what do children do with their time? In our society, they play, attend school, and watch a good deal of television. They also perform chores around the house and form at least some notions of what they will be when they grow up. All of these activities affect their later development.

Play

So important is play in the life of the child from age 2 to age 5 that these years are sometimes called "the play years." This is when children hop about the room shrieking with delight; don capes and go off on dragon hunts; and whip up cakes and cookies made of clay, sand, or thin air. We can detect two major changes in play between infancy and the age of 5: It becomes more social, and it becomes more imaginative. After age 5 or so, the exuberant and fanciful play of the preschool years gives way to somewhat more serious play in the elementary school years.

Play Becomes More Social

Many years ago, Mildred Parten (1932) devised a useful method for classifying the types of play engaged in by nursery school children. Her six categories of activity, arranged from least to most social, are as follows:

1. *Unoccupied play.* Children stand idly, look around, or engage in apparently aimless activities such as pacing.
2. *Solitary play.* Children play alone, typically with objects, and appear to be highly involved in what they are doing.
3. *Onlooker play.* Children watch others play, taking an active interest and perhaps even talking to the players, but not directly participating.
4. *Parallel play.* Children play next to one another, doing much the same thing, but they interact very little (for example, two girls might sit near each other, both drawing pictures, without talking to each other to any extent).
5. *Associative play.* Children interact by swapping materials, conversing, or following each other's lead, but they are not really united by the same goal (for example, our two girls may swap crayons and comment on each other's drawings as they draw).
6. *Cooperative play.* Children truly join forces to achieve a common goal; they act as a pair or group, dividing their labor and coordinating their activities in a meaningful way (for example, our two girls collaborate to draw a mural for their teacher).

The major message of Parten's study and others like it is that play becomes increasingly social from age 2 to age 5 (Barnes, 1971; Parten, 1932; Smith, 1978). Unoccupied and onlooker activities are quite rare at all ages, solitary and parallel play become less frequent with age, and associative and cooperative play (the most social of the types of play) become more frequent with age (see Figure 15.1). However, even though play becomes more social during the preschool years, solitary play still has its place. Indeed, older preschoolers who frequently engage in certain forms of solitary play (for example, making things) tend to be very socially competent (Rubin, 1982).

Play Becomes More Imaginative

Symbolic or pretend play truly blossoms during the preschool years, increasing dramatically in frequency and sophistication (Rubin, Fein, & Vandenberg, 1983). Such play continues to become more decentered (children can play heroes and heroines very different from themselves), decontextualized (few props are needed), and integrated (elaborate dramas can be enacted). Moreover, like children's play in general, pretend play becomes more social (Howes, 1985; Rubin, Watson, & Jambor, 1978). Children less often enact scenes on their own using dolls and other

[1]Parents who want practical guidelines for deciding which day-care settings are of high quality might consult Bradbard and Endsley (1979) or Scarr (1984).

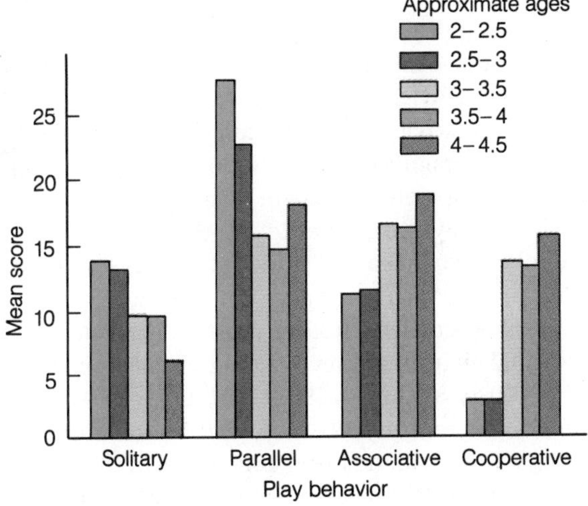

Figure 15.1 Frequency of activities engaged in by preschool children of different ages. With age, solitary and parallel play occur less frequently, while associative and cooperative play occur more frequently. (Adapted from Barnes, 1971)

toys and more often cooperate with playmates to enact their dramas.

Interestingly, many preschoolers, especially those who do not have much access to other children who can join them in pretend play, use their symbolic capacity to invent playmates—**imaginary companions** (Manosevitz, Prentice, & Wilson, 1973; Pines, 1978). Donna, age 4, actually invented *five* imaginary husbands who joined her in meals, conversations on her toy telephone, and school bus rides, during which they enjoyed throwing salt at cars (Pines, 1978). Although these pretend companions are often very vivid and real to their inventors, they are not a sign of emotional disturbance. Instead, they are just another sign of the imaginative powers of young children. Moreover, they serve the useful functions of reducing loneliness and providing comfort and security.

Play in the Elementary School Years

Children engage less frequently in symbolic play after they enter school (Fein, 1981). Instead, school-aged children spend more of their time playing organized games with rules—board games, games of tag and hide-and-seek, organized sports, and so on (Athey, 1984). They also develop individual hobbies such as building model cars or making scrapbooks that allow them to develop skills and gain knowledge.

According to Jean Piaget (1965), it is not until children enter the stage of concrete-operational thought at about age 6 or 7 that they become capable of abiding by the rules of games. They then view rules as sacred and unalterable, and they are quick to accuse one another of cheating if they detect the slightest infraction of the rules. Older children—11- and 12-year-olds who are entering the stage of formal-operational thought—gain a more flexible concept of rules, recognizing that rules are arbitrary agreements that can be changed so long as everybody concerned (or at least the majority) agrees to the changes.

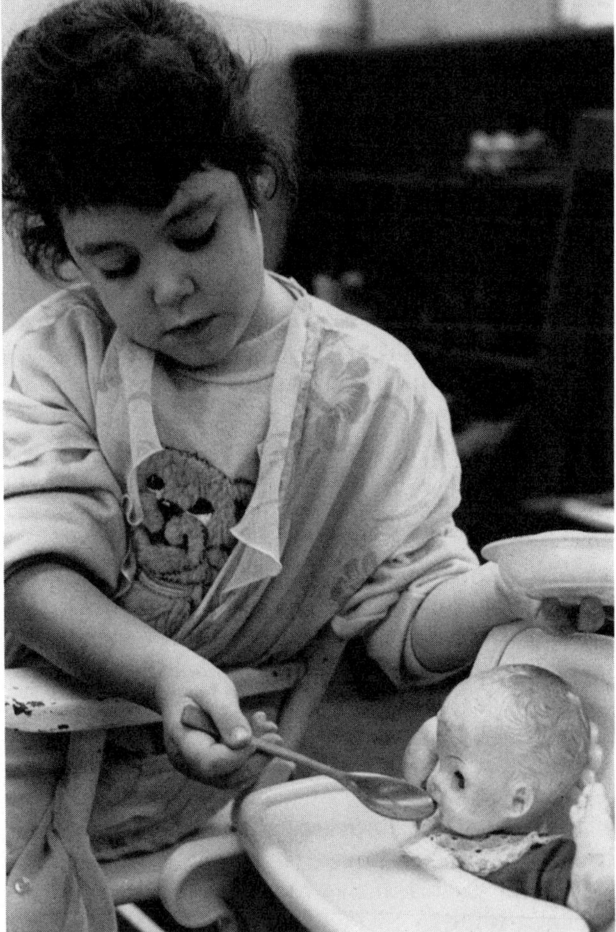

There seems to be no limit to the imaginative capacities of 4- and 5-year-olds.

Partly because of cognitive gains, then, the play of the school-aged child is more organized and rule governed—and less fanciful—than that of the preschool child.

WHAT GOOD IS PLAY?

We have said that play is activity done for its own sake. In this sense, it really does not need a larger purpose to be of interest to children—or to us. Yet in some historical periods and cultures—in 19th-century America, for example—play was often discouraged because it was viewed as a frivolous waste of time (Athey, 1984). Now we know better. Play contributes to virtually all areas of children's development. Indeed, the fact that playful activity occurs among the young of so many species strongly suggests that it prepares the young for adult life (Vandenberg, 1986).

Irene Athey (1984) has summarized some of the ways in which play activities contribute to physical, intellectual, social, and emotional development (Athey, 1984). The contributions of play to physical development are clear enough. Through play, infants can practice body movements, preschoolers get physical exercise and opportunities to improve their manipulation skills and coordination, and school-aged children involved in organized sports and games receive both exercise and skill training.

Intellectually, play provides a context for using language to communicate and for using the mind to imagine fantasy situations, plan strategies, and solve problems. As it turns out, preschool children who engage in a great deal of symbolic play perform in more mature ways on tests of Piagetian cognitive development than children who rarely pretend (Connolly, 1982). Moreover, they display greater creativity, coming up with novel ways to use objects such as clothespins, matchboxes, and paper clips (Christie & Johnsen, 1983; Dansky, 1980). Apparently children who use their minds playfully learn to use their minds more logically and creatively.

The contributions of play to social development are also important. To carry off a coherent episode of social pretend play, children must adopt different roles, act in character, mesh their own behavior with that of their playmates, and resolve conflicts (Giffin, 1984). It just won't work if one child is saying "We're going to catch the robber now" while another is saying "I'm sick, so go get the doctor." Children may also be learning about and preparing for adult roles when they "play house" and step into the shoes of their mothers and fathers. Perhaps due to the social experience they gain, preschool children who engage in a great deal of social pretend play tend to be more popular and socially mature than children who do not (Connolly & Doyle, 1984; Rubin et al., 1983). Similarly, playing organized games with rules fosters social development by encouraging children to adopt the perspectives of others and cooperate with them (Piaget, 1965).

Finally, play contributes to healthy emotional development, as psychoanalytic theorists such as Erik Erikson have emphasized. Through play, children can express feelings that bother them, resolve unresolved conflicts, and master challenges that they may not be able to master in real life (Curry & Arnaud, 1984; Fein, 1986). If Danny, for example, has recently been scolded by his mother for drawing on the wall, he may gain control of the situation by scolding his "child" for doing the same thing. Interestingly, children who are suffering from emotional disturbances not only reveal their concerns through their play but have difficulty playing in mature and creative ways. For example, Mavis Hetherington and her colleagues (Hetherington, Cox, & Cox, 1979) compared the play of preschool children who were experiencing their parents' divorce with that of children from intact families. The children from divorcing families had a restricted style of play: They acted out fewer different themes, had difficulty using props in multiple ways or getting by without realistic props, and adopted fewer roles. Moreover, the many aggressive themes in their play reflected their angers and anxieties about divorce.

Let it never be said, then, that play is useless. While children play because it is fun, not because it sharpens their skills, they indirectly contribute to their own development—physical, intellectual, social, and emotional—by doing so. In this sense, play truly is the child's work.

School

Starting at age 6, the typical child in the United States spends about five hours each weekday at school. Today, the vast majority of children begin their school careers earlier than that, at least by attending kindergarten as 5-year-olds. Let's ask three major questions about the role of schooling in child development:

1. Is it beneficial for preschool children to attend school?
2. What makes for an effective school?
3. How successfully are schools meeting the needs of

children who are culturally different or who have developmental disabilities?

Should Preschool-Aged Children Attend School?

In recent years, children in our society have begun their schooling earlier and earlier. Not only is kindergarten compulsory in most states, but there is talk of requiring school for 4-year-olds (Zigler, 1987). Already, many preschoolers spend full days in day-care settings or attend nursery schools or early education programs for part of the day (Clarke-Stewart, 1982). In either day-care centers or nursery schools, children have opportunities to play with a wide range of toys and equipment; to sing, hear stories, draw pictures; and to do other sorts of things that preschoolers enjoy doing. Some programs not only encourage play and social adjustment but have a strong academic emphasis and attempt to prepare children for school. Indeed, some wealthy parents will do almost anything to get their youngsters into the "right" preschools in the hope that early learning experiences will start them on their way to Harvard or Yale; in New York City, some parents even enroll their toddlers in courses that prepare them for admission interviews with exclusive nursery schools (Geist, 1985)!

Is attending preschool indeed beneficial? Most children who attend preschool programs are no more or less intellectually advanced than preschoolers who remain at home (Clarke-Stewart & Fein, 1983). But economically disadvantaged preschoolers who attend Head Start programs especially designed to prepare them for school experience *more* cognitive growth and achieve *more* success in school than similarly disadvantaged children who stay at home or attend other kinds of preschools (Burchinal, Lee, & Ramey, 1989; Lazar & Darlington, 1982; Lee, Brooks-Gunn, & Schnur, 1988; and see Chapter 9).

Moreover, children who attend preschool programs tend to be advanced in some aspects of their social development (Clarke-Stewart & Fein, 1983). Daily interactions with peers may allow them to develop social skills rather early. Because they are more socially mature, perhaps, these same children are also sometimes more aggressive with peers and less cooperative with adults than children who spend their time at home (Clarke-Stewart & Fein, 1983; Schenck & Grusec, 1987).

In sum, attending a preschool program can be at least as positive an experience as staying home for middle-class children and can be superior to staying at home for economically disadvantaged children. Even so, developmentalists such as Edward Zigler (1987) and David Elkind (1981), author of *The Hurried Child*, believe that the push for early education may be going too far. They fear that young children today are not given enough time simply to be children—to play and socialize as they choose. Elkind even worries that children may lose their self-initiative and enjoyment of learning when their lives are orchestrated by parents who pressure them to achieve at early ages. Whether it is possible for children to receive too much education too early remains to be seen.

What Makes for an Effective School?

Elementary and secondary schools can potentially contribute in a variety of ways to child development. Obviously, today's children acquire a good deal of basic knowledge and many academic skills at school: reading, writing, and arithmetic—and much more. They also acquire general strategies for learning new information and thinking about problems. Children in developing countries who are exposed to formal education pick up many cognitive skills at school (for example, effective memorization strategies) that similar children who do not attend school lack (Rogoff, 1981). Schools also expose children to an informal curriculum that teaches them how to fit into their culture. Children learn to obey rules, to cooperate with their classmates, to respect authority, and otherwise to behave as good citizens. Moreover, schools instill basic democratic and social values and provide moral guidance with respect to such social problems as racism, drug abuse, and sexual irresponsibility. Like families, then, schools serve as socialization agents, potentially affecting children's social and emotional development as well as providing them with knowledge and skills that will allow them to lead productive lives.

What makes some schools more effective at socialization than others? What might parents look for if they want their children to obtain the best education possible? In his review of research on education, Michael Rutter (1983) has defined *effective schools* as those that promote academic achievement, social skills, polite and attentive behavior, positive attitudes toward learning, low absenteeism, continuation of education beyond the age at which attendance is mandatory, and the acquisition of skills that will enable students to find and hold jobs. Rutter concludes that some schools are clearly more effective at accomplishing these objectives than others are, regardless of students' racial, ethnic, or socioeconomic backgrounds. Indeed, in Rutter's own study of 12 secondary schools, initially low-achieving students in "better" schools ended up scoring just as well on a final test of academic progress as initially high-achieving students in the least effective schools (Rutter, Maughan, Mortimore, Ouston, & Smith, 1979). Yet you may be surprised by some of the factors that do and do not have a bearing on how "effective" a school is.

FACTORS THAT HAVE LITTLE TO DO WITH A SCHOOL'S EFFECTIVENESS Surprising as it may seem, a school's *level of support* has little to do with the quality of education its students receive. The amount of money spent per pupil, the number of books in the school library, teachers' salaries, and teachers' academic credentials play only a minor role in determining student outcomes (Rutter, 1983). To be sure, some minimal level of support must exist for a school to be effective. Once this minimum is exceeded, however, it seems unlikely that merely adding extra dollars to a school's budget will substantially improve the quality of education (Rutter, 1983).

Another factor that has relatively little to do with a school's effectiveness is *average class size* (Rutter, 1983). Within a range of from 20 to 40 students per class, reducing class sizes from, say, 36 to 24 students is unlikely to increase student achievement. When smaller classes do prove to be beneficial, it is in the primary grades when children are just learning to read and do arithmetic problems (Educational Research Service, 1978) or when students are academically delayed.

Nor does it seem to matter whether or not a school uses **ability tracking**, in which students are grouped according to ability and then taught in classes or work groups with others of similar academic or intellectual standing. The pros and cons of ability tracking have been debated for years. On one side, we hear that teachers teach best and students learn best when students function at about the same level; on the other, we are told that tracking undermines the self-esteem of low-ability students and actually contributes to their poor performance. Rutter (1983) concluded that neither ability tracking nor mixed-ability grouping has decisive advantages. If any students benefit from ability tracking, it is likely to be the higher-ability students (Kulik & Kulik, 1982). When low-ability students are denied access to the most effective teachers and are stigmatized as "dummies," they sometimes suffer (Rutter, 1983).

These, then, are examples of school characteristics that do *not* seem to contribute a great deal to effective education. A school that has quite limited financial support (assuming it surpasses a basic minimum), places students in relatively large classes, and places students in mixed-ability learning groups or classes is often just as effective as another school that has ample financial resources, small classes, and ability tracking. So what *does* influence how well children perform?

FACTORS THAT MATTER To understand why some schools are more effective than others, we must consider characteristics of the student body, characteristics of the learning environment, and the interaction between student and environment. First, a school's effectiveness is a function of what it has to work with. On the average, academic achievement tends to be low in schools with a preponderance of economically disadvantaged students, and *any* child is likely to make more academic progress in a school with a high concentration of intellectually capable peers (Brookover, Beady, Flood, Schweitzer, & Wisenbaker, 1979; Rutter, 1983). However, this does *not* mean that schools are only as good as the students they serve. Many schools that draw heavily from disadvantaged minority populations are highly effective at motivating students and preparing them for jobs or further education (Rutter, 1983).

So what is it about the learning environment of some schools that allows them to be effective, even when many of their students are not very academically competent to begin with? Basically, the effective school environment is a comfortable but businesslike setting in which students are motivated to learn. More specifically, Rutter concludes that in effective schools teachers:

1. Strongly emphasize academics (they expect a lot of their students, regularly assign homework, and work hard to achieve their objectives in the classroom)
2. Manage classroom activities effectively to create a task oriented but comfortable atmosphere (for example, they waste little time on getting activities started or dealing with distracting discipline problems, provide clear instructions and feedback, and encourage and reward good work)

In a comfortable and task-oriented classroom, children are motivated to learn.

3. Manage discipline problems effectively (for example, they enforce the rules on the spot rather than sending offenders to the principal's office, and they avoid the use of physical punishment, which often only compounds discipline problems and creates a tense, negative atmosphere that is hardly conducive to learning)
4. Work with other faculty as a team—one that jointly decides on the curriculum and on approaches to discipline

One more point must be made: *Characteristics of students and the school environment often interact to affect student outcome.* Much educational research has been based on the assumption that *one* teaching method, organizational system, or philosophy of education will prove superior for all students. This assumption is often wrong. Instead, many educational practices are highly effective with *some* kinds of students but quite ineffective with other students. Consider an example: Jere Brophy (1979) concludes that teachers get the most out of high-ability students by moving at a quick pace and insisting on high standards of performance—that is, by challenging these students. By contrast, low-ability students do not respond well to this approach; they react much more favorably to slower-paced instruction from a teacher who is warm and encouraging rather than highly demanding or "pushy." Thus it may be the *fit* between student and classroom environment that matters most (Lerner & Lerner, 1983).

In sum, some students (for example, those from advantaged homes) do typically outperform others, and some learning environments (especially those in which teachers create a motivating, comfortable, and task-oriented setting) are generally more conducive to learning than others are. Still, what works best for one kind of student may not work as well with another kind of student. Here, then, we have another nice example of a recurring theme in this book: the importance of the *interaction* between individuals and their environments.

How Can Schools Meet the Needs of All Students?

Public schools in the United States are middle-class institutions staffed by middle-class instructors who preach middle-class values. What does this mean for the child who comes from a lower socioeconomic background and a minority subculture?

Schools are also geared to teach "normal" children the material that is considered to be manageable at each grade level. What, then, becomes of students with developmental disabilities who cannot learn at the same pace or in the same way as other students do?

Many lower-income and minority students do have difficulties in school, often earning poor marks and getting into trouble with school authorities. Why is this? In part, it is due to a poor fit between the student's home culture and the culture of the school. For one thing, many lower-income and minority group parents do not stress doing well in school to the extent that middle-class parents do and are less supportive of the school's mission. Children of lower-class parents who *are* interested and involved in their children's education do much better in school (Brookover et al., 1979; Hess & Holloway, 1984). In addition, educational materials that center on middle-class people leading middle-class lives may seem irrelevant to children from minority subcultures and may therefore fail to motivate them (Kagan & Zahn, 1975). Finally, teachers are likely to form negative impressions and low expectancies of children who deviate from their own middle-class standards (Minuchin & Shapiro, 1983).

The problem of teacher expectations is a significant one. As early as the first couple of weeks of kindergarten, and before teachers know much of anything about their students' competencies, many teachers are already placing children into ability groups for reading on the basis of cues to socioeconomic status: grooming, the quality of their clothing, and their mastery of standard English (Rist, 1970). Unfortunately, these ability labels tend to stick, so that once a child is placed in the "clowns" reading group rather than the "cardinals" reading group, he or she is likely to remain a "clown" and will be expected to perform like one.

In a classic study, Robert Rosenthal and Lenore Jacobson (1968) demonstrated that a teacher's expectancies about a student can influence that student's ultimate achievement. Through what they called the **Pygmalion effect**, or the teacher-expectancy effect, students actually perform better when they are expected to do well than when they are expected to do poorly: Teacher expectancies can become self-fulfilling prophecies.[2] To demonstrate this, Rosenthal and Jacobson gave each elementary school teacher in their study a list of five students who were supposed to be "rapid bloomers." In fact, the so-called rapid bloomers had been randomly selected from class rosters. Yet planting these high (though false) expectancies in the minds of teachers was sufficient to cause so-called rapid bloomers to show greater gains on measures of IQ and reading achievement than their unlabeled classmates.

By now, the Pygmalion effect has been demonstrated in many studies. How exactly does it work? It seems that teachers who expect great things of a student are warmer, expose the student to more material and more difficult material, interact with the student more often and give him or her many opportunities to respond, and accept more of the student's ideas (Harris & Rosenthal, 1986). Meanwhile, a Mexican-American or black student from a poverty area might be tagged by a teacher as a low-ability student, might then be treated in ways that do not facilitate learning, and might end up fulfilling the teacher's low expectancies as a result (see Sorensen & Hallinan, 1986). As early as first grade, children are aware of their teachers' expectations; with age, children increasingly expect of themselves the performance that their teachers expect of them (Weinstein, Marshall, Sharp, & Botkin, 1987).

For many American black students in the past, additional barriers to school success were created by school segregation. Black children in many states were forced to attend "black schools" that were clearly inferior to "white schools." In its landmark decision in the case of *Brown v. Board of Education* in 1954, the Supreme Court ruled that segregated schools were "inherently unequal" and declared that they must be desegregated. What have we learned since this ruling?

Walter Stephan (1978) concluded from his review of the research that the effects of school integration on children's racial attitudes, self-esteem, and school achievement have been disappointing. Black students' prejudice toward white students decreased in 50% of the studies reviewed, but white prejudice toward black students decreased in only 13% of the studies. It was not at all uncommon for students in integrated schools, especially white students, to be *more* negative toward the other racial group than students in segregated schools were. In addition, the self-esteem of black children in integrated schools was no higher than that of black children in segregated schools. The most encouraging news was that minority students tended to achieve more in integrated classrooms, especially if they began to attend them early in their academic careers (St. John, 1975). Moreover, these modest gains in the achievement of black students occurred without harming the performance of white children.

Similarly mixed results have come from studies of children who have developmental disabilities (mental retardation, physical disabilities, blindness, deafness, and so on) and who are integrated into regular classrooms through a practice called **mainstreaming**. Compared with similar students who attend segregated special education classes, these mainstreamed youngsters sometimes fare better academically and socially but sometimes do not (Gottlieb, 1978; Karnes & Lee, 1979; Madden & Slavin, 1983; Zigler & Muenchow, 1979). What we seem to be learning is that both racial integration and mainstreaming can have positive, negative, or nonexistent effects depending on the circumstances. Putting diverse students in the same schools and classrooms accomplishes little by itself. Instead, something special must be done to ensure that students do in fact interact in positive ways and also learn what they are supposed to be learning.

What techniques for facilitating integration *have* proved successful? Robert Slavin (1986) and his colleagues have had much success using **cooperative learning methods** in which students of different races or ability levels are

---

[2]According to Greek myth, the sculptor Pygmalion fell so in love with his statue of a beautiful woman that she came to life (with a little divine intervention from the goddess Aphrodite). The myth served as the basis for George Bernard Shaw's play *Pygmalion*, which in turn inspired the musical and movie *My Fair Lady*, in which Henry Higgins's high hopes for the lowly Eliza Doolittle became a reality.

assigned to work teams and are reinforced for performing well *as a team*. For example, each member of a math team is given problems to solve that are appropriate to his or her ability level. Yet members of a work team also monitor one another's progress and offer one another aid when needed. To encourage this cooperation, the teams that complete the most math units are rewarded—for example, with special certificates that designate them as "superteams." Here, then, is a formula for ensuring that children of different races and ability levels will interact in a context where the efforts of even the least capable team members are important to the group's success.

Slavin finds that elementary school students come to like math better and learn more about it when they participate in cooperative learning groups than when they receive traditional math instruction. Moreover, team members gain self-esteem from their successes, and minority group members and students with developmental disabilities are more fully accepted by their peers (see also Johnson, Johnson, & Maruyama, 1983). In short, racial integration and mainstreaming *can* succeed if educators deliberately design learning experiences that encourage students from different backgrounds to pool their individual efforts in order to achieve common goals.

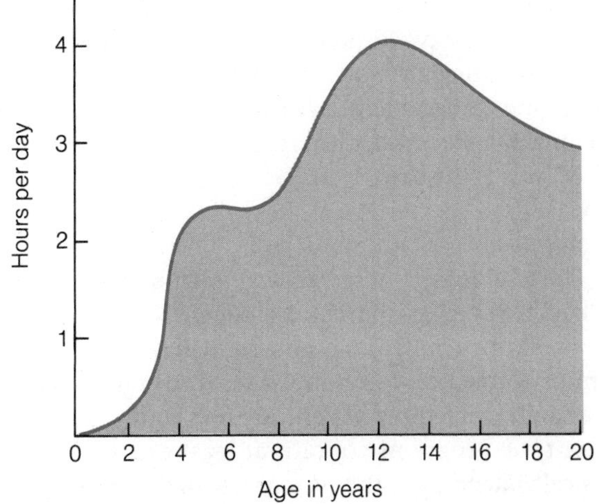

Figure 15.2 Average number of hours per day that children and adolescents in the United States spend watching television. (From Comstock, 1978)

The Changing Context of Child Development

The lifestyles of children are shaped not only by the schooling they receive but by the broader cultural context in which they live. Imagine being a child growing up in 18th-century America: You would have had heavy work responsibilities, no compulsory schooling, and no TV (much less MTV)! As we keep saying, human development takes place in an ever-changing social context. It makes sense to ask, then, how today's children may be affected by some of the major technological changes that have occurred in this century.

It is hard to believe that television did not even exist in the lives of children growing up before the late 1940s. Now virtually all homes have televisions, and children between the ages of 3 and 11 watch an average of three to four hours of TV a day. As we see in Figure 15.2, time spent in front of the TV gradually increases until about age 12 and then declines somewhat during adolescence. By age 18, a child born today will have spent more time watching television than in any other single activity except sleeping (Liebert & Sprafkin, 1988). Is all this time in front of the tube damaging to children's cognitive, social, and emotional growth?

Television and Children's Lifestyles

One way to answer that question is to find out whether the lifestyles of children who have access to television differ from those of children in remote areas who do not have television. One early survey found that after families purchased a set, parents and children spent less time together in leisure activities such as playing games and going on family outings (Johnson, 1967). Generally, however, children seem to substitute TV viewing for similar activities such as reading comics, going to movies, or listening to radio (Huston & Wright, 1982; Schramm, Lyle, & Parker, 1961). Apparently they do not spend any less time playing with peers, doing homework, or engaging in leisure reading (if we exclude comic books). Moreover, the introduction of television into an area does not seem to affect children's cognitive abilities one way or the other (Lonner, Thorndike, Forbes, & Ashworth, 1985). In moderate doses, at least, television does not seem to deaden young minds, although children who watch far more television than their peers do perform less well in school (Keith, Reimers, Fehrmann, Pottebaum, & Aubey, 1986).

In sum, the overall effects of exposure to television do not appear to be as negative as some critics have charged.

But isn't something missing if we focus only on whether or not children have *access* to television? Shouldn't we be asking what they are watching? Viewing a steady diet of murder and carnage may have quite different effects from watching *Sesame Street* and other educational programs. Indeed, this is the case.

Television as a Negative Force

The workings of observational learning (as discussed in Chapter 8) suggest that children might learn a variety of antisocial or socially unacceptable behaviors by seeing them performed on television. As it turns out, American television is incredibly violent: By one count, 80% of all prime-time programs contain at least one incident of physical violence, and the average rate of violent acts is 7.5 per hour (Gerbner, Gross, Morgan, & Signorelli, 1980). By one estimate, the average 16-year-old will have witnessed more than 13,000 killings on television (Waters & Malamud, 1975). Nor are Saturday-morning "children's" programs any better, for cartoon shows contain nearly 25 violent incidents per hour (Gerbner et al., 1980)!

Research has clearly established that watching violence on television can cause children to behave more aggressively. Actually, the relationship is circular: Watching violent TV increases children's aggressive tendencies, and aggressive children watch more and more violence on television, coming to prefer those sorts of programs, and in turn being further influenced by them (Eron, 1982). Moreover, televised violence desensitizes children to violence—that is, it makes them less emotionally upset by and more tolerant of violent acts in real life (Drabman & Thomas, 1974; Thomas, Horton, Lippincott, & Drabman, 1977).

Parents who are concerned about the amount of violence on TV can express their feelings to television stations and networks and can attempt to restrict their children's viewing of violent programs. They also have what may be a more realistic option: They can convert these viewing sessions into positive learning experiences. They can, for example, point out subtleties that young viewers often miss—for example, the aggressor's motives and intentions, and the unpleasant consequences that perpetrators suffer as a result of their aggressive acts (Collins, Sobol, & Westby, 1981). When adults highlight this information while expressing their disapproval of aggressive behavior—and, even better, when they point out more constructive approaches to solving problems than violence—children are less affected by the violence they view (Corder-Bolz & O'Bryant, 1977; Horton & Santogrossi, 1978).

Just as television may influence children to be more aggressive and more tolerant of aggression than they otherwise might be, it can have the unfortunate effect of reinforcing a variety of social stereotypes. For example, male characters on TV are often portrayed as more powerful, dominant, rational, and intelligent than women (Gerbner et al., 1980; Liebert & Sprafkin, 1988). Not surprisingly, children who watch a lot of commercial television are likely to hold more stereotyped views of masculinity and femininity than their classmates who watch little television (Frueh & McGhee, 1975). Television can teach children negative stereotypes of minority group members in much the same manner (Liebert & Sprafkin, 1988).

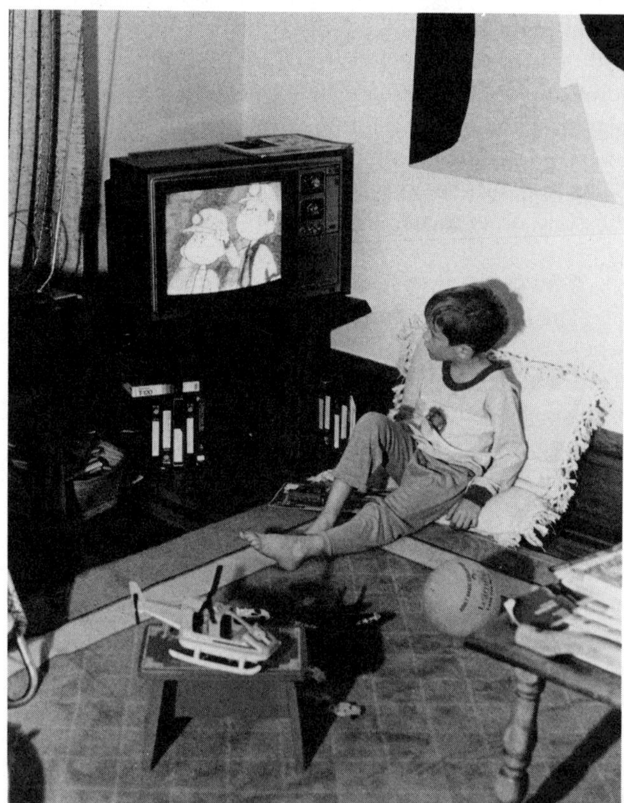

Watching aggressive acts, even when the perpetrators are cartoon characters rather than real people, can increase children's own aggressive tendencies.

Television as a Positive Force

Just as some kinds of television programs can foster unacceptable attitudes and behaviors in children, other kinds of programs can help parents and educators achieve their socialization goals. For example, if children watch **prosocial behavior** (positive social acts such as helping and cooperation) on television, they are likely to behave more prosocially themselves. In one study, 8- to 10-year-olds who had watched a *Waltons* episode that showed characters cooperating to solve a conflict later behaved more cooperatively while playing a game than age mates who had seen a noncooperative film or no film (Baran, Chase, & Courtright, 1979). Moreover, programs designed to counteract gender stereotypes or racial stereotypes by presenting women or minority group members in positive ways are effective at doing just that (Johnston, Ettema, & Davidson, 1980; Liebert & Sprafkin, 1988; Rossenwasser, Lingenfelter, & Harrington, 1989). In short, television can work to strengthen children's positive social tendencies and alter their social attitudes for the better.

Finally, television has the potential to contribute to children's cognitive development and school achievement. This is well illustrated by the success of *Sesame Street*, the immensely popular educational program created by the Children's Television Workshop. Typical episodes combine fast action and humor with a curriculum carefully designed to teach letters of the alphabet, numbers, counting, vocabulary, and many social and emotional lessons. In a major evaluation of *Sesame Street* in five areas of the United States during its first season, 3- and 5-year-old children were given a pretest to measure their cognitive skills and academic knowledge (Ball & Bogatz, 1970, cited in Liebert & Sprafkin, 1988; Bogatz & Ball, 1972). At the end of the season, they were given the same test again. The more frequently children watched *Sesame Street*, the better they performed on the overall test and the more often they knew such things as letters of the alphabet and how to write their names. Moreover, in a follow-up assessment of disadvantaged children who had taken part in the original study, heavy viewers of *Sesame Street* not only posted large cognitive gains, but they were rated by their teachers as better prepared for school and more interested in school activities than their classmates who rarely watched the program (Bogatz & Ball, 1972).

Is television a positive or a negative force in child development, then? It seems that the medium itself is not so influential as the message. This 20th-century invention has changed the ways in which recent generations of children spend their time, but television viewing, at least in moderate doses, does not seem to be keeping most children from other developmentally important activities. On the other hand, children are clearly affected by *what they watch* on television. Television has the capacity to teach children attitudes and behaviors that we would rather not have them learn, but at the same time it has the potential to join forces with parents and educators in helping children grow in positive directions.

Child Development in the Computer Age

Another technology that is beginning to affect the lifestyles of children in our society is the computer. Adults who grew up without computers—and are sometimes not sure what to make of them—are now buying them for their children, and schools are increasingly building computers into the educational process. Advertisements on television even hint that parents will ruin their children's chances of success if they do not rush out to buy a home computer! As Mark Lepper (1985) points out, the computer revolution is raising a host of interesting questions that demand answers: Do computers really help children learn? Do they increase interest in learning or distract young learners? How are they changing children's lifestyles?

Researchers have begun to ask whether students learn more when they receive **computer-assisted instruction**

The computer has begun to alter the experience of childhood.

than when they receive traditional instruction. Some computer-assisted instruction is simply drill (for example, of math problems), although computer-drill programs can diagnose learning problems, provide individually designed instruction, and give instantaneous feedback, much as a human tutor might. Other, more elaborate forms of computer-assisted instruction allow students to learn academic material by playing highly motivating and thought-provoking games. James Kulik and his associates (Kulik, Bangert, & Williams, 1983) concluded on the basis of several studies that computer-assisted instruction is indeed effective—more effective than traditional instruction—and that it is especially helpful at promoting learning among disadvantaged and low-ability students.

Douglas Clements (1986) has concluded that teaching students to program the computer provides even greater benefits. He taught first and third graders to use Logo, a computer language that allows them to make drawings on the screen once they learn the requisite problem-solving skills. Compared with children who participated in computer-assisted drills and children who received the usual classroom instruction, the "Logo" children performed no better or worse on academic achievement tests but made greater advances in Piagetian concrete operational abilities, metacognition (the ability to think about their own thinking), and even creativity. Demonstrations like this suggest that computers not only can drill children in academic material but can help them *think* in new ways. One of the computer's greatest strengths is that it fascinates children and increases their motivation to learn (Kee, 1986).

Are there any danger signs? Will children become computer "hackers" and social isolates who miss out on play with their peers? Daniel Kee (1986) has casually observed that children simply build the computer into their play with friends, as if it were any other toy, and classroom research suggests that children who are learning Logo engage in *more* collaborative conversations than children who work in a traditional manner (Hawkins, Sheingold, Gearhart, & Berger, 1982).

Will some children be left behind as the computer revolution unfolds? Children from economically disadvantaged homes may be exposed to computers in school but are unlikely to have computers at home. And at this point, boys are far more likely than girls to take an interest in computers and sign up for computer courses and camps, perhaps because computers are often viewed as involving mathematics, a traditionally "masculine" endeavor (Lepper, 1985). Also, many of the currently available game programs—space war games, for example—appeal to boys more than girls.

Although much more needs to be learned about the pros and cons of raising and educating children in a computer world, a good bet is that computers, like television sets, can be either a positive influence or a negative one depending on how they are used. If children hole up in their bedrooms playing aggressive search-and-destroy games, perhaps the effects will be bad, but if children use computers as tools to help them play with each other and learn in more creative and effective ways, the news may be quite positive.

Work: What Do You Want to Be When You Grow Up?

We usually think of choosing a vocation as a developmental task of adolescence. We ask young children what they want to be when they grow up but rarely take their answers seriously. In fact, children's vocational choices are based more on fantasy than on a realistic assessment of their own capabilities and the job opportunities available to them (Ginzberg, 1984). And yet, children *are* learning about the world of work and are beginning to figure out which kinds of jobs are and are not desirable to them. Career development is truly a lifelong process that begins in childhood (Grotevant & Cooper, 1988; Vondracek, Lerner, & Schulenberg, 1986).

For example, Table 15.1 lists answers Jo Ann Nelson (1978) obtained when she asked middle-class nursery school children and third graders what they would like to be when they grow up. Do you detect any developmental trends in these choices? In describing how children progressively narrow their vocational choices, Linda Gottfredson (1981) proposes that the first thing children realize is that they are headed for lives as adults. They learn that it will not do to aspire toward being a bunny rabbit, Cookie Monster, or ape! Instead, preschool children increasingly begin to identify with their parents and other adults who are competent and powerful and to want to be like them.

A second step in narrowing the field of choices is to favor occupations that are considered gender appropriate and to reject those that are supposedly for the other sex. Table 15.1 shows that boys establish a strong preference for masculine-stereotyped occupations very early, and that girls increasingly choose feminine-stereotyped occupations (notably nursing and teaching) as they get older. By the time they enter school, children express interest in occupations that seem to fit their emerging self-concepts as either males or females (Gottfredson, 1981; Henderson, Hesketh, & Tuffin, 1988). Finally, children narrow their vocational choices still further in late elementary school, when they begin to understand that some jobs are valued more highly by society than others are (Gottfredson, 1981). Young children tend to view a wide range of jobs as appealing; being a hamburger chef or a janitor may seem as fascinating as being a doctor or a lawyer. Older children begin to focus in on jobs that have high prestige in their society and socioeconomic group and that would allow them to feel good about themselves.

In short, long before adolescence, children are beginning to narrow the field of potential choices to jobs that could potentially express their emerging self-concepts—jobs that reflect an understanding that they will become adults, jobs that are compatible with their identities as males or females, and jobs that would allow them to gain approval or prestige. As adolescents, they will then face the difficult task of narrowing this range of acceptable options to specific choices that reflect their identities as individuals.

Table 15.1 Responses of nursery school and third-grade children to the question "What would you like to be when you are grown up?"

	NURSERY SCHOOL		THIRD GRADERS	
	3–4 years	4–5 years	Approx. 8 years	
Girls				
Nurse	0	6	Nurse	8
Teacher	0	1	Teacher	11
Clean house, take care of babies	2	1	Housework	1
Doctor	1	1	Doctor	3
"Firelady"	1	1	Artist	2
Princess	1	2	Athlete	4
Ticket lady	1	0	Veterinarian	2
Policeman	1	0	Art teacher	1
Ghost	1	0	Stewardess	1
Cookie Monster	1	0	Mother	2
"To play"	1	0	Train horses	1
Bunny rabbit	1	0	Musician	1
Red Riding Hood	1	0	Senator	1
			Camera "man"	1
			Waitress	1
Boys				
Football, baseball player	0	1	Athlete	4
Doctor	2	3	Doctor	3
Fireman	4	5	Veterinarian	5
Policeman	2	4	Fireman	2
Farmer	0	2	Actor	1
Ditch, dirt digger	1	1	Policeman	5
Build blocks	1	0	"Army man"	2
Engineer, railroad	0	1	Builder	3
Pilot	0	1	Steward	1
Drive dump truck	1	0	Scientist	3
Cowboy	2	0	Racer	1
Carpenter	0	1	Motorcyclist	1
Ape	0	1	Inventor	1
			Potter/artist	1
			Mailman	1
			Pilot	1
			"Like father"	1

Note: There were twelve 3- to 4-year-olds, twelve 4- to 5-year-olds, and twenty-four third graders (or 8-year-olds), and each child could name more than one occupation.
Source: From Nelson, 1978.

THE ADOLESCENT

Many of the lifestyle choices of children are made for them by adults. Adolescents must increasingly make their own choices about such matters as how much time to devote to studying, whether to work part time after school, whether to go to college, what kind of college or university to attend, and, perhaps most significantly, what to be when they grow up. Adolescents become more capable of making these educational and vocational choices as their cognitive and social skills expand; in turn, the choices they make shape their future development.

Adolescent Lifestyles and Leisure Activities

What do adolescents do with themselves? Some interesting answers come from a study in which Mihaly Csikszentmihalyi and Reed Larson (1984) equipped 75 students in a high school near Chicago with electronic pagers, buzzed them at random times during weekdays and weekends, and had them report on what they were doing and how they felt. In Figure 15.3, you can see how the average adolescent divided his or her waking hours among productive activities such as schoolwork, maintenance activities such as grooming and chores, and leisure. Surprisingly little time is devoted to schoolwork. On the other hand, adolescents have a considerable amount of leisure time—more such time than is available to the typical

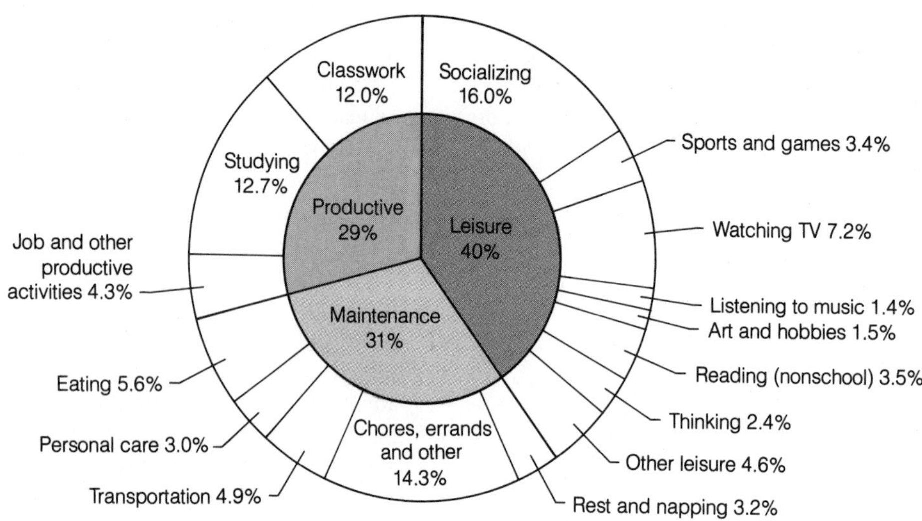

Figure 15.3 How high school students divide their waking hours among activities in a typical week. (From Csikszentmihalyi & Larson, 1984)

adult. Moreover, notice that the most common leisure activity is socializing with friends. Not surprisingly, as adolescents get older, they increasingly want to spend their time with their friends, and ultimately with dating partners (Smith, 1987).

How do adolescents experience their activities? Csikszentmihalyi and Larson (1984) found that adolescents often report being bored when they are doing the very things that are most relevant to preparing for adulthood—doing homework, attending classes, or working. They are the most intrinsically motivated and happy when they are engaged in leisure activities away from adult control. However, certain leisure pursuits such as sports, games, art, and hobbies seem to combine the best features of leisure and work (Kleiber, Larson, & Csikszentmihalyi, 1986). Adolescents are not only happy and intrinsically motivated when they pursue these activities, but they feel challenged and must exert effort to succeed, just as they must when they are doing schoolwork. Possibly, then, *challenging* leisure activities of this sort help adolescents make the transition from a child's world of play to an adult's world of work (Kleiber et al., 1986).

School: Paths to Adulthood

The educational paths and attainments of adolescents are already partially determined long before they enter junior high school. Many individuals' intelligence test scores remain quite stable from childhood on, so some children enter adolescence with more aptitude for schoolwork than others do (see Chapter 9). Moreover, some students enter adolescence with a stronger need for achievement than others do (see Chapter 12). Quite clearly a bright and achievement-oriented student is more likely to obtain good grades and go on to college and is less likely to drop out of school than a student with less ability and less need to achieve. Indeed, Dee Lloyd (1978) was able to predict accurately in three out of four cases which *third graders* would eventually graduate from high school and which would drop out. As youngsters, the future dropouts were distinguished by their lower IQ and achievement test scores, poorer grades, a tendency to have been held back a grade, lower socioeconomic status, and experience of divorce or family disruption.

This does *not* mean that adolescents' fates are sealed in childhood; experiences during adolescence still make a difference. Some adolescents make the most of their intellectual abilities, whereas others who have the ability to do well in school drop out or obtain poor grades. The impacts of school quality or "climate" are the same for adolescents as for children. For example, academic achievement is greater in schools where most students value academic achievement highly than in schools where such things as athletic achievements and extracurricular involvements are more decisive in determining how popular students are (Coleman, 1961). Even a capable student will find it hard to perform well where scholars are viewed as "nerds" and schoolwork is considered a waste of time. So, ability and motivation are not the only influences on educational achievement during adolescence; the social and intellectual climate of the school also helps to determine which adolescents will succeed and which will not.

The stakes are high. Students who achieve good grades in school are more likely than those who do not to be among the nearly half of adolescents who pursue their schooling after high school. These youth, in turn, are likely to end up in higher-status occupations than their peers who do not attend college (Featherman, 1980; Maruyama, Finch, & Mortimer, 1985). In a very real sense, then, individuals are steered along "high success" or "low success" routes in life from childhood on. Depending on their own choices and the influences of their home and school environments, adolescents are even more distinctly "sorted out" in ways that will affect their adult lifestyles, income levels, and adjustment.

Work: Vocational Exploration and Choice

How do adolescents decide what they want to do with their lives? According to a developmental theory of vocational choice proposed by Eli Ginzberg and his colleagues (see Ginzberg, 1972, 1984), vocational choice unfolds through three stages. Children, who are in the *fantasy stage* of vocational development, base their choices primarily on wishes and whims, wanting to be zookeepers, pro basketball players, fire fighters, performers, or whatever else strikes them as glamorous and exciting. From about age 11 to age 18, adolescents are in a *tentative stage* of vocational choice in which they begin to weigh factors other than their wishes and to make preliminary decisions. At first, they consider their *interests* (Would I enjoy counseling people?); then they consider their *capacities* (Am I skilled at relating to people, or am I too shy and insecure for this kind of work?); and finally they also think about their *values* (Is it really important to me to help people, or do I value power, money, or intellectual challenge more?). Adolescents base their vocational choices more on their values and capacities and less on their fantasies and interests as they get older (Kelso, 1977).

According to Ginzberg (1972, 1984), as adolescents leave this tentative stage, they also begin to take into account the realities of the job market and of alternative occupations. They might now consider the availability of job openings in a field such as psychological counseling, the years of education required, the work conditions, and so on. Finally, during the third stage of vocational choice, a *realistic stage* spanning the college years, the individual is likely to narrow things down to a specific choice based on interests, capacities, values, and available opportunities. Now serious preparation for a chosen occupation begins.

The main developmental trend evident in Ginzberg's stages is increasing realism about what one can be. Adolescents narrow down career choices in terms of both internal factors (their own interests, capacities, and values) and external factors (the opportunities available and the realities of the job market). The ultimate goal is to apply all these considerations, achieving an optimal fit between oneself and an occupation. Similarly, other theorists describe vocational choice as a matter of finding a good match between one's self-concept or personality and an occupation (Holland, 1973, 1985; Super, 1957, 1980, 1984).

The major criticism of theories of vocational choice is that they place too much emphasis on how the individual's qualities affect his or her decisions and too little on environmental influences (Brown, 1984). For example, as they get older, adolescents from lower-income families begin to aspire toward less prestigious occupations than middle-class youth do (Gottfredson, 1981; Hannah & Kahn, 1989; Henderson, Hesketh, & Tuffin, 1988). It seems likely that these youth come to believe that they can never attain high-status jobs and begin to make compromises in their career plans. When over 40% of black youths in our society are unemployed (Sum, Harrington, & Goedicke, 1987), it is little wonder that many low-income youth are more concerned about simply finding a job than about exploring many careers to find the one that best matches their interests, capabilities, and values (Grotevant & Cooper, 1988).

Similarly, the vocational choices of females have been and continue to be constrained by traditional gender norms. Females, especially college women, are increasingly aspiring toward high-status jobs that have traditionally been male dominated (Filorentine, 1988), but many girls continue aiming toward feminine-stereotyped, and often lower-status, occupations (Lueptow, 1981; Reid & Stephens, 1985). One reason is that female adolescents, unlike male adolescents, perceive a need to coordinate their ca-

Box 15.1
Should Adolescents Work?

Most adolescents in North America work part time for at least a portion of their high school careers. It makes sense to think that this early work experience influences adolescent development, just as experiences in the family, peer group, and school do. Laurence Steinberg (1984), collaborating with Ellen Greenberger and others, has attempted to find out just how adolescents are affected by their work experience. The research involved comparing working and nonworking high school students, as well as conducting a follow-up of nonworkers who either did or did not begin working during a year's time. Among the aspects of adolescent functioning measured were academic involvement and performance, work attitudes, and personal and social responsibility.

Overall, Steinberg reports more bad news than good. On the positive side, working students were more knowledgeable than nonworking students about the world of work, consumer issues, and financial management. They also had a stronger work orientation (for example, a sense of pride in doing a good job) and, especially if they were girls, a stronger sense of self-reliance. On the negative side, working adolescents also picked up some rather cynical attitudes toward work and became tolerant of unethical practices such as misreporting one's hours of work.

Most discouraging was the finding that adolescents who worked 15 or more hours a week were less involved in school than students who worked only a few hours a week or not at all. Those

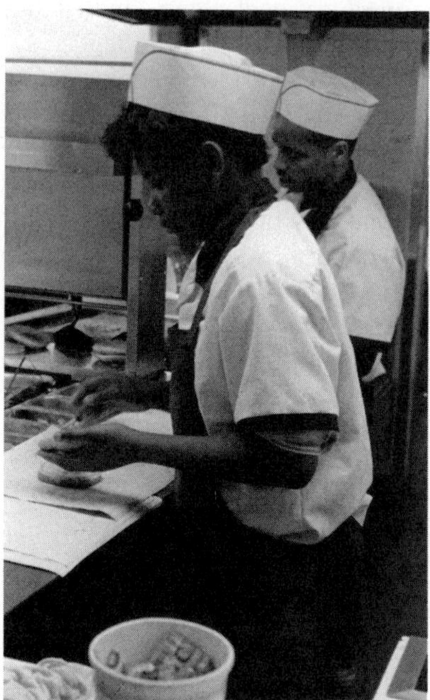

who worked long hours had lower attendance rates, spent less time on homework, participated less often in extracurricular activities, enjoyed school less—and, yes, received lower grades. Moreover, working tended to decrease some teenagers' involvement with family and peers. Other researchers find that adolescents who work long hours also use drugs more frequently (Bachman, 1987).

How do we explain these rather gloomy findings? Why doesn't gaining work experience speed up the process of becoming an adult? Perhaps because teenagers typically work in food service jobs (for example, pouring soft drinks behind the counter at McDonald's, scooping ice cream, waiting on tables, and the like), perform manual labor (especially cleaning or janitorial work), or serve as clerks or cashiers in stores. Steinberg and his colleagues found that these routine and repetitive jobs offered few opportunities for self-direction or decision making and only rarely called on academic skills such as reading and math. In short, they were simply not the kinds of jobs that you would expect to "build character" or teach new skills—although they might well motivate adolescents to stay in school so that they can get better jobs!

Steinberg concludes that many adolescents in our complex and rapidly changing society might be better off postponing work so that they can concentrate on obtaining a solid education, growing as individuals in their relationships with family and peers, and exploring the many career options available to them. However, he does acknowledge that working fewer than about 15 hours a week can foster knowledge of work and positive work attitudes without compromising school performance. And, on the basis of other research, he concludes that *school-based* work experience programs are especially likely to make a positive contribution to adolescent development. In such programs, students receive classroom instruction that can help them benefit from their trial work experiences, and they can blend their roles as students and workers rather than having one role competing with the other for time.

reer plans with their family plans (Aneshensel & Rosen, 1980; Leslie, 1986; O'Connell, Betz, & Kurth, 1989). Although many believe that they can "have it all" (O'Connell, Betz, & Kurth, 1989), those who come from lower socioeconomic backgrounds and have adopted traditional gender norms and expect to marry and launch families early in adulthood are especially likely to set their vocational sights low (Aneshensel & Rosen, 1980; Hannah & Kahn, 1989).

In short, societal influences discourage many low-income youth and females from seriously considering many options that might well fit their interests, capacities, and values. They are not alone, however. Many other adolescents of both sexes simply do not do what vocational theorists advise them to do: explore a wide range of occupations, gather information, and then rationally make a choice (Super, 1984). Those who *do* consider a wide range of options are more likely than those who entertain few possibilities to choose careers that fit their personalities well (Grotevant, Cooper, & Kramer, 1986). Just as Erik Erikson claimed, then, it is through questioning, exploring, and experimenting that adolescents achieve an identity. Yet too often adolescents simply drift into one field or another or make impulsive decisions. And too often they are quite uninformed about the occupations they do choose (Grotevant & Durrett, 1980).

Would adolescents be able to make more informed and rational choices if they had more experience in the world of work? As things stand, the large majority of adolescents do work part time during their high school career. But as Box 15.1 demonstrates, there are both pros and cons to obtaining early work experience, and it can be argued that adolescents in our complex, technological society may be better off concentrating on their schooling than taking on major job responsibilities.

In sum, as adolescents progress from the fantasy stage through the tentative and realistic stages of vocational development, they increasingly make realistic choices that take into account their own interests, competencies, and values as well as the opportunities available to them. The choices of low-income youth and of girls of all socioeconomic levels are often limited by external realities. But even when adolescents have considerable freedom in choosing a career, they often do not engage in a careful process of career exploration and planning that would give them a comprehensive knowledge of the options available to them. The saving grace is that vocational choice is not just one binding decision made in adolescence. We have many opportunities as adults to change our minds and chart new life courses.

THE ADULT

The lifestyles of adults are dominated by work—paid or unpaid, outside the home or within the home. So central is work to an adult's identity and development that we will want to look very closely at the "work life cycle" and its implications for men and women. But it is the total lifestyle of an adult that often determines how satisfied he or she is with life, so the way in which work is intertwined with participation in family roles and leisure activities is significant.

Daniel Levinson's Conception of Adult Development

Daniel Levinson and his colleagues (1978, 1986) have proposed an influential stage theory of adult development that can aid us in organizing our examination of adult career paths and lifestyles. The stages, which were based on interviews with 40 men aged 35 to 45 from four occupational groups (executives, biologists, novelists, and factory workers), describe the unfolding of what Levinson calls the individual's **life structure**. This is an overall pattern of life that reflects the person's priorities and relationships with other people and the larger society. Central to the life structure are family and work roles. Levinson proposes that adults go through a repeated process of first building a life structure and then questioning and altering it. Structure-building periods alternate with transitional or question-raising periods throughout adulthood. Box 15.2 lists Levinson's stages.

Although Levinson did not interview men in their 50s and 60s, he speculates that the same alternating periods of structure building and structure questioning continue into later life. Moreover, he claims that women experience the same stages that men do (Levinson, 1986). In fact, Levinson is convinced that his stages are maturational in nature and universal. Environmental factors will influence the specifics of an adult's life, but the basic pattern of building, questioning, and rebuilding will still be evident under the surface. Levinson's perspective has gained much attention as a way of conceptualizing how adults progress in their careers and how they change as individuals. Let's see how well the theory fares when we match it up with research on vocational development during the adult years.

Work: Career Paths During Adulthood

Not all research supports Levinson's theory in all its details, but much research suggests that young, middle-aged, and older adults confront different issues in their roles as workers. After engaging in much experimentation

Box 15.2
Daniel Levinson's Stages of Adult Development

Early adult transition (ages 17 to 22)
Make the transition from adolescence to early adulthood. Try to establish independence from parents and explore possibilities for an adult identity. Form *the dream*, a vision of your life goals.

Entering the adult world (ages 22 to 28)
Build your first life structure, often by making and testing out a career choice and getting married. Do your best to succeed. Find people who can support your development—a "special woman" (normally a man's wife) and/or a **mentor** (a guide or advisor, perhaps a trusted faculty member or a supervisor at work). Do not question your life; work hard to get off to a good start as an adult, though always with the idea of keeping doors of opportunity open.

Age-30 transition (ages 28 to 33)
Ask whether what you are doing is really what you want. Are you becoming locked in to a poor career choice or an unsatisfying marriage? If any uncomfortable feelings arise from your questioning, either ignore them and plug away, make small adjustments in your life structure, or plan a more major life change (for example, a job change, a divorce, or a decision to return to school).

Settling down (ages 33 to 40)
Build a new, and often somewhat different, life structure; "make it," or realize your Dream. Outgrow your need for a mentor and "become your own man." As in the structure-building period of Entering the Adult World, be ambitious, task-oriented, and unreflective.

Midlife transition (ages 40 to 45)
Begin all over again to question what you have built and where you are heading. If you have been a success, ask whether the dream you formulated as a young adult was really a worthy goal; if you have not achieved your dream, face the fact that you may never achieve it. Confront the facts of aging and ask what you really want for the future. Possibly make major changes in your life structure. Assuming you successfully confront and resolve midlife issues, you may gain self-understanding, a capacity for mentoring younger adults at work, and a deeper concern for your family—much like the middle-aged adult whom Erik Erikson describes as having a sense of generativity.

as young adults, people settle down into a chosen occupation and ultimately prepare for the end of their careers and make the transition into retirement. Notice as we proceed that most of the research that reveals these patterns has focused on men. We will look more closely at women's work lives later.

Early Adulthood: Exploration and Establishment

According to Levinson, early adulthood is a time for launching careers, making tentative commitments, revising them if necessary, seeking advancement, and establishing oneself firmly in what one hopes is a suitable occupation. Levinson's views are supported fairly well by Donald Super's influential theorizing and research (1957, 1980, 1984, 1985). Super, like Levinson and Eli Ginzberg, whose stages of vocational growth we examined earlier, describes adolescence as a time for career *exploration*. Exploration paves the way for Super's stage of career *establishment*, which spans the years from roughly 25 to 45 and is divided into two subphases. Early in the establishment stage, adults are in a *trial* period (not unlike Levinson's stage of Entering the Adult World) in which they make only tentative commitments to occupations and specific jobs and are willing to change jobs if they are dissatisfied. Assuming that they find a satisfying vocation, young adults enter a more settled phase of *stabilization* (similar to Levinson's Settling Down period) in their 30s and become committed to advancing in their chosen fields.

This pattern of career development can be seen in a longitudinal study in which boys were tracked from adolescence to age 36 (see Super, 1985). Using Super's data, Susan Phillips (1982) examined whether men's decisions about jobs at different ages were tentative and exploratory (for example, "to see if I really liked that kind of work") or more final (for example, "to get started in a field I wanted"). The proportion of decisions that were predominantly exploratory was 80% at age 21, 50% at age 25, and 37% at age 36. In other words, young adults progress from wide-open exploration, to tentative or trial commitments, to a stabilization of their choices. Yet notice that even in their mid-30s, many men were still trying to figure out what they wanted to be when they grew up! So common was experimentation that these men held an average of *seven* full-time jobs or training positions between the ages of 18 and 36, and 30% of them not only changed jobs but changed *fields* between ages 25 and 36 (Phillips, 1982). Women are also highly likely to change their career goals after they leave school (Jenkins, 1989). In short, we may make vocational choices as adolescents, but we are obviously very open to making new choices as young adults.

Once a person enters a particular career path, the degree of early success attained greatly affects later outcomes. Douglas Bray and Ann Howard (1983), in longitudinal studies of men who started out as beginning managers at AT&T and remained with the company until middle age, found that it became apparent quite early who was on the "fast track" destined for success and who was not. The successes, those who rose quickly to higher management levels, tended to be college graduates who were bright, aggressive, and achievement oriented. Their successes motivated them all the more, their job satisfaction increased, and their work became increasingly central in their lives. Less successful managers continued to be motivated to do their jobs well but lost much of their motivation to advance, perhaps because they realized that they had little chance of doing so. Work became less central in their lives; instead, family, religion, and other nonvocational concerns assumed greater importance (see Figure 15.4). Interestingly, successful and less successful managers were equally satisfied with their lives in general, but they apparently found very different sources of satisfaction.

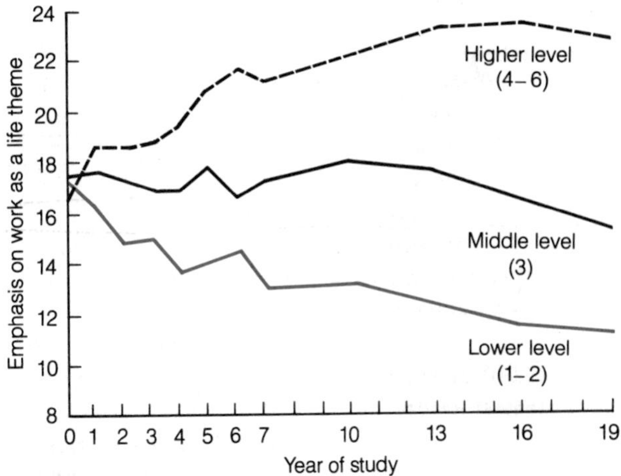

Figure 15.4 The extent to which successful ("higher-level") and less successful managers view work as a central theme in their lives over the course of their careers. (From Bray & Howard, 1983)

In sum, the adolescent's initial vocational choices and priorities are by no means the adult's final choices and priorities. As Levinson and Super theorize, adults seem to start out by formulating a career plan (or dream), engage in much questioning and make trial commitments early in their careers, and eventually settle into a particular career and lifestyle. Apparently, many young adults find that their first jobs are not what they hoped they would be. They then change jobs, or they stay in the same organization but begin to view other aspects of life as more important to them than work. Other adults achieve early success and become even more committed to advancing their careers.

Middle Adulthood: Is There a Midlife Crisis?

According to Levinson, the midlife transition period from age 40 to 45 is developmentally critical, a time of **midlife crisis**—of questioning one's entire life structure, including one's career, and raising unsettling issues about where one has been and where one is heading. True, most of Levinson's middle-aged men did not seek divorces, quit their jobs, buy red sports cars, and behave like adolescents, as popular images of the midlife crisis might suggest. However, Levinson characterized 80% of the men in his study as having experienced a bona fide crisis, a period of intense inner struggles and disturbing realizations in their early 40s. What have other researchers concluded about the midlife crisis?

Most everyone seems to agree that middle age is a time when many important issues arise and many pressures are experienced (Farrell & Rosenberg, 1981). Yet many researchers seriously doubt that the midlife "crisis" is really a crisis and doubt that it occurs in a narrowly defined age range. For example, George Vaillant (1977), in his longitudinal study of Harvard men, found that many middle-aged men were evaluating their lives but that virtually none could be described as experiencing a painful upheaval. Bonnie Hedlund and Peter Ebersole (1983) found that only about 20% of middle-aged men were reevaluating their dreams or raising questions about the meaning of their lives, suggesting that this sort of soul-searching is far from universal. What's more, midlife questioning was not restricted to the early 40s, as Levinson claims. Instead, men questioned their lives at a variety of ages, often in response to specific life events such as getting married, changing jobs, or experiencing marital problems.

If midlife "crisis" were widespread, we might expect that adults would experience personality changes at midlife or display symptoms of emotional disturbance. This does not seem to be the case for either men or women (Costa, MacCrae, & Arenberg, 1983; Costa et al., 1986). Finally, if midlife crisis were widespread, we might expect middle-aged adults to be dissatisfied with their work. Instead, middle-aged men and women are generally *more* satisfied with their jobs than younger adults are (Rhodes, 1983). In sum, Levinson seems to have overestimated the extent to which midlife crisis occurs. It would seem more appropriate to call the phenomenon midlife *questioning* than to call it midlife crisis and to recognize that it can occur at a variety of ages and is not typically emotionally wrenching.

How, then, should we evaluate Levinson's theory overall? He has certainly stimulated much thought and research by suggesting that people experience stagelike changes in their life structures during adulthood, and he has captured the flow of vocational development in early adulthood (for men, at least) quite well. However, as we have seen previously throughout this book, adults are so varied that it is difficult to fit them into a series of universal stages that unfold at predictable ages. The changes that adults experience seem to be timed by the life events that they experience more than by how old they are. Thus some 25-year-olds may well be entering the adult world and building preliminary life structures, but others may still be wondering what they want to do in life, and still others may be reevaluating their dreams because they dread going to work each morning. The broad themes and developmental trends that Levinson identifies are supported by research, but whether most adult lives change in precisely the ways and at precisely the times that he claims they do has not been established. And how well Levinson's stages fit women, blue-collar men, and men or women in other cultures remains to be found out.

Later Adulthood: Aging and Retirement

Our society tends to assume that older workers will begin to perform their work less capably than they did when they were younger (Bird & Fisher, 1986). But as Box 15.3 illustrates, most research flatly contradicts this assumption, indicating instead that most workers continue to be strongly motivated and effective on the job well into their 50s and 60s. Nevertheless, the large majority of men and women in our society retire from work sometime in their 60s.

Earlier in this century, most workers continued working until they simply could not work. Indeed, as late as 1930, over half of the relatively few men who survived to age 65 or older were still working (Palmore, Burchett, Fillenbaum, George, & Wallman, 1985). The introduction of Social Security in 1933 and the increased availability of private pension plans changed all that, making it financially possible for more men and women to retire. These programs have also reflected society's judgment that older workers *should* retire. Only about 10% to 15% of people age 65 and older currently work during a given year (Morrison, 1986).

How do people adjust to the final chapter of the work life cycle? Robert Atchley (1976) has proposed that adults progress through a series of phases as they make the transition from worker to retired person. The process of adjustment begins with a *preretirement phase* in which workers increasingly gather information and plan for the future as they near retirement (Evans, Ekerdt, & Bossé, 1985). Just after they retire, they often experience a *honeymoon phase* when they relish their newfound freedom and perhaps head for the beach, golf course, or camping grounds. Then, according to Atchley, many enter a *disenchantment phase* as the novelty wears off and later move on to a *reorientation phase* in which they begin to put together a realistic and satisfying lifestyle. Research supports this view: David Ekerdt and his colleagues (Ekerdt, Bossé, & Levkoff, 1985) found that men who had been retired only a few months were indeed in a honeymoon period in which they were highly satisfied with life and optimistic about the future, that men who had been retired 13 to 18 months were rather disenchanted with life, and that men who had been retired for longer periods were relatively satisfied once again.

After retirees have adapted to being retired, are they worse off than they were before they retired? Negative images of the retired person abound in our society: He or she supposedly ends up feeling useless, old, bored, sickly, and generally dissatisfied with life. Erdman Palmore and his

Box 15.3
Are Older Workers Inferior Workers?

Do we lose our capacities to perform effectively on the job or become less motivated to perform well as we get older? We can easily think of occupations in which age is definitely a liability. Kareem Abdul Jabbar, for example, was able to continue the strenuous work of playing pro basketball until age 42, but most pro athletes retire earlier than that. Aging workers who perform heavy physical labor may also find their work increasingly difficult. And we can probably all think of middle-aged adults who have lost their fire. But do most adults reach a point at which they are simply over the hill?

Susan Rhodes (1983) reviewed research on the relationship between age and work attitudes and behavior. In terms of actual work performance or productivity, workers in their 50s and 60s are inferior to younger workers in some job settings, superior to them in others, and, overall, not very different from them. David Waldman and Bruce Avolio (1986), analyzing many of the same studies, add that it matters how job performance is measured and what kind of jobs workers hold. Older workers often *outperform* younger workers when performance is measured in terms of productivity (for example, numbers of units of goods produced). By contrast, supervisors tend to rate younger workers as somewhat more effective than older workers, raising the possibility that supervisors may be biased in their judgments of older workers. In addition, aging professionals and managers are more likely to outperform their younger counterparts than aging nonprofessionals are.

Older workers generally have positive attitudes toward work as well (Rhodes, 1983). Indeed, they are more satisfied with their jobs than younger workers are, are more involved in their work, and are less interested in finding a new job. Why? We have seen that young adults are often in an exploratory or trial phase of their careers, and so many of them may not yet feel that they have found the right niche. Moreover, as Rhodes notes, young adults are likely to have less responsible and involving jobs than older workers do. In addition, older workers may have found jobs that suit them better, or may have learned to settle for less than ideal jobs, suspecting that it would be difficult for them to change jobs. It could also be that younger and older generations apply different standards when they evaluate their jobs.

We must conclude from these studies that, on the average, workers in their 50s and 60s at least equal—and sometimes surpass—younger workers in motivation, satisfaction, and performance. The federal government seems to be taking this message to heart, for it has passed legislation to raise or eliminate mandatory retirement ages and to protect older workers from age discrimination in hiring and retention. Nonetheless, many older workers continue to face subtle forms of discrimination in the workplace.

colleagues (1985) have analyzed seven longitudinal studies of retiring men and women. Their main message is that retirement has few effects at all on men and even fewer on women!

Retirement's most consistent impact is to reduce the individual's income—on average, to about three-fourths of what it was before retirement. The precise effects depend on a worker's socioeconomic status (Palmore et al., 1985). Workers who were living below the poverty line before they retired actually have more money after retirement than they had before because they become eligible for government programs for the aging poor. High-income individuals have less money after retirement but apparently have enough to satisfy them. Hardest hit are workers whose incomes were below average, but above the poverty line, before they retired. They tend to become dissatisfied with their financial situations when they see their already meager incomes drop considerably.

Retired people generally do *not* experience a decline in their health simply because they retire. Their activity patterns obviously change because they do not work (or work fewer hours), but despite some increase in solitary activities, people do not alter their involvement in social activities much at all. Finally, retirement has little effect on life satisfaction and attitudes. Overall, then, most retirees seem to adapt quite easily to retirement and to the drop in income that it typically involves. However, there are wide individual differences in adjustment. Some adults, especially those who retire involuntarily because of poor health and who have limited incomes, tend to fare poorly, while other adults, especially those who retire voluntarily and have the financial resources to create satisfying lifestyles for themselves, actually enjoy life more than ever after they retire (Palmore et al., 1985).

Women, Work, and the Family

In our account of the work life cycle to this point, we have had to draw primarily on studies of men. There is a simple reason for this: Men have traditionally been viewed as the major breadwinners in the family and have traditionally dominated the labor force. All that has rapidly changed. Now researchers are looking more closely at *women's* careers to find out whether the same principles that apply to men also apply to women. Most of the trends in vocational development already described are valid for both sexes, but women's careers also differ from men's in significant ways.

Women today are gradually "breaking through" in traditionally male-dominated fields.

The employment patterns of women have changed considerably in recent decades. Elizabeth Waldman (1985), drawing on U.S. Department of Labor statistics, concludes that one trend has been truly dramatic: Many more women are working now than in the past. For example, in 1950 about 34% of women were in the labor force; in 1984 the proportion was 54%. During this same period, the proportion of men in the labor force actually fell off from 86% to 78%, largely because many men were opting to retire early. Similarly, the average number of years that a woman spends working outside the home has climbed to 26 years, while the parallel figure for men is down to 37 years. Finally, women are now entering a wide range of fields that were formerly male dominated or even closed to women: coal mining, truck driving, engineering, and medicine to name a few.

At the same time, Waldman (1985) emphasizes that some things have not changed much at all. For example, there were about 100,000 female lawyers in 1984, about five times as many as there had been a decade earlier, but nearly *4 million* women were secretaries (and 99% of all secretaries are women). The fact is that the largest proportions of women still work in traditionally female-dominated and low-paying jobs. Moreover, the gap between women's and men's earnings has not narrowed much: Across all jobs, a woman averages about 66 cents for every dollar a man earns. So why aren't women achieving more in the workplace than they are? To answer that question, we must focus on two major barriers to women's career achievement: sex discrimination and conflicts between work and family.

Sex Discrimination

It may be difficult for today's young adults to appreciate that not so long ago women were simply barred from entering many occupations or were forbidden to work by their husbands, who viewed a wife's "having" to work as a sign that they had failed as breadwinners. Today, women cannot legally be denied entry into prestigious, male-dominated occupations, but they continue to face discrimination in the labor force. It is no accident, for example, that traditional "female" jobs often pay less than "male" jobs, that secretaries sometimes earn less than janitors in the same building. There is still a tendency to view "women's work" as less valuable and to assume that a woman somehow needs less money because her husband is the family's major earner. Moreover, traditional gender roles continue to operate in the workplace, pressuring women to be "feminine" rather than to display the so-called masculine behaviors that often lead to career advancement (Gutek, 1985; Gutek & Cohen, 1987; Larwood & Gutek, 1987).

Traditional gender roles also make it difficult for women to obtain the same support for their career ambitions that men receive (Gutek & Larwood, 1987). First, many women do not receive the mentoring that Daniel Levinson and others have found to be so important to vocational success (Roberts & Newton, 1987). In many companies, an "old boy network" helps promising young men make the right connections and rise quickly to the top. However, since few women have made it to the top in business and industry, a comparable "old girl network" does not yet exist. In addition, many working women do not receive as much support from their husbands as Levinson's men receive from their "special women" (Roberts & Newton, 1987). A woman's career still tends to be viewed as less important than her husband's (Gutek & Larwood, 1987).

Role Conflict

A second major barrier to women's career achievement is rooted in the conflicting demands of work and family. Society continues to view women as the primary keepers of home and family life. Despite changes in gender attitudes, two-thirds of what gets done at home today is done by women (Pleck, 1985). For many working wives, then, career must often take a back seat to family responsibilities, and career advancement is often sacrificed in the process. The main problem is this: Whether a worker is male or female, steady movement up the career ladder is most likely to occur when a worker works full time and continuously in the same organization (Larwood & Gutek, 1987; Van Velsor & O'Rand, 1984). However, few married women have followed this traditional male route to success; instead, they have often interrupted their careers to bear and raise children (Moen, 1985; Sorenson, 1983; Waite, Haggstrom, & Kanouse, 1986). In one study of retired elderly women, for example, 55% of the single women but *none* of the married women had worked continuously throughout their adult lives (Keating & Jeffrey, 1983). And when Phyllis Moen (1985) charted the career changes experienced by a national sample of women over a five-year period, she found that only 23% worked full time throughout the period studied. Married women with young children were particularly likely to leave their jobs or switch to part-time work.

Women who do take part-time jobs or interrupt their careers to raise children clearly damage their chances of rising to highly paid, responsible positions. This is especially true if they either postpone starting their careers until after they have had a family or switch to a new occupation (rather than returning to the same one) after taking time out for child rearing (Van Velsor & O'Rand, 1984). Meanwhile, the women who *do* make it to the top of the career ladder, especially in male-dominated fields, are more likely than most working women to be divorced or separated or, if they are married, to remain childless or have small families (Jenkins, 1989; Tangri & Jenkins, 1986; Valdez & Gutek, 1987).

The phenomenon behind these findings is **role conflict**—the feeling of being pulled in different directions by the competing demands of different roles (here, family roles and work roles). Apparently some women cope with role conflict by making sacrifices in their careers so that they can concentrate on family goals. Other women seem to do the opposite, limiting their involvements in marriage and family so that they can give full attention to their careers. Studies based on Levinson's model of adult development suggest that many women reevaluate their priorities during an "Age 30 Transition" (Roberts & Newton, 1987). Women who had emphasized marriage and family in their 20s sometimes set individual career goals for themselves, whereas career-oriented women sometimes find themselves longing to get married or to have children. For women, more than for men, recurring struggles with the issue of how to balance career and family goals characterize the adult years (Roberts & Newton, 1987). Does this mean that it is impossible for young women to "have it all"—to combine marriage, family, and a full-time, uninterrupted career? Aren't women who attempt to have it all likely to experience extraordinary role conflict? Moreover, won't they also experience the related problem of **role overload**—the problem of simply having too much to do, and too little time to do it?

It is curious that this question did not come up in early studies of men's vocational development. Instead, it was assumed—and research supports this assumption—that men are best off psychologically when they participate in multiple roles: when they are workers, husbands, *and* fathers (Baruch, Biener, & Barnett, 1987). Is it different for women? Grace Baruch and Rosalind Barnett (1986) examined relationships between middle-aged women's lifestyles and their self-esteem, happiness, and level of depression. They compared women who did or did not participate in each of three central roles: worker, spouse, and parent. Moreover, they asked these women about the rewards and concerns or problems they encountered in each of their roles.

As it turned out, the number of roles a woman played had little impact on her well-being. Although working outside the home tended to be associated with high self-esteem, women who were wives, mothers, *and* workers were generally neither worse off nor better off than women who played fewer roles and who would be expected to experience less role conflict and overload. Instead, it was the *quality of the individual's experience* in work and family roles that was most closely associated with well-being. Women experienced greater happiness and self-esteem, and less depression, when the rewards they gained from whatever roles they played outweighed the hassles. It is now clear that women do not necessarily suffer when they combine roles as paid workers, wives, and mothers (Baruch et al., 1987). Indeed, they sometimes benefit, especially if they are career-oriented individuals who view their work as more than "just a job" (Pietromonaco, Manis, & Markus, 1987), and especially if they and their husbands feel good about their working (Spitze, 1988).

These findings by no means suggest that barriers to women's career success caused by sex discrimination and role conflict have ceased to exist. However, women's and men's lives *are* becoming more similar than they used to be. According to Joseph Pleck (1985), many women of the 1960s and 1970s did indeed experience quite a bit of role conflict and overload because both they and their husbands believed that they should continue to fulfill their traditional family responsibilities even though they were working full time. More recently, Pleck concludes, role conflict and role overload have decreased, mostly because women are spending less time on family tasks, but partly because men are ever so slowly increasing their involvement in household tasks and child care. Both men and women are also more supportive of the idea that women should have careers than they used to be (Stroud, 1981). Perhaps as a result, today's women do not suffer poor mental health simply because they combine work and family, and they even *benefit* psychologically when they hold fulfilling jobs. If present trends continue, we will see more and more families in which *both* men and women are attempting to balance and integrate their central roles as workers, spouses, and parents—and are faring well psychologically when they find gratification in each of these roles.

What Does Work Contribute to Adult Development?

If play and schooling contribute to a child's development, how does work affect an adult's adjustment and personal growth? First of all, an adult's occupation is a central part of his or her identity. It means a great deal to people to say they are psychologists, electricians, or nurses. Meanwhile, the experience of being fired or laid off is often highly damaging to an adult's self-esteem and mental health (Cavanaugh, 1990; Warr, 1982). Moreover, work provides many personal rewards besides money—for example, opportunities to master challenges, gain status, and form enjoyable relationships (Havighurst, 1982). Just as obviously, work can be a source of stress that spills over into nonwork hours and in some cases causes physical or mental disorders.

If play and school can stretch children's minds, can certain kinds of work stretch the capacities of adults? Melvin Kohn, Carmi Schooler, and their colleagues believe so (see Kohn & Schooler, 1982, 1983). In their research, they have focused on the **substantive complexity** of a job, or the extent to which it provides opportunities for using one's mind and making independent judgments. For example, a secretary with a substantively complex job would do more than merely perform whatever typing assignments are placed on her desk. She might also handle the department budget and decide what office supplies are needed; interact with the public; assign tasks to clerical helpers; and, in general, take the initiative for making a large number of complex decisions every day.

Kohn and Schooler find that substantively complex or intellectually challenging work is associated with greater intellectual flexibility (an ability to handle intellectual problems adeptly and to keep an open mind about issues) and with greater self-direction (a tendency to be self-confident, independent-minded, responsible, and tolerant of others). By contrast, people who engage in intellectually unchallenging work tend to be relatively ineffective thinkers, are negative toward themselves and conforming in relation to others, and are often psychologically distressed as well. It is true that people who are already intellectually capable and self-directed are especially likely to land substantively complex jobs. However, Kohn and his colleagues demonstrate that the quality of one's job also influences one's subsequent personal qualities.

As a rule, the jobs held by middle-class white-collar workers and professionals offer more opportunities for intellectual and personal growth than working-class jobs. However, Kohn and his colleagues also find that the relationship between substantively complex work and intellectual and personal development holds up at every socioeconomic level. Moreover, secondary school and college students who take intellectually demanding courses and must complete complex assignments using their own judgment about how to proceed display more intellectual flexibility and self-direction than students whose work in school is less challenging (Miller, Kohn, & Schooler, 1986).

So, the way in which we pass our days as adults can have long-term implications for intellectual and personality functioning. We might imagine that those youth who are intellectually challenged in school are likely to develop the intellectual and personal qualities that will allow them to land substantively complex jobs—and that their initial strengths will be further enhanced by their daily work activities. In short, the notion that work builds character seems to have a good deal of truth to it!

Leisure

As noted earlier, adults typically have less time for leisure activities than adolescents do because they are so heavily involved in their work and family roles. Moreover, we know far more about adults' work lives than about their leisure lives, probably because work is considered more valuable. However, adults do manage to find time to play and to enrich themselves. More and more adults today seek further education; school is no longer "just for kids" (Moody, 1986; Willis, 1985). Moreover, the leisure interests and activities of adults change in interesting ways over the years. Chad Gordon, Charles Gaitz, and Judith Scott (1976), for example, found that older adults in Houston were more likely than younger adults to spend time in relaxing and solitary activities and less likely to pursue more active recreational pasttimes outside the home (for example, dancing and physically exerting sports activities). Other leisure activities—for example, watching television, conversing, entertaining, participating in organizations, watching sports events, and gardening or improving the home—were just as common in later adulthood as in early adulthood. Apparently, then, adults cut down on physically demanding recreational pursuits as they get older, but they continue to enjoy socializing with friends and relaxing at home (Kelly, Steinkamp, & Kelly, 1986).

Surprisingly, most adults do *not* increase their involvement in enjoyable leisure activities much after they retire, even though they have more time on their hands (Bossé & Ekerdt, 1981; Parnes & Less, 1985). They apparently find plenty of work around the house or in the community to fill their time. This pattern of adjustment to retirement may be due to the influence of the **Protestant Work Ethic**, a powerful norm in our society that makes us suspicious that "idleness is the devil's workshop" and convinced that honest labor makes people morally worthy. In one study, the elderly adults who were the most dissatisfied with retirement were those who believed most strongly in the Protestant Work Ethic and viewed their current activities as quite useless, perhaps because these pursuits were not "worklike" enough (Hooker & Ventis, 1984). Those retired (and, for that matter, nonretired) older adults who *do* value leisure and devote a good deal of time to it are more satisfied with their lives than those who rarely take time to play (Palmore, 1979; Parnes & Less, 1985).

The Keys to Successful Aging: Activity or Disengagement?

Our discussion of retirement and leisure in old age may have led you to conclude that elderly people are likely to be better off if they remain active as they age—if they continue to play productive roles in the family, work on a paid or volunteer basis, and develop meaningful leisure activities. Indeed, this is the message expressed by one theory of successful aging. **Activity theory** holds that aging adults will find their lives satisfying to the extent that they can maintain their preexisting activity levels, either by continuing old activities or by finding substitutes—for example, by replacing work with golf, volunteer work, and other stimulating pursuits (Havighurst, Neugarten, & Tobin, 1968). This theory holds that psychological needs do not really change as people enter old age, and that most aging individuals continue to want an active lifestyle.

Other theorists have taken almost precisely the opposite stand on the keys to successful aging. **Disengagement theory** claims that successful aging involves a mutual withdrawal of the aging individual and society (Cumming & Henry, 1961). According to this view, the aging individual *does* have capacities and needs different from those she or he once had and seeks to leave old roles behind and *reduce* activity. Meanwhile, society encourages and benefits from the older person's disengagement.

Which is it? Throughout this text, we have seen evidence that individuals who remain active in old age benefit from their activity. Those who are physically active maintain their health longer than those who lead sedentary lives (see Chapter 5). Those who are intellectually active are likely to maintain their cognitive functions longer (see Chapter 9, and our earlier discussion of the cognitive benefits of complex work). Finally, those who participate in meaningful social relationships are likely to be more satisfied with life than those who are socially isolated (see Chapter 13). In other words, there is more support for activity theory than for disengagement theory.

But before we conclude that activity theory tells us all we need to know about successful aging, let's add three qualifications. First, the relationship between sheer level of activity and life satisfaction or well-being is often quite weak. Apparently many individuals who are quite inactive are nonetheless satisfied with their lives, whereas many who are very busy are nonetheless unhappy. This suggests that the *quality* of one's activity is probably more important than the quantity of it. Second, some features of disengagement theory have merit. As we saw in Chapter 10, for example, older adults sometimes adopt a more passive stance toward the world around them and become more introspective than they were earlier in life. This sort of psychological withdrawal could be viewed as a kind of disengagement. Moreover, most older people today do withdraw from certain roles and cut down on at least some leisure activities. Most impressively, older adults—and younger members of society as well—are very supportive of the concept of retirement, suggesting that disengagement from work roles is mutually satisfying to the aging person and to society.

But third, and perhaps most important, neither activity theory *nor* disengagement theory adequately allows for individual differences in personality traits and preferences. Activity theorists assume that most people will benefit from maintaining an active lifestyle; disengagement theorists assume that most people will be best off if they disengage. Instead, it appears that people are most satisfied in old age when they can adopt whatever lifestyle suits their individual personality best, when they can be as active or inactive as they wish to be (Seleen, 1982). An energetic and outgoing woman might not be happy in old age unless she is on the go; if she is denied chances to maintain her active lifestyle, she may be quite miserable. By contrast, a man who earlier in life found work to be a hassle might like nothing better in his retirement years than to take it easy, do a little fishing, and sit on the porch. He

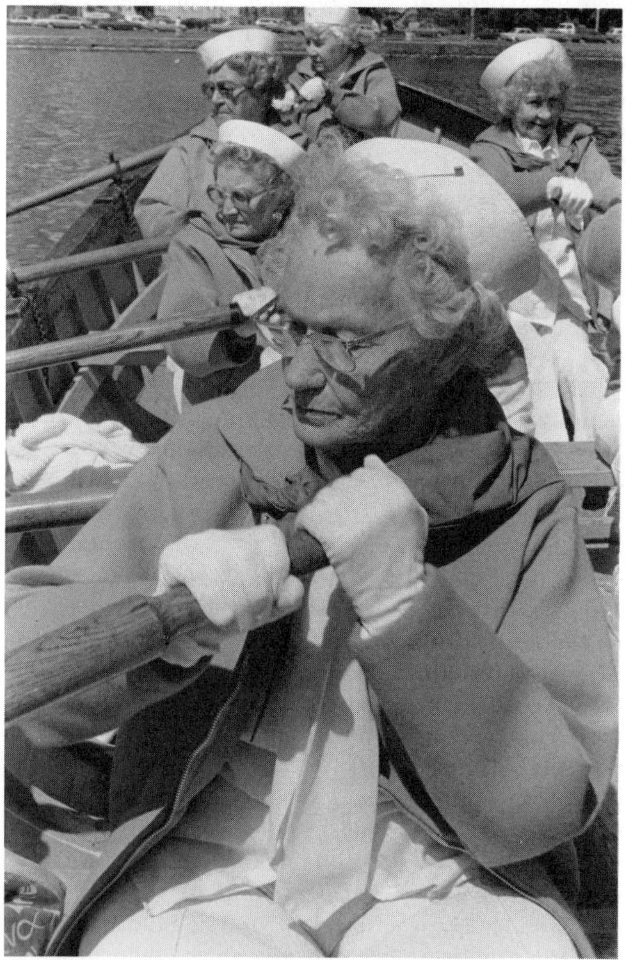

Many older adults subscribe to the activity theory of aging, although others find happiness through disengagement.

might well be miserable if he were forced to continue working or if he found himself in a nursing home where he was pestered daily to participate in planned recreational activities. In short, we cannot assume, as both activity theory and disengagement theory do, that what suits one is likely to suit all. Instead, what matters most is the "fit" between person and lifestyle.

APPLICATIONS: ENHANCING LIFESTYLES

Quite obviously, developmental research has much to contribute to the improvement of education. Practices in the schools have been greatly influenced by studies of how children of different ages learn and think, what motivates them, and how their achievement and adjustment to school can be enhanced. Developmental research is also useful to vocational educators and counselors who help children, adolescents, and adults prepare for and adjust to the world of work (see Vondracek, Lerner, & Schulenberg, 1986).

It may not have occurred to you, however, that developmentalists have also taken on the practical goal of enhancing the capacity for play. Now, why would anyone think that children need training in how to play? Don't they just naturally play? They certainly do, but some children, particularly disadvantaged youngsters, often seem to play less creatively and imaginatively than others do (McLoyd, 1986). These children also perform poorly on many measures of cognitive ability. Could it be, then, that encouraging such children to engage in symbolic play might increase their cognitive skills?

Eli Saltz, David Dixon, and James Johnson (1977) tested this hypothesis by launching a year-long play-training program for disadvantaged preschool children. Children were divided into four groups. One group listened to fairy tales (for example, *Little Red Riding Hood*) and then were asked to act out the parts in the stories. A second group also engaged in pretend play activities but acted out less fanciful scenes drawn from their everyday experience (for example, taking trips). The third group, like the first group, listened to fairy tales, but they discussed them instead of acting them out. And the final group, another control group, engaged in typical preschool activities such as cutting and pasting that did not call upon imaginative capacities.

The findings were striking: Children who participated in pretend play activities exceeded those who did not on a wide range of developmental measures. Most notably, their intellectual functioning improved, they had a greater capacity for empathy (experiencing another's emotions), and they were more able to control their impulses by resisting the temptation to play with a toy that they were told not to play with. Interestingly, the children who acted out fairy tales showed larger gains than the children who acted out everyday experiences. As Saltz and his colleagues note, this could be because taking on such roles as those of the wolf or the grandmother in *Little Red Riding Hood* requires using one's mind to step far outside one's usual role (that is, it involves a greater degree of decentration than playing more familiar roles). Simply being exposed to fairy tales clearly did not account for the developmental gains achieved by these children, for those in the group that merely listened to and discussed fairy tales were largely indistinguishable from the control children who participated in routine preschool activities.

Thus, involvement in symbolic play activities, especially those that require children to take on roles considerably different from their own, enhances development. After reviewing many other studies indicating that experience with symbolic or dramatic play can improve children's logical thinking, creativity, and social competence, James Christie and E. P. Johnsen (1983) wondered if the "back to basics" movement in education might not be a mistake. By stressing "the three R's" and cutting out such "frills" in the curriculum as art, music, dance, and drama, schools could well be eliminating symbolic activities that contribute far more to intellectual development than many educators realize.

Do adults also need help in learning how to play? Perhaps so. Richard MacNeil and Michael Teague (1987), for example, argue that many young and middle-aged adults have overdeveloped "work" selves and underdeveloped "leisure" selves and could use help in developing a satisfying range of leisure interests. Moreover, adults facing retirement are often unsure about what they will do with "all that time" ahead or are so committed to the Protestant Work Ethic that they resist doing anything that does not feel like work to them. MacNeil and Teague believe that leisure education and counseling for adults is best approached on an individual basis. Depending on their personalities, some adults may want help in finding new opportunities for stimulation and personal growth, while others may simply want advice on how to "pass the time" in a more relaxing way (MacNeil & Teague, 1987). What is clear is that humans of any age can thrive on a healthy dose of "play" in their lives.

REFLECTIONS

You have heard the saying "You are what you eat." Perhaps the moral of this chapter is that "You are what you *do*." Across the life span, we are clearly affected by the lifestyles that we lead. If all goes well, the developing person moves from a stimulating home (and perhaps stimulating day-care and preschool settings) in which the capacity for play is nurtured through a series of effective schools in which important life skills, values, and goals are acquired. He or she then establishes a satisfying and stimulating blend of education, work, and leisure as an adult, experiencing still further growth as a result.

Person and environment interact to determine whether a growth-enhancing or growth-inhibiting lifestyle is led. Environmental influences are perhaps strongest during childhood, since children's lifestyle decisions are often made for them by adults. Those children who, through no fault of their own, receive inadequate care early in life and go on to attend ineffective schools suffer for it later in life. Although we continue to be influenced by environmental forces as adolescents and adults, we are freer than children are to make our own decisions and to select our own activities—to take jobs, quit jobs, develop new hobbies, obtain further education, and so on. Our capabilities, traits, motives, and values both influence and are influenced by the decisions we make.

As we go about fashioning our lifestyles, however, we are often oblivious to the fact that the options we can even contemplate depend on the time and culture in which we live. Like children of the past in our own society, children in some societies of the world today do not attend school, have never seen television sets or computers, and are content to know that they will work alongside their parents in the fields when they grow up. How different it is to have one's childhood learning experiences structured by professional educators, to live daily with modern technology, and to face an almost unlimited array of career options as an adolescent. Or consider the differences between the vocational choices available to women today and those available to women of the not so distant past. Most girls of the 1940s knew precisely what their future career was to be: that of wife and mother. Today's young women can think about being lawyers or welders. And tomorrow? It's likely that some of the options available to us will have become outmoded, to be replaced by educational experiences, job opportunities, and leisure pursuits that we can only imagine.

So we progress through a series of choice points, at each of which it is decided where we will spend our days and how we will spend them. Sometimes the choices are our own; sometimes they are made for us; and always, the array of choices available to us depends on the culture and era in which we live. However our choices are fashioned, they matter. ❦

SUMMARY POINTS

1. Human beings pursue both play and work. Play is activity that is enjoyable and absorbing, intrinsically motivating, and unrealistic in quality; work is goal-directed activity that produces something of use or contributes to subsistence. The balance of work and play changes over the life span, and our development is influenced by the activities that form our ever-changing lifestyles.
2. As infants' cognitive abilities unfold, their play becomes increasingly sophisticated and varied; symbolic play, which emerges at about the age of 1, becomes increasingly decentered, decontextualized, and integrated.
3. Infants whose lifestyles include alternative care are often no less competent or well-adjusted than infants who are raised at home *if* they receive high-quality substitute care and responsive parenting at home.
4. The increasingly social and imaginative play of the preschool years and the organized games of the school years contribute to physical, intellectual, social, and emotional development.
5. Attending early day-care or nursery school programs is associated with intellectual growth among disadvantaged children and advanced social behavior (both positive and negative) among children of all family backgrounds. Elementary and secondary school children perform best when (a) they are intellectually capable and motivated; (b) their teachers create a learning environment that is comfortable, task-oriented, and motivating; and (c) there is a good "fit" between their own characteristics and the kind of instruction they receive.
6. The benefits of racial integration and mainstreaming can be enhanced through cooperative learning methods.
7. Although the availability of television has done little to alter children's participation in developmentally important activities, what children watch is highly important in either increasing aggressive tendencies and negative social attitudes or fostering prosocial behavior, positive social attitudes, and academic learning.

8. Children begin to prepare for vocational roles by increasingly narrowing their ideas about future careers to those that fit their self-concepts.

9. Adolescents are likely to benefit from leisure activities that are both enjoyable and challenging and from schools in which academic achievement is valued. According to Ginzberg, adolescents become increasingly realistic as they progress through the fantasy, tentative, and realistic stages of vocational choice, but social factors sometimes constrain the choices made by females and low-income youth of both sexes, and many adolescents do not engage in enough systematic career exploration.

10. Daniel Levinson's theory that adults go through a recurring process of building life structures and revising them is supported by evidence that young adults engage in much career exploration, but midlife crisis and upheaval in one's early 40s does not seem to be universal.

11. Retiring workers go through an adjustment process that extends from a preretirement phase to honeymoon, disenchantment, and reorientation phases after retirement and typically experience a drop in income but little change in health or psychological well-being.

12. Despite dramatic changes, most women continue to work in traditionally female and low-paying jobs, owing in part to sex discrimination and conflict between work and family roles. Yet women, like men, typically suffer no damage and can potentially benefit from adding work roles to their other roles, especially if their work is substantively complex.

13. Involvement in leisure activities does not change much over the adult years, even after retirement, though participation in more active pursuits does decline. Neither activity theory nor disengagement theory places enough emphasis on the fact that older adults are likely to be most satisfied when their lifestyles match their personalities and preferences.

14. Developmental research has contributed to the improvement of education and career education and counseling, and can also enhance the capacity for play.

KEY TERMS

ability tracking
activity theory
computer-assisted instruction
cooperative learning methods
disengagement theory
imaginary companions
leisure
life structure
mainstreaming
mentor
midlife crisis
play
prosocial behavior
Protestant Work Ethic
Pygmalion effect
role conflict
role overload
substantive complexity
symbolic capacity
symbolic play
work

CHAPTER

16

Psychological Disorders Throughout the Life Span

One-year-old Katie has not been eating well and is now noticeably small for her age. Tim, age 6, is wetting the bed almost every night and is in terror that his mother will be kidnapped. Just after she turned 16, Laurie came home drunk from a party; her parents do not know it, but it's far from the first time she has been drunk. Beth, a 28-year-old housewife and mother, has become overwhelmed by her responsibilities and has taken to staring out the window, crying, and letting the children fend for themselves. And Alvin, at 73, is getting more than a little forgetful, his wife and children say. The other day, he left the water running in the bathtub and flooded the second floor. ❦

It is the rare human being who makes it through the life span without having at least some difficulty adapting to the challenges of living. Each phase of the life span has its own unique challenges, and some of us inevitably run into trouble mastering them. This chapter is about some of the ways in which human development can go awry; it views developmental problems and psychological disorders as departures from the normal course of human development that have the potential to alter future development. By learning more about abnormal patterns of development, we can gain new perspectives on the forces that guide and channel—or block and distort—human development more generally.

WHAT MAKES BEHAVIOR ABNORMAL?

It is the job of clinical psychologists, school psychologists, psychiatrists, and other mental health professionals to decide who has a psychological disorder and who does not. How do these professionals—indeed, how do we—define the line between normal and abnormal behavior?

Criteria for Diagnosing Psychological Disorders

Three broad criteria are often applied in diagnosing psychological disorders:

1. *Statistical deviance: Does the person's behavior fall outside the normal range of behavior?* This is the criterion used when individuals are identified as mentally retarded, partly on the basis of their subaverage IQ scores. In other situations, a disorder is said to exist when otherwise normal behavior occurs with great frequency, severity, or persistence. Thus, a mild and temporary case of the "blahs" or "blues" would not be diagnosed as clinical depression because it is so statistically common, but a more enduring and severe case might be.
2. *Maladaptiveness: Does the person's behavior interfere with personal and social adaptation or pose a danger to self or others?* Two men might have the same thirst for a few beers after work, but one might be able to perform his job effectively and maintain close social relationships, whereas the other might repeatedly lose jobs and alienate family members because of his drinking. Maladaptive behavior also includes endangering others by behaving aggressively, as well as endangering oneself by attempting suicide.
3. *Personal distress: Does the behavior cause personal anguish or discomfort?* Many common psychological disorders—for example, depression, anxiety disorders (general states of extreme worrying and apprehension), and phobias (unreasonably intense fears of specific objects or situations)—clearly involve a good deal of personal suffering. They are of concern for that reason alone.

Although these guidelines are a start at defining abnormal behavior, you may have noticed that they are not very specific. That is, they do not tell us precisely where the dividing line between normal and abnormal behavior can be found. What's more, we must ask *which* forms of statistical deviation, *which* failures of adaptation, or *which* kinds of personal distress are most significant. To define psychological disorder more precisely, we must consider more specific standards of behavior—namely, those specified by *social norms* and *age norms*.

Social Norms

Behaviors are considered abnormal or normal only in some social context. **Social norms** are the expectations about how to behave that prevail in a particular social context, whether it is a culture, subculture, or everyday setting. Thus, hearing the "spirits" speak or seeing visions is defined as abnormal in the mainstream culture of North America, but among the Plains Indians these "symptoms" have been defined as valued skills (Wrightsman, Sigelman, & Sanford, 1979). Similarly, a child's screaming and shouting may be viewed as quite appropriate on the playground or in the backyard but may raise eyebrows when it is inappropriate *in context*—for example, when it occurs in the classroom or at church. Definitions of abnormal behavior vary from culture to culture, from subculture to subculture, and from one historical period to another. In a very real sense, then, abnormality is in the eye of a particular group of beholders.

Age Norms

Second—and this point is particularly important from a life-span developmental perspective—abnormal behavior must be defined in relation to **age norms**, or societal expectations about what behavior is appropriate or normal at various ages. The 4-year-old boy who frequently cries, acts impulsively, wets his bed, and talks to his imaginary friend may be perceived as—and may be—perfectly normal. The 40-year-old who does the same things has a problem! We simply cannot define abnormal behavior and development without having a solid grasp of *normal* behavior and development. Box 16.1 reinforces this point.

Specific Diagnostic Criteria

Psychologists and psychiatrists would not be able to diagnose and treat psychological disorders without more specific diagnostic criteria than we have outlined thus far. The most widely used diagnostic system is the *Diagnostic and Statistical Manual of Mental Disorders* published by the American Psychiatric Association (1987). The latest version of this manual—known as *DSM-III-R* because it is a revision of the third edition—spells out defining features and symptoms for the whole range of psychological disorders.

DSM-III-R defines depression—a very familiar psychological disorder that we will highlight in this chapter—as a variety of distinct affective or mood disorders, some relatively mild and some severe. One of the most common is **major depression**, which is defined as at least one episode of feeling profoundly depressed, sad, and hopeless, and/or losing interest in and the ability to derive pleasure from almost all activities, for at least two weeks (American Psychiatric Association, 1987). More specifically, a major depressive episode cannot be diagnosed unless the individual meets the criteria listed in Box 16.2.

A young man suffering from major depression might, for example, feel extremely discouraged and "down in the dumps"; no longer seem to care about his job or even about sexual relations with his wife; lose weight or have difficulty sleeping; speak and move very slowly, as though lacking the energy to perform even the simplest actions; have trouble paying attention to his work or making simple decisions; dwell on how guilty he feels about his many failings; and even begin to think he would be better off dead. Note that major depression would *not* be diagnosed if this young man were going through the normal grieving process after the death of a loved one (although a minority of grieving individuals display major depression in addition to their normal grief reactions).

This definition of major depression is intended to be applied to individuals of all ages. In other words, *DSM-III-R* takes the position that depression in a child is basically similar to depression in a young adult or in an elderly adult, even though it is acknowledged that children may express their depression somewhat differently than adults do. As we will see shortly, there are still many unanswered questions about whether the symptoms and significance of major depression—and other psychological disorders as well—change over the life span. Fortunately, there is now keen interest in exploring the relationships between psychological disorder and human development.

Developmental Psychopathology

In recent years, psychologists have become increasingly aware of the need to adopt a developmental per-

Box 16.1 Childhood as a Psychological Disorder

What might happen if we failed to take developmental norms into account in defining what is normal and what is not? Tongue in cheek, Jordan Smoller (1986) throws developmental norms out the window and attempts to show us that we might well view *childhood* as a disorder if we judged children entirely by the yardsticks we use to evaluate adult behavior. How do we know when someone is suffering from the disorder called "childhood"? Why, says Smoller, we look for the following defining features: congenital onset (one is usually born with the condition), dwarfism (unusually short stature), emotional lability and immaturity (a criterion that leads to the misdiagnosis of many adults as children), knowledge deficits (for example, gross ignorance of politics), and legume anorexia (a refusal to eat vegetables).

What causes this condition? Children, says Smoller, may learn to be children because they are treated as children—but childhood may also have a biological basis. Not only does it typically begin at birth, but genetic researchers find that if one identical twin is diagnosed as suffering from childhood, the other almost always has the same condition.

The seriousness of "childhood" and the difficulties psychologists face in treating it are illustrated by the case of Billy:

> Billy J., age 8, was brought to treatment by his parents. Billy's affliction was painfully obvious. He stood only 4′3″ high and weighed a scant 70 pounds, despite the fact that he ate voraciously. Billy presented a variety of troubling symptoms. His voice was noticeably high for a man. He displayed legume anorexia and, according to his parents, often refused to bathe. His intellectual functioning was also below normal—he had little general knowledge and could barely write a structured sentence. Social skills were also deficient. He often spoke inappropriately and exhibited "whining behavior." His sexual experience was non-existent. Indeed, Billy considered women "icky." . . . After years of painstaking treatment, Billy improved gradually. At age 11, his height and weight have increased, his social skills are broader, and he is now functional enough to hold down a paper route [Smoller, 1986, p. 9].

While this profile of childhood is grim indeed, Smoller reports encouraging new evidence: The vast majority of victims of childhood overcome the disorder, even without treatment, after many years have passed! Enough said: We simply cannot define abnormal behavior at any point in the life span without knowing what is normal at that same age.

spective on abnormal behavior (Gelfand & Peterson, 1985; Rutter, 1989). A new field called **developmental psychopathology** has emerged. As defined by Alan Sroufe and Michael Rutter (1984), developmental psychopathology is the study of the origins and course of maladaptive behavior. Developmental psychopathologists are well aware of the need to evaluate abnormal behavior in the context of normal development, and they are especially interested in finding out how psychological disorders evolve and how they affect later development.

The issues of concern to developmental psychopathologists are the same developmental issues that have concerned us throughout this book—most notably, the nature/nurture issue and the issue of continuity and discontinuity in development. Addressing the nature/nurture issue requires asking important questions such as:

> How do heredity and experience interact to give rise to psychological disorders?
>
> Why do some children who grow up in problem-ridden families develop psychological disorders while others in similar circumstances seem to be invulnerable to the stresses they experience?

Questions about the continuity or discontinuity of maladaptive behavior include:

> To what extent can we predict in childhood which individuals will have problems as adults?
>
> Are most childhood problems passing things that have no bearing on adult adjustment, or do poorly functioning children become poorly functioning adults?
>
> How do the symptoms of a particular disorder change as the developmental status of the individual changes?
>
> Do specific problems persist over the years, or might a problem adapting early in life predict the emergence of a quite different form of maladapted behavior later in life?

Box 16.2
Symptoms of a Major Depressive Episode

The *DSM-III-R* defines a major depressive episode by the criteria listed below. At least five of these symptoms, including one or the other of the first two, must be present during the same two-week period for major depression to be diagnosed.

1. Depressed mood (or can be irritable mood in children and adolescents) most of the day, nearly every day, as indicated either by subjective account or observation by others
2. Markedly diminished interest or pleasure in all, or almost all, activities most of the day, nearly every day (as indicated either by subjective account or observation by others of apathy most of the time)
3. Significant weight loss or weight gain when not dieting (e.g., more than 5% of body weight in a month), or decrease or increase in appetite nearly every day (in children, consider failure to make expected weight gains)
4. Insomnia or hypersomnia nearly every day
5. Psychomotor agitation or retardation nearly every day (observable by others, not merely subjective feelings of restlessness or being slowed down)
6. Fatigue or loss of energy nearly every day
7. Feelings of worthlessness or excessive or inappropriate guilt (which may be delusional) nearly every day (not merely self-reproach or guilt about being sick)
8. Diminished ability to think or concentrate, or indecisiveness, nearly every day (either by subjective account or as observed by others)
9. Recurrent thoughts of death (not just fear of dying), recurrent suicidal ideation without a specific plan, or a suicide attempt or a specific plan for committing suicide

Source: From American Psychiatric Association (1987), *Diagnostic and Statistical Manual of Mental Disorders* (3rd ed., rev.) *DSM-III-R*. Washington, DC: Author, p. 222.

These are important questions to answer if we want to gain a more complete understanding of the development of psychological disorders—and indeed, of development more generally. Some of them are addressed in this chapter. Specifically, this chapter will introduce a small sampling of the developmental problems that can arise during infancy, childhood, adolescence, and adulthood. The focus is on disorders that are closely associated with each developmental period—for example, on infantile autism to illustrate disorders of infancy, anorexia nervosa to illustrate disorders of adolescence, and Alzheimer's disease to illustrate disorders of old age. In addition, we will look into research on depression in *every* developmental period in order to see whether this widespread disorder is indeed the same phenomenon at any age or whether its symptoms and significance change over the life span. Finally, we will see that the successful treatment of psychological disorders requires a sensitivity to developmental issues.

THE INFANT

Adults worry about infants who do not eat properly, who cry endlessly, or who seem overly withdrawn and timid. Fortunately, infant development is strongly channeled by biological maturation. As a result, very few infants develop severe psychological problems. However, psychopathology does exist in infancy, and its effects can be tragic.

Infantile Autism

Perhaps no condition better illustrates how severely disturbed infant development can potentially be than **infantile autism**, a disorder first identified and described by Leo Kanner (1943). It is an example of what the American Psychiatric Association (1987) calls a "pervasive developmental disorder," a severe disorder associated with gross abnormalities in several areas of development. Fortunately, autism is rare, affecting about 4 or 5 of every 10,000 children, and 3 or 4 boys for every girl (American Psychiatric Association, 1987).

To appreciate how very different the autistic child is from the normally developing child, picture the typical infant that we have described in this book—a very social being who responds to others and forms close attachments starting at 6 or 7 months of age; a linguistic being who babbles and later uses one- and two-word sentences to converse; and a curious being who is fascinated by new experiences. Now consider the key features of infantile autism (see Rutter & Schopler, 1987):

1. *Onset before 30 months of age.* Autistic children are believed to be autistic from birth; they can be distinguished from other severely disordered children who at first develop normally and only later become disturbed.

2. *Deviant social development.* Autistic children seem unable to form normal social relationships or to respond appropriately to social cues. They do not make eye contact, seek other people for comfort, snuggle when held, participate in secure attachment relationships, or play cooperatively with peers. In short, autistic children, in stark contrast to normal children, seem to find social contact aversive rather than pleasurable.

3. *Deviant language and communication skills.* Many autistic children are mute, while others acquire limited language skills but cannot really converse with their companions. Among the unusual features of the autistic child's speech are a very flat, robotlike tone; pronoun reversals (for example, the use of "you" to refer to the self); and **echolalia** (a parroting back of what someone else says). Even those autistic children who have mastered basic sentence structure or grammar have difficulty using language in true give-and-take social exchanges. More generally, autistic children are deficient in their ability to use symbols, not only in language but in gesture and symbolic play (Atlas & Lapidus, 1987).

4. *Repetitive, stereotyped behavior.* Autistic children have an obsessive need for sameness and can become terribly upset by novelty or change. They engage in stereotyped behaviors such as rocking, flapping their hands, and spinning toys; become strongly attached to particular objects; and become highly distressed when their physical environment is altered (for example, when a chair in the living room is moved a few feet). Very possibly, it is the changeability of human beings that makes interacting with them so unpleasant for autistic children.

Some of these characteristics of autism can also be observed in severely or profoundly mentally retarded children. Yet the mentally retarded child is developmentally delayed or slow to develop, whereas the autistic child's development is clearly *deviant* or distorted (Rutter & Schopler, 1987). It was originally thought that autistic children had normal intellectual functioning. As it turns out, however, at least half of them are also mentally retarded and so display both the deviant behaviors associated with autism and the developmental delays associated with mental retardation (Quay, Routh, & Shapiro, 1987).

What causes infantile autism? Unfortunately, we are not yet sure. Early theorists suggested that rigid and cold parenting caused the disorder, but this harmful myth has been put to rest (Achenbach, 1982). The fact that autism is such a severe disorder present so early in life strongly suggests that it has an organic or physical basis (Rutter & Schopler, 1987). Indeed, autistic children display several neurological abnormalities, but it is not yet clear which of them are most important or how they arise (Volkmar & Cohen, 1988). There is evidence that genes contribute to autism. It is more likely that two identical twins will both be autistic if one is autistic than that two fraternal twins will both have the condition, and even when only one identical twin is autistic, the other twin is likely to have cognitive or linguistic deficits (Folstein & Rutter, 1977; Steffenburg et al., 1989). However, the fact that one identical twin can be autistic when the other is not indicates that early environmental influences must also contribute to autism. Indeed, some cases of autism have been linked to prenatal exposure to rubella (German measles) and to other prenatal or perinatal problems that can damage the brain (Chess, Fernandez, & Korn, 1978; Gillberg & Gillberg, 1983; Steffenburg et al., 1989). So autism seems to have many possible causes, both genetic and environmental.

What becomes of autistic children as they get older? The long-term outcome has usually been poor, undoubtedly because autism is such a pervasive and severe disorder and because it is so often accompanied by mental retardation. For example, when Christopher Gillberg and Suzanne Steffenburg (1987) reassessed autistic and other severely disturbed children when they were 16 to 23 years old, they found signs of improvement in many autistic individuals, but they judged the outcomes of almost half to be poor or very poor, indicating that these individuals were still severely handicapped and often in need of institutional care. What's more, many individuals actually became worse, sometimes temporarily and sometimes more permanently, after they reached puberty. Yet a minority of autistic children have become adults capable of living independently and holding jobs (Kanner, 1971). Good outcomes are most likely among those who have normal IQ scores and who can communicate using speech before they are 6 years old (Gillberg & Steffenburg, 1987).

Many individuals with infantile autism continue to function poorly as adolescents and adults, but some improve with age. One "improver," Jerry, described his childhood as a reign of "confusion and terror" in which "nothing seemed constant; everything was unpredictable and strange" (Bemporad, 1979, p. 192).

What can be done to treat autistic children? Researchers continue to search for a drug that will correct the suspected brain dysfunctions of these children, and they have had some success using drugs to correct problems such as hyperactive behavior. Yet they are a long way from discovering the "magic pill" to cure the condition (Quay et al., 1987; Rutter & Schopler, 1987). At present, the most effective treatment approach is intensive behavioral training. Ivar Lovaas and his colleagues have pioneered the use of reinforcement principles to shape social and language skills in autistic children. As we'll see at the end of this chapter, Lovaas (1987) has recently reported remarkably good adjustment among autistic children who received very intensive behavioral training starting early in life. Thus it could well be that the futures of autistic children who have had the benefit of today's more powerful intervention programs may be brighter than those of autistic children of the past.

In sum, infantile autism is one of the most vivid examples we have of human development gone awry. The profound problems that autistic children display in their social interactions and responses to the physical environment make it clear that their development is deviant and not merely delayed. Moreover, most of them remain disordered, at least to some extent, throughout their lives. Yet we can be encouraged by recent reports of the long-term benefits of early behavioral intervention, and we can also hope that researchers will eventually pinpoint the brain dysfunctions responsible for this disorder and develop effective drug treatments to correct them.

Depression in Infancy

Box 16.2 (p. 509) listed the *DSM-III-R* criteria for major depressive disorder, but did it occur to you that infants might display these symptoms? Can infants be depressed? It certainly seems impossible for infants to experience the sorts of cognitions that are common among depressed adults — feelings of low self-esteem, guilt, worthlessness, hopelessness, and so on (Garber, 1984). After all, young infants have not yet acquired the capacity for symbolic thought that would allow them to reflect on their experience. Yet infants *can* exhibit some of the behavioral and somatic (or bodily) symptoms of depression — for example, loss of interest in activities, loss of weight, or disruption of normal sleep patterns. Researchers dispute whether true depressive disorders can occur in infancy (Garber, 1984), but infants can and do experience *depression-like* states and symptoms. These symptoms are most likely to be observed in infants who lack a secure attachment relationship or who experience a disruption of their all-important emotional bonds (Trad, 1986).

Some years ago, Rene Spitz (1946) identified a syndrome among infants in institutions that he called **anaclitic depression**, or depression associated with the loss of an attachment figure. Infants suffering from this syndrome — always in response to being separated from their mothers in the second half of their first year of life — often had sad faces and were weepy, underweight, listless, unresponsive, and withdrawn. Moreover, their development was delayed in almost every way. And, as we will see in Chapter 17, infants who are 6 months of age and older also display many depression-like symptoms when they are permanently separated from a parent who dies.

In addition, infants who are neglected, abused, separated from attachment figures, or otherwise raised in a stressful or unaffectionate manner sometimes develop a related condition called **failure to thrive**: They fail to grow normally, lose weight, and become seriously underweight for their age. In some cases, an organic or biological cause such as an illness or heart defect can be found. More intriguing are those cases in which the cause seems to be emotional rather than physical. Infants who fail to thrive (as well as older children described as suffering from "psychosocial dwarfism") also often show many of the symptoms of depression, as well as delays in their cognitive and social development and bizarre behaviors such as drinking from toilets (Green, 1986).

Lytt Gardner (1972) identified several cases of the failure to thrive syndrome, one of which involved twins—a boy and a girl—who grew normally for the first four months of life. Soon afterwards, their father lost his job, their mother became pregnant with an unwanted baby, and the parents blamed each other for the family's problems. When the father moved out, the mother focused her resentment on her infant son. She fed him and tended to his physical care but became emotionally unresponsive to him. Although his sister continued to grow normally, the boy twin at 13 months of age was about the size of an average 7-month-old.

What is striking about this boy and infants like him, whose failure to thrive is not organically caused, is that their weight rapidly climbs and their depression-like emotional symptoms usually disappear almost immediately when they are removed from their homes (Green, 1986). How can we explain this rapid recovery? It appears that emotional traumas interfere with the production of growth hormone by the pituitary gland and that the secretion of growth hormone resumes when these infants (or young children) begin to receive affectionate care (Tanner, 1978). Yet failure-to-thrive infants may relapse if they are returned to their homes unless the family environment is changed and their parents learn more positive and responsive styles of child rearing (Brinich, Drotar, & Brinich, 1989; Lachenmeyer & Davidovicz, 1987; Singer, 1987). It is significant that a decrease in growth hormone production has also been observed in depressed children and adults (Puig-Antich, 1986). This suggests that there is a correspondence between failure to thrive in infancy and depression later in life.

Finally, developmentalists have been concerned about the possibility that infants whose parents are depressed and therefore emotionally unresponsive will become depressed themselves. In one project, children with a depressed parent were assessed from infancy to the age of 5 or 6 (Zahn-Waxler, Cummings, Iannotti, & Radke-Yarrow, 1984). Some of these children showed depression-like symptoms such as apathy and sadness. Many of them also seemed to be highly sensitive to the emotional distress of others but kept their own emotions under tight control. Finally, perhaps because their mothers are unresponsive or unpredictable, these infants are less likely to be securely attached than infants whose mothers are not depressed (Radke-Yarrow, Cummings, Kuczynski, & Chapman, 1985). It is not yet clear whether the young children of depressed parents will become clinically depressed themselves, but if their parents interact with them in negative ways, they are likely to develop emotional problems that could well be forerunners of later depression (Cytryn, McKnew, Zahn-Waxler, & Gershon, 1986; Goldstein, 1988).

In sum, it seems that even infants can display many of the symptoms of depression but that depression in an infant is not equivalent to depression in an adult (Garber, 1984; Trad, 1986). Most notably, young infants do not have the cognitive capacity to think depressive thoughts but can show many of the behavioral and physical symptoms of "adult" depression and experience disruptions of their physical growth and psychological development. The anaclitic depression observed in infants who are separated from their attachment figures, the failure to thrive observed in some infants with unresponsive or rejecting parents, and the restricted emotional expression observed in the infants of depressed parents all suggest that infants can become depressed, in their own way, when their social and emotional needs are unmet.

THE CHILD

Many children experience developmental problems of one sort or another—fears, recurring stomachaches, temper tantrums, and so on. A smaller proportion are officially diagnosed as having one of the psychological disorders associated with infancy, childhood, or adolescence—or as having a psychological disorder such as major depression that can occur at any age. Table 16.1 lists childhood disorders as categorized in *DSM-III-R*. Many developmental problems can also be placed in one or the other of two broad categories: problems of undercontrol and problems of overcontrol (Achenbach & Edelbrock, 1978).

Undercontrolled disorders are also called *externalizing* problems, for children with these disorders "act out" in ways that disturb other people and place them in conflict with social expectations. Undercontrolled children may be aggressive, disobedient, difficult to control, or disruptive. If their problems are severe enough, they may be diagnosed as having a "conduct disorder" or as being "hyperactive."

Overcontrolled disorders or *internalizing* problems involve inner distress, are more disruptive to the child than to other people, and include anxiety disorders (such as persistent worrying about being separated from loved ones), phobias, severe shyness or withdrawal, and depression.

Generally, undercontrolled disorders are more common among boys, whereas overcontrolled problems are more prevalent among girls (Achenbach et al., 1987; Lambert, Weisz, & Knight, 1989; Ostrov, Offer, & Howard, 1989). Cultural influences on these disorders are also evident. In Jamaica, where parents strongly discourage children from behaving aggressively and defiantly and strongly encourage them to be quiet and submissive, undercontrolled disorders are less common and overcontrolled disorders are more common than they are in the United States, where parents are more willing to put up with their children's acting out (Lambert et al., 1989). To give you a feel for these two categories of childhood disorder, we will look at one problem of undercontrol—hyperactivity—and one problem of overcontrol—depression.

Table 16.1 Psychological disorders associated with infancy, childhood, or adolescence

DSM CATEGORY	MAJOR EXAMPLES
Mental retardation	Subaverage general intellectual functioning (mild, moderate, severe, and profound levels)
Pervasive developmental disorders	Autism and similarly severe conditions
Specific developmental disorders	Learning disabilities in the areas of arithmetic, writing, or reading; language and speech disorders; motor skill disorder
Disruptive behavior disorders	Attention-deficit hyperactivity disorder; conduct disorders (persistent antisocial behavior); oppositional defiant behavior.
Anxiety disorders	Separation anxiety disorder, avoidant disorder (extreme fear of strangers), overanxious disorder (diffuse fears)
Eating disorders	Anorexia nervosa, bulimia nervosa, pica (eating nonnutritive substances such as paint or sand)
Gender identity disorders	Confusion concerning gender identity, transsexualism
Tic disorders	Tourette's disorder, chronic motor or vocal tics or involuntary movements
Elimination disorders	Enuresis (inappropriate urination), encopresis (inappropriate defecation)

Source: Based on *DSM-III-R*, American Psychiatric Association, 1987.

Hyperactivity

A 5-year-old boy in Florida got up at 5 o'clock one morning and went to the refrigerator (Renner, 1985). He broke raw eggs on the floor, poured beer on them, and then decided he had better mop up the mess. But once in the garage, he forgot that he had come for a mop, for he spotted some paint cans and commenced to paint. The day continued from there. Perhaps you can appreciate why the "undercontrolled" behavior of some hyperactive children is disturbing to other people!

When it was first identified, hyperactivity was defined principally as a problem of excess motor activity, and the term was used to describe children who could not seem to sit still or were continually on the go. Now hyperactivity is viewed as first and foremost an *attention* deficit. According to *DSM-III-R* criteria, a child has **attention-deficit hyperactivity disorder** if three symptoms are present:

1. *Inattention* (for example, the child does not seem to listen, has difficulty concentrating, and does not stick to activities or finish tasks)
2. *Impulsivity* (for example, the child acts before thinking and cannot inhibit an urge to blurt something out in class or have a turn in a group activity)
3. *Hyperactivity* (the perpetual motion, fidgeting, and restlessness that adults find so difficult to tolerate)

As many as 3% of children are diagnosable as hyperactive, and there are about three hyperactive boys for every hyperactive girl (American Psychiatric Association, 1987). As you might expect, hyperactive children have difficulty performing well in school. They also irritate both adults and peers by failing to comply with requests and disrupting others' activities.

You may also have noticed that many of the behaviors displayed by hyperactive children can readily be observed in normal preschool children. We are usually struck by how energetic preschool children are and how quickly their attention flits from one activity to another. Here, then, is a prime example of how critical it is to view abnormal behavior in the context of developmental norms. A child's attention deficits, impulsivity, and hyperactivity simply must be developmentally inappropriate for a diagnosis of hyperactivity to be justified (American Psychiatric Association, 1987). Otherwise, we might well mistake most average 3- and 4-year-olds for hyperactive children!

It is also clear that hyperactivity expresses itself in somewhat different ways at different ages. The condition often reveals itself first in infancy. Many parents of hyperactive children report that their children were very active, had difficult temperaments, or had irregular feeding and sleeping patterns as infants (Crook, 1980; Stewart, Pitts, Craig, & Dieruf, 1966). In the preschool years, perpetual and seemingly haphazard motor activity is the most noticeable sign of this disorder (American Psychiatric Association, 1987). However, in the grade school years, the hyperactive child may not be overactive so much as fidgety, restless, and inattentive to schoolwork (American Psychiatric Association, 1987).

What causes this disorder? We do not yet have a clear answer (see Achenbach, 1982; Prior & Sanson, 1986). Among other things, hyperactivity has been linked to a brain dysfunction, a delay in the development of the brain, birth complications, genetic makeup, and food allergies. In Box 16.3, we see that some of the theories that have been proposed have not been supported well by research. So hyperactivity remains somewhat of a mystery (Prior & Sanson, 1986).

What can be done to help hyperactive children? Many of them are given stimulant drugs such as Ritalin. It is not clear exactly why stimulants work, but they do seem to make most hyperactive children less distractible and disruptive in class (Dulcan, 1986) and can positively affect how their classmates view them (Whalen et al., 1989). However, stimulant drugs alone do not do much to help hyperactive children perform better academically (Dulcan, 1986). Here, behavioral or cognitive-behavioral treatment approaches offer some promise. For example, Sheryl Chase and Paul Clement (1985) treated hyperactive boys with either Ritalin or a cognitive-behavioral program in which they learned self-reinforcement techniques. Boys were taught to decide how many questions about their reading assignments they would answer each day and to then give themselves points to be exchanged for reinforcers if they met their goals for the day. Self-reinforcement was more effective than stimulant medication in increasing the amount of work boys did and the correctness of their answers. However, learning performance improved most with a *combination* of the two approaches, suggesting that many hyperactive children may benefit from both drug treatment and behavior modification.

What becomes of hyperactive children later in life? It used to be thought that hyperactive children outgrew their problems. Now we know that many of them continue to have difficulties adapting, even though they usually do outgrow their overactive behavior (Brown & Borden, 1986; Wallander & Hubert, 1985). As adolescents, hyperactive children frequently have difficulty attending to their academic work and continue to behave impulsively, often performing poorly in school or dropping out and often committing reckless delinquent acts without thinking about the consequences (Wallander & Hubert, 1985). The picture is more positive by early adulthood, for hyperactive individuals seem to adjust well to their jobs and obtain supervisor evaluations just as high as those of nonhyperactive adults. However, young adults who were diagnosed as hyperactive during childhood are likely to be restless, to be involved in more than their share of car accidents, to lack self-esteem, and to have personality problems (Wallander & Hubert, 1985). Later adjustment is especially poor among hyperactive children who are also aggressive (Milich & Loney, 1979).

In one study, young adults whose hyperactivity had been treated with Ritalin during childhood had higher self-esteem and somewhat fewer problems than those whose hyperactivity was not treated (Hechtman, Weiss, & Perlman, 1984). Whether treated or untreated, however, hyperactive young adults still had more emotional problems and made more impulsive changes in their lives than their nonhyperactive peers. It seems that neither stimulant drugs nor behavioral treatments fully resolve the longer-term problems of many hyperactive individuals, even though they can clearly improve functioning in the short term (Dulcan, 1986).

Box 16.3 Clearing Away the Misconceptions About Hyperactivity

Developmentalists do not fully understand what causes attention-deficit hyperactivity disorder, but we are at least weeding out some incorrect ideas about this condition. Initially, it was thought that hyperactive children had suffered some sort of "minimal brain damage." But researchers could find no evidence of brain damage in most hyperactive children, nor could they establish that most children who suffer brain damage become hyperactive (Achenbach, 1982). Researchers are still convinced that the brains of hyperactive children process stimulation differently than the brains of nonhyperactive children, but they are now looking for subtle differences in brain chemistry rather than for physical brain damage.

After it was discovered that stimulant drugs made hyperactive children less active, researchers were even more convinced that hyperactive children had a brain dysfunction that the drugs corrected. Since stimulants make adults more energetic and active than they would otherwise be, the tendency of these drugs to make hyperactive children *settle down* was paradoxical. Why would a stimulant quiet down children who already seemed overstimulated? One hypothesis was that hyperactive children might have underaroused brains and might be attempting to arouse their nervous systems by being so overactive (Achenbach, 1982). Stimulant drugs therefore would eliminate this need. There was just one small flaw with this theory. When Judy Rapoport and her colleagues (1978) studied the effects of stimulant drugs on normal boys, they discovered a new paradox. Normal boys responded to stimulants just as hyperactive boys did! If both hyperactive and nonhyperactive children calm down after taking stimulants, it makes a good deal less sense to argue that stimulants correct a brain disorder peculiar to hyperactive children.

The notion that particular foods and food additives cause or at least aggravate hyperactivity has also run into some difficulty. When Dr. Benjamin Feingold (1975) recommended placing hyperactive children on a diet free of chemical food additives, many parents soon became convinced that the diet achieved miracles. But perhaps these parents expected good results and treated their children differently after they launched the special diet. Controlled studies in which children and the adults who are evaluating them do not know whether they are getting the Feingold diet or a diet containing food additives indicate that food additives have little apparent effect on most hyperactive children (Gross, Tofanelli, Butzirus, & Snodgrass, 1987; Harley et al., 1978).

What about sugar, then? Many parents of hyperactive children believe their children immediately become worse after they eat sweets, but again, research evidence fails to support the idea, at least for most hyperactive children (Milich, Wolraich, & Lindgren, 1986). For example, Richard Milich and William Pelham (1986) had hyperactive boys drink either sugary drinks or drinks with the sugar substitute aspartame. Sugar seemed to have no negative effects on these boys' behavior or performance in learning situations. These researchers suggest an interesting explanation for the common observation that sugar makes hyperactive children more hyperactive. Perhaps these children simply cannot reorganize their activity after the disruption of stopping to eat a snack, sugary or otherwise. Some hyperactive children may well have allergic reactions to sugar, food additives, or other foods, however, so this hypothesis is still being pursued.

As you can see, misconceptions about hyperactivity have abounded. The story of changing understandings of hyperactivity illustrates how hard it can be to narrow in on the truth about what causes psychological disorders. Only carefully conducted studies can lead us nearer to the truth and to ways of preventing and treating those disorders.

In sum, attention-deficit hyperactivity disorder interferes with cognitive, social, and emotional development from the early years of life into the adult years. A difficult infant may become an uncontrollable and overactive preschooler, an inattentive grade school student, a low-achieving and delinquent adolescent, and even an impulsive and restless adult. True, many hyperactive children adapt well later in life, but perhaps even more will do so as we learn more about this disorder.

Depression in Childhood

As we saw earlier, there is some doubt that the depression-like symptoms displayed by deprived or traumatized infants really qualify as major depressive disorders. So now our question must be this: Can *children* experience true clinical depression? For years, many psychologists and psychiatrists, especially those influenced by psychoanalytic theory, argued that young children simply could not be depressed. Feelings of worthlessness, hopelessness, and self-blame were not believed to be possible until the child formed a strong superego, or internalized moral standards (Garber, 1984).

Once it was appreciated that children *could* become depressed, some researchers argued that depression in children is qualitatively different from depression in adults. Specifically, children were believed to display **masked depression**, or depression in the guise of symptoms other than those we associate directly with it (Quay et al., 1987). For example, a depressed child would not talk about being sad; instead, he or she might express depression indirectly by behaving aggressively or being very anxious. The problem with this "masked depression" hypothesis is that it could lead us to view almost any behavior problem as a sign of underlying depression—without much justification (Garber, 1984).

It is now clear that young children can meet the same criteria for major depression that are used in diagnosing adults—and as early as age 3 (Kashani & Carlson, 1985). True, depression in children is rarer than depression in adolescents and adults, but it exists (Rutter, 1986). Many depressed children are also aggressive or anxious, but these symptoms of "masked depression" are accompanied by *direct* evidence of depression (Puig-Antich, 1982; Ryan et al., 1987).

But doesn't depression express itself at least somewhat differently in a young child than in an adult? Yes. A depressed preschool child *is* less likely than a depressed adult to talk about feeling sad and is likely to seem very irritable (American Psychiatric Association, 1987; and see Box 16.2, p. 509). The child is more likely to display the behavioral and somatic symptoms of depression than to display the cognitive symptoms such as hopelessness and excessive guilt (American Psychiatric Association, 1987). Thus, like a depressed adult, a depressed preschooler might lose interest in everyday activities, eat poorly, and sleep restlessly. A young child is unlikely to feel hopeless, however, because young children lack the cognitive capacity to conceptualize the future and to draw the conclusion that present difficulties will persist (Garber, 1984).

Even school-aged children do not express their depression in precisely the way that adults do, although they are not as difficult to diagnose as preschool children are (Emde, Harmon, & Good, 1986; Garber, 1984; Puig-Antich, 1986). Like preschoolers, they often show their depression more clearly in how they act than in what they say (Bemporad & Wilson, 1978). Later in elementary school, depressed children are more likely to display the cognitive symptoms of depression: They will express feelings of low self-esteem and, later still, overwhelming feelings of guilt and self-blame (McConville, Boag, & Purohit, 1973). For example, one 11-year-old who attempted suicide said, "The devil is in me"; another claimed, "I'm a burden on the family" (Kosky, 1983, p. 459). One thing is clear: Parents and other adults need to become more aware that childhood is not always a happy, carefree time and that children *can* develop serious depressive disorders.

If you are still not completely convinced that even very young children can suffer from severely depressed moods, contemplate this finding: Perihan and Stuart Rosenthal (1984) report that children as young as age 2½ or 3 are capable of attempting suicide! At the tender age of 2½, for example, Elizabeth, reacting to her parents' divorce, a string of many different babysitters, and a depressed mother, ate a bottle of aspirin the day her mother returned from a brief hospital stay. While pretending to feed her doll aspirin, Elizabeth said, "The baby is going to the hospital because she died today" (p. 522). Other children who came to the attention of the Rosenthals reportedly jumped from high places, ran into traffic, threw themselves down stairs, and even stabbed themselves, often in response to abuse, rejection, or neglect. Suicide attempts in childhood are rare, though some apparent accidents may actually be suicide attempts: Children's claims that they want to die should be taken seriously (Pfeffer, 1986; Rosenthal & Rosenthal, 1984).

Do depressed children tend to become depressed adolescents and adults? Certainly many children outgrow mild bouts of sadness. However, most clinically depressed children have recurring episodes of serious depression during childhood and adolescence (Kovacs et al., 1984) and even during adulthood (Zeitlin, cited in Rutter, 1986). Fortunately, depressed children respond well to the antidepressant drugs that have proved so successful in helping adults through episodes of major depression (Cytryn et al., 1986), and they can also benefit from psychotherapy (Weisz, Weiss, Alicke, & Klotz, 1987).

In sum, children, even young ones, can become clinically depressed and even suicidal, though rarely. Moreover, depression in childhood is very similar to depression in adulthood, but depression manifests itself at least somewhat differently as the developing person gains new cognitive capacities. If adults become more sensitive to signs of depression in children, they will be more able to offer appropriate treatment and perhaps reduce the odds of recurrences later in life.

Childhood Disorders and the Family

Most of us have a strong belief in the power of the social environment, particularly the family, to shape child development. This often leads us to blame parents if their child is sad and withdrawn, uncontrollable and "bratty," or otherwise different from most children. We assume that these parents must have done something wrong. Parents whose children develop problems often draw the very same conclusion, feeling guilty because they assume they are responsible.

It is indeed essential to view developmental disorders from a family systems perspective and to appreciate how emerging problems affect and are affected by family interactions. In a thoughtful analysis of the influence of family environment on a number of childhood disorders, however, Jacob Sines (1987) warns that the power of parents to influence their children's adjustment may not be nearly so great as many of us believe. True, children with psychological disorders often come from problem-ridden families. For example, both depressed children and hyperactive children are more likely than children without these disorders to have rejecting or hostile parents. In addition, children with psychological disorders are more likely than most children to have parents and other relatives who have histories of psychological disorder themselves—and who even have histories of the same disorder the child has. Surely this means that children develop problems because they live in conflict-ridden family environments with adults whose own psychological problems make it difficult for them to parent effectively.

Or are there other interpretations? As Sine notes, we cannot be sure that unfavorable home environments *cause* childhood disorders. One alternative explanation is a genetic one. We know, for example, that some individuals are genetically predisposed to become clinically depressed and suicidal (Allen, 1976; Wender, Kety, Rosenthal, Schulsinger, Ortmann, & Lunde, 1986). Perhaps the son of a depressed mother becomes depressed not so much because his mother was unresponsive or rejecting as because he inherited her genetic predisposition to become depressed.

Nor can we be sure that "poor parenting" is the cause of a childhood disorder, since it could also be partly the *effect* of the disorder. As we have seen many times in this book, children contribute to their own development by shaping their social environment. Parental rejection might well contribute to the development of hyperactivity, but we cannot ignore the possibility that hyperactive behavior may make loving parents more tense and hostile than they would be if they were interacting with an easy-to-manage child. Both normal and abnormal development are affected by *reciprocal* influences within the family system.

Do not mistake us: Disruption, conflict, and hostility in the family *do* contribute to causing or aggravating many childhood problems. But many of these problems may be partially rooted in genetic endowment and may be the cause as well as the effect of disturbances in parent/child relationships. It is high time to move beyond the simple view that parents are to blame for all their children's problems. We must take seriously the notion that abnormal development, like normal development, is the product of both nature and nurture and of a history of complex transactions between child and social environment.

Do Childhood Problems Persist?

The parents of children who develop psychological problems very much want to know this: Will my child outgrow these problems, or will they persist? Parents are understandably concerned with the issue of continuity versus discontinuity in development. We have already seen that infantile autism, hyperactivity, and clinical depression *do* tend to persist beyond childhood, particularly if these conditions are inadequately treated. But we have also seen that *some* children with these disorders become competent and well-adjusted adults. So far, then, we have seen evidence of both continuity and change in the lives of children with psychological disorders.

To answer the continuity/discontinuity question more fully, we should consider the entire spectrum of childhood problems. Recall the distinction between undercontrolled or externalizing problems and overcontrolled or internalizing problems. As it turns out, undercontrolled problems such as aggression are more likely to persist into adolescence and adulthood than are overcontrolled problems such as anxiety and phobias or shyness and social withdrawal (Eron, 1987; Fischer, Rolf, Hasazi, & Cummings, 1984; Robins, 1966, 1979). Mariellen Fischer and her colleagues (1984) asked parents to complete checklists

Table 16.2 Odds of having a problem at ages 9 to 15 if the same problem was or was not evident in preschool

Status in Preschool	Problem Later
EXTERNALIZING PROBLEMS	
Problems	
Boys	25 out of 100
Girls	34 out of 100
No problems	
Boys	10 out of 100
Girls	10 out of 100
INTERNALIZING PROBLEMS	
Problems	
Boys	23 out of 100
Girls	14 out of 100
No problems	
Boys	14 out of 100
Girls	10 out of 100

Source: Based on Fischer, Rolf, Hasazi, & Cummings, 1984.

describing the behavior problems displayed by their children during the preschool years and seven years later when they were 9 to 15 years of age. The researchers then calculated the probability that a child who did or did not have severe problems during the preschool years would also have severe problems seven years later. As Table 16.2 shows, preschool children with severe undercontrolled or externalizing problems were almost three times as likely as preschool children without such problems to continue to be "acting out" later in childhood. By contrast, preschool children who were anxious, shy, and socially withdrawn were really *no more likely* than their peers without such internalizing problems to display these same problems seven years later.

Another message of this study is equally important: Overall, problems of early childhood were more likely to disappear than to persist. In other words, discontinuity was the rule, and continuity was the exception to the rule. Even the preschool children with severe problems of undercontrol had only about a 3 out of 10 chance of continuing to be severely antisocial and difficult children at follow-up. Similarly encouraging news comes from a study analyzing hospital records to determine which children in a Swedish community received psychiatric treatment at some point in their lives (von Knorring, Andersson, & Magnusson, 1987). Only 11% of children who had contact with psychiatric services before age 10 were still receiving psychiatric care in their early 20s. Again, then, having serious psychological problems as a child does not doom an individual to a life of maladjustment.

As Norman Garmezy (1987; Garmezy, Masten, & Tellegen, 1984) and Michael Rutter (1979, 1987) emphasize, children seem to be remarkably resilient. They very often outgrow early problems or survive stressful experiences. Some youngsters have even been described as "invulnerable children" because they seem to thrive despite the worst of odds. Such children appear to be protected from damage by their own competencies (especially intellectual ability and social skills) and by strong social support (especially from at least one caring parent figure).

At the same time, many adults with serious psychological problems had problems as children. Again, this is particularly true with respect to antisocial behavior. Chronic and serious delinquents and criminals are highly likely to have been children who behaved antisocially in a variety of ways in a variety of settings, starting at an early age (Loeber, 1982). Such individuals may trade picking fistfights for stealing wallets, but their underlying pattern of antisocial behavior carries over into later life. In short, many individuals overcome problems they displayed as children, but many adolescents and adults who do have severe problems, particularly those who are clearly antisocial, are continuing to act out a pattern of maladjusted behavior that took form much earlier in life. Fortunately, few of us have problems that persist for a lifetime.

THE ADOLESCENT

If any age group has a reputation for having problems and causing trouble, it is adolescents. This is supposedly the time when angelic children suddenly become emotionally unstable, unruly, problem-ridden monsters. The view that adolescence is a time of emotional **storm and stress** was set forth by the founder of developmental psychology, G. Stanley Hall (1904). It has been with us ever since.

Is Adolescence Really a Period of Storm and Stress?

Are adolescents really more likely to experience psychological problems than either children or adults? Our conclusion is that adolescents have a far worse reputation than they deserve. It is simply not true that most adolescents are emotionally disturbed or that most develop significant problems such as drug abuse and chronic delinquency. Instead, significant psychopathology characterizes only a minority of adolescents, and many of them were maladjusted before they reached puberty and continue to be maladjusted during adulthood (Strober, 1986). In a comprehensive survey of mental health on the Isle of Wight, for example, Michael Rutter and his associates (Rutter, Graham, Chadwick, & Yule, 1976) discovered that about 10% of a sample of 14-year-olds appeared to have serious psychological disorders and another 10% could be described as very miserable and negative about themselves. Rates of diagnosed psychological disorder were only slightly higher in this population of 14-year-olds than among a group of 10-year-olds or among the parents of the youngsters studied.

Yet adolescence *is* a period of heightened vulnerability to some forms of psychological disorder (Kashani, Orvaschel, Rosenberg, & Reid, 1989). After all, adolescents must cope with physical maturation, the emergence of new cognitive abilities, dating, changes in family dynamics, moves to new and more complex school settings, societal demands to become more responsible and to assume adult roles, and more (Petersen & Hamburg, 1986). Most adolescents seem to cope with these challenges remarkably well and undergo impressive psychological growth, although it is not unusual for them to feel depressed, anxious, and irritable now and then (Strober, 1986; Tolan, Miller, & Thomas, 1988). For a minority, the stresses of adolescence can precipitate serious psychological disorders (Petersen, 1988; Strober, 1986).

In sum, it can be a mistake to either overestimate or underestimate psychopathology among adolescents. If we cling too strongly to the storm and stress view of adolescence, we may misinterpret serious and potentially long-lasting problems as simply a normal "phase kids go through." In fact, parents and teachers often do fail to notice it when adolescents are severely depressed and even suicidal (Rutter et al., 1976). Perhaps adults too often assume that adolescents are supposed to be "down in the dumps" and will "outgrow it." Of course, we can also go wrong if we ignore the fact that serious and long-lasting disorders sometimes emerge during adolescence.

What special mental health risks *do* adolescents face? Among adolescent females, eating disorders such as anorexia nervosa and bulimia can make the adolescent period treacherous indeed. In addition, many adolescents of both sexes get themselves into trouble by engaging in delinquent behavior, including the illegal use of drugs. Finally, rates of depression do increase dramatically from childhood to adolescence, and suicide rates climb accordingly. These sorts of adolescent problems become far more understandable when we view them in the context of normal adolescent development.

Eating Disorders

Perhaps no psychological disorders are more unique to the period of adolescence than the eating disorders that afflict adolescent girls and young women. Both anorexia nervosa and bulimia have become more common in recent years (Halmi, 1987; Jones, Fox, Babigian, & Hutton, 1980). And both are serious—indeed, potentially fatal—conditions that are difficult to cure (Thompson & Gans, 1985).

Anorexia nervosa, which literally means nervous loss of appetite, has been defined as a refusal to maintain a weight that is at least 85% of the expected weight for one's height and age (American Psychiatric Association, 1987). Anorexic individuals are also characterized by a strong fear of becoming overweight; a distorted body image (a tendency to view themselves as fat even when they are emaciated); and, if they are females, an absence of regular menstrual cycles. Up to 1% of adolescent girls suffer from this condition, and 95 out of 100 of its victims are females (American Psychiatric Association, 1987).

Bulimia nervosa, the so-called binge/purge syndrome, is also rooted in a strong "fear of fat"; its victims believe they are far fatter than they are and want to be far thinner (Williamson, Davis, Goreczny, & Blouin, 1989). Bulimia is more prevalent than anorexia, affecting up to about 5% of high school and college females (Howat & Saxton, 1988; Johnson, Lewis, Love, Lewis, & Stuckey, 1984). Although males can also become bulimic, about 90% of the victims are adolescent or adult females, and that is whom re-

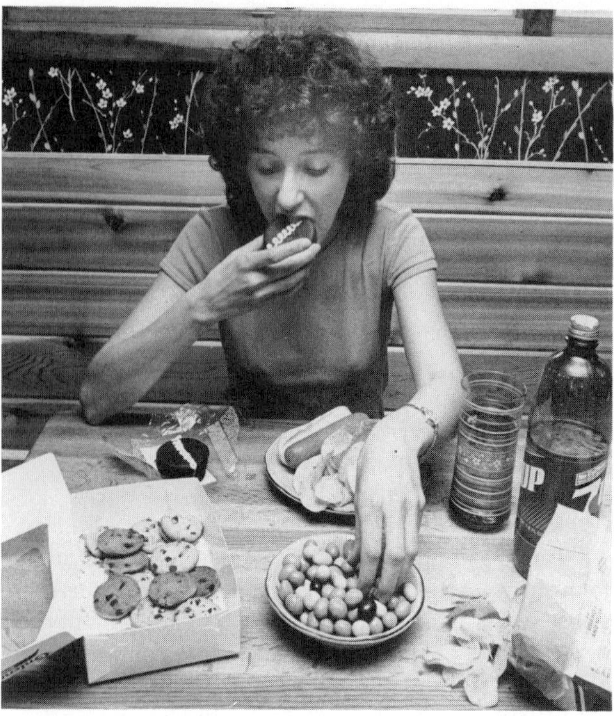

Bulimia can be life-threatening.

searchers have studied (Striegel-Moore, Silberstein, & Rodin, 1986).

Bulimia involves recurrent episodes of consuming huge quantities of food followed by purging activites such as self-induced vomiting, use of laxatives, or rigid dieting and fasting (American Psychiatric Association, 1987). A bulimic girl or woman typically binges on the very foods that are taboo to dieters, eating whole half gallons of ice cream, multiple bags of cookies and potato chips, or whole pies and cakes—as much as *55,000 calories* worth in a single binge session (Johnson, Stuckey, Lewis, & Schwartz, 1982). Not surprisingly, bulimic individuals experience a good deal of anxiety and depression in connection with their binge eating. They may learn to engage in purging activities to relieve these negative feelings (Hinz & Williamson, 1987).

Since anorexic females are, by definition, underweight, they are more "successful," in a perverse way, at avoiding fat than bulimic females are. Indeed, bulimic individuals can be found in all weight ranges (American Psychiatric Association, 1987). However, as many as half of anorexic patients are also bulimic, so the two disorders can coexist in the same person (Polivy & Herman, 1985).

What causes these eating disorders? Part of the problem is our society's obsession with thinness as the standard of physical attractiveness. Well before they reach puberty, girls in our society are socialized to want to be attractive to other people, to associate being thin with being attractive, and even to put themselves on strict diets to enhance their attractiveness (Streigel-Moore, Silberstein, & Rodin, 1986). As girls experience pubertal changes, they naturally gain fat and also face the pressures of succeeding in the world of dating (Streigel-Moore et al., 1986). In other words, they have more reason than ever to be obsessed with controlling their weight, which helps explain why adolescence is a prime time for the emergence of eating disorders (Attie & Brooks-Gunn, 1989).

The dieting so common among females in our society is clearly a risk factor for eating disorders. Anorexia nervosa can, of course, be viewed as dieting carried to an extreme. Moreover, Janet Polivy and Peter Herman (1985) have argued that attempts to diet may contribute to binge eating. Animals and humans are biologically programmed to compensate for a severe restriction of food intake by overeating. The bulimic individual desperately attempts to fight biology by controlling her eating, but one little lapse from a rigid diet is enough to loosen this control and precipitate serious binging. Stressful events or depressed moods can also undermine the bulimic individual's usual restraints on eating. In all seriousness, Polivy and Herman (1985) conclude that "perhaps dieting is the disorder that we should be attempting to cure" (p. 200).

But why do relatively few adolescent females become anorexic or bulimic, even though almost all of them experience social pressure to be thin? Michael Strober and Laura Humphrey (1987) have pieced together an answer. To begin with, genes predispose some individuals to develop an eating disorder, possibly by influencing their personalities (Holland, Hall, Murray, Russell, & Crisp, 1984; Scott, 1986). Anorexic females tend to be introverted young women who worry a good deal and are perfectionists. Bulimic women also appear to be insecure and are vulnerable to other problems such as depression and alcohol or drug abuse (Streigel-Moore et al., 1986).

Yet an eating disorder may not emerge unless a susceptible girl experiences disturbed family relationships—that is, unless heredity and environment interact in an unfavorable way. Salvador Minuchin and his colleagues (Minuchin, Rosman, & Baker, 1978) discovered that anorexic females have difficulty with the adolescent task of forming an identity separate from their parents because their families tend to be "enmeshed" or overly interdependent. These parents are overprotective and do not allow their daughters to argue or to express negative emotions. The result may be a young woman who is afraid of growing up but who also strongly desires to establish some sense of control over her life (which she can do by dieting). Bulimic females also appear to grow up in enmeshed families, but they are more likely than anorexic females to experience conflict and a lack of affection or support in their homes (Scalf-McIver & Thompson, 1989; Strober & Humphrey, 1987).

Here, then, is a dramatic example of how characteristics of the person, family, and wider social environment can interact to produce developmental problems. The young woman who is at risk for eating disorders may be predisposed, partly owing to her genetic makeup, to have difficulty coping with the pressures of adolescence, maintaining self-esteem, and establishing autonomy. However, she may not actually develop an eating disorder unless she also grows up in a culture that overvalues thinness and in a family that makes it hard for her to express her feelings and establish her own identity as an individual.

Juvenile Delinquency

Another problem that we closely associate with adolescence is **juvenile delinquency**, or lawbreaking by a minor. Of course, part of the reason that juvenile delinquency is an adolescent problem is that adolescents are minors and adults are not. Some forms of juvenile delinquency—called *status offenses*—are unlawful *only* if one is a minor (for example, drinking under age, truancy, and, in the past at least, a wide range of behaviors that adults frowned upon such as not obeying one's parents or being sexually promiscuous). Status offenses can be distinguished from delinquent behaviors that are crimes at any age.

Let us ask you a blunt question: Did you, as a minor, ever drink or smoke under age, use an illegal drug such as marijuana, swipe something from a store or from school, deface someone's property, or do anything else that you knew to be illegal? It would be surprising if you had not! Summarizing the research on juvenile delinquency, Martin Gold and Richard Petronio (1980) indicate that over 80% of adolescents admit to some sort of wrongdoing. The peak age for delinquent acts is about age 15 or 16, and this seems to be true in a variety of cultures, social classes, and ethnic groups (Shavit & Rattner, 1988). Boys are more likely than girls to commit delinquent acts, but girls are increasingly doing their share (Gold & Petronio, 1980). Moreover, while youth from low-income homes, especially minority youth, are disproportionately represented in official delinquency statistics, they are really not much more likely than advantaged youth to report engaging in delinquent acts (Gold & Petronio, 1980). In short, occasional delinquent behavior appears to be a normal part of the adolescent experience—common among most youths from all sorts of backgrounds, especially in midadolescence.

Why is delinquent behavior so common, and why does it peak when it does? Gold and Petronio (1980) suggest that committing delinquent acts bolsters self-esteem and status in the peer group. The large majority of delinquent acts are committed *with* peers and *for* peers. As discussed in Chapter 13, age 15 or 16 is not only the peak age for delinquent behavior but is also an age at which youth are especially dependent on peer approval and likely to conform to peer influence. Delinquent acts are often carefully chosen so that they will impress peers:

> A 15 year old who litters or scrawls graffiti on public walls presents little evidence of his courage, independence, or skill. On the other hand, a 15 year old who burns down a barn containing live animals is likely to be regarded as terribly disturbed or vicious ("kooky") even by heavily delinquent peers. But if a 15 year old manages somehow to steal the red flasher (the "bubble gum machine") off a police scout car, that act is a genuine bid for glory [Gold & Petronio, 1980, p. 525].

In short, it appears to be entirely normal to engage in a minor delinquent act on occasion in order to "fit in," feel good about oneself, and perhaps ultimately find an identity of one's own, but it is *not* normal to engage repeatedly in serious criminal acts—to commit armed robberies, assault people, or otherwise go far beyond the "optimal" range of youthful wrongdoing. The most serious juvenile offenders very often have troubled or disrupted family lives and poor relationships with their parents (Gold & Petronio, 1980). Fortunately, the large majority of delinquents do not go on to criminal careers as adults; for them, life as a delinquent is truly a phase they pass through. However, the child or adolescent who repeatedly engages in

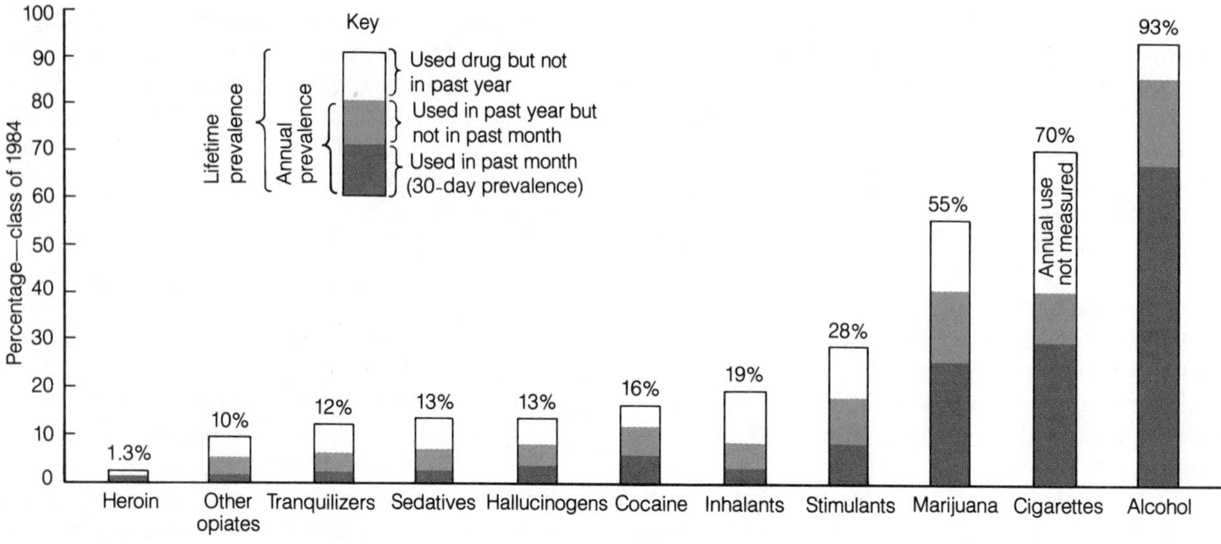

Figure 16.1 Percentages of high school seniors using various drugs. (From Johnston, O'Malley, & Bachman, 1985)

serious law-breaking and aggression is likely to continue to behave antisocially in adulthood and is in need of treatment (Eron, 1987; Robins, 1966).

Drinking and Drug Use

We can further appreciate just how statistically normal delinquent behavior is by looking at the percentages of adolescents who use alcohol and other drugs, as reported by Lloyd Johnston and his colleagues (Johnston et al., 1985). As Figure 16.1 illustrates, alcohol is by far the most widely used drug among adolescents. Indeed, not only have over 90% of the high school seniors surveyed tried alcohol, but 39% reported at least one episode of "party drinking" (five or more drinks in a row) within the past two weeks. Most seniors have tried marijuana or experimented with other illegal substances as well. Use of virtually all of these substances increased through the 1970s and then leveled off and in some cases even declined in the 1980s (Johnston, O'Malley, & Bachman, 1985). The junior high school years stand out as an especially dangerous time, for adolescents typically begin their experimentation with alcohol and other substances before they enter high school (Johnston et al., 1985). It is typical for adolescents to try alcohol before they try marijuana, and to try marijuana before they experiment with other illegal drugs (Yamaguchi & Kandel, 1984).

Why do some adolescents go beyond experimentation and end up abusing drugs? In offering a model to explain the origins of several adolescent problems, Richard Jessor (1987) assumes that adolescent problem behaviors are learned ways of achieving important goals. Two goals that are especially important during adolescence are achieving academic success and establishing autonomy or independence. Some adolescents may view problem behaviors such as drinking as ways of asserting their independence from parents and becoming more adultlike by doing the things that adults often do. Problem behaviors may also be learned ways of coping with the frustrations that come from failing to attain goals by more conventional means.

Jessor and his colleagues conducted a 12-year longitudinal study of problem drinking that started with 13- to 15-year-olds and tracked them until they were age 25 to 27. Problem drinkers got drunk an average of about 20 times a year and experienced problems that stemmed from their drinking. They were compared with abstainers and adolescents who drank but did so in moderation. Three general factors distinguished problem drinkers from other adolescents: their personal qualities, their social environment, and their other patterns of behavior.

With respect to their *personal qualities*, problem drinkers were likely to place little value on academic achievement and much value on independence. They had low expectations of academic achievement, were relatively unreligious, and were generally tolerant of deviant behavior. In short, they tended to be alienated from conventional values such as those promoted by schools and churches and were open to being nonconformists. Second, problem drinkers perceived their *social environment* differently from other adolescents. They saw large gaps between their parents' values and their friends' values, felt that they were more influenced by friends than parents, and had friends who also drank and approved of it. In other words, many of the problem drinkers had unsupportive parents with little impact on them while having peers who modeled and reinforced problem behaviors.

Third, Jessor stresses that drinking problems occurred within the context of the adolescent's *other behavior*. Specifically, problem drinkers were more likely than other adolescents to engage in other problem behaviors (smoking, using marijuana, committing delinquent acts, and having sexual intercourse) and were *less* likely to engage in conventional behaviors (studying and attending worship services). More generally, any particular adolescent problem is likely to be part of a larger *syndrome* of unconventional and norm-breaking behavior (see also Osgood, Johnston, O'Malley, & Bachman, 1988; Rowe, Rodgers, Meseck-Bushey, & St. John, 1989). Consequently, the same personality characteristics and features of the perceived social environment that predict adolescent problem drinking tend to predict other adolescent problem behaviors, as well as the continuation of drinking problems into adulthood (Jessor, 1987). More generally, Jessor's model gives us insights into how a wide range of adolescent problems may originate and suggests that preventing and treating such problems may require changing the values of adolescents themselves *and* altering the ways in which their parents and peers influence them.

Depression and Suicidal Behavior in Adolescence

Although adolescents are quite a bit more vulnerable to depression than children are, we cannot be sure why this is so (Rutter, 1986). It may be that adults fail to recognize many cases of depression in childhood. Or it could be that diagnosable depression is more likely to occur once the adolescent has developed advanced cognitive abilities and is more self-reflective. Or perhaps adolescents experience more stressful life events than children do. In one study, about 9% of junior and senior high school students were depressed enough to be diagnosed as suffering from major depression—a rate fairly similar to the rate among adults (Kaplan, Hong, & Weinhold, 1984).

We can appreciate that adolescents have one foot in childhood and the other in adulthood when we look at the ways in which depression is manifested during this period. Depressed adolescents display many of the same cognitive symptoms of depression that depressed adults display: Sad moods, hopelessness, feelings of worthlessness, and suicidal thoughts are common (Garber, 1984). Yet, like depression in childhood, depression in adolescence is sometimes masked by behavior problems that do not seem to be signs of depression. The depressed adolescent may, for example, get into trouble with the law, abuse drugs, and become sulky, grouchy, and even aggressive (American Psychiatric Association, 1987). Such a teenager may look more like a budding juvenile delinquent than like a victim of depression! Thus, diagnosing depression during adolescence can still be tricky, for adolescents share some of the qualities of both depressed adults and depressed children.

As depression becomes more common from childhood to adolescence, so do suicidal thoughts, suicide attempts, and actual suicides. Moreover, rates of suicide have been increasing in the adolescent age group, especially among 15- to 24-year-old males (Rosenberg, Smith, Davidson, & Conn, 1987). As a result, suicide has become the third leading cause of death for this age group, far behind accidents and just behind homicides (National Center for Health Statistics, 1988). For every adolescent suicide, there are many unsuccessful attempts—as many as 50 or 100 by some estimates (Petti & Larson, 1987; Smith & Crawford, 1986). Moreover, suicidal thoughts that may or may not lead to action are shockingly common during this period (Dubow, Kausch, Blum, Reed, & Bush, 1989; Smith & Crawford, 1986). In one survey of high school students, 62.6% reported at least one instance of suicidal thinking, and 10.5% had actually attempted suicide (Smith & Crawford, 1986).

Before we conclude that adolescence is the peak time for suicidal behavior, however, let's consider the suicide rates for different age groups presented in Figure 16.2. It is clear that *adults* are more likely to commit suicide than adolescents are. The suicide rate for females peaks in middle age, and the suicide rate for white males (though not for black males) climbs throughout adulthood, making elderly white men the group most likely to commit suicide (Rosenberg et al., 1987). Overall, males are more likely to commit suicide than females are—by a ratio of about 3 to 1. When we look at suicide *attempts*, this ratio is reversed, females leading males by a ratio of about 3 to 1. Apparently, then, females attempt suicide more often than males do, but males more often succeed when they try, most probably because they use more lethal techniques (especially guns).

What is really unique about suicidal behavior in adolescence, then? It is the fact that adolescents attempt suicide relatively frequently but are far less likely than adults to succeed at killing themselves when they try. For this reason, the typical adolescent suicide attempt has been characterized as a "cry for help," a desperate effort to get others to respond and help resolve problems that have become unbearable (Berman, 1986). The adolescent who attempts suicide often wants a better life, whereas the adult who attempts suicide is more often determined to end his or her life. This by no means suggests that adolescent suicide attempts should be taken lightly. Their message is clear: "I've got serious problems; wake up and help me!" The attempter is often depressed, has often experienced deteriorating relationships with parents and peers and suffered academic and social failures, and increasingly feels incapable of coping (Berman, 1986; Rubenstein, Heeren, Housman, Rubin, & Stechler, 1989). And because the adolescent who attempts suicide is at risk to commit it in the future, psychological help is definitely needed.

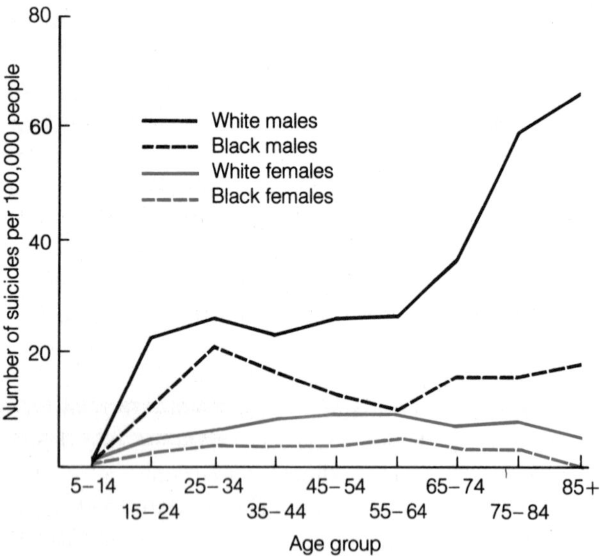

Figure 16.2 Number of suicides per 100,000 people by age, sex, and race in the United States in 1986. (Data from National Center for Health Statistics, 1986)

All in all, adolescence does appear to be a potentially treacherous period of the life span. However, let's remind ourselves that the large majority of adolescents, even though they commit an illegal act or think a depressive thought now and then, emerge from this period as well-adjusted and competent young adults. They will face new challenges adapting to the demands of adult life.

THE ADULT

At any age, psychological problems such as depression and anxiety, and physical illnesses as well, sometimes occur when an individual is unable to cope with stressful events. The developmental tasks and daily pressures of adult life *are* stress producing, so it is time for us to examine the relationship between stress and psychopathology. We will also continue our exploration of depression across the life span, and we will delve into the special problems of elderly adults who suffer from Alzheimer's disease and other serious brain disorders.

Stress and Coping in Adulthood

According to Richard Lazarus (Lazarus & DeLongis, 1983; Lazarus & Folkman, 1984), **stress** is a state that occurs when we perceive events to strain our coping capacities and threaten our well-being. What determines whether or not an experience is stressful, then, is the person's *appraisal* of an event in relation to his or her coping capacities. From this perspective, Sally may find giving birth to be a very stressful experience, while Meg may experience little stress at all in response to this same event because she is confident that she can manage.

What sorts of life experiences create stress and place the person at risk for developing problems? Most of the attention has focused on major life events, which may be *normative transitions*—events that are typical at certain ages such as marrying, becoming a parent, and retiring from work—or *nonnormative transitions*—unusual and unforeseen events that can happen at any age such as being in a car accident, undergoing surgery, or divorcing. Normative life events, because they can be anticipated, are less likely than nonnormative, unscheduled events to be stressful and to cause psychological problems such as anxiety and depression (Brim & Ryff, 1980; Pearlin, 1980). For example, retiring typically has little effect on mental health, but being unexpectedly laid off or demoted at work takes a psychological toll (Pearlin, 1980). Not surprisingly, undesirable life events are also more likely than desirable life events to be stressful and psychologically disturbing (Vinokur & Selzer, 1975).

Yet even nonnormative major life events do not seem to have as many implications for psychological well-being as ongoing life strains. Richard Lazarus and his colleagues, for example, have focused attention on the significance of *daily hassles*, chronic strains or everyday annoyances that may range in magnitude from repeatedly misplacing one's belongings to facing strong pressures to succeed, being trapped in a conflict-ridden relationship, worrying about bills, or living with a chronic illness (Kanner, Coyne, Schaefer, & Lazarus, 1981). The number of daily hassles that an adult is experiencing is actually a better predictor of his or her level of psychological distress than the number of major life events he or she has encountered (Kanner et al., 1981). Morton Lieberman (1983) puts it well: "We are done in more by the drips than by the floods" (p. 133).

In sum, the extent to which people experience stress and its potentially damaging effects depends on both the kinds of events they encounter and the way in which they appraise them. People generally seem to cope quite well with major life events that are a normal and expected part of adult development and occur on schedule. Symptoms of anxiety, depression, and other psychological problems are more likely to occur after nonnormative life events—particularly negative ones—that one did not expect to occur and is not prepared to manage. Yet the most stress-producing experiences of all may be those "little" daily hassles that, when added up, can make everyday life seem unbearable.

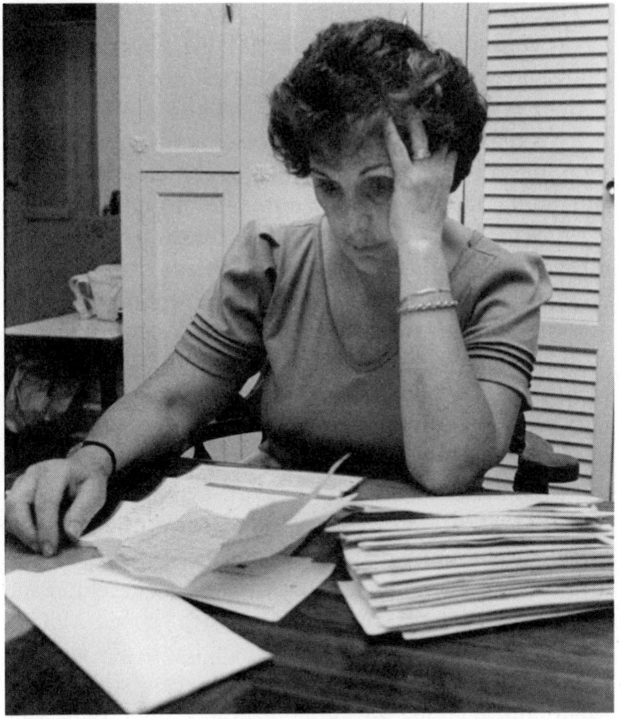

A daily life filled with hassles can contribute to psychological problems such as depression and anxiety.

Age and Stressful Experiences

When in their lives do you think adults are most likely to experience stressful events? It seems difficult to decide. After all, young adults face the struggles of building a life—of starting careers, finding mates, marrying, and having children. Yet middle-aged adults are involved in many roles and have heavy burdens of responsibility, and elderly adults often experience losses as their health declines, as they leave behind roles they played earlier in life, and as they watch loved ones die. As it turns out, adults experience the greatest number of life changes and strains in early adulthood (McLanahan & Sorensen, 1985; Pearlin, 1980). Life strains decrease from early adulthood to middle adulthood, perhaps as adults settle into more stable lifestyles. And elderly adults report even fewer hassles than middle-aged adults do, perhaps because they have fewer roles and responsibilities to juggle or because they appraise events differently and no longer perceive as many events as stressful (Folkman, Lazarus, Pimley, & Novacek, 1987; Lieberman, 1983).

Age and Coping Capacities

If young adults have more to cope with than older adults, do they also have more effective coping capacities at their disposal? Unless they do, they would be at high risk for mental health problems. Some researchers have proposed that coping capacities are at their peak in early and middle adulthood and deteriorate with age. According to this regression hypothesis, older adults cope with stressful events less actively and effectively than younger adults do (Pfeiffer, 1977). Other researchers, however, propose a "growth" hypothesis of coping, arguing that coping capacities *improve* with age (Vaillant, 1977).

Which is it? As it turns out, neither the regression hypothesis nor the "growth" hypothesis is very well supported. Instead, people of different ages are typically far more similar than different in their coping styles (Folkman & Lazarus, 1980; McCrae, 1982). However, a few signs of *both* growth and regression have been identified, and they carry an interesting message about adult development.

First consider some signs of growth. Robert McCrae (1982), for example, asked adults ranging in age from 24 to 91 to describe their responses to a recent stressful life event. Although few age differences in coping styles were detected, young adults were more likely than middle-aged and elderly adults to use immature and usually ineffective coping techniques such as expressing hostility and escaping problems through fantasy. Moreover, George Vaillant (1977) found that the men in his longitudinal study, who had relied quite heavily on these immature coping techniques in college, used more mature coping mechanisms such as humor and realistic planning in middle age. Here, then, is some support for the growth hypothesis (see also Felton & Revenson, 1987; Irion & Blanchard-Fields, 1987).

Now consider some evidence that might be interpreted as regression. Susan Folkman and her colleagues (Folkman, Lazarus, Pimley, & Novacek, 1987) compared the coping strategies of middle-aged and elderly adults and found that elderly adults were more passive in some respects. Middle-aged adults were likely to confront people when they became involved in interpersonal problems, to actively plan ways to solve problems, and to seek social support. By comparison, elderly adults were more likely to try to distance themselves from their problems or to make the best of unpleasant situations.

We might be tempted to conclude, then, that middle-aged and elderly adults have grown when they manage to deal with stressful events without venting anger or escaping their problems through fantasy as younger adults more often do. And we might view elderly adults as having regressed when they do not actively try to change their situations and instead try to live with them. But it may be more accurate to conclude, as Folkman and her colleagues do, that these few age differences in coping styles reflect *neither* growth nor regression. It may make sense, for example, for a young or middle-aged woman to confront her misbehaving child or her lazy co-worker if she believes that she can change their behavior. But it may make just as much sense for an elderly man to accept and make the best of an incurable illness. In other words, both younger and older adults may cope in ways that are appropriate to their stages in life and to the kinds of stressful events they are most likely to encounter (Folkman et al., 1987). Adults of different ages sometimes seem to have different coping styles partly because they encounter different kinds of life events. When facing similar kinds of crises, younger and older adults cope in quite similar ways (Folkman & Lazarus, 1980; McCrae, 1982).

If young adults experience more major life events and more ongoing hassles than older adults do, but do not differ greatly from older adults in their coping capacities, shouldn't they also be more susceptible to psychological disorders than older adults?

When Coping Fails: Age and Sex Differences in Psychopathology

When in adulthood *are* people most likely to suffer from psychological disorders? Which sorts of disorders predominate in different age groups, which among men, and which among women? The National Institute of Mental Health surveyed community mental health in New Haven, Baltimore, and St. Louis (Myers et al., 1984). Adults aged 18 or older were interviewed in their homes about the psychological symptoms they were experiencing. Estimates were made of the percentages of respondents who would meet the criteria set out in *DSM-III* for several psychological disorders.

Overall, a fairly large proportion of adults—15% to 22% of those surveyed in each city—were judged to have suffered from a diagnosable psychological disorder in the previous six months. Figure 16.3 shows how prevalent two very common types of disorder proved to be among men and women of different ages. Notice that both affective disorders (major depression and related mood disorders) and alcohol abuse and dependence affected a larger percentage of young adults than middle-aged or elderly adults. Indeed, the incidence of several other disorders examined in this study, including schizophrenia, anxiety disorders, and antisocial personality, decreased with age. The exception was cognitive impairment, which increased with age, undoubtedly because small minorities of older individuals were falling victim to Alzheimer's disease and other organic brain disorders (see later discussion). Otherwise, the stresses of early adulthood do seem to take a toll on mental health.

Figure 16.3 also reveals that men and women are vulnerable to different sorts of problems. Men are far more likely to abuse alcohol (and other drugs as well) than women are, whereas women are more likely to report symptoms of depression and other affective disorders (and phobias as well). Yet because some disorders are more prevalent among men while others are more prevalent among women, the two sexes have very similar overall rates of diagnosable psychological disorder. Possible reasons for age and sex differences in psychopathology will become clearer as we examine depression in adulthood.

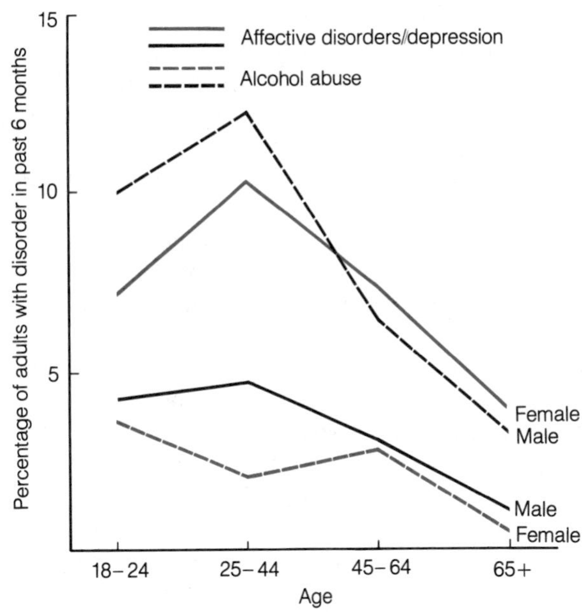

Figure 16.3 Percentage of adults of different ages displaying affective disorders or alcohol abuse/dependence in the past six months. (Adapted from Myers et al., 1984)

Depression in Adulthood

It has been estimated that about one of five adults will suffer from a serious affective disorder at some point in life (Hirschfeld & Cross, 1982). As we have just seen, young adults, especially young women, are especially vulnerable.

Age and Sex Differences

As Figure 16.3 revealed, some researchers have found that rates of clinical depression decrease from early adulthood to late adulthood (Myers et al., 1984). Other researchers find that the rates do not differ much among age groups (Bolla-Wilson & Bleecker, 1989; Feinson & Thoits, 1986). Neither pattern of findings supports the stereotyped notion that elderly adults are far more depressed than the rest of the population (Feinson & Thoits, 1986; Newmann, 1989).

Perhaps the question we should ask is this: Why *aren't* more elderly people clinically depressed? Perhaps they experience fewer stress-producing events than younger adults do—or perhaps they are less likely to *appraise* events as stressful (Folkman et al., 1987). But there is another possibility: Perhaps depression is actually quite common among the elderly but often goes undetected (La Rue, Dessonville, & Jarvik, 1985; Weiss, Nagel, & Aronson, 1986).

Recall that some researchers argue that depressed children may often go undiagnosed as such because children express their depression somewhat differently than adults do. Much the same argument has been made about depression in old age. Think about it: Symptoms of depression include fatigue, difficulty sleeping, cognitive deficits, and somatic (bodily) complaints. What if clinicians noted these symptoms in an elderly person but interpreted them as nothing more than normal aging, or as the result of the chronic illnesses that are so common in the elderly population? Then a case of depression might easily be missed. Elderly adults who are depressed are also less likely than younger adults to *admit* feeling sad or depressed (Klerman, 1983; Weiss, Nagel, & Aronson, 1986). This too could lead to underdiagnosis of depression in the elderly population. Yet *over*diagnosis of depression in older adults may also occur if bodily complaints attributable to aging and disease are uncritically accepted as evidence of depression (Bolla-Wilson & Bleecker, 1989; Newmann, 1989).

There is currently no reason to conclude that depression in elderly individuals is so different from depression in young and middle-aged adults that entirely different criteria must be developed to detect it (La Rue et al., 1985). Still, there may be subtle differences across the life span in how depression reveals itself. Clinicians need to be sensitive to the differences between normal aging processes and psychopathology. Moreover, they should evaluate the health status of elderly individuals, the drugs prescribed for them, and their eating habits to better distinguish between depression and ailments associated with poor health, the side effects of drugs, or poor nutrition (Zarit, Eiler, & Hassinger, 1985). Finally, the fact that elderly people are, if anything, less subject to severe or clinical forms of depression than younger adults are should not blind us to the fact that perhaps a fourth of elderly people are demoralized or are experiencing at least some of the symptoms of depression (Belsky, 1990; Blazer, Hughes, & George, 1987).

As we have also seen, women are more likely than men to be diagnosed as depressed—by a margin of about two to one (Nolen-Hoeksema, 1987). Interestingly, this gender gap is not evident in childhood. It first emerges during adolescence, reaches a peak in the 30-to-60 age range, and becomes less pronounced or even disappears in old age (Jorm, 1987). How can we explain this trend? Biological explanations centering on the influence of female hormones are not well suported (Nolen-Hoeksema, 1987). Instead, it could be that young and middle-aged women simply have more to cope with and more to be depressed about than men do because they carry the burden of responsibility for raising children and holding their families together (Jorm, 1987; Veroff, Douvan, & Kulka, 1981).

Alternatively, women and men may differ not so much in the likelihood that they will experience symptoms of depression as in the likelihood that they will report their symptoms or seek help (see Nolen-Hoeksema, 1987). Or it could be that men and women have been socialized to express their psychological distress in different ways, so that men externalize their problems by behaving antisocially or abusing drugs, whereas women have more often been socialized to internalize their distress (Dohrenwend & Dohrenwend, 1976; Horwitz & White, 1987; Stapley & Haviland, 1989). Finally, it has been suggested that socialized sex differences in coping styles are responsible. When they are depressed, men tend to avoid thinking about it and to engage in activities such as sports to help them forget their problems, whereas women are more likely to tell friends about their feelings and ruminate about why they are depressed (Nolen-Hoeksema, 1987). In this way, men may sidestep or minimize their depression, whereas women may actually aggravate their symptoms. Any of these factors may contribute to sex differences in rates of depression, and we are not yet sure which are most important.

How Does Depression Come About?

A **diathesis/stress model** of psychopathology has proved very useful in understanding how many psychological problems arise. This model proposes that psychopathology results from the interaction of a predisposition or vulnerability to psychological disorder (diathesis) and the experience of stressful events. As we have already seen, certain people are predisposed by their genetic makeup to become depressed. According to the diathesis/stress model, many individuals who experience high levels of stress will not become depressed because they do not have an inherited vulnerability to depression. Similarly, individuals whose families have a history of depression may not become depressed unless they also experience significant losses or other stressful events.

So depression evolves from the interaction of person and environment. To explain more precisely why some individuals become depressed and others do not, we must consider:

1. The individual's *personal resources* (personality traits, coping styles, and the like)
2. The *stressful events* with which he or she must cope
3. The person's *social environment* (particularly the availability of social support)

Personal resources include enduring personality traits, styles of interpreting events, and coping strategies. Individuals who cope effectively with stress typically possess many positive personality traits, which could be the product of both genes and experience. For example, effective copers are self-confident and have an easygoing disposition (Holahan & Moos, 1986; Pagel & Becker, 1987). They tend to be extraverted rather than introverted, and they are even-keeled rather than neurotic or easily upset (McCrae & Costa, 1986). People who are vulnerable to depression lack these protective personality traits.

Effective copers also have healthy *attribution styles*, or ways of explaining good and bad events in their lives. Martin Seligman and his colleagues (see Peterson & Seligman, 1984) have emphasized the importance of attribution styles in their theory of **learned helplessness**. Learned helplessness, which Seligman views as closely akin to depression, is a sense that one cannot control one's outcomes in life. Those individuals who are the least vulnerable to learned helplessness or depression cite internal factors such as their own skills as the causes of their triumphs but blame external factors for their failures and setbacks. By contrast, individuals who are prone to depression do just the opposite, feeling personally responsible when bad things happen to them but citing external causes when good things happen. Not only do depression-prone individuals blame themselves when negative life events occur, but they tend to see the internal causes they identify as global ("I'm generally a loser") and stable ("I'll always be this way"). This unhealthy pattern of internal, global, and stable attributions for bad outcomes appears to be an enduring aspect of personality (Burns & Seligman, 1989). Moreover, both children and adults who adopt this unhealthy attribution style *and* experience many stressful life events are especially likely to become helpless and depressed (Nolen-Hoeksema, Girgus, & Seligman, 1986; Peterson & Seligman, 1984).

Enduring personality traits and attribution styles influence the specific *coping strategies* that people use to deal with stressful life events. For example, self-confident, easygoing individuals make heavy use of **active-behavioral coping strategies**, taking positive action to work out their problems (Holahan & Moos, 1986, 1987). Faced with divorce, such individuals might seek help from friends or lawyers and devise and carry out realistic plans for reorganizing their lives. By contrast, depression-prone individuals are likely to make heavy use of **avoidance coping strategies**, trying to escape the problem and failing to take constructive actions. Avoidance strategies include taking one's feelings out on others, isolating oneself from others, denying that the situation is bad, and trying to reduce tension by drinking, smoking, or taking drugs.

According to the diathesis/stress model, individuals whose personal resources for coping are limited must experience *stressful life events* before they will become depressed. The odds of becoming depressed increase as the number of negative life events and daily hassles experienced by the individual mount (Aneshensel & Stone, 1982; Billings, Cronkite, & Moos, 1983). One stressful life event such as the death of a loved one or a divorce is usually insufficient to trigger major depression, but when bad events pile up or, more important, when everyday strains or hassles become overwhelming, a person may succumb (Lieberman, 1983).

Finally, the individual's *social environment* can affect his or her vulnerability to depression in response to stress. As we saw in Chapter 13, social support is a powerful contributor to well-being, and supportive family relationships are especially important. For example, men and women facing stressful life events are far more likely to become depressed if they lack an intimate and supportive relationship than if they enjoy one (Brown & Harris, 1978; Campbell, Cope, & Teasdale, 1983; Holahan & Holahan, 1987; Lieberman, 1983).

In sum, depression is indeed an outgrowth of the ongoing interaction between person and environment, just as the diathesis/stress model of psychopathology suggests. Some people are more vulnerable to depression than others, partly because of their genetic inheritance and partly because of their socialization experiences. These individuals lack the personal resources—the personality traits, attribution styles, and effective coping strategies—

Drinking away one's problems is an avoidance-coping strategy rather than an active-behavioral coping strategy and is rarely effective.

that can help them weather stressful times. Yet even these depression-prone individuals are unlikely to become clinically depressed unless they are also bombarded by multiple stress-producing events and must attempt to cope without adequate social support. These same generalizations seem to hold true for children as well as adults, and for many psychological problems besides depression.

Old Age and Dementia

Perhaps nothing scares us more about aging than the thought that we will become "senile." Let's immediately correct a common misconception: Becoming "senile" is *not* a normal part of the aging process. Instead, roughly 5% of the 65-and-older population suffers from moderate or severe **dementia** (La Rue, Dessonville, & Jarvik, 1985). Dementia, the technical term for "senility," is a progressive loss of cognitive capacities that leads to severe declines in tested intellectual ability; to impaired memory, poor judgment, and difficulty thinking abstractly; and often to personality changes as well. Although dementia is not a part of normal aging, it is one of the few psychological disorders that can be viewed as a problem of later life.

Dementia is not a single disorder. Indeed, much damage can be done by labeling any older person with cognitive impairments "senile" and then assuming that the problems will only get worse and that nothing can be done to restore functioning. Many different conditions can produce the symptoms we associate with "senility," and some of them are curable or reversible. It is also a mistake to assume that any elderly person who becomes somewhat forgetful or absentminded—who occasionally misplaces keys or cannot come up with people's names—is becoming senile. As we saw in Chapter 8, small declines in memory capacities in later life are common and usually do not have much effect on daily functioning. If this were all it took to warrant a diagnosis of dementia, many young and middle-aged adults would qualify too!

True dementia is a far more serious disorder. The most common cause of dementia is by now a household word—**Alzheimer's disease**, a condition that can strike in middle age but becomes increasingly likely with advancing age (Hyman, Damasio, Damasio, & Van Hoesen, 1989). The disease causes the formation in the brain of senile plaques (masses of dead cell material surrounding neurons) and neurofibrillary tangles (twisted strands of neural fibers within the bodies of neural cells). The result is a progressive—and irreversible or incurable—deterioration of neurons and increasingly impaired mental functioning.

An elderly man with Alzheimer's disease may at first just experience memory lapses now and then and find this upsetting. As the disorder progresses, he may have trouble coming up with the words he wants during conversations or forget what he is supposed to do next midway through making a sandwich. If tested, he may be unable to answer simple questions about where he is, what the date is, and who the president of the United States is (Kahn, Goldfarb, Pollack, & Peck, 1960). Eventually he will become incapable of caring for himself, lose all verbal abilities, and die five or so years after the disease took hold (Zarit, Orr, & Zarit, 1985). Not only do patients with Alzheimer's disease become increasingly unable to function, but they often test the patience of caregivers by wandering away and getting lost, becoming agitated and uncontrollable, accusing people of stealing the items they have misplaced, experiencing hallucinations, or taking off their clothes in public.

What causes Alzheimer's disease? Many cases, especially those that begin in middle age and are therefore said to have a presenile onset, appear to have a hereditary basis. Alzheimer's disease does strike repeatedly in some families, and in these same families, *Down syndrome*—the chromosome disorder that is one of the causes of mental retardation—is also prevalent (Heston, Mastri, Anderson, & White, 1981; Heyman et al., 1983). Recently, genetic researchers, by analyzing blood samples from families with high rates of Alzheimer's disease, have located a gene for the disease on the 21st pair of chromosomes and have suggested that anyone who inherits just one of these apparently dominant genes will eventually develop the disease (St. George-Hyslop et al., 1987). Not coincidentally, individuals with Down syndrome have three rather than the normal two 21st chromosomes and are also highly likely to develop Alzheimer's disease by age 40. So great progress is being made in understanding how genes may contribute to *some* cases of Alzheimer's disease.

However, other individuals fall prey to Alzheimer's disease even though there is no history of it in their families, so the search for causes continues. Among the hypotheses have been a deficit in neurotransmitter chemicals essential for normal learning and memory, improper functioning of the immune system, and a slow-working virus (Zarit et al., 1985). The slow-acting virus hypothesis was recently given a boost by preliminary evidence that injecting blood from Alzheimer's patients and their relatives into hamsters sometimes causes degeneration of the hamsters' brains about a year later (Manuelidis et al., 1988). This does not mean that Alzheimer's disease, like the common cold, can be spread from person to person. Instead, a virus responsible for Alzheimer's disease may lie dormant in most people, and genes or life experiences may somehow activate the virus in some people later in life (Manuelidis et al., 1988). It has already been established that a slow-working virus is responsible for Jakob-Creutzfeldt disease, another cause of dementia.

The second most common type of irreversible dementia is **multi-infarct dementia**, which is caused by a series of minor strokes that cut off the blood supply to areas of the brain. Whereas Alzheimer's disease usually progresses slowly and steadily, multi-infarct dementia often progresses in a steplike manner as each small stroke rather quickly brings about a new deterioration in functioning (American Psychiatric Association, 1987). Huntington's disease (a genetic disorder described in Chapter 3), Pick's disease, Parkinson's disease, Jakob-Creutzfeldt disease, and even AIDS are among the other possible causes of dementia (American Psychiatric Association, 1987).

However, a minority of cases of dementia—perhaps 10% to 20%—are not related to any of these causes and, more important, are *reversible* or curable (La Rue et al., 1985). Such problems as alcoholism, toxic reactions to medication, infections, metabolic disorders, and malnutrition can lead to the symptoms of dementia. If these problems are corrected—for example, if the individual is taken off a recently prescribed medicine or is placed on a proper diet—a once "senile" person can be restored to normal mental functioning. By contrast, if that same person is written off as "senile" or as a victim of Alzheimer's disease, a potentially curable condition may become a progressively worse and irreversible one.

Similarly, elderly adults may be mistakenly diagnosed as suffering from irreversible dementia when they are actually experiencing **delirium**, a reversible "clouding of consciousness" characterized by periods of disorientation and confusion alternating with periods of coherence (American Psychiatric Association, 1987). The same factors that can cause reversible forms of dementia, as well as stressful events such as moving or undergoing surgery, can result in delirium, so here too it is essential to look carefully for such causes and treat them (Zarit et al., 1985). Finally, elderly adults who are depressed are all too frequently misdiagnosed as suffering from dementia because they too often seem forgetful and mentally slow (Esser & Vitaliano, 1988; Zarit et al., 1985). Treatment with antidepressant drugs and psychotherapy can dramatically improve the functioning of such individuals. However, if their depression goes undetected and they are written off as "senile," they are likely to deteriorate further.

The moral is clear: It is absolutely critical to distinguish among irreversible dementias (notably, dementia of the Alzheimer's type and multi-infarct dementia), reversible dementias, delirium, depression, and other conditions that may be mistaken for irreversible dementias—including old age itself (Zarit et al., 1985). Only after all other causes (especially potentially treatable ones) have been ruled out should a diagnosis of Alzheimer's disease be made. But even if such a diagnosis is made, and deterioration leading to death must be expected, much can be done to help family members understand and cope with the Alzheimer's patient and improve his or her functioning using behavioral management techniques (Cavanaugh, 1990; Chiverton & Caine, 1989; Zarit et al., 1985).

APPLICATIONS

It can be discouraging to read about the countless ways in which human development can go awry. Yet many psychological disorders and developmental problems can be treated successfully, as we have already seen in this chapter. We cannot possibly review all of applied psychology and psychiatry here. Instead, being developmentalists, we would like to address these questions: What special challenges arise in working with either very young or very old clients? And just how much can be accomplished?

Treating Children and Adolescents

Treating children and adolescents differs in several ways from treating adults. First, children rarely seek treatment on their own (Johnson, Rasbury, & Siegel, 1986). Instead, they are referred for treatment by adults, usually parents, who are disturbed by their behavior. This means that therapists must view children *and* their parents as the "client." Second, children's therapeutic outcomes often depend greatly on the cooperation of their parents. Whether or not a disturbed family environment has contributed to a child's problem, the participation of parents in treatment is likely to be critical in resolving the problem (Gelfand & Peterson, 1985). Sometimes all members of the family must be treated for any enduring change in the child's behavior to occur—a principle underlying the use of family therapy as a treatment approach.

Third—and this is a point very familiar to students of human development—children function at very different levels of cognitive and emotional development than adults do, and interventions for them must be designed accordingly (Johnson et al., 1986; Kendall, Lerner, & Craighead, 1984). Just think about normal preschool children: Can they easily participate in therapy that requires them to verbalize their problems and gain insight into the causes of their behavior? Techniques that work with cognitively mature adults sometimes prove unworkable with young children (Kendall et al., 1984). Instead, therapists working with children must often devise techniques that are tailor-made for children (Gelfand & Peterson, 1985). In play therapy, for example, disturbed children are encouraged to act out in their play concerns that they cannot easily express in words. All things considered, then, treating children with psychological disorders is particularly challenging. Treatment must involve the family rather than the client alone, and it must be sensitive to the developmental competencies of that client.

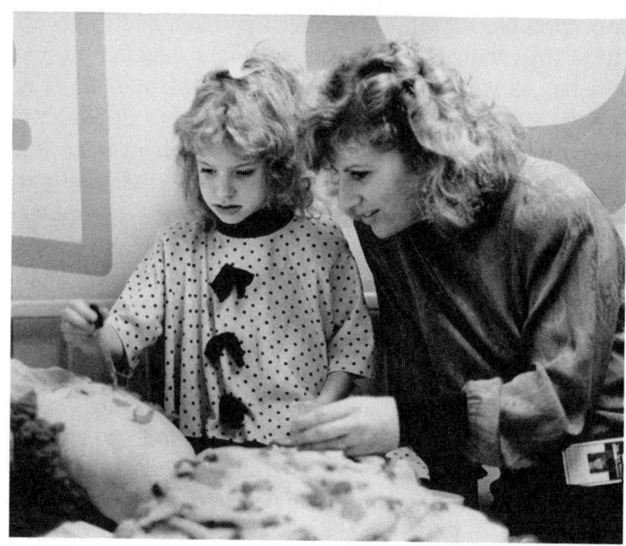

Play therapy can help young children who lack verbal skills express their feelings. Here it is used to help a girl deal with her anxieties about being hospitalized.

Does Psychotherapy Work?

Recently John Weisz and his colleagues (Weisz, Weiss, Alicke, & Klotz, 1987) reviewed over one hundred studies of the effectiveness of psychotherapy in treating problems of childhood and adolescence. Two major categories of psychotherapy were compared: (1) behavioral therapies (e.g., those in which reinforcement principles and modeling techniques are used to alter maladaptive behaviors and teach more adaptive ones); and (2) nonbehavioral therapies (primarily psychoanalytic therapies based on Freudian theory and other "talking cures" in which therapists help clients to express, understand, and solve their problems). These studies examined a wide range of problems (both undercontrolled problems and overcontrolled problems) and measured a wide range of outcomes (for example, anxiety, cognitive skills and school achievement, personality and self-concept, and social adjustment).

So does psychotherapy work with children and adolescents? Indeed it does—at least as well as it works with adults. The average child who received some form of psychotherapy functioned better than almost 80% of the untreated children who served as control subjects in the studies, and these benefits of treatment appeared to be lasting. Moreover, undercontrolled or externalizing problems such as hyperactivity and aggression were just as responsive to treatment as overcontrolled disorders such as phobias and social withdrawal, suggesting that problems of undercontrol need not persist if they are effectively treated. Finally, behavioral therapies proved to be more effective than nonbehavioral therapies, even though these alternative forms of therapy have often proved to be equally effective in treating adults. Very possibly, this is because children *do* have limited cognitive capacities. Consequently they may have difficulty participating in "talk therapies" but can respond well to direct attempts to alter their behavior or teach them new skills.

A Success Story: Behavioral Treatment of Autism

There may be no more stunning example of the power of the behavioral approach to treating childhood disorders than the work of O. Ivar Lovaas and his colleagues with autistic children. As we saw earlier, autistic children have long been considered to be very difficult to treat and often have severe deficits throughout their lives. Lovaas (1987), who pioneered the use of behavioral treatment with autistic children, has recently described the status at age 6 to 7 of two groups of autistic children treated at UCLA. Nineteen children received intensive treatment—more than 40 hours of one-on-one treatment a week for two or more years during their preschool years. Trained student therapists worked with these children using reinforcement principles to reduce their aggressive and self-stimulatory behavior and to teach them developmentally appropriate skills such as how to imitate others, play with toys and with peers, use language, and master academic concepts. Moreover, parents were taught to use the same behavioral techniques at home, and these children were mainstreamed into preschools serving normal children. The children who received this intensive treatment were compared with similarly disturbed children who, because of staff shortages or transportation problems, received a similar treatment program but were exposed to it for 10 hours or less a week.

The intensively trained group and the less intensively trained group were similar in almost all ways before they began the program. In the intensively trained group, for example, all but two children scored in the mentally retarded range on tests of intellectual functioning; none engaged in pretend play; and most were mute. How different these children were at age 6 to 7! Their IQ scores averaged 83—about 30 points higher than the average in the control group. Indeed, 9 of the 19 (47%) not only obtained average or above average IQ scores at follow-up but had successfully mastered the regular first-grade curriculum. Eight others were making good progress in classes for children with language disorders, and only two were in classes for autistic/retarded children. Lovaas informally reports that these educational benefits of early intensive training have lasted, so that the children who were able to make it in regular classrooms as first graders have continued to function well in regular classrooms. In contrast, none of the children in the comparison group had achieved both an average IQ score and success in a regular first-grade classroom. Instead, these children displayed the usual intellectual deficits of autistic children, and most attended special classes for autistic and retarded children.

These are truly remarkable and very encouraging findings. They suggest that many autistic children may have an as yet unrecognized potential to develop normally, both intellectually and socially. However, it appears that autistic children are apt to realize their potential only if society is willing to invest in carefully planned, round-the-clock behavioral training for them starting early in life. As Lovaas argues, the cost of a full-time special education teacher for two years during the preschool period is quite trivial compared with the costs of institutionalizing a severely handicapped autistic individual for a lifetime.

Treating Elderly Adults

Just as treating children appropriately is challenging, so is meeting the needs of elderly people with psychological problems. Perhaps the greatest problem is that elderly individuals are less likely than younger adults to seek and obtain psychological treatment (Belsky, 1990; Gatz, Popkin, Pino, & VandenBos, 1985; Lasoski & Thelen, 1987). For example, it is estimated that fewer than one out of four depressed elderly people receive treatment (Klerman, 1983). Possibly these data reflect characteristics of today's elderly generation. For example, they grew up in a time when a social norm of self-reliance was stronger than it is today and when there was less concern about or knowledge of psychological problems and ways of treating them (Gatz et al., 1985; Lasoski & Thelen, 1987). But another barrier may be *ageism* in the mental health care system: negative attitudes among mental health professionals that cause them to prefer working with younger people, to perceive elderly individuals as untreatable, or to misdiagnose their problems (Gatz & Pearson, 1988; Gatz et al., 1985).

What happens when elderly adults do seek treatment? Are they too old to change their ways, or can they benefit from psychotherapy? Research indicates that elderly adults are every bit as responsive to a wide range of psychotherapies as younger adults are (Gatz et al., 1985; Thompson, Gallagher, & Breckenridge, 1987). These findings underscore the importance of encouraging elderly people with psychological problems to seek treatment and should help to convince mental health professionals that working with these individuals can be rewarding. In Box 16.4, we provide an example of how even a very brief and simple intervention can dramatically improve the mental and physical well-being of elderly adults in nursing homes. Such demonstrations carry a larger message: Just as human beings can fall prey to psychological problems at any point in the life span, they have an impressive capacity throughout the life span to overcome problems and to experience new growth.

Box 16.4
Helping Nursing Home Residents Toward a Sense of Control

Some years ago, Ellen Langer and Judith Rodin (1976) began to suspect that declines in physical health and psychological well-being among nursing home residents might not be entirely due to the ravages of age and illness. Instead, they argued that elderly adults placed in nursing homes may lose the feeling that they are in control of their lives and become passive and helpless in consequence. Their argument is supported by evidence that elderly adults often do suffer a loss of perceived control (Arling, Harkins, & Capitman, 1986) and even an increased risk of death when they are institutionalized (Pastalan, 1983).

Langer and Rodin decided to increase residents' sense of personal control in a Connecticut nursing home. The nursing home administrator gave different talks to the residents of two floors of the facility. An experimental group (residents of the fourth floor) heard a responsibility-inducing speech. The administrator said it was their responsibility to make their wishes known and to make decisions about how to live their lives. He also offered the residents plants, made it clear that it was their choice whether they wanted to take one and which one they wanted, and emphasized that the plants were theirs to care for as they would like. Finally, these residents were given a choice about whether and when to see a movie. Residents living on the second floor served as the control group and re-

ceived the message that the *staff* was responsible for their well-being and would do everything possible to see to their needs. They were given a plant and were told that the nurses would care for it and that they would be scheduled to see a movie on a particular night.

How much difference did it make whether residents were led to believe that responsibility for their lives lay with them or with their caretakers? After three weeks, 93% of the experimental group members were rated as improved by nurses unfamiliar with the experimental manipulation. Judging from the nurses' ratings and the residents' own responses, these residents felt happier, were more mentally alert, and were more involved in activities than control residents, 71% of whom were judged to have deteriorated during the study period.

Even more impressive were the results of a follow-up study conducted 18 months later (Rodin & Langer, 1977). The responsibility-induced group was still at an advantage compared to the staff-reliant group, for they were rated more sociable, active, interested in their environment, and self-initiating. They were also judged by a physician to be enjoying better health than they had before the study began. Most notably, 30% of the control group members had died in the 18-month period following the experiment, compared with only half as many (15%) of the responsibility group.

It seems hard to believe that a brief speech, a plant to care for, and the opportunity to choose to see a movie could have so many beneficial effects on physical health and psychological well-being. Rodin and Langer believe that their treatment fostered a generalized sense of control that made residents feel competent to make any number of day-to-day decisions. Studies like this one suggest that human beings, including elderly ones, are far better able to cope with life's strains when they believe that they are in command of their own life course than when they feel pushed and pulled by external forces.

REFLECTIONS

Analogies are always dangerous, but likening life to a hurdles race seems a good way to put abnormal human development in perspective. The "hurdles" we must jump are the normal developmental tasks of each period of the life span, plus any stressful events that come our way. What is expected of us is fairly clear: We must move along at a good pace, stay on the right course, and avoid stumbling as we cross each hurdle.

Why do some of us set Olympic records while others of us cannot even finish the race? The hurdler's success in the race depends on both native endowment and environment (proper nutrition, good training, favorable track conditions, and so on). Similarly, our success in adapting to life's challenges depends on both nature and nurture—

on whether we are genetically hardy or genetically predisposed to develop problems and on whether we are nurtured by a supportive social environment or damaged by a destructive one. As we have seen throughout this book, it is naive to assume that either nature or nurture is solely responsible when development proceeds well or poorly; instead, it is the ongoing interaction between heredity and environment that is significant. So, for example, children and adults who are for whatever reasons vulnerable to depression may or may not become depressed depending on the number and height of the hurdles placed in their path. Notice that the race that developing persons run is a bit odd as hurdles races go: It's not entirely fair, since some of us have more to hurdle than others do, and have a greater chance of falling as a result.

There's another interesting difference between life and a hurdles event, this time a more heartening one: It seems that we can, in the course of living our lives, stumble over a hurdle or two and still win the race in the end. True, a few of us may be destined to falter fairly consistently, and others of us breeze all the way through. That is, there is some continuity in an individual's ability to adapt over the life span. However, discontinuity in adaptation over the life span is even more striking. Many of us, it seems, succumb to the challenges of one developmental period or another and yet go on to adapt successfully to later challenges, especially with social support and professional help. Indeed, some of us even *grow* as a result of our experiences with stressful events. If we take this message seriously, we quickly realize that children and adults with psychological disorders are not all that different from their more "normal" peers. Pick the right moment in the race, and almost any of us might be caught in the act of stumbling. ❦

SUMMARY POINTS

1. To study developmental psychopathology and diagnose many psychological disorders, psychologists and psychiatrists consider the broad criteria of statistical deviance, maladaptiveness, and personal distress and judge behavior in light of social norms and age norms. The *Diagnostic and Statistical Manual of Mental Disorders (DSM-III-R)* spells out specific diagnostic criteria for a wide range of psychological disorders.

2. Infantile autism, which begins before the age of 30 months, is characterized by deviant social responses, language and communication deficits, and repetitive behavior. Genetic endowment and prenatal or perinatal hazards contribute to it, and many victims remain impaired in later life.

3. Some infants who have been emotionally starved or separated from attachment figures—infants suffering from anaclitic depression or failure to thrive and children whose parents are depressed—display many depression-like symptoms, if not true clinical depression.

4. Children with attention-deficit hyperactivity disorder, an undercontrolled (externalizing) disorder, display inattention, impulsivity, and hyperactivity; they can be helped through a combination of stimulant drugs and behavioral training but often do not entirely outgrow their problems.

5. Depression, an overcontrolled (internalizing) childhood disorder, manifests itself differently at different ages, tends to recur, and can be treated with antidepressant drugs and psychotherapy.

6. It is too simple to view "bad" parenting as the cause of all childhood problems; heredity may also contribute, and children's problems can be partly the cause as well as the effect of disturbed parent/child relationships. Fortunately, most childhood problems, especially problems of overcontrol, are only temporary.

7. Contrary to the "storm and stress" view, adolescents are really not much more vulnerable to psychological disorders than children or adults are. Anorexia nervosa and bulimia, both serious eating disorders, seem to arise when a vulnerable adolescent, typically a girl, is raised in an enmeshed family and in a society that strongly encourages dieting. Minor delinquent behavior and experimentation with drugs are statistically normal during adolescence, but youth who develop more serious problem behaviors often have unconventional values, perceive their peers as encouraging deviance and their parents as unsupportive, and display multiple problems.

8. Risks of depression and suicide also rise during adolescence; depressed adolescents resemble both depressed adults and depressed children, and adolescents are more likely to attempt but less likely to commit suicide than adults are.

9. Stressful daily hassles are more likely to cause psychological problems than major life events, even nonnormative ones, are. Young adults experience more such life strains than older adults do but have no greater coping capacities, and therefore are more vulnerable to many psychological disorders.

10. Depression, which tends to be most common in early adulthood and among women, results, according to a diathesis/stress model, when a vulnerable individual who lacks positive coping resources experiences multiple stresses without adequate social support.

11. The most common forms of dementia, a progressive loss of cognitive capacities affecting about 5% of the elderly population, are Alzheimer's disease and multi-infarct dementia. These irreversible dementias must be carefully distinguished from cor-

rectable conditions such as reversible dementias, delirium, and depression.

12. Treating children and adolescents with psychological problems is especially challenging but often effective; O. Ivar Lovaas has had dramatic success applying intensive behavioral techniques to autistic children. Elderly adults with psychological disorders also pose special challenges but can benefit just as much from psychotherapy as younger adults can.

KEY TERMS

active-behavioral coping strategies
age norm
Alzheimer's disease
anaclitic depression
anorexia nervosa
attention-deficit hyperactivity disorder
avoidance coping strategies
bulimia nervosa
daily hassles
delirium
dementia
developmental psychopathology
diathesis/stress model
echolalia
failure to thrive
infantile autism
juvenile delinquency
learned helplessness
major depression
masked depression
multi-infarct dementia
overcontrolled disorders
social norm
status offense
stress
undercontrolled disorders

CHAPTER

17

THE FINAL CHALLENGE: DEATH AND DYING

Jessica was five. She showed her mother the picture she had painted. There were black clouds, dark trees, and large red splashes.

"My," said her mother. "Tell me all about this, Jess." Jessica pointed to the red splashes. "That's blood," she said. "And these are clouds." "Oh," said her mother. "See," said Jessica, "the trees are very sad. The clouds are black. They are sad too." "Why are they sad?" asked her mother. "They are sad because their Daddy has died," said Jessica, the tears slowly running down her cheeks. "Sad like us since Daddy died," said her mother and held her closely, and they wept [Raphael, 1983, p. 138].

Death hurts. One can be 5, 35, or 85 when death strikes a loved one, and still it hurts. By adulthood, most of us have experienced a significant loss, even if it was "only" the death of a beloved pet. Even when death is not striking so closely, it is there lurking somewhere in the background as we go about the tasks of living—in the newspaper, on television, or flitting ever so quickly through our minds. And sooner or later, we all face the ultimate developmental task: the task of dying.

Our task in this chapter is to understand death and its place in life-span human development. The chapter begins by examining the basic facts of death—what it is and what causes it. Then it offers some broad perspectives on the psychological experiences of dying and of losing a loved one to death. Next it puts death and dying in the context of life-span development, asking what death means and how it is experienced during infancy, childhood, adolescence, and adulthood. We will also try to understand why some individuals cope far more successfully with death than others do. We will discover that death is part of the human experience throughout the life span, but that each person's experience of it depends on his or her level of development, personality, and life circumstances. Finally, we'll close the chapter on a practical note, seeing what can be done to help dying and bereaved individuals through their ordeals.

LIFE AND DEATH ISSUES

What is death, really? When are we most vulnerable to it, and what kills us? And why is it that all of us eventually die of "old age" if we do not die earlier? These "life and death" questions serve to introduce the topic of death and dying.

What Is Death?

As you have probably noticed, there is a good deal of confusion in our society today about when life begins and when it ends. Proponents and opponents of legalized abortion argue vehemently about when life really begins. And we hear similarly heated debates about whether a person who lapses into an irreversible coma is truly alive or whether a terminally ill patient who is in agonizing pain should be kept alive with the help of life support machines or allowed to die naturally.

It used to be easy enough to tell that someone was dead: There was no breathing, no heartbeat, no sign of responsiveness. These criteria of biological death are still useful today. However, technological breakthroughs have forced the medical community to rethink what it means to say that someone is dead. The problem is that biological death is not a single event but a *process*. That is, different systems of the body die at different rates. Some individuals who have stopped breathing and who lack a heartbeat or pulse can now be revived before their brains cease to func-

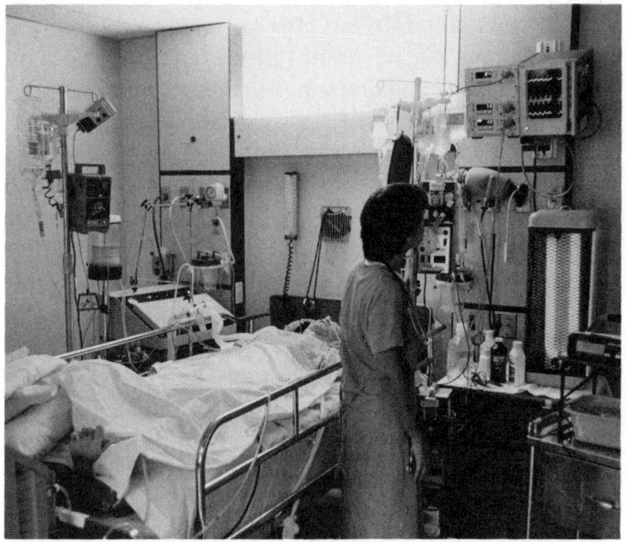

Life-support technologies can keep coma victims alive for years, but many people wonder whether it might not be better to let such patients die naturally.

tion. Moreover, basic bodily processes such as respiration and blood circulation can be maintained by life support machines in patients who have fallen into a coma and whose brains have ceased to function. Is the person whose brain cannot control breathing but who breathes with the aid of a "respirator" (actually a mechanical ventilator) alive or dead?

In 1968, an ad hoc committee of the Harvard Medical School offered a definition of death that it hoped would resolve the then new controversies about when a person is dead—a definition that has indeed gained widespread acceptance. This group defined biological death as **total brain death**: an irreversible loss of functioning in the entire brain, both the higher centers of the cerebral cortex that are involved in thought and the lower centers of the brain that control basic life processes such as breathing. Specifically, to be judged dead a person must:

1. Be totally unresponsive to stimuli, including painful ones
2. Fail to move for one hour and fail to breathe for three minutes after being removed from a ventilator
3. Have no reflexes (for example, no eye blink and no constriction of the eye's pupil in response to light)
4. Register a flat electroencephalogram (EEG), indicating an absence of electrical activity in the cortex of the brain

As an additional precaution, the testing procedure is repeated 24 hours later. Moreover, since coma is sometimes reversible if the cause is either an overdose of drugs or hypothermia (a body temperature below 90 degrees Farenheit), these conditions must be ruled out before a coma victim is ruled dead.

Now consider some of the life and death issues that have revolved around alternative definitions of biological death. A well-known controversy centered on Karen Ann Quinlan, a young woman who lapsed into a coma at a party in 1975, probably because of the combination of alcohol and tranquilizers that she had consumed (see Kastenbaum, 1986). Ms. Quinlan was totally unconscious, but her bodily functioning was maintained with the aid of a ventilator and other life support systems. After she had lain wasting away in a fetal position for weeks, her parents finally wanted to end her suffering and asked that the devices be turned off. The doctors declined to do this, the case went to court, and the court finally ruled that the respirator could be turned off. Much to everyone's surprise, Ms. Quinlan continued to breathe even without the mechanical assistance. She lived on in a vegetative state, lacking all consciousness and eating through a tube, until she died in 1985.

This famous case highlights at least three quite different positions that we might take on the issue of when a person is dead. First, there is the position laid out in the Harvard definition of total brain death. By this criterion, because the lower portions of Ms. Quinlan's brain were still functioning enough to support breathing, she was not dead either before or after her respirator was removed. But there are other points of view. Some experts think that the Harvard definition is too strict; instead, a person should be declared dead when the cerebral cortex is irreversibly dead, even if bodily functioning is still maintained by the more primitive portions of the brain. After all, is a person really a person if he or she lacks any awareness and if there is no hope that conscious mental activity will be restored? Still other experts would argue that even if a person's brain is totally dead, he or she should not be declared dead until even the best that medical technology has to offer fails to maintain basic bodily processes. After all, what if we discovered how to revive or cure seemingly hopeless patients?

So there is still plenty of room for debate about when death has occurred. The Harvard total brain death definition takes a middle ground between a very strict definition of death in which one is not dead until there is no functioning even with the aid of machines and a more liberal definition in which only the cortex of the brain, rather than the entire brain, must cease to function for the individual to be deemed dead. A very strict definition means a prolonged and difficult death for hopeless coma victims—at great expense to society and at great emotional cost to the families involved. But using a more liberal definition of death means that a mistake might occasionally be made; a seemingly irreversible loss of consciousness might turn out to be reversible.

The Quinlan case also focuses attention on the controversy surrounding **euthanasia**—a term meaning "happy" or "good" death that usually refers to hastening the death of someone who is suffering from an incurable illness or injury. Actually there are two very different forms of euthanasia. *Active euthanasia*, or "mercy killing," is deliberately causing a person's death—for example, by administering a lethal dose of drugs to a pain-wracked patient in the late stages of a terminal illness. *Passive euthanasia*, by contrast, means allowing a person to die—for example, by withholding life-saving treatments from an individual who is clearly expected to die. In the Quinlan case, the court actually endorsed a form of passive euthanasia when it agreed that Ms. Quinlan could be removed from the respirator, knowing that she was likely to die without this artificial life support.

There is overwhelming support among medical personnel and members of the general public for passive euthanasia (Carey & Posavac, 1978–1979). As a result, many states haved passed laws making it legal to withhold life-saving treatments from terminally ill patients and to "pull the plug" on life support equipment when that is the wish of the dying person or the immediate family (Aiken, 1985). The "right to die" or "death with dignity" movement has lobbied for such laws. You may be familiar with another product of this movement, the **Living Will**, a document in which a person states in advance that he or she does not wish to have extraordinary medical procedures applied if he or she is hopelessly ill (see Figure 17.1).

Although passive euthanasia with proper legal safeguards is widely accepted now, active euthanasia is still widely condemned. In fact, the law views it as murder. Right-to-die advocates believe that the law should be changed so that an incurable patient who is suffering from excruciating pain can ask for assistance in committing suicide and receive it. Right-to-life advocates often argue the opposite side of the euthanasia issue, claiming that everything possible should be done to maintain life and that nothing should be done to cut it short.

Life and death decisions such as these are not easy ones. They are particularly agonizing for people like the Quinlans who must confront them personally. Our society will continue to grapple with defining life and death and deciding what forms of euthanasia are or are not morally and legally acceptable, and will undoubtedly find that new issues arise as new medical technologies are introduced.

So far, we have looked at death from a purely biological perspective. However, death is more than a biological process; it is a psychological and social process as well. The social meanings attached to death vary immensely from historical era to historical era and from culture to culture. Indeed, what we have just discovered is that *society* defines who is dead and who is alive! In Box 17.1, we look into the remarkably different ways in which different societies interpret and respond to death.

What Kills Us and When?

How long are we likely to live, when is death most likely to occur, and what are the leading causes of death? In the United States, the **life expectancy** at birth—the average number of years a newborn can be expected to live—is 75 years (U.S. Bureau of the Census, 1989). This *average* life expectancy disguises important differences between males and females and between racial and ethnic groups. The life expectancy for white males is almost 72, whereas the life expectancy for white females is almost 79. Women's female hormones seem to protect them from high blood pressure and heart problems; avoiding health hazards and performing less dangerous work may also help women live longer. Meanwhile, life expectancies for black Americans, who often encounter health hazards associated with poverty, are a good deal lower than those for white Americans: 65 for males, 74 for females.

Life expectancies have increased dramatically over the course of history. The average life expectancy in ancient Greece is believed to have been around 20 years (Lehr, 1982). In the United States in 1900, the life expectancy at

My Living Will
To My Family, My Physician, My Lawyer and All Others Whom It May Concern

Death is as much a reality as birth, growth, maturity and old age—it is the one certainty of life. If the time comes when I can no longer take part in decisions for my own future, let this statement stand as an expression of my wishes and directions, while I am still of sound mind.

If at such a time the situation should arise in which there is no reasonable expectation of my recovery from extreme physical or mental disability, I direct that I be allowed to die and not be kept alive by medications, artificial means or "heroic measures". I do, however, ask that medication be mercifully administered to me to alleviate suffering even though this may shorten my remaining life.

This statement is made after careful consideration and is in accordance with my strong convictions and beliefs. I want the wishes and directions here expressed carried out to the extent permitted by law. Insofar as they are not legally enforceable, I hope that those to whom this Will is addressed will regard themselves as morally bound by these provisions.

(Optional specific provisions to be made in this space)

DURABLE POWER OF ATTORNEY (optional)

I hereby designate ________________ to serve as my attorney-in-fact for the purpose of making medical treatment decisions. This power of attorney shall remain effective in the event that I become incompetent or otherwise unable to make such decisions for myself.

Optional Notarization:

"Sworn and subscribed to

before me this ________ day

of __________, 19______."

____

Notary Public
(seal)

Signed ______________________

Date ______________________

Witness ______________________

____
Address

Witness ______________________

____
Address

Copies of this request have been given to ______________________

______________________ ______________________

(Optional) My Living Will is registered with Concern for Dying (No. ________)

Figure 17.1 The Living Will. (Courtesy of Concern for Dying, 250 West 57th Street, New York, NY 10107)

Box 17.1
Death in a Social Context

All people everywhere die, and all people everywhere grieve in some fashion. Moreover, all societies have evolved some manner of reacting to this universal experience—of interpreting its meaning, disposing of corpses, and expressing grief. Beyond these universals, the similarities end.

As Phillippe Ariès (1981) has shown, the social meanings of death have changed over the course of history. During the Middle Ages, for example, people were expected to recognize that their deaths were approaching so that they could bid their farewells and die with dignity surrounded by loved ones. Survivors freely and publicly expressed their grief after the death. Since the late 19th century, Ariès argues, death has been denied and avoided in Western societies. We have taken death out of the home and put it in the hospital and funeral parlor; we have shifted responsibility for the care of the dying from family and friends to the "experts"—physicians and funeral directors. We have made death a medical failure rather than a natural part of the life cycle. And we have dispensed with many standard mourning rituals such as the wearing of armbands or black clothing and have frowned upon open expressions of grief.

Is this Western way of managing death changing? Ariès believes so. Indeed, in the past couple of decades, "right to die" and "death with dignity" advocates have argued forcefully that we should return to some of the old ways, bringing death out in the open rather than avoiding all mention of it, allowing it to occur more naturally, and making it once again an experience to be shared within the family.

If we look at how people in other cultures interpret and manage death, we quickly realize how many alternatives there are to our Western ways (Huntington & Metcalf, 1979; Leming & Dickinson, 1985). Some people remain solemn after a death; others wail; others partake in rowdy celebrations. Some mourn for months or years; some conclude their mourning rituals within hours. Corpses are treated in a remarkable number of ways: They "are burned or buried, with or without animal or human sacrifice; they are preserved by smoking, embalming, or pickling; they are eaten—raw, cooked, or rotten; they are ritually exposed as carrion or simply abandoned; or they are dismembered and treated in a variety of these ways" (Huntington & Metcalf, 1979, p. 1). In most societies, there is some concept of spiritual immortality, yet here, too, there is much variety, from concepts of heaven and hell to the idea of reincarnation to the belief in ancestral ghosts (Leming & Dickinson, 1985).

In short, the experiences of dying individuals and of the survivors of a death are very much shaped by the historical and cultural context in which they occur. Death may be universal, but our experiences of death and dying are not. Moreover, within any society, there are subcultural and individual differences in the meanings people attach to death and the ways in which they deal with it. Death is truly what we humans make of it.

birth was only 47 years (Yin & Shine, 1985), not much different than the current life expectancy in some underdeveloped countries (Lehr, 1982). However, this does not mean that most people at the turn of the century died in their 40s. Instead, many more individuals in the past did not survive infancy and early childhood, and these early deaths pulled the average life expectancy down. Figure 17.2 shows the number of deaths per 1000 individuals in each age group in two years, 1900 and 1986. As you can see, infants were highly vulnerable beings in 1900; they were even more vulnerable in previous centuries. Difficulties surrounding birth and a host of infectious diseases such as measles and scarlet fever that are now under control used to make infancy and early childhood treacherous. Infants continue to be somewhat vulnerable, but by the mid-1980s infant mortality had fallen to about 10 out of 1000 live births (U.S. Bureau of the Census, 1989). Assuming that we survive infancy, we have little chance of dying during childhood, adolescence, and early adulthood. Death rates then climb steadily during middle age and old age.

In short, the main reason that the average life expectancy has increased dramatically in this century is that fewer people are dying very young. However, adults are also living longer than adults of the past did (Manton, 1986). They generally enjoy better health, and when they develop problems, they can be kept going with the aid of heart surgery, cancer treatments, kidney dialysis, and

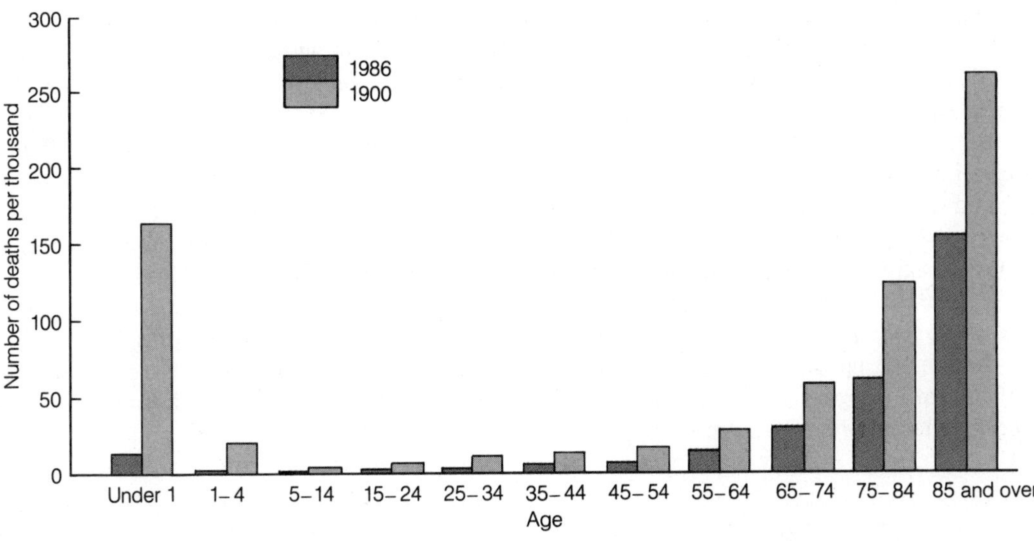

Figure 17.2 Rates of death by age group in 1900 and 1986. (Data from U.S. Bureau of the Census, 1975; National Center for Health Statistics, 1988)

other medical advances. Perhaps what is most intriguing about these changes in life expectancies is that we, more than people of the past, have come to associate death almost exclusively with old age (Kastenbaum, 1985). One can only wonder what it might have been like to live in the Middle Ages, when one-third to two-thirds of newborns never made it past infancy and when major infectious diseases such as the bubonic plague wiped out whole villages (Borstelmann, 1983). Perhaps we have the luxury of taking death lightly until we reach old age. Perhaps we stigmatize elderly people partly because they remind us of our own mortality (Kastenbaum, 1985).

What kills us? Information collected by the National Center for Health Statistics (1988) indicates that the leading causes of death change dramatically over the life span. Infant deaths are mainly associated with problems originating in the period surrounding birth or with congenital abnormalities that infants bring with them to life. The leading cause of death among children is accidents (especially car accidents but also poisonings, falls, fires, drownings, and so on). A few children also die from cancer and a wide range of acute diseases. Adolescence and early adulthood appear to be periods of good health but vulnerability to violent deaths. Accidents (especially car accidents), homicides, and suicides are the leading killers. Starting in the 35–44 age group, chronic diseases—notably diseases of the heart and cardiovascular system and cancers or tumors—begin to appear at the top of our perverse "hit parade" of leading killers. The incidence of these chronic conditions climbs steadily with age, raising overall death rates considerably. Among adults over the age of 55, heart diseases, cancers, and cerebrovascular diseases (strokes and related conditions)—in that order—are the top three killers. Among individuals age 65 to 74, for example, 37% of deaths are attributed to heart disease, 30% to cancer, and 6% to cerebrovascular diseases (National Center for Health Statistics, 1988).

In sum, the life expectancy is higher than it has ever been, primarily because fewer people are dying young but also because those people who do not die young are living longer. After we make it through the vulnerable period of infancy, we are at low risk of death through early adulthood and are most likely to die suddenly because of an accident if we do die. As we age, we become more and more vulnerable to death—particularly to death caused by chronic diseases. This is useful information so far as it goes, but it does not answer a more fundamental question: Why is it that all of us eventually die? Why is it that chronic killer diseases become more and more common with age? Why does no one live to be 150 or 200? To understand why death is an inevitable part of human development, we need the help of theories of aging.

Theories of Aging: But Why Do We Age and Die?

There is no simple answer to the question of why we ultimately age and die. However, several promising theories have been proposed, and each of them says something important about the aging process. In his survey of theories of aging and efforts to increase longevity, Roy Walford (1983) divided these theories into two main categories: **programmed theories of aging** that emphasize the systematic genetic control of aging processes, and **damage theories of aging** that emphasize the more haphazard processes that cause cells and organ systems to deteriorate.

Programmed Theories of Aging

Human beings, like other species, have a characteristic **maximum life span** — a ceiling on the number of years that anyone lives. For a time, it was believed that so-called "long-lived people" in the village of Vilcabamba in Ecuador and in areas of the Soviet Union lived to such incredible ages as 165 or even 195. Now we know that these life spans are indeed incredible: They reflect the tendency of people who value long life greatly to exaggerate their ages (Bennett & Garson, 1986; Mazess & Forman, 1979). (It's odd that adults in our society more often do the reverse, claiming to be age 39 eternally!) Although there may well be someone by now who has lived slightly longer, Fanny Thomas, a Californian, was verified to be 113 years (and 215 days) old when she died in 1980 (Walford, 1983). She attributed her long life to eating applesauce three times a day and never marrying. The few individuals who live as long as Ms. Thomas are the basis for setting the maximum human life span at 110–120. Interestingly, this maximum has not changed much over the centuries, even though the average life expectancy has been increasing dramatically.

We are long-lived compared to most species. The maximum life span for the mouse is 3½ years, for the dog 20, for the chimpanzee 50, and for the long-lived Galapagos tortoise 150 (Walford, 1983). The very fact that each species has its own characteristic maximum life span should convince us that species-wide genes have something to do with controlling how long individuals live. Moreover, we know that an individual's hereditary endowment influences his or her susceptibility to many killer diseases, and we know that some genetic conditions such as *progeria* speed up certain aging processes and result in premature death (these genetic aspects of aging were discussed in Chapter 3).

So we have good reason to believe that aging and death are genetically controlled. But how, exactly, do genes control aging? This is what is not yet known. Possibly there is an overall genetic program for development that is responsible for timing both maturational changes and aging. If genes can "turn on" or "turn off" to bring about maturational changes during infancy, or at puberty and menopause, why couldn't genes bring about aging and death in the same way? Alternatively, a genetic program that promotes longevity could eventually just run out (McClearn & Foch, 1985).

A programmed theory of aging that highlights changes within individual cells has been offered by Leonard Hayflick (1976). Hayflick grew cells in cultures, allowed them to divide or double, and measured the number of doublings that occurred. He discovered that cells from human embryos could double only a certain number of times — 50 times, plus or minus 10, to be exact — an estimate now referred to as the **Hayflick limit**. Hayflick also demonstrated that cells taken from human adults divide fewer times than this, presumably because they have already used up some of their capacity for reproducing themselves. Moreover, the maximum life span of a species is related to the number of cell divisions characteristic of that species: The short-lived mouse's cells can go through only 14 to 28 doublings; the very long-lived Galapagos tortoise's cells can manage 90 to 125. Presumably, cells that are approaching or have exceeded their limit cease to function effectively, die, and ultimately cause the organism to die. In Hayflick's (1976) words, "cells may be programmed simply to run out of program" (p. 1308).

It is not yet certain that Hayflick's limit applies to cells in living organisms in the same way it applies to cells grown in cultures, or that it applies to all kinds of cells, or that we actually run out of viable cells at a very old age (Hart & Turturro, 1983). Still, there is indeed a kind of genetic "aging clock" operating within individual body cells, and researchers are working hard to understand it better (Cristofalo, 1985).

Another programmed theory of aging implicates the neuroendocrine system, the complex control system consisting of the brain and the endocrine glands. According to an **endocrine theory** of aging, the genes program hormonal changes that bring about death. Consider Pacific salmon. Shortly after they swim back upstream to their place of birth and spawn, the endocrine glands of these fish release a massive dose of hormones that causes them to die (Walford, 1983). Could something similar happen to humans? We know that the hypothalamus of the brain, guided by a genetic program, sets in motion the hormonal changes responsible for puberty and menopause (see Chapter 5). Possibly the hypothalamus also serves as an aging clock, systematically altering levels of hormones and brain chemicals in later life so that bodily functioning is no longer regulated properly and we ultimately die (Finch, 1976). Possibly there are aging clocks in both the hypothalamus *and* the individual cells (Rosenfeld, 1985).

Finally, still another programmed theory of aging, the **immune system theory**, focuses on age-related changes in the body's ability to defend itself against potentially life-threatening foreign agents such as infections. The immune system, whose functioning is genetically controlled, clearly functions less effectively as we age. Two major changes are evident. First, the aging immune system becomes less able to detect and fight off foreign "invaders" that can damage the body. Thus, an older body is less able than a younger body to mobilize the body's immune defenses against cancer cells, infectious agents, or donated organs (Walford, 1983). Second, the immune system increasingly mistakes normal cells for enemies through what are called **autoimmune reactions**. That is, the immune system actually produces antibodies to attack and kill normal body cells, as illustrated by autoimmune diseases such as rheumatoid arthritis. These age-related changes in immune system functioning do seem to be genetically controlled. For example, hereditary differences among strains of mice in the genes that control the immune system are systematically linked to differences in the longevity of these strains (Smith & Walford, 1977). Thus immune system theory, like the Hayflick limit hypothesis and the endocrine theory, hold that aging and dying are the inevitable result of our biological endowment as human beings.

Damage Theories of Aging

Damage theories of aging generally propose that an accumulation of damage to cells and organs over the years ultimately causes death. Aging and death may not be written in the genetic code from conception on; rather, we are the victims of random destructive processes or errors that accumulate while we live. One early explanation of aging was a "wear-and-tear" theory proposing that organs simply wear out through use, much as shoes do. We now know that this view is naive. Indeed, using the body (as in regular aerobic exercise) often *improves* functioning rather than damaging it. Nonetheless, more modern versions of the wear-and-tear theory seem to have merit.

According to a **DNA repair theory** of aging, the genetic material DNA is damaged over the years as the cells metabolize nutrients and are increasingly exposed to environmental agents such as pesticides, pollution, and radiation. Cells are equipped to cope with these insults by repairing defective segments of DNA. However, it appears that long-lived species have a greater capacity for repairing DNA than shorter-lived species, and that the cells of younger individuals repair damaged DNA faster than those of older individuals do (Hart & Setlow, 1974; Walford, 1983). Over time, then, the basic genetic material of more and more cells becomes damaged, and the mechanisms for repairing such damage simply cannot keep up with the chaos. More and more cells would then function improperly or cease to function, and the organism would eventually die.

A second damage theory of aging is the **cross-linkage theory**. It has been observed that, as we age, molecules of the protein collagen, the major connective tissue between cells, become interlinked or coupled. As this cross-linkage of collagen molecules proceeds, the visible result is leathery, wrinkled skin that is not as pliable as the skin of a younger person. Stiff joints and arteriosclerosis (so-called "hardening of the arteries") are also due to cross-linkage. It is possible that this increasing cross-linkage of collagen and other connective tissues interferes with cell functioning. It is even possible that DNA molecules become cross-linked and that the genetic instructions that guide normal cell functioning become scrambled as a result (Walford, 1983).

Finally, a third damage theory of aging centers on the destructive effects of **free radicals**, molecules that have an extra or "free" electron, that are chemically unstable, and that react with other molecules in the body to produce substances that damage normal cells (Harman, 1981). "Age spots" on the skin of older people are one effect of free radicals (Hart & Turturro, 1983). We cannot live and breathe without producing these molecules, for they are a

Box 17.2
Searching for the Fountain of Youth

Throughout the ages, human beings have searched for the fountain of youth, the secret to a longer and healthier life. The Spanish explorer Ponce de León literally searched for a fountain of youth in Florida, as do countless retirees these days. Others, guided by the mistaken theory that decreases in levels of sex hormones were responsible for aging, transplanted ape testicles into old men in an effort to prolong their lives (Walford, 1983). The most effective way to lengthen life would be to discover the basic genetic mechanisms behind aging and then intervene to alter the genetic code. Then the maximum human life span might actually be raised. Lacking this knowledge, about the best we can do is to help people avoid dying young so that they can come closer to achieving the present maximum life span.

How, then, can one live a longer life? We cannot do anything about the genetic endowments we inherit at conception. Some individuals, by virtue of their genetic makeup, are more susceptible to killer diseases than others are. What we can control are aspects of our lifestyles. In particular, we can exert some control over the aging process by changing our diets, exercising, and avoiding known health risks.

At this point, the intervention that has most clearly been shown in laboratory studies to increase average longevity—and even the maximum life span—is dietary restriction (Masoro, 1988; Schneider & Reed, 1985; Walford, 1983). Specifically, rats placed on diets in which they receive severely restricted amounts of very nourishing food live longer on average and achieve greater maximum ages than rats who are free to eat as much as they choose. Moreover, rats who are placed on a restricted diet as adults seem to derive as much benefit as those who start the diet when they are very young (Yu, Masoro, & McMahan, 1985). Roy Walford (1983) emphasizes that a severely restricted diet must be adopted gradually over a number of years and that it must be exceptionally high in nutritional value. Walford follows such a diet himself, finding it easiest to fast two days a week and eat a very healthy daily diet of about 2100 calories on the remaining five days.

At this point, however, it has not yet been demonstrated conclusively that severe calorie restriction will actually extend the lives of humans as successfully as it has extended the lives of rats. Nor is it clear exactly what calorie counts and what combinations of nutrients are optimal (Schneider & Reed, 1985). Simply going on a starvation diet without knowing what one is doing is a good way to shorten one's life, so beware! Most current evidence suggests that people whose weight is moderate live longer than individuals who are either seriously overweight or seriously underweight (Kaplan et al., 1987). We can at least be confident that proper nutrition contributes to a long life.

Walford and others also believe that taking "antioxidants" such as vitamin E and selenium can lengthen life, for these substances neutralize potentially destructive free radicals. However, research here is mixed (Schneider & Reed, 1985). Besides, taking megadoses of vitamins, including vitamin E, can be dangerous (Schneider & Reed, 1985), and selenium is a poison.

How about regular exercise? As we saw in Chapter 5, regular aerobic exercise can improve the functioning of the cardiovascular system, possibly postpone the onset of heart disease, and contribute to psychological well-being. It is not as clear that exercise can slow all aging processes or extend life beyond its normal maximum (Schneider & Reed, 1985). Finally, we can extend our lives by avoiding known health risks (Cavanaugh, 1990; Walford, 1983). We can stop smoking, drink only in moderation, try our best to avoid life-threatening pollutants or toxins, and either reduce the stresses in our lives or learn to cope with stress more effectively, perhaps with the help of a strong support network. We need not wait until the mysteries of aging are unraveled before doing what we can to avoid dying young.

by-product of the metabolism of oxygen (Walford, 1983). The cells of the body routinely produce enzymes that defend against free radicals, but as in the case of DNA repair, there may come a time when the body's resources for fighting accumulating damage are no longer up to the task.

These, then, are some of the most promising explanations of why we age and die. The programmed theories of aging generally claim that aging and dying are as much a part of nature's plan as sprouting teeth or uttering one's first words. The Hayflick limit on cell reproduction, changes in endocrine functioning, and declines in the effectiveness of the immune system are believed to be genetically controlled. The damage theories suggest that we eventually succumb to haphazard destructive processes—increasingly faulty DNA that cannot be repaired, cross-linkage of the body's molecules, and an accumulation of free radicals. None of these specific theories of aging has proved to be *the* explanation (Shock, 1977). It is more likely that several of these mechanisms of aging ultimately make death inevitable, though some of them may prove to be more basic than others. For example, particular clusters of genes may well control many aging processes, *including* a decline in the ability of the body to keep accumulating damage under control (Walford, 1983).

Genetic researchers are making remarkable progress. It is not at all unthinkable that they might soon unlock the secrets of aging and dying. In the meantime, if we as individuals change our habits, we can reduce our chances of dying young. Box 17.2 describes what the never-ending search for the fountain of youth has yielded: ways to live longer. But none of this changes the fact that we will all die at some time, and so it is time we turned to the question of how humans cope with death and dying.

WHAT IS IT LIKE TO BE DYING?

People who die suddenly may well be blessed, for those who develop life-threatening illnesses face the challenge of coping with the knowledge that they are seriously ill and are likely to die. Perhaps no one has done more to focus attention on the emotional needs of dying patients than psychiatrist Elisabeth Kübler-Ross (1969, 1974), whose "stages of dying" are widely known.

Kübler-Ross's Stages of Dying

In interviews with over 200 terminally ill patients, Kübler-Ross (1969) detected a common sequence of emotional responses to the knowledge that one has a serious, and probably fatal, illness. She believed that similar reactions might occur in response to any major loss, so bear in mind that the family and friends of the dying person might experience some of these same emotional reactions during the illness of a loved one and after the death. Kübler-Ross's five stages of dying are as follows:

1. *Denial and isolation.* A common first response to dreadful news is to say, "No! It can't be!" **Denial** is a defense mechanism in which anxiety-provoking thoughts are kept out of, or "isolated" from, conscious awareness. A woman who has just been diagnosed as having lung cancer may insist that the diagnosis is wrong—or accept that she is ill but be convinced that she will beat the odds and recover. Denial can be a marvelous coping device: It can get us through a time of acute crisis until we are ready to cope more constructively. Even after dying patients face the facts and become ready to talk about dying, those around them often engage in their own denial, saying such things as, "Don't be silly; you'll be well in no time."
2. *Anger.* As the bad news begins to register, the dying person asks, "Why me?" Feelings of rage or resentment may be directed at anyone who is handy—doctors, nurses, or family members. Kübler-Ross advises those close to the dying person to be sensitive to this stage so that they do not avoid this irritable person or take the anger personally (unless, of course, it is deserved).
3. *Bargaining.* When the dying person bargains, he or she says, "Okay—me, but please . . ." The bargainer asks for some concession from God, the medical staff, or someone else. A woman with lung cancer may beg for a cure—or perhaps simply for a little more time, a little less pain, or a chance to ensure that her children will be taken care of after she dies.
4. *Depression.* When the dying person becomes even more aware of the reality of the situation, depression, despair, and a sense of hopelessness become the predominant emotional responses. Grief focuses on the losses that have already occurred (for example, the loss of the ability to function as one once did) and the losses to come (separation from loved ones, the inability to achieve one's dreams, and so on).
5. *Acceptance.* Assuming that the dying person is able to work through all the complex emotional reactions of the preceding stages, he or she may come to accept the inevitability of death in a calm and peaceful manner. Kübler-Ross (1969) describes the acceptance stage this way: "It is almost void of feelings. It is as if the pain had gone, the struggle is over, and there comes a time for 'the final rest before the long journey,' as one patient phrased it" (p. 100).

In addition to these five "stages of dying," Kübler-Ross emphasizes a sixth response that runs throughout the stages: *Hope.* She believes that it is essential for terminally ill patients to retain some sense of hope, even if it is only the hope that they can die with dignity.

Other Perspectives on the Process of Dying

Kübler-Ross deserves immense credit for sensitizing our society to the emotional needs of dying persons and convincing medical professionals to emphasize *caring* rather than curing. At the same time, there are flaws in her account of the dying person's experience (Retsinas, 1988; Schulz & Aderman, 1974; Schulz & Schlarb, 1987–1988). Among the most important criticisms are these: Kübler-Ross speaks of "stages" when it would be better not to do so, she largely ignores the course of the individual's illness, and she makes little of individual differences in emotional responses to dying.

The major problem with Kübler-Ross's "stages" is that they appear not to be stages at all. Research suggests that the dying process is simply not stagelike (Baugher, Burger, Smith, & Wallston, 1989–1990; Schulz & Aderman, 1974). Although it is common for dying patients to be depressed as death nears, the other emotional reactions Kübler-Ross describes seem to affect only minorities of individuals (Schulz & Aderman, 1974). Moreover, when these responses do occur, they do not unfold in a set order. Even Kübler-Ross (1974) herself acknowledged that her "stages" do not necessarily follow one another in a lock-step fashion.

As you are by now well aware, developmentalists speak of stages only when most individuals demonstrably proceed through a series of distinct or qualitatively different phases, *in order*. It might have been better if Kübler-Ross had, from the start, described her "stages" simply as common emotional reactions to dying. Unfortunately, some overzealous medical professionals, excited by these "stages," have misused them by trying to push patients through them in order, believing that dying patients would never come to accept death unless they experienced the "right" emotions at the "right" times (Kastenbaum, 1986).

Offering an alternative to the idea of stages of dying, Edwin Shneidman (1973, 1980) argues that dying patients experience a complex and ever-changing interplay of emotions and that they alternate between denial and acceptance. One day, a patient may express a recognition that death is imminent; the next day, he or she may talk of going home. Along the way, many reactions—disbelief, hope, fear, bewilderment, rage, apathy, and others as well—come and go and are even experienced simultaneously. Such a complex interplay of emotions cannot be reduced to stages. In other words, dying people experience many unpredictable ups and downs.

A second major problem in Kübler-Ross's theory is that it pays little attention to how emotional responses are shaped by the course of an illness and the specific events that occur along the way. Barney Glaser and Anselm Strauss (1968), for example, have analyzed the emotional reactions of dying patients and those around them in relationship to what they call the **dying trajectory**—the perceived shape and duration of the path that the individual is following from life to death. For example, one patient may be on a *lingering* trajectory, slowly and gradually worsening over time. The patient, family members, and staff all have a good deal of time to become accustomed to the fact that death lies ahead. Another patient may be following an *erratic* dying trajectory in which he or she is expected to go through a series of relapses and remissions before dying. Here emotional ups or downs are likely each time the patient's condition takes a turn for better or worse.

It is *perceptions* of the course of illness that matter most. A patient who expects to rebound may become enraged when told that he needs major surgery, whereas a patient who expects to deteriorate may accept the same news gracefully. It is generally more difficult to cope with surprises than to cope with a course of dying that is predictable and proceeds according to expectation. According to Glaser and Strauss, then, the perceived dying trajectory, along with actual changes in a patient's condition, will greatly influence the dying person's experiences. Kübler-Ross, by contrast, expects different patients to experience similar responses even if their dying trajectories are different.

Finally, by proposing a set of stages presumed to describe most dying people, Kübler-Ross has overlooked the fact that each individual's personality influences how he or she experiences dying. People cope with dying much as they have coped with the problems of living (Schulz & Schlarb, 1987–1988). For example, John Hinton (1975) found that cancer patients who, according to their spouses, had always faced life's problems directly and effectively, had been satisfied with their lives, and had maintained good interpersonal relationships *before* they became ill displayed less anger and irritability and were less depressed and withdrawn during their illnesses than patients who had previously avoided problems, had been unfulfilled, and had had difficulty maintaining good relationships with others. Depending on their predominant personality traits, coping styles, and social competencies, some dying persons may deny until the bitter end, some may "rage against the dying of the light," some may quickly be crushed by despair, still others may face reality and display incredible strength, and most will display combinations of these responses, each in their own unique way.

In sum, the experiences of dying persons are far more complex than Kübler-Ross's five "stages" of dying suggest. As Shneidman emphasizes, there is likely to be a complex interplay of many emotions and thoughts, with swings back and forth between acceptance and denial. Moreover, to understand which emotions will predominate and how these emotions will be patterned over time, we must take into account the perceived and actual course of the individual's condition (the dying trajectory) and the individual's prior personality and coping style.

WHAT IS IT LIKE TO LOSE A LOVED ONE?

Most of us know a good deal more about the process of grieving a death than about the process of dying. To describe responses to the death of a loved one, we must distinguish among three terms. **Bereavement** is a state of loss, **grief** is the emotional response to loss, and **mourning** consists of culturally prescribed ways of displaying one's reactions. Thus we can speak of a bereaved person who grieves by experiencing such emotions as sadness, anger, and guilt—and who mourns by attending the funeral and laying flowers on the grave each year.

Unless a death is sudden, relatives and friends, like the dying person, have been experiencing many painful emotions *before* the death. They too may alternate between acceptance and denial; they may take hope that the illness can be halted only to despair once more. Moreover, they often engage in what has been termed **anticipatory grief**, grieving before death occurs for what is happening and for what lies ahead (Rando, 1986).

Yet no amount of preparation and anticipatory grief can eliminate the need to grieve after the death actually occurs. How, then, do we grieve? Much of our information about the grieving process comes from studies of widows and widowers conducted by Colin Murray Parkes and his colleagues (Parkes, 1970, 1986; Parkes & Weiss, 1983). Parkes has been highly influenced by the thinking of John Bowlby (1980), whose theory of infant attachment was outlined in Chapter 13. Both Parkes and Bowlby have conceptualized grieving as a reaction to separation from a loved one. In other words, the grieving adult can be likened to the infant who experiences separation anxiety when his or her mother disappears from view.

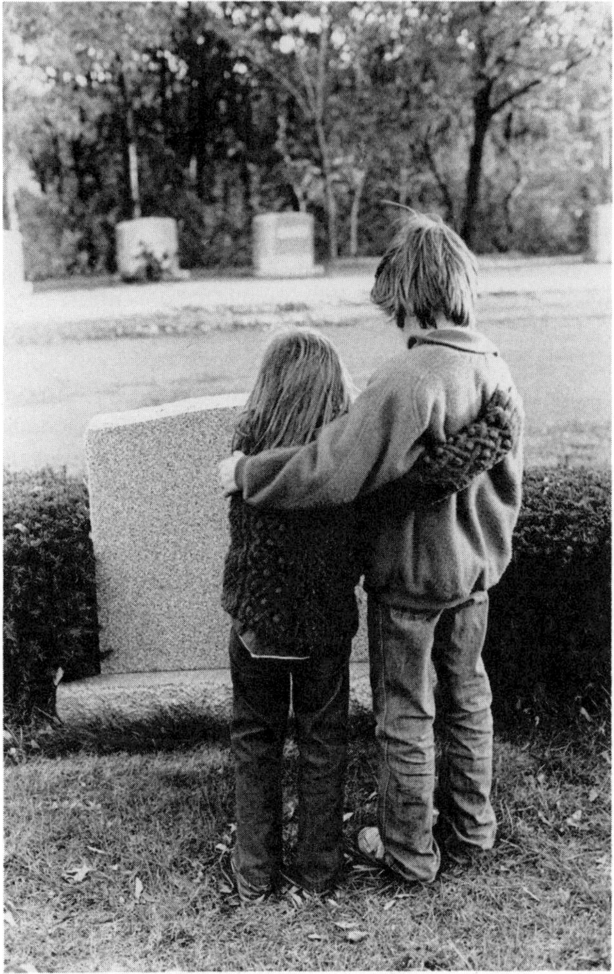

Grief is expressed through mourning behaviors such as visiting the cemetery.

The Parkes-Bowlby model of the grieving process describes four predominant reactions that overlap considerably and that therefore should not be viewed as clearcut "stages," even though the balances among them do change over time: numbness, yearning, disorganization and despair, and reorganization.

1. *Numbness.* In the first few hours or days after the death, the bereaved person is often in a daze—gripped by a sense of unreality and disbelief and almost empty of feelings. Underneath this state of numbness and shock is a sense that one is on the verge of bursting, and occasionally

painful emotions do break through. The bereaved person is struggling to defend himself or herself against the full weight of the loss. The bad news has not fully registered.

2. *Yearning.* As this numbing sense of shock and disbelief diminishes, the bereaved person experiences more and more agony. Grief comes in pangs or waves that typically are most severe from 5 to 14 days after the death. The grieving person has feelings of panic, bouts of uncontrollable weeping, and physical aches and pains. He or she is likely to be extremely restless, unable to concentrate or to sleep, and preoccupied with thoughts of the loved one and of the events leading to the death.

According to Parkes and Bowlby, the reaction that most clearly makes bereavement different from other kinds of emotional distress is separation anxiety, the distress of being parted from the object of one's attachment. The bereaved person pines and yearns for the loved one and actually searches for the deceased, as if the finality of the loss has not yet been accepted. As one London widow put it, "I go to the grave . . . but he's not there. It's as if I was drawn towards him" (Parkes, 1986, p. 65). A widow may think she heard her husband's voice or saw him in a crowd; she may actually sense his presence in the house and draw comfort from it; she may be drawn to his favorite chair or wear his bathrobe. Ultimately, of course, the quest to be reunited is doomed to fail.

Both anger and guilt are also common reactions during these early weeks and months of bereavement. Bereaved people often feel irritable and on edge and sometimes experience intense rage—at the loved one for dying, at the doctors for not doing a better job, and so on. To make sense of the death, they seem to need to pin blame somewhere. Unfortunately, they often find reason to blame themselves—to feel guilty. It does not take much to trigger guilt feelings in the bereaved. A widower may claim that he should have been more forceful with the doctors who were treating his wife; a mother may say she should have reminded her son to fasten his seat belt; or the friend of an adolescent who commits suicide may feel that she should have noticed the warning signs. One of the London widows studied by Parkes actually felt guilty because she never made her husband bread pudding!

3. *Disorganization and despair.* As time passes, pangs of intense grief and yearning become less frequent, though they still occur now and then. As it sinks in that a reunion with the loved one is impossible, depression, despair, and apathy increasingly predominate. During most of the first year after the death, and longer in many cases, bereaved individuals often feel apathetic or even defeated. They may have difficulty managing their lives or taking interest in activities. As one widow said nine months after her husband died, "I don't want to fight it any more" (Parkes, 1986, p. 105).

4. *Reorganization.* Eventually, bereaved persons begin to pull themselves together again as their pangs of grief and periods of apathy become less frequent. They increasingly cut the ties that bound them so closely to the loved one. If married, they begin to make the transition from being a wife or husband to being a widow or widower, slowly shedding their old identities as married persons and forging new identities as individuals. They begin to feel ready for new activities and for new relationships or attachments.

The grieving process described by Parkes is portrayed visually in Figure 17.3 (and see Jacobs et al., 1987–1988). After a death, numbness and disbelief quickly wane, but we may continue to shake our heads in disbelief occasionally even later on. Yearning and pining in response to separation are most intense in the first few months after the death, but these reactions also continue to plague us now and then in later months. Finally, as we gradually accept the finality of death, despair and depression increasingly overwhelm us, until these reactions too give way and we begin to reorganize or recover.

Some researchers would disagree with the specifics of this view of the bereavement process. However, there is

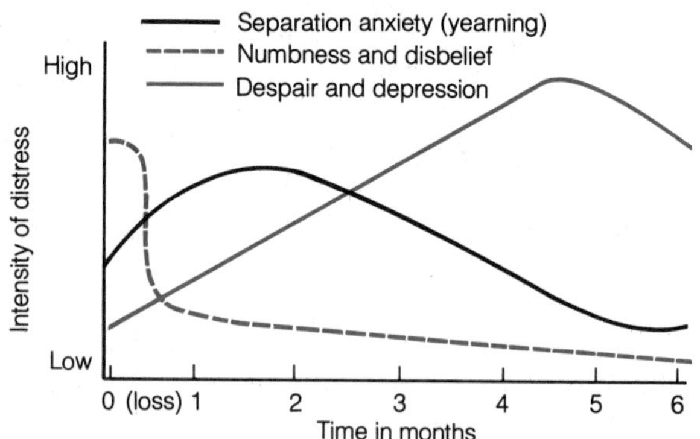

Figure 17.3 A portrayal of the overlapping phases of the grieving process over time. (From Jacobs, Kosten, Kasl, Ostfeld, Berkman, & Charpentier, 1987–1988)

widespread agreement on one point: *It takes a long time to get over the death of a loved one.* We are very sympathetic toward the bereaved immediately after a death, eager to help in any way we can. Too often, though, we quickly grow weary of someone who is depressed, irritable, or preoccupied. We begin to think, sometimes after only a few weeks, that it is time for the bereaved person to cheer up and get on with life. We are wrong! When people suffer a major loss, recovery typically is not evident until a year or more after the death (Murrell & Himmelfarb, 1989; Schulz, 1978), and full recovery can take years.

We have now presented some of the major theories of how people experience dying and bereavement. Notice, however, that these theories have been based on the responses of adults. How do infants, children, and adolescents respond to death? What does death even mean to very young children? A life-span perspective on death and dying is needed. So let us see how infants, children, and adolescents come to understand and cope with death and dying. Then we can look more closely at variations in the adult's experience of death.

THE INFANT

Do infants have any awareness at all of death? Certainly they do not comprehend death as the cessation of life. However, they do seem to gain an understanding of concepts that may pave the way for an understanding of death. Adah Maurer (1961) has suggested that infants gradually grasp the concepts of being and nonbeing from such experiences as watching objects and people appear and disappear, playing peek-a-boo, and even going to sleep and "coming alive" again in the morning. As infants begin to acquire the concept of object permanence described by Piaget, they search for missing or hidden objects and can become quite frustrated when those objects are "all gone." Very possibly, then, infants form a global category of things that are "all gone" and later divide it into subcategories, one of which is "dead" (Kastenbaum, 1985). Thus early experiences with the appearance and disappearance of objects and people may contribute to a later grasp of the distinction between life and death.

The experience that is most directly relevant to an emerging concept of death is the disappearance, for whatever reason, of a loved one. It is here that John Bowlby's influential theory of attachment is helpful. Infants form their first attachments at about the age of 6 or 7 months, and soon begin to display signs of separation anxiety or protest when their beloved caregivers leave them. They have now begun to grasp the concept that objects (or more specifically, persons) have permanent existence, and they expect a loved one who has disappeared to reappear. According to Bowlby, they are biologically programmed to protest separations by crying, searching for their loved one, or attempting to follow, for these behaviors increase the chances that they will be reunited with a caregiver and protected from harm.

Bowlby (1980) goes on to show that infants separated from their attachment figures display many of the same reactions that bereaved adults do. Whether the cause of separation from a parent is death or vacation trip, infants first engage in vigorous *protest*—yearning and searching for the loved one and expressing outrage when they fail. One 17-month-old girl said only, "Mum, Mum, Mum" for three days after her mother died and was willing to sit on a nurse's lap but would turn her back, as if she did not want to see that the nurse was not "Mum" (Freud & Burlingham, cited in Bowlby, 1980). If, after a week or so of protest, they have not succeeded in finding the loved one, infants begin to *despair*; they lose hope, end their searches, and become apathetic and sad. Their grief may be reflected in a poor appetite, a change in sleeping patterns, excessive clinginess, or a loss of language capabilities and other signs of regression to less mature behavior (Furman, 1984; Raphael, 1983). Ultimately, such infants begin to seek new relationships and will recover from their loss most completely if they can count on an existing attachment figure (for example, the surviving parent) or can attach themselves to someone new.

Clearly, then, infants who are at least 6 months of age or so and who have formed genuine attachment bonds are old enough to experience intense grief and depression-like symptoms when a parent or other loved one dies (see also Spitz, 1946, and Chapter 16's discussion of depression in infancy). Moreover, the responses they display—the protest and anger, the yearning and searching, the despair and depression—are the same sorts of responses that bereaved adults display. What is the difference? It is mainly that infants lack the concept that death means permanent separation or loss. Lacking the cognitive powers to interpret what has happened, an infant whose mother has died may have little idea why she is gone, where she is, or when she will return. As we will see later, such painful and confusing early experiences of loss sometimes leave a mark on the personality and make it difficult for the individual to cope with loss later in life.

THE CHILD

Much as many parents would like to shelter their children from death and other unpleasant life experiences, children do encounter death in their early years. For many, the brush with death may be little more than seeing dead insects on the windowsills or dead animals along the roadside. For some, death strikes much closer, taking a grandparent, parent, or sibling—or even the child himself or herself.

Grasping the Concept of Death

Contrary to what many adults would like to believe, young children are highly curious about death, think about it with some frequency, and are quite willing to talk about it (Kastenbaum, 1986; Stambrook & Parker, 1987). Yet their beliefs about death are often considerably different from those that prevail among adults in Western societies. In our society, a "mature" understanding of death has several components (Hoffman & Strauss, 1985; Speece & Brent, 1984): Death is (1) the *cessation* of life (and of all life processes such as movement, sensation, and thought), and it is characterized by (2) *irreversibility* (it is final and cannot be undone), (3) *universality* (it is inevitable and happens to all living beings), and (4) *internal or biological causality* (it is the result of natural processes internal to the organism, even if external causes set off these internal changes).

Researchers have studied children's conceptions of death by asking them the sorts of questions contained in Table 17.1, or by asking children to draw pictures of their images of death. Research on the topic was pioneered by Maria Nagy (1948), who studied Hungarian children ranging in age from 3 to 10. Nagy and other researchers since have found that children between the ages of 3 and 5 are a long way from having a mature concept of death. Rather than viewing death as a complete cessation of life, they tend to think that the dead retain at least some of their capacities. According to preschoolers, the dead may not be as lively and capable as the living, but they may well be able to move around a bit, hear what is going on outside their coffins, experience hunger, and think and dream. Young children give up the notion that the dead can engage in overt behavior such as moving around before they abandon the idea that they can think and dream (Hoffman & Strauss, 1985).

Preschool-aged children also tend to view death as reversible rather than irreversible. They liken it to a sleep (from which one can awaken) or to a trip (from which one can return). With the right medical care, the proper foods, or a bit of magic, a dead person might be brought back to life (Speece & Brent, 1984). As one youngster put it, "Help them, give them hot food, and keep them healthy so it won't happen again" (Koocher, 1974, p. 408). In addition, young children are not always sure that death is universal; among those who can avoid death may be people who are very clever—or the child and his or her loved ones (Speece & Brent, 1984). Finally, young children think death is caused by one concrete and external agent or another. One may say that people die because they eat aluminum foil; another may say the cause is eating a dirty bug or Styrofoam cups (Koocher, 1974)!

Much progress is made between the ages of 5 and 7 in acquiring a mature concept of death (see Figure 17.4). By the age of 7, most children in our society do understand that death involves a cessation of life functions, that it is irreversible, and that it is universal (Speece & Brent, 1984).

Table 17.1 Western children's concepts of death and questions pertaining to them

CONCEPT	QUESTIONS
Cessation of life	Can a dead person move? Get hungry? Speak? Think? Dream? Do dead people know that they are dead?
Irreversibility	Can a dead person become a live person again? Is there anything that could make a dead animal come back to life?
Universality	Does everyone die at some time? Will your parents die someday? Your friends? Will you die?
Biological causality	What makes a person die? Why do animals die?

Source: Based on Hoffman & Strauss, 1985; Florian & Kravetz, 1985; and other sources.

By the age of 5 or 6, most of them even understand that they will die, at least in the remote future (Reilly, Hasazi, & Bond, 1983). What is left for children to accomplish after the age of 7 or so, then? They must still gain a fuller understanding of the causality of death. In the early elementary school years, they can catalog a number of concrete causes of death (guns, knives, poison, illness, and so on), but they fail to appreciate that all deaths ultimately involve a failure of internal biological processes (Hoffman & Strauss, 1985; Koocher, 1974; Orbach, Gross, Glaubman, & Berman, 1986). Paula, age 12, had mastered this concept: "When the heart stops, blood stops circulating, you stop breathing and that's it. . . . there's lots of ways it can get started, but that's what really happens" (Koocher, 1974, pp. 407–408).

Some children have far more sophisticated understandings of death than their age mates. Why might this be? Children's concepts of death appear to be a function of both their level of cognitive development and their life experiences. Notice that major breakthroughs in the understanding of death occur in about the 5-to-7 age range—precisely the time that children are making the transition from Piaget's preoperational stage of cognitive development to the concrete-operational stage. Apparently children's understandings of death, like their understandings of many other concepts, become more adultlike when they begin to master important logical operations. Children who perform well on Piagetian cognitive tasks or on tests of verbal intelligence tend to express more mature concepts of death than their less cognitively capable peers (Koocher, 1973; Orbach et al., 1986; Speece & Brent, 1984).

Figure 17.4 Young children can talk about and draw pictures of death, but they do not yet understand that it is internally caused. This drawing by a 5-year-old boy focuses on one specific external cause of death—a knife. (From Wenestam & Wass, 1987)

However, children's concepts of death are also influenced by their specific life experiences—by the cultural and religious beliefs to which they are exposed and by their own personal encounters with death (Stambrook & Parker, 1987). For example, Jewish and Christian children in Israel, who are exposed to our Western concept of death, provide more "mature" answers to questions about death than Druze children, who are taught to believe in reincarnation (Florian & Kravetz, 1985). It only makes sense that a child who learns that people are reincarnated after they die might not view death as a final cessation of all life processes. Some children may also acquire sophisticated concepts of death quite early because they encounter death firsthand. Interestingly, preschool children growing up in conflict-torn areas of Belfast, Northern Ireland, where violent deaths are routine, seem to have a more mature concept of death than children in more peaceful neighborhoods (McWhirter, Young, & Majury, 1983).

Within our own culture as well, each child's understandings of death will be influenced by social learning experiences (Kane, 1979). How is a young child to overcome the belief that death is temporary, for example, if parents and other adults claim that relatives who have died are "asleep"? Isn't it also understandable that such a child might become afraid of going to bed at night? We must also wonder about statements that liken death to a journey, as in "Grandma has gone to Heaven." For all the young child knows, Heaven might be a hop, skip, and jump from Chicago—and surely one can purchase a round-trip ticket and return! So why doesn't Grandma come back? Experts on death insist that adults only make death more confusing and frightening to young children when they use such euphemisms (Kastenbaum, 1986; Osterweis, Solomon, & Green, 1984). They recommend that parents give children honest but simple answers to the many questions they naturally ask about death. If children are given misleading explanations, they will believe them. If their questions are dodged and they are told nothing, they will invent their own ideas, possibly ones that are more disturbing than the truth.

In sum, young children are naturally curious about death and form ideas about it from an early age. During the preschool years, they are likely to view death as only a lessening of life processes rather than a cessation of them, and to view death as reversible, selective, and attributable to any number of very concrete external causes. By about the age of 7, they have mastered the concept that death is the cessation of all life functions, and that it is irreversible and universal. Later they come to appreciate that death is ultimately due to a failure of internal biological processes. Each child's grasp of death will depend on his or her level of cognitive development and death-related experience. What does this all mean for those children who are actually dying?

The Dying Child

It is one thing to understand death but quite another to experience it directly. As Robert Kastenbaum (1986) emphasizes, children need not possess a fully mature concept of death in order to suffer when death threatens or strikes. How do children react when they have a terminal illness such as cancer? Do they understand that they are dying, or do they assume that they will get well? Do they face their problems stoically, or do they crumble in the face of their stressful experiences?

Parents and doctors often assume that terminally ill children are unaware that they will die and are better off remaining ignorant. Yet research shows that dying children are far more aware of what is happening to them than adults realize; their tragic experience makes them "grow up" early (Spinetta, 1974; Waechter, 1984). Consider what Myra Bluebond-Langner (1977) found when she carefully observed children ranging in age from 2 to 14 who had leukemia. Even preschool children arrived, over time, at an understanding that they were going to die and that death is irreversible. Even though adults were secretive, these children were closely attuned to what was going on around them. They noticed changes in their treatments and subtle changes in the way adults interacted with them, and, perhaps most important, they learned from the fates of other children who had the same disease and were receiving the same treatments. They progressed from seeing themselves as well, to thinking that they were ill but would recover, to realizing that they would never get well and would die. Over time, many of these ill children stopped talking about the long-term future and wanted to have holidays such as Christmas early. A doctor trying to get one boy to cooperate with a procedure said, "I thought you would understand, Sandy. You told me once you wanted to be a doctor." Sandy threw an empty syringe at the doctor and screamed, "I'm not going to be anything!" (p. 59).

How do terminally ill children cope with the knowledge that they are dying? They are not all the models of bravery that some people suppose them to be. Instead, they experience the wide range of emotions that dying adults experience—the anger, the depression, and the anxieties over being separated from loved ones, experiencing pain, and wondering what lies ahead. In her studies of dying children, Eugenia Waechter (1984) found that terminally ill children have higher levels of anxiety—especially about death, mutilation, and loneliness or separation—than either healthy children or chronically ill children who are not expected to die.

Waechter also found that preschool children respond differently to terminal illness than school-aged children do. For example, preschool children do not often talk about dying. Instead, their behavior reveals their fears; they may fly into temper tantrums or portray violent acts in their pretend play. They very much need reassurance that they are still loved and that their illness is not a punishment for bad behavior. By comparison, school-aged children understand more about their situation and can talk about their feelings if they are given an opportunity to do so. They very much want to participate in normal activities so that they will not feel inadequate compared with their peers, and they want to maintain a sense of control or mastery, even if the best they can do is to take charge of deciding which finger should be pricked to take a blood sample. They also have more sophisticated coping skills than preschool children do. Frances Worchel and her colleagues (Worchel, Copeland, & Barker, 1987), for example, found that young children with cancer try to exert control through behavioral means (for example, by struggling to get away from the nurse administering shots). Older children use more cognitive coping strategies (for example, by asking questions, thinking positive thoughts, and making decisions themselves).

In short, children with terminal illnesses often become very aware of the fact that they are dying and of what that really means. Quite naturally, then, they experience a full range of unpleasant emotions and reveal in their behavior, if not in their words, that they are anxious and upset. What, then, can be done to help children cope with dying? Quite obviously, they need the love and support of parents, siblings, and other significant individuals in their lives. Children with cancer who seem to be adjusting well emotionally to their ordeal have a strong sense that their parents are in control of the situation (Worchel et al., 1987), and they also have opportunities to talk with adults about their anxieties (Waechter, 1984). In other words, they are not the victims of a well-intentioned but ultimately counterproductive conspiracy of silence on the part of parents and medical care providers.

The Bereaved Child

Children's coping capacities are also tested when they lose a parent, sibling, pet, or other loved one to death. Three major messages have emerged from studies of bereaved children:

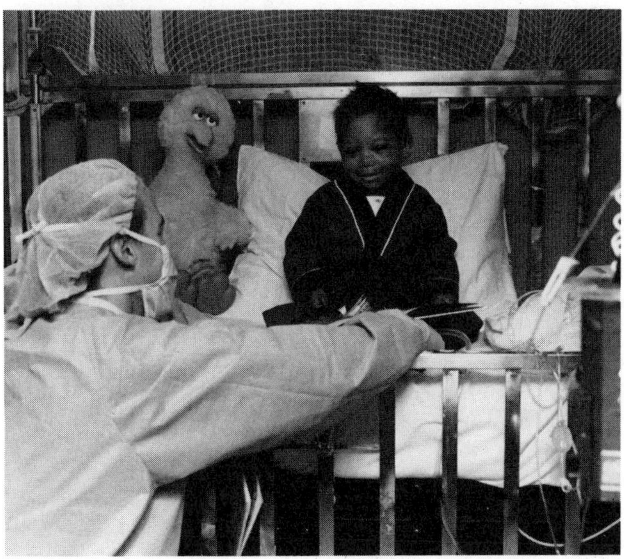

Children who are dying of cancer often become painfully aware that they are dying and that death is irreversible.

1. Children most certainly grieve.
2. They express their grief differently than adults do.
3. They are especially vulnerable to long-term negative effects of bereavement (Osterweis et al., 1984).

Consider some of the reactions that have been observed in young children whose parents have died (Osterweis et al., 1984; Raphael, 1983). These children often misbehave or strike out at their surviving parent in their rage. They ask endless questions: Where is Daddy? When is he coming back? Will I get a new Daddy? Still others go about their activities as if nothing had happened. You can readily see how a parent might be disturbed by some of these behaviors—the seemingly inexplicable tantrums, the distressing questions, or, worse, the child's apparent lack of concern about the death. Yet all of these behaviors indicate that the loss is affecting the child greatly. Even an apparent lack of concern may be the child's attempt to deny and avoid emotions that are simply too overwhelming to face (Osterweis et al., 1984). It is important, then, for adults to recognize that children express their grief in ways that reflect their level of development.

What grief symptoms do children most commonly experience? In the first weeks and months after the death, they are likely to be "sad, angry, and fearful; their behavior includes appetite and sleep disturbance, withdrawal, concentration difficulties, dependency, regression, restlessness, and learning difficulties" (Osterweis et al., 1984, p. 104). The preschool child's grief is likely to manifest itself in problems with sleeping, eating, toileting, and other daily routines. Negative moods, temper tantrums, and bedwetting episodes are common (Van Eerdewegh, Clayton, & Van Eerdewegh, 1985). Older children often become either withdrawn or aggressive and experience academic and social difficulties at school (Osterweis et al., 1984).

Remember, children are highly dependent on their parents. Moreover, they simply do not have the coping capacities that adults do. As a result, children often take years to recover fully from the death of a parent (Osterweis et al., 1984). Well beyond the first year after the death, many bereaved children continue to be unhappy, to have difficulty in school, or to engage in delinquent acts. Moreover, studies of adults who suffer from chronic depression and related forms of psychopathology suggest that these adults are more likely than most adults to have experienced the death of a parent in early childhood (Bowlby, 1980; Osterweis et al., 1984). However, as we will see later, many bereaved children—especially those who have positive coping skills and a good deal of social support—overcome their losses quite successfully.

THE ADOLESCENT

Adolescents typically understand death as the irreversible cessation of biological processes, and they can express more abstract concepts of death once they attain Piaget's stage of formal operations (Koocher, 1973; and see Figure 17.5). Some adolescents even use their new cognitive capacities to ponder the big questions of life and to contemplate the meaning of death (Gordon, 1986). Interestingly, adolescents are *less* likely than 7-year-olds to view death as nothing but a cessation of life; instead, most adolescents, influenced by religious teachings, conceptualize some sort of spiritual continuation after death (McIntyre, Angle, & Struempler, 1972).

Children's reactions to death and dying clearly reflect their developmental capacities and needs. Similarly, adolescents who become terminally ill are likely to be concerned about the issues that are most central during adolescence (Adams & Deveau, 1986; Waechter, 1984). Concerned about their body images as they experience physical and sexual maturation, they may be acutely disturbed if their illness alters their appearance. Concerned about being accepted by peers, they may feel like "freaks" and be upset when friends who do not know what to say or do abandon them (Adams & Deveau, 1986). Concerned about establishing their independence, they may be distressed by having to depend on parents and medical personnel and may struggle to assert their wills and maintain a sense of control. As one put it, "After all, it's my body and my life. . . ." (Adams & Deveau, 1986, p. 85). Concerned about establishing their identities and charting future goals, adolescents may be angry and bitter at having their dreams snatched from them. And cognitively equipped to think about others' feelings toward them, they, more than children, may worry about the impact of their death on loved ones (Tobin & Treloar, cited in Raphael, 1983).

Similarly, the reactions of an adolescent to the death of a family member or friend are likely to reflect the themes of the adolescent period. Some studies suggest that early adolescence, like early childhood, is a period of special vulnerability to the negative effects of bereavement (Osterweis et al., 1984). Possibly this is because young adolescents have so many maturational changes and social pressures to cope with already. Even though adolescents are becoming increasingly independent of their parents, they still depend quite heavily on them and take the death of a parent hard. And given the importance of peers in this developmental period, it is not surprising that adolescents are sometimes devastated when a friend dies in a car accident, commits suicide, or succumbs to a deadly disease.

For the most part, adolescents grieve much as adults do. However, they are sometimes reluctant to express their emotions for fear of seeming abnormal or losing control (Osterweis et al., 1984). For example, the adolescent who yearns for a dead parent may feel that he or she is being

Figure 17.5 Compared to children, adolescents often express very abstract concepts of death that are influenced by their religious training. The 16-year-old girl who drew this picture explained, "The water represents the depth of death. The bubbles represent the releasing of the soul. The tree represents the memories we leave behind. The flame represents Hell and the halo represents Heaven." (From Wenestam & Wass, 1987)

sucked back into the dependency of childhood and may lock these painful feelings inside:

> "When my mother died I thought my heart would break," recalled Geoffrey, age fourteen. "Yet I couldn't cry. It was locked inside. It was private and tender and sensitive like the way I loved her. They said to me, 'You're cool man, real cool, the way you've taken it,' but I wasn't cool at all. I was hot—hot and raging. All my anger, all my sadness was building up inside me. But I just didn't know any way to let it out" [Raphael, 1983, p. 176].

In sum, by the time children reach adolescence, they have acquired a mature concept of death, understanding it as a natural, irreversible, and universal process and thinking more abstractly about it. Whereas young children often express their grief indirectly through their behavior (by wetting their beds, throwing tantrums, and so on), older children and adolescents more directly experience and express painful thoughts and emotions. However, they are also better equipped to cope with these emotions. In each period of development, children's concerns about death also reflect their major needs. Thus, when a life-threatening illness strikes, the young child may most want reassurance of parental love and protection, and the school-aged child may hope to keep up with peers in school, but the adolescent may want to maintain a sense of independence.

Even though concepts of death and reactions to it change with age, encounters with death are painful and potentially damaging at any age. Bereaved infants, children, and adolescents are all at risk to develop long-lasting problems. Knowing this, it becomes all the more important to ensure that these youngsters receive love and consistent support. They cannot be sheltered from death's blows; instead, their parents and other adults need to help them cope with their very real emotional reactions to death and dying.

THE ADULT

How do we cope with death and dying as adults? We have already introduced models of adults' experiences of dying and bereavement that partially answer that question. Here, we'll elaborate by examining attitudes toward death and dying during the adult years, responses to bereavement in the context of the family life cycle, and factors that determine whether an individual grieves "normally" or pathologically.

Death Anxiety

Adults in our society know full well that death is an irreversible cessation of life processes. However, this by no means suggests that they have mastered their fears of death. **Death anxiety** is a complex set of concerns about death and dying. The person who is highly anxious about death does not want to think about it or be reminded of it, dreads developing a serious illness and facing the pain and stress that dying may entail, and strongly senses that life is too short (Lonetto & Templer, 1986).

Who is most or least anxious about death? On death anxiety scales, men tend to express less death anxiety than women do, although it is possible that they are merely less willing to admit their fears (Hickson, Housley, & Boyle, 1988; Lonetto & Templer, 1986; Pollack, 1979–1980). Strongly religious individuals also tend to be less afraid of death than other people (Lonetto & Templer, 1986). However, merely participating in organized religion does not necessarily protect adults from death anxiety. Indeed, in some studies, individuals who are only somewhat religious actually fear death more than *either* nonbelievers or strong believers do, possibly because they fear punishment in an afterlife (Kalish, 1963; McMordie, 1981). In addition, personality has a bearing on death anxiety. Those individuals who have high self-esteem, a sense of mastery, and a sense of meaning and purpose in their lives are likely to be less anxious about death and dying than individuals who lack confidence, do not have a sense of fulfillment, or show signs of personality disturbance (Pollack, 1979–1980).

The relationship between age and death anxiety is of special interest to us. Do adults become more and more anxious as they reach ages at which death is more probable, or do they become less anxious as they work through their fears and accept the inevitable? Research suggests that death anxiety tends to be lower among elderly adults than among young or middle-aged adults (Lonetto & Templer, 1986; Pollack, 1979–1980; Reker, Peacock, & Wong, 1987) and may be highest among middle-aged adults (Gesser, Wong, & Reker, 1987–1988). Elderly adults may think about their own deaths more frequently than younger adults do, but they seem to have resolved some of their fears (Kalish & Reynolds, 1977).

Or is it just that older adults are less willing to admit to fears that may still lurk within them? Herman Feifel and Allan Branscomb (1973) present some intriguing evidence that this may be the case. They used both direct and indirect methods to assess the death anxieties of people ranging in age from 10 to 89. Asked directly whether they were afraid of death, 71% of this sample said no, and elderly adults were particularly unwilling to admit any fear. However, these researchers also attempted to assess feelings below the level of awareness. They asked respondents to come up with word associations for death-related terms such as "coffin" and neutral words such as "baggage." People took longer to generate associations to death terms than to neutral terms, and this was interpreted as betraying their anxieties about death. Moreover, older adults (and also highly religious ones, by the way) revealed just as much death anxiety on this measure as young adults (and less religious ones) did. This study, then, warns us that many individuals who do not directly admit to death anxiety nonetheless may harbor it. It is a mistake to assume that most elderly people have entirely mastered the fear of death and dying, even though they may have resolved some aspects of their anxiety. Instead, anxieties about death and dying appear to be a fundamental part of the human experience at all ages (Lonetto & Templer, 1986).

Even if adults of different ages do not differ greatly in their levels of death anxiety, is it still possible that they differ in what concerns them the most about dying? Richard Kalish and David Reynolds (1977) base their belief that this is the case on surveys of four different ethnic groups in the Los Angeles area. Table 17.2 shows what these adults said they would want to do if they knew they had only six months to live. Notice that young adults seemed to want to "grab all the gusto" they could—to have experiences that would otherwise be forgone, to see some of their plans and goals realized. Young adults who are dying are especially likely to feel angry and cheated (Kalish, 1981). Middle-aged adults were not as intent on seeking out new experiences or changing their lives, but they were highly concerned about their relationships. Indeed, among people who are parents, concerns about the welfare of family members are often most troublesome (Diggory & Rothman, 1961). By contrast, the elderly adults in this survey seemed to have realized enough goals and no longer had children depending on them so much. They appeared to place more importance on being able to put the meaning of their lives in perspective through contemplation—perhaps to engage in the process of *life review* that we discussed in Chapter 10.

Table 17.2 If you were told you had a terminal disease and six months to live, how would you want to spend your time until you died? (N = 434)

RESPONSES	YOUNG (%)	MIDDLE-AGED (%)	OLD (%)
Marked change in lifestyle, self-related (travel, sex, drugs, experiences)	24	15	9
Withdrawal (read, contemplate, pray)	14	14	37
Focus concern on others, be with loved ones	29	25	12
Complete projects, tie up loose ends	11	10	3
No change in lifestyle	17	29	31
Other/DK	5	6	8

Source: From Kalish & Reynolds, 1977.

In sum, death anxiety appears to be part of the human condition throughout the life span. It is likely to be lowest among men, strongly religious individuals, and people who are relatively well adjusted. Moreover, elderly adults are less likely to say that they are anxious about death than younger adults are, even though they may be more anxious than they admit. In addition, major concerns about dying appear to reflect the central developmental themes of each period of adulthood. Young adults may find it especially threatening to be unable to complete plans, to experience what life has to offer, and to maintain important relationships. Concerns about the welfare of one's family are prominent among middle-aged adults, and elderly adults seem to be especially concerned about making sense of their lives before they die. Notice the echoes of Erik Erikson here: identity and intimacy concerns in early adulthood, issues of generativity and caring for the younger generation in middle adulthood, and the quest for a sense of integrity in old age.

Death and the Family Life Cycle

Given the importance of family attachments throughout the life span, it is not surprising that the deaths of fam-

this table can serve as a handy description of normal human development, we need to supplement it by turning to some of the processes and themes behind these changes.

MAJOR THEMES IN HUMAN DEVELOPMENT

Another way in which to leave you with the big picture is by highlighting some major generalizations about human development. Some of these larger themes are incorporated in the life-span developmental perspective introduced in Chapter 1 or represent stands on the developmental issues laid out in Chapter 2; many have been echoed throughout this book. We leave you with the following thoughts:

We Are Indeed Whole Beings Throughout the Life Span

As our review of major developments in each life phase should make clear, it is the intermeshing of physical, cognitive, personal, and social development that gives each period of the life span—and each individual human—a distinctive and coherent quality. Thus, for example, the fact that 7-month-old infants become attached to their caregivers is not just a milestone in social development divorced from other aspects of development. The maturation of sensory and motor abilities permits infants to crawl after their parents to maintain the proximity they desire, and their cognitive growth makes them aware that caregivers continue to exist when they leave the room (and

PERSONAL DEVELOPMENT	SOCIAL DEVELOPMENT
Acquisition of sense of self, self-recognition, and awareness of gender identity. Temperament as basis of personality. Trust versus mistrust conflict.	Social from birth. Attachment to caregiver at 7 months; separation and stranger anxiety follow. Increased social skills with parents and peers; capacity for simple pretend play. Family-centered lifestyle.
Concrete, physical self-concept. Rapid acquisition of gender role. Simple notions of morality. Conflicts of autonomy versus shame and initiative versus guilt.	Parent/child relationship still central in social world. Increased social-cognitive abilities, though egocentric in some ways. More cooperation with peers; social pretend play blossoms. Exposure to schooling.
Self-concept includes psychological traits. Personality "jells." Strong gender typing. Internalization of moral standards, shift from preconventional to conventional morality. Much social comparison and conflict of industry versus inferiority.	Increased involvement with same-sex peers; formation of close chumships. Role-taking skills advance. Play centers on organized games with rules. School and television are important socialization agents.
More abstract and integrated self-concept. Adjustment to sexuality and gender role. Conventional moral reasoning. Conflict of identity versus role confusion.	Peak peer involvement and conformity. More emotionally intimate friendships; dating relationships begin. Parent/child relationship becomes more equal; autonomy increases. Involved in school and career exploration.
Continued work on identity. Some shift to postconventional moral reasoning. Increased confidence. Divergence of roles in family according to sex. Personality fairly stable. Conflict of intimacy versus isolation.	Social networks continue to expand, and romantic relationships are formed. Most establish families and take on roles as spouses and parents. Careers are launched; much job switching. Period of much life change; high risk of divorce and psychological problems.
Continued personality stability, but possible midlife questioning and androgyny shift. Conflict of generativity versus stagnation.	Relations center within family. The nest empties and the grandparent role is often added to existing roles. High responsibility for younger and older generations. Career is more stable, and peak success is attained. Family and work roles dominate.
Most maintain characteristic personality traits, self-esteem, and life satisfaction. Philosophical and moral growth for some as they resolve conflict of integrity versus despair.	Continued close ties to family and friends; loneliness is rare. Generally smooth adjustment to retirement, and maintenance of social activities. For women especially, adjustment to loss of spouse.

therefore can be retrieved). Moreover, the emergence of attachment bonds in turn affects development in other areas: by providing toddlers with the security they need in order to explore the world around them and, in the process, to develop their motor skills and cognitive capacities all the more.

With Age, Behavior Becomes More Complex and Organized

Heinz Werner (1957), a pioneering and influential developmental theorist, summarized much of what he had observed of human development in what he termed the **orthogenetic principle**: "Wherever development occurs it proceeds from a state of relative globality and lack of differentiation to a state of increasing differentiation, articulation, and hierarchical integration" (p. 126). That is, developing humans increasingly master more and more specific responses and organize these responses into more integrated and coherent patterns. The companion processes of differentiation and integration, Werner believed, were central to human development.

The orthogenetic principle is indeed a useful way of thinking about many aspects of human development, particularly from infancy to adulthood. Lacking voluntary motor control, for example, the young infant often flails its whole body when pinched on the arm (global response); the older child is able to move specific parts of the body on command (differentiation); and this child may eventually coordinate separate movements to dance the latest dance or build a birdhouse (integration). Similarly, young children describe other people's personalities in only the most global terms ("He's nice" "She's mean"); school-aged children develop a more differentiated vocabulary of trait labels to use in characterizing their companions; and adolescents become true personality theorists, integrating all they have learned about their companions, contradictions included, into coherent theories of how these people tick.

Differentiation and integration are undoubtedly part of the reason that adults seem so much more competent to deal with the world than infants do. As global capacities are converted into a wide range of specific capacities, humans become more able to adapt their behavior to the demands of specific situations. The infant is a bit like a golfer with only one, all-purpose golf swing; the older individual has a whole arsenal of distinctive "swings" and the ability to choose the right swing for the right occasion. As differentiated responses are integrated into coherent wholes, behavior also becomes more consistent or coherent. The preschool child may flit from one activity to another without finishing any; the adult can mobilize many capacities to see a task through to completion. So we become more complex beings as we get older, and while we are whole beings at every age, there is a sense in which we become more whole with age.

Development Proceeds in Multiple Directions

Werner's orthogenetic principle summarizes *one* important direction of human development, but not all of human development is a matter of becoming more and more capable or of progressing toward some "mature" endpoint. True, we cannot help but be impressed by all the maturing that takes place during the first 20 years of life. Yet human development involves not only gains but losses, as well as systematic changes that make us neither better nor worse than we were before but simply different.

When we think of losses, of course, we think first of declines in capacities late in life. Yet loss is by no means restricted to old age; it is common, for example, for children to lose some of their intrinsic motivation to learn as they progress through school. Moreover, growth is not restricted to childhood, for many middle-aged and elderly adults continue to accumulate knowledge, refine their capacities to master everyday challenges, and gain new insights into their lives. We simply must abandon the traditional view that human development consists of growth or improvement up to adulthood; stability into middle age; and decline in old age. Instead, there are gains, losses, and just plain changes during all phases of the life span. What's more, we do not all move along the same developmental paths. The older adult who is healthy, well educated, and active is likely to be maintaining or strengthening many capacities in old age that his or her less healthy, less educated, and less active agemate is losing.

There Is Both Continuity and Discontinuity in Development

As we have seen throughout this book, developmentalists have long grappled with the issue of *continuity versus discontinuity* in human development. We can appreciate the wisdom of staking out a middle ground on the continuity/discontinuity issue by considering whether development is or is not stagelike, whether our early traits predict our later traits, and whether our early experiences have lasting impacts.

Do we merely accumulate (or lose) knowledge and skills as we develop (and therefore undergo *quantitative* change), or do we progress through distinct stages (each of which is a *qualitatively* distinct reorganization of capacities)? Consider what we know about cognitive development. There is some support for Piaget's claim that children progress through distinct stages of cognitive development. At the same time, transitions between stages of cognitive development occur quite gradually, and children who can perform some of the tasks that are supposedly mastered during a "stage" often fail other such tasks, suggesting that cognitive development is less stagelike than Piaget believed and depends on experience with particular kinds of problems (Flavell, 1985). Some aspects of cognitive growth are not very stagelike at all. For example, the fact that older children know more words than younger children do is the result of continuous or gradual vocabulary building. Development often involves *both* stagelike discontinuity and continuous, gradual change.

Another question of continuity and discontinuity in development is this: Do we retain the same standings relative to our age mates on various trait dimensions as we get older, or is it quite possible for the shy and intelligent child to become an outgoing and not-so-intelligent adult? Here we have seen evidence that *some* early predispositions carry over into later life. Children who are relatively intelligent and relatively introverted compared with other children are indeed likely to become relatively intelligent and introverted adolescents and adults, whereas their less intelligent and more extraverted agemates are likely to retain those traits. However, this continuity or consistency is far from perfect, and there is ample room for change. For example, a bright child may suffer a loss of intellectual capacity if he or she is abused and neglected at home and attends inferior schools, or an introverted child may gain confidence and blossom into a more outgoing individual with the aid of supportive friends. We do seem to carry many predispositions with us through the life span, and this gives each of us a sense of being basically the same person. Yet many of us undergo significant changes during our lives. That is why predicting the character of the adult from knowledge of the child is still a risky business.

Finally, a third important variation on the continuity/discontinuity issue centers on this question: Do early experiences have relatively permanent effects on us, or can their effects be undone by later experiences? Contrary to what Sigmund Freud believed, early experiences rarely make or break us. True, the child who is exposed to rubella prenatally or who suffers severe oxygen deprivation at birth may be permanently handicapped. More often, however, early damage can be undone if a child experiences a more favorable environment in subsequent years. For this reason, developmentalists such as Jerome Kagan (1986) emphasize that humans are remarkably resilient, or capable of rebounding from adverse experiences early in life. Perhaps the soundest conclusion is that early experiences *influence but do not determine* later outcomes. If adverse early experiences are followed by adverse later experiences, we can expect poor outcomes, but if potentially damaging early experiences are offset by favorable later experiences, we can expect developing humans to display a good deal of resilience.

Nature and Nurture Truly Interact

Although the *nature/nurture issue* may never be fully resolved, it is clear that multiple forces, both within the person and outside the person, conspire to determine human development. Heredity and environment jointly explain both universal developmental trends and individual differences in development. Consider a universal accomplishment such as acquiring language. Biological maturation, guided by a species-wide genetic blueprint, clearly makes this achievement possible, for no amount of stimulation from adults can make a 1-month-old infant speak sentences. Yet once an infant is maturationally ready, language skills will not be acquired without the necessary input from the environment—specifically, opportunities to converse with speakers of the language. So it goes for many other developmental milestones: Nothing much happens unless the child is maturationally ready to learn *and* has the requisite learning experiences. It is the combination of a maturational plan specified by the genes and universal features of human experience that accounts for the many similarities in human development across cultures.

And why do individuals differ from one another? Why, for example, can one high school student speak, read, and write so much more effectively than a classmate? We could argue that the two inherited different intellectual potentials, but we would have to recognize that a genetic potential for high intelligence will never be realized if a child grows up in a closet, deprived of linguistic stimulation. We could stress the importance of linguistic stimulation at home and at school, but we would have to acknowledge that children with the genes for high intelligence are more likely to actively seek out, elicit, and profit from such stimulation than children with limited genetic potential. In short, the experiences we have influence whether our genetic potentials are realized or not, and the genes we inherit influence what experiences we will seek out and have and how we will respond to them. Depending on which aspect of human development we study, we may find that either heredity or environment is more influential than the other, but we cannot escape the conclusion that there would be no development without the ongoing contributions of *both*.

We Are Individuals, Becoming Even More Diverse with Age

In any human development textbook, there is a tendency to emphasize developmental phenomena that are shared by all or most individuals—to highlight the regularities and commonalities. We do indeed share a good deal with our fellow developing humans. But let us not lose sight of the fact that each of us is truly one of a kind. Indeed, the diversity of developing humans is so impressive that it often seems impossible to generalize about them.

Individuality is apparent starting at birth if we look closely at each infant's temperament, daily rhythms, and rate of development. Yet young infants are not nearly the individuals that they will become. Early development is strongly channeled by a species-wide genetic blueprint and unfolds in a remarkably predictable way. All that seems necessary is a reasonably adequate environment: a nourishing womb, opportunities to explore the world through one's senses and actions, and social interactions with caregivers. Maturation and experience will then ensure that virtually all infants progress through similar milestones at similar ages. Scientists delight in such predictability.

Ah, but human development becomes less and less predictable as time passes. The universal forces of biological maturation become less powerful than they were in infancy (McCall, 1981), although they continue to guide development throughout the life span. Instead, our *individual* genetic endowments express themselves more fully, and, partly influenced by our individual heredities, we increasingly accumulate our own unique histories of life experiences. As social/environmental influences become more significant over the years, we may still detect psychological similarities between individuals of similar ages *if* these individuals experience similar life events and role transitions at similar ages. However, there will not be much regularity at all if different adults experience events such as leaving school, marrying, and becoming parents at widely different ages and if they also experience their own idiosyncratic or nonnormative life events such as divorces, car accidents, and promotions. This diversity of experience is a reality in adulthood. The result? We know a good deal about a person knowing that he or she is 2 weeks or 2 years old, whereas we know very little indeed about a person simply knowing that he or she is 25 or 65. Indeed, elderly adults are as diverse a group of human beings as one can find.

In sum, we can draw some generalizations about different phases of the life span, but we must avoid stereotyping human beings based on age. Our "stereotypes" of infants are quite accurate, but the generalizations we make about elderly people may not fit any particular elderly person very well. The fact that different individuals follow different developmental pathways over a lifetime is challenging to developmentalists who study adult development, for they rarely detect the sorts of universal, age-related stages that students of infant and child development have described. Instead, it becomes necessary to look more closely at the major life events that individuals experience, regardless of how old they are at the time, and to trace the implications of these events for later functioning.

We Develop in a Cultural and Historical Context

Life-span developmentalists have begun to include in their definition of "environment" not only the individual's immediate context (home, classroom, workplace, and so on) but the broader social context in which he or she develops. As we saw in Chapter 4, human development does take different forms depending on how a particular culture carves up the life span into meaningful age groups and what it expects people of different ages to do. Moreover, human development in the 17th century was different from human development in the 20th century, and our development as individuals is influenced by social changes and historical events occurring during our lifetimes. The implication? Much as we may lament it, a good deal of the research described in this book is culture bound and time bound. Research findings that are most often based on children and adults in Western societies in the 20th century (most often middle-class, white children and adults, at that) may not generalize to humans in non-Western societies or other historical eras.

Yet by systematically studying the influence on development of where and when people are born, we gain insights into how important the context of development is. Already, for example, it is clear that today's cohorts of adults are functioning better intellectually and maintaining their intellectual capacities longer than adults who were born early in this century and who received less education and poorer health care (Schaie, 1983). What this suggests is that our current picture of functioning in old age may be overpessimistic. Future cohorts of elderly people are more likely than today's elderly people to enjoy good health and to maintain a high level of intellectual functioning well into old age. Changes in the family and in men's and women's roles, technological innovations such as the computer, and significant events yet to take place may make human development in the 21st century quite different from human development today.

We Are Active in Our Own Development

Early developmental theorists tended to view human beings as passively shaped by forces beyond their control. Sigmund Freud viewed the developing child as driven by biological urges and molded by early experiences in the family. John Watson and other early learning theorists emphasized that humans merely respond to the stimuli that their environments provide. Jean Piaget did much to alter this image of developing humans by emphasizing how children *actively* explore the world around them and *actively* invent their own understandings rather than merely absorbing lessons spoonfed to them by adults. Piaget's insights about the developing child are now firmly embedded in our assumptions about human development at all ages. To be sure, infants are influenced by their caregivers, but they also elicit more or less responsive care from adults depending on their own temperaments and behaviors. Children, in a very real sense, tell their parents how to parent them and, by doing so, contribute to their own development. With age, we only become more active in our own development, for we have more freedom and ability to seek out the experiences we want and to influence those around us. It is the ongoing, dynamic transaction between an active person and a changing environment, each influencing the other in a reciprocal way, that steers our development.

Development Is Best Viewed from a Life-Span Perspective

Developmentalists have never before been as aware of the importance of understanding linkages between earlier and later development as they are today. It is valuable, of course, to study infancy, adolescence, or any other developmental period in its own right. But it is more valuable still to view behavior during any one phase of life from a life-span perspective. It is revealing, for example, to appreciate that the teenage girl who bickers with her parents about house rules started out as an infant securely attached to these individuals; gained from her attachment the sense of security she needed to assert her autonomy as a 2- and 3-year-old; and has been building ever since toward the time when she can forge her own identity. It is important too to recognize that this adolescent's quest for a separate identity and increased independence will help her arrive at the point when she is ready to launch a career, commit herself to an intimate relationship, and perhaps nurture children of her own.

Much Remains to Be Learned

Often it seems that the more one learns about a topic the more one realizes how much more there is to learn. This is certainly true of human development. As our discussion here reveals, developmentalists have abandoned simple models in favor of more complex ones. They appreciate, for example, that development is not the result of nature *or* nurture working alone, but that it is instead the product of the ongoing transactions between a changing person and a changing world. They appreciate that human development can take a variety of routes depending on how a maturing individual and his or her ever-changing environments affect one another. In short, developmentalists are increasingly adopting the sophisticated *contextual/dialectical* model of human development that we introduced in Chapter 2, and this is prompting them to ask questions that would not even have been raised in the past. How, for example, do children who are predisposed to be either sociable or shy really influence the behavior of their parents, peers, and teachers over time, and how are changes in the ways in which others treat them linked to changes in their behavior? We have barely scratched the surface in our efforts to find out how developing humans shape and are shaped by the immediate and broader contexts in which they develop, and how relationships between person and environment change over the years. We need more long-term longitudinal studies in order to truly capture the *process* of development, and we need to consider a wider range of influences on development, if we can ever hope for a better explanation of human development and its many variations.

For developmentalists, then, there are always more questions than answers. We find this to be both a humbling and an inspiring thought. And we hope that you too feel both humbled and inspired as you complete your introduction to life-span human development. For much as you may have learned, there is much more to be discovered. We hope that you are intrigued enough to observe more closely your own development and that of those around you or even to take further coursework. We hope that you will use what you learn to steer your own development and that of others in more productive directions. Yet no matter how much any of us learns about human development, life will still offer us challenges and surprises. The 17th-century French sage François La Rochefoucauld put it nicely: "We come newborn to every milestone of life's journey, and often act like novices at each, no matter what our age" (La Rochefoucauld, 1959, p. 108).

Glossary

A, not B, error The tendency of 8- to 12-month-old infants to search for a hidden object in the place where they last found it (A) rather than in its new hiding place (B).

ability tracking The practice in education of grouping students according to ability and then educating them in classes with students of comparable academic or intellectual standing.

accommodation In Piaget's cognitive-developmental theory, the process of modifying existing schemata in order to incorporate or adapt to new experiences; in vision, changes in the shape of the eye's lens to bring objects at differing distances into focus.

active-behavioral coping strategies Methods of dealing with stressful events that involve taking positive action of some sort in an effort to resolve problems.

activity theory A perspective holding that aging adults will find satisfaction to the extent that they maintain an active lifestyle. Contrast to *disengagement theory.*

adaptation In Piaget's cognitive-developmental theory, one's inborn tendency to adjust to the demands of the environment, consisting of the complementary processes of assimilation and accommodation.

adolescent egocentrism A characteristic of adolescent thought that involves difficulty differentiating between one's own thoughts and feelings and those of other people; evident in the *personal fable* and *imaginary audience* phenomena.

adolescent growth spurt The rapid increase in physical growth that occurs during adolescence.

affiliative motive A desire to interact with other human beings or to form and maintain social relationships.

age by treatment experiment A special experiment in which a researcher studies differences between age groups in their responses to an experimental treatment or manipulation.

age grades Socially defined age groups or strata, each with different statuses, roles, privileges, and responsibilities in society.

age-irrelevant society A society in which age norms have loosened, and many behaviors are acceptable at a wide range of ages.

age norm Expectations about what people should be doing or how they should behave at different points in the life span.

age of viability A point (currently between about the 24th and 28th prenatal weeks) when a fetus may survive outside the uterus if excellent medical care is available.

ageism Prejudice and discrimination directed at older people.

aging To the biologist, deterioration of the organism that leads inevitably to death; to most developmentalists, positive, negative, or neutral changes in the *mature* organism.

alternative birth center A birthing room or facility that provides a homelike atmosphere but still makes medical technology available.

altruism Behavior such as helping or sharing that is motivated by concern for the welfare of another person rather than by self-interest.

Alzheimer's disease A pathological condition of the nervous system that results in an irreversible loss of cognitive capacities; the leading cause of dementia.

amniocentesis A method of extracting amniotic fluid from a pregnant woman so that fetal body cells within the fluid can be tested for chromosomal abnormalities and other genetic defects.

amnion A watertight membrane that surrounds the developing embryo, serving to regulate its temperature and to cushion it against injuries.

amoral Lacking any sense of morality; without standards of right and wrong.

anaclitic depression Sadness, withdrawal, and developmental delay associated with the loss of an attachment figure during infancy.

anal stage Freud's second stage of psychosexual development (from 1 to 3 years of age), in which anal activities such as defecation become the primary methods of gratifying the sex instinct.

androgenized females Genetic females who were exposed to male sex hormones during the prenatal period and therefore developed malelike external genitals and some masculine behaviors.

androgens Male hormones that help trigger the adolescent growth spurt, as well as the development of the male sex organs, secondary sex characteristics, and sexual motivation.

androgyny A gender-role orientation in which the person possesses *both* masculine-stereotyped and feminine-stereotyped personality traits.

animism The attribution of life and lifelike qualities to inanimate objects.

anorexia nervosa A life-threatening eating disorder characterized by failure to maintain a normal weight, a strong fear of weight gain, and a distorted body image; literally, "nervous lack of appetite."

anoxia A lack of sufficient oxygen to the brain; may result in neurological damage or death.

anticipatory grief Grieving before death occurs for what is happening and for what lies ahead.

Apgar test A test that is routinely used to assess a newborn's heart rate, respiration, color, muscle tone, and reflexes immediately after birth and then 5 minutes later; used to identify high-risk babies.

assimilation Piaget's term for the process by which children interpret new experiences by incorporating them into their existing schemata.

attachment A strong affectional tie that binds a person to an intimate companion; characterized by affection and a desire to maintain proximity.

attention The focusing of perception and cognition on something in particular.

attention-deficit hyperactivity disorder A childhood disorder characterized by inattention or attention deficits, impulsive behavior, and overactive or fidgety behavior.

attribution theory A theory of motivation emphasizing that explanations or causal attributions for outcomes influence future expectancies of success and motivation to succeed.

authoritarian parenting A restrictive style of parenting in which adults impose many rules, expect strict obedience, and often rely on power tactics rather than explanations to elicit compliance.

authoritative parenting A flexible style of parenting in which adults lay down clear rules but also grant a fair amount of autonomy to their children and explain the rationale for their restrictions.

autism See *infantile autism.*

autoimmune reactions Processes in which the immune system produces antibodies to attack and kill normal body cells; involved in rheumatoid arthritis and other diseases and possibly in aging and dying.

automatization The process by which information processing becomes effortless and highly efficient as a result of continued practice or increased expertise.

autonomous morality Piaget's second stage of moral development, in which children, starting at age 10 or 11, realize that rules are agreements between individuals that can be changed by consensus.

autonomy The capacity to make decisions independently, serve as one's own source of emotional strength, and otherwise manage life tasks without being overdependent on other people; an important developmental task of adolescence.

autonomy versus shame and doubt Psychosocial conflict in which toddlers attempt to demonstrate their independence from and control over other people; second of Erikson's stages.

avoidance coping strategies Methods of dealing with stressful events that involve denying or escaping one's problems rather than taking constructive action.

babbling An early form of vocalization that appears between 4 and 6 months of age and involves repeating consonant–vowel combinations such as "baba" or "dadada."

baby biographies Carefully recorded observations of the growth and development of children by their parents over a period of time. The first scientific investigations of development.

behavior genetics The scientific study of how genotype interacts with environment to determine behavioral attributes such as intelligence, temperament, and personality.

behavior modification The systematic application of learning principles to change behavior in desirable directions.

behaviorism A school of thinking in psychology that holds that conclusions about human development should be based on controlled observations of overt behavior rather than on speculation about unconscious motives or other unobservable phenomena; the philosophical underpinning for early theories of learning.

bereavement A state of loss that provides the occasion for grief and mourning.

blastula A hollow sphere of about 100 to 150 cells that the zygote forms by rapid cell division as it moves through the fallopian tube.

breech presentation A delivery in which the fetus emerges feet first or buttocks first rather than head first.

bulimia nervosa A life-threatening eating disorder characterized by recurrent eating binges followed by purging activities such as vomiting.

carrier In genetics, an individual who possesses a recessive gene associated with a disease and who, while he or she does not have the disease, can transmit the gene for it to offspring.

case study A research method in which the investigator gathers extensive information about the life of a single individual and then tests hypotheses by analyzing this information.

cataracts A pathologic condition of the eye involving opacification (clouding) of the lens that can impair vision or cause blindness.

catch-up growth A phenomenon in which children who have experienced growth deficits will grow very rapidly to "catch up to" the growth trajectory that they are genetically programmed to follow.

categorical self A person's classification of the self along socially significant dimensions such as age and sex.

centration The tendency to focus on only one aspect of a problem when two or more aspects are relevant.

cephalocaudal direction The principle that growth proceeds from the head (cephalic region) to the tail (caudal region).

cerebral cortex The convoluted outer covering of the brain that is involved in voluntary body movements, perception, and higher intellectual functions such as learning, thinking, and speaking.

Cesarean section A surgical procedure in which an incision is made in the mother's abdomen and uterus so that the baby can be removed through the abdomen.

chorion A membrane that surrounds the amnion and becomes attached to the uterine lining to gather nourishment for the embryo.

chorionic villus biopsy An alternative to amniocentesis in which a catheter is inserted through the cervix to withdraw fetal cells from the chorion for prenatal testing to detect genetic defects.

chromosome A threadlike structure made up of genes; in humans, there are 46 chromosomes in the nucleus of each cell.

chromosomal abnormalities Conditions in which a child has too few, too many, or incomplete chromosomes because of errors in the formation of sperm or ova.

chumship A close friendship with a peer of the same sex that emerges at about age 9 to 12, according to Sullivan.

class inclusion The logical understanding that parts or subclasses are included in the whole class and that the whole is therefore greater than any of its parts.

classical conditioning A type of learning in which a stimulus that intially had no effect on the individual comes to elicit a response owing to its association with a stimulus that already elicits the response.

climacteric The loss of reproductive capacity in either sex in later life.

clinical method An interview procedure used by Jean Piaget in which a child's response to each successive question (or problem) determines what the investigator will ask next; that is, an unstandardized questioning procedure.

clique A small friendship group that interacts frequently.

codominance In genetics, an instance in which two different but equally powerful genes produce a phenotype in which both genes are equally expressed.

cognition The activity of knowing and the processes through which knowledge is acquired (e.g., attending, perceiving, remembering, and thinking).

cognitive style An individual's characteristic ways of approaching problems and processing information, as illustrated by the dimensions of field independence/dependence and reflectivity/impulsivity.

cohabitation The living together of two single adults as an unmarried couple.

cohort A group of people born at the same time; a particular generation of people, whose development may differ from that of other cohorts.

computer-assisted instruction Learning activities conducted with the aid of a computer, ranging from simple drills to elaborate problem-solving activities.

conception The moment of fertilization, when a sperm penetrates an ovum, forming a zygote.

concordance rate The percentage of cases in which a particular attribute is present for both members of a pair of people (e.g., twins) if it is present for one member.

concrete operations stage Piaget's third stage of cognitive development, lasting from about age 7 to age 11, when children are acquiring logical operations and can reason effectively about real objects and experiences.

conditioned response (CR) A learned response to a stimulus that was not originally capable of producing the response.

conditioned stimulus (CS) An initially neutral stimulus that comes to elicit a particular response after being paired with an unconditioned stimulus that always elicits the response.

confidant A spouse, relative, or friend to whom a person feels emotionally close and with whom he or she can share thoughts and feelings.

conformity The tendency to go along with the opinions or wishes of someone else or to yield to group pressures.

conservation The recognition that certain properties of an object or substance do not change when its appearance is altered in some superficial way.

constraint-seeking questions In the Twenty Questions Task and similar hypothesis-testing tasks, questions that rule out more than one answer to narrow the field of possible choices rather than asking about only one hypothesis at a time.

contact comfort The pleasurable tactile sensations provided by a parent or a soft, terry cloth mother substitute; believed to foster attachments in infant monkeys and possibly humans.

contextual-dialectical theories Theoretical perspectives that hold that development arises from the ongoing interrelationships between a changing organism and a changing world.

continuity/discontinuity issue The debate among theorists about whether human development is best characterized as gradual and continuous or abrupt and stagelike.

continuous reinforcement A schedule of reinforcement in which every occurrence of an act is reinforced.

contour The amount of light/dark transition or boundary area in a visual stimulus.

conventional morality Kohlberg's term for the third and fourth stages of moral reasoning in which societal values are internalized and judgments are based on a desire to gain approval or uphold law and social order.

convergent thinking Thinking that involves "converging" on the one best answer to a problem and that is precisely what IQ tests measure. Contrast with *divergent thinking.*

cooing An early form of vocalization that involves repeating vowel-like sounds.

cooperative learning methods Procedures that involve assigning students, usually of different races or ability levels, to work teams that are reinforced for performing well as teams and that therefore encourage cooperation among teammates.

correlation A relationship or association between two variables, the strength and direction of which is expressed as a correlation coefficient.

correlation coefficient A measure, ranging from +1.00 to −1.00, of the extent to which two variables or attributes are systematically related to each other in either a positive or a negative way.

correlational method A research technique that involves determining whether two or more variables are related to one another. It cannot indicate that one thing caused another, but it can *suggest* that a causal relationship exists or allows us to predict one characteristic from our knowledge of another.

counterconditioning A treatment based on classical conditioning principles in which the goal is to extinguish an undesirable response to a person, object, or situation and replace it with a new and more adaptive response.

creativity The ability to produce novel responses or works.

critical period A defined period in the development of an organism when it is particularly sensitive to certain environmental influences; outside this period, the same influences will have far less effect.

cross-cultural comparison A research method that compares the behavior and/or development of people from different cultural backgrounds.

crossing over A process in which genetic material is exchanged between pairs of chromosomes during meiosis.

cross-linkage theory Theory of aging focusing on the increased interlinking or coupling of molecules of collagen or other substances.

cross-modal perception The ability to use one sensory modality to identify a stimulus or pattern of stimuli that is already familiar through another modality.

cross-sectional design A developmental research design in which different age groups are studied at the same point in time and compared.

crowd A network of heterosexual cliques that forms during adolescence and serves to arrange mixed-sex social activities.

crystallized intelligence Those aspects of intellectual functioning that involve making use of knowledge acquired through experience. Contrast with *fluid intelligence.*

cultural/familial retardation Mental retardation that appears to be due to some combination of low genetic potential and a poor family environment rather than to a specific biological cause. Contrast with *organic retardation.*

cultural relativity The principle that a person's behavior can be understood only within the context of his or her cultural environment.

culture A system of meanings shared by a population of people and transmitted to future generations.

culture bias The situation that arises in testing when one cultural or subcultural group is more familiar with test items than another group and therefore has an unfair advantage.

cumulative-deficit hypothesis The notion that impoverished environments inhibit intellectual growth and that these inhibiting effects accumulate over time.

daily hassles Everyday annoyances or chronic life strains that can mount up and cause psychological distress or physical illness.

damage theories of aging Theories that emphasize a number of haphazard processes that cause cells and organ systems to deteriorate; contrast to *programmed theories.*

dark adaptation The process by which the eyes become more sensitive to light over time as they remain in the dark.

death anxiety A complex set of concerns about death and dying.

decentration The ability to focus on two or more dimensions of a problem at one time.

defense mechanisms Mechanisms used by the ego to defend itself against anxiety caused by conflict between the id's impulses and social demands.

deferred imitation The imitation of models who are no longer present.

delirium A clouding of consciousness characterized by alternating periods of disorientation and coherence.

dementia A progressive loss of cognitive capacities such as memory and judgment that affects some aging individuals and that has a variety of causes.

denial A defense mechanism in which anxiety-provoking thoughts are kept out of, or isolated from, conscious awareness.

dependent variable The aspect of behavior that is measured in an experiment and that is assumed to be under the control of, or "dependent" on, the independent variable.

depression See *major depression.*

development Systematic changes in the individual occurring between conception and death; such changes can be positive, negative, or neutral.

developmental psychology A discipline that seeks to describe, explain, and optimize changes in individuals and in their relationships with other people from conception until death.

developmental psychopathology A field of study concerned with the origins and course of maladaptive or psychopathological behavior.

developmental quotient (DQ) A numerical measure of an infant's performance on a developmental test relative to the performance of other infants the same age.

developmental stage A distinct phase within a larger sequence of development; a period characterized by a particular set of abilities, motives, behaviors, or emotions that occur together and form a coherent pattern.

dialectical theory The view, set forth by Klaus Riegel, that development results from the continuous dialogues between a changing person and a changing world.

dialectical thinking The ability to uncover and resolve contradictions between opposing ideas.

diathesis/stress model The view that psychopathology results from the interaction of a person's predisposition to psychological problems and the experience of stressful events.

differentiation theory A perspective holding that perception involves detecting distinctive features or cues that are contained in the sensory stimulation we receive. Contrast with *enrichment theory.*

diffusion status Identity status characterizing individuals who are not questioning who they are and have not committed themselves to an identity.

disengagement theory A perspective that holds that successful aging involves a mutually satisfying withdrawal of the aging individual and society from one another. Contrast to *activity theory.*

display rules Socially defined rules specifying what emotions should or should not be expressed under what circumstances.

distinctive feature Any dimension on which two or more objects differ and can be discriminated.

divergent thinking Thinking that requires coming up with a variety of ideas or solutions to a problem when there is no one right answer. Contrast with *convergent thinking.*

DNA repair theory Theory of aging that focuses on the deterioration of the genetic material, DNA, and the body's diminished ability to repair this damage.

dominant gene A relatively powerful gene that is expressed phenotypically and masks the effect of a less powerful, recessive gene.

double standard The view that sexual behavior appropriate for members of one gender is inappropriate for members of the other.

Down syndrome A chromosomal abnormality in which the child has inherited an extra 21st chromosome and is, as a result, mentally retarded; also called trisomy 21.

dying trajectory The perceived shape and duration of the path that the dying individual is following from life to death.

echolalia The repetition of sounds, as when an autistic child parrots back what someone else says.

eclectic In the context of science, an individual who recognizes that no single theory can explain everything but that each has something to contribute to our understanding.

ecological approach Bronfenbrenner's view emphasizing that the developing person is embedded in a series of environmental systems (microsystem, mesosystem, exosystem, and macrosystem).

effectance motivation A motive to display competence, master challenges, and affect the world around one.

ego Psychoanalytic term for the rational component of the personality.

egocentrism The tendency to view the world from one's own perspective while failing to recognize that others may have different points of view.

elaboration A strategy for remembering that involves adding something to or creating meaningful links between the bits of information one is trying to retain.

Electra complex Female version of the Oedipus complex, in which a 4- to 6-year-old girl is said to envy her father for possessing a penis and would choose him as a sex object in the hope of sharing this valuable organ that she lacks.

empathy The vicarious experiencing of another person's feelings.

empirical-inductive reasoning A style of problem solving in which one induces or draws general conclusions based on specific observations.

empty nest Term used to describe the family after the last child departs the household.

encoding The first step in learning and remembering something. It is the process of getting information into the information-processing system or learning it and organizing it in a form suitable for storing.

endocrine gland Type of gland that secretes chemicals called hormones directly into the bloodstream. Endocrine glands play critical roles in stimulating growth and regulating bodily functions.

endocrine theory Theory of aging claiming that the genes program hormonal changes that bring about death.

engrossment Parents' fascination with their neonate; a desire to touch, hold, caress, and talk to the newborn baby.

enrichment theory A perspective on perception holding that we must "add to" sensory stimulation by drawing on stored knowledge in order to perceive a meaningful world. Contrast with *differentiation theory*.

environment Events or conditions outside the person that are presumed to influence, or be influenced by, the individual.

equity A balance of contributions and gains in a social relationship that results in neither partner feeling over- or underbenefited.

estrogen The female hormone responsible for the development of the breasts and the female sex organs and secondary sex characteristics as well as the beginning of menstrual cycles.

ethology A discipline that studies the evolved behavior of a species in its natural surroundings.

euthanasia Literally, "good death"; specifically, hastening the death of someone who is suffering from an incurable illness or injury.

exosystem In Bronfenbrenner's ecological approach, settings not experienced directly by the individual that still influence his or her development (e.g., effects of events at a parent's workplace on a child's development).

experiment A research strategy in which the investigator manipulates or alters some aspect of a person's environment in order to measure what effect it has on the individual's behavior or development.

experimental control The holding of all other factors besides the independent variable in an experiment constant, so that any changes in the dependent variable can be said to be caused by the manipulation of the independent variable.

expressive role A pattern of behavior, usually instilled in females, that stresses being kind, nurturant, cooperative, and sensitive to the needs of others.

extended family A family unit composed of parents and children and other kin such as grandparents, aunts and uncles, cousins, and so on, especially when living together.

extinction The gradual weakening and disappearance of a learned response when it is no longer reinforced.

extraversion/introversion A personality dimension indicating the extent to which a person is outgoing and socially oriented as opposed to shy, retiring, and uncomfortable around other people.

factor analysis A technique that identifies clusters of tasks or test items (called factors) that are highly correlated with one another and unrelated to other items.

failure to thrive A condition observed in infants who are emotionally deprived and characterized by stunted growth, weight loss, and delays in cognitive and socioemotional development.

faith The ways in which we make or find meaning in our lives, within or outside the context of organized religion.

family life cycle The sequence of changes in family composition, roles, and relationships that occurs from the time people marry until they die.

fetal alcohol syndrome A group of congenital problems commonly observed in the offspring of mothers who use alcohol heavily during pregnancy.

field dependent A dimension of cognitive style that involves being highly dependent on or influenced by the surrounding context.

field independent A dimension of cognitive style that involves being relatively undistracted by the surrounding context and able to analyze complex stimuli.

filter model of mate selection Model proposed by Udry that views partner selection as a process of narrowing the field of possible partners by means of considerations of propinquity, attractiveness, social background, and so on.

5-to-7 shift The dramatic changes in cognition and problem solving that occur between ages 5 and 7.

fixation In psychoanalytic theory, a defense mechanism in which development is arrested and part of the libido remains tied to an early stage of development.

fluid intelligence Those aspects of intelligence that involve actively thinking and reasoning to solve novel problems. Contrast with *crystallized intelligence.*

foreclosure status Identity status characterizing individuals who appear to have committed themselves to a life direction but who have adopted an identity prematurely, without much thought.

formal operations stage Piaget's fourth and final stage of cognitive development (from age 11 or 12 and beyond), when the individual begins to think more rationally and systematically about abstract concepts and hypothetical ideas.

fraternal twins Twins that are not identical and that result when a mother releases two ova at roughly the same time and each is fertilized by a different sperm.

free radicals Molecules that have an extra or "free" electron, are chemically unstable, and react with other molecules in the body to produce substances that damage normal cells; a possible factor in aging and death.

functional grammar An analysis of the semantic relations (meanings) that children express in their earliest sentences.

gender consistency The stage of gender typing in which children realize that one's sex is stable across situations or despite changes in activities or appearance.

gender identity One's awareness that one is either a male or a female.

gender-role norms Society's expectations or standards concerning what males and females should be like and how they should behave.

gender-role stereotypes Overgeneralized and largely inaccurate beliefs about what males and females are like.

gender roles A pattern of behaviors and traits that defines how to act the part of a female or a male in a particular society.

gender schemas Organized sets of beliefs and expectations about males and females that guide information processing.

gender stability The stage of gender typing in which children realize that sex remains stable over time.

gender typing The process by which children become aware of their gender and acquire the motives, values, and behaviors considered appropriate for members of their biological sex.

gene A functional unit of heredity made up of DNA and transmitted from generation to generation.

generation gap The discrepancy or difference between the attitudes and values of older and younger generations.

generativity versus stagnation The psychosocial conflict in which middle-aged adults must gain the sense that they have produced something that will outlive them and genuinely care for younger generations in order to avoid self-preoccupation; seventh of Erikson's stages.

genetic counseling A service designed to inform prospective parents about genetic conditions and to help them determine the likelihood that they would transmit such disorders to their children.

genital stage Freud's fifth and final stage of psychosexual development (from puberty onward), in which the underlying aim of the sex instinct is to establish an erotic relationship with another adult and to have children.

genotype The genetic endowment that an individual inherits; contrast with *phenotype.*

germinal period First phase of prenatal development, lasting for about two weeks from conception until the developing organism becomes attached to the wall of the uterus.

gerontology The study of aging and old age.

Gestalt psychology A school of psychology emphasizing organization, patterning, and wholeness in human experience, especially innate principles for organizing visual stimuli into coherent patterns.

giftedness The possession of unusually high general intellectual potential or of special abilities in such areas as creativity, mathematics, or the arts.

goal-corrected partnership John Bowlby's term for parent/child attachments starting at about age 3, when children can adjust their behavior to the goals and plans of their attachment objects.

grief The emotional response to loss.

growth The physical changes that occur from conception to maturity.

habituation A simple form of learning that involves learning *not* to respond to a stimulus that is repeated over and over; learning to be bored by the familiar.

Hayflick limit The estimate that human cells can double only 50 times, plus or minus 10, and then will die.

heritability The amount of variability in a population on some trait dimension that is attributable to genetic differences among those individuals.

heteronomous morality Piaget's first stage of moral development, in which children view the rules of authority figures as sacred and unalterable.

heterozygous Having inherited two genes that have different effects (e.g., one gene for straight hair, one for curly hair).

holophrase A single-word utterance used by an infant that represents an entire sentence's worth of meaning.

HOME inventory A widely used instrument that allows an observer to determine just how intellectually stimulating or impoverished a home environment is.

homozygous Having inherited two genes for an attribute that are identical in their effects.

horizontal decalage An inability to solve certain problems even though one can solve similar problems presumably requiring the same mental operations; unevenness in the emergence of related abilities.

hospice A program that supports dying persons and their families through a philosophy of "caring" rather than "curing," either in a facility or at home.

hot flashes Sudden experiences of warmth and sweating, often followed by a cold shiver, that occur in menopausal women.

human growth hormone The pituitary hormone that stimulates the rapid growth and development of body cells.

Huntington's disease A genetic disease caused by a single, dominant gene that strikes in middle age to produce a deterioration of physical and mental abilities and premature death.

hyperactivity See *attention-deficit hyperactivity disorder.*

hypothesis A theoretical prediction about what will hold true if we observe a phenomenon.

hypothetical-deductive reasoning A style of problem solving in which one starts with general or abstract ideas and deduces or traces their specific implications; "if/then" thinking.

id Psychoanalytic term for the inborn component of the personality that is driven by the instincts or selfish urges.

ideational fluency The most common measure of creativity; the sheer number of different, including novel, ideas that one can generate.

identical twins Monozygotic twins who develop from a single zygote that later divides to form two genetically identical individuals.

identification Freud's term for the individual's tendency to emulate, or adopt the attitudes and behaviors of, another person, particularly his or her same-sex parent.

identity One's self-definition or sense of who one is, where one is going, and how one fits into society.

identity achievement status Identity status characterizing individuals who have carefully thought through identity issues and made commitments or resolved their identity issues.

identity versus role confusion The psychosocial conflict in which adolescents must form a coherent self-definition or else remain confused about their life directions; fifth of Erickson's stages.

idiot savant A person who has an extraordinary talent but who is otherwise mentally retarded.

imaginary audience A form of adolescent egocentrism that involves confusing your own thoughts with the thoughts of a hypothesized audience for your behavior and concluding that others share your preoccupations.

imaginary companions Pretend playmates invented by many preschool children during the peak of symbolic play.

immanent justice In Piaget's heteronomous stage of moral development, the belief that rule violations will invariably be punished, that justice is ever present in the world.

immune system theory Theory of aging focusing on declines in the body's ability to defend itself successfully against potentially life-threatening foreign agents such as infection, and on autoimmune reactions that jeopardize normal body cells.

imprinting An innate form of learning in which the young of certain species will follow and become attached to moving objects (usually their mothers) during a critical period early in life.

impulsivity A cognitive style characterized by quick responding to problems, often based on the first hypothesis or answer that comes to mind. Contrast with *reflectivity.*

incomplete dominance Condition in which a stronger gene fails to mask all the effects of a weaker partner gene; a phenotype results that is similar but not identical to the effect of the stronger gene.

independent variable The aspect of the environment that a researcher deliberately changes or manipulates in an experiment in order to see what effect it has on behavior; a causal variable. Contrast to *dependent variable.*

indirect effects Instances in which the relationship between two individuals in a family is modified by the behavior or attitudes of a third family member.

individuative-reflective faith In Fowler's theory of the development of faith, the stage that involves reflecting on the meaning of life and developing a belief system that is uniquely one's own.

induction A form of discipline that involves explaining why a child's behavior is wrong and should be changed by emphasizing its effects on other people.

industry versus inferiority Psychosocial conflict in which school-aged children must master important cognitive and social skills or else feel incompetent; fourth of Erikson's stages.

infant states The different levels of consciousness such as sleep, alert inactivity, and crying that young infants experience during a day.

infantile amnesia A lack of memory for the early years of one's life.

infantile autism A pervasive and severe developmental disorder that begins in infancy and is characterized by such problems as an aversion to social contact, deviant communication or mutism, and repetitive, stereotyped behavior.

information-processing approach An approach to cognition that emphasizes the fundamental mental processes involved in attention, perception, memory, and decision making.

initiative versus guilt Psychosocial conflict in which preschool children must learn to initiate new activities and pursue bold plans or else become self-critical; third of Erikson's stages.

insecure-avoidant attachment An infant/caregiver bond or intimate relationship characterized by little separation protest and a tendency to avoid or ignore the attachment object.

insecure-resistant attachment An anxious and ambivalent infant/caregiver bond or intimate relationship in which the individual may strongly protest separations but resist contact upon reunion.

instinct An inborn biological force assumed to motivate a particular response or class of responses.

instrumental role A pattern of behavior, usually instilled in males, that stresses being dominant, independent, assertive, and competitive.

integrity versus despair Psychosocial conflict in which elderly adults attempt to find a sense of meaning in their lives and to accept the inevitability of death; eighth of Erikson's stages.

intelligence According to Piaget, a basic life function that helps an organism adapt to its environment; more generally, mental abilities that permit humans to learn and solve problems.

intelligence quotient (IQ) A numerical measure of a person's performance on an intelligence test relative to the performance of other examinees of the same age, typically with a score of 100 defined as average.

internalization The process of adopting as one's own the attributes or standards of other people.

intimacy versus isolation Psychosocial conflict in which young adults must commit themselves to a shared identity with another person or else remain aloof and unconnected to others; sixth of Erikson's stages.

Just Community An approach to moral education advocated by Lawrence Kohlberg in which students and teachers jointly and democratically deal with the moral issues facing them.

juvenile delinquency Lawbreaking behavior by a minor.

karyotype A chromosomal portrait created by staining chromosomes, photographing them under a high power microscope, and arranging them into a predetermined pattern.

kinship The extent to which two individuals share genes in common; degree of genetic relatedness.

Klinefelter syndrome A sex chromosome abnormality in which males inherit two or more X chromosomes (XXY or XXXY); these males fail to develop secondary sex characteristics and often show deficiencies on tests of verbal abilities.

knowledge base One's existing information about a content area, significant for its influence on how well one can learn and remember.

Lamaze method Prepared childbirth in which parents attend classes and learn mental exercises and relaxation techniques to ease delivery.

language A symbolic system in which a limited number of signals can be combined according to rules to produce an infinite number of messages.

language acquisition device (LAD) A set of linguistic processing skills that nativists believe to be innate; presumably the LAD enables a child to infer the rules governing others' speech and then to use these rules to produce language.

latency period Freud's fourth stage of psychosexual development (age 6 to puberty), in which sexual desires are repressed and all the child's available libido is channeled into socially acceptable outlets such as schoolwork or rigorous play.

lateralization The specialization of the two hemispheres of the cerebral cortex of the brain.

learned helplessness A crippling inability to act based on the sense that one cannot control one's outcomes in life.

learning A relatively permanent change in behavior (or behavior potential) that results from one's experiences or practice.

leisure Time that is one's own, free of obligations.

libido Freud's term for the biological energy of the sex instinct.

life expectancy The average number of years a newborn baby today can be expected to live; almost 75 years at present in the United States.

life review Process in which elderly adults reflect on unresolved conflicts of the past and evaluate their lives; it may contribute to a sense of integrity and readiness for death.

life-span perspective An emerging view that development occurs throughout the life span, is very much affected by the historical context in which it occurs, can take many different directions, is influenced by many interacting causal factors, and can best be understood if changes during one period of life are viewed in relation to changes during other periods of life.

life structure In Levinson's theory of adult development, an overall pattern of life that reflects the person's priorities and relationships.

Living Will A document in which a person states in advance that he or she does not wish to have extraordinary medical procedures applied if he or she is hopelessly ill.

locus of control A personality dimension differentiating between people who assume they are personally responsible for their life outcomes (internal locus) and people who believe that their outcomes depend on forces outside themselves (external locus).

logical operation A type of cognitive schema in which an internal mental activity is performed on the objects of thought; an action such as mental addition or classification.

longitudinal design A developmental research design in which one group of subjects is studied repeatedly over a period of months or years.

long-term memory The third memory store in information processing, in which information that has been examined and interpreted is stored relatively permanently for future use.

looking-glass self The idea that a person's self-concept is largely a reflection of the ways in which other people respond to him or her.

love withdrawal A form of discipline that involves withholding attention, affection, or approval after a child misbehaves.

macrosystem In Bronfenbrenner's ecological approach, the larger cultural or subcultural context of development.

mainstreaming The educational practice of integrating handicapped students into regular classrooms rather than placing them in segregated special education classes.

major depression An affective or mood disorder characterized by at least one episode of feeling profoundly sad and hopeless and/or losing interest in almost all activities.

masked depression Depression, particularly in a child, that seems to manifest itself more in problems such as aggression and anxiety than in overtly depressed behavior, and that is therefore "disguised" as problems other than depression.

maturation Developmental changes that are biologically programmed by genes rather than being caused by learning, injury, illness, or some other life experience.

maximum life span A ceiling on the number of years that any member of a species lives; 110 to 120 for humans.

mechanistic model A world view underlying certain theories that regards human beings as machines shaped by outside forces and analyzable into their parts. Contrast with *organismic model.*

meiosis The process in which a germ cell divides, producing gametes (sperm or ova), each containing half of the parent cell's original complement of chromosomes; in humans, the products of meiosis normally contain 23 chromosomes.

menarche A female's first menstrual period.

menopause The ending of a woman's menstrual periods and reproductive capacity in midlife.

mental age (MA) A measure of intellectual development that reflects the level of age-graded problems that a child is able to solve; the age at which a child functions intellectually.

mental retardation Significant subaverage general intellectual functioning associated with impairments in adaptive behavior and manifested during the developmental period.

mentor A guide or adviser who provides consultation and practical aid to a younger person.

mesosystem In Bronfenbrenner's ecological approach, interrelationships between microsystems or immediate environments (e.g., ways in which events in the family affect a child's interactions at a day-care center).

metacognition The ability to engage in thinking about thinking.

metalinguistic awareness Knowledge of and an ability to think about language and its properties (as illustrated by an appreciation of double meanings and metaphors).

metamemory One's knowledge about memory and memory processes.

microsystem In Bronfenbrenner's ecological approach, the immediate settings in which the person functions (e.g., the family).

"middle generation squeeze" Expression describing the phenomenon in which middle-aged adults sometimes experience heavy responsibilities for both the younger and older generations in the family.

midlife crisis A period of major questioning, inner struggle, and re-evaluation hypothesized to occur in an adult's early forties.

mitosis The process in which a cell duplicates its chromosomes and then divides into two genetically identical daughter cells.

modified extended family Term used to describe an arrangement in which nuclear families that are related by kinship maintain separate households but frequently interact with one another rather than functioning in isolation.

moral affect The emotional component of morality, including feelings of guilt, shame, and pride in ethical conduct.

moral reasoning The cognitive component of morality; the thinking that occurs when people decide whether various acts are right or wrong.

moral rules Standards of conduct that focus on the basic rights and privileges of individuals. Contrast with *social-conventional rules.*

morality The ability to distinguish right from wrong and to act on this distinction. Morality has affective, cognitive, and behavioral components.

moratorium status Identity status characterizing individuals who are currently experiencing an identity crisis or period of questioning but have not yet resolved the issues they have raised.

morpheme One of the smallest meaningful units of language; these include words and grammatical markers such as prefixes, suffixes, and verb tense modifiers (for example, -ed, -ing).

motherese Baby talk, or the short, simple, high-pitched, and often repetitive sentences that adults use when talking with young children.

motive An energizing state that directs a person's behavior toward a particular kind of goal.

mourning Culturally prescribed ways of displaying one's reactions to a loss.

multi-infarct dementia A progressive loss of cognitive capacities caused by a series of minor strokes.

mutation A change in the structure or arrangement of one or more genes that produces a new phenotype.

myelin A waxy substance that insulates neural axons and thereby speeds the transmission of neural impulses.

natural selection The evolutionary principle that individuals who have characteristics advantageous for survival in a particular environment are the ones who are most likely to survive and reproduce. Over many generations, this process of "survival of the fittest" will lead to changes in a species and the development of new species.

naturalistic observation A research method in which the scientist tests hypotheses by observing people as they engage in common everyday activities in their natural habitats.

nature/nurture issue The debate within developmental psychology over the relative importance of biological predispositions (nature) and environmental influences (nurture) as determinants of human development.

need for achievement (n Ach) A motive to compete and strive for success whenever one's behavior can be evaluated against a standard of excellence.

negative reinforcement The process in operant conditioning whereby a response is strengthened or made more probable when its consequence is the removal of an unpleasant stimulus from the situation.

neonate A newborn infant from birth to approximately 1 month of age.

neuron The basic unit of the nervous system; a nerve cell.

neuroticism A personality dimension indicating the extent to which a person is psychologically stable or unstable (e.g., anxious, easily upset, depressed).

nonnormative transition A life event that is idiosyncratic to the individual or that only a minority of people experience.

nonreversal shift A type of learning problem in which subjects who have learned to respond to one aspect of a dimension (for example, large on the size dimension) must now learn to respond to some aspect of a different dimension (for example, black on a color dimension). Contrast with *reversal shift.*

normal distribution A symmetrical (bell-shaped) curve that describes the variability of characteristics within populations; most people fall at or near the average score, with relatively few high or low scores.

normative transition Life event or transition that is normal or typical in a society and that is experienced by most people.

nuclear family A family unit consisting of husband/father, wife/mother, and at least one child. Contrast to *extended family*.

object permanence The understanding that objects continue to exist when they are no longer visible or otherwise detectable to the senses; fully mastered by the end of infancy.

observational learning Learning that results from observing the behavior of other people; emphasized in Bandura's social learning theory.

Oedipus complex Freud's term for the conflict that 4- to 6-year-old boys experience when they develop an incestuous desire for their mothers and, at the same time, a jealous and hostile rivalry with their fathers.

olfaction The sense of smell, made possible by sensory receptors in the nasal passage that react to chemical molecules in the air.

operant conditioning A form of learning in which freely emitted acts (or "operants") become either more or less probable depending on the consequences they produce.

oral stage Freud's first stage of psychosexual development (from birth to 1 year), in which children gratify the sex instinct by stimulating the mouth, lips, teeth, and gums.

organic retardation Mental retardation due to some identifiable biological cause associated with hereditary factors, diseases, or injuries. Contrast with *cultural-familial retardation*.

organismic model A world view underlying certain theories that regards human beings as whole, living organisms who are active in their own development and change in a stagelike manner. Contrast with *mechanistic model*.

organization In Piaget's cognitive-developmental theory, one's inborn tendency to combine and integrate available schemes into more coherent and complex systems or bodies of knowledge; in information-processing theory, a strategy for remembering that involves grouping or classifying stimuli into meaningful (or manageable) clusters.

orthogenetic principle Werner's principle that development proceeds from global and undifferentiated states toward more differentiated and integrated patterns of response.

osteoporosis A disease in which bone tissue is lost, leaving bones fragile and easily fractured.

overcontrolled disorders Childhood behavior problems that involve internalizing difficulties in ways that cause anxiety, depression, and other forms of inner distress.

overextension The young child's tendency to use a word to refer to a wider set of objects, actions, or events than adults do (for example, using the word *car* to refer to all motor vehicles).

overregularization The overgeneralization of observed grammatical rules to irregular cases to which the rules do not apply (for example, saying "mouses" rather than "mice").

parental imperative The notion that the demands of parenthood cause men and women to adopt distinct roles and psychological traits.

partial reinforcement A schedule of reinforcement in which only some occurrences of a particular act are reinforced, often on an unpredictable schedule.

peer A social equal; one who functions at a level of behavioral complexity similar to that of the self, often someone of similar age.

perception The interpretation of sensory input.

perinatal environment The environment surrounding birth.

period of the embryo Second phase of prenatal development, lasting from the third through the eighth prenatal week, during which the major organs and anatomical structures begin to develop.

period of the fetus Third phase of prenatal development, lasting from the ninth prenatal week until birth; during this period, the major organ systems begin to function and the fetus grows rapidly.

permissive parenting A lax style of parenting in which adults make few demands on their children and rarely attempt to control their behavior.

permissiveness/restrictiveness dimension A dimension of parenting that describes the amount of autonomy, or freedom from rules and demands, that parents allow their children.

personal fable A form of adolescent egocentrism that involves thinking that oneself and one's thoughts and feelings are unique or special.

personality The organized combination of attributes, motives, values, and behaviors that is unique to each individual.

phallic stage Freud's third stage of psychosexual development (from 3 to 6 years of age), in which children gratify the sex instinct by fondling their genitals and developing an incestuous desire for the parent of the other sex.

phenotype The way in which a person's genotype is actually expressed in observable or measurable characteristics.

phenylketonuria (PKU) A genetic disease in which the child is unable to metabolize phenylalanine; if left untreated, it soon causes hyperactivity and mental retardation.

phoneme One of the basic units of sound used in a particular spoken language.

phonology The sound system of a language and the rules for combining these sounds to produce meaningful units of speech.

pincer grasp A grasp in which the thumb is used in opposition to the fingers, enabling an infant to become more dexterous at lifting and manipulating objects.

pituitary gland The "master gland" located at the base of the brain that regulates the other endocrine glands and produces growth hormone.

placenta An organ, formed from the chorion and the lining of the uterus, that provides for the nourishment of the unborn child and the elimination of its metabolic wastes.

plasticity An openness of the brain cells to positive and negative environmental influence, especially characteristic of immature brains.

play Activity that is enjoyable, that is intrinsically motivated, and that has an unrealistic quality.

polygenic trait A characteristic that is influenced by the action of many gene pairs rather than a single pair.

positive reinforcement The process in operant conditioning whereby a response is strengthened when its consequence is a pleasant event.

postconventional morality Kohlberg's term for the fifth and sixth stages of moral reasoning, in which moral judgments are based on a more abstract understanding of democratic social contracts or on universal principles of justice that have validity apart from the views of particular authority figures.

postpartum blues Feelings of sadness, resentment, and depression that mothers may experience following a birth.

power assertion A form of discipline that involves the use of superior power to administer spankings, withhold privileges, and so on.

pragmatics Rules specifying how language is to be used appropriately in different social contexts to achieve goals.

preconventional morality Kohlberg's term for the first two stages of moral reasoning, in which society's rules are not yet internalized and judgments are based on the punishing or rewarding consequences of an act.

premenstrual syndrome (PMS) A number of symptoms experienced shortly before each menstrual period that include having tender breasts and a bloated feeling, as well as being irritable and moody.

premoral period Piaget's term for the period up to about age 6 in which children have little concern for or awareness of rules and are not yet really moral beings.

prenatal environment The environment surrounding an organism between conception and birth.

preoperational stage Piaget's second stage of cognitive development, lasting from about age 2 to age 7, when children think at a symbolic level but have not yet mastered logical operations.

presbycusis Problems of the aging ear, especially a loss of sensitivity to high frequency sounds.

presbyopia Problems of the aging eye, especially a loss of near vision caused by a decreased ability of the lens to accommodate to objects that are close to the eye.

primary circular reaction A pleasurable action, centered on an infant's own body, that is discovered by chance and performed over and over.

problem-finding stage According to Arlin, a stage beyond formal operations in which the individual becomes capable of using knowledge to ask new questions and to define new problems.

problem solving The use of the information-processing system to achieve a goal or arrive at a decision.

production deficiency A failure to spontaneously generate the mediators or strategies that would improve memory even though one has the capacity to benefit from doing so.

progeria A genetic disorder that results in premature aging and death in children.

programmed theories of aging Theories that emphasize the systematic genetic control of aging processes; compare to *damage theories of aging.*

prosocial behavior Positive actions toward other people such as helping and cooperating.

Protestant Work Ethic The norm in many Western societies that associates work with moral worth and idleness with moral failing.

proximodistal direction In development, the principle that growth proceeds from the center of the body (or the proximal region) to the extremities (or distal regions).

psychoanalytic theory The theoretical perspective associated with Freud and his followers that emphasizes unconscious motivations for behavior, conflicts within the personality, and stages of psychosexual development.

psychometric approach The research tradition that spawned standardized tests of intelligence and that views intelligence as a trait or a set of traits that can be measured and that varies from person to person.

puberty The point at which a person reaches sexual maturity and is physically capable of conceiving a child.

punisher Any consequence of an act that suppresses that act and/or decreases the probability that it will recur.

punishment The process by which the consequence of an act suppresses the response and decreases the probability that it will recur.

Pygmalion effect The tendency of teacher expectancies to become self-fulfilling prophecies, causing students to perform better or worse depending on their teacher's estimation of their potential.

questionnaire A research instrument that asks the individuals being studied to respond to a number of written questions.

random assignment A technique in which research participants are assigned to experimental conditions in an unbiased or random way so that the resulting groups are not systematically different from one another.

random sample A sample that is formed by identifying all members of a larger population of interest and then selecting a portion of them in an unbiased or random way to participate in the study.

range of reaction principle The idea that genotype sets limits on the range of possible phenotypes that a person might display in response to different environmental influences.

recall memory Recollecting or actively retrieving objects, events, and experiences when examples or cues are not provided. Contrast with *recognition memory.*

recessive gene A less powerful gene that is not expressed phenotypically when paired with a dominant gene.

reciprocal determinism The notion in social learning theory that the flow of influence between people and their environments is a two-way street; the environment may affect the person, but the person's characteristics and behavior will also influence the environment.

recognition memory Identifying an object or event that one experiences as

recognition memory *(continued)* one that has been experienced before, as when one must select the correct answer from several options. Contrast with *recall memory*.

reconstituted family A new family that forms after the remarriage of a single parent, sometimes involving the blending of two families into a new one.

reflectivity A cognitive style characterized by relatively slow and deliberate responding based on a careful evaluation of alternative hypotheses. Contrast with *impulsivity*.

reflex An unlearned and automatic response to a stimulus.

regression A defense mechanism that involves retreating to an earlier, less traumatic stage of development.

rehearsal A strategy for remembering that involves repeating the items one is trying to retain.

reinforcer Any consequence of an act that increases the probability that the act will recur.

relativism The belief that knowledge depends on the subjective perspective of the knower or that what is found to be true depends on one's initial assumptions.

reliability The extent to which a research measure yields consistent information from occasion to occasion or yields agreement between different observers.

REM sleep A state of active, irregular sleep associated with dreaming; named for the rapid eye movements associated with it.

remote long-term memory Memory for the distant past, as opposed to recent events.

repression A type of motivated forgetting in which anxiety-provoking thoughts and conflicts are forced out of conscious awareness.

research ethics Standards of conduct that investigators are ethically bound to honor in order to protect their research participants from physical or psychological harm.

retrieval The process of getting information out of long-term memory when it is needed.

reversal shift A type of learning problem in which subjects who have learned to respond to one aspect of a dimension (for example, large) must now learn to respond to the opposite aspect of the same dimension (small). Contrast with *nonreversal shift*.

reversibility The ability to reverse or negate an action by mentally performing the opposite action.

rites of passage Rituals that signify the passage from one stage of life to another; for example, puberty rites.

role conflict The sense of being pulled in different directions by the competing demands of different roles or activities.

role overload The sense of having too much to do in carrying out one's major roles or life activities.

rubella A disease that has little effect on a pregnant woman but may cause a number of serious birth defects such as blindness, deafness, and mental retardation in unborn children who are exposed in the first 3 to 4 months of gestation; German measles.

sample The group of individuals chosen to be the subjects of a study.

scheme (or schema; plural, schemes or schemata) A cognitive structure or organized pattern of action or thought that is used to deal with experiences.

schizophrenia A serious form of mental illness characterized by disturbances in logical thinking, emotional expression, and interpersonal behavior.

scientific method An attitude or value about the pursuit of knowledge that dictates that investigators must be objective and must allow their data to decide the merits of their theorizing.

secondary circular reaction A pleasurable response, centered on an object in an infant's environment, that is discovered by chance and performed over and over.

secular trend A trend in industrialized society toward earlier maturation and greater body size now than in the past.

secure attachment An infant/caregiver bond or intimate relationship in which the individual welcomes close contact, uses the attachment object as a source of comfort, and dislikes but can manage separations.

secure base A point of safety, represented by an infant's attachment figure, that permits exploration of the environment.

selective breeding A method of studying genetic influence that involves deliberately determining whether a trait can be bred in animals through selective mating.

self-concept One's perceptions of one's unique attributes or traits.

self-esteem One's overall evaluation of one's worth as a person based on an assessment of the qualities that make up the self-concept.

semantics The aspect of language centering on meanings.

sensation The process by which information is detected by the sensory receptors and transmitted to the brain.

sensorimotor stage Piaget's first stage of cognitive development, spanning the first two years of life, in which infants rely on their senses and motor behaviors in adapting to the world around them.

sensory register The first memory store in information processing, in which stimuli are noticed and are very briefly available for further processing.

sensory threshold The point at which low levels of stimulation can be detected.

separation anxiety A wary or fretful reaction that infants display when they are separated from their attachment objects.

sequential design A developmental research design that combines the cross-sectional approach and the longitudinal approach in a single study to compensate for the weaknesses of each.

seriation A logical operation that allows one to mentally order a set of stimuli along a quantifiable dimension such as height or weight.

sex-linked characteristic An attribute determined by a gene that appears on one of the two types of sex chromosomes, usually the X chromosome.

shaping A method of teaching complex patterns of behavior by reinforcing successively closer approximations of these responses.

short gestation baby A baby born more than three weeks before his or her due date.

short-term memory The second memory store in information processing, in which stimuli are retained for several seconds and operated upon (also called working memory).

sibling rivalry A spirit of competition, jealousy, or resentment that may arise between two or more brothers or sisters.

sickle cell disease A genetic blood disease in which red blood cells assume an unusual sickled shape and become inefficient at distributing oxygen throughout the body.

single gene-pair inheritance Genetic mechanism through which a characteristic is influenced by only one pair of genes, one gene from the mother and its partner from the father.

size constancy The tendency to perceive an object as the same size despite changes in its distance from the eyes.

small for date Babies born close to their due dates but weighing less than 2500 grams.

social clock A personal sense of when things should be done in one's life and when one is ahead of or behind the schedule dictated by age norms.

social cognition Thinking about the thoughts, feelings, motives, and behavior of the self and other people.

social comparison The process of defining and evaluating oneself by comparing oneself to other people.

social-conventional rules Standards of conduct determined by social consensus that indicate what is appropriate within a particular social setting. Contrast with *moral rules*.

social learning theory Bandura's theory that children and adults can learn novel responses merely by observing the behavior of a model, making mental notes on what they have seen, and then using these mental representations to reproduce the model's behavior at some future time; more broadly, a learning perspective that emphasizes the cognitive processing of social experiences.

social norm A socially defined expectation about how people should behave.

social referencing The process, evident starting in infancy, of reading the emotional reactions of other people and using this information to guide one's own behavior in ambiguous situations.

social support The several forms of assistance from other people that bolster individuals and protect them from stress.

socialization The process by which individuals acquire the beliefs, values, and behaviors judged important in their society.

sociobiology The study of the influence of biological evolution on social behavior.

sociometric techniques Methods for determining who is well liked and popular and who is disliked or neglected in a group.

species heredity The genetic endowment that members of a particular species have in common; responsible for universal species traits and patterns of maturation.

status offense An act that is unlawful only if the perpetrator has the status of a minor (for example, drinking under age).

storage In information processing, the holding of information in the long-term memory store.

storm and stress G. Stanley Hall's term for the emotional ups and downs and rapid changes that he believed characterize adolescence.

Strange Situation test A series of mildly stressful situations to which infants are exposed to determine the quality of their attachments.

stranger anxiety A wary or fretful reaction that infants often display when approached by an unfamiliar person.

stress An aversive state brought about by events that seem to strain the person's coping capacities and threaten his or her well-being.

structure-of-intellect model Guilford's factor-analytic model of intelligence, which proposes that there are 120 distinct mental abilities.

substantive complexity The extent to which a job or activity provides opportunities for using one's mind and making independent judgments.

sudden infant death syndrome (SIDS) The unexplained death of a sleeping infant who suddenly stops breathing.

superego Psychoanalytic term for the component of the personality that consists of one's internalized moral standards.

symbolic capacity The capacity to use symbols such as words, images, or actions to represent or stand for objects and experiences; representational thought.

symbolic play Pretend play; play in which one actor, object, or action represents another.

synapse The point at which the axon or dendrite of one neuron makes a connection with another neuron.

syntax Rules specifying how words can be combined to form meaningful sentences in a language.

syphilis A common sexually transmitted disease that may cross the placental barrier in the middle and later stages of pregnancy, causing miscarriage or serious birth defects.

tabula rasa The idea that the mind of an infant is a "blank slate" and that all knowledge, abilities, behaviors, and motives are acquired through experience.

telegraphic speech Early sentences that consist primarily of content words and omit the less meaningful parts of speech such as articles, prepositions, pronouns, and auxiliary verbs.

temperament A pattern of tendencies to respond in predictable ways; building blocks of personality such as activity level, sociability, and emotionality.

teratogen Any disease, drug, or other environmental agent that can harm a developing fetus.

terminal drop A rapid decline in intellectual abilities that people who are within a few years of dying often experience.

tertiary circular reaction An exploratory scheme in which an infant devises a new method of acting on objects to produce interesting results.

test norms Standards of normal performance on psychometric instruments that

test norms *(continued)* are based on the average scores and range of scores obtained by a large, representative sample of test takers.

testosterone The most important of the male hormones or androgens; essential for normal prenatal development and sexual development at puberty.

thalidomide A mild tranquilizer that, taken early in pregnancy, can produce a variety of malformations of the limbs, eyes, ears, and heart.

theory A set of concepts and propositions designed to organize, describe, and explain a set of observations.

time of measurement The period of time in history when developmental data are collected. Historical events and changes in the social climate can influence conclusions about development.

time out A behavior modification technique in which the individual is removed temporarily from the situation in which misbehavior is being positively reinforced.

total brain death An irreversible loss of functioning in the entire brain, both the higher centers of the cerebral cortex that are involved in thought and the lower centers of the brain that control basic life processes such as breathing.

transductive reasoning Reasoning from the particular to the particular, so that events that merely occur together are assumed to be causally related.

transformational grammar Rules of syntax that allow one to transform declarative statements into questions, negatives, imperatives, and other kinds of sentences.

transitivity The ability to recognize the necessary or logical relations among elements in a serial order (for example, if A>B and B>C, then A>C).

triarchic theory of intelligence An information-processing theory of intelligence that emphasizes three aspects of intelligent behavior: the context in which people display intelligence, the previous experience they have with cognitive tasks, and the information-processing components they use to go about solving problems.

trust versus mistrust Psychosocial conflict of infancy, in which infants must learn to trust others to meet their needs in order to trust themselves; first stage in Erikson's theory.

Turner syndrome A sex chromosome abnormality in which females inherit only one X chromosome (XO); they remain small in stature, fail to develop secondary sex characteristics, and may show some mental deficiencies.

ultrasound Method of examining physical organs by scanning them with sound waves—for example, scanning the womb and thereby producing a visual outline of the fetus to detect gross abnormalities.

umbilical cord A soft tube containing blood vessels that connects the embryo to the placenta and serves as a source of oxygen and nutrients and as a vehicle for the elimination of wastes.

unconditioned response (UCR) The unlearned response elicited by an unconditioned stimulus.

unconditioned stimulus (UCS) A stimulus that elicits a particular response without any prior learning.

unconscious motivation Freud's term for feelings, experiences, and conflicts that influence a person's thinking and behavior, even though they cannot be recalled.

undercontrolled disorders Childhood behavior problems that involve externalizing or acting out difficulties in ways that disturb other people.

underextension The young child's tendency to use general words to refer to a smaller set of objects, actions, or events than adults do (for example, using *candy* to refer only to mints).

vaginal atrophy A condition in which the walls of the vagina become thinner and dryer; often a symptom of menopause.

validity The extent to which a research instrument measures what it is intended to measure rather than something else.

verbal mediation The process of using language as a tool of thought, as by verbally labeling aspects of task stimuli that seem important.

visual acuity The ability to perceive detail in a visual stimulus.

visual cliff An elevated glass platform that creates an illusion of depth, used to test the depth perception of infants.

warmth/hostility dimension A dimension of parenting that describes the amount of affection and approval parents display toward their children.

work Activity that is goal directed or aimed toward producing something of use or contributing to subsistence.

X chromosome The longer of the two sex chromosomes; normal females have two X chromosomes, whereas normal males have but one.

Y chromosome The shorter of the two sex chromosomes; normal males have one Y chromosome, whereas females have none.

zygote A single cell formed at conception from the union of a sperm and an ovum.

References

Chapter 1: Understanding Life-Span Human Development

American Psychological Association. (1982). *Ethical principles in the conduct of research with human participants.* Washington, DC: Author.

Aries, P. (1962). *Centuries of childhood.* New York: Knopf.

Baltes, P. B. (1983). Life-span developmental psychology: Observations on history and theory revisited. In R. M. Lerner (Ed.), *Developmental psychology: Historical and philosophical perspectives.* Hillsdale, NJ: Erlbaum.

Baltes, P. B. (1987). Theoretical propositions of life-span developmental psychology: On the dynamics between growth and decline. *Developmental Psychology, 23,* 611–626.

Baltes, P. B., Reese, H. W., & Lipsitt, L. P. (1980). Life-span developmental psychology. *Annual Review of Psychology, 31,* 65–110.

Bengtson, V. L., Cuellar, J. B., & Ragan, P. K. (1977). Stratum contrasts and similarities in attitudes toward death. *Journal of Gerontology, 32,* 76–88.

Biesele, M., & Howell, N. (1981). "The old people give you life": Aging among !Kung hunter-gatherers. In P. T. Amoss & S. Harrell (Eds.), *Other ways of growing old: Anthropological perspectives.* Stanford, CA: Stanford University Press.

Birren, J. E., & Zarit, J. M. (1985). Concepts of health, behavior, and aging. In J. E. Birren & J. Livington (Eds.), *Cognition, stress, and aging.* Englewood Cliffs, NJ: Prentice-Hall.

Borstelmann, L. J. (1983). Children before psychology: Ideas about children from antiquity to the late 1800s. In W. Kessen (Vol. Ed.; P. H. Mussen, General Ed.), *Handbook of child psychology: Vol. 1. History, theory, and methods* (4th ed.). New York: Wiley.

Bronfenbrenner, U. (1979). *The ecology of human development. Experiments by nature and design.* Cambridge, MA: Harvard University Press.

Charlesworth, R., & Hartup, W. W. (1967). Positive social reinforcement in the nursery school peer group. *Child Development, 38,* 993–1002.

Clayton, V. P., & Birren, J. E. (1980). The development of wisdom across the life span: A reexamination of an ancient topic. In P. B. Baltes & O. G. Brim, Jr. (Eds.), *Life-span development and behavior* (Vol. 3). New York: Academic.

Coates, B., & Hartup, W. W. (1969). Age and verbalization in observational learning. *Developmental Psychology, 1,* 556–562.

Cohen, J. (1957). The factorial structure of the WAIS between early adulthood and old age. *Journal of Consulting Psychology, 21,* 283–290.

Cooke, R. A. (1982). The ethics and regulation of research involving children. In B. B. Wolman (Ed.), *Handbook of developmental psychology.* Englewood Cliffs, NJ: Prentice-Hall.

Darwin, C. A. (1877). A biographical sketch of an infant. *Mind, 2,* 285–294.

deMause, L. (1974). The evolution of childhood. In L. deMause (Ed.), *The history of childhood.* New York: The Psychohistory Press.

Despert, J. L. (1965). *The emotionally disturbed child: Then and now.* New York: Brunner/Mazel.

Dublin, L. I., & Lotka, A. J. (1936). *Length of life. A study of the life table.* New York: Ronald Press.

Elder, G. H., Jr. (1974). *Children of the Great Depression.* Chicago: University of Chicago Press.

Elder, G. H., Jr. (1979). Historical change in life patterns and personality. In P. B. Baltes & O. G. Brim, Jr. (Eds.), *Life-span development and behavior* (Vol. 2). New York: Academic.

Elder, G. H., Jr. (1980). Adolescence in historical perspective. In J. Adelson (Ed.), *Handbook of adolescent psychology.* New York: Wiley.

Elder, G. H., Jr., Liker, J. K., & Cross, C. E. (1984). Parent–child behavior in the Great Depression: Life course and intergenerational influences. In P. B. Baltes & O. G. Brim, Jr. (Eds.), *Life-span development and behavior* (Vol. 6). Orlando, FL: Academic.

Friedrich, L. K., & Stein, A. H. (1973). Aggressive and prosocial television programs and the natural behavior of preschool children. *Monographs of the Society for Research in Child Development, 38* (4, Serial No. 51).

Fry, C. L. (1985). Culture, behavior, and aging in the comparative perspective. In J. E. Birren & K. W. Schaie (Eds.), *Handbook of the psychology of aging* (2nd ed.). New York: Van Nostrand Reinhold.

Guemple, L. (1983). Growing old in Inuit society. In J. Sokolovsky (Ed.), *Growing old in different societies. Cross-cultural perspectives.* Belmont, CA: Wadsworth.

Haan, N. (1981). Common dimensions of personality development: Early adolescence to middle life. In D. H. Eichorn, J. A. Clausen, N. Haan, M. P. Honzik, & P. H. Mussen (Eds.), *Present and past in middle life.* New York: Academic.

Hall, G. S. (1891). The contents of children's minds on entering school. *Pedagogical Seminary, 1,* 139–173.

Hall, G. S. (1904). *Adolescence* (2 vols.). New York: Appleton.

Hall, G. S. (1922). *Senescence: The last half of life.* New York: Appleton.

Hareven, T. (1986). Life-course transitions and kin assistance in old age: A cohort comparison. In D. Van Tassel & P. N. Stearns (Eds.), *Old age in a bureaucratic society. The elderly, the experts, and the state of American history.* Westport, CT: Greenwood Press.

Helmreich, R. L., Spence, J. T., & Gibson, R. H. (1982). Sex-role attitudes: 1972–1980. *Personality and Social Psychology Bulletin, 8,* 656–663.

Kagan, J. (1986). Presuppositions in developmental inquiry. In L. Cirillo & S. Wapner (Eds.), *Value presuppositions in theories of human development.* Hillsdale, NJ: Erlbaum.

Kaplan, B. (1983). A trio of trials. In R. M. Lerner (Ed.), *Developmental psychology: Historical and philosophical perspectives.* Hillsdale, NJ: Erlbaum.

Kean, A. W. G. (1937). The history of the criminal liability of children. *Law Quarterly Review, 3,* 364–370.

Keith, J. (1985). Age in anthropological research. In R. H. Binstock & E. Shanas (Eds.), *Handbook of aging and the social sciences* (2nd ed.). New York: Van Nostrand Reinhold.

Keniston, K. (1970). Youth: A "new" stage of life. *American Scholar, 39,* 631–654.

Kett, J. F. (1977). *Rites of passage. Adolescence in America 1790 to the present.* New York: Basic Books.

McCall, R. B. (1977). Challenges to a science of developmental psychology. *Child Development, 48,* 333–344.

Mead, M. (1935). *Sex and temperament in three primitive societies.* New York: William Morrow.

Miller, S. A. (1987). *Developmental research methods.* Englewood Cliffs, NJ: Prentice-Hall.

Neugarten, B. L. (1975). The future and the young-old. *Gerontologist, 15* (Part 2), 4–9.

Neugarten, B. L., & Neugarten, D. A. (1986). Changing meanings of age in the aging society. In A. Pifer & L. Bronte (Eds.), *Our aging society. Paradox and promise.* New York: Norton.

Pifer, A., & Bronte, L. (1986). Introduction: Squaring the pyramid. In A. Pifer & L. Bronte (Eds.), *Our aging society. Paradox and promise.* New York: Norton.

Plomin, R. (1990) *Nature and nurture. An introduction to human behavioral genetics.* Pacific Grove, CA: Brooks/Cole.

Ratzan, R. M. (1986). Communication and informed consent in clinical geriatrics. *International Journal of Aging and Human Development, 23,* 17–26.

Reinert, G. (1979). Prolegomena to a history of life-span developmental psychology. In P. B. Baltes & O. G. Brim, Jr. (Eds.), *Life-span development and behavior* (Vol. 2). New York: Academic.

Rice, D. P., & Feldman, J. J. (1983). Living longer in the United States: Demographic changes and health needs of the elderly. *Milbank Memorial Fund Quarterly, 61,* 362–396.

Rosenmayr, L. (1985). Changing values and positions of aging in Western culture. In J. E. Birren & K. W. Schaie (Eds.), *Handbook of the psychology of aging* (2nd ed.). New York: Van Nostrand Reinhold.

Schaie, K. W. (1965). A general model for the study of developmental problems. *Psychological Bulletin, 64,* 91–107.

Schaie, K. W. (1983). The Seattle longitudinal study: A 21-year exploration of psychometric intelligence in adulthood. In K. W. Schaie (Ed.), *Longitudinal studies of adult psychological development.* New York: Guilford.

Schaie, K. W. (1986). Beyond calendar definitions of age, time, and cohort: The general developmental model revisited. *Developmental Review, 6,* 252–277.

Schaie, K. W., & Hertzog, C. (1985). Measurement in the psychology of adulthood and aging. In J. E. Birren & K. W. Schaie (Eds.), *Handbook of the psychology of aging* (2nd ed.). New York: Van Nostrand Reinhold.

Singer, J. L., & Singer, D. G. (1981). *Television, imagination, and aggression: A study of preschoolers.* Hillsdale, NJ: Erlbaum.

Weiss, K. M. (1981). Evolutionary perspectives on human aging. In P. T. Amoss & S. Harrell (Eds.), *Other ways of growing old. Anthropological perspectives.* Stanford, CA: Stanford University Press.

Willems, E. P., & Alexander, J. L. (1982). The naturalistic perspective in research. In B. B. Wolman (Ed.), *Handbook of developmental psychology.* Englewood Cliffs, NJ: Prentice-Hall.

Chapter 2: Theories of Human Development

Babikian, H. M., & Goldman, A. (1971). A study of teen-age pregnancy. *American Journal of Psychiatry, 128,* 755–760.

Baltes, P. B. (1983). Life-span developmental psychology: Observations on history and theories revisited. In R. M. Lerner (Ed.), *Developmental psychology: Historical and philosophical perspectives.* Hillsdale, NJ: Erlbaum.

Bandura, A. (1977). *Social learning theory.* Englewood Cliffs, NJ: Prentice-Hall.

Bandura, A. (1986). *Social foundations of thought and action. A social cognitive theory.* Englewood Cliffs, NJ: Prentice-Hall.

Bandura, A. (1989). Social cognitive theory. In R. Vasta (Ed.), *Annals of child development: Vol. 6. Theories of child development: Revised formulations and current issues.* Greenwich, CT: JAI Press.

Bijou, S. W., & Baer, D. M. (1961). *Child development: Vol. 1. A systematic and empirical theory.* New York: Appleton-Century-Crofts.

Bowlby, J. (1969). *Attachment and loss: Vol. 1. Attachment.* New York: Basic.

Bowlby, J. (1973). *Attachment and loss: Vol. 2. Separation.* New York: Basic.

Brooks-Gunn, J., & Furstenberg, F. F., Jr. (1989). Long-term implications of fertility-related behavior and family formation on adolescent mothers and their children. In K. Kreppner & R. M. Lerner (Eds.), *Family systems and life-span development.* Hillsdale, NJ: Erlbaum.

Chilman, C. S. (1986). Some psychological aspects of adolescent sexual and contraceptive behaviors in a changing American society. In J. B. Lancaster & B. A. Hamburg (Eds.), *School-age pregnancy and parenthood. Biosocial dimensions.* New York: Aldine DeGruyter.

Cobliner, W. G. (1974). Pregnancy in the single adolescent girl: The role of cognitive functions. *Journal of Youth and Adolescence, 3,* 17–29.

Dawson, D. A. (1986). The effects of sex education on adolescent behavior. *Family Planning Perspectives, 18,* 162–170.

Erikson, E. H. (1950). In M. J. E. Senn (Ed.), *Symposium on the healthy personality.* New York: Josiah Macy, Jr., Foundation.

Erikson, E. H. (1963). *Childhood and society* (2nd ed.). New York: Norton.

Erikson, E. H. (1968). *Identity. Youth and crisis.* New York: Norton.

Erikson, E. H. (1982). *The life cycle completed. A review.* New York: Norton.

Eron, L. D., Huesmann, L. R., Brice, P., Fischer, P., & Mermelstein, R. (1983). Age trends in the development of aggression, sex-typing, and related television habits. *Developmental Psychology, 19,* 71–77.

Fabes, R. A., & Strouse, J. (1984). Youth's perceptions of models of sexuality: Implications for sex education. *Journal of Sex Education and Therapy, 10,* 33–37.

Finkel, M. L., & Finkel, D. J. (1978). Male adolescent contraceptive utilization. *Adolescence, 13,* 443–451.

Fisher, S., & Greenberg, R. P. (1977). *The scientific credibility of Freud's theories and therapy.* New York: Basic Books.

Freud, S. (1933). *New introductory lectures in psychoanalysis.* New York: Norton.

Freud, S. (1961). The dissolution of the Oedipus complex. In J. Strachey (Ed.), *The standard edition of the complete psychological works of Sigmund Freud* (Vol. 19). London: Hogarth Press. (Original work published 1924)

Freud, S. (1964). An outline of psychoanalysis. In J. Strachey (Ed.), *The standard edition of the complete psychological works of Sigmund Freud* (Vol. 23). London: Hogarth Press. (Original work published 1940)

Furstenberg, F. F., Jr., Brooks-Gunn, J., & Morgan, S. P. (1987). *Adolescent mothers in later life.* New York: Cambridge University Press.

Furstenberg, F. F., Jr., Lincoln, R., & Menken, J. (Eds.). (1981). *Teenage sexuality, pregnancy, and childbearing.* Philadelphia, PA: University of Pennsylvania Press.

Gesell, A., & Ilg, F. L. (in collaboration with Ames, L. B., Learned, J., & Bullis, G. E.) (1949). *Child development. An introduction to the study of human growth. I. Infant and child in the culture of today. II. The child from five to ten.* New York: Harper & Brothers.

Hamburg, B. A. (1986). Subsets of adolescent mothers: Developmental, biomedical, and psychosocial issues. In J. B. Lancaster & B. A. Hamburg (Eds.), *School-age pregnancy and parenthood. Biosocial dimensions.* New York: Aldine DeGruyter.

Hatcher, S. L. M. (1973). The adolescent experience of pregnancy and abortion: A developmental analysis. *Journal of Youth and Adolescence, 2,* 53–102.

Hazan, C., & Shaver, P. (1987). Romantic love conceptualized as an attachment process. *Journal of Personality and Social Psychology, 52,* 511–524.

Hefner, R., Rebecca, M., & Oleshansky, B. (1975). Development of sex-role transcendence. *Human Development, 18,* 143–158.

Hinde, R. A. (1983). Ethology and child development. In M. M. Haith & J. J. Campos (Vol. Eds; P. H. Mussen, General Ed.), *Handbook of child psychology: Vol. 2. Infancy and developmental psychobiology* (4th ed.). New York: Wiley.

Hinde, R. A. (1989). Ethological and relationships approaches. In R. Vasta (Ed.), *Annals of child development: Vol. 6. Theories of child development: Revised formulations and current issues.* Greenwich, CT: JAI Press.

Inhelder, B., & Piaget, J. (1958). *The growth of logical thinking from childhood to adolescence: An essay on the construction of formal operational structures* (A. Parsons & S. Milgram, Trans.). New York: Basic Books.

Kagan, J. (1980) Perspectives on continuity. In O. G. Brim, Jr., & J. Kagan (Eds.), *Constancy and change in human development.* Cambridge, MA: Harvard University Press.

Kaplan, B. (1983). A trio of trials. In R. M. Lerner (Ed.), *Developmental psychology: Historical and philosophical perspectives.* Hillsdale, NJ: Erlbaum.

Katcher, A. (1955). The discrimination of sex differences by young children. *Journal of Genetic Psychology, 87,* 131–143.

Kirby, D. (1985). The effects of selected sexuality education programs: Toward a more realistic view. *Journal of Sex Education and Therapy, 11,* 28–37.

Lancaster, J. B., & Hamburg, B. A. (1986). The biosocial dimensions of school-age pregnancy and parenthood: An introduction. In J. B. Lancaster & B. A. Hamburg (Eds.), *School-age pregnancy and parenthood. Biosocial dimensions.* New York: Aldine DeGruyter.

Lerner, R. M. (1982). Children and adolescents as producers of their own development. *Developmental Review, 2,* 342–370.

Lerner, R. M., & Kauffman, M. B. (1985). The concept of development in contextualism. *Developmental Review, 5,* 309–333.

Lorenz, K. Z. (1937). The companion in the bird's world. *Auk, 54,* 245–273.

Marsiglio, W., & Mott, F. L. (1986). The impact of sex education on sexual activity, contraceptive use and premarital pregnancy among American teenagers. *Family Planning Perspectives, 18,* 151–162.

McGillicuddy-DeLisi, A. V. (1985). The relationship between parental beliefs and children's cognitive level. In I. E. Sigel (Ed.), *Parental belief systems. The psychological consequences for children.* Hillsdale, NJ: Erlbaum.

Miller, S. A. (1988). Parents' beliefs about children's cognitive development. *Child Development, 59,* 259–285.

Morrison, D. M. (1985). Adolescent contraceptive behavior: A review. *Psychological Bulletin, 98,* 538–568.

Overton, W. F. (1984). World views and their influence on psychological theory and research: Kuhn-Lakatos-Lauden. In H. W. Reese (Ed.), *Advances in child development and behavior* (Vol. 18). New York: Academic.

Phipps-Yonas, S. (1980). Teenage pregnancy and motherhood: A review of the literature. *American Journal of Orthopsychiatry, 50,* 403–431.

Piaget, J. (1950). *The psychology of intelligence.* New York: Harcourt Brace & World.

Piaget, J. (1952). *The origins of intelligence in children.* New York: International Universities Press.

Plomin, R. (1990). *Nature and nurture. An introduction to human behavioral genetics.* Pacific Grove, CA: Brooks/Cole.

Proctor, S. E. (1986). A developmental approach to pregnancy prevention with early adolescent females. *Journal of School Health, 56,* 313–316.

Reese, H. W., & Overton, W. F. (1970). Models of development and theories of development. In L. R. Goulet & P. B. Baltes (Eds.), *Life-span developmental psychology: Research and theory.* New York: Academic.

Reppen, J. (Ed.). (1985). *Beyond Freud. A study of modern psychoanalytic theorists.* Hillsdale, NJ: The Analytic Press (distributed by Erlbaum).

Riegel, K. F. (1976). The dialectics of human development. *American Psychologist, 31,* 689–700.

Riegel, K. F. (1979). *Foundations of dialectical psychology.* New York: Academic.

Sameroff, A. (1975). Transactional models in early social relations. *Human Development, 18,* 65–79.

Sameroff, A. J. (1983). Developmental systems: Contexts and evolution. In W. Kessen (Vol. Ed.; P. H. Mussen, General Ed.), *Handbook of child psychology: Vol. 1. History, theory, and methods* (4th ed.). New York: Wiley.

Schaffer, C., & Pine, F. (1972). Pregnancy, abortion, and the developmental tasks of adolescence. *Journal of the American Academy of Child Psychiatry, 11,* 511–536.

Skinner, B. F. (1953). *Science and human behavior.* New York: Macmillan.

Steinlauf, B. (1979). Problem-solving skills, locus of control, and contraceptive effectiveness of young women. *Child Development, 50,* 268–271.

Thompson, L., & Spanier, G. B. (1978). Influence of parents, peers, and partners on the contraceptive use of college men and women. *Journal of Marriage and the Family, 40,* 481–492.

Vaillant, G. E. (1983). Childhood environment and maturity of defense mechanisms. In D. Magnusson & V. L. Allen (Eds.), *Human development. An interactional perspective.* New York: Academic.

Vygotsky, L. S. (1962). *Thought and language.* Cambridge, MA: MIT Press.

Vygotsky, L. S. (1978). *Mind in society. The development of higher psychological processes.* (Ed. by M. Cole, V. John-Steiner, S. Scribner, & E. Souberman). Cambridge, MA: Harvard University Press.

Watson, J. B. (1913). Psychology as the behaviorist views it. *Psychological Review, 20,* 158–177.

Watson, J. B. (1925). *Behaviorism.* New York: Norton.

Watson, J. B., & Raynor, R. (1920). Conditioned emotional reactions. *Journal of Experimental Psychology, 3,* 1–14.

Weisberg, P. (1963). Social and nonsocial conditioning of infant vocalization. *Child Development, 34,* 377–388.

Weisfeld, G. E., & Billings, R. L. (1988). Observations on adolescence. In K. B. MacDonald (Ed.), *Sociobiological perspectives on human development.* New York: Springer-Verlag.

Whitbourne, S. K., & Tesch, S. A. (1985). A comparison of identity and intimacy statuses in college students and alumni. *Developmental Psychology, 21,* 1039–1044.

Chapter 3: The Genetics of Life-Span Development

Ahern, F. M., Johnson, R. C., Wilson, J. R., McClearn, G. E., & Vandenberg, S. G. (1982). Family resemblances in personality. *Behavior Genetics, 12,* 261–280.

Anastasi, A. (1958). Heredity, environment, and the question, "how?" *Psychological Review, 65,* 197–208.

Apgar, V., & Beck, J. (1974). *Is my baby all right?* New York: Pocket Books.

Baker, L. A., Mack, W., Moffitt, T. E., & Mednick, S. (1989). Sex differences in property crime in a Danish adoption cohort. *Behavior Genetics, 19,* 355–370.

Bateson, P. (1985). Problems and possibilities in fusing developmental and evolutionary thought. In G. Butterworth, J. Rutkowska, & M. Scaife (Eds.), *Evolution and developmental psychology.* Brighton, England: Harvester.

Baird, P. A., Anderson, T. W., Newcombe, H. B., & Lowry, R. B. (1988). Genetic disorders in children and young adults: A population study. *American Journal of Human Genetics, 42,* 677–693.

Begley, S., Carey, J., & Katz, S. (1984, March 5). The genetic counselors. *Newsweek,* p. 69.

Bishop, J. A., & Cooke, L. M. (1975). Moths, melanism and clean air. *Scientific American, 232* (1), 90–99.

Bonner, J. T. (1980). *The evolution of culture in animals.* Princeton, NJ: Princeton University Press.

Bouchard, T. J., Jr. (1984). Twins reared together and apart: What they tell us about human diversity. In S. W. Fox (Ed.), *Individuality and determinism. Chemical and biological bases.* New York: Plenum.

Bouchard, T. J., Jr., & McGue, M. (1981). Family studies of intelligence: A review. *Science, 212,* 1055–1059.

Bowlby, J. (1969). *Attachment and loss: Vol. 1. Attachment.* London: Hogarth Press.

Brown, W. T. (1985). Genetics of aging. In M. P. Janicki & H. M. Wisniewski (Eds.), *Aging and developmental disabilities. Issues and approaches.* Baltimore, MD: Paul H. Brookes.

Burns, G. W. (1976). *The science of genetics.* New York: Macmillan.

Buss, A. H., & Plomin, R. (1984). *Temperament: Early developing personality traits.* Hillsdale, NJ: Erlbaum.

Daniels, D. (1986). Differential experiences of siblings in the same family as predictors of adolescent sibling personality differences. *Journal of Personality and Social Psychology, 51,* 339–346.

Daniels, D., & Plomin, R. (1985). Differential experience of siblings in the same family. *Developmental Psychology, 21,* 747–760.

Darwin, C. (1859). *The origin of species.* New York: Modern Library.

DeBusk, F. L. (1972). The Hutchinson-Gilford progeria syndrome. Report of 4 cases and review of the literature. *Journal of Pediatrics, 80,* 697–724.

Draper, P., & Harpending, H. (1988). A sociobiological perspective on the development of human reproductive strategies. In K. B. MacDonald (Ed.), *Sociobiological perspectives on human development.* New York: Springer-Verlag.

Dunn, J., & Stocker, C. (1989). The significance of differences in siblings' experiences within the family. In K. Kreppner & R. M. Lerner (Eds.), *Family systems and life-span development.* Hillsdale, NJ: Erlbaum.

Fairweather, D. V. I. (1978). Techniques and safety of amniocentesis. In D. V. I. Fairweather & T. K. A. B. Eskes (Eds.), *Amniotic fluid: Research and clinical application.* Amsterdam: Elsevier.

Farber, S. L. (1981). *Identical twins reared apart. A reanalysis.* New York: Basic Books.

Fischbein, S. (1981). Heredity–environment influences on growth and development during adolescence. In L. Gedda, P. Parisi, & W. E. Nance (Eds.), *Twin research 3: Part B, Intelligence, personality, and development.* New York: Alan R. Liss.

Floderus-Myhred, B., Pedersen, N., & Rasmuson, I. (1980). Assessment of heritability for personality, based on a short-form of the Eysenck Personality Inventory: A study of 12,898 twin pairs. *Behavior Genetics, 10,* 153–162.

Foch, T. T., & Plomin, R. (1980). Specific cognitive abilities in 5- to 12-year-old twins. *Behavior Genetics, 10,* 507–520.

Fuller, J. L. (1983). Sociobiology and behavior genetics. In J. L. Fuller & E. C. Simmel (Eds.), *Behavior genetics. Principles and applications.* Hillsdale, NJ: Erlbaum.

Fuller, J. L., & Thompson, W. R. (1978). *Genetic basis of behavior.* St. Louis: Mosby.

Goldsmith, H. H. (1983). Genetic influences on personality from infancy to adulthood. *Child Development, 54,* 331–355.

Goldsmith, H. H., & Campos, J. J. (1986). Fundamental issues in the study of early temperament: The Denver twin temperament study. In M. E. Lamb, A. L. Brown, & B. Rogoff (Eds.), *Advances in developmental psychology* (Vol. 4). Hillsdale, NJ: Erlbaum.

Gottesman, I. I. (1963). Heritability of personality: A demonstration. *Psychological Monographs, 77* (Whole No. 572).

Gottesman, I. I., & Shields, J. (1973). Genetic theorizing and schizophrenia. *British Journal of Psychiatry, 122,* 17–18.

Gusella, J. F., Wexler, N. S., Conneally, P. M., Naylor, S. L., Anderson, M. A., Tanzi, R. E., Watkins, P. C., Ottina, K., Wallace, M. R., Sakaguchi, A. Y., Young, A. B., Shoulson, I., Bonilla, E., & Martin, J. B. (1983). A polymorphic DNA marker genetically linked to Huntington disease. *Nature, 306,* 234–238.

Hamilton, W. D. (1964). The genetical evolution of social behavior, I & II. *Journal of Theoretical Biology, 7,* 1–52.

Hearnshaw, L. S. (1979). *Cyril Burt. Psychologist.* Ithaca, NY: Cornell University Press.

Heath, A. C., Kendler, K. S., Eaves, L. J., & Markell, D. (1985). The resolution of cultural and biological inheritance: Informativeness of different relationships. *Behavior Genetics, 15,* 439–465.

Hebb, D. O. (1970). A return to Jensen and his social science critics. *American Psychologist, 25,* 568.

Hendin, D., & Marks, J. (1978). *The genetic connection. How to protect your family against hereditary disease.* New York: Signet.

Heston, L. L. (1970). The genetics of schizophrenia and schizoid disease. *Science, 167,* 249–256.

Hinde, R. A. (1983). Ethology and child development. In M. M. Haith & J. J. Campos (Vol. Eds.; P. H. Mussen, General Ed.), *Handbook of child psychology: Vol. 2. Infancy and developmental psychobiology* (4th ed.). New York: Wiley.

Holtzman, N. A., Kronmal, R. A., Van Doorninck, W., Azen, C., & Koch, R. (1986). Effect of age at loss of dietary control on intellectual performance and behavior of children with phenylketonuria. *New England Journal of Medicine, 314,* 593–598.

Jarvik, L. F., & Bank, L. (1983). Aging twins: Longitudinal psychometric data. In K. W. Schaie (Ed.), *Longitudinal studies of adult psychological development.* New York: Guilford.

Kallmann, F. J., & Jarvik, L. F. (1959). Individual differences in constitution and genetic background. In J. E. Birren (Ed.), *Handbook of aging and the individual. Psychological and biological aspects.* Chicago: University of Chicago Press.

Kallmann, F. J., & Sander, G. (1949). Twin studies on senescence. *American Journal of Psychiatry, 106,* 29–36.

Kessler, S. (1975). Psychiatric genetics. In D. A. Hamburg & K. Brodie (Eds.), *American handbook of psychiatry: Vol. 6. New psychiatric frontiers.* New York: Basic Books.

Kettlewell, H. B. D. (1959). Darwin's missing evidence. *Scientific American, 200* (3), 48–53.

Lewontin, R. C., Rose, S., & Kamin, L. J. (1984). *Not in our genes: Biology, ideology, and human nature.* New York: Pantheon.

Loehlin, J. C. (1982). Are personality traits differentially heritable? *Behavior Genetics, 12,* 417–428.

Loehlin, J. C. (1985). Fitting heredity–environment models jointly to twin and adoption data from the California Psychological Inventory. *Behavior Genetics, 15,* 199–221.

Loehlin, J. C., & Nichols, R. C. (1976). *Heredity, environment, and personality.* Austin, TX: University of Texas Press.

Loehlin, J. C., Willerman, L., & Horn, J. M. (1985). Personality resemblance in adoptive families when the children are late-adolescent or adult. *Journal of Personality and Social Psychology, 48,* 376–392.

Lykken, D. T., Tellegen, A., & Iacono, W. G. (1982). EEG spectra in twins: Evidence for a neglected mechanism of genetic determination. *Physiological Psychology, 10,* 60–65.

Lytton, H. (1977). Do parents create, or respond to, differences in twins? *Developmental Psychology, 13,* 456–459.

MacDonald, K. B. (Ed.). (1988). *Sociobiological perspectives on human development.* New York: Springer-Verlag.

Magenis, R. E., Overton, K. M., Chamberlin, J., Brady, T., & Lorrien, E. (1977). Parental origin of the extra chromosome in Down's syndrome. *Human Genetics, 37,* 7–16.

Martin, N. G., Oakeshott, J. G., Gibson, J. B., Starmer, G. A., Perl, J., & Wilkers, A. V. (1985). A twin study of psychomotor and physiological responses to an acute dose of alcohol. *Behavior Genetics, 15,* 305–347.

McCall, R. B. (1981). Nature–nurture and the two realms of development: A proposed integration with respect to mental development. *Child Development, 52,* 1–12.

McCall, R. B. (1983). Environmental effects on intelligence: The forgotten realm of discontinuous nonshared within-family factors. *Child Development, 54,* 408–415.

McClearn, G., & Foch, T. T. (1985). Behavioral genetics. In J. E. Birren & K. W. Schaie (Eds.), *Handbook of the psychology of aging* (2nd ed.). New York: Van Nostrand Reinhold.

Mednick, S. A., Gabrielli, W. F., Jr., & Hutchings, B. (1984). Genetic influences in criminal convictions: Evidence from an adoption cohort. *Science, 224,* 891–894.

Morrison, J. R., & Stewart, M. A. (1973). The psychiatric status of the legal families of adopted hyperactive children. *Archives of General Psychiatry, 28,* 888–891.

Neale, M. C., & Martin, N. G. (1989). The effects of age, sex, and genotype on self-report drunkenness following a challenge dose of alcohol. *Behavior Genetics, 19,* 63–78.

Novitski, E. (1982). *Human genetics* (2nd ed.). New York: Macmillan.

O'Connor, M., Foch, T., Sherry, T., & Plomin, R. (1980). A twin study of specific behavioral problems of socialization as viewed by parents. *Journal of Abnormal Child Psychology, 8,* 189–199.

Omenn, G. S. (1983). Medical genetics, genetic counseling, and behavior genetics. In J. L. Fuller & E. C. Simmel (Eds.), *Behavior genetics. Principles and applications.* Hillsdale, NJ: Erlbaum.

Pedersen, N. L., McClearn, G. E., Plomin, R., & Friberg, L. (1985). Separated fraternal twins: Resemblance for cognitive abilities. *Behavior Genetics, 15,* 407–419.

Plomin, R. (1986). *Development, genetics, and psychology.* Hillsdale, NJ: Erlbaum.

Plomin, R. (1990). *Nature and nurture. An introduction to human behavioral genetics.* Pacific Grove, CA: Brooks/Cole.

Plomin, R., & DeFries, J. C. (1980). Genetics and intelligence: Recent data. *Intelligence, 4,* 15–24.

Plomin, R., & DeFries, J. C. (1985). *Origins of individual differences in infancy. The Colorado adoption project.* Orlando, FL: Academic.

Plomin, R., DeFries, J. C., & Loehlin, J. C. (1977). Genotype–environment interaction and correlation in the analysis of human behavior. *Psychological Bulletin, 84,* 309–322.

Plomin, R., DeFries, J. C., & McClearn, G. E. (1989). *Behavioral genetics: A primer* (2nd ed.). New York: W. H. Freeman.

Plomin, R., Pedersen, N. L., McClearn, G. E., Nesselroade, J. R., & Bergeman, C. S. (1988). EAS temperaments during the last half of the life span: Twins reared apart and twins reared together. *Psychology and Aging, 3,* 43–50.

Plomin, R., & Thompson, L. (1988). Life-span developmental behavioral genetics. In P. B. Baltes, D. L. Featherman, & R. M. Lerner (Eds.), *Life-span development and behavior* (Vol. 8). Hillsdale, NJ: Erlbaum.

Reznikoff, M., Domino, G., Bridges, C., & Honeyman, M. (1973). Creative abilities in identical and fraternal twins. *Behavior Genetics, 3,* 365–377.

Rose, R. J., Koskenvuo, M., Kaprio, J., Sarna, S., & Langinvainio, H. (1988). Shared genes, shared experiences, and similarity of personality: Data from 14,288 adult Finnish co-twins. *Journal of Personality and Social Psychology, 54,* 161–171.

Rovet, J., & Netley, C. (1982). Processing deficits in Turner's syndrome. *Developmental Psychology, 18,* 77–94.

Rowe, D. C. (1983). Biometrical genetic models of self-reported delinquent behavior: A twin study. *Behavior Genetics, 13,* 473–489.

Rowe, D. C., & Plomin, R. (1981). The importance of nonshared (E1) environmental influences in behavioral development. *Developmental Psychology, 17,* 517–531.

Scarr, S., & Carter-Saltzman, L. (1983). Genetics and intelligence. In J. L. Fuller & E. C. Simmel (Eds.), *Behavior genetics. Principles and applications.* Hillsdale, NJ: Erlbaum.

Scarr, S., & Kidd, K. K. (1983). Developmental behavior genetics. In M. M. Haith & J. J. Campos (Vol. Eds.; P. H. Mussen, General Ed.), *Handbook of child psychology: Vol. 2. Infancy and developmental psychobiology* (4th ed.). New York: Wiley.

Scarr, S., & McCartney, K. (1983). How people make their own environments: A theory of genotype → environment effects. *Child Development, 54,* 424–435.

Scarr, S., Webber, P. L., Weinberg, R. A., & Wittig, M. A. (1981). Personality resemblance among adolescents and their parents in biologically related and adoptive families. *Journal of Personality and Social Psychology, 40,* 885–898.

Scarr, S., & Weinberg, R. A. (1976). IQ test performance of black children adopted by white families. *American Psychologist, 31,* 1159–1166.

Scarr, S., & Weinberg, R. A. (1978). The influence of family background on intellectual attainment. *American Sociological Review, 43,* 674–692.

Scarr, S., & Weinberg, R. A. (1983). The Minnesota adoption studies: Genetic differences and malleability. *Child Development, 54,* 260–267.

Schaeffer, C. (1987, March). Will the baby be okay? *Changing Times, 41,* 97–103.

Stern, C. (1956). Hereditary factors affecting adoption. In *A study of adoption practices* (Vol. 2). New York: Child Welfare League of America.

Stunkard, A. J., Sorensen, T. I., Hanis, C., Teasdale, T. W., Chakraborty, R., Schull, W. J., & Schulsinger, F. (1986). An adoption study of human obesity. *New England Journal of Medicine, 314,* 193–198.

Tanner, J. M. (1978). *Fetus into man: Physical growth from conception to maturity.* Cambridge, MA: Harvard University Press.

Thompson, R. F. (1975). *Introduction to physiological psychology.* New York: Harper & Row.

Trivers, R. L., & Hare, H. (1976). Haplodiploidy and the evolution of social insects. *Science, 191,* 249–263.

Tryon, R. C. (1940). Genetic differences in maze learning in rats. *Yearbook of the National Society for Studies in Education, 39,* 111–119.

Watson, J. D., Tooze, J., & Kurtz, D. T. (1983). *Recombinant DNA. A short course.* New York: Scientific American Books (distributed by W. H. Freeman).

Wilson, E. O. (1975). *Sociobiology: The new synthesis.* Cambridge, MA: Belknap Press, Harvard University Press.

Wilson, R. S. (1978). Synchronies in mental development: An epigenetic perspective. *Science, 202,* 939–948.

Wilson, R. S. (1983). The Louisville twin study: Developmental synchronies in behavior. *Child Development, 54,* 298–316.

Wilson, R. S., & Matheny, A. P., Jr. (1986). Behavior-genetics research in infant temperament: The Louisville twin study. In R. Plomin & J. Dunn (Eds.), *The study of temperament: Changes, continuities and challenges.* Hillsdale, NJ: Erlbaum.

Chapter 4: Environment and Life-Span Development

Abel, E. L. (1980). Fetal alcohol syndrome: Behavioral teratology. *Psychological Bulletin, 87,* 29–50.

Abel, E. L. (1981). Behavioral teratology of alcohol. *Psychological Bulletin, 90,* 564–581.

Achenbaum, W. A. (1985). Societal perceptions of the aging and the aged. In R. H. Binstock & E. Shanas (Eds.), *Handbook of aging and the social sciences* (2nd ed.). New York: Van Nostrand Reinhold.

Adler, J., & Carey, J. (1982, January 11). But is it a person? *Newsweek,* p. 44.

Ainsworth, M. D. S. (1967). *Infancy in Uganda: Infant care and the growth of love.* Baltimore, MD: Johns Hopkins University Press.

Allen, M. C., & Capute, A. J. (1986). Assessment of early auditory and visual abilities of extremely premature infants. *Developmental Medicine and Child Neurology, 28,* 458–466.

Amoss, P. T. (1981). Coast Salish elders. In P. T. Amoss, & S. Harrell (Eds.), *Other ways of growing old. Anthropological perspectives.* Stanford, CA: Stanford University Press.

Amoss, P. T., & Harrell, S. (1981). Introduction: An anthropological perspective. In P. T. Amoss, & S. Harrell (Eds.), *Other ways of growing old. Anthropological perspectives.* Stanford, CA: Stanford University Press.

Apgar, V., & Beck, J. (1974). *Is my baby all right?* New York: Pocket Books.

Baird, P. A., Anderson, T. W., Newcombe, H. B., & Lowry, R. B. (1988). Genetic disorders in children and young adults: A population study. *American Journal of Human Genetics, 42,* 677–693.

Baker, R. L., & Mednick, B. R. (1984). *Influences on human development. A longitudinal perspective.* Boston: Kluwer Nijhoff Publishing.

Barnard, K. E., & Bee, H. L. (1983). The impact of temporally patterned stimulation on the development of preterm infants. *Child Development, 54,* 1156–1167.

Barol, B. (with Prout, L. R., Fitzgerald, K., Katz, S., & King, P.). (1986, July 28). Cocaine babies: Hooked at birth. *Newsweek,* pp. 56–57.

Barrera, M. E., Rosenbaum, P. L., & Cunningham, C. E. (1986). Early home interventions with low-birth-weight infants and their parents. *Child Development, 57,* 20–33.

Barry, H., Child, I. L., & Bacon, M. K. (1959). The relation of child training to subsistence economy. *American Anthropologist, 61,* 51–63.

Beckwith, L., & Parmelee, A. H., Jr. (1986). EEG patterns of preterm infants, home environment, and later IQ. *Child Development, 57,* 777–789.

Beidelman, T. O. (1971). *The Kagura. A matrilineal people of East Africa.* New York: Holt, Rinehart & Winston.

Belsky, J. (1985). Experimenting with the family in the newborn period. *Child Development, 56,* 407–414.

Belsky, J., & Tolan, W. J. (1981). Infants as producers of their own development: An ecological analysis. In R. M. Lerner, & N. A. Busch-Rossnagel (Eds.), *Individuals as producers of their development. A life-span perspective.* New York: Academic.

Benedict, R. (1934). *Patterns of culture.* Boston: Houghton Mifflin.

Bengtson, V. L., Dowd, J. J., Smith, D. H., & Inkeles, A. (1975). Modernization, modernity, and perceptions of aging: A cross-cultural study. *Journal of Gerontology, 30,* 688–695.

Biesele, M., & Howell, N. (1981). "The old people give you life": Aging among !Kung hunter-gatherers. In P. T. Amoss & S. Harrell (Eds.), *Other ways of growing old.* Stanford, CA: Stanford University Press.

Bochner, S., & David, K. H. (1968). Delay of gratification, age, and intelligence in Aboriginal culture. *International Journal of Psychology, 3,* 167–174.

Brackbill, Y. (1979). Obstetrical medication and infant behavior. In J. D. Osofsky (Ed.), *Handbook of infant development.* New York: Wiley.

Brackbill, Y., McManus, K., & Woodward, L. (1985). *Medication in maternity: Infant exposure and maternal information.* Ann Arbor: University of Michigan Press.

Brazelton, T. B. (1979). Behavioral competence of the newborn infant. *Seminars in Perinatology, 3,* 35–44.

Bronfenbrenner, U. (1979). *The ecology of human development. Experiments by nature and design.* Cambridge, MA: Harvard University Press.

Bronfenbrenner, U. (1989). Ecological systems theory. In R. Vasta (Ed.), *Annals of child development: Vol. 6. Theories of child development: Revised formulations and current issues.* Greenwich, CT: JAI Press.

Bronfenbrenner, U., & Crouter, A. C. (1983). The evolution of environmental models in developmental research. In W. Kessen (Vol. Ed.; P. H. Mussen, General Ed.), *Handbook of child psychology: Vol. 1. History, theory, and methods* (4th ed.). New York: Wiley.

Brown, S. S. (Ed.). (1988). *Prenatal care: Reaching mothers, reaching infants.* Washington, DC: National Academy Press.

Browne, J. C., & Dixon, G. (1978). *Antenatal care.* Edinburgh: Churchill Livingstone.

Callahan, E. J., & McClusky, K. A. (Eds.). (1983). *Life-span developmental psychology. Nonnormative life events.* New York: Academic.

Cohen, S. E., & Parmelee, A. H. (1983). Prediction of five-year Stanford-Binet scores in preterm infants. *Child Development, 54,* 1242–1253.

Cohen, S. E., Parmelee, A. H., Jr., Beckwith, L., & Sigman, M. (1986). Cognitive development in preterm infants: Birth to 8 years. *Developmental and Behavioral Pediatrics, 7,* 102–110.

Colombo, J. (1982). The critical period concept: Research, methodology, and theoretical issues. *Psychological Bulletin, 91,* 260–275.

Corah, N. L., Anthony, E. J., Painter, P., Stern, J. A., & Thurston, D. L. (1965). The effects of perinatal anoxia after seven years. *Psychological Monographs, 79* (Whole No. 596).

Cotterell, J. L. (1986). Work and community influences on the quality of child rearing. *Child Development, 57,* 362–374.

Curtiss, S. (1977). *Genie: A psycholinguistic study of a modern day "wild child."* New York: Academic.

Dalton, K. (1980). *Depression after childbirth.* Oxford: Oxford University Press.

Datan, N., & Ginsberg, L. H. (Eds.). (1975). *Life-span developmental psychology: Normative life crises.* New York: Academic.

Dick-Read, G. (1972). *Childbirth without fear: The original approach to natural childbirth* (Rev. ed.). New York: Harper & Row. (Original work published 1933)

Dixon, S. D., LeVine, R. A., Richman, A., & Brazelton, T. B. (1984). Mother–child interaction around a teaching task: An African–American comparison. *Child Development, 55,* 1252–1264.

Dowd, J. J., & Bengston, V. L. (1978). Aging in minority populations: An examination of the double jeopardy hypothesis. *Journal of Gerontology, 33,* 427–436.

Edwards, M., & Waldorf, M. (1984). *Reclaiming birth: History and heroines of American childbirth reform.* Trumansburg, NY: The Crossing Press.

Field, T. M. (1984). Early interactions between infants and their postpartum depressed mothers. *Infant Behavior and Development, 7,* 517–522.

Field, T., Sandberg, D., Garcia, R., Vega-Lahr, N., Goldstein, S., & Guy, L. (1985). Pregnancy problems, postpartum depression, and early mother–infant interactions. *Developmental Psychology, 21,* 1152–1156.

Finley, G. E. (1982). Modernization and aging. In T. M. Field, A. Huston, H. C. Quay, L. Troll, & G. E. Finley (Eds.), *Review of human development.* New York: Wiley-Interscience.

Finster, M., Pedersen, H., & Morishima, H. O. (1984). Principles of fetal exposure to drugs used in obstetric anesthesia. In B. Krauer, F. Krauer, F. E. Hytten, & E. del Pozo (Eds.), *Drugs and pregnancy. Maternal drug handling—fetal drug exposure.* Orlando, FL: Academic.

Fried, P. A. (1980). Marijuana use by pregnant women: Neurobehavioral effects on neonates. *Drug and Alcohol Dependence, 6,* 415–424.

Fry, C. L. (1985). Culture, behavior, and aging in the comparative perspective. In J. E. Birren, & K. W. Schaie (Eds.), *Handbook of the psychology of aging* (2nd ed.). New York: Van Nostrand Reinhold.

Fuhrmann, W., & Vogel, F. (1976). *Genetic counseling.* New York: Springer-Verlag.

Garmezy, N. (1987). Stress, competence, and development: Continuities in the study of schizophrenic adults, children vulnerable to psychopathology, and the search for stress-resistant children. *American Journal of Orthopsychiatry, 57,* 159–174.

Glass, P., Avery, G. B., Subramanian, K. N. S., Keys, M. P., Sostek, A. M., & Friendly, D. S. (1985). Effects of bright light in the hospital nursery on the incidence of retinopathy of prematurity. *New England Journal of Medicine, 313,* 401–404.

Goldberg, S. (1983). Parent–infant bonding: Another look. *Child Development, 54,* 1355–1382.

Goodstein, A., & Goldstein, S. (1986). The challenge of an aging population: The case of the People's Republic of China. *Research on Aging, 8,* 179–200.

Gottlieb, S. E., & Barrett, D. E. (1986). Effects of unanticipated cesarian section on mothers, infants, and their interaction in the first month of life. *Developmental and Behavioral Pediatrics, 7,* 180–185.

Greenberg, M., & Morris, N. (1974). Engrossment: The newborn's impact upon the father. *American Journal of Orthopsychiatry, 44,* 520–531.

Greenberg, M. T., & Crnic, K. A. (1988). Longitudinal predictors of developmental status and social interaction in premature and full-term infants at age two. *Child Development, 59,* 554–570.

Grossman, F. K., Eichler, L. S., Winickoff, S. A., & Associates (1980). *Pregnancy, birth, and parenthood: Adaptations of mothers, fathers, and infants.* San Francisco: Jossey-Bass.

Grossmann, K., Thane, K., & Grossman, K. E. (1981). Maternal tactual contact of the newborn after various postpartum conditions of mother–infant contact. *Developmental Psychology, 17,* 158–169.

Guemple, L. (1983). Growing old in Inuit society. In J. Sokolovsky (Ed.), *Growing old in different societies. Cross-cultural perspectives.* Belmont, CA: Wadsworth.

Gunderson, V., & Sackett, G. P. (1982). Paternal effects on reproductive outcome and developmental risk. In M. E. Lamb & A. L. Brown (Eds.), *Advances in developmental psychology* (Vol. 2). Hillsdale, NJ: Erlbaum.

Half our pregnancies are unintentional. (1983, October 10). *Newsweek,* p. 37.

Hamm, A. C. (1981). *Questions and answers about DES exposure during pregnancy and birth.* NIH Pub. No. 81-1118. Washington, DC: National Institutes of Health, U.S. Department of Health and Human Services.

Hareven, T. (1986). Life-course transitions and kin assistance in old age: A cohort comparison. In D. Van Tassel & P. N. Stearns (Eds.), *Old age in a bureaucratic society. The elderly, the experts, and the state of American history.* Westport, CT: Greenwood Press.

Harrell, S. (1981). Growing old in rural Taiwan. In P. T. Amoss, & S. Harrell (Eds.), *Other ways of growing old: Anthropological perspectives.* Stanford, CA: Stanford University Press.

Heinonen, O. P., Slone, D., & Shapiro, S. (1977). *Birth defects and drugs in pregnancy.* Littleton, MA: Publishing Sciences Group.

Henneborn, W. J., & Cogan, R. (1975). The effect of husband participation on reported pain and probability of medication during labor and birth. *Journal of Psychosomatic Research, 19,* 215–222.

Hess, R. D. (1970). Social class and ethnic influences upon socialization. In P. H. Mussen (Ed.), *Carmichael's manual of child psychology* (Vol. 2). New York: Wiley.

Howard, R. B., & Cronk, C. (1983). Nutrition and development. In M. D. Levine, W. B. Carey, A. C. Crocker, & R. T. Gross (Eds.), *Developmental-behavioral pediatrics.* Philadelphia: W. B. Saunders.

Jacobson, C. B., & Berlin, C. M. (1972). Possible reproductive detriment in LSD users. *Journal of the American Medical Association, 222,* 1367–1373.

Jacobson, J. L., Jacobson, S. W., Fein, G. G., Schwartz, P. M., & Dowler, J. K. (1984). Prenatal exposure to an environmental toxin. *Developmental Psychology, 20,* 523–532.

Jacobson, S. W., Fein, G. G., Jacobson, J. L., Schwartz, P. M., & Dowler, J. K. (1984). Neonatal correlates of exposure to smoking, caffeine, and alcohol. *Infant Behavior and Development, 7,* 253–265.

Johnson, D. L., Teigen, K., & Davila, R. (1983). Anxiety and social restriction. A study of children in Mexico, Norway, and the United States. *Journal of Cross-Cultural Psychology, 14,* 439–454.

Jones, K. L., Smith, D. W., Ulleland, C. N., & Streissguth, A. P. (1973). Pattern of malformation in offspring of chronic alcoholic mothers. *Lancet, 1,* 1267–1271.

Kagan, J. (1986). Rates of change in psychological processes. *Journal of Applied Developmental Psychology, 7,* 125–130.

Kagan, S., & Masden, M. C. (1972). Rivalry in Anglo-American and Mexican children of two ages. *Journal of Personality and Social Psychology, 24,* 214–220.

Kahn, R. L. (1979). Aging and social support. In M. W. Riley (Ed.), *Aging from birth to death: Interdisciplinary perspectives.* Boulder, CO: Westview.

Kaplan, B. J. (1986). A psychobiological review of depression during pregnancy. *Psychology of Women Quarterly, 10,* 35–48.

Keith, J. (1985). Age in anthropological research. In R. H. Binstock & E. Shanas (Eds.), *Handbook of aging and the social sciences* (2nd ed.). New York: Van Nostrand Reinhold.

Kennell, J. H., Voos, D. K., & Klaus, M. H. (1979). Parent–infant bonding. In J. D. Osofsky (Ed.), *Handbook of infant development.* New York: Wiley.

Kessner, D. M. (1973). *Infant death: An analysis by maternal risk and health care.* Washington, DC: National Academy of Sciences.

Kett, J. F. (1977). *Rites of passage: Adolescence in America 1790 to the present.* New York: Basic Books.

Klaus, M. H., & Kennell, J. H. (1976). *Maternal–infant bonding.* St Louis: C. V. Mosby.

Klee, L. (1986). Home away from home: The alternative birth center. *Social Science and Medicine, 23,* 9–16.

Kohn, M. L. (1969). *Class and conformity: A study of values.* Homewood, IL: Dorsey Press.

Kolata, G. B. (1979). Scientists attack report that obstetrical medications endanger children. *Science, 204,* 391–392.

Konner, M. J. (1976). Maternal care, infant behavior and development among the !Kung. In R. B. Lee & I. DeVore (Eds.), *Kalahari hunter-gatherers. Studies of the !Kung San and their neighbors.* Cambridge, MA: Harvard University Press.

Konner, M. J. (1981). Evolution of human behavior development. In R. H. Munroe, R. L. Munroe, & B. B. Whiting (Eds.), *Handbook of cross-cultural human development.* New York: Garland STPM Press.

Kopp, C. B., & Krakow, J. B. (1983). The developmentalist and the study of biological risk: A view of the past with an eye toward the future. *Child Development, 54,* 1086–1108.

Kopp, C. B., & Parmelee, A. H. (1979). Prenatal and perinatal influences on infant behavior. In J. D. Osofsky (Ed.), *Handbook of infant development.* New York: Wiley.

Kraus, M. A., & Redman, E. S. (1986). Postpartum depression: An interactional view. *Journal of Marital and Family Therapy, 12,* 63–74.

Lefkowitz, M. M. (1981). Smoking during pregnancy: Long-term effects on offspring. *Developmental Psychology, 17,* 192–194.

Lamaze, F. (1958). *Painless childbirth: Psychoprophylactic method.* London: Burke.

Leroy, M. (1988). *Miscarriage.* London: Macdonald & Company.

Lester, B. M., Als, H., & Brazelton, T. B. (1982). Regional obstetric anesthesia and newborn behavior: A reanalysis toward synergistic effects. *Child Development, 53,* 687–692.

LeVine, R. A. (1974). Parental goals: A cross-cultural view. *Teachers College Record, 76,* 226–239.

MacDonald, K. (1986). Early experience, relative plasticity, and cognitive development. *Journal of Applied Developmental Psychology, 7,* 101–124.

MacFarlane, A. (1977). *The psychology of childbirth.* Cambridge, MA: Harvard University Press.

Markides, K. S., Boldt, J. S., & Ray, L. A. (1986). Sources of helping and intergenerational solidarity: A three-generations study of Mexican-Americans. *Journal of Gerontology, 41,* 506–511.

McKinney, J. P. (1984). Becoming an adult in the 1980s. In R. P. Boger, G. E. Blom, & L. E. Lezotte (Eds.), *Child nurturance: Vol. 4. Child nurturing in the 1980s.* New York: Plenum.

McLanahan, S. S., & Sorensen, A. B. (1985). Life events and psychological well-being over the life course. In G. H. Elder, Jr. (Ed.), *Life course dynamics. Trajectories and transitions, 1968–1980.* Ithaca, NY: Cornell University Press.

Mead, M. (1978). *Culture and commitment: The new relationships between the generations in the 1970s* (Rev. & Updated Ed.). Garden City, NY: Anchor Press.

Miller, S. S. (1976). *Symptoms: The complete home medical encyclopedia.* New York: Thomas Y. Crowell.

Mischel, W., & Metzner, R. (1962). Preference for delayed reward as a function of age, intelligence, and length of delay interval. *Journal of Abnormal and Social Psychology, 64,* 425–431.

Money, J., & Ehrhardt, A. (1972). *Man and woman, boy and girl.* Baltimore, MD: Johns Hopkins University Press.

Moore, K. L (1977). *The developing human.* Philadelphia: W. B. Saunders.

Murray, A. D., Dolby, R. M., Nation, R. L., & Thomas, D. B. (1981). Effects of epidural anesthesia on newborns and their mothers. *Child Development, 52,* 71–82.

Myers, B. J. (1982). Early intervention using Brazelton training with middle-class mothers and fathers of newborns. *Child Development, 53,* 462–471.

Myers, R. E. (1980). Reply to Drs. Kron and Brackbill. *American Journal of Obstetrics and Gynecology, 136,* 819–820.

Myers, R. E., & Myers, S. E. (1979). Use of sedative, analgesic, and anesthetic drugs during labor and delivery: Bane or boon. *American Journal of Obstetrics and Gynecology, 133,* 83–104.

Neugarten, B. L. (1968). Adult personality: Toward a psychology of the life cycle. In B. L. Neugarten (Ed.), *Middle age and aging. A reader in social psychology.* Chicago: University of Chicago Press.

Neugarten, B. L. (1975). The future and the young-old. *Gerontologist, 15,* (Part II), 4–9.

Neugarten, B. L., Moore, J. W., & Lowe, J. C. (1965). Age norms, age constraints, and adult socialization. *American Journal of Sociology, 70,* 710–717.

Neugarten, B. L., & Neugarten, D. A. (1986). Changing meanings of age in the aging society. In A. Pifer & L. Bronte (Eds.), *Our aging society. Paradox and promise.* New York: W. W. Norton.

Ogbu, J. U. (1981). Origins of human competence: A cultural-ethological perspective. *Child Development, 52,* 413–429.

Osako, M. M., & Liu, W. T. (1986). Intergenerational relations and the aged among Japanese Americans. *Research on Aging, 8,* 128–155.

Paige, K. E., & Paige, J. M. (1981). *The politics of reproductive ritual.* Berkeley, CA: University of California Press.

Palkovitz, R. (1985). Fathers' birth attendance, early contact, and extended contact with their newborns: A critical review. *Child Development, 56,* 392–406.

Peterson, G. H., Mehl, L. E., & Liederman, P . H. (1979). The role of some birth-related variables in father attachment. *American Journal of Orthopsychiatry, 49,* 330–338.

Pines, M. (1981, September). Update: The civilizing of Genie. *Psychology Today,* pp. 28–34.

Planned Parenthood Federation of America. (1976). *11 million teenagers: What can be done about the epidemic of adolescent pregnancies in the United States?* New York: Alan Guttmacher Institute.

Plath, D., & Ikada, K. (1975). After coming of age: Adult awareness of age norms. In T. R. Williams (Ed.), *Socialization and communication in primary groups.* The Hague: Mouton.

Radke-Yarrow, M., Cummings, E. M., Kuczynski, L., & Chapman, M. (1985). Patterns of attachment in two- and three-year-olds in normal families and families with parental depression. *Child Development, 56,* 884–893.

Ragozin, A. S., Basham, R. B., Crnic, K. A., Greenberg, M. T., & Robinson, N. M. (1982). Effects of maternal age on parenting role. *Developmental Psychology, 18,* 627–634.

Rauh, V. A., Achenbach, T. M., Nurcombe, B., Howell, C. T., & Teti, D. M. (1988). Minimizing adverse effects of low birthweight: Four-year results of an early intervention. *Child Development, 59,* 544–553.

Roberts, C. J., & Lowe, C. R. (1975). Where have all the conceptions gone? *Lancet, 1,* 498–499.

Rode, S. S., Chang, P., Fisch, R. O., & Sroufe, L. A. (1981). Attachment patterns of infants separated at birth. *Developmental Psychology, 17,* 188–191.

Rohner, R. P. (1984). Toward a conception of culture for cross-cultural psychology. *Journal of Cross-Cultural Psychology, 15,* 111–138.

Rosow, I. (1985). Status and role change through the life cycle. In R. H. Binstock & E. Shanas (Eds.), *Handbook of aging and the social sciences* (2nd ed.). New York: Van Nostrand Reinhold.

Rowles, G. D. (1981). Geographical perspectives on human development. *Human Development, 24,* 67–76.

Rutter, M. (1980). Raised lead levels and impaired cognitive/behavioral functioning: A review of the evidence. *Developmental Medicine and Child Neurology, 22* (Suppl. 42), 1–26.

Sameroff, A. J. (1983). Developmental systems: Contexts and evolution. In W. Kessen (Vol. Ed.; P. H. Mussen, General Ed.), *Handbook of child psychology: Vol. 1. History, theory, and methods* (4th ed.). New York: Wiley.

Sameroff, A. J., & Chandler, M. J. (1975). Reproductive risk and the continuum of caretaking casualty. In F. D. Horowitz, M. Hetherington, S. Scarr-Salapatek, & G. Siegel (Eds.), *Review of child development research* (Vol. 4). Chicago: University of Chicago Press.

Scafidi, F. A., Field, T. M., Schanberg, S. M., Bauer, C. R., Vega-Lahr, N., Garcia, R., Poirier, J., Nystrom, G., & Kuhn, C. M. (1986). Effects of tactile/kinesthetic stimulation on the clinical course and sleep/wake behavior of preterm neonates. *Infant Behavior and Development, 9,* 91–105.

Schardein, J. L. (1985). *Chemically induced birth defects.* New York: Dekker.

Schaefer, M., Hatcher, R. P., & Barglow, P. D. (1980). Prematurity and infant stimulation: A review of research. *Child Psychiatry and Human Development, 10,* 199–212.

Sontag, L. W. (1941). The significance of fetal environmental differences. *American Journal of Obstetrics and Gynecology, 42,* 996–1003.

Spreen, O., Tupper, D., Risser, A., Tuokko, H., & Edgell, D. (1984). *Human developmental neuropsychology.* New York: Oxford University Press.

Stein, Z. A., & Susser, M. W. (1976). Prenatal nutrition and mental competence. In J. D. Lloyd-Still (Ed.), *Malnutrition and intellectual development.* Littleton, MA: Publishing Sciences Group.

Stein, Z. A., Susser, M. W., Saenger, G., & Marolla, F. (1975). *Famine and human development: The Dutch hunger winter of 1944–1945.* New York: Oxford University Press.

Stern, M., & Hildebrandt, K. A. (1986). Prematurity stereotyping: Effects on mother–infant interaction. *Child Development, 57,* 308–315.

Stewart, A. J., Sokol, M., Healy, J. M., Jr., & Chester, N. L. (1986). Longitudinal studies of psychological consequences of life changes in children and adults. *Journal of Personality and Social Psychology, 50,* 143–151.

Stott, D. H., & Latchford, S. A. (1976). Prenatal antecedents of child health, development, and behavior: An epidemiological report of incidence and association. *Journal of the American Academy of Child Psychiatry, 15,* 161–190.

Streissguth, A. P., Barr, H. M., & Martin, D. C. (1983). Maternal alcohol use and neonatal habituation assessed by the Brazelton scale. *Child Development, 54,* 1109–1118.

Streissguth, A. P., Barr, H. M., Sampson, P. D., Darby, B. L., & Martin, D. C. (1989). IQ at age 4 in relation to maternal alcohol use and smoking during pregnancy. *Developmental Psychology, 25,* 3–11.

Streissguth, A. P., Herman, C. S., & Smith, D. W. (1978). Stability of intelligence in the fetal alcohol syndrome: A preliminary report. *Alcoholism: Clinical and Experimental Research, 2,* 165–170.

Super, C. M., & Harkness, S. (1981). Figure, ground, and Gestalt: The cultural context of the active individual. In R. M. Lerner & N. A. Busch-Rossnagel (Eds.), *Individuals as producers of their development. A life-span perspective.* New York: Academic.

Tinklenberg, J. R. (1975). *Marijuana and health hazards: Methodological issues in current research.* New York: Academic.

U.S. Bureau of the Census. (1987). *Statistical abstract of the United States: 1988* (108th ed.). Washington, DC: Author.

U.S. Department of Health, Education and Welfare. (1979). *Smoking and health: A report to the Surgeon General.* DHEW Pub. no. PHS 79-50066. Washington, DC: U.S. Government Printing Office.

Valsiner, J., & Benigni, L. (1986). Naturalistic research and ecological thinking in the study of child development. *Developmental Review, 6,* 203–223.

Van Gennep, A. (1960). *The rites of passage* (M. B. Vizedom & G. L. Caffee, Trans.). Chicago: University of Chicago Press. (Original work published 1908)

Vorhees, C. V., & Mollnow, E. (1987). Behavioral teratogenesis: Long-term influences on behavior from early exposure to environmental agents. In J. D. Osofsky (Ed.), *Handbook of infant development* (2nd ed.). New York: Wiley.

Werner, E. E. (1989). High-risk children in young adulthood: A longitudinal study from birth to 32 years. *American Journal of Orthopsychiatry, 59,* 72–81.

Werner, E. E., & Smith, R. S. (1982). *Vulnerable but invincible. A longitudinal study of resilient children and youth.* New York: McGraw-Hill.

Whiting, B. B., & Edwards, C. P. (1988). *Children of different worlds. The formation of social behavior.* Cambridge, MA: Harvard University Press.

Whiting, B. B., & Whiting, J. W. M. (1975). *Children of six cultures.* Cambridge, MA: Harvard University Press.

Wideman, M. V., & Singer, J. E. (1984). The role of psychological mechanisms in preparation for childbirth. *American Psychologist, 39,* 1357–1371.

Widmayer, S., & Field, T. (1980). Effects of Brazelton demonstrations on early interactions of preterm infants and their teenage mothers. *Infant Behavior and Development, 3,* 79–89.

Wilson, R. S. (1985). Risk and resilience in early mental development. *Developmental Psychology, 21,* 795–805.

Winick, M. (1976). *Malnutrition and brain development.* New York: Oxford University Press.

Worobey, J., & Brazelton, T. B. (1986). Experimenting with the family in the newborn period: A commentary. *Child Development, 57,* 1298–1300.

Zepelin, H., Sills, R. A., & Heath, M. W. (1986–1987). Is age becoming irrelevant? An exploratory study of perceived age norms. *International Journal of Aging and Human Development, 24,* 241–256.

Chapter 5: The Physical Self

Adams, P., Davies, G. T., & Sweetnam, P. (1970). Osteoporosis and the effects of ageing on bone mass in elderly men and women. *Quarterly Journal of Medicine, 39,* 601–615.

Andres, R., & Tobin, J. D. (1977). Endocrine systems. In C. E. Finch & L. Hayflick (Eds.), *Handbook of the biology of aging.* New York: Van Nostrand Reinhold.

Asso, D. (1983). *The real menstrual cycle.* Chichester, England: Wiley.

Bafitis, H., & Sargent, F., II. (1977). Human physiological adaptability through the life sequence. *Journal of Gerontology, 32,* 402–410.

Bartus, R. T., Dean, R. L., III, Beer, B., & Lippa, A. S. (1982). The cholingeric hypothesis of geriatric memory dysfunction. *Science, 217,* 408–417.

Berg, W. K., Adkinson, C. D., & Strock, B. D. (1973). Duration and frequency of periods of alertness in neonates. *Developmental Psychology, 9,* 434.

Berg, W. K., & Berg, K. M. (1979). Psychological development in infancy: State, sensory function, and attention. In J. D. Osofsky (Ed.), *Handbook of infant development.* New York: Wiley.

Bennett, E. L., Diamond, M. C., Krech, D., & Rosenzweig, M. R. (1964). Chemical and anatomical plasticity of the brain. *Science, 146,* 610–619.

Berscheid, E., Walster, E., & Bohrnstedt, G. (1973, June). The happy American body: A survey report. *Psychology Today,* pp. 119–131.

Birren, J. E., Butler, R. N., Greenhouse, S. W., Sokoloff, L., & Yarrow, M. R. (Eds.). (1963). *Human aging: A biological and behavioral study.* Washington DC: U.S. Government Printing Office.

Birren, J. E., Woods, A. M., & Williams, M. V. (1980). Behavioral slowing with age: Causes, organization, and consequences. In L. W. Poon (Ed.), *Aging in the 1980s.* Washington, DC: American Psychological Association.

Boismier, J. D. (1977) Visual stimulation and the wake–sleep behavior in human neonates. *Developmental Psychobiology, 10,* 219–227.

Bondareff, W. (1985). The neural basis of aging. In J. E. Birren & K. W. Schaie (Eds.), *Handbook of the psychology of aging* (2nd ed.). New York: Van Nostrand Reinhold.

Botwinick, J. (1984). *Aging and behavior. A comprehensive integration of research findings* (3rd ed.). New York: Springer.

Bower, T. G. R. (1982). *Development in infancy* (2nd ed.). San Francisco: Freeman.

Brierley, J. (1976). *The growing brain.* London: NFER Publishing.

Brooks-Gunn, J., & Warren, M. P. (1988). The psychological significance of secondary sexual characteristics in nine- to eleven-year-old girls. *Child Development, 59,* 1061–1069.

Brooks-Gunn, J., & Zahaykevich, M. (1989). Parent-daughter relationships in early adolescence: A developmental perspective. In K. Kreppner & R. M. Lerner (Eds.), *Family systems and life-span development.* Hillsdale, NJ: Erlbaum.

Brown, J. L. (1964). States in newborn infants. *Merrill-Palmer Quarterly, 10,* 313–327.

Brown, M. A., & Woods, N. F. (1986). Sex role orientation, sex typing, occupational traditionalism, and perimenstrual symptoms. In V. L. Olesen & N. F. Woods (Eds.), *Culture, society, and menstruation.* Washington, DC: Hemisphere.

Buell, S. J., & Coleman, P. D. (1979). Dendritic growth in the aged human brain and failure of growth in senile dementia. *Science, 206,* 854–856.

Buskirk, E. R. (1985). Health maintenance and longevity: Exercise. In C. E. Finch & E. L. Schneider (Eds.), *Handbook of the biology of aging* (2nd ed.). New York: Van Nostrand Reinhold.

Cherry, K. E., & Morton, M. R. (1989). Drug sensitivity in older adults: The role of physiologic and pharmacokinetic factors. *International Journal of Aging and Human Development, 28,* 159–174.

Clarkson-Smith, L., & Hartley, A. A. (1989). Relationships between physical exercise and cognitive abilities in older adults. *Psychology and Aging, 4,* 183–189.

Connor, J. R., Jr., Diamond, M. C., & Johnson, R. E. (1980). Aging and environmental influences on two types of dendritic spines in the rat occipital cortex. *Experimental Neurology, 70,* 371–379.

Corbin, C. (1973). *A textbook of motor development.* Dubuque, Iowa: William C. Brown.

Coren, S., Porac, C., & Duncan, P. (1981). Lateral preference behaviors in preschool children and young adults. *Child Development, 52,* 443–450.

Cowan, W. M. (1979). The development of the brain. *Scientific American, 241*(3), 112–133.

Crawford, M. P., & Hooper, D. (1973). Menopause, ageing and family. *Social Science and Medicine, 7,* 469–482.

Cunningham, D. A., Rechnitzer, P. A., Pearce, M. E., & Donner, A. P. (1982). Determinants of self-selected walking pace across ages 19 to 66. *Journal of Gerontology, 37,* 560–564.

Davidson, J. M., Chen, J. J., Crapo, L., Gray, G. D., Greenleaf, W. J., & Catania, J. A. (1983). Hormonal changes and sexual function in aging men. *Journal of Clinical Endocrinology and Metabolism, 57,* 71–77.

Davis, M. A., Murphy, S. P., & Neuhaus, J. M. (1988). Living arrangements and eating behavior of older adults in the United States. *Journal of Gerontology: Social Sciences, 43,* S96–S98.

Davis, M. A., Randall, E., Forthofer, R. N., Lee, E. S., & Margen, S. (1985). Living arrangements and dietary patterns of older adults in the United States. *Journal of Gerontology, 40,* 434–442.

Dennis, W. (1960). Causes of retardation among institutional children: Iran. *Journal of Genetic Psychology, 96,* 47–59.

Dorfman, P. W. (1977). Timing and anticipation: A developmental perspective. *Journal of Motor Behavior, 9,* 67–79.

Duncan, P. D., Ritter, P. L., Dornbusch, S. M., Gross, R. T., & Carlsmith, J. M. (1985). The effects of pubertal timing on body image, school behavior, and deviance. *Journal of Youth and Adolescence, 14,* 227–235.

Dyer, K. F. (1977). The trend of the male–female performance differential in athletics, swimming and cycling 1948–1976. *Journal of Biosocial Science, 9,* 325–338.

Eichorn, D. H. (1979). Physical development: Current foci of research. In J. D. Osofsky (Ed.), *Handbook of infant development.* New York: Wiley.

Englander-Golden, P., Sonleitner, F. J., Whitmore, M. R., & Corbley, G. J. M. (1986). Social and menstrual cycles: Methodological and substantive findings. In V. L. Olesen & N. F. Woods (Eds.), *Culture, society, and menstruation.* Washington, DC: Hemisphere.

Epstein, H. T. (1974). Phrenoblysis: Special brain and mind growth periods. I. Human brain and skull development. *Developmental Psychobiology, 7,* 207–216.

Epstein, H. T. (1980). EEG developmental stages. *Developmental Psychobiology, 13,* 629–631.

Faust, M. S. (1960). Developmental maturity as a determinant of prestige in adolescent girls. *Child Development, 31,* 173–184.

Faust, M. S. (1977). Somatic development of adolescent girls. *Monographs of the Society for Research in Child Development, 42,* (Whole No. 169).

Fentress, J. C., & McLeod, P. J. (1986). Motor patterns in development. In E. M. Blass (Ed.), *Handbook of behavioral neurobiology: Vol. 8. Developmental psychobiology and developmental neurobiology.* New York: Plenum.

Fischer, K. W. (1987). Relations between brain and cognitive development. *Child Development, 58,* 623–632.

Flint, M. (1982). Male and female menopause: A cultural put-on. In A. M. Voda, M. Dinnerstein, & S. R. O'Donnell (Eds.), *Changing perspectives on menopause.* Austin, TX: University of Texas Press.

Fries, J. F., & Crapo, L. M. (1981). *Vitality and aging: Implications of the rectangular curve.* San Francisco: W. H. Freeman.

Frisch, R. E. (1983). Fatness, puberty, and fertility. The effects of nutrition and physical training on menarche and ovulation. In J. Brooks-Gunn & A. C. Petersen (Eds.), *Girls at puberty, Biological and psychosocial perspectives.* New York: Plenum.

Frisch, R. E., & McArthur, J. W. (1974). Menstrual cycles: Fatness as a determinant of minimum weight for height necessary for their maintenance or onset. *Science, 185,* 949–951.

Frisch, R. E., Wyshak, G., & Vincent, L. (1980). Delayed menarche and amenorrhea of ballet dancers. *New England Journal of Medicine, 303,* 17–19.

Gaddis, A., & Brooks-Gunn, J. (1985). The male experience of pubertal change. *Journal of Youth and Adolescence, 14,* 61–69.

Goldman-Rakic, P. S., Isseroff, A., Schwartz, M. L.; & Bugbee, N. M. (1983). The neurobiology of cognitive development. In M. M. Haith & J. J. Campos (Vol. Eds.; P. H. Mussen, General Ed.), *Handbook of child psychology: Vol. 2. Infancy and developmental psychobiology* (4th ed.). New York: Wiley.

Greene, J. G. (1984). *The social and psychological origins of the climacteric syndrome.* Hants, Eng. & Brookfield, VT: Gower.

Greenough, W. T. (1986). What's special about development? Thoughts on the bases of experience-sensitive synaptic plasticity. In W. T. Greenough & J. M. Juraska (Eds.), *Developmental neuropsychobiology.* Orlando, FL: Academic.

Greif, E. B., & Ulman, K. J. (1982). The psychological impact of menarche on early adolescent females: A review. *Child Development, 53,* 1413–1430.

Guigoz, Y., & Munro, H. N. (1985). Nutrition and aging. In C. E. Finch & E. L. Schneider (Eds.), *Handbook of the biology of aging* (2nd ed.). New York: Van Nostrand Reinhold.

Gustafson, G. E. (1984). Effects of the ability to locomote on infants' social and exploratory behaviors. *Developmental Psychology, 20,* 397–405.

Halverson, H. M. (1931). An experimental study of prehension in infants by means of systematic cinema records. *Genetic Psychology Monographs, 10,* 107–286.

Harman, S. M., & Talbert, G. B. (1985). Reproductive aging. In C. E. Finch & E. L. Schneider (Eds.), *Handbook of the biology of aging* (2nd ed.). New York: Van Nostrand Reinhold.

Harman, S. M., & Tsitouras, P. D. (1980). Reproductive hormones in aging men. I. Measurement of sex steroids, basal luteinizing hormone, and Leydig cell response to human chorionic gonadotropin. *Journal of Clinical Endocrinology and Metabolism, 51,* 35–40.

Harris, C. S. (1978). *Fact book on aging: A profile of America's older population.* Washington, DC: National Council on Aging.

Haywood, K. M. (1986). *Life span motor development.* Champaign, IL: Human Kinetics Publishers.

Heath, G. W., Hagberg, J. M., Ehsani, A. A., & Holloszy, J. O. (1981). A physiological comparison of young and older endurance athletes. *Journal of Applied Physiology, 51,* 634–640.

Herkowitz, J. (1978). Sex-role expectations and motor behavior of the young child. In M. V. Ridenour (Ed.), *Motor development: Issues and applications.* Princeton, NJ: Princeton Book Company.

Hill, J. P. (1988). Adapting to menarche: Familial control and conflict. In M. R. Gunnar & W. A. Collins (Eds.), *Development during the transition to adolescence: Vol. 21. Minnesota symposia on child psychology.* Hillsdale, NJ: Erlbaum.

Hill, J. P., Holmbeck, G. N., Marlow, L., Green, T. M., & Lynch, M. E. (1985). Menarcheal status and parent–child relations in families of seventh-grade girls. *Journal of Youth and Adolescence, 14,* 301–316.

Hill, J. P., & Lynch, M. E. (1983). The intensification of gender-related role expectations during early adolescence. In J. Brooks-Gunn & A. C. Petersen (Eds.), *Girls at puberty: Biological and psychosocial perspectives.* New York: Plenum.

Hofsten, C. von (1982). Eye–hand coordination in the newborn. *Developmental Psychology, 18,* 450–461.

Hofsten, C. von (1984). Developmental changes in the organization of prereaching movements. *Developmental Psychology, 20,* 378–388.

Hutt, S. J., Lenard, H. G., & Prechtl, H. E. R. (1969). Psychophysiology of the newborn. In L. P. Lipsitt & H. W. Reese (Eds.), *Advances in child development and behavior.* New York: Academic.

Huttenlocher, P. R. (1979). Synaptic density in human frontal cortex—developmental changes and effects of aging. *Brain Research, 163,* 195–205.

Janowsky, J. S., & Finlay, B. L. (1986). The outcome of perinatal brain damage:

The role of normal neuron loss and axon retraction. *Developmental Medicine and Child Neurology, 28,* 375–389.

Johnston, C. C., Jr., Hui, S. L., Witt, R. M., Appledorn, R., Baker, R. S., & Longcope, C. (1985). Early menopausal changes in bone mass and sex steroids. *Journal of Clinical Endocrinology and Metabolism, 61,* 905–911.

Jones, M. C. (1965). Psychological correlates of somatic development. *Child Development, 36,* 899–911.

Jones, M. C., & Bayley, N. (1950). Physical maturing among boys as related to behavior. *Journal of Educational Psychology, 41,* 129–148.

Jones, M. C., & Mussen, P. H. (1958). Self-conceptions, motivations, and interpersonal attitudes of early- and late-maturing girls. *Child Development, 29,* 491–501.

Keough, J., & Sugden, D. (1985). *Movement skill development.* New York: Macmillan.

Kermoian, R., & Campos, J. J. (1988). Locomotor experience: A facilitator of spatial cognitive development. *Child Development, 59,* 908–917.

Kinsbourne, M., & Hiscock, M. (1983). The normal and deviant development of functional lateralization of the brain. In M. M. Haith & J. J. Campos (Vol. Eds.; P. H. Mussen, General Ed.), *Handbook of child psychology: Vol. 2. Infancy and developmental psychobiology* (4th ed.). New York: Wiley.

Konner, M. J. (1976). Maternal care, infant behavior and development among the !Kung. In R. B. Lee & I. DeVore (Eds.), *Kalahari hunter-gatherers. Studies of the !Kung San and their neighbors.* Cambridge, MA: Harvard University Press.

Kron, R. E. (1966). Instrumental conditioning of nutritive sucking behavior in the newborn. *Recent Advances in Biological Psychiatry, 9,* 295–300.

Lakatta, E. G. (1985). Heart and circulation. In C. E. Finch & E. L. Schneider (Eds.), *Handbook of the biology of aging* (2nd ed.). New York: Van Nostrand Reinhold.

Lamy, P. P. (1986). The elderly and drug interactions. *Journal of the American Geriatrics Society, 34,* 586–592.

Lenneberg, E. H. (1967). *Biological foundations of language.* New York: Wiley.

Livson, N., & Peskin, H. (1980). Perspectives on adolescence from longitudinal research. In J. Adelson (Ed.), *Handbook of adolescent psychology.* New York: Wiley.

Magnusson, D., Stattin, H., & Allen, V. L. (1985). Biological maturation and social development: A longitudinal study of some adjustment processes from mid-adolescence to adulthood. *Journal of Youth and Adolescence, 14,* 267–283.

Marsh, R. W. (1985). Phrenoblysis: Real or chimera? *Child Development, 56,* 1059–1061.

Marshall, W. A. (1977). *Human growth and its disorders.* New York: Academic.

Masters, W. H., & Johnson, V. E. (1966). *Human sexual response.* Boston: Little, Brown.

Mayer, J. (1975). Obesity during childhood. In M. Winick (Ed.), *Childhood obesity.* New York: Wiley.

McGandy, R. B., Barrows, C. H., Spanias, A., Meredith, A., Stone, J. L., & Norris, A. H. (1966). Nutrient intakes and energy expenditure in men of different ages. *Journal of Gerontology, 21,* 581–587.

McGanity, W. J. (1976). Problems of nutritional evaluation of the adolescent. In J. I. McKigney & H. N. Munro (Eds.), *Nutritional requirements in adolescence.* Cambridge, MA: MIT Press.

Mendelson, B. K., & White, D. R. (1985). Development of self-body-esteem in overweight youngsters. *Developmental Psychology, 21,* 90–96.

Michel, G. F. (1981). Right-handedness: A consequence of infant supine head-orientation preference. *Science, 212,* 685–687.

Montoye, H. J., & Lamphiear, D. E. (1977). Grip and arm strength in males and females, age 10 to 69. *Research Quarterly for Exercise and Sport, 48,* 108–120.

Munro, H. N. (1985). Nutritional aspects of ageing: Present status and implications. In J. A. M. Gray (Ed.), *Prevention of disease in the elderly.* Edinburgh & New York: Churchill Livingstone.

Murray, M. P., Duthie, E. H., Jr., Gambert, S. R., Sepic, S. B., & Mollinger, L. A. (1985). Age-related differences in knee muscle strength in normal women. *Journal of Gerontology, 40,* 275–280.

Murray, M. P., Kory, R. C., & Clarkson, B. H. (1969). Walking patterns in healthy old men. *Journal of Gerontology, 24,* 169–178.

National Center for Health Statistics. (1983). Americans assess their health: United States, 1978. *Vital and Health Statistics,* Series 10 (No. 142).

Neugarten, B. L., Wood, V., Kraines, R. J., & Loomis, B. (1963). Women's attitudes toward the menopause. *Vita Humana, 6,* 140–151.

Neyzi, O., Saner, G., Alp, H., Binyildiz, P., Yazicioglu, S., Emre, S., & Gurson, C. T. (1976). Relationships between body weight in infancy and weight in later childhood and adolescence. In Z. Laron (Ed.), *The adipose child.* New York: Karger.

Ochs, A. L., Newberry, J., Lenhardt, M. L., & Harkins, S. W. (1985). Neural and vestibular aging associated with falls. In J. E. Birren & K. W. Schaie (Eds.), *Handbook of the psychology of aging* (2nd ed.). New York: Van Nostrand Reinhold.

Peskin, H. (1973). Influence of the developmental schedule of puberty on learning and ego functioning. *Journal of Youth and Adolescence, 2,* 273–290.

Prechtl, H. F. R. (1981). The study of neural development as a perspective of clinical problems. In K. J. Connolly & H. F. R. Prechtl (Eds.), *Maturation and development.* Philadelphia: Lippincott.

Ramsay, D. S. (1984). Onset of duplicated syllable babbling and unimanual handedness in infancy: Evidence for developmental change in hemispheric specialization? *Developmental Psychology, 20,* 64–71.

Ramsay, D. S. (1985). Fluctuations in unimanual hand preference in infants following the onset of duplicated syllable babbling. *Developmental Psychology, 21,* 318–324.

Roche, A. F. (1981). The adipocyte-number hypothesis. *Child Development, 52,* 31–43.

Roffwarg, H. P., Muzio, J. W., & Dement, W. C. (1966). Ontogenetic development of the human sleep–dream cycle. *Science, 152,* 604–619.

Rosenzweig, M. R., & Leiman, A. L. (1982). *Physiological psychology.* Lexington, MA: Heath.

Rowe, J. W. (1985). Interaction of aging and disease. In C. M. Gaitz & T. Samorajski (Eds.), *Aging 2000: Our health care destiny: Vol. 1. Biomedical issues.* New York: Springer-Verlag.

Ruble, D. N., & Brooks-Gunn, J. (1982). The experience of menarche. *Child Development, 53,* 1557–1566.

Salthouse, T. A. (1984). Effects of age and skill in typing. *Journal of Experimental Psychology: General, 113,* 345–371.

Scammon, R. E. (1930). The measurement of the body in childhood. In J. A. Harris, C. M. Jackson, D. G. Paterson, & R. E. Scammon (Eds.), *The measurement of man.* Minneapolis: University of Minnesota Press.

Scarrone, L. A. (1976). Nutritional and deficiency disorders. In S. S. Miller (Ed.), *Symptoms: The complete home medical encyclopedia.* New York: Thomas Y. Crowell.

Schaie, K. W. (1983). The Seattle longitudinal study: A 21-year exploration of psychometric intelligence in adulthood. In K. W. Schaie (Ed.), *Longitudinal studies of adult psychological development.* New York: Guilford.

Scheibel, M. E., Lindsay, R. D., Tomiyasu, U., & Scheibel, A. B. (1975). Progressive dendritic changes in aging human cortex. *Experimental Neurology, 47,* 392–403.

Severne, L. (1982). Psychosocial aspects of the menopause. In A. M. Voda, M. Dinnerstein, & S. R. O'Donnell (Eds.), *Changing perspectives on menopause.* Austin, TX: University of Texas Press.

Shanas, E., & Maddox, G. L. (1985). Health, health resources, and the utilization of care. In R. H. Binstock & E. Shanas (Eds.), *Handbook of aging and the social sciences* (2nd ed.). New York: Van Nostrand Reinhold.

Shephard, R. J. (1978). *Physical activity and aging.* Chicago: Year Book Medical Publishers.

Shephard, R. J. (1985). The cardiovascular benefits of exercise in the elderly. *Topics in Geriatric Rehabilitation, 1,* 1–10.

Shephard, R. J., & Montelpare, W. (1988). Geriatric benefits of exercise as an adult. *Journal of Gerontology, 43,* M86–M90.

Shepherd, G. M. (1988). *Neurobiology.* New York: Oxford University Press.

Sherman, B. M., & Korenman, S. G. (1975). Hormonal characteristics of the human menstrual cycle throughout reproductive life. *Journal of Clinical Investigation, 55,* 699–706.

Shinohara, Y. (1985). Effects of aging and hypertension on cerebral blood flow and autoregulation in normal subjects and CVD patients. In C. M. Gaitz & T. Samorajski (Eds.), *Aging 2000: Our health care destiny: Vol. 1. Biomedical issues.* New York: Springer-Verlag.

Shirley, M. M. (1933). *The first two years: A study of 25 babies: Vol. 1. Postural and locomotor development.* Minneapolis: University of Minnesota Press.

Sigelman, C. K., Miller, T. E., & Whitworth, L. A. (1986). The early development of stigmatizing reactions to physical differences. *Journal of Applied Developmental Psychology, 7,* 17–32.

Soules, M. R., & Bremner, W. J. (1982). The menopause and climacteric: Endocrinologic basis and associated symptomatology. *Journal of the American Geriatrics Society, 30,* 547–561.

Spirduso, W. W. (1980). Physical fitness, aging, and psychomotor speed: A review. *Journal of Gerontology, 35,* 850–865.

Spreen, O., Tupper, D., Risser, A., Tuokko, H., & Edgell, D. (1984). *Human developmental neuropsychology.* New York: Oxford University Press.

Staffieri, J. R. (1967). A study of social stereotype of body image in children. *Journal of Personality and Social Psychology, 7,* 101–104.

Steinberg, L. (1988). Reciprocal relation between parent–child distance and pubertal maturation. *Developmental Psychology, 24,* 122–128.

Steinberg, L. D. (1981). Transformations in family relations at puberty. *Developmental Psychology, 17,* 833–840.

Stelmach, G. E., Phillips, J., DiFabio, R. P., & Teasdale, N. (1989). Age, functional postural reflexes, and voluntary sway. *Journal of Gerontology: Biological Sciences, 44,* B100–B106.

Stones, M. J., & Kozma, A. (1985). Physical performance. In N. Charness (Ed.), *Aging and human performance.* Chichester, England, & New York: Wiley.

Tanner, J. M. (1962). *Growth at adolescence* (2nd Ed.). Oxford, England: Blackwell.

Tanner, J. M. (1978). *Fetus into man: Physical growth from conception to maturity.* Cambridge, MA: Harvard University Press.

Tanner, J. M. (1981). Growth and maturation during adolescence. *Nutrition Review, 39,* 43–55.

Thelen, E. (1984). Learning to walk: Ecological demands and phylogenetic constraints. In L. P. Lipsitt & C. Rovee-Collier (Eds.), *Advances in infancy research* (Vol. 3). Norwood, NJ: Ablex.

Thomas, J. R., Gallagher, J. D., & Purvis, G. J. (1981). Reaction time and anticipation time: Effects of development. *Research Quarterly for Exercise and Sport, 52,* 359–367.

Treloar, A. E. (1982). Predicting the close of menstrual life. In A. M. Voda, M. Dinnerstein, & S. R. O'Donnell (Eds.), *Changing perspectives on menopause.* Austin, TX: University of Texas Press.

Tsitouras, P. D., Martin, C. E., & Harman, S. M. (1982). Relationship of serum testosterone to sexual activity in healthy elderly. *Journal of Gerontology, 37,* 288–293.

Weg, R. B. (1983). Changing physiology of aging. In D. S. Woodruff & J. E. Birren (Eds.), *Aging. Scientific perspectives and social issues.* Pacific Grove, CA: Brooks/Cole.

Welford, A. T. (1984). Between bodily changes and performance: Some possible reasons for slowing with age. *Experimental Aging Research, 10,* 73–88.

Whitbourne, S. K. (1985). *The aging body. Physiological changes and psychological consequences.* New York: Springer-Verlag.

Wilkinson, R. T., & Allison, S. (1989). Age and simple reaction time: Decade differences for 5,325 subjects. *Journal of Gerontology: Psychological Sciences, 44,* P29–P35.

Willemsen, E. (1979). *Understanding infancy.* San Francisco: W. H. Freeman.

Winick, M. (1976). *Malnutrition and brain development.* New York: Oxford University Press.

Witelson, S. F. (1987). Neurobiological aspects of language in children. *Child Development, 58,* 653–688.

Wolff, P. H. (1966). The causes, controls, and organization of behavior in the neonate. *Psychological Issues, 5* (1, Whole No. 17).

Woods, N. F., Most, A., & Dery, G. K. (1982). Prevalence of perimenstrual symptoms. *American Journal of Public Health, 72,* 1257–1264.

Woollacott, M. H., Shumway-Cook, A., & Nashner, L. M. (1986). Aging and posture control: Changes in sensory organization and muscular coordination. *International Journal of Aging and Human Development, 23,* 97–114.

Wright, A. L. (1982). Variation in Navajo menopause: Toward an explanation. In A. M. Voda, M. Dinnerstein, & S. R. O'Donnell (Eds.), *Changing perspectives on menopause.* Austin, TX: University of Texas Press.

Yamaura, H., Ito, M., Kubota, K., & Matsuzawa, T. (1980). Brain atrophy during aging: A quantitative study with computed tomography. *Journal of Gerontology, 35,* 492–498.

Zack, P. M., Harlan, W. R., Leaverton, P. E., & Cornoni-Huntley, J. (1979). A longitudinal study of body fatness in childhood and adolescence. *Journal of Pediatrics, 95,* 126–130.

Zelazo, P. R. (1984). "Learning to walk": Recognition of higher order influences? In L. P. Lipsitt & C. Rovee-Collier (Eds.), *Advances in infancy research* (Vol. 3). Norwood, NJ: Ablex.

Zelazo, P. R., Zelazo, N. A., & Kolb, S. (1972). "Walking" in the newborn. *Science, 176,* 314–315.

Zeskind, P. S., & Ramey, C. T. (1978). Fetal malnutrition: An experimental study of its consequences in two caregiving environments. *Child Development, 49,* 1155–1162.

Zeskind, P. S., & Ramey, C. T. (1981). Preventing intellectual and interactional sequelae of fetal malnutrition: A longitudinal, transactional, and synergistic approach to development. *Child Development, 52,* 213–218.

Chapter 6: Perception

Anderson, D. R., Lorch, E. P., Field, D. E., Collins, P. A., & Nathan, J. G. (1986). Television viewing at home: Age trends in visual attention and time with TV. *Child Development, 57,* 1024–1033.

Aslin, R. N. (1987). Visual and auditory development in infancy. In J. D. Osofsky (Ed.), *Handbook of infant development* (2nd ed.). New York: Wiley.

Aslin, R. N., Pisoni, D. B., & Jusczyk, P. W. (1983). Auditory development and speech perception in infancy. In M. M. Haith & J. J. Campos (Eds.), *Handbook of child psychology: Vol. 2. Infancy and developmental psychobiology* (4th ed.). New York: Wiley.

Axelrod, S., & Cohen, L. D. (1961). Senescence and embedded-figure performance in vision and touch. *Perceptual and Motor Skills, 12,* 283–288.

Baltes, P. B., Reese, H. W., & Nesselroade, J. R. (1977). *Life-span developmental psychology: Introduction to research methods.* Pacific Grove, CA: Brooks/Cole.

Banks, M. S. (1980). The development of visual accommodation during early infancy. *Child Development, 51,* 646–666.

Banks, M. S., & Ginsburg, A. P. (1985). Infant visual preferences: A review and new theoretical treatment. In H. W. Reese (Ed.), *Advances in child development and behavior* (Vol. 19). Orlando, FL: Academic.

Banks, M. S., in collaboration with Salapatek, P. (1983). Infant visual perception. In M. M. Haith & J. J. Campos (Eds.; P. H. Mussen, Gen. Ed.), *Handbook of child psychology: Vol. 2. Infancy and developmental psychobiology* (4th ed.). New York: Wiley.

Barrera, M. E., & Maurer, D. (1981a). Discrimination of strangers by the three-month-old. *Child Development, 52,* 558–563.

Barrera, M. E., & Maurer, D. (1981b). Recognition of mother's photographed face by the three-month-old infant. *Child Development, 52,* 714–716.

Bartoshuk, L. M., Rifkin, B., Marks, L. E., & Bars, P. (1986). Taste and aging. *Journal of Gerontology, 41,* 51–57.

Beall, C. M., & Goldstein, M. C. (1986). Age differences in sensory and cognitive function in elderly Nepalese. *Journal of Gerontology, 41,* 387–389.

Bergman, M. (1980). *Aging and the perception of speech.* Baltimore, MD: University Park Press.

Bergman, M., Blumenfeld, V. G., Cascardo, D., Dash, B., Levitt, H., & Margulies, M. K. (1976). Age-related decrement in hearing for speech: Sampling and longitudinal studies. *Journal of Gerontology, 31,* 533–538.

Bertenthal, B. I., Proffitt, D. R., Kramer, S. J., & Spetner, N. B. (1987). Infants' encoding of kinetic displays varying in relative coherence. *Developmental Psychology, 23,* 171–178.

Bess, F. H., & McConnell, F. E. (1981). *Audiology, education, and the hearing impaired child.* St Louis: C. V. Mosby.

Bornstein, M. H., Ferdinandsen, K., & Gross, C. G. (1981). Perception of symmetry in infancy. *Developmental Psychology, 17,* 82–86.

Bornstein, M. H., Kessen, W., & Weiskopf, S. (1976). Color vision and hue categorization in young human infants. *Journal of Experimental Psychology: Human Perception and Performance, 2,* 115–129.

Botwinick, J. (1984). *Aging and behavior. A comprehensive integration of research findings* (3rd ed.). New York: Springer.

Bower, T. G. R. (1982). *Development in infancy* (2nd ed.). San Francisco: W. H. Freeman.

Bower, T. G. R., Broughton, J. M., & Moore, M. K. (1970a). The coordination of vision and tactile input in infancy. *Perception and Psychophysics, 8,* 51–53.

Bower, T. G. R., Broughton, J. M., & Moore, M. K. (1970b). Infant responses to approaching objects: An indicator of response to distal variables. *Perception and Psychophysics, 9,* 193–196.

Burg, A. (1966). Visual acuity as measured by dynamic and static tests: A comparative evaluation. *Journal of Applied Psychology, 50,* 460–466.

Burg, A. (1968). Lateral visual field as related to age and sex. *Journal of Applied Psychology, 52,* 10–15.

Bushnell, E. W., Shaw, L., & Strauss, D. (1985). Relationship between visual and tactual exploration by 6-month-olds. *Developmental Psychology, 21,* 591–600.

Butler, R. N., & Lewis, M. I. (1977). *Aging and mental health* (2nd ed.). St Louis: C. V. Mosby.

Butterfield, E. C., & Siperstein, G. N. (1972). Influence of contingent auditory stimulation upon non-nutritional suckle. In J. F. Bosma (Ed.), *Third symposium on oral sensation and perception: The mouth of the infant.* Springfield, IL: Charles C Thomas.

Campos, J. J., Hiatt, S., Ramsay, D., Henderson, C., & Svejda, M. (1978). The emergence of fear on the visual cliff. In M. Lewis & L. Rosenblum (Eds.), *The origins of affect.* New York: Plenum.

Campos, J. J., Langer, A., & Krowitz, A. (1970). Cardiac responses on the visual cliff in prelocomotor human infants. *Science, 170,* 196–197.

Cernoch, J. M., & Porter, R. H. (1985). Recognition of maternal axillary odors by infants. *Child Development, 56,* 1593–1598.

Chall, J. S. (1967). *Learning to read: The great debate.* New York: McGraw-Hill.

Chang, H. W., & Trehub, S. E. (1977). Infants' perception of temporal grouping in auditory patterns. *Child Development, 48,* 1666–1670.

Chapman, M., & Lindenberger, U. (1988). Functions, operations, and decalage in the development of transitivity. *Developmental Psychology, 24,* 542–551.

Clark, W. C., & Mehl, L. (1971). Thermal pain: A sensory decision theory–analysis of the effect of age and sex on d', various response criteria, and 50% pain threshold. *Journal of Abnormal Psychology, 78,* 202–212.

Clarkson, M. G., & Berg, W. K. (1983). Cardiac orienting and vowel discrimination in newborns: Crucial stimulation parameters. *Child Development, 54,* 162–171.

Cohen, L. B., DeLoache, J. S., & Strauss, M. S. (1979). Infant visual perception. In J. Osofsky (Ed.), *Handbook of infant development.* New York: Wiley.

Colombo, J. (1986). Recent studies in early auditory development. In G. J. Whitehurst (Ed.), *Annals of child development. A research annual* (Vol. 3). Greenwich, CT: JAI Press.

Corso, J. F. (1963). Aging and auditory thresholds in men and women. *Archives of Environmental Health, 6,* 350–356.

Corso, J. F. (1981). *Aging sensory systems and perception.* New York: Praeger.

Crook, C. K. (1978). Taste perception in the newborn infant. *Infant Behavior and Development, 1,* 52–69.

Dannemiller, J. L., & Stephens, B. R. (1988). A critical test of infant pattern preference models. *Child Development, 59,* 210–216.

Davis, A. (1983). The epidemiology of hearing disorders. In R. Hinchcliffe (Ed.), *Hearing and balance in the elderly.* Edinburgh: Churchill Livingstone.

Day, R. H., & McKenzie, B. E. (1981). Infant perception of the invariant size of approaching and receding objects. *Developmental Psychology, 17,* 670–677.

DeCasper, A. J., & Fifer, W. P. (1980). Of human bonding: Newborns prefer their mothers' voices. *Science, 208,* 1174–1176.

DeCasper, A. J., & Spence, M. J. (1986). Prenatal maternal speech influences newborns' perception of speech sounds. *Infant Behavior and Development, 9,* 133–150.

Descartes, R. (1965). *La dioptrique.* In R. J. Herrnstein & E. G. Boring (Eds.), *A sourcebook in the history of psychology.* Cambridge, MA: Harvard University Press. (Original work published 1638)

Doty, R. L., Shaman, P., Applebaum, S. L., Giberson, R., Siksorski, L., & Rosenberg, L. (1984). Smell identification ability: Changes with age. *Science, 226,* 1441–1443.

Eimas, P. D. (1975a). Auditory and phonetic cues for speech: Discrimination of thė (r-l) distinction by young infants. *Perception and Psychophysics, 18,* 341–347.

Eimas, P. D. (1975b). Speech perception in early infancy. In L. B. Cohen & P. Salapatek (Eds.), *Infant perception: From sensation to cognition.* New York: Academic.

Eimas, P. D. (1985). The perception of speech in early infancy. *Scientific American, 252,* 46–52.

Engen, T. (1977). Taste and smell. In J. E. Birren & K. W. Schaie (Eds.), *Handbook of the psychology of aging.* New York: Van Nostrand Reinhold.

Fantz, R. L. (1961). The origin of form perception. *Scientific American, 204,* 66–72.

Fantz, R. L. (1963). Pattern vision in newborn infants. *Science, 140,* 296–297.

Fantz, R. L., & Fagan, J. F. (1975). Visual attention to size and number of pattern details by term and preterm infants during the first six months. *Child Development, 46,* 3–18.

Farkas, M. S., & Hoyer, W. J. (1980). Processing consequences of perceptual grouping in selective attention. *Journal of Gerontology, 35,* 207–216.

Field, J., Muir, D., Pilon, R., Sinclair, M., & Dodwell, P. (1980). Infants' orientation to lateral sounds from birth to three months. *Child Development, 51,* 295–298.

Ganchrow, J. R., Steiner, J. E., & Daher, M. (1983). Neonatal facial expressions to different qualities and intensities of gustatory stimuli. *Infant Behavior and Development, 6,* 189–200.

Gibson, E. J. (1969). *Principles of perceptual learning and development.* New York: Appleton-Century-Crofts.

Gibson, E. J. (1987). Introductory essay: What does infant perception tell us about theories of perception? *Journal of Experimental Psychology: Human Perception and Performance, 13,* 515–523.

Gibson, E. J., Gibson, J. J., Pick, A. D., & Osser, H. A. (1962). A developmental study of the discrimination of letter-like forms. *Journal of Comparative and Physiological Psychology, 55,* 897–906.

Gibson, E. J., & Levin, H. (1975). *The psychology of reading.* Cambridge, MA: M.I.T. Press.

Gibson, E. J., & Spelke, E. S. (1983). The development of perception. In J. H. Flavell & E. M. Markman (Eds., P. H. Mussen, Gen. Ed.), *Handbook of child psychology: Vol. 3. Cognitive development* (4th ed.). New York: Wiley.

Gibson, E. J., & Walk, R. D. (1960). The "visual cliff." *Scientific American, 202,* 64–71.

Gibson, E. J., & Walker, A. S. (1984). Development of knowledge of visual-tactile affordances of substance. *Child Development, 55,* 453–460.

Greenberg, D. A., & Branch, L. G. (1982). A review of methodological issues concerning incidence and prevalence data of visual deterioration in elders. In R. Sekuler, D. Kline, & K. Dismukes (Eds.), *Aging and human visual function.* New York: Alan R. Liss.

Haith, M. M. (1980). Visual competence in early infancy. In R. Held, H. Liebowitz, & H. R. Teuber (Eds.), *Handbook of sensory physiology* (Vol. 8). Berlin: Springer-Verlag.

Harkins, S. W., Price, D. D., & Martelli, M. (1986). Effects of age on pain perception: Thermonociception. *Journal of Gerontology, 41,* 58–63.

Held, R., & Hein, A. (1963). Movement-produced stimulation in the development of visually guided behavior. *Journal of Comparative and Physiological Psychology, 56,* 872–876.

Herbst, K. G. (1983). Psycho-social consequences of disorders of hearing in the elderly. In R. Hinchcliffe (Ed.), *Hearing and balance in the elderly.* Edinburgh: Churchill Livingstone.

Hills, B. L. (1980). Vision, visibility, and perception in driving. *Perception, 9,* 183–216.

Hudson, W. (1960). Pictorial depth perception in sub–cultural groups in Africa. *Journal of Social Psychology, 52,* 183–208.

Hull, R. H. (1980). Hull's thirteen commandments for talking to the hearing-impaired older person. *ASHA, 22,* 427.

Hutchinson, K. M. (1989). Influence of sentence context on speech perception in young and older adults. *Journal of Gerontology: Psychological Sciences, 44,* P36–P44.

James, W. (1890). *Principles of psychology* (2 vols.). New York: Holt.

Kagan, J. (1971). *Change and continuity in infancy.* New York: Wiley.

Kahn, H. A., Leibowitz, H. M., Ganley, J. P., Kini, M. M., Colton, T., Nickerson, R. S., & Dawber, T. R. (1977). The Framingham eye study. I. Outline and major prevalence findings. *American Journal of Epidemiology, 106,* 17–32.

Kant, I. (1958). *Critique of pure reason.* New York: Modern Library. (Original work published 1781)

Kaufmann-Hayoz, R., Kaufmann, F., & Stucki, M. (1986). Kinetic contours in infants' visual perception. *Child Development, 57,* 292–299.

Kellman, P. J., & Spelke, E. S. (1983). Perception of partly occluded objects in infancy. *Cognitive Psychology, 15,* 483–524.

Kellman, P. J., Spelke, E. S., & Short, K. R. (1986). Infant perception of object unity from translatory motion in depth and vertical translation. *Child Development, 57,* 72–86.

Kenshalo, D. R. (1977). Age changes in touch, vibration, temperature, kinesthesis and pain sensitivity. In J. E. Birren & K. W. Schaie (Eds.), *Handbook of the psychology of aging.* New York: Van Nostrand Reinhold.

Kisilevsky, B. S., & Muir, D. W. (1984). Neonatal habituation and dishabituation to tactile stimulation during sleep. *Developmental Psychology, 20,* 367–373.

Kleinman, J. M., & Brodzinsky, D. M. (1978). Haptic exploration in young, middle-aged, and elderly adults. *Journal of Gerontology, 33,* 521–527.

Kline, D. W., & Schieber, F. (1985). Vision and aging. In J. E. Birren & K. W. Schaie (Eds.), *Handbook of the psychology of aging* (2nd ed.). New York: Van Nostrand Reinhold.

Kogan, N. (1983). Stylistic variation in childhood and adolescence: Creativity, metaphor, and cognitive styles. In J. H. Flavell & E. M. Markman (Eds.), *Handbook of child psychology: Vol. 3. Cognitive development* (4th ed.). New York: Wiley.

Kosnik, W., Winslow, L., Kline, D., Rasinski, K., & Sekuler, R. (1988). Visual changes in daily life throughout adulthood. *Journal of Gerontology: Psychological Sciences, 43,* P63–P70.

Kremenitzer, J. P., Vaughn, H. G., Jr., Kurtzberg, D., & Dowling K. (1979). Smooth-pursuit eye movements in the newborn infant. *Child Development, 50,* 442–448.

Lebo, C. P., & Reddell, R. C. (1972). The presbycusis component in occupational hearing loss. *Laryngoscope, 82,* 1399–1409.

Lipsitt, L. P., & Levy, N. (1959). Electrotactual threshold in the neonate. *Child Development, 30,* 547–554.

Locke, J. (1939). An essay concerning human understanding. In E. A. Burtt (Ed.), *The English philosophers from Bacon to Mill.* New York: Modern Library. (Original work published 1690)

Maccoby, E. E. (1967). Selective auditory attention in children. In L. P. Lipsitt & C. C. Spiker (Eds.), *Advances in child development and behavior.* New York: Academic.

MacFarlane, A. (1977). *The psychology of childbirth.* Cambridge, MA: Harvard University Press.

Maurer, D. (1985). Infants' perception of facedness. In T. M. Fields & N. A. Fox (Eds.), *Social perception in infants.* Norwood, NJ: Ablex.

Maurer, D., & Salapatek, P. (1976). Developmental changes in the scanning of faces by young infants. *Child Development, 47,* 523–527.

McDowd, J. M., & Craik, F. I. M. (1988). Effects of aging and task difficulty on divided attention. *Journal of Experimental Psychology: Human Perception and Performance, 14,* 267–280.

Meltzoff, A. N., & Borton, R. W. (1979). Intermodal matching by human neonates. *Nature, 282,* 403–404.

Miller, P. H., & Weiss, M. G. (1981). Children's attention allocation, understanding of attention, and performance on the incidental learning task. *Child Development, 52,* 1183–1190.

Mitchell, D. E., Freeman, R. D., Millodot, M., & Haegerstrom, G. (1973). Meridional amblyopia: Evidence for modification of the human visual system by early visual experience. *Vision Research, 13,* 535–558.

Miyawaki, K., Strange, W., Verbrugge, R., Liberman, A. M., Jenkins, J. J., & Fujimura, D. (1975). An effect of linguistic experience: The discrimination of [r] and [l] by native speakers of Japanese and English. *Perception and Psychophysics, 18,* 331–340.

Morrison, F. J. (1984). Reading disability: A problem in rule learning and word decoding. *Developmental Review, 4,* 36–47.

Muir, D. W. (1985). The development of infants' auditory spatial sensitivity. In S. E. Trehub & B. Schneider (Eds.), *Advances in the study of communication and affect: Vol. 10. Auditory development in infancy.* New York: Plenum.

Murphy, C. (1985). Cognitive and chemosensory influences on age-related changes in the ability to identify blended foods. *Journal of Gerontology, 40,* 47–52.

National Center for Health Statistics, G. S. Poc. (1983). Eye care visits and use of eyeglasses or contact lenses: United States, 1979 and 1980. *Vital and Health Statistics,* Series 10 (No. 145).

Nissen, M. J., & Corkin, S. (1985). Effectiveness of attentional cueing in older and younger adults. *Journal of Gerontology, 40,* 185–191.

Ochs, A. L., Newberry, J., Lenhardt, M. L., & Harkins, S. W. (1985). Neural and vestibular aging associated with falls. In J. E. Birren & K. W. Schaie (Eds.), *Handbook of the psychology of aging* (2nd ed.). New York: Van Nostrand Reinhold.

Olsho, L. W., Harkins, S. W., & Lenhardt, M. L. (1985). Aging and the auditory system. In J. E. Birren & K. W. Schaie (Eds.), *Handbook of the psychology of aging* (2nd ed.). New York: Van Nostrand Reinhold.

Panek, P. E. (1985). Age differences in field-dependence/independence. *Experimental Aging Research, 11,* 97–99.

Peeples, D. R., & Teller, D. Y. (1975). Color vision and brightness discrimination in two-month-old human infants. *Science, 189,* 1102–1103.

Piaget, J. (1954). *The construction of reality in the child.* New York: Basic Books.

Piaget, J. (1960). *Psychology of intelligence.* Paterson, NJ: Littlefield, Adams.

Pitts, D. G. (1982). The effects of aging on selected visual functions: Dark adaptation, visual acuity, stereopsis, and brightness contrast. In R. Sekuler, D. Kline, & K. Dismukes (Eds.), *Aging and human visual function.* New York: Alan R. Liss.

Planek, T. W. (1974). Factors influencing the adaptation of the aging driver to today's traffic. *Clinical Medicine, 81* (5), 36–43.

Plude, D. J., & Hoyer, W. J. (1981). Adult age differences in visual search as a function of stimulus mapping and processing load. *Journal of Gerontology, 36,* 598–604.

Plude, D. J., & Hoyer, W. J. (1985). Attention and performance: Identifying and localizing age deficits. In N. Charness (Ed.), *Aging and human performance.* Chichester, England: Wiley.

Popelka, G. R. (1984). Improving the hearing of the elderly. In R. E. Dunkle, M. R. Haug, & M. Rosenberg (Eds.), *Communication technology and the elderly. Issues and forecasts.* New York: Springer.

Porter, F. L., Miller, R. H., & Marshall, R. E. (1986). Neonatal pain cries: Effects of circumcision on acoustic features and perceived urgency. *Child Development, 57,* 790–802.

Powers, M. K., Schneck, M., & Teller, D. Y. (1981). Spectral sensitivity of human infants at absolute visual threshold. *Vision Research, 21,* 1005–1016.

Pratt, K. C. (1954). The neonate. In L. Carmichael (Ed.), *Manual of child psychology* (2nd ed.). New York: Wiley.

Pulling, N. H., Wolf, E., Sturgis, S. P., Vaillancourt, D. R., & Dolliver, J. J. (1980). Headlight glare resistance and driver age. *Human Factors, 22,* 103–112.

Rader, N., Bausano, M., & Richards, J. E. (1980). On the nature of the visual-cliff–avoidance response in human infants. *Child Development, 51,* 61–68.

Rango, N. (1985). The social epidemiology of accidental hypothermia among the aged. *Gerontologist, 25,* 424–430.

Reese, H. W. (1963). Perceptual set in young children. *Child Development, 34,* 151–159.

Riesen, A. H. (1965). Effects of visual deprivation on perceptual function and the neural substrate. In J. deAjuriaguerra (Ed.), *Dessaferentation experimental et clinique.* Geneva: Georg.

Riesen, A. H., Chow, K. L., Semmes, J., & Nissen, H. W. (1951). Chimpanzee vision after four conditions of light deprivation. *American Psychologist, 6,* 282.

Rieser, J., Yonas, A., & Wilkner, K. (1976). Radial localization of odors by human newborns. *Child Development, 47,* 856–859.

Rose, S. A., Gottfried, A. W., & Bridger, W. H. (1981). Cross-modal transfer in 6-month-old infants. *Developmental Psychology, 17,* 661–669.

Rovee, C. K., Cohen, R. Y., & Shlapack, W. (1975). Life-span stability in olfactory sensitivity. *Developmental Psychology, 11,* 311–318.

Salapatek, P. (1975). Pattern perception in early infancy. In L. B. Cohen & P. Salapatek (Eds.), *Infant perception: From sensation to cognition* (Vol. 1). New York: Academic.

Salthouse, T. A. (1982). *Adult cognition. An experimental psychology of human aging.* New York: Springer-Verlag.

Samuels, C. A., & Ewy, R. (1985). Aesthetic perception of faces during infancy. *British Journal of Developmental Psychology, 3,* 221–228.

Schiff, A. R., & Knopf, I. J. (1985). The effect of task demands on attention allocation in children of different ages. *Child Development, 56,* 621–630.

Schiffman, S. (1977). Food recognition by the elderly. *Journal of Gerontology, 32,* 586–592.

Schiffman, S., & Pasternak, M. (1979). Decreased discrimination of food odors in the elderly. *Journal of Gerontology, 34,* 73–79.

Sharpe, J. A., & Sylvester, T. O. (1978). Effect of aging on horizontal smooth pursuit. *Investigative Ophthalmology and Visual Science, 17,* 465–468.

Sivak, M., Olson, P. L., & Pastalan, L. A. (1981). Effect of driver's age on nighttime legibility of highway signs. *Human Factors, 23,* 59–64.

Slater, A., Morison, V., & Rose, D. (1983). Perception of shape by the new-born baby. *British Journal of Developmental Psychology, 1,* 135–142.

Slater, A., Morison, V., Town, C., & Rose, D. (1985). Movement perception and identity constancy in the new-born baby. *British Journal of Developmental Psychology, 3,* 211–220.

Smith, F. (1977). Making sense of reading—and of reading instruction. *Harvard Educational Review, 47,* 386–395.

Spelke, E. S., von Hofsten, C., & Kestenbaum, R. (1989). Object perception in infancy: Interaction of spatial and kinetic information for object boundaries. *Developmental Psychology, 25,* 185–196.

Spitzer, M. E. (1988). Taste acuity in institutionalized and noninstitutionalized elderly men. *Journal of Gerontology: Psychological Sciences, 43,* P71–P74.

Steiner, J. E. (1979). Human facial expressions in response to taste and smell stimulation. In H. W. Reese & L. P. Lipsitt (Eds.), *Advances in child development and behavior* (Vol. 13). New York: Academic.

Stevens, J. C., & Cain, W. S. (1987). Old-age deficits in the sense of smell as gauged by thresholds, magnitude matching, and odor identification. *Psychology and Aging, 2,* 36–42.

Streri, A., & Pecheux, M. (1986a). Tactual habituation and discrimination of form in infancy: A comparison with vision. *Child Development, 57,* 100–104.

Streri, A., & Pecheux, M. (1986b). Vision-to-touch and touch-to-vision transfer of form in 5-month-old infants. *British Journal of Developmental Psychology, 4,* 161–167.

Strutt, G. F., Anderson, D. R., & Well, A. D. (1975). A developmental study of the effects of irrelevant information on speeded classification. *Journal of Experimental Child Psychology, 20,* 127–135.

Stryker, M. P., Sherk, H., Leventhal, A. G., & Hirsch, V. H. B. (1978). Physiological consequences for the cat's visual cortex of effectively restricting early visual experience with oriented contours. *Journal of Neurophysiology, 41,* 896–909.

Trehub, S. E. (1985). Auditory pattern perception in infancy. In S. E. Trehub & B. Schneider (Eds.), *Advances in the study of communication and affect: Vol. 10. Auditory development in infancy.* New York: Plenum.

Trehub, S. E., Bull, D., Schneider, B. A., & Morrongiello, B. A. (1986). PESTI: A procedure for estimating individual thresholds in infant listeners. *Infant Behavior and Development, 9,* 107–118.

Treiber, F., & Wilcox, S. (1980). Perception of a "subjective contour" by infants. *Child Development, 51,* 915–917.

Van Giffen, K., & Haith, M. M. (1984). Infant visual response to Gestalt geometric forms. *Infant Behavior and Development, 7,* 335–346.

Vandenberg, B. (1984). Developmental features of exploration. *Developmental Psychology, 20,* 3–8.

Verrillo, R. T. (1982). Effects of aging on the suprathreshold responses to vibration. *Perception and Psychophysics, 32,* 61–68.

Verrillo, R. T., & Verrillo, V. (1985). Sensory and perceptual performance. In N. Charness (Ed.), *Aging and human performance.* Chichester, England: Wiley.

Vlietstra, A. G. (1982). Children's responses to task instructions: Age changes and training effects. *Child Development, 53,* 534–542.

Vurpillot, E. (1968). The development of scanning strategies and their relation to visual differentiation. *Journal of Experimental Child Psychology, 6,* 632–650.

Walk, R. D. (1981). *Perceptual development.* Pacific Grove, CA: Brooks/Cole.

Weiffenbach, J. M., Cowart, B. J., & Baum, B. J. (1986). Taste intensity perception in aging. *Journal of Gerontology, 41,* 460–468.

Wellman, H. M. (Ed.). (1985). *Children's searching: The development of search skill and spatial representation.* Hillsdale, NJ: Erlbaum.

Werker, J. F., Gilbert, J. H. V., Humphrey, K., & Tees, R. C. (1981). Developmental aspects of cross-language speech perception. *Child Development, 52,* 349–355.

Werker, J. F., & Tees, R. C. (1984). Cross-language speech perception: Evidence for perceptual reorganization during the first year. *Infant Behavior and Development, 7,* 49–63.

Werner, E. E. (1979). *Cross-cultural child development. A view from the planet earth.* Pacific Grove, CA: Brooks/Cole.

Wertheimer, M. (1923). Untersuchungen zur Lehre von der Gestalt. II. *Psychologische Forschung, 4,* 301–350.

Whitbourne, S. K. (1985). *The aging body. Physiological changes and psychological consequences.* New York: Springer-Verlag.

Williams, A. F., & Carsten, O. (1989). Driver age and crash involvement. *American Journal of Public Health, 79,* 326–327.

Williams, J. (1979). Reading instruction today. *American Psychologist, 34,* 917–922.

Wingfield, A., Poon, L. W., Lombardi, L., & Lowe, D. (1985). Speed of processing in normal aging: Effects of speech rate, linguistic structure, and processing time. *Journal of Gerontology, 40,* 579–595.

Witkin, H. A. (1959). The perception of the upright. *Scientific American, 200,* 50–56.

Witkin, H. A., & Berry, J. W. (1975). Psychological differentiation in cross-cultural perspective. *Journal of Cross-Cultural Psychology, 6,* 4–87.

Witkin, H. A., & Goodenough, D. R. (1977). Field dependence and interpersonal behavior. *Psychological Bulletin, 84,* 661–689.

Witkin, H. A., & Goodenough, D. R. (1981). *Cognitive styles: Essence and origins.* New York: International Universities Press.

Yendovitskaya, T. V. (1971). Development of attention. In A. V. Zaporozhets & D. B. Elkonin (Eds.), *The psychology of preschool children.* Cambridge, MA: M.I.T. Press.

Yonas, A., Pettersen, L., & Lockman, J. J. (1979). Young infants' sensitivity to optical information for collision. *Canadian Journal of Psychology, 33,* 268–276.

Zaporozhets, A. V. (1965). The development of perception in the preschool child. *Monographs of the Society for Research in Child Development, 30* (2, Serial No. 100, pp. 82–101).

Zichenko, V. P., Van Chzhi-tsin, & Tarakanov, V. (1963). The formation and development of perceptual activity. *Soviet Psychology and Psychiatry, 2,* 3–12.

Chapter 7: Cognition and Language

Ackerman, B. P. (1982). Contextual integration and utterance interpretation: The ability of children and adults to interpret sarcastic utterances. *Child Development, 53,* 1075–1083.

Acredolo, L., & Goodwyn, S. (1988). Symbolic gesturing in normal infants. *Child Development, 59,* 450–466.

Arlin, P. K. (1975). Cognitive development in adulthood: A fifth stage? *Developmental Psychology, 11,* 602–606.

Arlin, P. K. (1977). Piagetian operations in problem finding. *Developmental Psychology, 13,* 297–298.

Arlin, P. K. (1984). Adolescent and adult thought: A structural interpretation. In M. L. Commons, F. A. Richards, & C. Armon (Eds.), *Beyond formal operations. Late adolescent and adult cognitive development.* New York: Praeger.

Baillargeon, R., & Graber, M. (1988). Evidence of location memory in 8-month-old infants in a nonsearch AB task. *Developmental Psychology, 24,* 502–511.

Bandura, A. (1971). An analysis of modeling processes. In A. Bandura (Ed.), *Psychological modeling.* New York: Lieber-Atherton.

Basseches, M. (1984). *Dialectical thinking and adult development.* Norwood, NJ: Ablex.

Bates, E., & MacWhinney, B. (1982). Functionalist approaches to grammar. In E. Wanner & L. Gleitman (Eds.), *Language acquisition: The state of the art.* Cambridge, England: Cambridge University Press.

Bates, E., O'Connell, B., & Shore, C. (1987). Language and communication in infancy. In J. D. Osofsky (Ed.), *Handbook of infant development* (2nd ed.). New York: Wiley.

Beal, C. R. (1987). Repairing the message: Children's monitoring and revision skills. *Child Development, 58,* 401–408.

Beal, C. R., & Flavell, J. H. (1983). Young speakers' evaluations of their listener's comprehension in a referential communication task. *Child Development, 54,* 148–153.

Belmore, S. M. (1981). Age-related changes in processing explicit and implicit language. *Journal of Gerontology, 36,* 316–322.

Benedict, H. (1979). Early lexical development: Comprehension and production. *Journal of Child Language, 6,* 183–200.

Berg, C. A., & Sternberg, R. J. (1985). A triarchic theory of intellectual development during adulthood. *Developmental Review, 5,* 334–370.

Blackburn, J. (1984). The influence of personality, curriculum, and memory correlates on formal reasoning in young adults and elderly persons. *Journal of Gerontology, 39,* 207–209.

Bloom, L. (1970). *Language development: Form and function in emerging grammars.* Cambridge, MA: M.I.T. Press.

Bloom L., Hood, L., & Lightbown, P. (1974). Imitation in language development: If, when and why. *Cognitive Psychology, 6,* 380–420.

Bohannon, J. N., III, & Warren-Leubecker, A. (1985). Theoretical approaches to language acquisition. In J. Berko Gleason (Ed.), *The development of language.* Columbus, OH: Merrill.

Bower, T. G. R. (1982). *Development in infancy.* San Francisco: W. H. Freeman.

Braine, M. D. S. (1963). The ontogeny of English phrase structure: The first phrase. *Language, 39,* 1–13.

Brainerd, C. J. (1978). The stage question in cognitive-developmental theory. *Behavioral and Brain Sciences, 2,* 173–213.

Brown, R., & Hanlon, C. (1970). Derivational complexity and order of acquisition. In J. R. Hayes (Ed.), *Cognition and the development of language.* New York: Wiley

Brown R., Cazden, C., & Bellugi, U. (1969). The child's grammar from I–III. In J. P. Hill (Ed.), *Minnesota Symposia on Child Psychology* (Vol. 2). Minneapolis: University of Minnesota Press.

Bruner, J. S. (1983). *Child's talk: Learning to use language.* New York: Norton.

Carey, S. (1977). The child as word learner. In M. Halle, J. Bresnan, & G. A. Miller (Eds.), *Linguistic theory and psychological reality.* Cambridge, MA: M.I.T. Press.

Case, R. (1985). *Intellectual development: Birth to adulthood.* Orlando, FL: Academic.

Cavanaugh, J. C., Kramer, D. A., Sinnott, J. D., Camp, C. J., & Markley, R. P. (1985). On missing links and such: Interfaces between cognitive research and everyday problem-solving. *Human Development, 28,* 146–168.

Chapman, M., & Lindenberger, U. (1988). Functions, operations, and decalage in the development of transitivity. *Developmental Psychology, 24,* 542–551.

Chomsky, C. S. (1969). *The acquisition of syntax in children from 5 to 10.* Cambridge, MA: M.I.T. Press.

Chomsky, N. (1968). *Language and mind.* New York: Harcourt Brace & World.

Chomsky, N. (1975). *Reflections on language.* New York: Pantheon Books.

Clark, H. H., & Clark, E. V. (1977). *Psychology and language: An introduction to psycholinguistics.* New York: Harcourt Brace Jovanovich.

Clarke-Stewart, K. A. (1973). Interactions between mothers and their young children: Characteristics and consequences. *Monographs of the Society for Research in Child Development, 38* (Serial No. 153).

Commons, M. L., Richards, F. A., & Armon, C. (Eds.). (1984). *Beyond formal operations. Late adolescent and adult cognitive development.* New York: Praeger.

Commons, M. L., Richards, F. A., & Kuhn, D. (1982). Systematic and metasystematic reasoning: A case for levels of reasoning beyond Piaget's stage of formal operations. *Child Development, 53,* 1058–1069.

Cornelius, S. W., & Caspi, A. (1987). Everyday problem solving in adulthood and old age. *Psychology and Aging, 2,* 144–153.

Corso, J. F. (1977). Auditory perception and communication. In J. E. Birren & K. W. Schaie (Eds.), *Handbook of the psychology of aging.* New York: Van Nostrand.

Cowan, P. A. (1978). *Piaget: With feeling.* New York: Holt, Rinehart & Winston.

Dale, P. S. (1976). *Language development: Structure and function.* New York: Holt, Rinehart & Winston.

De Boysson-Bardies, B., Sagart, L., & Durand, C. (1984). Discernible differences in the babbling of infants according to target language. *Journal of Child Language, 11,* 1–16.

DeLisi, R., & Staudt, J. (1980). Individual differences in college students' performance on formal operations tasks. *Journal of Applied Developmental Psychology, 1,* 163–174.

Denney, N. W. (1982). Aging and cognitive changes. In B. B. Wolman (Ed.), *Handbook of developmental psychology.* Englewood Cliffs, NJ: Prentice-Hall.

de Villiers, P. A., & de Villiers, J. G. (1979). *Early language.* Cambridge, MA: Harvard University Press.

Diamond, A. (1985). The development of the ability to use recall to guide action, as indicated by infants' performance on AB. *Child Development, 56,* 868–883.

Eimas, P. D. (1975). Speech perception in early infancy. In L. B. Cohen & P. Salapatek (Eds.), *Infant perception: From sensation to cognition* (Vol. 2). New York: Academic.

Elkind, D. (1967). Egocentrism in adolescence. *Child Development, 38,* 1025–1034.

Elkind, D., & Bowen, R. (1979). Imaginary audience behavior in children and adolescents. *Developmental Psychology, 15,* 38–44.

Enright, R., Lapsley, D., & Shukla, D. (1979). Adolescent egocentrism in early and late adolescence. *Adolescence, 14,* 687–695.

Field, D. (1981). Can preschool children really learn to conserve? *Child Development, 52,* 326–334.

Field, T. M., Woodson, R., Greenberg, R., & Cohen, D. (1982). Discrimination and imitation of facial expressions by neonates. *Science, 218,* 179–181.

Fischer, K. W. (1980). A theory of cognitive development: The control and construction of hierarchies of skills. *Psychological Review, 87,* 477–531.

Fischer, K. W., Hand, H. H., & Russell, S. (1984). The development of abstractions in adolescence and adulthood. In M. L. Commons, F. A. Richards, & C. Armon (Eds.), *Beyond formal operations. Late adolescent and adult cognitive development.* New York: Praeger.

Fischer, K. W., & Lazerson, A. (1984). *Human development. From conception through adolescence.* New York: W. H. Freeman.

Flavell, J. H. (1963). *The developmental psychology of Jean Piaget.* New York: Van Nostrand Reinhold.

Flavell, J. H. (1985). *Cognitive development* (2nd ed.). Englewood Cliffs, NJ: Prentice-Hall.

Flavell, J. H., Everett, B. H., Croft, K., & Flavell, E. R. (1981). Young children's knowledge about visual perception: Further evidence for the level 1–level 2 distinction. *Developmental Psychology, 17,* 99–103.

Flavell, J. H., & Wohlwill, J. F. (1969). Formal and functional aspects of cognitive development. In D. Elkind & J. H. Flavell (Eds.), *Studies in cognitive development: Essays in honor of Jean Piaget.* New York: Oxford University Press.

Freedle, R., & Lewis, M. (1977). Prelinguistic conversation. In M. Lewis & L. Rosenblum (Eds.), *Interaction, conversation, and the development of language.* New York: Wiley.

Gallagher, J. M., & Easley, J. A., Jr. (Eds.). (1978). *Knowledge and development (Vol. 2). Piaget and education.* New York: Plenum.

Gauvain, M., & Rogoff, B. (1989). Collaborative problem-solving and children's planning skills. *Developmental Psychology, 25,* 139–151.

Gelman, R. (1972). The nature and development of early number concepts. In H. W. Reese (Ed.), *Advances in child development and behavior* (Vol. 7). New York: Academic.

Gelman, R. (1978). Cognitive development. *Annual Review of Psychology, 29,* 297–332.

Gelman, R., & Shatz, M. (1977). Appropriate speech adjustments: The operation of conversational constraints on talk to two-year-olds. In M. Lewis & L. Rosenblum (Eds.), *Interaction, conversation, and the development of language.* New York: Wiley.

Gray, W. M., & Hudson, L. M. (1984). Formal operations and the imaginary audience. *Developmental Psychology, 20,* 619–627.

Greenfield, P. M., & Smith, J. H. (1976). *The structure of communication in early language development.* New York: Academic.

Grieser, D. L., & Kuhl, P. K. (1988). Maternal speech to infants in a tonal language: Support for universal prosodic features in motherese. *Developmental Psychology, 24,* 14–20.

Harter, S. (1982). Cognitive-developmental considerations in the conduct of play therapy. In C. E. Schaefer & K. J. O'Connor (Eds.), *Handbook of play therapy.* New York: Wiley

Hoff-Ginsberg, E. (1986). Function and structure in maternal speech: Their relation to the child's development of syntax. *Developmental Psychology, 22,* 155–163.

Hooper, F. H., Hooper, J. O., & Colbert, K. K. (1985). Personality and memory correlates of intellectual functioning in adulthood: Piagetian and psychometric assessments. *Human Development, 28,* 101–107.

Hooper, F. H., & Sheehan, N. W. (1977). Logical concept attainment during the aging years. Issues in the neo-Piagetian research literature. In W. F. Overton & J. M. Gallagher (Eds.), *Knowledge and development (Vol. 1). Advances in research and theory.* New York: Plenum.

Horn, J. L., & Donaldson, G. (1980). Cognitive development in adulthood. In O. G. Brim, Jr., and J. Kagan (Eds.), *Constancy and change in human development.* Cambridge, MA: Harvard University Press.

Hunt, K. W. (1970). Syntactic maturity in schoolchildren and adults. *Monographs of the Society for Research in Child Development, 35* (1, Serial No. 134).

Inhelder, B. (1966). Cognitive development and its contribution to the diagnosis of some phenomena of mental deficiency. *Merrill-Palmer Quarterly, 12,* 299–319.

Inhelder, B., & Piaget, J. (1964). *Early growth of logic in the child: Classification and seriation.* New York: Harper & Row.

Kahan, L. D., & Richards, D. D. (1986). The effects of context on referential communication strategies. *Child Development, 57,* 1130–1141.

Kaye, K., & Marcus, J. (1981). Infant imitation: The sensorimotor agenda. *Developmental Psychology, 17,* 258–265.

Keating, D. P. (1980). Thinking processes in adolescence. In J. Adelson (Ed.), *Handbook of adolescent psychology.* New York: Wiley.

Kemler Nelson, D. G., Hirsh-Pasek, K., Jusczyk, P. W., & Cassidy, K. W. (1989). How the prosodic cues in motherese might assist in language learning. *Journal of Child Language, 16,* 55–68.

Kenny, S. L. (1983). Developmental discontinuities in childhood and adolescence. In K. W. Fischer (Ed.), *Levels and transitions in children's development* (No. 21, New Directions for Child Development Series). San Francisco: Jossey-Bass.

Kitchener, K. S., & King, P. M. (1981). Reflective judgment: Concepts of justification and their relationship to age and education. *Journal of Applied Developmental Psychology, 2,* 89–116.

Kitchener, K. S., King, P. M., Wood, P. K., & Davison, M. L. (1989). Sequentiality and consistency in the development of reflective judgment: A six-year longitudinal study. *Journal of Applied Developmental Psychology, 10,* 73–95.

Krauss, R. M., & Glucksberg, S. (1977). Social and nonsocial speech. *Scientific American, 236,* 100–105

Kuhn, D. (1988). Cognitive development. In M. H. Bornstein & M. E. Lamb (Eds.), *Developmental psychology: An advanced textbook.* Hillsdale, NJ: Erlbaum.

Labouvie-Vief, G. (1984). Logic and self-regulation from youth to maturity: A model. In M. L. Commons, F. A. Richards, & C. Armon (Eds.), *Beyond formal operations: Late adolescent and adult cognitive development.* New York: Praeger.

Labouvie-Vief, G. (1985). Intelligence and cognition. In J. E. Birren & K. W. Schaie (Eds.), *Handbook of the psychology of aging* (2nd ed.). New York: Van Nostrand Reinhold.

Labouvie-Vief, G., Adams, C., Hakim-Larson, J., & Hayden, M. (April 1983). *Contexts of logic: The growth of interpretation from pre-adolescence to mature adulthood.* Paper presented at the biennial meeting of the Society for Research in Child Development, Detroit, Michigan.

Lapsley, D. K., Milstead, M., Quintana, S. M., Flannery, D., & Buss, R. R. (1986). Adolescent egocentrism and formal operations: Tests of a theoretical assumption. *Developmental Psychology, 22,* 800–807.

Lapsley, D. K., & Murphy, M. N. (1985). Another look at the theoretical assumptions of adolescent egocentrism. *Developmental Review, 5,* 201–217.

Lechner, C. R., & Rosenthal, D. A. (1984). Adolescent self-consciousness and the imaginary audience. *Genetic Psychology Monographs, 110*(2), 289–305.

Leonard, L. B., Chapman, K., Rowan, L. E., & Weiss, A. L. (1983). Three hypotheses concerning young children's imitations of lexical items. *Developmental Psychology, 19,* 591–601.

Martorano, S. C. (1977). A developmental analysis of performance on Piaget's formal operations tasks. *Developmental Psychology, 13,* 666–672.

McGhee, P. E. (1979). *Humor. Its origin and development.* San Francisco: W. H. Freeman.

McGhee, P. E., & Chapman, A. J. (1980). *Children's humour.* London: Wiley.

McNeill, D. (1970). *The acquisition of language.* New York: Harper & Row.

Meltzoff, A. N. (1988a). Infant imitation after a 1-week delay: Long-term memory for novel acts and multiple stimuli. *Developmental Psychology, 24,* 470–476.

Meltzoff, A. N. (1988b). Infant imitation and memory: Nine-month-olds in immediate and deferred tests. *Child Development, 59,* 217–225.

Meltzoff, A. N., & Moore, M. K. (1983). Newborn infants imitate adult facial gestures. *Child Development, 54,* 702–709.

Mervis, C. B., & Mervis, C. A. (1982). Leopards are kitty-cats: Object labeling by mothers for their thirteen-month-olds. *Child Development, 53,* 267–273.

Molfese, D. L. (1977). Infant cerebral asymmetry. In S. J. Segalowitz & F. A. Gruber (Eds.), *Language development and neurological theory.* New York: Academic.

Nagy, P., & Griffiths, A. K. (1982). Limitations of recent research relating Piaget's theory to adolescent thought. *Review of Educational Research, 52,* 513–556.

Neimark, E. D. (1975). Longitudinal development of formal operations thought. *Genetic Psychology Monographs, 91,* 171–225.

Neimark, E. D. (1979). Current status of formal operations research. *Human Development, 22,* 60–67.

Nelson, K. (1973). Structure and strategy in learning to talk. *Monographs of the Society for Research in Child Development, 38* (Serial No. 149).

Nelson, K. E. (1977). Facilitating children's syntax acquisition. *Developmental Psychology, 13,* 101–107.

Newport, E. L., Gleitman, H., & Gleitman, L. R. (1977). Mother, I'd rather do it myself: Some effects and noneffects of maternal speech style. In C. E. Snow & C. A. Ferguson (Eds.), *Talking to children: Language input and acquisition.* Cambridge,England: Cambridge University Press.

Norman-Jackson, J. (1982). Family interactions, language development, and primary reading achievement of Black children in families of low income. *Child Development, 53,* 349–358.

Obler, L. K., & Albert, M. L. (1985). Language skills across adulthood. In J. E. Birren & K. W. Schaie (Eds.), *Handbook of the psychology of aging* (2nd ed.). New York: Van Nostrand Reinhold.

Oller, D. K., & Eilers, R. E. (1988). The role of audition in infant babbling. *Child Development, 59,* 441–449.

Olsho, L. W., Harkins, S. W., & Lenhardt, M. L. (1985). Aging and the auditory system. In J. E. Birren & K. W. Schaie (eds.), *Handbook of the psychology of aging* (2nd ed.). New York: Van Nostrand Reinhold.

Owens, R. E., Jr. (1984). *Language development. An introduction.* Columbus, OH: Merrill.

Patterson, C. J., O'Brien, C. O., Kister, M. C., Carter, D. B., & Kotsonis, M. E. (1981). Development of comprehension monitoring as a function of context. *Developmental Psychology, 17,* 379–389.

Pearce, K. A., & Denney, N. W. (1984). A lifespan study of classification preference. *Journal of Gerontology, 39,* 458–464.

Penner, S. G. (1987). Parental responses to grammatical and ungrammatical child utterances. *Child Development, 58,* 376–384.

Perry, W. G., Jr. (1970). *Forms of intellectual and ethical development in the college years: A scheme.* New York: Holt, Rinehart & Winston.

Piaget, J. (1926). *Language and thought in the child.* London: Routledge & Kegan Paul.

Piaget, J. (1929). *The child's conception of the world.* New York: Harcourt, Brace & World.

Piaget, J. (1951). *Play, dreams, and imitation in childhood.* New York: Norton.

Piaget, J. (1952). *The origins of intelligence in children.* New York: International Universities Press.

Piaget, J. (1954). *The construction of reality in the child.* New York: Basic Books.

Piaget, J. (1970). Piaget's theory. In P. H. Mussen (Ed.), *Carmichael's manual of child psychology* (Vol. 1). New York: Wiley.

Piaget, J. (1972). Intellectual evolution from adolescence to adulthood. *Human Development, 15,* 1–12.

Piaget, J. (1977). The role of action in the development of thinking. In W. F. Overton & J. M. Gallagher (Eds.), *Knowledge and development* (Vol. 1). New York: Plenum.

Piaget, J. (1985). *The equilibration of cognitive structures. The central problem of intellectual development.* (Trans. by T. Brown & K. J. Thampy). Chicago: University of Chicago Press.

Piaget, J., & Inhelder, B. (1956). *The child's conception of space.* New York: Norton.

Prawat, R. S., & Wildfong, S. (1980). The influence of functional context on children's labeling responses. *Child Development, 51,* 1057–1060.

Price, G. C., Hess, R. D., & Dickson, W. P. (1981). Processes by which verbal-educational abilities are affected when mothers encourage preschool children to verbalize. *Developmental Psychology, 17,* 554–564.

Reeder, K. (1981). How young children learn to do things with words. In P. S. Dale & D. Ingram (Eds.), *Child language—An international perspective.* Baltimore: University Park Press.

Reynolds, R. E., & Ortony, A. (1980). Some issues in the measurement of children's comprehension of metaphorical language. *Child Development, 51,* 1110–1119.

Rice, M. L., & Kemper, S. (1984). *Child language and cognition.* Baltimore: University Park Press.

Rice, M. L., & Woodsmall, L. (1988). Lessons from television: Children's word learning when viewing. *Child Development, 59,* 420–429.

Richards, F. A., & Commons, M. L. (1984). Systematic, metasystematic, and cross-paradigmatic reasoning: A case for stages of reasoning beyond formal operations. In M. L. Commons, F. A. Richards, & C. Armon (Eds.), *Beyond formal operations. Late adolescent and adult cognitive development.* New York: Praeger.

Riegel, K. F. (1973). Dialectic operations: The final period of cognitive development. *Human Development, 16,* 346–370.

Riley, T., Adams, G. R., & Nielsen, E. (1984). Adolescent egocentrism: The association among imaginary audience behavior, cognitive development, and parental support and rejection. *Journal of Youth and Adolescence, 13,* 401–417.

Rogoff, B., & Lave, J. (Eds.). (1984). *Everyday cognition: Its development in social context.* Cambridge, MA: Harvard University Press.

Rogoff, B., & Wertsch, J. V. (Eds.). (1984). *Children's learning in the "zone of proximal development."* (No. 23, New Directions for Child Development Series). San Francisco: Jossey-Bass.

Rondal, J. A. (1980). Fathers' and mothers' speech in early language development. *Journal of Child Language, 7,* 353–369.

Rondal, J. A. (1985). *Adult–child interaction and the process of language acquisition.* New York: Praeger.

Rosenthal, M. K. (1982). Vocal dialogues in the neonatal period. *Developmental Psychology, 18,* 17–21.

Ruffman, T. K., & Olson, D. R. (1989). Children's ascriptions of knowledge to others. *Developmental Psychology, 25,* 601–606.

Sachs, J. (1985). Prelinguistic development. In J. Berko Gleason (Ed.), *The development of language.* Columbus, OH: Merrill.

Saltz, R. (1979). Children's interpretation of proverbs. *Language Arts, 56,* 508–514.

Schaie, K. W. (1977/78). Toward a stage theory of adult cognitive development. *International Journal of Aging and Human Development, 8,* 129–138.

Schaie, K. W. (1983). The Seattle longitudinal study: A 21-year exploration of psychometric intelligence in adulthood. In K. W. Schaie (Ed.), *Longitudinal studies of adult psychological development.* New York: Guilford.

Schieffelin, B. B., & Ochs, E. (1983). A cultural perspective on the transition from prelinguistic to linguistic communication. In R. M. Golinkoff (Ed.), *The transition from prelinguistic to linguistic communication.* Hillsdale, NJ: Erlbaum.

Scribner, S. (1984). Studying working intelligence. In B. Rogoff & J. Lave (Eds.), *Everyday cognition: Its development in social context.* Cambridge, MA: Harvard University Press.

Sedlak, A. J., & Kurtz, S. T. (1981). A review of children's use of causal inference principles. *Child Development, 52,* 759–784.

Selzer, S. C., & Denney, N. W. (1980). Conservation abilities among middle-aged and elderly adults. *International Journal of Aging and Human Development, 11,* 135–146.

Shatz, M. (1983). Communication. In P. H. Mussen (ed.), *Handbook of child psychology* (Vol. 3). New York: Wiley.

Sinnott, J. D. (1984). Postformal reasoning: The relativistic stage. In M. L. Commons, F. A. Richards, & C. Armon (Eds.), *Beyond formal operations. Late adolescent and adult cognitive development.* New York: Praeger.

Skinner, B. F. (1957). *Verbal behavior.* New York: Appleton-Century-Crofts.

Slobin, D. I. (1979). *Psycholinguistics.* Glenview, IL: Scott, Foresman.

Snow, C. E., Arlman-Rupp, A., Hassing, Y., Jobse, J., Joosken, J., & Vorster, J. (1976). Mother's speech in three social classes. *Journal of Psycholinguistic Research, 5,* 1–20.

Sonnenschein, S. (1986). Development of referential communication skills: How familiarity with a listener affects a speaker's production of redundant messages. *Developmental Psychology, 22,* 549–555.

Sternberg, R. J. (Ed.). (1984). *Mechanisms of cognitive development.* New York: W. H. Freeman.

Stone, C. A., & Day, M. D. (1978). Levels of availability of a formal operational strategy. *Child Development, 49,* 1054–1065.

Thomas, D., Campos, J. J., Shucard, D. W., Ramsay, D. S., & Shucard, J. (1981). Semantic comprehension in infancy: A signal detection approach. *Child Development, 52,* 798–803.

Thompson, J. R., & Chapman, R. S. (1977). Who is "Daddy" revisited? The status of two-year-olds' overextended words in use and comprehension. *Journal of Child Language, 4,* 359–375.

Tomlinson-Keasey, C., Eisert, D. C., Kahle, L. R., Hardy-Brown, K., & Keasey, B. (1979). The structure of concrete-operational thought. *Child Development, 50,* 1153–1163.

Trabasso, T. (1975). Representation, memory, and reasoning: How do we make transitive inferences? In A. D. Pick (Ed.), *Minnesota symposia on child psychology* (Vol. 9). Minneapolis: University of Minnesota Press.

Tulkin, S. R., & Konner, M. J. (1973). Alternative conceptions of intellectual functioning. *Human Development, 16,* 33–52.

Vygotsky, L. S. (1962). *Thought and language.* Cambridge, MA: M.I.T. Press.

Vygotsky, L. S. (1978). *Mind in society. The development of higher psychological processes.* (Ed. by M. Cole, V. John-Steiner, S. Scribner, & E. Souberman). Cambridge, MA: Harvard University Press.

Weir, R. H. (1966). Some questions on the child's learning of phonology. In F. Smith & G. Miller (Eds.), *The genesis of language.* Cambridge, MA: M.I.T. Press.

Werker, J. F., Gilbert, J. H. V., Humphrey, K., & Tees, R. C. (1981). Developmental aspects of cross-language speech perception. *Child Development, 52,* 349–355.

Whitehurst, G. J., Falco, F. L., Lonigan, C. J., Fischel, J. E., DeBaryshe, B. D., Valdez-Menchaca, M. C., & Caulfield, M. (1988). Accelerating language development through picture book reading. *Developmental Psychology, 24,* 552–559.

Whitehurst, G. J., & Valdez-Menchaca, M. C. (1988). What is the role of reinforcement in early language acquisition? *Child Development, 59,* 430–440.

Wilkinson, L. C., & Rembold, K. L. (1981). The form and function of children's gestures accompanying verbal directives. In P. S. Dale & D. Ingram (Eds.), *Child language: An international perspective.* Baltimore: University Park Press.

Willis, S. L. (1985). Towards an educational psychology of the older adult learner: Intellectual and cognitive bases. In J. E. Birren & K. W. Schaie (Eds.), *Handbook of the psychology of aging* (2nd ed.). New York: Van Nostrand Reinhold.

Wishart, J. G., & Bower, T. G. R. (1985). A longitudinal study of the development of the object concept. *British Journal of Developmental Psychology, 3,* 243–258

Wolff, P. H. (1969). The natural history of crying and other vocalizations in early infancy. In B. M. Foss (Ed.), *Determinants of infant behavior* (Vol. 4). London: Methuen.

Yalisove, D. (1978). The effect of riddle structure on children's comprehension of riddles. *Developmental Psychology, 14,* 173–180.

Chapter 8: Learning and Information Processing

Abravanel, E., & Gingold, H. (1985). Learning via observation during the 2nd year of life. *Developmental Psychology, 21,* 614–623.

Abravanel, E., & Sigafoos, A. D. (1984). Exploring the presence of imitation during early infancy. *Child Development, 55,* 381–392.

Arenberg, D. (1982). Changes with age in problem solving. In F. I. M. Craik & S. Trehub (Eds.), *Aging and cognitive processes.* New York: Plenum.

Ashmead, D. H., & Perlmutter, M. (1980). Infant memory in everyday life. In M. Perlmutter (Ed.), *New directions for child development: Vol. 10. Children's memory.* San Francisco: Jossey-Bass.

Atkinson, R. C., & Shiffrin, R. M. (1968). Human memory: A proposed system and its control processes. In K. W. Spence & J. T. Spence (Eds.), *The psychology of learning and motivation: Advances in research and theory* (Vol. 2). New York: Academic.

Bahrick, H. P., Bahrick, P. O., & Wittlinger, R. P. (1975). Fifty years of memory for names and faces: A cross-sectional approach. *Journal of Experimental Psychology: General, 104,* 54–75.

Baker, L., & Brown, A. L. (1984). Metacognitive skills and reading. In P. D. Pearson (Ed.), *A handbook of reading research.* New York: Longman.

Baltes, M. M., & Barton, E. M. (1979). Behavioral analysis of aging: A review of the operant model and research. *International Journal of Behavioral Development, 2,* 297–320.

Bandura, A. (1965). Influence of models' reinforcement contingencies on the acquisition of imitative responses. *Journal of Personality and Social Psychology, 1,* 589–595.

Bandura, A. (1977). *Social learning theory.* Englewood Cliffs, NJ: Prentice-Hall.

Bandura, A. (1986). *Social foundations of thought and action. A social cognitive theory.* Englewood Cliffs, NJ: Prentice-Hall.

Barrett, T. R., & Watkins, S. K. (1986). Word familiarity and cardiovascular health as determinants of age-related recall differences. *Journal of Gerontology, 41,* 222–224.

Barrett, T. R., & Wright, M. (1981). Age-related facilitation in recall following semantic processing. *Journal of Gerontology, 36,* 194–199.

Bellucci, G., & Hoyer, W. J. (1975). Feedback effects on the performance and self-reinforcing behavior of elderly and young adult women. *Journal of Gerontology, 30,* 456–460.

Berg, C. A. (1989). Knowledge of strategies for dealing with everyday problems from childhood through adolescence. *Developmental Psychology, 25,* 607–618.

Bjorklund, D. F. (1985). The role of conceptual knowledge in the development of organization in children's memory. In C. J. Brainerd & M. Pressley (Eds.), *Basic processes in memory development. Progress in cognitive development research.* New York: Springer-Verlag.

Bjorklund, D. F. (1987). How age changes in knowledge base contribute to the development of children's memory: An interpretive review. *Developmental Review, 7,* 93–130.

Bjorklund, D. F., & Zeman, B. R. (1982). Children's organization and metamemory awareness in their recall of familiar information. *Child Development, 53,* 799–810.

Botwinick, J. (1984). *Aging and behavior. A comprehensive integration of research findings* (3rd ed.). New York: Springer.

Botwinick, J., & Storandt, M. (1974). *Memory, related functions and age.* Springfield, IL: Charles C Thomas.

Bray, N. W., Hersh, R. E., & Turner, L. A. (1985). Selective remembering during adolescence. *Developmental Psychology, 21,* 290–294.

Bray, N. W., Justice, E. M., & Zahm, D. N. (1983). Two developmental transitions in directed forgetting strategies. *Journal of Experimental Child Psychology, 36,* 43–55.

Brown, A. L. (1975). The development of memory: Knowing, knowing about knowing, and knowing how to know. In H. W. Reese (Ed.), *Advances in child development and behavior* (Vol. 10). New York: Academic.

Brown, A. L., Bransford, J. D., Ferrara, R. A., & Campione, J. C. (1983). Learning, remembering and understanding. In J. H. Flavell & E. M. Markman (Eds.), *Handbook of child psychology: Vol. 3. Cognitive development* (4th ed.). New York: Wiley.

Brown, A. L., Day, J. D., & Jones, R. S. (1983). The development of plans for summarizing texts. *Child Development, 54,* 968–979.

Brown, A. L., & Smiley, S. S. (1978). The development of strategies for studying text. *Child Development, 49,* 1076–1088.

Campione, J. L., Brown, A. L., & Bryant, N. R. (1985). Individual differences in learning and memory. In R. J. Sternberg (Ed.), *Human abilities. An information-processing approach.* New York: W. H. Freeman.

Canestrari, R. E. (1963). Paced and self-paced learning in young and elderly adults. *Journal of Gerontology, 18,* 165–168.

Case, R. (1984). The process of stage transition: A neo-Piagetian view. In R. J. Sternberg (Ed.), *Mechanisms of cognitive development.* New York: W. H. Freeman.

Case, R. (1985). *Intellectual development: Birth to adulthood.* Orlando, FL: Academic.

Cavanaugh, J. C. (1983). Comprehension and retention of television programs by 20- and 60-year-olds. *Journal of Gerontology, 38,* 190–196.

Cavanaugh, J. C., Grady, J. G., & Perlmutter, M. (1983). Forgetting and use of memory aids in 20 to 70 year olds' everyday life. *International Journal of Aging and Human Development, 17,* 113–122.

Cavanaugh, J. C., & Perlmutter, M. (1982). Metamemory: A critical examination. *Child Development, 53,* 11–28.

Cavanaugh, J. C., & Poon, L. W. (1989). Metamemorial predictors of memory performance in young and older adults. *Psychology and Aging, 4,* 365–368.

Cerella, J. (1985). Information processing rates in the elderly. *Psychological Bulletin, 98,* 67–83.

Chi, M. T. H. (1978). Knowledge structures and memory development. In R. Siegler (Ed.), *Children's thinking: What develops?* Hillsdale, NJ: Erlbaum.

Chi, M. T. H., Glaser, R., & Rees, E. (1982). Expertise in problem solving. In R. J. Sternberg (Ed.), *Advances in the psychology of human intelligence* (Vol. 1). Hillsdale, NJ: Erlbaum.

Chi, M. T. H., Hutchinson, J. E. & Robin, A. F. (1989). How inferences about novel domain–related concepts can be constrained by structured knowledge. *Merrill–Palmer Quarterly, 35,* 27–62.

Coates, B., & Hartup, W. W. (1969). Age and verbalization in observational learning. *Developmental Psychology, 1,* 556–562.

Collins, W. A., Wellman, H., Keniston, A. H., & Westby, S. D. (1978). Age-related aspects of comprehension and inference from a televised dramatic narrative. *Child Development, 49,* 389–399.

Cornelius, S. W., & Caspi, A. (1987). Everyday problem solving in adulthood and old age. *Psychology and Aging, 2,* 144–153.

Craik, F. I. M. (1977). Age differences in human memory. In J. E. Birren & K. W. Schaie (Eds.), *Handbook of the psychology of aging.* New York: Van Nostrand Reinhold.

Cunningham, J. G., & Weaver, S. L. (1989). Young children's knowledge of their memory span: Effects of task and experience. *Journal of Experimental Child Psychology, 48,* 32–44.

Daehler, M. W., & Greco, C. (1985). Memory in very young children. In M. Pressley & C. J. Brainerd (Eds.), *Cognitive learning and memory in children. Progress in cognitive development research.* New York: Springer-Verlag.

Davis, J. M., & Rovee-Collier, C. K. (1983). Alleviated forgetting of a learned contingency in 8-week-old infants. *Developmental Psychology, 19,* 353–365.

Dempster, F. N. (1981). Memory span: Sources of individual and developmental differences. *Psychological Bulletin, 89,* 63–100.

Dempster, F. N. (1985). Short-term memory development in childhood and adolescence. In C. J. Brainerd & M. Pressley (Eds.), *Basic processes in memory development. Progress in cognitive development research.* New York: Springer-Verlag.

Denney, N. W. (1980). Task demands and problem-solving strategies in middle-aged and older adults. *Journal of Gerontology, 35,* 559–564.

Denney, N. W. (1982). Aging and cognitive changes. In B. B. Wolman (Ed.), *Handbook of developmental psychology.* Englewood Cliffs, NJ: Prentice-Hall.

Denney, N. W. (1985). A review of life span research with the Twenty Questions Task: A study of problem-solving ability. *International Journal of Aging and Human Development, 21,* 161–173.

Denney, N. W., Jones, F. W., & Krigel, S. W. (1979). Modifying the questioning strategies of young children and elderly adults with strategy-modeling techniques. *Human Development, 22,* 23–36.

Dixon, R. A., & Hultsch, D. F. (1983a). Metamemory and memory for text relationships in adulthood: A cross-validation study. *Journal of Gerontology, 38,* 689–694.

Dixon, R. A., & Hultsch, D. F. (1983b). Structure and development of metamemory in adulthood. *Journal of Gerontology, 38,* 682–688.

Domjan, M., & Burkhard, B. (1982). *The principles of learning and behavior.* Pacific Grove, CA: Brooks/Cole.

Ellis, N. R., Palmer, R. L., & Reeves, C. L. (1988). Developmental and intellectual differences in frequency processing. *Developmental Psychology, 24,* 38–45.

Erber, J. T. (1981). Remote memory and age: A review. *Experimental Aging Research, 1,* 189–199.

Erber, J. T., Herman, T. G., & Botwinick, J. (1980). Age differences in memory as a function of depth of processing. *Experimental Aging Research, 6,* 341–348.

Ericsson, K. A., Chase, W. G., & Faloon, S. (1980). Acquisition of a memory skill. *Science, 208,* 1181–1182.

Fagan, J. F., Jr. (1984). Infant memory. History, current trends, relations to cognitive psychology. In M. Moscovitch (Ed.), *Infant memory. Its relation to normal and pathological memory in humans and other animals.* New York: Plenum.

Field, T. M., Woodson, R., Greenberg, R., & Cohen, D. (1982). Discrimination and imitation of facial expressions by neonates. *Science, 218,* 179–181.

Fitzgerald, H. E., & Brackbill, Y. (1976). Classical conditioning in infancy: Development and constraints. *Psychological Bulletin, 83,* 353–376.

Flavell, J. H. (1985). *Cognitive development* (2nd ed.). Englewood Cliffs, NJ: Prentice-Hall.

Flavell, J. H., Beach, D. H., & Chinsky, J. M. (1966). Spontaneous verbal rehearsal in a memory task as a function of age. *Child Development, 37,* 283–299.

Flavell, J. H., & Wellman, H. M. (1977). Metamemory. In R. V. Kail & J. W. Hagen (Eds.), *Perspectives on the development of memory and cognition.* Hillsdale, NJ: Erlbaum.

Friedman, S. B. (1972). Habituation and recovery of visual response in the alert human newborn. *Journal of Experimental Child Psychology, 13,* 339–349.

Gardner, H. (1985). *The mind's new science. A history of the cognitive revolution.* New York: Basic.

Guttentag, R. E. (1985). Memory and aging: Implications for theories of memory development during childhood. *Developmental Review, 5,* 56–77.

Hasher, L., & Zacks, R. T. (1979). Automatic and effortful processes in memory. *Journal of Experimental Psychology: General, 108,* 356–388.

Hasher, L., & Zacks, R. T. (1984). Automatic processing of fundamental information. The case of frequency of occurrence. *American Psychologist, 39,* 1372–1388.

Hertzog, C., Hultsch, D. F., & Dixon, R. A. (1989). Evidence for the convergent validity of two self-report metamemory questionnaires. *Developmental Psychology, 25,* 687–700.

House, B. J. (1982). Learning processes: Developmental trends. In J. Worell (Ed.), *Psychological development in the elementary years.* New York: Academic.

Howard, L., & Polich, J. (1985). P300 latency and memory span development. *Developmental Psychology, 21,* 283–289.

Hulicka, I. M. (1967). Age differences in retention as a function of interference. *Journal of Gerontology, 22,* 180–184.

Hultsch, D. F. (1971). Adult age differences in free classification and free recall. *Developmental Psychology, 4,* 338–342.

Hultsch, D. F., & Dixon, R. A. (1984). Memory for text materials in adulthood. In P. B. Baltes & O. G. Brim, Jr. (Eds.), *Life-span development and behavior* (Vol. 6). New York: Academic.

Jones, M. C. (1924). A laboratory study of fear: The case of Peter. *Pedagogical Seminary, 31,* 308–315.

Justice, E. M. (1985). Categorization as preferred memory strategy: Developmental changes during elementary school. *Developmental Psychology, 21,* 1105–1110.

Kail, R. (1988). Developmental functions for speeds of cognitive processes. *Journal of Experimental Child Psychology, 45,* 339–364.

Kaitz, M., Meschulach-Sarfaty, O., Auerbach, J., & Eidelman, A. (1988). A reexamination of newborns' ability to imitate facial expressions. *Developmental Psychology, 24,* 3–7.

Kee, D. W., & Bell, T. S. (1981). The development of organizational strategies in the storage and retrieval of categorical items in free-recall learning. *Child Development, 52,* 1163–1171.

Keil, F. C. (1984). Mechanisms of cognitive development and the structure of knowledge. In R. J. Sternberg (Ed.), *Mechanisms of cognitive development.* New York: W. H. Freeman.

Kemler, D. G. (1978). Patterns of hypothesis testing in children's discriminative learning: A study of the development of problem-solving strategies. *Developmental Psychology, 14,* 653–673.

Kendler, H. H., & Kendler, T. S. (1975). From discrimination learning to cognitive development: A neobehavioristic odyssey. In K. W. Estes (Ed.), *Handbook of learning and cognitive processes* (Vol. 1). Hillsdale, NJ: Erlbaum.

Kendler, T. S. (1979). Toward a theory of mediational development. In H. W. Reese & L. P. Lipsitt (Eds.), *Advances in child development and behavior* (Vol. 13). New York: Academic.

Kendler, T. S., Kendler, H. H., & Leonard, B. (1962). Mediated responses to size and brightness as a function of age. *American Journal of Psychology, 75,* 571–586.

Klahr, D., & Robinson, M. (1981). Formal assessment of problem-solving and planning processes in preschool children. *Cognitive Psychology, 13,* 113–148.

Klahr, D., & Wallace, J. C. (1976). *Cognitive development: An information-processing view.* Hillsdale, NJ: Erlbaum.

Kreutzer, M. A., Leonard, C., & Flavell, J. H. (1975). An interview study of children's knowledge about memory. *Monographs of the Society for Research in Child Development, 40* (1, Serial No. 159).

Kron, R. E. (1966). Instrumental conditioning of nutritive sucking behavior in the newborn. *Recent Advances in Biological Psychiatry, 9,* 295–300.

Labouvie-Vief, G., & Schell, D. A. (1982). Learning and memory in later life. In B. B. Wolman (Ed.), *Handbook of developmental psychology.* Englewood Cliffs, NJ: Prentice-Hall.

Lachman, J. L., & Lachman, R. (1980). Age and the actualization of world knowledge. In L. W. Poon, J. L. Fozard, L. S. Cermak, D. Arenberg, & L. W. Thompson (Eds.), *New directions in memory and aging.* Hillsdale, NJ: Erlbaum.

Leech, S., & Witte, K. L. (1971). Paired-associate learning in elderly adults as related to pacing and incentive conditions. *Developmental Psychology, 5,* 174–180.

Lesgold, A. M. (1984). Acquiring expertise. In J. R. Anderson & S. M. Kosslyn (Eds.), *Tutorials in learning and memory. Essays in honor of Gordon Bower.* San Francisco: W. H. Freeman.

Liberty, C., & Ornstein, P. A. (1973). Age differences in organization and recall: The effects of training in categorization. *Journal of Experimental Child Psychology, 15,* 169–186.

Lipsitt, L. P., & Kaye, H. (1964). Conditioned sucking in the human newborn. *Psychonomic Science, 1,* 29–30.

Little, A. H., Lipsitt, L. P., & Rovee-Collier, C. K. (1984). Classical conditioning and retention of the infant's eyelid response: Effects of age and interstimulus interval. *Journal of Experimental Child Psychology, 37,* 512–524.

Luria, A. R. (1961). *The role of speech in the regulation of normal and abnormal behavior.* New York: Liveright.

Mayer, R. E. (1985). Mathematical ability. In R. J. Sternberg (Ed.), *Human abilities. An information-processing approach.* New York: W. H. Freeman.

McCall, R. B., Parke, R. D., & Kavanaugh, R. D. (1977). Imitation of live and televised models by children one to three years of age. *Monographs of the Society for Research in Child Development, 42* (Serial No. 173).

Meltzoff, A. N. (1988). Infant imitation and memory: Nine-month-olds in immediate and deferred tests. *Child Development, 59,* 217–225.

Meltzoff, A. N., & Moore, M. K. (1983). Newborn infants imitate adult facial gestures. *Child Development, 54,* 702–709.

Miller, P. H., & Weiss, M. G. (1981) Children's attention allocation, understanding of attention, and performance on the incidental learning task. *Child Development, 52,* 1183–1190.

Mitchell, D. B., & Perlmutter, M. (1986). Semantic activation and episodic memory: Age similarities and differences. *Developmental Psychology, 22,* 86–94.

Nelson, K. (1984). The transition from infant to child memory. In M. Moscovitch (Ed.), *Infant memory. Its relation to normal and pathological memory in humans and other animals.* New York: Plenum.

Newell, A., & Simon, H. A. (1961). Computer simulation of human thinking. *Science, 134,* 2011–2017.

Offenbach, S. I. (1974). A developmental study of hypothesis testing and cue selection strategies. *Developmental Psychology, 10,* 484–490.

Ornstein, P. A., Medlin, R. G., Stone, B. P., & Naus, M. J. (1985). Retrieving for rehearsal: An analysis of active rehearsal in children's memory. *Developmental Psychology, 21,* 633–641.

Ornstein, P. A., Naus, M. J., & Liberty, C. (1975). Rehearsal and organizational processes in children's memory. *Child Development, 46,* 818–830.

Papousek, H. (1967). Experimental studies of appetitional behavior in human newborns and infants. In H. W. Stevenson, E. H. Hess, & H. L. Rheingold (Eds.), *Early behavior: Comparative and developmental approaches.* New York: Wiley.

Paris, S. G., & Oka, E. R. (1986). Children's reading strategies, metacognition, and motivation. *Developmental Review, 6,* 25–56.

Parke, R. D. (1977). Some effects of punishment on children's behavior—revisited. In E. M. Hetherington & R. D. Parke (Eds.), *Contemporary readings in child psychology.* New York: McGraw-Hill.

Pascual-Leone, J. (1970). A mathematical model for the transition rule in Piaget's developmental stages. *Acta Psychologica, 32,* 301–345.

Pascual-Leone, J. (1984). Attentional, dialectic, and mental effort: Toward an organismic theory of life stages. In M. L. Commons, F. A. Richards, & C. Armon (Eds.), *Beyond formal operations. Late adolescent and adult cognitive development.* New York: Praeger.

Perlmutter, M. (1986). A life-span view of memory. In P. B. Baltes, D. L. Featherman, & R. M. Lerner (Eds.), *Life-span development and behavior* (Vol. 7). Hillsdale, NJ: Erlbaum.

Poon, L. W. (1985). Differences in human memory with aging: Nature, causes, and clinical implications. In J. E. Birren & K. W. Schaie (Eds.), *Handbook of the psychology of aging* (2nd ed.). New York: Van Nostrand Reinhold.

Poon, L. W., Fozard, J. L., Paulshock, D. R., & Thomas, J. C. (1979). A questionnaire assessment of age differences in retention of recent and remote events. *Experimental Aging Research, 5,* 401–411.

Pressley, M. (1982). Elaboration and memory development. *Child Development, 53,* 296–309.

Pressley, M. (1983). Making meaningful materials easier to learn: Lessons from cognitive strategy research. In M. Pressley & J. R. Levin (Eds.), *Cognitive strategy research. Educational applications.* New York: Springer-Verlag.

Pressley, M., Forrest-Pressley, D. L., Elliott-Faust, D., & Miller, G. (1985). Children's use of cognitive strategies, how to teach strategies, and what to do if they can't be taught. In M. Pressley & C. J. Brainerd (Eds.), *Cognitive learning and memory in children. Progress in cognitive development research.* New York: Springer-Verlag.

Pressley, M., & Levin, J. R. (1980). The development of mental imagery retrieval. *Child Development, 51,* 558–560.

Rabinowitz, J. C. (1986). Priming in episodic memory. *Journal of Gerontology, 41,* 204–213.

Reder, L. M., Wible, C., & Martin, J. (1986). Differential memory changes with age: Exact retrieval versus plausible inference. *Journal of Experimental Psychology: Learning, Memory, and Cognition, 12,* 72–81.

Reese, H. W., & Rodeheaver, D. (1985). Problem solving and complex decision making. In J. E. Birren & K. W. Schaie (Eds.), *Handbook of the psychology of aging* (2nd ed.). New York: Van Nostrand Reinhold.

Reissland, N. (1988). Neonatal imitation in the first hour of life: Observations in rural Nepal. *Developmental Psychology, 24,* 464–469.

Rovee-Collier, C. (1987). Learning and memory in infancy. In J. D. Osofsky (Ed.), *Handbook of infant development* (2nd ed.). New York: Wiley.

Salatas, H., & Flavell, J. H. (1976). Behavioral and metamnemonic indicators of strategic behaviors under remember instructions in first grade. *Child Development, 47,* 81–89.

Salthouse, T. (1985). *A theory of cognitive aging.* Amsterdam: North Holland, Elsevier.

Schaie, K. W. (1977/1978). Toward a stage theory of adult cognitive development. *International Journal of Aging and Human Development, 8,* 129–138.

Schaie, K. W., & Willis, S. L. (1986). *Adult development and aging* (2nd ed.). Boston: Little, Brown.

Schneider, W., & Sodian, B. (1988). Metamemory–memory behavior relationships in young children: Evidence from a memory-for-location task. *Journal of Experimental Child Psychology, 45,* 209–233.

Schneider, W., Korkel, J., & Weinert, F. E. (1989). Domain-specific knowledge and memory performance: A comparison of high- and low-aptitude children. *Journal of Educational Psychology, 81,* 306–312.

Scogin, F., Storandt, M., & Lott, L. (1985). Memory-skills training, memory complaints, and depression in older adults. *Journal of Gerontology, 40,* 562–568.

Sheingold, K., & Tenney, Y. J. (1982). Memory for a salient childhood event. In U. Neisser (Ed.), *Memory observed. Remembering in natural contexts.* San Francisco: W. H. Freeman.

Siegler, R. S. (1981). Developmental sequences within and between concepts. *Monographs of the Society for Research in Child Development, 46* (Serial No. 189).

Skinner, B. F. (1953). *Science and human behavior.* New York: Macmillan.

Skinner, B. F. (1983). Intellectual self-management in old age. *American Psychologist, 38,* 239–244.

Somerville, S. C., Wellman, H. M., & Cultice, J. C. (1983). Young children's deliberate reminding. *Journal of Genetic Psychology, 143,* 87–96.

Sophian, C. (1980). Habituation is not enough: Novelty preferences, search, and memory in infancy. *Merrill-Palmer Quarterly, 26,* 239–257.

Spilich, G. J., Vesonder, G. T., Chiesi, H. L., & Voss, J. F. (1979). Text processing of domain-related information for individuals with high and low domain knowledge. *Journal of Verbal Learning and Verbal Behavior, 18,* 275–290.

Sullivan, M. W. (1982). Reactivation: Priming forgotten memories in human infants. *Child Development, 53,* 516–523.

Sunderland, A., Watts, K., Baddeley, A. D., & Harris, J. E. (1986). Subjective memory assessment and test performance in elderly adults. *Journal of Gerontology, 41,* 376–384.

Tumblin, A., & Gholson, B. (1981). Hypothesis theory and the development of conceptual learning. *Psychological Bulletin, 90,* 102–124.

Vander Linde, E., Morrongiello, B. A., & Rovee-Collier, C. (1985). Determinants of retention in 8-week-old infants. *Developmental Psychology, 21,* 601–613.

Verna, G. B. (1977). The effects of a four-hour delay of punishment under two conditions of verbal instruction. *Child Development, 48,* 621–624.

Vinter, A. (1986). The role of movement in eliciting early imitations. *Child Development, 57,* 66–71.

Waddell, K. J., & Rogoff, B. (1981). Effect of contextual organization on spatial memory of middle-aged and older women. *Developmental Psychology, 17,* 878–885.

Wagner, D. A. (1978). Memories of Morocco: The influence of age, schooling, and environment on memory. *Cognitive Psychology, 10,* 1–28.

Watson, J. B., & Raynor, R. (1920). Conditioned emotional reactions. *Journal of Experimental Psychology, 3,* 1–14.

Wellman, H. M. (1977). Preschoolers' understanding of memory relevant variables. *Child Development, 48,* 1720–1723.

Wellman, H. M., Ritter, K., & Flavell, J. H. (1975). Deliberate memory behavior in the delayed reactions of very young children. *Developmental Psychology, 11,* 780–787.

White, S. H., & Pillemer, D. B. (1979). Childhood amnesia and the development of a socially accessible memory system. In J. F. Kihlstrom & F. J. Evans (Eds.), *Functional disorders of memory.* Hillsdale, NJ: Erlbaum.

Whitney, P. (1986). Developmental trends in speed of semantic memory retrieval. *Developmental Review, 6,* 57–79.

Willemsen, E. (1979). *Understanding infancy.* San Francisco: Freeman.

Yesavage, J. A., Rose, T. L., & Bower, G. H. (1983). Interactive imagery and affective judgments improve face–name learning in the elderly. *Journal of Gerontology, 38,* 197–203.

Yussen, S. R., & Levy, V. M. (1975). Developmental changes in predicting one's own memory span of short-term memory. *Journal of Experimental Child Psychology, 19,* 502–508.

Zivian, M. T., & Darjes, R. W. (1983). Free recall by in-school and out-of-school adults. Performance and metamemory. *Developmental Psychology, 19,* 513–520.

Chapter 9: Mental Abilities

Alpaugh, P. K., & Birren, J. E. (1977). Variables affecting creative contributions across the adult life span. *Human Development, 20,* 240–248.

Baumeister, A. A. (1973). Mental retardation—Social artifact. *Contemporary Psychology, 18,* 342–343.

Bayley, N. (1968). Behavioral correlates of mental growth: Birth to thirty-six years. *American Psychologist, 23,* 1–17.

Bayley, N. (1969). *Bayley Scales of Infant Development.* New York: Psychological Corporation.

Baenninger, M., & Newcombe, N. (1989). The role of experience in spatial test performance: A meta-analysis. *Sex Roles, 20,* 327–344.

Baltes, P. B., Sowarka, D., & Kliegl, R. (1989). Cognitive training research on fluid intelligence in old age: What can older adults achieve by themselves? *Psychology and Aging, 4,* 217–221.

Bee, H. L., Barnard, K. E., Eyres, S. J., Gray, C. A., Hammond, M. A., Spietz, A. L., Snyder, C., & Clark, B. (1982). Prediction of IQ and language skill from perinatal status, child performance, family characteristics, and mother–infant interaction. *Child Development, 53,* 1134–1156.

Belmont, L., & Marolla, F. A. (1973). Birth order, family size, and intelligence. *Science, 182,* 1096–1101.

Berbaum, M. L., & Moreland, R. L. (1980). Intellectual development within the family: A new application of the confluence model. *Developmental Psychology, 16,* 506–518.

Berrueta-Clement, J. R., Schweinhart, L. J., Barnett, S. W., Epstein, A. S., & Weikart, D. P. (1984). *Changed lives: The effects of the Perry Preschool Program on youths through age 19.* Ypsilanti, MI: High/Scope Press.

Bornstein, M. H., & Sigman, M. D. (1986). Continuity in mental development from infancy. *Child Development, 57,* 251–274.

Botwinick, J. (1984). *Aging and behavior. A comprehensive integration of research findings* (3rd ed.). New York: Springer.

Bradley, R. H., & Caldwell, B. M. (1976). Early home environment and changes in mental test performance in children from 6 to 36 months. *Developmental Psychology, 12,* 93–97.

Bradley, R. H., & Caldwell, B. M. (1984). 174 children: A study of the relationship between home environment and cognitive development during the first 5 years. In A. W. Gottfried (Ed.), *Home environment and early cognitive development. Longitudinal research.* Orlando, FL: Academic.

Bradley, R. H., Caldwell, B. M., & Rock, S. L. (1988). Home environment and school performance: A ten-year follow-up and examination of three models of environmental action. *Child Development, 59,* 852–867.

Bradley, R. H., Caldwell, B. M., Rock, S. L., Ramey, C. T., Barnard, K. E., Gray, C., Hammond, M. A., Mitchell, S., Gottfried, A. W., Siegel, L., & Johnson, D. L. (1989). Home environment and cognitive development in the first 3 years of life: A collaborative study involving six sites and three ethnic groups in North America. *Developmental Psychology, 25,* 217–235.

Brody, E. B., & Brody, N. (1976). *Intelligence: Nature, determinants, and consequences.* New York: Academic.

Busse, E. W., & Maddox, G. L. (1985). *The Duke longitudinal studies of normal aging. 1955–1980. Overview of history, design, and findings.* New York: Springer.

Caldwell, B. M., & Bradley, R. H. (1978). *Manual for the Home Observation for Measurement of the Environment.* Little Rock: University of Arkansas at Little Rock.

Cattell, R. B. (1963). Theory of fluid and crystallized intelligence: A critical experiment. *Journal of Educational Psychology, 54,* 1–22.

Cole, N. (1981). Bias in testing. *American Psychologist, 36,* 1067–1077.

Coleman, L. J. (1985). *Schooling the gifted.* Menlo Park, CA: Addison-Wesley.

Cornelius, S. W. (1984). Classic pattern of intellectual aging: Test familiarity, difficulty, and performance. *Journal of Gerontology, 39,* 201–206.

Cox, C. M. (1926). *Genetic studies of genius. Vol. 2: The early mental traits of three hundred geniuses.* Stanford, CA: Stanford University Press.

Crockenberg, S. (1983). Early mother and infant antecedents of Bayley Scale performance at 21 months. *Developmental Psychology, 19,* 727–730.

Cunningham, W. R., & Owens, W. A., Jr. (1983). The Iowa State study of the adult development of intellectual abilities. In K. W. Schaie (Ed.), *Longitudinal studies of adult psychological development.* New York: Guilford.

Demming, J. A., & Pressey, S. L. (1957). Tests "indigenous" to the adult and older years. *Journal of Counseling Psychology, 2,* 144–148.

Dennis, W. (1966). Creative productivity between the ages of 20 and 80 years. *Journal of Gerontology, 21,* 1–8.

Dixon, R. A., Kramer, D. A., & Baltes, P. B. (1985). Intelligence: A life-span developmental perspective. In B. B. Wolman (Ed.), *Handbook of intelligence. Theories, measurements, and applications.* New York: Wiley.

Eichorn, D. H., Hunt, J. V., & Honzik, M. P. (1981). Experience, personality, and IQ: Adolescence to middle age. In D. H. Eichorn, J. A. Clausen, N. Haan, M. P. Honzik, & P. H. Mussen (Eds.), *Present and past in middle life.* New York: Academic.

Escalona, S. (1968). *The roots of individuality: Normal patterns of individuality.* Chicago: Aldine.

Fagan, J. F., III, & McGrath, S. K. (1981). Infant recognition memory and later intelligence. *Intelligence, 5,* 121–130.

Fagan, J. F., III, & Singer, L. T. (1983). Infant recognition memory as a measure of intelligence. In L. P. Lipsitt & C. K. Rovee-Collier (Eds.), *Advances in infancy research* (Vol. 2). Norwood, NJ: Ablex.

Falbo, T., & Polit, D. F. (1986). Quantitative review of the only child literature: Research evidence and theory development. *Psychological Bulletin, 100,* 176–189.

Feldman, D. H. (1980). *Beyond universals in cognitive development.* Norwood, NJ: Ablex.

Feldman, D. H. (1982). A developmental framework for research with gifted children. In D. H. Feldman (Ed.), *New directions for child development: No. 17. Developmental approaches to giftedness and creativity.* San Francisco: Jossey-Bass.

Feldman, D. H. (1986). *Nature's gambit. Child prodigies and the development of human potential.* New York: Basic Books.

Feldman, R. D. (1982). *Whatever happened to the Quiz Kids? Perils and profits of growing up gifted.* Chicago: Chicago Review Press.

Feuerstein, R. (1979). *The dynamic assessment of retarded performers: The learning potential assessment device. Theory, instruments, and techniques.* Baltimore: University Park Press.

Feuerstein, R., Miller, R., Hoffman, M. B., Rand, Y., Mintzker, Y., & Jensen, M. R. (1981). Cognitive modifiability in adolescence: Cognitive structure and the effects of intervention. *Journal of Special Education, 15,* 269–287.

Fincher, J. (1973). The Terman study is 50 years old: Happy anniversary and pass the ammunition. *Human Behavior, 2,* 8–15.

Fisher, M. A., & Zeaman, D. (1970). Growth and decline of retardate intelligence. In N. R. Ellis (Ed.), *International review of research in mental retardation* (Vol. 4). New York: Academic.

Gardner, H. (1983). *Frames of mind: The theory of multiple intelligences.* New York: Basic.

Getzels, J. W., & Jackson, P. W. (1962). *Creativity and intelligence: Explorations with gifted children.* New York: Wiley.

Gottfried, A. W. (1984). Home environment and early cognitive development: Integration, meta-analyses, and conclusions. In A. W. Gottfried (Ed.), *Home environment and early cognitive development. Longitudinal research.* Orlando, FL: Academic.

Gottfried, A. W., & Gottfried, A. E. (1984). Home environment and cognitive development in young children of middle-socioeconomic-status families. In A. W. Gottfried (Ed.), *Home environment and early cognitive development. Longitudinal research.* Orlando, FL: Academic.

Gray, S. W., Ramsey, B. K., & Klaus, R. A. (1982). *From 3 to 20: The early training project.* Baltimore: University Park Press.

Gribbin, K., Schaie, K. W., & Parham, I. A. (1980). Complexity of life style and maintenance of intellectual abilities. *Journal of Social Issues, 36,* 47–61.

Grossman, H. J. (1983). *Classification in mental retardation.* Washington, DC: American Association on Mental Deficiency.

Gruber, H. E. (1982). On the hypothesized relation between giftedness and creativity. In D. H. Feldman (Ed.), *New directions for child development: No. 17. Developmental approaches to giftedness and creativity.* San Francisco: Jossey-Bass.

Guilford, J. P. (1967). *The nature of human intelligence.* New York: McGraw-Hill.

Harrell, T. W., & Harrell, M. S. (1945). Army General Classification Test scores for civilian occupations. *Educational and Psychological Measurement, 5,* 229–239.

Harrington, D. M., Block, J. H., & Block, J. (1983). Predicting creativity in preadolescence from divergent thinking in early childhood. *Journal of Personality and Social Psychology, 45,* 609–623.

Harrington, D. M., Block, J. H., & Block, J. (1987). Testing aspects of Carl Rogers's theory of creative environments: Child-rearing antecedents of creative potential in young adolescents. *Journal of Personality and Social Psychology, 52,* 851–856.

Hayslip, B., Jr. (1989). Alternative mechanisms for improvements in fluid ability performance among older adults. *Psychology and Aging, 4,* 122–124.

Hayslip, B., Jr., Fish, M., & Wilson, R. (1989). The Kendrick Battery: Sensitivity to survival effects. *International Journal of Aging and Human Development, 28,* 227–237.

Hennessey, B. A., & Amabile, T. M. (1988). The conditions of creativity. In R. J. Sternberg (Ed.), *The nature of creativity. Contemporary psychological perspectives.* Cambridge, England: Cambridge University Press.

Hertzog, C. (1989). Influences of cognitive slowing on age differences in intelligence. *Developmental Psychology, 25,* 636–651.

Honzik, M. P. (1983). Measuring mental abilities in infancy. The value and limitations. In M. Lewis (Ed.), *Origins of intelligence: Infancy and early childhood* (2nd ed.). New York: Plenum.

Honzik, M. P., Macfarlane, J. W., & Allen, L. (1948). The stability of mental test performance between two and eighteen years. *Journal of Experimental Education, 17,* 309–324.

Horn, J. L. (1982). The theory of fluid and crystallized intelligence in relation to concepts of cognitive psychology and aging in adulthood. In F. I. M. Craik & S. Trehub (Eds.), *Advances in the study of communication and affect: Vol. 8. Aging and cognitive processes.* New York: Plenum.

Horn, J. L., & Cattell, R. B. (1967). Age differences in fluid and crystallized intelligence. *Acta Psychologica, 26,* 107–129.

Horner, K. L., Rushton, J. P., & Vernon, P. A. (1986). Relation between aging and research productivity of academic psychologists. *Psychology and Aging, 1,* 319–324.

Howieson, N. (1981). A longitudinal study of creativity: 1965–1975. *Journal of Creative Behavior, 15,* 117–134.

Hunt, J. McV., & Paraskevopoulos, J. (1980). Children's psychological development as a function of the inaccuracy of their mothers' knowledge of their abilities. *Journal of Genetic Psychology, 136,* 285–298.

Janos, P. M., & Robinson, N. M. (1985). Psychosocial development in intellectually gifted children. In F. D. Horowitz & M. O'Brien (Eds.), *The gifted and talented: Developmental perspectives.* Washington, DC: American Psychological Association.

Jaquish, G. A., & Ripple, R. E. (1981). Cognitive creative abilities and self-esteem across the adult life-span. *Human Development, 24,* 110–119.

Jarvik, L. F., & Bank, L. (1983). Aging twins: Longitudinal psychometric data. In K. W. Schaie (Ed.), *Longitudinal studies of adult psychological development.* New York: Guilford.

Jayanthi, M., & Rogoff, B. (1985). A cultural perspective on the development of talent. In F. D. Horowitz & M. O'Brien (Eds.), *The gifted and talented. Developmental perspectives.* Washington, DC: American Psychological Association.

Jensen, A. R. (1969). How much can we boost IQ and scholastic achievement? *Harvard Educational Review, 39,* 1–123.

Jensen, A. R. (1977). Cumulative deficit in the IQ of blacks in the rural South. *Developmental Psychology, 13,* 184–191.

Jensen, A. R. (1980). *Bias in mental testing.* New York: Free Press.

Jones, L. V. (1984). White–black achievement differences. The narrowing gap. *American Psychologist, 39,* 1207–1213.

Kail, R. (1988). Developmental functions for speeds of cognitive processes. *Journal of Experimental Child Psychology, 45,* 339–364.

Kaufman, A. S., & Kaufman, N. L. (1983). *Kaufman assessment battery for children: Interpretive manual.* Circle Pines, MN: American Guidance Service.

Kleemeier, R. W. (1962). Intellectual change in the senium. *Proceedings of the Social Statistics Section of the American Statistical Association,* 290–295.

Klineberg, O. (1963). Negro–white differences in intelligence test performance: A new look at an old problem. *American Psychologist, 18,* 198–203.

Kogan, N. (1983). Stylistic variation in childhood and adolescence: Creativity, metaphor, and cognitive styles. In J. H. Flavell & E. H. Markman (Eds.), *Handbook of child psychology: Vol. 3. Cognitive development* (4th ed.). New York: Wiley.

Labouvie-Vief, G. (1985). Intelligence and cognition. In J. E. Birren & K. W. Schaie (Eds.), *Handbook of the psychology of aging* (2nd ed.). New York: Van Nostrand Reinhold.

Lazar, I., & Darlington, R. (1982). Lasting effects of early education: A report from the Consortium for Longitudinal Studies. *Monographs of the Society for Research in Child Development, 47* (2–3, Serial No. 195).

Lehman, H. C. (1953). *Age and achievement.* Princeton, NJ: Princeton University Press.

Levenstein, P. (1970). Cognitive growth in preschoolers through verbal interaction with mothers. *American Journal of Orthopsychiatry, 40,* 426–432.

Lewis, M., & Michalson, L. (1985). The gifted infant. In J. Freeman (Ed.), *The psychology of gifted children. Perspectives on development and education.* Chichester, England: Wiley.

Lewontin, R. C. (1976). Race and intelligence. In N. J. Block & G. Dworkin (Eds.), *The IQ controversy.* New York: Pantheon.

Linn, M. C., & Petersen, A. C. (1985). Emergence and characterization of sex differences in spatial ability: A meta-analysis. *Child Development, 56,* 1479–1498.

Loehlin, J. C., Lindzey, G., & Spuhler, J. N. (1975). *Race differences in intelligence.* San Francisco: W. H. Freeman.

Longstreth, L., Davis, B., Carter, L., Flint, D., Owen, J., Rickert, M., & Taylor, E. (1981). Separation of home intellectual environment and maternal IQ as determinants of child IQ. *Developmental Psychology, 17,* 532–541.

MacPhee, D., Ramey, C. T., & Yeates, K. O. (1984). Home environmental and early cognitive development: Implications for intervention. In A. W. Gottfried (Ed.), *Home environment and early cognitive development. Longitudinal research.* Orlando, FL: Academic.

Manton, K. G., Siegler, I. C., & Woodbury, M. A. (1986). Patterns of intellectual development in later life. *Journal of Gerontology, 41,* 486–499.

Markus, G. B., & Zajonc, R. B. (1977). Family configuration and intellectual development: A simulation. *Behavioral Science, 22,* 137–142.

Marlowe, H. A., Jr. (1986). Social intelligence: Evidence for multidimensionality and construct independence. *Journal of Educational Psychology, 78,* 52–58.

McCall, R. B. (1981). Nature–nurture and the two realms of development: A proposed integration with respect to mental development. *Child Development, 55,* 1–12.

McCall, R. B. (1983). A conceptual approach to early mental development. In M. Lewis (Ed.), *Origins of intelligence: Infancy and early childhood* (2nd ed.). New York: Plenum.

McCall, R. B., Applebaum, M. I., & Hogarty, P. S. (1973). Developmental changes in mental test performance. *Monographs of the Society for Research in Child Development, 38* (3, Serial No. 150).

McCall, R. B., Eichorn, D. H., & Hogarty, P. S. (1977). Transitions in early mental development. *Monographs of the Society for Research in Child Development, 42,* (Serial No. 171).

McCrae, R. R., Arenberg, D., & Costa, P. T., Jr. (1987). Declines in divergent thinking with age: Cross-sectional, longitudinal, and cross-sequential analyses. *Psychology and Aging, 2,* 130–137.

Miller, S. A. (1986). Parents' beliefs about their children's cognitive abilities. *Developmental Psychology, 22,* 276–284.

Minton, H. L., & Schneider, F. W. (1980). *Differential psychology.* Pacific Grove, CA: Brooks/Cole.

Moore, E. G. J. (1986). Family socialization and the IQ test performance of traditionally and transracially adopted black children. *Developmental Psychology, 22,* 317–326.

Mumford, M. D., & Gustafson, S. B. (1988). Creativity syndrome: Integration, application, and innovation. *Psychological Bulletin, 103,* 27–43.

Newcombe, N., & Bandura, M. M. (1983). Effect of age at puberty on spatial ability in girls: A question of mechanism. *Developmental Psychology, 19,* 215–224.

Newcombe, N., Dubas, J. S., & Baenninger, M. (1989). Associations of timing of puberty, spatial ability, and lateralization in adult women. *Child Development, 60,* 246–254.

Oakland, T., & Parmelee, R. (1985). Mental measurement of minority-group children. In B. B. Wolman (Ed.), *Handbook of intelligence. Theories, measurements, and applications.* New York: Wiley.

Over, R. (1989). Age and scholarly impact. *Psychology and Aging, 4,* 222–225.

Owens, W. A., Jr. (1953). Age and mental abilities: A longitudinal study. *Genetic Psychology Monographs, 48,* 3–54.

Piaget, J. (1950). *The psychology of intelligence.* New York: Harcourt Brace & World.

Plomin, R., & DeFries, J. C. (1980). Genetics and intelligence: Recent data. *Intelligence, 4,* 15–24.

Popkin, S. J., Schaie, K. W., & Krauss, I. K. (1983). Age-fair assessment of psychometric intelligence. *Educational Gerontology, 9,* 47–55.

Quay, L. C. (1971). Language dialect, reinforcement, and the intelligence-test performance of Negro children. *Child Development, 42,* 5–15.

Ramey, C. T., & Haskins, R. (1981). The modification of intelligence through early experience. *Intelligence, 5,* 5–19.

Reynolds, C. R., & Kaufman, A. S. (1985). Clinical assessment of children's intelligence with the Wechsler Scales. In B. B. Wolman (Ed.), *Handbook of intelligence. Theories, measurements, and applications.* New York: Wiley.

Richards, J. M., Jr., Holland, J. L., & Lutz, S. W. (1967). Prediction of student accomplishment in college. *Journal of Educational Psychology, 58,* 343–355.

Robinson, N. M., & Janos, P. M. (1986). Psychological adjustment in a college-level program of marked academic acceleration. *Journal of Youth and Adolescence, 15,* 51–60.

Robinson, N. M., & Robinson, H. B. (1982). The optimal match: Devising the best compromise for the highly gifted student. In D. H. Feldman (Ed.), *Developmental approaches to giftedness and creativity* (New Directions for Child Development, No. 17). San Francisco: Jossey-Bass.

Rose, S. A., Feldman, J. F., Wallace, I. F., & McCarton, C. (1989). Infant visual attention: Relation to birth status and developmental outcome during the first 5 years. *Developmental Psychology, 25,* 560–576.

Ross, R. T., Begab, M. J., Dondis, E. H., Giampiccolo, J. S., Jr., & Meyers, C. E. (1985). *Lives of the mentally retarded. A forty-year follow-up study.* Stanford, CA: Stanford University Press.

Rothbart, M. K. (1971). Birth order and mother–child interaction in an achievement situation. *Journal of Personality and Social Psychology, 17,* 113–120.

Sacks, E. L. (1952). Intelligence scores as a function of experimentally established social relationships between child and examiner. *Journal of Abnormal and Social Psychology, 47,* 354–358.

Sanders, B., & Soares, M. P. (1986). Sexual maturation and spatial ability in college students. *Developmental Psychology, 22,* 199–203.

Scarr, S., & Weinberg, R. A. (1976). IQ test performance of black children adopted by white families. *American Psychologist, 31,* 726–739.

Scarr, S., & Weinberg, R. A. (1977). Intellectual similarities within families of both adopted and biological children. *Intelligence, 32,* 170–191.

Scarr, S., & Weinberg, R. A. (1983). The Minnesota adoption studies: Genetic differences and malleability. *Child Development, 54,* 260–267.

Schaie, K. W. (1983). The Seattle longitudinal study: A 21-year exploration of psychometric intelligence in adulthood. In K. W. Schaie (Ed.), *Longitudinal studies of adult psychological development.* New York: Guilford.

Schaie, K. W. (1984). Midlife influences upon intellectual functioning in old age. *International Journal of Behavioral Development, 7,* 463–478.

Schaie, K. W., & Hertzog, C. (1983). Fourteen-year cohort-sequential analyses of adult intellectual development. *Developmental Psychology, 19,* 531–543.

Schaie, K. W., & Hertzog, C. (1986). Toward a comprehensive model of adult intellectual development: Contributions of the Seattle longitudinal study. In R. J. Sternberg (Ed.), *Advances in the psychology of human intelligence* (Vol. 3). Hillsdale, NJ: Erlbaum.

Schaie, K. W., & Willis, S. L. (1986). *Adult development and aging* (2nd ed.). Boston: Little, Brown.

Schaie, K. W., & Willis, S. L. (1986). Can decline in adult intellectual functioning be reversed? *Developmental Psychology, 22,* 223–232.

Shepard, R. N., & Metzler, J. (1971). Mental rotation of three-dimensional objects. *Science, 171,* 701–703.

Siegler, I. C. (1983). Psychological aspects of the Duke longitudinal studies. In K. W. Schaie (Ed.), *Longitudinal studies of adult psychological development.* New York: Guilford.

Siegler, I. C., & Costa, P. T., Jr. (1985). Health behavior relationships. In J. E. Birren & K. W. Schaie (Eds.), *Handbook of the psychology of aging* (2nd ed.). New York: Van Nostrand Reinhold.

Signorella, M. L., Jamison, W., & Krupa, M. H. (1989). Predicting spatial performance from gender stereotyping in activity preferences and in self-concept. *Developmental Psychology, 25,* 89–95.

Simonton, D. K. (1975). Age and literary creativity: A cross-cultural and transhistorical survey. *Journal of Cross-Cultural Psychology, 6,* 259–277.

Simonton, D. K. (1984). *Genius, creativity, and leadership. Historiometric inquiries.* Cambridge, MA: Harvard University Press.

Simonton, D. K. (1985). Quality, quantity, and age: The careers of ten distinguished psychologists. *International Journal of Aging and Human Development, 21,* 241–255.

Simonton, D. K. (1989). Age and creative productivity: Nonlinear estimation of an information-processing model. *International Journal of Aging and Human Development, 29,* 23–37.

Skodak, M., & Skeels, H. M. (1949). A final follow-up study of children in adoptive homes. *Journal of Genetic Psychology, 75,* 85–125.

Smith, G., & Carlsson, I. (1985). Creativity in middle and late school years. *International Journal of Behavioral Development, 8,* 329–343.

Spearman, C. (1927). *The abilities of man.* New York: Macmillan.

Sternberg, R. J. (1985). *Beyond IQ: A triarchic theory of human intelligence.* Cambridge, MA: Cambridge University Press.

Sternberg, R. J., & Berg, C. A. (1986). Quantitative integration: Definitions of intelligence: A comparison of the 1921 and 1986 symposia. In R. J. Sternberg, & D. K. Detterman (Eds.), *What is intelligence? Contemporary viewpoints on its nature and definition.* Norwood, NJ: Ablex.

Sternberg, R. J., Conway, B. E., Ketron, J. L., & Bernstein, M. (1981). People's conceptions of intelligence. *Journal of Personality and Social Psychology, 41,* 37–55.

Terman, L. M. (1954). The discovery and encouragement of exceptional talent. *American Psychologist, 9,* 221–238.

Terman, L. M., & Merrill, M. A. (1972). *Stanford-Binet Intelligence Scale—Manual for the Third Revision.* Boston: Houghton Mifflin.

Terman, L. M., & Oden, M. H. (1959). *The gifted group at mid-life.* Stanford, CA: Stanford University Press.

Thorndike, R. L., Hagen, E. P., & Sattler, J. M. (1986). *The Stanford-Binet Intelligence Scale* (4th ed.). Chicago: Riverside Publishing.

Thurstone, L. L. (1938). *Primary mental abilities.* Chicago: University of Chicago Press.

Thurstone, L. L., & Thurstone, T. G. (1941). Factorial studies of intelligence. *Psychometric Monographs,* No. 2.

Torrance, E. P. (1975). Creativity research in education: Still alive. In I. A. Taylor & J. W. Getzels (Eds.), *Perspectives in creativity.* Chicago: Aldine-Atherton.

Torrance, E. P. (1988). The nature of creativity as manifest in its testing. In R. J. Sternberg (Ed.), *The nature of creativity. Contemporary psychological perspectives.* Cambridge, England: Cambridge University Press.

Waber, D. P. (1977). Sex differences in mental abilities, hemispheric lateralization, and rate of physical growth at adolescence. *Developmental Psychology, 13,* 29–38.

Waddell, K. J., & Rogoff, B. (1981). Effect of contextual organization on spatial memory of middle-aged and older women. *Developmental Psychology, 17,* 878–885.

Wallace, A. (1986). *The prodigy. A biography of William Sidis.* New York: Dutton.

Wallach, M. A. (1971). *The intelligence–creativity distinction.* Morristown, NJ: General Learning Press.

Wallach, M. A. (1985). Creativity testing and giftedness. In F. D. Horowitz & M. O'Brien (Eds.), *The gifted and talented. Developmental perspectives.* Washington, DC: American Psychological Association.

Wallach, M. A., & Kogan, N. (1965). *Thinking in young children.* New York: Holt, Rinehart & Winston.

Wechsler, D. (1967). *Wechsler Preschool and Primary Scale of Intelligence.* New York: Psychological Corporation.

Wechsler, D. (1974). *Wechsler Intelligence Scale for Children—Revised.* New York: Psychological Corporation.

Wechsler, D. (1981). *Wechsler Adult Intelligence Scale—Revised.* New York: Psychological Corporation.

Westling, D. L. (1986). *Introduction to mental retardation.* Englewood Cliffs, NJ: Prentice-Hall.

White, K. R. (1985–1986). Efficacy of early intervention. *Journal of Special Education, 19,* 401–416.

Willis, S. L. (1985). Towards an educational psychology of the older adult learner: Intellectual and cognitive bases. In J. E. Birren & K. W. Schaie (Eds.), *Handbook of the psychology of aging.* New York: Van Nostrand Reinhold.

Yeates, K. O., MacPhee, D., Campbell, F. A., & Ramey, C. T. (1983). Maternal IQ and home environment as determinants of early childhood intellectual competence: A developmental analysis. *Developmental Psychology, 19,* 731–739.

Yerkes, R. M. (1921). Psychological examining in the U.S. Army. *Memoirs: National Academy of Science, 15,* 1–890.

Zajonc, R. B., & Markus, G. B. (1975). Birth order and intellectual development. *Psychological Review, 82,* 74–88.

Zigler, E., Abelson, W. D., Trickett, P. K., & Seitz, V. (1982). Is an intervention program necessary to improve economically disadvantaged children's IQ scores? *Child Development, 53,* 340–348.

Chapter 10: Self-Conceptions, Personality, and Emotional Expression

Adams, G. R., & Fitch, S. A. (1982). Ego stage and identity status development: A cross-sequential analysis. *Journal of Personality and Social Psychology, 43,* 574–583.

Archer, S. L. (1982). The lower age boundaries of identity development. *Child Development, 53,* 1551–1556.

Bandura, A. (1982). The psychology of chance encounters and life paths. *American Psychologist, 37,* 747–755.

Belsky, J. K. (1990). *The psychology of aging.* Pacific Grove, CA: Brooks/Cole.

Bengtson, V. L., Reedy, M. N., & Gordon, C. (1985). Aging and self-conceptions: Personality processes and social contexts. In J. E. Birren & K. W. Schaie (Eds.), *Handbook of the psychology of aging* (2nd ed.). New York: Van Nostrand Reinhold.

Bernstein, R. M. (1980). The development of the self-system during adolescence. *Journal of Genetic Psychology, 136,* 231–245.

Berthenthal, B. I., & Fischer, K. W. (1978). Development of self-recognition in the infant. *Developmental Psychology, 14,* 44–50.

Bilsker, D., Schiedel, D., & Marcia, J. (1988). Sex differences in identity status. *Sex Roles, 18,* 231–236.

Block, J. (1981). Some enduring and consequential structures of personality. In A. I. Rabin, J. Aronoff, A. M. Barclay, & R. A. Zucker (Eds.), *Further explorations in personality.* New York: Wiley.

Block, J. H. (1971). *Lives through time.* Berkeley, CA: Bancroft Books.

Boylin, W., Gordon, S. K., & Nehrke, M. F. (1976). Reminiscing and ego integrity in institutionalized elderly males. *The Gerontologist, 16,* 118–124.

Breytspraak, L. M. (1984). *The development of self in later life.* Boston: Little, Brown.

Brooks-Gunn, J., & Lewis, M. (1981). Infant social perception: Responses to pictures of parents and strangers. *Developmental Psychology, 17,* 647–649.

Buss, A. H., & Plomin, R. (1984). *Temperament: Early developing personality traits.* Hillsdale, NJ: Erlbaum.

Butler, R. N. (1963). The life review: An interpretation of reminiscence in the aged. *Psychiatry, 26,* 65–76.

Butler, R. N. (1975). *Why survive? Being old in America.* New York: Harper & Row.

Campbell, E., Adams, G. R., & Dobson, W. R. (1984). Familial correlates of identity formation in late adolescence: A study of the predictive utility of connectedness and individuality in family relations. *Journal of Youth and Adolescence, 13,* 509–525.

Chess, S., & Thomas, A. (1984). *Origins and evolution of behavior disorders: From infancy to early adult life.* New York: Brunner/Mazel.

Cole, P. M. (1985). Display rules and the socialization of affective displays. In G. Zivin (Ed.), *The development of expressive behavior. Biology-environment interactions.* Orlando, FL: Academic.

Conley, J. J. (1985). Longitudinal stability of personality traits: A multitrait-multimethod-multioccasion analysis. *Journal of Personality and Social Psychology, 49,* 1266–1282.

Cooley, C. H. (1902). *Human nature and the social order.* New York: Scribner's.

Coopersmith, S. (1967). *The antecedents of self-esteem.* San Francisco: W. H. Freeman.

Costa, P. T., Jr., & McCrae, R. R. (1988). Personality in adulthood: A six-year longitudinal study of self-reports and spouse ratings on the NEO Personality Inventory. *Journal of Personality and Social Psychology, 54,* 853–863.

Costa, P. T., Jr., McCrae, R. R., & Arenberg, D. (1980). Enduring dispositions in adult males. *Journal of Personality and Social Psychology, 38,* 793–800.

Costa, P. T., Jr., McCrae, R. R., & Arenberg, D. (1983). Recent longitudinal research on personality and aging. In K. W. Schaie (Ed.), *Longitudinal studies of adult psychological development.* New York: Guilford.

Costa, P. T., Jr., McCrae, R. R., Zonderman, A. B., Barbano, H. E., Lebowitz, B., &

Larson, D. M. (1986). Cross-sectional studies of personality in a national sample: 2. Stability in neuroticism, extraversion, and openness. *Psychology and Aging, 1,* 144–149.

Cote, J. E., & Levine, C. (1988). A critical examination of the ego identity status paradigm. *Developmental Review, 8,* 147–184.

Damon, W., & Hart, D. (1982). The development of self-understanding from infancy through adolescence. *Child Development, 53,* 841–864.

Denham, S. A. (1989). Maternal affect and toddlers' social-emotional competence. *American Journal of Orthopsychiatry, 59,* 368–376.

Douglas, K., & Arenberg, D. (1978). Age changes, cohort differences, and cultural change on the Guilford-Zimmerman Temperament Survey. *Journal of Gerontology, 33,* 737–747.

Dusek, J., & Flaherty, J. (1981). The development of the self-concept during the adolescent years. *Monographs of the Society for Research in Child Development, 46* (4, Serial No. 191).

Dweck, C. S., & Elliott, E. S. (1983). Achievement motivation. In E. M. Hetherington (Vol. Ed.; P. H. Mussen, General Ed.), *Handbook of child psychology: Vol. 4. Socialization, personality, and social development* (4th ed.). New York: Wiley.

Erikson, E. H. (1963). *Childhood and society* (2nd ed.). New York: Norton.

Erikson, E. H. (1968). *Identity. Youth and crisis.* New York: Norton.

Erikson, E. H. (1982). *The life cycle completed: A review.* New York: Norton.

Finn, S. E. (1986). Stability of personality self-ratings over 30 years: Evidence for an age/cohort interaction. *Journal of Personality and Social Psychology, 50,* 813–818.

Frey, K. S., & Ruble, D. N. (1985). What children say when the teacher is not around: Conflicting goals in social comparison and performance assessment in the classroom. *Journal of Personality and Social Psychology, 48,* 550–562.

Gallup, G. G., Jr. (1979). Self-recognition in chimpanzees and man: A developmental and comparative perspective. In M. Lewis & L. A. Rosenblum (Eds.), *Genesis of behavior: Vol. 2. The child and its family.* New York: Plenum.

Gambria, L. M. (1979–1980). Sex differences in daydreaming and related mental activity from the late teens to the early nineties. *International Journal of Aging and Human Development, 10,* 1–34.

George, L. K., & Okun, M. A. (1985). Self-concept content. In E. Palmore, E. W. Busse, G. L. Maddox, J. B. Nowlin, & I. C. Siegler (Eds.), *Normal aging III.* Durham, NC: Duke University Press.

Glick, M., & Zigler, E. (1985). Self-image: A cognitive-developmental approach. In R. L. Leahy (Ed.), *The development of the self.* Orlando, FL: Academic.

Goldsmith, H. H., Buss, A. H., Plomin, R., Rothbart, M. K., Thomas, A., Chess, S., Hinde, R. A., & McCall, R. B. (1987). Roundtable: What is temperament? Four approaches. *Child Development, 58,* 505–529.

Grotevant, H. D., & Cooper, C. R. (1986). Individuation in family relations. A perspective on individual differences in the development of identity and role-taking skills in adolescence. *Human Development, 29,* 82–100.

Haan, N. (1981). Common dimensions of personality development: Early adolescence to middle life. In D. H. Eichorn, J. A. Clausen, N. Haan, M. P. Honzik, & P. H. Mussen (Eds.), *Present and past in middle life.* New York: Academic.

Haight, B. K. (1988). The therapeutic role of a structured life review process in homebound elderly subjects. *Journal of Gerontology: Psychological Sciences, 43,* P40–P44.

Halberstadt, A. G. (1984). Family expression of emotion. In C. Z. Malatesta & C. E. Izard (Eds.), *Emotion in adult development.* Beverly Hills, CA: Sage.

Harris, P. L., Olthof, T., & Terwogt, M. M. (1981). Children's knowledge of emotion. *Journal of Child Psychology and Psychiatry, 22,* 247–261.

Harter, S. (1982a). A cognitive-developmental approach to children's understanding of affect and trait labels. In F. C. Serafica (Ed.), *Social-cognitive development in context.* New York: Guilford.

Harter, S. (1982b). The perceived competence scale for children. *Child Development, 53,* 87–97.

Harter, S. (1983). Developmental perspectives on the self-system. In E. M. Hetherington (Vol. Ed; P. H. Mussen, General Ed.), *Handbook of child psychology: Vol. 4. Socialization, personality, and social development* (4th ed.). New York: Wiley.

Harter, S. (1986). Cognitive-developmental processes in the integration of concepts about emotions and the self. *Social Cognition, 4,* 119–151.

Harter, S., & Pike, R. (1984). The pictorial scale of perceived competence and social acceptance for young children. *Child Development, 55,* 1969–1982.

Hill, S. D., & Tomlin, C. (1981). Self-recognition in retarded children. *Child Development, 52,* 145–150.

Isberg, R. S., Hauser, S. T., Jacobson, A. M., Powers, S. I., Noam, G., Weiss-Perry, B., & Follansbee, D. (1989). Parental contexts of adolescent self-esteem: A developmental perspective. *Journal of Youth and Adolescence, 18,* 1–23.

Izard, C. E. (1982). *Measuring emotions in infants and children.* New York: Cambridge University Press.

Johnson, W., Emde, R. N., Pannabecker, B., Stenberg, C., & Davis, M. (1982). Maternal perception of infant emotion from birth through 18 months. *Infant Behavior and Development, 5,* 313–322.

Kagan, J. (1983). Developmental categories and the premise of connectivity. In R. M. Lerner (Ed.), *Developmental psychology. Historical and philosophical perspectives.* Hillsdale, NJ: Erlbaum.

Kagan, J. (1989). Temperamental contributions to social behavior. *American Psychologist, 44,* 668–674.

Kagan, J., & Moss, H. A. (1962). *Birth to maturity.* New York: Wiley.

Kahn, S., Zimmerman, G., Csikszentmihalyi, M., & Getzels, J. M. (1985). Relations between identity in young adulthood and intimacy at midlife. *Journal of Personality and Social Psychology, 49,* 1316–1322.

Keller, A., Ford, L. H., Jr., & Meachum, J. A. (1978). Dimensions of self-concept in preschool children. *Developmental Psychology, 14,* 483–489.

Kroger, J. (1988). A longitudinal study of ego identity status interview domains. *Journal of Adolescence, 11,* 49–64.

Kagan, J., Reznick, J. S., Snidman, N., Gibbons, J., & Johnson, M. O. (1988). Childhood derivatives of inhibition and lack of inhibition to the unfamiliar. *Child Development, 59,* 1580–1589.

Leon, G. R., Gillum, B., Gillum, R., & Gouze, M. (1979). Personality stability and change over a 30-year period—middle age to old age. *Journal of Consulting and Clinical Psychology, 47,* 517–524.

Lerner, J. V., & Lerner, R. M. (1983). Temperament and adaptation across life: Theoretical and empirical issues. In P. B. Baltes & O. G. Brim, Jr. (Eds.), *Life-span development and behavior* (Vol. 5). New York: Academic.

Lewis, M., & Brooks-Gunn, J. (1979). *Social cognition and the acquisition of self.* New York: Plenum.

Lewis, M., & Michalson, L. (1983). *Children's emotions and moods: Developmental theory and measurement.* New York: Plenum.

Lewis, M., Stanger, C., & Sullivan, M. W. (1989). Deception in 3-year-olds. *Developmental Psychology, 25,* 439–443.

Lewis, M., Sullivan, M. W., Stanger, C., & Weiss, M. (1989). Self-development and self-conscious emotions. *Child Development, 60,* 146–156.

Livesley, W. J., & Bromley, D. B. (1973). *Person perception in childhood and adolescence.* London: Wiley.

Livson, F. B. (1976). Patterns of personality in middle-aged women: A longitudinal study. *International Journal of Aging and Human Development, 7,* 107–115.

Livson, F. B. (1981). Paths to psychological health in the middle years: Sex differences. In D. H. Eichorn, J. A. Clausen, N. Haan, M. P. Honzik, & P. H. Mussen (Eds.), *Present and past in middle life.* New York: Academic.

Mahler, M. S., Pine, F., & Bergman, A. (1975). *The psychological birth of the infant.* New York: Basic Books.

Malatesta, C. Z. (1981). Affective development over the lifespan: Involution or growth? *Merrill-Palmer Quarterly, 27,* 145–173.

Malestesta, C. Z., Grigoryev, P., Lamb, C., Albin, M., & Culver, C. (1986). Emotional socialization and expressive development in preterm and full-term infants. *Child Development, 57,* 316–330.

Malatesta, C. Z., & Haviland, J. M. (1982). Learning display rules: The socialization of emotion expression in infancy. *Child Development, 53,* 991–1003.

Malatesta, C. Z., & Izard, C. E. (1984). The facial expression of emotion. Young, middle-aged, and older adult expressions. In C. Z. Malatesta & C. E. Izard (Eds.), *Emotion in adult development.* Beverly Hills, CA: Sage.

Malatesta, C. Z., Izard, C. E., Culver, C., & Nicolich, M. (1987). Emotion communication skills in young, middle-aged, and older women. *Psychology and Aging, 2,* 193–203.

Malatesta, C. Z., & Kalnok, M. (1984). Emotional experience in younger and older adults. *Journal of Gerontology, 39,* 301–308.

Marcia, J. E. (1966). Development and validation of ego identity status. *Journal of Personality and Social Psychology, 3,* 551–558.

Marsh, H. W. (1989). Age and sex effects in multiple dimensions of self-concept: Preadolescence to early adulthood. *Journal of Educational Psychology, 81,* 417–430.

McCarthy, J. D., & Hoge, D. R. (1982). Analysis of age effects in longitudinal studies of adolescent self-esteem. *Developmental Psychology, 18,* 372–379.

McCrae, R. R., & Costa, P. T., Jr. (1984). *Emerging lives, enduring dispositions. Personality in adulthood.* Boston: Little, Brown.

McGuire, W. J., McGuire, C. V., Child, P., & Fujioka, T. (1978). Salience of ethnicity in the spontaneous self-concept as a function of one's ethnic distinctiveness in the social environment. *Journal of Personality and Social Psychology, 36,* 511–520.

Mead, G. H. (1934). *Mind, self, and society.* Chicago: University of Chicago Press.

Meilman, P. W. (1979). Cross-sectional age changes in ego identity status during adolescence. *Developmental Psychology, 15,* 230–231.

Michalson, L., & Lewis, M. (1985). What do children know about emotions and when do they know it? In M. Lewis & C. Saarni (Eds.), *The socialization of emotions.* New York: Plenum.

Molinari, V., & Reichlin, R. E. (1984–1985). Life review reminiscence in the elderly: A review of the literature. *International Journal of Aging and Human Development, 20,* 81–92.

Montemayor, R., & Eisen, M. (1977). The development of self-conceptions from childhood to adolescence. *Developmental Psychology, 13,* 314–319.

Mortimer, J. T., Finch, M. D., & Kumka, D. (1982). Persistence and change in development: The multidimensional self-concept. In P. B. Baltes & O. G. Brim, Jr. (Eds.), *Life-span development and behavior* (Vol. 4). New York: Academic.

Moss, H. A., & Susman, E. J. (1980). Longitudinal study of personality development. In O. G. Brim, Jr., & J. Kagan (Eds.), *Constancy and change in human development.* Cambridge, MA: Harvard University Press.

Munro, G., & Adams, G. R. (1977). Ego-identity formation in college students and working youth. *Development Psychology, 13,* 523–524.

Mussen, P., Eichorn, D. H., Honzik, M. P., Bieber, S. L., & Meredith, W. M. (1980). Continuity and change in women's characteristics over four decades. *International Journal of Behavioral Development, 3,* 333–347.

Nelson, C. A. (1987). The recognition of facial expressions in the first two years of life: Mechanisms of development. *Child Development, 58,* 889–909.

Neugarten, B. L. (1977). Personality and aging. In J. E. Birren & K. W. Schaie (Eds.), *Handbook of the psychology of aging.* New York: Van Nostrand Reinhold.

Neugarten, B. L., & Gutman, D. L. (1958). Age-sex roles and personality in middle age: A thematic apperception study. *Psychological Monographs: General and Applied, 17* (Whole No. 470).

Ochse, R., & Plug, C. (1986). Cross-cultural investigation of the validity of Erikson's theory of personality development. *Journal of Personality and Social Psychology, 50,* 1240–1252.

Offer, D., Ostrov, E., & Howard, K. I. (1984). The self-image of normal adolescents. In D. Offer, E. Ostrov, & K. I. Howard (Eds.), *Patterns of adolescent self-image* (New Directions for Mental Health Services, No. 22). San Francisco: Jossey-Bass.

O'Malley, P. M., & Bachman, J. G. (1983). Self-esteem: Change and stability between ages 13 and 23. *Developmental Psychology, 19,* 257–268.

Orlofsky, J. L., Marcia, J. E., & Lesser, I. M. (1973). Ego identity status and the intimacy versus isolation crisis of young adulthood. *Journal of Personality and Social Psychology, 27,* 211–219.

Raskin, P. M. (1986). The relationship between identity and intimacy in early adulthood. *Journal of Genetic Psychology, 147,* 167–181.

Reznick, J. S., Kagan, J., Snidman, N., Gersten, M., Baak, K., & Rosenberg, A. (1986). Inhibited and uninhibited children: A follow-up study. *Child Development, 57,* 660–680.

Rodin, J., & Langer, E. (1980). Aging labels: The decline of control and the fall of self-esteem. *Journal of Social Issues, 36* (2), 12–29.

Rosenholtz, S. J. (1977). The multiple abilities curriculum: An intervention against the self-fulfilling prophecy. Unpublished doctoral dissertation, Stanford University, Stanford, CA.

Rosenholtz, S. J. (1985). Modifying status expectations in the traditional classroom. In J. Berger & M. Zelditch, Jr. (Eds.), *Status, rewards, and influence.* San Francisco: Jossey-Bass.

Ruble, D. N. (1983). The development of comparison processes and their role in achievement-related self-socialization. In E. T. Higgins, D. N. Ruble, & W. W. Hartup (Eds.), *Social cognition and social development: A sociocultural perspective.* New York: Cambridge University Press.

Ryff, C. D., & Heincke, S. G. (1983). Subjective organization of personality in adulthood and aging. *Journal of Personality and Social Psychology, 44,* 807–816.

Saarni, C. (1984). An observational study of children's attempts to monitor their expressive behavior. *Child Development, 55,* 1504–1513.

Savin-Williams, R. C., & Demo, D. H. (1984). Developmental change and stability in adolescent self-concept. *Developmental Psychology, 20,* 1100–1110.

Schaie, K. W., & Parham, I. A. (1976). Stability of adult personality traits: Fact or fable? *Journal of Personality and Social Psychology, 34,* 146–158.

Secord, P. F., & Peevers, B. H. (1974). The development and attribution of person concepts. In T. Mischel (Ed.), *Understanding other persons.* Totowa, NJ: Rowman & Littlefield.

Selman, R. L. (1980). *The growth of interpersonal understanding.* New York: Academic.

Simmons, R. G., Blyth, D. A., Van Cleave, E. F., & Bush, D. M. (1979). Entry into adolescence: The impact of school structure, puberty, and early dating on self-esteem. *American Sociological Review, 44,* 948–967.

Simmons, R. G., Rosenberg, F., & Rosenberg, M. (1973). Disturbance in self-image at adolescence. *American Sociological Review, 38,* 553–568.

Slugoski, B. R., Marcia, J. E., & Koopman, R. F. (1984). Cognitive and social interactional characteristics of ego identity statuses in college males. *Journal of Personality and Social Psychology, 47,* 646–661.

Stern, D. N. (1983). The early development of schemas of self, other, and "self with other." in J. D. Lictenberg & S. Kaplan (Eds.), *Reflections on self psychology.* Hillsdale, NJ: Erlbaum.

Stevens, D. P., & Truss, C. V. (1985). Stability and change in adult personality over 12 and 20 years. *Developmental Psychology, 21,* 568–584.

Stipek, D. J. (1983). A developmental analysis of pride and shame. *Human Development, 26,* 42–54.

Tesch, S. A. (1985). Psychosocial development and subjective well-being in an age cross-section of adults. *International Journal of Aging and Human Development, 21,* 109–120.

Thomas, A., & Chess, S. (1977). *Temperament and development.* New York: Brunner/Mazel.

Thomas, A., & Chess, S. (1986). The New York longitudinal study: From infancy to early adult life. In R. Plomin & J. Dunn (Eds.), *The study of temperament: Changes, continuities, and challenges.* Hillsdale, NJ: Erlbaum.

Thomas, A., Chess, S., & Birch, H. G. (1970). The origin of personality. *Scientific American, 223,* 102–109.

Vaillant, G. E. (1977). *Adaptation to life.* Boston: Little, Brown.

Vaillant, G. E. (1983). Childhood environment and maturity of defense mechanisms. In D. Magnusson & V. L. Allen (Eds.), *Human development. An interactional perspective.* New York: Academic.

Vaillant, G. E., & Milofsky, E. (1980). Natural history of male psychological health. IX: Empirical evidence for Erikson's model of the life cycle. *American Journal of Psychiatry, 137,* 1348–1359.

Veroff, J., Douvan, E., & Kulka, R. A. (1981). *The inner American. A self-portrait from 1957 to 1976.* New York: Basic Books.

Ward, R. A. (1977). The impact of subjective age and stigma on older persons. *Journal of Gerontology, 32,* 227–232.

Waterman, A. S. (1982). Identity development from adolescence to adulthood: An extension of theory and a review of research. *Developmental Psychology, 18,* 341–358.

Waterman, A. S. (1984). *The psychology of individualism.* New York: Praeger.

Waterman, A. S. (1988). Identity status theory and Erikson's theory: Communalities and differences. *Developmental Review, 8,* 185–208.

Wells, L. E., & Stryker, S. (1988). Stability and change in the self over the life course. In P. B. Baltes, D. L. Featherman, & R. M. Lerner (Eds.), *Life-span development and behavior* (Vol. 8). Hillsdale, NJ: Erlbaum.

Whitbourne, S. K. (1986). *The me I know: A study of adult identity.* New York: Springer-Verlag.

Whitbourne, S. K., & Tesch, S. A. (1985). A comparison of identity and intimacy statuses in college students and alumni. *Developmental Psychology, 21,* 1039–1044.

Whitbourne, S. K., & Waterman, A. S. (1979). Psychosocial development during the adult years: Age and cohort comparisons. *Developmental Psychology, 15,* 373–378.

Woodruff, D. S., & Birren, J. E. (1972). Age changes and cohort differences in personality. *Developmental Psychology, 6,* 252–259.

Wrightsman, L. S. (1988). *Personality development in adulthood.* Newbury Park, CA: Sage.

Chapter 11: Gender Roles and Sexuality

Abrahams, B., Feldman, S. S., & Nash, S. C. (1978). Sex role self-concept and sex role attitudes: Enduring personality characteristics or adaptations to changing life situations? *Developmental Psychology, 14,* 393–400.

Alpert, D., & Breen, D. T. (1989). "Liberality" in children and adolescents. *Journal of Vocational Behavior, 34*, 154–160.

Atkinson, J., & Huston, T. L. (1984). Sex role orientation and division of labor early in marriage. *Journal of Personality and Social Psychology, 46*, 330–345.

Bakwin, H. (1973). Erotic feelings in infants and young children. *American Journal of Diseases of Children, 126*, 52–54.

Bandura, A. (1977). *Social learning theory*. Englewood Cliffs, NJ: Prentice-Hall.

Barry, H., III., Bacon, M. K., & Child, I. L. (1957). A cross-cultural survey of some sex differences in socialization. *Journal of Abnormal and Social Psychology, 55*, 327–332.

Baruch, G. K., & Barnett, R. C. (1986). Father's participation in family work and children's sex-role attitudes. *Child Development, 57*, 1210–1223.

Baumrind, D. (1982). Are androgynous individuals more effective persons and parents? *Child Development, 53*, 44–75.

Beach, F. A. (1965). *Sex and behavior*. New York: Wiley.

Bell, R. Q., Weller, G. M., & Waldrip, M. F. (1971). Newborn and preschooler: Organization of behavior and relations between periods. *Monographs of the Society for Research in Child Development, 36* (1–2, Serial No. 142).

Bem., S. L. (1974). The measurement of psychological androgyny. *Journal of Consulting and Clinical Psychology, 42*, 155–162.

Bem, S. L. (1975). Sex-role adaptability: One consequence of psychological androgyny. *Journal of Personality and Social Psychology, 31*, 634–643.

Bem, S. L. (1978). Beyond androgyny: Some presumptuous prescriptions for a liberated sexual identity. In J. A. Sherman & F. L. Denmark (Eds.), *The psychology of women: Future directions in research*. New York: Psychological Dimensions.

Bem, S. L. (1979). Theory and measurement of androgyny: A reply to the Podhazer-Tetenbaum and Locksley-Colten critiques. *Journal of Personality and Social Psychology, 37*, 1047–1054.

Bem, S. L. (1989). Genital knowledge and gender constancy in preschool children. *Child Development, 60*, 649–662.

Bernstein, A. C., & Cowan, P. A. (1975). Children's concepts of how people get babies. *Child Development, 46*, 77–91.

Best, D. L., Williams, J. E., Cloud, J. M., Davis, S. W., Robertson, L. S., Edwards, J. R., Giles, H., & Fowles, J. (1977). Development of sex-trait stereotypes among young children in the United States, England, and Ireland. *Child Development, 48*, 1375–1384.

Bilsker, D., Schiedel, D., & Marcia, J. (1988). Sex differences in identity status. *Sex Roles, 18*, 231–236.

Blakemore, J. E. O., LaRue, A. A., & Olejnik, A. B. (1979). Sex-appropriate toy preference and the ability to conceptualize toys as sex-role related. *Developmental Psychology, 15*, 339–340.

Block, J. H. (1976). Issues, problems, and pitfalls in assessing sex differences: A critical review of *The psychology of sex differences. Merrill-Palmer Quarterly, 22*, 283–308.

Bradbard, M. R., Martin, C. L., Endsley, R. C., & Halverson, C. F. (1986). Influence of sex stereotypes on children's exploration and memory: A competence versus performance distinction. *Developmental Psychology, 22*, 481–486.

Broderick, C. B. (1982). Adult sexual development. In B. B. Wolman (Ed.), *Handbook of developmental psychology*. Englewood Cliffs, NJ: Prentice-Hall.

Broderick, C. B., & Rowe, G. P. (1968). A scale of preadolescent heterosexual development. *Journal of Marriage and the Family, 30*, 97–101.

Brooks-Gunn, J., & Furstenberg, F. F., Jr. (1989). Long-term implications of fertility-related behavior and family formation on adolescent mothers and their children. In K. Kreppner & R. M. Lerner (Eds.), *Family systems and life-span development*. Hillsdale, NJ: Erlbaum.

Brooks-Gunn, J. & Lewis, M. (1981). Infant social perception: Responses to pictures of parents and strangers. *Developmental Psychology, 17*, 647–649.

Broverman, I. K., Vogel, S. R., Broverman, D. M., Clarkson, F. E., & Rosenkrantz, P. S. (1972). Sex-role stereotypes: A current appraisal. *Journal of Social Issues, 28*, 59–78.

Caplan, P. J., MacPherson, G. M., Tobin, P. (1985). Do sex-related differences in spatial abilities exist? *American Psychologist, 40*, 786–799.

Carroll, J. L., Volk, K. D., & Hyde, J. S. (1985). Differences between males and females in motives for engaging in sexual intercourse. *Archives of Sexual Behavior, 14*, 131–139.

Carroll, L. (1988). Concern with AIDS and the sexual behavior of college students. *Journal of Marriage and the Family, 50*, 405–411.

Carter, D. B., & McCloskey, L. A. (1983–1984). Peers and the maintenance of sex-typed behavior: The development of children's conceptions of cross-gender behavior in their peers. *Social Cognition, 2*, 294–314.

Carter, D. B., & Patterson, C. J. (1982). Sex roles as social conventions: The development of children's conceptions of sex-role stereotypes. *Developmental Psychology, 18*, 812–824.

Coles, R., & Stokes, G. (1985). *Sex and the American teenager*. New York: Harper & Row.

Comfort, A. (1974). Sexuality in old age. *Journal of the American Geriatrics Society, 22*, 440–442.

Condry, J., & Condry, S. (1976). Sex differences: A study in the eye of the beholder. *Child Development, 47*, 812–819.

Cowan, C. P., & Cowan, P. A. (1987). A preventive intervention for couples becoming parents. In C. F. Z. Boukydis (Ed.), *Research on support for parents and infants in the postnatal period*. New York: Ablex.

Cunningham, J. D., & Antill, J. K. (1984). Changes in masculinity and femininity across the family life cycle: A reexamination. *Developmental Psychology, 20*, 1135–1141.

Damon, W. (1977). *The social world of the child*. San Francisco: Jossey-Bass.

Darling, C. A., & Hicks, M. W. (1982). Parental influence on adolescent sexuality: Implications for parents and educators. *Journal of Youth and Adolescence, 11*, 231–245.

Darling, C. A., Kallen, D. J., & VanDusen, J. E. (1984). Sex in transition, 1900–1980. *Journal of Youth and Adolescence, 13*, 385–399.

Deaux, K. (1984). From individual differences to social categories. Analysis of a decade's research on gender. *American Psychologist, 39*, 105–116.

DeLamater, J., & MacCorquodale, P. (1979). *Premarital sexuality: Attitudes, relationships, behavior*. Madison, WI: University of Wisconsin Press.

Diamond, M. (1982). Sexual identity, monozygotic twins reared in discordant sex roles and a BBC follow up. *Archives of Sexual Behavior, 11*, 181–186.

Douvan, E., & Adelson, J. (1966). *The adolescent experience*. New York: Wiley.

Dreyer, P. H. (1982). Sexuality during adolescence. In B. B. Wolman (Ed.), *Handbook of developmental psychology*. New York: Wiley.

Dweck, C. S., Davidson, W., Nelson, S., & Enna, B. (1978). Sex differences in learned helplessness: II. The contingencies of evaluative feedback in the classroom, and III. An experimental analysis. *Developmental Psychology, 14*, 268–276.

Dweck, C. S., & Elliott, E. S. (1983). Achievement motivation. In E. M. Hetherington (Vol. Ed.; P. H. Mussen, General Ed.), *Handbook of child psychology: Vol. 4. Socialization, personality, and social development* (4th ed.). New York: Wiley.

Eaton, W. O., & Enns, L. R. (1986). Sex differences in human motor activity level. *Psychological Bulletin, 100*, 19–28.

Ehrhardt, A. A. (1985). The psychobiology of gender. In A. S. Rossi (Ed.), *Gender and the life course*. New York: Aldine.

Ehrhardt, A. A., & Baker, S. W. (1974). Fetal androgens, human central nervous system differentiation, and behavioral sex differences. In R. C. Friedman, R. M. Rickard, & R. L. Van de Wiele (Eds.), *Sex differences in behavior*. New York: Wiley.

Elias, J., & Gebhard, P. (1969). Sexuality and sexual learning in childhood. *Phi Delta Kappan, 50*, 401–405.

Emmerich, W. (1959). Parental identification in young children. *Genetic Psychology Monographs, 60*, 257–308.

Emmerich, W., & Shepard, K. (1982). Development of sex-differentiated preferences during late childhood and adolescence. *Developmental Psychology, 18*, 406–417.

Etaugh, C., Levine, D., & Mennella, A. (1984). Development of sex biases in children: 40 years later. *Sex Roles, 10*, 911–922.

Fagot, B. I. (1978). The influence of sex of child on parental reactions to toddler children. *Child Development, 49*, 459– 465.

Fagot, B. I. (1985). Beyond the reinforcement principle: Another step toward understanding sex-role development. *Developmental Psychology, 21*, 1097–1104.

Fagot, B. I., Leinbach, M. D., & Hagan, R. (1986). Gender labeling and the adoption of sex-typed behaviors. *Developmental Psychology, 22*, 440–443.

Feingold, A. (1988). Cognitive gender differences are disappearing. *American Psychologist, 43*, 95–103.

Feldman, S. S., Biringen, Z. C., & Nash, S. C. (1981). Fluctuations of sex-related self-attributions as a function of stage of family life cycle. *Developmental Psychology, 17*, 24–35.

Felstein, I. (1983). Dysfunction: Origins and therapeutic approaches. In R. B. Weg (Ed.), *Sexuality in the later years. Roles and behavior*. New York: Academic.

Ford, C. S., & Beach, F. A. (1951). *Patterns of sexual behavior*. New York: Harper & Row.

Forisha, B. L., & Goldman, B. H. (1981). *Outsiders on the inside: Women & organizations*. Englewood Cliffs, NJ: Prentice-Hall.

Frueh, T., & McGhee, P. H. (1975). Traditional sex-role development and the amount of time spent watching television. *Developmental Psychology, 11*, 109.

Furstenberg, F. F., Jr., Brooks-Gunn, J., & Morgan, S. P. (1987). *Adolescent mothers in later life*. New York: Cambridge University Press.

Furstenberg, F. F., Jr., Lincoln, R., & Menken, J. (Eds.). (1981). *Teenage sexuality, pregnancy, and childbearing*. Philadelphia: University of Pennsylvania Press.

Gagnon, J. H. (1985). Attitudes and responses of parents to pre-adolescent masturbation. *Archives of Sexual Behavior, 14*, 451–466.

George, L. K., & Weiler, S. J. (1981). Sexuality in middle and late life. The effects of age, cohort, and gender. *Archives of General Psychiatry, 38*, 919–923.

Goldman, R., & Goldman, J. (1982). *Children's sexual thinking. A comparative study of children aged 5 to 15 years in Australia, North America, Britain and Sweden*. London: Routledge and Kegan Paul.

Greenblat, C. S. (1983). The salience of sexuality in the early years of marriage. *Journal of Marriage and the Family, 45*, 289–299.

Grotevant, H. D., & Thorbecke, W. (1982). Sex differences in styles of occupational identity formation in late adolescence. *Developmental Psychology, 18*, 396–405.

Gullotta, T. P., Adams, G. R., & Alexander, S. J. (1986). *Today's marriages and families. A wellness approach*. Pacific Grove, CA: Brooks/Cole.

Gutmann, D. (1975). Parenthood: Key to the comparative psychology of the life cycle? In N. Datan & L. H. Ginsberg (Eds.), *Life span developmental psychology: Normative life crises*. New York: Academic.

Gutmann, D. (1977). The cross-cultural perspective: Notes toward a comparative psychology of aging. In J. E. Birren & K. W. Schaie (Eds.), *Handbook of the psychology of aging*. New York: Van Nostrand Reinhold.

Guttentag, M., & Bray, H. (1976). *Undoing sex stereotypes. Research and resources for educators*. New York: McGraw-Hill.

Hannah, J. S., & Kahn, S. E. (1989). The relationship of socioeconomic status and gender to the occupational choices of grade 12 students. *Journal of Vocational Behavior, 34*, 161–178.

Hass, A. (1979). *Teenage sexuality: A survey of teenage sexual behavior*. New York: Macmillan.

Hetherington, E. M., & Frankie, G. (1967). Effect of parental dominance, warmth, and conflict on imitation in children. *Journal of Personality and Social Psychology, 6*, 119–125.

Hill, J. P., & Lynch, M. E. (1983). The intensification of gender-related role expectations during early adolescence. In J. Brooks-Gunn & A. C. Petersen (Eds.), *Girls at puberty. Biological and psychosocial perspectives*. New York: Plenum.

Hiller, D. V., & Philliber, W. W. (1986). The division of labor in contemporary marriage: Expectations, perceptions, and performance. *Social Problems, 33*, 191–201.

Hodgson, J. W., & Fischer, J. L. (1979). Sex differences in identity and intimacy development in college youth. *Journal of Youth and Adolescence, 8*, 37–50.

Hunt, M. (1974). *Sexual behavior in the 1970s*. Chicago: Playboy Press.

Huston, A. C. (1983). Sex-typing. In E. M. Hetherington (Vol. Ed.; P. H. Mussen, General Ed.), *Handbook of child psychology: Vol. 4. Socialization, personality, and social development.* New York: Wiley.

Huston, A. C. (1985). The development of sex typing: Themes from recent research. *Developmental Review, 5,* 1–17.

Hutt, C. (1972). *Males and females.* Baltimore: Penguin Books.

Hyde, J. S. (1981). How large are cognitive gender differences? A meta-analysis using w^2 and d. *American Psychologist, 36,* 892–901.

Hyde, J. S. (1984). How large are sex differences in aggression? A developmental meta-analysis. *Developmental Psychology, 20,* 722–736.

Hyde, J. S., & Linn, M. C. (1988). Gender differences in verbal ability: A meta-analysis. *Psychological Bulletin, 104,* 53–69.

Hyde, J. S., Rosenberg, B. G., & Behrman, J. A. (1977). Tomboyism. *Psychology of Women Quarterly, 2,* 73–75.

Imperato-McGinley, J., Peterson, R. E., Gautier, T., & Sturla, E. (1979). Androgens and the evolution of male gender identity among male pseudohermaphrodites with 5a-reductase deficiency. *New England Journal of Medicine, 300,* 1233–1237.

Intons-Peterson, M. J., & Reddel, M. (1984). What do people ask about a neonate? *Developmental Psychology, 20,* 358–359.

Jacklin, C. N., & Maccoby, E. E. (1978). Social behavior at 33 months in same-sex and mixed-sex dyads. *Child Development, 49,* 557–569.

Jasso, G. (1985). Marital coital frequency and the passage of time: Estimating the separate effects of spouses' ages and marital duration, birth and marriage cohorts, and period influences. *American Sociological Review, 50,* 224–241.

Jung, C. G. (1933). *Modern man in search of a soul* (W. S. Dell & C. F. Baynes, Trans.). New York: Harcourt, Brace and Company.

Katcher, A. (1955). The discrimination of sex differences by young children. *Journal of Genetic Psychology, 87,* 131–143.

Katz, P. A. (1979). The development of female identity. *Sex Roles, 5,* 155–178.

Katz, P. A. (1986). Modification of children's gender-stereotyped behavior: General issues and research considerations. *Sex Roles, 14,* 591–602.

Kinsey, A. C., Pomeroy, W. B., Martin, C. E. (1948). *Sexual behavior in the human male.* Philadelphia: W. B. Saunders.

Kinsey, A. C., Pomeroy, W. B., Martin, C. E., & Gebhard, P. H. (1953). *Sexual behavior in the human female.* Philadelphia: W. B. Saunders.

Kohlberg, L. (1966). A cognitive-developmental analysis of children's sex-role concepts and attitudes. In E. E. Maccoby (Ed.), *The development of sex differences.* Stanford, CA: Stanford University Press.

Kuhn, D., Nash, S. C., & Brucken, L. (1978). Sex-role concepts of two- and three-year-olds. *Child Development, 49,* 445–451.

Lamb, M. E. (1981). *The role of the father in child development.* New York: Wiley.

Langlois, J. H., & Downs, A. C. (1980). Mothers, fathers, and peers as socialization agents of sex-typed play behaviors in young children. *Child Development, 51,* 1237–1247.

Lenney, E. (1977). Women's self-confidence in achievement settings. *Psychological Bulletin, 84,* 1–13.

Lenney, E. (1981). What's fine for the gander isn't always good for the goose: Sex differences in self-confidence as a function of ability area and comparison with others. *Sex Roles, 7,* 905–924.

Lewin, M., & Tragos, L. M. (1987). Has the feminist movement influenced adolescent sex role attitudes? A reassessment after a quarter century. *Sex Roles, 16,* 125–135.

Lewis, M., & Brooks-Gunn, J. (1979). *Social cognition and the acquisition of self.* New York: Plenum.

Lewis, M., & Weinraub, M. (1979). Origins of early sex-role development. *Sex Roles, 5,* 135–153.

Liebert, R. M., & Sprafkin, J. (1988). *The early window. Effects of television on children and youth* (3rd ed.). New York: Pergamon.

Linn, M. C., & Petersen, A. C. (1985). Emergence and characterization of sex differences in spatial ability: A meta-analysis. *Child Development, 56,* 1479–1498.

Livson, F. B. (1983). Gender identity: A lifespan view of sex-role development. In R. B. Weg (Ed.), *Sexuality in the later years. Roles and behavior.* New York: Academic.

Lockheed, M. E. (1986). Reshaping the social order: The case of gender segregation. *Sex Roles, 14,* 617–628.

Lorber, J. (1986). Dismantling Noah's ark. *Sex Roles, 14,* 567–580.

Lott, B. (1985). The potential enrichment of social/personality psychology through feminist research and vice versa. *American Psychologist, 40,* 155–164.

Lueptow, L. B. (1981). Sex-typing and change in the occupational choices of high school seniors: 1964–1975. *Sociology of Education, 54,* 16–24.

Maccoby, E. E. (1980). *Social development.* New York: Harcourt Brace Jovanovich.

Maccoby, E. E., & Jacklin, C. N. (1974). *The psychology of sex differences.* Stanford, CA: Stanford University Press.

Maccoby, E. E., & Jacklin, C. N. (1980). Sex differences in aggression: A rejoinder and reprise. *Child Development, 51,* 964–980.

MacFarlane, A. (1977). *The psychology of childbirth.* Cambridge, MA: Harvard University Press.

Maier, R. A. (1984). *Human sexuality in perspective.* Chicago: Nelson-Hall.

Major, B., Carnevale, P. J. D., & Deaux, K. (1981). A different perspective on androgyny: Evaluations of masculine and feminine personality characteristics. *Journal of Personality and Social Psychology, 41,* 988–1001.

Mancini, J. A., & Orthner, D. K. (1978). Recreational sexuality preferences among middle-class husbands and wives. *Journal of Sex Research, 14,* 96–106.

Marcus, D. E., & Overton, W. F. (1978). The development of cognitive gender constancy and sex-role preferences. *Child Development, 49,* 434–444.

Markides, K. S., & Vernon, S. W. (1984). Aging, sex-role orientation, and adjustment: A three-generations study of Mexican Americans. *Journal of Gerontology, 39,* 586–591.

Martin, C. L. (1989). Children's use of gender-related information in making social judgments. *Developmental Psychology, 25,* 80–88.

Martin, C. L., & Halverson, C. F., Jr. (1981). A schematic processing model of sex typing and stereotyping in children. *Child Development, 52,* 1119–1134.

Martin, C. L., & Halverson, C. F., Jr. (1983). The effects of sex-typing schemas on young children's memory. *Child Development, 54*, 563–574.

Massad, C. M. (1981). Sex-role identity and adjustment during adolescence. *Child Development, 52*, 1290–1298.

Masters, J. C., Ford, M. E., Arend, R., Grotevant, H. D., & Clark, L. V. (1979). Modeling and labeling as integrated determinants of children's sex-typed imitative behavior. *Child Development, 50*, 364–371.

Masters, W. H., & Johnson, V. E. (1966). *Human sexual response*. Boston: Little, Brown.

Masters, W. H., & Johnson, V. E. (1970). *Human sexual inadequacy*. Boston: Little, Brown.

McGhee, P. E., & Frueh, T. (1980). Television viewing and the learning of sex-role stereotypes. *Sex Roles, 6*, 179–188.

Mead, M. (1928). *Coming of age in Samoa*. New York: William Morrow.

Mead, M. (1935). *Sex and temperament in three primitive societies*. New York: William Morrow.

Mischel, W. (1970). Sex-typing and socialization. In P. H. Mussen (Ed.), *Carmichael's manual of child psychology* (Vol. 2). New York: Wiley.

Mobarak, A., & Shamoian, C. A. (1985). Aging and sexuality. In Z. DeFries, R. C. Friedman, & R. Corn (Eds.), *Sexuality. New perspectives*. Westport, CT: Greenwood Press.

Money, J., & Ehrhardt, A. (1972). *Man and woman, boy and girl*. Baltimore: Johns Hopkins University Press.

Money, J., & Tucker, P. (1975). *Sexual signatures: On being a man or a woman*. Boston: Little, Brown.

Morrison, D. M. (1985). Adolescent contraceptive behavior: A review. *Psychological Bulletin, 98*, 538–568.

Moss, H. A. (1967). Sex, age, and state as determinants of mother–infant interaction. *Merrill-Palmer Quarterly, 13*, 19–36.

Munroe, R. H., Shimmin, H. S., & Munroe, R. L. (1984). Gender understanding and sex-role preferences in four cultures. *Developmental Psychology, 20*, 673–682.

Mussen, P. H., & Rutherford, E. (1963). Parent–child relations and parental personality in relation to young children's sex-role preferences. *Child Development, 34*, 589–607.

O'Connell, A. N. (1976). The relationship between life style and identity synthesis in traditional, neotraditional, and nontraditional women. *Journal of Personality, 44*, 675–688.

Olweus, D., Mattsson, A., Schalling, D., & Low, H. (1980). Testosterone, aggression, physical and personality dimensions in normal adolescent males. *Psychosomatic Medicine, 42*, 253–269.

Orlofsky, J. L. (1979). Parental antecedents of sex-role orientation in college men and women. *Sex Roles, 5*, 495–512.

Orlofsky, J. L., & O'Heron, C. A. (1987). Stereotypic and nonstereotypic sex role trait and behavior orientations: Implications for personal adjustment. *Journal of Personality and Social Psychology, 52*, 1034–1042.

Parsons, J. E., Kaczala, C. M. & Meese, J. L. (1982). Socialization of achievement attitudes and beliefs: Classroom influences. *Child Development, 53*, 322–339.

Parsons, T. (1955). Family structure and the socialization of the child. In T. Parsons & R. F. Bales (Eds.), *Family socialization and interaction processes*. Glencoe, IL: Free Press.

Pfeiffer, E., Verwoerdt, A., & Davis, G. C. (1972). Sexual behavior in middle life. *American Journal of Psychiatry, 128*, 1262–1267.

Pleck, J. H. (1981). *The myth of masculinity*. Cambridge, MA: MIT Press.

Pleck, J. H. (1985). *Working wives/working husbands*. Beverly Hills, CA: Sage.

Reid, P. T., & Stephens, D. S. (1985). The roots of future occupations in childhood: A review of the literature on girls and careers. *Youth and Society, 16*, 267–288.

Rheingold, H. L., & Cook, K. V. (1975). The contents of boys' and girls' rooms as an index of parents' behavior. *Child Development, 46*, 459–463.

Richardson, J. G., & Simpson, C. H. (1982). Children, gender, and social structure: An analysis of the contents of letters to Santa Claus. *Child Development, 53*, 429–436.

Richmond-Abbott, M. (1983). *Masculine and feminine. Sex roles over the life cycle*. Reading, MA: Addison-Wesley.

Robinson, C. C., & Morris, J. T. (1986). The gender-stereotyped nature of Christmas toys received by 36-, 48-, and 60-month-old children: A comparison between nonrequested vs requested toys. *Sex Roles, 15*, 21–32.

Robinson, I. E., & Jedlicka, D. (1982). Change in sexual attitudes and behavior of college students from 1965 to 1980: A research note. *Journal of Marriage and the Family, 44*, 237–240.

Robinson, P. K. (1983). The sociological perspective. In R. B. Weg (Ed.), *Sexuality in the later years. Roles and behavior*. New York: Academic.

Rose, R. M., Bernstein, I. S., & Gordon, T. P. (1975). Consequences of social conflict on plasma testosterone levels in rhesus monkeys. *Psychosomatic Medicine, 37*, 50–61.

Rosen, R., & Hall, E. (1984). *Sexuality*. New York: Random House.

Rosenwasser, S. M., Lingenfelter, M., & Harrington, A. F. (1989). Nontraditional gender role portrayals on television and children's gender role perceptions. *Journal of Applied Developmental Psychology, 10*, 97–105.

Rubin, J. Z., Provenzano, F. J., & Luria, Z. (1974). The eye of the beholder: Parents' views on sex of newborns. *American Journal of Orthopsychiatry, 44*, 512–519.

Ruble, D. N. (1988). Sex-role development. In M. H. Bornstein & M. E. Lamb (Eds.), *Developmental psychology: An advanced textbook*. Hillsdale, NJ: Erlbaum.

Ruble, D. N., Balaban, T., & Cooper, J. (1981). Gender constancy and the effects of sex-typed televised toy commercials. *Child Development, 52*, 667–673.

Ruble, T. L. (1983). Sex stereotypes: Issues of change in the 1970s. *Sex Roles, 9*, 397–402.

Safir, M. P. (1986). The effects of nature or of nurture on sex differences in intellectual functioning. *Sex Roles, 14*, 581–590.

Schiedel, D. G., & Marcia, J. E. (1985). Ego identity, intimacy, sex role orientation, and gender. *Developmental Psychology, 21*, 149–160.

Serbin, L. A., & Sprafkin, C. (1986). The salience of gender and the process of sex typing in three- to seven-year-old children. *Child Development, 57*, 1188–1199.

Serbin, L. A., Tonick, I. J., & Sternglanz, S. H. (1977). Shaping cooperative cross-sex play. *Child Development, 48*, 924–929.

Shaffer, D. R., & Johnson, R. D. (1980). Effects of occupational choice and sex-role preferences on the attractiveness of competent men and women. *Journal of Personality, 48*, 505–519.

Sigelman, C. K., Carr, M. B., & Begley, N. L. (1986). Developmental changes in the influence of sex-role stereotypes on person perception. *Child Study Journal, 16*, 191–205.

Slaby, R. G., & Frey, K. S. (1975). Development of gender constancy and selective attention to same-sex models. *Child Development, 46*, 849–856.

Smith, P. K., & Daglish, L. (1977). Sex differences in parent and infant behavior in the home. *Child Development, 48*, 1250–1254.

Spence, J. T., & Helmreich, R. L. (1978). *Masculinity and femininity: Their psychological dimensions, correlates, and antecedents*. Austin, TX: University of Texas Press.

Starr, B. D., & Weiner, M. B. (1981). *The Starr-Weiner report on sex and sexuality in the mature years*. New York: Stein & Day.

Stein, S. L., & Weston, L. C. (1982). College women's attitudes toward women and identity achievement. *Adolescence, 17*, 895–899.

Stevens, D. P., & Truss, C. V. (1985). Stability and change in adult personality over 12 and 20 years. *Developmental Psychology, 21*, 568–584.

Stoddart, T., & Turiel, E. (1985). Children's concepts of cross-gender activities. *Child Development, 56*, 1241–1252.

Terborg, J. R., & Ilgen, D. R. (1975). A theoretical approach to sex discrimination in traditionally masculine occupations. *Organizational Behavior and Human Performance, 13*, 352–376.

Tesch, S. A., & Whitbourne, S. K. (1982). Intimacy and identity status in young adults. *Journal of Personality and Social Psychology, 43*, 1041–1051.

Thompson, A. P. (1983). Extramarital sex: A review of the research literature. *Journal of Sex Research, 19*, 1–22.

Thompson, S. K. (1975). Gender labels and early sex-role development. *Child Development, 46*, 339–347.

Thorne, B., & Luria, Z. (1986). Sexuality and gender in children's daily worlds. *Social Problems, 33*, 176–190.

Turner, B. F. (1982). Sex-related differences in aging. In B. B. Wolman (Ed.), *Handbook of developmental psychology*. New York: Wiley.

Urberg, K. A. (1979). Sex-role conceptualization in adolescents and adults. *Developmental Psychology, 15*, 90–92.

Weizman, R., & Hart, J. (1987). Sexual behavior in healthy married elderly men. *Archives of Sexual Behavior, 16*, 39–44.

Westoff, C. F. (1974). Coital frequency and contraception. *Family Planning Perspectives, 6*, 136–141.

White, M. J., Kruczek, T. A., Brown, M. T., & White, G. B. (1989). Occupational sex stereotypes among college students. *Journal of Vocational Behavior, 34*, 289–298.

Whiting, B. B., & Edwards, C. P. (1988). *Children of different worlds. The formation of social behavior*. Cambridge, MA: Harvard University Press.

Whitley. B. E., Jr. (1983). Sex-role orientation and self-esteem: A critical meta-analytic review. *Journal of Personality and Social Psychology, 44*, 765–778.

Wielandt, H., & Boldsen, J. (1989). Age at first intercourse. *Journal of Biosocial Science, 21*, 169–177.

Wilkinson, L. C., & Marrett, C. B. (Eds.). (1985). *Gender influences in classroom interaction*. Orlando, FL: Academic.

Windle, M. (1986). Sex role orientation, cognitive flexibility, and life satisfaction among older adults. *Psychology of Women Quarterly, 10*, 263–273.

Young, W. C., Goy, R. W., & Phoenix, C. H. (1964). Hormones and sexual behavior. *Science, 143*, 212–218.

Zelnik, M., & Shah, F. (1983). First intercourse among young Americans. *Family Planning Perspectives, 15*, 64–70.

Zern, D. S. (1984). Relationships among selected child-rearing variables in a cross-cultural sample of 110 societies. *Developmental Psychology, 20*, 683–690.

Chapter 12: Choices: Motives and Morals

Ainlay, S. C., & Smith, D. R. (1984). Aging and religious participation. *Journal of Gerontology, 39*, 357–363.

Arend, A., Gove, F. L., & Sroufe, L. A. (1979). Continuity of individual adaptation from infancy to kindergarten: A predictive study of ego-resiliency and curiosity in preschoolers. *Child Development, 50*, 950–959.

Aronfreed, J. (1976). Moral development from the standpoint of a general psychological theory. In T. Lickona (Ed.), *Moral development and behavior*. New York: Holt, Rinehart & Winston.

Atkinson, J. W. (1964). *An introduction to motivation*. Princeton, NJ: Van Nostrand.

Bandura, A. (1986). *Social foundations of thought and action. A social cognitive theory*. Englewood Cliffs, NJ: Prentice-Hall.

Baruch, R. (1967). The achievement motive in women: Implications for career development. *Journal of Personality and Social Psychology, 5*, 260–267.

Battle, E. S. (1966). Motivational determinants of academic competence. *Journal of Personality and Social Psychology, 4*, 634–642.

Benenson, J. F., & Dweck, C. S. (1986). The development of trait explanations and self-evaluations in the academic and social domains. *Child Development, 57*, 1179–1187.

Berkowitz, M. W. (1985). The role of discussion in moral education. In M. W. Berkowitz & F. Oser (Eds.), *Moral education: Theory and application*. Hillsdale, NJ: Erlbaum.

Berkowitz, M. W., & Gibbs, J. C. (1983). Measuring the developmental features of moral discussion. *Merrill-Palmer Quarterly, 29*, 399–410.

Bielby, D. D., & Papalia, D. E. (1975). Moral development and perceptual role-taking egocentrism: Their development and interrelationship across the life-span. *International Journal of Aging and Human Development, 6*, 293–308.

Blasi, A. (1980). Bridging moral cognition and moral action: A critical review of the literature. *Psychological Bulletin, 88*, 1–45.

Blasi, A. (1984). Moral identity: Its role in moral functioning. In W. M. Kurtines & J. L. Gewirtz (Eds.), *Morality, moral behavior, and moral development*. New York: Wiley.

Blazer, D., & Palmore, E. (1976). Religion and aging in a longitudinal panel. *Gerontologist, 16,* 82–85.

Boldizar, J. P., Wilson, K. L., & Deemer, D. K. (1989). Gender, life experiences, and moral judgment development: A process-oriented approach. *Journal of Personality and Social Psychology, 57,* 229–238.

Brabeck, M. (1983). Moral judgment: Theory and research on differences between males and females. *Developmental Review, 3,* 274–291.

Brody, G. H., & Shaffer, D. R. (1982). Contributions of parents and peers to children's moral socialization. *Developmental Review, 2,* 31–75.

Bullock, M., & Lutkenhaus, P. (1988). The development of volitional behavior in the toddler years. *Child Development, 59,* 664–674.

Burton, R. V. (1963). The generality of honesty reconsidered. *Psychological Review, 70,* 481–499.

Burton, R. V. (1976). Honesty and dishonesty. In T. Lickona (Ed.), *Moral development and behavior.* New York: Holt, Rinehart & Winston.

Burton, R. V. (1984). A paradox in theories and research in moral development. In W. M. Kurtines & J. L. Gewirtz (Eds.), *Morality, moral behavior, and moral development.* New York: Wiley.

Cassidy, J. (1986). The ability to negotiate the environment: An aspect of infant competence as related to quality of attachment. *Child Development, 57,* 331– 337.

Chap, J. B. (1985–1986). Moral judgment in middle and late adulthood: The effects of age-appropriate moral dilemmas and spontaneous role taking. *International Journal of Aging and Human Development, 22,* 161–171.

Colby, A., Kohlberg, L., Gibbs, J., & Lieberman, M. (1983). A longitudinal study of moral judgment. *Monographs of the Society for Research in Child Development, 48* (Nos. 1–2, Serial No. 200).

Coleman, J. S. (1961). *The adolescent society. The social life of the teenager and its impact on education.* Glencoe, IL: Free Press.

Crandall, V. C. (1967). Achievement behavior in young children. In *The young child: Reviews of research.* Washington, DC: National Association for the Education of Young Children.

Crandall, V. C. (1969). Sex differences in expectancy of intellectual and academic reinforcement. In C. P. Smith (Ed.), *Achievement-related motives in children.* New York: Russell Sage Foundation.

Damon, W. (1977). *The social world of the child.* San Francisco: Jossey-Bass.

Damon, W. (1984). Self-understanding and moral development from childhood to adolescence. In W. M. Kurtines & J. L. Gewirtz (Eds.), *Morality, moral behavior, and moral development.* New York: Wiley.

Deci, E. L., & Ryan, R. M. (1985). *Intrinsic motivation and self-determination.* New York: Plenum.

de Vries, B., & Walker, L. J. (1986). Moral reasoning and attitudes toward capital punishment. *Developmental Psychology, 22,* 509–513.

Dweck, C. S. (1975). The role of expectations and attributions in the alleviation of learned helplessness. *Journal of Personality and Social Psychology, 31,* 674–685.

Dweck, C. S. (1978). Achievement. In M. E. Lamb (Ed.), *Social and personality development.* New York: Holt, Rinehart & Winston.

Dweck, C. S., Davidson, W., Nelson, S., & Enna, B. (1978). Sex differences in learned helplessness: II. The contingencies of evaluative feedback in the classroom, and III. An experimental analysis. *Developmental Psychology, 14,* 268–276.

Dweck, C. S., & Elliot, E. S. (1983). Achievement motivation. In E. M. Hetherington (Vol. Ed.; P. H. Mussen, General Ed.), *Handbook of child psychology: Vol. 4. Socialization, personality, and social development* (4th ed.). New York: Wiley.

Dweck, C. S., & Leggett, E. L. (1988). A social-cognitive approach to motivation and personality. *Psychological Review, 95,* 256–273.

Findley, M. J., & Cooper, H. M. (1983). Locus of control and academic achievement: A literature review. *Journal of Personality and Social Psychology, 44,* 419–427.

Finkelstein, N. W., & Ramey, C. T. (1977). Learning to control the environment in infancy. *Child Development, 48,* 806–819.

Fischer, K. W., & Lazerson, A. (1984). *Human development. From conception through adolescence.* New York: W. H. Freeman.

Fischer, W. F. (1963). Sharing in preschool children as a function of the amount and type of reinforcement. *Genetic Psychology Monographs, 68,* 215–245.

Ford, M. E., & Thompson, R. A. (1985). Perceptions of personal agency and infant attachment: Toward a life-span perspective on competence development. *International Journal of Behavioral Development, 8,* 377–406.

Ford, M. R., & Lowery, C. R. (1986). Gender differences in moral reasoning: A comparison of the use of justice and care orientations. *Journal of Personality and Social Psychology, 50,* 777–783.

Fowler, J. W. (1981). *Stages of faith. The psychology of human development and the quest for meaning.* San Francisco: Harper & Row.

Freud, S. (1960). *A general introduction to psychoanalysis.* New York: Washington Square Press. (Original work published 1935)

Gibbs, J. C. (1979). Kohlberg's moral stage theory. A Piagetian revision. *Human Development, 22,* 89–112.

Gibbs, J. C., & Schnell, S. V. (1985). Moral development "versus" socialization. A critique. *American Psychologist, 40,* 1071–1080.

Gilligan, C. (1977). In a different voice: Women's conceptions of self and morality. *Harvard Educational Review, 47,* 481–517.

Gilligan, C. (1982). *In a different voice: Psychological theory and women's development.* Cambridge, MA: Harvard University Press.

Green, M. (1989). *Theories of human development. A comparative approach.* Englewood Cliffs, NJ: Prentice-Hall.

Grolnick, W. S., & Ryan, R. M. (1989). Parent styles associated with children's self-regulation and competence in school. *Journal of Educational Psychology, 81,* 143–154.

Grusec, J. E., Kuczynski, L., Rushton, J. P., Simutis, Z. (1979). Learning resistance to temptation through observation. *Developmental Psychology, 15,* 233–240.

Haan, N., Aerts, E., & Cooper, B. A. B. (1985). *On moral grounds. The search for practical morality.* New York: New York University Press.

Harkness, S., Edwards, C. P., & Super, C. M. (1981). Social roles and moral reasoning: A case study in a rural African community. *Developmental Psychology, 17,* 595–603.

Harter, S. (1981). A new self-report scale of intrinsic versus extrinsic orientation in the classroom: Motivational and informational components. *Developmental Psychology, 17,* 300–312.

Harter, S. (1982). The perceived competence scale for children. *Child Development, 53,* 87–97.

Hartshorne, H., & May, M. S. (1928–1930). *Studies in the nature of character: Vol. 1. Studies in deceit. Vol. 2. Studies in self-control. Vol. 3. Studies in the organization of character.* New York: Macmillan.

Heckhausen, H. (1986). Achievement and motivation through the life span. In A. B. Sorensen, F. E. Weinert, & L. R. Sherrod (Eds.), *Human development and the life course: Multidisciplinary perspectives.* Hillsdale, NJ: Erlbaum.

Helkama, K. (1988). Two studies of Piaget's theory of moral judgment. *European Journal of Social Psychology, 18,* 17–38.

Helmreich, R. L., Sawin, L. L., & Carsrud, A. L. (1986). The honeymoon effect in job performance: Temporal increases in the predictive power of achievement motivation. *Journal of Applied Psychology, 71,* 185–188.

Hoffman, M. L. (1970). Moral development. In P. H. Mussen (Ed.), *Carmichael's manual of child psychology* (Vol. 2). New York: Wiley.

Hoffman, M. L. (1981). Is altruism part of human nature? *Journal of Personality and Social Psychology, 40,* 121–137.

Hoffman, M. L. (1983). Affective and cognitive processes in moral internalization. In E. T. Higgins, D. N. Ruble, & W. W. Hartup (Eds.), *Social cognition and social development: A sociocultural perspective.* Cambridge, England: Cambridge University Press.

Hoffman, M. L. (1988). Moral development. In M. H. Bornstein & M. E. Lamb (Eds.), *Developmental psychology: An advanced textbook* (2nd ed.). Hillsdale, NJ: Erlbaum.

Kagan, J., & Moss, H. A. (1962). *Birth to maturity.* New York: Wiley.

Keasey, C. B. (1971). Social participation as a factor in the moral development of preadolescents. *Developmental Psychology, 5,* 216–220.

Kohlberg, L. (1963). The development of children's orientations toward a moral order: I. Sequence in the development of moral thought. *Vita Humana, 6,* 11–33.

Kohlberg, L. (1973). Continuities in childhood and adult moral development revisited. In P. B. Baltes & K. W. Schaie (Eds.), *Life-span developmental psychology: Personality and socialization.* New York: Academic.

Kohlberg, L. (1975, June). The cognitive-developmental approach to moral education. *Phi Delta Kappan,* pp. 670–677.

Kohlberg, L. (1981). *Essays on moral development: Vol. 1. The philosophy of moral development.* San Francisco: Harper & Row.

Kohlberg, L. (1984). *Essays on moral development: Vol. 2. The psychology of moral development.* San Francisco: Harper & Row.

Kohlberg, L. (1985). The just community approach to moral education in theory and practice. In M. W. Berkowitz & F. Oser (Eds.), *Moral education: Theory and application.* Hillsdale, NJ: Erlbaum.

Kohlberg, L., & Candee, D. (1984). The relationship of moral judgment to moral action. In W. M. Kurtines & J. L. Gewirtz (Eds.), *Morality, moral behavior, and moral development.* New York: Wiley.

Krogh, K. M. (1985). Women's motives to achieve and to nurture in different life stages. *Sex roles, 12,* 75–90.

Kruger, A. C., & Tomasello, M. (1986). Transactive discussions with peers and adults. *Developmental Psychology, 22,* 681–685.

Kurtines, W. M. (1986). Moral behavior as rule governed behavior: Person and situation effects on moral decision making. *Journal of Personality and Social Psychology, 50,* 784–791.

Lapsley, D. K., Harwell, M. R., Olson, L. M., Flannery, D., & Quintana, S. M. (1984). Moral judgment, personality, and attitude toward authority in early and late adolescence. *Journal of Youth and Adolescence, 13,* 527–542.

Leon, M. (1984). Rules mothers and sons use to integrate intent and damage information in their moral judgments. *Child Development, 55,* 2106–2113.

Linn, R. (1989). Hypothetical and actual moral reasoning of Israeli selective conscientious objectors during the war in Lebanon (1982–1985). *Journal of Applied Developmental Psychology, 10,* 19–36.

Lyons, N. P. (1983). Two perspectives: On self, relationships, and morality. *Harvard Educational Review, 53,* 125–145.

MacTurk, R. H., McCarthy, M. E., Vietze, P. M., & Yarrow, L. J. (1987). Sequential analysis of mastery behavior in 6- and 12-month-old infants. *Developmental Psychology, 23,* 199–203.

Maehr, M. L., & Kleiber, D. A. (1981). The graying of achievement motivation. *American Psychologist, 36,* 787–793.

Malatesta, C. Z., & Culver, L. C. (1984). Thematic and affective content in the lives of adult women. In C. Z. Malatesta & C. E. Izard (Eds.), *Emotion in adult development.* Beverly Hills, CA: Sage.

Malinowski, C. I., & Smith, C. P. (1985). Moral reasoning and moral conduct: An investigation prompted by Kohlberg's theory. *Journal of Personality and Social Psychology, 49,* 1016–1027.

Martin, G. B., & Clark, R. D., III. (1982). Distress crying in neonates: Species and peer specificity. *Developmental Psychology, 18,* 3–9.

Matas, L., Arend, R. A., & Sroufe, L. A. (1978). Continuity of adaptation in the second year: The relationship between quality of attachment and later competence. *Child Development, 49,* 547–556.

McClelland, D. C. (1985). How motives, skills, and values determine what people do. *American Psychologist, 40,* 812–825.

McClelland, D. C., Atkinson, J. W., Clark, R. A., & Lowell, E. L. (1953). *The achievement motive.* New York: Appleton-Century-Crofts.

Mellinger, J. C., & Erdwins, C. J. (1985). Personality correlates of age and life roles in adult women. *Psychology of Women Quarterly, 9,* 503–514.

Messer, D. J., McCarthy, M. E., McQuiston, S., MacTurk, R. H., Yarrow, L. J., & Vietze, P. M. (1986). Relation between mastery behavior in infancy and competence in early childhood. *Developmental Psychology, 22,* 366–372.

Miller, A. (1985). A developmental study of the cognitive basis of performance impairment after failure. *Journal of Personality and Social Psychology, 49,* 529–538.

Mischel, W. (1974). Processes in the delay of gratification. In L. Berkowitz (Ed.), *Advances in experimental social psychology* (Vol. 7). New York: Academic.

Moberg, D. O. (1965). Religiosity in old age. *Gerontologist, 5,* 78–87.

Nelson, E. A., Grinder, R. E., & Biaggio, A. M. B. (1969). Relationships between behavioral, cognitive-developmental, and self-report measures of morality and personality. *Multivariate Behavioral Research, 4,* 483–500.

Nelson, E. A., Grinder, R. E., & Mutterer, M. L. (1969). Sources of variance in behavioral measures of honesty in temptation situations: Methodological analyses. *Developmental Psychology, 1,* 265–279.

Nelson, S. A. (1980). Factors influencing young children's use of motives and outcomes as moral criteria. *Child Development, 51,* 823–829.

Nelson-Le Gall, S. A. (1985). Motive–outcome matching and outcome foreseeability: Effects on attribution of intentionality and moral judgments. *Developmental Psychology, 21,* 332–337.

Nicholls, J. G. (1978). The development of the concepts of effort and ability, perception of academic attainment, and the understanding that difficult tasks require more ability. *Child Development, 49,* 800–814.

Nicholls, J. G., & Miller, A. T. (1984). Reasoning about the ability of self and others: A developmental study. *Child Development, 55,* 1990–1999.

Nisan, M., & Kohlberg, L. (1982). Universality and variation in moral judgment: A longitudinal and cross-sectional study in Turkey. *Child Development, 53,* 865–876.

Nucci, L. P., & Nucci, M. S. (1982). Children's responses to moral and social conventional transgressions in free-play settings. *Child Development, 53,* 1337–1342.

Palmore, E. (1981). *Social patterns in normal aging: Findings from the Duke Longitudinal Study.* Durham, NC: Duke University Press.

Parke, R. D. (1977). Some effects of punishment on children's behavior—revisited. In E. M. Hetherington & R. D. Parke (Eds.), *Contemporary readings in child psychology.* New York: McGraw-Hill.

Perry, D. G., & Parke, R. D. (1975). Punishment and alternative response training as determinants of response inhibition in children. *Genetic Psychology Monographs, 91,* 257–279.

Perry, L. C., Perry, D. G., & Weiss, R. J. (1986). Age differences in children's beliefs about whether altruism makes the actor feel good. *Social Cognition, 4,* 263–269.

Phillips, D. (1984). The illusion of incompetence among academically competent children. *Child Development, 55,* 2000–2016.

Piaget, J. (1965). *The moral judgment of the child.* New York: Free Press. (Original work published 1932)

Power, C. (1985). Democratic moral education in the large public high school. In M. W. Berkowitz & F. Oser (Eds.), *Moral education: Theory and application.* Hillsdale, NJ: Erlbaum.

Pratt, M. W., Golding, G., & Hunter, W. J. (1983). Aging as ripening: Character and consistency of moral judgment in young, mature, and older adults. *Human Development, 26,* 277–288.

Pratt, M. W., Golding, G., Hunter, W., & Norris, J. (1988). From inquiry to judgment: Age and sex differences in patterns of adult moral thinking and information-seeking. *International Journal of Aging and Human Development, 27,* 109–124.

Pratt, M. W., Golding, G., & Kerig, P. (1987). Lifespan differences in adult thinking about hypothetical and personal moral issues: Reflection or regression? *International Journal of Behavioral Development, 10,* 359–375.

Raynor, J. O. (1970). Relationships between achievement-related motives, future orientation, and academic performance. *Journal of Personality and Social Psychology, 15,* 28–33.

Raynor, J. O. (1982). A theory of personality functioning and change. In J. O. Raynor & E. E. Entin, *Motivation, career striving, & aging.* Washington, DC: Hemisphere.

Reker, G. T., Peacock, E. J., & Wong, P. T. P. (1987). Meaning and purpose in life and well-being: A life-span perspective. *Journal of Gerontology, 42,* 44–49.

Rest, J. R., & Thoma, S. J. (1985). Relation of moral judgment development to formal education. *Developmental Psychology, 21,* 709–714.

Rosen, B. C., & D'Andrade, R. (1959). The psychosocial origins of achievement motivation. *Sociometry, 22,* 185–218.

Rosenholtz, S. J., & Simpson, C. (1984). The formation of ability conceptions: Developmental trend or social construction? *Review of Educational Research, 54,* 31–63.

Rosenkoetter, L. I. (1973). Resistance to temptation: Inhibitory and disinhibitory effects of models. *Developmental Psychology, 8,* 80–84.

Rushton, J. P. (1980). *Altruism, socialization, and society.* Englewood Cliffs, NJ: Prentice-Hall.

Rybash, J. M., Roodin, P. A., & Hoyer, W. J. (1983). Expressions of moral thought in later adulthood. *Gerontologist, 23,* 254–260.

Santrock, J. W. (1975). Moral structure: The interrelations of moral behavior, moral judgment, and moral affect. *Journal of Genetic Psychology, 127,* 201–213.

Schaffer, H. R., & Emerson, P. E. (1964). The development of social attachments in infancy. *Monographs of the Society for Research in Child Development, 29* (3, Serial No. 94).

Schlaefli, A., Rest, J. R., & Thoma, S. J. (1985). Does moral education improve moral judgment? A meta-analysis of intervention studies using the Defining Issues Test. *Review of Educational Research, 55,* 319–352.

Sears, R. R., Maccoby, E. E., & Levin, H. (1957). *Patterns of child rearing.* New York: Harper & Row.

Selman, R. L. (1980). *The growth of interpersonal understanding.* New York: Academic.

Smetana, J. G. (1981). Preschool children's conceptions of moral and social rules. *Child Development, 52,* 1333–1336.

Smetana, J. G. (1985). Preschool children's conceptions of transgressions: Effects of varying moral and conventional domain-related attributes. *Developmental Psychology, 21,* 18–29.

Smetana, J. G. (1989). Toddlers' social interactions in the context of moral and conventional transgressions in the home. *Developmental Psychology, 25,* 499–508.

Snarey, J. R. (1985). Cross-cultural universality of social–moral development: A critical review of Kohlbergian research. *Psychological Bulletin, 97,* 202–232.

Snarey, J. R., Reimer, J., & Kohlberg, L. (1985). Development of social–moral reasoning among kibbutz adolescents: A longitudinal cross-cultural study. *Developmental Psychology, 21,* 3–17.

Spence, J. T. (1985). Achievement American style. The rewards and costs of individualism. *American Psychologist, 40,* 1285–1295.

Stevens, D. P., & Truss, C. V. (1985). Stability and change in adult personality over 12 and 20 years. *Developmental Psychology, 21,* 568–584.

Stipek, D. J. (1984). The development of achievement motivation. In R. Ames & C. Ames (Eds.), *Research on motivation in education* (Vol. 1). Orlando, FL: Academic.

Stipek, D. J., Roberts, T. A., & Sanborn, M. E. (1984). Preschool-age children's performance expectations for themselves and another child as a function of the incentive value of success and the salience of past performance. *Child Development, 55,* 1983–1989.

Surber, C. F. (1982). Separable effects of motives, consequences, and presentation order on children's moral judgments. *Developmental Psychology, 18,* 257–266.

Tellis-Nayak, V. (1982). The transcendent standard: The religious ethos of the rural elderly. *Gerontologist, 22,* 359–363.

Thoma, S. J. (1986). Estimating gender differences in the comprehension and preference of moral issues. *Developmental Review, 6,* 165–180.

Tietjen, A. M., & Walker, L. J. (1985). Moral reasoning and leadership among men in a Papua New Guinea society. *Developmental Psychology, 21,* 982–992.

Tisak, M. S. (1986). Children's conceptions of parental authority. *Child Development, 57,* 166–176.

Tomlinson-Keasey, C., & Keasey, C. B. (1974). The mediating role of cognitive development in moral judgment. *Child Development, 45,* 291–298.

Toner, I. J., Parke, R. D., & Yussen, S. R. (1978). The effect of observation of model behavior on the establishment and stability of resistance to deviation in children. *Journal of Genetic Psychology, 132,* 283–290.

Toner, I. J., & Potts, R. (1981). Effect of modeled rationales on moral behavior, moral choice, and level of moral judgment in children. *Journal of Psychology, 107,* 153–162.

Turiel, E. (1978). The development of concepts of social structure: Social convention. In J. Glick & A. Clarke-Stewart (Eds.), *The development of social understanding.* New York: Gardner Press.

Turiel, E. (1983). *The development of social knowledge. Morality and convention.* Cambridge, England: Cambridge University Press.

Veroff, J., Atkinson, J. W., Feld, S. C., & Gurin, G. (1960). The use of thematic apperception to assess motivation in a nationwide interview study. *Psychological Monographs, 74* (12, Whole No. 499).

Veroff, J., Reuman, D., & Feld, S. (1984). Motives in American men and women across the adult life span. *Developmental Psychology, 20,* 1142–1158.

Veroff, J., & Veroff, J. B. (1980). *Social incentives. A life-span developmental approach.* New York: Academic.

Walker, L. J. (1980). Cognitive and perspective-taking prerequisites of moral development. *Child Development, 51,* 131–139.

Walker, L. J. (1984). Sex differences in the development of moral reasoning: A critical review. *Child Development, 55,* 677–691.

Walker, L. J. (1986). Experiential and cognitive sources of moral development in adulthood. *Human Development, 29,* 113–124.

Walker, L. J. (1989). A longitudinal study of moral reasoning. *Child Development, 60,* 157–166.

Watson, J. S., & Ramey, C. T. (1972). Reactions to response-contingent stimulation in early infancy. *Merrill–Palmer Quarterly, 18,* 219–228.

Weiner, B. (1974). *Achievement and attribution theory.* Morristown, NJ: General Learning Press.

Weiner, B. (1986). *An attributional theory of motivation and emotion.* New York: Springer-Verlag.

Weiner, I. B. (1980). Psychopathology in adolescence. In J. Adelson (Ed.), *Handbook of adolescent psychology.* New York: Wiley.

White, R. W. (1959). Motivation reconsidered: The concept of competence. *Psychological Review, 66,* 297–333.

Winterbottom, M. (1958). The relation of need for achievement to learning experiences in independence and mastery. In J. Atkinson (Ed.), *Motives in fantasy, action, and society.* Princeton, NJ: Van Nostrand.

Yarrow, L. J., MacTurk, R. H., Vietze, P. M., McCarthy, M. E., Klein, R. P., & McQuiston, S. (1984). Developmental course of parental stimulation and its relationship to mastery motivation during infancy. *Developmental Psychology, 20,* 492–503.

Young, G., & Dowling, W. (1987). Dimensions of religiosity in old age: Accounting for variation in types of participation. *Journal of Gerontology, 42,* 376–380.

Zahn-Waxler, C., Radke-Yarrow, M., & King, R. A. (1979). Child rearing and children's prosocial initiations toward victims of distress. *Child Development, 50,* 319–330.

Chapter 13: Participation in the Social World

Adams, R. G. (1985–1986). Emotional closeness and physical distance between friends: Implications for elderly women living in age-segregated and age-integrated settings. *International Journal of Aging and Human Development, 22,* 55–76.

Ainsworth, M. D. S. (1973). The development of infant–mother attachment. In B. M. Caldwell & H. N. Ricciuti (Eds.), *Review of child development research* (Vol. 3). Chicago: University of Chicago Press.

Ainsworth, M. D. S. (1979). Attachment as related to mother–infant interaction. In J. G. Rosenblatt, R. A. Hinde, C. Beer, & M. Busnel (Eds.), *Advances in the study of behavior* (Vol. 9). New York: Academic.

Ainsworth, M. D. S. (1989). Attachments beyond infancy. *American Psychologist, 44,* 709–716.

Ainsworth, M. D. S., Blehar, M., Waters, E., & Wall, S. (1978). *Patterns of attachment.* Hillsdale, NJ: Erlbaum.

Alexander, B. K., & Harlow, H. F. (1965). Social behavior in juvenile rhesus monkeys subjected to different rearing conditions during the first 6 months of life. *Zoologische Jarbücher Physiologie, 60,* 167–174.

Allan, G. (1986). Friendship and care for elderly people. *Ageing and Society, 6,* 1–12.

Allen, J. P., Weissberg, R. P., & Hawkins, J. A. (1989). The relation between values and social competence in early adolescence. *Developmental Psychology, 25,* 458–464.

Alley, T. R. (1981). Head shape and the perception of cuteness. *Developmental Psychology, 17,* 650–654.

Ambrose, J. A. (1963). The concept of a critical period in the development of social responsiveness in early infancy. In B. M. Foss (Ed.), *Determinants of infant behavior* (Vol. 2). London: Methuen.

Antonucci, T. C. (1985). Personal characteristics, social support, and social behavior. In R. H. Binstock & E. Shanas (Eds.), *Handbook of aging and the social sciences* (2nd ed.). New York: Van Nostrand Reinhold.

Arend, R., Gove, F. L., & Sroufe, L. A. (1979). Continuity of individual adaptation from infancy to kindergarten: A predictive study of ego-resiliency and curiosity in preschoolers. *Child Development, 50,* 950–959.

Arling, G. (1976). The elderly widow and her family, neighbors and friends. *Journal of Marriage and the Family, 38,* 757–768.

Arling, G. (1987). Strain, social support, and distress in old age. *Journal of Gerontology, 42,* 107–113.

Asher, S. R. (1986). An overview of intervention research with unpopular children. In S. R. Asher & J. Coie (Eds.), *Assessment of children's social status.* New York: Cambridge University Press.

Athey, I. (1984). Contributions of play to development. In T. D. Yawkey & A. D. Pelligrini (Eds.), *Child's play: Developmental and applied.* Hillsdale, NJ: Erlbaum.

Babchuk, N. (1978–1979). Aging and primary relations. *International Journal of Aging and Human Development, 9,* 137– 151.

Barenboim, C. (1981). The development of person perception in childhood and adolescence: From behavioral comparisons to psychological constructs to psychological comparisons. *Child Development, 52,* 129–144.

Belsky, J. (1980). Child maltreatment: An ecological integration. *American Psychologist, 35,* 320–335.

Belsky, J. (1981). Early human experience: A family perspective. *Developmental Psychology, 17,* 3–23.

Belsky, J., Rovine, M., & Taylor, D. G. (1984). The Pennsylvania infant and family development project, III: The origins of individual differences in infant–mother attachment: Maternal and infant contributions. *Child Development, 55,* 718–728.

Berndt, T. J. (1979). Developmental changes in conforming to peers and parents. *Developmental Psychology, 15,* 608–616.

Berndt, T. J. (1982). The features and effects of friendship in early adolescence. *Child Development, 53,* 1447–1460.

Berndt, T. J., & Hoyle, S. G. (1985). Stability and change in childhood and adolescent friendships. *Developmental Psychology, 21,* 1007–1015.

Bierman, K. L. (1986). Process of change during social skills training with preadolescents and its relation to treatment outcome. *Child Development, 57,* 230–240.

Bierman, K. L., & Furman, W. (1984). The effects of social skills training and peer involvement on the social adjustment of preadolescents. *Child Development, 55,* 151–162.

Bixenstine, V. C., DeCorte, M. S., & Bixenstine, B. A. (1976). Conformity to peer-sponsored misconduct at four grade levels. *Developmental Psychology, 12,* 226–236.

Blanchard-Fields, F. (1986a). Attributional processes in adult development. *Educational Gerontology, 12,* 291–300.

Blanchard-Fields, F. (1986b). Reasoning on social dilemmas varying in emotional saliency: An adult developmental perspective. *Psychology and Aging, 1,* 325–333.

Boccia, M., & Campos, J. (1983, April). *Maternal emotional signalling: Its effects on infants' reactions to strangers.* Paper presented at the biennial meeting of the Society for Research in Child Development, Detroit, MI.

Bower, T. G. R. (1982). *Development in infancy.* San Francisco: W. H. Freeman.

Bowlby, J. (1969). *Attachment and loss: Vol. 1. Attachment.* New York: Basic.

Bowlby, J. (1973). *Attachment and loss: Vol. 2. Separation.* New York: Basic.

Bowlby, J. (1980). *Attachment and loss: Vol. 3. Loss, sadness and depression.* New York: Basic.

Brackbill, Y. (1958). Extinction of the smiling response to infants as a function of reinforcement schedule. *Child Development, 29,* 114–124.

Bretherton, I., Stolberg, U., & Kreye, M. (1981). Engaging strangers in proximal interaction: Infants' social initiative. *Developmental Psychology, 17,* 746–755.

Bronfenbrenner, U. (1970). *Two worlds of childhood: U.S. and U.S.S.R.* New York: Russell Sage Foundation.

Brook, J. S., Whiteman, M., & Gordon, A. S. (1983). Stages of drug use in adolescence: Personality, peer, and family correlates. *Developmental Psychology, 19,* 269–277.

Brown, B. B., & Lohr, M. J. (1987). Peer-group affiliation and adolescent self-esteem: An integration of ego-identity and symbolic-interaction theories. *Journal of Personality and Social Psychology, 52,* 47–55.

Brownell, C. A. (1986). Convergent developments: Cognitive-developmental correlates of growth in infant/toddler peer skills. *Child Development, 57,* 275– 286.

Buhrmester, D., & Furman, W. (1986). The changing functions of friends in childhood: A neo-Sullivanian perspective. In V. J. Derlega & B. A. Winstead (Eds.), *Friendship and social interaction.* New York: Springer-Verlag.

Buss, D. M. (1985). Human mate selection. *American Scientist, 73,* 47–51.

Carlson, V., Cicchetti, D., Barnett, D., & Braunwald, K. (1989). Disorganized/disoriented attachment relationships in maltreated infants. *Developmental Psychology, 25,* 525–531.

Chatters, L. M., Taylor, R. J., & Jackson, J. S. (1986). Aged blacks' choices for an informal helper network. *Journal of Gerontology, 41,* 94–100.

Clark, E. A., & Hanisee, J. (1982). Intellectual and adaptive performance of Asian children in adoptive American settings. *Developmental Psychology, 18,* 595–599.

Clarke, A. M., & Clarke, A. D. B. (1976). *Early experience: Myth and evidence.* New York: Free Press.

Clasen, D. R., & Brown, B. B. (1985). The multidimensionality of peer pressure in adolescence. *Journal of Youth and Adolescence, 14,* 451–468.

Coie, J. D., & Dodge, K. A. (1983). Continuities and changes in children's social status: A five-year longitudinal study. *Merrill–Palmer Quarterly, 29,* 261–282.

Coie, J. D., Dodge, K. A., & Coppotelli, H. (1982). Dimensions and types of social status: A cross-age perspective. *Developmental Psychology, 18,* 557–570.

Coie, J. D., & Kupersmidt, J. B. (1983). A behavioral analysis of emerging social status in boys' groups. *Child Development, 54,* 1400–1416.

Cowen, E. L., Pederson, A., Babigian, H., Izzo, L. D., & Trost, M. A. (1973). Long-term follow-up of early detected vulnerable children. *Journal of Consulting and Clinical Psychology, 41,* 438–446.

Crockenberg, S. B. (1981). Infant irritability, mother responsiveness, and social support influences on the security of infant–mother attachment. *Child Development, 52,* 857–865.

Davis, K. E. (1985, February). Near and dear: Friendship and love compared. *Psychology Today,* pp. 22–30.

de Jong-Gierveld, J. (1986). Loneliness and the degree of intimacy in interpersonal relationships. In R. Gilmour & S. Duck (Eds.), *The emerging field of personal relationships.* Hillsdale, NJ: Erlbaum.

Denney, N. W. (1982). Aging and cognitive changes. In B. B. Wolman (Ed.), *Handbook of developmental psychology.* Englewood Cliffs, NJ: Prentice–Hall.

Dennis, W. (1973). *Children of the creche.* New York: Appleton-Century-Crofts.

Diaz, R. M., & Berndt, T. J. (1982). Children's knowledge of a best friend: Fact or fancy? *Developmental Psychology, 18,* 787–794.

Dickens, W. J., & Perlman, D. (1981). Friendship over the life cycle. In S. Duck & R. Gilmour (Eds.), *Personal relationships: Vol. 2. Developing personal relationships.* London, New York: Academic.

Dickinson, G. E. (1975). Dating behavior of black and white adolescents before and after desegregation. *Journal of Marriage and the Family, 37,* 602–608.

Dickstein, S., & Parke, R. D. (1988). Social referencing in infancy: A glance at fathers and marriage. *Child Development, 59,* 506–511.

Dodge, K. A. (1983). Behavioral antecedents of peer social status. *Child Development, 54,* 1386–1399.

Dolen, L. S., & Bearison, D. J. (1982). Social interaction and social cognition in aging. *Human Development, 25,* 430–442.

Douvan, E., & Adelson, J. (1966). *The adolescent experience.* New York: Wiley.

Dunphy, D. C. (1963). The social structure of urban adolescent peer groups. *Sociometry, 26,* 230–246.

Egeland, B., & Farber, E. A. (1984). Mother–infant attachment: Factors related to its development and changes over time. *Child Development, 55,* 753–771.

Elkind, D. (1980). Strategic interactions in early adolescence. In J. Adelson (Ed.), *Handbook of adolescent psychology.* New York: Wiley.

Ellis, S., Rogoff, B., & Cromer, C. C. (1981). Age segregation in children's social interactions. *Developmental Psychology, 17,* 399–407.

Feinman, S., & Lewis, M. (1983). Social referencing at 10 months: A second-order effect on infants' responses to strangers. *Child Development, 54,* 878–887.

Field, D., & Minkler, M. (1988). Continuity and change in social support between young-old and old-old or very-old age. *Journal of Gerontology: Psychological Sciences, 43,* P100–P106.

Fischer, C. S., & Phillips, S. L. (1982). Who is alone? Social characteristics of people with small networks. In L. A. Peplau & D. Perlman (Eds.), *Loneliness. A sourcebook of current theory, research and therapy.* New York: Wiley-Interscience.

Fischer, J. L., Sollie, D. L., Sorell, G. T., & Green, S. K. (1989). Marital status and career stage influences on social networks of young adults. *Journal of Marriage and the Family, 51,* 521–534.

Fitzgerald, J. M., & Martin-Louer, P. (1983–1984). Person perception in adulthood: A categories analysis. *International Journal of Aging and Human Development, 18,* 197–205.

Flavell, J. H. (1985). *Cognitive development* (2nd ed.). Englewood Cliffs, NJ: Prentice-Hall.

Fox, M., Gibbs, M., & Auerbach, D. (1985). Age and gender dimensions of friendship. *Psychology of Women Quarterly, 9,* 489–502.

Freud, A., & Dann, S. (1951). An experiment in group upbringing. In R. Eisler, A. Freud, H. Hartmann, & E. Kris (Eds.), *The psychoanalytic study of the child* (Vol. 6). New York: International Universities Press.

Freud, S. (1930). *Three contributions to the theory of sex.* New York: Nervous and Mental Disease Publishing Company. (Original work published 1905)

Furman, W., & Bierman, K. L. (1983). Developmental changes in young children's conceptions of friendship. *Child Development, 54,* 549–556.

Furman, W., & Buhrmester, D. (1985). Children's perceptions of the personal relationships in their social networks. *Developmental Psychology, 21,* 1016–1024.

Furman, W., Rahe, D. F., & Hartup, W. W. (1979). Rehabilitation of socially withdrawn preschool children through mixed-age and same-age socialization. *Child Development, 50,* 915–922.

Gavin, L. A., & Furman, W. (1989). Age differences in adolescents' perceptions of their peer groups. *Developmental Psychology, 25,* 827–834.

Gewirtz, H. B., & Gewirtz, J. L. (1968). Caretaking settings, background events, and behavior differences in four Israeli child-rearing environments: Some preliminary trends. In B. M. Foss (Ed.), *Determinants of infant behavior* (Vol. 4). London: Methuen.

Gnepp, J. (1989). Personalized inferences of emotions and appraisals: Component processes and correlates. *Developmental Psychology, 25,* 277–288.

Gnepp, J., & Chilamkurti, C. (1988). Children's use of personality attributions to predict other people's emotional and behavioral reactions. *Child Development, 59,* 743–754.

Goldberg, S. (1983). Parent–infant bonding: Another look. *Child Development, 54,* 1355–1382.

Goldberg, S., Perrotta, M., Minde, K., & Corter, C. (1986). Maternal behavior and attachment in low-birth-weight twins and singletons. *Child Development, 57*, 34–46.

Goldfarb, W. (1943). The effects of early institutional care on adolescent personality. *Journal of Experimental Education, 12*, 107–129.

Goldfarb, W. (1945). Effects of psychological deprivation in infancy and subsequent stimulation. *American Journal of Psychiatry, 102*, 18–33.

Goldfarb, W. (1947). Variations in adolescent adjustment in institutionally reared children. *Journal of Orthopsychiatry, 17*, 449–457.

Goldsmith, H. H., & Alansky, J. A. (1987). Maternal and infant temperamental predictors of attachment: A meta-analytic review. *Journal of Consulting and Clinical Psychology, 55*, 805–816.

Green, K. D., Forehand, R., Beck, S. J., & Vosk, B. (1980). An assessment of the relationship among measures of children's social competence and children's academic achievement. *Child Development, 51*, 1149–1156.

Greene, J. G., Fox, N. A., & Lewis, M. (1983). The relationship between neonatal characteristics and three-month mother–infant interaction in high-risk infants. *Child Development, 54*, 1286–1296.

Harkness, S., & Super, C. M. (1985). The cultural context of gender segregation in children's peer groups. *Child Development, 56*, 219–224.

Harlow, H. F., & Harlow, M. K. (1977). The young monkeys. In *Readings in developmental psychology today* (3rd ed.). Del Mar, CA: CRM Books.

Harlow, H. F., & Zimmerman, R. R. (1959). Affectional responses in the infant monkey. *Science, 130*, 421–432.

Hartup, W. W. (1983). Peer relations. In M. Hetherington (Ed.; P. H. Mussen, General Ed.), *Handbook of child psychology: Vol. 4. Socialization, personality, and social development* (4th ed.). New York: Wiley.

Hay, D. F. (1985). Learning to form relationships in infancy: Parallel attainments with parents and peers. *Developmental Review, 5*, 122–161.

Hay, D. F., Nash, A., & Pedersen, J. (1983). Interaction between six-month-old peers. *Child Development, 54*, 557–562.

Hazan, C., & Shaver, P. (1987). Romantic love conceptualized as an attachment process. *Journal of Personality and Social Psychology, 52*, 511–524.

Hodges, J., & Tizard, B. (1989). IQ and behavioural adjustment of ex-institutional adolescents. *Journal of Child Psychology and Psychiatry, 30*, 53–75.

Holahan, C. K., & Holahan, C. J. (1987). Self-efficacy, social support, and depression in aging: A longitudinal analysis. *Journal of Gerontology, 42*, 65–68.

Howes, C. (1983). Patterns of friendship. *Child Development, 54*, 1041–1053.

Hudson, L. M., Forman, E. R., & Brion-Meisels, S. (1982). Role-taking as a predictor of prosocial behavior in cross-age tutors. *Child Development, 53*, 1320–1329.

Huston, T. L., Surra, C. A., Fitzgerald, N. M., & Cate, R. M. (1981). From courtship to marriage: Mate selection as an interpersonal process. In S. Duck & R. Gilmour (Eds.), *Personal relationships: Vol. 2. Developing personal relationships*. London, New York: Academic.

Ingersoll-Dayton, B., & Antonucci, T. C. (1988). Reciprocal and nonreciprocal social support: Contrasting sides of intimate relationships. *Journal of Gerontology: Social Sciences, 43*, S65–S73.

Isabella, R. A., Belsky, J., & von Eye, A. (1989). Origins of infant–mother attachment: An examination of interactional synchrony during the infant's first year. *Developmental Psychology, 25*, 12–21.

Jacobson, J. L., & Wille, D. E. (1986). The influence of attachment pattern on developmental changes in peer interaction from the toddler to the preschool period. *Child Development, 57*, 338–347.

Jones, W. H., Hobbs, S. A., & Hockenbury, D. (1982). Loneliness and social skill deficits. *Journal of Personality and Social Psychology, 42*, 682–689.

Kagan, J. (1972). Do infants think? *Scientific American, 226*, 74–82.

Kagan, J. (1976). Emergent themes in human development. *American Scientist, 64*, 186–196.

Kahn, R. L., & Antonucci, T. C. (1980). Convoys over the life course: Attachment, roles, and social support. In P. B. Baltes & O. G. Brim, Jr. (Eds.), *Life-span development and behavior* (Vol. 3). New York: Academic.

Kavanaugh, R., & McCall, R. (1983). Social influencing among 2-year-olds: The role of affiliative and antagonistic behaviors. *Infant Behavior and Development, 6*, 39–52.

Keating, D., & Clark, L. V. (1980). Development of physical and social reasoning in adolescence. *Developmental Psychology, 16*, 23–30.

Kendig, H. L., Coles, R., Pittelkow, Y., & Wilson, S. (1988). Confidants and family structure in old age. *Journal of Gerontology: Social Sciences, 43*, S31–S40.

Kessen, W. (1975). *Childhood in China*. New Haven, CT: Yale University Press.

Klaus, H. M., & Kennell, J. H. (1976). *Maternal–infant bonding*. St. Louis: C. V. Mosby.

Kobak, R. R., & Sceery, A. (1988). Attachment in late adolescence: Working models, affect regulation, and representations of self and others. *Child Development, 59*, 135–146.

Kohlberg, L. (1969). Stage and sequence: The cognitive-developmental approach to socialization. In D. A. Goslin (Ed.), *Handbook of socialization theory and research*. Chicago: Rand McNally.

Kramer, D. A. (1986). A life-span view of social cognition. *Educational Gerontology, 12*, 277–289.

Krause, N., Liang, J., & Yatomi, N. (1989). Satisfaction with social support and depressive symptoms: A panel analysis. *Psychology and Aging, 4*, 88–97.

Kurdek, L. A., & Krile, D. (1982). A developmental analysis of the relation between peer acceptance and both interpersonal understanding and perceived social self-competence. *Child Development, 53*, 1485–1491.

Ladd, G. W. (1981). Effectiveness of a social learning method for enhancing children's social interaction and peer acceptance. *Child Development, 52*, 171–178.

Ladd, G. W., Price, J. M., & Hart, C. H. (1988). Predicting preschoolers' peer status from their playground behaviors. *Child Development, 59*, 986–992.

Lamb, M. E. (1987). Predictive implications of individual differences in attachment. *Journal of Consulting and Clinical Psychology, 55*, 817–824.

Langlois, J. H. (1986). From the eye of the beholder to behavioral reality: Development of social behaviors and social relations as a function of physical attractiveness. In C. P. Herman, M. P. Zanna, & E. T. Higgins (Eds.), *Physical appearance, stigma, and social behavior: The Ontario Symposium, Volume 3.* Hillsdale, NJ: Erlbaum.

Larson, R., Zuzanek, J., & Mannell, R. (1985). Being alone versus being with people: Disengagement in the daily experience of older adults. *Journal of Gerontology, 40,* 375–381.

LeMare, L. J., & Rubin, K. H. (1987). Perspective taking and peer interaction: Structural and developmental analyses. *Child Development, 58,* 306–315.

Lerner, R. M., & Ryff, C. D. (1978). Implementation of the life-span view of human development: The sample case of attachment. In P. B. Baltes (Ed.), *Life-span development and behavior* (Vol. 1). New York: Academic.

Lester, B. M., Kotelchuck, M., Spelke, E., Sellers, M. J., & Klein, R. E. (1974). Separation protest in Guatemalan infants: Cross-cultural and cognitive findings. *Developmental Psychology, 10,* 79–85.

Lever, J. (1976). Sex differences in the games children play. *Social Problems, 23,* 478–487.

Levy-Shiff, R. (1983). Adaptation and competence in early childhood: Communally-raised kibbutz children versus family raised children in the city. *Child Development, 54,* 1606–1614.

Lewis, M., & Rosenblum, M. A. (1975). *Friendship and peer relations.* New York: Wiley.

Liang, J., Dvorkin, L., Kahana, E., & Mazian, F. (1980). Social integration and morale: A re-examination. *Journal of Gerontology, 35,* 746–757.

Livesley, W. J., & Bromley, D. B. (1973). *Person perception in childhood and adolescence.* London: Wiley.

Lorenz, K. Z. (1937). The companion in the bird's world. *Auk, 54,* 245–273.

Louis Harris and Associates (1981). *Aging in the eighties: America in transition.* Washington, DC: National Council on Aging.

Lowenthal, M. F., & Haven, C. (1968). Interaction and adaptation: Intimacy as a critical variable. *American Sociological Review, 33,* 20–30.

Main, M., & Cassidy, J. (1988). Categories of response to reunion with the parent at age 6: Predictable from infant attachment classifications and stable over a 1-month period. *Developmental Psychology, 24,* 415–426.

Main, M., Kaplan, N., & Cassidy, J. (1985). Security in infancy, childhood, and adulthood: A move to the level of representation. In I. Bretherton & E. Waters (Eds.), *Growing points of attachment theory and research. Monographs of the Society for Research in Child Development, 50,* (1–2, Serial No. 209), 66–104.

Main, M., & Weston, D. R. (1981). The quality of the toddler's relationship to mother and to father: Related to conflict and the readiness to establish new relationships. *Child Development, 52,* 932–940.

Matejcek, Z., Dytrych, Z., & Schuller, V. (1979). The Prague study of children born from unwanted pregnancies. *International Journal of Mental Health, 7,* 63–74.

Matthews, S. H. (1986). *Friendships through the life course. Oral biographies in old age* (Vol. 161, Sage Library of Social Research). Beverly Hills, CA: Sage.

McDavid, J. W., & Harari, H. (1966). Stereotyping of names and popularity in grade school children. *Child Development, 37,* 453–459.

McGuire, K. D., & Weisz, J. R. (1982). Social cognition and behavior correlates of preadolescent chumship. *Child Development, 53,* 1478–1484.

Miller, B. C., McCoy, J. K., & Olson, T. D. (1986). Dating age and stage as correlates of adolescent sexual attitudes and behavior. *Journal of Adolescent Research, 1,* 361–371.

Morgan, D. L. (1988). Age differences in social network participation. *Journal of Gerontology: Social Sciences, 43,* S129–S137.

Morgan, G. A., & Ricciuti, H. N. (1969). Infants' responses to strangers during the first year. In B. M. Foss (Ed.), *Determinants of infant behavior* (Vol. 4). London: Methuen.

Mueller, E., & Lucas, T. (1975). A developmental analysis of peer interactions among toddlers. In M. Lewis & L. Rosenblum (Eds.), *Friendship and peer relations.* New York: Wiley.

Mueller, E., & Vandell, D. (1979). Infant-infant interaction. In J. Osofsky (Ed.), *Handbook of infant development.* New York: Wiley.

Murstein, B. I. (1980). Mate selection in the 1970s. *Journal of Marriage and the Family, 42,* 777–792.

Norris, J. E., & Rubin, K. H. (1984). Peer interaction and communication: A life-span perspective. In P. B. Baltes & O. G. Brim, Jr. (Eds.), *Life-span behavior and development* (Vol. 6). New York: Academic.

Novak, M. A. (1979). Social recovery of monkeys isolated for the first year of life: II. Long-term assessment. *Developmental Psychology, 15,* 50–61.

Oden, S., & Asher, S. R. (1977). Coaching children in social skills for friendship making. *Child Development, 48,* 495–506.

O'Mahony, J. F. (1986). Development of person description over adolescence. *Journal of Youth and Adolescence, 15,* 389–403.

Parlee, M. B., & the Editors of *Psychology Today* (1979, October). The friendship bond. *Psychology Today,* pp. 42–54, 113.

Peevers, B. H., & Secord, P. F. (1973). Developmental changes in attribution of descriptive concepts to persons. *Journal of Personality and Social Psychology, 27,* 120–128.

Piaget, J. (1965). *The moral judgment of the child.* New York: Free Press. (Original work published 1932)

Pihlblad, C. T., & Adams, D. L. (1972). Widowhood, social participation and life satisfaction. *International Journal of Aging and Human Development, 3,* 323–330.

Pilisuk, M., & Minkler, M. (1980). Supportive networks: Life ties for the elderly. *Journal of Social Issues, 36* (2), 95–116.

Place, D. M. (1975). The dating experience for adolescent girls. *Adolescence, 10,* 157–174.

Powers, E. A., & Bultena, G. L. (1976). Sex differences in intimate friendships of old age. *Journal of Marriage and the Family, 38,* 739–747.

Provence, S., & Lipton, R. C. (1962). *Infants in institutions.* New York: International Universities Press.

Putallaz, M. (1987). Maternal behavior and children's sociometric status. *Child Development, 58,* 324–340.

Putallaz, M., & Gottman, J. M. (1981). An interactional model of children's entry into peer groups. *Child Development, 52*, 986–994.

Putallaz, M., & Wasserman, A. (1989). Children's naturalistic entry behavior and sociometric status: A developmental perspective. *Developmental Psychology, 25*, 297–305.

Rabiner, D., & Coie, J. (1989). Effect of expectancy inductions on rejected children's acceptance by unfamiliar peers. *Developmental Psychology, 25*, 450–457.

Radke-Yarrow, M., Cummings, E. M., Kuczynski, L., & Chapman, M. (1985). Patterns of attachment in two- and three-year-olds in normal families and families with parental depression. *Child Development, 56*, 884–893.

Rholes, W. S., Jones, M., & Wade, C. (1988). Children's understanding of personal disposition and its relationship to behavior. *Journal of Experimental Child Psychology, 45*, 1–17.

Rholes, W. S., & Ruble, D. N. (1984). Children's understanding of dispositional characteristics of others. *Child Development, 55*, 550–560.

Roberto, K. A., & Kimboko, P. J. (1989). Friendships in later life: Definitions and maintenance patterns. *International Journal of Aging and Human Development, 28*, 9–19.

Roberto, K. A., & Scott, J. P. (1986). Equity considerations in the friendships of older adults. *Journal of Gerontology, 41*, 241–247.

Rode, S. S., Chang, P., Fisch, R. O., & Sroufe, L. A. (1981). Attachment patterns of infants separated at birth. *Developmental Psychology, 17*, 188–191.

Roff, M. F., Sells, S. B., & Golden, M. M. (1972). *Social adjustment and personality development in children*. Minneapolis: University of Minnesota Press.

Roodin, P. A., Rybash, J. M., & Hoyer, W. J. (1986). Qualitative dimensions of social cognition in adulthood. *Educational Gerontology, 12*, 301–311.

Rook, K. S. (1984). Promoting social bonding. Strategies for helping the lonely and socially isolated. *American Psychologist, 39*, 1389–1407.

Rubin, Z., & Sloman, J. (1984). How parents influence their children's friendships. In M. Lewis (Ed.), *Beyond the dyad*. New York: Plenum.

Rutter, M. (1979). Maternal deprivation, 1972–1978: New findings, new concepts, new approaches. *Child Development, 50*, 283–305.

Schaffer, H. R. (1971). *The growth of sociability*. Baltimore: Penguin Books.

Schaffer, H. R. (1977). *Mothering*. Cambridge, MA: Harvard University Press.

Schaffer, H. R., & Emerson, P. E. (1964). The development of social attachments in infancy. *Monographs of the Society for Research in Child Development, 29*, (3, Serial No. 94).

Sebald, H. (1986). Adolescents' shifting orientation toward parents and peers: A curvilinear trend over recent decades. *Journal of Marriage and the Family, 48*, 5–13.

Selman, R. L. (1976). Social-cognitive understanding: A guide to educational and clinical experience. In T. Lickona (Ed.), *Moral development and behavior: Theory, research and social issues*. New York: Holt, Rinehart & Winston.

Selman, R. L. (1980). *The growth of interpersonal understanding*. New York: Academic.

Selman, R. L., Beardslee, W., Schultz, L. H., Krupa, M., & Podorefsky, D. (1986). Assessing adolescent interpersonal negotiation strategies: Toward the integration of structural and functional models. *Developmental Psychology, 22*, 450–459.

Shantz, C. U. (1987). Conflicts between children. *Child Development, 58*, 283–305.

Sharabany, R., Gershoni, R., & Hofman, J. E. (1981). Girlfriend, boyfriend: Age and sex differences in intimate friendship. *Developmental Psychology, 17*, 800–808.

Shea, L., Thompson, L., & Blieszner, R. (1988). Resources in older adults' old and new friendships. *Journal of Social and Personal Relationships, 5*, 83–96.

Shulman, N. (1975). Life-cycle variations in patterns of close relationships. *Journal of Marriage and the Family, 37*, 813–821.

Singer, L. M., Brodzinsky, D. M., Ramsay, D., Steir, M., & Waters, E. (1985). Mother–infant attachments in adoptive families. *Child Development, 56*, 1543–1551.

Skolnick, A. (1986). Early attachment and personal relationships across the life course. In P. B. Baltes, D. L. Featherman, & R. M. Lerner (Eds.), *Life-span development and behavior* (Vol. 7). Hillsdale, NJ: Erlbaum.

Snow, R., & Crapo, L. (1982). Emotional bondedness, subjective well-being, and health in elderly medical patients. *Journal of Gerontology, 37*, 609–615.

Spitz, R. A. (1945). Hospitalism: An inquiry into the genesis of psychiatric conditions in early childhood. In A. Freud (Ed.), *The psychoanalytic study of the child* (Vol. 1). New York: International Universities Press.

Sprunger, L. W., Boyce, W. T., & Gaines, J. A. (1985). Family–infant congruence: Routines and rhythmicity in family adaptations to a young infant. *Child Development, 56*, 564–572.

Sroufe, L. A. (1977). Wariness of strangers and the study of infant development. *Child Development, 48*, 1184–1199.

Sroufe, L. A., Fox, N. E., & Pancake, V. R. (1983). Attachment and dependency in developmental perspective. *Child Development, 54*, 1615–1627.

Sroufe, L. A., Waters, E., & Matas, L. (1974). Contextual determinants of infant affectional response. In M. Lewis & L. A. Rosenblum (Eds.), *The origins of fear*. New York: Wiley.

Steele, B. F., & Pollack, C. B. (1974). A psychiatric study of parents who abuse infants and small children. In R. E. Helfer & C. H. Kempe (Eds.), *The battered child*. Chicago: University of Chicago Press.

Steinberg, L., & Silverberg, S. B. (1986). The vicissitudes of autonomy in early adolescence. *Child Development, 57*, 841–851.

Stern, D. (1977). *The first relationship: Infant and mother*. Cambridge, MA: Harvard University Press.

Sternberg, R. J., & Grajek, S. (1984). The nature of love. *Journal of Personality and Social Psychology, 47*, 312–329.

Stevenson, M. B., VerHoeve, J. N., Roach, M. A., & Leavitt, L. A. (1986). The beginning of conversation. Early patterns of mother–infant vocal responsiveness. *Infant Behavior and Development, 9*, 423–440.

Styczynski, L. E., & Langlois, J. H. (1977). The effects of familiarity on behavioral stereotypes associated with physical attractiveness in young children. *Child Development, 48*, 1137–1141.

Sullivan, H. S. (1953). *The interpersonal theory of psychiatry*. New York: Norton.

Suomi, S. J., & Harlow, H. F. (1972). Social rehabilitation of isolate reared monkeys. *Developmental Psychology, 6*, 487–496.

Suomi, S. J., & Harlow, H. F. (1975). The role and reason of peer relationships in rhesus monkeys. In M. Lewis & L. A. Rosenblum (Eds.), *Friendship and peer relations*. New York: Wiley.

Suomi, S. J., & Harlow, H. F. (1978). Early experience and social development in rhesus monkeys. In M. E. Lamb (Ed.), *Social and personality development*. New York: Holt, Rinehart & Winston.

Tesch, S. A. (1983). Review of friendship development across the life span. *Human Development, 26*, 266–276.

Thoman, E. B., Acebo, C., & Becker, P. T. (1983). Infant crying and stability in the mother–infant relationship: A systems analysis. *Child Development, 54*, 653–659.

Thompson, R. A., & Lamb, M. E. (1984). Continuity and change in socioemotional development during the second year. In R. N. Emde & R. J. Harmon (Eds.), *Continuities and discontinuities in development*. New York: Plenum.

Tietgen, A. M. (1982). The social networks of preadolescent children in Sweden. *International Journal of Behavioral Development, 5*, 111–130.

Tizard, B. (1977). *Adoption: A second chance*. London: Open Books.

Udry, J. R. (1971). *The social context of marriage* (2nd ed.). Philadelphia: J. B. Lippincott.

Vandell, D. L., & Wilson, K. S. (1987). Infants' interactions with mother, sibling, and peer: Contrasts and relations between interaction systems. *Child Development, 58*, 176–186.

Vandell, D. L., Wilson, K. S., & Buchanan, N. R. (1980). Peer interaction in the first year of life: An examination of its structure, content, and sensitivity to toys. *Child Development, 51*, 481–488.

Van Ijzendoorn, M. H., & Kroonenberg, P. M. (1988). Cross-cultural patterns of attachment: A meta-analysis of the Strange Situation. *Child Development, 59*, 147–156.

Vaughn, B. E., Egeland, B. R., Sroufe, L. A., & Waters, E. (1979). Individual differences in infant–mother attachment at twelve and eighteen months: Stability and change in families under stress. *Child Development, 50*, 971–975.

Veroff, J., Douvan, E., & Kulka, R. A. (1981). *The inner American. A self-portrait from 1957 to 1976*. New York: Basic Books.

Vygotsky, L. S. (1978). *Mind in society. The development of higher psychological processes* (Ed. by M. Cole, V. John-Steiner, S. Scribner, & E. Souberman). Cambridge, MA: Harvard University Press.

Walster, E., Walster, G. W., & Berscheid, E. (1978). *Equity: Theory and research*. Boston: Allyn & Bacon.

Ward, R. A., Sherman, S. R., & LaGory, M. (1984). Subjective network assessments and subjective well-being. *Journal of Gerontology, 39*, 93–101.

Waters, E., Vaughn, B. E., & Egeland, B. R. (1980). Individual differences in mother–infant attachment relationships at age one: Antecedents in neonatal behavior in an urban, economically disadvantaged sample. *Child Development, 51*, 208–216.

Waters, E., Wippman, J., & Sroufe, L. A. (1979). Attachment, positive affect, and competence in the peer group: Two studies in construct validation. *Child Development, 50*, 821–829.

Watson, J. S., Hayes, L. A., Vietze, P., & Becker, J. (1979). Discriminative infant smiling to orientations of talking faces of mother and stranger. *Journal of Experimental Child Psychology, 28*, 92–99.

Weber, R. A., Levitt, M. J., & Clark, M. C. (1986). Individual variation in attachment security and Strange Situation behavior: The role of maternal and infant temperament. *Child Development, 57*, 56–65.

Weinraub, M., & Lewis, M. (1977). The determinants of children's responses to separation. *Monographs of the Society for Research in Child Development* (4, Serial No. 172).

Wheeler, L., Reis, H., & Nezlek, J. (1983). Loneliness, social interaction, and sex roles. *Journal of Personality and Social Psychology, 45*, 943–953.

Whiting, B. B., & Edwards, C. P. (1988). *Children of different worlds. The formation of social behavior*. Cambridge, MA: Harvard University Press.

Wilks, J. (1986). The relative importance of parents and friends in adolescent decision making. *Journal of Youth and Adolescence, 15*, 323–334.

Winstead, B. A. (1986). Sex differences in same-sex friendships. In V. J. Derlega & B. A. Winstead (Eds.), *Friendship and social interaction*. New York: Springer-Verlag.

Wolff, P. H. (1963). Observations on the early development of smiling. In B. M. Foss (Ed.), *Determinants of infant behavior* (Vol. 2). London: Methuen.

Wright, P. H. (1982). Men's friendships, women's friendships and the alleged inferiority of the latter. *Sex Roles, 8*, 1–20.

Yeates, K. O., & Selman, R. L. (1989). Social competence in the schools: Toward an integrative developmental model for intervention. *Developmental Review, 9*, 64–100.

Youniss, J. (1980). *Parents and peers in social development. A Sullivan–Piaget perspective*. Chicago: University of Chicago Press.

Youniss, J., & Smollar, J. (1985). *Adolescent relations with mothers, fathers, and friends*. Chicago: University of Chicago Press.

Zaslow, M. (1980). Relationships among peers in kibbutz toddler groups. *Child Psychiatry and Human Development, 10*, 178–189.

Chapter 14: The Family

Abbott, D. A., & Brody, G. H. (1985). The relation of child age, gender, and number of children to the marital satisfaction of wives. *Journal of Marriage and the Family, 47*, 77–91.

Abramovitch, R., Corter, C., & Pepler, D. J. (1980). Observations of mixed-sex sibling dyads. *Child Development, 51*, 1268–1271.

Abramovitch, R., Corter, C., Pepler, D. J., & Stanhope, L. (1986). Sibling and peer interaction: A final follow-up and a comparison, *Child Development, 57*, 217–229.

Ainsworth, M. D. S. (1979). Attachment as related to mother–infant interaction. In J. S. Rosenblatt, R. A. Hinde, C. Beer, & M. Busnel (Eds.), *Advances in the study of behavior* (Vol. 9). New York: Academic Press.

Aizenberg, R., & Treas, J. (1985). The family in later life: Psychosocial and demographic considerations. In J. E. Birren & K. W. Schaie (Eds.), *Handbook of the psychology of aging* (2nd ed.). New York: Van Nostrand Reinhold.

Aldous, J. (1985). Parent–adult child relations as affected by the grandparent status. In V. L. Bengtson & J. F. Robertson (Eds.), *Grandparenthood*. Beverly Hills, CA: Sage.

Allison, P. D., & Furstenberg, F. F., Jr. (1989). How marital dissolution affects children: Variations by age and sex. *Developmental Psychology, 25*, 540–549.

Anderson, K. E., Lytton, H., & Romney, D. M. (1986). Mothers' interactions with normal and conduct-disordered boys: Who affects whom? *Developmental Psychology, 22*, 604–609.

Atkinson, M. P., Kivett, V. R., & Campbell, R. T. (1986). Intergenerational solidarity: An examination of a theoretical model. *Journal of Gerontology, 41*, 408–416.

Balswick, J. O., & Macrides, C. (1975). Parental stimulus for adolescent rebellion. *Adolescence, 10*, 253–266.

Barnett, R. C., & Baruch, G. K. (1987). Determinants of father's participation in family work. *Journal of Marriage and the Family, 49*, 29–40.

Baskett, L. M., & Johnson, S. M. (1982). The young child's interaction with parents versus siblings: A behavioral analysis. *Child Development, 53*, 643–650.

Baumrind, D. (1967). Child care practices anteceding three patterns of preschool behavior. *Genetic Psychology Monographs, 75*, 43–88.

Baumrind, D. (1977, March). *Socialization determinants of personal agency*. Paper presented at the biennial meeting of the Society for Research in Child Development, New Orleans.

Becker, W. C. (1964). Consequences of different kinds of parental discipline. In M. L. Hoffman & L. W. Hoffman (Eds.), *Review of child development research* (Vol. 1). New York: Russell Sage Foundation.

Beckman, L. J. (1981). Effects of social interaction and children's relative inputs on older women's psychological wellbeing. *Journal of Personality and Social Psychology, 41*, 1075–1086.

Bell, A. P., & Weinberg, M. S. (1978). *Homosexualities: A study of diversity among men and women*. New York: Simon & Schuster.

Bell, R. Q., & Chapman, M. (1986). Child effects in studies using experimental or brief longitudinal approaches to socialization. *Developmental Psychology, 22*, 595–603.

Bell, R. Q., & Harper, L. V. (1977). *Child effects on adults*. Hillsdale, NJ: Erlbaum.

Belsky, J. (1980). Child mistreatment: An ecological integration. *American Psychologist, 35*, 320–335.

Belsky, J. (1981). Early human experience: A family perspective. *Developmental Psychology, 17*, 3–23.

Belsky, J., Gilstrap, B., & Rovine, M. (1984). The Pennsylvania infant and family development project, I: Stability and change in mother–infant and father–infant interaction in a family setting at one, three, and nine months. *Child Development, 55*, 692–705.

Belsky, J., & Isabella, R. A. (1985). Marital and parent–child relationships in family of origin and marital change following the birth of a baby: A retrospective analysis. *Child Development, 56*, 342–349.

Belsky, J., Lang, M. E., & Rovine, M. (1985). Stability and change in marriage across the transition to parenthood: A second study. *Journal of Marriage and the Family, 47*, 855–865.

Belsky, J. K. (1990). *The psychology of aging*. Pacific Grove, CA: Brooks/Cole.

Bennett, N. G., Blanc, A. K., & Bloom, D. E. (1988). Commitment and the modern union: Assessing the link between premarital cohabitation and subsequent marital stability. *American Sociological Review, 53*, 127–138.

Berger, R. M. (1982). *Gay and gray. The older homosexual man*. Urbana, IL: University of Illinois Press.

Block, J. H., Block, J., & Gjerde, P. F. (1986). The personality of children prior to divorce: A prospective study. *Child Development, 57*, 827–840.

Bloom, D. E., & Pebley, A. R. (1982). Voluntary childlessness: A review of the evidence and implications. *Population Research and Policy Review, 1*, 203–224.

Blumstein, P., & Schwartz, P. (1983). *American couples. Money, work, sex*. New York: Morrow.

Bradley, R. H., Caldwell, B. M., & Elardo, R. (1979). Home environment and cognitive development in the first 2 years: A cross-lagged panel analysis. *Developmental Psychology, 15*, 246–250.

Brody, E. M. (1981). "Women in the middle" and family help to older people. *Gerontologist, 21*, 471–480.

Brody, E. M. (1985). Parent care as a normative family stress. *Gerontologist, 25*, 19–29.

Brody, E. M., Johnsen, P. T., & Fulcomer, M. C. (1984). What should adult children do for elderly parents? Opinions and preferences of three generations of women. *Journal of Gerontology, 39*, 736–746.

Brody, G. H., Neubaum, E., & Forehand, R. (1988). Serial marriage: A heuristic analysis of an emerging family form. *Psychological Bulletin, 103*, 211–222.

Bronfenbrenner, U. (1979). Contexts of child rearing: Problems and prospects. *American Psychologist, 34*, 844–850.

Bronfenbrenner, U. (1989). Ecological systems theory. In R. Vasta (Ed.), *Annals of child development: Vol. 6. Theories of child development: Revised formulations and current issues*. Greenwich, CT: JAI Press.

Brooks-Gunn, J., Zahaykevich, M. (1989). Parent-daughter relationships in early adolescence: A developmental perspective. In K. Kreppner & R. M. Lerner (Eds.), *Family systems and life-span development*. Hillsdale, NJ: Erlbaum.

Buehler, C. A., Hogan, M. J., Robinson, B. E., & Levy, R. J. (1985–1986). The parental divorce transition: Divorce-related stressors and well-being. *Journal of Divorce, 9*, 61–81.

Bugental, D. B., Blue, J., & Cruzcosa, M. (1989). Perceived control over caregiving outcomes: Implications for child abuse. *Developmental Psychology, 25*, 532–539.

Campbell, A. (1981). *The sense of well-being in America. Recent patterns and trends*. New York: McGraw-Hill.

Cargan, L. (1981). Singles: An examination of two stereotypes. *Family Relations, 30*, 377–385.

Cassidy, J. (1986). The ability to negotiate the environment: An aspect of infant competence as related to quality of attachment. *Child Development, 57*, 331–337.

Cavanaugh, J. C. (1990). *Adult development and aging*. Belmont, CA: Wadsworth.

Cherlin, A., & Furstenberg, F. F., Jr. (1986). *The new American grandparent. A place in the family, a life apart*. New York: Basic Books.

Chiriboga, D. A. (1982). Adaptation to marital separation in later and early life. *Journal of Gerontology, 37*, 109–114.

Cicirelli, V. G. (1982). Sibling influence throughout the life span. In M. E. Lamb & B. Sutton- Smith (Eds.), *Sibling relationships: Their nature and significance across the lifespan*. Hillsdale, NJ: Erlbaum.

Cicirelli, V. G. (1989). Feelings of attachment to siblings and well-being in later life. *Psychology and Aging, 4*, 211–216.

Clingempeel, W. G., Ievoli, R., & Brand, E. (1984). Structural complexity and the quality of stepparent–stepchild relationships. *Family Processes, 23*, 547–560.

Clingempeel, W'. G., & Segal, S. (1986). Stepparent–stepchild relationships and the psychological adjustment of children in stepmother and stepfather families. *Child Development, 57*, 474–484.

Coverman, S., & Sheley, J. F. (1986). Change in men's housework and child-care time, 1965–1975. *Journal of Marriage and the Family, 48*, 413–422.

Cowan, C. P., & Cowan, P. A. (1987). A preventive intervention for couples becoming parents. In C. F. Z. Boukydis (Ed.), *Research on support for parents and infants in the postnatal period*. New York: Ablex.

Crnic, K. A., Greenberg, M. T., Ragozin, A. S., Robinson, N. M., & Basham, R. B. (1983). Effects of stress and social support on mothers and premature and full-term infants. *Child Development, 54*, 209–217.

Deimling, G. T., & Bass, D. M. (1986). Symptoms of mental impairment among elderly adults and their effects on family caregivers. *Journal of Gerontology, 41*, 778–784.

DeMaris, A., & Leslie, G. R. (1984). Cohabitation with the future spouse: Its influence upon marital satisfaction and communication. *Journal of Marriage and the Family, 46*, 77–84.

Demo, D. H., & Acock, A. C. (1988). The impact of divorce on children. *Journal of Marriage and the Family, 50*, 619–648.

Desimone-Luis, J., O'Mahoney, K., & Hunt, D. (1979). Children of separation and divorce: Factors influencing adjustment. *Journal of Divorce, 3*, 37–42.

Dornbusch, S. M., Carlsmith, J. M., Bushwall, S. J., Ritter, P. L., Leiderman, H., Hastorf, A. H., & Gross, R. T. (1985). Single parents, extended households, and the control of adolescents. *Child Development, 56*, 326–341.

Dunn, J. (1984). Sibling studies and the development impact of critical incidents. In P. B. Baltes & O. G. Brim, Jr. (Eds.), *Life-span development and behavior* (Vol. 6). New York: Academic.

Dunn, J., & Kendrick, C. (1981). Interaction between young siblings: Association with the interaction between mother and firstborn child. *Developmental Psychology, 17*, 336–343.

Dunn, J., & Kendrick, C. (1982). *Siblings: Love, envy, and understand*. Cambridge, MA: Harvard University Press.

Dunn, J., & Munn, P. (1985). Becoming a family member: Family conflict and the development of social understanding in the second year. *Child Development, 56*, 480–492.

Duvall, E. M. (1977). *Marriage and family development* (5th ed.). Philadelphia: J. B. Lippincott.

Egeland, B. (1979). Preliminary results of a prospective study of the antecedents of child abuse. *International Journal of Child Abuse and Neglect, 3*, 269–278.

Egeland, B., Jacobvitz, D., & Sroufe, L. A. (1988). Breaking the cycle of abuse. *Child Development, 59*, 1080 – 1088.

Egeland, B., & Sroufe, L. A. (1981). Attachment and early maltreatment. *Child Development, 52*, 44–52.

Egeland, B., Sroufe, L. A., & Erickson, M. (1983). The developmental consequences of different patterns of maltreatment. *International Journal of Child Abuse and Neglect, 7*, 459–469.

Egerton, J. (1983). *Generations. An American family*. Lexington, KY: University Press of Kentucky.

Essex, M. J., & Nam, S. (1987). Marital status and loneliness among older women: The differential importance of close family and friends. *Journal of Marriage and the Family, 49*, 93–106.

Falbo, T., & Polit, D. F. (1986). Quantitative review of the only child literature: Research evidence and theory development. *Psychological Bulletin, 100*, 176–189.

Feldman, R. S., Devin-Sheehan, L., & Allen, V. L. (1976). Children tutoring children: A critical review of research. In V. L. Allen (Ed.), *Children as teachers: Theory and research on tutoring*. New York: Academic.

Feldman, S. S., & Gehring, T. M. (1988). Changing perceptions of family cohesion and power across adolescence. *Child Development, 59*, 1034–1045.

Fischer, C. S., & Phillips, S. L. (1982). Who is alone? Social characteristics of people with small networks. In L. A. Peplau & D. Perlman (Eds.), *Loneliness. A sourcebook of current theory, research and therapy*. New York: Wiley-Interscience.

Frodi, A. M., & Lamb, M. E. (1980). Child abusers' responses to infant smiles and cries. *Child Development, 51*, 238–241.

Furman, W., & Buhrmester, D. (1985a). Children's perceptions of the personal relationships in their social networks. *Developmental Psychology, 21*, 1016–1024.

Furman, W., & Buhrmester, D. (1985b). Children's perceptions of the qualities of sibling relationships. *Child Development, 56*, 448–461.

Garbarino, J., & Sherman, D. (1980). High-risk neighborhoods and high-risk families: The human ecology of child maltreatment. *Child Development, 51*, 188–198.

Gelles, R. J. (1973). Child abuse as psychopathology: A sociological critique and reformulation. *American Journal of Orthopsychiatry, 43*, 611–621.

Gerstel, N. (1988). Divorce and kin ties: The importance of gender. *Journal of Marriage and the Family, 50*, 209–219.

Gil, D. G. (1970). *Violence against children*. Cambridge, MA: Harvard University Press.

Gjerde, P. F. (1986). The interpersonal structure of family interaction settings: Parent–adolescent relations in dyads and triads. *Developmental Psychology, 22*, 297–304.

Glass, J., Bengtson, V. L., & Dunham, C. C. (1986). Attitude similarity in three-generation families: Socialization, status inheritance, or reciprocal influence. *American Sociological Review, 51*, 685–698.

Glenn, N. D. (1975). Psychological well-being in the postparental stage: Some evidence from national surveys. *Journal of Marriage and the Family, 37*, 105–110.

Glenn, N. D. (1985, June). Children of divorce. *Psychology Today*, pp. 68–69.

Glenn, N. D., & McLanahan, S. (1981). The effects of offspring on the psychological well-being of older adults. *Journal of Marriage and the Family, 43*, 409–421.

Glenn, N. D., & McLanahan, S. (1982). Children and marital happiness: A further specification of the relationship. *Journal of Marriage and the Family, 44*, 63–72.

Glenn, N. D., & Weaver, C. N. (1988). The changing relationship of marital status to reported happiness. *Journal of Marriage and the Family, 50*, 317–324.

Glick, P. C. (1984a). American household structure in transition. *Family Planning Perspectives, 16*, 205–211.

Glick, P. C. (1984b). Marriage, divorce, and living arrangements: Prospective changes. *Journal of Family Issues, 5*, 7–26.

Goetting, A. (1986). The developmental tasks of siblingship over the life cycle. *Journal of Marriage and the Family, 48*, 703–714.

Gold, D. T. (1989). Sibling relationships in old age: A typology. *International Journal of Aging and Human Development, 28*, 37–51.

Greene, A. L., & Boxer, A. M. (1986). Daughters and sons as young adults: Restructuring the ties that bind. In N. Datan, A. L. Greene, & H. W. Reese (Eds.), *Life-span developmental psychology. Intergenerational relations*. Hillsdale, NJ: Erlbaum.

Greene, J. G., Fox, N. A., & Lewis, M. (1983). The relationship between neonatal characteristics and three-month mother–infant interactions in high-risk infants. *Child Development, 54*, 1286–1296.

Grolnick, W. S., & Ryan, R. M. (1989). Parent styles associated with children's self-regulation and competence in school. *Journal of Educational Psychology, 81*, 143–154.

Grossman, F. K., Eichler, L. S., Winickoff, S. A., & Associates (1980). *Pregnancy, birth, and parenthood: Adaptations of mothers, fathers, and infants*. San Francisco: Jossey-Bass.

Grotevant, H. D., & Cooper, C. R. (1986). Individuation in family relations. A perspective on individual differences in the development of identity and role-taking skills in adolescence. *Human Development, 29*, 82–100.

Gwartney-Gibbs, P. A. (1986). The institutionalization of premarital cohabitation: Estimates from marriage license applications, 1970–1980. *Journal of Marriage and the Family, 48*, 423–434.

Hagestad, G. O. (1985). Continuity and connectedness. In V. L. Bengtson & J. F. Robertson (Eds.), *Grandparenthood*. Beverly Hills, CA: Sage.

Hagestad, G. O. & Burton, L. M. (1986). Grandparenthood, life context, and family development. *American Behavioral Scientist, 29*, 471–484.

Haggstrom, G. W., Kanouse, D. E., & Morrison, P. A. (1986). Accounting for the educational shortfalls of mothers. *Journal of Marriage and the Family, 48*, 175–186.

Harkins, E. B. (1978). Effects of empty nest transition on self-report of psychological and physical well-being. *Journal of Marriage and the Family, 40*, 549–556.

Hart, S. N., & Brassard, M. R. (1987). A major threat to children's mental health. Psychological maltreatment. *American Psychologist, 42*, 160–165.

Helmreich, R. L., Spence, J. T., & Gibson, R. H. (1982). Sex-role attitudes: 1972–1980. *Personality and Social Psychology Bulletin, 8*, 656–663.

Henton, J., Cate, R., Koval, J., Lloyd, S., & Christopher, S. (1983). Romance and violence in dating relationships. *Journal of Family Issues, 4*, 467–482.

Hess, R. D., & Camara, K. A. (1979). Post divorce family relationships as mediating factors in the consequences of divorce for children. *Journal of Social Issues, 35*, 79–96.

Hetherington, E. M. (1981). Children and divorce. In R. W. Henderson (Ed.), *Parent–child interaction: Theory, research and prospects*. New York: Academic.

Hetherington, E. M. (1987). Family relations six years after divorce. In K. Pasley & M. Ihinger-Tollman (Eds.), *Remarriage and stepparenting today: Current research and theory*. New York: Guilford.

Hetherington, E. M. (1989). Coping with family transitions: Winners, losers, and survivors. *Child Development, 60*, 1–14.

Hetherington, E. M., & Camara, K. A. (1984). Families in transition: The processes of dissolution and reconstitution. In R. D. Parke (Ed.), *Review of child development research: Vol. 7. The family*. Chicago: University of Chicago Press.

Hetherington, E. M., Cox, M., & Cox, R. (1982). Effects of divorce on parents and children. In M. E. Lamb (Ed.), *Nontraditional families*. Hillsdale, NJ: Erlbaum.

Hetherington, E. M., & Frankie, G. (1967). Effect of parental dominance, warmth, and conflict on imitation in children. *Journal of Personality and Social Psychology, 6*, 119–125.

Hill, J. P., Holmbeck, G. N., Marlow, L., Green, T. M., & Lynch, M. E. (1985). Menarcheal status and parent–child relations in families of seventh-grade girls. *Journal of Youth and Adolescence, 14*, 301–316.

Hill, R. (1986). Life cycle stages for types of single parent families: Of family development theory. *Family Relations, 35*, 19–29.

Hoffman, L. W., & Manis, J. D. (1979). The value of children in the United States: A new approach to the study of fertility. *Journal of Marriage and the Family, 41*, 583–596.

Hudson, M. F. (1986). Elder mistreatment: Current research. In K. A. Pillemer & R. S. Wolf (Eds.), *Elder abuse. Conflict in the family*. Dover, MA: Auburn House.

Huston, T. L., McHale, S. M., & Crouter, A. C. (1986). When the honeymoon's over: Changes in the marriage relationship over the first year. In R. Gilmour & S. Duck (Eds.), *The emerging field of personal relationships*. Hillsdale, NJ: Erlbaum.

Kandel, D. B., & Lesser, G. S. (1972). *Youth in two worlds: United States and Denmark*. San Francisco: Jossey-Bass.

Keith, V. M., & Finlay, B. (1988). The impact of parental divorce on children's educational attainment, marital timing, and likelihood of divorce. *Journal of Marriage and the Family, 50*, 797–809.

Keller, B. B., & Bell, R. Q. (1979). Child effects on adult's method of eliciting altruistic behavior. *Child Development, 50*, 1004–1009.

Kempe, R. S., & Kempe, C. H. (1978). *Child abuse*. Cambridge, MA: Harvard University Press.

Kinard, E. M. & Reinherz, H. (1986). Effects of marital disruption on children's school aptitude and achievement. *Journal of Marriage and the Family, 48*, 285–293.

Kitson, G. C., Babri, K. B., & Roach, M. J. (1985). Who divorces and why. A review. *Journal of Family Issues, 6*, 255–293.

Kitson, G. C., & Raschke, H. J. (1981). Divorce research: What we know; what we need to know. *Journal of Divorce, 4*, 1–37.

Kitson, G., & Sussman, M. B. (1982). Marital complaints, demographic characteristics, and symptoms of mental distress in divorce. *Journal of Marriage and the Family, 44*, 87–101.

Kline, M., Tschann, J. M., Johnston, J. R., & Wallerstein, J. S. (1989). Children's adjustment in joint and sole physical custody families. *Developmental Psychology, 25*, 430–438.

Klineberg, S. L. (1984). Social change, world views, and cohort succession: The United States in the 1980s. In K. A. McCluskey & H. W. Reese (Eds.), *Life-span developmental psychology. Historical and generational effects*. Orlando, FL: Academic.

Kreppner, K., Paulsen, S., & Schuetze, Y. (1982). Infant and family development: From triads to tetrads. *Human Development, 25*, 373–391.

Kurdek, L. A., & Schmitt, J. P. (1986). Early development of relationship quality in heterosexual married, heterosexual cohabiting, gay, and lesbian couples. *Developmental Psychology, 22*, 305–309.

Lamb, M. E. (1981). *The role of the father in child development*. New York: Wiley.

Lamb, M. E., & Elster, A. B. (1985). Adolescent mother–infant–father relationships. *Developmental Psychology, 21*, 768–773.

Larson, P. C. (1982). Gay male relationships. In W. Paul, J. D. Weinrich, J. C. Gonsiorek, & M. E. Hotvedt (Eds.), *Homosexuality. Social, psychological, and biological issues*. Beverly Hills, CA: Sage.

Lauer, R. H., & Lauer, J. C. (1986). Factors in long-term marriages. *Journal of Family Issues, 7*, 382–390.

Lee, G. R. (1988). Marital satisfaction in later life: The effects of nonmarital roles. *Journal of Marriage and the Family, 50*, 775–783.

Lewis, R. A., Freneau, P. J., & Roberts, C. L. (1979). Fathers and the postparental transition. *Family Coordinator, 28*, 514–520.

Litwak, E. (1960). Geographic mobility and extended family cohesion. *American Sociological Review, 25*, 385–394.

Long, N., Slater, E., Forehand, R., & Fauber, R. (1988). Continued high or reduced interparental conflict following divorce: Relation to young adolescent adjustment. *Journal of Consulting and Clinical Psychology, 56*, 467–469.

Maccoby, E. E., & Martin, J. A. (1983). Socialization in the context of the family: Parent–child interaction. In E. M. Hetherington (Ed.; P. H. Mussen, General Ed.), *Handbook of child psychology: Vol. 4. Socialization, personality, and social development* (4th ed.). New York: Wiley.

MacKinnon, C. E. (1989). An observational investigation of sibling interactions in married and divorced families. *Developmental Psychology, 25*, 36–44.

Macklin, E. D. (1978). Review of research on nonmarital cohabitation in the United States. In B. I. Murstein (Ed.), *Exploring intimate life styles*. New York: Springer.

Main, M., & Weston, D. R. (1981). The quality of the toddler's relationship to mother and to father: Related to conflict and the readiness to establish new relationships. *Child Development, 52*, 932–940.

Markides, K. S., Boldt, J. S., & Ray, L. A. (1986). Sources of helping and intergenerational solidarity: A three-generations study of Mexican Americans. *Journal of Gerontology, 41*, 506–511.

Matejcek, Z., Dytrych, Z., & Schuller, V. (1979). The Prague study of children born from unwanted pregnancies. *International Journal of Mental Health, 7*, 63–74.

Matthews, S. H., & Sprey, J. (1984). The impact of divorce on grandparenthood: An exploratory study. *Gerontologist, 24*, 41–47.

Matthews, S. H., & Sprey, J. (1985). Adolescents' relationships with grandparents: An empirical contribution to conceptual clarification. *Journal of Gerontology, 40*, 621–626.

McLanahan, S. S., & Sorenson, A. B. (1985). Life events and psychological well-being over the life course. In G. H. Elder, Jr. (Ed.), *Life course dynamics. Trajectories and transitions, 1968–1980*. Ithaca, NY: Cornell University Press.

Menaghan, E. (1983). Marital stress and family transitions: A panel analysis. *Journal of Marriage and the Family, 45*, 371–386.

Menaghan, E. G., & Lieberman, M. A. (1986). Changes in depression following divorce: A panel study. *Journal of Marriage and the Family, 48*, 319–328.

Montemayor, R. (1982). The relationship between parent–adolescent conflict and the amount of time adolescents spend alone and with parents and peers. *Child Development, 53*, 1512–1519.

Moore, D. (1987). Parent–adolescent separation: The construction of adulthood by late adolescents. *Developmental Psychology, 23*, 298–307.

Myers-Walls, J. A. (1984). Balancing multiple roles responsibilities during the transition to parenthood. *Family Relations, 33*, 267–271.

Neugarten, B. L. (1970). Adaptation and the life cycle. *Journal of Geriatric Psychiatry, 4*, 71–87.

Neugarten, B. L., & Weinstein, K. (1964). The changing American grandparent. *Journal of Marriage and the Family, 26*, 199–204.

Newcomb, P. R. (1979). Cohabitation in America: An assessment of consequences. *Journal of Marriage and the Family, 41*, 597–603.

Nock, S. L. (1987). *Sociology of the family*. Englewood Cliffs, NJ: Prentice-Hall.

Norman-Jackson, J. (1982). Family interactions, language development, and primary reading achievement of Black children in families of low income. *Child Development, 53*, 349–358.

Norton, A. J., & Moorman, J. E. (1987). Current trends in marriage and divorce among American women. *Journal of Marriage and the Family, 49*, 3–14.

Nydegger, C. N. (1986). Asymmetrical kin and the problematic son-in-law. In N. Datan, A. L. Greene, & H. W. Reese (Eds.), *Life-span developmental psychology. Intergenerational relations*. Hillsdale, NJ: Erlbaum.

Oates, K. (1986). *Child abuse and neglect: What happens eventually?* New York: Brunner/Mazel.

Offer, D., Ostrov, E., & Howard, K. I. (1981). *The adolescent. A psychological self-portrait.* New York: Basic Books.

Ogbu, J. U. (1981). Origins of human competence: A cultural-ethological perspective. *Child Development, 52,* 413–429.

Okraku, I. O. (1987). Age and attitudes toward multigenerational residence, 1973 to 1983. *Journal of Gerontology, 42,* 280–287.

Olson, D. H., & Lavee, Y. (1989). Family systems and family stress: A family life cycle perspective. In K. Kreppner & R. M. Lerner (Eds.), *Family systems and life-span development.* Hillsdale, NJ: Erlbaum.

Orthner, D. K. (1975). Leisure activity patterns and marital satisfaction over the marital career. *Journal of Marriage and the Family, 37,* 91–102.

Palkovitz, R. (1984). Parental attitudes and fathers' interactions with their 5-month-old infants. *Developmental Psychology, 20,* 1054–1060.

Parke, R. D. (1979). Perspectives on father–infant interaction. In J. Osofsky (Ed.), *Handbook of infant development.* New York: Wiley.

Parke, R. D., & Lewis, N. G. (1981). The family in context: A multilevel interactional analysis of child abuse. In R. W. Henderson (Ed.), *Parent–child interaction: Theory, research, and prospects.* New York: Academic.

Parke, R. D., & Sawin, D. B. (1976). The father's role in infancy: A reevaluation. *Family Coordinator, 25,* 365–371.

Parke, R. D., & Tinsley, B. R. (1984). Fatherhood: Historical and contemporary perspectives. In K. A. McCluskey & H. W. Reese (Eds.), *Life-span developmental psychology. Historical and generational effects.* Orlando, FL: Academic.

Patterson, G. R., & Stouthamer-Loeber, M. (1984). The correlation of family management practices and delinquency. *Child Development, 55,* 1299–1307.

Paul, W., & Weinrich, J. D. (1982). Whom and what we study. Definition and scope of sexual orientation. In W. Paul, J. D. Weinrich, J. C. Gonsiorek, & M. E. Hotvedt (Eds.), *Homosexuality. Social, psychological, and biological issues.* Beverly Hills, CA: Sage.

Paulhus, D., & Shaffer, D. R. (1981). Sex differences in the impact of number of older and number of younger siblings on scholastic aptitude. *Social Psychology Quarterly, 44,* 363–368.

Pedersen, F., Anderson, B., & Cain, R. (1977, March). *An approach to understanding linkages between parent–infant and spouse relationships.* Paper presented at the biennial meeting of the Society for Research in Child Development, New Orleans.

Pedro-Carroll, J. L., & Cowen, E. L. (1985). The children of divorce intervention program: An investigation of the efficacy of a school-based prevention program. *Journal of Consulting and Clinical Psychology, 53,* 603–611.

Peplau, L. A., & Amaro, H. (1982). Understanding lesbian relationships. In W. Paul, J. D. Weinrich, J. C. Gonsiorek, & M. E. Hotvedt (Eds.), *Homosexuality. Social, psychological, and biological issues.* Beverly Hills, CA: Sage.

Peterson, J. L., & Zill, N. (1986). Marital disruption, parent–child relationships, and behavior problems in children. *Journal of Marriage and the Family, 48,* 295–307.

Pulkinnen, L. (1982). Self-control and continuity from childhood to adolescence. In P. B. Baltes & O. G. Brim, Jr. (Eds.), *Life-span development and behavior* (Vol. 4). New York: Academic.

Rebelsky, F., & Hanks, C. (1971). Father verbal interaction with infants in the first three months of life. *Child Development, 42,* 63–68.

Rempel, J. (1985). Childless elderly: What are they missing? *Journal of Marriage and the Family, 47,* 343–348.

Richards, L. N., Bengtson, V. L., & Miller, R. B. (1989). The "generation in the middle": Perceptions of changes in adults' intergenerational relationships. In K. Kreppner & R. M. Lerner (Eds.), *Family systems and life-span development.* Hillsdale, NJ: Erlbaum.

Rollins, B. C., & Feldman, H. (1970). Marital satisfaction over the family life cycle. *Journal of Marriage and the Family, 32,* 20–28.

Rosen, R. (1979). Some crucial issues concerning children of divorce. *Journal of Divorce, 3,* 19–26.

Ross, H. G., & Milgram, J. I. (1982). Important variables in adult sibling relationships: A qualitative study. In M. E. Lamb & B. Sutton-Smith (Eds.), *Sibling relationships: Their nature and significance across the lifespan.* Hillsdale, NJ: Erlbaum.

Rossi, A. S. (1986). Gender and parenthood. In A. S. Rossi (Ed.), *Gender and the life course.* New York: Aldine.

Ryan, R. M., & Lynch, J. H. (1989). Emotional autonomy versus detachment: Revisiting the vicissitudes of adolescence and young adulthood. *Child Development, 60,* 340–356.

Santrock, J. W., & Warshak, R. A. (1979). Father custody and social development in boys and girls. *Journal of Social Issues, 35,* 112–125.

Santrock, J. W., Warshak, R. A., Lindbergh, C., & Meadows, L. (1982). Childrens' and parents' observed social behavior in stepfather families. *Child Development, 53,* 472–480.

Schaefer, E. S. (1959). A circumplex model for maternal behavior. *Journal of Abnormal and Social Psychology, 59,* 226–235.

Schaefer, E. S., & Bayley, N. (1963). Maternal behavior, child behavior, and their intercorrelations from infancy through adolescence. *Monographs of the Society for Research in Child Development, 28* (3, Serial No. 87).

Schinke, S. P., Schilling, R. F., II., Barth, R. P., Gilchrist, L. D., & Maxwell, J. S. (1986). Stress-management intervention to prevent family violence. *Journal of Family Violence, 1,* 13–26.

Schumm, W. R., & Bugaighis, M. A. (1986). Marital quality over the marital career: Alternative explanations. *Journal of Marriage and the Family, 48,* 165–168.

Seltzer, J. A., & Bianchi, S. M. (1988). Children's contact with absent parents. *Journal of Marriage and the Family, 50,* 663–677.

Shanas, E. (1980). Older people and their families: The new pioneers. *Journal of Marriage and the Family, 42,* 9–15.

Sherrod, K. B., O'Connor, S., Vietze, P. M., & Altemeier, W. A., III. (1984). Child health and maltreatment. *Child Development, 55,* 1174–1183.

Sigelman, C. K., Berry, C. J., & Wiles, K. A. (1984). Violence in college students' dating relationships. *Journal of Applied Social Psychology, 14,* 530–548.

Singh, B. K., & Williams, J. S. (1981). Childlessness and family satisfaction. *Research on Aging, 3,* 218–227.

Sirignano, S. W., & Lachman, M. E. (1985). Personality change during the transition to parenthood: The role of perceived infant temperament. *Developmental Psychology, 21,* 558–567.

Skolnick, A. (1981). Married lives: Longitudinal perspectives on marriage. In D. H. Eichorn, J. A. Clausen, N. Haan, M. P. Honzik, & P. H. Mussen (Eds.), *Present and past in middle life.* New York: Academic.

Snow, M. E., Jacklin, C. N., & Maccoby, E. E. (1983). Sex-of-child differences in father–child interaction at one year of age. *Child Development, 54,* 227–232.

Spanier, G. B. (1983). Married and unmarried cohabitation in the United States: 1980. *Journal of Marriage and the Family, 45,* 277–288.

Starr, R. H., Jr. (1979). Child abuse. *American Psychologist, 34,* 872–878.

Steele, B. F., & Pollack, C. B. (1974). A psychiatric study of parents who abuse infants and small children. In R. E. Hefler & C. H. Kempe (Eds.), *The battered child.* Chicago: University of Chicago Press.

Steinberg, L. (1981). Transformations in family relations at puberty. *Developmental Psychology, 17,* 833–840.

Steinberg, L. (1985). *Adolescence.* New York: Knopf.

Steinberg, L. (1988). Reciprocal relation between parent–child distance and pubertal maturation. *Developmental Psychology, 24,* 122–128.

Stemp, P. S., Turner, J., & Noh, S. (1986). Psychological distress in the postpartum period: The significance of social support. *Journal of Marriage and the Family, 48,* 271–277.

Stevenson, M. R., & Black, K. N. (1988). Paternal absence and sex-role development: A meta-analysis. *Child Development, 59,* 793–814.

Stewart, R. B., & Marvin, R. S. (1984). Sibling relations: The role of conceptual perspective-taking in the ontogeny of sibling caregiving. *Child Development, 55,* 1322–1332.

Stewart, R. B., Mobley, L. A., Van Tuyl, S. S., & Salvador, M. A. (1987). The firstborn's adjustment to the birth of a sibling: A longitudinal assessment. *Child Development, 58,* 341–355.

Stolberg, A. L., & Garrison, K. M. (1985). Evaluating a primary prevention program for children of divorce. *American Journal of Community Psychology, 13,* 11–124.

Stoneman, Z., & Brody, G. H. (1981). Two's company, three makes a difference: An examination of mothers' and fathers' speech to their young children. *Child Development, 52,* 705–707.

Straus, M. A. (1980). A sociological perspective on the causes of family violence. In M. R. Green (Ed.), *Violence and the family* (AAAS Selected Symposium No. 47). Boulder, CO: Westview.

Straus, M. A., & Gelles, R. J. (1986). Societal change and change in family violence from 1975 to 1985 as revealed by two national surveys. *Journal of Marriage and the Family, 48,* 465–479.

Stroebe, W., & Stroebe, M. S. (1986). Beyond marriage: The impact of partner loss on health. In R. Gilmour & S. Duck (Eds.), *The emerging field of personal relationships.* Hillsdale, NJ: Erlbaum.

Stull, D. E., & Scarisbrick-Hauser, A. (1989). Never-married elderly. A reassessment with implications for long-term care policy. *Research on Aging, 11,* 124–139.

Sullivan, K., & Sullivan, A. (1980). Adolescent–parent separation. *Developmental Psychology, 16,* 93–99.

Summers, M. (1987, April). *Imitation, dominance, agonism and prosocial behavior: A meta-analysis of sibling behavior.* Paper presented at the biennial meeting of the Society for Research in Child Development, Baltimore, MD.

Sweet, J. A., & Bumpass, L. L. (1987). *American families and households.* New York: Russell Sage Foundation.

Tanfer, K. (1987). Patterns of premarital cohabitation among never-married women in the United States. *Journal of Marriage and the Family, 49,* 483–497.

Thomas, J. L. (1986). Gender differences in satisfaction with grandparenting. *Psychology and Aging, 1,* 215–219.

Tietjen, A. M., & Bradley, C. F. (1985). Social support and maternal psychosocial adjustment during the transition to parenthood. *Canadian Journal of Behavioral Science, 17,* 109–121.

Trickett, P. K., & Susman, E. J. (1988). Parental perceptions of child-rearing practices in physically abusive and nonabusive families. *Developmental Psychology, 24,* 270–276.

U.S. Bureau of the Census. (1989). *Statistical abstract of the United States, 1989* (109th ed.). Washington, D.C.: U.S. Government Printing Office.

Veroff, J., Douvan, E., & Kulka, R. A. (1981). *The inner American. A self-portrait from 1957 to 1976.* New York: Basic Books.

Wagner, M. E., Schubert, H. J. P., & Schubert, D. S. P. (1985). Effects of sibling spacing on intelligence, interfamilial relations, psychosocial characteristics, and mental and physical health. In H. W. Reese (Ed.), *Advances in child development and behavior* (Vol. 19). New York: Academic.

Wallerstein, J. S. (1984). Children of divorce: Preliminary report of a ten-year follow-up of young children. *American Journal of Orthopsychiatry, 54,* 444–458.

Wallerstein, J. S. (1987). Children of divorce: Report of a ten-year follow-up of early latency-age children. *American Journal of Orthopsychiatry, 57,* 199–211.

Wallerstein, J. S., & Kelly, J. B. (1980). *Surviving the breakup: How children and parents cope with divorce.* New York: Basic Books.

Waters, E., Wippman, J., & Sroufe, L. A. (1979). Attachment, positive affect, and competence in the peer group: Two studies in construct validation. *Child Development, 50,* 821–829.

Weisner, T. S., & Gallimore, R. (1977). My brother's keeper: Child and sibling caretaking. *Current Anthropology, 18,* 169–190.

Whitbourne, S. K. (1986). *The me I know: A study of adult identity.* New York: Springer-Verlag.

White, K., Speisman, J. C., & Costos, D. (1983). Young adults and their parents: Individuation to mutuality. In H. D. Grotevant & C. R. Cooper (Eds.), *Adolescent development in the family* (New Directions for Child Development, No. 22). San Francisco: Jossey-Bass.

Widmayer, S., & Field, T. (1980). Effects of Brazelton demonstrations on early interactions of preterm infants and their teen-age mothers. *Infant Behavior and Development, 3,* 79–89.

Wilkie, C. F., & Ames, E. W. (1986). The relationship of infant crying to parental stress in the transition to parenthood. *Journal of Marriage and the Family, 48*, 545–550.

Wilson, M. N. (1986). The black extended family: An analytical consideration. *Developmental Psychology, 22*, 246–258.

Wolfe, D. A., Edwards, B., Manion, I., & Koverola, C. (1988). Early intervention for parents at risk of child abuse and neglect: A preliminary investigation. *Journal of Consulting and Clinical Psychology, 56*, 40–47.

Wright, P. J., Henggeler, S. W., & Craig, L. (1986). Problems in paradise?: A longitudinal examination of the transition to parenthood. *Journal of Applied Developmental Psychology, 7*, 277–291.

Youniss, J., & Smollar, J. (1985). *Adolescent relations with mothers, fathers, and friends*. Chicago: University of Chicago Press.

Zaslow, M. J. (1989). Sex differences in children's response to parental divorce: 2. Samples, variables, ages, and sources. *American Journal of Orthopsychiatry, 59*, 118–141.

Chapter 15: Lifestyles: Play, School, and Work

Aneshensel, C. S., & Rosen, B. C. (1980). Domestic roles and sex differences in occupational expectations. *Journal of Marriage and the Family, 42*, 121–131.

Atchley, R. C. (1976). *The sociology of retirement*. Cambridge, MA: Schenkman.

Athey, I. (1984). Contributions of play to development. In T. D. Yawkey & A. D. Pelligrini (Eds.), *Child's play: Developmental and applied*. Hillsdale, NJ: Erlbaum.

Bachman, J. G. (1987, July). Adolescence. An eye on the future. *Psychology Today*, pp. 6–8.

Bammel, G., & Burris-Bammel, L. L. (1982). *Leisure and human behavior*. Dubuque, IA: William C. Brown.

Baran, S. J., Chase, L. J., & Courtright, J. A. (1979). Television drama as a facilitator of prosocial behavior: "The Waltons." *Journal of Broadcasting, 23*, 277–284.

Barglow, P., Vaughn, B. E., & Molitor, N. (1987). Effect of maternal absence due to employment on the quality of infant–mother attachment in a low-risk sample. *Child Development, 58*, 945–954.

Barnes, K. E. (1971). Preschool play norms: A replication. *Developmental Psychology, 5*, 99–103.

Baruch, G. K., & Barnett, R. (1986). Role quality, multiple role involvement, and psychological well-being in midlife women. *Journal of Personality and Social Psychology, 51*, 578–585.

Baruch, G. K., Biener, L., & Barnett, R. C. (1987). Women and gender in research on work and family stress. *American Psychologist, 42*, 130–136.

Belsky, J. (1984). Two waves of day care research: Developmental effects and conditions of quality. In R. C. Ainslie (Ed.), *The child and the day care setting. Quality variations and development*. New York: Praeger.

Belsky, J., & Most, R. (1981). From exploration to play: A cross-sectional study of infant free-play behavior. *Developmental Psychology, 17*, 630–639.

Belsky, J., & Rovine, M. J. (1988). Nonmaternal care in the first year of life and the security of infant–parent attachment. *Child Development, 59*, 157–167.

Benn, R. K. (1986). Factors promoting secure attachment relationships between employed mothers and their sons. *Child Development, 57*, 1224–1231.

Bird, C. P., & Fisher, T. D. (1986). Thirty years later: Attitudes toward the employment of older workers. *Journal of Applied Psychology, 71*, 515–517.

Bogatz, G. A., & Ball, S. (1972). *The second year of* Sesame Street: *A continuing evaluation*. Princeton, NJ: Educational Testing Service.

Bossé, R., & Ekerdt, D. J. (1981). Changes in self-perception of leisure activities with retirement. *Gerontologist, 21*, 650–654.

Bradbard, M. R., & Endsley, R. C. (1979). What do licensers say to parents who ask their help with selecting quality day care? *Child Care Quarterly, 8*, 307–312.

Bray, D. W., & Howard, A. (1983). The AT&T longitudinal studies of managers. In K. W. Schaie (Ed.), *Longitudinal studies of adult psychological development*. New York: Guilford.

Brookover, W., Beady, C., Flood, P., Schweitzer, J., & Wisenbaker, J. (1979). *School social systems and student achievement: Schools can make a difference*. New York: Praeger.

Brophy, J. (1979). Teacher behavior and its effects. *Journal of Educational Psychology, 71*, 733–750.

Brown, D. (1984). Summary, comparison, and critique of major theories. In D. Brown, L. Brooks, & Associates (Eds.), *Career choice and development*. San Francisco: Jossey-Bass.

Brownell, C. A. (1988). Combinatorial skills: Converging developments over the second year. *Child Development, 59*, 675–685.

Burchinal, M., Lee, M., & Ramey, C. (1989). Type of day-care and preschool intellectual development in disadvantaged children. *Child Development, 60*, 128–137.

Burud, S. L., Aschbacher, P. R., & McCroskey, J. (1984). *Employer-supported child care. Investing in human resources*. Boston, MA: Auburn House.

Cavanaugh, J. C. (1990). *Adult development and aging*. Belmont, CA: Wadsworth.

Christie, J. F., & Johnsen, E. P. (1983). The role of play in social-intellectual development. *Review of Educational Research, 53*, 93–115.

Clarke-Stewart, A. (1982). *Daycare*. Cambridge, MA: Harvard University Press.

Clarke-Stewart, K. A., & Fein, G. G. (1983). Early childhood programs. In M. M. Haith & J. J. Campos (Eds.; P. H. Mussen, General Ed.), *Handbook of child psychology: Vol. 2. Infancy and developmental psychobiology* (4th ed.). New York: Wiley.

Clements, D. H. (1986). Effects of Logo and CAI environments on cognition and creativity. *Journal of Educational Psychology, 78*, 309–318.

Coleman, J. (1961). *The adolescent society*. New York: Free Press.

Collins, W. A., Sobol, B. L., & Westby, S. (1981). Effects of adult commentary on children's comprehension and inferences about a televised aggressive portrayal. *Child Development, 52*, 158–163.

Comstock, G. (1978). *Television and human behavior*. New York: Columbia University Press.

Connolly, J. (1982). Social pretend play and social competence in preschoolers. In D. J. Pepler & K. Rubin (Eds.), *The play of children: Current theory and research*. Basil: Karger.

Connolly, J. A., & Doyle, A. B. (1984). Relation of social fantasy play to social competence in preschoolers. *Developmental Psychology, 20*, 797–806.

Corder-Bolz, C. R., & O'Bryant, S. (1977, August). *Significant other modification of the impact of televised programming upon young children*. Paper presented at the annual meeting of the American Psychological Association, San Francisco.

Corrigan, R. (1987). A developmental sequence of actor–object pretend play in young children. *Merrill–Palmer Quarterly, 33* 87–106.

Costa, P. T., Jr., McCrae, R. R., & Arenberg, D. (1983). Recent longitudinal research on personality and aging. In K. W. Schaie (Ed.), *Longitudinal studies of adult psychological development*. New York: Guilford.

Costa, P. T., Jr., McCrae, R. R., Zonderman, A. B., Barbano, H. E., Lebowitz, B., & Larson, D. M. (1986). Cross-sectional studies of personality in a national sample: 2. Stability in neuroticism, extraversion, and openness. *Psychology and Aging, 1*, 144–149.

Csikszentmihalyi, M., & Larson, R. (1984). *Being adolescent. Conflict and growth in the teenage years*. New York: Basic Books.

Cumming, E., & Henry, W. E. (1961). *Growing old: The process of disengagement*. New York: Basic Books.

Curry, N. E., & Arnaud, S. H. (1984). Play in developmental preschool settings. In T. D. Yawkey & A. D. Pelligrini (Eds.), *Child's play: Developmental and applied*. Hillsdale, NJ: Erlbaum.

Dansky, J. (1980). Make-believe: A mediator of the relationship between play and associative fluency. *Child Development, 51*, 576–579.

Drabman, R. S., & Thomas, M. H. (1974). Does media violence increase children's tolerance of real-life aggression? *Developmental Psychology, 10*, 418–421.

Educational Research Service. (1978). *Class size: A summary of research*. Arlington, VA: Author.

Ekerdt, D. J., Bossé, R., & Levkoff, S. (1985). Empirical test for phases of retirement: Findings from the Normative Aging Study. *Journal of Gerontology, 40*, 95–101.

Elkind, D. (1981). *The hurried child: Growing up too fast too soon*. Reading, MA: Addison-Wesley.

Eron, L. D. (1982). Parent–child interaction, television violence, and aggression of children. *American Psychologist, 37*, 197–211.

Etaugh, C. (1980). Effects of nonmaternal care on children. Research evidence and popular views. *American Psychologist, 35*, 309–319.

Evans, L., Ekerdt, D. J., & Bossé, R. (1985). Proximity to retirement and anticipatory involvement: Findings from the Normative Aging Study. *Journal of Gerontology, 40*, 368–374.

Farrell, M. P., & Rosenberg, S. D. (1981). *Men at midlife*. Dover, MA: Auburn House.

Featherman, D. L. (1980). Schooling and occupational careers: Constancy and change in worldly success. In O. G. Brim, Jr., & J. Kagan (Eds.), *Constancy and change in human development*. Cambridge, MA: Harvard University Press.

Fein, G. G. (1981). Pretend play: An integrative review. *Child Development, 52*, 1095–1118.

Fein, G. G. (1986). The affective psychology of play. In A. W. Gottfried & C. C. Brown (Eds.), *Play interactions. The contributions of play material and parental involvement to children's development*. Lexington, MA: Lexington Books.

Fiorentine, R. (1988). Increasing similarity in the values and life plans of male and female college students? Evidence and implications. *Sex Roles, 18*, 143–158.

Frueh, T., & McGhee, P. H. (1975). Traditional sex-role development and the amount of time spent watching television. *Developmental Psychology, 11*, 109.

Geist, W. E. (1985, November 3). New Yorkers trying to stop nursery school madness. *Lexington Herald-Leader*, p. A14.

Gerbner, G., Gross, L., Morgan, M., & Signorelli, N. (1980). The "mainstreaming" of America: Violence profile no. 11. *Journal of Communication, 30*, 10–29.

Giffin, H. (1984). The coordination of meaning in the creation of a shared make-believe reality. In I. Bretherton (Ed.), *Symbolic play: The development of social understanding*. Orlando, FL: Academic.

Ginzberg, E. (1972). Toward a theory of occupational choice: A restatement. *Vocational Guidance Quarterly, 20*, 169–176.

Ginzberg, E. (1984). Career development. In D. Brown, L. Brooks, & Associates (Eds.), *Career choice and development*. San Francisco: Jossey-Bass.

Gordon, C., Gaitz, C. M., & Scott, J. (1976). Leisure and lives: Personal expressivity across the life span. In R. H. Binstock & E. Shanas (Eds.), *Handbook of aging and the social sciences*. New York: Van Nostrand Reinhold.

Gottfredson, D. C. (1985). Youth employment, crime, and schooling: A longitudinal study of a national sample. *Developmental Psychology, 21*, 419–432.

Gottfredson, L. S. (1981). Circumscription and compromise: A developmental theory of occupational aspirations. *Journal of Counseling Psychology, 28*, 545–579.

Gottlieb, J. (1978). Observing social adaptation in schools. In G. P. Sackett (Ed.), *Observing behavior*. Baltimore: University Park Press.

Grotevant, H. D., & Cooper, C. R. (1988). The role of family experience in career exploration: A life-span perspective. In B. B. Baltes, D. L. Featherman, & R. M. Lerner (Eds.), *Life-span development and behavior* (Vol. 8). Hillsdale, NJ: Erlbaum.

Grotevant, H. D., Cooper, C. R., & Kramer, K. (1986). Exploration as a predictor of congruence in adolescents' career choices. *Journal of Vocational Behavior, 29*, 201–215.

Grotevant, H. D., & Durrett, M. E. (1980). Occupational knowledge and career development in adolescence. *Journal of Vocational Behavior, 17*, 171–182.

Gutek, B. A. (1985). *Sex and the workplace*. San Francisco: Jossey-Bass.

Gutek, B. A., & Cohen, A. G. (1987). Sex ratios, sex role spillover, and sex at work: A comparison of men's and women's experiences. *Human Relations, 40*, 97–115.

Gutek, B. A., & Larwood, L. (1987). Introduction. In B. A. Gutek & L. Larwood (Eds.), *Women's career development*. Newbury Park, CA: Sage.

Hannah, J. S., & Kahn, S. E. (1989). The relationship of socioeconomic status and gender to the occupational choices of grade 12 students. *Journal of Vocational Behavior, 34,* 161–178.

Harris, M. J., & Rosenthal, R. (1986). Four factors in the mediation of teacher expectancy effects. In R. S. Feldman (Ed.), *The social psychology of education. Current research and theory.* Cambridge, England: Cambridge University Press.

Havighurst, R. J. (1982). The world of work. In B. B. Wolman (Ed.), *Handbook of developmental psychology.* Englewood Cliffs, NJ: Prentice-Hall.

Havighurst, R. J., Neugarten, B. L., & Tobin, S. S. (1968). Disengagement and patterns of aging. In B. L. Neugarten (Ed.), *Middle age and aging.* Chicago: University of Chicago Press.

Hawkins, J., Sheingold, K., Gearhart, M., & Berger, C. (1982). Microcomputers in schools: Impact on the social life of elementary classrooms. *Journal of Applied Developmental Psychology, 3,* 361–373.

Hedlund, B., & Ebersole, P. (1983). A test of Levinson's mid-life reevaluation. *Journal of Genetic Psychology, 143,* 189–192.

Henderson, S., Hesketh, B., & Tuffin, K. (1988). A test of Gottfredson's theory of circumscription. *Journal of Vocational Behavior, 32,* 37–48.

Hess, R. D., & Holloway, S. D. (1984). Family and school as educational institutions. In R. D. Parke (Ed.), *Review of child development research: Vol. 7. The family.* Chicago: University of Chicago Press.

Hetherington, E. M., Cox, M., & Cox, R. (1979). Play and social interaction in children following divorce. *Journal of Social Issues, 35,* 26–49.

Holland, J. L. (1973). *Making vocational choices. A theory of careers.* Englewood Cliffs, NJ: Prentice-Hall.

Holland, J. L. (1985). *Making vocational choices: A theory of vocational personalities and work environments* (2nd ed.). Englewood Cliffs, NJ: Prentice-Hall.

Hooker, K., & Ventis, D. G. (1984). Work ethic, daily activities, and retirement satisfaction. *Journal of Gerontology, 39,* 478–484.

Horton, R., & Santogrossi, O. (1978, August). *Mitigating the impact of televised violence through concurrent adult commentary.* Paper presented at the annual meeting of the American Psychological Association, Toronto.

Howes, C. (1985). Sharing fantasy: Social pretend play in toddlers. *Child Development, 56,* 1253–1258.

Huston, A., & Wright, J. C. (1982). Effects of communications media on children. In C. B. Kopp & J. B. Krakow (Eds.), *The child: Development in a social context.* Reading, MA: Addison-Wesley.

Jenkins, S. R. (1989). Longitudinal prediction of women's careers: Psychological, behavioral, and social-structural influences. *Journal of Vocational Behavior, 34,* 204–235.

Johnson, D. W., Johnson, R. T., & Maruyama, G. (1983). Interdependence and interpersonal attraction among heterogeneous and homogeneous individuals: A theoretical formulation and a meta-analysis of the research. *Review of Educational Research, 53,* 5–54.

Johnson, N. (1967). *How to talk back to your television.* Boston: Little, Brown.

Johnston, J., Ettema, J., & Davidson, T. (1980). *An evaluation of "Freestyle": A television series designed to reduce sex-role stereotypes.* Ann Arbor, MI: Institute for Social Research.

Kagan, J., Kearsley, R. B., & Zelazo, P. R. (1978). *Infancy: Its place in human development.* Cambridge, MA: Harvard University Press.

Kagan, S., & Zahn, G. L. (1975). Field dependence and the school achievement gap between Anglo-American and Mexican- American children. *Journal of Educational Psychology, 67,* 643–650.

Karnes, M. B., & Lee, R. C. (1979). Mainstreaming in the preschool. In L. G. Katz (Ed.), *Current topics in early childhood education* (Vol. 2). Norwood, NJ: Ablex.

Keating, N., & Jeffrey, B. (1983). Work careers of ever married and never married retired women. *Gerontologist, 23,* 416–421.

Kee, D. W. (1986). Computer play. In A. W. Gottfried & C. C. Brown (Eds.), *Play interactions. The contribution of play materials and parental involvement to children's development.* Lexington, MA: Lexington Books.

Keith, T. Z., Reimers, T. M., Fehrmann, P. G., Pottebaum, S. M., & Aubey, L. W. (1986). Parental involvement, homework, and TV time: Direct and indirect effects on high school achievement. *Journal of Educational Psychology, 78,* 373–380.

Kelly, J. R., Steinkamp, M. W., & Kelly, J. R. (1986). Later life leisure: How they play in Peoria. *Gerontologist, 26,* 531–537.

Kelso, G. I. (1977). The relation of school grade to ages and stages in vocational development. *Journal of Vocational Behavior, 10,* 287–301.

Kleiber, D., Larson, R., & Csikszentmihalyi, M. (1986). The experience of leisure in adolescence. *Journal of Leisure Research, 18,* 169–176.

Klein, R. P. (1985). Caregiving arrangements by employed women with children under 1 year of age. *Developmental Psychology, 21,* 403–406.

Kohn, M. L., & Schooler, C. (1982). Job conditions and personality: A longitudinal assessment of their reciprocal effects. *American Journal of Sociology, 87,* 1257–1286.

Kohn, M. L., & Schooler, C. (in collaboration with J. Miller, K. A. Miller, C. Schoenbach, & R. Schoenberg). (1983). *Work and personality: An inquiry into the impact of social stratification.* Norwood, NJ: Ablex.

Kulik, C. C., & Kulik, J. A. (1982). Effects of ability grouping on secondary school students: A meta-analysis of evaluation findings. *American Educational Research Journal, 19,* 415–428.

Kulik, J. A., Bangert, R. L., & Williams, G. W. (1983). Effects of computer-based teaching on secondary school students. *Journal of Educational Psychology, 75,* 19–26.

Lamb, M. E., Hwang, C., Bookstein, F. L., Broberg, A., Hult, G., & Frodi, M. (1988). Determinants of social competence in Swedish preschoolers. *Developmental Psychology, 24,* 58–70.

Larwood, L., & Gutek, B. A. (1987). Working toward a theory of women's career development. In B. A. Gutek & L. Larwood (Eds.), *Women's career development.* Newbury Park, CA: Sage.

Lazar, I., & Darlington, R. (1982). Lasting effects of early education: A report from the Consortium for Longitudinal Studies. *Monographs of the Society for Research in Child Development 47* (2–3, Serial No. 195).

Lee, V. E., Brooks-Gunn, J., & Schnur, E. (1988). Does Head Start Work? A 1- year follow-up comparison of disadvantaged children attending Head Start, no preschool, and other preschool programs. *Developmental Psychology, 24,* 210–222.

Lepper, M. R. (1985). Microcomputers in education. Motivational and social issues. *American Psychologist, 40,* 1–18.

Lerner, J. V., & Lerner, R. M. (1983). Temperament and adaptation across life: Theoretical and empirical issues. In P. B. Baltes & O. G. Brim, Jr. (Eds.), *Life-span development and behavior* (Vol. 5). New York: Academic.

Leslie, L. A. (1986). The impact of adolescent females' assessments of parenthood and employment on plans for the future. *Journal of Youth and Adolescence, 15,* 29–49.

Levinson, D. J. (1986). A conception of adult development. *American Psychologist, 41,* 3–13.

Levinson, D. J., with Darrow, C. N., Klein, E. B., Levinson, M. H., & McKee, B. (1978). *The seasons of a man's life.* New York: Ballantine Books.

Liebert, R. M., & Sprafkin, J. (1988). *The early window: Effects of television on children and youth* (3rd ed.). New York: Pergamon.

Lloyd, D. N. (1978). Prediction of school failure from third-grade data. *Educational and Psychological Measurement, 38,* 1193–1200.

Lonner, W. J., Thorndike, R. M., Forbes, N. E., & Ashworth, C. (1985). The influence of television on measured cognitive abilities. A study with native Alaskan children. *Journal of Cross-Cultural Psychology, 16,* 355–380.

Lueptow, L. B. (1981). Sex-typing and change in the occupational choices of high school seniors: 1964–1975. *Sociology of Education, 54,* 16–24.

MacNeil, R. D., & Teague, M. L. (1987). *Aging and leisure: Vitality in later life.* Englewood Cliffs, NJ: Prentice-Hall.

Madden, N. A., & Slavin, R. E. (1983). Mainstreaming students with mild handicaps: Academic and social outcomes. *Review of Educational Research, 53,* 519–569.

Manosevitz, M., Prentice, N. M., & Wilson, F. (1973). Individual and family correlates of imaginary companions in preschool children. *Developmental Psychology, 8,* 72–79.

Maruyama, G., Finch, M. D., & Mortimer, J. T. (1985). Processes of achievement in the transition to adulthood. In Z. S. Blau (Ed.), *Current perspectives on aging and the life cycle* (Vol. 1). Greenwich, CT: JAI Press.

McCune- Nicolich, L., & Fenson, L. (1984). Methodological issues in studying early pretend play. In T. D. Yawkey & A. D. Pellegrini (Eds.), *Child's play: Developmental and applied.* Hillsdale, NJ: Erlbaum.

McGuire, F. A., Dottavio, D., & O'Leary, J. T. (1986). Constraints to participation in outdoor recreation across the life span: A nationwide study of limitors and prohibitors. *Gerontologist, 26,* 538–544.

McLoyd, V. C. (1986). Social class and pretend play. In A. W. Gottfried & C. C. Brown (Eds.), *Play interactions. The contributions of play materials and parental involvement to children's development.* Lexington, MA: Lexington Books.

Miller, K. A., Kohn, M. L., & Schooler, C. (1986). Educational self-direction and personality. *American Sociological Review, 51,* 372–390.

Minuchin, P. P., & Shapiro, E. K. (1983). The school as a context for social development. In E. M. Hetherington (Ed; P. H. Mussen, General Ed.), *Handbook of child psychology. Vol 4: Socialization, personality, and social development.* New York: Wiley.

Moen, P. (1985). Continuities and discontinuities in women's labor force activity. In G. H. Elder, J. (Ed.), *Life course dynamics. Trajectories and transitions, 1968–1980.* Ithaca, NY: Cornell University Press.

Moody, H. R. (1986). Education as a lifelong process. In A. Pifer & L. Bronte (Eds.), *Our aging society. Paradox and promise.* New York: Norton.

Morrison, M. H. (1986). Work and retirement in an older society. In A. Pifer & L. Bronte (Eds.), *Our aging society. Paradox and promise.* New York: Norton.

Neff, W. S. (1985). *Work and human behavior* (3rd ed.). New York: Aldine.

Nelson, J. N. (1978). Age and sex differences in the development of children's occupational reasoning. *Journal of Vocational Behavior, 13,* 287–297.

Nicolich, L. M. (1977). Beyond sensorimotor intelligence: Assessment of symbolic maturity through analysis of pretend play. *Merrill–Palmer Quarterly, 23,* 89–99.

O'Connell, B., & Bretherton, I. (1984). Toddler's play, alone and with mother: The role of maternal guidance. In I. Bretherton (Ed.), *Symbolic play: The development of social understanding.* Orlando, FL: Academic.

O'Connell, L., Betz, M., & Kurth, S. (1989). Plans for balancing work and family life: Do women pursuing nontraditional and traditional occupations differ? *Sex Roles, 20,* 35–45.

Palmore, E. (1979). Predictors of successful aging. *Gerontologist, 19,* 427–431.

Palmore, E. B., Burchett, B. M., Fillenbaum, G. G., George, L. K., & Wallman, L. M. (1985). *Retirement. Causes and consequences.* New York: Springer.

Parnes, H. S., & Less, L. (1985). Variation in selected forms of leisure activity among elderly males. In Z. S. Blau (Ed.), *Current perspectives on aging and the life cycle: Vol. 1. Work, retirement and social policy.* Greenwich, CT: JAI Press.

Parten, M. B. (1932). Social participation among preschool children. *Journal of Abnormal and Social Psychology, 27,* 243–269.

Pence, A. R. (1986). Infant schools in North America, 1825–1840. In S. Kilmer (Ed.), *Advances in early education and day care. A research annual* (Vol. 4). Greenwich, CT: JAI Press.

Phillips, D., McCartney, K., & Scarr, S. (1987). Child-care quality and children's social development. *Developmental Psychology, 23,* 537–543.

Phillips, S. D. (1982). Career exploration in adulthood. *Journal of Vocational Behavior, 20,* 129–140.

Piaget, J. (1962). *Play, dreams and imitation in childhood.* New York: Norton. (Original work published 1951)

Piaget, J. (1965). *The moral judgment of the child.* New York: Free Press. (Original work published 1932)

Pietromonaco, P. R., Manis, J., & Markus, H. (1987). The relationship of employment to self-perception and well-being in women: A cognitive analysis. *Sex Roles, 17,* 467–477.

Pines, M. (1978, September). Invisible playmates. *Psychology Today*, pp. 38–42, 106.

Pleck, J. H. (1985). *Working wives/working husbands*. Beverly Hills, CA: Sage.

Ramey, C. T., Bryant, D. M., & Snarez, T. M. (1985). Preschool compensatory education and the modifiability of intelligence: A critical review. In D. K. Detterman (Ed.), *Current topics in human intelligence: Vol. 1. Research methodology*. Norwood, NJ: Ablex.

Reid, P. T., & Stephens, D. S. (1985). The roots of future occupations in childhood. A review of the literature on girls and careers. *Youth and Society, 16*, 267–288.

Rhodes, S. R. (1983). Age-related differences in work attitudes and behavior: A review and conceptual analysis. *Psychological Bulletin, 93*, 328–367.

Rist, R. C. (1970). Student social class and teacher expectations: The self-fulfilling prophecy in ghetto education. *Harvard Educational Review, 40*, 411–451.

Roberts, P., & Newton, P. M. (1987). Levinsonian studies of women's adult development. *Psychology and Aging, 2*, 154–163.

Rogoff, B. (1981). Schooling and the development of cognitive skills. In H. C. Triandis & A. Heron (Eds.), *Handbook of cross-cultural psychology: Vol. 4. Developmental psychology*. Boston: Allyn & Bacon.

Rosenthal, R., & Jacobson, L. (1968). *Pygmalion in the classroom*. New York: Holt, Rinehart & Winston.

Rosenwasser, S. M., Lingenfelter, M., & Harrington, A. F. (1989). Nontraditional gender role portrayals and children's gender role perceptions. *Journal of Applied Developmental Psychology, 10*, 97–105.

Ross, H. S., & Lollis, S. P. (1987). Communication within infant social games. *Developmental Psychology, 23*, 241–248.

Rubin, K. H. (1982). Nonsocial play in preschoolers: Necessarily evil? *Child Development, 53*, 651–657.

Rubin, K. H., Fein, G., & Vandenberg, B. (1983). Play. In E. M. Hetherington (Ed.; P. H. Mussen, General Ed.), *Handbook of child psychology: Vol. 4: Socialization, personality, and social development*. New York: Wiley.

Rubin, K. H., Watson, K. S., & Jambor, T. W. (1978). Free-play behaviors in preschool and kindergarten children. *Child Development, 49*, 534–536.

Rudman, W. J. (1986). Sport as part of successful aging. *American Behavioral Scientist, 29*, 453–470.

Rutter, M. (1983). School effects on pupil progress: Research findings and policy implications. *Child Development, 54*, 1–29.

Rutter, M., Maughan, B., Mortimore, P., Ouston, J., & Smith, A. (1979). *Fifteen thousand hours: Secondary schools and their effects on children*. Cambridge, MA: Harvard University Press.

Saltz, E., Dixon, D., & Johnson, J. (1977). Training disadvantaged preschoolers on various fantasy activities: Effects on cognitive functioning and impulse control. *Child Development, 48*, 367–380.

Scarr, S. (1984). *Mother care/other care*. New York: Basic Books.

Schenk, V. M., & Grusec, J. E. (1987). A comparison of prosocial behavior of children with and without day care experiences. *Merrill–Palmer Quarterly, 33*, 231–240.

Schramm, W., Lyle, J., & Parker, E. B. (1961). *Television in the lives of our children*. Stanford, CA: Stanford University Press.

Seleen, D. R. (1982). The congruence between actual and desired use of time by older adults: A predictor of life satisfaction. *Gerontologist, 22*, 95–99.

Shore, C. (1986). Combinatorial play, conceptual development, and early multiword speech. *Developmental Psychology, 22*, 184–190.

Shore, C., O'Connell, B., & Bates, E. (1984). First sentences in language and symbolic play. *Developmental Psychology, 20*, 872–880.

Slade, A. (1987). Quality of attachment and early symbolic play. *Developmental Psychology, 23*, 78–85.

Slavin, R. E. (1986). Cooperative learning: Engineering social psychology in the classroom. In R. S. Feldman (Ed.), *The social psychology of education. Current research and theory*. Cambridge, England: Cambridge University Press.

Smith, D. M. (1987). Some patterns of reported leisure behavior of young people. A longitudinal study. *Youth and Society, 18*, 255–281.

Smith, P. K. (1978). A longitudinal study of social participation in preschool children: Solitary and parallel play reexamined. *Developmental Psychology, 14*, 517–523.

Sorensen, A. (1983). Women's employment patterns after marriage. *Journal of Marriage and the Family, 45*, 311–321.

Sorensen, A. B., & Hallinan, M. T. (1986). Effects of ability grouping on growth in academic achievement. *American Educational Research Journal, 23*, 519–542.

Spitze, G. (1988). Women's employment and family relations: A review. *Journal of Marriage and the Family, 50*, 595–618.

Steinberg, L. (1984). The varieties and effects of work during adolescence. In M. E. Lamb, A. L. Brown, & B. Rogoff (Eds.), *Advances in developmental psychology* (Vol. 3). Hillsdale, NJ: Erlbaum.

Stephan, W. G. (1978). School desegregation: An evaluation of the predictions made in *Brown vs. Board of Education. Psychological Bulletin, 85*, 217–238.

St. John, N. H. (1975). *School desegregation: Outcomes for children*. New York: Wiley.

Stroud, J. G. (1981). Women's careers: Work, family, and personality. In D. H. Eichorn, J. A. Clausen, N. Haan, M. P. Honzik, & P. H. Mussen (Eds.), *Present and past in middle life*. New York: Academic.

Sum, A. M., Harrington, P. E., & Goedicke, W. (1987). One-fifth of the nation's teenagers. Employment problems of poor youth in America, 1981–1985. *Youth and Society, 18*, 195–237.

Super, D. E. (1957). *The psychology of careers*. New York: Harper & Row.

Super, D. E. (1980). A life-span, life-space, approach to career development. *Journal of Vocational Behavior, 13*, 282–298.

Super, D. E. (1984). Career and life development. In D. Brown, L. Brooks, & Associates (Eds.), *Career choice and development*. San Francisco: Jossey-Bass.

Super, D. E. (1985). Coming of age in Middletown. Careers in the making. *American Psychologist, 40*, 405–414.

Tangri, S. S., & Jenkins, S. R. (1986). Stability and change in role innovation and life plans. *Sex Roles, 14*, 647–662.

Thomas, M. H., Horton, R. W., Lippincott, E. C., & Drabman, R. S. (1977). Desensitization to portrayals of real-life aggression as a function of exposure to television violence. *Journal of Personality and Social Psychology, 35*, 450–458.

Vaillant, G. E. (1977). *Adaptation to life*. Boston, MA: Little, Brown.

Valdez, R. L., & Gutek, B. A. (1987). Family roles. A help or a hindrance for working women? In B. A. Gutek & L. Larwood (Eds.), *Women's career development*. Newbury Park, CA: Sage.

Vandenberg, B. R. (1986). Beyond the ethology of play. In A. W. Gottfried & C. C. Brown (Eds.), *Play interactions. The contributions of play materials and parental involvement to children's development*. Lexington, MA: Lexington Books.

Van Velsor, E., & O'Rand, A. M. (1984). Family life cycle, work career patterns, and women's wages at midlife. *Journal of Marriage and the Family, 46*, 365–373.

Vaughan, B. E., Gove, F. L., & Egeland, B. R. (1980). The relationship between out-of-home care and the quality of infant–mother attachment in an economically disadvantaged population. *Child Development, 51*, 1203–1214.

Vondracek, F. W., Lerner, R. M., & Schulenberg, J. E. (1986). *Career development: A life-span developmental approach*. Hillsdale, NJ: Erlbaum.

Waite, L. J., Haggstrom, G., & Kanouse, D. E. (1986). The effects of parenthood on the career orientation and job characteristics of young adults. *Social Forces, 65*, 43–73.

Waldman, D. A., & Avolio, B. J. (1986). A meta-analysis of age differences in job performance. *Journal of Applied Psychology, 71*, 33–38.

Waldman, E. (1985). Today's girls in tomorrow's labor force. Projecting their participation and occupations. *Youth and Society, 16*, 375–392.

Warr, P. (1982). Job loss, unemployment, and psychological well-being. In V. L. Allen & van de Vliert, E. (Eds.), *Role transitions. Explorations and explanations*. New York: Plenum.

Waters, H. F., & Malamud, P. (1975, March 10). Drop that gun, Captain Video. *Newsweek*, pp. 81–82.

Weinstein, R. S., Marshall, H. H., Sharp, L., & Botkin, M. (1987). Pygmalion and the student: Age and classroom differences in children's awareness of teacher expectations. *Child Development, 58*, 1079–1093.

Weisner, T. S. (1984). Ecocultural niches of middle childhood: A cross-cultural perspective. In W. A. Collins (Ed.), *Development during middle childhood. The years from six to twelve*. Washington, DC: National Academy Press.

Willis, S. L. (1985). Towards an educational psychology of the older adult learner: Intellectual and cognitive bases. In J. E. Birren & K. W. Schaie (Eds.), *Handbook of the psychology of aging* (2nd ed.). New York: Van Nostrand Reinhold.

Zigler, E. F. (1987). Formal schooling for four-year-olds? No. *American Psychologist, 42*, 254–260.

Zigler, E. F., & Muenchow, S. (1979). Mainstreaming: The proof is in the implementation. *American Psychologist, 34*, 993–996.

Chapter 16: Psychological Disorders Throughout the Life Span

Achenbach, T. M. (1982). *Developmental psychopathology* (2nd ed.). New York: Wiley.

Achenbach, T. M., & Edelbrock, C. S. (1978). The classification of child psychopathology: A review and analysis of empirical efforts. *Psychological Bulletin, 85*, 1275–1301.

Achenbach, T. M., Verhulst, F. C., Edelbrock, C., Baron, G. D., & Akkerhuis, G. W. (1987). Epidemiological comparisons of American and Dutch children: II. Behavioral/emotional problems reported by teachers for ages 6 to 11. *Journal of the American Academy of Child Psychiatry, 26*, 326–332.

Allen, M. G. (1976). Twin studies of affective illness. *Archives of General Psychiatry, 33*, 1476–1478.

American Psychiatric Association. (1987). *Diagnostic and statistical manual of mental disorders (3rd ed., rev.) DSM-III-R*. Washington, DC: Author.

Aneshensel, C. S., & Stone, J. D. (1982). Stress and depression. A test of the buffering model of social support. *Archives of General Psychiatry, 39*, 1392–1396.

Arling, G., Harkins, E. B., & Capitman, J. A. (1986). Institutionalization and personal control. A panel study of impaired older people. *Research on Aging, 8*, 38–56.

Atlas, J. A., & Lapidus, L. (1987). Patterns of symbolic expression in subgroups of the childhood psychoses. *Journal of Clinical Psychology, 43*, 177–188.

Attie, I., & Brooks-Gunn, J. (1989). Development of eating problems in adolescent girls: A longitudinal study. *Developmental Psychology, 25*, 70–79.

Belsky, J. K. (1990). *The psychology of aging*. Pacific Grove, CA: Brooks/Cole.

Bemporad, J. R. (1979). Adult recollections of a formerly autistic child. *Journal of Autism and Developmental Disorders, 9*, 179–197.

Bemporad, J. R., & Wilson, A. (1978). A developmental approach to depression in childhood and adolescence. *Journal of the American Academy of Psychoanalysis, 6*, 325–352.

Berman, A. L. (1986). Helping suicidal adolescents: Needs and responses. In C. A. Corr & J. N. McNeil (Eds.), *Adolescence and death*. New York: Springer.

Billings, A. G., Cronkite, R. C., & Moos, R. H. (1983). Social-environmental factors in unipolar depression. *Journal of Abnormal Psychology, 92*, 119–133.

Blazer, D., Hughes, D. C., & George, L. K. (1987). The epidemiology of depression in an elderly community population. *Gerontologist, 27*, 281–287.

Bolla-Wilson, K., & Bleecker, M. L. (1989). Absence of depression in elderly adults. *Journal of Gerontology: Psychological Sciences, 44*, P53–P55.

Brim, O. G., Jr., & Ryff, C. D. (1980). On the properties of life events. In P. B. Baltes & O. G. Brim, Jr. (Eds.), *Life-span development and behavior* (Vol. 3). New York: Academic.

Brinich, E., Drotar, D., & Brinich, P. (1989). Security of attachment and outcome of preschoolers with histories of nonorganic failure to thrive. *Journal of Clinical Child Psychology, 18*, 142–152.

Brown, G. W., & Harris, T. O. (1978). *Social origins of depression*. New York: Free Press.

Brown, R. T., & Borden, K. A. (1986). Hyperactivity at adolescence: Some misconceptions and new directions. *Journal of Clinical Child Psychology, 15,* 194–209.

Burns, M. O., & Seligman, M. E. P. (1989). Explanatory style across the life span: Evidence for stability over 52 years. *Journal of Personality and Social Psychology, 56,* 471–477.

Campbell, E. A., Cope, S. J., & Teasdale, J. D. (1983). Social factors and affective disorder: An investigation of Brown and Harris's model. *British Journal of Psychiatry, 143,* 548–553.

Cavanaugh, J. C. (1990). *Adult development and aging.* Belmont, CA: Wadsworth.

Chase, S. N., & Clement, P. W. (1985). Effects of self-reinforcement and stimulants on academic performance in children with attention deficit disorder. *Journal of Clinical Child Psychology, 14,* 323–333.

Chess, S., Fernandez, P., & Korn, S. (1978). Behavioral consequences of congenital rubella. *Journal of Pediatrics, 93,* 699–703.

Chiverton, P., & Caine, E. D. (1989). Education to assist spouses in coping with Alzheimer's disease. *Journal of the American Geriatrics Society, 37,* 593–598.

Crook, W. G. (1980). Can what a child eats make him dull, stupid, or hyperactive? *Journal of Learning Disabilities, 13,* 53–58.

Cytryn, L., McKnew, D. H., Zahn-Waxler, C., & Gershon, E. S. (1986). Developmental issues in risk research: The offspring of affectively ill parents. In M. Rutter, C. E. Izard, & P. B. Read (Eds.), *Depression in young people. Developmental and clinical perspectives.* New York: Guilford.

Dohrenwend, B. P., & Dohrenwend, B. S. (1976). Sex differences in psychiatric disorders. *American Journal of Sociology, 81,* 1447–1454.

Dubow, E. F., Kausch, D. F., Blum, M. C., Reed, J., & Bush, E. (1989). Correlates of suicidal ideation and attempts in a community sample of junior high and high school students. *Journal of Clinical Child Psychology, 18,* 158–166.

Dulcan, M. K. (1986). Comprehensive treatment of children and adolescents with attention deficit disorders: The state of the art. *Clinical Psychology Review, 6,* 539–569.

Emde, R. N., Harmon, R. J., & Good, W. V. (1986). Depressive feelings in children: A transactional model for research. In M. Rutter, C. E. Izard, & P. B. Read (Eds.), *Depression in young people. Developmental and clinical perspectives.* New York: Guilford.

Eron, L. D. (1987). The development of aggressive behavior from the perspective of a developing behaviorism. *American Psychologist, 42,* 435–442.

Esser, S. R., & Vitaliano, P. P. (1988). Depression, dementia, and social supports. *International Journal of Aging and Human Development, 26,* 289–301.

Feingold, B. F. (1975). *Why your child is hyperactive.* New York: Random House.

Feinson, M. C., & Thoits, P. A. (1986). The distribution of distress among elders. *Journal of Gerontology, 41,* 225–233.

Felton, B. J., & Revenson, T. A. (1987). Age differences in coping with chronic illness. *Psychology and Aging, 2,* 164–170.

Fischer, M., Rolf, J. E., Hasazi, J. E., & Cummings, L. (1984). Follow-up of a preschool epidemiological sample: Cross-age continuities and predictions of later adjustment with internalizing and externalizing dimensions of behavior. *Child Development, 55,* 137–150.

Folkman, S., & Lazarus, R. S. (1980). An analysis of coping in a middle-aged community sample. *Journal of Health and Social Behavior, 21,* 219–239.

Folkman, S., Lazarus, R. S., Pimley, S., & Novacek, J. (1987). Age differences in stress and coping processes. *Psychology and Aging, 2,* 171–184.

Folstein, S., & Rutter, M. (1977). Infantile autism: A genetic study of 21 twin pairs. *Journal of Child Psychology and Psychiatry, 18,* 297–321.

Garber, J. (1984). The developmental progression of depression in female children. In D. Cicchetti & K. Schneider-Rosen (Eds.), *Childhood depression* (New Directions for Child Development, No. 26). San Francisco: Jossey-Bass.

Gardner, L. J. (1972). Deprivation dwarfism. *Scientific American, 227,* 76–82.

Garmezy, N. (1987). Stress, competence, and development: Continuities in the study of schizophrenic adults, children vulnerable to psychopathology, and the search for stress-resistant children. *American Journal of Orthopsychiatry, 57,* 159–174.

Garmezy, N., Masten, A. S., & Tellegen, A. (1984). The study of stress and competence in children: A building block for developmental psychopathology. *Child Development, 55,* 97–111.

Gatz, M., & Pearson, C. G. (1988). Ageism revised and the provision of psychological services. *American Psychologist, 43,* 184–188.

Gatz, M., Popkin, S. J., Pino, C. D., & VandenBos, G. R. (1985). Psychological interventions in older adults. In J. E. Birren & K. W. Schaie (Eds.), *Handbook of the psychology of aging* (2nd ed.). New York: Van Nostrand Reinhold.

Gelfand, D. M., & Peterson, L. (1985). *Child development and psychopathology.* Beverly Hills, CA: Sage.

Gillberg, C., & Gillberg, I. C. (1983). Infantile autism: A total population study of reduced optimality in the pre-, peri-, and neonatal period. *Journal of Autism and Developmental Disorders, 13,* 153–166.

Gillberg, C., & Steffenburg, S. (1987). Outcome and prognostic factors in infantile autism and similar conditions: A population-based study of 46 cases followed through puberty. *Journal of Autism and Developmental Disorders, 17,* 273–287.

Gold, M., & Petronio, R. J. (1980). Delinquent behavior in adolescence. In J. Adelson (Ed.), *Handbook of adolescent psychology.* New York: Wiley-Interscience.

Goldstein, M. J. (1988). The family and psychopathology. *Annual Review of Psychology, 39,* 283–299.

Green, W. H. (1986). Psychosocial dwarfism: Psychological and etiological considerations. In B. B. Lahey & A. E. Kazdin (Eds.), *Advances in clinical child psychology* (Vol. 9). New York: Plenum.

Gross, M. D., Tofanelli, R. A., Butzirus, S. M., & Snodgrass, E. W. (1987). The effect of diets rich in and free from additives on the behavior of children with hyperkinetic and learning disorders. *Journal of the American Academy of Child and Adolescent Psychiatry, 26,* 53–55.

Hall, G. S. (1904). *Adolescence* (2 vols). New York: Appleton.

Halmi, K. A. (1987). Anorexia nervosa and bulimia. In V. B. Van Hasselt & M. Hersen (Eds.), *Handbook of adolescent psychology.* New York: Pergamon.

Harley, J. P., Ray, R. S., Tomasi, L., Eichman, P. L., Matthews, C. G., & Chun, R. (1978). Hyperkinesis and food additives: Testing the Feingold hypothesis. *Pediatrics, 61*, 818–828.

Hechtman, L., Weiss, G., & Perlman, T. (1984). Young adult outcomes of hyperactive children who received long-term stimulant treatment. *Journal of the American Academy of Child Psychiatry, 23*, 261–269.

Heston, L. L., Mastri, A. R., Anderson, E., & White, J. (1981). Dementia of the Alzheimer type. Clinical genetics, natural history, and associated conditions. *Archives of General Psychiatry, 38*, 1085–1090.

Heyman, A., Wilkinson, W. E., Hurwitz, B. J., Schmechel, D., Sigmon, A. H., Weinberg, T., Helms, M. J., & Swift, M. (1983). Alzheimer's disease: Genetic aspects and associated clinical disorders. *Annals of Neurology, 14*, 507–515.

Hinz, L. D., & Williamson, D. A. (1987). Bulimia and depression: A review of the affective variant hypothesis. *Psychological Bulletin, 102*, 150–158.

Hirschfeld, R. M. A., & Cross, C. K. (1982). Epidemiology of affective disorders. *Archives of General Psychiatry, 39*, 35–46.

Holahan, C. J., & Moos, R. H. (1986). Personality, coping, and family resources in stress resistance: A longitudinal analysis. *Journal of Personality and Social Psychology, 51*, 389–395.

Holahan, C. J., & Moos, R. H. (1987). Personal and contextual determinants of coping strategies. *Journal of Personality and Social Psychology, 52*, 946–955.

Holahan, C. K., & Holahan, C. J. (1987). Self-efficacy, social support, and depression in aging: A longitudinal analysis. *Journal of Gerontology, 42*, 65–68.

Holland, A. J., Hall, A., Murray, K., Russell, G. F. M., & Crisp, A. H. (1984). Anorexia nervosa: A study of 34 twin pairs and one set of triplets. *British Journal of Psychiatry, 145*, 414–419.

Horwitz, A. V., & White, H. R. (1987). Gender role orientations and styles of pathology among adolescents. *Journal of Health and Social Behavior, 28*, 158–170.

Howat, P. M., & Saxton, A. M. (1988). The incidence of bulimic behavior in a secondary and university population. *Journal of Youth and Adolescence, 17*, 221–231.

Hyman, B. T., Damasio, H., Damasio, A. R., & Van Hoesen, G. W. (1989). Alzheimer's disease. *Annual Review of Public Health, 10*, 115–140.

Irion, J. C., & Blanchard-Fields, F. (1987). A cross-sectional comparison of adaptive coping in adulthood. *Journal of Gerontology, 42*, 502–504.

Kashani, J. H., Orvaschel, H., Rosenberg, T. K., & Reid, J. C. (1989). Psychopathology in a community sample of children and adolescents: A developmental perspective. *Journal of the American Academy of Child and Adolescent Psychiatry, 28*, 701–706.

Jessor, R. (1987). Problem-behavior theory, psychosocial development, and adolescent problem drinking. *British Journal of Addiction, 82*, 331–342.

Johnson, C., Lewis, C., Love, S., Lewis, L., & Stuckey, M. (1984). Incidence and correlates of bulimic behavior in a female high school population. *Journal of Youth and Adolescence, 13*, 15–26.

Johnson, C. L., Stuckey, M. K., Lewis, L. D., & Schwartz, D. M. (1982). Bulimia: A descriptive survey of 316 cases. *International Journal of Eating Disorders, 2*, 3–16.

Johnson, J. H., Rasbury, W. C., & Siegel, L. J. (1986). *Approaches to child treatment. Introduction to theory, research, and practice.* New York: Pergamon.

Johnston, L. D., O'Malley, P. M., & Bachman, J. G. (1985). *Use of licit and illicit drugs by America's high school students 1975–1984* (DHHS Publication No. ADM 85-1394). Rockville, MD: National Institute on Drug Abuse.

Jones, D. J., Fox, M. M., Babigian, H. M., & Hutton, H. E. (1980). Epidemiology of anorexia nervosa in Monroe County, New York: 1960–1976. *Psychosomatic Medicine, 42*, 551–558.

Jorm, A. F. (1987). Sex and age differences in depression: A quantitative synthesis of published research. *Australian and New Zealand Journal of Psychiatry, 21*, 46–53.

Kahn, R. L., Goldfarb, A. I., Pollack, M., & Peck, A. (1960). Brief objective measures for the determination of mental status in the aged. *American Journal of Psychiatry, 117*, 326–328.

Kanner, A. D., Coyne, J. C., Schaefer, C., & Lazarus, R. S. (1981). Comparison of two modes of stress measurement: Daily hassles and uplifts versus major life events. *Journal of Behavioral Medicine, 4*, 1–39.

Kanner, L. (1943). Autistic disturbances of affective contact. *Nervous Child, 2*, 217–250.

Kanner, L. (1971). Follow-up study of eleven autistic children originally reported in 1943. *Journal of Autism and Childhood Schizophrenia, 1*, 119–145.

Kaplan, S. L., Hong, G. K., & Weinhold, C. (1984). Epidemiology of depressive symptomatology in adolescents. *Journal of the American Academy of Child Psychiatry, 23*, 91–98.

Kashani, J. H., & Carlson, G. A. (1985). Major depressive disorder in a preschooler. *Journal of the American Academy of Child Psychiatry, 24*, 490–494.

Kashani, J. H., Orvaschel, H., Rosenberg, T. K., & Reid, J. C. (1989). Psychopathology in a community sample of children and adolescents: A developmental perspective. *Journal of the American Academy of Child and Adolescent Psychiatry, 28*, 701–706.

Kendall, P. C., Lerner, R. M., & Craighead, W. E. (1984). Human development and intervention in childhood psychopathology. *Child Development, 55*, 71–82.

Klerman, G. L. (1983). Problems in the definition and diagnosis of depression in the elderly. In L. D. Breslau & M. R. Haug (Eds.), *Depression and aging. Causes, care, and consequences.* New York: Springer.

Kosky, R. (1983). Childhood suicidal behavior. *Journal of Child Psychology and Psychiatry, 24*, 457–468.

Kovacs, M., Feinberg, T. L., Crouse-Novak, M., Paulauskas, S. L., Pollock, M., & Finkelstein, R. (1984). Depressive disorders in childhood: II. A longitudinal study of the risk for a subsequent major depression. *Archives of General Psychiatry, 41*, 643–649.

Lachenmeyer, J. R., & Davidovicz, H. (1987). Failure to thrive. A critical review. In B. B. Lahey & A. E. Kazdin (Eds.), *Advances in clinical child psychology* (Vol. 10). New York & London: Plenum.

Lambert, M. C., Weisz, J. R., & Knight, F. (1989). Over- and undercontrolled clinic referral problems of Jamaican and American children and adolescents: The culture general and the culture specific. *Journal of Consulting and Clinical Psychology, 57*, 467–472.

Langer, E. J., & Rodin, J. (1976). The effects of choice and enhanced personal responsibility for the aged: A field experiment in an institutional setting. *Journal of Personality and Social Psychology, 34*, 191–198.

La Rue, A., Dessonville, C., & Jarvik, L. F. (1985). Aging and mental disorders. In J. E. Birren & K. W. Schaie (Eds.), *Handbook of the psychology of aging* (2nd ed.). New York: Van Nostrand Reinhold, 1985.

Lasoski, M. C., & Thelen, M. H. (1987). Attitudes of older and middle-aged persons toward mental health intervention. *Gerontologist, 27*, 288–292.

Lazarus, R. S., & DeLongis, A. (1983). Psychological stress and coping in aging. *American Psychologist, 38*, 245–254.

Lazarus, R. S., & Folkman, S. (1984). *Stress, appraisal, and coping*. New York: Springer.

Lieberman, M. A. (1983). Social contexts of depression. In L. D. Breslau & M. R. Haug (Eds.), *Depression and aging. Causes, care, and consequences*. New York: Springer.

Loeber, R. (1982). The stability of antisocial and delinquent child behavior: A review. *Child Development, 53*, 1431–1446.

Lovaas, O. I. (1987). Behavioral treatment and normal educational and intellectual functioning in young autistic children. *Journal of Consulting and Clinical Psychology, 55*, 3–9.

Manuelidis, E. E., De Figueiredo, J. M., Kim, J. H., Fritch, W. W., & Manuelidis, L. (1988). Transmission studies from blood of Alzheimer disease patients and healthy relatives. *Proceedings of the National Academy of Sciences, 85*, 4898–4901.

McConville, B. J., Boag, L. C., & Purohit, A. P. (1973). Three types of childhood depression. *Canadian Psychiatric Association Journal, 18*, 133–138.

McCrae, R. R. (1982). Age differences in the use of coping mechanisms. *Journal of Gerontology, 37*, 454–460.

McCrae, R. R., & Costa, P. T., Jr. (1986). Personality, coping, and coping effectiveness in an adult sample. *Journal of Personality, 54*, 385–405.

McLanahan, S. S., & Sorensen, A. B. (1985). Life events and psychological well-being over the life course. In G. H. Elder, Jr. (Ed.), *Life course dynamics. Trajectories and transitions, 1968–1980*. Ithaca, NY: Cornell University Press.

Milich, R., & Loney, J. (1979). The role of hyperactive and aggressive symptomology in predicting adolescent outcome among hyperactive children. *Journal of Pediatric Psychology, 4*, 93–112.

Milich, R., & Pelham, W. E. (1986). Effects of sugar ingestion on the classroom and playgroup behavior of attention deficit disordered boys. *Journal of Consulting and Clinical Psychology, 54*, 714–718.

Milich, R., Wolraich, M., & Lindgren, S. (1986). Sugar and hyperactivity: A critical review of empirical findings. *Clinical Psychology Review, 6*, 493–513.

Minuchin, S., Rosman, B. L., & Baker, L. (1978). *Psychosomatic families: Anorexia nervosa in context*. Cambridge, MA: Harvard University Press.

Myers, J. K., Weissman, M. M., Tischler, G. L., Holzer, C. E., III, Leaf, P. J., & Orvaschel, H. (1984). Six-month prevalence of psychiatric disorders in three communities. *Archives of General Psychiatry, 41*, 959–967.

National Center for Health Statistics. (1988). *Vital statistics of the United States, 1986: Vol. 2, Mortality, Part A* (DHHS Publication No. PHS 88-1122). Washington, DC: U.S. Government Printing Office.

Newmann, J. P. (1989). Aging and depression. *Psychology and Aging, 4*, 150–165.

Nolen-Hoeksema, S. (1987). Sex differences in unipolar depression: Evidence and theory. *Psychological Bulletin, 101*, 259–282.

Nolen-Hoeksema, S., Girgus, J. S., & Seligman, M. E. P. (1986). Learned helplessness in children. A longitudinal study of depression, achievement, and explanatory style. *Journal of Personality and Social Psychology, 51*, 435–442.

Osgood, D. W., Johnston, L. D., O'Malley, P. M., & Bachman, J. G. (1988). The generality of deviance in late adolescence and early adulthood. *American Sociological Review, 53*, 81–93.

Ostrov, E., Offer, D., & Howard, K. I. (1989). Gender differences in adolescent symptomatology: A normative study. *Journal of the American Academy of Child and Adolescent Psychiatry, 28*, 394–398.

Pagel, M., & Becker, J. (1987). Depressive thinking and depression: Relations with personality and social resources. *Journal of Personality and Social Psychology, 52*, 1043–1052.

Pastalan, L. A. (1983). Environmental displacement: A literature reflecting old-person–environment transactions. In G. D. Rowles & R. J. Ohta (Eds.), *Aging and milieu. Environmental perspectives on growing old*. New York: Academic.

Pearlin, L. I. (1980). Life strains and psychological distress among adults. In N. J. Smelser & E. H. Erikson (Eds.), *Themes of work and love in adulthood*. Cambridge, MA: Harvard University Press.

Petersen, A. C. (1988). Adolescent development. *Annual Review of Psychology, 39*, 583–607.

Petersen, A. C., & Hamburg, B. A. (1986). Adolescence: A developmental approach to problems and psychopathology. *Behavior Therapy, 17*, 480–499.

Peterson, C., & Seligman, M. E. P. (1984). Causal explanations as a risk factor for depression: Theory and evidence. *Psychological Review, 91*, 347–374.

Petti, T. A., & Larson, C. N. (1987). Depression and suicide. In V. B. Van Hasselt & M. Hersen (Eds.), *Handbook of adolescent psychology*. New York: Pergamon.

Pfeffer, C. R. (1986). *The suicidal child*. New York: Guilford.

Pfeiffer, E. (1977). Psychopathology and social pathology. In J. E. Birren & K. W. Schaie (Eds.), *Handbook of the psychology of aging*. New York: Van Nostrand Reinhold.

Polivy, J., & Herman, C. P. (1985). Dieting and binging. A causal analysis. *American Psychologist, 40*, 193–201.

Prior, M., & Sanson, A. (1986). Attention deficit disorder with hyperactivity: A critique. *Journal of Child Psychology and Psychiatry, 27*, 307–319.

Puig-Antich, J. (1982). Major depression and conduct disorder in prepuberty. *Journal of the American Academy of Child Psychiatry, 21*, 118–128.

Puig-Antich, J. (1986). Psychobiological markers: Effects of age and puberty. In M. Rutter, C. E. Izard, & P. B. Read (Eds.), *Depression in young people. Developmental and clinical perspectives.* New York: Guilford.

Quay, H. C., Routh, D. K., & Shapiro, S. K. (1987). Psychopathology of childhood: From description to validation. *Annual Review of Psychology, 38,* 491–532.

Radke-Yarrow, M., Cummings, E. M., Kuczynski, L., & Chapman, M. (1985). Patterns of attachment in two- and three-year-olds in normal families and families with parental depression. *Child Development, 56,* 884–893.

Rapoport, J. L., Buchsbaum, M. S., Zahn, T. P., Weingartner, H., Ludlow, C., & Mikkelsen, E. J. (1978). Dextroamphetamine: Cognitive and behavioral effects in normal prepubertal boys. *Science, 199,* 560–563.

Renner, L. (1985, March 2). Hyperactivity difficult to diagnose, control. *Lexington Herald-Leader,* p. B6.

Robins, L. N. (1966). *Deviant children grow up: A sociological and psychiatric study of sociopathic personality.* Baltimore: Williams & Wilkins.

Robins, L. N. (1979). Follow-up studies. In H. C. Quay & J. S. Werry (Eds.), *Psychopathological disorders of childhood* (2nd ed.). New York: Wiley.

Rodin, J., & Langer, E. J. (1977). Long-term effects of a control-relevant intervention with the institutionalized aged. *Journal of Personality and Social Psychology, 35,* 897–902.

Rosenberg, M. L., Smith, J. C., Davidson, L. E., & Conn, J. M. (1987). The emergence of youth suicide: An epidemiologic analysis and public health perspective. *Annual Review of Public Health, 8,* 417–440.

Rosenthal. P. A., & Rosenthal, S. (1984). Suicidal behavior by preschool children. *American Journal of Psychiatry, 141,* 520–525.

Rowe, D. C., Rodgers, J. L., Meseck-Bushey, S., & St. John, C. (1989). Sexual behavior and nonsexual deviance: A sibling study of their relationship. *Developmental Psychology, 25,* 61–69.

Rubenstein, J. L., Heeren, T., Housman, D., Rubin, C., & Stechler, G. (1989). Suicidal behavior in "normal" adolescents: Risk and protective factors. *American Journal of Orthopsychiatry, 59,* 59–71.

Rutter, M. (1979). Protective factors in children's responses to stress and disadvantage. In M. W. Kent & J. E. Rolf (Eds.), *Primary prevention of psychopathology: Vol. 3. Social competence in children.* Hanover, NH: University Press of New England.

Rutter, M. (1986). The developmental psychopathology of depression: Issues and perspectives. In M. Rutter, C. E. Izard, & P. B. Read (Eds.), *Depression in young people. Developmental and clinical perspectives.* New York: Guilford.

Rutter, M. (1987). Psychosocial resilience and protective mechanisms. *American Journal of Orthopsychiatry, 57,* 316–331.

Rutter, M. (1989). Pathways from childhood to adult life. *Journal of Child Psychology and Psychiatry, 30,* 23–51.

Rutter, M., Graham, P., Chadwick, O. F. D., & Yule, W. (1976). Adolescent turmoil: Fact or fiction? *Journal of Child Psychology and Psychiatry, 17,* 35–56.

Rutter, M., & Schopler, E. (1987). Autism and pervasive developmental disorders: Concepts and diagnostic issues. *Journal of Autism and Developmental Disorders, 17,* 159–186.

Ryan, N. D., Puig-Antich, J., Ambrosini, P., Rabinovich, H., Robinson, D., & Nelson, B. (1987). The clinical picture of major depression in children and adolescents. *Archives of General Psychiatry, 44,* 854–861.

Scalf-McIver, L., & Thompson, J. K. (1989). Family correlates of bulimic characteristics in college females. *Journal of Clinical Psychology, 45,* 467–472.

Scott, D. W. (1986). Anorexia nervosa: A review of possible genetic factors. *International Journal of Eating Disorders, 5,* 1–20.

Shavit, Y., & Rattner, A. (1988). Age, crime, and the early life course. *American Journal of Sociology, 93,* 1457–1470.

Singer, L. (1987). Long-term hospitalization of nonorganic failure-to-thrive infants: Patient characteristics and hospital course. *Journal of Developmental and Behavioral Pediatrics, 8,* 25–31.

Sines, J. O. (1987). Influence of the home and family environment on childhood dysfunction. In B. B. Lahey & A. E. Kazdin (Eds.), *Advances in clinical child psychology* (Vol. 10). New York & London: Plenum.

Smith, K., & Crawford, S. (1986). Suicidal behavior among "normal" high school students. *Suicide and Life-Threatening Behavior, 16,* 313–325.

Smoller, J. W. (1986). The etiology and treatment of childhood. In G. C. Ellenbogen (Ed.), *Oral sadism and the vegetarian personality. Readings from the Journal of Polymorphous Perversity.* New York: Brunner/Mazel. (Originally published by Wry-Bred Press)

Spitz, R. A. (1946). Anaclitic depression: An inquiry into the genesis of psychiatric conditions in early childhood, II. *Psychoanalytic Study of the Child, 2,* 313–342.

Sroufe, L. A., & Rutter, M. (1984). The domain of developmental psychopathology. *Child Development, 55,* 17–29.

St. George-Hyslop, P. H., Tanzi, R. E., Polinsky, R. J., Haines, J. L., Nee, L., & Watkins, P.C. (1987). The genetic defect causing familial Alzheimer's disease maps on chromosome 21. *Science, 235,* 885–889.

Stapley, J. C., & Haviland, J. M. (1989). Beyond depression: Gender differences in normal adolescents' emotional experiences. *Sex Roles, 20,* 295–308.

Steffenburg, S., Gillberg, C., Hellgren, L., Andersson, L., Gillberg, I. C., Jakobsson, G., & Bohman, M. (1989). A twin study of autism in Denmark, Finland, Iceland, Norway, and Sweden. *Journal of Child Psychology and Psychiatry, 30,* 405–416.

Stewart, M. A., Pitts, F. N., Craig, A. G., & Dieruf, W. (1966). The hyperactive child syndrome. *American Journal of Orthopsychiatry, 36,* 861–867.

Striegel-Moore, R. H., Silberstein, L. R., & Rodin, J. (1986). Toward an understanding of risk factors for bulimia. *American Psychologist, 41,* 246–263.

Strober, M. (1986). Psychopathology in adolescence revisited. *Clinical Psychology Review, 6,* 199–209.

Strober, M., & Humphrey, L. L. (1987). Familial contributions to the etiology and course of anorexia nervosa and bulimia. *Journal of Consulting and Clinical Psychology, 55,* 654–659.

Tanner, J. M. (1978). *Fetus into man: Physical growth from conception to maturity.* Cambridge, MA: Harvard University Press.

Thompson, L. W., Gallagher, D., & Breckenridge, J. S. (1987). Comparative effectiveness of psychotherapies for depressed elders. *Journal of Consulting and Clinical Psychology, 55*, 385–390.

Thompson, M. G., & Gans, M. T. (1985). Do anorexics and bulimics get well? In S. W. Emmett (Ed.), *Theory and treatment of anorexia nervosa and bulimia. Biomedical, sociocultural, and psychological perspectives.* New York: Brunner/Mazel.

Tolan, P., Miller, L., & Thomas, P. (1988). Perception and experience of types of social stress and self-image among adolescents. *Journal of Youth and Adolescence, 17*, 147–163.

Trad, P. V. (1986). *Infant depression. Paradigms and paradoxes.* New York: Springer.

U.S. Bureau of the Census. (1986). *Statistical abstract of the United States: 1987* (107th ed.). Washington, DC: Author.

Vaillant, G. E. (1977). *Adaptation to life.* Boston: Little, Brown.

Veroff, J., Douvan, E., & Kulka, R. A. (1981). *The inner American. A self-portrait from 1957 to 1976.* New York: Basic Books.

Vinokur, A., & Selzer, M. L. (1975). Desirable vs. undesirable life events: Their relationship to stress and mental distress. *Journal of Personality and Social Psychology, 32*, 329–337.

Volkmar, F. R., & Cohen, D. J. (1988). Neurobiologic aspects of autism. *New England Journal of Medicine, 318*, 1390–1392.

Von Knorring, A., Andersson, O., & Magnusson, D. (1987). Psychiatric care and course of psychiatric disorders from childhood to early adulthood in a representative sample. *Journal of Child Psychology and Psychiatry, 28*, 329–341.

Wallander, J. L., & Hubert, N. C. (1985). Long-term prognosis for children with attention deficit disorder with hyperactivity (ADD/H). In B. B. Lahey & A. E. Kazdin (Eds.), *Advances in clinical child psychology* (Vol. 8). New York: Plenum.

Weiss, I. K., Nagel, C. L., & Aronson, M. K. (1986). Applicability of depression scales to the old person. *Journal of the American Geriatrics Society, 34*, 215–218.

Weisz, J. R., Weiss, B., Alicke, M. D., & Klotz, M. L. (1987). Effectiveness of psychotherapy with children and adolescents: A meta-analysis for clinicians. *Journal of Consulting and Clinical Psychology, 55*, 542–549.

Wender, P. H., Kety, S. S., Rosenthal, D., Schulsinger, F., Ortmann, J., & Lunde, I. (1986). Psychiatric disorders in the biological and adoptive families of adopted individuals with affective disorders. *Archives of General Psychiatry, 43*, 923–929.

Whalen, C. K., Henker, B., Buhrmester, D., Hinshaw, S. P., Huber, A., & Laski, K. (1989). Does stimulant medication improve the peer status of hyperactive children? *Journal of Consulting and Clinical Psychology, 57*, 545–549.

Williamson, D. A., Davis, C. J., Goreczny, A. J., & Blouin, D. C. (1989). Body-image disturbances in bulimia nervosa: Influences of actual body size. *Journal of Abnormal Psychology, 98*, 97–99.

Wrightsman, L. S., Sigelman, C. K., & Sanford, F. H. (1979). *Psychology. A scientific study of human behavior.* Pacific Grove, CA: Brooks/Cole.

Yamaguchi, K., & Kandel, D. B. (1984). Patterns of drug use from adolescence to young adulthood: II. Sequences of progression. *American Journal of Public Health, 74*, 668–672.

Zahn-Waxler, C., Cummings, E. M., Iannotti, R. J., & Radke-Yarrow, M. (1984). Young offspring of depressed parents: A population at risk for affective problems. In D. Cicchetti & K. Schneider-Rosen (Eds.), *Childhood depression* (New Directions for Child Development, No. 26). San Francisco: Jossey-Bass.

Zarit, S. H., Eiler, J., & Hassinger, M. (1985). Clinical assessment. In J. E. Birren & K. W. Schaie (Eds.), *Handbook of the psychology of aging* (2nd ed.). New York: Van Nostrand Reinhold.

Zarit, S. H., Orr, N. K., & Zarita, J. M. (1985). *The hidden victims of Alzheimer's disease. Families under stress.* New York: New York University Press.

Chapter 17: The Final Challenge: Death and Dying

Adams, D. W., & Deveau, E. J. (1986). Helping dying adolescents: Needs and responses. In C. A. Corr & J. N. McNeil (Eds.), *Adolescence and death.* New York: Springer.

Adams, D. W., & Deveau, E. J. (1987). When a brother or sister is dying of cancer: The vulnerability of the adolescent sibling. *Death Studies, 11*, 279–295.

Ad Hoc Committee of the Harvard Medical School to Examine the Definition of Brain Death. (1968). A definition of irreversible coma. *Journal of the American Medical Association, 205*, 337–340.

Aiken, L. R. (1985). *Dying, death, and bereavement.* Boston: Allyn & Bacon.

Akiyama, H., Holtzman, J. M., & Britz, W. E. (1986–1987). Pet ownership and health status during bereavement. *Omega, 17*, 187–193.

Ariès, P. (1981). *The hour of our death* (H. Weaver, Trans.). New York: Knopf. (Original work published 1977)

Balk, D. (1983). Adolescents' grief reactions and self-concept perceptions following sibling death: A study of 33 teenagers. *Journal of Youth and Adolescence, 12*, 137–161.

Ball, J. F. (1976–1977). Widow's grief: The impact of age and mode of death. *Omega, 7*, 307–333.

Bankoff, E. A. (1983). Aged parents and their widowed daughters: A support relationship. *Journal of Gerontology, 38*, 226–230.

Barrett, C. J., & Schneweis, K. M. (1980–1981). An empirical search for stages of widowhood. *Omega, 11*, 97–104.

Bass, D. M. (1985). The hospice ideology and success of hospice care. *Research on Aging, 7*, 307–327.

Baugher, R. J., Burger, C., Smith, R., & Wallston, K. (1989–1990). A comparison of terminally ill persons at various time periods to death. *Omega, 20*, 103–115.

Becker, D., & Margolin, F. (1967). How surviving parents handled their young children's adaptation to the crisis of loss. *American Journal of Orthopsychiatry, 37*, 753–757.

Bennett, N. G., & Garson, L. K. (1986). Extraordinary longevity in the Soviet Union: Fact or artifact. *Gerontologist, 26*, 358–361.

Black, D. & Urbanowicz, M. A. (1987). Family intervention with bereaved children. *Journal of Child Psychology and Psychiatry, 28*, 467–476.

Bluebond-Langner, M. (1977). Meanings of death to children. In H. Feifel (Ed.), *New meanings of death.* New York: McGraw-Hill.

Borstelmann, L. J. (1983). Children before psychology: Ideas about children from antiquity to the late 1800s. In W. Kessen (Vol. Ed.; P. H. Mussen, General Ed.), *Handbook of child psychology: Vol. 1. History, theory, and methods* (4th ed.). New York: Wiley.

Bowlby, J. (1980). *Attachment and loss: Vol. 3. Loss, sadness and depression.* New York: Basic Books.

Bowling, A. (1987). Mortality after bereavement: A review of the literature on survival periods and factors affecting survival. *Social Science and Medicine, 24,* 117–124.

Brown, G. W., Harris, T. O., & Bifulco, A. (1986). Long-term effects of early loss of parent. In M. Rutter, C. E. Izard, & P. B. Read (Eds.), *Depression in young people. Developmental and clinical perspectives.* New York: Guilford.

Bunch, J. (1972). Recent bereavement in relation to suicide. *Journal of Psychosomatic Research, 16,* 361–366.

Burks, V. K., Lund, D. A., Gregg, C. H., & Bluhm, H. P. (1988). Bereavement and remarriage for older adults. *Death Studies, 12,* 51–60.

Butterfield-Picard, H., & Magno, J. B. (1982). Hospice the adjective, not the noun. The future of a national priority. *American Psychologist, 37,* 1254–1259.

Carey, R. G., & Posavac, E. J. (1978–1979). Attitudes of physicians on disclosing information to and maintaining life for terminal patients. *Omega, 9,* 67–77.

Cavanaugh, J. C. (1990). *Adult development and aging.* Belmont, CA: Wadsworth.

Cole, D. (1987, July). It might have been: Mourning the unborn. *Psychology Today,* pp. 64–65.

Coleman, F. W., & Coleman, W. S. (1984). Helping siblings and other peers cope with dying. In H. Wass & C. A. Corr (Eds.), *Childhood and death.* Washington, DC: Hemisphere.

Cristofalo, V. J. (1985). The destiny of cells: Mechanisms and implications of senescence. *Gerontologist, 25,* 577–583.

DeFrain, J., Taylor, J., & Ernst, L. (1982). *Coping with sudden infant death.* Lexington, MA: Lexington Books.

Diggory, J. C., & Rothman, D. Z. (1961). Values destroyed by death. *Journal of Abnormal and Social Psychology, 63,* 205–210.

Durlak, J. A. (1978–1979). Comparison between experiential and didactic methods of death education. *Omega, 9,* 57–66.

Elizur, E., & Kaffman, M. (1983). Factors influencing the severity of childhood bereavement reactions. *American Journal of Orthopsychiatry, 53,* 668–676.

Feifel, H., & Branscomb, A. B. (1973). Who's afraid of death? *Journal of Abnormal Psychology, 81,* 282–288.

Finch, C. E. (1976). The regulation of physiological changes during mammalian aging. *Quarterly Review of Biology, 51,* 49–83.

Florian, V., & Kravetz, S. (1985). Children's concepts of death. A cross-cultural comparison among Muslims, Druze, Christians, and Jews in Israel. *Journal of Cross-Cultural Psychology, 16,* 174–189.

Furman, E. (1984). Children's patterns in mourning the death of a loved one. In H. Wass & C. A. Corr (Eds.), *Childhood and death.* Washington, DC: Hemisphere.

Gesser, G., Wong, P. T. P., & Reker, G. T. (1987–1988). Death attitudes across the life-span: The development and validation of the Death Attitude Profile (DAP). *Omega, 18,* 113–128.

Glaser, B. G., & Strauss, A. L. (1968). *Time for dying.* Chicago: Aldine.

Graham-Pole, J., Wass, H., Eyberg, S., Chu, L., & Olejnik, S. (1989). Communicating with dying children and their siblings: A retrospective analysis. *Death Studies, 13,* 463–483.

Gordon, A. K. (1986). The tattered cloak of immortality. In C. A. Corr & J. N. McNeil (Eds.), *Adolescence and death.* New York: Springer.

Haas-Hawkings, G., Sangster, S., Ziegler, M., & Reid, D. (1985). A study of relatively immediate adjustment to widowhood in later life. *International Journal of Women's Studies, 8,* 158–166.

Harman, D. (1981). The aging process. *Proceedings of the National Academy of Sciences of the USA, 78,* 7124–7128.

Hart, R. W., & Setlow, R. B. (1974). Correlation between deoxyribonucleic acid excision-repair and life-span in a number of mammalian species. *Proceedings of the National Academy of Sciences of the USA, 71,* 2169–2173.

Hart, R. W., & Turturro, A. (1983). Theories of aging. In M. Rothstein (Ed.), *Review of biological research in aging* (Vol. 1). New York: Alan R. Liss.

Hayflick, L. (1976). The cell biology of human aging. *New England Journal of Medicine, 295,* 1302–1308.

Helsing, K. J., Szklo, M., & Comstock, G. W. (1981). Factors associated with mortality after widowhood. *American Journal of Public Health, 71,* 802–809.

Hickson, J., Housley, W. F., & Boyle, C. (1988). The relationship of locus of control, age, and sex to life satisfaction and death anxiety in older persons. *International Journal of Aging and Human Development, 26,* 191–199.

Hinton, J. (1975). The influence of previous personality on reactions to having terminal cancer. *Omega, 6,* 95–111.

Hoffman, S. I., & Strauss, S. (1985). The development of children's concepts of death. *Death Studies, 9,* 469–482.

Huntington, R., & Metcalf, P. (1979). *Celebrations of death: The anthropology of mortuary ritual.* Cambridge, England: Cambridge University Press.

Jacobs, S. C., Kosten, T. R., Kasl, S. V., Ostfeld, A. M., Berkman, L., & Charpentier, P. (1987–1988). Attachment theory and multiple dimensions of grief. *Omega, 18,* 41–52.

Kalish, R. A. (1963). An approach to the study of death attitudes. *American Behavioral Scientist, 6*(9), 68–70.

Kalish, R. A. (1981). *Death, grief, and caring relationships.* Pacific Grove, CA: Brooks/Cole.

Kalish, R. A., & Reynolds, D. K. (1976). *Death and ethnicity: A psychocultural study.* Los Angeles: Ethel Percy Andrus Gerontology Center, University of Southern California.

Kalish, R. A., & Reynolds, D. K. (1977). The role of age in death attitudes. *Death Education, 1,* 205–230.

Kane, B. (1979). Children's concepts of death. *Journal of Genetic Psychology, 134,* 141–153.

Kaplan, G. A., Seeman, T. E., Cohen, R. D., Knudsen, L. P., & Guralnik, J. (1987). Mortality among the elderly in the Alameda County study: Behavioral and demographic risk factors. *American Journal of Public Health, 77,* 307–312.

Kaprio, J., Koskenvuo, M., & Rita, H. (1987). Mortality after bereavement: A prospective study of 95,647 widowed persons. *American Journal of Public Health, 77,* 283–287.

Kastenbaum, R. (1985). Dying and death: A life-span approach. In J. E. Birren & K. W. Schaie (Eds.), *Handbook of the psychology of aging* (2nd ed.). New York: Van Nostrand Reinhold.

Kastenbaum, R. J. (1986). *Death, society, and human experience* (3rd ed.). Columbus, OH: Charles E. Merrill.

Klenow, D. J., & Youngs, G. A., Jr. (1987). Changes in doctor/patient communication of a terminal prognosis: A selective review and critique. *Death Studies, 11*, 263–277.

Knapp, R. J. (1986). *Beyond endurance. When a child dies.* New York: Schocken.

Koocher, G. P. (1973). Childhood, death, and cognitive development. *Developmental Psychology, 9*, 369–375.

Koocher, G. P. (1974). Talking with children about death. *American Journal of Orthopsychiatry, 44*, 404–411.

Kübler-Ross, E. (1969). *On death and dying.* New York: Macmillan.

Kübler-Ross, E. (1974). *Questions and answers on death and dying.* New York: Macmillan.

Lehman, D. R., Ellard, J. H., & Wortman, C. B. (1986). Social support for the bereaved: Recipients' and providers' perspectives on what is helpful. *Journal of Consulting and Clinical Psychology, 54*, 438–446.

Lehman, D. R., Wortman, C. B., & Williams, A. F. (1987). Long-term effects of losing a spouse or child in a motor vehicle crash. *Journal of Personality and Social Psychology, 52*, 218–231.

Lehr, U. M. (1982). Social-psychological correlates of longevity. In C. Eisdorfer (Ed.), *Annual review of gerontology and geriatrics* (Vol. 3). New York: Springer.

Leming, M. R., & Dickinson, G. E. (1985). *Understanding dying, death, and bereavement.* New York: Holt, Rinehart & Winston.

Lesher, E. L., & Bergey, K. J. (1988). Bereaved elderly mothers: Changes in health, functional activities, family cohesion, and psychological well-being. *International Journal of Aging and Human Development, 26*, 81–90.

Leviton, D., & Forman, E. C. (1974). Death education for children and youth. *Journal of Clinical Child Psychology, 3*, 8–10.

Lieberman, M. A., & Videka-Sherman, L. (1986). The impact of self-help groups on the mental health of widows and widowers. *American Journal of Orthopsychiatry, 56*, 435–449.

Littlefield, C. H., & Rushton, J. P. (1986). When a child dies: The sociobiology of bereavement. *Journal of Personality and Social Psychology, 51*, 797–802.

Lonetto, R., & Templer, D. I. (1986). *Death anxiety.* Washington, DC: Hemisphere.

Lopata, H. Z. (1973). *Widowhood in an American city.* Cambridge, MA: Schenkman.

Lopata, H. Z. (1979). Widowhood and husband sanctification. In L. A. Bugen (Ed.), *Death and dying. Theory, research, practice.* Dubuque, IA: William C. Brown.

Lund, D. A., Dimond, M. F., Caserta, M. S., Johnson, R. J., Poulton, J. L., & Connelly, J. R. (1985–1986). Identifying elderly with coping difficulties after two years of bereavement. *Omega, 16*, 213–224.

Manton, K. G. (1986). Past and future life expectancy increases at later ages: Their implications for the linkage of chronic morbidity, disability, and mortality. *Journal of Gerontology, 41*, 672–681.

Masoro, E. J. (1988). Minireview: Food restriction in rodents—An evaluation of its role in the study of aging. *Journal of Gerontology: Biological Sciences, 43*, B59–B64.

Maurer, A. (1961). The child's knowledge of non-existence. *Journal of Existential Psychiatry, 2*, 193–212.

Mazess, R. B., & Forman, S. H. (1979). Longevity and age exaggeration in Vilcabamba, Ecuador. *Journal of Gerontology, 34*, 94–98.

McClearn, G., & Foch, T. T. (1985). Behavioral genetics. In J. E. Birren & K. W. Schaie (Eds.), *Handbook of the psychology of aging* (2nd ed.). New York: Van Nostrand Reinhold.

McIntosh, J. L., & Wrobleski, A. (1988). Grief reactions among suicide survivors: An exploratory comparison of relationships. *Death Studies, 12*, 21–39.

McIntyre, M. S., Angle, C. R., & Struempler, L. J. (1972). The concept of death in midwestern children and youth. *American Journal of Diseases of Children, 123*, 527–532.

McMordie, W. R. (1981). Religiosity and fear of death: Strength of belief system. *Psychological Reports, 49*, 921–922.

McWhirter, L., Young, V., & Majury, J. (1983). Belfast children's awareness of violent death. *British Journal of Social Psychology, 22*, 81–92.

Metzger, A. M. (1979–1980). A Q-methodology study of the Kübler-Ross stage theory. *Omega, 10*, 291–301.

Murphy, S. A. (1986). Stress, coping, and mental health outcomes following a natural disaster. Bereaved family members and friends compared. *Death Studies, 10*, 411–429.

Murrell, S. A., & Himmelfarb, S. (1989). Effects of attachment bereavement and pre-event conditions on subsequent depressive symptoms in older adults. *Psychology and Aging, 4*, 166–172.

Nagy, M. (1948). The child's theories concerning death. *Journal of Genetic Psychology, 73*, 3–27.

National Center for Health Statistics. (1988). *Vital statistics of the United States, 1986: Vol. 2, Mortality, Part A* (DHHS Publ. No. 88-1122). Washington, DC: U.S. Government Printing Office.

Oken, D. (1961). What to tell cancer patients. *Journal of the American Medical Association, 175*, 1120–1128.

Orbach, I., Gross, Y., Glaubman, H., & Berman, D. (1986). Children's perception of various determinants of the death concept as a function of intelligence, age, and anxiety. *Journal of Clinical Child Psychology, 15*, 120–126.

Osterweis, M., Solomon, F., & Green, M. (Eds.). (1984). *Bereavement. Reactions, consequences, and care.* Washington, DC: National Academy Press.

Owen, G., Fulton, R., & Markusen, E. (1982–1983). Death at a distance: A study of family survivors. *Omega, 13*, 191–225.

Parkes, C. M. (1970). "Seeking" and "finding" a lost object. *Social Science and Medicine, 4*, 187–201.

Parkes, C. M. (1986). *Bereavement. Studies of grief in adult life* (2nd ed.). London & New York: Tavistock.

Parkes, C. M. (1987–1988). Research: Bereavement. *Omega, 18*, 45–56.

Parkes, C. M., & Weiss, R. S. (1983). *Recovery from bereavement.* New York: Basic Books.

Pennebaker, J. W., & O'Heeron, R. C. (1984). Confiding in others and illness rate among spouses of suicide and accidental-death victims. *Journal of Abnormal Psychology, 93*, 473–476.

Peppers, L. G. (1987–1988). Grief and elective abortion: Breaking the emotional bond? *Omega, 18*, 1–12.

Pollack, J. M. (1979–1980). Correlates of death anxiety: A review of empirical studies. *Omega, 10*, 97–121.

Rando, T. A. (1986). A comprehensive analysis of anticipatory grief: Perspectives, processes, promises, and problems. In T. A. Rando (Ed.), *Loss and anticipatory grief.* Lexington, MA: Lexington Books.

Raphael, B. (1983). *The anatomy of bereavement.* New York: Basic Books.

Reilly, T. P., Hasazi, J. E., & Bond, L. A. (1983). Children's conceptions of death and personal mortality. *Journal of Pediatric Psychology, 8*, 21–31.

Reker, G. T., Peacock, E. J., & Wong, P. T. P. (1987). Meaning and purpose in life and well-being: A life-span perspective. *Journal of Gerontology, 42*, 44–49.

Retsinas, J. (1988). A theoretical reassessment of the applicability of Kübler-Ross's stages of dying. *Death Studies, 12*, 207–216.

Rosen, H. (1986). *Unspoken grief. Coping with childhood sibling loss.* Lexington, MA: Lexington Books.

Rosenfeld, A. (1985). *Prolongevity II.* New York: Knopf.

Rosenheim, E., & Reicher, R. (1986). Children in anticipatory grief: The lonely predicament. *Journal of Clinical Child Psychology, 15*, 115–119.

Sanders, C. M. (1979–1980). A comparison of adult bereavement in the death of a spouse, child and parent. *Omega, 10*, 303–322.

Sanders, C. M. (1982–1983). Effects of sudden vs. chronic illness death on bereavement outcome. *Omega, 13*, 227–241.

Saunders, C. (1977). Dying they live: St. Christopher's Hospice. In H. Feifel (Ed.), *New meanings of death.* New York: McGraw-Hill.

Schneider, E. L., & Reed, J. D. (1985). Modulations of aging processes. In C. E. Finch & E. L. Schneider (Eds.), *Handbook of the biology of aging* (2nd ed.). New York: Van Nostrand Reinhold.

Schulz, R. (1978). *The psychology of death, dying, and bereavement.* Reading, MA: Addison-Wesley.

Schulz, R., & Aderman, D. (1974). Clinical research and the stages of dying. *Omega, 5*, 137–143.

Schulz, R., & Schlarb, J. (1988). Two decades of research on dying: What do we know about the patient? *Omega, 18*, 299–317.

Scott, J. P., & Kivett, V. R. (1985). Differences in the morale of older, rural widows and widowers. *International Journal of Aging and Human Development, 21*, 121–136.

Shanfield, S. B., Swain, B. J., & Benjamin, G. A. H. (1986–1987). Parents' responses to the death of adult children from accidents and cancer: A comparison. *Omega, 17*, 289–297.

Shneidman, E. S. (1973). *Deaths of man.* New York: Quadrangle.

Shneidman, E. S. (1980). *Voices of death.* New York: Harper & Row.

Shock, N. W. (1977). Biological theories of aging. In J. E. Birren & K. W. Schaie (Eds.), *Handbook of the psychology of aging.* New York: Van Nostrand Reinhold.

Silverman, P. R. (1969). The widow-to-widow program. An experiment in preventive intervention. *Mental Hygiene, 53*, 333–337.

Silverman, P. R. (1981). *Helping women cope with grief* (Sage Human Services Guide No. 25). Beverly Hills, CA: Sage.

Smith, G. S., & Walford, R. L. (1977). Influence of the main histocompatibility complex on aging in mice. *Nature, 270*, 727–729.

Speece, M. W., & Brent, S. B. (1984). Children's understanding of death: A review of three components of a death concept. *Child Development, 55*, 1671–1686.

Spinetta, J. J. (1974). The dying child's awareness of death: A review. *Psychological Bulletin, 81*, 256–260.

Spitz, R. A. (1946). Anaclitic depression: An inquiry into the genesis of psychiatric conditions in early childhood, II. *Psychoanalytic Study of the Child, 2*, 313–342.

Stambrook, M., & Parker, K. C. H. (1987). The development of the concept of death in childhood: A review of the literature. *Merrill–Palmer Quarterly, 33*, 133–157.

Stroebe, W., & Stroebe, M. S. (1986). Beyond marriage: The impact of partner loss on health. In R. Gilmour & S. Duck (Eds.), *The emerging field of personal relationships.* Hillsdale, NJ: Erlbaum.

Thomas, L. E., DiGiulio, R. C., & Sheehan, N. W. (1988). Identity loss and psychological crisis in widowhood: A re-evaluation. *International Journal of Aging and Human Development, 26*, 225–239.

U.S. Bureau of the Census. (1975). *Historical statistics of the United States, colonial times to 1970* (Part 1). Washington, DC: U.S. Government Printing Office.

U.S. Bureau of the Census. (1989). *Statistical abstract of the United States: 1989* (109th ed.). Washington, DC: U.S. Government Printing Office.

van der Wal, J. (1989–1990). The aftermath of suicide: A review of empirical evidence. *Omega, 20*, 149–171.

Van Eerdewegh, M. M., Clayton, P. J., & Van Eerdewegh, P. (1985). The bereaved children: Variables influencing early psychopathology. *British Journal of Psychiatry, 147*, 188–194.

Vess, J., Moreland, J., & Schwebel, A. I. (1985–1986). Understanding family role reallocation following a death: A theoretical framework. *Omega, 16*, 115–128.

Waechter, E. H. (1984). Dying children. Patterns of coping. In H. Wass & C. A. Corr (Eds.), *Childhood and death.* Washington, DC: Hemisphere.

Walford, R. L. (1983). *Maximum life span.* New York: Norton.

Weisman, A. D., & Worden, J. W. (1975). Psychosocial analysis of cancer deaths. *Omega, 6*, 61–75.

Wenestam, C., & Wass, H. (1987). Swedish and U.S. children's thinking about death: A qualitative study and cross-cultural comparison. *Death Studies, 11*, 99–121.

Worchel, F. F., Copeland, D. R., & Barker, D. G. (1987). Control-related coping strategies in pediatric oncology patients. *Journal of Pediatric Psychology, 12*, 25–38.

Yin, P., & Shine, M. (1985). Misinterpretations of increases in life expectancy in gerontology textbooks. *Gerontologist, 25*, 78–82.

Yu, B. P., Masoro, E. J., & McMahan, C. A. (1985). Nutritional influences on aging of Fischer 344 rats: I. Physical, metabolic, and longevity characteristics. *Journal of Gerontology, 40*, 657–670.

Chapter 18: Fitting the Pieces Together

Flavell, J. H. (1985). *Cognitive development* (2nd ed.). Englewood Cliffs, NJ: Prentice-Hall.

Kagan, J. (1986). Rates of change in psychological processes. *Journal of Applied Developmental Psychology, 7*, 125–130.

La Rochefoucauld, F. (1959). *The maxims of La Rochefoucauld* (L. Kronenberger, Trans.). New York: Vintage Books. (Original work published 1665)

McCall, R. B. (1981). Nature–nurture and the two realms of development: A proposed integration with respect to mental development. *Child Development, 52*, 1–12.

Schaie, K. W. (1983). The Seattle longitudinal study: A 21-year exploration of psychometric intelligence in adulthood. In K. W. Schaie (Ed.), *Longitudinal studies of adult psychological development*. New York: Guilford.

Werner, H. (1957). The concept of development from a comparative and organismic point of view. In D. B. Harris (Ed.), *The concept of development: An issue in the study of human behavior*. Minneapolis: University of Minnesota Press.

NAME INDEX

N

O

S

Subject Index

Page numbers in *italics* designate figures; page numbers followed by "t" designate tables; page numbers followed by "f" designate footnotes.

Q

R

T

CREDITS

These pages constitute an extension of the copyright page. We have made every effort to trace the ownership of all copyrighted material and to secure permission from copyright holders. In the event of any question arising as to the use of any material, we will be pleased to make the necessary corrections in future printings.

TABLES AND FIGURES

Chapter 1

4: Figure 1.2 from "Stratum Contrasts and Similarities in Attitudes Toward Death," by V. L. Bengtson, J. B. Cuellar, and P. K. Ragan, 1977, *Journal of Gerontology, 32.* Reprinted by permission. **23:** Figure 1.6 adapted from "Age and Verbalization in Observational Learning," by B. Coates and W. W. Hartup, 1969, *Developmental Psychology, 1,* pp. 556–562. Copyright 1969 by the American Psychological Association. Reprinted by permission.

Chapter 3

80: Table 3.2 adapted from "Genetic Counseling," by S. M. Pueschel and A. Goldstein. In J. L. Matson and J. A. Mulick (Eds.), *Handbook of Mental Retardation,* 1983. Copyright 1983 by Pergamon Press, Inc. Reprinted by permission. **85:** Figure 3.7 from "Behavior-Genetics Research in Infant Temperament: The Louisville Twin Study," by R. S. Wilson and A. P. Matheny, Jr. In R. Plomin and J. Dunn (Eds.), *The Study of Temperament: Changes, Continuities and Challenges,* 1986. Copyright 1986 by Lawrence Erlbaum Associates, Inc. Reprinted by permission. **86:** Figure 3.8 data from "The Louisville Twin Study: Developmental Synchronies in Behavior," by R. S. Wilson, 1983, *Child Development, 54,* pp. 298–316. © 1983 by The Society for Research in Child Development, Inc. Reprinted by permission.

Chapter 4

107: Figure 4.3 reprinted from "Infant Death: An Analysis by Maternal Risk and Health Care," by D. Kessner, 1973, with permission from the National Academy of Sciences, Washington, D.C. **109:** Figure 4.4 adapted from a figure in *The Developing Human,* by K. L. Moore, 1988 (4th ed.). Philadelphia, W. B. Saunders. Reprinted by permission. **117:** Figure 4.6 from "Risk and Resilience in Early Mental Development," by R. S. Wilson, 1985, *Developmental Psychology, 21,* p. 802. Copyright 1985 by the American Psychological Association. **124:** Table 4.4 adapted from "Age Norms, Age Constraints, and Adult Socialization," by B. L. Neugarten, J. W. Moore, and J. C. Lowe, 1965, *American Journal of Sociology, 70,* p. 712. Copyright 1965 by The University of Chicago Press. Reprinted by permission.

Chapter 5

135: Figure 5.1 from *Growth at Adolescence* (2nd ed.), by J. M. Tanner, 1962, Blackwell Scientific Publications Ltd., London; redrawn from "The Measurement of the Body in Childhood," by R. E. Scammon. In J. A. Harris, C. M. Jackson, D. G. Paterson, and R. E. Scammon (Eds.), *The Measurement of Man,* 1930, University of Minnesota Press. Reprinted by permission. **142:** Table 5.4 adapted from "The Denver Development Screening Test," by W. K. Frankenberg and J. B. Dodds, 1967, *Journal of Pediatrics, 71,* pp. 181–191. Reprinted by permission. **147:** Figure 5.4 adapted from *Archives of the Diseases of Childhood,* by J. M. Tanner, R. H. Whithouse, and A. Takaishi, 1966, *41,* pp. 454–471. Reprinted by permission. **148:** Figure 5.5 from "Somatic Development of Adolescent Girls," by M. S. Faust, 1977, *Monographs of the Society for Research in Child Development, 42* (Whole No. 169). © 1977 by The Society for Research in Child Development, Inc. Reprinted by permission. **152:** Figure 5.6 from *Science and Medicine of Exercise and Sport*, 2nd ed., edited by Warren K. Johnson and Elsworth R. Buskirk. Copyright © 1974 by Warren K. Johnson and Elsworth R. Buskirk. Reprinted by permission of Harper & Row, Publishers, Inc. **153:** Figure 5.8 data from "Human Physiological Adaptability Through the Life Sequence," by H. Bafitis and F. Sargent II, 1977, *Journal of Gerontology, 32.* Reprinted by permission.**155:** Table 5.5 data from "Prevalence of Perimenstrual Symptoms," by N. F. Woods, A. Most, and G. K. Dery, 1982, *American Journal of Public Health 72,* pp. 1257–1264. © 1982 American Journal of Public Health. Reprinted by permission. **160:** Figure in Box 5.3 from "Effects of Age and Skill in Typing," by T. A. Salthouse, 1984, *Journal of Experimental Psychology: General, 113,* pp. 345–371. Copyright 1984 by the American Psychological Association. Reprinted by permission.

Chapter 6

167: Figure 6.1 adapted from "Perceptual Set in Young Children," by H. W. Reese, 1963, *Child Development, 34.* © 1963 by The Society for Research in Child Development, Inc. Reprinted by permission. **170:** Figure 6.2 from "Infant Visual Perception," by M. S. Banks, in collaboration with P. Salapatek. In M. M. Haith & J. J. Campos (Eds.; P. H. Mussen, Gen. Ed.), *Handbook of Child Psychology: Vol. 2. Infancy and Developmental Psychobiology* (4th ed.), 1983. Copyright © 1983 by John Wiley & Sons, Inc. Reprinted by permission. **171:** Figure 6.3 adapted from "Pattern Perception in Infancy," by P. Salapatek. In L. B. Cohen and P. Salapatek (Eds.), *Infant Perception: From Sensation to Cognition,* Volume 1, 1975. Copyright 1975 by Academic Press, Inc. Reprinted by permission. **172:** Figure in Box 6.1 adapted from "Perception of Partly Occluded Objects in Infancy," by P. J. Kellman and E. S. Spelke, 1983, *Cognitive Psychology, 15,* pp. 483–524. Reprinted by permission of Academic Press. **181:** Figure 6.6 adapted from "A Developmental Study of the Discrimination of Letter-Like Forms," by E. J. Gibson, A. D. Pick, and H. A. Osser, 1962, *Journal of Comparative and Physiological Psychology, 55,* pp. 897–906. Copyright 1962 by the American Psychological Association. **188:** Table 6.1 from "Food Recognition by the Elderly," by S. Schiffman, 1977, *Journal of Gerontology, 32.* Reprinted by permission. **187:** Figure 6.8 from "Age-Related Decrement in Hearing for Speech: Sampling and Longitudinal Studies," by M. Bergman, V. G. Blumenfeld, D. Cascardo, B. Dash, H. Levitt, and M. K. Margulies, 1976, *Journal of Gerontology, 31.* Reprinted by permission. **191:** Figure 6.9 from "Pictorial Depth Perception in

Sub-cultural Groups in Africa," by W. Hudson, *Journal of Social Psychology, 52,* 1977, pp. 183–208. Reprinted with permission of the Helen Dwight Reid Educational Foundation. Published by Heldref Publications, 4000 Albemarle St., N.W., Washington, D.C. 20016. Copyright © 1960.

Chapter 7

208: Table 7.2 from *Psycholinguistics* by Dan I. Slobin. Copyright © 1979, 1974 by Scott, Foresman and Company. Reprinted by permission. **214:** Table 7.3 from *The Acquisition of Language,* by David McNeill. Copyright © 1970 by David McNeill. Reprinted by permission of Harper & Row, Publishers, Inc. **217:** Table 7.4 adapted from "Social and Non-Social Speech," by R. M. Krauss and S. Glucksberg, February 1977, *Scientific American, 236,* pp. 100–105. Copyright © 1977 by Scientific American, Inc. All rights reserved. **225:** Table 7.5 data from "Individual Differences in College Students' Performance on Formal Operations Tasks," by R. DeLisi and J. Staudt, 1980, *Journal of Applied Developmental Psychology, 1,* pp. 163–174. Reprinted by permission.

Chapter 8

240: Figure 8.2 adapted from "Influence of Models' Reinforcement Contingencies on the Acquisition of Imitative Responses," by A. Bandura, 1965, *Journal of Personality and Social Psychology, 1,* pp. 589–595. Copyright 1965 by the American Psychological Association. Reprinted by permission. **243:** Figure 8.3 adapted from "Human Memory: A Proposed System and Its Control Processes," by R. C. Atkinson and R. M. Shiffrin. In K. W. Spence and J. T. Spence (Eds.), *The Psychology of Learning and Motivation: Advances in Research and Theory,* (Vol. 2), 1968, Academic Press. **244:** Figure 8.4 adapted from "Memory Span: Sources of Individual and Developmental Differences," by F. N. Dempster, 1981, *Psychological Bulletin, 89,* pp. 63–100. Copyright 1981 by the American Psychological Association. Reprinted by permission; from J. Botwinick and M. Storandt, *Memory, Related Functions and Age,* 1974. Courtesy of Charles C Thomas, Publisher, Springfield, Illinois. **252:** Figure 8.7 from "Knowledge Structures and Memory Development," by M. T. H. Chi. In R. Siegler (Ed.), *Children's Thinking: What Develops?* 1978. Copyright 1978 by Lawrence Erlbaum Associates, Inc. Reprinted by permission. **253:** Figure 8.8 adapted from "Vertical and Horizontal Processes in Problem-Solving," by H. H. Kendler and T. S. Kendler, 1962, *Psychological Review, 69,* pp. 1–16. Copyright 1962 by the American Psychological Association. Reprinted by permission. **255:** Table 8.1 adapted from "Developmental Sequences Within and Between Concepts," by R. S. Siegler, 1981. *Monographs of the Society for Research in Child Development, 46* (Serial No. 189). © 1981 by The Society for Research in Child Development, Inc. Reprinted by permission. **261:** Figure 8.10 adapted from "Differential Memory Changes with Age: Exact Retrieval Versus Plausible Inference, by L. M. Reder, C. Wible, and J. Martin, 1986, *Journal of Experimental Psychology: Learning, Memory, and Cognition, 12,* p. 76. Copyright 1986 by the American Psychological Association. Adapted by permission.

Chapter 9

272: Figure 9.1 adapted from *The Nature of Human Intelligence,* by J. P. Guilford, 1967. New York: McGraw-Hill. Reprinted with permission of the publisher. **274:** Table 9.1 reprinted with permission of The Riverside Publishing Company from *Stanford-Binet Intelligence Scale: Fourth Edition* by R. L. Thorndike, E. P. Hagen, and J. M. Sattler. The Riverside Publishing Company, 8420 W. Bryn Mawr Avenue, Chicago, IL 60631. Copyright 1986. **276:** Figure 9.3 from "Measuring Mental Abilities in Infancy. The Value and Limitations," by M. P. Honzik, 1983. In M. Lewis (Ed.), *Origins of Intelligence. Infancy and Early Childhood* (2nd ed.), Plenum. Reprinted by permission.**278:** Table 9.2 from "The Stability of Mental Test Performance Between Two and Eighteen Years," by M. P. Honzik, J. W. MacFarlane, and L. Allen, 1948, *Journal of Experimental Education, 17,* pp. 309–324. **280:** Table 9.4 modified from "The Seattle Longitudinal Study: A 21-Year Exploration of Psychometric Intelligence in Adulthood," by K. W. Schaie, 1983, The Guilford Press. Reprinted by permission. **281:** Table 9.3 from "Army General Classification Test Scores for Civilian Populations," by T. W. Harrell and M. S. Harrell, 1945, *Educational and Psychological Measurement, 5,* pp. 229–239. Reprinted by permission. **286:** Table 9.5 from *Manual for Home Observation for Measurement of the Environment,* by B. M. Caldwell and R. H. Bradley, 1978, University of Arkansas Press. **288:** Figure 9.5 from "Birth Order, Family Size, and Intelligence," by L. Belmont and F. A. Marolla, 1973, *Science, 182,* pp. 1096–1101. Copyright 1973 by the AAAS. **294:** Figure 9.6 abridged Figure 2 from *Modes of Thinking in Young Children* by Michael A. Wallach and Nathan Kogan, copyright © 1965 by Holt, Rinehart and Winston, Inc., reprinted by permission of the publisher. **297:** Figure 9.7 data from "Creative Productivity Between the Ages of 20 and 80 Years," by W. Dennis, 1966, *Journal of Gerontology, 21,* p. 2. Reprinted by permission.**300:** Figure 9.8 from "Can Decline in Adult Intellectual Functioning Be Reversed?" by K. W. Schaie and S. L. Willis, 1986, *Developmental Psychology, 22,* p. 228. Copyright 1986 by the American Psychological Association. Reprinted by permission.

Chapter 10

313: Figure 10.1 adapted from *Birth to Maturity,* by K. Kagan and H. A. Moss, 1962. Copyright © 1962 by John Wiley & Sons, Inc. Reprinted by permission. **317:** Figure 10.2 adapted from "Cross-Sectional Age Changes in Ego Identity Status During Adolescence," by P. W. Meilman, 1979, *Developmental Psychology, 15,* pp. 230–231. Copyright 1979 by the American Psychological Association. Reprinted by permission. **330:** Figure 10.4 adapted from "An Observational Study of Children's Attempts to Monitor Their Expressive Behavior," by C. Saarni, 1984, *Child Development, 55,* pp. 1504–1513. © 1984 by The Society for Research in Child Development, Inc. Reprinted by permission.

Chapter 11

338: Table 11.1 adapted from *The Psychology of Sex Differences,* by E. E. Maccoby and C. N. Jacklin, 1974, Stanford University Press. Reprinted by permission of the publisher. **342:** Figure 11.1 based on "Social Behavior at 33 Months in Same-Sex and Mixed-Sex Dyads," by C. N. Jacklin and E. E. Maccoby, 1978, *Child Development, 49,* pp. 557–569. © 1978 by The Society for Research in Child Development, Inc. Reprinted by permission. **343:** Table 11.2 based on "Children, Gender, and Social Structure: An Analysis of the Contents of Letters to Santa Claus," by J. G. Richardson and C. H. Simpson, 1982, *Child Development, 53,* pp. 429–436. © 1982 by The Society for Research in Child Development, Inc. Reprinted by permission. **345:** Figure 11.2 adapted from *Man and Woman, Boy and Girl,* by J. Money and A. Ehrhardt, 1972, Johns Hopkins University Press. Reprinted by permission of the publisher. **354:** Figure 11.3 adapted from "Children's Concepts of Cross-Gender Activities," by T. Stoddart and E. Turiel, 1985, *Child Development, 56,* pp. 1241–1252. © 1985 by The Society for Research in Child Development, Inc. Reprinted by permission.

Chapter 12

384 : Figures 12.2 and 12.3 adapted from "Factors Influencing Young Children's Use of Motives and Outcomes as Moral Criteria," by S. A. Nelson, 1980, *Child Development, 51,* pp. 823–829. © 1980 by The Society for Research in Child Development, Inc. Reprinted by permission. **387:** Table 12.3 adapted from "Contributions of Parents and Peers to Children's Moral Socialization," by G. H. Brody and D. R. Shaffer, 1982, *Developmental Review, 2,* pp. 31–75. Reprinted by permission of Academic Press, Inc. **389:** Figure 12.4 from "A Longitudinal Study of Moral Judgment," by A. Colby, L. Kohlberg, J. Gibbs, and M. Lieberman, 1983, *Monographs of the Society for Research in Child Development, 48* (Nos. 1–2, Serial No. 200). © 1983 by The Society for Research in Child Development, Inc. Reprinted by permission. **390, 391:** Figures 12.5 and 12.6 data from "Motives in American Men and Women Across the Adult Life Span," by J. Veroff, D. Reuman, and S. Feld, 1984, *Developmental Psychology, 20,* pp. 1142–1158. Copyright 1984 by the American Psychological Association. Adapted by permission.

Chapter 13

420: Table 13.1 adapted from "Social-Cognitive Understanding: A Guide to Educational and Clinical Experience," by R. L. Selman. In T. Lickona (Ed.), *Moral Development and Behavior: Theory, Research, and Social Issues,* 1976, Holt, Rinehart and Winston, Inc.. Reprinted by permission. **421:** Figure 13.2 from "Age Segregation in Children's Social Interactions," by S. Ellis, B. Rogoff, and C. C. Cromer, *Developmental Psychology, 17,* pp. 399–407. Copyright 1981 by the American Psychological Association. **424:** Figure 13.3 from "The Social Structure of Urban Adolescent Peer Groups," by D. C. Dunphy, 1963, *Sociometry, 26,* pp. 230–246. Reprinted by permission. **426:** Figure 13.4 from "Girlfriend, Boyfriend: Age and Sex Differences in Intimate Friendship," by R. Sharabany, R. Gershoni, and J. E. Hofman, 1981, *Developmental Psychology, 17,* pp. 800–808. Copyright 1981 by the American Psychological Association. Reprinted by permission. **430:** Figure 13.5 from *The Social Context of Marriage,* 2nd ed. by J. Richard Udry. Copyright © 1971 by J. B. Lippincott Company. Reprinted by permission of Harper & Row, Publishers, Inc. **432:** Figure in Box 13.6 modified from "Romantic Love Conceptualized as an Attachment Process," by C. Hazan and P. Shaver, 1987, *Journal of Personality and Social Psychology, 52,* pp. 511–524. Copyright 1987 by the American Psychological Association. **434:** Figure 13.6 adapted from "Rehabilitation of Socially Withdrawn Preschool Children through Mixed-Age and Same-Age Socialization," by D. F. Rahe and W. W. Hartup, 1979, *Child Development,* pp. 915–992. © 1979 by The Society for Research in Child Development, Inc. Reprinted by permission.

Chapter 14

439: Figure 14.1 from "Early Human Experience: A Family Perspective," by J. Belsky, 1981, *Developmental Psychology, 17,* pp. 3–23. Copyright 1981 by the American Psychological Association. Reprinted by permission. **440:** Table 14.1 from *Marriage and Family Development,* by E. M. Duvall. Copyright © 1978 by J. B. Lippincott Company. Reprinted by permission of Harper & Row, Publishers, Inc. **450:** Table 14.2 adapted from *The Adolescent: A Psychological Self-Portrait,* by Daniel Offer, Eric Ostrov, and Kenneth I. Howard. Copyright © 1981 by Basic Books, Inc. Reprinted by permission of Basic Books, Publishers, New York. **457:** Figure 14.3 from "Marital Satisfaction over the Family Life Cycle," by B. C. Rollins and H. Feldman, 1970, *Journal of Marriage and the Family, 32,* pp. 20–28. Copyrighted 1970 by the National Council on Family Relations, 3989 Central Ave. N.E., Suite #550, Minneapolis, MN 55421. Reprinted by permission. **468:** Figure 14.4 adapted from "Child Abuse as Psychopathology: A Sociological Critique and Reformulation," by R. J. Gelles, 1973, *American Journal of Orthopsychiatry, 43,* pp. 611–621. Reprinted, with permission, from the American Journal of Orthopsychiatry. Copyright 1973 by the American Orthopsychiatric Association, Inc.

Chapter 15

477: Figure 15.1 adapted from "Preschool Play Norms: A Replication," by K. E. Barnes, 1971, *Developmental Psychology, 5,* pp. 99–103. Copyright 1971 by the American Psychological Association. Reprinted by permission. **483:** Figure 15.2 from *Television and Human Behavior,* by G. Comstock, 1978, Columbia University Press. **487:** Table 15.1 from "Age and Sex Differences in the Development of Children's Occupational Reasoning," by J. N. Nelson, 1978, *Journal of Vocational Behavior, 13,* pp. 287–297. Reprinted by permission of Academic Press, Inc. **488:** Figure 15.3 from *Being Adolescent,* by M. Csikszentmihalyi and R. Larson. Copyright © 1984 by Basic Books, Inc. Reprinted by permission of Basic Books, Inc., Publishers, New York. **493:** Figure 15.4 from "The AT&R Longitudinal Studies of Managers," by D. W. Bray and A. Howard. In K. W. Schaie (Ed.), *Longitudinal Studies of Adult Psychological Development,* 1983. Reprinted by permission of The Guilford Press.

Chapter 16

509: Figure in Box 16.2 from *Diagnostic and Statistical Manual of Mental Disorders (3rd ed., rev.) DSM-III-R,* 1987, American Psychiatric Association, Washington, D.C. **518:** Table 16.2 adapted from "Follow-up of a Preschool Epidemiological Sample: Cross-Age Continuities and Predictions of Later Adjustment with Internalizing and Externalizing Dimensions of Behavior," by M. Fischer, J. E. Rolf, J. E. Hasazi, and L. Cummings, 1984, *Child Development, 55,* pp. 137–150. © 1984 by The Society for Research in Child Development, Inc.. Reprinted by permission. **522:** Figure 16.1 from *Use of Licit and Illicit Drugs by America's High School Students 1975–1984,* by L. D. Johnston, P. M. O'Malley, and J. G. Bachman, 1985. (DHHS Publication No. ADM 85–1394). National Institute on Drug Abuse, Rockville, MD. **527:** Figure 16.3 adapted from "Six-Month Prevalence of Psychiatric Disorders in Three Communities," by J. K. Myers, et al., 1984, *Archives of General Psychiatry, 41,* pp. 959–967.

Chapter 17

550: Figure 17.3 reprinted with permission from *Omega, 18,* pp. 41–52, S. C. Jacobs, T. R. Kosten, S. V. Kasl, A. M. Ostfeld, L Berkman, and P. Charpentier, "Attachment Theory and Multiple Dimensions of Grief," Copyright 1987–1988, Pergamon Press, Inc. **552:** Table 17.1 adapted from "Development of Children's Concepts of Death," by S. I. Hoffman and S. Strauss, *Death Studies,* 1985, *9*(5–6), p. 475. Copyright 1985 by Hemisphere Publishing Corp. Adapted by permission; and "Children's Concepts of Death: A Cross-Cultural Comparison Among Muslims, Druze, Christians, and Jews in Israel," by V. Florian and S. Kravetz, 1985, *Journal of Cross-Cultural Psychology, 16,* pp. 174–189. Copyright 1985 by *Journal of Cross-Cultural Psychology.* Reprinted by permission of Sage Publications, Inc. **558:** Table 17.2 from "The Role of Age in Death Attitudes," by R. A. Kalish and D. K. Reynolds, *Death Education 1,* 1977, *1*(2), p. 225. Copyright 1977 by Hemisphere Publishing Corp. Reprinted by permission. **559:** Table 17.3 adapted from *Bereavement: Studies of Grief in Adult Life* (2nd ed.)., by C. M. Parkes, 1986, Tavistock Publications. Reprinted by permission of publisher.

PHOTO CREDITS

Chapter 1

6: *Don Baltasar Carlos with a Dwarf*, Diego Rodriguez de Silva y V. Velazquez, Spanish, 1599–1660. Oil on canvas: 50⅜ × 40⅛ in. Henry Lillie Pierce Fund. Courtesy, Museum of Fine Arts, Boston, Catalog #01.104; **11:** © Gale Zucker; **16:** Amazon Photos; **19:** Brown Brothers; **27:** Larry Hamill.

Chapter 2

33: © Gale Zucker; **40:** The Bettmann Archive; **45:** Harvard University Archives: **47:** Amazon Photos; **49:** Yves de Braine/Black Star; **54:** (*left*) courtesy of B. F. Skinner, (*right*) Chuck Painter/News and Publicatons Service, Stanford University; **55:** Nina Leen/*Life* Magazine, © 1964 Time Inc.; **59:** © Gale Zucker.

Chapter 3

74: Phototake/copyright © by Martin M. Rotker 1988, all rights reserved; **77:** G. W. Willis, © 1988/Biological Photo Service; **79:** © Gale Zucker; **87:** Courtesy of Professor E. Novitzski; 90: Courtesy of *Washington Post*; **91:** Courtesy of Frank L. DeBusk, University of Florida College of Medicine.

Chapter 4

101: © Gale Zucker; 106: Landrum B. Shettles, M.D.; 111: From J. M. Graham, Jr., "Congenital Anomalies." In M. D. Levin, W. B. Carey, A. C. Crocker, and R. T. Gross (Eds.), *Developmental Behavioral Pediatrics* (Philadelphia: Saunders, 1983), 363–389; **120:** © Ulrike Welsch 1987; **126:** © 1980 Larry Hamill; **128:** © Martha Tabor/Working Images Photographs.

Chapter 5

139: © Gale Zucker; **144:** Amazon Photos; **146:** © Gale Zucker; **150:** © Elizabeth Crews/Stock, Boston; **153:** Jacques M. Chenet, all rights reserved/Woodfin Camp; **157:** Mimi Forsyth/Monkmeyer Press Photo Service; **162:** © Rameshwar Das 1985/Monkmeyer Press Photo Service.

Chapter 6

173: William Vandivert; **176, 178, 181, 186:** Amazon Photos.

Chapter 7

199: © Gale Zucker; **203, 216, 219:** Amazon Photos; **227:** © Gale Zucker; **228:** Amazon Photos; **230:** © Gale Zucker.

Chapter 8

241: From "Imitation of Film-Mediated Aggressive Models" by A. Bandura, D. Ross, and S. A. Ross, 1963, *Journal of Abnormal and Social Psychology*, pp. 3–11. Copyright 1963 by the American Psychological Association; **245:** Amazon Photos; **252:** Mimi Forsyth/Monkmeyer Press Photo Service; **256:** Amazon Photos; **258:** © Tim Davis/Photo Researchers, Inc.; **259:** Courtesy of B. F. Skinner.

Chapter 9

271: Amazon Photos; **285:** © Gale Zucker; **291, 298:** Amazon Photos.

Chapter 10

307: Amazon Photos; **318:** © Ulrike Welsch 1987; **323:** Amazon Photos; **327:** Larry Busacca/Retna Ltd.; **328:** C. E. Izard, University of Delaware; **330:** © Gale Zucker; **331:** Amazon Photos.

Chapter 11

340, 352, 356: Amazon Photos; **361, 364, 371:** © Gale Zucker.

Chapter 12

379, 380: David Shaffer; **387:** © Alexander Lowry, 1987/Photo Researchers, Inc.; **394:** Jean-Claude Lejeune/Stock, Boston; **397:** Amazon Photos.

Chapter 13

406: © Gale Zucker; **408:** Amazon Photos; **410:** © Gale Zucker; **412:** University of Wisconsin, Harlow Primate Laboratory; **418:** Amazon Photos; **428:** © Gale Zucker; **433:** Amazon Photos.

Chapter 14

439: Al Clayton; **443:** © Gale Zucker; **448:** Amazon Photos; **452, 453:** © Gale Zucker; **459, 466:** Amazon Photos.

Chapter 15

473: George Bellerose/Stock, Boston; **477, 481, 484, 485, 490:** Amazon Photos; **496:** © Gale Zucker; **500:** © 1987 Peter Menzel/Stock, Boston.

Chapter 16

511: Meri Houtchens-Kitchen/The Picture Cube; **520, 525:** © Gale Zucker; **529:** Amazon Photos; **532, 534:** © Gale Zucker.

Chapter 17

539: Mike Kagan/Monkmeyer Press Photo Service; **542:** © Magnum Photos; **549:** © Gale Zucker; **553, 556:** From Claes-Göran Wenestam and Hannelore Wass, "Swedish and U.S. Children's Thinking About Death," *Death Studies*, 1987, Vol. 11, pp. 109 and 111; **555:** © David M. Grossman; **564:** Amazon Photos; **565:** Alan Oddie/Photo Edit.

Chapter 18

570–577: Bettie Lou courtesy of Bettie Lou Sjoberg; Jay courtesy of Larry Hamill.